THE OXFORD HANDBOOK OF

CHARLES DICKENS

THE OXFORD HANDBOOK OF

CHARLES DICKENS

Edited by
ROBERT L. PATTEN
JOHN O. JORDAN
and
CATHERINE WATERS

OXFORD
UNIVERSITY PRESS

OXFORD
UNIVERSITY PRESS

Great Clarendon Street, Oxford, OX2 6DP,
United Kingdom

Oxford University Press is a department of the University of Oxford.
It furthers the University's objective of excellence in research, scholarship,
and education by publishing worldwide. Oxford is a registered trade mark of
Oxford University Press in the UK and in certain other countries

© the several contributors 2018

The moral rights of the authors have been asserted

First Edition published in 2018

Impression: 1

All rights reserved. No part of this publication may be reproduced, stored in
a retrieval system, or transmitted, in any form or by any means, without the
prior permission in writing of Oxford University Press, or as expressly permitted
by law, by licence or under terms agreed with the appropriate reprographics
rights organization. Enquiries concerning reproduction outside the scope of the
above should be sent to the Rights Department, Oxford University Press, at the
address above

You must not circulate this work in any other form
and you must impose this same condition on any acquirer

Published in the United States of America by Oxford University Press
198 Madison Avenue, New York, NY 10016, United States of America

British Library Cataloguing in Publication Data

Data available

Library of Congress Control Number: 2018939911

ISBN 978-0-19-874341-5

Printed and bound by
CPI Group (UK) Ltd, Croydon, CR0 4YY

Links to third party websites are provided by Oxford in good faith and
for information only. Oxford disclaims any responsibility for the materials
contained in any third party website referenced in this work.

Acknowledgements

First and foremost, the editors want to recognize the professionalism of all the contributors to the Handbook. They have collectively provided energy and inspiration, teaching us anew the breadth and depth of Dickens's achievement and worldwide impact. We are very grateful for their participation in this tribute.

Next, credit must be given to Andrew McNeillie and Pamela Dalziel, who initiated this project and brought it far enough along that Oxford University Press saw fit to continue developing it. Thereafter Jacqueline Norton, OUP commissioning editor for English literature, took charge and mentored us in responding to panels of review that urged us to think about the remit more ambitiously. To the scholars who comprised those several nameless review panels and brought so many valuable suggestions for improvement to our attention, we, and this Handbook, owe much.

In the process of preparing this manuscript for the Press, two facilitators deserve special commendation. Tara Thomas, an advanced graduate student in the Literature Department at the University of California, Santa Cruz, spent ten weeks checking each quotation from Dickens's texts and correspondence in every essay; she embarrassed us all by finding so many errors, and cheered us by correcting them. At the Press, Aimee Wright has proved invaluable, educating us about OUP's unique protocols, orthography, and punctuation, assisting us in obtaining appropriate illustrations, and then overseeing the copy-editing of 50 different essays by authors trained in many alternative styles and protocols. Whatever semblance of standardization we have achieved is due in large part to Aimee's educated and rigorous eyes.

We have benefited from the unstinted cooperation and wisdom of the following: Malcolm Andrews, His Honour Derwin Hope, His Honour Judge Iain Hughes QC, Carolyn Lagattuta, Courtney Mahaney, Kay McStay, Michael Slater, Claire Wood.

For permission to quote from or reproduce materials in their possession, we gratefully acknowledge these institutions: the Berg Collection of the New York Public Library, Astor, Lenox and Tilden Foundations; Commander Mark Dickens; the *Dickensian*; The Pickwick Bicycle Club, Fareham, Hampshire; Faber & Faber, Farrar Strauss and Giroux, McHenry Library Special Collections, University of California, Santa Cruz; Xavier University Library.

And for providing copies of needed books, we are grateful to Interlibrary Loan at University of California, Santa Cruz.

Finally, the editors wish to thank our families, who must often have wondered whether we would ever get the work–life balance righted, but who supplied only support and encouragement nonetheless.

Robert L. Patten, John O. Jordan, and Catherine Waters

Contents

List of Illustrations — xiii
List of Contributors — xv
Dickens Timeline — xxvii
Dickens Family Tree — xxxiii

Introduction — 1
ROBERT L. PATTEN, JOHN O. JORDAN, AND CATHERINE WATERS

PART I PERSONAL AND PROFESSIONAL LIFE

1. Biographical Dickens — 9
ROSEMARIE BODENHEIMER

2. Dickens's Lifetime Reading — 25
LEON LITVACK

3. Dickens as Professional Author — 43
JOHN BOWEN

4. Dickens as a Public Figure — 59
TONY WILLIAMS

PART II THE WORKS

5. Dickens's Early Sketches — 79
PAUL SCHLICKE

6. *Pickwick Papers*: The Posthumous Life of Writing — 92
JEREMY TAMBLING

7. *Oliver Twist*: Urban Aesthetics and the Homeless Child — 105
GALIA BENZIMAN

8. *Nicholas Nickleby*: Equity vs Law — 119
   JON MICHAEL VARESE

9. *The Old Curiosity Shop* and *Master Humphrey's Clock* — 134
   SARAH WINTER

10. *Barnaby Rudge* and the Jesuit Menace — 153
    MARK ESLICK

11. *Martin Chuzzlewit* — 166
    LOGAN DELANO BROWNING

12. *Dombey and Son* and the Question of Reproduction — 179
    MICHAL PELED GINSBURG

13. Christmas Books and Stories — 191
    RUTH GLANCY

14. *David Copperfield* — 207
    PHILIP DAVIS

15. *Bleak House* — 220
    KATE FLINT

16. *Hard Times* for our Times — 233
    GRAHAME SMITH

17. *Little Dorrit* — 245
    FRANCESCA ORESTANO

18. *A Tale of Two Cities* — 260
    NATHALIE VANFASSE

19. *Great Expectations* — 273
    MARY HAMMOND

20. *Our Mutual Friend* — 285
    IAN DUNCAN

21. *The Mystery of Edwin Drood* — 299
    PETE ORFORD

22. 'Milestones on the Dover Road': Dickens and Travel — 312
    MICHAEL HOLLINGTON

23. Journalism and Correspondence 324
    HAZEL MACKENZIE

24. Charles Dickens and the 'Dark Corners' of Children's Literature 337
    MOLLY CLARK HILLARD

PART III THE SOCIO-HISTORICAL CONTEXTS

25. The Trouble with Angels: Dickens, Gender, and Sexuality 357
    JAMES ELI ADAMS

26. Domesticity and Queer Theory 372
    HOLLY FURNEAUX

27. Psychology, Psychiatry, Mesmerism, Dreams, Insanity, and Psychoanalytic Criticism 388
    TYSON STOLTE

28. Dickens and Astronomy, Biology, and Geology 404
    JONATHAN SMITH

29. Social Reform 420
    DAVID VINCENT

30. Dickens, Industry, and Technology 436
    RICHARD MENKE

31. Material Culture 452
    CLAIRE WOOD

32. Dickens and Affect 468
    WENDY PARKINS

33. History and Change: Dickens and the Past 484
    DAVID PAROISSIEN

34. Class and its Distinctions 501
    CHRIS R. VANDEN BOSSCHE

35. Race, Imperialism, Colonialism, Postcolonialism, and Cosmopolitanism 517
    JAMES BUZARD

36. Dickens, Political Economy, and Money 532
    AYŞE ÇELIKKOL

37. Dickens and Animal Studies 550
    JENNIFER MCDONELL

38. Dickens and the Environment 566
    ALLEN MACDUFFIE

39. Dickens and Religion 581
    JENNIFER GRIBBLE

40. Drinking in Dickens 597
    HELENA MICHIE

41. Cognitive Dickens 613
    CHIP BADLEY AND KAY YOUNG

PART IV THE LITERARY AND CULTURAL CONTEXTS

42. Dickens's Language 631
    DANIEL TYLER

43. Genres: *Auctor Ludens*, or Dickens at Play 647
    ROBERT TRACY

44. Dickens and the Theatre 666
    JOHN GLAVIN

45. Dickens's Visual Mediations 682
    HELEN GROTH

PART V DICKENS RE-VISIONED

46. Dickens's World-System: Globalized Modernity as Combined and Uneven Development 703
    PAUL YOUNG

47. Dickens's Global Circulation 722
    REGENIA GAGNIER

48. Adopting and Adapting Dickens since 1870: Stage, Film, Radio, Television 738
SHARON ARONOFSKY WELTMAN

49. Crowdsourced Dickens: Adapting and Adopting Dickens in the Internet Age 756
JULIET JOHN

Index 775

List of Illustrations

1.1	Felix Mendelssohn Bartholdy, pen-and-ink drawing of Birmingham, September 1840	10
2.1	Dummy book backs from Gad's Hill Library	41
4.1	'In Memory of Charles Dickens', *Illustrated Police News*, 16 June 1870	60
5.1	George Cruikshank, frontispiece to *Sketches by Boz*, first series, Volume 1, etching	85
7.1	George Cruikshank, 'Oliver Twist at Mrs. Maylie's Door', *Oliver Twist*, etching	110
7.2	George Cruikshank, 'Monks and the Jew', *Oliver Twist*, etching	116
8.1	First page of Articles of Agreement	127
8.2	Handwritten legal opinion from Richard Bentley's lawyer, Sutton Sharpe	130
9.1	Samuel Williams, 'Nell in bed', *The Old Curiosity Shop*, wood engraving	135
9.2	George Cattermole, 'The ruin in snow', *The Old Curiosity Shop*, wood engraving	143
9.3	George Cattermole, 'Nell dead', *The Old Curiosity Shop*, wood engraving	146
9.4	Hablot K. Browne, 'Quilp beating the figurehead', *The Old Curiosity Shop*, wood engraving	148
10.1	Hablot K. Browne, 'The Secretary's Watch', *Barnaby Rudge*, wood engraving	161
13.1	John Leech, 'Trotty Veck', *The Chimes*, wood engraving	195
13.2	Richard Doyle, 'The Dinner on the Steps', *The Chimes*, wood engraving	196
13.3	John Leech, 'Scrooge and Bob Cratchit', *A Christmas Carol*, wood engraving	198
17.1	Hablot K. Browne, wrapper design for *Little Dorrit*, steel etching	246
17.2	Advertisement for the London Stereoscopic Company, 'Little Dorrit Advertiser', *Little Dorrit*, wood engraving	256
18.1	Fred Barnard, 'La Carmagnole', *A Tale of Two Cities*, wood engraving	269
43.1	Hablot K. Browne, 'Mr. Pecksniff on his Mission', *Martin Chuzzlewit*, steel etching	651
43.2	Hablot K. Browne, 'Mrs. Gamp makes Tea', *Martin Chuzzlewit*, steel etching	653

43.3	Hablot K. Browne, 'Mrs. Gamp propoges a toast', *Martin Chuzzlewit*, steel etching	654
43.4	Hablot K. Browne, detail of frontispiece, Mrs. Gamp dancing, *Martin Chuzzlewit*, steel etching	655
43.5	Hablot K. Browne, 'Under the Microscope', *Little Dorrit*, steel etching	658
43.6	Hablot K. Browne, 'Five and Twenty', *Little Dorrit*, steel etching	661
45.1	Hablot K. Browne, 'Tom all Alone's', *Bleak House*, steel etching	685
45.2	Hablot K. Browne, wrapper design for *Dombey and Son*, steel etching	688
49.1	The Pickwick Bicycle Club's bicentenary ride to the Birthplace Museum	771

List of Contributors

James Eli Adams is Professor of English and Comparative Literature at Columbia University. He is the author of *Dandies and Desert Saints: Styles of Victorian Masculinity* (Cornell University Press, 1995) and *A History of Victorian Literature* (Wiley-Blackwell, 2009), as well as the co-editor, with Andrew Miller, of *Sexualities in Victorian Britain* (Indiana University Press, 1996) and the general editor of *The Encyclopedia of the Victorian Era* (Grolier, 2004). He is also a former editor of the journal *Victorian Studies*.

Chip Badley is a Ph.D. candidate in the English department at the University of California, Santa Barbara. A graduate research assistant of the Literature and the Mind initiative, he is pursuing an emphasis in the Cognitive Science Program. His dissertation considers neuroaesthetics and in nineteenth-century American literature.

Galia Benziman is Associate Professor at the Hebrew University of Jerusalem and specializes in British literature of the long nineteenth century. Her research focuses on Dickens, Thomas Hardy, and the history of childhood. Her book *Narratives of Child Neglect in Romantic and Victorian Culture* was published in 2012 (Palgrave Macmillan), and her second book, *Codes of Bereavement: Thomas Hardy's Elegiac Poetry and Prose* was published in 2018 (Palgrave Macmillan). She has published essays on Romantic and Victorian literature in *Dickens Studies Annual, Dickens Quarterly, Studies in the Novel, Women's Studies, SEL Studies in English Literature 1500–1900, Partial Answers: Journal of Literature and the History of Ideas, JNT: Journal of Narrative Theory, Victorian Literature and Culture* (forthcoming), and other journals.

Rosemarie Bodenheimer is Professor of English Emerita at Boston College. She is the author of *Knowing Dickens* (Cornell University Press, 2007) and numerous articles on Victorian novelists. Much of her work, including *The Real Life of Mary Ann Evans: Her Letters and Fiction* (Cornell University Press, 1994), explores the relationships among letters, biography, and imaginative fiction. She is currently doing some work on Felix Mendelssohn's family.

John Bowen is Professor of Nineteenth-Century Literature at the University of York, and a Fellow of the English Association. He has written widely on nineteenth- and twentieth-century fiction, and his books include *Other Dickens: Pickwick to Chuzzlewit* (Oxford University Press, 2000), *Palgrave Advances in Charles Dickens Studies* (co-edited with Robert L. Patten, 2005), and editions of Dickens's *Barnaby Rudge* (Penguin, 2003) and Anthony Trollope's *Phineas Redux* (2011) and *Barchester Towers* (2014, both Oxford World's Classics). A former President of the Dickens Society and Co-Director of the University of California Dickens Project, he is the President of the Dickens Fellowship 2017–19. He is a member of the Advisory Boards of the British Library 'Discovering Literature' website and of the Oxford Dickens Editions; he has made many broadcasts for the BBC and has reviewed frequently for the *Times Literary Supplement*. He is currently writing *Reading Charles Dickens* for Cambridge as well as editing *Bleak House* for Norton and George Orwell's *1984* for Oxford World's Classics.

Logan Delano Browning is Publisher and Executive Editor of *SEL Studies in English Literature 1500–1900* and Professor in the Practice of English and Humanities at Rice University, Houston, Texas. He has contributed to the *Oxford Reader's Companion to Dickens* (Oxford University Press, 1999), *Dickens Quarterly*, and a variety of other periodicals and reference works. He is working on a book about the literature and culture of New Orleans.

James Buzard teaches Literature at the Massachusetts Institute of Technology and is the author of *Disorienting Fiction: The Autoethnographic Work of 19th-Century British Novels* (Princeton University Press, 2005) and *The Beaten Track: European Tourism, Literature, and the Ways to 'Culture', 1800–1918* (Oxford University Press, 1993), as well of numerous articles on nineteenth- and twentieth-century British literature and culture.

Ayşe Çelikkol is Assistant Professor in the Department of English Language and Literature at Bilkent University, Turkey. She is the author of *Romances of Free Trade: British Literature, Laissez-Faire, and the Global Nineteenth Century* (Oxford University Press, 2011). Her work on Dickens, Alfred Tennyson, Edward FitzGerald, Walter Scott, Elizabeth Stoddard, and other nineteenth-century authors has appeared in journals such as *ELH*, *American Literature*, *Partial Answers*, and *Victorian Poetry*. She is a contributor to *The Oxford Handbook of Victorian Literary Culture*.

Philip Davis is Professor of Literature and Director of the Centre for Research into Reading, Literature and Society (CRILS) at the University of Liverpool. His publications include *Memory and Writing* (Liverpool University Press, 1983), *The Experience of Reading* (Routledge, 1992), *Real Voices: On Reading* (Macmillan, 1997), *The Victorians 1830–1880*, Oxford English Literary History volume 8 (Oxford University Press, 2002), *Why Victorian Literature Still Matters* (Blackwell, 2008), *Reading and the Reader* (Oxford University Press, 2013), *Bernard Malamud: A Writer's Life* (Oxford University Press, 2007), and *The Transferred Life of George Eliot* (Oxford University Press, 2017), He has also published books on Shakespeare and Samuel Johnson, and articles on reading and brain-imaging. He is editor of *The Reader* magazine and general editor of The *Literary Agenda* Series, on the future of Literary Studies in the twenty-first century, from Oxford.

Ian Duncan is Florence Green Bixby Professor of English at the University of California, Berkeley, where he works on the novel, Scottish literature, Romanticism, and Victorian literature and culture. He is the author of *Scott's Shadow: The Novel in Romantic Edinburgh* (Princeton University Press, 2007) and *Modern Romance and Transformations of the Novel* (Cambridge University Press, 1992), a co-editor of *Scotland*

and the Borders of Romanticism (Cambridge University Press, 2004) and *The Edinburgh Companion to James Hogg* (Edinburgh University Press, 2012), and a general editor of the Collected Works of James Hogg as well as of a new monograph series, *Edinburgh Critical Studies in Romanticism*. He is completing a book on the novel and the science of man in Europe from Buffon to Darwin.

Mark Eslick is the Science and Engineering Careers Manager at the University of Brighton. His primary research interest is in nineteenth-century fiction and religion, especially the work of Charles Dickens and his relationship with Catholicism. His publications on Dickens include essays on 'Agnes Wickfield and the Victorian Madonna' and 'Dickens's *Pictures from Italy*' for Oxford University Press. He also has an interest in creative writing and is currently working on a collection of short stories called 'Seven Sacraments'.

Kate Flint is Provost Professor of Art History and English at the University of Southern California, having previously taught at Rutgers, Oxford, and Bristol Universities. Her research is in nineteenth- and early twentieth-century cultural, literary, and art history, both British and transatlantic. She has published *Flash! Photography, Writing, and Surprising Illumination* (Oxford University Press, 2017), *The Transatlantic Indian 1776–1930* (Princeton University Press, 2008), *The Victorians and the Visual Imagination* (Cambridge University Press, 2000), *The Woman Reader 1837–1914* (Oxford University Press, 1993), and *Dickens* (Harvester, 1986), as well as editing *The Cambridge History of Victorian Literature* (Cambridge University Press, 2012). Editor of *Pictures from Italy* (Penguin, 1998), *Hard Times* (Penguin, 1995), and *Great Expectations* (Oxford World's Classics, 1994), she has written widely on Dickens, especially on Dickens and the visual arts. Her current work explores Victorian environmentalism, the detail and the local, and she is embarking on a longer-term project involving late nineteenth- and early twentieth-century cultural history.

Holly Furneaux is Professor of English at Cardiff University. Her latest book is *Military Men of Feeling: Emotion, Touch and Masculinity in the Crimean War* (Oxford University Press, 2016). She is also author of *Queer Dickens: Erotics, Families, Masculinities* (Oxford University Press, 2009), co-editor, with Sally Ledger, of *Dickens in Context* (Cambridge University Press, 2011), and editor of John Forster's *Life of Dickens* (Sterling, 2011). She is now working on projects exploring queer Dickens afterlives and late Victorian imperial masculinities.

Regenia Gagnier is Professor of English at the University of Exeter, Editor of the Global Circulation Project of *Literature Compass*, and Senior Research Fellow in Egenis, the Centre for the Study of Life Sciences. Her books include *Idylls of the Marketplace: Oscar Wilde and the Victorian Public* (Stanford University Press 1986); *Subjectivities: A History of Self-Representation in Britain 1832–1920* (Oxford University Press, 1991), *The Insatiability of Human Wants: Economics and Aesthetics in Market Society* (University of Chicago Press, 2000). *Individualism, Decadence and Globalization: On the Relationship of Part to Whole 1859–1920* (Palgrave Macmillan, 2010). Her recent co-edited books include *The Politics of Gender in Anthony Trollope's Novels: New Readings for the Twenty-First Century* (Ashgate, 2009) and *The Palgrave Sourcebook on Victorian Literature* (Palgrave Macmillan, 2012). Her book on the global circulation of the literatures of liberalization is forthcoming in 2019 in the Palgrave series New Comparisons in World Literature. From 2009 to 2012 she was President of the British Association for Victorian Studies.

Michal Peled Ginsburg is Professor Emerita of French and Comparative Literature at Northwestern University. She is the author of books on the nineteenth-century novel in England and France, including *Economies of Change: Form and Transformation in the Nineteenth-Century Novel* (Stanford University Press, 1996). She is also the author of numerous articles and essays on Dickens's novels. Her most recent book is *Portrait Stories* (Fordham University Press, 2015).

Ruth Glancy is professor emerita at Concordia University of Edmonton. Her publications include editions of Dickens's Christmas writings and several annotated bibliographies of Dickens's works as well as student companions and handbooks. She is currently preparing an edition of the complete Christmas numbers for the Oxford Edition of Dickens and an annotated bibliography of *Little Dorrit*.

John Glavin is Professor of English and Director of the Office of Fellowships, Awards and Resources for Undergraduates at Georgetown University. His publications include *After Dickens: Reading, Adaptation and Performance* (Cambridge University Press, 1999), *Dickens on Screen* (Cambridge University Press, 2003), and *Dickens Adapted* (Ashgate, 2012). His memoir *The Good New: Tuscany in 2000*, an account of teaching Shakespeare's Italian plays in Italy, was published by New Academia Press (dated 2018). At Georgetown he offers courses in Writing for the Screen. As John G. he is also the namesake of the villain in the award-winning film *Memento* (2000), written by his former student Jonathan Nolan.

Jennifer Gribble is Honorary Associate Professor of English at the University of Sydney. Her publications include *The Lady of Shalott in the Victorian Novel* (Macmillan, 1983), an edition of George Eliot's *Scenes of Clerical Life* for Penguin (1998), and a recent series of articles and book chapters on Dickens. She is currently working on a study of Dickens and the Bible.

Helen Groth is Professor of English and Associate Dean of Arts and Social Sciences, University of New South Wales. Her publications include *Victorian Photography and Literary Nostalgia* (Oxford University Press, 2004), *Moving Images: Nineteenth-Century Reading and Screen Practices* (Edinburgh University Press, 2013) and, with Natalya Lusty, *Dreams and Modernity: A Cultural History* (Routledge, 2013). She has recently co-edited two collections, *Sounding Modernism* (Edinburgh University Press, 2017) and *Mindful Aesthetics: Literature and the Science of Mind* (Bloomsbury, 2013), and has published on Victorian visual culture, literature and dreams, and, more recently, sound and literature. Forthcoming are a chapter on rioting in *Barnaby Rudge* in *Sound, Space and Civility in the British World, c.1700–1900*, edited by Bruce Buchan et al. (Palgrave, 2018), and a chapter on 'Charlotte Brontë and the Listening Reader' in *The Brontës and the Idea of the Human*, edited by Alexandra Lewis (Cambridge University Press, 2019). She has two current book projects, one on 'The Listening Reader' and another on rioting in the literary archive from 1780 to the present.

Mary Hammond is Professor of English and Book History at the University of Southampton, UK, and founding Director of the Southampton Centre for Nineteenth-Century Research. Her books include *Reading, Publishing and the Formation of Literary Taste in England, 1880–1914* (Ashgate, 2006), *Charles Dickens's Great Expectations: A Cultural Life 1860–2012* (Ashgate, 2015), and a number of co-edited collections including *Publishing in the First World War* (Palgrave, 2007), *Books Without Borders* (2 volumes, Palgrave, 2008), *Rural–Urban Relationships in the Nineteenth Century: Uneasy Neighbours* (Routledge, 2016), and *The Edinburgh History of Reading: A World Survey from Antiquity to the Present* (2 volumes, Edinburgh University Press, forthcoming in 2019).

Molly Clark Hillard is Associate Professor of English at Seattle University, specializing in Victorian literature. She is the author of *Spellbound: The Fairy Tale and the Victorians* (Ohio State University Press, 2014). Her essays have appeared in such venues as *Narrative, SEL, Partial Answers, Boundary II Online, RaVoN*, and *Dickens Studies Annual*. She is at work on her next book project, about the networking of Victorian and twenty-first-century literatures.

Michael Hollington is currently Honorary Research Fellow at the University of Kent Canterbury and in the past has been Professor at the University of New South Wales, at the University of Toulouse-Le Mirail, and elsewhere. He is best known as a Dickensian for his book *Dickens and the Grotesque* (Routledge, 1984; reissued 2014) and two edited collections, *Charles Dickens: Critical Assessments* (Helm Information, 1995: 4 vols) and *The Reception of Charles Dickens in Europe* (Bloomsbury, 2013: 2 vols), but he has published books and articles on many other writers including Katherine Mansfield and Günter Grass.

Juliet John is Hildred Carlile Chair of English Literature at Royal Holloway, University of London and Head of the Department of English. She has published widely on Victorian literature and culture. Her books include *Dickens and Mass Culture* (Oxford University Press, 2010; paperback 2013), *Dickens's Villains: Melodrama, Character, Popular Culture* (Oxford University Press, 2001; paperback 2003), and *The Oxford Handbook of Victorian Literary Culture* (Oxford University Press, 2016). She is Editor-in-Chief of *Oxford Bibliographies: Victorian Literature*.

John O. Jordan is Research Professor of Literature at the University of California, Santa Cruz, and Director of the Dickens Project. He is the author of *Supposing* Bleak House (University of Virginia Press, 2011), editor of the *Cambridge Companion to Charles Dickens* (Cambridge University Press, 2001), co-editor, with Nirshan Perera, of *Global Dickens* (Ashgate, 2012), and co-editor, with Robert L. Patten, of *Literature in the*

Marketplace: Nineteenth-Century British Publishing and Reading Practices (Cambridge University Press, 1995).

Leon Litvack is Professor of Victorian Studies at the Queen's University of Belfast, Northern Ireland. He is Principal Editor of the Charles Dickens Letters Project, and a world authority on Dickens's manuscripts, handwriting, and photographic portraits. His publications have revolved around historical and visual approaches to the author. This has led him to produce intricately researched studies on Dickens's interest in Australia and the convict experience; his passion for education; his lifetime reading; his intimate knowledge of the topography of London and south-east England; his life at his home, Gad's Hill; his photographic portraits and the cultivation of celebrity; his methods of composition; his journalism; and his death and funeral. He is the author of the comprehensive annotated bibliography of *Dombey and Son*, and is currently working on two book-length projects: a volume of essays entitled *Reading Dickens Differently*, and the authoritative Oxford edition of *Our Mutual Friend*.

Allen MacDuffie is an Associate Professor in the English Department at the University of Texas at Austin. His first book, *Victorian Literature, Energy, and the Ecological Imagination*, was published by Cambridge University Press in 2014, and won the Sonya Rudikoff Award for best first scholarly book in the field of Victorian Studies. His essays on Victorian fiction and poetry have appeared in *Representations*, *ELH*, *PMLA*, and *Philological Quarterly*, and his most recent work, on the television series *Breaking Bad* and contemporary serial narrative, is forthcoming from *Cultural Critique*.

Hazel Mackenzie is Lecturer and Research Lead for English Literature at the University of Buckingham. Her speciality is Victorian periodical studies. She has published essays on the journalism of Charles Dickens, William Makepeace Thackeray, Anthony Trollope, and George Eliot. She is currently working on a research companion to Dickens's *The Old Curiosity Shop* for Liverpool University Press.

Jennifer McDonell is a Senior Lecturer at the University of New England (Australia). She has published on Robert Browning and Elizabeth Barrett Browning in such journals as *Modern Language Quarterly*, *Critical Survey*, and *Australian Literary Studies*. Chapters on Dickens have been published in *Animals in Victorian Literature and Culture* (Palgrave, 2017) and *Reading Literary Animals: Medieval to Modern* (Routledge, forthcoming 2018). Jennifer is also the author of 'The Animal Turn, Literary Studies, and the Academy', *Literary Theory: An Anthology*, 3rd edition, ed. Julie Rivkin and Michael Ryan (Blackwell, 2017) and 'Animals' in *The Encyclopedia of Victorian Literature* (Blackwell, 2015).

Richard Menke, Associate Professor of English at the University of Georgia, is the author of *Telegraphic Realism: Victorian Fiction and Other Information Systems* (Stanford University Press, 2008). His essays on nineteenth-century literature, science, and technology have appeared in journals such as *ELH*, *PMLA*, *Critical Inquiry*, *English Language Notes*, *Victorian Periodicals Review*, and *Victorian Studies*.

Helena Michie is the author of five books in Victorian Studies and the study of gender and sexuality. Her most recent, *Love Among the Archives: Writing the Lives of Sir George Scharf, Victorian Bachelor*, with Robyn Warhol (Edinburgh University Press. 2015), won the North American Victorian Studies Association's 2015 Best Book of the Year prize. Some of her other works include *Victorian Honeymoons: Journeys to the Conjugal* (Cambridge University Press, 2006); *The Flesh Made Word: Female Figures and Women's Bodies* (Oxford University Press, 1987); and *Sororophobia: Differences among Women in Literature and Culture* (Oxford University Press, 1991). Professor Michie teaches courses in feminist theory, literary theory, and Victorian literature and culture at Rice University. She also teaches classes and workshops on professional writing. Her current project, *Homing*, is about the historical emergence of the modern concept of home, and comes out of her interest in the long and wide nineteenth century.

Francesca Orestano, Professor of English Literature at the University of Milan, is the author of *Dal neoclassico al classico* (Compostampa, 1990), on John Neal and the American Renaissance; *Paesaggio e finzione: William Gilpin e il pittoresco* (Unicopli, 2000); *La parola e lo sguardo* (Adriatica, 2005); and editor of *Strange Sisters: Literature and Aesthetics in the XIX c.* (Lang, 2009). She works on John Ruskin, art criticism, chemistry, and the reception of the Italian Renaissance; on history, biography, and Virginia Woolf. In the field of children's literature, she has worked on Maria Edgeworth, Charles and Mary Lamb, Charles Darwin and animal stories, and the First World War. She has written on Dickens and American landscape, the magic lantern, *A Holiday Romance*, Dickens's tramps, Dickens and blindness, and Dickens and Virginia Woolf; and edited with Michael Hollington *Dickens and Italy* (Cambridge Scholars, 2009). With Michael Vickers she has edited *Not Just Porridge: English Literati at Table* (Archaeopress, 2017), a gastronomic history of English literature from Chaucer to the present time.

Dr Pete Orford is Course Director of the MA by Research in Charles Dickens Studies at the University of Buckingham, and an Academic Associate of the Charles Dickens Museum. He created the Drood Inquiry (<http://www.droodinquiry.com>), an open-access, interactive exploration of potential endings to *The Mystery of Edwin Drood*, and curated the exhibition 'Solving *Edwin Drood*: A Dickensian Whodunnit' at the Charles Dickens Museum. His book, *The Mystery of Edwin Drood: Charles Dickens' Unfinished Novel and our Endless Attempts to End it*, is due for publication with Pen and Sword Books in 2018.

Wendy Parkins is Professor of Victorian Literature at the University of Kent. She has published several articles on Dickens, emotion, and the ethics of vulnerability. She is the author of *Jane Morris: The Burden of History* (Edinburgh University Press, 2013) and *Mobility and Modernity in British Women's Novels, 1850s–1930s* (Palgrave Macmillan, 2009).

David Paroissien is Professorial Research Fellow, Buckingham University and Emeritus Professor of English, University of Massachusetts, Amherst. Recent publications include: ' "Dedlocked": The Case Against the Past in *Bleak House* and *A Child's History* *of England'*, in Christine Huguet (ed.), *Charles Dickens: L'Inimitable/The Inimitable* (Democratic Books, 2011), 123–61; 'Our Island's Story: Dickens's Search for a National Identity', in Hazel Mackenzie and Ben Winyard (eds), *Charles Dickens and the Mid-Victorian Press, 1850–1870* (University of Buckingham Press, 2013), 297–304; 'Dickens and the Voices of History', in Christine Huguet and Nathalie Vanfasse (eds), *Charles Dickens: Modernism, Modernity*, Colloque de Cerisy (Édition du Sagittaire, 2014), 103–18; and 'Dickens the Historian, Carlyle the Novelist, and Dickens, Carlyle and the French Revolution', in Alexander Lyon Macfie (ed.), *The Fiction of History* (Routledge, 2015), 72–82.

Robert L. Patten is Senior Research Scholar at the Institute of English Studies, School of Advanced Study, University of London, and a Corresponding Fellow of the English Association, though he mainly works from home in New Mexico. He has written extensively about Dickens and the graphic artists Hablot Knight Browne ('Phiz') and George Cruikshank, and also published essays on Charlotte Brontë, Alfred, Lord Tennyson, William Makepeace Thackeray, Victorian illustration, nineteenth-century print culture, nineteenth-century European 'realism', and the concept of authorship. He has served as Chair of the Victorian Division of the MLA and as President of the Society for the History of Authorship, Reading and Publishing. *Charles Dickens and 'Boz'* (Cambridge University Press, 2012) was accorded the Colby Prize from the Research Society for Victorian Periodicals, and an enlarged reprint of a 1978 book, *Charles Dickens and his Publishers*, was issued from Oxford in 2017. He is now editing the Oxford Edition of Dickens's Christmas books.

Paul Schlicke retired in 2010 from the University of Aberdeen, where he taught from 1971. He is author of *Dickens and Popular Entertainment* (Allen and Unwin, 1985, 2016), *Coffee with Dickens* (Duncan Baird, 2008), and *Simply Dickens* (Simply Charly, 2016) as well as many articles and reviews, primarily in *The Dickensian* and *Dickens Quarterly*. He is editor of six Dickens titles (*Pickwick, Nickleby, The Old Curiosity Shop, Hard Times, Sketches of Young Gentlemen*, and *Sketches of Young Couples*) and of *The Oxford Companion to Charles Dickens* (Oxford University Press, 1999, 2011). He is compiler of *The Old Curiosity Shop: An Annotated Bibliography* (Garland, 1988) and of the Dickens entry in the *Cambridge Bibliography of English Literature*, 3rd edn (Cambridge University Press, 1999). He is past president of the Dickens Society and of the Dickens Fellowship, and former chair of the board of the Charles Dickens Museum. His Oxford edition of *Sketches by Boz* is in production.

Grahame Smith retired in 2000 as Emeritus Professor of English Studies at the University of Stirling, having previously held appointments at UCLA and the University of Wales, and a two-year secondment from Stirling to the University of Malawi. In addition to numerous articles and essays on Dickens and on film, his major publications are *Dickens, Money and Society* (University of California Press, 1968); *The Novel and Society: Defoe to George Eliot* (Batsford, 1984); *Charles Dickens: A Literary Life* (St. Martin's Press, 1996); and *Dickens and the Dream of Cinema* (Manchester University

Press, 2003). He also edited *Hard Times* for the 1994 Everyman Dickens for which the General Editor was Professor Michael Slater. From 2009 to 2011 he was President of the Dickens Fellowship.

Jonathan Smith is William E. Stirton Professor of English at the University of Michigan-Dearborn. He has published numerous works on Victorian literature and science, including *Charles Darwin and Victorian Visual Culture* (Cambridge University Press, 2006) and *Fact and Feeling: Baconian Science and the Nineteenth-Century Literary Imagination* (Wisconsin University Press, 1994). He is also the editor, with Piers Hale, of *Negotiating Boundaries* (Pickering and Chatto, 2011), volume 1 of *Victorian Science and Literature*. His essay on 'The Victorian Novel and Science' appeared in *The Oxford Handbook of the Victorian Novel* (Oxford University Press, 2013).

Tyson Stolte is a Professor in the Department of English at New Mexico State University. He has published essays on the connections between Dickens's fiction and Victorian psychological debate in *Victorian Review, Novel: A Forum on Fiction*, and *Victorian Literature and Culture*, and his articles on other topics have appeared in *Dickens Studies Annual* and *Victorian Poetry*. He is currently at work on a monograph about Dickens, first-person narration, and nineteenth-century mental science.

Jeremy Tambling, formerly Professor of Literature at Manchester University, and of Comparative Literature, University of Hong Kong, is author of books on literary and cultural theory. Amongst his recent books are *Dickens' Novels as Poetry: Allegory and Literature of the City* (Routledge, 2014) and *Histories of the Devil: From Marlowe to Mann and the Manichees* (Palgrave, 2017). He edited *The Palgrave Handbook of Literature and the City* (2017).

Robert Tracy is Emeritus Professor of English and Celtic Studies at the University of California, Berkeley. He has been a Visiting Professor at the University of Leeds, Wellesley College, and Trinity College, Dublin, a frequent lecturer at University of California Santa Cruz's annual Dickens Universe, and is an Advisory Editor of *Dickens Studies Annual* and *LIST*. His publications include *Trollope's Later Novels* (University of California Press, 1978), *Stone* (Princeton University Press, 1981, a translation of 81 poems by the Russian poet Osip Mandelstam), *The Unappeasable Host: Studies in Irish Identities* (University College Dublin Press, 1998), and articles about William Butler Yeats, James Joyce, Dickens, William Trevor, Brian Friel, and Seamus Heaney. He has also edited Anthony Trollope's *The MacDermotts of Ballycloran* and Sheridan Le Fanu's *In a Glass Darkly* for the Oxford's World Classics series. In 2008–9 he was President of the Dickens Society.

Daniel Tyler is a Fellow and Director of Studies at Trinity Hall, Cambridge University. He is the editor of *Dickens's Style* (Cambridge University Press, 2013) and Dickens's *The Uncommercial Traveller* (Oxford University Press, 2015).

Chris R. Vanden Bossche is Professor Emeritus, University of Notre Dame. His work on Dickens and class includes a chapter on *Barnaby Rudge* in his book *Reform Acts: Chartism, Social Agency and the Victorian Novel, 1832–1867* (Johns Hopkins

University Press, 2014) as well as articles on *David Copperfield* and *Bleak House* in, respectively, *Dickens Studies Annual* and *Victorian Studies*.

Nathalie Vanfasse is Professor of English at Aix-Marseille Université, France. She graduated from the École Normale Supérieure in Paris and the Paris School of Political Science (Institut d'Études Politiques de Paris) and holds a Ph.D. from the University of Paris IV-Sorbonne. Her monograph *Dickens entre normes et déviance* (Publications de l'Université de Provence) was short-listed for the 2008 prize of the SAES/AFEA (French Society for British and American Academic Studies), and she is the author of articles and chapters on Dickens's work and on nineteenth-century travel writing. She has co-edited special issues on *Dickens Matters, Dickens His/story* (*Dickens Quarterly*, 2012); *Dickens in the New Millennium* (*Les Cahiers Victoriens et Edouardiens*, 2012); and two volumes on *Charles Dickens, Modernism, Modernity: Colloque de Cerisy* (Éditions du Sagittaire, 2014). Her new monograph entitled *La plume et la route: Charles Dickens écrivain-voyageur* (Presses de l'Université de Provence, 2017) won the 2018 SELVA Prize (Société d'Etude de la Littérature de Voyage du Monde Anglophone).

Jon Michael Varese is the Director for Public Outreach at the Dickens Project, where he has worked for two decades to bring Dickens and Victorian Literature to audiences beyond the traditional academy. He is the editor of the 2012 Barnes and Noble Signature edition of *Great Expectations*, and his popular work on Dickens and the Victorians has appeared in the *Guardian* UK online and the *San Francisco Chronicle*.

David Vincent is Emeritus Professor of Social History, The Open University. His recent publications include *The Culture of Secrecy: Britain 1832–1998* (Oxford University Press, 1998), *The Rise of Mass Literacy. Reading and Writing in Modern Europe* (Polity Press, 2000), '*I Hope I Don't Intrude': Privacy and its Dilemmas in Nineteenth-Century Britain* (Oxford University Press, 2015), and *Privacy: A Short History* (Polity Press, 2016).

Catherine Waters is Professor of Victorian Literature and Print Culture at the University of Kent. She is the author of *Dickens and the Politics of the Family* (Cambridge University Press, 1997) and *Commodity Culture in Dickens's* Household Words: *The Social Life of Goods* (Ashgate, 2008). She is series editor of the six-volume collection *A Library of Essays on Charles Dickens* (Ashgate, 2012) and has co-edited several essay collections devoted to Dickens, the most recent being *Dickens and the Imagined Child*, co-edited with Peter Merchant (Ashgate, 2015). She is a member of the editorial advisory board of the *Dickens Journals Online* project and a vice-president of the Canterbury branch of the Dickens Fellowship.

Sharon Aronofsky Weltman is William E. 'Bud' Davis Alumni Professor of English at Louisiana State University. Her *Ruskin's Mythic Queen: Gender Subversion in Victorian Culture* (Ohio University Press, 1999) was named an Outstanding Academic Book by *Choice* magazine in 1999. She wrote *Performing the Victorian: John Ruskin and Identity in Theater, Science, and Education* (Ohio State University Press, 2007) and in 2011 guest-edited the 1847 melodrama *The String of Pearls* (*Sweeney Todd*) for *Nineteenth-Century Theatre and Film*, which she now co-edits. Her essay on performing Jewishness in *Oliver!* appeared in *Dickens Adapted: Best Essays*, edited by John Glavin (Ashgate, 2012). In 2014, she directed a National Endowment for the Humanities Summer Seminar for College and University Teachers on Dickens and adaptation. Her current book project, *Victorians on Broadway*, examines adaptations of Victorian literature to the popular stage and other media in the nineteenth and twentieth centuries (especially Broadway musicals), including two chapters on Dickens.

Tony Williams was President of The Dickens Fellowship from 2015 to 2017. He is Associate Editor of the Fellowship's journal, *The Dickensian*, and a Senior Honorary Research Fellow in Humanities at the University of Buckingham. A graduate of the University of Wales, Swansea, and of Birkbeck College, University of London, he taught English in state schools in England from 1969 to 1997 and is a frequent speaker on Dickens-related topics in the United Kingdom and elsewhere. He is an Honorary Academic Advisor to the Charles Dickens Museum in London and worked with the Museum of London on its Dickens bicentenary exhibition including co-authoring with Alex Werner *Dickens's Victorian London 1839–1901* (Random House, 2012).

Sarah Winter is Professor of English and Comparative Literary and Cultural Studies at the University of Connecticut, Storrs. She has published two books, *The Pleasures of Memory: Learning to Read with Charles Dickens* (Fordham University Press, 2011) and *Freud and the Institution of Psychoanalytic Knowledge* (Stanford University Press, 1999), as well as articles on Charles Darwin's theories of emotional expression, language, and race; on the novel and human rights; and on Victorian ethnography and pedagogy. Her current book project, supported by a US National Endowment for the Humanities Fellowship for 2016–17, focuses on the history of habeas corpus, human rights, and the novel, and includes a chapter on Dickens's stories about insolvent debtors and political prisoners.

Dr Claire Wood is Lecturer in Victorian Literature at the University of Leicester. She is the author of *Dickens and the Business of Death* (Cambridge University Press, 2015), a Trustee of the Dickens Society, and part of the Editorial Board for *Dickens Quarterly*. Her research interests include Victorian death culture, materiality, and afterlives. In 2013 she completed a postdoc at the Charles Dickens Museum, London, investigating the reach and diversity of activities organized to celebrate the Dickens 2012 Bicentenary. Her current research explores different forms of death comedy in the work of Dickens and other nineteenth-century writers.

Kay Young is Professor of English and Comparative Literature and Director of the Literature and Mind programme at the University of California, Santa Barbara. From 2005 to 2010, she was on an academic fellowship at the Institute of Contemporary Psychoanalysis in Los Angeles. Her books include *Ordinary Pleasures: Couples, Conversation, and Comedy* (Ohio State University Press, 2001) and *Imagining Minds: The Neuro-Aesthetics* *of Austen, Eliot, and Hardy* (Ohio State University Press, 2010). Currently, she is writing on attachment theory and the verbal arts.

Paul Young is Senior Lecturer in Victorian Literature and Culture in the Department of English, University of Exeter. His first book, entitled *Globalization and the Great Exhibition: The Victorian New World Order*, was published as part of the Palgrave Studies in Nineteenth-Century Writing and Culture Series in 2009. Building upon this work, he has continued to explore cultural dimensions of Victorian imperialism and globalization, publishing articles and essays that consider how different literary and cultural forms—from the Gothic mode to the Adventure story to geographical board games—can be understood with relation to nineteenth-century Britain's global expansion. He is currently working on his new monograph project, entitled *Carnivorous Empire: Adventure Fiction and the Global Growth of Britain's Meat Markets, 1865–1915*, which is contracted to appear with Johns Hopkins University Press.

Dickens Timeline

1812 7 Feb.	CD born in Portsmouth, Hampshire
1816 Apr.	Dickens family moves to London
1817 ?June	Dickens family moves to Chatham
?1821–Dec. 1822	CD at Revd William Giles's school, Chatham
1822–3	Dickens family moves back to London
?1823–4	CD employed at Warren's Blacking Factory
1824 Mar.–May	John Dickens in the Marshalsea Debtors' Prison
1824–7	CD at Wellington House Academy, London
1827–8	CD employed as a solicitor's clerk at Ellis and Blackmore, then by Charles Molloy
?1829–?1831	CD a shorthand reporter at Doctors' Commons
1830 8 Feb.	CD admitted as a reader to the British Museum
?1831	CD joins staff of the *Mirror of Parliament*
1832 ?Mar.	CD becomes a parliamentary reporter on the *True Sun*
1833 1 Dec.	'A Dinner at Poplar Walk' published in the *Monthly Magazine*
1834–6	CD publishes further stories in the *Morning* and *Evening Chronicle*, *Bell's Life in London*, and elsewhere
1834 Aug.	CD becomes a news reporter and sometime drama critic on the *Morning Chronicle* and later *Evening Chronicle*
1835 ?May	CD engaged to Catherine Hogarth
1836 Feb.	*Sketches by Boz*, First Series in two volumes, published by John Macrone
31 Mar.	*Pickwick Papers* Part I, 'edited' by 'Boz', in 20 as 19 monthly numbers dated from April to November 1837, published by Chapman and Hall
2 Apr.	CD marries Catherine Hogarth
June	*Sunday Under Three Heads*, CD using pseudonym of 'Timothy Sparks', published by Chapman and Hall
Sept.–Dec.	Two theatrical productions, *The Strange Gentleman* and *The Village Coquettes*, staged and published

4 Nov.	CD signs Agreement with Richard Bentley to edit *Bentley's Miscellany* from Jan. 1837; subsequently CD resigns from the *Morning Chronicle*
17 Dec.	*Sketches by Boz*, Second Series in one volume, published by John Macrone
1836–7 Winter	CD meets John Forster
1837 31 Jan.	*Oliver Twist* chapter 1 published in *Bentley's Miscellany*; runs for 24 monthly instalments dated from February 1837 to April 1839
Apr.	CD family moves into 48 Doughty Street
7 May	Mary Hogarth dies; publication of *Pickwick* and *Oliver Twist* suspended for a month
1 Nov.	*Pickwick* XIX/XX published; first number of Chapman and Hall 20 Part *Sketches by Boz* published, to June 1839
17 Nov.	*Pickwick Papers* published by Chapman and Hall in one volume
1838 10 Feb.	*Sketches of Young Gentlemen*, anonymous, published by Chapman and Hall
26 Feb.	*Memoirs of Joseph Grimaldi*, 'edited' by 'Boz', published by Richard Bentley
31 Mar.	*Nicholas Nickleby* Part I, by 'Boz', in 20 as 19 monthly numbers dated from April 1838 to October 1839, published by Chapman and Hall
9 Nov.	*Oliver Twist* published by Richard Bentley in three volumes; subsequent editions give both CD and 'Boz' as author
1839 31 Jan.	CD resigns editorship of *Bentley's Miscellany*
23 Oct.	*Nicholas Nickleby* published by Chapman and Hall in one volume
Dec.	CD family moves to 1 Devonshire Terrace
1840 10 Feb.	*Sketches of Young Couples*, anonymously, published by Chapman and Hall
4 Apr.	*Master Humphrey's Clock* No. 1 published by Chapman and Hall; runs to 4 Dec. 1841 in weekly numbers
25 Apr.	First instalment of *The Old Curiosity Shop* published in *Master Humphrey's Clock*; runs uninterruptedly from No. 12 (20 June)
15 Oct.	*Master Humphrey's Clock* Vol. 1 published by Chapman and Hall
1841 6 Feb.	Final instalment of *The Old Curiosity Shop* published
13 Feb.	First instalment of *Barnaby Rudge* published in *Master Humphrey's Clock*; runs uninterruptedly through 42 weekly numbers
Apr.	*Master Humphrey's Clock* Vol. 2 published by Chapman and Hall

4 Dec.	Final number of *Master Humphrey's Clock*
15 Dec.	*Master Humphrey's Clock* Vol. 3, and one-volume editions of *The Old Curiosity Shop* and *Barnaby Rudge*, published by Chapman and Hall
1842 Jan.–June	CD and Catherine travel to America and Canada
19 Oct.	*American Notes* is published by Chapman and Hall
31 Dec.	*Martin Chuzzlewit* Part I, 'edited' by 'Boz', in 20 as 19 monthly numbers dated from January 1843 to July 1844, published by Chapman and Hall
1843	CD publishes various articles in the *Examiner*
19 Dec.	*A Christmas Carol* is published by Chapman and Hall
1844 30 June	Final number of *Martin Chuzzlewit*, and one-volume edition, published by Chapman and Hall
2 July	CD family travels to Italy; CD stays there, with brief trips to France and London, until 3 July 1845
16 Dec.	*The Chimes* is published by Chapman and Hall, and Bradbury and Evans
1845–9	CD drafts his 'Autobiographical Fragment' at various times and shares some early memories with Forster; portions adapted for *David Copperfield* and others later published in first volume of Forster's biography
20 Sept.	First performance by CD's troupe, the Company of Amateurs, of Ben Jonson's *Every Man in his Humour*
20 Dec.	*The Cricket on the Hearth* is published by Bradbury and Evans
31 Dec.	*Oliver Twist*, revised, is published in ten monthly parts dated from January 1846 to October by Bradbury and Evans
1846 Jan.–Mar.	CD editor of the *Daily News* (deed of partnership 21 Jan.), resigns editorship 9 Feb.; publishes 'Travelling Letters' (from Italy)
24 Jan.–11 Mar.	CD contributes verses and articles to the *Daily News* to Mar.
18 May	*Pictures from Italy* published by Bradbury and Evans
31 May	CD family departs for Switzerland, later Paris, until Feb. 1847
summer	CD writes for and reads to his children 'The Children's New Testament', published 1934 as *The Life of Our Lord*
30 Sept.	*Dombey and Son* Part I, in 20 as 19 monthly numbers, dated from October 1846 to April 1848, published by Bradbury and Evans
19 Dec.	*The Battle of Life* is published by Bradbury and Evans
1847 27 Mar.	First instalment of the Cheap Edition of CD's works published by Chapman and Hall, and Bradbury and Evans; continues throughout his lifetime and beyond

5 June	CD arranges lease of Urania Cottage, opens in Nov.
1848 Apr.	*Dombey and Son* published in one volume by Bradbury and Evans
19 Dec.	*The Haunted Man* published by Bradbury and Evans
1849 30 Apr.	*David Copperfield* Part I, in 20 as 19 monthly numbers dated from May 1849 to November 1850, published by Bradbury and Evans
1850 27 Mar.	*Household Words* first weekly number; CD 'conductor' and contributor
Nov.	CD's Company of Amateurs perform Jonson's *Every Man in his Humour*
1 Nov.	*David Copperfield* published in one volume by Bradbury and Evans
1850s	CD in great demand as a speaker at celebratory dinners; with Bulwer Lytton organizes Guild of Literature and Art
1851 15 Jan.	The Company of Amateurs perform at Rockingham Castle
Jan.	*A Child's History of England* begins irregular serialization in *Household Words*; completed in 39 episodes, 10 Dec. 1853
31 Mar.	Death of John Dickens
14 Apr.	Death of Dora Annie Dickens
May	The Company of Amateurs perform Bulwer Lytton's *Not So Bad as We Seem* at Devonshire House before Queen Victoria, following with public performances in London and other cities to 3 Sept. 1853
1852 28 Feb.	*Bleak House* Part I, in 20 as 19 monthly numbers dated from March 1852 to September 1853, published by Bradbury and Evans
1853 31 Aug.	*Bleak House* XIX/XX published; one-volume edition follows shortly thereafter
Dec.	CD begins Public Readings with *Carol* and *Cricket on the Hearth*
1854 1 Apr.	First instalment of *Hard Times* in *Household Words*; continues weekly to 12 Aug.; one-volume edition follows shortly thereafter
1855 June	Performances of Wilkie Collins's *The Lighthouse* at Tavistock House and elsewhere
30 Nov.	*Little Dorrit* Part I, in 20 as 19 monthly numbers dated from December 1855 to July 1857, published by Chapman and Hall
1856 14 Mar.	CD concludes purchase of Gad's Hill Place
1857 Jan.	The Company of Amateurs perform Wilkie Collins's *The Frozen Deep* at Tavistock House; further performances in other locations through August, including one before Queen Victoria on 4 July

13 Feb.	CD takes possession of Gad's Hill
30 June	*Little Dorrit* XIX/XX published; one-volume edition published shortly thereafter
21–4 Aug.	Ternans join the Company of Amateurs for Manchester performances of *The Frozen Deep*
3–31 Oct.	*The Lazy Tour of Two Idle Apprentices* by CD and Wilkie Collins published in weekly instalments in *Household Words*
1858 29 Apr.	CD's first paid Reading for his own benefit in St Martin's Hall; series of 17 continues until 22 July
7 June	CD's 'personal' statement about his separation from Catherine published in *The Times*
2 Aug.	Commencement of first Reading tour; 85 performances ending 13 Nov.
16 Aug.	The 'Violated Letter' published in *New York Tribune*; reprinted in UK newspapers on 31 Aug.
24 Dec.	First series of eight Christmas Readings in St Martin's Hall; continued to 10 Feb. 1859
1859 30 Apr.	First issue of *All the Year Round*, which CD 'conducts' and contributes to; *A Tale of Two Cities* appears weekly until 26 Nov. and is reprinted in monthly parts and published in one volume on 21 Nov. by Chapman and Hall
28 May	Final number of *Household Words*
1860 28 Jan.	CD commences 'The Uncommercial Traveller' papers, published in *All the Year Round* irregularly and collected into volumes on 15 Dec. 1860 (1861 on title page), and in 1865 and 1874.
Oct.	Final move into Gad's Hill
1 Dec.	*Great Expectations* commences in weekly numbers in *All the Year Round* until 3 Aug. 1861
1861	CD gives further Readings, Mar.–Apr. 1861 and Oct. 1861–Jan. 1862
5 July	Three-volume edition of *Great Expectations* published
1862–3	From 20 June 1862 until 16 Feb. 1863, CD and members of his family live mainly in France
1863 12 Sept.	Elizabeth (Mrs John) Dickens, CD's mother, dies
1864 30 Apr.	*Our Mutual Friend* Part I, in 20 as 19 monthly numbers dated from May 1864 to November 1865, published by Chapman and Hall
1865 31 Jan.	*Our Mutual Friend* Vol. 1 published by Chapman and Hall
9 June	CD involved in railway accident at Staplehurst, Kent

Nov	*Our Mutual Friend* Vol. 2 published by Chapman and Hall
1866 10 Apr.	First provincial and London Reading tour organized by George Dolby; concludes 12 June
1867–8	Diamond Edition of CD's works, 14 volumes, published in Boston by Ticknor and Fields
1867 15 Jan.	Second provincial, Ireland, and London Reading tour managed by Dolby; concludes 13 May
end May	*Pickwick Papers*, Vol. 1 of Charles Dickens Edition, published by Chapman and Hall; Edition concludes posthumously in 1875
9 Nov.	CD sails from Liverpool to Boston for American Reading tour
1868 Jan.–Feb.	'George Silverman's Explanation' published in three instalments in the *Atlantic Monthly*, and in Feb. in *All the Year Round*
Jan.–Apr.	'Holiday Romance' published in Ticknor and Fields's *Our Young Folks* in four instalments, and Jan.–Apr. in *All the Year Round*
2 May	CD arrives in London at conclusion of his second American tour
19 Sept.	CD announces abolition of the Christmas numbers of *All the Year Round*
6 Oct.	CD commences Farewell provincial Reading tour of 72 performances
1869 22 Apr.	CD collapses at Preston; cancels rest of Reading tour
Nov.	As literary executor, CD publishes *Religious Opinions of the Late Chauncy Hare Townshend*
1870 Jan.–June	CD rents 5 Hyde Park Place, London
11 Jan.	CD commences Farewell Readings in London
15 Mar.	Final Reading of the series; two other morning Readings given, 14 and 21 Mar., for a theatrical charity
31 Mar.	*The Mystery of Edwin Drood*, Part I, dated April, published by Chapman and Hall; monthly parts concluded, unfinished, 31 Aug., dated September.
8 June	CD suffers a stroke; does not regain consciousness
9 June	CD dies
14 June	Private burial ceremony in Westminster Abbey
12 Aug.	One-volume *Drood* published
1871–3	Forster's three-volume biography published in annual instalments, Nov. 1871, Nov. 1872, and Dec. 1873, but dated as following years, 1872, 1873, and 1874

DICKENS FAMILY TREE

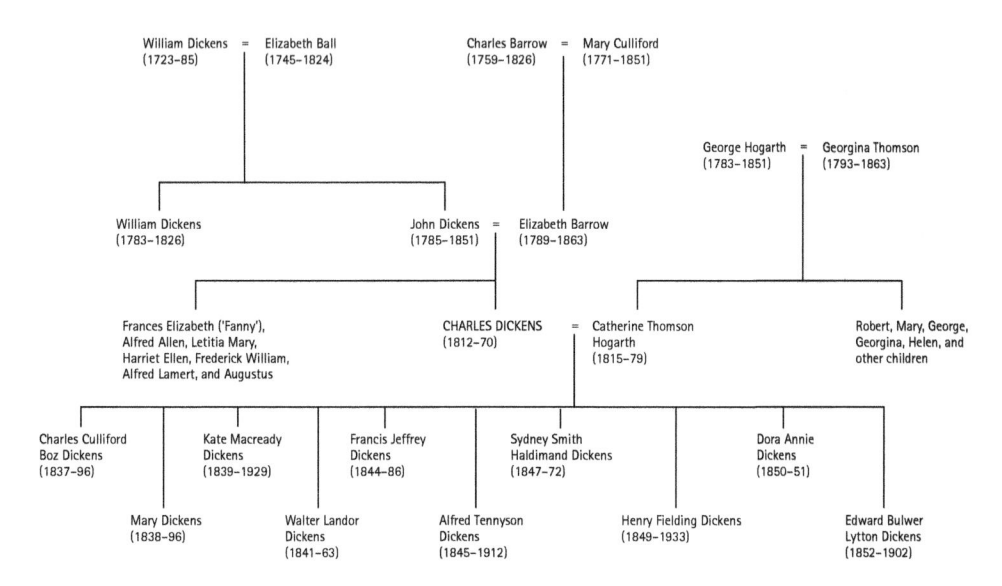

- William Dickens (1723–85) = Elizabeth Ball (1745–1824)
- Charles Barrow (1759–1826) = Mary Culliford (1771–1851)
- George Hogarth (1783–1851) = Georgina Thomson (1793–1863)

Children of William Dickens and Elizabeth Ball:
- William Dickens (1783–1826)
- John Dickens (1785–1851) = Elizabeth Barrow (1789–1863) [daughter of Charles Barrow and Mary Culliford]

Children of John Dickens and Elizabeth Barrow:
- Frances Elizabeth ('Fanny'), Alfred Allen, Letitia Mary, Harriet Ellen, Frederick William, Alfred Lamert, and Augustus
- CHARLES DICKENS (1812–70) = Catherine Thomson Hogarth (1815–79)

Children of George Hogarth and Georgina Thomson:
- Catherine Thomson Hogarth (1815–79)
- Robert, Mary, George, Georgina, Helen, and other children

Children of Charles Dickens and Catherine Thomson Hogarth:
- Charles Culliford Boz Dickens (1837–96)
- Mary Dickens (1838–96)
- Kate Macready Dickens (1839–1929)
- Walter Landor Dickens (1841–63)
- Francis Jeffrey Dickens (1844–86)
- Alfred Tennyson Dickens (1845–1912)
- Sydney Smith Haldimand Dickens (1847–72)
- Henry Fielding Dickens (1849–1933)
- Dora Annie Dickens (1850–51)
- Edward Bulwer Lytton Dickens (1852–1902)

INTRODUCTION

When Dickens published *Pictures from Italy* (1846), the account of his travels undertaken in Italy with his family throughout 1844, he clearly intended to depart from the genre of the handbook as popularized by John Murray's series of *Handbooks for Travellers*, begun in 1836. While Murray provided practical advice to travellers regarding recommended routes, sight-seeing, transport, hotels, and so on, Dickens instead offered his readers 'a series of faint reflections—mere shadows in the water': a form of virtual travel designed not just to inform, but to immerse the reader in an imaginary journey.[1] Dickens's title for the volume aptly signals the graphic power of his descriptions of Italy which, he declares, 'were written on the spot', or 'were at least penned in the fullness of the subject, and with the liveliest impressions of novelty and freshness'. The book is, he says, 'made as accessible as possible, because it would be a great pleasure to me if I could hope, through its means, to compare impressions with some among the multitudes who will hereafter visit the scenes described with interest and delight'.[2] *The Oxford Handbook of Charles Dickens* seeks to emulate the accessibility, innovativeness, and imaginative interest inspired by its inimitable subject.

The chapters collected here, all originally composed for this Handbook, comprise three constituents: (1) a survey of some of the principal lines of reception and critical interpretation of Charles Dickens's writings from the time of their publication to the present; (2) the authors' readings of the topic in ways that are innovative and original; and (3) prompts to readers to explore the topic further, perhaps along lines that the author suggests might be fruitful and valuable. Our contributors include leading international experts as well as emerging scholars in the field of Dickens studies. They reflect the transnational reach of scholarship on Dickens, coming from Australia, Canada,

---

[1] Eleanor McNees discusses the connection with Murray's Handbooks in 'Reluctant Source: Murray's Handbooks and *Pictures from Italy*', *Dickens Quarterly* 24, 4 (December 2007): 211–29. For a recent book on Dickens's travel narratives and his efforts to write both as a sceptical, fact-seeking journalist and as an empathetic, participatory storyteller, consult Nathalie Vanfasse, *La plume et la route: Charles Dickens écrivain-voyageur* (Aix-en-Provence: Presses Universitaires de Provence, 2017).

[2] *American Notes and Pictures from Italy*, introd. Sacheverell Sitwell, New Oxford Illustrated Dickens (London: Oxford University Press, 1957), 'The Reader's Portrait', 260–1.

France, Israel, Italy, Turkey, the United Kingdom, and the USA. The ambitious scope of this Handbook is elicited by the range of variety and diversity of its titular subject.

In accordance with the aims of the *Oxford Handbooks Online* series, this volume provides ready reference, information about a subject, and guidance for readers. A handbook is designed to be easily consulted and to be authoritative about its subject. To these ends we have sought to provide essays that will be 'accessible' (to use Dickens's term) to specialists and novices alike. Since the readership is likely to be global, and thus to reach consumers whose first language may not be English and whose library resources might differ significantly from those of our authors, we have made all citations as universally applicable as possible. Therefore, quotations from Dickens's fiction are cited by volume or book, chapter, and page in an authoritative edition. But lacking that, a reader should be able to find the quotation from the other information even if the page differs. And in the case of articles, we provide the full page range, so that readers can order a copy from a depository library if their local institutions do not hold the periodical.

While no brief essay can encompass the whole of Dickens's life and career, the chapters in Part I address the ways he understood his life and communicated it to his audiences, his vast reading and borrowing from English and European literary and artistic forebears, his practice and credo as a popular writer in an age of significant cultural, political, scientific, industrial, and philosophical transition, and his impact as an entertainer, social and political commentator, philanthropist, and advocate for justice, sympathy, honesty, the poor, children, outcasts, and the precepts of the New Testament, especially the gospel of Luke, over against the Utilitarian and Malthusian calculations of a nascent capitalist era.

Part II supplies chapters on Dickens's major works. In any one of these chapters readers will find particular instances of how Dickens's commitments and convictions are formulated and dramatized in inventive ways to entertain and educate his audience. The substance, artistry, and print formats of these works are all considered. For anyone reading these chapters consecutively, the overarching effect might be to glimpse the development, experimentation, reconceptualization, and refinement of Dickens's metier. He never simply repeated. His convictions altered in some ways, grew weaker or stronger; each new title impresses his world view freshly and originally. His lifetime journalism and correspondence also exhibit his changing ideas on a host of subjects, from politics to aesthetics, capitalism to charity, and England compared to America and Western Europe.

Part III then takes up particular aspects of that world view. How did Dickens's works address issues concerning families, parents and children, their gendered organization and relationship to social structures of work, education, finance, classes, race, religion, and empire? How did Dickens's fictions conceive of, understand, and value contemporary industrialization and technology? What do they record of the transformation of Britain from an agrarian and mercantile economy to one fuelled by manufacturing, banking, borrowing, and stock markets, energy production and consumption, and science? How did the 'modern industrial era' as he understood it deal with environmental degradation and improvements; pollution and toxic foods, drinks, air, and contagion? Did he keep up with and record imaginatively new scientific findings about the body and the mind, the life cycle, birth and death? How should the law, based on late medieval foundations, be adjusted to encompass new forms of credit, organization, property, entitlement, charity, and civic responsibility? What was the age doing to communicate among its populations? How were Dickens's writings engaging affect, material possessions, memory, faith, varieties of thinking and believing, and expressing selfhood and otherness, different races, foreigners and foreign countries, imperial conquest, colonial subjection and rebellion, and contamination from sources outside 'little Britain'? What was the history of this island kingdom, how did Dickens represent that past, and in what ways did the UK's history impact the Victorian present?

In Part IV, these issues are expanded into four general categories of manifestation: his language and immense rhetorical range, the genres he deployed to create reading experiences that articulated selfhood, romance, realism, imagination, distress and sorrow, violence, and humour; the role that theatre going, theatrical inheritance, and writing, producing, and acting in dramas played in shaping Dickens's imagination; and how he and his world came to understand the visual as not simply sensations yielding aesthetic pleasure and pain, but also as systems embedding information as fossils and stars embed the history of eons.

Finally, opening up the perspectives to even wider visions, the last Part investigates the effects Dickens's creations have had on global culture. What did other civilizations take up from his writings and transmit, transformed? How have twentieth- and twenty-first-century media adopted and adapted Dickens to different formats and situations? What does it mean to be a 'popular' writer, second only to Shakespeare in English, according to many now? In what ways have contemporary modes of communication, from heritage sites recovering and recasting history to the internet and instant communication across vast spaces, affected the absorption of Dickens into today's hugely varied cultures?

Cross-referencing ideas in these chapters is another way of discovering *connections*, a key term that appears in many essays and contexts. These connections are valuable not only for the ways Dickens employed them in thinking and writing about the human condition, but also for us, as we explore the connections between his century and ours. Readers of print editions of this Handbook will find in the Index keywords and concepts that show up repeatedly. Using this aid a reader could, for example, explore all the facets of Dickens's treatment of children and childhood, and the frameworks within which these vulnerable members of society are imagined and assessed. Or, if a reader is interested in industrialism—still an important basis of many developing nations—and how together with science, finance, and technology it transformed Victorian lives, the environment, and values, Index entries will enable a search for the many ways Dickens's writings viewed, critiqued, and imagined the future of nascent capitalist production and consumption.

Readers of the print editions have other aids of comprehension. A Time Line will enable them to fix a particular date or event within the span of Dickens's life. This is important not only for comprehending the moment, but also for gathering the ways in which any particular episode might be refigured in his fictions, his journalism, his theatrics, or the projections of his own life that he shared with, or concealed from, his public, and in some cases even from his family. And a genealogical chart of that family, reproduced from Paul Schlicke's *Oxford Reader's Companion to Dickens*, will help readers to identify and keep straight the many children and relatives of Charles and Catherine whose lives were so entangled with their father's career and fame.[3]

Within each chapter citations provide full bibliographic information. Given this complete reference, we hope readers who wish to follow up can locate the necessary sources in some collection or library. In addition, authors supplement the material they reference with suggestions for Further Reading. These are works that might put the topic into a broader perspective, or offer a different interpretation, or drill down into very specific and richly complex instances of what the chapter must of necessity treat more generally.

Recognizing that some will access these chapters on small screens, our authors have attempted to make their points clearly. At the start chapters often map how the exposition will progress. Strong topic sentences enable paragraphs to be grasped more easily. And sentences shorter than some of those Dickens and other Victorians composed—which often confound contemporary readers—should aid in comprehension. The printed text and its ebook version contain a List of Contributors. This list provides current information about each writer, so that someone interested in a particular voice and perspective can discover other works by the same person. And for those interested in obtaining individual chapters when they become available, the Oxford Handbooks Online website will provide an Abstract and a list of keywords that will enable some of the same kinds of searching as an index.

From November 2011 to December 2012 Britain celebrated the 200th anniversary of Charles Dickens. A diverse programme of over 1,200 events globally exceeded expectations (which were great to begin with) in scale, range, creativity, and numbers of participants. Within Great Britain there were exhibitions in museums and libraries, dramatizations and Public Readings, participatory reading groups, competitions, festivals, tours, and much new work released in radio, television, film, and print mediums. The British Film Institute circulated a film retrospective of Dickens's screen adaptations, and some of those films were shown in cinemas worldwide. The British Council facilitated outreach globally: 68 countries participated. Westminster Abbey hosted memorial services on Dickens's birthday, 7 February (1812), and his death day, 9 June (1870). Members of the royal family attended both events. A reception on the terrace of the House of Commons commemorating the 200th birthday launched a new schools programme about copyright, called 'What the Dickens?' On Valentine's Day, 14 February, Her Majesty the Queen and HRH the Duke of Edinburgh received descendants of Dickens, representatives from the Dickens Fellowship both within the UK and from the Commonwealth, staff at the Charles Dickens Museum, academics, and stars of Dickens films and television productions, in the Picture Gallery and the Blue Drawing Room of Buckingham Palace. Throughout the bicentennial year a Global Readathon, consisting of interactive staged readings of his novels, was conducted in 24 participating countries, including such diverse non-anglophone cultures as those in Argentina, Korea, and Iraq.[4]

---

[3] Ibid.
[4] Dr Claire Wood, 'Dickens 2012: Recording Commemorative Events in the Digital Age', a report prepared for the Archives & Records Association of the UK and Northern Ireland, and archived by the Charles Dickens Museum, section 2, 'Background to Dickens 2012', pp. 4–8.

Anticipating these celebrations, the Oxford commissioning editor for literature, Andrew McNeillie, asked Dr Pamela Dalziel, Distinguished University Scholar at the University of British Columbia and then responsible for further editions of the Clarendon Dickens, to prepare a proposal for a Handbook of Dickens, in conjunction with an advisory editor of her choice. Dr Robert L. Patten, then Lynette S. Autrey Professor in Humanities at Rice University and Senior Research Fellow, Institute of English Studies, School of Advanced Study, University of London, agreed to join her in this undertaking. In consultation with others, including Tyson Stolte, a contributor to this book, Dalziel and Patten prepared a syllabus that was sent out by McNeillie to a panel of readers for advice. It came back with many suggestions. The plan was revised and sent out again, and about that time Jacqueline Norton took over the project. Eventually she forwarded a proposal to the Delegates of the Press, who oversee its publications on behalf of the university of which it is a department. The Delegates solicited the opinion of further outside readers, and as the project became more comprehensive and global in reach, mirroring the breadth of coverage instantiated in the bicentenary events, additional changes resulted in an expansion to 50 chapters, including this Introduction, and to over 350,000 words. Professor Dalziel's other commitments proved too imperative for her to continue; but the fundamental structures and philosophy of this volume retain her vision. Two co-editors joined the team, Dr Catherine Waters, Professor of Victorian Literature and Print Culture in the School of English, University of Kent, and Dr John Jordan, Research Professor in the Literature Department at the University of California, Santa Cruz, and Director of the Dickens Project there. With the approval of the Delegates, and under the direction of Jacqueline Norton, the Dickens Handbook was contracted in the summer of 2015. The editors hope that the result adequately meets the vision of Dickens 2012 and fulfils the expectations of its many creators.

The proof will be if readers find that these chapters inspire new work and wonder. Dickens is inexhaustible.

The Editors

PART I

PERSONAL AND PROFESSIONAL LIFE

CHAPTER 1

BIOGRAPHICAL DICKENS

ROSEMARIE BODENHEIMER

In September 1840, the German composer Felix Mendelssohn appeared at the Birmingham Music Festival to conduct a newly completed choral work. He was travelling with his friend Ignaz Moscheles, a Prague-born pianist and composer who had settled in London in 1825, where he taught Charles Dickens's sister Fanny during her studies at the Royal College of Music.[1] Soon after their arrival in Birmingham, Mendelssohn wrote a letter to Moscheles's wife Charlotte, including a pen-and-ink sketch of Birmingham's features to amuse her young daughters (Figure 1.1). The sketch is a composite, including a toy-like railway carriage, a giant archway, the Town Hall where the music festival was held, and several factories with smoking chimneys. The real surprise of the sketch, however, is a low building in the foreground with 'Warren's Blacking' written across its front in large black lettering.[2]

What was Warren's Blacking, that dark secret of Charles Dickens's childhood, doing in Mendelssohn's playful sketch? In 1840, Dickens had not yet revealed his humiliating childhood employment in the boot-blacking factory to his best friend John Forster. More than another 30 years were to pass before Forster opened Dickens's memories to the general public in the first two chapters of *The Life of Charles Dickens*.[3] Did Warren's Blacking have a life of its own, unconnected to the traumatic memory of a single, temporary child worker? Why was its name, so deeply associated in Dickens biography with a rat-infested warehouse on Hungerford Stairs in mid-1820s London, inscribed on a building in Birmingham?

Mendelssohn's sketch can lead us directly into some of the unsolved mysteries of Dickens's life story. In the decades since Forster's account, Dickens has appeared in many contradictory guises: abandoned child, self-pitying adult, generous champion

---

[1] William J. Carlton, 'Fanny Dickens: Pianist and Vocalist', *Dickensian* 53, 3 (September 1957): 34.
[2] Mendelssohn's sketch is reproduced as illustration 14 in R. Larry Todd's *Mendelssohn: A Life in Music* (Oxford: Oxford University Press, 2003). The sketch is held at the Mendelssohn-Archiv at the Staatsbibliotek zu Berlin. Ms. autogr S10 (Album Emily Moscheles), fol. 31.
[3] John Forster, *The Life of Charles Dickens* (1872–4), ed. J. W. T. Ley (London: Cecil Palmer, 1928).

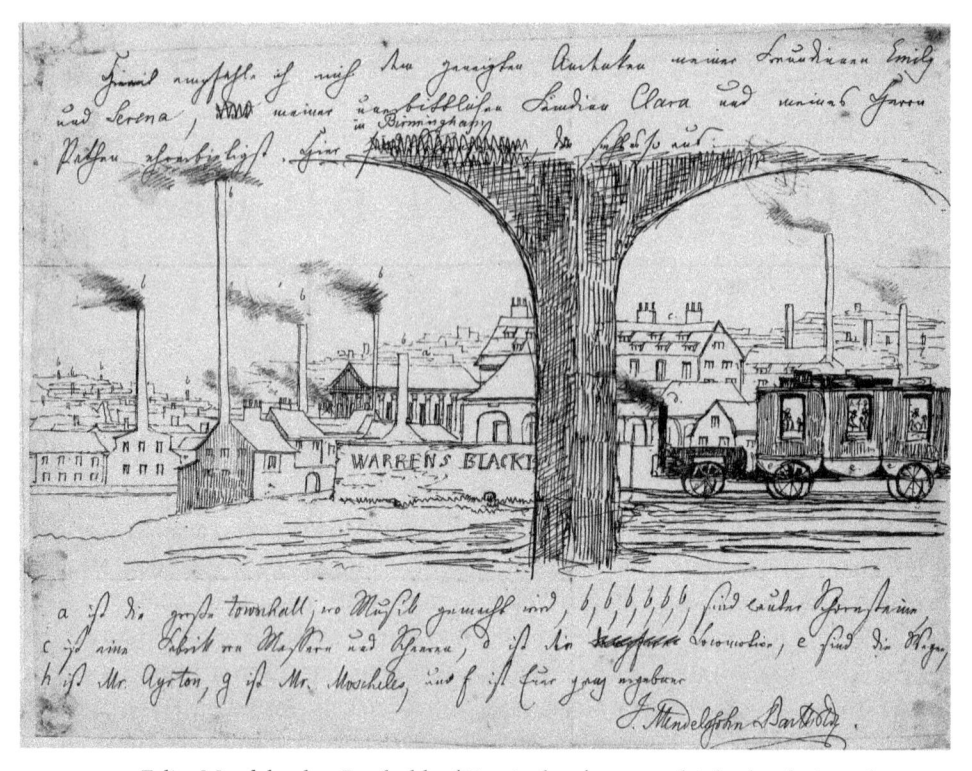

FIGURE 1.1 Felix Mendelssohn Bartholdy, 'Birmingham', pen-and-ink sketch in a letter to Charlotte Moscheles, September 1840. Staatsbibliotek zu Berlin, Musikabteilung mit Mendelssohn Archiv. Mus. Ms.

autograph S 10, fol 31 (Album Emily Moscheles)

of the poor, radical social critic, conservative Victorian, narcissistic charmer and control freak, haunted melancholic, spirited celebrator, family man, family tormentor. His ability to play all of these characters, at different times and in different moods, makes him an especially fascinating subject of biography, and guarantees that new attempts on his life (as he once put it) will continue into the future.[4] Bypassing chronology, this chapter will treat the two most contested episodes in Dickens's life, his stint as a child labourer at Warren's Blacking in 1824, and the breakup of his marriage to Catherine Hogarth Dickens in 1858. Both occasions prompted Dickens to write autobiographically in ways intended to control the way his life would be interpreted by others. The blacking warehouse memories were shaped 24 years after the childhood experience in

---

[4] By February 1842 Dickens was joking about writing a memoir to counter misrepresentations of his life: 'I may one of these days be induced to lay violent hands upon myself—in other words attempt my own life.' *The Letters of Charles Dickens*, ed. Madeline House, Graham Storey, et al., Pilgrim/British Academy Edition, 12 vols (Oxford: Clarendon Press, 1965–2002). Henceforth *PLets* followed by volume:page number(s), and if required hn. for headnote, n. or nn. numbered for footnotes, with page range given before page cited. Here, 3:61.

a document privately given to Forster, who was asked to withhold the story until after Dickens's death. The banishment of Catherine was written up in the heat of the moment, in letters to friends and justifications published in newspapers. The circumstances were very different, yet both these attempts at information control help to shed light on Dickens's characteristic ways of managing his image, and on the subsequent evolution of Dickens biography.

BLACKING, WRITING

In the nearly 150 years since Forster published Dickens's so-called autobiographical fragment, the biographical record reveals how successfully Dickens set the terms by which he would come to be understood. A rough outline of shifts in biographical fashion and method may be charted through four major life-and-work studies considered standard biographies for their times. These include John Forster's *The Life of Charles Dickens* (1872–4), Edgar Johnson's *Charles Dickens: His Tragedy and Triumph* (1952), Peter Ackroyd's *Dickens* (1990), and Michael Slater's *Charles Dickens* (2009).[5] Published soon after Dickens's death, Forster's book remains to this day the indispensable source for later biographers. His narrative encompasses a life-in-letters and a memoir of professional and personal friendship, as well as a portrait of the artist at work. As a Victorian biographer, Forster was naturally concerned to protect his subject's reputation and the sensitivities of Dickens's living wife and children, so he toned down his friend's excesses and elided his relationship with Ellen Ternan, with whom Dickens had a 12-year affair after Catherine was ejected from their home. Although new facts have come to light in the interval, the authority of Forster's work has never been superseded, nor have its depths been fully explored.[6]

The opening scoop of Forster's work was his revelation of John Dickens's three-month imprisonment for debt in the Marshalsea Prison in early 1824, and Charles Dickens's unhappy employment at Warren's Blacking before, during, and after his father's incarceration. Although Dickens deliberately concealed this past from all would-be biographers during his lifetime, he entrusted his best friend Forster with a memoir of that period, probably in bursts of spoken and written confidences between May 1847 and January 1849.[7] On 22 April 1848, writing to praise Forster's new biography of Oliver Goldsmith, he made Forster his designated biographer: 'I desire no better for my fame when my

---

[5] Edgar Johnson, *Charles Dickens: His Tragedy and Triumph* (New York: Simon and Schuster, 1952); Peter Ackroyd, *Dickens* (New York: HarperCollins 1991); and Michael Slater, *Charles Dickens* (New Haven and London: Yale University Press, 2009).

[6] For a brief account of Dickens biographers from John Forster to Edmund Wilson, see Rosemarie Bodenheimer, 'Dickens and the Writing of a Life', in John Bowen and Robert L. Patten (eds), *Palgrave Advances in Charles Dickens Studies* (Houndmills: Palgrave Macmillan, 2006), 48–68.

[7] See Slater, *Charles Dickens*, on the probable dates of the fragment/s, 278–9 and 283–4.

personal dustyness shall be past the controul of my love of order, than such a biographer and such a Critic.'[8] The phrasing quietly requests Forster to carry on that love of orderly control for the sake of his friend's posthumous fame.

Presenting the blacking warehouse episode through quotations from a fragmentary narrative partially incorporated into *David Copperfield*, Forster created some tantalizing biographical dilemmas that have never been adequately resolved. The manuscript, or manuscripts, of Dickens's reminiscences did not—according to Forster—survive intact, and Forster's account managed to blur the boundaries between the childhoods of Dickens and his character David. Thus, it has remained difficult to untangle all the facts of Dickens's case from the fictions of Copperfield's, or to separate what Dickens wrote down from what Forster claimed to recall despite an occasional 'blank' in the written narrative.[9] Forster's tendency to revise or delete portions of the Dickens letters he quoted in his narrative adds to the uncertainties raised by his account.[10] Because there is no independent source of evidence about Dickens's employment at Warren's, and no firm dating for either the blacking period or the composition of the fragment, our biographical castles have necessarily been built on somewhat shaky ground.

Edgar Johnson's two-volume work marks an American phase in Dickens biography, and, as the subtitle *His Tragedy and Triumph* suggests, a fashion for evocative emotional narration. Johnson had access to a range of unpublished Dickens letters, and he brought Ellen Ternan into his story without moral apologies.[11] Leading his audience to identify with Dickens in both suffering and success, his utterly sympathetic re-creation of the autobiographical fragment treated it as straightforward biographical evidence. During that mid-twentieth-century period, American critics tended to treat the blacking warehouse as a formative event and a fundamental key to Dickens's creative imagination. Interpretations of the wounded child's trauma by Edmund Wilson, Steven Marcus, Robert Newsom, and others drew on Freudian methodologies to understand the psychodynamics of Dickens's art.[12] By 1987, however, Alexander Welsh was reconsidering the fragment as a document that suggested more about the prideful mid-life Dickens who wrote it than about the child's experience 24 years earlier.[13] That shift marked an important and necessary turn towards rhetorical readings of Dickens's reminiscences, in which the 36-year-old writer became as important as the 12-year-old child.

---

[8] *PLets* 5:288–90, 290.

[9] Forster, *Life*, 29.

[10] For efforts to sort out the puzzles of the fragment, see Nina Burgis, 'Introduction' to *David Copperfield* (Oxford: Clarendon Press, 1981), xv–xxii, and Philip Collins, 'Dickens's Autobiographical Fragment and *David Copperfield*', *Cahiers Victoriens et Edouardiens* 20 (1984): 87–96.

[11] A moralistic account of Dickens's affair with Ellen Ternan was first made public in Thomas Wright's *The Life of Charles Dickens* (London: Herbert Jenkins, 1935), 241–73.

[12] Edmund Wilson, 'Dickens: The Two Scrooges', in *The Wound and the Bow* (New York: Oxford University Press, 1947), 1–104; Steven Marcus, 'Who Is Fagin?' in *Dickens from Pickwick to Dombey* (New York: Simon and Schuster, 1965), 358–78; and Robert Newsom, 'The Hero's Shame', *Dickens Studies Annual* 11 (1983): 1–24.

[13] Alexander Welsh, *From Copyright to Copperfield* (Cambridge, MA: Harvard University Press, 1987), 108, 156–72.

By 1990, when Peter Ackroyd published his *Dickens*, biographical evidence was readily available: half the Dickens letters had been published in the Pilgrim Edition, and most of the rest were held in archives. Though he frequently warned his readers that 'apparent childhood memories' appearing in Dickens's fictions and journalism were 'not necessarily to be taken literally', Ackroyd drew liberally on brief quotations from anywhere in Dickens's work to enhance the flavour of a particular biographical moment.[14] His leisurely, talkative narration elaborates on Dickens as a haunter of the London places he knew so intimately, and emphasizes the troubled strangeness of the man. When it comes to the blacking period, Ackroyd imagines the child's resentments and fears, but also calls attention to the retrospective darkening in the adult's account of his childhood. Of the fragment itself, he writes, 'This pitiable and self-pitying account is perhaps too carefully crafted to be altogether true,' though he goes on to assert that 'for the first time he was separated entirely from his family ... and left to fend for himself.'[15] The fragment itself shows that Dickens was not entirely separated from his family, who continued to support him with lodging, clothes, and company during John Dickens's stay in the Marshalsea, but in the fluidity of his narrative Ackroyd remains open to a range of emotional possibilities. His book is especially valuable for its emphasis on Dickens as a man who believed that what he felt at any moment was entirely true, that he was in the right and others to blame in any conflict. This pattern of feeling helps to place the autobiographical fragment as one instance among many in Dickens's habitual spinning of his life story for the consumption of others.[16]

Ackroyd's book also reflects a shift in approach to one unsolved problem: how long did Dickens work for Warren's Blacking? 'I have no idea how long it lasted; whether for a year, or much more, or less', Dickens wrote.[17] Previous biographers assumed a period of five or six months, lasting from around the time of Dickens's 12th birthday (7 February 1824) until June or July of that same year.[18] In 1988 Michael Allen suggested that Dickens had remained at Warren's for 13 months or more, until March or April 1825. In 2011 he

---

[14] Ackroyd, *Dickens*, 33.
[15] Ibid. 75.
[16] Ackroyd, *Dickens*, 492.
[17] Forster, *Life*, 35.
[18] According to this timing, John Dickens entered the Marshalsea on 20 February, about two weeks after Charles went to work. Charles continued to live with his family in the Gower Street house they had taken in the vain hope that Elizabeth Dickens could start a school there. After Lady Day (25 March), when the Gower Street lease ran out, the rest of the family moved into the Marshalsea, placing Charles in lodgings kept for children by Mrs Roylance in Camden Town. After perhaps a month, Charles objected to this arrangement, and the family found him a room with a kindly landlord on Lant Street close to the prison. John Dickens applied for insolvency and was released on 28 May, but Charles was not allowed to stop working. He and his family boarded temporarily with Mrs Roylance and then moved to a nearby house in Johnson Street, Somers Town. At some point Warren's moved from Hungerford Stairs to better quarters on Chandos Street, where Charles and the other boys worked at a window visible to passers-by. Sometime during that summer his father provoked a quarrel with James Lamert, the cousin by marriage who had hired Charles at the Hungerford Warren's. As a result, Charles was sent home. He bitterly recalled that his mother wanted him to return to work, but his father put his foot down, and sent him back to school (Forster, *Life*, 34–5).

revised his theory, but remained devoted to the notion that Dickens had spent at least a year at Warren's, this time beginning in September 1823 and lasting until August 1824. Both speculations were based on inconclusive archival evidence about when the family moved to Somers Town and when the factory moved from Hungerford Stairs to Chandos Street. Although Allen himself admitted that 'firm conclusions cannot be drawn', he nevertheless drew his conclusion. The 12-or-13-month theory, though not the 1823 start date, was quietly adopted by Ackroyd and most subsequent Dickens biographers.[19]

Does the length of time matter? Dickens's own uncertainty about dates seems the most convincing to me, exactly because it conveys the idea that it does not. Six additional months does not equal a greater amount of suffering, or require a larger portion of sympathy on the reader's part. What did matter was the shock of declassing, the loss of school and schoolmates, the painful contrast with sister Fanny, who was studying and winning prizes at the Royal Academy of Music, and the despairing feeling that there was no end in sight. 'My rescue from this kind of existence I considered quite hopeless, and abandoned as such, altogether', Dickens wrote.[20] Unlike some of the more outraged and accusatory sentences in the fragment, this one has a painful accuracy that implies several inner phases of accommodation: the hope of rescue, the father's shaming incompetence and public downfall, the abandonment of faith in his parents, the shutting down. A few months would be sufficient for a child to suffer a sequence of that sort, and then bounce back to youthful exuberance after his release into more familiar situations. George Gissing, who probably knew more about the experience of abrupt declassing than any other Dickens biographer, got it right. 'Imagine Charles Dickens kept in the blacking warehouse for ten years', he wrote, conjuring up an image of genius squandered in despair. Luckily, 'it did not last long enough to corrupt the natural sweetness of his mind'.[21]

Michael Allen's work does, however, afford a refreshing perspective on the independent history of Warren's Blacking, which had a troubled story of its own that extended for years before and after Charles Dickens's brief appearance as a labeller of blacking pots. As Dickens noted in the memories quoted by Forster, he had been employed not at the thriving business run by Robert Warren at 30 Strand, but at the Hungerford Stairs factory originally owned by Robert's uncle Jonathan Warren, who claimed to have invented the Warren's blacking formula, and who carried on an imitative advertising campaign designed to confuse the rival establishments in the public mind.[22] Allen's research has uncovered a number of claims and counter-claims between the rival firms, brought in the Court of Chancery. Allen also showcases Robert Warren's

---

[19] See Michael Allen, *Charles Dickens's Childhood* (New York: St Martin's Press, 1988), 100, and *Charles Dickens and the Blacking Factory* (St Leonards, UK: Oxford-Stockley Publications, 2011), 92–5.

[20] Forster, *Life*, 29.

[21] George Gissing, *Charles Dickens: A Critical Study* (1898; repr. New York: Dodd, Mead and Company, 1904), 20–1.

[22] Forster, *Life*, 24.

lavish, inventive advertising, which included posters, placards, poems, tokens given out to customers, and men dressed as blacking bottles roaming the streets of London. Both firms extended their reach to cities across England, where agents would spread the word and take orders.[23] Felix Mendelssohn's 1840 sketch suggests his fascination with the advertising posters he saw both in London and, presumably, in Birmingham.

Dickens himself was clearly delighted by the opportunity to make fun of Warren's advertising jingles in print, knowing that they would be a familiar sight to many Londoners. Sam Weller enters in the fourth number of *Pickwick Papers* blacking boots 'with a polish which would have struck envy to the soul of the amiable Mr Warren, (for they used Day and Martin at the White Hart)', and his father Tony later makes fun of Warren's poets.[24] Did Dickens write such jingles himself? John Drew suggests that he very likely did, during his brief association with the young newspaper *The True Sun* in 1832.[25] There is no definitive proof. If he did, however, Dickens was probably earning his few shillings from Robert Warren, not from the struggling rival firm where he had toiled eight years earlier, and the parodic verse may have been fired by the pleasure of a small comic revenge.[26]

Michael Slater's richly authoritative *Charles Dickens* (2009) is notable for its minimization of the blacking warehouse episode. Slater concentrates on Dickens as a professional writer, and his 'originary document' is not the autobiographical fragment but the first piece of Dickens's childhood writing that we possess. His Dickens is no haunted man, but an astonishingly productive whirlwind of literary energy and accomplishment, whose life experiences are instantly transformed into writing. Quick to note 'the problematic nature of attempting any sort of objective account of Dickens's life during 1822–24', Slater draws on previous accounts of the Dickens family situation with a judiciousness that characterizes his treatment of contested moments in Dickens's personal history.[27] Significantly, his account of the autobiographical fragment occurs not in connection with the family crisis of 1822–4, but in a chapter devoted to the years 1848–9, where he takes up the question of how and when Forster came to know about Dickens's childhood.[28] Slater's approach might be taken to signal a more general twenty-first-century cooling of the psychological temperature about Dickens's months as a child worker.[29]

---

[23] Allen, *Blacking Factory*. Allen details three Chancery cases brought by rival owners of the two firms, based on records held at The National Archives at Kew. The advertising campaigns are described on pp. 50–63.

[24] *The Pickwick Papers*, ed. James Kinsley (Oxford: Clarendon Press, 1986), 138, 496. See also Mr Slum the blacking poet in *The Old Curiosity Shop*, ed. Elizabeth M. Brennan (Oxford: Clarendon Press, 1997), chapter 28.

[25] John M. L. Drew, *Dickens the Journalist* (Houndmills: Palgrave Macmillan, 2003), 17–19.

[26] Forster (*Life*, 36) notes that the rival firm had been sold during Dickens's lifetime to Robert Warren, 'and he had made an excellent bargain of it'.

[27] Slater, *Charles Dickens*, 15.

[28] Ibid. 278–9.

[29] Robert L. Patten also challenges the Warren's Blacking trauma diagnosis, presenting the autobiographical fragment as just one of many Dickens stories that elaborated and revised his image as an author during the 1840s. See 'Whitewashing the Blacking Factory', *Dickens Studies Annual* 46 (2015): 1–22.

Revisiting Dickens's memory fragment in the light of this cooling, I also find myself reconsidering the vocabulary of trauma that has long been applied to Dickens's childhood situation as if it held an explanatory key to his creative and personal lives.[30] It is entirely imaginable that Dickens would have been the Dickens we know without the blacking warehouse experience. It was indeed that very Dickens who, at 12, observed and recalled the details of food, shillings and pence, streets, shops, work skills, and people that composed his life during the months at Warren's, and provided the material for his written reminiscences. It was the same Dickens who loved to wander and observe in the Seven Dials and other dicey London neighbourhoods, even before he was sent to work. As a diagnosis, trauma can suggest an experience that changes a personality in destructive ways, one that ever after intrudes itself upon its unwilling victim and affects his or her ability to flourish. There is no evidence that his time at Warren's did that to Dickens, who went into the factory a sensitive, self-conscious, proud, and brilliant child, and came out the same. Nowhere in the autobiographical fragment does Dickens say, 'everything changed at that moment', or suggest an equivalent transformation.

To say this is not to diminish the reality, the pain, or the importance of Warren's Blacking in Dickens's life. Even the most sceptical reader of the autobiographical fragment does not doubt that it happened as he said it did. Quite understandably, the interlude was afterwards unmentioned between Dickens and his parents; similar silences form around painful or shameful episodes in the pasts of many families. For Dickens, I suggest, it was the kind of experience that crops up in the psyche at moments of vulnerability, or when some reminder triggers a painful memory generally ignored in daily consciousness. In the creative life such an experience acts as an irritant, like the proverbial grains of sand around which pearls form in the oyster. Once the first layer of pearl goes on, each creative act takes its own course, and establishes its own shape.

It is also important to separate Dickens's great drive, ambition, and achievement from those months at Warren's. Had he not already contained those energies, he would not have suffered as much as he did when they were temporarily thwarted. His sensitivity to any imagined slight from others was not created during those months, nor was his refusal to imagine that he could be in the wrong. These characteristics were his, and they manifested themselves over and over in situations ranging from love relationships to edits of others' work. His touchiness about his family's shaky class position was nurtured by his father's genteel fantasies and failures, long before Charles was 12 years old. The Warren's Blacking episode would enclose those feelings in an especially intense set of circumstances, as if they had been condensed into a bad dream. When confronted with other historical figures who are driven, restless, productive, and engaged in multiple activities, we do not automatically assume that they are attempting to overcome or flee from some originary trauma; some, in fact, sport quite luxurious childhoods. Warren's

---

[30] I drew on a version of trauma theory in my previous reading of the fragment: see Rosemarie Bodenheimer, *Knowing Dickens* (Ithaca, NY: Cornell University Press, 2007), 68–73.

Blacking was a crucial memory for Dickens, but it does not explain the resilience with which he turned every aspect of his experience into artistic gold.

With such thoughts in mind, the emphasis can shift to the circumstances of 1847–8 under which Dickens wrote the fragment for Forster. How might we begin to explain what writing those paragraphs did for Dickens at that time? Rhetorically, the passages Forster quoted fall into three main types. Of these, the detailed evocations of daily rituals are by far the most persuasive parts. The child's attempts to make his six (later, seven) shillings cover his bits of food for the week, his lonely walks and dinner hours, his lodgings, his proud attempts to hold his own among the other working boys, and his keen memories of observed street scenes and Marshalsea characters—all of this is brilliantly done. Then there are moments in which the successful 36-year-old writer dramatizes himself seeing himself as a child, while the child encounters strangers in public spaces. The depicted child wonders self-consciously how he looks to others from the outside, and invents lies to prevent them from knowing his shameful situation. Placed near the end of Forster's chapter, these passages bleed into the *Copperfield* mode of memory narration, and may mark a transition between personal memoir and early experiments for the new novel.

Finally, there are the passages everyone quotes, the ones in which the adult writer interrupts the detailed memories to express his outrage and an extremity of pain, despair, and shame. 'It is wonderful to me how I could have been so easily cast away at such an age.' 'No words can express the secret agony of my soul'; 'I know that, but for the mercy of God, I might easily have been, for any care that was taken of me, a little robber or a little vagabond.'[31] Full of unmediated rage at his parents, especially unforgiving to his mother, such interventions have been taken as the primary evidence of ongoing trauma in Dickens's adult psyche. It is also possible that some of them were written after Dickens had decided to encase his memories in the fiction of *David Copperfield*, releasing a rhetorical display that he might not have indulged in memoir. Whatever the case, I will reconsider them here as indications that events of the late 1840s had triggered newly complicated feelings about ongoing family relationships with his parents, his older sister Fanny, his younger brother Fred, and his eldest son Charley.

Restless in 1846, Dickens launched *The Daily News*, a Liberal newspaper he intended to edit. He hired several family members, including his father John Dickens, who was to manage the team of parliamentary reporters. It was as if Dickens were revisiting the very early days of his journalistic career, when his father's reporting had paved the way for his own. Could he now pave the way to salary and respectability for his father? John was controversial on *The Daily News*, earning criticism from some quarters and praise from others, and Dickens felt he had to defend him.[32]

His editorship lasted all of three weeks. Resigning abruptly on 9 February 1846, he handed the paper over to Forster and, soon thereafter, fled to Switzerland with his

---

[31] Forster, *Life*, 25, 26, 28.
[32] Ackroyd, *Dickens*, 480–2; Slater, *Charles Dickens*, 242.

household, where he planned to write *Dombey and Son*. The quick exit is to some extent understandable—there was a new novel brewing—but every biographer has been struck by its suddenness; 9 February 1824 is the date most often suggested as the day on which Dickens had started working at Warren's. Was he suddenly overwhelmed with revulsion when that date came around in 1846? Was he horrified to be back in the business of shoring up and protecting his father's name, or simply by working alongside him on a daily basis? These questions remain unanswerable, but they do suggest that it was not just old memories that fired the angers enclosed in the autobiographical fragment.

The parents' unreliability also meant that Dickens had to play father and financier for his younger brothers. Eight years younger than Charles, Frederick Dickens was close to his brother and had spent many of his younger years living in his household. By the mid-1840s his resemblance to their father was becoming ever more apparent, as Fred went into debt and adopted John's habit of borrowing money from Dickens's friends. In early 1847 he was determined to marry Anna Weller, the younger sister of the pianist Christiana Weller, with whom Charles had briefly fallen in love three years earlier when she performed onstage with him in Liverpool.[33] Fred insisted on marrying Anna over the strong objections of her father and Dickens, who wrote long, exasperated, lecturing letters attempting to discipline Fred's feelings and forbid the marriage.[34] The fact that Fred's rash behaviour was a discomforting mirror of his own recent infatuation with Christiana could not have made matters any easier for Dickens.

At about the same time, Dickens was forcibly reminded that his own eldest son had the power to wrench his parents' lives and emotions out of shape. Charley had been placed at the King's College School in Wimbledon, to prepare him for Eton. On 8 March 1847 the Dickens family sojourn in Paris was abruptly interrupted when the 9-year-old was taken ill with scarlet fever. His parents returned instantly to London. Though they were not allowed to visit Charley because of Catherine's pregnancy, they hovered nearby as their son gradually recovered.[35] As Charley neared the age when Dickens himself was taken out of school and allowed to roam the streets of London, his anxiously nurtured health and education would have struck Dickens by contrast with his own parents' insensitivities to his needs at that age.

The most important familial spur to the autobiographical fragment was the illness and death of Fanny Dickens Burnett, the elder sister with whom Charles had shared the most during their youth. Born two years apart, Fanny and Charles were natural companions during a happy early childhood; the next surviving sibling, Letitia Dickens, was born four years after Charles. After the family's move to London and economic decline in 1822, Fanny's musical talent offered hope of her earning power, and John Dickens paid the fees for her to study piano as a boarder at the newly founded Royal Academy of Music, where she was admitted on 9 April 1823.[36] Once Charles was earning

---

[33] I tell this story in *Knowing Dickens*, 101–5.
[34] *PLets* 5:17–18, 22–3, 26.
[35] *PLets* 5:32–3, 36, 50–1, 62–3.
[36] My account of Fanny Dickens is based on Carlton, 'Fanny Dickens', 33–43.

his weekly shillings at Warren's, and after Elizabeth Dickens moved into the Marshalsea with Letitia, Fred, and Alfred, Charles picked up Fanny every Sunday morning at the Hanover Square music school, and they walked to the prison to spend the day with their family. Did Fanny tell her mentors and fellow-students where she was going, during those three months of Sundays? Did she share her brother's barely concealed shame, on their walks to and from the Marshalsea? Certainly, as the two responsible eldest children out on their own, they would have talked about their work and their family situation in ways that would not be communicated to other family members. When Dickens wrote that 'no word of that part of my childhood ... has passed my lips to any human being', and that 'my father and my mother have been stricken dumb upon it', he left out the sister who would always have remembered with him, even if they had ceased to discuss that painful period when it was over.[37] Most likely, Fanny Dickens Burnett had already died when he wrote those words.

Fanny and her singer-husband pursued successful musical careers in London and Manchester, but by early 1846 her health was in decline. Charles and Catherine Dickens began to arrange consultations with London doctors for her. In the winter of 1847 she broke down while performing at a party, and was diagnosed with tuberculosis. In June 1848 her doctors gave up hope, and 38-year-old Fanny remained, dying, in London, visited regularly by her parents and other family members. On 5 July 1848 Dickens had a long private talk with her, which he was moved to describe in a letter to Forster. 'I don't know why I write this before going to bed', he wrote. 'I only know that in the very pity and grief of my heart, I feel as if it were doing something.' He felt himself to have been present at a turning point in her illness: 'Her cough suddenly ceased almost, and, strange to say, she immediately became aware of her hopeless state; to which she resigned herself, after an hour's unrest and struggle, with extraordinary sweetness and constancy.'[38] Full of sentiment, Dickens's letter reflects Fanny's religious piety and hope in the world to come. It also reveals his feeling that writing was a way of 'doing something' about a hopeless personal situation.

Fanny died on 2 September 1848. The day before, Dickens had written intimately to Catherine, 'No words can express the terrible aspect of suffering and suffocation—the appalling noise in her throat—and the agonized look around, which lasted, I should think a quarter of an hour'.[39] 'No words can express the secret agony of my soul as I sunk into this companionship', he wrote in the fragment, referring to his lower-class co-workers.[40] It was an emotional time. The day after Fanny's death, Dickens wrote another angry letter to his brother Fred, shocked to hear that Fred was planning a December wedding while still substantially in debt.[41] The painful old story was renewing itself, in close conjunction with the loss of the one family member who had not needed to

---

[37] Forster, *Life*, 35.
[38] *PLets* 5:362–3.
[39] *PLets* 5:399–400, 399.
[40] Forster, *Life*, 26.
[41] *PLets* 5:400–1.

rely on him. With fresh anger and resentment brewing, Fanny's illness and death may have propelled Dickens to tell the blacking story his own way, unmediated by Fanny's memories and her tendency to put the best face on things.

As Fanny faded away, Dickens chose Forster to safeguard those memories, probably because his friend had already heard something about them.[42] In March or April of 1847, Forster mentioned that a Mr Dilke recalled meeting the child Dickens with his father in the street, during his employment at Warren's.[43] Hearing this, Dickens's need for information control went into high gear. Had Dilke told the story to anyone else? How much did he know? If the shame of that early period existed in another memory, Dickens's strongest instinct was to write his own version for posterity. As I have suggested, however, his manner of telling the story was likely affected by family emotions much closer to hand.

The Erasure of Catherine

Ten years after Dickens turned the blacking episode into the story of an abandoned but resilient child, he was busy destroying his marriage. By giving Forster the autobiographical narrative, he had hoped to control the reception of facts about his childhood that could be revealed after his death. Now he attempted to rewrite the story of his relationship with Catherine so that he would again be seen as the well-meaning, patient victim of a woman's failure to fulfil adequately the roles of wife and mother. Both family crises created shame; they put Dickens in positions he did not wish others to associate with the person he thought himself to be. Neither event was respectable. Writing in self-defence was, as usual, the way to redeem his image.

Of course, there were differences. The breakup with Catherine, a sustained act of will on Dickens's part, involved many other people, each of whom would have a different perspective on the painful process. Their children were enjoined to remain silent as his family of origin had earlier been, but there were plenty of people who would, and did, gossip freely. His own guilty responsibility for the breakup was evident to many observers. Because Dickens was so eager to deny this to his beloved public-at-large, he wrote two versions of the separation that appeared in newspapers, as well as letters to some dubious friends.

By all accounts Dickens was beside himself during the events of 1857 and 1858; words like 'frenzied', 'hysterical', and 'restless' appear over and over in the biographical record. He had often been flirtatious with young women, especially if they were lively

---

[42] Dickens probably read the fragment to Catherine after Forster had seen it. According to Charles Dickens Jr, she advised him not to publish it because he had written so harshly of his parents. Nina Burgis quotes to this effect from Charley's 1892 introduction to the Macmillan edition of *David Copperfield*: Charles Dickens, *David Copperfield*, ed. Nina Burgis (Oxford: Clarendon Press, 1981), xxi.

[43] Forster, *Life*, 23.

performers like himself and his sister, but something bigger overcame him in the case of the young actress Ellen Ternan. In the summer of 1857 Dickens met the Ternan family of actresses when they took part in a Manchester performance of his play *The Frozen Deep*. Early in September Dickens ran after them, in the hope of seeing Ellen when she and her sisters appeared at Doncaster during Race Week. He cloaked his pursuit in the guise of a working tour with Wilkie Collins, which produced *The Lazy Tour of Two Idle Apprentices* for *Household Words*. Before leaving, he explained to Forster that he and Catherine were incompatible, and had always been so, since the birth of their second child Mamie.[44] The campaign to backdate his marital unhappiness had begun.

What Dickens would write about Catherine's responsibility for the failure of their marriage was to have a long shelf life in twentieth-century biography. Most biographers took Dickens at his word about the long-standing unhappiness of the union, casting Catherine as a clumsy, silly, and unsuitable partner for a great novelist. Attempting to turn the tide in *Dickens and Women* (1983), Michael Slater argued persuasively that Dickens had misrepresented the marriage in retrospect. 'Once we know how a story ends, we can never again read its beginning with an open mind', he noted, alluding to the many biographical narratives that followed Dickens by foreshadowing the end of the marriage while describing its early stages.[45] In 2012, Slater pursued the subject in *The Great Charles Dickens Scandal*, which details evolving representations of Catherine Dickens and Ellen Ternan in Dickens biography and journalism from Forster to the present. As he recounts all of the rumour, scandal, revelation, speculation, and cover-up surrounding these matters, Slater acknowledges that the absence of decisive evidence means that both the quality of the marriage and the relationship with Ellen Ternan remain open to endless speculation.[46]

The actual breakup occurred in May–June 1858, when Dickens took decisive action to formalize his separation from Catherine. After much wrangling with members of Catherine's outraged family, they finally signed a legal separation agreement. He would continue to support her in a house on Gloucester Crescent, while the children (with the exception of Charley) were to live with him at Gad's Hill under the familiar care of their aunt Georgina Hogarth. After the breakup Dickens burned Catherine's letters to him, along with the rest of his correspondence, as part of his effort to negate 20 years of intimacy. We know no more about what actually happened between husband and wife than we know about the tenor of the Dickens family life during the period described in the autobiographical fragment.[47]

---

[44] *PLets* 8:430–1.

[45] Michael Slater, *Dickens and Women* (Stanford, CA: Stanford University Press, 1983), 103.

[46] Michael Slater, *The Great Charles Dickens Scandal* (New Haven and London: Yale University Press, 2012). See also the excellent chapter 19, 'Writing off a Marriage', in Slater's *Charles Dickens*.

[47] For a discussion of the breakup as it affected Catherine, see Lilian Nayder, *The Other Dickens: A Life of Catherine Hogarth* (Ithaca, NY, and London: Cornell University Press, 2011), 250–76. Nayder effectively creates Catherine's reality as a person in her own right, but Catherine left so few traces that the narrative is necessarily dominated by Dickens's actions and words.

Dickens's self-justifications depended upon the audience he was addressing. In the September 1857 letter to Forster, who liked and defended Catherine, he writes as if her suffering in the marriage were as acute as his own: 'God knows she would have been a thousand times happier if she had married another kind of man, and that her avoidance of this destiny would have been at least equally good for us both.'[48] Adjusting to life with a man as controlling and wilful as Dickens would be difficult for any woman, but Catherine had managed to do it through twenty years and ten childbirths. Was Dickens now making her into a character he invented for his own purposes, or was there some truth in his version of what she had become during those years? For other friends, Dickens emphasized Catherine's lifelong jealousy of a wholly innocent husband, forgetting for the moment the many infatuations and flirtations in which he had indulged. By far the most melodramatic of his stories was the bad mother narrative. Early in May 1858, he tried to persuade Angela Burdett-Coutts that Catherine had been an unnatural mother from the very beginning, failing to attach her children to her or to play with them in their infancy. His daughters, he wrote, 'harden into stone figures of girls when they can be got to go near her, and have their hearts shut up in her presence as if they closed by some horrid spring'.[49] The Gothic fiction makes melodramatic characters of everyone except his observing, narrating self.

The two published narratives were unsuccessful attempts to douse the flames of malicious gossip.[50] The so-called 'Violated Letter' was written on 25 May 1858 for Arthur Smith, the manager of Dickens's Public Readings, who was given permission to show it 'to any one who wishes to do me right, or to any one who may have been misled into doing me wrong'.[51] (It made its way into the *New York Tribune* on 16 August, and then appeared in other American and British papers.) Its main purpose was to declare that Dickens and Catherine had been unhappy together for many years, that they had separated amicably, and that the separation had been instigated by Catherine, on the grounds that 'she felt herself unfit for the life she had to lead as my wife and that she would be better far away'. The heroine of the piece is Georgina Hogarth, brought in as a witness to the marital misery, and as the saviour of the marriage, since the 'peculiarity of [Catherine's] character has thrown all the children on someone else'. Forster is cast as the adviser who first recommends a separation. The children are with Dickens all the way, 'as though we were brothers and sisters'. All the active parties are other people, while Dickens is placed with the children, who look on sadly but truthfully as it all transpires around them. Shades of the blacking warehouse begin to emerge.

Dickens's second public stand was the Personal Statement he published in *The Times* on 7 June and in *Household Words* on 12 June. In its rather abstract rhetoric, 'the Public' becomes Dickens's true wife. 'Three-and-twenty years have passed since I entered on

---

[48] *PLets* 8:429–30, 430.
[49] *PLets* 8:558–60, 559.
[50] See *PLets* 8:739–51 for texts of the 'Violated Letter', the Personal Statement, and other documents generated by the separation process.
[51] *PLets* 8:568.

my present relations with the Public', it begins. 'Through all that time I have tried to be as faithful to the Public, as they have been to me.' A spouse of longer standing than Catherine, the Public knows Dickens the way he wants to be understood. 'Those who know me and my nature, need no assurance under my hand that such calumnies are as irreconcilable with me, as they are, in their frantic incoherence, with one another.' The take-home message is simple: whatever you may have heard is 'abominably false'. A good many readers, beyond the circles of literary gossip, may have wondered what he was talking about, but they continued to attend his Readings.

As for Catherine, Dickens later claimed to have erased her from his memory. When Angela Burdett-Coutts suggested reconciliation and forgiveness in February 1864, he wrote 'that a page in my life which once had writing on it, has become absolutely blank, and that it is not in my power to pretend that it has a solitary word upon it'.[52] The weird image leaves Dickens apparently helpless, at the mercy of a self-whitening page. In its conflation of life with writing, however, it retains a kind of mystery. Had Dickens come to believe that what he wrote constituted his actual life?

After the marital breakup, Dickens claimed to be suffering a recurrence of the helpless misery he associated with his blacking days. At least for Forster, who knew the story, he pulled the old strings in June of 1862: 'The never-to-be-forgotten misery of that old time bred a certain shrinking sensitiveness in a certain ill-clad, ill-fed child, that I have found come back in the never-to-be-forgotten misery of this later time.'[53] In his mind, something profoundly wrong had happened to him on both occasions. Aligning those shrinking sensitivities, he refused to see the difference between the child's compliance with his family of origin and the adult's frantic decision to dismantle his own marriage. Yet the connection is profound in another way. The blacking warehouse briefly forced the middle-class child into a prematurely independent working-class existence. The marital separation was also a kind of declassing, as if Dickens could no longer tolerate the demands of the bourgeois life he had so carefully cultivated during his rise to fame. He was now free to roam, to hide, to come and go in the guises he might invent for each occasion. In each case, he had found it necessary to break his allegiance to a family situation that was, he felt, restricting his capacities.

After both episodes Dickens was moved to write accounts intended to silence anyone who might pass an independent judgement on those shaming episodes, when his life had spun out of control in ways that were visible to others. His ability to arouse both compassion and incredulity in his future biographers attests to the power of those representations. However we believe or judge him, Dickens established the terms for our responses. Further investigations of these and other episodes in Dickens's written biographical revelations might produce other insights about relations between his life and his accounts of it. But the Inimitable so often anticipates us. Beating the sceptical reader to his target, he slipped a wry comment about the dubiousness of his account into

---

[52] *PLets* 10:355–9, 356.
[53] *PLets* 10:97–8, 98.

the autobiographical fragment itself. In a small comic scene, a kindly pub owner and his wife observe the child Dickens as he orders a glass of their very best ale on some special occasion. 'They asked me a good many questions, as what my name was, how old I was, where I lived, how I was employed, &c. &c. To all of which, that I might commit nobody, I invented appropriate answers.'[54]

Further Reading

Robert Douglas-Fairhurst, *Becoming Dickens: The Invention of a Novelist* (Cambridge, MA and London: The Belknap Press of Harvard University Press, 2011)
Albert D. Hutter, 'Reconstructive Autobiography: The Experience at Warren's Blacking', *Dickens Studies Annual* 6 (1977): 1–14
Fred Kaplan, *Dickens: A Biography* (New York: Avon Books, 1988)
Robert Newsom, 'The Hero's Shame', *Dickens Studies Annual* 11 (1983): 1–24
Claire Tomalin, *The Invisible Woman: The Story of Nelly Ternan and Charles Dickens* (New York: Alfred A. Knopf, 1991)

---

[54] Forster, *Life*, 32.

CHAPTER 2

DICKENS'S LIFETIME READING

LEON LITVACK

In order to assess what Dickens read from childhood onward, and to determine how this vast and varied storehouse contributed to his imaginative output, journalism, speeches, and other forms of public pronouncement, it is reasonable to consider the records of volumes he purchased and possessed at various points in his life. Evidence comes primarily from three sources: the inventory of the contents of his house in Devonshire Terrace, completed in 1844 before his departure for Italy;[1] the 'book accounts' with his publishers, stretching from 1844 to 1858, which served as a convenient credit facility for purchasing volumes directly through the book trade;[2] and the catalogue of the library at his last home, Gad's Hill, compiled before the final sale in 1878.[3] Among the topics that feature are the following: English and American fiction, poetry, and drama of various periods; the classics; collections of essays; French and Italian literature; biography; books about London; science and industry; sociology and social reform; parliamentary reports; art; adventure and shipwrecks; travel; dreams and the occult; criminal, naval, and military trials; and standard reference works, including encyclopedias, dictionaries, and books of phrases, quotations, and slang. These three sources, while significant, do

---

[1] *The Letters of Charles Dickens*, ed. Madeline House, Graham Storey, et al., Pilgrim/British Academy Edition, 12 vols (Oxford: Clarendon Press, 1965–2002). Subsequent citations: *PLets* followed by volume:page range, page, and hn. for headnote, n. or nn. for footnotes, with page range given before page cited. Here, 4:711–25; hereafter 'Devonshire Inventory'.

[2] See Leon Litvack, 'What Books did Dickens Buy and Read? Evidence from the Book Accounts with his Publishers', *Dickensian* 94, 2 (Summer 1998): 85–130); hereafter 'Book Accounts'.

[3] *Catalogue of the Library of Charles Dickens from Gadshill, reprinted from Sotheran's 'Price Current of Literature' Nos. CLXXIV and CLXXV, Catalogue of his Pictures and Objects of Art, sold by Messrs. Christie, Manson & Woods, July 9, 1870, Catalogue of the Library of W. M. Thackeray, sold by Messrs. Christie, Manson & Woods, March 18 1864, and Relics from his Library, Comprising Books Enriched with his Characteristic Drawings, reprinted from Sotheran's 'Price Current of Literature' No. CLXXVII*, ed. J. H. Stonehouse (London: Piccadilly Fountain Press, 1935), 5–120; hereafter 'Stonehouse'.

not provide a comprehensive picture of the wealth of printed material that Dickens absorbed, then employed intelligently and imaginatively, to create those monumental works for which he is best remembered. Rather, they serve as a convenient checklist for confirming that individual intertextual references may be related to volumes Dickens is known to have had in his library. They are, perhaps, most useful when considered in outline, rather than in detail.

From his earliest years Dickens was an avid reader. He vividly recalled the mnemonics and rhymes through which he learned the alphabet,[4] and referred to himself as 'a GREAT reader of good fiction at an unusually early age',[5] who became anxious when he had no reading material to hand.[6] His childhood experiences provided fertile ground for nourishing the life of his imagination,[7] and he continually returned to them for inspiration. Even before he could read, his nursemaid Mary Weller (who lived with the Dickens family in the years 1817–22) related to him such gruesome stories as Captain Murderer, which Dickens claims to have heard '[h]undreds of times' from this 'female bard', who had a 'fiendish enjoyment' of the young boy's 'terrors'.[8] Dickens also reminisced about 'the most astonishing picture-books' he had devoured as a child, which were 'all about scimitars and slippers and turbans, and dwarfs and giants and genii and fairies, and blue-beards and bean-stalks and riches and caverns and forests ... all new and all true'.[9] His literary adviser and biographer Forster remarked that 'No one was more intensely fond than Dickens of old nursery tales',[10] and he read this type of literature into adulthood, in such collections as *The Child's Fairy Library*.[11] Nursery tales and nursery rhymes were infused into his work in both casual and fundamental ways.[12] For example, in *Great Expectations* one of Mr Jaggers's clients is described as 'pulling a lock of hair in the middle of his forehead, like the Bull in Cock Robin pulling at the bell-rope';[13] in *Our Mutual Friend*, 'a pretty little dead bird' in Mr Venus's shop is likened to 'Cock Robin, the hero of the Ballad'.[14] Such incidental references demonstrate Dickens's easy familiarity with tales and legends that were at the bedrock of English culture, and

---

[4] See *Bleak House*, ed. George Ford and Sylvère Monod, Norton Critical Edition (New York: W. W. Norton, 1999), chapter 8, page 88, and [Charles Dickens,] 'A Christmas Tree', *Household Words*, 21 December 1850. Subsequent references to *Bleak House* are inserted parenthetically in the text by *BH* chapter, page.

[5] [Charles Dickens], 'New Uncommercial Samples: Mr. Barlow', *All the Year Round*, 16 January 1869.

[6] See *PLets* 9:519–20, 519.

[7] See Michael Slater, *Charles Dickens* (New Haven and London: Yale University Press, 2009), 6.

[8] [Dickens], 'The Uncommercial Traveller', *All the Year Round*, 8 September 1860.

[9] [Dickens], 'The Child's Story', *Household Words*, 25 December 1852.

[10] John Forster, *The Life of Charles Dickens*, ed. J. W. T. Ley (London: Cecil Palmer, 1928), 317.

[11] See *PLets* 6:164–5, 165.

[12] For a more comprehensive treatment of Dickens's interest in fairy tales see Elaine Ostry, *Social Dreaming: Dickens and the Fairy Tale* (New York and London: Routledge, 2002).

[13] *Great Expectations*, ed. Margaret Cardwell (Oxford: Clarendon Press, 1993), II:1, 167. Subsequent references are inserted parenthetically in the text by *GE* volume:chapter, page.

[14] *Our Mutual Friend*, ed. Michael Cotsell, Oxford World's Classics (Oxford: Oxford University Press, 1998), I:7, 78–9. Subsequent references are inserted parenthetically in the text by *OMF* Book:chapter, page.

could be alluded to casually in order to add imaginative colour to his narratives. In other cases nursery stories that Dickens knew were put to more extended use; for example, in *Dombey and Son* the story of Dick Whittington (who rises to become a wealthy merchant and Lord Mayor of London) serves as the model for the progress of the hero, Walter Gay—particularly in the early portion of the novel.[15] His uncle, Solomon Gills, imagines his nephew's prospects: 'Why it may be his House one of these days, in part. Who knows? Sir Richard Whittington married his master's daughter.'[16] This iconic self-help story is treated with humour and a modicum of irony by Dickens, so that it never appears didactic; it is an example of the sophisticated way in which he uses a well-loved legend to infuse his narrative with playful satire, while at the same time enhancing Walter's character by anchoring him to a popular touchstone of English culture.

Dickens was intimately familiar with other well-known tales, including Bluebeard, Dick Turpin, Tom Thumb, Jack the Giant Killer, Sleeping Beauty, Hansel and Gretel, Little Red Riding Hood, Cinderella, Babes in the Wood, Puss in Boots, and Cock Robin. He encountered them in various forms, including chapbooks, those small, cheaply produced paper booklets (printed on a single sheet then folded), which formed the staple reading material of those with little money to spare, and which, Dickens wrote in his journalistic piece 'Out of the Season', 'were infinite delights to me'.[17] He mentioned the tales fancifully in correspondence; for example, in a letter to his friend William Charles Macready he makes reference to Cinderella: 'You ... have flung away your glass slipper, and changed your triumphal coach into a seedy old pumpkin.'[18] He was able to use details from grisly narratives like that of the wife-killer Bluebeard for comic purposes; in *Pickwick Papers,* for instance, Sam Weller jokes, 'I think he's the wictim o' connubiality, as Blue Beard's domestic chaplain said, with a tear of pity, ven he buried him.'[19] Such details came effortlessly to Dickens, and confirm how fluently—and widely—he ranged across the literature he knew from early childhood, and employed creatively throughout the course of his career. These fairy tales also served as an important touchstone for his complex emotional life. In December 1857 he delved deeply into this wellspring of his imagination to express the torment he felt in his burgeoning love for the young Ellen Ternan:

> I wish I had been born in the days of Ogres and Dragon-guarded Castles. I wish an Ogre with seven heads (and no particular evidence of brains in the whole lot of

---

[15] For Dickens's intended alteration of Walter's fate (that is, to have him 'disappoint all the expectations' and regress 'from that love of adventure and boyish light-heartedness, into negligence, idleness, dissipation, dishonesty, and ruin') see Forster, *Life*, 473, and *PLets* 4:589–93, 593.

[16] *Dombey and Son*, ed. Alan Horsman (Oxford: Clarendon Press, 1974), 4, 45. Subsequent references are inserted parenthetically in the text by *DS* chapter, page. On Whittington see also 6, 78; 9, 112; 10, 136; 15, 209; and 17, 227.

[17] [Dickens], 'Out of the Season', *Household Words*, 28 June 1856.

[18] *PLets* 4:9–13, 11.

[19] *Pickwick Papers*, ed. James Kinsley (Oxford: Clarendon Press, 1986), 20, 300. Subsequent references are inserted parenthetically in the text by *PP* chapter, page. See also *PLets* 5:152–3.

them) had taken the Princess whom I adore—you have no idea how intensely I love her!—to his stronghold on the top of a high series of Mountains, and there tied her up by the hair. Nothing would suit me half so well this day, as climbing after her, sword in hand, and either winning her or being killed.—*There's* a state of mind for you, in 1857.[20]

As Dickens grew, and began to attend the school run by William Giles, his reading widened to include, as Forster notes, 'not only ... the famous books that David Copperfield specially names, of *Roderick Random, Peregrine Pickle, Humphrey Clinker, Tom Jones,* the *Vicar of Wakefield, Don Quixote, Gil Blas, Robinson Crusoe,* the *Arabian Nights* and the *Tales of the Genii*,[21] but also ... the *Tatler,* the *Spectator,* the *Idler,* the *Citizen of the World,* and Mrs. Inchbald's *Collection of Farces*'.[22] The last of these volumes is especially noteworthy, given the great significance of the drama in Dickens's imaginative development. He not only attended the theatre from an early age,[23] and saw such plays as Shakespeare's *Richard III* and *Macbeth*;[24] he also read cheap periodicals featuring popular burlesques, including the *Portfolio of Entertaining and Instructive Varieties.*[25] Dickens owned a toy theatre,[26] replete (as he later recalled) with 'its familiar proscenium, and ladies in feathers, in the boxes'.[27] He made use of the texts of juvenile dramas, such as *The Miller and his Men* (which featured a sensational explosion) and stage performances,[28] and made reference to this play in, for example, *Dombey and Son* (12, 154). Given Dickens's extraordinary powers of recollection, such childhood reading and performing constituted for him 'a teeming world of fancies so suggestive and all-embracing', to the extent that in later years he could maintain the 'charming' and immediate effect of these early experiences 'as with the freshest garlands of the rarest flowers'.[29]

Dickens's school days were also occupied with the study of standard educational texts, like Lindley Murray's *English Grammar*—a volume he often derided and parodied. In *Nicholas Nickleby,* for example, Squeers responds to Peg Sliderskew's question ('Is that you?'), in these words:

---

[20] *PLets* 8:487–9, 488. See also Michael Slater, *Dickens and Women* (London: J. M. Dent & Sons, 1983), 202–17.
[21] See *David Copperfield,* ed. Nina Burgis (Oxford: Clarendon Press, 1981), 4, 48. Subsequent references are inserted parenthetically in the text by *DC* chapter, page.
[22] Forster, *Life,* 8. He adds that these volumes were, for Dickens, 'a host of friends when he had no single friend'.
[23] See ibid. 7.
[24] [Dickens], 'The Uncommercial Traveller', *All the Year Round,* 30 June 1860.
[25] Forster, *Life,* 27. See also Robert Langton, *The Childhood and Youth of Charles Dickens* (London: Hutchinson & Co., 1912), 77–8.
[26] Forster, *Life,* 10.
[27] [Dickens], 'A Christmas Tree', *Household Words,* 21 December 1850.
[28] Forster recalls that Dickens performed in *The Miller and his Men* at Wellington House Academy, *Life,* 44.
[29] 'A Christmas Tree'.

'Ah! it's me, and me's the first person singular, nominative case, agreeing with the verb "it's", and governed by Squeers understood, as a acorn, a hour; but when the h is sounded, the a only is to be used, as a and, a art, a ighway,' replied Mr Squeers, quoting at random from the grammar.[30]

He was also familiar with Francis Walkingame's pervasive arithmetic text, *The Tutor's Assistant*, which he also treated with disdain (*NN* 78, 82).[31] His Latin training was sound:[32] he knew Ovid and Virgil,[33] and wrote about Paul Dombey's experiences at Dr Blimber's school with sensitivity and humour (*DS* 11–12, 142–62). Dickens also had experience of devotional works like Isaac Watts's *Divine Songs, Attempted in Easy Language for the Use of Children*, evoked through hypocrites like Pecksniff, who recalls one of the poems Dickens himself recited with '*such* action and *such* attitudes':[34] "Tis the voice of the sluggard; I hear him complain; you have woke me too soon; I must slumber again.'[35] Dickens passionately opposed the dreary and ridiculous attitudes these texts often adopted towards their young readers. For him the epitome of such wrongheaded, patronizing didacticism was Mr Barlow, the '[i]rrepressible instructive monomaniac' in the popular children's book *The History of Sandford and Merton*, who 'never made, or took, a joke', forced upon the young 'a cold shower-bath of explanations and experiments', and stifled all imaginative thought.[36]

Yet relief was provided by other writers—particularly the eighteenth-century English essayists—whose works the schoolboy Dickens read many times before the age of 11. When he moved from Chatham to London in 1822 his schoolmaster William Giles gave him a copy of Oliver Goldsmith's journal *The Bee*, which Dickens 'kept for his sake, and its own, a long time afterwards'.[37] He recalled this volume, and others like it, in his plans for a new journal in 1839: 'The best general idea of the plan of the work might be given perhaps by reference to *The Tatler*, *The Spectator*, and Goldsmith's *Bee*; but it would be far more popular both in the subjects of which it treats and its mode of treating them.'[38] Though his design did not come to fruition until 1850, with the establishment of *Household Words*,[39] Dickens clearly bore in mind the example of figures like Addison's

---

[30] *Nicholas Nickleby*, ed. Paul Schlicke, Oxford World's Classics (Oxford: Oxford University Press, 2009), chapter 57, page 750. Subsequent references are inserted parenthetically in the text by *NN* chapter, page.

[31] Despite his contempt for Walkingame, Dickens purchased a copy in 1847—probably for the use of his children (see Litvack, 'Book Accounts', 108–9).

[32] See Forster, *Life*, 4.

[33] [Dickens], 'A Christmas Tree'.

[34] Langton, *Childhood*, 26. See also Slater, *Charles Dickens*, 8.

[35] *Martin Chuzzlewit*, ed. Margaret Cardwell (Oxford: Clarendon Press, 1982), 9, 153. Subsequent references are inserted parenthetically in the text by *MC* chapter, page.

[36] [Dickens], 'New Uncommercial Samples: Mr. Barlow', 16 January 1869.

[37] Forster, *Life*, 8. See also *PLets* 5:432–3.

[38] *PLets* 1:562–5, 563.

[39] See *PLets* 5:621–3.

Spectator; as he wrote to Forster, 'If the mark between a sort of *Spectator*, and a different sort of *Athenæum*, could be well hit, my belief is that a deal might be done.'[40]

The evocative passage on childhood reading, from the fourth chapter of *David Copperfield*, is often taken as evidence of how such early experiences contributed centrally to the imaginative life of the author.[41] Dickens confirms, through David, that 'When I think of it, the picture always rises in my mind, of a summer evening, the boys at play in the churchyard, and I sitting on my bed, reading as if for life' (*DC* 4, 48). Forster unambiguously asserts that 'Every word of this personal recollection had been written down as fact.'[42] Dickens depended for his creative sustenance upon such works as Alain René Lesage's *Gil Blas*, Oliver Goldsmith's *The Vicar of Wakefield*, Daniel Defoe's *Robinson Crusoe*, and especially the *Arabian Nights*,[43] which, even when he was at the height of his fame, continued to occupy 'far too high a place in the imagination to be burlesqued and parodied'.[44]

The first indication of Dickens's wish to systematize as a reader was his application for a ticket at the British Museum, the day after his 18th birthday in 1830. The few surviving library slips indicate that his course of miscellaneous reading included Goldsmith's *History of England*, Joseph Addison's *Miscellaneous Works*, engravings of Hans Holbein's *The Dance of Death*, and, most notably, the *Life* and *Dramatic Works* of Shakespeare.[45] This Elizabethan dramatist, with whom Dickens had a deep and abiding familiarity, proved to be a greater creative stimulus to him than any other single author. Not only did he possess several editions of the plays and poems; his library was also stocked with works of Shakespearian biography, bibliography, and textual annotation.[46] He called Shakespeare 'the noblest of all dramatists',[47] and considered his plays 'an unspeakable source of delight'.[48] When he travelled to the United States in 1842, he took with him a one-volume edition of Shakespeare, which, he told Forster, 'I constantly carry in my great-coat pocket'.[49] Dickens referred to Shakespeare constantly in correspondence, speeches, and journalism, as well as in fiction.[50] The playwright was constantly before him at his home, Gad's Hill: as Dickens delighted in informing visitors, the house was built 'on the identical spot where Falstaff ran away'.[51] To emphasize the point, Dickens

---

[40] *PLets* 4:658–60, 660.
[41] See Slater, *Charles Dickens*, 11.
[42] Forster, *Life*, 6.
[43] For a catalogue of emotional reminiscences of the *Arabian Nights* see 'A Christmas Tree'.
[44] [Dickens], 'Where We Stopped Growing', *Household Words*, 1 January 1853.
[45] See William Miller, 'Dickens Reads at the British Museum', *Dickensian* 43, 2 (Spring 1947): 84, and Slater, *Charles Dickens*, 32.
[46] See Devonshire Inventory, 716, 725; and Stonehouse, 22, 24, 87, 100–1.
[47] *The Speeches of Charles Dickens*, ed. K. J. Fielding (Oxford: Clarendon Press, 1960), 231; hereafter *Speeches*.
[48] *PLets* 3:165–6, 165.
[49] Ibid.
[50] See Valerie Gager, *Shakespeare and Dickens: The Dynamics of Influence* (Cambridge: Cambridge University Press, 1996), 251–369.
[51] *PLets* 8:328–9, 329; 333–4, 334.

displayed a framed plaque on the upstairs landing; it opened thus: 'THIS HOUSE, GADSHILL PLACE, stands on the summit of Shakespeare's Gadshill, ever memorable for its association with Sir John Falstaff in his noble fancy.'[52] *Henry IV*, parts I and II held a special attraction for Dickens on account of Falstaff, and he delighted in recalling him, for example, at the opening of a speech for the establishment of the Shakespeare Foundation Schools in 1864. He said, referring to himself, 'it is the duty of the chairman on an occasion of this nature, to be very careful that he does not anticipate those speakers who come after him. Like Falstaff, with a considerable difference, he has to be the cause of speaking in others'.[53] He used this favourite character in fiction as well; 'Mr. Dombey', Dickens writes, 'seemed to grow, like Falstaff's assailants, and instead of being one man in buckram, to become a dozen' (*DS* 8, 53).

Dickens ranged widely across the Shakespearian oeuvre in his allusions. *Henry V* and *Othello* inspired the titles of *Household Words* and *All the Year Round*, respectively.[54] Lines from *The Merchant of Venice* are artfully used in his critique of the design competition for the fresco *The Spirit of Chivalry*: 'Hath not a commissioner eyes? Hath not a commissioner hands, organs, dimensions, senses, affections, passions? Does he lose them all in the Commission Room, and dwindle into a mere polite machine: a deferential and obsequious instrument?'[55] He frequently referred to the apothecary episode from *Romeo and Juliet* Act 5, Scene 1; for example, in *Nicholas Nickleby*, Mr Crummles suggests that Smike should be cast in the role, and when the unfortunate boy delivers the line 'Who calls so loud?', he is acclaimed, 'alike by audience and actors, the very prince and prodigy of Apothecaries' (*NN* 25, 330). Years later, in 1865, he referred to a chemist's shop as being 'very like the apothecary's in Romeo and Juliet'.[56]

Dickens drew on other plays, including *A Midsummer Night's Dream*, *The Tempest*, *King Lear*, and *As You Like It* for elements of structure.[57] But the two Shakespearian works that appealed to him most were *Macbeth* and *Hamlet*. He was fascinated by the three witches in the first Act of *Macbeth*, and recalled them in such texts as *Great Expectations*, where Pip describes the 'diseased affection of the heart' on the visage of a Soho housekeeper: 'I had been to see Macbeth at the theatre, a night or two before, and … her face looked to me as if it were all disturbed by fiery air, like the faces I had seen rise out of the Witches' caldron' (*GE* II:7, 212). In *David Copperfield* several characters

---

[52] Forster, *Life*, 652.

[53] *Speeches*, 333.

[54] *Henry V*, Act 4, Scene 3, supplied the motto for *Household Words* ('Familiar in his mouth as household words'); *Othello*, Act 1, Scene 3, inspired the motto for *All the Year Round* ('The story of our lives from year to year').

[55] [Dickens], 'The Spirit of Chivalry', in *The Dent Uniform Edition of Dickens' Journalism*, ed. Michael Slater and John Drew, 4 vols (London: J. M. Dent, Columbus: Ohio State University Press, 1993–2000), 2:79. These lines were excised at proof stage. Subsequent references to these volumes are inserted parenthetically in the text as Dent volume:title, page.

[56] *PLets*, 11:30–1, 31.

[57] On *King Lear* see, for example, Alexander Welsh, *From Copyright to Copperfield: The Identity of Dickens* (Cambridge, MA: Harvard University Press, 1987), 87–99.

poignantly quote from *Macbeth*. For example, the impecunious Wilkins Micawber animates his correspondence with a single word: 'If any drop of gloom were wanting in the overflowing cup, which is now "commended" (in the language of an immortal Writer) to the lips of the undersigned' (*DC* 28, 366). James Steerforth recalls Macbeth's interruption of a gathering, after the departure of the Ghost, from Act 3 Scene 4; he says, '"Why, being gone, I am a man again", like Macbeth. And now for dinner! If I have not (Macbeth-like) broken up the feast with most admired disorder, Daisy' (*DC* 22, 275). Dickens referred to *Macbeth* freely in correspondence; for example, in 1842, when he visited President John Tyler in the White House, he shaped his reaction so as to employ Macbeth's inability to utter 'amen' after the murder of Duncan: 'He expressed great surprise at my being so young. I would have returned the compliment; but he looked so jaded, that it stuck in my throat like Macbeth's amen.'[58] In writing to his sister-in-law Georgina Hogarth about the 'emulative moustaches' of his close friends, he notes that the whiskers of Augustus Egg 'are not near his nose, but begin at the corners of his mouth, like those of the Witches in Macbeth'.[59]

Dickens's allusions to *Hamlet* are equally pervasive. In a speech at the Conversazione of the Birmingham Polytechnic Institution in 1844 he concluded with an appeal for comprehensive liberal education, by adapting Hamlet's address to Yorick's skull in Act 5, Scene 1: 'Now hie thee to the council chamber, and tell them, though they lay it on in sounding language and fine words an inch thick, to this complexion they must come at last.'[60] In his recollections of his time at Wellington House Academy he described the Latin master as being 'solemn as the ghost in Hamlet'.[61] In *The Old Curiosity Shop* Dick Swiveller and Mr Chuckster (both members of the 'Lodge of Glorious Apollos') exchange lines based on Hamlet's soliloquy in Act 3, Scene 2: ' "Tis now the witching—' | 'Hour of night!' | 'When churchyards yawn,' | 'And graves give up their dead.'[62] Dickens also demonstrated his knowledge of *Hamlet* in performance, in chapter 31 of *Great Expectations*: Mr Wopsle (the parish clerk with theatrical ambitions) stages a wretched—though hilarious—performance of the play. Dickens writes: 'Whenever that undecided Prince had to ask a question or state a doubt, the public helped him out with it. As for example; on the question whether 'twas nobler in the mind to suffer, some roared yes, and some no, and some inclining to both opinions said "Toss up for it;" and quite a Debating Society arose' (*GE* II:12, 254). These examples attest to the author's deep and abiding love of Shakespeare—both in outline and in detail. In his public life he supported the efforts of the London Shakespeare Committee (of which Forster was chairman) to purchase the birthplace in Stratford, and his amateur dramatic company's performances of *The Merry Wives of Windsor* contributed to the endowment of a curatorship.[63] He also

---

[58] *PLets* 3:109–12, 111.
[59] *PLets* 7:175–6, 175.
[60] *Speeches*, 64.
[61] [Dickens], 'Our School', *Household Words*, 11 October 1851.
[62] *The Old Curiosity Shop*, ed. Elizabeth M. Brennan (Oxford: Clarendon Press, 1998), 56, 432–3. Subsequent references are inserted parenthetically in the text by *OCS* chapter, page.
[63] See, for example, *PLets* 5:277–9, 278–9; 315–16, 315.

counted among his close associates the leading Shakespeare scholars and actors of the day, including Charles Knight and Macready. For him Shakespeare was, without doubt, 'the great master who knew everything'.[64]

In terms of the sheer number of references discernible in Dickens's output, Shakespeare is far outweighed by the Bible and the Anglican Prayer Book. While he cannot be described as an overtly religious man, he did have clear ideas about the merit and import of religious—particularly Christian—sentiments.[65] In 1853 he wrote to his friend Clarkson Stanfield on the death of the artist's son: 'I heartily sympathize with you my dear friend in resigning him to the mercy of God and that blessed Saviour in whom we all trust humbly, according to our several ways.'[66] The last phrase is significant: Dickens's own way was to trust and abide by the example of the historical Jesus. When his youngest son Edward (affectionately known as Plorn), was departing for Australia in 1868, Dickens wrote to say that while he didn't wish to harass his family about 'religious observances, or mere formalities', he nevertheless had put a New Testament among the books his son was to take with him, 'for the very same reasons, and with the very same hopes that made me write an easy account of it for you,[67] when you were a little child; because it is the best book that ever was or will be known in the world, and because it teaches you the best lessons by which any human creature who tries to be truthful and faithful to duty can possibly be guided'. Dickens also beseeched his dear boy: 'Never abandon the wholesome practice of saying your own private prayers, night and morning. I have never abandoned it myself, and I know the comfort of it.'[68]

Though scholars have attempted to catalogue the references in Dickens's fiction to the Old and New Testaments and the *Book of Common Prayer*,[69] such efforts represent only a small portion of the thousands of allusions in his work. What is clear, however, is that his familiarity with these texts derived from direct reading. References to the Old Testament outweigh those to the New, and he used the Hebrew and Christian Scriptures in different ways. He employed the Old Testament for diverse effects: its narratives, images, and language (in the Authorized, or King James, Version) were recalled easily. Thus in *David Copperfield* Ham Peggotty refers to the Book of Job (3:17) in his plea to David to say to Little Em'ly 'anything as might bring her to believe as I was not tired of my life, and yet was hoping fur to see her without blame, wheer the wicked cease from troubling and the weary are at rest' (*DC* 51, 631). Belshazzar's feast, from Daniel chapter 5, is the inspiration for Dickens's fascinating description of Rosa Dartle's facial

---

[64] [Dickens], 'The Uncommercial Traveller', *All the Year Round*, 21 July 1860.
[65] See Dennis Walder, *Dickens and Religion* (London: George Allen & Unwin, 1981).
[66] *PLets* 7:17.
[67] *The Life of Our Lord*, written in 1846, but only published in 1934, after the death of Dickens's last surviving child, Henry. See Gary Colledge, *Dickens, Christianity, and The Life of Our Lord* (London: Continuum, 2009).
[68] *PLets* 12:187–8, 188. On the 'biblical Dickens' see Janet L. Larson, *Dickens and the Broken Scripture* (Athens, GA: University of Georgia Press, 1985), 6–14.
[69] See, for example, Nicholas Bentley, Michael Slater, and Nina Burgis, *The Dickens Index* (Oxford: Oxford University Press, 1988), 20–1, 28–9, and Larson, *Dickens and the Broken Scripture*.

scar: 'There was a little altercation between her and Steerforth about a cast of the dice at back-gammon—when I thought her, for one moment, in a storm of rage; and then I saw it [the scar] start forth like the old writing on the wall' (*DC* 20, 252). Dickens occasionally combined Old Testament allusions for comic effect: in *Martin Chuzzlewit*, for example, General Choke tells Martin, 'Well! you come from an old country: from a country, sir, that has piled up golden calves as high as Babel, and worshipped 'em for ages. We are a new country, sir; ... we have no false gods; man, sir, here, is man in all his dignity' (*MC* 21, 348). This passage fuses Genesis 11 with Exodus 32, and supplements them with an allusion to the Ten Commandments (from Exodus 20:1–17 and Deuteronomy 4:4–21), in order to emphasize the ridiculousness of a character who is ironically called '[o]ne of the most remarkable men in the country' (*MC* 21, 347).[70]

There were certain Old Testament stories that Dickens used repeatedly; among them was Noah's Ark—particularly through associations with childhood. In 'A Christmas Tree' he recalled a boyhood toy, 'the wonderful Noah's Ark! It was not found seaworthy when put in a washing-tub, and the animals were crammed in at the roof, and needed to have their legs well shaken down before they could be got in'. His son Plorn also had such a plaything: 'a Noah's Ark with all the animals out walking, in company with Noah Ham, Shem, and Japhet, Mrs. N, Mrs. H, Mrs. S, and Mrs. J'.[71] Toy arks also feature in his fiction: in Esther's narrative in *Bleak House*, Peepy Jellyby takes a Noah figurine 'out of an ark I had given him before we went to church', and '*would* dip him head first into the wine-glasses and then put him in his mouth' (*BH* 30, 376), thus playing out Noah's drunkenness from Genesis 9:18–23; in *Our Mutual Friend* the Boffins purchase a toy Noah's ark for little Johnny (*OMF* II:9, 326). Dickens also alludes to the ark in *American Notes*, where he describes a night steamer on the Potomac River as 'not unlike a child's Noah's ark in form, with the machinery on the top of the roof'.[72] In *Great Expectations*, after the recapturing of Magwitch, the young Pip likens 'the black Hulk lying out a little way from the mud of the shore' to 'a wicked Noah's ark' (*GE* I:5, 41). Such passages indicate how wonderfully evocative the Old Testament could be for Dickens, especially when viewed through the lens of childhood.

Whereas the author's versatile allusions to the Hebrew Scriptures tended to derive from cheerful juvenile habituation and a genuine love of story, his references to the Christian Scriptures, and to some extent the *Book of Common Prayer*, were more directly inspired by a wish to teach and comfort. Particularly noteworthy in this regard are the set-piece deathbeds of such characters as Jo the crossing sweeper, where he and Allan Woodcourt recite the Lord's Prayer (from Matthew 6:9–13, and Luke 11:1–4); this is followed by the omniscient narrator's stark admonition: 'Dead, your Majesty. Dead, my lords and gentlemen. Dead, Right Reverends and Wrong Reverends of every order. Dead, men and women, born with Heavenly compassion in your hearts. And dying

---

[70] The epithet is also used of Jefferson Brick and other American characters (see *MC* 16, 272).
[71] *PLets* 7: 563–4, 564.
[72] *American Notes*, ed. Patricia Ingham, 2 vols (London: Penguin, 2000), II:1, 145. Subsequent references are inserted parenthetically in the text by *AN* volume:chapter, page.

thus around us, every day' (*BH* 47, 572). Likewise, in an attempt to lend solemnity and purpose to the death of Magwitch, Pip recalls—and Dickens slightly misquotes[73]—the episode of the Pharisee and the Publican from Luke 13:18: 'Mindful, then, of what we had read together, I thought of the two men who went up into the Temple to pray, and I knew there were no better words that I could say beside his bed, than "O Lord, be merciful to him, a sinner!"' (*GE* III:17, 456–7). Sidney Carton's approaching death in *A Tale of Two Cities* is imbued with pathos, through four occurrences of a poignant phrase from the Anglican burial service: 'I am the resurrection and the life, saith the Lord: he that believeth in me, though he were dead, yet shall he live: and whosoever liveth and believeth in me, shall never die.'[74] These lines echo the more general theme of resurrection in the text,[75] and reinforce that some aspect of Carton will live on, in the family of Charles Darnay and Lucie Manette.

Dickens was especially fascinated by Jesus's utterance beginning 'Suffer the little children', which appears in Matthew 19:14 ('Suffer little children, and forbid them not, to come unto me: for of such is the kingdom of heaven') and Mark 10:14 ('Suffer the little children to come unto me, and forbid them not: for of such is the kingdom of God'). When the daughter of Maria Winter died in 1855, he wrote to say, 'The simplest and most affecting passage in all the noble history of our Great Master, is his consideration for little children. And in reference to yours, as many millions of bereaved mothers poor and rich will do in reference to theirs until the end of time, you may take the comfort of the gracious words "And he took a child, and set it in the midst of them."'[76] He used this image for similar purposes in *Bleak House*, where Esther Summerson and Ada Clare try to comfort Jenny, the brickmaker's wife, whose baby has died: 'we whispered to her what Our Saviour said of children' (*BH* 8, 100). The idea of hope in the face of adversity is also present in *Hard Times*, when Louisa Gradgrind thinks back on her old home and the dreams of childhood, 'so good to be remembered when outgrown, for then the least among them rises to the stature of a great Charity in the heart, suffering little children to come into the midst of it.'[77]

Whereas Dickens tended to treat the New Testament with veneration and seriousness, he treated the Prayer Book with more latitude, and a modicum of humour. At Paul Dombey's christening, for example, 'Miss Tox kept her Prayer-book open at the Gunpowder Plot, and occasionally read responses from that service' (*DS* 5, 60). In the same novel, Captain Cuttle conflates the service of baptism with both the Ten Commandments and the banns of marriage. He says, 'Wal'r, my lad … prowiding as there is any just cause or impediment why two persons should not be jined together in the

---

[73] On this misquotation see Edgar Rosenberg's comment in *Great Expectations*, Norton Critical Edition (New York and London: W. W. Norton, 1999), 452–3.

[74] *A Tale of Two Cities*, ed. Andrew Sanders, Oxford World's Classics (Oxford: Oxford University Press, 1988), III:9, 301, 302; III:15, 360.

[75] See Andrew Sanders, *Charles Dickens: Resurrectionist* (London: Macmillan, 1982), 166–70.

[76] *PLets* 7:648–9, 648.

[77] *Hard Times*, ed. Fred Kaplan, 4th edn, Norton Critical Edition (New York: W. W. Norton, 2016), book 2, chapter 9, page 159.

house of bondage, for which you'll overhaul the place and make a note, I hope I should declare it as promised and wowed in the banns' (*DS* 50, 670). For the wedding of Bella Wilfer and John Harmon in *Our Mutual Friend*, the text of the service is inordinately compressed: 'Who taketh? I, John, and so do I, Bella. Who giveth? I, R. W. Forasmuch, Gruff and Glum, as John and Bella have consented together in holy wedlock, you may (in short) consider it done, and withdraw your two wooden legs from this temple. To the foregoing purport, the Minister speaking, as directed by the Rubric, to the People, selectly represented in the present instance by G. and G. above mentioned' (*OMF* IV:4, 665–6). Dickens clearly did value the *Book of Common Prayer*, and recommended it for daily use by the inmates of Urania Cottage.[78] As with the Bible, it was an important element of the cultural currency of nineteenth-century English life, and thus merited a place of significance in his imaginative storehouse.

Dickens's working knowledge of prose fiction was immense. He was, for example, intimately familiar with works produced at the inception of the genre, including John Bunyan's *Pilgrim's Progress*. He did not, however, appreciate the volume for its devotional or moralistic elements;[79] instead he valued its imagery and its peripatetic structure, which he used as a frame for *Oliver Twist* (subtitled '*The Parish Boy's Progress*'), and for *The Old Curiosity Shop*, in which Nell says to her grandfather, 'I feel as if we were both Christian, and laid down on this grass all the cares and troubles we brought with us; never to take them up again' (*OCS* 15, 126). The works of Defoe (whom he called 'that wonderful genius for the minutest details in a narrative')[80] were also among his favourites—particularly *Robinson Crusoe*, the work that 'kept alive' David Copperfield's 'fancy, and my hope of something beyond that place and time' (*DC* 4, 48). Dickens strongly defended Defoe's text in his polemical piece 'Frauds on the Fairies'.[81] He also loved the work of Swift (which he recalled reading 'with a delicious laziness')[82]— particularly *Gulliver's Travels*, with its satire, which he poignantly employed to describe the aims of Americans, in their consumption of food: 'to empty, each creature, his Yahoo's trough as quickly as he can, and then slink sullenly away' (*American Notes*, II:4, 189).

Dickens's debt to Henry Fielding (after whom he named his eighth child) was significant. He called him 'one of the greatest English writers', particularly for his 'profound knowledge of human nature'.[83] He drew on the mock heroic (evident in Fielding's *Joseph Andrews*) for the early portions of *Pickwick Papers*, such as the opening of chapter 2: 'THAT punctual servant of all work, the sun, had just risen, and begun to strike a light on the morning of the thirteenth of May, one thousand eight hundred and twenty-seven, when Mr. Samuel Pickwick burst like another sun from his slumbers,

---

[78] *PLets* 5:192.
[79] See *PLets* 6:783.
[80] *PLets* 8:62–3, 62.
[81] [Dickens], 'Frauds on the Fairies', *Household Words*, 1 October 1853.
[82] *PLets* 2:238–9, 238.
[83] *PLets* 7:648–9, 648; 5:651–4, 652.

threw open his chamber window, and looked out upon the world beneath' (*PP* 2, 7–8). *Tom Jones* was also a greatly beloved text, and provided some inspiration for *Great Expectations*, in terms of the developing relationship between Pip and Estella: two characters from widely divergent social classes.

In 'The Holly Tree Inn' Dickens claimed to know 'every word' of Laurence Sterne's *A Sentimental Journey* and Tobias Smollett's *Peregrine Pickle*.[84] Sterne (whose *Tristram Shandy* was also a favourite) inspired Dickens's treatment of sentimental scenes, like the deaths of Little Nell and Paul Dombey. Dickens recalled Sterne often in his work, as in 'Shops and their Tenants' from *Sketches by Boz*: 'What inexhaustible food for speculation do the streets of London afford! We never were able to agree with Sterne in pitying the man who could travel from Dan to Beersheba, and say that all was barren' (Dent 1: 'Shops and their Tenants', 61). From Smollett, through such texts as *Roderick Random* and *Humphry Clinker*,[85] Dickens appreciated the techniques of the grotesque, particularly in physiognomy; the construction of characters like Sam Weller from *Pickwick Papers* demonstrates how Dickens adapted from Smollett elements of the picaresque,[86] a feature he also admired in Cervantes's *Don Quixote*, in which he found 'some of the finest things'.[87]

Dickens's reading in writers of the eighteenth century exercised an inordinate influence on his output—particularly up to 1848, with the completion of *Dombey and Son* and the Christmas Books. He did, of course, read and appreciate a wide range of later, nineteenth-century prose fiction—particularly authors like Walter Scott, whom he called 'Foremost and unapproachable in the bright world of fiction'.[88] He read *Kenilworth* 'with greater delight than ever',[89] and used this and other historical novels, including *Waverley* and *The Heart of Midlothian*, as models for *Barnaby Rudge*.[90] Dickens spoke out of deep familiarity with the Waverley novels when he told an Edinburgh audience in 1841 that Scott ('the mighty genius') was 'equally at home in the wild grandeur of Highland scenery or the burning sands of Syria, and in the low haunts of London life'.[91]

As a professional writer and editor, Dickens's sensibilities were highly sensitized to the output of his contemporaries. He followed literary trends with interest, and in writing such works as *Oliver Twist* he was conscious of its resemblance to Newgate novels[92] like *Paul Clifford*, by Edward Bulwer Lytton, and *Rookwood*, by William Harrison Ainsworth, whose *Jack Sheppard* Dickens published in *Bentley's Miscellany* in 1839. This first outing as the editor of a periodical obliged Dickens to read a host of (then) popular authors, including James Sheridan Knowles, Francis Mahony ('Father Prout'), Edward

---

[84] [Dickens], 'The Holly-Tree Inn: The Guest', *Household Words* Christmas number, 15 December 1855.
[85] See *PLets* 7:458.
[86] See, for example, *PP* 10, 137–48; 16, 230–41.
[87] *PLets* 8:153–5, 153.
[88] [Dickens], 'Review of Lockhart's Life of Sir Walter Scott', in Dent 2:37.
[89] *PLets* 1:576.
[90] See Andrew Sanders, *The Victorian Historical Novel, 1840–1880* (London: Macmillan, 1978), 68–96.
[91] *Speeches*, 12.
[92] See Dickens's 1841 Preface to the third edition of *Oliver Twist*, lxiii.

and Henry Mayhew, Samuel Lover, Gilbert À Beckett, and Richard Harris Barham ('Thomas Ingoldsby'). While he published all of these authors, there were others whose contributions did not make it into *Bentley's*, or into his subsequent journals, *Household Words* and *All the Year Round*.[93] Dickens's editorial reading was extremely laborious: the scale of it is demonstrated in an 1853 article by the author and Henry Morley, who note that in 1852, 'we read nine hundred manuscripts, of which eleven were available for this journal, after being entirely re-written';[94] in one case, Dickens's efforts to 'hack and hew' a single piece into shape for his journal made the proofs look like 'an inky fishing-net'.[95] It should not, of course, be assumed that such reading and editing necessarily translated into literary influence; however Dickens was clearly attuned to the efforts of novelists like William Makepeace Thackeray, whose *Vanity Fair* appeared around the same time as *Dombey and Son*. Indeed in 1848 Dickens confessed to Thackeray, concerning an article by the latter in the satirical journal *Punch*, 'I cried most bitterly over [it] ... and shall never forget it.'[96]

In later years some writers he published were subjected to high levels of scrutiny, and indeed intervention in their creative processes. In the case of Harriet Martineau (a writer Dickens described as 'grimly bent upon the enlightenment of mankind')[97] Dickens fundamentally disagreed with her approach to such subjects as education and factory legislation, and excised from her work passages he believed did not subscribe to the ethos of the journal.[98] He wrangled with Elizabeth Gaskell, a regular contributor to *Household Words*, particularly about her novel *North and South*, which he was publishing in the journal. In a later moment of intense frustration he burst out, 'If I were Mr. G. O Heaven how I would beat her!'[99]

Dickens of course read across many genres, including poetry, and his library featured numerous anthologies, such as *The British Poets*, and many books about poetry such as *Sketches of the Poetical Literature of the Past Half-Century*, and Johnson's *Lives of the Poets*.[100] He frequently alludes to John Milton's *Paradise Lost*, for example in chapter 58 of *Great Expectations*, where Pip serves as a type of Adam, gaining knowledge of good and evil.[101] There are also many references to Alexander Pope's *Essay on Man*, such as in *Little Dorrit*, where Mrs Merdle recalls Epistle I when she says to Amy Dorrit, 'There used to be a poem when I learnt lessons, something about Lo the poor Indians whose

---

[93] See John Drew, *Dickens the Journalist* (London: Palgrave Macmillan, 2003), 181–2, and Kathryn Chittick, *Dickens and the 1830s* (Cambridge: Cambridge University Press, 1990), 92–113.

[94] [Dickens and Henry Morley], 'H. W.', *Household Words*, 16 April 1853.

[95] *PLets* 8:139.

[96] *PLets* 5:227–8, 228.

[97] *PLets* 7:438–40, 438.

[98] See Drew, *Dickens the Journalist*, 125–8.

[99] *PLets* 7:699–700, 700 and n. 1. The humorous outburst concerned a story by Gaskell, 'Half a Lifetime Ago'. On *North and South* see, for example, *PLets* 7:417–18, 417 and n.

[100] Stonehouse, 15, 81, 94.

[101] See Jerome Meckier, *Dickens's Great Expectations: Misnar's Pavilion versus Cinderella* (Lexington, Ky: University Press of Kentucky, 2002), 178.

something mind!'[102] Thomas Gray's 'Elegy Written in a Country Churchyard' is quoted in Dickens's fiction, and he wrote a parody of the poem for Mary Boyle in 1849.[103] He knew Robert Burns's songs and poems, including 'Auld Lang Syne',[104] and he often referred to and sang the *Irish Melodies* of Thomas Moore.[105]

Dickens drew inspiration from Romantic poets such as Samuel Taylor Coleridge, and compared his own photographic portrait by John Watkins to the Ancient Mariner, on account of his 'grim and wasted aspect'.[106] He purchased a copy of Wordsworth's *Prelude* at about the time he composed David Copperfield's retrospective self-examination, set in the Alps,[107] and referred to the last line of the 'Immortality' Ode in a letter to Forster: 'there *are* thoughts, you know, that lie too deep for words'.[108] The works of Byron held a particular attraction for him—especially *Don Juan* and *Childe Harold's Pilgrimage*, both of which he employed satirically. In 'The Boarding-House' from *Sketches by Boz*, Mr Hicks 'could not resist the singularly appropriate quotation, beginning "But beef is rare within these oxless isles"', from the second canto of *Don Juan* (Dent 1:280). Dickens also used the motif of the Byronic Hero in his portrayals of Steerforth in *David Copperfield* and Eugene Wrayburn in *Our Mutual Friend*.[109]

Dickens read the poetry of his contemporaries, and particularly appreciated the work of Tennyson, after whom he named his fourth son. He considered *Idylls of the King* 'all wonderfully fine—chivalric, imaginative, passionate, admirable',[110] and told listeners at the Liverpool Mechanics' Institution that Tennyson 'is one of us', and 'uses his great gifts ... for the general welfare'.[111] Dickens also enjoyed the poetry of Edward Bulwer Lytton with 'deepest interest, admiration and delight',[112] and published works by Coventry Patmore, Elizabeth Barrett Browning, and George Meredith in *Household Words*.[113]

There are, of course, new possibilities for researching this broad, deep, and above all endlessly captivating subject, which adds so significantly to the vast storehouse of influences on Dickens's creative impulse. Fresh opportunities are offered by the ongoing

---

[102] *Little Dorrit*, ed. Harvey Peter Sucksmith (Oxford: Clarendon Press, 1979), volume I, chapter 20, 237.

[103] See, for example, *DC* 49, 608, where Micawber quotes from the poem ('Each in his narrow cell ...'). The parody for Boyle is printed in *PLets* 5:708–9.

[104] See *DC* 17, 225, and 49, 608; and *OMF* IV:6, 477.

[105] See *PLets* 2:79 and nn. 1, 3. See also Leon Litvack, 'Dickens, Ireland and the Irish Part I', *Dickensian* 99, 1 (Spring 2003): 36–41.

[106] *PLets* 9:465–6, 466. See also *PLets* 2:103–4, 103.

[107] See Litvack, 'Book Accounts', 94–5, 103. See also *DC* 58, 697–8.

[108] *PLets* 3:204–11, 211. Wordsworth's line is 'thoughts that do often lie too deep for tears'.

[109] See William R. Harvey, 'Charles Dickens and the Byronic Hero', *Nineteenth-Century Fiction* 24 (1969–70): 307–13.

[110] *PLets* 9:106–7, 107.

[111] *Speeches*, 56.

[112] *PLets* 5:500–1, 500.

[113] See, for example, Patmore's 'The Golden Age', in *Household Words*, 2 November 1850; E. B. Browning's sonnet 'Hiram Power's Greek Slave', in *Household Words*, 26 October 1850; and Meredith's 'Monmouth', in *Household Words*, 1 November 1856.

digitization of the periodicals that Dickens edited, and to which he contributed—not only *Household Words* and *All the Year Round*, but also *The Morning* and *Evening Chronicle*, *Bell's Life in London*, *Bentley's Miscellany*, *The Daily News*, and others. It is also important to recall that he amended (in an unacknowledged fashion) the contributions of others to his journals; further examination of these might well reveal undocumented intertexts. Substantial work also needs to be carried out on the influences of another of his favourite authors, Ben Jonson: Dickens cast himself in both *Every Man in his Humour* and *The Alchemist*,[114] and he was to have written a 'jeu d'esprit' on the occasion of his amateur company's theatrical tour in 1847, in which Mrs Gamp would have provided 'her critical opinion of Ben Jonson as a literary character'.[115] Sustained analysis is also wanted on contemporary American writers, including Washington Irving (one of his favourites), to whom he intimated that 'everything' he had written was 'upon my shelves, and in my thoughts, and in my heart of hearts'.[116] Dickens spoke French well, and carefully read such authors as Voltaire, whose work he took with him to Italy in 1844;[117] there has been little investigation of how Dickens uses *Candide*, or Lesage's *Gil Blas*, which he knew from an early age.[118]

Many of Dickens's works display evidence of substantial research; for example, the death of Krook in *Bleak House* from spontaneous combustion was, in the author's estimation, an extrapolation based on reliable scientific evidence.[119] While this particular turn of plot may fall into the realm of pseudo-science, Dickens's appreciation of more widely acknowledged advancements may be judged from the great variety of articles by others that he published in his journals; they treated such topics as evolutionary biology, conservation, steam-powered machinery, medicine, astronomy, photography, thermodynamics, and chemistry. Dickens owned and used a variety of reference works: encyclopedias;[120] dictionaries (of e.g. pronunciation, Latin phrases, biography, antiquities, nautical terms, human and comparative anatomy, 'universal knowledge', and the United States Congress);[121] chronicles of London (manners and customs, history, prisons, water supplies, sanitation, diseases, pauperism, night scenes, 'underground' life, and the 'vulgar tongue');[122] and official reports (on e.g. slavery, insanity, immigration, education, agriculture, urban burial, anaesthetics, and capital punishment).[123] All of these could bear closer scrutiny.

---

[114] On *Every Man in his Humour* see PLets 4:332–3; 347–8, 347; 359–60, 359; 364–5; 377–8, 377; on *The Alchemist* see PLets 4:441; 5:195 n. 5, 202, and 242 n. 2; 6:256–9, 258 and n. 3, and 7:881 n. 5.
[115] PLets 5:140–1, 141.
[116] PLets 2:267–9, 267.
[117] PLets 4:174–5, 174 and n. 2.
[118] [Dickens], 'The Uncommercial Traveller', Dent 4:172.
[119] See BH 32, 403. See also PLets 7:22–3.
[120] See, for example, Stonehouse, 42, 83.
[121] See ibid. 6, 11, 14, 42, 47, 51, 62, 66, 71, 96, 103, 116, 119.
[122] Ibid. 9, 15, 25, 41, 45, 60, 74, 82, 88–9, 104, 116.
[123] Ibid. 61, 87–9.

FIGURE 2.1 *The Wisdom of our Ancestors*, from the dummy book backs in Dickens's study, Gad's Hill Place, Higham, Kent.

© Leon Litvack, 2017

What appears above is a representative summary of the main areas of influence that books exercised over Dickens's life and work. Yet to appreciate fully the breadth and depth of Dickens's reading, it is necessary to consider carefully and comprehensively the references and subjects (not all of them overt) in his works, his vast correspondence, his speeches, his library listings, and the comments of his friends, family, and professional contacts. One could also add to this impressive list those book titles that were never intended as reading material, but only as fictitious (often satirical) volumes that Dickens invented for the dummy book backs he had constructed to line the Gad's Hill library walls (Figure 2.1); these included *Hansard's Guide to Refreshing Sleep* (many volumes); *Noah's Arkitecture* [sic], 2 vols; *Malthus's Nursery Songs*; and *The Wisdom of our Ancestors. I.—Ignorance; II.—Superstition. III.—The Block. IV.—The Stake. V.—The Rack. VI.—Dirt. VII.—Disease*.[124] Even then one would still wonder at the inventive and tireless reading potential and experience of a man who possessed an exceptional memory, carried all that he knew effortlessly, and was gifted with an imagination that

---

[124] See Langton, *Childhood*, 122–7.

naturalized everything and transformed it into serviceable material. Dickens cannot, then, simply be considered a 'literary' writer, but rather one whose creative efforts emerged from a lifelong habit of reading that was active, perceptive, and incessantly productive.

Further Reading

Philip Collins, 'Dickens's Reading', *Dickensian* 60, 3 (Autumn 1964): 136–51

T. W. Hill, 'Books that Dickens Read', *Dickensian* 45, 2 (Spring 1949): 81–90; 45, 3 (Summer 1949): 201–7

Norbert Lennartz and Dieter Koch (eds), *Texts, Contexts, and Intertextuality: Dickens as a Reader* (Göttingen: V&R Unipress, 2014)

George Henry Lewes, 'Dickens in Relation to Criticism', *Fortnightly Review* 11 (1872): 141–54

Harry Stone, *Dickens and the Invisible World: Fairy Tales, Fantasy, and Novel-Making* (Bloomington: Indiana University Press, 1979)

CHAPTER 3

DICKENS AS PROFESSIONAL AUTHOR

JOHN BOWEN

A Different Author

DICKENS was a very different author from those who had come before him and, despite his enormous influence, from his contemporaries. Rapid changes in the technologies and economics of publishing and printing, and in the class-composition of the United Kingdom, gave new possibilities for authorial self-creation, control, and circulation, which Dickens developed and exploited in novel and creative ways. His astonishing European and North American, if not global, success as an author was built on an intimate understanding of the possibilities of literary markets, in which he played a shaping role through his innovative use of serial publication of his novels, the editing and part-ownership of the journals *Household Words* (1850–9) and *All the Year Round* (1859–70), and through his often conflicted relationships with publishers. This chapter examines how these forces shaped his fiction, journalism, and other writings, and his identity and self-presentation as an author.

We are fortunate to have a large archive of material that shows just how active and inventive a participant in the literary marketplace and profession Dickens was. It includes his prefaces, letters, speeches, manuscripts, publishers' accounts, and proofs. We know who wrote for the magazines he edited, the kinds of revisions he made to their work, and how he saw—and sought to transform—the calling or profession to which he gave his life. His friend John Forster was given the majority of Dickens's manuscripts and proofs, which he in turn bequeathed to the South Kensington Museum, now the V&A. These, together with the archives of Dickens's publishers Chapman and Hall, give an unparalleled insight into the context and material circumstances in and through which his writings became print. Dickens's letters, of which nearly 15,000 survive, are an equally rich resource, from which we can gain an exceptionally detailed picture of his private and public roles as author, editor, speechmaker, and man of letters. In letters to authors and aspiring authors, to his sub-editor at *Household Words* and *All the Year Round*, W. H. Wills, and in his negotiations with publishers and collaborators, we see the depth of his interest not only in the material form and fate of his own writings but also in such topics as copyright reform, theatrical adaptation, and the status and moral purpose of the professional author in modern society.[1]

The professionalism of Dickens's writing life was driven above all by his creativity and restless literary ambition, his determination to write what he wanted and to be justly rewarded for it. Writing and print were there almost from the start of his life: his maternal uncle was an unsuccessful novelist (author of *Emir Malek, Prince of the Assassins*, 1827) and successful editor of Hansard's great rival, *The Mirror of Parliament*; and his father John had journalistic ambitions and was later chief reporter on the *Daily News*, which Dickens briefly edited. In the early and mid-nineteenth century, literary life was an economically precarious one. Dickens's father-in-law, George Hogarth, for example, despite being a successful lawyer, friend of Sir Walter Scott, magazine editor, and music critic, nevertheless suffered recurrent financial difficulties, went bankrupt, and was imprisoned for debt, as were many of his literary precursors, including Henry Fielding, Tobias Smollett, and his beloved Oliver Goldsmith.[2] Scott himself, the dominant literary figure of the generation preceding Dickens's and an important role model for him, was ruined by the economic crisis of 1825 and the collapse of a printing business in which he had a share.[3] For the rest of his life, Scott worked like a dog to pay off the massive debts that ensued.

The literary, theatrical, and journalistic worlds that Dickens inhabited were full of unfortunates of many sorts—chancers, bankrupts, casualties, and failures—and he was determined not to be one of them. He could be a ruthless negotiator and in his early years reneged on numerous contracts and agreements with publishers that he felt did not do him justice. The fear that underpinned these quarrels is rawly evident in a letter that he wrote to Forster about Richard Bentley ('The Brigand of Burlington Street'), the publisher of *Oliver Twist* (1837–9; volume publication 1838) which contrasts

> The immense profits which Oliver has realised to its publisher, and is still realising; the paltry, wretched, miserable sum it brought to me (not equal to what is every day paid for a novel that sells fifteen hundred copies at most); ... I have still the slavery and drudgery of another work on the same journeyman-terms ... my books are

---

[1] See in particular Robert L. Patten, *Charles Dickens and his Publishers* (Oxford: Clarendon Press, 1978), and Michael Slater, *Charles Dickens: A Life Defined by Writing* (New Haven: Yale University Press, 2009).

[2] On George Hogarth, see William F. Long, 'Passages in the Life of Mr George Hogarth—2: Mr Hogarth goes to prison', *Dickensian* 112, 2 (Summer 2016): 118–29. On debt and literary authorship, see Margot Finn, *The Character of Credit: Personal Debt in English Culture 1740–1914* (Cambridge: Cambridge University Press, 1993), 51–8.

[3] For the consequences of the collapse of Archibald Constable and Company, see Joanne Shattock, 'The Publishing Industry', in John Kucich and Jenny Bourne Taylor (eds), *Oxford History of the Novel in English: Volume 3: The Nineteenth-Century Novel 1820–1880* (Oxford: Oxford University Press, 2011), 4–5.

enriching everybody connected with them but myself, and ... I, with such a popularity as I have acquired, am struggling in old toils, and wasting my energies in the very height and freshness of my fame, and the best part of my life, to fill the pockets of others.[4]

Dickens knew he was not a 'journeyman' and was determined not to be paid like one. But if it was not the work of a journeyman, what was it? A business, career, profession, trade, calling; all of the above; or something else entirely?

It was inventive, for a start. The most striking thing about Dickens's relation to the literary profession is how much and how deeply he reshaped it. The major literary figures of the generation before Dickens were mainly poets (William Blake, Lord Byron, Percy Shelley, William Wordsworth, John Keats, Samuel Coleridge); only Jane Austen and Frances Burney were solely novelists. By the time of his death, the novel was the dominant literary and cultural form. Serial publication of the sort that Dickens pioneered in the *Pickwick Papers* (1836–7) barely existed as a significant mode of publication before then. Afterwards, it shaped strongly the careers of most of his important contemporaries and successors, including George Eliot, Anthony Trollope, Elizabeth Gaskell, William Makepeace Thackeray, and Thomas Hardy. Readerships for fiction expanded greatly in his lifetime, driven by technological changes in printing and paper technology, the growth of advertising, and through many innovations by writers and publishers in the ways in which fictions were created and distributed.[5]

Dickens was at the forefront of many of these changes, and there was remarkable variety in the modes by which his work reached the public. His first book *Sketches by Boz* (1836), for example, collected (and revised) an array of different kinds of articles and stories that had originally appeared in important newspapers (*Morning Chronicle* and *Evening Chronicle*), a Sunday sporting paper (*Bell's Life in London*), and monthly magazines with much smaller circulations: the *Monthly Magazine*, the *Library of Fiction*, and the *Carlton Chronicle*. We think of Dickens primarily as a novelist, but he was also a miscellaneous writer throughout his career, able to turn from *Pickwick Papers* or *Little Dorrit* to add yet another item to the 'truly prodigious amount of other writing ... short stories, topical journalism, essays, travel writings and writings for children, polemical pieces in verse as well as prose' that he also wrote.[6] Throughout his working life, the great novels were interwoven with a mass of other writings, which sometimes distracted Dickens but more often spurred him to greater inventiveness. Of his first six books, from

---

[4] *The Letters of Charles Dickens*, ed. Madeline House, Graham Storey, et al., Pilgrim/British Academy Edition, 12 vols (Oxford: Clarendon Press, 1965–2002). Future citations: *PLets* followed by volume:page range, page, and hn. for headnote, n. or nn. for footnotes, with page range given before page. Here, 1:493–4.

[5] See David Finkelstein, 'Publishing and the Materiality of the Book', in Kate Flint (ed.), *Cambridge History of Victorian Literature* (Cambridge: Cambridge University Press, 2012), 15–33, and David McKitterick (ed.), *Cambridge History of the Book in Britain Volume 6: 1830–1914* (Cambridge: Cambridge University Press, 2010).

[6] Slater, *Dickens*, 20.

Sketches by Boz to *Barnaby Rudge*, it was only the latter that began life as a through-plotted novel, and even that had several false starts. In the early years, the genesis and execution of his works were often brilliantly imaginative messes: *Pickwick* was first intended to be a kind of magazine or miscellany, and *Oliver Twist* and *The Old Curiosity Shop* began as short stories.

After a serious wobble following the suicide of its illustrator (and inaugurator) Robert Seymour (1798–1836) and some initial uncertainty, Dickens and his publishers established what was to be his favourite publication format with *Pickwick Papers*: a novel produced in 20 monthly instalments (19 in fact, as the final one was invariably a double number), each of 32 pages of text, together with two illustrations, each instalment to be sold for a shilling, the double number retailing for 2 shillings. *Pickwick* was followed by *Oliver Twist*, again in monthly instalments, but contained within *Bentley's Miscellany*, a miscellaneous magazine that Dickens himself edited. It was not a happy experience. Dickens quarrelled badly with its publisher Bentley. After the return to the *Pickwick* format for *Nickleby* (which he wrote simultaneously with the later stages of *Oliver*, which had begun as he was still finishing *Pickwick*), *Barnaby Rudge* and *Old Curiosity Shop* appeared in *Master Humphrey's Clock* (1840–1), a threepenny weekly journal edited, and in fact entirely written, by Dickens. This was one of his more important publishing adventures, showing how quickly he could respond to market demands. His initial plan was for an illustrated miscellany, with contributions both by himself and others. The public disliked it, and after an initial éclat, sales dropped. Dickens responded by rapidly expanding a short story into *The Old Curiosity Shop*, which became a triumphant success and raised his reputation to new heights.

Barnaby Rudge (1841) immediately followed over subsequent weeks, after which Dickens returned to monthly numbers, which became the way in which many of his most important works entered the world, including *Nicholas Nickleby* (1838–9), *Martin Chuzzlewit* (1843–4), *Dombey and Son* (1846–8), *David Copperfield* (1849–50), *Bleak House* (1852–3), *Little Dorrit* (1855–7), and *Our Mutual Friend* (1864–5). This revolutionary format, which significantly cheapened the price and enlarged the readership of new fiction, ran from the beginning to the very end of his career. *The Mystery of Edwin Drood* (1870) had a similar but shorter pattern of publication: intended to be in 12 monthly instalments, it was curtailed by Dickens's sudden death to a fragmentary six. Although the price of one shilling per instalment, a pound in total, was markedly less than the standard three-volume novel price of 31*s.* 6*d.*, it was still not a negligible amount. Scrooge's clerk, Bob Cratchit, for example, earned 15 shillings per week, so even a single instalment would be a significant purchase for a working-class or lower-middle-class family.

Throughout his career, Dickens continued to innovate, and *Hard Times* (1854), *A Tale of Two Cities* (1859), and *Great Expectations* (1860–1) appeared in weekly instalments of the twopenny magazines, *Household Words* and *All the Year Round*, which he founded and over which he had complete control. For the latter, whose weekly sales were a more-than-healthy 100,000, he was also its publisher. It is hard to get reliable figures for Dickens's overall circulation in the often swashbuckling world of Victorian print culture, although we know that it began small, quickly got big, and eventually became enormous. A few hundred readers for the first few monthly instalments of *Pickwick Papers* grew to 40,000 or so by the end of the run, with a triumphant 100,000 weekly copies sold by the end of *The Old Curiosity Shop* and nearly 300,000 for some of the late Christmas stories in *All the Year Round* such as *Mrs Lirriper's Lodgings* (1863).[7] These numbers are the tip of a much larger iceberg, that of cheap reprinting, which has still to be accurately measured. Although it was only later in the century that a mass working-class readership was reached, knowledge of Dickens's work through cheap plagiarisms and continuations, theatrical and fictional adaptations, illustrations, and Public Readings would have been wide. Progressively cheaper editions ensured that with each decade of his life, his work came within the budget of more and more readers. It was profitable for him and for his publishers, and in its cross-class readership and appeal, culturally transforming. As his works began to come out of copyright in the 1880s, a freshly illustrated *Pickwick Papers* could be bought for sixpence, less than 2 per cent of its price at first publication.

Dickens was also always an international author in his readership and increasingly in his subject matter and sense of authorial identity. He was translated early and often into many European languages: the first German translation of Dickens (*Pickwick Papers*) was as early as 1837 and by 1842 it was joined by French, Danish, Czech, Italian, Polish, Swedish, Hungarian, and Norwegian translations of his work.[8] These could often be partial or misleading—*A Christmas Carol* (1843), for example, appeared in a Bulgarian translation in 1860 (re-translated from the Russian) under the magnificently point-missing title *Glorious Resurrection or a Tale of Easter* (1860)—but they testify to the scale and range of cultural portability that Dickens's work inspired in the ever-growing print- and translation-culture of the nineteenth century. *Pickwick Papers* was pirated in Van Diemen's Land (Tasmania) in 1838 but Dickens received no financial reward from this and little more from his millions of readers in the USA.[9] Despite his efforts to change the law through confronting his adoring readers with the question of copyright on his 1842 North American tour, the 'culture of reprinting' proved too strong even for him.[10] There were important things in Dickens's professional life that even he not could control. We will never know how many people read his works in the United States and Europe, freely and promiscuously translated, reprinted, and excerpted as they were in thousands of obscure newspapers, editions, and magazines. But new digital technologies have hugely increased our ability to map the millions of readers, quoters, reviewers, publishers,

---

[7] Patten, *Charles Dickens and his Publishers*, 68, 110, 301.
[8] *The Reception of Charles Dickens in Europe, Volume 1*, ed. Michael Hollington (London: Bloomsbury, 2013), xxv–xxvi.
[9] Charles Dickens, *The Posthumous Papers of the Pickwick Club* (Launceston: Henry Dowling, 1838).
[10] Meredith McGill, *American Literature and the Culture of Reprinting, 1834–1853* (Philadelphia: University of Pennsylvania Press, 2007), 109–40.

printers, and plagiarists around the world and the often imaginative ways in which they used his work.[11]

LABOURER IN ART

The many ways in which Dickens's works appeared in print had consequences for the creative life and writing discipline from which they came, in which we can see a complex mix of constraint and improvisational possibility. Throughout his life, his gift for multitasking and inspired spontaneity never left him: in the middle of working on *Our Mutual Friend*, his last complete novel, for example, he could still surprise himself with an idea for that year's Christmas story, *Doctor Marigold's Prescriptions*:

> I sat down to cast about for an idea, with a depressing notion that I was, for the moment, overworked. Suddenly, the little character [Sophy, Dr Marigold's daughter] ... and all belonging to it came flashing up in the most cheerful manner, and I had only to look on and leisurely describe it.[12]

This need to stir his own creativity may explain why Dickens never settled to what has historically been the more usual pattern of novel writing, that of completing and revising the work entirely before publication. Instead, he clearly relished the technically difficult demands that a regular, unbreakable publication schedule of exactly the same number of pages created. Indeed, he would crank up the level of difficulty for himself, not only through the characteristically large number of characters, multiple plots, and entangled back-stories that he had to manage, but also through such extraordinary formal innovations as the dual narration of *Bleak House*. He could chafe at times at the constraints of weekly publication, which he told Forster 'drive me frantic', but there is a distinctive tightness to the three later novels, *Hard Times*, *Great Expectations*, and *A Tale of Two Cities*, written in this way.[13]

After the scurrying and scrambling of the early years of his career, when he seemed able to write in all sorts of places and times, the printer's boy at his metaphorical elbow, Dickens increasingly settled into more routinized patterns of working that he sustained through the extraordinary array of other activities—charitable, theatrical, familial—that he undertook. He would usually write in the morning, with the afternoon reserved for long, often solitary, walks at four miles an hour. There was a parallel sedimenting of the

---

[11] See, for example, Hannah Crafts, *The Bondwoman's Narrative*, ed. Henry Louis Gates Jr (New York: Warner, 2003), and Gill Ballinger, Tim Lustig, and Dale Townshend, 'Missing Intertexts: Hannah Crafts's "The Bondwoman's Narrative" and African American Literary History', *Journal of American Studies* 39, 2 (August 2005): 207–37.

[12] *PLets* 11:105.

[13] *PLets* 9:91–2, 92.

planning and structuring of the novels. In a major departure from the initial conception of *Martin Chuzzlewit*, the titular character, for example, had suddenly headed off to the United States, seriously dislocating the novel's central section and movement. Dickens never changed horses in midstream in such a dramatic way again, but the openness of his working practices meant that he could stop Walter Gay going to the bad and Edith Dombey from sleeping with Carker in *Dombey and Son*, could revise the character of Miss Mowcher in *David Copperfield* in response to a distressed letter from the woman (Jane Seymour Hill) on whom she was evidently based, and rewrite the final chapter of *Great Expectations* at the urging of his friend and fellow-novelist Edward Bulwer Lytton.

Robert L. Patten has rightly seen the years from Dickens's first appearance in print ('A Dinner at Poplar Walk', *Monthly Magazine*, December 1833) to the winding up of *Master Humphrey's Clock* in 1841 as decisive for his understanding of the role of a successful professional writer in the modern world. For Patten he was both pioneer and archetype of the 'industrial age author', taking control of his name, persona, and publishing career and, in doing so, decisively changing the role of the author and the complicated set of networks—economic, social, publishing, readerly—within which he or she moved.[14] He was a competitive and market-savvy writer, who battled hard with his publishers for control and artistic integrity, but behind the embattled brinkman was a private writing self, whom we can sometimes glimpse, as his daughter Mamie did one day when she was ill:

> I was lying on the sofa endeavouring to keep perfectly quiet, while my father wrote busily and rapidly at his desk, when he suddenly jumped from his chair and rushed to a mirror which hung near, and in which I could see the reflection of some extraordinary facial contortions which he was making. He returned rapidly to his desk, wrote furiously for a few moments, and then went again to the mirror. The facial pantomime was resumed, and then turning toward, but evidently not seeing, me, he began talking rapidly in a low voice. Ceasing this soon, however, he returned once more to his desk, where he remained silently writing until luncheon time.[15]

His talking aloud, use of the mirror, and 'facial pantomime' have often been remarked upon, but busy, absorbed silence is the heart of this scene of writing. Dickens became, as Mamie put it, 'in action, as in imagination, the creature of his pen'.[16]

The first six novels (of 14) were written at high speed, back to back for the most part, by the time Dickens was 32. After that, he became a more careful and considered artist, who liked to plan ahead and to have several instalments in hand before launching a new work upon the public. Some planning notes for *Old Curiosity Shop* and *Martin Chuzzlewit* survive, and his manuscripts from *Dombey and Son* onwards contain detailed and

---

[14] Robert L. Patten, *Charles Dickens and 'Boz': The Making of the Industrial-Age Author* (Cambridge: Cambridge University Press, 2012).
[15] Mary Dickens, *My Father As I Recall Him* (London: Roxburghe, 1902), 47–8.
[16] Ibid., 49.

fascinating memoranda to himself, with trial titles, possible names for characters, alternative possibilities for plot development, calculations of timing and of characters' ages, and innumerable demonstrations of the thought and care with which he wrote. We witness processes of internal debate and decision in these 'number plans', which are sometimes brutally direct (of the end of Merdle, the crooked financier of *Little Dorrit*, he writes 'Merdles? <u>Yes. His suicide and demolition</u>') but more often point us to the nuances of his art: 'Lead through to <u>Dorrit</u>—Can she have anything to do with it? Watch her'; 'Condense, if possible, the whole fatherly character'; 'From her own point of view. Dissect it'; 'Scene (<u>reserve carefully till now</u>) between Little Dorrit and Arthur'; '<u>Pave the way</u>'; 'Tell the whole story, <u>working it out as much as possible through Mrs. Clennam herself</u>'; 'Very quiet conclusion'.[17]

Dickens was essentially a producer of written texts which became part of a rich, multi-dimensional cultural form. The novels were all (with the significant exceptions of *Hard Times* and *Great Expectations*) illustrated on their first publication. Dickens had an active and shaping role in their visual appearance, suggesting subjects, directing his illustrators, and at times revising or rejecting what they offered. He had the good fortune to be illustrated by one of the great graphic artists of the century, George Cruikshank (1792–1878), for *Sketches by Boz* and *Oliver Twist* and when the first of these was published, Cruikshank was the better known of the collaborators. Although their friendship survived until the 1850s, their creative relationship did not last, as both men wanted control. With 'Phiz', Hablot K. Browne, however, Dickens built a long-term partnership that lasted from *Pickwick* until *A Tale of Two Cities*, when Phiz sadly wrote to a friend that 'Dickens probably thinks a new hand would give his old puppets a fresh look.'[18]

Phiz defined for many generations of readers the physical appearance of many of Dickens's most famous characters including Micawber, Sam Weller, Mrs Gamp, and Chadband, but perhaps his finest work is found in the suggestive, ominous recessions of the 'dark plates' of *Little Dorrit* and *Bleak House*. For *Our Mutual Friend*, Dickens chose the much younger and more 'realist' Marcus Stone (1840–1921), whose wood engravings gave a very different, more contemporary, visual appearance to the novel, as did the work of Luke Fildes (1844–1927) for the unfinished *Mystery of Edwin Drood*. But it was not just the novels that were illustrated. Dickens's other writings were accompanied and interpreted by, among others, William Blake's pupil Samuel Palmer, John Leech, best known for his work for *Punch* magazine, Dickens's close friends the painters Clarkson Stanfield and Daniel Maclise, George Cattermole, and Marcus Stone's father Frank.

---

[17] Charles Dickens, *Little Dorrit*, ed. Harvey Peter Sucksmith (Oxford: Clarendon Press, 1979), 806–28. Dickens uses a mixture of single, double, and triple underlining. All the underlined passages quoted here are in fact doubly underlined with the exception of 'reserve carefully till now' which is singly underlined. See also *Dickens' Working Notes for his Novels*, ed. Harry Stone (Chicago: University of Chicago Press, 1987).

[18] Undated letter to his friend and assistant Robert Young, quoted in Frederic G. Kitton, *Charles Dickens and his Illustrators* (London: George Redway, 2nd edn, 1899), 113.

The most important of their work was for the annual Christmas books, which began with the brilliantly (and expensively) illustrated *A Christmas Carol* (1843), followed by *The Chimes* (1844), *The Cricket on the Hearth* (1845), *The Battle of Life* (1846), and *The Haunted Man* (1848). These were integrally and memorably illustrated, sold substantial numbers, and were rapidly imitated by other authors, increasingly displacing the aristocratic annuals that until that point had hitherto held sway over the festive season.[19] As with serial publication, these writings had a distinctive and new publication rhythm, allied to the calendar.

Dickens collaborated with his illustrators while ensuring that he retained overall control, and we can see a similar pattern to his work as an editor. He was hard-working and highly interventionist; a characteristic letter to Forster recounts that he had

> a story to hack and hew into some form for *Household Words* this morning, which has taken me four hours of close attention. And I am perfectly addled by its horrible want of continuity after all, and the dreadful spectacle I have made of the proofs—which look like an inky fishing-net.[20]

His many editorial projects, which included not only his four magazines but also his brief inaugural editorship of the *Daily News* (1846), were collaborative in nature, but in strictly controlled ways: every page of *Household Words* had the words 'Conducted by Charles Dickens' on it, although much of it was written, of course, by others. Although he published the work of many women authors in its pages, fostering their careers and showing personal kindness to them, his essential collaborative and friendship networks were with men. George Eliot (1819–80), despite her admiration for Dickens, resisted his attempts to get her to write for *Household Words*. But he was more successful with Elizabeth Gaskell (1810–65); Dickens published more than two-thirds of the articles and stories that she wrote between 1850 and her death.[21] Gaskell increasingly resented his editorial interventions, particularly his attempts to compress and revise her novel *North and South* (1854–5), although she did contribute to the collaborative Christmas numbers of his magazines, including *A Round of Stories by the Christmas Fire* (1852) and *Mrs Lirriper's Lodgings* (1863). For these, Dickens would create a framework to which he and a range of other authors would contribute stories that were more or less related to the frame.

Even if Dickens had never written a word of fiction, he would have been a major figure as both journalist and editor. Understanding his practice as editor, particularly for the two journals he created and 'conducted', *Household Words* and *All the Year Round*, is immensely revealing of his professional networks, his political and social concerns and

---

[19] See Katherine D. Harris, *Forget Me Not: The Rise of the British Literary Annual, 1823–1835* (Athens, OH: Ohio University Press, 2015).
[20] *PLets* 8:139.
[21] Paul Schicke (ed.), *Oxford Reader's Companion to Dickens* (Oxford: Oxford University Press, 1999), 247.

causes, and his aesthetic and fictional preferences and ideals. There is a substantial trove of collaborative journalism by Dickens and his junior colleagues at *Household Words*, in which one can see close up the sometimes brilliant transformation of everyday Victorian print by Dickens.[22] The recent discovery of a marked set of *All the Year Round* identifies many hitherto-unknown or misidentified contributors and has the potential to transform our understanding of the social and professional networks within which Dickens worked in the latter stages of his career.[23] Much work on this topic remains to be done. These local, national, and international networks were complex, extensive, and interlocking, and they plugged the little editorial office in Wellington Street, a stone's throw from Chandos Place where Dickens had worked as a child labourer, into an unprecedentedly global and transnational print, information, and fiction-reading culture.[24]

However much he relished the role of editor, Dickens found the management of such essentially miscellaneous fictional works as the Christmas numbers an increasingly frustrating business. They did lead, however, to his most important and innovative collaborative works, written with his younger colleague and friend Wilkie Collins (1824–89). Collins, author of *The Woman in White* (*All the Year Round*, 1859–60) and *The Moonstone* (*All the Year Round*, 1868), had begun as a kind of protégé or 'sorcerer's apprentice' to the older writer in such stories as *The Wreck of the Golden Mary* and *The Perils of Certain English Prisoners* (their jointly authored Christmas stories for 1856 and 1857). But by the time of *A Message from the Sea* (1860) and *No Thoroughfare* (1867), he was a major novelist in his own right, and an equal contributor to the joint works.

The grafting of voices that we find in collaborative writing can be unsettling to critical norms that assume the uniqueness and coherence of the writing self, and Dickens's collaborative work with Collins is not easily assimilated to conventional accounts of their literary careers. But Collins's most important innovation in fictional form, that of telling a story through sequential, partial narrators in *The Woman in White* and *The Moonstone*, derived directly from the practice of their collaborative Christmas numbers. For Dickens too, collaborative work could be as important as his solitary labour. Writing to Sir James Emerson Tennant about his elaborate stage production of Collins's *The Frozen Deep* (in which he also starred), he spoke of deriving

> a strange feeling out of it, like writing a book in company. A satisfaction of a most singular kind, which has no exact parallel in my life. A something that I suppose to belong to the life of a Labourer in Art, alone, and which has to me a conviction of its

---

[22] Harry Stone (ed.), *The Uncollected Writings of Charles Dickens: Household Words 1850–1859* (London: Allen Lane, 1969).

[23] See Jeremy Parrott, 'The Annotated Set of *All the Year Round*: Questions, Answers and Conjectures', *Dickensian* 112, 1 (Spring 2016): 10–21.

[24] See Lauren M. E. Goodlad, *The Victorian Geopolitical Aesthetic: Realism, Sovereignty, and Transnational Experience* (Oxford: Oxford University Press, 2015).

being actual Truth without its pain, that I never could adequately state if I were to try never so hard.[25]

For such a uniquely imaginative author as Dickens, at the height of his powers, it is a remarkable thing to say. Finding in a theatrical collaboration the satisfaction of the 'Truth' of 'Art ... without its pain' shows how Dickens saw in collaborative relationships not the dilution but the consolidation and strengthening of his creative life. It is highly distinctive: none of his fictional contemporaries collaborated as much or as often as he did, and we have to look to much earlier practices in theatre such as Shakespeare's collaborations with John Fletcher on *Two Noble Kinsmen* and *Henry VIII* to find such a major literary figure collaborating in maturity.

'What I profess'

John Forster (1812–76) was the single most important figure within Dickens's professional life and, with the possible exceptions of his wife Catherine Dickens and companion Ellen Ternan, the person who knew him best. Forster, the son of a Newcastle butcher, had a highly successful career as journalist, editor, biographer, and man of letters. He was the close confidant of several major literary figures of the period, including Leigh Hunt, Charles Lamb, Edward Bulwer Lytton, Walter Savage Landor, and Robert Browning. Trained in the law, he was a skilled adviser and robust negotiator on their behalf. His friendship with Dickens was trusting and intimate from early in their careers. He negotiated his contracts, corrected his proofs, and became the custodian of his manuscripts and secrets, preserving a great deal of revealing, if judiciously weeded, material. His biography of Dickens (1872–4) is a uniquely insightful, but censored, account of Dickens's life and a vivid invocation of his presence. Forster was a consummate literary professional: hard-working, punctual, and assertive, he had a shaping role in Dickens's own career and professional journey. It was Forster, for example, who was able to discourage Dickens from fatally naming his new magazine *Household Harmony* in 1859, not long after the excruciating and public breakup of his marriage.[26]

He was unsuccessful, though, in trying to dissuade Dickens from becoming a paid reader and performer of his own writing. This became a major (and extremely lucrative) preoccupation of the last 12 years of his life, and a way for him to redefine his art and public self. For Forster the work of a performer, even one as talented as Dickens, was intrinsically less dignified than authorship, 'a substitution', as he put it, 'of lower aims for higher: a change to commonplace from more elevated pursuits'.[27] But the Public Readings encapsulated Dickens's belief in the essentially performative nature of social

---

[25] *PLets* 8:255–6, 256.
[26] *PLets* 9:15–16, 15.
[27] John Forster, *The Life of Charles Dickens*, ed. J. W. T. Ley (London: Cecil Palmer, 1928), 641.

being, and triumphantly confirmed his intimate and affectionate relationship with his readers. Some of his deepest explorations of both writing and performance come from this period of his life, in the abandoned writings that become the stories of *Somebody's Luggage* (1862) and in the patter of Dr Marigold, the showman of *Dr Marigold's Prescriptions*.

Forster did succeed, though, in preserving an almost overwhelmingly full record of Dickens's creative process for posterity through his generous bequest of the manuscripts and proofs of the majority of Dickens's works to the South Kensington Museum. These provide the necessary materials not simply for definitive editions of the novels, such as the Oxford Edition, but many other possible research projects into both the gestation and nuances of Dickens's art and practice of writing. They have a good claim to form the most important manuscript collection by a single author in English and reveal the extraordinary care that Dickens took, from inaugurating decisions about character, title, and plot in the notes to the detailed shaping of phrase and idiom. Together with this treasury of 'number plans', preliminary planning notes, manuscripts, and proofs, a unique 'Book of Memoranda' by Dickens also survives, full of names and ideas for characters, novels, and stories.[28] Many of these chips from Dickens's workshop find their way into his later fiction. But in their original form they seem even more mysteriously suggestive, seeds or pips that will grow into some of Dickens's most celebrated stories and afterlives.

Fiction in the nineteenth century aspired to greatness and immortality, while seeming to be irredeemably embedded in the low, ephemeral, and vulgar. Dickens had an ambivalent relationship to these two essential aspects of his art. He was drawn in his life both to the bohemian and the respectable worlds, and in his art to understanding their relationship. He knew much about the life of the poor and socially marginal from his own disordered and indebted childhood, when at 12 years old he worked at Warren's Blacking Warehouse, visited his family in prison, and walked the streets of London. As a talented and successful male, he could move easily between dinners with the aristocracy, backstage encounters at theatres, and expeditions to low-life haunts and opium dens with the newly formed detective police. He was deeply aware of the equivocal and potentially vulnerable positions in which writers, artists, and performers were often placed by the officiousness of public morality. So he worked hard to preserve his artistic freedom and to defend, as he did in *Hard Times* and elsewhere, the 'bohemian' world against the censure of Gradgrinds and Bounderbys. His fiction constantly drew on low and unrespectable life for its subject matter, but he insisted in his own person and public utterances that 'Literature was a dignified profession.'[29] Dickens refused three times to meet Queen Victoria after a performance in his stage clothes and make-up, for example; however much he knew and wrote about the criminal, marginal, and bohemian worlds,

---

[28] *Charles Dickens' Book of Memoranda*, ed. Fred Kaplan (New York: New York Public Library, 1981).
[29] *The Speeches of Charles Dickens*, ed. K. J. Fielding (Oxford: Clarendon Press, 1960), 389.

however brilliant and committed a stage performer he was, he would only meet the queen as a gentleman.

In a bravura passage from the *Eighteen Brumaire of Louis Bonaparte*, Dickens's admirer and contemporary Karl Marx (1818–83) ransacked the languages of Europe to characterize 'the whole indefinite, disintegrated mass, thrown hither and thither, which the French call *la bohème*':

> decayed roués with dubious means of subsistence and of dubious origin, alongside ruined and adventurous offshoots of the bourgeoisie ... vagabonds, discharged soldiers, discharged jailbirds, escaped galley slaves, swindlers, mountebanks, lazzaroni, pickpockets, tricksters, gamblers, *maquereaux* [pimps], brothel keepers, porters, literati, organ grinders, ragpickers, knife grinders, tinkers, beggars—in short, the whole indefinite, disintegrated mass, thrown hither and thither, which the French call *la bohème*.[30]

This was a world with which Dickens was intimately familiar, as he showed through the many debtors, performers, and working poor in his novels. But he is less contemptuous of it than Marx, and dramatized not only the difficulty of such people's lives, but also their value, both in themselves and for the hard truths they reveal about the lives of the genteel, privileged, and secure.

To write about such material in novels and stories that were designed to be read by as wide a readership as possible was difficult in the often-censorious world of Victorian public discourse. Some of the hostility that his work engendered can be seen in an early criticism by Thackeray (1811–63) of the portrayal of the prostitute Nancy in *Oliver Twist*. Thackeray, who became Dickens's great rival with the publication of *Vanity Fair* (1847-8), criticized Dickens for a lack of moral courage in his writing that he felt showed a fundamental aesthetic untruthfulness.

> Bah! what figments these novelists tell us! Boz, who knows life well, knows that his Miss Nancy is the most unreal fantastical personage possible; no more like a thief's mistress than one of Gesner's shepherdesses resembles a real country wench. He dare not tell the truth concerning such young ladies.[31]

For Thackeray, the sympathetic depiction of the criminal poor in fiction inevitably led to the condoning of immorality: 'in the sorrows of Nancy', he wrote, 'there is no ... lurking moral, as far as we have been able to discover; we are asked for downright sympathy'.[32]

---

[30] Karl Marx, *The Eighteen Brumaire of Louis Bonaparte*, in *Surveys from Exile*, trans. Ben Fowkes, ed. and introd. David Fernbach (Harmondsworth: Penguin, 1973), 142–249, 197.

[31] William Makepeace Thackeray, 'Going to See a Man Hanged', in *Sketches and Travels in London and Miscellaneous Contributions to 'Punch'* (London: Smith, Elder, 1899), 227–43, 236, first published in *Fraser's Magazine* 22 (August 1840): 150–8.

[32] William Makepeace Thackeray, *Catherine: A Story*, ed. Sheldon F. Goldfarb (Ann Arbor: University of Michigan Press, 1999), 133; first published in *Fraser's Magazine* 19–21 (May 1839–February 1840).

Dickens's response, in his preface to *Oliver Twist*, one of his most important expressions of artistic intent, was to insist both on the truthfulness of his novel and its moral purpose: the novel depicted, he claimed, the 'stern and plain truth' in order to draw 'a lesson of the purest good ... from the vilest evil'.[33] So far, so unsurprising. But Dickens went on to make a more radical claim in his assertion that 'It is useless to discuss whether the conduct and character of the girl [Nancy] seems natural or unnatural, probable or improbable, right or wrong. IT IS TRUE.' In making this claim, Dickens asserts that the criteria by which we judge the truth of literature should be radically different from those of ethical judgement, probability, or truth to 'nature'.[34] Such a belief was an essential part of his credo.

Questions of the moral effect and purpose of literature came to focus increasingly at mid-century in charged debates about the social role of the writer. The 'Dignity of Literature' debate saw Forster and Dickens strongly committed to the 'dignity' of literature, in opposition to Thackeray, who 'was never quite sure that it was proper for a gentleman to live by his pen'.[35] A complex set of questions about class identity, moral purpose, and aesthetic dedication were embedded in their controversies. Was 'the trade of literature ... a craft as any other', as Thackeray put it, or in such remarks did he, as Dickens put it in his obituary, feign 'a want of earnestness' and make 'a pretence of under-valuing his art'?[36] We should be wary, though, of seeing Dickens simply as a 'professional author' as opposed to the gentlemanly amateur Thackeray, as this too neatly divides aspects of his life and work that were deeply bound together. To a degree, of course, the distinction holds: Dickens's theatrical company was called the 'Company of Amateurs' and the gentlemanly actors were not paid (although the actresses were), whereas his books were a serious business in which Dickens took a lively interest in the income they brought, carefully scrutinized the six-monthly accounts of his publishers, and repeatedly demanded changes to his contracts to improve his earnings. But the way that Dickens managed his amateur actors was very 'professional'—disciplined, systematic, and committed—and behind all the organized business of publishing lay the unsystematic creative processes that Dickens summoned up in his study and on his long solitary walks.

Indeed, the successes of his 'amateur' theatrical company led to plans to form 'The Provident Union of Literature, Science, and Art', a scheme to help writers and artists in

---

[33] Charles Dickens, *Oliver Twist*, ed. Kathleen Tillotson (Oxford: Clarendon Press, 1966), lxiii, lxi.

[34] See John Bowen, *Other Dickens: Pickwick to Chuzzlewit* (Oxford: Oxford University Press, 2000), 82–4, and Martin Heidegger, 'The Origin of the Work of Art', in *Off the Beaten Track*, trans. and introd. Julian Young and Kenneth Haynes (Cambridge: Cambridge University Press, 2002), 27–9 and 33–6.

[35] *PLets* 5:ix–x.

[36] William Makepeace Thackeray, 'A Brother of the Press on the History of a Literary Man, Laman Blanchard, and the Chances of the Literary Profession', *Fraser's Magazine* 33 (March 1846): 332–42. Charles Dickens, 'In Memoriam: W. M. Thackeray', *The Dent Uniform Edition of Dickens's Journalism: 'The Uncommercial Traveller' and Other Papers 1859–1870*, vol. 4, ed. Michael Slater and John Drew (London: J. M. Dent; Columbus: Ohio State University Press, 2000), 326–30, 328; first published in the *Cornhill* 9, 50 (February 1864): 129–32. Subsequent references to Dent are by volume:title, page.

difficulty. This in turn led to the creation of the 'Guild of Literature and Art', which was intended to be simultaneously a professional association, a mutual aid society, and an insurance scheme for writers.[37] The intention was to assist writers in financial difficulties without the element of aristocratic patronage that infected the help given by the Royal Literary Fund, and to build a set of cottages for them on land given to the Guild by Bulwer Lytton. Like Dickens's and Forster's attempts to reform the Royal Literary Fund, however, the Guild did not succeed. A contemporary review in the *Spectator* captured well the fundamental contradiction of the project:

> we have great doubts as to the practicability of making the gipsy race of men serving 'the liberal arts' amenable to laws of commercial society,—unless you convert them altogether into traders, and then they will be no longer servants of the liberal arts.[38]

Gipsies, artists, or tradesmen? Dickens had all these sides to his working life. Although the idea of literary professionalism could sometimes reconcile the conflicts among them, he rarely uses the word 'professional' in his fiction without irony. Jingle, the con-man of *Pickwick Papers*, for example, speaks with a 'professional (i.e. theatrical) air'; Tony Weller, the coach driver in the same novel, makes a 'parental and professional joke'; Mr Bung, a brokers' man in *Sketches by Boz*, retails his 'professional anecdotes'. The odious 'professional philanthropist' Mr Honeythunder in *The Mystery of Edwin Drood* nicely embodies the ambivalence of the term: he is a full-time, hard-working philanthropist, but the suspicion is that he only helps others for the money.[39] Dickens could admire the professionalism of doctors such as Allan Woodcourt in *Bleak House*, but the moral imperative that underpins so much of his work—the obligation selflessly to heed the serious needs of others—inevitably requires much more than professionalism. Indeed, *Bleak House* is the novel most concerned with the limits of professional identity, which we see both in Richard Carstone's increasingly desperate attempts to launch a professional career and in the indifference to suffering that characterizes the 'professionalism' of the book's many lawyers. The deadly and interminable court case of Jarndyce and Jarndyce 'is a joke in the profession'.[40]

Here, as elsewhere, the issues that dominated Dickens's dealings with the worlds of publishing and professional life also often appear in his novels. Questions of literary value and of the uniqueness or singularity of the writing self are the topics of Dickens's negotiations with his publishers and his battles over rewards and copyright, but they are also central topics of his fiction. There are many writers and aspiring writers in his

---

[37] See Richard Salmon, *The Formation of the English Literary Profession* (Cambridge: Cambridge University Press, 2013), 102–34.

[38] 'The Guild of Literature and Art', *Spectator*, 26 April 1851, 12.

[39] *Pickwick Papers*, ed. James Kinsley (Oxford: Clarendon Press, 1986), chapter 8, page 122 and chapter 23, 245; *Sketches by Boz*, Dent 1:SB 'The Broker's Man', 29; *The Mystery of Edwin Drood*, ed. Margaret Cardwell (Oxford: Clarendon Press, 1972), chapter 17, page 151.

[40] Charles Dickens, *Bleak House*, ed. George Ford and Sylvère Monod (New York: Norton, 1977), chapter 1, page 8.

fiction, most notably in the quasi-autobiographical *David Copperfield*. Although David's own writing career as a successful author is the heart and destination of the book, it is rarely treated directly. Instead, a host of too-amateur (Julia Mills, Micawber) or too-professional (Traddles, Heep) writers reflect and refract the questions of copying and creativity, purpose and professionalism that were at the heart of David's (and Dickens's) working life. Although Dickens often reflected on the nature of his writing, he never did so in a systematic or formal way, but rather in letters, reviews, prefaces, and journalism.

No single passage can epitomize the complexity of his relationship to his own labour, profession, or calling, but a letter of advice to a contributor to one of his journals is particularly revealing:

> It does not seem to me to be enough to say of any description that it is the exact truth. The exact truth must be there; but the merit or art in the narrator, is the manner of stating the truth. As to which thing in literature, it always seems to me that there is a world to be done. And in these times, when the tendency is to be frightfully literal and catalogue like—to make the thing in short a sum in reduction that any miserable creature can do it in that way—I have an idea (really founded on the love of what I profess) that the very holding of popular literature through a kind of popular dark age, may depend on such fanciful treatment.[41]

There is much to note about this passage, in particular the emphasis placed on the exact truth in literature and the 'fanciful treatment' that must accompany it; on the seriousness of the work required to state the truth within 'frightfully literal and catalogue like' times; and, above all, on the need to hold fast to the creation of popular literature within 'a kind of popular dark age'. But it is the final phrase in brackets (which work to emphasize, not subordinate their content) that is most telling: Dickens's invocation of 'the love of what I profess', a love that, as it professes, goes well beyond professionalism.

Further Reading

Peter Ackroyd, *Dickens* (London: Sinclair-Stevenson, 1990)
Rosemarie Bodenheimer, *Knowing Dickens* (Ithaca, NY: Cornell University Press, 2007)
Charles Dickens, *The Christmas Stories*, ed. Ruth Glancy (London: Everyman, 1996)
John M. L. Drew, *Dickens the Journalist* (London: Palgrave, 2003)
Lillian Nayder, *Unequal Partners: Charles Dickens, Wilkie Collins, and Victorian Authorship* (Ithaca, NY: Cornell University Press, 2002)
Robert L. Patten, *George Cruikshank's Life, Times, and Art* (New Brunswick, NJ: Rutgers University Press, 1992 and 1996)
Michael Steig, *Dickens and Phiz* (Bloomington: Indiana University Press, 1978)

---

[41] Forster, *Life*, 727–8.

CHAPTER 4

DICKENS AS A PUBLIC FIGURE

TONY WILLIAMS

Posthumous Tributes: Britannia Mourns Dickens's Passing

Soon after Charles Dickens died on 9 June 1870 obituaries began to appear in the press testifying to the many ways he was regarded by his contemporaries (Figure 4.1). *The Times* obituary on 12 June 1870 gave an account of Dickens's life and writings, concentrating on the early works, and particularly praising *The Pickwick Papers*, whilst listing everything from *Dombey* to *Drood* in one sentence. It mentioned his journalism, commended his philanthropic work for the Guild of Literature and Art and the Royal Literary Fund, and referred to his Public Readings. *Nicholas Nickleby* and *Oliver Twist* were singled out for revealing his powerful pathos and his 'sympathy for the poor, the suffering, and the oppressed which took all hearts by storm. This power of sympathy it was, no doubt, which has made his name a household word in English homes. How many a phase of cruelty and wrong his pen exposed, and how often he stirred others to try at least to lessen the amount of evil and suffering which must be ever abroad in the world, will never be fully known. There was always a lesson beneath his mirth'. Dickens was 'the dear friend of men, women and children, even as he was the strong warm friend of humanity'. *The Times* emphasized that Dickens's name would live on through his characters, humour, social awareness, and campaigning for reforms.[1]

The Dean of Westminster Abbey, the Very Reverend Arthur Stanley, said that he 'made Englishmen feel more as one family than they had ever felt before'.[2] The *Daily*

---

[1] Reprinted in *Great Victorian Lives*, ed. Andrew Sanders (London: Times Books, 2007), 80–4.
[2] *Sunday Times*, 2 June 1870, reprinted in *Charles Dickens: A Critical Anthology*, ed. Stephen Wall (Harmondsworth: Penguin, 1970), 176.

FIGURE 4.1 'In Memory of Charles Dickens', *Illustrated Police News*, 16 June 1870, page 1.

© The British Library Board. *Illustrated Police News*, 16 June 1870, page 1

News wrote on 10 June 1870 of another important aspect of Dickens's work: 'He was emphatically the novelist of his age. In his pictures of contemporary life posterity will read, more clearly than in contemporary records, the character of nineteenth century life.' This observation echoed the sentiment expressed by the journalist and economist Walter Bagehot in 1858 that Dickens was 'a special correspondent for posterity', capturing his age for subsequent generations.[3]

On Monday 20 June 1870, *The Times* printed the text of the sermon that the liberal theologian and Regius chair of Greek at Oxford, Benjamin Jowett, had delivered at the memorial service in Westminster Abbey the previous Sunday.[4] It emphasized the personal relationship existing between the author and his public, something which he had himself identified as being 'like no other man's'. Jowett's remarks captured the

[3] Walter Bagehot, 'Charles Dickens', review of the Library Edition of Dickens's works, *National Review*, October 1858, 459–86.
[4] Benjamin Jowett, *The Times*, 20 June 1870.

astonishing depth of feeling which Dickens evoked in those who knew him. And everyone felt they knew him, from the creations of his mind and heart presented in his writings.

> [H]e whose loss we now mourn occupied a greater space than any other writer in the minds of Englishmen during the last thirty-five years. We read him, talked about him, acted him; we laughed with him, we were roused by him to a consciousness of the misery of others, and to a pathetic interest in human life. The workhouse child, the cripple, and half-clothed and half-starved inhabitant of a debtors' prison found a way to his heart, and through the exertions of his genius, to touch our hearts also. Works of fiction would be intolerable if they attempted to be sermons directly to instruct us; but indirectly they are great instructors of this world, and we can hardly exaggerate the debt of gratitude which is due to a writer who has led us to sympathise with these good, true, sincere, honest English characters of ordinary life, and to laugh at the egotism, the hypocrisy, the false respectability of religious professors and others ... Men seem to have lost, not a great writer only, but one whom they had personally known.

One of the most moving items to appear in the press at this time was Sir Luke Fildes's engraving 'The Empty Chair'. It appeared in the *Graphic* the day after Dickens's death, showing his desk and vacant chair in his study at Gad's Hill: it was reprinted worldwide. The writer was gone. The Dickens of social campaigning and sympathy for the oppressed, Dickens the great creator of characters who live on eternally, emerges from both the obituaries and Jowett's sermon. His presence as a public figure, his unforgettable portrayals of Christmas over more than a quarter of a century, his articulation of his writer's role and his journalism more generally, his public involvement in social reform and the commemoration of British writers, his wide-ranging philanthropy, his memorable speeches and Readings that endeared him to a public not only in the UK but also in France and the USA, and his careful cultivation of his professional and personal image, persisted as defining characteristics of Dickens through his lifetime, after his death, and on into our own times.

The Public Figure

All writers are public figures insofar as they reach out to an audience for their work. But the extent to which such writers engage more widely with the age in which they write defines the nature of their public image. The case of Charles Dickens is that of a writer for whom that involvement was extensive and deep. It is also the case that he devoted considerable effort to the creation of the image he wished to project, which was in many ways identifiable with the reality of his life and personality.

Early on Dickens established an identity that persisted throughout his lifetime. His works engaged with real contemporary social issues, beginning with a critique of the

New Poor Law in *Oliver Twist* and a denunciation of cruel Yorkshire schools in *Nicholas Nickleby*, and continuing on through to his great mid-century condition-of-England novel *Bleak House*, and to the late visions of the dark modern city in *Our Mutual Friend*. Dickens's writing demonstrates a deep and sincere involvement with the sufferings of the poor and marginalized in society, and especially with the lives of suffering children. He strives to make his readership aware of these problems and to consider ways in which they could move to action for change. Often it was a particular feature of contemporary society—a corrupt institution or a tradition which needed reforming—that inspired his passion. One that he shared with his audience then and now was the observance and importance of Christmas.

CHRISTMAS

From 1843 onwards Dickens's Christmas books and stories became a powerfully significant part of his output and established a special relationship with his readership which he was keen to foster and develop. He believed that special relationship conferred a great responsibility on him to satisfy audience expectations; he did not wish to leave 'any gap at Christmas firesides which I ought to fill.'[5] When Dickens died, a coster barrow girl who sold fruits and vegetables in Covent Garden Market is reported to have said, on hearing the news: 'Dickens dead? Then will Father Christmas die too?'[6] Recalling this incident in 1907, the writer Theodore Watts-Dunton remarked: 'It was from her I learnt that there were at the time thousands and thousands of the London populace who never read a line of Dickens—who never, indeed, had had an opportunity of reading a line—but who were, nevertheless, familiar with his name. They looked upon Dickens as the spirit of Christmas incarnate: as being, in a word, Father Christmas himself.'[7] Watts-Dunton's observations remind us how wide was Dickens's appeal, including those who could not read him but could listen to him being read. His public range was enormous.

A Christmas Carol had emerged from Dickens's engagement with public events. Personally he was actively engaged in one of his regular philanthropic concerns—the plight of children. In the 1840s there was no such thing as a state education system; schools were either endowed by churches or individuals, or supported through

---

[5] *The Letters of Charles Dickens*, ed. Madeline House, Graham Storey, et al., Pilgrim/British Academy Edition, 12 vols (Oxford: Clarendon Press, 1965–2002). Subsequent citations: *PLets* followed by volume:page range, page, and hn. for headnote, n. or nn. for footnotes, with page range given before page cited. Here, *PLets* 5:165–6, 165.

[6] Quoted in Catherine Waters, *Dickens and the Politics of the Family* (Cambridge: Cambridge University Press, 1997), 83.

[7] Theodore Watts-Dunton, 'Dickens and Father Christmas: A Yule-Tide Approach for the Babes of Famine Street', *The Nineteenth Century and After* 62 (16 December 1907): 1014–29, 1016.

voluntary contributions. Dickens visited Field Lane Ragged School in September 1843 at the behest of the heiress Angela Burdett-Coutts, who was considering giving money to the institution. So called 'Ragged Schools' were set up often by religious organizations, who saw them as a missionary act, taking Christian doctrine and basic education into uncivilized parts of London—and they really were uncivilized. Field Lane was a notorious criminal area, at the end of Saffron Hill where it joined Holborn. Dickens had used it as the setting for the criminal activities of Fagin and Bill Sikes in *Oliver Twist*. He was appalled by what he discovered at the school: 'My heart so sinks within me when I go into these scenes', he reported to Miss Coutts, 'that I almost lose the hope of ever seeing them changed.'[8]

Dickens had also been shocked by reading the 1842 and 1843 Reports of the Children's Employment Commission that detailed the appalling conditions of child labour in mines and manufactories. Thus the *Carol* is a text written in response to specific social concerns—ignorance and want—that outraged the writer, who believed they needed to be exposed to general awareness. But it reaches wider and deeper than that, in its response to the whole social atmosphere of the time.

The 1840s were without doubt very difficult and potentially dangerous years. Nineteenth-century England was in the throes of moving from an agrarian to an industrial economy. That shift entailed massive social dislocation and rising distress among the labouring population. Political and social measures such as the establishment of the Metropolitan Police in 1829, the Reform Act of 1832, the New Poor Law of 1834, and other forces later, were changing the way society was organized in an attempt to respond to the needs of this rapidly changing world. Economic shifts brought large numbers of rural workers and immigrants into English cities, already under considerable strain from the urbanizing transformations earlier that resulted from the industrial revolution.

Framed by those conditions, the 12 days of Christmas for the early Victorians embodied the values of a past world, a settled, ordered, idyllic rural past, where people came together in celebration of traditions enshrining something important for the community. The 1840s seemed not to offer much chance or hope for such community of shared values and traditions. In *A Christmas Carol* Dickens, economically and skilfully, managed to use the human yearning, indeed the human need, for tradition, community, and celebration, as a means of challenging and indicting contemporary attitudes in his overwhelming call for change. The little book established his public involvement in important social movements as well as becoming a lasting literary achievement. William Makepeace Thackeray, Dickens's friend and fellow journalist and writer, called it 'a national benefit, and to every man or woman who reads it a personal kindness'.[9]

---

[8] *PLets* 3:562–4, 564.
[9] M. A. T. [W. M. Thackeray], 'A Box of Novels', *Fraser's Magazine* 39 (February 1844): 166–9, 167.

Role of the Writer

Dickens's relationship with his reading public was a special one, developed through the medium of serial publication, month by month or week by week, creating a particular bond of communication, where readers could influence the progress of the work in question and Dickens as the writer could respond to these reactions: the works become almost collaborative, conversational.

He also had a very strong sense of the importance of the writer's calling. He argued for better copyright arrangements to protect authors' work and for increasing recognition of the status of the literary profession, properly established and self-supporting. When he wrote to a former girlfriend, Maria Winter, on 3 April 1855, he told her that he held his 'inventive capacity on the stern condition that it must master my whole life... Whoever is devoted to an Art must be content to deliver himself wholly up to it, and to find his recompense in it'.[10] An interesting example of this professionalism occurs in the publication of *Little Dorrit*. Dickens had completed writing the novel on 9 May 1857. Two days before, he had visited the site of the Marshalsea Prison and found 'the rooms that arose in my mind's-eye when I became Little Dorrit's biographer'.[11] His account of this visit is included in his Preface of May 1857 and, to contemporary readers, would have seemed an example of a writer's professionalism in going to check the accuracy of his imaginative vision. Dickens's authorized biographer John Forster, to whom Dickens wrote of this visit on 7 May, knew differently, of course, and so, with the benefit of hindsight, do we. When Dickens writes in his Preface of 'the crowding ghosts of many miserable years' (*LD* 'Preface', lx), we can apprehend, to some small degree, what the force of the phrase was to him, a 'son' of the Marshalsea when his father was incarcerated there. We can do so especially when we recall that his visit took place on the 20th anniversary of the fatal collapse of his beloved sister-in-law Mary Hogarth who died on 7 May 1837. This provides one example of Dickens's construction of his public image: apparently a conscientious author checking his facts. At the same time, however, as will be considered in more detail further on, he suppresses facts about his childhood and later life.

Journalism

Dickens's public image was closely connected to and abetted by his involvement with the press. The success of *Sketches by Boz* tempted him away from the *Morning Chronicle* in November 1836 to become editor of *Bentley's Miscellany*: Richard Bentley wanted to

---

[10] *PLets* 7:583–4, 584.
[11] Charles Dickens, 'Preface', *Little Dorrit*, ed. Harvey Peter Sucksmith (Oxford: Clarendon Press, 1979), lix.

exploit the name 'Boz'.[12] Although the periodical provided him with a place to publish his novel *Oliver Twist*, he never felt he had adequate editorial control, and so resigned from editing it in 1839. He tried a similar miscellany approach himself with *Master Humphrey's Clock* (1840–1), eventually using it to publish *The Old Curiosity Shop* and *Barnaby Rudge*. Once again, the format didn't work for him. During the early 1840s he published in the Radical weekly paper the *Examiner*, which was sub-edited and later edited by his friend John Forster; he penned over 40 articles, revealing his commitment to liberal reform, expressing aesthetic opinions through theatre reviews, and taking up social issues.

However, he was never other than an occasional—if powerful—contributor and wanted to be more of a direct influence on opinion. He attempted this by accepting the editorship of the newly created 'Morning Newspaper of Liberal Politics and Thorough Independence', the *Daily News*, launched on 21 January 1846. It was a post which he relinquished very quickly, after 17 days. Dickens did not have, at that point, the skill, experience, attention, or patience to manage a daily.

At mid-century, in 1850 Dickens began another kind of journalism. Until near the end of his life, in addition to writing seven novels, annual Christmas stories, and miscellaneous articles, some gathered under the title of *The Uncommercial Traveller*, he published and 'conducted' two weekly journals: *Household Words* (1850–9) and its very similar successor *All the Year Round*, which ran from 1859 and after Dickens's death continued under the editorship of his son. The pages of Dickens's journals offer an unequalled window into the world of mid-Victorian England in its 'summer-dawn of time': its concerns and its achievements, its national and international affairs, unfolded week by week.[13] The hearty success of these ventures demonstrates Dickens's public prominence and the extent of his popular appeal. From March 1850 to July 1870 there were 1,061 weekly issues, over 23 million words, well over 6,000 articles, poems, serial fiction instalments, and 380 contributors, over 90 of them women. Dickens himself supplied 108 articles to *Household Words* and 49 to *All the Year Round*, in addition to three novels: *Hard Times* (1854), *A Tale of Two Cities* (1859), and *Great Expectations* (1860–1).

Household Words was for Dickens, aged 38 in 1850, the fulfilment of a dream. Setting up his own 24-page weekly journal gave him the measure of editorial control he had long wanted. Now he was no longer dependent on other publishers for handling his works, though they did continue to do so: he was a profitable commodity. He could publish, as well as edit and write, and use the medium for his own purposes. He established an office at 16 Wellington Street North, near Covent Garden, in London: a Spartan, business-like set of rooms, but a place in central London where he could stay overnight if he wished and where he could entertain guests as well as work. He gathered together a staff of very talented young men, and used a number of other established writers too, such as the

---

[12] *Bentley's Miscellany* entry in *Oxford Reader's Companion to Dickens*, ed. Paul Schlicke (Oxford: Oxford University Press, 1999), 38–41, 38.

[13] *Household Words*, 'A Preliminary Word', 30 March 1850, 1. Henceforth *HW*, 'title', date, and page inserted parenthetically in the text or partly provided in the text itself.

novelists Elizabeth Gaskell and later Wilkie Collins. The periodical was very strictly under Dickens's control: there were no bylines on the articles to identify the writers (though we do know their identities from the account books kept showing payments to contributors). The whole enterprise was advertised on the first page of every weekly issue as 'Conducted by Charles Dickens': usually enough to guarantee sales. Dickens's stance and attitudes permeate every issue. His friend Douglas Jerrold called it not anonymous but 'mononymous': there was no doubt who was behind every word that was written. *Household Words* dealt with topics of the day such as sanitation and housing, poverty and education; 'process' articles on scientific and technological developments in layman's language; factory conditions; and governmental inadequacy. As well as discussing national issues, the journal expanded into the wider world, with articles on the Crimean War, the Indian Mutiny, Italy, and America.

When Dickens created *All the Year Round* in 1859, he followed the same template. In these later years he depended more on a team of talented writers both for individual articles and for collaborative anonymous pieces, especially in the Christmas numbers.[14] A divergence from the earlier publication, instituted to keep pace with rival magazines of the 1860s, was to open each number with a serialized fiction. One of the most successful of these was Wilkie Collins's mystery *The Woman in White*.

Public Involvement

In addition to covering a wide range of contemporary topics in the pages of his journals, Dickens also contributed to public events in other ways. He was indirectly associated with postal reforms, and more directly involved in commemorations of Shakespeare and the Great Exhibition of 1851.

Debates about reforming the inefficient and expensive British postal system heightened during the later 1830s. At that time, namely from January 1838 to October 1839, Dickens was working on and publishing his third novel, *The Life and Adventures of Nicholas Nickleby*. In format it duplicated *Pickwick* and thus regularized his 20-part monthly serial: 32 pages of text customarily divided into three or four chapters and two illustrations, all encased in a paper illustrated wrapper that also contained advertisements. *Nickleby* was popular from the beginning. Almost 50,000 copies were sold of the first instalment, and the sales held up strongly throughout its serial run.[15] It was the great popular success of its time.

Meanwhile, an enthusiastic supporter of Rowland Hill's proposed postal reforms, Henry Cole (later Sir Henry), had been busily devising ways of promoting those reforms

---

[14] The recent discovery by Dr Jeremy Parrott of a marked set of *All the Year Round* may enable us to confirm the author of each article in the journal. See Parrott, 'The Annotated Set of *All the Year Round*: Questions, Answers and Conjectures', *Dickensian*, 112, 1 (Spring 2016): 10–21.

[15] *PLets* 1:569–70.

to a wider public. He wrote a short playlet in 1838 called *A Report of an Imaginary Scene at Windsor Castle* respecting the proposed Uniform Penny Postage that had a wide circulation. But then he hit on the idea of increasing even that distribution: he arranged with Dickens's publishers Chapman and Hall to have the script stitched into a monthly instalment of *Nickleby*. Thus, at the end of March 1839 when the 13th monthly part of the novel (chapters 40–2, dated April) was published, readers found in that issue of the accompanying *Nickleby Advertiser* Cole's two-page playlet.[16] It was a stroke of brilliance: the most popular writer of the time seemed here to be lending his support to the campaign, just as Cole has, in his play, Queen Victoria strongly in favour of a standard-rate sender-paid postage. While the insertion, whether Dickens approved of it or not, reflects his concern with campaigning designed to correct social injustices, the main thing from Cole's viewpoint was to take advantage of the enormously wide circulation of Dickens's serial.

In the 1840s Dickens became involved with Shakespeare's house in Stratford-upon-Avon, which had been purchased for the nation in 1843. These events brought together his enormous admiration for Shakespeare with his own delight in performance. He served on the London Shakespeare Committee and in 1847–8 was the driving force behind a move to raise funds for the establishment of a curatorial post, to be first given to the playwright James Sheridan Knowles, who had fallen into straitened circumstances. He threw himself into service with his customary enthusiasm. The Amateur Company he assembled, acted in, and directed produced *The Merry Wives of Windsor* at the Haymarket Theatre in London and then in various other venues, including Manchester, Liverpool, Edinburgh, Glasgow, and Birmingham.

Nearly two decades later Dickens visited Stratford during the 1864 celebrations for the tercentenary of Shakespeare's birth. One of the aims of these events was to raise funds for a new permanent memorial to Shakespeare. A statue was planned, but Dickens's sentiment that 'Shakespeare's best monument is his works' held sway, eventually leading to the building of the Shakespeare Memorial Theatre in 1879.

A third set of public events with which Dickens became associated was the Great Exhibition of 1851. His enthusiasm for this cause was more overt than that for postal reform, but less energetic than his commemorations of his Elizabethan fellow author. Though interested in and supportive of some of the age's technological developments, Dickens was never a wholesale admirer either of industrialization or the British government. He was a friend and supporter of Joseph Paxton, designer of the great glass conservatory housing the exhibition, and of Prince Albert who with Henry Cole organized the event. Dickens joined the Central Working Classes Committee of the Great Exhibition in May of 1850, but was quickly convinced that because this committee was not recognized by the superintending Royal Commission, it could achieve very little. His somewhat ambivalent attitude towards the project can be seen in 'The Last

---

[16] [Henry Cole], 'Queen Victoria and the Uniform Penny Postage', reproduced in Charles Dickens, *Nicholas Nickleby*, ed. Michael Slater (London: Scolar Press, 1982), in advertising section following chapter 13, page 416.

Words of the Old Year', published in *Household Words* on 4 January 1851 (*HW* 337–9). In it, the narrator imagines the dying year, 1850, speaking about the events over which his successor will preside:

> 'I have seen,' he presently said, 'a project carried into execution for a great assemblage of the peaceful glories of the world. I have seen a wonderful structure, reared in glass, by the energy and skill of a great natural genius... Which of my children shall behold the Princes, Prelates, Nobles, Merchants, of England, equally united, for another Exhibition—for a great display of England's sins and negligences, ... this dark Exhibition of the bad results of our doings! Where shall we hold it? When shall we open it? What courtier speaks? (338)

Other public causes to which Dickens contributed, and for which during his lifetime he was sometimes assailed and sometimes hailed, included opposition to public hangings, criticizing the government's conduct of the Crimean War in leading articles published in *Household Words*, and helping to furnish Florence Nightingale's hospital at Scutari with bed linen, clothing, and bandages. He was invited to stand for election as one of Birmingham's Members of Parliament in 1868 alongside John Bright and George Dixon, Liberals whom he respected. He declined. In a letter to James Freeman on 19 April 1869 he explained 'that my mind was thoroughly made up never to enter the House of Commons, and that I had satisfied myself to rest content with my present sphere of usefulness and occupation'.[17]

Philanthropy

As is evident in the quotation from the Old Year 1850, Dickens's creative output is full of encouragement for his fellow subjects to be aware of the suffering of others and by implication to take action about it. His own philanthropic outlook was focused on what he could do directly and personally, rather than at a remote distance. It is a sentiment echoed in John Jarndyce's words in *Bleak House*: 'he had remarked that there were two classes of charitable people: one, the people who did a little and made a great deal of noise; the other, the people who did a great deal and made no noise at all'.[18]

One of the outstanding philanthropists of the Victorian era was Angela Burdett-Coutts. She inherited the wealth of the great Coutts banking house and for her charitable activities was in 1871 raised by Queen Victoria to the peerage as Baroness Burdett-Coutts. She first met Dickens in 1837. They became great friends and collaborated on a number of philanthropic endeavours: Ragged Schools, housing for the poor, and from

---

[17] *PLets* 12:337.
[18] *Bleak House*, ed. George Ford and Sylvère Monod, Norton Critical Edition (New York: W. W. Norton, 1999), chapter 8, page 93.

1847 the Home for Homeless Women in Shepherd's Bush, London, known as Urania Cottage. The relationship virtually ended in 1858 as a result of Dickens's separation from his wife Catherine.

But for 20 years she and Dickens partnered on many projects. To take the most lasting example: in May 1846 he sent her detailed plans for a scheme to rescue women from the streets and a life of crime and to offer them a domestic setting in which to learn self-respect, to work in a community with others, and to acquire skills and education. By establishing a wholesome and cheerful domestic residence, Dickens wanted the women to be, as he put it, 'tempted to virtue'.[19] Eventually they might escape their past by emigrating to the colonies. Other institutions which existed for prostitutes like the Magdalen Hospital and Homes (1758 onwards) were much more prison-like and stressed punishment and guilt. This was to be different. Dickens, after consulting people he knew in the prison service, established a clear system of marks for rewards and loss of them when the women transgressed.

Miss Burdett-Coutts provided the financial backing for the enterprise, which opened in 1847, and was enthusiastically supportive of all its aims. Dickens had the highest praise for her at all times. He handled the day-to-day running of the Home and the range of his activities in connection with it is, simply, staggering. He wrote 'An Appeal to Fallen Women' and arranged for its circulation to potential inmates, as well as visiting prisons and other institutions in search of those who might benefit from the opportunity to reform. He planned the routines and chose the wallpaper and the material for the inmates' clothing, insisting on bright colours to bring cheer into their lives. He served on an administrative committee, which he established, attended regular meetings, managed the accounts, and interviewed staff and young women for admission. He dealt with day-to-day running and with the wide range of problems which occurred, ranging from recalcitrant inmates to clogged drains.

Whilst many of the young women were highly appreciative of the chances they were given, they were by no means angels nor did they change overnight. They robbed the home, damaged the fixtures and fittings, ganged up against the staff, stole out overnight, and sneaked men into the home behind the backs of the staff. Dickens dealt with all the cases of indiscipline and transgression and had no reluctance about sending them packing if they did not behave. He had no illusions, saying of one especially difficult inmate, 'she would corrupt a Nunnery in a fortnight'.[20]

He wrote an account of the Home's activities in 'Home for Homeless Women', published in *Household Words* on 23 April 1853. By that date, 57 or 58 women had passed through Urania Cottage. Thirty of these had gone to Australia or elsewhere and done well. Seven left the Home during the probationary period, seven ran away, ten were expelled, and three relapsed on the passage out to Australia. There are no final figures for the Home when it closed in 1862, but if the same success rate was maintained as in the

---

[19] *PLets* 5:181–8, 183.
[20] *PLets* 5:641.

first five years then about 100 young women would have been enabled to establish new lives overseas.

So much is striking about this act of mid-Victorian benevolence. No one would argue that Urania Cottage was anything but a drop in the ocean so far as dealing with the great social evil of prostitution in the nineteenth century was concerned. But it gave new hope for those young women who could take advantage of it. This endeavour displays that concern with individual need that is so much a part of Dickens's approach to philanthropy.[21] For the 11 years or so in which he was directly involved with its operation he was of course expending his phenomenal energy in other areas as well.

Another long-term effort involved hospitals for children. The Foundling Hospital was a near neighbour when the Dickens family occupied 48 Doughty Street between 1837 and 1839. The Hospital had been established in 1739 as the result of strenuous efforts by Thomas Coram, a retired sea-captain, horrified by what he saw of abandoned children in eighteenth-century London. Dickens wrote about its work and was one of its greatest supporters. He attended services in the Hospital Chapel, which became a very popular place of worship in the 1840s.

Justly famous as a writer about the sufferings of children, Dickens was notably drawn to support the work of a new hospital for sick children that opened on 14 February 1852 close to the site of Coram's Hospital and Dickens's former Doughty Street residence. It is better known to us now as Great Ormond Street Hospital for Sick Children. He was a friend of Dr Charles West, one of the Hospital's founders, who called him 'the children's friend'. There was no hospital in London devoted specifically to the care of children. In an article called 'Drooping Buds' published in *Household Words* just six weeks after the hospital started work, Dickens made a compelling case for its support (*HW*, 3 April 1852, 45–8).

Nonetheless, by 1858 the hospital was experiencing a financial crisis. Dickens agreed to speak at its Festival Dinner on 9 February that year, two days after his birthday. His speech about the sufferings alleviated by the hospital's work was so powerful that it raised, as he described it, the 'unprecedented sum of £3,000', including a remarkable £500 donation from a lady known simply as 'Mary Jane'.[22] Shortly afterwards he was invited to become one of the Honorary Governors of the Hospital which, he wrote on 17 February, gave him 'great pleasure'. He assured the Committee of Management 'of the gratification I derive from their generous recognition of my most willingly rendered services'.[23] When his friend William Macready, the great actor and theatre manager, sent him a donation for the hospital's work, he replied on 15 March 1858: 'You may be sure that it is a good and kind Charity. It is amazing to me that it is not at this day ten times as large and rich as it is. But I hope and trust that I have happily been able to give it a good thrust

---

[21] For further information, consult Jenny Hartley, *Charles Dickens and the House of Fallen Women* (London: Methuen, 2009).
[22] *PLets* 8:517 and nn.
[23] *PLets* 8:520–1, 520.

onward into a great course.' Although at the time upwards of 21,000 children under the age of 10 died annually, the hospital still had only 31 beds.[24]

Indeed, Dickens's charitable activities raised enough money to enable it to buy adjoining property and increase its bed capacity from 20 to 75. In addition, financial support made it possible to provide facilities and accommodation for the training of nurses to work with the children. The most important factor militating against recovery was poverty and poor living conditions: many patients just required good food and a healthy environment. Dickens's involvement and patronage gave at least some of them a chance.

As a public figure, recognized for his social concerns and his sympathy with the poor and underprivileged, Dickens became the target for begging letters, importuning him for financial or other assistance. He writes about this in a *Household Words* piece, 'The Begging-Letter Writer'. Though a generous man, willing to help financially and other ways in cases of genuine need, Dickens grew intensely angry when, approached by a correspondent exploiting barefaced lies, he reflected on 'the immeasurable harm he does to the deserving,—dirtying the stream of true benevolence' (*HW*, 18 May 1850, 169–72, 169). In his last years Dickens developed a system whereby those who called on him for help at Gad's Hill would be given a token that they could exchange for food at the inn Sir John Falstaff which stood across the road from his home.

In March of 1858, having given a very successful public Reading of the *Carol* to raise funds for the Great Ormond Street facility, Dickens considered embarking on a career as a professional reader. He consulted the doubtful John Forster in a letter on 30 March: 'Will you then try to think of this reading project (as I do) apart from all personal likings and dislikings, and solely with a view to its effect on that peculiar relation (personally affectionate, and like no other man's) which subsists between me and the public?'[25] Though Forster remained critical of the project, Dickens then embarked on the first of a series of Public Readings adapted from his own works that eventually took him to France and the United States. He became his own scriptwriter, adapter, stage-manager, performer, and theatrical impresario all rolled into one, acting his own writing, and satisfying his need for audience approval. We are fortunate to have eyewitness accounts of these performances from an American, his friend Kate Field, and from two countrymen, George Dolby his agent for the Readings, and the Roman Catholic Charles Kent, friend, journalist, and contributor to *All the Year Round*.

In a review of the early Readings, the *Illustrated London News*, in July 1858, gave this picture of him:

> Mr. Charles Dickens is an excellent reader. He uses little action, but he can make his features eloquent. He is far from monotonous, and throws an alteration of light and shade, so to speak, into his reading, by means of a rapid or slow utterance, according to the character or importance of the passages read. He, therefore, maintains the

[24] *PLets* 8:531–2, 531 and n. 3.
[25] *PLets* 8:539–40, 539.

interest of his subject for two hours with comparative ease, and carries his audience with him by means of the variety which he imparts to his entertainment. Without any aid from costume, or any extravagance of motion, by the mere power of facial expression, he impersonates the different characters of his stories and brings them ideally, but vividly, before the spectator's mind. Mr. Dickens has invented a new medium for amusing an English audience, and merits the gratitude of an intelligent public.[26]

Charles Kent wrote of a later performance that 'whilst he stood there unmistakably before his audience ... that earnest, animated, mobile, delightful face ... altogether disappeared, and we were as conscious as though we saw them, of the bald head, the spectacles, and the little gaiters of Mr. Pickwick—of the snuffy tones, the immense umbrella, and the voluminous bonnet and gown of Mrs. Gamp'.[27]

One further form of performance to which Dickens made an enormous contribution was the making of speeches. He often spoke on behalf of charitable activities, adult education, hospitals, and special social celebrations. They were reported assiduously in newspapers by reporters who attended their presentation and wrote them down verbatim. Some were then published as printed pamphlets. Dickens never read a script and rarely used notes. His memory was so phenomenal that he could write out a speech he had given, afterwards, from memory.[28]

As well as being before the public eye in all of these ways, Dickens was represented in painting and portraits, in sculpture and in published engravings in the press, sometimes in caricature and sometimes for purposes of advertisement. Starting with images on the wrappers or in the frontispiece of early publications, Dickens's features were well known and widely publicized, particularly through the development of photography from 1839 onwards.[29]

Correspondence

Dickens's correspondence also contributes to our knowledge of him as a public figure and underscores many of the themes that emerge in his life. Letters he wrote to family

---

[26] *Illustrated London News*, 31 July 1858. For more on the strategies of presentation and effects on his audience, see Malcolm Andrews, *Charles Dickens and his Performing Selves* (Oxford: Oxford University Press, 2006).

[27] Charles Kent, *Charles Dickens as a Reader* (London: Chapman and Hall, 1872), 32.

[28] These speeches are collected and introduced by K. J. Fielding (ed.), *The Speeches of Charles Dickens* (Oxford: Clarendon Press, 1960).

[29] Recent articles on this topic by Leon Litvack have been published in the *Dickensian*: 'Dickens's Dream and the Conception of Character', *Dickensian* 103, 1 (Spring 2007): 5–36 and 'A Dickens Photographer Identified: Adolphe Naudin', *Dickensian* 111, 2 (Summer 2015): 130–41. He has also published 'Dickens in the Eye of the Beholder: The Photographs of Robert Hindry Mason', *Dickens Studies Annual* 47 (2016): 166–99.

and friends whilst travelling in America and Italy in the 1840s were borrowed back on his return and incorporated in *American Notes* (1842) and *Pictures from Italy* (1846), thereby emphasizing that they were written with a possible view to publication. When composing the posthumous *Life of Charles Dickens* (1872–4), John Forster drew significantly on the correspondence he had received from Dickens throughout their friendship.

The first attempt to publish the letters, in 1880 and 1882, was intended to supplement Forster's *Life*; they were issued by Dickens's publisher Chapman and Hall and appeared in a binding similar to that used for Forster's biography. The edition was compiled by Dickens's daughter Mary ('Mamie') and his sister-in-law Georgina Hogarth. As editors they were very selective and omitted much that they felt was inappropriate. They also exercised their blue pencils freely, cutting out phrases and sentences, combining parts of one letter with another, and even adding pieces themselves.

The next major attempt to publish a collected edition came in 1938, when three volumes of the lavishly produced and expensive Nonesuch edition were devoted to the letters, edited by the great Dickensian Walter Dexter and comprising 5,811 letters to 1,000 correspondents. Unfortunately, this collection, only available to purchasers of the complete edition of the novels, perpetuated many of the errors and anomalies in Mamie and Georgina's edition.

It was in 1951 that the scholar Humphry House suggested the publication of a full and properly edited edition.[30] Despite his untimely death in 1955 this scheme was set in motion and eventually became the monumental Pilgrim/British Academy edition, published from 1965 to 2002 in 12 hefty volumes, comprising some 14,252 pieces of correspondence Dickens wrote from the earliest known items of the 1820s through to the final letters written—one to Charles Kent on the day before he died. The edition is meticulously annotated and researched.[31]

The publication of Dickens's correspondence provides an intimate view of his activities and opinions. Even though they were, for the most part, written to individuals and considered to be private, from early on Dickens was aware enough of their importance in conveying who he was that, even in spontaneous moments, he projected an indelible personality. The letters cover a huge range of subjects and occasions—business, family affairs, the lives and needs of friends. He writes letters home whilst travelling, and letters from home and office about his writing and editing work. There are letters organizing and reporting on his performing and charitable acts; long or short notes in times of personal crisis, births, and bereavements; invitations to hundreds of parties and gatherings; accounts of the development and education of his children; stories regarding relationships of love and friendship; fulminations about his dislikes; details of financial

---

[30] Humphry House, *All in Due Time* (London: Rupert Hart-Davis, 1955), 221–9.
[31] Since 2000 new discoveries have been published in the *Dickensian*, the journal of the Dickens Fellowship. These are now available online at <http://dickensfellowship.org/dickens-letters-supplements>. The Clarendon Press has commissioned a 13th volume that will contain these.

and legal affairs; reports on housing, permanent and temporary; statements concerning his reactions to international and national politics; explanations of the collapse of his and Catherine's marriage: the entire spectrum of topics in a life of colossal energy and appetite for living. It is undoubtedly the case that Rowland Hill's postal reforms played a major role in facilitating this voluminous correspondence.

Since Dickens became famous at such a young age—24—his outgoing mail was often saved by the recipients. However, the correspondence Dickens received was burnt when he moved into Gad's Hill Place in 1860. He wrote to his sub-editor W. H. Wills on 4 September 1860: 'Yesterday I burnt, in the field at Gad's Hill, the accumulated letters and papers of twenty years. They sent up a smoke like the Genie when he got out of the casket on the seashore; and as it was an exquisite day when I began, and rained very heavily when I finished, I suspect my correspondence of having overcast the face of the Heavens.'[32] He is alleged to have said, 'Would to God every letter I had ever written was on that pile' as the last ones went up in smoke. Later, in 1864 he was approached by the Revd S. R. Hole for any correspondence he had from his artist friend John Leech who had recently died; Hole was writing a biography. Dickens told him: 'A year or two ago, shocked by the misuse of the private letters of public men, which I constantly observed, I destroyed a very large and very rare mass of correspondence. It was not done without pain, you may believe, but, the first reluctance conquered, I have steadily abided by my determination to keep no letters by me, and to consign all such papers to the fire.'[33]

Preserving the Image

Although Dickens was in the public eye for 35 years, much about him remained unknown to all but Forster and Catherine. *The Times* obituary of June 1870 gave very little information about his family background. He did on a number of occasions respond to letters requesting information about his early life. But he concealed his boyhood experiences of employment and his father's incarceration in a debtors' prison. It was left to John Forster in his 1872–4 biography to reveal to the world the information about Dickens's 'Hard Experiences in Boyhood'. Forster's biography emphasizes the heroic achievements of Dickens's childhood and subsequent career; it also deploys material from Dickens's own 'Autobiographical Fragment' which he consigned to Forster, and from which he himself drew in writing *David Copperfield*.

Thus, whilst the public projections of Dickens made people feel he was personally known to them, there ran alongside a depth of privacy and indeed secrecy about

---

[32] *PLets* 9:302–4, 304.
[33] *PLets* 10: 464–5, 465.

certain aspects of his personal life. Dickens's public image was damaged by the separation from his wife Catherine in May 1858. Since he was a celebrity, wild rumours about his marital troubles circulated throughout England and abroad. To correct the most egregious of these, he published an explanation in an article entitled 'Personal' which appeared in *Household Words* on 12 June 1858 (*HW* 601). This did nothing to quell curiosity, which continued to discomfort him and make him wary of public disclosure. He was seriously alarmed when, on returning from a visit to France on 9 June 1865, he was involved in a rail accident at Staplehurst in Kent. His travelling companions were Ellen Ternan, with whom Dickens had commenced an affair after his marital breakup, and her mother. He made sure to get them both away from the scene of the disaster before involving himself in working amongst the injured and dying. He made it clear in subsequent correspondence that he did not wish to be involved in ensuing enquiries about the episode. Any revelations about his relationship with Ellen Ternan were severely and effectively suppressed through to the end of his life and beyond, into the twentieth century.[34]

Conclusion

Dickens's writing forces his readers or hearers to engage with the world as it is and to reject conventional responses. He often does this through the use of sentiment as a powerful weapon, urging us to show compassion for other human beings. He aimed at arousing the conscience of his age, to keep the poor, the suffering, the marginalized, and the rejected ever before us, through his fiction, his journalism, his Public Readings, and also his acts of personal benevolence and genuine philanthropy. The public image which he painstakingly developed during the course of doing all this reflects the reality and sincerity of his actions. But the dark episodes in his own personal and professional life that he remained so reticent and secretive about have produced on later generations, as these affairs came to light, some discordance. Who was Dickens? How can we understand the relationship between all the appeals he made during his public lifetime and his own personal embarrassments and violations of the hearth and home he so volubly celebrated? To what extent can we read his life into his fiction and role as 'the strong warm friend of humanity' to which he was consigned at his burial? There is much work still to be done on these issues.

---

[34] For further information, readers are referred to the research undertaken by Claire Tomalin in *The Invisible Woman* (London: Penguin, 1991), Michael Slater in *The Great Charles Dickens Scandal* (New Haven: Yale University Press, 2012), and Patrick Leary, 'How the Dickens Scandal went Viral', in Hazel Mackenzie and Ben Winyard (eds), *Charles Dickens and the Mid-Victorian Press, 1850–1870* (Buckingham: University of Buckingham Press, 2013), 305–23.

Further Reading

Malcolm Andrews, *Charles Dickens and his Performing Selves* (Oxford: Oxford University Press, 2006)

John M. L. Drew, *Dickens the Journalist* (Houndmills: Palgrave Macmillan, 2003)

K. J. Fielding, *The Speeches of Charles Dickens* (Oxford: Clarendon Press, 1960)

Leon Litvack, '*Dickens's Dream* and the Conception of Character', *Dickensian* 103, 1 (Spring 2007): 5–36

Michael Slater, *Charles Dickens* (New Haven: Yale University Press, 2009)

PART II
THE WORKS

CHAPTER 5

DICKENS'S EARLY SKETCHES

PAUL SCHLICKE

Dickens's early sketches are largely undiscovered territory, wildly popular when published but unjustifiably denigrated by Dickens himself and largely ignored by subsequent commentators. This material is worthy of new consideration, and with the advent of the forthcoming Oxford edition students will have all the evidence they need to reconsider how Dickens learned his art: its topics, treatments, and popular impact.

The subtitle of *Sketches by Boz*, 'Every-Day Life and Every-Day People', identifies the distinctive subject matter of Dickens's early sketching. His focus is on insecurely respectable and decidedly lower-class characters of the circles in which Dickens himself then moved. Just as Wordsworth's *Lyrical Ballads* staked a claim for the inherent dignity of a lowly shepherd such as Michael, so too Dickens's focus on unexceptional men and women articulated his convictions that such people were worthy of respect, and that condescending prejudice against them deserved nothing but contempt. Dickens's comedy serves not only to ridicule pretensions, but to relish the insouciance of the likes of Horatio Sparkins and the Theatrical Young Gentleman. Writing during the Reform era, moreover, Dickens's stance was emphatically political: attacking the 'bleared eyes of bigotry and gloom', he endorses the right of ordinary people to the innocent pleasures and activities of their daily lives.[1]

The sketches reveal Dickens's deepest convictions about class, even as the poised narration prefigures the artistry of his maturity. Hallmarks of his style appear in sharp relief: the distinctive narrative voice, modulating between droll detachment, easy familiarity, and earnest engagement; the sharp eye for telling details and the knack of introducing surprising comparisons through metaphor and simile, making a character utterly unique even as it is at the same time representative; the energy and range of expression, moving rapidly from ironic detachment to pathos, horror, or fascination.

Dickens wrote the 60 short imaginative articles which became *Sketches by Boz* between 1833 and 1836. All but four of these first appeared in newspapers or periodicals;

---

[1] [Charles Dickens,] 'The Queen's Coronation', *Examiner*, 1 July 1838, p. 403.

eight were combined into four two-part sketches, bringing the total in the final collected arrangement to 56. The first six appeared without by-line; the remainder appeared under one or the other of two pseudonyms, 'Boz' and 'Tibbs'. Dickens's name did not appear on the title page of any authorized edition of *Sketches by Boz* until 1843,[2] and although it was advertised to be his work long before that, its significance as his first published volume was largely eclipsed by the phenomenal fame of *Pickwick* (1836–7). Twelve more early character sketches were published anonymously as *Sketches of Young Gentlemen* in 1838, and a further 11, also anonymously, appeared as *Sketches of Young Couples* in 1840. Dickens's authorship of *Young Gentlemen* and *Young Couples* was never publicly acknowledged during his lifetime, and they have been noticed only rarely. Although it would be exaggeration to say that all of the sketches sank without trace, their reputation (when they have been remarked upon at all) has ranged largely between the perfunctory and the dismissive.

Dickens himself is partly to blame for the neglect of his sketches. The three prefaces which he wrote for the selections published by John Macrone, while not negative, are humble statements of aspiration. Thereafter, however, Dickens becomes explicitly apologetic for obtruding inferior work on the public. The 'advertisement' to the first complete edition (1839) describes the sketches as 'the earliest productions of their Author, written from time to time to meet the exigencies of a Newspaper or a Magazine'. And the Preface to the 1850 'Cheap' edition, reprinted in every authorized edition to appear for the rest of Dickens's life, is positively dismissive. 'I am conscious', he wrote, 'of their being extremely crude and ill-considered, and bearing obvious marks of haste and inexperience.' Later letters confirm that this was his final verdict.[3]

Following on from their purchase of *Sketches by Boz* from Macrone, Chapman and Hall brought out another volume of sketches in 1837, *Sketches of Young Ladies*. Illustrated by his *Pickwick* artist, Hablot Browne ('Phiz'), it was attributed to 'Quiz', the pseudonym of a young Oxford graduate named Edward Caswall, and sold very well, going through some 11 editions. Caswall was commissioned to write a sequel, but abandoned it, entering the church instead (he later followed Cardinal Newman into the Roman

---

[2] Baron Tauchnitz published an authorized English-language edition for the continental market only, entitled *Sketches by Charles Dickens* in 1843, but the work did not appear with attribution to Dickens for domestic readers until published by Chapman and Hall in 1850 as a title in the Cheap Edition of Dickens's works.

[3] When initial sales of the Cheap Edition fell below expectation, Dickens promptly decided to delay publication of *Sketches by Boz*, originally planned to be the third volume in the series: 'It is clear to me', he wrote to Edward Chapman, 'that we must go on, in the cheap Edition, with the Stories, and not take in the Sketches yet' (*The Letters of Charles Dickens*, British Academy/Pilgrim edition, 12 vols, ed. Madeline House, Graham Storey, et al. (Oxford: Clarendon Press, 1965–2002), 5:246–7, 247). Subsequent citations: *PLets* followed by volume: page range, page, and hn. for headnote, n. or nn. for footnotes, with page range given before page cited. *Sketches by Boz* eventually appeared in the Cheap Edition as volume 8 of the original series of 9. Letters to Louis Hachette (*PLets* 8:22–3) and to Antonin Roche (*PLets* 11:254) corroborate this judgement.

Catholic Church, and became a prolific and admired author of hymns).[4] Dickens stepped in to fill the gap. *Sketches of Young Gentlemen* was published on 10 February 1838, advertised as a companion volume to *Young Ladies*, and illustrated (like *Young Ladies*) by Browne. Also like the earlier work, it went into several editions, but not before a rival publisher, William Kidd, brought out a version of his own, *Characteristic Sketches of Young Gentlemen*, by Quiz, Jun., illustrated by Cruikshank (artist for *Sketches by Boz*), claiming that this was the original work, 'fraudulently imitated' by Chapman and Hall.[5] Dickens's *Young Gentlemen* appeared without attribution, presumably because he was explicitly prohibited in his contracts with Richard Bentley from writing anything besides *Nicholas Nickleby* for any publisher besides Bentley.[6] Dickens confided to his diary that he was pleased to have earned £120 for a work not generally known to be his, but he never publicly acknowledged authorship.[7] Two years later, his imagination tickled by news of the queen's engagement to be married, he wrote a further volume, *Sketches of Young Couples*, published—also anonymously—on the queen's wedding day (10 February 1840), dedicated to her, and illustrated once again by Browne. Privately, he wrote a series of madcap letters to friends, announcing that he was himself madly in love with the queen and proposing to run off with a maid of honour, to hang himself from the pear tree in the garden, or to turn Chartist.[8] He was proud enough of *Young Couples* to inscribe copies for friends,[9] but he never publicly acknowledged authorship, and it was sometimes supposed that he had written *Young Ladies* as well as *Young Gentlemen* and *Young Couples*; they were advertised as companion volumes, and the confusion was redoubled when an edition containing all three works came out in a single volume in 1843.[10] These sketches have remained generally unknown among Dickens's works, rarely mentioned by scholars, and infrequently republished.

If *Sketches of Young Gentlemen* and *Sketches of Young Couples* have sunk virtually without trace, *Sketches by Boz* has fared only a very little better. Largely ignored or only perfunctorily noted by Dickens critics, the work has rarely received more than passing notice. George Gissing and G. K. Chesterton both offered guarded verdicts, acknowledging limited achievement but dismissing the sketches overall as apprentice work, a verdict corroborated by Virgil Grillo and Duane DeVries in the only book-length studies of the sketches. Major Dickens critics of the twentieth century were silent about them, and only a scattering of essays has appeared. There are a few notable exceptions. Attesting to the 'sheer merit' of the sketches, Kathleen Tillotson in 1957

---

[4] See Nancy Marie De Flon, *Edward Caswell: Newman's Brother and Friend* (Leominster: Gracewing, 2005).

[5] *Operative*, 4 November 1838; see *PLets* 1:434n.

[6] 'Agreements with Publishers', *PLets* 1:648–50, 649.

[7] Diary entry for Monday 8 January 1838; *PLets* 1:630.

[8] *PLets* 2:23–9.

[9] Inscribed copies went to William Giles, Daniel Maclise, and W. C. Macready. *PLets* 1:429; 2:27–9, 27n.; 240 and 241n.

[10] See *PLets* 1:429; 2:1, 213 and n. 3. The three titles were later republished together in 1869, 1875, and most recently in 2012.

provided a prolegomena to a scholarly edition of the sketches—a call which still has not been met over half a century later.[11] J. Hillis Miller, in a bold and challenging reading (1970), contested the accepted view of the sketches as realism,[12] and there is useful historical contextualization in books by Kathryn Chittick and Fred Schwarzbach. But that is pretty much all.

The present chapter deplores this situation, on five major grounds. First, the consensus ignores Dickens's own initial enthusiasm for the sketches. Just as he was later to re-create the early days of his marriage in the months leading up to the separation from Catherine, his later pronouncements about the sketches contradict his estimate of them when he was first writing, publishing, and collecting them into volumes. Second, the neglect contrasts radically with the initial reception of them by Dickens's first readers. Contrary to the received wisdom that it was *Pickwick* which launched Dickens's career, for the several months before readers began to marvel over the Pickwickians and Wellers, Dickens was already receiving stupendous celebrity for *Sketches by Boz*. The press was full of enthusiastic endorsements, and the collection of individual magazine and newspaper pieces into volumes, accompanied by George Cruikshank's illustrations, was greeted with acclaim. Third, avoidance ignores the single most important evidence which we have of Dickens's development as a writer. He extensively revised the sketches on at least five separate occasions over 17 years, and meticulous documentation of the evolution gives precise, detailed information as to how he conceived of his own writing. Fourth, to overlook the sketches is to miss a particularly rich source for an understanding of the very texture of life in London in the 1830s. Dickens was there, documenting trends, developments, conventions, attitudes, and multiple additional aspects of the spirit of the age. And finally, to neglect the sketches is to disregard their intrinsic worth, 'the first sprightly runnings of his genius', as Forster eloquently put it.[13]

Dickens did not always have a negative view of the sketches. Indeed, all the surviving evidence indicates that his initial attitude was one of pride, satisfaction, good humour, and optimism that they would be the foundation for later achievement. As the first sketches began appearing, he wrote frequent letters to his friend Henry Kolle, who had recently married Anne Beadnell, older sister of Maria Beadnell, with whom Dickens had been passionately in love. It was in the months following his abandonment of pursuit of Maria, with time on his hands, that he started writing and publishing sketches,

---

[11] Kathleen Tillotson, '*Sketches by Boz*, Collection and Revision', in John Butt and Kathleen Tillotson, *Dickens at Work* (London: Methuen, 1957), 35–61, 35.

[12] As proposed, for example, in the introductions to modern editions of the sketches, by Thea Holme, Oxford Illustrated Edition (Oxford: Oxford University Press, 1957), p. vii; and Dennis Walder (London: Penguin, 1995), p. xvi. Cf. Michael Slater's introduction to volume 1 of *The Dent Uniform Edition of Dickens' Journalism*, ed. Michael Slater and John Drew, 4 vols (London: J. M. Dent, Columbus: Ohio State University Press, 1993–2000), xiii. J. Hillis Miller, 'The Fiction of Realism: *Sketches by Boz, Oliver Twist*, and Cruikshank's Illustrations', in *Charles Dickens and George Cruikshank*, introd. Ada Nisbet (Los Angeles: William Andrews Clark Library, University of California Press, 1971), 1–69.

[13] John Forster, *Life of Charles Dickens*, ed. J. W. T. Ley (London: Cecil Palmer, 1928), 76.

and his persistent drawing them to the attention of Anne was no doubt partly intended to show the Beadnells 'the quality of man they trifled with'.[14] As soon as 'A Dinner at Poplar Walk' was published in the *Monthly Magazine* (December 1833), Dickens wrote to Kolle with the 'important announcement' of its appearance, 'the first of a series', he boasted. A week later he wrote again, reporting that the sketch had been pirated in a magazine called *The Thief*, intimating that he had been approached for more sketches by the *Monthly*, and outlining his plans for future publications. Further letters to Kolle offer to show subsequent sketches to him and his wife.[15] A few months later, having learned that a dramatization loosely based on his sketch 'The Bloomsbury Christening' had been staged without authorization or acknowledgement, he wrote to the editor of the *Monthly* to protest, and his letter was duly published. Meantime, he wrote a surprisingly generous review of the production for the *Morning Chronicle*, in which he laconically observed that 'the characters are old and very particular friends of ours'.[16] Further indication of his delight in his role as a published author is a passing remark in 'The Steam Excursion' which declared that a character in that tale had appeared in a newspaper report—written not coincidentally by Dickens (without by-line, of course).[17] It is clear from the evidence of these letters that Dickens was enjoying seeing his work in print, and eager to let others know.

It was during the time these sketches were appearing that Dickens met and became engaged to Catherine Hogarth, and his letters to her reveal another side of his authorship, not simply enjoyment, but also concerted dedication to his writing. The letters reveal a significantly different kind of relationship to her from that to Maria Beadnell: instead of passionate yearning, Dickens wrote to Catherine with affection and anticipation of their coming marriage, but above all with determination to let nothing interfere with his commitment to authorship. The letters contain frequent excuses for missed opportunities to meet with Catherine on the grounds that he must press on with his sketches. He frequently mentions how hard he is working, often how tired he is, and above all the priority he gives to writing his sketches.

His correspondence with his publisher, John Macrone, and with his illustrator, George Cruikshank, confirms this dedication. The first surviving letter to Macrone details arrangements for collecting copies of sketches for the proposed volume. A few days later, in vibrant prose, he describes himself as being in a 'fever of anxiety' to see the first evidence of progress towards publication.[18] His enthusiasm is testimony to his buoyant mood at the time.

On 5 November 1835 he visited Newgate prison with Macrone and an American journalist, Nathaniel Parker Willis. Reporting to Kate that he was 'intensely interested' in

---

[14] Dickens adopts this phrase to describe Dick Swiveller's reaction at being snubbed by Sophy Wackles and her sisters in *The Old Curiosity Shop* (chapter 8).

[15] *PLets* 1:32, 33–4, 39, and nn.

[16] *PLets* 1:42 and nn.

[17] 'The Steam Excursion', *Monthly Magazine* NS 18 (October 1834): 375.

[18] *PLets* 1:88–9, 89.

what he saw, he promptly showed his account to others and was intensely gratified with their response; 'It would "make" any book,' according to Hogarth.[19] Working closely with Cruikshank, he continued to express eagerness to see the pictures and the proofs.[20] He worried over advertisements and was disappointed when Macrone distributed copy too late for immediate review.[21]

But once the first series appeared, he proudly distributed presentation copies, and wrote to his uncle Thomas Culliford Barrow, announcing the 'great success of my book, and the name it has established for me among the Publishers'.[22] In under six months the First Series went into a second edition, and within a year a Second Series appeared; by two or three years later at least ten unauthorized English-language editions were published in America, France, Germany, and India, plus translations into German, Swedish, and Dutch (Figure 5.1).

All the evidence of the time, in short, categorically proves that Dickens was dedicated first to the publication of sketches in newspapers and magazines, and then to the production of his first volume. Famously, a decade later in the Preface to the 1847 Cheap edition of *Pickwick* he looked back and nostalgically recalled his pride at seeing the first of his sketches in print.[23] Recently Robert L. Patten has deconstructed that statement, demonstrating convincingly that it misrepresents the experience in virtually every detail.[24] What is not in doubt, however, is the pride which it records: when he was initially writing, publishing, and collecting his sketches, Dickens was fully committed to them. He worked hard to make them as artistically excellent as he possibly could, and took great satisfaction in his achievement in so doing.

Within a few months, however, his attitude changed dramatically. He was approached by Chapman and Hall to join Robert Seymour in the project which became *Pickwick*. That work took some months to establish itself, but by the autumn of 1836 it was achieving unprecedented recognition, and at the same time Dickens signed contracts to edit a new miscellany for Richard Bentley, the foremost publisher of fiction of the day, and to write two novels for him. Fired by this success, Dickens resigned from his job on the *Morning Chronicle*, reneged on a contract to write a novel for Macrone, and only by gathering together previously rejected sketches and a handful which he had managed to write since Macrone's first volumes appeared in February did he manage to assemble sufficient material for the Second Series of *Sketches by Boz*, in a single volume rather than the projected two. Macrone, having wrested the copyright in return for release

---

[19] *PLets* 1:97–8, 103–4, 115–16. He showed the sketch to George Hogarth, soon to be his father-in-law, who had commissioned the series for the *Evening Chronicle*; to John Black, his editor on the *Morning Chronicle*; to Harrison Ainsworth, his fellow novelist, who had introduced him to Macrone initially; and to Macrone.
[20] *PLets* 1:112.
[21] *PLets* 1:130.
[22] *PLets* 1:144.
[23] 1847 Preface, *The Pickwick Papers*, ed. James Kinsley (Oxford: Clarendon Press, 1986), 884.
[24] Robert L. Patten, *Charles Dickens and 'Boz': The Birth of the Industrial-Age Author* (Cambridge: Cambridge University Press, 2012), 91–4.

FIGURE 5.1 George Cruikshank, frontispiece to *Sketches by Boz*, First Series, Volume 1, etching, 1836.

from the contract to write *Gabriel Varden*, proceeded to bring out a third edition of the First Series and a second edition of the Second Series that winter. Having parted with the copyrights, Dickens had no control over that, and when Macrone next proposed to bring out a serialized version of the sketches, simultaneous with the runs of both *Pickwick* and *Oliver Twist*, Dickens, with Forster's help, arranged for Chapman and Hall to buy the copyrights and back copy of all the sketches from Macrone. To recoup their outlay—*over 20 times* the price Dickens had accepted for the copyright alone a mere six months previously—Chapman and Hall themselves brought out a serialized version of the sketches, gathered at the completion of its run into the 1839 single-volume edition, with the previously noted apologetic preface.

If Dickens took an unimpressed view of *Sketches by Boz*, however, his readers did not. There was a positive deluge of praise in the press. Unauthorized reprintings of entire sketches, extensive excerpting of passages, and enthusiastic commentary filled newspapers and journals of the day, praising sketches individually and enthusing about them as a collection. The British Library online newspaper archive, massively expanded in recent years, reveals over *700* references to the sketches in the decade following the appearance of the first one in 1833. With few exceptions, notices were brief, generally devoting more space to quotation than to analysis. But they were almost invariably complimentary, praising Boz for the fidelity of his observation of scenes, manners, and morals. They admired the theatricality of his tales, the freshness, humour, and pathos of the writing, and marvelled at the range of tone. Comparisons were made to writers as diverse as Washington Irving, Victor Hugo, Henry Fielding, Tobias Smollett, Oliver Goldsmith, Joseph Addison, and Miguel de Cervantes. Marvelling at the visual quality of his writing, they commented on the aptness of combination with the illustrations of George Cruikshank, and evoked William Hogarth as a worthy comparison. It is remarkable that the various commentators singled out *every one* of the collected sketches for comment, and praised Boz's range of tone.

It can hardly be stated too emphatically: *Sketches by Boz* launched Dickens's career. Whereas early sales and reviews of *Pickwick* were few and unenthusiastic, the reception of *Sketches by Boz* was widespread and dithyrambic. Months after the first numbers of *Pickwick* were issued, catapulting Dickens's fame even higher, his reputation was already firmly established. When the First Series of sketches was published in February 1836, reviewers noted their familiarity with the earlier newspaper and magazine versions and applauded the decision to collect them into volumes. 'He is an old favourite of ours,' wrote the *Court Journal* (20 February 1836); 'We were struck by some of these sketches when we first read them in the publications in which they originally appeared, and a second perusal has strengthened the favourable impression', said the *Examiner* (28 February 1836). It was on the strength of the sketches that Bentley hired Boz to edit his new journal; it was on the strength of the sketches that other publishers sought him.[25] Months before the autumn of 1836, when the popularity of *Pickwick* was rising, Boz was the talk of the town. His name was appearing in competing advertisements by Bentley and Macrone; the Second Series was on the brink of publication; *Oliver Twist* was imminent. The celebrity which was to last his lifetime and beyond was well and truly established.

But, as we have seen, Dickens quickly became dissatisfied with his sketches. Having revised them extensively in the autumn of 1835 for the First Series, he revised them

---

[25] Thomas Frost tried unsuccessfully to lure Dickens back to the *Monthly*; Thomas Tegg approached him to write a children's story; Percival Banks recruited him to write for the *Carlton Chronicle*; and John Macrone fought unsuccessfully to retain him for writing to follow the sketches.

again for a second edition, and he undertook some of his most extensive revision for the Second Series. When Chapman and Hall issued the sketches serially, starting in 1837, he rearranged them into the four-section division in which they have appeared ever since, and once more revised heavily. The parts were then assembled unchanged to make up the one-volume edition of 1839. Finally, for the delayed publication of the sketches in the Cheap edition of 1850, Dickens undertook by far the most extensive revision of all, changing punctuation, words, sentences, and whole paragraphs.[26] Thereafter, he left the text largely unchanged for future editions, not because he was at last satisfied, but because he no longer could be bothered to try any further to improve it.

When the Oxford edition eventually appears, it will systematically chart the full extent of Dickens's revisions. For present purposes, it is sufficient to glance at the kinds of changes which he made. All of the sketches underwent some revision. The move from cramped newspaper columns allowed space for more generous paragraphing. Dickens rephrased and repunctuated sentences. He changed a number of titles, and renamed several characters. He systematically expanded contractions, and cut a number of slang expressions. He also cleaned up stylistic indelicacies and profanity, and removed ephemeral and political allusions. Changes of this nature are to be found in all of the sketches.[27]

Two of the more interesting areas of revision were the persona of his narrator, and his response to the evolving spirit of the age. Whereas the Boz of the newspapers (and Tibbs, narrator of the *Bell's Life* sketches) was an insouciant young man, cheerfully buttonholing his reader, as when he quaffs grog while welcoming in the new year, and when he sneaks into a private chamber in the Houses of Parliament, in later versions he is more proper, attending to his writing and behaving more circumspectly. The sketches all first appeared before Victoria came to the throne, and their tone, while not quite equalling the raffishness of the Regency (such as that found in Pearce Egan), would nevertheless bring the occasional blush to the cheek of the young person. It is fascinating to note that this robustness remained virtually unchanged when Dickens first collected the sketches, but about 50 per cent of the profanity in the original versions was excised for the 1839 edition, and it was almost totally eliminated in 1850, as was reference to a brothel (in 'The Great Winglebury Duel'). In revision the sketches remain lively and frequently amusing, never descending into high Victorian earnestness, but later versions target a wider, more family-oriented audience than the predominantly male readers who first saw the sketches in periodicals and newspapers. The revisions speak volumes about the emerging spirit of the Victorian age.

---

[26] Dickens's final major revision took place around the time he was launching *Household Words*, with possibly reciprocal influence on his reworking of old sketches and undertaking new essays for his periodical. See Paul Schlicke, '"Our Hour": Dickens's Shifting Authorial Personae', in Hazel Mackenzie and Ben Winyard (eds), *Charles Dickens and the Mid-Victorian Press 1850–1870* (Buckingham: University of Buckingham Press, 2013), 261–75.

[27] This paragraph repeats conclusions in an earlier essay, Paul Schlicke, 'Revisions to *Sketches by Boz*', *Dickensian* 101, 1 (spring 2005): 29–38.

A salient feature of the sketches is their topicality.[28] Saturated with contemporary detail, they provide a vivid panorama of London in the 1830s, and the realism with which they evoke that setting has from the start been one of their foremost attractions. But it needs stressing just how minutely engaged Dickens was with the rapidly evolving social climate. Two aspects stand out particularly: transport and Reform.

In the space of only a few years in the 1820s and 1830s, the process of moving about in London transformed utterly. Historically up to 1823 there had been a monopoly of hackney carriages, big, lumbering four-wheeled carriages, often discarded vehicles previously run privately by wealthy owners. Strictly limited in number to 1,200, they provided the only means of getting about the metropolis, other than walking or riding a horse. But from that date cabriolets, or cabs, light, two-wheeled horse-drawn carriages, were licensed to carry passengers for hire; and in 1829 George Shillibeer introduced the first omnibus, initially limited to a single route between Paddington and Bank and restricted from entering central London, skirting round the City via the Angel, a coaching inn in Islington. In 1831 limitations on numbers and routes were lifted; soon buses and cabs were ubiquitous, fares were fixed by Parliament, and the days of the dominance of hackney coaches were finished. More legislation followed, but congestion was an increasing problem, and the uncouth behaviour of drivers and cads led to widespread complaint. Competition, including buses racing up and down crowded thoroughfares, led to injuries and fatalities. Dickens records all of this: throughout the sketches characters get from one place to another by means of a variety of vehicles and with varying degrees of satisfaction. The vicissitudes of Minns and Dumps, and most notably, the behaviour of 'aggerawatin' Bill Barker in 'The Last Cab Driver, and the First Omnibus Cad', hilariously chronicle the situation. At the conclusion of that sketch Dickens reflects on the way things have changed:

> We have spoken of Mr. Barker and of the red cab driver, in the past tense. Alas! Mr. Barker has again become an absentee; and the class of men to which they both belonged are fast disappearing. Improvement has peered beneath the aprons of our cabs, and penetrated to the very innermost recesses of our omnibuses. Dirt and fustian will vanish before cleanliness and livery. Slang will be forgotten when civility becomes general: and that enlightened, eloquent, sage, and profound body, the Magistracy of London, will be deprived of half their amusement, and half their occupation.[29]

The nostalgia is tongue in cheek, but Dickens accurately records the profound transformation of London transport taking place even as he was composing the sketches.

---

[28] See Paul Schlicke and William F. Long, 'The Topicality of *Sketches by Boz*', in Christine Huguet and Nathalie Vanfasse (eds), *Dickens, Modernism, Modernity: Colloque de Cerisy*, 2 vols (Paris: Éditions du Sagittaire, 2014), 2:11–28.

[29] *Sketches by Boz*, second series (London: John Macrone, 1837 (for 1836)), 283–308, 308.

An even more pervasive area of topicality is the political dimension of Dickens's sketches, written in an era of great ferment. It was the time of Reform, as the unenfranchised majority of the population contested vigorously with vested interests, who were determined to block any incursion into their traditional privileges. The issues were highly contentious. All of the newspapers and journals to which Dickens contributed (with the sole exception of the Tory *Carlton Chronicle*) were outspoken in their reformist perspective. It needs stressing that Dickens's stance of taking seriously the lives of ordinary people was emphatically to situate him on the side of Reform, every bit as much in his sketches as in his news reporting. Although he cheerfully ridicules the pretensions of social climbers such as the Malderdons in 'Horatio Sparkins' and the Tuggses during their visit to Ramsgate, he champions the right of folk unpretentiously to carry on their daily lives, dining, attending the circus, going to the fair, or simply pottering in their garden. He is outspoken that he considers drunkenness to be the result rather than the cause of poverty, and he is confident that most people, given the opportunity, will behave responsibly. As he says in 'London Recreations' (*Evening Chronicle*, 17 Mar. 1835, p. 3, cols 3–4), 'Whatever be the class, or whatever the recreation, so long as it does not render a man absurd himself, or offensive to others, we hope it will never be interfered with, either by a misdirected feeling of propriety on the one hand, or detestable cant on the other.'[30]

He knew what he was talking about: having lived through the traumas of his father's imprisonment for debt and his own youthful employment in the blacking factory, he had personal experience of poverty and social humiliation. He was a parliamentary reporter during the debates as the Reform Bill was passing through the legislature; he covered election hustings, and followed closely the crises as the king dissolved Parliament, and politicians jockeyed to form a government either to block or to pass the Reform Bill. Overtly, 'A Parliamentary Sketch' and 'Bellamy's' deal directly with politics; the case recounted in 'Doctors' Commons' concerns a legal action (for which Dickens served as amanuensis) arising from an altercation between supporters and opponents of Reform.[31] And it has not previously been noticed that, although all of the 'Our Parish' sketches deal directly with political manoeuvrings at a local level, one sketch in particular, 'The Election for Beadle', provides a kind of allegory of the aftermath of Reform, ridiculing the triviality and inconsequence of the parish election, in which the two candidates base their campaign for election not on competence for the job but, absurdly, on the number of children they have sired. At the time Dickens wrote this sketch (July 1835) the reformed Parliament had been in office for long enough for Dickens to perceive that the great new legislation had left matters pretty much where they were, with regard to pettifogging and dissipation of idealism; the only consolation being that (as we learn

---

[30] This paragraph was eliminated in subsequent editions and does not appear in Dent.
[31] See William F. Long and Paul Schlicke, 'Bumple against Sludberry Revisited', *Dickens Quarterly* 32 (2015): 181–98.

in another Parish Sketch, 'The Broker's Man') the obviously more competent candidate is elected.[32]

At the end of the day, however, it is not for their record of the age, or the evidence they provide of Dickens's artistic development, that we should return to Dickens's sketches, but for their marvellous artistic achievement. There is not room in the present chapter to make a case for their excellence, but a glance at two of the sketches, one from *Sketches by Boz*, the other from *Sketches of Young Couples*, can serve to give the flavour. 'Meditations in Monmouth Street' is characteristic of the methods of *Sketches by Boz*. Dickens the *flâneur*, loitering along the streets of lower-class London—in this case, the very lowest slum of them all, the rookery around Seven Dials—pauses to look round himself. Seeing old clothes for sale on racks outside a shop, he turns observation into imagination, and builds a life history of the supposed wearer of some of the clothes he sees. In miniature, the sketch depicts the characteristic stance of Dickens's work: responding to the world about him not simply with vivid accuracy, but, more importantly, with an overflow of joyful meditation, generating that frisson between mundane reality and fantasy which lies at the core of his artistry.

'The Young Couple' is the first sketch in the latest volume, *Young Couples*. It portrays a youthful housemaid, who is filled with wonder at the preparations for the wedding of the young lady of the house on the corner. The girl, agog with the excitement of the impending event, eagerly witnesses the breakfast table, the bride's family, and even the bride herself. 'What daydreams of hope and happiness', Dickens exclaims. The sketch is truly magical: in the little girl's eyes, the house is 'enchanted'.[33] She imagines herself as a bride, but there is no envy in this, only delight at being vouchsafed a glimpse of the occasion. The delicacy with which Dickens writes evokes the happiness of the event, alert to the class and gender issues in ways that recognize life's complexities even as they contribute to the joyfulness. It is a minor masterpiece that deserves to be better known. It has a poignant aftermath, disclosed in the final sketch in the volume, where we learn that the dreamy young housemaid marries not long after the event in the first sketch, but with 'a bad husband who used her ill', and by the time of the later sketch ('The Old Couple') has long since died in Lambeth workhouse.[34] The juxtaposition of that outcome with the idyllic beauty of the scene here described is a tremendous early illustration of Dickens's power.

---

[32] See William F. Long and Paul Schlicke, 'Bung against Spruggins: Reform in "Our Parish"', *Dickens Quarterly* 34, 1 (March 2017): 5–13.

[33] Charles Dickens, *Sketches of Young Gentlemen and Young Couples*, introd. Paul Schlicke (Oxford and New York: Oxford University Press, 2012), 'The Young Couple', 157–63, 157.

[34] 'The Old Couple', 213–19, 215.

Further Reading

John Butt and Kathleen Tillotson, *Dickens at Work* (London: Methuen, 1957)

G. K. Chesterton, *Charles Dickens* (London: Methuen, 1906)

Kathryn Chittick, *Dickens and the 1830s* (Cambridge: Cambridge University Press, 1990)

Charles Dickens, *Sketches by Boz*, ed. Paul Schlicke (Oxford: Oxford University Press, forthcoming)

Duane DeVries, *Dickens's Apprentice Years: The Making of a Novelist* (Brighton: Harvester Press, 1976)

George Gissing, *Dickens: A Critical Study* (London: Blackie and Son, 1898)

Virgil Grillo, *Charles Dickens' Sketches by Boz: End in the Beginning* (Boulder, CO: Colorado Associated University Press, 1974)

Tim Killick, *British Short Fiction in the Early Nineteenth Century: The Rise of the Tale* (Aldershot: Ashgate, 2008)

Martina Lauster, *Sketches of the Nineteenth Century: European Journalism and Its Physiologies, 1830–1850* (Houndmills: Palgrave Macmillan, 2007)

F. S. Schwarzbach, *Dickens and the City* (London: Athlone Press, 1979)

CHAPTER 6

PICKWICK PAPERS
The Posthumous Life of Writing

JEREMY TAMBLING

Seymour and Dickens

To start with how it was written.

The initiative began with Robert Seymour (1798–1836), artist, illustrator, and caricaturist, friend of Cruikshank, colleague of Gilbert à Beckett and later of Henry Mayhew on *Figaro in London* (1831–9).[1] To Richard Penn's text, Seymour had produced *Maxims and Hints for an Angler and Miseries of Fishing* (1833), memoirs of the 'Houghton Fishing Club', with a Pickwick-figure, like the fisherman in Seymour's cover-design for *Pickwick Papers*. There was also *The Book of Christmas* (1835–6; text by Thomas K. Hervey), and *The Squib Annual of Poetry, Politics, and Personalities*, published by Chapman and Hall, whom Seymour approached in November 1835 with sketches for a 'Nimrod Club' of Cockney sportsmen. Nimrod (see Genesis 10:9) was the pen-name of C. J. Apperley (1779–1843), gentleman hunting-correspondent of the *Sporting Magazine*.[2] R. S. Surtees, editing the rival *New Sporting Magazine*, had created the Cockney huntsman Jorrocks in articles between 1831 and 1834; it became *Jorrocks' Jaunts and Jollities* (1838). Surtees parodied Nimrod ('Pomponious Ego') in *Handley Cross* (1843). In February 1836, Chapman and Hall, approving Seymour's proposal, engaged Dickens at £14 3s. 6d. per month to provide text (letterpress) accompanying four Seymour woodcuts for a series of monthly illustrated paper parts. The first instalment appeared on 31 March.

Dickens's advertisement in the *Athenaeum* on 26 March shows him altering things.[3] It said the Pickwick Club had been founded in 1822, and that 'The Pickwick Travels, the

---

[1] M. Dorothy George, *English Political Caricature 1793–1832* (Oxford: Clarendon Press, 1959), 248–56.
[2] Norman Gash, *Robert Surtees and Early Victorian Society* (Oxford: Clarendon Press, 1993), 17.
[3] Charles Dickens, *Pickwick Papers*, ed. James Kinsley (Oxford: Clarendon Press, 1986), xx–xxi. Subsequent references are inserted parenthetically in the text, by *PP* chapter, page.

Pickwick Diary, the Pickwick Correspondence—in short the whole of the Pickwick Papers'—had been bought from the secretary and placed in the hands of Boz, author of 'Sketches Illustrative of Every Day Life and Every Day People', for Seymour to illustrate. Further, 'it is presumed that the series will be completed in about twenty numbers'. Whereas the Advertisement indicates that the series will show an 'insatiable thirst for Travel', the dreaming fisherman in the boat near London's Putney Bridge for the cover-design is motionless, but provides a frequent Dickensian motif: a text being dreamed while the protagonist sleeps, like the story of the Bagman's Uncle (*PP* 49, 752–3). Birds raid Pickwick's lunch-basket; above the title, another mocks Mr Winkle's attempt to shoot (the illustration pairs the fat and the thin man). The travel-motif references Smollett, whose Preface to *Roderick Random* says that 'North Britons' are 'addicted to travelling' which 'justifies my conduct in deriving an adventurer from that country'.[4] Adventure and travel pair, as both 'random'. Reference to *Sketches by Boz* hint that the *Pickwick Papers* will be more urban than travel oriented: not Seymour's idea. The title, *The Posthumous Papers of the Pickwick Club, Containing a Faithful Record of the Perambulations, Perils, Travels, Adventures and Sporting Transactions of the Corresponding Members Edited by 'Boz'*, indicates that the club, mocking a learned society (not Seymour's idea), has been wound up, as the last chapter shows: the novel records its last year, starting 13 May 1827. Writing becomes 'posthumous', a historical reconstruction from surviving papers; it lacks a father, that is, any originating authority from the past (David Copperfield was 'a posthumous child').[5] The Club is gone, inaccessible apart from these 'papers', which must be 'edited'.

As Scott's *The Antiquary* (1816) satirizes Jonathan Oldbuck's identification of a historical battle site, having found a stone marked A.D.L.L. which he thinks is Latin, till told it means 'Aiken Drum's Lang Ladle', so Dickens, using Scott, satirizes Pickwick's antiquarianism when he finds, and creates a history through misreading, the inscription 'Bill Stumps his Mark' (*PP* 11, 157, 167–9).[6] Thus mocked, Pickwick, sensibly, hires Sam Weller, with his 'extensive and peculiar' knowledge (*PP* 20, 296), not just of London; Weller guides him into new experiences until this is bounded by the prison, after which travel functions only to conclude the tale.

'Pickwick' derived from a Bath family with a stage-coaching business: 'Moses Pickwick'. Dickens had visited Bath in November 1835, and the coincidence of names, where life precedes art, is noted by Weller (*PP* 35, 540), his father a stage-coachman. Sam finds this rivalry, and lowering of Pickwick's uniqueness, offensive; and since 'Moses' was a source for 'Boz' (see Dickens's 1847 Preface [*PP* 886]), it intrudes Dickens, the non-'slow coach' (*PP* 34, 521) autobiographically into the text. John Forster, who met Dickens at the end of 1836, becoming his literary adviser and biographer, seems to be Dowler in

---

[4] Tobias Smollett, *Roderick Random* (London: Everyman, 1927), 5.
[5] Dickens, *David Copperfield*, ed. Nina Burgis (Oxford: Clarendon Press, 1981), chapter 1, page 2. See Jeremy Tambling, *Becoming Posthumous: Life and Death in Literary and Cultural Studies* (Edinburgh: Edinburgh University Press, 2001), 59–87.
[6] Walter Scott, *The Antiquary*, ed. David Punter (Harmondsworth: Penguin, 1998), 28–31.

Pickwick Papers, a fierce ex-army man of 45 (*PP* 35, 538).[7] Weller senior's veracity as a typical stage-coachman in what he calls the 'golden age' of the fast stage-coach is defended in a background study to the novel's rural aspects: *The England of Nimrod and Surtees*, which notes the prejudice suffered by 'Cockney' hunters, like Jorrocks, joining country hunts.[8] If Seymour thought of Pickwick as thin, reversing his earlier sketches, that might have fitted with Pickwick as the pedantic lean scholar, like Dr Syntax with his horse Grizzle in William Combe's and Thomas Rowlandson's *Doctor Syntax's Tour in Search of the Picturesque* (1812), inspired by Cervantes and *Hudibras*. Did any Dickens memory inform *Pickwick Papers* of the Pic Nic Society and newspaper that Combe (1742–1823) ran in 1802–3? Combe was a debtor in the King's Bench prison from 1799 until his death.[9] But the thin/fat antithesis altered: according to Edward Chapman: Pickwick's 'present immortal' image Dickens 'made from my description of a friend of mine at Richmond, a fat old beau who would wear, in spite of the ladies' protests, drab tights and black gaiters. His name was John Foster'.[10] Chapman confirmed Dickens's account, in the 1847 Preface, of the 'origins' of *Pickwick Papers*: Dickens saying: 'I thought of Mr Pickwick' (*PP* 885), so that Seymour created a rotund Pickwick (like Seymour's own early idea), from the first chapter's description of the Club.[11]

The first number contained four Seymour plates: Pickwick addressing 12 disciple-like members of the Club; 'The Pugnacious Cabman'; 'The Sagacious Dog'; and 'Dr Slammer's defiance of Jingle'. The May number contained 'The Dying Clown'; about this Dickens asked Seymour for minor changes.[12] Seymour had also completed 'Mr Pickwick in chase of his Hat' and 'Mr Winkle soothes the refractory Steed', but he shot himself on 20 April, having met Dickens once, three days before. He left 'Arrival at Manor Farm' or 'The Pickwickians in Mr. Wardle's Kitchen', a finished sketch (i.e. the etching could be made from it; only background was needed to be filled in more thoroughly). Dickens then did not invent the conclusion of Part 2 (chapter 5).[13]

Seymour had considerable talent. Charles Baudelaire, discussing some lithographs, *Sketches by Seymour*, comments on his fishing and hunting caricatures, as comprising 'the double epic of cranks', noting a characteristic English 'violence and love of the excessive', saying that in caricature, the English are extremists. He notes 'The deep deep sea' where the enthusiastic fat husband in the boat on a river-jaunt has not seen that

---

[7] James A. Davies, *John Forster: A Literary Life* (Leicester: Leicester University Press, 1983), 174–5.

[8] E. W. Bovill, *The England of Nimrod and Surtees, 1815–1854* (Oxford: Oxford University Press, 1959), 170–3, 128–32, 105–15.

[9] Harlan W. Hamilton, *Doctor Syntax: A Silhouette of William Combe, Esq. (1742–1823)* (London: Chatto and Windus, 1969), 213–24, 240–61; John Harvey, *Victorian Novelists and their Illustrators* (London: Sidgwick and Jackson, 1970), 65.

[10] *The Letters of Charles Dickens*, ed. Madeline House, Graham Storey, et al., Pilgrim/British Academy Edition, 12 vols (Oxford: Clarendon Press, 1965–2002), 5:574–6, 575–6 n. 6. Subsequent citations: *PLets* followed by volume:page range, page, and hn. for headnote, n. or nn. for footnotes, with page range given before page cited.

[11] See David Parker, 'The *Pickwick* Prefaces', *Dickens Studies Annual* 43 (2012): 67–80.

[12] *PLets* 1:145–6.

[13] Joseph Grego (ed.), *Pictorial Pickwickiana*, 2 vols (London: Chapman and Hall, 1899), 1:80.

his wife, equally fat to judge from the legs, all that is visible of her, has disappeared into the water.[14] There is nothing sentimental about Seymour's pictures: guns go off unexpectedly; husbands and wives together are mocked; their subject is mutual stupidity. Michele Hannoosh thinks that bourgeois hunting (Surtees describes both, admiring especially Jorrocks, the grocer), images, for Seymour, middle-class fears and uncertainty, fears of impotence. More pronounced than in Surtees (a country squire), this intensifies Seymour's satire.[15] The Dickens/Seymour contention needs revisiting: more could be done on English caricature in the 1830s (e.g. *Figaro in London*).[16] Comparative work with French caricature would help; critical idealizing of the goodwill within *Pickwick Papers* has obscured the presence in Seymour of another, different voice.[17]

Writing and Reception

Once Seymour died, Dickens's freedom to use his own reading and ideas became more apparent.

Seymour's June replacement was Robert William Buss (1804–75), with 'The Cricket Match' and 'The Arbour Scene'.[18] July, and all later work was by Hablot Knight Browne (1815–82) who called himself Nemo; then, in Part 5, Phiz. By then, Dickens was in editorial control: the contract now being 32, not 24, pages of letterpress plus two illustrations per month, costing one shilling per part. By July (Part 4), the time of the number's appearance and the narrative's time of year had coincided, increasing the sense of immediacy, and of the author intervening, commenting on the seasons, especially Christmas.[19] Notably, Dickens retained Seymour's stress on sport.[20]

Unlike Surtees, Dickens integrated the monthly parts with each other from the beginning: note the endings of Part 1 (*PP* 3, 41), Part 2 (*PP* 5, 78), and especially Part 3 (*PP* 8, 125). Part 4 changes, returning to London, and introducing Weller. In Part 5, chapter 12, with Mrs Bardell in Mr Pickwick's arms, the plot—the lawsuit, the imprisonment—begins, and the novel gains a unifying subject-element, anticipated by Part 4 in the

---

[14] Charles Baudelaire, *Selected Writings on Art and Artists*, trans. P. E. Charvet (Harmondsworth: Penguin, 1972), 233–4.

[15] Michele Hannoosh, *Baudelaire and Caricature* (Philadelphia: Pennsylvania State University Press, 1992), 202–4.

[16] Brian Maidment, *Comedy, Caricature, and the Social Order, 1820–50* (Manchester and New York: Manchester University Press 2013), 144–76 discusses Seymour.

[17] See Stephen Jarvis's novel, *Death and Mr Pickwick* (London: Random, 2015) and my review, *Dickensian* 111, 3 (Winter 2015): 269–71.

[18] See Walter Dexter and J. W. T. Ley, *The Origin of Pickwick: New Facts Now First Published in the Year of the Centenary* (London: Chapman and Hall, 1936).

[19] David M. Bevington, 'Seasonal Relevance in the *Pickwick Papers*', *Nineteenth-Century Fiction* 13 (1961): 219–30.

[20] David Parker, 'Mr Pickwick and the Horses', *Dickensian* 85, 2 (Summer 1989): 82–98.

Jingle/Miss Wardle elopement and the Doctors' Commons satire. October introduces Mr Weller senior, who, while having a marital sub-plot involving the Revd Stiggins, joins Pickwick's narrative in chapter 22 (November); at this stage, Dickens solidifies his relationships with Chapman and Hall, his 'periodical publishers',[21] indicating that *more* sets of 20 numbers, that is other novels, would succeed *Pickwick Papers*, now specifically called a novel.[22] Here Dickens uses the adjective 'Pickwickian', as he had earlier;[23] leading to the mythologizing of text, characters, situations, and the period, sometimes beyond criticism.

Integration continued. By December, revenge on Job Trotter and Jingle becomes a sub-plot, and the legal process shapes everything. The Christmas number, Part 10, contains an address undertaking to end within 20 numbers. The editor becomes a 'Stage-Manager', adding words concluding each performance John Richardson (1766–1836) masterminded in his 'Richardson's Shows' (plays at fairs): 'we shall keep perpetually going on beginning again, regularly, until the end of the fair' (*PP* 882). Dickens assumes Richardson's role, in this intervention ending chapter 28 (*PP* 432). The only month missed was June 1837, mourning Mary Hogarth who died on 7 May. Serialization ended with a double-issue (November 1837), and front matter including the dedication to T. N. Talfourd (a model for Tommy Traddles in *David Copperfield*). For those who could not afford the shilling cost of a monthly number (Weller is paid £12 per annum), there were cheaper popularizations of the adventures of Weller, and theatrical presentations.[24]

Reviews of *Pickwick Papers*, which by September 1836, were warm, apart from those finding it vulgar and common, found influences from William Hogarth, Shakespeare, Henry Fielding, and Tobias Smollett. The impact of each of these predecessors on Dickens remains a subject for research; with Smollett, we could start with the prison-scenes, as Forster noted.[25] The *Athenaeum* called it 'two pounds of Smollett, three ounces of Sterne, a handful of Hook, and a dash of a grammatical Pierce Egan'.[26] Egan's *Life in London* (1820–1), treating the aristocracy and the poor in the 'back-slums', influenced Dickens incalculably.[27] Theodore Hook (1788–1841), contemporary of Byron, entertainer, dramatist, and journalist, moved from 'silver-fork' novels to sketches from life, with incessant punning; the change underlining then contemporary moves

---

[21] *PLets* 1:188–9, 189.
[22] Kathryn Chittick, *Dickens and the 1830s* (Cambridge: Cambridge University Press, 1990), 72–3.
[23] *PLets* 1:132.
[24] See Louis James's researches on these independent popularizations. I am grateful to him for an unpublished version of 'Sam Weller's *Pickwick*', a lecture given at 'Privacy, Literacy, and the Self: Conference in Honour of David Vincent', Open University, 27 June 2015.
[25] John Forster, *The Life of Charles Dickens*, ed. J. W. T. Ley (London: Cecil Palmer 1928), 90.
[26] Quoted, Philip Collins (ed.), *Charles Dickens: The Critical Heritage* (New York: Barnes and Noble, 1971), 32.
[27] Pierce Egan, *Tom and Jerry: Life in London* (reprint London: John Camden Hotten, 1969), 322. See J. C. Reid, *Bucks and Bruisers: Pierce Egan and Regency England* (London: Routledge and Kegan Paul, 1971), 203–18.

away from the aristocracy, also evident in Surtees.[28] The novel's biggest shift was from its initial situation of four males (Pickwick, Winkle, Snodgrass, Tupman, all indebted to Seymour's conception) all liable to affairs of the heart and embarrassments over women, especially widows, derivative from the eighteenth century (e.g. Widow Wadman in *Tristram Shandy*), to something more staidly middle-class: a Christmas wedding (chapter 28); Sam writing a Valentine (chapter 32).[29] Two Pickwickians marry; two remain bachelors, Tupman in lodgings in Richmond, Pickwick in a house in Dulwich, tended by the married Sam and Mary. Winding up the Club codifies sexuality: if Jingle and Trotter formed an odd couple, they have been exported to Guyana, as Jingle's other friend, Job's brother, has absconded to America (*PP* 53, 816–19)—where Weller Senior wanted Pickwick to escape, evading imprisonment (*PP* 45, 700).

DICKENS, CARNIVAL, CERVANTES

We can now turn to some contexts with which to read the novel.

It has always, uniquely, attracted readers.[30] Every area of interest in it, assuming that all was drawn from life, came within the scope of Percy Fitzgerald in 1891. And in 1921, B. W. Matz, editor of the *Dickensian*, wrote *The Inns and Taverns of* Pickwick, finding factual locations for these, down to the particular room Pickwick slept in.[31] In Chapman and Hall's centenary *A Pickwick Portrait Gallery* (1936), characters are assumed to be real, subjects of imaginary conversations, as in Bernard Darwin's chapter on Sergeant Buzfuz.[32] That devoted readership has not disappeared, nor G. K. Chesterton's celebratory style, treating Dickens's characters as part of a mythology about an undying real and innocent life, which is also idealized, so that the 'sceptic' is 'cast out by it'.[33] Gissing's descriptively useful Introduction to *Pickwick Papers* is not substantially different.[34]

Contemporary criticism is more apt to be intently historical in detail, as with Robert L. Patten on Dickens's emergence as a writer, discussing the material conditions of the text's production, though, with Patten, also speculating, as on the significance of the 'posthumous', which he takes as the author's way of extending the life of 'Boz' beyond the

---

[28] Elliot Engel and Margaret King, *The English Novel Before Victoria* (London: Macmillan, 1984), 120–34; see the anonymous Memoir in *Choice Humourous Works of Theodore Hook* (London: Chatto and Windus, 1902), 3–38.

[29] J. Hillis Miller, 'Sam Weller's Valentine: Dickens', *Topographies* (Stanford, CA: Stanford University Press, 1995), 105–33.

[30] Malcolm Andrews, 'Dickens and his Critics', in Andrews (ed.), *Charles Dickens: The Pickwick Papers* (London: Everyman, 1998), 824–35.

[31] Percy Fitzgerald, *The History of Pickwick* (London: Chapman and Hall, 1891); B. W. Matz, *The Inns and Taverns of Pickwick* (London: Cecil Palmer, 1921).

[32] Chapman and Hall, *A Pickwick Portrait Gallery* (London: Chapman and Hall, 1936), 136–47.

[33] G. K. Chesterton, 'The *Pickwick Papers*', in George H. Ford and Lauriat Lane Jr (eds), *The Dickens Critics* (Ithaca, NY: Cornell University Press, 1961), 109–21.

[34] George Gissing, *The Immortal Dickens* (London: Cecil Palmer, 1925), 41–62.

text. Dickens writes the text; Boz, posthumously, edits it. Patten also finds significant the number of deaths in the novel.[35]

Yet the mythological has not disappeared in post-1960s criticism. It is described by John Bowen, noting the book's fascination with language as something distinctive within it, potentially deconstructive.[36] Language, which often recalls Dickens's writing as a parliamentary reporter for the Benthamite *Morning Chronicle*, from 1834 to November 1836, is used in a way called 'Pickwickian' (*PP* 1, 7) (compare 'parliamentary'); that is, a word that can mean what the speaker wants.[37] Hence, Weller's Valentine is signed 'Your love-sick Pickwick' (*PP* 33, 500). Language's referentiality is subordinated to the allegorical. Mr Pott, whom Phiz seems first to have illustrated, Seymour-style, as the Whig politician Henry Brougham (1778–1868),[38] is a 'walking allegory' when dressed as a Russian officer of justice (*PP* 15, 220) in Eatanswill. The text, which the *Oxford English Dictionary* gives for a first citation of 'prosy' (*PP* 31, 472), notes language's evasions and shiftiness, as when discussing whether something is 'perjury' or a 'legal fiction' (*PP* 40, 623), knowing that all language-uses may be fictional; its attention to such doubleness makes that its focus (less mechanical, more sophisticated than Hook's punning).

Reading for something allegorical, 'other', within the text, gives hints for a criticism using certain emphases in Walter Benjamin on reading as allegorical, and within Mikhail Bakhtin on the carnivalesque and the dialogic.[39] These make *Pickwick Papers* primarily comic, affirmatory, plural in its range of significances; though these effects remain almost Chestertonian, especially when *Pickwick Papers* is regarded as the exceptional novel, larger than life. Perhaps Chesterton's 'mythos' associates with some of the implications of carnival-time, which Benjamin calls a time of exception, when things happen outside what can be planned; which celebrates exaggeration; and which is innocent.[40] Carnival exploits antitheses between life-affirming fatness and Lenten thinness. As Cervantes's Don Quixote (1605–15) is thin, Sancho Panza fat, so that contrast obtains here.[41] With the Wellers: father is fat; son, thin.

---

[35] Robert L. Patten, *Charles Dickens and his Publishers* (Oxford: Clarendon Press, 1978), 45–74, and *'Boz': The Birth of the Industrial-Age Author* (Cambridge: Cambridge University Press, 2012), 78–133, specifically 116–17. See also Patten's introduction and notes to *Pickwick Papers* (Harmondsworth: Penguin, 1972).

[36] John Bowen, *Other Dickens: Pickwick to Chuzzlewit* (Oxford: Oxford University Press, 2000), 44–81.

[37] Matthew Bevis, 'Temporising Dickens', *Review of English Studies* 52 (2001): 171–91, especially 183.

[38] Robert L. Patten, 'Portraits of Pott: Lord Brougham and the *Pickwick Papers*', *Dickensian* 66, 3 (Autumn 1970): 205–24.

[39] Mikhail Bakhtin, *Rabelais and his World*, trans. Hélène Iswolsky (Cambridge, MA: MIT Press, 1968) and *The Dialogic Imagination: Four Essays*, trans. Caryl Emerson and Michael Holquist (Austin: University of Texas Press, 1981).

[40] Walter Benjamin, 'Conversations above the Corso: Recollections of Carnival-Time in Nice', *Selected Writings Vol 3: 1935–1938*, ed. Marcus Bullock and Michael W. Jennings (Cambridge, MA: Harvard University Press, 2002), 25–32.

[41] Juliet McMaster, 'Visual Design in *Pickwick Papers*', *SEL Studies in English Literature* 23, 4 (Autumn 1983): 595–614.

Chapman's 'fat beau' and Jo the 'fat boy' go together. Combined, fatness and thinness suggest carnival, like Richardson's show which culminated at Bartholomew Fair, an occasion for London's carnivalesque (held annually after 24 August in Smithfield). Bartholomew Fair is the name for the worst—most anarchic—parts of the Fleet Prison, which Mr Roker calls the Fair (*PP* 41, 630).[42] Not *all* carnivalesque drinking is celebratory: 'treating' the electorate to drink is a voting tactic (*PP* 13, 181). This bribery has a long literary and artistic history behind it, including Hogarth, Smollett, and Oliver Goldsmith.[43]

Future research could relate *Pickwick Papers* to Carnival versus Lent, but not simply keying into the fat/thin distinction. Mr Fogg, half of the firm that prosecutes the breach of promise suit, is 'an elderly pimply-faced, vegetable-diet sort of man, in a black coat, dark mixture trousers, and small black gaiters; a kind of being who seemed to be an essential part of the desk at which he was writing', whereas his partner Dodson is 'a plump, portly, stern-looking man, with a loud voice' (*PP* 20, 293). The vegetable diet suggests Lent, the plumpness carnival, but too much should not be made of that, any more than with the turnkeys, where a 'stout' one is replaced by 'a long thin man' (*PP* 40, 626). Fatness and thinness, carefully portrayed in Phiz's picture 'Mr Pickwick "sits for his Portrait"', are equally unpleasant, caricatures, suggesting that all bodies are strange, uncanny; that Dickens has no thought of the 'natural'.

Noting the novel's different language registers and uses should be supplemented by examining its poetry: not just the 'Ode to an expiring Frog' (*PP* 15, 215–16). Even the discussions of poetic language (*PP* 33, 496–500) are significant. Linguistic styles are burlesqued, as with the 'Report of the Committee of the Brick Lane Branch of the United Grand Junction Ebenezer Temperance Association' (*PP* 33, 504–7). This comes as the report of the Report read out by the secretary, Mr Humm, comprising minutes, including interruptions. Are these latter from the previous meeting, set down here, or are they interruptions as the Report is read out and now incorporated into the minutes, as if the Report is now becoming the minutes for the *next* meeting? In that case, the narrative will never end, as long as the Temperance Association survives, because each past Report will have to include a present Report, which will become a past one—like the continuous narrative of the Arabian Nights. The ambiguity, intentionally or not, confuses historical chronology, as a paradigm of what Pickwickian writing does. The proceedings turn to a song, 'Who hasn't heard of a Jolly Young Waterman', written by the entertainer Charles Dibdin (1740–1814) for his opera *The Waterman* (Haymarket Theatre, 1774). It is given a burlesque allegorization, since history is rewritten making Dibdin to have written it to acclaim Temperance, and the song is made to fit the hymn-tune the Old Hundredth. A 'waterman' becomes someone who does not touch alcohol. 'He was always first oars with the fine city ladies' becomes:

---

[42] See 'The Humours of the Fleet' (poem, 1749), in John Ashton, *The Fleet, its River, Prison and Marriages* (London: T. Fisher Unwin, 1888), 288.

[43] Steven Earnshaw, *The Pub in Literature* (Manchester: Manchester University Press, 2000), 198–9.

> The soft sex to a man—[Mr Humm] begged pardon, to a female—rallied round the young waterman, and turned with disgust from the drinker of spirits (cheers). The Brick Lane Branch brothers were watermen (cheers and laughter). That room was their boat; that audience were the maidens; and he (Mr Anthony Humm), however unworthily, was 'first oars' (unbounded applause). (*PP* 33, 506)

The layerings of different language-uses and punning show 'rational and moral enjoyment' (*PP* 33, 506) replacing the popular/carnivalesque; and of 'Temperance' allying itself with Mr Stiggins's Evangelicalism. He appears during the singing of Dibdin's song and brings the proceedings to a carnival end by being, hypocritically, drunk. Meanwhile, the Wellers, father and son, note ambiguities contained in the word 'soft'.

Attention to these different textual modes is basic to Bakhtinian criticism. It requires attention to the eighteenth-century novel and to Cervantes, whose significance in Dickens has been underdiscussed.[44] Dickens read Cervantes as a child.[45] Forster calls Sam Weller and Mr Pickwick 'the Sancho and the Quixote of Londoners, and as little likely to pass away as the old city itself', while Washington Irving, in 1841, called 'Old Pickwick the Quixote of commonplace life', adding 'as with the Don, we begin by laughing at him and end by loving him'.[46] Dostoevsky, writing *The Idiot*, paired Don Quixote with Mr Pickwick, as 'positively good', comparing them with Christ. Dostoevsky thought that Pickwick had succeeded because he was ridiculous, which makes Pickwick a holy fool, even mad.[47] Perhaps Pickwick is mad (*PP* 22, 342; 45, 704). Yet Anthony Close notes that the 'Romantic' approach to *Don Quixote*, idealizing the hero, and anticipated in Henry Fielding's idealizing 'Quixotic' Parson Adams in *Joseph Andrews*, misses Cervantes's burlesque and satire (note that Hogarth, Seymour, and Cruikshank all illustrated Cervantes).[48] Smollett's Preface to *Roderick Random* is nearer the mark than Fielding: 'Cervantes, by an inimitable piece of ridicule, reformed the taste of mankind, representing chivalry in the right point of view', and so 'point[ing] out the follies of ordinary life'.[49]

Overlapping readings of Cervantes were thus available to Dickens; while they cannot be sharply differentiated as to which author used which, it seems that one tradition treats Cervantes in broadly 'realist' terms, while another, more Sterne-like, reads more metatextually, responding to Cervantes's games about authorship, as when Part 1 chapter 9 introduces Cid Hamet Ben Engeli, the supposed 'author' of *Don Quixote*, whose Arabic must be translated into Spanish, and whose veracity is in question, but

---

[44] Alexander Welsh, *Reflections on the Hero as Quixote* (Princeton: Princeton University Press, 1981) and Walter L. Reed, *An Exemplary History of the Novel: The Quixotic versus the Picaresque* (Chicago: University of Chicago Press, 1981).

[45] Forster, *Life*, 8.

[46] Ibid. 92; *PLets* 2:269–70 n. 1.

[47] Quoted, Steven Marcus, *Dickens from Pickwick to Dombey* (New York: W. W. Norton, 1985), 13.

[48] Anthony Close, *The Romantic Approach to Don Quixote* (Cambridge: Cambridge University Press, 1977), 1–28.

[49] *Roderick Random*, 4.

whose posthumous papers—the Quixote Papers—'Cervantes' has to buy, making the hermeneutical point, that all readings depend upon a history or origin lacking attribution or authority. Cervantes and Dickens play with the 'papers' only existing as language, so that, in parodic, comic mode, each subverts literary genres having pretentions to 'truth'. *Pickwick Papers* is thus both realist and subversive of realism, in order to introduce wonderfully extravagant truths.

Contrasting with festivities associated with the Pickwickians, whether at Dingley Dell (chapter 6); at Muggleton (chapters 7 and 8); with Mr Tupman at the Leather Bottle at Cobham (*PP* 11, 155–6); with Mr Pickwick's cold punch (chapter 19), and especially the Christmas scenes (chapter 28), followed by the medical students' drunkenness, there appear interpolated narratives, often tragic, where a distinction appears between a tale *told* and a manuscript *read*: 'The Stroller's Tale' (told *and* read, chapter 3); 'The Story of the Convict's Return' (told, after a poetry recital, by an extraneous clergyman, chapter 6), and 'A Madman's Manuscript' (chapter 11—a manuscript given by the old clergyman). The next two are comic: 'The Bagman's Tale' (chapter 14: retold from an account by the bagman's uncle about a friend of his, 80 years ago, i.e. 1747, in the decisive decade for the English novel); and 'The Parish Clerk' (chapter 17; written by Pickwick and then told, from conversations with Sam). There follow the Old Man's stories about the Inns of Court, and the 'Queer Client' (chapter 21). Then come 'The Story of the Goblins who stole a Sexton' (told on Christmas Eve by Mr Wardle, chapter 29), 'Prince Bladud' (36, a manuscript which Mr Pickwick finds and reads in his Bath lodgings), and 'The Bagman's Uncle', another story by the 'vun-eyed' bagman, whom Weller says is 'a gammonin'' that 'ere landlord ... till he don't rightly know vether he's a standing on the soles of his boots or the crown of his hat' (*PP* 48, 746). The bagman is a caricatural figure inducing dispossession, turning the world upside down. Carnival possibilities in the *narrative* meet those in the interpolated *stories*. This re-meeting of the bagman, and these and other stories told by a recurring antiquarian character, challenging German tales of the uncanny à la E. T. A. Hoffmann (*PP* 21, 307), relate to a broader significance deriving from Cervantes's interpolated stories in *Don Quixote* and 'Exemplary Stories' (*Novelas ejemplares*). One, 'Rinconete and Cortadilio', may be source-material for *Oliver Twist*: Dickens could have read it in Thomas Roscoe's translation: *The Spanish Novelists: A Series of Tales from the Earliest Period to the Close of the Seventeenth Century* (1832).[50]

These tales create a 'thick' sense of a history, eighteenth century and earlier; and question the concept of an author, in claiming an age exceeding personal memory (*PP* 29, 432). They threaten to make all narrative posthumous, not least because so many of them centre on their subjects' deaths, and introduce uncanny, ghostly elements, like the first 'Bagman's Tale', deepening the text, giving Shakespearian antecedents, as with the fairy references (*PP* 28, 422). They distinguish between festivity and the Lenten mood, especially with Gabriel Grub's pre-Scrooge-like moroseness. Dickens reworks Grub into

---

[50] Pamela H. Long, 'Dickens, Cervantes, and the Pick-pocketing of an Image', in J. A. Garillo Ardila (ed.), *The Cervantean Heritage: Reception and Influence of Cervantes in Britain* (Oxford: Legenda, 2009), 190–5.

a 'Dance of Death' narrative, a medieval theme he often evokes: the goblin on the tombstone anticipates Mr Punch similarly positioned in *The Old Curiosity Shop* (chapter 16). Grub's return echoes Washington Irving's Rip Van Winkle (a name already recalled in Mr Winkle, another fantasist in his own world). That gives a sense of the anachronistic: all narrative times embedding other times within them.

INNS AND PRISONS

I want now to turn as a context for the book to a more specific topic. Commenting in 1840, Thackeray says that in a hundred years' time, a historian 'would do wrong to put the great contemporary history of *Pickwick* aside, as a frivolous work. It contains true character ... and gives us a better idea of the state and ways of the people than one could get from any more pompous or authentic histories'.[51] He is right, though *Pickwick Papers* does not start from an immediate social history. For example, B. W. Matz notes for *Pickwick Papers* some 12 London inns: see chapters 3, 10, 20, 22, 26, 33, 42, 46, 54, and 57. Matz cites some 23 others, outside London, such as the Great White Horse at Ipswich (chapter 22), whose Fieldingesque echoes are discussed by H. M. Daleski in an essay using Marcus's seminal, Freudian, reading.[52] (Goldsmith's comedy *She Stoops to Conquer* (1773), the 'mistakes of a night' as it was first called, is also present.) Matz's necessarily incomplete list indicates the novel's backbone, and articulates it with carnivalesque tavern dining. Few actions happen outside such temporary accommodations, which include Pickwick's lodgings in Goswell Street, Garroway's Coffee-house (*PP* 34, 521), and Inns of Court lodgings. Bob Sawyer's lodgings at Lant Street, with personal resonances for Dickens when he stayed there during his father's imprisonment, appear in chapter 32. Last, there are '[u]nfurnished lodgings': the dry arches of Waterloo Bridge, and the lodgings called 'the twopenny rope' which Sam's poverty experienced (*PP* 16, 231–2).

Inns evoke travel in the episodic novel, or novel of the road, which overlaps here with the 'picaresque novel', the 'picaro' being the vagabond who gave his name to 'Figaro', who, via Pierre Beaumarchais, passes, as an image of freedom and free speech, into Seymour's *Figaro in London*.[53] Coaches, and waiting-rooms at coaching-inns, also figure; inn-sign descriptions show awareness of this England's visual culture. Much of the description of the Fleet concentrates on its various quarters, and on finding living-space.

---

[51] Quoted, Collins, *Critical Heritage*, 44.
[52] H. M. Daleski, *Dickens and the Art of Analogy* (London: Faber and Faber, 1970), 17–48; Marcus, *Dickens from* Pickwick *to* Dombey, 13–53. For Cervantes in Fielding, see Ronald Paulson, *Don Quixote in England: The Aesthetics of Laughter* (Baltimore: Johns Hopkins University Press, 1998).
[53] See J. A. Garrido Ardila (ed.), *The Picaresque Novel in Western Literature* (Cambridge: Cambridge University Press, 2015), 23.

From John Gay's *Beggar's Opera* Dickens could have noted how much the tavern and the prison are, for thieves gathering from all stations of society, alternative locations, almost heterotopias. Sam tells a story about a prisoner who drinks nightly at a public-house until the turnkey tells him he is getting into bad company (*PP* 46, 635). The Fleet, anticipated earlier with the tale about the Marshalsea (*PP* 21, 311), whose prisoners, when John Dickens was imprisoned, were made over into the descriptions of the Fleet is a logical final 'inn'; even yields a tale, via the cobbler, the Chancery prisoner (*PP* 44, 679–81). Did Pickwick derive from John Dickens?

The prison clinches the point, evident in *Don Quixote* Part One, where chapters 32 to 46 take place inside one inn, that inns are both the place for adventure, and where adventure is narrated.[54] Inns, in *Pickwick Papers*, serving coach travel, suggest a different sense of time, contrasting with *Dombey and Son*'s 'railway-time'. Thomas Rowlandson's *Drawings for a Tour in a Post Chaise* indicates how, in 1784, going from London to Salisbury (80 miles) meant rising at four to get to Salisbury by nightfall: a post coach (a private means of conveyance, as opposed to the public stage-coach) compassed London to Exeter (158 miles) in two days.[55] Similar indications of journey-times appear in going to and from Birmingham in *Pickwick Papers*, written one year before the railway joined London and Birmingham. After that, the country was more networked, interconnected, and the novel of the road, its inns having separate times, no central organized time, becomes impossible, though Jonathan Grossman thinks that stage-coaches also evoked speed and networking.[56] *Pickwick Papers* records not chronological, but festal time, as with Christmas. Distances are accepted. Inns make narrative grow out of chance meetings, where class, that new word of the nineteenth century, is transcended: a person's class cannot be deduced from their arrival at an inn. Jingle, of 'No Hall, Nowhere' (*PP* 7, 105), exists on his own credit. Inns produce changes of fortune and station, as at the Great White Horse: all stations in life 'must expect reverses' (*PP* 41, 642), as in the prison, where the reality is money.

The Fleet was a mile from Furnival's Inn, where Dickens began writing. Hogarth sets the penultimate *Rake's Progress* (1735) picture there: the ultimate in Bedlam. *Life in London* culminates with Bob Logic in the Fleet, which imprisons so many it might 'be denominated a small map of London' (*Life in London*, 384). Who could have anticipated Pickwick in the Fleet? James Kinsley's Clarendon edition records Dickens's 'source' for the Fleet, F. W. N. Bayley's *Scenes and Stories by a Clergyman in Debt, Written during his Confinement in the Debtors' Prisons* (1835), plus Nimrod's biography (1835) of the

---

[54] See Will McMorran, *The Inn and the Traveller: Digressive Topographies in the Early Modern European Novel* (Oxford: Legenda, 2002), 39–76.

[55] Robert R. Wark (ed.), *Rowlandson's Drawings for a Tour in a Post Chaise* (San Marino: Huntington Library, 1963), 8.

[56] Jonathan H. Grossman, *Charles Dickens's Networks: Public Transport and the Novel* (Oxford: Oxford University Press, 2012), 10–90; see especially 37.

Regency squire from Shropshire, Jack Mytton (1796–1834), who died, mad, in the King's Bench (*PP*, lxxvii–lxxv).[57] Mytton in Dickens becomes

> a strong-built countryman, flicking with a worn-out hunting-whip the top-boot that adorned his right foot: his left being thrust into an old slipper. Horses, dogs, and drink had brought him there pell-mell. There was a rusty spur on the solitary boot, which he occasionally jerked into the empty air, at the same time giving the boot a smart blow, and muttering some of the sounds by which a sportsman encourages his horse. He was riding, in imagination, some desperate steeple-chace at that moment. Poor wretch! He never rode a match on the swiftest animal in his costly stud, with half the speed at which he had torn along the course that ended in the Fleet. (*PP* 42, 657)

Sport begins and ends the novel; Nimrod calls the dying Mytton 'an old-young man'.[58] Phiz's illustration indicates that this prisoner will die here or in Bedlam; like the Chancery Prisoner, he lacks Mytton's braggadocio. The Fleet levels Regency blades; experience is dwarfed, useless. Pickwick removes himself from circulation in the prison to survive (*PP* 45, 707), so threatening to end the narrative, until a contingency makes Mrs Bardell join him. When the text opens up to such abysses, Dickens becomes the artist whose writing shrinks from nothing. How much he has learned from other writers: how much he embeds in it. And what of Dickens's personal history lies recorded, posthumously? A topic for more investigation!

Further Reading

John Butt and Kathleen Tillotson, *Dickens at Work* (London: Methuen, 1957)
James Kincaid, *Dickens and the Rhetoric of Laughter* (Oxford: Clarendon Press, 1971)
Ruth Livesey, *Writing the Stage Coach Nation: Locality on the Move in Nineteenth-Century British Literature* (Oxford: Oxford University Press, 2016)
Steven Marcus, 'Language into Structure: *Pickwick* Revisited', *Daedalus* 101 (1972): 183–202
Jeremy Tambling, *Reading Dickens' Novels as Poetry: Allegory, and the Literature of the City* (London: Routledge, 2014)
Julian Wolfreys, *The Old Story, With a Difference: Pickwick's Vision* (Columbus: Ohio State University Press, 2006)

---

[57] H. P. Sucksmith, 'The Identity and Significance of the Mad Huntsman in *Pickwick Papers*', *Dickensian* 68, 1 (Spring 1972): 109–14.
[58] 'Nimrod', *The Life of John Mytton, Esq. of Halson, Shropshire* (London: Routledge, 1870), 179; and Part Four.

CHAPTER 7

OLIVER TWIST
Urban Aesthetics and the Homeless Child

GALIA BENZIMAN

ONE of Dickens's most popular works, *Oliver Twist* (1837–39) has received abundant critical attention, with scholars assessing the novel's role in Dickens's formation as an author and its treatment of social issues such as the New Poor Law, criminality, destitute children, prostitution, and anti-Semitism. In recent decades there has been much interest in the novel's publication history and its part in the commodification of culture within the market economy of the early Victorian period.

Early twentieth-century critics who found fault with *Oliver Twist* pointed to the novel's generic shifts from realism to sentimentality and melodrama as well as its allegedly flat characters, especially the protagonist. In the 1930s and later, the novel's social vision was attacked by those who purportedly revealed Dickens's limitations as a social critic.[1] Among the significant recent changes in the critical understanding of *Oliver Twist* is a growing appreciation of Dickens's early work. John Bowen's *Other Dickens* (2000) established the early novels as worthy of serious study in their own right and proposed to read them not in order to show Dickens's subsequent 'growth to maturity', but to acknowledge 'each text's singular force'.[2] Redeeming *Oliver Twist* from its label of immaturity, subsequent studies emphasized the continuities rather than differences between the periods.[3] As part of the revaluation of those very aspects that had made early critics frown on *Oliver Twist*, Dickens's use of popular aspects of melodrama was now construed as no less radical than his realism.[4]

---

[1] Among such early readings, see George Orwell's 1939 'Charles Dickens', in *A Collection of Essays* (New York: Doubleday Anchor Books, 1954); Edmund Wilson, 'Dickens: The Two Scrooges', in *The Wound and the Bow* (New York: Oxford University Press, 1965); Humphry House, *The Dickens World* (London: Oxford University Press, 1960); and Arnold Kettle, *An Introduction to the British Novel* (London: Hutchinson University Library, 1972).

[2] John Bowen, *Other Dickens: Pickwick to Chuzzlewit* (Oxford: Oxford University Press, 2000), 2.

[3] Among these see Juliet John, *Dickens's Villains* (Oxford: Oxford University Press, 2001); Amanpal Garcha, *From Sketch to Novel* (Cambridge: Cambridge University Press, 2009); and Robert L. Patten, *Charles Dickens and 'Boz': The Birth of the Industrial Age Author* (Cambridge: Cambridge University Press, 2012).

[4] See in particular Sally Ledger, *Dickens and the Popular Radical Imagination* (Cambridge: Cambridge University Press, 2007).

Much has been written of both Dickens's treatment of childhood and his depiction of the city, yet *Oliver Twist* requires a parallel discussion of these two topics, informed by the recent developments. The London of early Dickens is often read as a place of squalor, alienation, and danger, a 'negative system of indifference', a 'city of destruction', a 'literal hell', an 'infernal labyrinth', a 'bottomless pit of mud and darkness', and 'a threat to a life of genuine meaning',[5] while the countryside serves as a bucolic place of retreat, setting up *Oliver Twist*'s dichotomy of urban vs rural.[6] Within this binary, the child is understood as an emblem of innocence, immune to the corrupting influence of the city. Placing the novel within a conceptual framework that acknowledges greater complexity, we may observe London's positive contribution to the protagonist's growth.[7] Challenging the rigid city–country binary, a re-examination of the child's agency and freedom of choice undermines the contention that he is but a static pawn in the hands of others.[8]

OLIVER IN THE CITY

Critics have repeatedly regarded the image of the city in *Oliver Twist* as negative. While Romantic paradigms clearly influenced Dickens's depiction of the city—for instance, the filth, stench, and danger of the London slum as first revealed in chapter 8—those same paradigms promoted the child, the epitome of moral innocence, as linked to Nature. Oliver's fortuitous removal to the Maylies' country house in chapter 32 suggests that the child is alien to the city and must be rescued from it.

---

[5] Quotes are, in order of appearance, from Raymond Williams, *The Country and the City* (London: Chatto and Windus, 1973), 154; Alexander Welsh, *The City of Dickens* (London: Oxford University Press, 1971), 142; F. S. Schwarzbach, *Dickens and the City* (London: Athlone Press, 1979), 16; J. Hillis Miller, *Charles Dickens: The World of his Novels* (Cambridge, MA: Harvard University Press, 1958), 58, 59; and Burton Pike, *The Image of the City in Modern Literature* (Princeton: Princeton University Press, 1981), 68.

[6] See Justin Eichenlaub, 'The Infrastructural Uncanny: *Oliver Twist* in the Suburbs and Slums', *Dickens Studies Annual* 44 (2013): 1–27; and Joseph Duffy, 'Another Version of Pastoral: *Oliver Twist*', *ELH* 35, 3 (1968): 403–21. Along with the rural, the domestic hearth is regarded as a place of retreat; see Welsh, *The City*, 1971; and Patten, '"A Surprising Transformation": Dickens and the Hearth', in U. C. Knoepflmacher and G. B. Tennyson (eds), *Nature and the Victorian Imagination* (Berkeley: University of California Press, 1977), 153–70.

[7] Helpful here is Julian Wolfreys's reading, cautioning against the accepted idea that in Dickens the city is a problem, 'merely the place of particular oppressive forces' ('Dickensian Architextures or, the City and the Ineffable', in Jeremy Tambling (ed.), *A Library of Essays on Charles Dickens: Dickens and the City* (Farnham: Ashgate, 2012), 323–68, 344). Another reading that underlines the city's sustaining side is Murray Baumgarten's 'Reading Dickens Writing London', *Partial Answers* 9, 2 (June 2011): 219–31.

[8] Among the numerous readings of Oliver as a pawn, see Steven Marcus, *Dickens: From Pickwick to Dombey* (London: Chatto and Windus, 1965), 74–80; Hillis Miller, *World of his Novels*, 43; James Eli Adams, *A History of Victorian Literature* (Malden: Wiley-Blackwell, 2012), 64–5; and James Kincaid, 'Dickens and the Construction of the Child', in Wendy Jacobson (ed.), *Dickens and the Children of Empire* (Basingstoke: Palgrave, 2000), 29–42.

The reading of the city in *Oliver Twist* as negative is corroborated by modern conceptualizations of the city as a site of alienation and struggle. In Georg Simmel's classic essay 'The Metropolis and Mental Life' (1903), indifference is cited as the city's defining characteristic. Metropolitan man psychologically adjusts to the urban environment; the cut-throat struggle for survival precludes deep emotional relationships, and incessant stimuli make people apathetic.[9] In a similar vein, Louis Wirth characterizes urban relations as 'impersonal, superficial, transitory, and segmental'. Due to the enormous population, communication is reduced to its most elementary level, and 'the reserve of unattached individuals toward one another... gives rise to loneliness'.[10]

However, more recent environmentalist approaches discern different effects of the city, showing how urban alienation allows for pluralistic accommodation of multiple identities. In *The Country and the City* (1973), Raymond Williams suggests that alongside the loneliness and oppression depicted in Victorian fiction, the varied urban experience offers vitality and opportunities for development. As Ian Watt asserts, the rise of the novel is related to the emergence of the metropolis: 'the world of the novel is essentially the world of the modern city'.[11] This is even more clearly the case in the Victorian period. Jeremy Tambling argues that the Victorian city became a textual site of new communications, which enabled new forms of discourse to emerge.[12]

Murray Bookchin argues further that the growth of the modern city provided the basis for ethical relations. His theory of 'social ecology' postulates that the rise of urban cosmopolitanism led to the 'shift from blind custom to a commanding morality, and finally, to a rational ethics ... Humanity, gradually disengaging itself from the biological facts of blood ties, began to admit the "stranger" and increasingly recognize itself as a shared community of human beings rather than an ethnic folk'.[13]

These diverse conceptualizations of urbanity find their expression in Dickens, where the city allows some characters growth and vitality, undermining the binary of sustaining rurality vs oppressive city. David Craig maintains that in early Dickens, the city is extrinsic to the self, unlike the later novels wherein city and self are fused.[14] According to such readings, Oliver, like little Nell in *The Old Curiosity Shop* (1840–1), is a mere spectator, so pure that the city cannot touch him. Yet even in the early novels the city serves as a trope for the subject's fluid self, epitomized by the homeless child. The urban experience penetrates Oliver's innermost core, acting as a catalyst for his *Bildung*, or process of self-formation. Dickens uses the allegory of the child's absorption into

---

[9] *The Sociology of Georg Simmel*, ed. and trans. Kurt H. Wolff (Glencoe, IL: The Free Press, 1950), 409–24.

[10] Louis Wirth, *On Cities and Social Life* (Chicago: University of Chicago Press, 1964), 75.

[11] Ian Watt, *The Rise of the Novel: Studies in Defoe, Richardson and Fielding* (Berkeley: University of California Press, 2001), 185.

[12] Tambling, *Library of Essays*, xxi.

[13] Murray Bookchin, 'What Is Social Ecology?', in David Keller (ed.), *Environmental Ethics: The Big Questions* (Malden: Wiley-Blackwell, 2010), 268–74, 271.

[14] David Craig, 'The Interplay of City and Self in *Oliver Twist, David Copperfield,* and *Great Expectations*', *Dickens Studies Annual* 16 (1987): 17–38, 17.

the metropolis to revise the moral paradigm of nature vs city. *Oliver Twist* is suffused with a mixed, in many respects benign, urban ecology. The city is not necessarily a dangerous place; it is a substrate for moral growth that enables ethical relations with the homeless, the prostitute, the excluded. As much as there is a positive, pluralistic side to the menacing urban setting, so does the rural world of *Oliver Twist* emerge as hermetic, monologic, and homogeneous.

London was a source of inspiration for Dickens, whose literary career virtually grew out of the streets. In *Oliver Twist* the city itself is a text, a welter of signs needing to be deciphered. Yet the city also stands for childhood trauma; from the Autobiographical Fragment it emerges as a place of exploitation and loneliness. The venue of trauma somehow becomes immensely productive for the author-to-be and likewise for his fictional children. In Dickens it seems almost a constant that children must be urbanized in order to survive and grow, though that has not been the prevailing reading of the urban innocent and could be profitably explored in greater detail in many of the novels. For good or for bad, the urban labyrinth accommodates the child and is integrated into his formation. Constructing the criminal slum not as extrinsic but as the formative milieu for the protagonist, Dickens undermines the rigid binaries of rural/urban, good/evil, bourgeois/criminal, which seem to provide the organizing theme of his novel.

The city of the Victorian period conveys a far more diverse social reality than in previous centuries. Besides its association with empire and capital, it is also related to youth as metaphor for newness, search, progress. Franco Moretti sees this as accounting for the growing popularity of the *Bildungsroman* (novel of education and formation) in the nineteenth century.[15] Given that the child is a subject in the making, there is positive value to the unsettling encounter with the city that further deconstructs the child's amorphous identity. According to Robert L. Patten, some of Dickens's authorial anxieties as well as the collective concerns of his culture are embedded in *Oliver Twist*'s probe of the portability and theft of identity. Identities can be easily performed in the city, which upsets the reliability of habitual identity markers.[16]

Dickens shapes Oliver's childhood as a socializing *Bildung* process that requires mastering the codes of the city. Resisting his oppression, Oliver runs away and then decides to go to London—an active choice of survival. Had Oliver been a static character he would have ended up like Dick, his workhouse friend who opts for a more passive escape—early death. Dick's decline (like little Nell's) is marked by his refusal to leave with Oliver; Nell chooses death when, with her senile grandfather, she turns her back on the city.

This is how Oliver chooses to go to London:

> The stone by which he was seated, bore, in large characters, an intimation that it was just seventy miles from that spot to London. The name awakened a new train of

---

[15] Franco Moretti, *The Way of the World: The Bildungsroman in European Culture* (London: Verso, 2000), 10–11.

[16] Patten, *Charles Dickens and 'Boz'*, 162–3, 167–8.

ideas in the boy's mind. London!—that great large place!—nobody – not even Mr. Bumble—could ever find him there! ... It was the very place for a homeless boy, who must die in the streets, unless some one helped him. As these things passed through his thoughts, he jumped upon his feet, and again walked forward.[17]

The initial representation of the city in *Oliver Twist* is nominal and textual, hence both symbolic and not easily accessible. It is accessible to Oliver, though, because unlike little Dick he is literate. Oliver's understanding of the road sign extends beyond mechanic recognition of letters; he grasps the semantic implications of 'London' and realizes the city's potential to alter his position. If Oliver can gain mastery over the codes of modern society, he will survive. As the starting point of his *Bildung*, his choosing London for his destination calls into question the truism that Oliver is a passive pawn.

Critics have queried Oliver's ability to read, given his background of neglect.[18] It is of equal interest to ask *why* Dickens wanted Oliver to be literate, a child with the ability to make out not only texts, but also non-verbal signs and situations. What Oliver knows and what he fails to know is a matter for discussion. Often labelled as simple due to his profound goodness, Oliver manifests sharp acuity in reading certain situations. He responds strongly to the portrait of the unknown woman—his mother—because he intuitively perceives what redeeming powers lie waiting there: 'the eyes look so sorrowful; and where I sit, they seem fixed upon me. It makes my heart beat, ... as if it was alive, and wanted to speak to me, but couldn't' (*OT* 12, 71). As part of his reading of situations, during the break-in at the Maylies' Oliver wisely schemes to wake up the family; he later saves himself by knocking on their door to beg for mercy, as shown in Cruikshank's illustration (Figure 7.1).

Alongside these moments of penetration, Oliver often fails in decoding social situations. Yet, as in any process of learning, mistakes are an important part of *Bildung*. Oliver's cluelessness sometimes verges on imbecility: how can he fail to understand what 'the Jew' and the boys are rehearsing? A possible explanation is that he is intuitively able to discern only the supportive forces around him while mentally rejecting the harmful ones, until he learns how to cope with them. In this respect, his blindness to the nature of the thieves' profession is a survival mechanism, hence a sign of strength. Indeed, it is this blindness that saves him from becoming a convicted criminal: 'The robbery was committed by another boy. I saw it done; and I saw that this boy was perfectly amazed and stupefied by it' (*OT* 11, 65)—so testifies the bookstall keeper, who rushes to court

---

[17] Charles Dickens, *Oliver Twist*, ed. Kathleen Tillotson (London: Oxford University Press, 1966), chapter 8, 44. Subsequent references are inserted parenthetically in the text by *OT* chapter, page. See pp. 369–71 of Tillotson edition for instalment and chapter divisions in *Bentley's Miscellany* and 1838 three-volume edition.

[18] See Patrick Brantlinger, 'How Oliver Twist Learned to Read, and What He Read', in Robert L. Patten (ed.), *Dickens and Victorian Print Cultures* (Farnham: Ashgate, 2012), 381–403; and Kenneth Sroka, 'Dickens' Metafiction: Readers and Writers in *Oliver Twist, David Copperfield*, and *Our Mutual Friend*', *Dickens Studies Annual* 22 (1993): 35–66.

FIGURE 7.1 George Cruikshank, 'Oliver Twist at Mrs. Maylie's Door', *Oliver Twist*, etching, in *Bentley's Miscellany*, April 1838.

all in a sweat in order to acquit the unfamiliar boy just because of his expression of utter shock.

Oliver's physical collapse at court is not only caused by the chase and the accusations levelled against him. It is also the result of his loss of faith in his friends. Oliver has to register and process new information about Fagin and the boys. He acquires knowledge of the world by degrees, an agonizing and destabilizing process that enables his psychological growth. This process continues throughout Dickens's corpus for many other characters; more could be done to assess the changes in the valence of the city between early novels and later ones, and to compare the challenges and costs to survival across Dickens's work.

Oliver's errors are empowering. Although unsettling, being lost creates the confusion and disorientation that are essential for gaining knowledge. The city is both the figurative and literal setting for this process. The social and topographical diversity of the urban maze allows the child's fluid self to find a route, but only after a phase of going astray. The scene of Oliver's abduction illustrates how moments of weakness are opportunities for empowerment that gradually enable Oliver to invent himself anew:

> Oliver Twist, little dreaming that he was within so very short a distance of the merry old gentleman, was on his way to the book-stall. When he got into Clerkenwell, he accidentally turned down a by-street which was not exactly in his way; but not discovering his mistake until he had got half-way down it, and knowing it must lead in the right direction, he did not think it worth while to turn back...
> He was walking along; thinking how happy and contented he ought to feel; and how much he would give for only one look at poor little Dick: who, starved and beaten, might be weeping bitterly at that very moment; when he was ... stopped by having a pair of arms thrown tight round his neck. (*OT* 15, 95)

We should first note that Oliver is not entirely 'happy and contented' but only thinks he 'ought to feel' this way. His position as Mr Brownlow's protégé is too tentative for him to feel secure. Indeed, the events that immediately follow demonstrate how shaky his social placement is. Oliver's turning the wrong way anticipates the lot of other children who go astray in the urban labyrinth, a recurrent motif in Dickens. Little Nell is first described as being lost; forced to put her trust in strangers, she luckily confides in Dickens's harmless narrator:

> I turned hastily round and found at my elbow a pretty little girl, who begged to be directed to a certain street at a considerable distance, and indeed in quite another quarter of the town.... 'I am a little frightened now, for I have lost my road.'
> 'And what made you ask it of me? Suppose I should tell you wrong'...
> She put her hand in mine as confidingly as if she had known me from her cradle, and we trudged away together ... I observed that every now and then she stole a curious look at my face as if to make quite sure that I was not deceiving her.[19]

Yet even Dickens's harmless narrator deceives her, using the girl's vulnerability to satisfy his curiosity. Fearing that she might run off as soon as she sees a familiar road, he takes her through less frequented paths, increasing her dependence upon him for his own purposes. Florence Dombey—another of Dickens's lost children—loses her way and meets a less benign stranger, Good Mrs Brown, who robs her of her nice clothes. The desperate girl's surprising encounter with and rescue by Walter only emphasize how unexpected the city's social itinerary is.

Jeremy Tambling observes that there is 'no reason why Oliver should go down the wrong road: it does not make his abduction any more likely to happen'.[20] True, yet the

---

[19] Charles Dickens, *The Old Curiosity Shop*, ed. Elizabeth Brennan (Oxford: Oxford University Press, 1999), chapter 1, 7–8. Subsequent references are inserted parenthetically in the text by *OCS* chapter, page.

[20] Tambling, 'Dangerous Crossings: Dickens, Digression, and Montage', *Yearbook of English Studies* 26 (1996): 43–53, 50.

very redundancy of detail suggests its significance. The wrong turn demonstrates how errors are intrinsic to Oliver's position. The wrong turn has the same artistic function as his abduction. These are all mischances that contribute to his *Bildung*. His mistaken turn shows how, as a child, he is always entrapped at crossroads of diverse and conflicting selves.

Underneath all the mechanisms of control exerted upon the child—by the parish, the bourgeoisie, the criminals, the Law—there is the child's fragile yet budding agency. The anonymous faces in the street, which are among the features of the urban setting, have just as much power as Fagin's gang to determine the boy's identity. As in the 'Stop thief' chase, the crowd of strangers is convinced that Nancy is speaking the truth when she says that Oliver is her runaway brother who broke their mother's heart. This in turn compels Oliver to half believe it himself. The same is true of Florence Dombey's experience following her robbery by Good Mrs Brown. Her weeping protestations that she is not really a beggar are disregarded by passers-by who deem them a trained waif's attempts to elicit pity. In both cases, the false identity imposed by the crowd affects the child's self-perception.

This kind of error metonymically represents deep mental and social processes. Florence's episode as a street beggar resembles and reveals her devalued position in the degrading emotional economy of her wealthy father's household. Oliver's kidnapping highlights the issue of his stolen identity and the mystery of his class affiliation, the underlying theme of the novel. The tentative acceptance of erroneous identities attached to them by the crowd is an important phase in these children's process of learning who they really are. 'Weak with recent illness; stupefied by the blows and the suddenness of the attack; ... and overpowered by the conviction of the bystanders that he really was the hardened little wretch he was described to be; what could one poor child do!' (*OT* 15, 97). The alienated urban environment misreads the child, and, overwhelmed by what the crowd sees in him, the child becomes a stranger to himself. Yet the abduction, while undermining Oliver's fragile sense of selfhood, does not obliterate it. Within the helplessness of being dragged away, he finds the strength to assert: 'I don't know her ... I live at Pentonville' (*OT* 15, 96). Though disregarded, his assertion reflects his motivation to determine where he belongs—significant progress, even if not yet supported by sufficient social force for it to be realized.

Florence, like Oliver, will later use the knowledge acquired during the degrading experience of her own abduction to flee her father's house and turn to the streets—once so menacing and alien—for her rescue. 'Where to go? Still somewhere, anywhere! still going on; but where! She thought of the only other time she had been lost in the wild wilderness of London—though not lost as now—and went that way.'[21] Gradually mastering the codes of the city, Florence turns her early disorientation to her own advantage.

---

[21] Charles Dickens, *Dombey and Son*, ed. Alan Horsman (Oxford: Oxford University Press, 2001), chapter 48, 638. Subsequent references are inserted parenthetically in the text by *DS* chapter, page.

Thanks to its diversity, the city continually opens up vistas where one's social position may change. Nancy, for example, gets to meet Rose Maylie and is given a chance to save herself. For Nancy it is too late to adopt a new self. One has to be a child—a vacant, fluid self—in order to be able to undergo such transformation. It is not accidental that Oliver's first initial is an O, as determined by Mr Bumble's ingenious system of naming: a round cipher with a hollow interior. The major theme of *Oliver Twist* is how this hollowness is to be filled, emptied out, and refilled over and over again—either with food or with social affiliation. The child does not merely represent an empty stomach that has to be fed; he is a vacant self that has to acquire substance.[22]

The abduction episode is an important juncture in the protagonist's career, as also suggested by the fact that just before his new Pentonville self is messed up by Nancy, Oliver reminds himself of little Dick. It is while thinking that he 'ought to feel' happy and contented that he recalls, with guilt, his friend and alter-ego, the boy who stands for his famished workhouse self. The fluidity of Oliver's conflicting selves makes Dick rise vividly to his mind, for Dick illustrates what might have become of Oliver had he stayed behind.

Critics tend to see the contrast between the two boys as indicating Dickens's class conservatism: the lower-class child dies in poverty, while Edwin Leeford's son survives and inherits wealth. The fact that Dick dies before Oliver can share his fortune with him suggests that Dick, 'lacking Oliver's genteel parentage and in spite of his moral perfections, was never a candidate for gentility'.[23] Yet the difference is not only the result of birth. Dick and Oliver represent two optative selves of contrasting temperaments: one manifests active choice, while the other stands for passive resignation and stasis.

As John Bowen points out, Dickens often called himself 'Dick'.[24] Indeed, this minor character in *Oliver Twist* embodies the poor, declassed, and oppressed self that haunts Dickens. We see this alternative self in the career of the fictional Oliver, and encounter it again in the Autobiographical Fragment, whose protagonist is anxious that he might become lower class and ignorant.

In Dickens, children who turn their backs on the city—like little Nell and little Dick—cannot grow up, as the epithet 'little' implies. Whoever goes to the city—Oliver, Florence, Pip, or the autobiographical Dickens—survives, even if the price of survival is ongoing dissonance, epitomized in the urban diversity of sounds, sights, smells, identities. The city is a variegated mix, for not far from the slum with its heaps of dirty children, where everyone 'wallow[s] in the filth' (*OT* 8, 49), we see clean, wide roads, elegant houses, lovely gardens. Andrew Sanders states that, contrary to commonly held belief, there was

---

[22] See Galia Benziman, 'Who Stole the Child? Missing Babies and Blank Identities in Early Dickens', in Peter Merchant and Catherine Waters (eds), *Dickens and the Imagined Child* (Farnham: Ashgate, 2015), 27–41.
[23] Sarah Gilead, 'Liminality, Anti-Liminality, and the Victorian Novel', *ELH* 53, 1 (1986): 183–97, 189.
[24] Bowen, *Other Dickens*, 39.

no rigid residential segregation among different economic groups in Victorian London, and pockets of real poverty were retained amidst the prosperity.[25]

The open-endedness of London, with the multiplicity of selves it spews out, appears as a dark possibility in Dickens's memoir. Describing himself aimlessly wandering the streets—hungry part of the time, lonely all the time—he states: 'I know that, but for the mercy of God, I might easily have been ... a little robber or a little vagabond.'[26] The criminal self, another potential identity, is a major theme in *Oliver Twist*. Here, too, Dickens creates a doppelgänger for Oliver. Noah Claypole, escaping from the undertaker Sowerberry straight into Fagin's den, mirrors Oliver's earlier emigration. Dick, Noah, and Oliver represent various routes; this variety indicates that each child has freedom of choice. Together, these boys form a split self, torn between conflicting subject positions.

Noah, rephrasing Oliver's fantasy of anonymity expressed at the milestone in chapter 8, goes to London declaring: 'I shall go and lose myself among the narrowest streets I can find, and not stop till we come to the very out-of-the-wayest house I can set eyes on' (*OT* 42, 285). He, too, cannot yet read the codes of the city, and he, too, as a green newcomer, makes mistakes.[27] Yet unlike Oliver, he chooses to integrate within the world of crime. By giving him the name of a biblical survivor, Dickens hints that Noah resembles Oliver. A boy who goes to the city is a boy who wants to live.

There is constant tension between the agency implied in the state of unsupervised anonymity and the threat that this condition imposes. Lacking class affiliation, the child's alleged agency clashes with the city's arbitrary power to determine his identity. The similar yet diametrically opposed careers of Oliver and Noah suggest that this duality is an enabling condition. While the city exerts arbitrary power, it still permits freedom of choice, which Oliver and Noah use creatively. This creativity should not be disregarded. In the Autobiographical Fragment, young Dickens's painful loneliness among strangers allows for an imaginative identity-game to take place. Ashamed of his father's arrest, he pretends that he lives in a respectable house and produces a false name and a series of lies that anticipate the identity switches of many future fictional characters. Obscurity in the city inspires a playful impulse to transform and disguise one's identity. This creativity is part of the process of *Bildung*.

When Dickensian children lack the acrobatic ability to 'read' the multiple identities available in the city, they might as well withdraw to an isolated position, away from the social and from the city. Before she physically flees the metropolis, little Nell retreats to

---

[25] Andrew Sanders, 'London: Residential Segregation', in Paul Schlicke (ed.), *The Oxford Reader's Companion to Dickens* (Oxford: Oxford University Press, 1999), 358–9.

[26] John Forster, *The Life of Charles Dickens*, ed. J. W. T. Ley (London: Cecil Palmer, 1928), 28.

[27] See Michal Peled Ginsburg, 'Truth and Persuasion: The Language of Realism and of Ideology in *Oliver Twist*', *Novel* 20, 3 (1987): 220–36, 227–8.

her eccentric interiority, projecting her inner world onto the blurred nocturnal street scene, as envisaged through her window:

> She would take her station here at dusk, and watch the people as they passed up and down the street, or appeared at the windows of the opposite houses ... There was a crooked stack of chimneys on one of the roofs, in which by often looking at them she had fancied ugly faces that were frowning over at her and trying to peer into the room, and she felt glad when it grew too dark to make them out ... [L]ooking out into the street again, [she] would perhaps see a man passing with a coffin on his back, ... which made her shudder. (OCS 9, 79)

Alexander Welsh defines the Dickensian home as a sanctuary. The 'domestic scenes, the firesides and family circles that are defended against the surrounding city' are a refuge from the malign influence of urban reality where 'the streets are places of alienation or even physical danger'.[28] Yet the home, like the rural environment, is also a suffocating, constricted place. Nell in this passage exists in a monologic space, her paranoid projections enabled by the anonymity of strange faces in the big city. In such scenes, retreating indoors suggests a regression into one's secluded psychic space. Dickens shows this to be pathological. For him, watching through a window rather than risking an actual encounter with the Real prevents the child from experiencing the city's power and leads to a misreading of its signs. The young, secluded Florence, in chapter 23 of *Dombey and Son*, is trapped in her subjectivity instead of getting out and plunging into the streets—as she will do much later, in the passage already cited. Alone at her London home, Florence seems 'shut up in the heart of a thick wood'; no forest 'was ever more solitary and deserted to the fancy, than was her father's mansion in its grim reality ... Shadowy company attended Florence up and down the echoing house, and sat with her in the dismantled rooms. As if her life were an enchanted vision, there arose out of her solitude ministering thoughts, that made it fanciful and unreal' (DS 23, 311–13). Watching other people's windows and imagining the domestic happiness that they must be enjoying (DS 24, 334–5), Florence remains a static spectator until her plunge into the streets much later.

Likewise Oliver: incarcerated alone in Fagin's solitary apartment filled 'with strange shadows', he peers through the back-garret window. He 'often gazed with a melancholy face for hours together; but nothing was to be descried from it but a confused and crowded mass of house-tops, blackened chimneys, and gable-ends' (OT 18, 115). Indoors, the child's chances to learn from experience, read the codes of his environment, and grow up are precluded. The window serves as an emblem of the isolated eccentricity that prevents actual contact with the pulsating city, that is, with the Real. Unlike the semiotic readings offered by earlier critics, the city thus perceived suggests that those who are distanced from it are locked in their interiority, trapped in their fantasies and fears.

---

[28] Welsh, *The City of Dickens*, 143.

Oliver in the Country

Dickens further interrogates this position in the mysterious countryside scene where Oliver—half in a dream, half in reality—sees the faces of Fagin and Monks through the window (Figure 7.2). This scene coalesces the domestic and pastoral sanctuaries that supposedly offer a refuge from the city. The countryside chapters in the novel are notorious for their tedium, and there is a consensus that in the prose of these sections, Dickens is not at his best. We may attribute this drop in rhetorical prowess to the fact that Dickens does not see the countryside as a desirable solution.

The city–country dichotomy created in these chapters is usually taken at face value. Oliver is rescued from the defiling urban surroundings and brought to a blissful rural shelter as a reward for his goodness. His sense of security and peace of mind once in the

FIGURE 7.2 George Cruikshank, 'Monks and the Jew', *Oliver Twist*, etching, in *Bentley's Miscellany*, June 1838.

countryside are a marked contrast to his perpetual anxiety in the city. Yet the possibility that the soothing countryside is after all harmful is already suggested in the praise of the rural scenery. Although Dickens refers here to the city as a site of exploitation and hard labour, in accordance with the Romantic paradigm, his prose extolling the healing freedom of the country includes some morbid imagery:

> Who can describe the pleasure and delight: the peace of mind and soft tranquillity: the sickly boy felt in the balmy air, and among the green hills and rich woods, of an inland village! Who can tell how scenes of peace and quietude sink into the minds of pain-worn dwellers in close and noisy places, and carry their own freshness, deep into their jaded hearts! Men who have lived in crowded, pent-up streets, ... even they, with the hand of death upon them, have been known to yearn at last for one short glimpse of Nature's face; and carried, far from the scenes of their old pains and pleasures, have seemed to pass at once into a new state of being; and crawling forth, from day to day, to some green sunny spot, ... they have sunk into their tombs as peacefully as the sun: ... The memories which peaceful country scenes call up, are not of this world, nor its thoughts and hopes. Their gentle influence may teach us how to weave fresh garlands for the graves of those we loved. (*OT* 32, 210)

The country, depicted as serene and pure, is 'not of this world'. If one wants to be part of this world, one should hurry back to the city.

Oliver's enjoyment of the countryside has a lethargic quality to it. As part of his daily routine, he 'would sit by one of the windows, listening to the sweet music, in a perfect rapture' (*OT* 32, 211). It is during such vacant staring out of windows that the squalor of city life, in the shape of Fagin and Monks, suddenly emerges. Whether they come from the slum or from the depths of Oliver's unconscious is unclear. The scene is nightmarish, the two figures vanishing without a trace. Critics have read the scene as the uncanny return of the political repressed—the poverty and criminality of London that supposedly have no place in this middle-class rural idyll. The window scene reveals that Oliver's sense of protection is false. The threats of the city have not disappeared with Oliver's removal to the country. Fagin's den is not an alien venue, but rather an immanent risk that accompanies him wherever he turns.

This risk, however, is positive, because it embodies the secret of Oliver's identity—not just his stolen nominal and legal identity but the very core of his yet-embryonic and unknown potential existence. That explains why the view of Fagin and Monks through the window is 'as firmly impressed upon his memory, as if it had been deeply carved in stone, and set before him from his birth' (*OT* 34, 228). The city's invasion is positive, subverting the rigid moral and psychological allegory of the novel and allowing Oliver renewed contact with the Real.

Repressing social tensions, the rural world also checks the child's development. In the monotony of the countryside Oliver becomes docile and passive, his introversion suggested by his sitting by windows. The fading Rose in the next room provides another hint that the blooming setting, those 'clusters of jessamine and honeysuckle' (*OT* 34, 227) that creep over the casement, is sterile and deathly. What brings Oliver back to life and pulls him out of his stupor is the unexpected vision of the urban Real, which, though ugly, is energizing. Alarmed by the vision, Oliver regains his old vitality, 'leap[s] from the window into the garden, call[s] loudly for help' and returns to action (*OT* 34, 228). The leap recalls the weary boy's jump to his feet in chapter 8 upon seeing the word 'London' carved in another stone. With the hideous faces in the window presenting an unattractive vision of city life, Oliver is reminded that only his contact with the Real and a continued struggle for survival will enable him to decipher the hidden code of his existence.

Further Reading

Jim Barloon, 'The Black Hole of London: Rescuing Oliver Twist', *Dickens Studies Annual* 28 (1999): 1–12

Laura Berry, *The Child, the State, and the Victorian Novel* (Charlottesville: University Press of Virginia, 1999)

Rosemarie Bodenheimer, 'Dickens and the Art of Pastoral', *Centennial Review* 23 (1979): 452–67

John Lamb, 'Faces in the Window, Stains on the Rose: Grimaces of the Real in *Oliver Twist*', *Dickens Studies Annual* 34 (2004): 1–16

William Lankford, '"The Parish Boy's Progress": The Evolving Form of *Oliver Twist*', *PMLA* 93, 1 (1978): 20–32

Richard Lehan, *The City in Literature* (Berkeley: University of California Press, 1998)

Patrick Parrinder, '"Turn Again, Dick Whittington!" Dickens, Wordsworth, and the Boundaries of the City', *Victorian Literature and Culture* 32, 2 (2004): 407–19

Sambudha Sen, 'Hogarth, Egan, Dickens, and the Making of an Urban Aesthetic', *Representations* 103 (2008): 84–106

Aleksandar Stević, 'Fatal Extraction: Dickensian Bildungsroman and the Logic of Dependency', *Dickens Studies Annual* 45 (2014): 63–94

CHAPTER 8

NICHOLAS NICKLEBY
Equity vs Law

JON MICHAEL VARESE

NICHOLAS *Nickleby* is a novel about contracts—making them, breaking them, revising them, reconsidering them, validating, invalidating, reinterpreting, and re-examining them. It is a novel about contracts in the economic sphere (business, employment), as well as contracts that exist more informally, though no less importantly, within the larger social fabric (family and friendship). Indeed, the idea behind the contractual agreement, and what does and does not constitute a contract, is central to nearly every interaction, relationship, and decision that drives the plot of this seemingly disparate novel forward. As they do for businesses and families in the world at large, contracts, agreements, and promises act as the vehicles through which the social and economic relations of this novel ultimately find validity and coherence.

But when is a contract a contract, and when is it not? Does a contract, no matter the kind, need to be adhered to at any cost? What are the conditions under which a contract might be invalidated? And is there more to a contract than just the agreed-to terms? That is to say, does the equity—or fairness—aspect of a contract have the ability to compete with or even supersede the strict letter of the law? These are the questions that stand at the centre of *Nicholas Nickleby*, and at the centre of Dickens's business life in the 1830s. Only in reading the two alongside one another can we begin to understand what contracts meant for Dickens both inside and outside of the novel.

BUSINESS AND SOCIAL CONTRACTS IN *NICHOLAS NICKLEBY*

Nicholas Nickleby's first order of business puts forward a position on the validity of traditional contracts, and one's justification for making or breaking them. Part I (April

1838) introduces Ralph Nickleby, Nicholas Nickleby, and Wackford Squeers as parties to a particular set of agreements. The first agreement, between Nicholas and Ralph, is not explicitly a financial one, while the other agreement, between Nicholas and Squeers, is a traditional employment contract. Each of these agreements is wrapped up with the other—part of a scheme to rid the city of Nicholas as expeditiously as possible.

In short, these initial contracts go like this: if Nicholas agrees to leave London, and take up employment with Squeers in Yorkshire, Ralph Nickleby will 'provide for' Nicholas's mother and sister. In the related contract, Squeers agrees to pay Nicholas a salary of £5 per annum to fill the role of 'able assistant'.[1] The nature of the traditional employment contract is straightforward; the nature of Ralph's familial promise less so. Presumably, Ralph's responsibility involves supplying Kate and Mrs Nickleby with the means to a better life, *contingent on* Nicholas accepting Squeers's offer and leaving town. ('Your mother and sister, Sir,' replied Ralph, 'will be provided for in that case [not otherwise], by me, and placed in some sphere of life in which they will be able to be independent ... they will not remain as they are, one week after your departure ...' (*NN* 3, 27)). Nicholas, believing that all will be well if everyone upholds their part of the agreement, enthusiastically accepts his uncle's offer, and seals the deal with a handshake. But soon we discover that for Ralph and Squeers, relatives are nothing more than commodities to be bought and sold. And to ensure the success of their transactions, Ralph and Squeers must usher guardians and protectors off-stage.

These first issues of contract, of promise, bring to light the tensions between equity and law—the two opposing principles that inform all contractual relationships in this novel. If one sets out the terms of a contract, and adheres to the terms exactly, does that mean that the contract has been fulfilled? The novel will struggle with this question, along with the ones posed earlier, from its opening pages, down to the very last.

Squeers is of course the ultimate perversion of the honest agreement, breaking every rule of fair trade in the way he runs his academy. He equates boys with money ('I took down ten boys; ten twentys—two hundred pound' (*NN* 4, 31)), profits from taking in bastards and the unwanted ('What are these boys;—natural children?' (*NN* 4, 34)), and rules with outright violence ('Mr. Squeers looked at the little boy to see whether he was doing anything he could beat him for ...' (*NN* 4, 31)). Nicholas has no inkling as to the real nature of this business when he enters into his agreement(s) with his uncle and Squeers. On the contrary, his initial enthusiasm over gaining a position—any position—is sadly misguided. Soon though, he will become acquainted with the 'internal economy' of Dotheboys Hall, where the children have 'the countenances of old men' (*NN* 8, 88); where the diet, as the original employment advertisement proclaims, is indeed 'unparalleled' (*NN* 3, 26); and where the 'practical mode of teaching' ('C-l-e-a-n, clean, verb active, to make bright, to scour. W-i-n, win, d-e-r, der, winder, a casement. When the boy knows this out of book, he goes and does it' (*NN* 8, 90)), is more of an

---

[1] Charles Dickens, *Nicholas Nickleby*, ed. Paul Schlicke (Oxford: Oxford University Press, 2008), 26–7. Hereafter cited parenthetically in the text with *NN* chapter and page number.

introduction to the daily chores at Dotheboys Hall than it is real education. This is not what Nicholas signed up for, but he resolves to stay on in the job, knowing that 'at all events others depended too much on his uncle's favour to admit of his awakening his wrath' (*NN* 8, 96).

Nicholas remains agitated—and compliant—until Part IV (July 1838), which provides the novel's first breach of contract, and moves the story in a new direction. With his patience for Squeers worn through, particularly with regard to Smike, whose beatings have increased since Nicholas's arrival, Nicholas at last '[resolves] that the out-standing account between himself and Mr. Squeers should be settled rather more speedily than the latter anticipated' (*NN* 13, 152). The economic language ('out-standing account') is significant, for here language and the 'business' of the story unite to create what John Bowen has called 'a speculative economy governed by exploitative and ruthless exchange ... constantly entwining domestic and familial relations with those of economic success and failure'.[2] Nicholas's situation is about business, but it's also about family—it can't not be, given the nature of the agreements he has made. Furthermore, within the context of this commercial situation, Nicholas has actually increased his family (with Smike), and has, intentionally or unintentionally, taken on the role of father/brother in the absence of the blood relatives he would normally defend. 'Have a care,' Nicholas warns Squeers, 'for if you do raise the devil within me, the consequences shall fall heavily upon your own head.' Squeers does raise the devil with him, spitting on Nicholas and striking him across the face, at which point the novel's hero springs upon him and 'beat[s] the ruffian till he roar[s] for mercy' (*NN* 13, 155).

This pivotal moment in the novel represents the breaking of a contract (two really) in the direst circumstances, as well as the formation of a new one (again, with Smike). We never see the letter to which Nicholas earlier alludes, the letter in which he has 'begged forgiveness' for Smike (*NN* 13, 154), but the reference to it tells us that for Nicholas, attempts at negotiation with Squeers began long before this final confrontation. The break that Nicholas makes at this moment has its roots in Nicholas's general sense of indignation at the injustices he sees around him; but it's Smike, and the helplessness that Smike represents, that come to symbolize and legitimize Nicholas's reasons for striking out. Avenging not just Smike but all of the 'dastardly cruelties practiced on helpless infancy in this foul den', Nicholas refuses to continue to bear the conditions under which his uncle has placed him. Things have simply become too hot, and these contracts are no longer worth keeping. Ultimately, this interaction between schoolmaster and assistant demonstrates that when one party (in this instance, the demonized party) refuses to

---

[2] John Bowen, 'Performing Business, Training Ghosts: *Nicholas Nickleby*', *Other Dickens:* Pickwick *to* Chuzzlewit (Oxford: Oxford University Press, 2000), 119. According to Bowen, the language of business and economics in general permeates nearly every aspect of this novel: 'economic concerns, obsessions indeed, are at the centre of the novel, and almost every significant relationship (with the important exception of Kate and Nicholas) is at some point challenged, mediated, or enabled by economic demands or needs' (111). Likewise, Patten has exquisitely shown that 'every relationship entered into within the novel has an economic element'. See Robert L. Patten, *Charles Dickens and 'Boz'* (Cambridge: Cambridge University Press, 2012), 197 and ff.

negotiate with the party that stands on higher moral ground (Nicholas invokes the right of 'Heaven' earlier in his warning as well), it's time to break the contract. This framework, this encoded belief, defines not simply a guiding principle for relationships here, but for practically every relationship in the novel going forward.

As Nicholas departs from Dotheboys Hall, Smike secretly follows his guardian angel, hiding in the shadows until morning. His one desire, he tells Nicholas, is 'to go with you—anywhere—everywhere—to the world's end—to the churchyard grave' (*NN* 13, 159). Clinging to Nicholas's hand, he promises ardent devotion, if Nicholas will only take him on as a companion. 'May I—may I go with you?' Smike asks. 'I will be your faithful hard-working servant … I only want to be near you' (*NN* 13, 159). 'And you shall,' Nicholas cries out. 'And the world shall deal by you as it does by me, till one or both of us shall quit it for a better. Come!' This sentimental exchange, with its till-death-do-us-part-like promises, is almost something in the way of a marriage contract—a partnership that is established not on the precepts of financial gain (like the Nicholas–Squeers agreement) or financial conservation (like the Nicholas–Ralph agreement), but on a sort of higher emotional level, devoid of market value. The promissory words of this exchange create a palliative contract that soothes Nicholas in the wake of having to acknowledge the true terms of his earlier agreements. 'Taking his stick in one hand', Nicholas '[extends] the other to his delighted charge', concluding this negotiation not with the firm and business-like handshake that sealed the deal with his uncle, but with a tender and paternal gesture that leaves Nicholas and Smike walking, literally hand in hand, off into the sunrise together (*NN* 13, 159). Even at this very early point in the novel, we can see that these broader, more equitable contracts, as opposed to contracts that follow the strict letter of the law, are the kinds of contracts that Dickens favours.

Betrayal of the Social Contract

Back in London, there are problems, and other contracts are being broken—sort of. Ralph has been doing what he said he'd do, but not very well. He's placed Kate and Mrs Nickleby in 'a large old dingy house in Thames Street: the door and windows of which were so bespattered with mud, that it would have appeared to have been uninhabited for years' (*NN* 11, 131). 'This house depresses and chills one,' Kate tells Newman Noggs. 'If I were superstitious, I should be almost inclined to believe that some dreadful crime had been perpetrated within these old walls, and that the place had never prospered since. How frowning and dark it looks!' There is in fact a kind of crime going on here, as Ralph makes good on his end of the agreement, but only at the barest minimum. Using the same deceptive tactic that he used with his nephew, Ralph also arranges for Kate to work at Mrs Mantalini's millinery, where women of that occupation ostensibly 'make large fortunes, keep equipages, and become persons of great wealth and fortune' (*NN* 10, 120). The working environment there, however, quickly reveals itself to be less than pleasant under the repressive management of Miss Knag, and the harassment of the lascivious Mr Mantalini.

It gets worse though, and the real infidelity to the larger familial contract here is Ralph's dangling of his niece before Sir Mulberry Hawk and Lord Verisopht in an attempt to continue to secure Lord Verisopht's favour—and finances. Kate is wickedly abused by the Verisopht crowd, made the subject of a bet at dinner, and assaulted directly by Hawk in an upstairs room at her uncle's—all under the watchful eyes of Ralph, who dismisses the nobleman's behaviour with little concern. 'What is this?' Ralph asks when he walks in on Hawk's assault. 'It is this, Sir', Kate replies, 'that beneath the roof where I, a helpless girl, your dead brother's child, should most have found protection, I have been exposed to insult which should make you shrink to look upon me' (*NN* 19, 241). 'I wish ... I had never done this' Ralph later muses, after *increasing* Kate's exposure to harm by providing Verisopht with her location at the Wittiterlys'. 'And yet it will keep this boy to me, while there is money to be made. Selling a girl—throwing her in the way of temptation, and insult, and coarse speech. Nearly two thousand pounds profit from him already though. Pshaw! Match-making mothers do the same thing every day' (*NN* 26, 341). Ralph is perpetrating something awful here, and one can now see why it is all the more important that he keep his nephew out of London. Ralph's actions amount to a betrayal of the 'biological' contract between family members as he wilfully puts his niece into commercial circulation.[3] 'You would sell your flesh and blood for money', Hawk tells him (*NN* 19, 242). And indeed, this appears to be true.

The judgement of the novel is clear. These 'bad' kinds of contracts, which favour law over equity, exactitude over fairness, are bound to be broken, and broken justifiably. To that end, chapter 33, IN WHICH MR. RALPH NICKLEBY IS RELIEVED, BY A VERY EXPEDITIOUS PROCESS, FROM ALL COMMERCE WITH HIS RELATIONS, concludes the first half of the book. In the chapter's opening paragraphs, we learn that Nicholas, emboldened by the full knowledge of Ralph's treachery, is determined to sever all relations with his uncle ('My resolution is taken ... nothing will avail Ralph Nickleby now' (*NN* 33, 419)). His first move is to retrieve Kate from the house of the Wititterlys, where, as Nicholas has learned, she has been the object of pursuit by Hawk and Verisopht. Nicholas wastes no time breaking Kate's employment contract, a contract that she herself previously refused to dishonour, even when pushed to the breaking point by her uncle's unfeeling remarks. ('I will not disgrace your recommendation. I will remain in the house in which it placed me, until I am entitled to leave it by the terms of my engagement' (*NN* 28, 371–2)). Under such dire circumstances, however, Kate's situation is no longer negotiable, and Nicholas, with his 'whole blood on fire', announces his purpose to Mr. Wittiterly, 'and the impossibility of deferring it' (*NN* 33, 421–2).

---

[3] On the instability and redrawing of 'biological' family relationships, see Helena Michie, 'The Avuncular and Beyond: Family (Melo)drama in *Nicholas Nickleby*', in John Schad (ed.), *Dickens Refigured: Bodies, Desires and Other Histories* (Manchester: Manchester University Press, 1996), 80–97. Michie notes that 'Ralph's unprofessed but all-absorbing profession of usury links him to another figure in the Victorian avunculate: the pawnbroker, often referred to by his clients in Victorian times as "uncle". If the uncle does not produce children, he does produce money; if children traditionally serve as capital and labour, the uncle produces interest'. Ibid. 87.

With Kate secure, Nicholas next goes to collect his mother from his uncle's house, and charges Newman Noggs, now working in the full role of double-agent, with delivering a letter to Ralph. The letter is the formal written document that not only notifies Ralph of the cancellation of his agreement with his nephew, but also severs all relations between them.

> You are known to me now. There are no reproaches I could heap upon your head which would carry with them one thousandth part of the groveling shame that this assurance will awaken even in your breast.
> Your brother's widow and her orphan child spurn the shelter of your roof, and shun you with disgust and loathing. Your kindred renounce you, for they know no shame but the ties of blood which bind them in name with you.
> You are an old man, and I leave you to the grave. May every recollection of your life cling to your false heart, and cast their darkness on your death-bed. (*NN* 33, 425)

Ralph Nickleby's deceptive and unforgivable behaviour voids any agreement between himself and his nephew. The 'shelter' Ralph provided for Kate and Mrs Nickleby, once the physical manifestation of the terms to which Ralph had agreed, is now 'spurned', and the gratitude he enjoyed in the form of both Kate's discretion and Nicholas's self-imposed absence is now replaced with 'disgust and loathing'. The 'commerce' from which this chapter relieves Ralph is not simply financial, for in renouncing his uncle and breaking the family contract from the other side, Nicholas condemns Ralph to an emotionless life of figures and tables—to a lonely state of familial bankruptcy. How fitting then that the number concludes with Newman Noggs turning his back on Ralph to consult 'some figures in an Interest-table ... apparently quite abstracted from every other object' (*NN* 33, 425). Having helped orchestrate the renunciation of his boss, Newman is now an extended part of 'an ever-increasing adoptive family',[4] and the emotional loyalty toward the Nicklebys that he favours over the more professional allegiance he supposedly owes to Ralph presages the very different kinds of contracts that take shape in the second half of the novel.

Dickens and Contracts, Equity versus Law

To be sure, it is no accident that Dickens's 'theory of contract' should come out so forcefully in this novel, for the years and months before, during, and after *Nicholas Nickleby*'s composition mark a special period during which Dickens's own contracts—and by

---

[4] Ibid. 86. Michie uses the phrase in her discussion of the Cheerybles and their 'avuncular interventions'.

extension his artistic and commercial value—were being constantly re-evaluated and renegotiated. By the time the first number of *Nicholas Nickleby* appeared in April of 1838, Dickens's relations with the book's publishers, Chapman and Hall, had reached a near love affair state. During their brief partnership with him (beginning in February 1836), they had renegotiated Dickens's initial *Pickwick* agreement not once but *twice*, raising the author's payments from 9 guineas to 20 guineas, and eventually to £25 per part. Midway through *Pickwick*, in March of 1837, they gave Dickens an unsolicited £500 bonus and a set of Shakespeare. And then in the months that followed, they hosted a celebratory banquet in his honour (April), and gifted him a set of silver Pickwickian punch ladles (July). At the end of *Pickwick*'s run, as they were trying to secure Dickens for a follow-up serial, Chapman and Hall determined that Dickens should receive £2,000 for the *Pickwick Papers* in its entirety—the equivalent of £100 per number, nearly ten times the amount of the original agreed-to terms.[5] All of this had been offered coolly and willingly in light of Dickens's exorbitant success. 'With feelings most sensitive by nature to honorable and generous treatment', Dickens wrote, 'I am and shall ever be impressed with the highest possible sense of your unvarying conduct towards me.'[6] The relationship was one that seemed to be rewarding Dickens equitably at every turn, despite what had been agreed to formally or informally between the two parties.

In contrast to Chapman and Hall, there was also Richard Bentley—the publisher who haunted nearly every corner of Dickens's professional life during this time. Since August of 1836, Dickens had been signing and renegotiating numerous contracts with him as well: for an unnamed, three-volume novel at £500, as well as another novel on the same terms (August 1836); to edit Bentley's new *Miscellany* and to furnish his own writing for that publication (November 1836); for an increase in salary based on the *Miscellany*'s sales (March 1837); for material copyrights, more money, and a delineation as to how *Oliver Twist* and *Barnaby Rudge* would 'count' toward what Dickens owed Bentley (September 1837); to edit—and receive half profits for—the memoirs of Joseph Grimaldi (November 1837); to renegotiate the terms for *Oliver Twist* and *Barnaby Rudge* yet again (September 1838); to renegotiate the terms for *Oliver Twist* and *Barnaby Rudge* once more (gaining £500 and £2,000 for those novels respectively), and to cease editorship of the *Miscellany* (February 1839); and finally to buy out the copyright of *Oliver Twist* from Bentley, and have Bentley surrender any claims he still had on Dickens's writing (July 1840).[7] And while *all* of these negotiations, over time, turned out to work in Dickens's favour, we see throughout, and especially from September 1837 onward, an author–publisher relationship that is characterized by antagonism and combativeness.

---

[5] The details of these events are all covered in Robert L. Patten, *Charles Dickens and his Publishers* (Oxford: Clarendon Press, 1978), 60–74.

[6] Charles Dickens, *The Letters of Charles Dickens*, ed. Madeline House, Graham Storey, et al., Pilgrim/British Academy Edition, 12 vols (Oxford: Clarendon Press, 1965–2002), 1:288. Hereafter cited as *PLets* with volume and page number.

[7] See Patten, *Publishers*, 75–87.

There are no banquets with Richard Bentley, no bonuses, no punch ladles. There is rather a Dickens who is insistent on increasingly asking for more, and a publisher who is resistant to—even niggling about—those asks at every turn. Bentley's position on equity versus law could not have been more different from Chapman and Hall's. Whereas Chapman and Hall considered their agreements with Dickens a means to establishing a real, almost familial partnership with a writer, subject to modification or supplementation in particular circumstances, Bentley thought of agreements as something strict and enforceable, until he was repeatedly shown otherwise.

The problem with 'agreements' and 'contracts' in the early nineteenth century though, is that one was legally enforceable, and one was not. An agreement—that is, the concurrence of wills of two or more people with respect to some common matter, evidenced by acts or documents understood by each party—was by itself of no legal effect. In order to be enforceable, the agreement also needed to contain an intention to create legal relations and validity under the law.[8] Thus, all contracts were agreements, but not all agreements were contracts. What Dickens signed with his publishers, at least in name, were *agreements*, though if Bentley had tried to sue Dickens for damages (and there is strong indication that he could have) then Dickens's agreements would very likely have stood as contracts too, no matter how they had been titled (Figure 8.1).[9]

It is also likely, however, that Dickens, Bentley, and their respective lawyers all understood that in the context of the contemporary English court system, contracts were not as straightforwardly enforceable as they may have seemed.

Before the Judicature Acts of the 1870s, which consolidated England's exceedingly fragmented court system into the system that survives today, the law was administered under two parallel but distinct entities: the Court of Equity (Chancery) and the Common Law Courts. By the time Dickens's difficulties with Bentley began in the 1830s, this bifurcated system had existed for centuries, with the law courts having become notorious for basing everything they did on 'forms of action'—the strict, convoluted, and impenetrable series of requirements and procedures that one needed to follow in order to make any kind of legal claim. Equity, on the other hand, arose 'from the sulkiness and obstinacy of the Common Law Courts, which refused to suit

---

[8] His Honour Judge Iain Hughes QC, personal communication. I am deeply indebted to both Judge Hughes and His Honour Derwin Hope for their help in clarifying this historical distinction. While the idea of intention did not become an easily identifiable part of legal contract doctrine until the later nineteenth century, it was certainly being discussed and debated earlier in the century by legal philosophers, notably by Joseph Chitty in his influential *A Practical Treatise on the Law of Contracts* (1826, 1834, and ff.), and even as far back as the seventeenth century with the case of *Weeks v. Tybald* (1605). See A. W. B. Simpson, 'Innovations in Nineteenth Century Contract Law', *LQR* 91 (1975): 247–78, esp. 263–5.

[9] The Pilgrim editors title all of Dickens's contracts 'agreements'. See *PLets* 1:647 and ff. The terminology was used within, and to title, the agreements themselves.

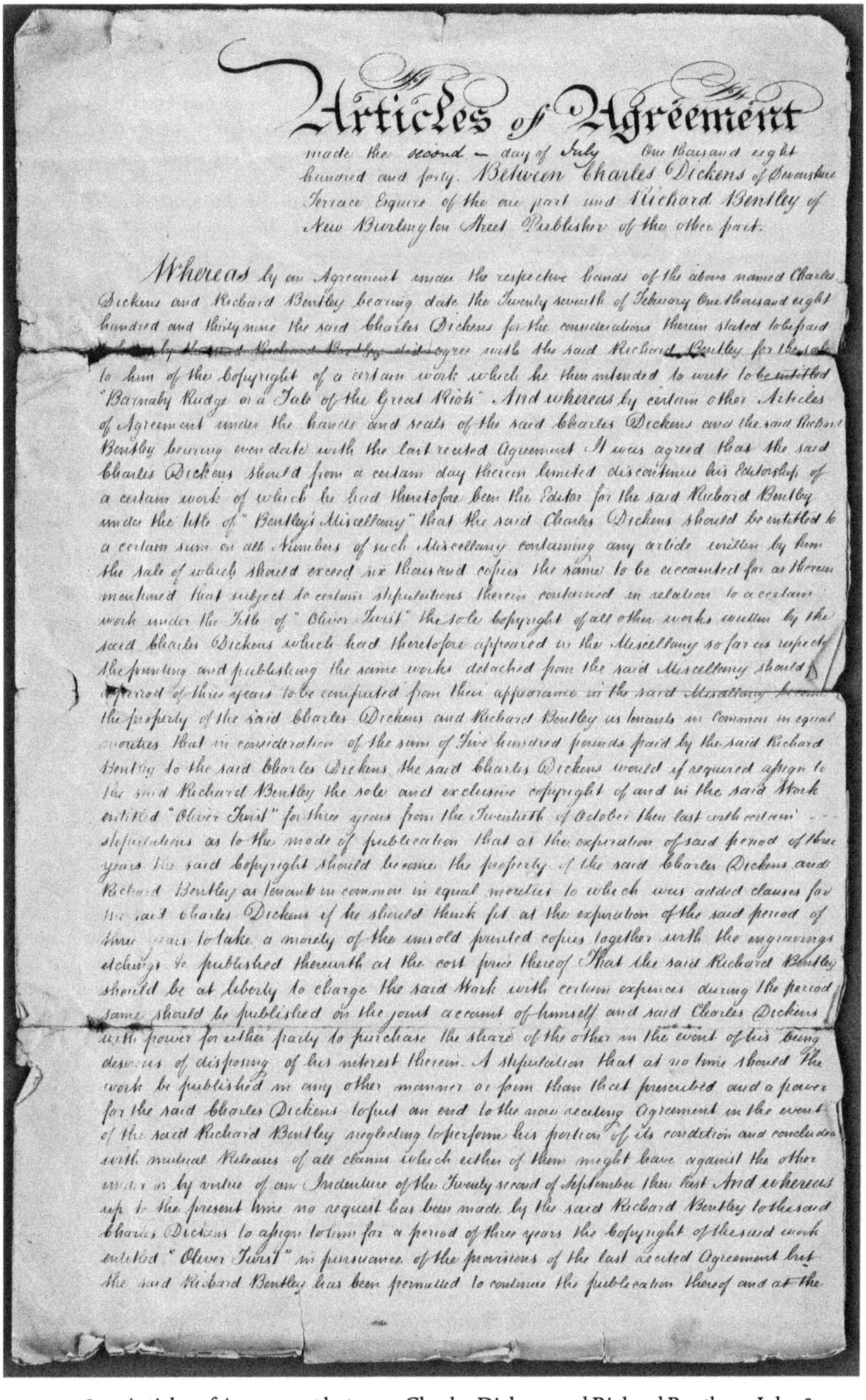

Articles of Agreement

made the second day of July One thousand eight hundred and forty. Between Charles Dickens of Devonshire Terrace Esquire of the one part and Richard Bentley of New Burlington Street Publisher of the other part.

Whereas by an Agreement under the respective hands of the above named Charles Dickens and Richard Bentley bearing date the Twenty seventh of February One thousand eight hundred and thirty nine the said Charles Dickens for the consideration therein stated to be paid by the said Richard Bentley did agree with the said Richard Bentley for the sale to him of the Copyright of a certain work which he then intended to write to be entitled "Barnaby Rudge or a Tale of the Great Riots" And whereas by certain other Articles of Agreement under the hands and seals of the said Charles Dickens and the said Richard Bentley bearing even date with the last recited Agreement It was agreed that the said Charles Dickens should from a certain day therein limited discontinue his Editorship of a certain work of which he had theretofore been the Editor for the said Richard Bentley under the title of "Bentley's Miscellany" that the said Charles Dickens should be entitled to a certain sum on all Numbers of such Miscellany containing any article written by him the sale of which should exceed six thousand copies the same to be accounted for as therein mentioned that subject to certain stipulations therein contained in relation to a certain work under the Title of "Oliver Twist" the sole Copyright of all other works written by the said Charles Dickens which had theretofore appeared in the Miscellany so far as respects the printing and publishing the same works detached from the said Miscellany should after a period of three years to be computed from their appearance in the said Miscellany become the property of the said Charles Dickens and Richard Bentley as tenants in common in equal moieties that in consideration of the sum of Five hundred pounds paid by the said Richard Bentley to the said Charles Dickens the said Charles Dickens would if required assign to the said Richard Bentley the sole and exclusive copyright of and in the said Work entitled "Oliver Twist" for three years from the Twentieth of October then last with certain stipulations as to the mode of publication that at the expiration of said period of three years the said Copyright should become the property of the said Charles Dickens and Richard Bentley as tenants in common in equal moieties to which was added clauses for the said Charles Dickens if he should think fit at the expiration of the said period of three years to take a moiety of the unsold printed copies together with the engravings etchings &c published therewith at the cost price thereof That the said Richard Bentley should be at liberty to charge the said Work with certain expences during the period same should be published on the joint account of himself and said Charles Dickens with power for either party to purchase the share of the other in the event of his being desirous of disposing of his interest therein. A stipulation that at no time should the work be published in any other manner or form than that prescribed and a power for the said Charles Dickens to put an end to the now reciting Agreement in the event of the said Richard Bentley neglecting to perform his portion of its condition and concluding with mutual Releases of all claims which either of them might have against the other under or by virtue of an Indenture of the Twenty second of September then last And whereas up to the present time no request has been made by the said Richard Bentley to the said Charles Dickens to assign to him for a period of three years the Copyright of the said work entitled "Oliver Twist" in pursuance of the provisions of the last recited Agreement but the said Richard Bentley has been permitted to continue the publication thereof and at the

FIGURE 8.1 Articles of Agreement between Charles Dickens and Richard Bentley, 2 July 1840.

Henry W. and Albert Berg Collection of English and American Literature, The New York Public Library, Astor, Lenox and Tilden Foundations themselves to the changes which took place in opinion and in the circumstances of society'.[10] In short, Equity was where one would have taken a case when the law courts offered no remedy. Because the Lord Chancellor was not bound by the medieval and often impossible-to-navigate forms of action that defined everything in Law, the subtler aspects of a plaintiff's or defendant's situation could be considered. While over time Chancery became plagued with its own bureaucracy and inefficiencies (later mocked by Dickens in *Bleak House*), it nonetheless offered an important alternative to the unyielding forms of action that prevented so many from even thinking about bringing a case before a court of law.[11]

Thus, the conflicts we see Dickens working out in *Nicholas Nickleby* manifest the very *structure* of the English court system in the 1830s. Whereas Bentley and Ralph embody the inflexibility and resistance of the law, Chapman and Hall, and as we shall see the Cheerybles and other extended family members, embody another kind of relationship, based on fairness, performance, and due consideration. Bentley's persistent interference in editorial matters, coupled with his tight-fisted way of doing business, riled Dickens continuously, and must have seemed that much pettier when viewed alongside the actions of Chapman and Hall, who rarely, if ever, tampered with Dickens's creativity, and who gave Dickens an unsolicited £300 bonus based on the sales of *Nicholas Nickleby* in January of 1839.[12] By the end of that month in fact, Dickens was writing to Forster again to say that he had had it with Bentley—'This net that has been wound about me so chafes me, so exasperates and irritates my mind, that to break it at whatever cost—*that* I should care nothing for—is my constant impulse.'[13] Dickens soon after resigned from the

---

[10] John Austin, *Lectures on Jurisprudence, or the Philosophy of Positive Law*, ed. Robert Campbell (London: John Murray, 1880), 311. Austin goes on to note that 'if the Courts of Common Law had not refused to introduce certain rules of law or of procedure which were required by the exigencies of society, the equitable or extraordinary jurisdiction of the Chancellor would not have arisen, and the distinction between Law and Equity would never have been heard of'.

[11] Ironically, Chancery was also the body that issued the writs (or opening pleadings) for those wishing to commence an action in a court of law. A plaintiff needed to pigeon-hole his writ into one of numerous categories (Trespass, Trover, Ejectment, Detinue, Replevin, Debt, Covenant, Special Assumpsit, amongst others) with no exceptions. Pollock and Maitland describe the degree of exactitude with which writs and actions needed to be adhered to and executed: 'The metaphor which likens the Chancery to a shop is trite; we will liken it to an armory. It contains every weapon of medieval warfare from the two-handed sword to the poniard. The man who has a quarrel with his neighbor comes thither to choose his weapon. The choice is large but he must remember that he will not be able to change weapons in the middle of the combat and also that every weapon has its proper use and may be put to none other. If he selects a sword, he must observe the rules of sword play; he must not try to use his crossbow as a mace. To drop metaphor, our plaintiff is *not merely choosing a writ; he is choosing an action*, and every action has its own rules.' Sir Frederick Pollock and Frederic William Maitland, *The History of English Law Before the Time of Edward I*, 1895. Quoted in R. Ross Perry, *Common-Law Pleading: Its History and Principles* (Boston: Little, Brown, and Company, 1897), 39.

[12] The first (of three) *Nickleby* bonuses (totalling £1,500) came on 3 January 1839. See Patten, *Publishers*, 100, and PLets 1:570.

[13] PLets 1:494.

Miscellany—permanently this time, and not coincidentally during the very same month that Ralph Nickleby is 'relieved from all commerce with his relations'. Bentley could have taken Dickens to court any number of times, but never did, most likely (at least in part) because of the countless obstacles posed by the forms of action requirements described above. Had prosecution been easier, Bentley almost certainly would have pursued legal action, as he had come to believe (through many other publishing disputes, and not just with Dickens) that a contract was a contract, no matter what the agreement might imply.[14]

For Dickens, things worked a bit differently. 'We may put our hands in our pockets,' he once wrote with regard to his legal squabbles with Bentley, 'and wait for the Dragon's approach with perfect philosophy'.[15] And in Dickens's mind, he had every right to do so. His gradual instigation of and withdrawal from 'the Dragon' was part of a more comprehensive process in which he was constantly reassessing his own market value in light of his ever-increasing commercial success. And so, by the time he came to sign the Articles of Agreement for *Nicholas Nickleby*—the first of Dickens's contracts to give him the perpetual copyright of one of his books in its entirety—contracts, in Dickens's estimation, had become pliable documents. For Dickens, contracts only remained contracts insofar as they compensated the author in an appropriate and reasonably equitable fashion. Like the manuscripts he was writing, contracts could be edited, altered, and revised, so long as there were 'justified' purposes for revising them. The battles that emerged in Dickens's business life during this time—between generosity and stinginess, amicability and irritability, faithfulness and unfaithfulness—imbued him with a sense of self-righteousness and authority that in turn became instrumental in defining how he thought about agreements and contracts. Those battles also contributed to a kind of script that outlined the very basics of what human transactions should look like—a script that rather quickly found its way into Dickens's fiction.

---

[14] For more on one of the later potential court cases, see To Edward Chapman, 27 December 1839, *PLets* 1:621 n. 8, and To W. C. Macready, [?23 February 1840], *PLets* 2:33 n. 2. In February 1840, Bentley had in fact sought counsel from Sutton Sharpe in Lincoln's Inn as to whether he might be able to bring an injunction against Dickens that would prohibit the author from publishing anything else before he delivered *Barnaby Rudge*. (This condition had been stipulated in a previous agreement, and Dickens had actively and knowingly been working in violation of it: '... the Sharks of Bedford Row are likely to bring it to a Compensation Question 'afore long'. See To Thomas Mitton, [29 January 1840], *PLets* 2:14.) Sharpe's reply to Bentley (Figure 8.2), citing important precedent, was that Chancery (the body that issued injunctions) would not side with Bentley, and stated that Bentley's agreement with Dickens was 'substantially of an active nature although guarded by the negative provision'. Under those circumstances, because a Court of Equity could not compel Dickens to write the work in question, it would not 'give partial relief by enforcing the negative stipulation but [would] leave the parties altogether to a Court of Law'. The manuscript of this opinion is in the Berg Collection, New York Public Library.

[15] *PLets* 2:35. Dickens's legal team had also received counsel from James Bacon in Chancery, who presumably told them, as Sutton Sharpe had told Bentley, that Bentley would not have won an injunction against Dickens.

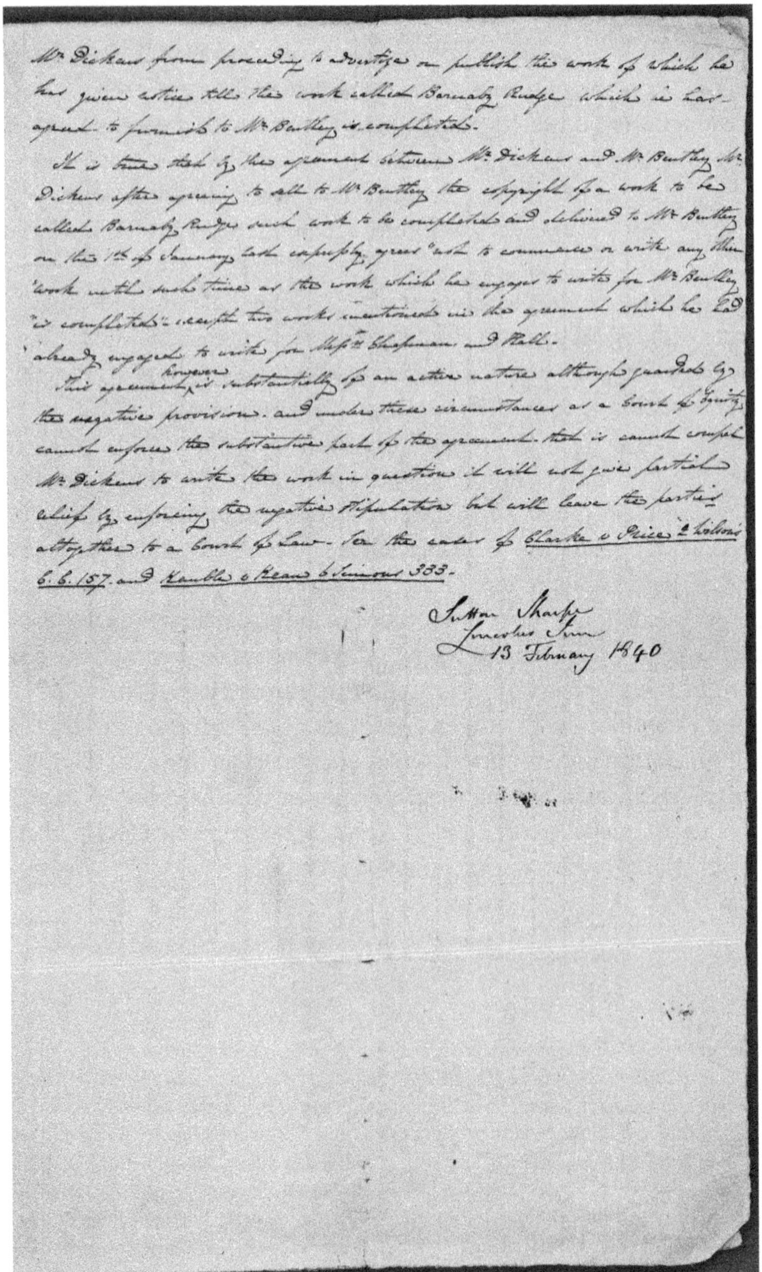

Mr Dickens from proceeding to advertize or publish the work of which he has given notice till the work called Barnaby Rudge which he has agreed to furnish to Mr Bentley is completed.

It is true that by the agreement between Mr Dickens and Mr Bentley Mr Dickens after agreeing to sell to Mr Bentley the copyright of a work to be called Barnaby Rudge such work to be completed and delivered to Mr Bentley on the 1st of January last expressly agrees "not to commence or write any other work until such time as the work which he engages to write for Mr Bentley is completed" except the two works mentioned in the agreement which he had already engaged to write for Messrs Chapman and Hall.

This agreement however is substantially of an active nature although guarded by the negative provision. and under these circumstances as a Court of Equity cannot enforce the substantive part of the agreement that is cannot compel Mr Dickens to write the work in question it will not give partial relief by enforcing the negative stipulation but will leave the parties altogether to a Court of Law. See the cases of Clarke v Price 2 Wilson's C.C. 157. and Kemble v Kean 6 Simons 333.

Sutton Sharpe
Lincolns Inn
13 February 1840

FIGURE 8.2 Legal opinion from Sutton Sharpe of Lincoln's Inn to Richard Bentley, written in Sharpe's hand, 13 February 1840. Because Bentley was unlikely to win a case against Dickens for failing to deliver *Barnaby Rudge*, Sharpe advised against prosecution. See footnote 14.

Henry W. and Albert Berg Collection of English and American Literature, The New York Public Library, Astor, Lenox and Tilden Foundations

Final Verdicts and Further Beginnings

The purpose of Parts XI–XX of *Nicholas Nickleby* is to replace the bad experience of having to break bad agreements with the more rewarding experience of keeping good ones. Whereas Nicholas's agreements with duplicitous businessmen bring him nothing but trouble and misery in the first half of the novel, the contracts that he keeps with others in the second half of the story bring him nothing less than pleasure, advantage, and a sense of moral righteousness. These new or 'good' agreements, which influence the plot of the second half of the novel from beginning to end, function in two major ways: first, they trump or supersede the bad agreements that are still alive and well in the story, serving as the mechanisms that expose and ultimately defeat the schemes that constantly threaten to undermine the promotion of honesty and moral virtue; and second, and perhaps more significantly for Dickens as an author, they bring a sense of unity to the plot hitherto not seen in any of Dickens's fiction. Unlike the contracts in the first half of the novel, which tend to move both Nicholas and the story almost erratically from place to place, the contracts in the second half of *Nicholas Nickleby* help create a larger, more complex, and more stabilizing fabric, the whole of which becomes greater than the sum of its parts.

While the opening of the second half of the novel makes clear that Ralph, Squeers, and others (Mantalini is present here too) are doomed to remain stuck in their 'flat' financial landscapes, something is about to change, and change dramatically. In chapter 35, Nicholas meets and becomes employed by the Cheeryble brothers, the beneficent twins who always seem to be donating to one charitable cause or another, and whose generosity is so abundant as to be practically unbelievable. Having lost one paternal figure by his own reckoning, Nicholas now gains two, and agrees to work as a kind of bookkeeper in the counting house of Cheeryble Brothers for £120 a year (*NN* 35, 457)—a salary 24 times that of the pittance he earned as an assistant schoolmaster in Yorkshire. The increase in pay is not merely coincidental. Chapman and Hall had, unprovoked, either increased or supplemented Dickens's salary numerous times by this point. As in Dickens's own career, the novel demonstrates that an increase in financial compensation accompanies the moral high ground—an idea that Dickens relentlessly plays out in this story as he simultaneously writes it into his own.[16] 'The twins,' as John Glavin has observed, 'turn their protégé to scribbling just as that other proto-lovable pair, Chapman and Hall, out of the blue, magically made the young Dickens into the author of *Pickwick*.'[17] The result of this turning point in the book, then, is an almost too serendipitous upward trajectory for Nicholas that's entirely in synch with that of his creator's.

---

[16] Patten writes about the 'moral code' embodied in literature—a code that has the potential to act as an agent of national unity. 'Dickens felt strongly, all his life, that literature should, and his did, serve this end.' See Patten, '*Boz*', 224 and ff.

[17] John Glavin, *After Dickens: Reading, Adaptation, and Performance* (Cambridge: Cambridge University Press, 1999), 128.

From the first two important transitions that take place in Part XI—namely the reallocation of Nicholas's services to a new job and his family's transfer to a new residence—we see that the Cheerybles' way of doing business is as different from Ralph's standard practice as Chapman and Hall's is from Bentley's. The Cheerybles' 'scheming'—advancing loans in secret, and manipulating matters financially so that it will actually cost them money rather than earn it—is something unheard of in the 'old' world (or Part I–X world) of making and breaking contracts, just as their munificent treatment of their 'faithful servant' Tim Linkinwater (they've pensioned his mother and sister, and purchased a burial plot for the family (*NN* 35, 454)), and the undying loyalty with which he repays them is something never witnessed in the sad universe of Newman Noggs.[18] Along with his devotion to Smike, the only good carry-over contract from the first half of the book, Nicholas's fortuitous agreement with the Cheeryble Brothers will drive the remainder of the narrative, allowing Dickens to develop what is certainly one of his first 'Dickensian' plots, replete with quintessential intricacies and coincidences. By the end of chapter 35, Nicholas and his family are comfortably positioned as the result of this agreement, and the 'editor' of these 'fortunes'[19] can pithily summarize the result of equitable negotiations: 'In short, the poor Nicklebys were social and happy; while the rich Nickleby was alone and miserable' (*NN* 35, 458). Ralph's fate at the end of a rope, in the very place where his dejected son Smike once rested, delivers the novel's final verdict on the guilt of those who refuse to see beyond their own financial gain and inflexibility.

There is not enough space here to reflect in detail on how contracts and relationships further define the second half of *Nicholas Nickleby*. Indeed, the Cheeryble–Linkinwater relationship, the Arthur Gride–Madeline Bray sub-plot, Nicholas's continued devotion to Smike, and even the bizarre re-emergence of Brooker, all provide opportunities to talk further about the inextricability of business and family, and the honouring or betraying of both commercial and social contracts. But it doesn't stop there. One might approach practically any novel in the Dickens oeuvre with questions of good and bad negotiations in mind—we can think back immediately to the many layers of avuncular relationships in *Oliver Twist* (1838), or ahead to the themes of apprenticeship and 'old style' fidelity in *Barnaby Rudge* (1841), where Dickens, ever conscious of commercial trends and how he could benefit from them, finally makes good on his promise to deliver a historical novel in the full manner of Sir Walter Scott. In these cases as in countless others, it's important to keep in mind how significantly the plots of these novels are intertwined with the negotiations that brought them into being. As the case of *Nicholas Nickleby* demonstrates, we must read the development of Dickens's fiction alongside

---

[18] Not just the 'old' world of the novel, but literally the late eighteenth and earlier nineteenth century: '[The Cheerybles] harken back to an earlier time, and Dickens' representation of them is redolent with nostalgia for an era in which competition was not valued over community.' Joseph W. Childers, 'Nicholas Nickleby's Problem of *Doux Commerce*', *Dickens Studies Annual* 25 (1996): 57.

[19] The full title of the novel, before its truncation in book form, was *The Life and Adventures of Nicholas Nickleby, Containing a Faithful Account of the Fortunes, Misfortunes, Uprisings, Downfallings, and Complete Career of the Nickleby Family*.

the development of the author himself, keeping the two in constant dialogue with each other, rather than going 'back and forth' between them.[20] Only then can we begin to untangle what Dickens's novels are really trying to say, as they struggle to clarify the innumerable and inevitable tensions between the menacing and the good, the commercial and the domestic.

Further Reading

Kathryn Chittick, *Dickens and the 1830s* (Cambridge: Cambridge University Press, 1990)

Eileen Cleere, *Avuncularism: Capitalism, Patriarchy, and Nineteenth-Century English Literature* (Stanford, CA: Stanford University Press, 2004)

Robert Douglas-Fairhurst, *Becoming Dickens: The Invention of a Novelist* (Cambridge, MA: The Belknap Press/Harvard University Press, 2011)

Michael Slater, 'The Composition and Monthly Publication of *Nicholas Nickleby*', in Michael Slater (ed.), *The Life and Adventures of Nicholas Nickleby* (Philadelphia: University of Pennsylvania Press, 1982), vii–lxxxiv

---

[20] The idea is Rosemarie Bodenheimer's, who has stated the situation of biographical criticism better than anyone else: 'We cannot go back and forth between life and work because we do not have a life; everything we know is on a written page. To juxtapose letters and fiction ... is to read one kind of text alongside another.' Rosemarie Bodenheimer, *Knowing Dickens* (Ithaca, NY: Cornell University Press, 2007), 16.

CHAPTER 9

THE OLD CURIOSITY SHOP AND *MASTER HUMPHREY'S CLOCK*

SARAH WINTER

THE OLD CURIOSITY SHOP, ALLEGORY, AND CAPITALISM

An early 1840 review of Charles Dickens's *The Old Curiosity Shop* highlights its incongruities: 'we do not know where we have met, in fiction, with a more striking and picturesque combination of images than is presented by the simple, childish figure of little Nelly, amidst a chaos of such obsolete, grotesque, old-world commodities as from the stock in trade of The Old Curiosity Shop'. Commenting on the illustration of this scene (Figure 9.1), the reviewer observes, 'it is like an Allegory of the peace and innocence of Childhood in the midst of Violence, Superstition, and all the hateful or hurtful Passions of the world'.[1] Appearing originally in the weekly *Master Humphrey's Clock*, edited and written by Dickens, *Shop* was published in 1841 as a single volume by Chapman and Hall. In this edition, Dickens incorporated the reviewer's observations in several paragraphs added to the conclusion of the first chapter, where the first-person narrator, Master Humphrey, considers the impression created by his glimpse of Little Nell through the window of the curiosity shop, sleeping amidst 'heaps of fantastic things':

> I had her image, without any effort of imagination, surrounded and beset by everything that was foreign to its nature, and furthest removed from the sympathies of her sex and age. If ... I had been forced to imagine her in a common chamber, with

---

[1] [Thomas Hood], '*Master Humphrey's Clock*. By "Boz"', *The Atheneum* 680 (7 November 1840): 887–8.

FIGURE 9.1 Samuel Williams, 'Nell in bed', *The Old Curiosity Shop*, wood engraving, in *Master Humphrey's Clock*, 25 April 1840.

General Collection, Beinecke Rare Book and Manuscript Library, Yale University

nothing unusual or uncouth in its appearance, it is very probable that I should have been less impressed with her strange and solitary state. As it was, she seemed to exist in a kind of allegory; and having these shapes about her, claimed my interest so strongly, that... I could not dismiss her from my recollection, do what I would.[2]

Via Dickens's revision, the early reviewer, later known to Dickens as the poet Thomas Hood, initiated a characterization of the allegorical mode of *Shop* that would remain vital to its critical reception as a serious work of art.

This revised passage, along with its accompanying illustration, also caught the attention of two early twentieth-century readers of Dickens who would become extraordinarily influential modern theorists of culture, history, the arts, and modern media. In a November 1930 letter, Walter Benjamin informed his friend Theodor W. Adorno that, following up on his recommendation, he was now 'absorbed' in reading Dickens's *Shop*

---

[2] Charles Dickens, *The Old Curiosity Shop*, ed. Elizabeth M. Brennan (Oxford: Clarendon Press, 1997), 1, 19. All further references to this edition will appear parenthetically in the text by chapter number (Arabic) and page number with the abbreviation *OCS*.

in German translation, *Der Raritätenladen*. Adorno had read the novel 'with enormous emotion' in September of that year, reporting to Siegfried Kracauer that it was 'a book of the very first rank—full of mysteries'.[3] In 1931, Adorno published an exegesis of the novel's allegorical response to modernity. After observing that the meaning of Dickens's novel 'has changed with time', Adorno argues that 'In Dickens's non-psychological method of illustrating and describing objective essences one can make out, not only evidence of a pre-bourgeois outlook, but of an artistic intention that goes beyond bourgeois practice... The pre-bourgeois form of Dickens's novels provides a way of unmasking that same bourgeois world that it serves to represent.'[4] *Shop*, for Adorno, presents a critical stance on capitalism that demonstrates the novel's prescience and continuing relevance to the twentieth century. Adorno's account also 'conformed to Benjamin's profound characterization of allegory as the form that embodies mourning, the melancholic condition of our [modern] existence'.[5]

Referring to Adorno's discussion of *Shop* in the section of his unfinished *Arcades Project* (*Das Passagen-Werk*, 1927–40) on 'The Collector', Benjamin too quotes Dickens's passage about allegory and positions the novel as a harbinger of relations to objects characteristic of modern capitalist culture. Like Master Humphrey in his inability to forget his allegorical vision of Nell, the 'collector' finds 'the world is present, and indeed ordered, in each of his objects. Ordered, however, according to a surprising and, for the profane understanding, incomprehensible connection'.[6] The image of Little Nell among the miscellaneous objects in the curiosity shop evokes a similar, involuntary response of recognition, thus making Dickens's novel a collection in Benjamin's sense.[7]

Dickens's *Shop* continues to pose intriguing conundrums for critical analysis in at least three of its elements: (1) its intricate plotting of Little Nell's arduous journey with

---

[3] Walter Benjamin, letter to Wiesengrund-Adorno, Berlin, 11 October 1930, in *Theodor Adorno and Walter Benjamin, The Complete Correspondence, 1928–1940*, ed. Henri Lonitz, trans. Nicholas Walker (Cambridge, MA: Harvard University Press, 1999), 7–8 n. 5.

[4] Theodor Adorno, 'An Address on Charles Dickens's *The Old Curiosity Shop*', in Michael Hollington, 'A Translation of Adorno's "Rede über den *Raritätenladen* von Charles Dickens"', *Dickens Quarterly* 6, 3 (September 1989): 95–101, 96; hereafter 'An Address'. Adorno's essay originally appeared in the *Frankfurter Zeitung* 75, 281 (8 April 1931): 1–2. Hollington translates the version revised by Adorno and appearing in *Gesammelte Schriften*, vol. 11, *Noten zur Literatur*, ed. Gretel Adorno and Rolf Tiedemann (Frankfurt am Main: Suhrkamp, 1973), 515–22.

[5] Michael Hollington, 'Adorno, Benjamin, and *The Old Curiosity Shop*', *Dickens Quarterly* 6, 3 (September 1999): 87–95, 91. The major work where Benjamin develops his theory of allegory is *Der Ursprung des deutschen Trauerspeils* (*The Origin of German Tragic Drama*) of 1925.

[6] Walter Benjamin, *The Arcades Project*, trans. Howard Eiland and Kevin McLaughlin (Cambridge, MA: Harvard University Press, 1999), H2, 7; H2a, 1; 207. Benjamin's *Das Passagen-Werk* is organized into 36 convolutes or files labelled with capital letters, arranged in alphabetical order, and further organized according to subheadings indicated by numbers and lower-case letters. The original text is published in Walter Benjamin, *Gesammelte Schriften*, vol. 5, ed. Rolf Tiedemann and Hermann Schweppenhaüser (Frankfurt am Main: Suhrkamp, 1982).

[7] See Kevin McLaughlin's related discussion of 'Boz' as a collector of texts in Benjamin's sense, in *Writing in Parts: Imitation and Exchange in Nineteenth-Century Literature* (Stanford, CA: Stanford University Press, 1995), chapter 2.

her grandfather, Old Trent, through an industrialized English landscape, and their pursuit by an array of London-based characters, including both ineffectual rescuers and a lecherous, malevolent, money-lending dwarf, Quilp; (2) in the wrenching emotional impact of Nell's death on Victorian readers; and (3) in its mixed critical reception after its enormous popularity among an international reading audience during its serial run.

The status of *Shop* as a Victorian best-seller devolved after Dickens's death into its reputation as unbearably maudlin and sentimental.[8] Building on important studies by Ian Duncan, Audrey Jaffe, Paul Schlicke, Hilary M. Schor, Garrett Stewart, Dennis Walder, and Alexander Welsh,[9] the recent scholarly discussion seeks not to debunk Victorian sentimentality, however, but rather to understand the novel's multi-faceted appeal in new ways. Dickens's original plan for *Clock* to satirize 'the administration of justice' and 'keep a special look-out upon the magistrates in town and country, and never to leave those worthies alone', also prompts investigation of connections between the legal satire in *Shop* and its framing narrative in *Clock*.[10] Despite the light-hearted rendering of Mr Pickwick and the Wellers as visitors to Master Humphrey's reading circle, Nell's Gothic tale seems to renew Dickens's attack in *The Pickwick Papers* (April 1836 to November 1837) on the inhumane procedures of the law, and thus to raise new questions about the critique of British government underlying both his humorous and his sentimental early fictions.

CLOCKS AND SERIAL FICTION: *MASTER HUMPHREY'S CLOCK*

After his break with publisher Richard Bentley and his replacement as editor of *Bentley's Miscellany* by Harrison Ainsworth in January 1839, Dickens continued writing his latest novel in monthly parts, *Nicholas Nickleby* (March 1838 to September 1839), for publishers Chapman and Hall. In July 1839, Dickens wrote a letter to his friend and close adviser

---

[8] For a detailed account of the popular and critical response to *The Old Curiosity Shop* through the mid-twentieth century, see Loralee MacPike, '"The Old Curiosity Shape": Changing Views of Little Nell, Part I', *Dickens Studies Newsletter* 12, 2 (1981): 33–8 and '"The Old Curiosity Shape": Changing Views of Little Nell, Part II', *Dickens Studies Newsletter* 12, 3 (1981): 70–6.

[9] Ian Duncan, *Modern Romance and Transformations of the Novel: The Gothic, Scott, Dickens* (Cambridge: Cambridge University Press, 1992); Audrey Jaffe, *Vanishing Points: Dickens, Narrative, and the Subject of Omniscience* (Ithaca, NY: Cornell University Press, 1991); Paul Schlicke, *Dickens and Popular Entertainment* (London: Allen and Unwin, 1985); Hilary M. Schor, *Dickens and the Daughter of the House* (Cambridge: Cambridge University Press, 1999); Garrett Stewart, *Dickens and the Trials of Imagination* (Cambridge, MA: Harvard University Press, 1974); Dennis Walder, *Dickens and Religion* (London: Allen and Unwin, 1981); Alexander Welsh, *The City of Dickens* (Oxford: Clarendon Press, 1971).

[10] Charles Dickens, Letter to John Forster, 14 July 1839, in *The Pilgrim Edition of the Letters of Charles Dickens*, vol. 1, 1820–1839, ed. Madeline House and Graham Storey (Oxford: Clarendon Press, 1965), 562–5, 564. Hereafter *PLets* volume:page range, page.

John Forster, envisioning a new publication—a weekly miscellany entirely under his editorial control and written by himself, though with the association of other contributors he chose. Costing only 3*d*. per issue, four of which would then be issued in monthly one-shilling instalments, this new cheaper format was intended to reach an even broader audience than his earlier novels. Dickens also negotiated much more favourable terms with Chapman and Hall than he had received from Bentley: £50 per number and a half-share of the profits. The bulk of the illustrations were drawn by George Cattermole and Hablot K. Browne ('Phiz') and then interspersed as wood engravings within, or as Dickens put it 'dropped into', the text they were depicting, rather than being reproduced on separate pages as in Dickens's monthly issues.[11]

Titled *Master Humphrey's Clock*, the first instalment (4 April 1840) opens with the first-person framing narrative of Master Humphrey, an elderly man 'misshapen' and 'deformed' from his youth, and residing in a rambling, antique house in 'a venerable suburb of London' with a group of male friends, who gather one night a week to read narratives that they have composed and stored in Humphrey's ornate old clock.[12] These interpolated narratives, set in London and its environs during the Elizabethan, Jacobean, and Stuart reigns, also include plots featuring abuses of power under an absolutist regime, including the Jacobean era's superstitions against witchcraft and public executions under Charles II, described by a character in one tale as '[t]he murders of state policy' (*MHC* III, 69–70). Jeremy Tambling has noted that in these antiquarian tales, which 'are not just for anecdotal interest, nor signs of nostalgia', 'Dickens identifies with the residual, and what modernity sets aside'.[13] Dickens also envisioned *Clock* as a kind of sequel that would reintroduce his popular characters Sam Weller, Mr Weller senior, and Mr Pickwick to Old Humphrey's reading circle, thus appealing to past readers of 'Boz'.[14] Master Humphrey's recognition of Mr Pickwick at their first meeting heightens the text's self-reflexivity by pointing to the 'reality' of Dickens's popular characters within the framing narrative: '"You knew me directly!" said Mr. Pickwick. "What a pleasure it is to think that you knew me directly!" I remarked that I had read his adventures very often, and his features were quite familiar to me from the published portraits' (*MHC* III, 53).

Selling almost 70,000 copies of the first number, the new serial declined in popularity until the resumption of Master Humphrey's tale of Little Nell, which had begun in the

---

[11] Elizabeth M. Brennan, *OCS* 'Introduction', iv–x; Robert L. Patten, *Charles Dickens and his Publishers* (Oxford: Clarendon Press, 1978), 110–11. See also Joan Stevens, '"Woodcuts dropped into the Text": The Illustrations in *The Old Curiosity Shop* and *Barnaby Rudge*', *Studies in Bibliography* 20 (1967): 113–34.

[12] Charles Dickens, *Master Humphrey's Clock and A Child's History of England*, introd. Derek Hudson, The Oxford Illustrated Dickens (Oxford: Oxford University Press, 1958), 1, 5–11. This *Clock* source provides excerpts from the periodical, and numbers them as chapters in Roman numerals. Chapter VI contains insertions of Humphrey's voice between instalments of the *Shop* that do not appear in the Clarendon edition, adds his voice (no longer in a 'chapter') at the end of *Clock* introducing *Barnaby Rudge*, and finally supplies the wind-up of the *Clock* after the conclusion of *Rudge*. All further references to this edition will appear parenthetically in the text by chapter number (Roman) and page number with the abbreviation *MHC*.

[13] Jeremy Tambling, *Going Astray: Dickens and London* (Harlow: Pearson Longman, 2009), 79.

[14] Brennan, *OCS* 'Introduction', xiv.

fourth weekly number published on 25 April 1840.[15] Returning in the seventh number (16 May 1840), Nell's story was interspersed among tales of Master Humphrey and the Pickwick characters until the 12th number (20 May 1840), after which *Shop* continued until its finish in number 45 (6 February 1841).[16] *Shop* became an international sensation; British sales of the final instalments reached 100,000 and it was equally popular in the United States.[17] *Barnaby Rudge*, Dickens's historical novel of the 1780 Gordon Riots in London, appeared in numbers 46 (13 February 1841) to 88 (4 December 1841), where Dickens also closed *Clock* by returning to the framing narrative to report Old Humphrey's death, followed by the breakup of the reading group and the stopping of his old clock (*MHC* VI, 110–17).

Recent criticism has drawn greater attention to *Clock* as an innovative publishing venture and intriguing narrative frame for the two novels Dickens published in its pages. By positing a kinship between Old Humphrey's clock and the clock in the tower of St Paul's cathedral (*MHC* VI, 108–9), Dickens's serial identifies the time of narration with national time, and therefore connects *Clock* itself to the collective reading time of its transnational audience. Robert L. Patten sees the emergence of *Shop* within *Clock*'s miscellaneous narratives as an expression of a highly lucrative version of authorship that Dickens developed in the relay between his earlier publishing persona as the editor 'Boz' and his growing authority over his own work (and its remuneration) as the famous popular novelist, 'Charles Dickens'.[18] Jonathan H. Grossman illuminates the structuring of *Shop*'s plot via the interconnected methods of early Victorian transportation—the stage-coaching system, canal-barge, horse-drawn carriage, and trekking on foot—exactly during the 1840s period that a standard railway time was also being extended, with 'London ... always a hub'. Grossman views the tragic plot's emphasis on transit and failed connections as creating a complex omniscient perspective representing the shared national clock time of the Victorian public transport network.[19] Holly Furneaux links the new critical approach of 'thing theory' to queer theory and age studies by accounting for Master Humphrey's affectionate treatment of his clock not as a commodity form but rather as a 'machine capable of fellow feeling', creating a relationship which functions, as its manuscripts are distributed from hand to hand, as a 'tactile and emotional conduit' joining the members of his reading circle of disabled, elderly men, and extending to *Clock*'s circulation among a larger reading audience.[20] Elaine Freedgood differentiates the 'Victorian thing culture' visible in Dickens's writings from commodity culture,

---

[15] Hudson, *MHC* 'Introduction', vi.
[16] Brennan, *OCS* 'Introduction', xl–xli.
[17] Patten, *Charles Dickens and his Publishers*, 110–11.
[18] Robert L. Patten, *Charles Dickens and 'Boz': The Birth of the Industrial-Age Author* (Cambridge: Cambridge University Press, 2012), chapter 6.
[19] Jonathan H. Grossman, *Charles Dickens's Networks: Public Transport and the Novel* (Oxford: Oxford University Press, 2012), 102; 153; 85.
[20] Holly Furneaux, 'Dickens, Sexuality, and the Body; or Clock Loving: Master Humphrey's Queer Objects of Desire', in Juliet John (ed.), *Dickens and Modernity* (Cambridge: D. S. Brewer, 2012), 41–59, 48, 45–6.

arguing that 'thing culture' is recognized by 'cultural practices' such as 'the keeping of keepsakes' or the love for a familiar old clock, where 'personal, random value trumps exchange value; apparently meaningless things can suddenly become legally legible, or luminous, or life-altering'.[21]

Curiosity, Gambling, Temporality

The theme of curiosity provides one of the most prominent examples of *Shop*'s tendency, as noted by Adorno, to interchange the objective and the subjective: 'whenever psychology seems to be appearing it gets taken up in the objective meanings that are on display'.[22] Just as Nell's unfinished story provokes the compelling curiosity that leads to its extension into a serial novel, so do the curious objects surrounding her provide an objective impulse for her trajectory within the narrative, and a material cause for her fate, as Master Humphrey's account of his own curiosity upon encountering Nell implies: 'It would be a curious speculation ... to imagine her in her future life, holding her solitary way among a crowd of wild grotesque companions; the only pure, fresh, youthful object in the throng. It would be curious to find—' (*OCS* 1, 19). Master Humphrey's body objectively motivates his desire to escape the attention which his deformity often attracts by wandering the streets of London at night, thus also allowing him to pursue his speculative reveries (*MHC* I, 7–9; *OCS* 1, 5–6). This habit fits the detached social profile of the *flâneur*, also shared by Dickens himself in his own habitual night walks and described by French writers such as Honoré de Balzac and Charles Baudelaire. The *flâneur* wanders through the city streets observing passing faces in crowds, but his distinctive approach involves not idleness or aimless curiosity but 'a kind of paradoxical form of activity, a kind of negative capability permitting a special heightened form of observation'.[23]

Pedagogical transactions and impulses of friendship form contrasting connotations of curiosity to the detachment of *flânerie*. For example, Dick Swiveller, an improvident law clerk, becomes curious about the 'small servant' of his employers, Sampson and Sally Brass, who is locked up in the cellar kitchen every night, beaten and starved, and whom he discovers 'looking through the keyhole for company' (*OCS* 57, 443) and watching him play cribbage against himself. Dick decides to call her the 'Marchioness', regales her with beef and purl (ale heated and mixed with gin, sugar, and ginger, consumed early in the morning by labourers), and joins her in the cellar, teaching her to play cribbage for imaginary stakes. Afterward, a theatrically inspired soliloquy reveals Swiveller's curiosity as the beginning of a friendship: 'This Marchioness ... is a very extraordinary

---

[21] Elaine Freedgood, 'Commodity Criticism and Victorian Thing Culture: The Case of Dickens', in Eileen Gillooly and Deirdre David (eds), *Contemporary Dickens* (Columbus: Ohio State University Press, 2009), 152–68, 157.
[22] Adorno, 'An Address', 96.
[23] Michael Hollington, 'Dickens the Flâneur', *The Dickensian* 77, 2 (Summer 1981): 71–87, 74.

person—surrounded by mysteries, ignorant of the taste of beer, unacquainted with her own name (which is less remarkable), and taking a limited view of society through the keyholes of doors—can these things be her destiny, or has some unknown person started an opposition to the decrees of fate? It is a most inscrutable and unmitigated staggerer!' (*OCS* 58, 448–9). She later escapes from the Brasses' custody in order to care for Swiveller during his long illness, thus rendering him, as she terms him, a 'Liverer' (*OCS* 64, 496). Their friendship based in a grateful return of care is possible in the comic London plot, which is divided by alternating instalments from Nell's tragic plot of flight from London with her grandfather and their long trek through the wasted industrial landscape of the West Midlands to Shropshire, followed by her premature death.

Shop's tragic plot revises the didactic strategies of Evangelical religious tracts, distributed by the millions to the poor, to produce a new form of narrative didacticism which replaces conversion and social deference with benevolent forms of curiosity. The scene of Nell's Bible reading in the Gothic chapel (*OCS* chapter 53), for example, remediates the pious reading associated with Victorian schooling, opening up the question of what other kinds of secularized reading practices, both individual and collective, became associated with Dickens's novels and how they competed with and adapted other forms of cheap publication and popular print genres.[24]

The novel's gambling theme also injects an anti-Providential stance into the allegorical plot described by Adorno, in which 'social criticism and the representation of objective realities coalesce'.[25] Old Trent imagines his gaming as a way to 'make amends' to Nell for their poverty and suffering: 'Patience—patience, and we'll right thee yet, I promise thee', he tells her, 'Lose today, win tomorrow. And nothing can be won without anxiety and care—nothing' (*OCS* 30, 234–5). In place of the gambler's self-serving logic, the implied author, in the wake of Nell's funeral in the final chapter, provides a different ethic of service that transforms the pain of loss into a multiplication of good deeds: 'When Death strikes down the innocent and young, for every fragile form from which he lets the panting spirit free, a hundred virtues rise, in shapes of mercy, charity, and love, to walk the world, and bless it' (*OCS* 72, 563). This moral chimes with Dickens's retrospective comments in an 1841 speech about his intentions in writing *Shop*: 'If I have put into my book anything which can fill the young mind with better thoughts of death, or soften the grief of older hearts; if I have written one word which can afford pleasure or consolation to old or young in time of trial, I shall consider it as something achieved—something which I shall be glad to look back upon in after life.'[26] This speech also shows the importance Dickens accorded to *Shop* as a model for his personal connection to his reading audience: 'I feel as if the deaths of the fictitious creatures, in which you have been kind enough to express an interest, had endeared us to each other as real afflictions

---

[24] See Sarah Winter, *The Pleasures of Memory: Learning to Read with Charles Dickens* (New York: Fordham University Press, 2011), chapters 3 and 4.

[25] Adorno, 'An Address', 97.

[26] Charles Dickens, speech on 25 June 1841, at a banquet in his honour at Edinburgh, in *The Speeches of Charles Dickens*, ed. K. J. Fielding (Oxford: Clarendon Press, 1960), 8–15, 10.

deepen friendships in actual life; I feel as if they had been real persons, whose fortunes we had pursued together in inseparable connexion, and that I had never known them apart from you.'[27]

In its treatment of the harm caused by gambling, *Shop* again exhibits its analytic grasp of mentalities associated with capitalist modernity, particularly the experience of new forms of temporality associated with risk. In his thoughts on gambling in *The Arcades Project*, Benjamin notes 'the significance of the temporal element in the intoxication of the gambler ... [which] depends on the peculiar capacity of the game to provoke presence of mind through the fact that, in rapid succession, it brings to the fore constellations which work—each one wholly independent of the others—to summon up in every instance a thoroughly new, original reaction from the gambler'.[28] In his discussion of the novel's theorization of money, Matthew Rowlinson calls its mystery 'the secret of an extravagant love that repeatedly sets its object at risk—a gambler's love, or a novelist's'.[29] Thomas Hood writes in 1840 of Old Trent's hypocrisy that 'No one ever played, as a practice, except for the sake of play; and the old man's gambling has just as much to do with his love of Nelly, as gambling on the turf with the love of horses, or on the Stock Exchange with the love of country'.[30] In juxtaposition to Benjamin's archival montage in *The Arcades Project*, Hood's comment on gambling not only illuminates the social criticism in *Shop*, but also indicates how future research in Victorian-era reviews and careful study of their styles of analysis can inform new readings of Dickens's fiction.

We also notice this heightened awareness of temporality in the sensory effects achieved through description, as when the group of rescuers, including Kit, the single gentleman (Old Trent's brother), and Mr Garland, finally arrive past midnight at the snowbound Gothic ruin of the church and adjoining buildings where Nell and her grandfather have found refuge (Figure 9.2):

> The old church tower, clad in a ghostly garb of pure cold white again rose up before them, and a few moments brought them close beside it. A venerable building—grey, even in the midst of the hoary landscape. An ancient sun-dial on the belfry wall was nearly hidden by the snow-drift, and scarcely to be known for what it was. Time itself seemed to have grown dull and old, as if no day were ever to displace the melancholy night. (*OCS* 70, 547)

Such mixed representations incorporating immediate sensory and more abstract temporal effects also create depictions of acute mental tension—in this case the agony and

---

[27] Ibid. 9.
[28] Benjamin, *The Arcades Project*, O12a, 2, 512–13. For further discussion of Old Trent's gambling in light of Benjamin's theories, see Gillian Piggott, *Dickens and Benjamin: Moments of Revelation, Fragments of Modernity* (Aldershot: Ashgate, 2012), 115–18.
[29] Matthew Rowlinson, *Real Money and Romanticism* (Cambridge: Cambridge University Press, 2010), 169.
[30] [Hood], '*Master Humphrey's Clock*. By "Boz"', 887.

FIGURE 9.2 George Cattermole, 'The ruin in snow', *The Old Curiosity Shop*, wood engraving, in *Master Humphrey's Clock*, 16 January 1841.

General Collection, Beinecke Rare Book and Manuscript Library, Yale University

suspense shared by the searchers for Nell and the reader—inviting further research into the novel's creation of reality effects through ostentatiously aesthetic means.

As Kit approaches the cottage, 'there was such a silence all around, that he felt sure he could have heard even the breathing of a sleeper, if there had been one there' (*OCS* 70, 549). Instead of the faint sound of breathing, however, Kit hears through the door

> a curious noise inside. It was difficult to determine what it was. It bore a resemblance to the low moaning of one in pain, but it was not that, being far too regular and constant. Now it seemed a kind of song, now a wail—seemed, that is, to his changing fancy, for the sound itself was never changed or checked. It was unlike anything he had ever heard, and in its tone there was something fearful, chilling, and unearthly. (*OCS* 70, 550)

Here we find another attribution of 'curious', this time to the extreme and strangely objectified suffering of Nell's grandfather—who resembles a broken mechanism—bemoaning and yet denying that there is no sleeper in the adjoining room, but the dead child: 'With limbs huddled together, head bowed down, arms crossed upon the breast, and fingers tightly clenched, [the figure] rocked to and fro upon its seat without a moment's pause, accompanying the action with the mournful sound he had heard' (*OCS* 71, 551). The topic of curiosity, far from having been exhausted in previous criticism, warrants further investigation, not least in regard to *Shop*'s insights into modern pathologies related to speculation, both monetary, epistemological, and ethical, and their linkage to the affects, rituals, and consolations surrounding death and mourning.

Nell too exhibits a benevolent and poignant curiosity through her peculiar habit during her stay with Mrs Jarley of following the poor apprentice teacher from Miss Monflathers's school and her younger sister after witnessing their emotional reunion: '[Nell] would often think, if she had such a friend as [the older sister] to whom to tell her griefs, how much lighter her heart would be—that if she were but free to hear that voice, she would be happier' (*OCS* 32, 250). In order to derive a shared 'consolation' from 'fictitious creatures'—to return to Dickens's hopes for *Shop*'s effects on readers—one should be able, like Nell, to believe in the possibility of non-exploitative imaginary friendships. As she was fading away, Nell finally voiced her desire to be identified to the sisters: 'She wished they could be told how much she thought about them, and how she had watched them as they walked together, by the river side at night' (*OCS* 72, 559). As an ideal reader of *Shop*'s exploration of the isolation and melancholy of modern life, Nell finds comfort in her 'sympathy with them and her recognition in their trials of something akin to her own loneliness of spirit' (*OCS* 42, 322).

The Dwarf and the Wax-Work Girl

Curiosity is also linked more threateningly to punitive or prurient forms of observation such as surveillance and voyeurism, both apparent in Nell's pursuit by and allegorical pairing with Quilp, who expresses sexual fantasies about Nell while observing her grandfather kissing her on the cheek: 'what a nice kiss that was—just upon the rosy part. What a capital kiss! ... Such a fresh, blooming, modest little bud, neighbour ... such a chubby, rosy, cosy, little Nell!' (*OCS* 9, 82). Both in London and while she is tramping through England and very vulnerable, Nell is in constant danger of being sexually trafficked. Pointing out that Master Humphrey first meets Nell near Covent Garden Market, where prostitutes were known to gather, Catherine Robson suggests that Quilp's overt lust for her is less disturbing to the reader than the ambiguous gazes of the novel's old men, evident in her grandfather's terrifying visit to her room at night to steal her money for his gambling. Robson argues that, although Nell's body is frequently depicted as 'supine' and in a kind of stasis unto death that seems meant to preserve her purity, 'in transferring working-class mobility to Nell, [Dickens] lays his heroine open to all kinds of threats' including 'a highly specific, body-centered eroticism'.[31] Examining the ubiquitous keyholes in *Shop* as 'a figure for certain openings in the body', William A. Cohen interprets the novel's exploration of sexuality in scenes of gazing, listening, and oral/aural interchange through apertures as a 'commingling' that also lends a queer erotic palpability to the reader's experience.[32]

Michael Hollington has observed 'how thoroughly and pervasively Dickens confuses the categories of persons and things'.[33] In addition to Nell's own appearance as a lifelike corpse displayed on her bed in Cattermole's illustration to the penultimate weekly instalment (30 January 1841) (Figure 9.3), *Shop* is replete with other artificial or inanimate human figures, including effigies on Gothic tombs, the replicas in Mrs Jarley's waxworks display, a ship's figurehead, Punch and Judy puppets, and even Quilp's 'deserted carcase' cast upon the bank of a 'dismal swamp' after his drowning in the Thames (*OCS* 67, 528). Katherine Inglis focuses on the automaton, 'a regular actor in Dickens's imaginative representations of the destabilization of human agency', appearing in *Shop* as the moving wax-work nun that Mrs Jarley installs above the door of the wax-works display to attract customers (*OCS* 32, 252). The nun automaton, according to Inglis, represents Nell in her role as an animated wax-works girl, and also links her 'with the characterization of female factory workers as docile automatous figures in contemporary discussions of machine-work', a further indication of Nell's loss of autonomy.[34] Disability studies also offer another important framework for innovative readings of *Shop*'s interrogations of prostheses and personhood. For example, Lara Karpenko points out that dwarfs, giants, and other unusual individuals were often exhibited at Victorian fairs as 'natural curiosities'. She argues that *Shop* contributed to 'a turning point in middle-class attitudes' in the 1840s 'from rejection of to emotional engagement with the freak', not least by depicting, through Quilp's evident 'sexual potency', the possibility of physical intimacy.[35] Heather Tilley has studied Dickens's gift in 1869 of 250 copies of *Shop* printed in embossed Boston type to American schools for the blind, focusing on educators' expectations that the novel's sentimental story would have a positive 'moralizing influence' on the purported 'emotional deficiencies' of students with visual impairments.[36]

---

[31] Catherine Robson, 'The Ideal Girl in Industrial England', *Journal of Victorian Culture* 3, 2 (1998): 197–233, 222–4.

[32] William A. Cohen, 'Interiors: Sex and the Body in Dickens', *Critical Survey* 17, 2 (2005): 5–19, 9, 13.

[33] Michael Hollington, 'The Voice of Objects in *The Old Curiosity Shop*', *Australasian Journal of Victorian Studies* 14, 1 (2009): 1–8, 1.

[34] Katherine Inglis, 'Becoming Automatous: Automata in *The Old Curiosity Shop* and *Our Mutual Friend*', *19: Interdisciplinary Studies in the Long Nineteenth Century* 6 (2008), <http://www.19.bbk.ac.uk>, 2–39, 1, 10. Accessed 6 June 2016.

[35] Lara Karpenko, '"Printed Words that Gave ... Pain": Embodied Response and Deformito-Mania in *The Old Curiosity Shop*', *Nineteenth-Century Studies* 24 (2010): 17–32, 17–18, 24.

[36] Heather Tilley, 'The Sentimental Touch: Dickens's *Old Curiosity Shop* and the Feeling Reader', *Journal of Victorian Culture* 16, 2 (August 2011): 226–41, 226.

FIGURE 9.3 George Cattermole, 'Nell dead', *The Old Curiosity Shop*, wood engraving, in *Master Humphrey's Clock*, 23 January 1841.

General Collection, Beinecke Rare Book and Manuscript Library, Yale University

Capitalism and the Law

Miss Monflathers, the school proprietress, also makes Nell into an object lesson for her female pupils: 'Don't you feel how naughty it is of you ... to be a wax-work child, when you might have the proud consciousness of assisting, to the extent of your infant powers, the manufactures of your country; of improving your mind by the constant contemplation of the steam-engine; and of earning a comfortable and independent subsistence of from two-and-nine-pence to three shillings per week?' (*OCS* 31, 244). This satire on didactic literature also foreshadows Nell's nightmare vision of poverty and unemployment in the tumultuous industrial town (*OCS* 45, 346–52), often viewed by critics as an allusion to Chartism, and revealing the exploitative logic of capitalism. Building on such approaches, we can understand how *Shop*'s critique of Victorian pedagogy's manufacturing of consent to the social order makes Nell a self-aware protagonist of literature targeted at the working classes. Hood observes that while Nell's character seems unlikely because she 'thinks, speaks, and acts in a style beyond her years', she accurately depicts how 'poverty and misfortune are apt to make advances of worldly knowledge to the young at a most ruinous discount—a painful sacrifice of the very capital of childhood'.[37] Hood's telling terms reveal that the 'capital of childhood', as source of her innocence and purity, also forms the basis of Nell's potential economic and sexual exploitation. Further connections between the novel's critique of industrial capitalism and studies of Victorian childhood and children's literature could follow from this configuration.

Nell's and her grandfather's flight from London is also an escape from Quilp—'the very epitome of the bourgeois profit seeker' according to Adorno—who takes ownership of the curiosity shop in forfeiture for Old Trent's gambling debts.[38] Adorno concludes that '[t]he crisis that this industrial world has engendered—identified as unemployment by Dickens—is decisive for Nell's life; she dies as a sacrificial victim ... atoning for the injustice that prevails here'.[39] Reconsidering Adorno's account, Andrew McCann investigates 'the way in which *Shop* carries within it a certain sort of self-consciousness about its own ability to make meaning out of the base materiality of the nineteenth century'.[40] Nell's passage through the devastated zones of the factory and industrial town, for McCann, poses the question: 'how can the material traces of the past articulate the matter and the lives destroyed in the course of their own production?'[41] The depictions in *Shop* of both historical ruins and the environmental destruction and refuse of industrialization, particularly in its striking illustrations, also prompt further analysis in light of the new field of ecocritcism. Emphasizing the importance of 'visual reading' in the Victorian response to the novel and its images, art historian Dominic Janes analyses the 'complexity of early Victorian attitudes to gothic material culture', as revealed by the 'divergent sensibilities' of the multiple illustrators of *Clock*.[42]

Shop also continues Dickens's satirical attacks on the legal system launched in *Pickwick*. The crime of 'combinings together of friends ... which the law terms conspiracies' (*OCS* 62, 479), and which Quilp's lawyer, Sampson Brass, and his sister Sally perpetrate against Kit by framing him for theft on Quilp's orders in revenge for Kit's insults and defiance, is one of multiple conspiracies in the novel. Kit's exoneration and Sampson Brass's punishment suggest that the legal system can correct its errors. However, Dickens's plan to attack the 'worthies' of law and state in *Clock* appears in a

---

[37] [Hood], '*Master Humphrey's Clock*. By "Boz"', 887.
[38] Adorno, 'An Address', 98.
[39] Adorno, 'An Address', 100.
[40] Andrew McCann, 'Ruins, Refuse, and The Politics of Allegory in *The Old Curiosity Shop*', *Nineteenth-Century Literature* 66, 2 (September 2011): 170–94, 174.
[41] Ibid., 189.
[42] Dominic Janes, 'The Gothic Arousal of Architecture in Dickens's *The Old Curiosity Shop* and its Illustrations', *Nineteenth-Century Contexts* 35, 3 (2013): 325–41, 327–8.

FIGURE 9.4 Hablot K. Browne, 'Quilp beating the figurehead', *The Old Curiosity Shop*, wood engraving, in *Master Humphrey's Clock*, 19 November 1840.

General Collection, Beinecke Rare Book and Manuscript Library, Yale University

more subtle and potent form in another scene of droning recitation, akin to Old Trent's mournful denials of Nell's death, but overheard by Sampson Brass on a visit to Quilp's ramshackle counting house next to the Thames.[43] On entering, Sampson perceives a ship's figurehead 'intended for the effigy of some famous admiral': ' "Is it like Kit—is it his picture, his image, his very self?" cried the dwarf, aiming a shower of blows at the insensible countenance, and covering it with deep dimples' (*OCS* 62, 477–9). As he whacks and brands this figurehead with a fragment of detritus, 'a rusty iron bar, which he used in lieu of a poker' (*OCS* 62, 478) (Figure 9.4), Quilp recites over and over in 'rather a kind of chant than a song; being a monotonous repetition of one sentence in a very rapid manner, with a long stress upon the last word, which he swelled into a dismal roar' the following words: 'The worthy magistrate, after remarking that the prisoner would find

[43] *PLets* 1:562–5, 564.

some difficulty in persuading a jury to believe his tale, committed him to take his trial at the approaching sessions; and directed the customary recognizances to be entered into for the pro-se-cu-tion' (*OCS* 62, 476).[44] Quilp is intoning a newspaper report on Kit's indictment that he has just been reading (*OCS* 62, 478). The conspiracy here connects the public's curiosity about press reports on criminal proceedings to both the magistrate's inability to credit Kit's protestations of innocence, and to Quilp's desire to destroy Kit by means of the law.

There is a violently pedagogical tendency to this satirical scene, like others in the novel in which figures from fairy tales or didactic literature—a dwarf, a naughty child sent to bed without her dinner, a cruel pedagogue or neglectful parent, and an honest apprentice fallen into the hands of villains—are arrayed in the grotesque tableaux noticed by Adorno.[45] In this instance, the dwarf, while flagrantly punishing a replica of Kit, is also indirectly inflicting a sadistic and vengeful object lesson in effigy on admirals and magistrates, the figureheads and authorities of the British state. Future work in the Victorian law and literature field could be alive to such intersections of legal, political, economic, and educational genres, concepts, and practices in Dickens's writings, particularly in their contestations of abuses of authority.

The Failed Rescue and Comparative Studies

G. K. Chesterton observed that the 'artistic idea' of *Shop* can be captured in the summation that 'all the good powers and personalities in the story should set out in pursuit of one insignificant child, to repair an injustice to her, should track her from town to town all over England with all the resources of wealth, intelligence, and travel, and should all—arrive too late'.[46] This narrative arc reappears in the twentieth-century German writer W. G. Sebald's *Austerlitz* (2001), an enigmatic narrative centred on the search for his lost identity of Jacques Austerlitz, who learns as an adult that he was evacuated from Prague to London on a *Kindertransport* in the summer of 1939 at the age of 4. As he pieces together his history, he discovers that his mother, Agáta, who had placed him on the train to rescue him, was deported by the Nazis during the winter of 1941 to the Theresienstadt Jewish ghetto. After her deportation, officials emptied out Agáta's and other deportees' apartments of their confiscated 'abandoned objects', which were taken away, meticulously sorted and catalogued, and warehoused.[47]

---

[44] Adorno, 'An Address', 98.
[45] Ibid., 97.
[46] G. K. Chesterton, *Appreciations and Criticisms of the Works of Charles Dickens* (1911; reprint New York: Haskell House, 1970), 53.
[47] W. G. Sebald, *Austerlitz*, trans. Anthea Bell (New York: Random House, 2001), 180.

Recounting to the unnamed narrator his visit to Prague in 1993, where a series of revelations about his identity occurred, Austerlitz describes his trip to Terezín, the town near the site of the Theresienstadt camp. He wanders through the deserted streets until he chances upon one of the few shops, 'THE ANTIKOS BAZAR'. He stands gazing through the afternoon into the large display windows, 'in what proved to be the vain hope that someone might arrive and open this curious emporium [*dieses seltsame Magazin aufschließen würde*]'.[48] Among the miscellaneous items in the window of this curiosity shop, Austerlitz sees a figurine, captured in one of the photographs 'dropped into' Sebald's text, and wonders

> [W]hat was the meaning of... the ivory-colored porcelain group of a hero on horseback turning to look back, as his steed rears up on its hindquarters, in order to raise up with his outstretched left arm an innocent girl already bereft of her last hope, and to save her from a cruel fate not revealed to the observer? They were all as timeless as that moment of rescue, perpetuated but forever just occurring, these ornaments, utensils, and mementoes stranded in the Terezín bazaar, objects that for reasons one could never know had outlived their former owners and survived the process of destruction, so that I could now see my own faint shadow image barely perceptible among them.[49]

Even though the figurine may represent Austerlitz's own ambiguous 'timeless moment of rescue', it is among the objects that evoke the unrescued dead of Theresienstadt and the ruins left behind by the Nazi genocide of the Jews. Thus this possible allusion to Dickens's novel 'full of mysteries' in Sebald's own mysterious text suggests that *Shop* is not just a sentimental or allegorical tale of sacrifice and atonement, but it also charts a persistent historical narrative of the collective failure to rescue the innocent from acts of violence and injustice. And like *Shop*, Sebald's narrative surrounds the figure of an 'insignificant' child—that is, anyone's very significant child—with 'stranded [*gestrandeten*]' objects that 'have outlived their owners [*ihre ehemaligen Besitzer überlebt ... hatten*]'.[50] In Austerlitz's case, such 'mementoes' recollect the confiscated belongings of the deported, and thus the loss of his mother. In seeing his reflection in the window, Austerlitz too, like the 'wax-works child', is incorporated among these objects that had 'survived the process of destruction [*den Prozeß der Zerstörung überdauert hatten*]'.[51] Sebald's ANTIKOS BAZAR, then, akin to Dickens's curiosity shop, is a memory place of solitude, incongruity, and melancholy, where persons and things have been equally reduced to remnants bereft of their identities and attachments.

Making this connection between Sebald and Dickens draws further attention to the sustained critical interest in comparative approaches to *Shop*, its influences, and

---

[48] Sebald, *Austerlitz*, trans. Anthea Bell, 194; W. G. Sebald, *Austerlitz* (Frankfurt am Main: Fischer, 2001), 281.
[49] Sebald, *Austerlitz*, trans. Anthea Bell, 197.
[50] Sebald, *Austerlitz* (Frankfurt am Main), 284–5.
[51] Ibid.

international dissemination, including Michael Hollington's translation of Adorno's essay. The novel also played a central role in Fyodor Dostoevsky's 'transmogrifications' of Dickens's plots and characters, according to Loralee MacPike.[52] Gillian Piggott's recent book *Dickens and Benjamin*, which traces intriguing affinities between the writings of Dickens and Benjamin, also centres on *Shop*. Richard Maxwell has explored the novel in the context of convergences between Dickens's mysteries of London and Victor Hugo's mysteries of Paris.[53] Matthew Beaumont has observed that the more sinister implications of Old Humphrey's night walking and interest in Nell reappear in novels by Robert Louis Stevenson, James Joyce, and Vladimir Nabokov.[54] Extending this trend and magnifying its scope, a three-volume collection of essays surveying European translations of and responses to Dickens's writings was published in 2013.[55] The literary and critical interest in *Shop* also extends beyond Europe and North America. Japanese writer Kenzaburo Oe published *Legion of Quilp*, a novel based on *Shop*, in 1988.[56] In terms similar to Adorno and Benjamin, Salman Rushdie has described how his own early novels were strongly influenced by Dickens's 'real innovation: namely, his unique combination of naturalistic backgrounds and surreal foregrounds', and he views Dickens as 'a quintessentially Indian writer' due to the ways that Dickensian London 'seemed to me to hold up the mirror to the pullulating cities of India'.[57] This sampling of both subtle echoes and overt reworkings of Dickens's fictions by an international group of writers and critics indicates that in future studies of the global reach of Dickens's writings and influence, *The Old Curiosity Shop*, 'full of [the] mysteries' and anachronisms of modernity, will continue to play a prominent role.[58]

Further Reading

John Bowen, 'Spirit and the Allegorical Child: Little Nell's Mortal Aesthetic', in Wendy S. Jacobson (ed.), *Dickens and the Children of Empire* (Basingstoke: Palgrave Macmillan, 2000), 13–28

Joel J. Brattin, 'Dick Swiveller's Bed', *Dickens Quarterly* 26, 3 (September 2009): 165–74

---

[52] Loralee MacPike, *Dostoevsky's Dickens: A Study of Literary Influence* (Totowa, NJ: Barnes and Noble Books, 1981), 1.

[53] Richard Maxwell, *The Mysteries of Paris and London* (Charlottesville, VA, and London: University Press of Virginia, 1992).

[54] Matthew Beaumont, 'The Mystery of Master Humphrey: Dickens, Nightwalking, and *The Old Curiosity Shop*', *The Review of English Studies*, new series, 65, 268 (2013): 118–36.

[55] Maxime Leroy (ed.), *Dickens and Europe*, 3 vols (Newcastle-upon-Tyne: Cambridge Scholars Publishing, 2013).

[56] See Masaie Matsumura, 'Dickens in Japan', in John O. Jordan and Nirshan Perera (eds), *Global Dickens* (London: Routledge, 2012), 59–63.

[57] Salman Rushdie, 'Salman Rushdie on Jane Austen, Charles Dickens, and Influence', *Signature*, 5 October 2015, <http://www.signature-reads.com/2015/10/salman-rushdie-on-charles-dickens-jane-austen-and-influence>. Accessed 8 July 2016.

[58] Qtd in Walter Benjamin, letter to Wiesengrund-Adorno, Berlin, 11 October 1930.

Gareth Cordery, 'Quilp, Commerce and Domesticity: Crossing Boundaries in *The Old Curiosity Shop*', *Dickens Quarterly* 26, 4 (December 2009): 209–33

Jacob Jewusiak, 'No Plots for Old Men', *Novel: A Forum on Fiction* 46, 2 (Summer 2013): 193–213

John B. Lamb, 'The Wax Girl: Molding Little Nell in *The Old Curiosity Shop*', *Dickens Studies Annual* 44 (2013): 127–42

Hilary M. Schor, *Curious Subjects: Women and the Trials of Realism* (Oxford: Oxford University Press, 1974)

Helen Small, 'The Bounded Life: Adorno, Dickens, and Metaphysics', *Victorian Literature and Culture* 32, 2 (2004): 547–56

Richard Walsh, 'Why We Wept for Little Nell: Character and Emotional Involvement', *Narrative* 5, 3 (1997): 302–32

CHAPTER 10

BARNABY RUDGE AND THE JESUIT MENACE

MARK ESLICK

Introduction

PUBLISHED in the short-lived weekly magazine *Master Humphrey's Clock* in 1841, *Barnaby Rudge*, a melodramatic tale based around the anti-Catholic Gordon Riots of 1780, was problematic in its inception, composition, and publication. Dickens first conceived the story (originally called 'Gabriel Vardon: The Locksmith of London') in 1836, but found it difficult to begin and repeatedly delayed writing. This long gestation period was further complicated as Dickens broke a series of agreements with different publishers he had promised the book to. When the novel finally appeared it was a notable departure from the works of vivid life that had catapulted Dickens to literary acclaim. *Barnaby Rudge* marked a shift in subject matter, style, and tone that many of his readers found unsatisfying. Sales of *Master Humphrey's Clock* dropped dramatically over the course of its serialization and *Barnaby Rudge* has remained the least read and least liked of Dickens's novels ever since. Yet it is a far better book than its reputation suggests. It is a work filled with murder, mystery, intrigue, hauntings, and psychosexual energies, and one in which a spectacular public uprising is portrayed with great dramatic force. *Barnaby Rudge* is an important book in other ways. It marks a crucial point in the development of Dickens's artistic method and provides intriguing insights into his often-complex attitudes to history and politics. A fascinating, disturbing power seems to reside in the many dark corners and unresolved tensions of *Barnaby Rudge*. But this is especially true in the moments Dickens engages with Catholicism. Strangely, the primary subject matter of the book has tended to be overlooked. *Barnaby Rudge* is a novel that is shaped by an ideal of religious tolerance and is influenced by the moderate Protestant faiths, such as Unitarianism, that affected Dickens's social gospel of his early to middle period. Yet *Barnaby Rudge* appeared at a time when fierce anti-Catholic feeling was once again escalating to become a prominent feature of English life. Dickens's tale of the riots of 'Eighty allowed him to focus and explore a potentially destructive religious force at work in contemporary society.

Critical Interpretations

Barnaby Rudge marks a departure from Dickens's early episodic books. However, Dickens's draughtsmanship of the novel is generally only gestured towards. The shape of *Barnaby Rudge*, for example, has been equally praised and disparaged, but mostly superficially. Two critics, though, have explored the craftsmanship and experimental achievement of *Barnaby Rudge* in some depth. Jack Lindsay has discussed how Dickens almost entirely defines the essence of violent social upheaval through a series of symbolic devices, dynamic chiaroscuro effects, and clusters of poetic imagery.[1] Thomas J. Rice has also considered Dickens's artistry and argues that *Barnaby Rudge* can be read as his first real work of maturity. Focusing on Dickens's extensive use of analogy, time as a structural and figurative device, and, lastly, the narrative point of view, Rice highlights how Dickens uses narrative techniques and images to produce a 'coherent, unified whole' that is a 'clear anticipation of the organically unified late novels'.[2]

Barnaby Rudge is certainly not without fault. Yet, as Lindsay and Rice show, it is important to recognize the successes of Dickens's innovations here. The mental processes of several characters, most notably Barnaby, are more fully developed than in Dickens's previous books. Also, there is a heavy reliance on images of pervading darkness to suggest dangerous forces. How an intricate network of relationships compensates for the absence of a central character is also an ambitious innovation. And the narrative point of view is particularly striking. 'Chroniclers', writes Dickens, 'are privileged to enter where they list, to come and go through keyholes, to ride upon the wind, to overcome, in their soarings up and down, all obstacles of distance, time and place.'[3] Free from such constraints, the omniscient eye in *Barnaby Rudge* arguably establishes the celebrated cinematic vision that is fully realized in *Bleak House*.

History, rather than the artistry of the novel, has been the dominant line of critical enquiry into *Barnaby Rudge*. A recurring critical view is that Dickens simply set himself the task of writing a serious historical novel early in his career to emulate Sir Walter Scott, and that he did not have any real interest in the complexities of historical processes. G. K. Chesterton, for example, believed that Dickens 'Undoubtedly ... knew no history'[4]

---

[1] See Jack Lindsay, 'Barnaby Rudge', in John Gross and Gabriel Pearson (eds), *Dickens and the Twentieth Century* (London: Routledge and Kegan Paul, 1966), 91–106.

[2] Thomas J. Rice, 'The End of Dickens's Apprenticeship: Variable Focus in *Barnaby Rudge*', *Nineteenth-Century Fiction*, 30, 2 (September 1975): 172–84.

[3] *Barnaby Rudge*, ed. Clive Hurst, Oxford World's Classics (Oxford: Oxford University Press, 2003), chapter 9, page 79. Subsequent references are inserted parenthetically in the text by *BR* chapter, page.

[4] G. K. Chesterton, *Chesterton on Dickens* (London: Dent, 1992), 70.

and many others have echoed this idea.[5] Admirers of the novel, however, have read it as a serious attempt by Dickens to articulate a philosophy of history. Patrick Brantlinger presents a strong case for Dickens's 'visionary intensity' and the way *Barnaby Rudge* tries to present a philosophy of 'grotesque populism'.[6] Dickens's portrayal of the 1780 Gordon Riots, at the time of writing 'the largest, deadliest and most protracted urban riots in British history',[7] certainly shows him having a far from shallow acquaintance with history and a keen interest in an important historical event that continued to resonate in the 1840s. His depiction of the events of the riots, in particular the graphic accounts of the burning of Langdale's distillery and the storming of Newgate Prison, show Dickens's flair for adapting historical action to demonstrate how a host of social and political abuses work to create a violent uprising. This promotes the simple historical vision he states in the preface, that the Gordon Riots 'teach a good lesson' (*BR* Preface, 6).

Yet, as John Bowen shows, *Barnaby Rudge* is 'an unusual and deviant example'[8] of the historical novel form. *Barnaby Rudge* shares many traits with the historical novels of Scott, William Harrison Ainsworth, and other nineteenth-century historical novelists. But it goes against the traditional historical form in certain ways, especially in its mingling of fact and fiction. Indeed, as Bowen notes, it is not until Chapter the Thirty-Fifth, with the introduction of Lord George Gordon, that 'anything remotely like an historical event takes place'.[9] It is, though, the uncanny effects the reader constantly encounters that are peculiarly innovative. They work to give *Barnaby Rudge* a far more intriguing sense and vision of history than is generally recognized. From the opening chapter's description of the Maypole Inn, with its emphasis on cycles of growth and decay that reflect the process of history itself, to the constant reiteration of time and the absurdity of turning the clock back, to the weird repetitions (of names, relations, events, dates, dreams, and so on), Dickens uses the Gothic mode to produce 'a more complex sense of the strangeness of historical events and the inability of human intentions and actions to influence them'.[10]

Another critical commonplace is that *Barnaby Rudge* is only superficially about the past and that it is really a 'tract for its time'. It is almost customary to say that by writing about the Gordon Riots Dickens was really writing about the charged political situation of 1840s England, especially the threat of Chartism. The five-year delay between Dickens's idea and the publication of *Barnaby Rudge* certainly increased its topicality. Between 1836 and 1841 Chartist agitation for political enfranchisement grew and led to widespread fears of social revolution. John Butt and Kathleen Tillotson, Steven Marcus, and others have therefore argued that Dickens progressively realized that the political

---

[5] See, for example, George Lukacs, *The Historical Novel* (Harmondsworth: Penguin, 1969), 290–2.
[6] Patrick Brantlinger, 'Did Dickens Have a Philosophy of History?', *Dickens Studies Annual* 30 (2001): 59–74.
[7] Linda Colley, *Britons: Forging the Nation 1707–1837* (London: Vintage, 1996), 352.
[8] John Bowen, 'Introduction' to *Barnaby Rudge*, ed. John Bowen (London: Penguin, 2003), xv.
[9] Ibid.
[10] Ibid., xvii.

conditions leading to the Gordon Riots were analogous to the potentially revolutionary situation in contemporary England.[11] *Barnaby Rudge*, this idea suggests, is a veiled commentary on Chartism as Chartist agitation formed the mental background of the author and his contemporary audience. Yet in the first full-length study of the novel, D. G. Paz's *Dickens and* Barnaby Rudge, the long-held critical claims that *Barnaby Rudge* is essentially about Chartism and is a political analogy have been carefully reconsidered.[12] Paz's detailed investigation shines an interesting light on the novel's critical history by showing that the supposed Chartist and political impulses behind the novel have been exaggerated or are unsupported by fact. Interestingly, Paz also highlights how the critical fixation with history and politics has obscured investigations into the central impulse of *Barnaby Rudge*: namely, the religious fanaticism that led to the anti-Catholic riots of 1780.

DICKENS, CATHOLICISM, AND THE JESUITICAL GASHFORD

Several studies have examined the importance of religion in Dickens's life and work. Dennis Walder's *Dickens and Religion*, for example, explores how Dickens's fundamental outlook as a liberal Protestant informs his writing and is expressed in remarkably different ways at different stages of his life.[13] And Janet L. Larson's *Dickens and the Broken Scripture* uncovers the pervasiveness and increasingly complex and dissonant role of religious allusions in Dickens's work.[14] But attacks on formal religion, or rather attacks on those who corrupt what Dickens believed to be true Christian values, are also a strong feature of his work. His antipathy to the spiritual gloominess of Dissent is well known. As early as 1836, in the anti-Sabbatarian pamphlet *Sunday Under Three Heads*, Dickens—publishing pseudonymously—charged Dissenting congregations as being 'stronghold[s] of intolerant zeal and ignorant enthusiasm'.[15] In his novels there are a number of fiercely satirical portraits of hypocritical Dissenters, the Reverends Stiggins in *The Pickwick Papers* and Chadband in *Bleak House* being among the more memorable, as well as a long line of zealous females, through which Dickens paints a wholly

---

[11] John Butt and Kathleen Tillotson, *Dickens at Work* (London: Methuen, 1957), 82–3; Steven Marcus, *Dickens: From Pickwick to Dombey* (London: W. W. Norton, 1965), 171–5.
[12] See D. G. Paz, *Dickens and* Barnaby Rudge (Monmouth: Merlin Press, 2006).
[13] Dennis Walder, *Dickens and Religion* (London: Allen and Unwin, 1981).
[14] Janet L. Larson, *Dickens and the Broken Scripture* (Athens: University of Georgia Press, 1985). Larson notes that Dickens alludes to the Bible and *The Book of Common Prayer* more than to any other texts.
[15] Timothy Sparks [Charles Dickens], *Sunday Under Three Heads* (London: Chapman and Hall, 1836), 8.

unflattering, though generally comic, portrait of Dissent as an abhorrent deviation from normative Anglicanism.

Roman Catholicism, though, is the religion widely considered to have aroused Dickens's strongest religious enmities. A consensus has formed among biographers and critics that he was staunchly anti-Catholic. Humphry House argues that 'In nothing was Dickens so much of an elementary John Bull as in his hatred of Roman Catholicism.' For Philip Collins the author had an 'ingrained English prejudice against ... the Catholic Church' that became 'an almost unqualified obsession'. Peter Ackroyd believes that Roman Catholicism was a 'pet hate' for Dickens. Andrew Sanders asserts that he had 'rooted anti-Catholic prejudices'; and Michael Slater speaks of his 'virulent anti-Catholicism'.[16] Yet up to the point of writing *Barnaby Rudge*, apart from admitting in the Preface that he 'has no sympathy with the Romish Church' (*BR* Preface, 6), very little anti-Catholic sentiment can be found in Dickens's letters, journalism, or fiction. He was certainly aware of the anti-Catholic sentiment that had become more pronounced in England since the 1820s. As a parliamentary reporter, Dickens followed the agitation over Catholic emancipation and subtle moments in his early novels suggest he was acutely aware of the general anti-Catholic feeling in the country.[17] As anti-Catholicism became a more pronounced feature of the social, cultural, and political landscape of England in the late 1830s and early 1840s, exacerbated by the rising prominence of the Anglo-Catholic Oxford Movement as well as mass Irish immigration, Dickens was alert to the ferocious cries of 'No Popery' that could again be heard on the streets. His tale of the 1780 riots therefore afforded him the opportunity to analyse a troubling force at work in contemporary society.

Barnaby Rudge is deeply sympathetic to victimized Catholics. Denying Catholics legal rights is shown to be absurd and unjust, especially through the principal Catholic character, Geoffrey Haredale, who suffers under these 'hard laws' (*BR* 43, 349). Sympathy for Catholic victims of the riots is even more pronounced. Catholic families 'terrified by the threats and warnings' (*BR* 61, 486) of their Protestant neighbours are shown fleeing their homes, and the reader is made to feel great pity for one family who sit 'trembling among their goods in the open street' as no one will hire them a cart because they 'professed the obnoxious religion' (*BR* 61, 486). Protestant extremism is condemned as the refuge of ignorant bigots who, for the most part, have no true religious feeling and who 'in their daily practice set at nought the commonest principles of right and wrong' (*BR* Preface, 6). The novel also registers scepticism about fears of a Catholic conspiracy. In Chapter the Thirty-Seventh, the popularity of Lord George Gordon's Protestant Association is attributed to the 'whispers of a confederacy among the Popish powers to degrade and enslave England, establish an inquisition in London, and turn the pens of Smithfield

---

[16] Humphry House, *The Dickens World* (London: Oxford University Press, 1941), 128; Philip Collins, *Dickens and Education* (London: Macmillan, 1965), 62–3; Peter Ackroyd, *Dickens* (Aylesbury: Minerva, 1991), 532; Andrew Sanders, *Charles Dickens* (Oxford: Oxford University Press, 2003), 144; Michael Slater, *Dickens and Women* (London: J. M. Dent, 1983), 86.

[17] Walder, *Dickens and Religion*, 95.

market into stakes and cauldrons' (*BR* 37, 294). But such whispers, we are told, are imaginary fears used only to incite religious hatred. They are 'by-gone bugbears which had lain quietly in their graves for centuries' and are only being 'raised again to haunt the ignorant and credulous' (*BR* 37, 294).

While the persecution of Catholics is condemned in *Barnaby Rudge*, Catholic characters are somewhat compromised and Catholicism is oddly constituted. Haredale, in particular, reflects negatively upon Catholicism. We never hear him talking about his faith or see him attending mass, but Dickens does include odd moments to give a sense of his Catholic frame of mind. Haredale, for example, warns Hugh, 'Gently with your light, friend. You swing it like a censer' (*BR* 34, 275) and he later muses on his home being 'another bead in the long rosary of his regrets' (*BR* 61, 490). Haredale's portrait suggests it is because of his Catholic faith that he has 'mused and brooded' when his 'spirit should have mixed with all God's great Creation' (*BR* 79, 631). Towards the end of the tale, Haredale atones for his sins by repairing to a presumably Catholic establishment 'known throughout Europe for the rigour and severity of its discipline' where he takes 'vows which ... shut him out from nature and his kind' and where he later dies and is 'buried in its gloomy cloisters' (*BR* The Last, 654). Asceticism is figured as unnatural and Dickens clearly feels the practice of seeking atonement through solitude is flawed.

Barnaby Rudge can therefore be read as deeply ambivalent towards Catholicism. Paradoxically, though, the novel plays upon fears about a nightmarish vision of a sinister network of Catholics conspiring to infiltrate, destabilize, and control England: the Protestant fantasy of the conspiring Jesuit. Judith Wilt has previously explored the idea of a Jesuitical presence in the novel. Wilt's fascinating reading argues that Sir John Chester is the novel's 'conspiring Jesuit' and that the continuing return of the Jesuit in literature 'plays out an English anxiety that the "Catholic" is in fact the authentic, and the "Protestant" a masquerade'.[18] But there is another character irrigated with classically Jesuitical qualities; a prevaricator and manipulator who orchestrates the Gordon Riots: Gashford, the secretary of Lord George Gordon. Gashford, though seemingly an extreme Protestant, is weirdly drawn through the language and images commonly used in anti-Jesuit literature and feeds into Victorian Protestant paranoia surrounding Jesuitical intrigue.

Jesuits loomed large in the Victorian Protestant imagination. Founded in 1540, the Society of Jesus had long been viewed by anti-Catholics as a secretive, militant organization bent upon Catholic world domination. Arriving in England in 1580, Jesuits were outlawed five years later as fears for English sovereignty focused on Jesuitism as a sign of religious and temporal invasion. Protestant propagandists throughout the seventeenth and eighteenth centuries continued to link the society to acts of conspiracy against the state, the most famous being the Gunpowder plot of 1605. The Jesuit order was suppressed by Pope Clement XIII in 1733, but its revival by Pope Pius VII in 1814 led to renewed and heightened suspicion of the figure of the Jesuit. The 1829 Catholic

---

[18] Judith Wilt, 'Masques of the English in *Barnaby Rudge*', *Dickens Studies Annual* 30 (2001): 75–94.

Emancipation Act encapsulated such fears. Jesuits were the only order to be named in the Act's legislation for 'the gradual Suppression and final Prohibition'[19] of all Catholic brotherhoods.

Victorian anti-Catholics inherited and cultivated these suspicions. Throughout the 1830s and 1840s Protestant Evangelicals created a wave of intense feeling against the society. Stories of Jesuitical intrigue were common in the mainstream press. *The Times*, for example, accused Newman, Pusey, and other prominent Tractarians of being 'Oxford Jesuits'[20] bent on corrupting the Established Church. Virulently anti-Catholic publications such as *The Bulwark, or, Reformation Journal* also printed rumours that Jesuits were living and working in every stratum of society, laying plots to subvert the constitution and destabilize the nation: 'Britain, ever since the Reformation, has been the especial object of Jesuitical craft and recklessness, and perhaps never more than at the present moment, … no means, foul or fair, will be left untried to subvert the Protestantism of this country'.[21] Anti-Catholic fiction fed into and fuelled fears of Jesuitical intrigue. Works such as the anonymous *The Jesuits Exposed* (1839) and *The Wandering Jew* (1844) by Eugene Sue crystallized the image of the Jesuit as an object of suspicion and fear. These and other sensationalized tales portrayed Jesuits as cunning, calculating, wicked men; suave masters of manipulation; sexually debauched lechers; and emissaries of Satan.[22] Such lurid tales heightened a feeling amongst the English that the Jesuits were a dangerous enemy in their midst.

A Victorian reader steeped in the anti-Jesuit literature of the day would have little trouble identifying Gashford as a Jesuitical figure.[23] Let us consider Dickens's first description of the character in *Barnaby Rudge*:

> Gashford, the secretary, was … angularly made, high shouldered, bony, and ungraceful. His dress, in imitation of his superior, was demure and staid in the extreme; his manner, formal and constrained. This gentleman had an overhanging brow, great hands and feet and ears, and a pair of eyes that seemed to have made an unnatural retreat into his head, and to have dug themselves a cave to hide in. His manner was smooth and humble, but very sly and slinking. He wore the aspect of a man who was always lying in wait for something that *wouldn't* come to pass; but he looked patient—very patient—and fawned like a spaniel dog. Even now, while he warmed

---

[19] Quoted in E. R. Norman, *Anti-Catholicism in Victorian England* (London: George Allen and Unwin, 1968), 138.

[20] *The Times*, 4 January 1839, p. 4.

[21] Anon., 'Popery Absolving Murders', *The Bulwark, or, Reformation Journal* 1 (1851–2): 212.

[22] For a survey of the language and images used to construct stereotypical evil Jesuits in Victorian fiction see Margaret M. Maison, *Search your Soul, Eustace* (London and New York: Sheed and Ward, 1961), 169–82.

[23] Gashford is a Dickensian invention, but his prototype, Dr Robert Watson, may have inspired Dickens to invest the character with Jesuitical qualities. Watson's life story, little of which can be verified, reads like that of a Jesuitical conspirator. For discussions of Watson as the inspiration for Gashford see W. Forbes Grey, 'The Prototype of "Gashford" in *Barnaby Rudge*', *Dickensian* 29, [227] (Summer 1933): 175–83 and Frank A. Gibson, 'Gashford and Gordon', *Dickensian* 44, [287] (Summer 1948): 124–9.

and rubbed his hands before the blaze, he had the air of one who only presumed to enjoy it in his degree as a commoner; and though he knew his lord was not regarding him, he looked into his face from time to time, and, with a meek and deferential manner, smiled as if for practice. (*BR* 35, 283)

Gashford is carefully invested with stock traits commonly associated with the figure of the Jesuit in anti-Catholic writing. Physically repulsive, unswervingly subservient, animalistic, hypocritical, devious, and manipulative: the character exudes Jesuitical qualities. Dickens's choice of adjectives—most notably, 'unnatural', 'smooth', 'sly', and 'slinking' (*BR* 35, 283)—have a strikingly familiar resonance with other contemporary representations of malevolent Jesuits. Indeed, throughout *Barnaby Rudge* Gashford's Jesuitness continues to be suggested through terms frequently employed by anti-Jesuit writers. Gashford is 'silky' (*BR* 35, 281), 'stealthy' (*BR* 36, 289), 'wily' (*BR* 37, 296), 'fawning' (*BR* 43, 343), 'servile, false' (*BR* 43, 349), 'crafty' (*BR* 49, 394), 'artful' (*BR* 50, 402), and 'cunning' (*BR* 53, 424).

Other stereotypical Jesuitical characteristics are grafted on to the character. His speech is almost always equivocal, particularly during his conversations with the deluded Lord George Gordon. He has more than a hint of sexual deviance. Haredale, for example, reveals that when Gashford was a young man he 'robbed his benefactor's daughter of her virtue' (*BR* 43, 349). And he is figured as Satanic: 'the secretary's face ... might have furnished a study for the devil's picture' (*BR* 44, 356).

Jesuitical tendencies are also suggested in the many references to the character's gaze. As Susan M. Griffin shows, in many Victorian anti-Catholic novels 'Jesuits keep custody of their eyes not in order to protect their own purity, but to mask their real identities.'[24] Gashford is constantly 'managing his eyes' (*BR* 37, 303) by either 'drawing his sleeve in a hasty way across his eyes' (*BR* 36, 290), or 'stealthily raising his eyes' only to let them 'drop again' when they meet another's 'steady gaze' (*BR* 43, 345). Furthermore, the narrator's frequent exposure of the seething hatred that lies just beneath the surface of Gashford's cool exterior resonates with a popular theme of anti-Jesuit literature: the idea of the Jesuit being 'exposed' or 'unmasked'.

Finally, there is a peculiar detail in Hablot K. Browne's illustration of Gashford entitled 'The Secretary's Watch' that reinforces the character's Jesuitness (Figure 10.1). We hear of the secretary's restlessness as he waits for the rioters to begin their destruction of the Warren, the home of Haredale: 'The secretary smiled, but he had other thoughts to dwell upon, and soon dismissed the topic. Dinner was brought him, but he sent it down untasted; and, in restless pacings up and down the room, and constant glances at the clock, and many futile efforts to sit down and read, or go to sleep, or look out of the window, consumed four weary hours. When the dial told him thus much time had crept away, he stole up stairs to the top of the house, and coming out upon the roof sat down, with his face towards the east' (*BR* 53, 427–8). Gashford is then pictured sitting on a rooftop and

---

[24] Susan M. Griffin, *Anti-Catholicism and Nineteenth-Century Fiction* (Cambridge: Cambridge University Press, 2004), 141.

FIGURE 10.1 Hablot K. Browne, 'The Secretary's Watch', *Barnaby Rudge*, wood engraving.

Illustration supplied courtesy of The British Library

somewhat strangely positioned behind him is a black cat that eerily mirrors his physical posture. Significantly, this is an image that Dickens would later use in *Pictures from Italy* when he condemns the Jesuits he encounters as power-hungry men who 'muster strong in the streets, and go slinking noiselessly about, in pairs, like black cats'.[25]

Representations of the Society of Jesus as loathsome primarily functioned as a Protestant tool to denigrate the Church of Rome. But the depiction of malevolent Jesuitical characters such as Gashford reveals a deeper anxiety that exceeds the question of denominational difference: the figure of the Jesuit embodies an anxiety concerning the fragility of England and English nationhood itself.

---

[25] *American Notes and Pictures from Italy*, introd. Sacheverell Sitwell, New Oxford Illustrated Dickens (London: Oxford University Press, 1957), chapter 5, page 296.

Victorian anti-Catholic writing frequently portrayed the Jesuit plot as a secular as well as religious menace. Jesuits were often associated with social destabilization and revolution, and Jesuitical incitement of unrest among the lower orders was a recurring theme of anti-Catholic literature. William Sewell's *Hawkstone; A Tale of and for England in 184–* (1846), for example, a text which places Jesuitism alongside anti-establishment movements such as Chartism and Fenianism, shows the villainous Jesuit Pearce cultivating upheaval and disruption among society's discontents.[26] Similarly, in *Barnaby Rudge*, Gashford preys upon the disenfranchised and incites their anarchic passions. He recruits and manipulates disillusioned characters such as Hugh through a cynical understanding of their frustrations. Gashford, the 'man that blows the fire' (*BR* 35, 288), also orchestrates the mob at every turn. During the attack on the Houses of Parliament he controls the violence of the mob with 'the gentlest motion of his arm' (*BR* 49, 394), and it is he who sets them upon their destruction of the Maypole and the Warren. Importantly, it is through Gashford's manipulation of the lower orders that the deep divisions within English society are exposed. As the mob he has incited gather at Westminster to present a petition against Catholic emancipation, the narrator tells us that although the crowd is 'sprinkled doubtless here and there with honest zealots' it was 'composed for the most part of the very scum and refuse of London, whose growth was fostered by bad criminal laws, bad prison regulations, and the worst conceivable police' (*BR* 49, 393).

Gashford's Jesuitical scheming therefore gives rise to reflection about the state of English society as the mob are shown to be easily susceptible to manipulation because they are completely dislocated from society. Hugh's cry to Gashford for him to 'Give us something to do with life in it—with life in it, Master' (*BR* 44, 354) is symbolic of the disenfranchisement of the rioters who are 'stimulated by their own headlong passions, by poverty, by ignorance, by the love of mischief, and the hope of plunder' (*BR* 53, 421). Detached from any sense of community, and without any formal political representation, the lower classes have been excluded from the fabric of society.

Barnaby Rudge's portrayal of a Jesuitical manipulator is central to the novel's theme of social fracture. It works to register disquiet about the alienating structure of English society. Conversely, though, the portrayal of a Jesuitical menace acts as a spur to the formation of English identity. As Maureen Moran argues, Victorian anti-Catholic portrayals of Jesuits created a 'figure of difference against which a healthy national identity can be imagined and articulated'.[27] Anti-Catholic literature did indeed tend to focus on the Jesuit as 'other' by positioning him outside normal boundaries. These characters were almost always invested with a mysterious aura, a sense of strangeness, or foreignness. One way anti-Catholic novelists created this sense of 'otherness' was by employing sinister images of spiders or serpents that dehumanized the Jesuit. For example, the anonymous

---

[26] See William Sewell, *Hawkstone; A Tale of and for England in 184–*, 2 vols (London: John Murray, 1846).

[27] Maureen Moran, *Catholic Sensationalism and Victorian Literature* (Liverpool: Liverpool University Press, 2007), 45.

writer of a later Victorian work called *A Glance at the Intrigues of the Jesuits, and their Allies, for the Humiliation of England, and the Extinction of the Protestant Religion*, one of the more unambiguously titled nineteenth-century anti-Jesuit texts, exemplified this trend by portraying Jesuits as 'deadly vipers in England's bosom ... twisting their horrid coils around her'.[28]

Barnaby Rudge plays upon this idea of the Jesuit as 'other'. Gashford is invested with a sense of strangeness. He is 'unnatural' (*BR* 35, 283) and, like many fictional Jesuits, he has an insect-like hideousness and a reptilian repulsiveness. Gashford has 'crawled and crept through life' (*BR* 43, 349) and has a 'cold insidious palm' (*BR* 48, 386). At times he even seems to be a pseudo-magical figure. During the riots he mysteriously vanishes from view and reappears from nowhere. This uncanny eeriness is noted by Dennis the hangman, who says, 'that 'ere quiet way of yours might almost wake a dead man' (*BR* 53, 422). By investing the Jesuitical Gashford with a strange sense of cultural otherness Dickens subtly reinforces Jesuit antipathy to English culture and, consequently, enables expression of normative English identity through opposition.

Gashford, then, is drawn through the anti-Jesuit language and imagery of the day that fuelled Victorian fears of the Society of Jesus. Dickens's Jesuitical figure, however, is a complex and over-determined one. Gashford may be Jesuitical, but he is never explicitly identified as a Jesuit. Indeed, a strange sense of ambiguity about his religious affiliations permeates the novel. Dickens achieves this ambiguity by playing upon what was arguably the dominant concern of anti-Jesuit propaganda: the idea of the Society of Jesus as a network of spies. Victorian anti-Jesuit narratives had an almost unqualified obsession with the idea of Jesuits being spies who were secretly infiltrating England. Gashford is similarly figured as a spy. During the riots he is seen walking 'stealthily about, listening to all he heard, and diffusing or confirming ... such false intelligence as suited his own purpose' (*BR* 50, 403). Moreover, his character is surrounded by the language of surveillance. Gashford is 'informed' (*BR* 50, 404), keeps a 'solitary watch' (*BR* 54, 429), and is a 'fit agent' (*BR* 81, 650). Towards the end of the novel it is no surprise that he has gathered information for nefarious political purposes and claims to have access to 'very important documents' which he has kept in 'secret drawers, and distributed in various places' (*BR* 71, 573–4). Crucially, however, the idea of Gashford being a spy for the 'Church of Rome' is disturbed when he ends his days working for the English Crown. Following his defeat by Edward Chester and Joe Willet, the secretary 'subsisted for a time upon his traffic in his master's secrets' and 'procured an appointment in the honourable corps of spies and eaves-droppers employed by the government' (*BR* The Last, 656).

Dickens also refuses to identify the character's faith in a stereotypical way. Gashford's life story *could* read like that of a conspiring Jesuit. Born and raised in the Catholic faith, he was educated by Jesuits at St Omer's College in France. His claim to have converted to Protestantism after having been 'stricken by the ... eloquence' of Lord George Gordon, a

---

[28] A Member of the University of Oxford, *A Glance at the Intrigues of the Jesuits, and their Allies, for the Humiliation of England, and the Extinction of the Protestant Religion* (Bristol: I. E. Chillcott, 1868), 5.

man he clearly regards with contempt, and immediately to have 'abjured the errors of the Romish church' (*BR* 35, 286), seems highly suspect. Cryptic moments in the text hint towards Gashford's Catholicity. For example, in the scene where his plan to kidnap Emma Haredale is thwarted we are told that, 'Gashford ... crouching yet malignant, raised his scowling face' (*BR* 71, 573). 'Malignant' is a term that carries a specifically religious meaning as it was used by early Protestants to describe the Roman Catholic Church.[29]

Yet Gashford, it seems, has been excommunicated from the Catholic Church. Haredale tells Gordon that the reason why the secretary converted to Protestantism is because he detests 'the altars where his vicious life was publicly denounced' (*BR* 43, 349). Early on in the novel it is actually suggested that Gashford has no religious affiliation whatsoever. Gordon tells the secretary of a dream he had of the two men becoming Jews. Speaking aloud to himself, Gashford scorns Gordon saying: 'Dreamed he was a Jew ... After a time ... I don't see why that religion shouldn't suit me as well as any other. There are rich men among the Jews; shaving is very troublesome;—yes, it would suit me well enough' (*BR* 37, 296). Purely motivated by power and greed, Gashford exploits religion, no matter what the form, for his own ends.

Barnaby Rudge, through the character of Gashford, the man at the heart of the anti-Catholic riots, strongly echoes contemporary anti-Catholic portraits of the Jesuit. And Dickens, by attaching such associations to Gashford, works to undermine his Protestant politics. Yet this is done in a rather strange, ambiguous way so that the novel also disrupts Protestant concerns of Catholic invaders seeking the destruction of English society. *Barnaby Rudge*, therefore, weirdly resists and revises the Victorian myth of Jesuitical nightmares.

A New Light on Dickens and Catholicism?

Barnaby Rudge's ambiguity towards Catholicism offers a fresh lens to view Dickens's relationship with the religion. From the early 1840s onwards Dickens's antipathies towards both Anglo-Catholicism and Roman Catholicism strengthened. He railed against the Catholic-flavoured ritualism of the Tractarians; in *Pictures from Italy* he attacked Roman Catholicism as a ridiculous, oppressive religion; and during the 1850 Papal Aggression his anti-Catholicism intensified to the point of him making pronouncements worthy of *The Protestant Magazine*.[30] Yet this should not overshadow the fact that in *Barnaby Rudge*

---

[29] See *Oxford English Dictionary* (Sense 6b). The only other occasion the word appears is when Gashford calls Gabriel Varden 'a malignant' who 'remains in outer darkness' (*BR* 36, 345) because of Varden's refusal to join the Protestant Association.

[30] For Dickens's opposition to the Oxford Movement see 'Report of the Commissioners', *The Examiner*, 3 June 1843. For his reaction to the Papal Aggressions see 'A Crisis in the Affairs of Mr John Bull', *Household Words*, 23 November 1850.

he supports tolerance for a persecuted Catholic minority. Importantly, neither should it obscure the fact that Catholicism spurs Dickens's creativity. Reading other moments in his fiction when he engages with Catholicism could therefore prove fruitful in understanding how these involve not only prejudices and anxieties, but also affirmations, identifications, and sympathies. Encountering such moments—Little Nell's deathbed surrounded by the vestiges of Catholicism, Jacob Marley seemingly existing in a purgatorial realm, Agnes Wickfield being heavily invested with Marian traits, and so on—we may begin to find a secret attraction to Catholic beliefs, rituals, and iconography that offer Dickens a rich source of imaginative and narrative possibilities through which he can explore ideas such as suffering, mortality, or motherhood in a context other than his own liberal Protestantism. Yet this secret attraction to Catholicism may not simply be a creative one, especially if we recall a 'curious dream' Dickens had while resident in Italy. Dickens's dream vision of his beloved sister-in-law, Mary Hogarth, dressed as the Madonna, who he asks ' "What is the True religion? ... perhaps the Roman Catholic is the best?" ', to which the spirit replied ' "for *you*, it is the best!" ',[31] surely suggests a deeply complex personal relationship with the Catholic religion.

Further Reading

Charles Dickens, *The Life of Our Lord* (London: Associated Newspapers, 1934)
Christopher Hibbert, *King Mob: The Story of Lord George Gordon and the London Riots of 1780* (London: Longman, 1958)
Myron Magnet, *Dickens and the Social Order* (Philadelphia: University of Pennsylvania Press, 1985)
Michael E. Schiefelbein, *The Lure of Babylon: Seven Protestant Novelists and Britain's Roman Catholic Revival* (Macob, GA: Mercer University Press, 2001)
Gauri Viswanathan, *Outside the Fold: Conversion, Modernity, and Belief* (Princeton: Princeton University Press, 1998)
Michael Wheeler, *The Old Enemies: Catholic and Protestant in Nineteenth-Century English Culture* (Cambridge: Cambridge University Press, 2006)

---

[31] *The Letters of Charles Dickens*, ed. Madeline House, Graham Storey, et al., Pilgrim/British Academy Edition, 12 vols (Oxford: Clarendon Press, 1965–2002). Here, 4: 196.

CHAPTER 11

MARTIN CHUZZLEWIT

LOGAN DELANO BROWNING

For many readers and scholars, *Martin Chuzzlewit* ranks dead last or next to last ahead of *Barnaby Rudge* in the Dickens canon, valued more for what Dickens seems to have learned from writing the novel than for what he achieves in its pages. Certainly, from the publication of the first monthly instalments in early 1843, the novel has spawned criticism ranging in tone from mild disappointment to outrage and dismissal. However, such negative verdicts have from the first elicited equally strong, if sometimes less numerous, defences and even celebrations of the novel's quality and value. Also from the first, despite the many negative readings and the relative unpopularity of the novel, particular characters almost instantly became part of familiar public discourse and developed extensive afterlives within that discourse. Accounting for these diverse reactions has perforce become an almost unavoidable concern for scholars assessing *Chuzzlewit*, and will be the first business of this chapter as well.

Dickens himself was among the first champions of the novel; in the face of disappointing sales and quarrels with the publishers Chapman and Hall arising from their lack of confidence in the novel, he declared to John Forster in November 1843 that even at that point *Chuzzlewit* was 'in a hundred points immeasurably the best of [his] stories' and lamented, 'How coldly did this very book go on for months, until it forced itself up in people's opinion, without forcing itself up in sale!'[1] The novel's most eloquent and effective champion of recent years has been John Bowen, who in *Other Dickens* ingeniously deploys a variety of theoretical methods and approaches (borrowed from Paul de Man, Sigmund Freud, Mikhail Bakhtin, Jacques Lacan, Michel Foucault, Jacques Derrida, Jonathan Culler, et al.) to argue for the unique greatness of all early Dickens novels up to *Chuzzlewit*. Bowen suggests that each of Dickens's early novels should be valued for its particular strangeness, its departure from or resistance to precedent or common practice: 'One is constantly struck', says Bowen, by 'how strongly his

---

[1] Charles Dickens, To John Forster [2 November 1843], *The Letters of Charles Dickens*, ed. Madeline House, Graham Storey, et al., Pilgrim/British Academy Edition, 12 vols (Oxford: Clarendon Press, 1965–2002) Subsequent citations: *PLets* followed by volume:page range, page. Here 3: 590–1, 590.

writing outplays and subverts the critical norms and presuppositions both of his day and our own.'[2] To Bowen, *Martin Chuzzlewit*, which challenges readers' expectations and standards in so many ways, thus stands as 'one of the most important of all nineteenth-century novels', 'one of the first and most prescient of modern novels, and a key harbinger of modernism', and a 'triumph of language'.[3]

Clearly, from Dickens's early insistence on the novel's quality to Bowen's enthusiastic advocacy, there is a genealogy of critical praise worth noting by students of this challenging text. However, it is a peculiar feature of much of this praise that it includes and often starts from the acknowledgement of a weakness or problematic element in the novel. For instance, G. K. Chesterton acknowledges incoherence, Sylvère Monod 'unevenness', and even Bowen acquiesces that the novel's plot 'is by common consent both non-existent and a mess'.[4]

Over time, many particular passages or elements of the novel have been both praised and condemned. The opening chapter of Chuzzlewit genealogy, for instance, is called 'one of the most remarkable of any novel' by Bowen, but he quotes numerous examples of the 'contempt with which it has been treated by most critics of the novel'.[5] The decision to shift the novel's setting from England to America by having Martin and then Mark Tapley decide to journey there has been thought unjustifiably abrupt, and to introduce questions about the plausibility of the plot (e.g. how can Martin make his fortune as an architect when he has had virtually no instruction before Pecksniff terminates their relationship and orders him out of the house?). The American episodes, essentially eight chapters, to these critics seem mere self-indulgence that allows Dickens to repurpose his accounts of America from *American Notes* and to vent his intense anger at the largely negative response of American readers to his highly critical portrait of their country and its culture. But others declare that the American chapters work deftly as parallels to the English chapters with which they are alternated, or they see powerful, effective satiric comedy, one critic going so far as to call the American scenes 'pure creative joy in grotesque invention'.[6] Jerome Meckier and Nancy Aycock Metz especially have each formulated powerful arguments for the importance of the American episodes both to the richness of *Martin Chuzzlewit* and to Dickens's developing world view.[7]

---

[2] John Bowen, *Other Dickens: Pickwick to Chuzzlewit* (Oxford: Oxford University Press, 2000), 4.

[3] Bowen, 'The Genealogy of Monsters: *Martin Chuzzlewit*', chapter 7 of *Other Dickens: Pickwick to Chuzzlewit*, 183–219, 183, 184–5, and 218.

[4] G. K. Chesterton, *Charles Dickens: A Critical Study* (London: Methuen, 1906), 242; Sylvère Monod, '*Martin Chuzzlewit*' (London: George Allen & Unwin, 1985), 149; and Bowen, *Other Dickens*, 215.

[5] Bowen, *Other Dickens*, 185.

[6] Albert J. Guerard, *The Triumph of the Novel: Dickens, Dostoevsky, Faulkner* (New York: Oxford University Press, 1976), 246; qtd in Monod, '*Martin Chuzzlewit*', 52.

[7] For the argument that Dickens's America was derived from and a response to a much more extensive reading of other travel accounts and contemporary periodical coverage than previously understood, see Jerome Meckier, *Innocent Abroad: Charles Dickens's American Engagements* (Lexington: University Press of Kentucky, 1990) and Nancy Aycock Metz, 'Introduction', 1–9, esp. 3–5, in Metz, *The Companion to 'Martin Chuzzlewit'* (Mountfield: Helm Information, 2001).

In a 1997 essay, 'Getting It Wrong Again and Again—Me and *Martin Chuzzlewit*', James Kincaid gives a wonderful sense of this lack of critical consensus when he describes the situation he faced when first attempting to write about the novel in the late 1960s and early 1970s:

> *Martin Chuzzlewit* had at the time been generally dismissed as a botch by the Dickens establishment, Bill Daleski and J. Hillis Miller aside. Barbara Hardy (who got lots of attention) represented pretty well for me (who got none) the maddeningly cocksure condescension shown toward the novel, Dickens, and the Victorians. Her interpretation... construed *Martin Chuzzlewit* as a disunified jumble, a tediously obvious exemplum on selfishness, and an artistic disaster. *Martin Chuzzlewit*, in other words, was what the modernists thought the Victorians were: simple-minded, hypocritical, and shallow.[8]

Kincaid suggests that his two attempts to correct that negative critical consensus were failures, but he ends the essay by intensifying his call for others to recognize that 'The challenge is not to understand *Martin Chuzzlewit* but to not understand it, to confront the price we are paying to maintain the illusions of understanding and to wonder if we can't stop paying and can start being paid, if we cannot, by being disobedient, discover the rules and see if they are worth obeying.'[9] In the nearly 20 years since Kincaid wrote those words, a number of scholars have responded to that challenge, and much can be learned from those responses, demonstrating as they often do the extraordinary way in which the novel's most remarkable attributes somehow derive from or are at least linked to its less successful or appealing ones. Surely Kincaid is right to suggest that the way forward in *Chuzzlewit* studies is to take the novel for what it is rather than to lament what it is not. Surely part of that way forward involves the analysis of how often what the novel lacks somehow generates what it ends up being.

There is an important qualification to the confusing critical polyphony associated with *Martin Chuzzlewit*, and contemporary academics and general readers should be aware of that exception before embarking on a study of the novel. Superb scholarly resources exist upon which to found further explorations. Of particular significance are the 1982 Clarendon Press edition of the novel edited meticulously by Margaret Cardwell; Robert E. Lougy's remarkable 1990 *'Martin Chuzzlewit': An Annotated Bibliography*; and the publication of *The Companion to 'Martin Chuzzlewit'* in 2001 by Nancy Aycock Metz, the novel's pre-eminent authority and most devoted student.[10]

---

[8] James Kincaid, 'Getting It Wrong Again and Again—Me and *Martin Chuzzlewit*', in Shlomith Rimmon-Kenan, Leona Toker, and Shuli Barzilai (eds), *Rereading Texts / Rethinking Critical Presuppositions: Essays in Honour of H. M. Daleski* (Frankfurt am Main: Peter Lang, 1997), 335–45, 337.

[9] Ibid. 345.

[10] Charles Dickens, *Martin Chuzzlewit*, ed. Margaret Cardwell (Oxford: Clarendon Press, 1982); Robert E. Lougy, *'Martin Chuzzlewit': An Annotated Bibliography* (New York and London: Garland Publishing, 1990); and Metz, *Companion*. Subsequent references to the text of *Martin Chuzzlewit* are to Cardwell's Clarendon edition and will appear parenthetically in the text by *MC* chapter, page.

Several recent essays stand out as examples of the successful conversion of an aspect of the novel thought to be a weakness when measured by one standard into a strength when measured by another. The description of these essays will be followed by an exploration of some additional approaches to the novel, which seem most likely to produce the richest possible readings of the work as well as a sophisticated, fully developed sense of what the novel meant to Dickens's development as an author.

Three of these notable studies take what has been deemed a weakness when viewing the novel through a narratological lens, and show how from a different theoretical perspective the feature becomes significantly valuable. An excellent essay by Adam Grener, 'Coincidence as Realist Technique: Improbable Encounters and the Representation of Selfishness in *Martin Chuzzlewit*', reassesses the extraordinary amount of coincidence in the novel (he counts 21 instances), converting a trait often deemed a weakness into 'an important and productive tool for realist representation'.[11] Grener shows how narrative coincidence is an especially 'apt mechanism for figuring reality in a way that enables the representation of both objective structures which shape individual experience and subjective responses to those structures'. Thus, he argues, 'what is perhaps most important about such [coincidental] encounters is not whether they are themselves "probable" or "realistic", but rather whether they create opportunities for the narrative to put readers into productive relationship with the particular social milieu represented'.[12] Coincidence turns out to be the most effective way for Dickens to show the evil of the varieties of selfishness manifested throughout the novel. Possible ways to extend and critique the implications of Grener's reassessment of coincidence are laid out in Paul Fyfe's brilliant *By Accident or Design: Writing the Victorian Metropolis*, which explores how '[t]he Victorians frequently looked to accident for its explanatory power in the face of uncertain logic of urban development and exchange', providing—though it only explicitly mentions a single relevant scene in *Martin Chuzzlewit*, the 'accidental' encounter between Tom Pinch, John Westlock, and Ruth Pinch—a superb vocabulary for anyone wishing to analyse the intersection of coincidence and accident in the novel.[13]

Jacob Jewusiak, in 'No Plots for Old Men', another repurposing essay that also treats *The Old Curiosity Shop* and *A Christmas Carol* extensively, takes the old characters of the novel (e.g. Jonas, old Martin, Chuffey, Sweedlepipe, Nadgett), usually defined as extraneous narrative capital for the *Bildungsroman* plot line of development and maturation, and argues that these (sometimes entirely off-stage) threats to the main plot are in *Chuzzlewit* ultimately its prime movers: 'development—for both the narrative and the characters—is wrought by the very means that forestall it'.[14] Jewusiak shows just how '*Martin Chuzzlewit* disables inheritance as a means of supporting masculine subjectivity

---

[11] Adam Grener, 'Coincidence as Realist Technique: Improbable Encounters and the Representation of Selfishness in *Martin Chuzzlewit*', *Narrative* 20, 3 (October 2012): 322–42, 323.

[12] Ibid., 339.

[13] Paul Fyfe, *By Accident or Design: Writing the Victorian Metropolis* (Oxford: Oxford University Press, 2015), 213.

[14] Jacob Jewusiak, 'No Plots for Old Men', *Novel: A Forum on Fiction* 46, 2 (2013): 193–213, 203.

in a society where male power is increasingly threatened by age; instead, the old man engages in acts of deferral that invest his aged frame with narrative control and social relevance.'[15]

In yet another repurposing of narrative features, William Kumbier shows in 'Dickens's Three-Part Invention: Tom Pinch and Musical Play in *Martin Chuzzlewit*' the richness of Dickens's obsessive doubling in the novel when viewed from a musicological perspective, thus enabling an uncomplicated appreciation of many previously undervalued parts of the novel, especially its concluding shift from true narrative to a poetic apostrophe (Dickens's own word in the text and one of the significant tropes in the novel that is examined by Bowen in *Other Dickens*)[16] directed at Tom Pinch.[17] These three recent essays, valuable in themselves as *Chuzzlewit* criticism, also point to avenues for further useful reassessment of the novel.

Ironically, it is John Lucas who points us to the richest possible path for study of the novel. In one of the harsher accounts of *Chuzzlewit*, he deplores, 'as an important cause of the muddles' he sees in the novel, Dickens's 'involvement with his characters': 'Dickens becomes so interested in his characters that he lets them take over the novel and therefore destroy any consistent rendering of his theme.'[18] Lucas's complaint, we shall see, which is rendered more fiercely than are many other attacks on a particular feature of *Chuzzlewit*, both reflects disagreement with earlier assessments that have celebrated the characterization in the novel, and at the same time points the way forward for profitable further study.

Ever since 1843–4, the tactic most often encountered in creative and critical attempts to praise or celebrate something about the novel has been founded or departs from an appreciation of Dickens's construction of individual characters. In the creative instances, particular characters—most often Seth Pecksniff and Sarah Gamp, but more lately, at least in critical discourse, Tom Pinch—are lifted from the maze of the novel's plot for use in another context or genre, thus demonstrating those characters' exquisite versatility and richness. I believe that careful study of these appropriations and adaptations offers as much promise as any other approach to provide new insight and appreciation of the novel. Besides the usual spate of dramatic adaptations that scavenged Dickens's prose for subjects and characters, political cartoonists and satirical writers in *Punch* and other magazines began 'before the intended full-length [was] much more than half-completed'[19] to draw frequently upon the images of Pecksniff and Gamp in order to deride political figures such as Robert Peel and periodicals such as the *Evening Standard*

---

[15] Ibid., 201.

[16] Bowen, *Other Dickens*, 208–10. Bowen discusses the use of irony, hyperbole, and prosopopoeia in the novel, as well as other rhetorical tropes.

[17] William Kumbier, 'Dickens's Three-Part Invention: Tom Pinch and Musical Play in *Martin Chuzzlewit*', *Dickens Quarterly* 30, 2 (June 2013): 104–13.

[18] John Lucas, *The Melancholy Man: A Study of Dickens's Novels* (London: Methuen, 1970), 118.

[19] Laman Blanchard, 'Review of *Martin Chuzzlewit* and *A Christmas Carol*', *Ainsworth's Magazine* (January 1844): 84–8, 86; qtd in Nancy Aycock Metz, 'Dickens, *Punch*, and Pecksniff', *Dickens Quarterly* 10, 1 (March 1993): 6–17, 6.

for their hypocrisy or ineffectiveness. F. G. Kitton notes that 'Mrs. Gamp was an especial favourite of Punch' and lists 'numerous verses published in the pages of *Punch*, purporting to be written by Sairey Gamp and Betsey Prig (and addressed to Gladstone, Disraeli, Churchill, and others), in the vernacular of those notorious midwives'.[20] Nancy Aycock Metz describes *Punch*'s appropriation of Pecksniff beginning in 1844 to ridicule, first, Sir Robert Peel, and, later, Samuel Carter Hall. In one marvellous bit of rich satire cutting in multiple directions, Douglas Jerrold, author of many of the Pecksniff takeoffs in *Punch*, even suggested in facetious sympathy with the prime minister that Peel should not worry about a rumour that Dickens might be suing him in Chancery for violation of the copyright held by Dickens on the character of Pecksniff: 'Sir Robert Peel is in a condition to prove that the part in question has been enacted by him for a long series of years, and was so, long before any of Mr. Dickens's work appeared; in short, that he, Sir Robert Peel, is the original Pecksniff.'[21] Dickens, by this time well known for his preoccupation with copyright guarantees and piracies of his literary property, and having only just been involved in a frustrating copyright infringement case over one especially egregious piracy, a *Christmas Carol* stage adaptation, resulting in his being left with a large bill for court costs and an award of damages that were never paid as the defendants immediately filed for bankruptcy, was here being skewered just as surely as Peel.[22]

The stage adaptations galore involving Pecksniff, Gamp, and many other characters were sometimes endorsed by Dickens and sometimes not.[23] But Dickens in fact makes the most extensive use of Gamp in his own staged readings, and he seems to have known from his first creation of her character how important Gamp would be to him, writing to John Forster as he prepared to introduce her to his readers in the eighth instalment of the novel that 'I mean to make my mark with her.'[24]

As Paul Schlicke has noted, Dickens's Gamp reading was 'unusual in being based not on a short work or a single episode from a longer one, but on selected passages from the entire novel; it was also the most revised of all his Public reading texts'.[25] It seems paradoxical, if not ironic, that Dickens appears unable to let Mrs Gamp disappear and instead chooses to resurrect her, creating new episodes and dialogue for her, when the last view of her at the end of *Martin Chuzzlewit* shows her in one of her infamous 'walking

---

[20] F. G. Kitton, 'Dickens and *Punch*', *English Illustrated Magazine* 8 (1890–1): 799–807, 805.

[21] [Douglas Jerrold], 'The Political Pecksniff', *Punch* (July–December 1844): 25; qtd in Metz, 'Dickens, *Punch*, and Pecksniff', 10.

[22] Making this connection as part of a much more extensive argument about Dickens's characters as projections of Dickens himself, Alexander Welsh notes a number of parallels between Dickens and Pecksniff (*From Copyright to Copperfield* (Cambridge, MA and London: Harvard University Press, 1987), chs 1–5, 1–73, especially 25–7).

[23] For a full list of such adaptations up until 1990 that includes Dickens's own Readings as well as musical and film adaptations, see Lougy, '*Martin Chuzzlewit*': *An Annotated Bibliography*, 33–58.

[24] Dickens, To Forster, July 1843, *PLets* 3:520.

[25] Paul Schlicke, '*Martin Chuzzlewit*', in Schlicke (ed.), *Oxford Reader's Companion to Charles Dickens* (Oxford: Oxford University Press, 1999), 366–71, 370.

swoons' after hearing Old Martin stridently warn her barber bird-fancier landlord Poll Sweedlepipe to

> take as much care of your lady-lodger as you can, and give her a word or two of good advice now and then. Such ... as hinting at the expediency of a little less liquor, and a little more humanity, and a little less regard for herself, and a little more regard for her patients, and perhaps a trifle of additional honesty. Or when Mrs. Gamp gets into trouble, Mr. Sweedlepipe, it had better not be at a time when I am near enough to the Old Bailey, to volunteer myself as a witness to her character. Endeavour to impress that upon her at your leisure, if you please. (*MC* 52, 810)

Dickens, apparently not as sanctimoniously contemptuous of the Falstaffian nurse as he makes Old Martin, gives her a great deal more to say and do in some later short bits of writing and in his amateur theatricals and Public Readings, but those make clear that she has not heeded Old Martin's warnings. Taryn Hakala notes that in the case of Dickens's *A New Piljians Projiss* (1847), Mrs Gamp not only speaks, but also takes over the narrative, and is said on the title page of the unfinished piece to be the author, leaving Charles Dickens as merely editor.[26] Dickens got the idea for *A New Piljians Projiss* when planning a theatrical benefit for Leigh Hunt (and, in later planning, also for John Poole), performed by amateurs, including Dickens, John Forster, John Leech, George Cruikshank, Douglas Jerrold, Mark Lemon, and George Henry Lewes. The featured plays were Jonson's *Every Man in his Humour* and Shakespeare's *Merry Wives of Windsor*. In the pamphlet Dickens imagined, intended by him to raise some additional money for the honourees, the idea was to have Mrs Gamp, who might in her nurse's role be needed to help with Catherine Dickens or Leech's wife Anne, both pregnant, travel with the 'strolling players' to Manchester and Liverpool and also narrate her experiences to Mrs Harris.

Gamp or her voice continues to be resurrected or borrowed by writers from Algernon Swinburne to E. M. Forster. Forster, in his delightful fantasy tale 'The Celestial Omnibus', has her *and* Mrs Harris appear to a young boy given rides on a magical omnibus driven by literary luminaries such as Sir Thomas Browne and Dante to a literary world where he sees and visits with fictional characters such as Gamp and Mrs Harris, but also Achilles, Tom Jones, and Wagner's Rhine Maidens. On a return visit, he is accompanied by an adult companion, the 'cultured' Mr Bons, who admonishes him for spending time with the vulgar characters like Mrs Gamp, Mrs Harris, and Tom Jones: 'Well, my lad, you have made a miserable mess of it. Think of a cultured person with your opportunities! A cultured person ... would not have wasted his time with a Mrs. Gamp or a Tom Jones. The creations of Homer, of Shakespeare, and of Him [Dante] who drives us now, would

---

[26] Taryn Hakala, 26 August 2016, email. Appendix G (857–64) of the Clarendon edition of *Chuzzlewit* is a version of 'A New Piljians Projiss' based primarily on proofs sent to Frank Stone that became part of the Suzannet collection at Dickens House. John Forster also includes a version of the fragment in his biography (*The Life of Charles Dickens*, ed. J. W. T. Ley (London, 1928; originally published London, 1872-6), 459–63).

alone have contented him.' But the sanctimonious Mr Bons cannot face the visionary community, and he attempts to flee; in London his body is 'found in a shockingly mutilated condition in the vicinity of the Bermondsey gas-works ... apparently ... hurled from a considerable height'.[27] Clearly, at least in Forster's imagination, it is not wise to condescend to Mrs Gamp.

One of the best explanations for the fascination of Dickens and so many others with the garrulous, malaprop-hurling nurse comes from William Faulkner in a 1955 interview. He claims he no longer reads his contemporaries' works but rereads those by 'old friends' such as Dickens almost exclusively. He goes on to name as first among his favourite fictional characters 'Sarah Gamp—a cruel, ruthless woman, a drunkard, opportunist, unreliable, most of her character was bad, but at least it was character ... Mrs. Gamp coped with life, didn't ask any favors, never whined.'[28] Many believe his perverse admiration for Gamp led him to model his irascible Memphis bordello owner Reba Rivers in *Sanctuary* (1931) on her. Faulkner's sense of Gamp's authenticity and vigour and their appeal is expressed in a more scholarly vein by Robert Polhemus, who has suggested that the appeal of Gamp (and Pecksniff as well) is due to '[a] pleasure principle, a kind of primitive comic drive that disdains conventional reality, animates their language, and their original tongues can sound like assertions of a lost individual freedom'. He explains further: 'The most powerful and funniest voices in the novel belong to Pecksniff and Mrs. Gamp. They express, in their manic verbal lives, certain essential realities in the nature of the Victorian world and in their author that moral convention and an internal censor sought to stifle but that Dickens was driven to voice somehow.'[29] Because this drive leading Dickens and so many others to give Gamp a life all her own has been so persistent, I believe a renewed focus on such characterological reading and reappropriation and conversion can be an especially rewarding approach to the novel for contemporary readers and critics. T. S. Eliot, in an oft-quoted comment, pronounced that 'Dickens excelled in character; in the creation of characters of greater intensity than human beings.'[30] In the same essay, he went on to say, 'Dickens's characters are real because there is no one like them.'[31] Analysing the afterlives of Dickens's *Chuzzlewit* characters should be an especially rich way to bring into focus this fecund aspect of Dickens's writing.

---

[27] E. M. Forster, 'The Celestial Omnibus', in *The Collected Tales of E. M. Forster* (New York: Borzoi/Alfred A. Knopf, 1947), 49–74, 69 and 74. This story is one of several instances where later authors talk about Mrs Harris as if she did exist and wasn't an imaginary character of Gamp's invention. Faulkner is another author who does this. And of course a number of the cartoons in *Punch* grant her substantiality.

[28] William Faulkner, Interview with Jean Stein vanden Heuvel (1956), in *Lion in the Garden: Interviews with William Faulkner, 1926–1962*, ed. James B. Meriwether and Michael Millgate (New York: Random House, 1968), 237–56, 251.

[29] Robert Polhemus, 'Dickens's *Martin Chuzzlewit*: The Comedy of Expression', in *Comic Faith: The Great Tradition from Austen to Joyce* (Chicago: University of Chicago Press, 1980), 88–123, 96, 99.

[30] T. S. Eliot, 'Wilkie Collins and Dickens', in *Selected Essays* (New York: Harcourt, Brace, and Co.; London: Faber, 1950), 410.

[31] Ibid., 411.

If characters in *Martin Chuzzlewit* have had extraordinary afterlives and generated parallel critical afterlives, so too have some of Dickens's places invented for the novel—none more so than 'M. Todgers's Commercial Boarding-House ... a house of that sort which is likely to be dark at any time' (*MC* 8, 126) and which is as notable for the difficulty of finding it as for its extraordinary situation and peculiar occupants. Dickens is never more hyperbolic than in describing Pecksniff's struggle to reach his London lodgings with his daughters: he

> dived across the street, and then across other streets, and so up the queerest courts, and down the strangest alleys and under the blindest archways, in a kind of frenzy: now skipping over a kennel, now running for his life from a coach and horses; now thinking he had lost his way, now thinking he had found it; now in a state of the highest confidence, now despondent to the last degree, but always in a great perspiration and flurry; until at length they stopped in a kind of paved yard near the Monument. That is to say, Mr. Pecksniff told [his daughters] so; for as to anything they could see of the Monument, or anything else but the buildings close at hand, they might as well have been playing blindman's buff at Salisbury. (*MC* 8, 125)

Once the Pecksniffs have been settled in their rooms by Mrs Todgers, Dickens's narrator takes on a voice familiar from Boz's urban sketches to convey the astonishing, unique difficulty of getting to the boarding house:

> You couldn't walk about in Todgers's neighbourhood... You groped your way for an hour through lanes and bye-ways, and court-yards and passages; and never once emerged upon anything that might be reasonably called a street. A kind of resigned distraction came over the stranger as he trod those devious mazes, and, giving himself up for lost, went in and out and round about, and quietly turned back again when he came to a dead wall or was stopped by an iron railing, and felt that the means of escape might possibly present themselves in their own good time, but that to anticipate them was hopeless. Instances were known of people who, being asked to dine at Todgers's, had travelled round and round it for a weary time, with its very chimney-pots in view; and finding it, at last, impossible of attainment, had gone home again with a gentle melancholy on their spirits, tranquil and uncomplaining. Nobody had ever found Todgers's on a verbal direction, though given within a minute's walk of it. Cautious emigrants from Scotland or the North of England had been known to reach it safely by impressing a charity boy, town-bred, and bringing him along with them; or by clinging tenaciously to the post-man; but these were rare exceptions, and only went to prove the rule that Todgers's was in a labyrinth, whereof the mystery was known but to a chosen few. (*MC* 9, 129)

Though many attempts exist to map Todgers's surrounding labyrinth and to assess the Dickensian narrator's dizzying prose, no critical essay devoted to *Martin Chuzzlewit* has had a more extraordinary afterlife and influence than the essay that manages this mapping and assessing better than any other, Dorothy Van Ghent's 'The Dickens World: A View from Todgers's', which first appeared in the *Sewanee Review* in 1950.

Virtually no essay or reference work treating *Martin Chuzzlewit* since fails to mention the piece, and in many cases subsequent criticism uses the essay as a primary departure point. Literary scholars working in urban studies and on 'city-in-literature' projects have also relied in significant ways upon its brief 20 pages for support and inspiration. Curiously, most of the essay is concerned with other Dickens novels, using the Todgers's scenes to understand key features of *Pickwick Papers, Great Expectations, Bleak House, Hard Times, Little Dorrit, David Copperfield,* and *Our Mutual Friend,* while managing allusions to works by Balzac, Sartre, and Molière along the way. But the essay's main achievement is its mapping of Todgers's location, the 'labyrinth, whereof the mystery was known but to a chosen few'. Van Ghent's charting of this microcosm of London, and indeed ultimately, of all urban environments, is in turn translated into an anatomy of Dickens's own 'imagination of a thoroughly nervous universe, whose ganglia spread through things and people alike, so that moral contagion, from its breeding center in the human, transforms also the non-human and gives it the aptitude of the diabolic'.[32] Within the Dickens corpus, the claustral unnatural environment so vividly captured in Todgers's 'baffling labyrinths, its animated chimneys, its illicit bacillary invasions, its hints and signals of a cancerous organization', is never 'healed' in the pages of *Martin Chuzzlewit,* but only, according to Van Ghent, much later with Pip's 'grotesque gesture' in *Great Expectations* as he bows down to 'the wounded, hunted, shackled man, Magwitch'.[33] Despite the extraordinary number of times that scholarship on *Martin Chuzzlewit* has relied on this essay as a foundation, I believe that further studies should explore in greater detail and with new approaches the significance of Todgers's to the novel, as well as considering its afterlife in other similar settings throughout the Dickens canon and Victorian and modern fiction more generally. Such efforts could profitably begin by thinking about the comparison between Todgers's and Pawkins's, the American boarding house where Martin and Mark Tapley find themselves just a few chapters after the first Todgers's episodes have concluded.

Though scholars have carefully studied the composition and serialization of *Martin Chuzzlewit,* and though many scholars from Steven Marcus to John Lucas to Bowen have believed that the novel somehow marks a key change or turning point in Dickens's writing, this is another vein of critical study where more work should be done. An excellent starting point for the further study of *Martin Chuzzlewit* in relation to the Dickens writing that preceded it would be Robert L. Patten's account of Dickens's career through the volume publication of *Barnaby Rudge* in December of 1841. Patten essentially closes his study as the author is about to depart for six months in the United States at the start of 1842, and he tantalizingly notes that '*Barnaby* doesn't just rewrite Dickens's earlier works; it burns them down as savagely as the rioters torched London'; the 'unwriting' in 'Dickens's scorched earth narrative' allows him the prospect of 'freedom from the

---

[32] Dorothy Van Ghent, 'The Dickens World: A View from Todgers's', *Sewanee Review* 58 (1950): 419–38; repr. in Martin Price (ed.), *Dickens: A Collection of Critical Essays* (Englewood Cliffs, NJ: Prentice-Hall, 1967), 24–38, 31.

[33] Ibid., 38.

shackles and confinement of serial cells' and for nearly a full year he has that freedom.[34] But in November 1842 just after the publication of the two-volume *American Notes*, Dickens returned to writing for the monthly number as he began *Chuzzlewit*. When the first monthly number appeared at the start of 1843, the cover illustration announced this work as 'Edited by BOZ' with no author listed, significantly not 'Charles Dickens', as had been the case with *American Notes* just six months earlier, and would be with *A Christmas Carol* in December 1843, and the volume edition of *Chuzzlewit* in July 1844. More scholarly attention should be devoted to sorting through this important transitional time before the widely acknowledged triumph to follow, *Dombey and Son*, for which Dickens seems to have settled securely and certainly into being the grand author Charles Dickens and to have left the ever-morphing Boz largely in his past.[35]

As noted earlier, many critics have debated the quality and effectiveness of the American episodes, and their placement in the novel. Ostensibly begun as a way to stimulate the slow sale of the first parts, the American chapters also seem to have helped Dickens to settle a grudge against the many critics of *American Notes*, which had been fiercely attacked by many of its American readers as ungrateful self-absorbed claptrap. Many scholars have also noted that Dickens composed and published *A Christmas Carol* while in the midst of *Chuzzlewit*'s serial publication. But more needs to be done to explore the implications of this overlap. When Dickens began the novel, he was generally perceived as an angry disappointed recent traveller to the United States, who had excoriated that culture for its crass materialism, vanity, greed, and intellectual obtuseness, and, in the case of the southern states, for the institution of slavery. He was also well known in literary circles as someone infuriated with the American disrespect for copyright. But after December 1843 he also became known by many as the author of *A Christmas Carol*, a work that was hailed extravagantly, described rapturously by Thackeray as 'a national benefit',[36] and offered to readers the prospects of profound moral conversion from one way of life to another. Dickens himself was well on the way to becoming virtually synonymous with Christmas to the British public. Much more needs to be done to evaluate the space between *Chuzzlewit* instalments that are pre-*Carol* and those that follow. To borrow an idea from recent narrative theory, we need to think not only about the content of each instalment or other grouping of reading material, but also about the lived experience of author and reader occupying the time between each reading or writing session. We need to think much more deeply about what the intervention of *Carol* in the monthly issues of the novel meant to Dickens the writer and to his readers.

---

[34] Robert L. Patten, *Charles Dickens and 'Boz': The Birth of the Industrial-Age Author* (Cambridge: Cambridge University Press, 2012), 309.

[35] The one-volume edition published by Bernard Tauchnitz retained the language of the monthly instalments, however, and its title page included the phrase 'Edited by Boz'. Lougy, 'Martin Chuzzlewit', 24, Item 45.

[36] William Makepeace Thackeray, 'A Box of Novels', *Fraser's Magazine* 29, 170 (February 1844): 153–69, 169. An instalment of Thackeray's *Barry Lyndon* appears in this same issue of *Fraser's*.

Critics of the novel could also fruitfully engage with some recent studies of Victorian fiction that do not spend much time if any in a direct consideration of *Chuzzlewit*, and apply their insights to the novel. Besides Fyfe's book already mentioned in relation to Grener's essay on coincidence, Talia Schaffer's *Romance's Rivals: Familiar Marriage in Victorian Fiction* would be an excellent takeoff point for additional work on the novel's construction, deconstruction, and reconstruction of family units. Schaffer's book looks at the extraordinary number of marriages or fantasies of marriage in Victorian fiction that show women marrying or wishing to marry for other reasons besides an individual desire for a sexually attractive mate; 'What would happen', she asks, 'if we read the history of the novel not as the inevitable triumph of individualism, but as a messy and imperfect, yet heartfelt attempt to retain sociality?'[37] I find it difficult to think of a novel more suited to being viewed through the lens of Schaffer's 'familiar marriage', especially as one considers that, as David Lodge noticed when preparing his television screenplay for it, English 'married life is conspicuous by its absence from the pages of *Martin Chuzzlewit* ... [W]hat an extraordinary number of orphans, widows, and widowers, bachelors and spinsters there are in this novel'. Lodge was so impressed by the undertaker Mould's family being the only English family portrayed with two parents and children, that he pushed very hard for the television version of the novel to end like a Shakespearian comedy with a quadruple marriage, relieving all tensions as obstacles to marriage are removed for John and Ruth, Martin and Mary, Mrs Lupin and Mark Tapley, with Mrs Todgers and Mr Jinkins thrown in for good measure.[38] How many of these marriages should be understood as versions of 'familiar' marriage available to Dickens's imagination in the 1840s? And why does he seem to turn away so forcefully in this novel from offering this sort of resolution to a number of characters for whom it seems ideally suited, especially Tom Pinch?

Several recent books share with Jewusiak an impatience with the restricting effect of the *Bildungsroman* plot, shutting off as it does the opportunity for lyric, suspense, and meditation to contribute to the novel's richness because of its inherent linear drive to a conclusion. Neither Elisha Cohn's *Still Life: Suspended Development in the Victorian Novel* nor Rebecca Rainof's *The Victorian Novel of Adulthood: Plot and Purgatory in Fictions of Maturity* themselves give specific attention to *Martin Chuzzlewit*, but each would make splendid departure points for further consideration of how to revalue important elements in the novel that have seemed to obfuscate or impede in the narratological context of the *Bildungsroman* plot, but which can take on new vigour viewed from other critical perspectives.[39]

---

[37] Talia Schaffer, *Romance's Rival: Familiar Marriage in Victorian Fiction* (New York: Oxford University Press, 2016), 23.

[38] David Lodge, 'Adapting *Martin Chuzzlewit*', in *The Practice of Writing* (New York: Allen Lane/Penguin Press, 1997), 230–59, 257 and 258.

[39] Elisha Cohn, *Still Life: Suspended Development in the Victorian Novel* (Oxford: Oxford University Press, 2016); Rebecca Rainof, *The Victorian Novel of Adulthood: Plot and Purgatory in Fictions of Maturity* (Athens: Ohio University Press, 2015).

These approaches and others like them seem to me a model for future criticism and study of *Martin Chuzzlewit*: a willingness to mine the novel for what is most interesting and provocative and then to repurpose, re-engineer, or recontextualize those treasures into new creative or critical or scholarly contexts without worrying about according a positive assessment to the novel as an organic whole. As Alexander Welsh puts it, starting any consideration of the novel with what it does well will be 'more rewarding of study than the novel's supposed absence of aesthetic form'.[40]

Further Reading

Ruth Livesey, 'Halting at the Fingerpost: Dickens, *Martin Chuzzlewit*, and the Railway Future', chapter 4 of *Writing the Stage Coach Nation: Locality on the Move in Nineteenth-Century British Literature* (Oxford: Oxford University Press, 2016), 122–52

Steven Marcus, 'The Self and the World', ch. 6 of *Dickens: From Pickwick to Dombey* (New York: Basic Books, 1965), 213–68

J. Hillis Miller, '*Martin Chuzzlewit*', chapter 4 of *Charles Dickens: The World of his Novels* (Cambridge, MA: Harvard University Press, 1958), 98–142

Robert L. Patten, 'Trouble in Eden: *American Notes* and *Martin Chuzzlewit*', chapter 7, and 'The Break', chapter 8, of *Charles Dickens and his Publishers* (Oxford: Clarendon Press, 1978), 119–56

---

[40] Welsh, *From Copyright to Copperfield*, 58.

CHAPTER 12

DOMBEY AND SON AND THE QUESTION OF REPRODUCTION

MICHAL PELED GINSBURG

Dombey and Son is a domestic novel, Dickens's first in that genre, and as such it has attracted considerable critical attention in recent decades to the way in which it represents the private and the public sphere as well as the relation between them. Special attention has been paid to the roles of both woman and man in the domestic sphere; the place of emotion and feelings; the role of family and family relations; constructions of femininity and masculinity; the association of family and home with nature; and the commodification or commercialization of family and home.[1]

Dickens's treatment of the relation between the private and public sphere in *Dombey and Son* is considerably more complex than what its main plot may suggest. While the latter dwells on Dombey's failure to appreciate the private sphere of family and home, the novel as a whole presents a more nuanced position by portraying different familial configurations and homes. For example, the Midshipman violates the separation of spheres just as does Dombey and Son, but with no disastrous effects; and the sub-plot

---

[1] On family and home, see Catherine Waters, *Dickens and the Politics of the Family* (Cambridge: Cambridge University Press, 1997), 38–57; on the gendering of the division between private and public spheres, see, among others, Lisa Surridge, 'Domestic Violence, Female Self-Mutilation, and the Healing of the Male in *Dombey and Son*', *Victorian Institute Journal* 25 (1997): 77–103; on the place of commodities in shaping interiors and the sexual struggle for control of domestic space, see Susan Nygaard, 'Redecorating Dombey: The Power of "A Woman's Anger" versus Upholstery in *Dombey and Son*', *Critical Matrix* 8 (1994): 40–80; on emotions and the family, see Jana Gohrisch, 'Familiar Excess? Emotion and the Family in Victorian Literature', *Yearbook of Research in English and American Literature* 16 (2000): 163–83; on the question of nature, see Paul Schacht, 'Dickens and the Uses of Nature', *Victorian Studies* 34 (1990): 77–102 as well as studies dealing with Polly's nursing (see n. 2); on the question of masculinity, see Rosemary Coleman, 'How *Dombey and Son* Thinks about Masculinities', *Dickens Studies Annual* 45 (2014): 125–45.

involving Cuttle and Mrs Mac Stinger parodies the idea of the home as a refuge by presenting it as a prison, with the angel in the house turned into a fury. More generally, any attempt to represent the domestic sphere as separate from or independent of the public sphere of commerce and power fails: even the Toodle family, wholesome as apples, is 'contaminated' and de-naturalized when Polly sells her milk.[2] To this extent, Dickens undermines the very premises of domestic ideology even as he promotes it. But at the same time—and this issue has received considerably less critical attention—by arguing for the importance of family and home 'negatively'—by representing, in the novel, dysfunctional families and unhappy homes while reserving the well-functioning, happy family for the novel's very end—Dickens is also complicit with domestic ideology. In placing the functional family 'beyond narrative', he reinforces the idea, promoted by domestic ideology, that family and home are stable and static, immune to both conflict and change. In so doing he renders invisible what domestic ideology itself seeks to hide: that the home and family relations, rather than being natural and spontaneous, need constant labour of maintenance and reproduction in order to survive.

In this chapter I propose to examine the role of reproduction and maintenance in the novel, as it pertains to both the domestic sphere and the public sphere of economic and social relations. I start with a brief analysis of two (out of many) alternative views of the relation between the private and the public spheres and the attendant question of social reproduction that can serve as particularly useful foils to my discussion of Dickens's novel. I then show how representing the care for family and home by the effects of its absence ends up conflicting with claims about the naturalness of family and home that support domestic ideology. I argue further that Dickens's representation of the firm of Dombey and Son also shows the need for, and the failure of, the labour of reproduction and maintenance.

Before approaching Dickens's representation of family and home in *Dombey and Son* it is useful to provide a (limited) foil that will highlight different options, available at different socio-historical moments. Oliver Goldsmith's *The Vicar of Wakefield* (1766) provides an example of how family and home may be perceived outside a domestic ideology that posits a rigid separation between the private and public sphere. Family and home, in the *Vicar*, are neither a shelter from a hostile world nor the site of quiescent unity and stability. The focus on family and home does not entail a valorization of privacy but rather of sociality, especially in the form of hospitality. Recalling

---

[2] Or, as Jules Law puts it, the selling of the milk shows 'the essentially social nature of the fluid exchanges that sustain the household economy'. *The Social Life of Fluids: Blood, Milk, and Water in the Victorian Novel* (Ithaca, NY: Cornell University Press, 2010), 34. Charles Hatten has argued that 'Polly's position is doubly problematic, for as a working mother she must work instead of mothering her own children, but her nursing of a bourgeois child transforms mothering into work'. *The End of Domesticity: Alienation from the Family in Dickens, Eliot, and James* (Newark: University of Delaware Press, 2010), 68. This description seems to ignore that mothering *is* work—which is what domestic ideology, insistent on separating the home from the outside world, does. The real opposition is not between mothering and work but between mothering and *paid* work. As unpaid work the labour of mothering—of maintaining life—remains invisible.

the many visitors they used to have, the Vicar explains: 'As we lived near the road, we often had the traveller or stranger come to taste our gooseberry wine.'[3] Hospitality opens up the home to the world at large; as a social practice, it is marked by indifference to both the merits of the guests and the quality of their reception. When the Vicar speaks of the 'vacant hilarity'[4] of their evening entertainment, his remark need not be interpreted as a sign of his moral failing (as has become routine in recent criticism). Rather, it can be interpreted as signalling that for the Vicar sociality is important in and of itself: the goal of sociality—the reproduction of social ties, of the social fabric—is inherent in the process. The Vicar has enough discrimination to tell the difference among his various guests, but this difference is not of the utmost importance since what occupies centre stage is the very process of sociality. Thus hospitality bridges between domestic and public rather than separating them and is practised for its own sake: the reproduction of social ties.

In the novels of Jane Austen, the new emphasis on individual desire, whose end and goal is marriage, does not exclude the representation of the process of reproducing social relations, which is, by definition, endless.[5] But there is already a difference: 'vacant hilarity' will not do for Austen's heroines, who are much more fastidious than the Vicar. While the company at Sir John's and Lady Middleton's meets 'for the sake of eating, drinking, and laughing together, playing at cards, or consequences, or any other game that was sufficiently noisy',[6] Elinor and Marianne are incapable of being pleased by those whose conversation is impoverished by 'want of sense, either natural or improved—want of elegance—want of spirits—or want of temper'.[7] This is because in Austen's novels the focus on the individual entails a shift from the question of social reproduction per se to the profit—material, intellectual, spiritual—the individual may gain from social relations. And yet the plot of marriage shows the continuing investment in the social: the process that leads to marriage is that of the socialization of a young adult, reconciling individual desire with social constraints, and its result is the creation of a new social cell. Moreover, in Austen's novels, family relations produced through marriage are seen as continuous with other social relations—with one's neighbours, friends, as well as the stranger who moves into the neighbourhood.

By the time we get to *Dombey and Son* things have further changed. The family, rather than being considered as the smallest social unit, and thus continuous with the social world at large, is now relegated to a domestic sphere, presumably separate from the social sphere. Though there is a marriage at the centre of the novel, it has nothing to do with the socialization of a young adult. Even the 'traffic in women', by which men give

---

[3] Goldsmith, *The Vicar of Wakefield and Other Writings*, ed. Frederick W. Hilles (New York: Modern Library, 1955), 306.

[4] Ibid., 321.

[5] D. A. Miller, *Narrative and its Discontents: Problems of Closure in the Traditional Novel* (Princeton: Princeton University Press, 1981), 42.

[6] Jane Austen, *Sense and Sensibility*, ed. Ros Ballaster (London: Penguin Classics, 1995), 136.

[7] Ibid., 220.

and receive in marriage and thus reproduce the social bond between them, is absent from the novel: the possibility of arranging a marriage for Florence that will strengthen his firm or create useful commercial ties is never entertained by Dombey. And when, after his marriage with Edith, Dombey opens his home to 'society', his understanding of what this means is limited to impressing his business associates with the richness of his home and the beauty of his wife.

Thus, if Goldsmith's novel shows the home as open to the social world and sociality as its own goal, and Austen's novels represent both social reproduction and individual desire, highlighting the continuity between them, in Dickens's first domestic novel the need for the reproduction of social and affective ties is mostly ignored, is present mainly through its absence. We will see this first in the representation of the domestic sphere and then in the representation of the socio-economic one.

The social function of the private sphere is to reproduce both the material home and the affective bonds that constitute and define the family. But though the nineteenth-century British novel often participates in celebrating family and home, the labour of maintaining them is considered 'un-narratable': according to convention, fed by an ideological perspective whose roots are in class and gender bias, this labour of maintenance is too boring to be narrated. The novel's fundamental strategy of making the case for the importance of the home by showing how ignoring it brings disaster derives from and reinforces the idea that there is no story to be told about the well-kept home and well-maintained family. This both idealizes the home (no labour is needed to reproduce it, it is not subject to change, to time) and discards the labour of its reproduction as unworthy of representation, devaluing it or, conversely, demonizing it (as we shall see in the case of Mrs Mac Stinger).

But the representation of the failure to maintain the home can end up undermining its idealization. In Dombey's eyes, the role of his wife is, by doing 'the honours of his house',[8] to represent him (and his other house, Dombey and Son) to the outside world. He considers Fanny as part of his 'plate and furniture' (*DS* 1, 5), suggesting that the house/home and all its furniture (human and non-human) are material tokens of his status. This explains why the material home plays such an important role in the novel, where descriptions of the house punctuate the narrative, appearing at each major turn of the plot.[9]

In rendering visible the changes that the house/home undergoes, Dickens shows it to be subject to decay brought about by time and thereby negatively demonstrates the need

---

[8] *Dombey and Son*, ed. Alan Horsman (Oxford: Clarendon Press, 1974), chapter 1, page 2. Subsequent references are inserted parenthetically in the text by *DS* chapter, page.

[9] For a fuller discussion of this question see my 'House and Home in *Dombey and Son*', *Dickens Studies Annual* 36 (2005): 57–73. For a different discussion of house and home see Patricia Michael, 'Varieties of House, Home, and Transformation in Dickens's *Dombey and Son*', in Francesca Saggini et al. (eds), *The House of Fiction as the House of Life: Representations of the House from Richardson to Woolf* (Newcastle-upon-Tyne: Cambridge Scholars Publishing, 2012), 101–107. For a different analysis of the changes to the house, see David Ellison, 'Mobile Homes, Fallen Furniture, and the Dickens Cure', *South Atlantic Quarterly* 108 (2009): 87–14.

for repeated acts of care to maintain it. In so doing, the narrator opposes Dombey's view that the reproduction of the same demands no labour, no effort. Identifying himself and Paul with the firm that has existed before either of them, and will, he believes, exist long after they are both gone, Dombey presents the continuity of the firm as produced not only without support from others, but also without any effort on the part of the principals: 'Paul and myself', he tells his sister, 'will be able, when the time comes, to hold our own—the House, in other words, will be able to hold its own, and maintain its own, and hand down its own of itself' (*DS* 2, 48). Since what Dombey desires is that there should always be Dombey and Son, that the same/the name should be preserved and repeated for ever, he seems to bracket time (which he believes can be skipped over or arrested) and thus to disregard both the ravages of time and the need for the labour of maintenance.

In the description of the house/home, the narrator undermines Dombey's belief that the effects of time can be neutralized. Following Fanny's funeral, Dombey's house takes on the appearance of an unoccupied house, its furniture all covered up to eliminate wear and tear in the absence of domestic care. But since the only family member to have departed is Fanny, it suggests that she had a role that was not visible, except now, through her absence. The need for the labour of maintenance can only be deduced here through negation: in Fanny's absence, apparently some measures have to be taken to fight against decay and, thus, artificially preserve what formerly was constantly (if invisibly) reproduced.

In the long description of the house in chapter 23 its deterioration seems at first to be a consequence of Dombey's departure, following Paul's death. Since Dombey's absence from the house could not have lasted more than a few months, the decay appears as a 'monstrous fantasy' (*DS* 23, 311), as if produced by fancy or magic: 'Mildew and mould began to lurk in closets. Fungus trees grew in corners of the cellars. … The grass began to grow upon the roof, and in the crevices of the basement paving. A scaly crumbling vegetation sprouted round the window-sills. Fragments of mortar lost their hold upon the insides of the unused chimneys, and came dropping down' (*DS* 23, 312). Only at the end of two long pages are we told that this decline has actually started a few years before, has been going on 'since the time when the poor lady died' (*DS* 23, 312). The decay of the house shows, as Paul's death already did, that Dombey's attempt at 'preservation' has not been successful. Indeed, Dombey's attempt to arrest time could succeed only in fairy tales, where 'the spell that used to set enchanted houses sleeping … left their waking freshness unimpaired' (*DS* 23, 311). But the house—a real one—could not be protected against the effects of neglect resulting from Fanny's death.

Following the description of the fall of the house of Dombey and Son, the narrator again provides a description of the changes in the house: 'CHANGES have come again upon the great house in the long dull street, once the scene of Florence's childhood and loneliness. It is a great house still, proof against wind and weather, without breaches in the roof, or shattered windows, or dilapidated walls; but it is a ruin none the less, and the rats fly from it' (*DS* 59, 786). By stating that 'changes have come again' and by referring to 'Florence's childhood and loneliness', the narrator invites us to see these changes as similar to those brought upon the house after Paul's death. But though the year that has passed was a year of neglect (following the departure of Edith and Florence 'Mr Dombey's servants are becoming ... quite dissipated, and unfit for ... service' (*DS* 51, 689)), we don't find in this description any signs of the decay that marked the description of the deserted house in that previous instance. Here the house seems to be immune to the elements (it is 'proof against wind and weather'), and its ruin seems to be moral or affective rather than physical. It is as though now the narrator, like Dombey before him, is confusing the 'great house in the long dull street' with the House—and the name—of Dombey and Son, since the latter can indeed be ruined without being dilapidated. The allusion to the rats flying away evokes the image of a sinking ship and thus again links the ruin of the house to the description of the demise of the firm, where the house of Dombey and Son was compared to a ship making battle against storms and tides. At the moment in which Dombey loses both firm and home, the two seem to be conflated. This conflation, however, cannot be attributed to Dombey's misguided view of family and home as the 'home department' of his firm; it is, rather, the result of the way *the narrator*, in his description of the changes brought about the house, dematerializes it.

Alone in the empty house after the bankruptcy, Dombey thinks about Florence and of 'what might have been' (*DS* 59, 797). With all the furniture gone, what is left is just an empty shell, and this evacuation of the house of all material goods causes Dombey to see it as the site of affective bonds (which are thus dematerialized): 'And now he felt that he had had two children born to him in that house, and that between him and the bare wide empty walls there was a tie, mournful, but hard to rend asunder, connected with a double childhood, and a double loss' (*DS* 59, 797). On the one hand, Dombey comes to realize that considering his home as but a conspicuous sign of his social status, commercial success, and wealth prevented him from developing ties of affection to members of his family; on the other hand, linking the birth of this consciousness to the disappearance of material objects implies that they were the root of the problem. Discovering the power of family ties in the empty house, Dombey (this time with the narrator's complicity) is led to dissociate them from all material reality and hence to see them as outside time and in no need of care.

This reasoning is implicit in Dombey's thoughts about the vanity of all worldly things: 'His boy had faded into dust, his proud wife had sunk into a polluted creature, his flatterer and friend had been transformed into the worst of villains, his riches had melted away' (*DS* 59, 796). Dombey realizes that matter is subject to decay and destruction; it is subject to change since it is subject to time. But rather than concluding that material possessions need to be cared for in order to be protected from such destruction and that family and social ties have to be cultivated and reproduced in order to endure, he concludes that he should have invested his attention in something that was not subject to time and change: his daughter Florence who 'alone had never changed' (*DS* 59, 796).

In the novel, Florence's love serves as the prime example of family ties as natural and self-perpetuating. Though her description 'alone in the great dreary house' (*DS* 23, 311) insists on the similarity between her and the house (both are 'solitary', deserted by

Dombey), the more Florence is made to resemble the princess or the abode of the legend, the less she resembles the house in its 'grim reality' (*DS* 23, 311). In an explicit contrast to the long description of the decay of the house we read: 'But Florence bloomed there, like the king's fair daughter in the story' (*DS* 23, 312). If the reference to her 'blooming' suggests that her natural growth and physical beauty are unimpeded, the reference to 'the blank walls [looking] down upon her with a vacant stare, as if they had a Gorgon-like mind to stare her youth and beauty into stone' (*DS* 23, 311) suggests that her feelings of love remain alive, in spite of her father's cruelty.[10]

Following Dombey's marriage with Edith, the house is renovated and is made to look like a palace. The transformation of the house is contrasted with Florence's unchanging love: 'ALTHOUGH the enchanted house was no more', Florence has not changed:

> In her thoughts of her new mother, and in the love and trust overflowing her pure heart towards her, Florence loved her own dead mother more and more. She had no fear of setting up a rival in her breast. The new flower sprang from the deep-planted and long-cherished root, she knew. Every gentle word that had fallen from the lips of the beautiful lady, sounded to Florence like an echo of the voice long hushed and silent. How could she love that memory less for living tenderness, when it was her memory of all parental tenderness and love! (*DS* 30, 406–7)

Florence's love for her mother is not subject to time; it need not be removed to make room for her new love for Edith, since her love 'springs' naturally (it is her nature to love) and because the love for her dead mother is subsumed in a generalized, abstract concept of 'all parental tenderness and love'. As Florence continues to 'bloom', like the princess in the fairy tale, the love that is deep-rooted in her heart gives repeatedly and effortlessly new blossoms. Her love maintains and reproduces itself in a manner analogous to the way Dombey hoped his name, his house, his money would—with little or no labour.

Only once in the novel does Florence judge Dombey by his behaviour—'his cruelty, neglect and hatred'—and concludes that this behaviour severs the familial tie: she 'had no father upon earth' (*DS* 47, 637). But when she returns, at the end of the novel, she repents of having left him, 'knowing' what a sorrow to a parent's love a child's departure must be (*DS* 59, 802). In order to reach this 'knowledge' Florence equates her own love for her child and her mother's love for her with Dombey's 'love'. In so doing she further separates love from behaviour and specific acts. Not only is love indestructible, it is also generalized and abstracted and thus not related to acts. It is simply there, like a natural or divine force, and no particular 'acts of affirmation and reinforcement'[11] are needed to create and recreate it, just as no acts of negation and destruction can undo it.

---

[10] The passage echoes Florence's meeting with her father just before he left, during which 'The glowing love within [her] breast' froze before his stare 'and she stood and looked at him as if stricken into stone' (*DS* 18, 252).

[11] Pierre Bourdieu, paraphrased by Gohrisch, 'Familiar Excess?', 168.

In undermining Dombey's belief that time can be neutralized (arrested or accelerated), that objects can be artificially preserved, Dickens has shown that the house/home is subject to decay brought about by time and thereby negatively demonstrated the need for the labour of maintenance. The house as a physical space, in other words, cannot be subjected to the fantasy of indestructible love, independent of circumstance and acts, reproduced without labour. The materiality of the home is put at odds with the idealization of family feelings as 'natural'. But while Dickens insists throughout the novel on the materiality of the home, he becomes complicit with the repentant Dombey's dematerialization of the home: Dombey's redemption requires that the house be emptied of all its material objects, indeed deprived of its materiality, thus transforming the home from a physical space to an idealized affective state. Perhaps this is why the idyll of family love at the end of the novel cannot take place in a real house where time and the need for maintenance to offset its effects are always present.

Recent interest in material culture has brought renewed attention to the representation of objects in the Victorian novel.[12] The representation of objects in *Dombey and Son*—dwelling on their being in time, subject to change—draws our attention to materiality as the very ground for any labour of reproduction, including the reproduction of social and affective ties. It thus provides another perspective from which materiality and material objects in his novels might be explored in future research.

The idea that the labour of maintaining the material home is 'un-narratable' repeats and reinforces the notion that this labour is best when invisible. Thus, the first-person narrator of *David Copperfield* praises Agnes for perfectly maintaining the home: '[T]he staid old house was, as to its cleanliness and order, still just as it had been when I first saw it ... [e]ven the old flowers [were] here' because Agnes 'found a pleasure ... in keeping everything as it used to be'.[13] And elsewhere he comments: 'I knew who had done all this, by its seeming to have quietly done itself' (*DC* 35, 440). To render housework visible means to utter the heterodox opinion that man, rather than being the one for whom the house is kept, 'is *so* in the way in the house' (as the ladies of Elizabeth Gaskell's *Cranford* put it on the novel's first page). How much this opinion is threatening to male sense of power, can be seen by the demonization of the woman who practises house work aggressively rather than gently and invisibly—the woman who does not remain invisible in the task that defines her. Thus Mrs Mac Stinger's house cleaning and housekeeping is presented as violent, unreasonable, ridiculous, since it is highly visible and totally ignores the man of the house (Captain Cuttle), whose comfort is supposedly the *raison d'être* of housekeeping.[14]

---

[12] See, for example, Elaine Freedgood, *The Ideas in Things: Fugitive Meaning in the Victorian Novel* (Chicago: Chicago University Press, 2006).

[13] *David Copperfield*, ed. Nina Burgis (Oxford: Clarendon Press, 1981), chapter 60, pages 717–19. Subsequent references are inserted parenthetically in the text by *DC* chapter, page.

[14] Harriet Carker occupies a median point: her housekeeping is decoupled from matrimony, but is still subordinated to a male presence and point of view. For a discussion of Harriet's housekeeping, see Rodney Stenning Edgecombe, 'The Heroine of Quiet Service in *Dombey and Son*', *Dickens Quarterly* 25 (2008): 73–89.

The marriage of Mrs Mac Stinger with Bunsby towards the end of the novel is the occasion for the staging of the most misogynistic sentiments in the novel. The scene is described from the point of view of Cuttle, who sees it as 'a procession of sacrifice' with Bunsby as the victim (*DS* 60, 813). Cuttle not only considers Mrs Mac Stinger as a man trapper but 'sees' man trapping as already present in her young daughter (thus depriving her of the innocence of childhood to which Dickens is otherwise ideologically committed) (*DS* 60, 904–5). We are miles away from either Florence's selfless, artless love or from Edith's diagnosis of female art as imposed upon women by social conditions, by their dependence on parents or spouses. Cuttle, the natural man of feeling, is afraid of women (his first reaction is to run away); he feels that woman's natural inclination is not to cater to man's comfort but to entrap him for her own selfish needs.

How can we explain this scene? For man to hold his place, woman's labour has to remain unrecognized: invisible or trivial. Conversely, rendering woman's labour of maintaining the home visible requires considering it as independent, rather than in the service, of men (or independent of the male hegemonic point of view that trivializes it in relation to supposedly more important concerns). Independent women, who have their own interests, are considered 'unnatural' women. Hence they are now seen not as angels but as demons—as man trappers.

The passage is surprising not only because of the mildness shown by Cuttle in the rest of the novel but also because the Midshipman, whose sole inhabitant Cuttle is for much of the novel, is routinely represented in the novel as both analogous and antithetical to Dombey and Son, both the firm and the family. The Midshipman violates the distinction between the private and the public sphere in quite the same way as Dombey and Son: it is both a store and a home. But, while Dombey thinks of his family as the 'home department' of his firm, the denizens of the Midshipman seem to go the opposite way: no business ever takes place in the store, which eventually becomes the refuge for Florence once she runs away from home. Especially under the care of Captain Cuttle, the store becomes a home.

Rather than considering the Midshipman a hopelessly anachronistic, and thus failed, business venture, one can argue that in actively withstanding change it shows itself to be an idealized home, a true haven from the changing, conflicted outside world. This is especially the case under the command of Cuttle. Unlike Sol Gills, the Instrument Maker, Cuttle has no clue as to the function and use of the instruments in the store, which therefore are treated as material objects that need to be taken care of (rather than either used or sold). He polishes them repeatedly just as one polishes the silver or dusts the furniture. It is worth noting that while the representation of the Midshipman renders visible (comparatively speaking) the labour of maintaining the material home and family/social bonds, it also dissociates them from women's sphere—the latter thus appearing as the condition of possibility of the former. It is also worth noting that by casting Cuttle as a somewhat ridiculous character, Dickens distances himself from this representation of the home.

The failure of reproduction is manifest also in the public sphere. Both aspects of this sphere—the economic and the social—are treated in the novel. In the first part the emphasis is on the firm of Dombey and Son; in the second part, beginning with Dombey's marriage to Edith, the emphasis shifts to the social world.

One of the contradictions at the centre of the firm of Dombey and Son is that by linking the survival of the firm to the presence of a son, who will take place of the father and, in his turn, will have a son, Dombey creates a situation where the survival of his firm depends on a process of reproduction of which he is not in complete control: he depends on a woman to reproduce his name and guarantee the continuity of the firm. Dombey minimizes the importance of this initial dependence. He is of the opinion that once Fanny gives birth to a male heir, her function is over and asserts the complete sufficiency of himself and his son to perpetuate the firm on their own, with no external help. In this he proves wrong since the process of reproduction does not end in giving birth; repeated acts of care are needed in order to maintain life (assure survival). Dombey's impotence in this important task of maintenance is first shown when he needs to engage a wet nurse (no, nothing can be done with a teapot even temporarily). And no matter how much he insists on the sufficiency of Dombey and Son to conquer the world with no help, again and again he is shown delegating the care of Paul to women: Polly and Florence, most obviously, but also Mrs Pipchin and Mrs Wickam; even in the male world of Mr Blimber's academy the young Paul is entrusted to Cornelia. Again and again Dombey is forced to face the need for the labour of reproduction to sustain both Paul's life and the firm, and this labour is one he cannot perform at home, where the labour of reproduction and maintenance is relegated to women.

Critics have long been puzzled by the way in which the male sphere of economic activity and relations is represented in the novel.[15] This on at least two grounds: first, that in the late 1840s the mercantilism represented by the firm of Dombey and Son has given way to industrial production and, second, that thinking of the continuity of the firm in terms of a relation to one's son is modelled on the relation of the aristocracy to land property. In other words, the firm of Dombey and Son is, on both counts, hopelessly out of synch with its time.

There is, however, another way of thinking about the firm of Dombey and Son and understanding Dickens's way of representing it. This is a shipping firm, engaged in the transport of goods. The little we see of the firm's activities, however, takes place in the 'counting-house' (*DS* 13, 170), that is, the part of the firm where the abstract labour of accounting takes place. The one person whom we actually see doing work in the firm is Carker, the Manager. Thus the firm's activities are neither production nor reproduction but rather exchange, accounting, and especially management—the modern, rather than archaic, activity of organization, coordination, and control:

> MR. CARKER the Manager sat at his desk ... reading those letters which were reserved for him to open, backing them occasionally with such memoranda and

---

[15] See, for example, F. S. Schwarzbach, *Dickens and the City* (London: Athlone Press, 1979), 106–7.

references as their business purport required, and parcelling them out into little heaps for distribution through the several departments of the House…

The general action of the man so engaged—pausing to look over a bundle of papers in his hand, dealing round in various portions, taking up another bundle and examining its contents with knitted brows and pursed-out lips—dealing, and sorting, and pondering by turns—would easily suggest some whimsical resemblance to a player at cards. (*DS* 22, 291–2)

While the analogy to a game, and the insistence on Carker's excellence in games, his talent in winning, suggests that management confers power on the person who exercises it, the description of Carker as he performs the task of management highlights its non-productive nature.

Following his marriage to Edith, Dombey's attention is focused on increasing his power and social status through social relations. For Dombey the social is mostly a spectacle, a display of power and riches by which he attempts to impress upon his business associates his grandeur. Though his scolding of Edith for failing to act as a hostess to his guests suggests that he understands that spectacle is not enough and that there is a labour needed to keep and reproduce social ties (e.g. through hospitality), he does not practise it himself, just as he fails to see that family ties partake of the social (marriage and the family are social institutions), and that these ties also have to be maintained.

Dombey's resorting to Carker the Manager to mediate between him and Edith shows how 'management' comes to operate also in the private sphere. Critics have argued that, as the faith in the ability of the angel in the house to take care of the family declines, rescuing the family is increasingly trusted to professionals.[16] Dickens's portrayal of Carker as a villain who ends up destroying the family may be read as resistance to this intrusion.

While critics' main interest has been in the way such professionals participate in the surveillance of the family and contribute to the incursion of modern power into the home, my reading of *Dombey and Son* suggests another aspect of this phenomenon. I have discussed the invisibility of the labour of maintaining and reproducing the material home and family bonds in the context of a domestic ideology that conceives of the home as a stable site—both free of conflict and moral ambiguities and unchanging. But the reproduction of family and home is also part of the larger process of maintaining and reproducing the social fabric. As *The Vicar of Wakefield* (as well as Gaskell's *Cranford*) demonstrates, this process is highly visible when the question of survival—of self, family, home, community—is experienced as real and concrete. What *Dombey and Son* suggests is that, as confidence in material survival grows, the processes of social reproduction begin to be taken for granted and thus both recede to the background and are devalued. The suspicion lingers, however, that social relations do not perpetuate

---

[16] For a review of recent work on the relation between the novel and the professions, see Jennifer Ruth, 'The Victorian Novel and the Professions', in Lisa Rodensky (ed.), *Oxford Handbook of the Victorian Novel* (Oxford: Oxford University Press, 2013), 397–412.

themselves naturally and spontaneously and that the disinvestment in the labour of reproduction creates a void. One of the 'cures' to this problem appears to be 'management', that is the non-productive organization and control of human 'resources'. The goal of management is not the maintenance of social ties, but rather increased efficiency and smooth functioning; its effect is the instrumentalization rather than the reproduction of the domestic sphere.[17] Ultimately, 'managing' the family (like managing a workplace) means discarding reformist agendas of transformation and betterment and replacing them with strategies for diffusing conflict—not in order to improve conditions but in order to increase the stability, and hence efficiency, of the social sphere. The representation of the 'Manager' in *Dombey and Son* thus can lead to renewed investigation of Dickens's relation to reform and his representation of conflict.

FURTHER READING

Robert Clark, 'Riddling the Family Firm: The Sexual Economy in *Dombey and Son*', *ELH* 51 (1984): 69–84

Kelly Hager, 'Making a Spectacle of Yourself, or, Marriage and Melodrama in *Dombey and Son*', *Dickens and the Rise of Divorce: The Failed Marriage Plot and the Novel Tradition* (Farnham: Ashgate, 2010), 91–130

Elizabeth Langland, *Nobody's Angels: Middle Class Women and Domestic Ideology in Victorian Culture* (Ithaca, NY: Cornell University Press, 1995)

Hilary Schor, '*Dombey and Son*: The Daughter's Nothing', *Dickens and the Daughter of the House* (Cambridge: Cambridge University Press, 2000), 49–69

---

[17] Andrew Elfenbein reads the role of Carker in the context of a conflict of power between capitalist and manager vis-à-vis the employees. 'Managing the House in *Dombey and Son*: Dickens and the Uses of Analogy', *Studies in Philology* 92 (1995): 361–82. Elfenbein, however, sees the family and home as 'managed' prior to and independent of Carker; he can thus speak of Florence's 'brand of emotional management' (366) and of Fanny as 'the figure who "naturally" ought to be in charge of managing Paul's development' (372). Rather than making a distinction between social reproduction and management, he sees an opposition between female and male management.

CHAPTER 13

CHRISTMAS BOOKS AND STORIES

RUTH GLANCY

Christmas Books

Dickens's five Christmas Books—*A Christmas Carol, The Chimes, The Cricket on the Hearth, The Battle of Life,* and *The Haunted Man*, written between 1843 and 1848—hold a contradictory position in Dickens's oeuvre. They are often regarded as minor works (even *A Christmas Carol*), written for a particular audience and too limited in intention and length to compete with the expansive canvas of the novels that Dickens's genius seemed to require. At the same time, however, they have long been recognized as being pivotal in Dickens's career and almost singly responsible for Dickens's worldwide reputation as a result of the remarkable success of *A Christmas Carol*. Almost from the beginning, they have been seen as the epitome of Dickens's social criticism, his 'philosophy of Christmas', as Louis Cazamian referred to it in 1903.[1] G. K. Chesterton declared that all of Dickens's books were Christmas books,[2] and in 1939 the French critic Alain agreed that Dickens's novels are variations on his Christmas themes as dramatized in the Christmas books.[3] They have also been recognized as teaching Dickens about plotting and coherence, the greater maturity of the later novels made possible in part by Dickens's artistic development in the years between *Martin Chuzzlewit* and *Dombey and Son*. The first critic to comment at length on this centrality was John Butt, who in 1954 argued that *A Christmas Carol* was 'the first occasion of Dickens discovering a plot sufficient to

---

[1] Louis Cazamian, 'Dickens: La Philosophie de Noël', in *Le Roman social en Angleterre 1830-1850: Dickens, Disraeli, Mrs. Gaskell, Kingsley* (Paris: Société nouvelle de librairie et d'édition, 1903).

[2] G. K. Chesterton, 'Introduction', in *Christmas Books* (London: J. M. Dent; New York: E. P. Dutton, 1907).

[3] Alain, 'Le Fantastique et le réel d'après les "Contes de Noel" de Dickens', *La Nouvelle Revue française* 53 (1939): 817–23.

carry his message, and a plot coterminous with his message, a plot, that is to say, the whole of which bears upon his message and does not overlap it'. Butt's 1951 lecture on the Christmas Books (a lecture not published until 1969) formed the foundation for much later criticism of the five books.[4]

The centrality of the Christmas writings, epitomized by *A Christmas Carol*, to Dickens's thought was acknowledged by Dickens himself, particularly in regard to his relationship with his readers, when in 1845 he proposed starting a cheap weekly paper that would contain '*Carol* philosophy, cheerful views, sharp anatomization of humbug, jolly good temper ... and a vein of glowing, hearty, generous, mirthful, beaming reference in everything to Home, and Fireside'.[5] When he sought to strengthen his ties with his readers by giving Public Readings, he began with the *Carol* in 1853, and it remained central to his immensely popular repertoire for the next 17 years. '*Carol* philosophy' was the essential Dickens also for two of the most influential critics of the twentieth century, G. K. Chesterton and Edmund Wilson. If Chesterton can be seen as representative of the early view of Dickens as cheerful, optimistic, and uncomplicated (in his many essays on Dickens and Christmas he joked that Scrooge had secretly been giving away turkeys all his life),[6] Wilson is usually credited with being the first to recognize the darker, more complex underside of Dickens's life and art. In his ground-breaking 1940 essay 'Dickens: The Two Scrooges', Wilson places Scrooge at the centre of his argument that Dickens was a dual personality and that Scrooge's redemption at the end of *A Christmas Carol* will be short lived.[7] If the general reader's impression of Dickens and Christmas is the Chestertonian one of conviviality, charity, and the domestic hearth, so memorably described in the Cratchits' Christmas dinner, scholars since Wilson have increasingly concentrated on the more complex vision evident in the figures of Ignorance and Want, the Waif in *The Haunted Man*, and the other representations of those excluded from the Christmas fireside.

The contemporary reviews of *A Christmas Carol* were almost uniformly glowing, recognizing its originality, timeliness, and morality: it was a 'national benefit' to William Makepeace Thackeray;[8] 'as charming a moral as could be desired in this cold-hearted utilitarian age' to C. W. Russell;[9] a 'noble book, finely felt, and calculated to work much social good'.[10] Comparing it to the usual Christmas literary offerings, one reviewer

---

[4] John E. Butt, '*A Christmas Carol*: Its Origin and Design', *Dickensian* 51, 1 (January 1955): 15–18; 'Dickens's Christmas Books', in *Pope, Dickens, and Others* (Edinburgh: Edinburgh University Press, 1969), 127–48.

[5] *The Letters of Charles Dickens*, ed. Madeline House, Graham Storey, et al., Pilgrim/British Academy Edition, 12 vols (Oxford: Clarendon Press, 1965–2002), 4:327–8, 328. Subsequent citations: PLets followed by volume:page range, page, and hn. for headnote, n. or nn. for footnotes, with page range given before page cited.

[6] G. K. Chesterton, 'Dickens and Christmas', in *Charles Dickens* (London: Methuen, 1906), 153–77.

[7] Edmund Wilson, 'Dickens: The Two Scrooges', *New Republic* 102 (1940): 297–300, 339–42; repr., rev., and enl. in *The Wound and the Bow* (Cambridge, MA: Houghton Mifflin, 1941), 1–104.

[8] [William Makepeace Thackeray], 'A Box of Novels', *Fraser's Magazine* 29 (February 1844): 153–69.

[9] [C. W. Russell], '*A Christmas Carol, In Prose*', *Dublin Review* 15 (December 1843): 510–29.

[10] Bon Gaultier, pseudonym [Theodore Martin], 'Bon Gaultier and his Friends', *Tait's Edinburgh Magazine* 11 (February 1844): 119–31.

argued that its value was 'enhanced by reflecting that people will resort to it, instead of to a certain class of trash, which is so copiously poured out at the Christmas season. Mr. Dickens's aims are most humane'.[11] A notable exception was the lawyer and economist Nassau Senior, who criticized Dickens for advocating a return to feudalism and famously pointed out that 'who went without turkey and punch in order that Bob Cratchit can get them ... is a disagreeable reflection kept wholly out of sight'.[12] This Utilitarian view of political economy led to Dickens's more overtly critical attack on that kind of thinking in the next Christmas book, *The Chimes*.

The economic argument in both books has been the source of much academic debate. The first major study of Scrooge as the exemplar of the capitalist driven by Mammon in the decade known as the Hungry Forties was Edgar Johnson's influential 1952 biography, *Charles Dickens: His Tragedy and Triumph*. Since then, Dickens has been seen as pre-Keynesian, embracing consumer spending in response to a depression,[13] as well as Marxian, although many Marxist critics regret that Scrooge just becomes a better capitalist at the end.[14] It has often been noted that there is an irony in Dickens's decrying Scrooge's miserly ways when one of his aims in writing *A Christmas Carol* was to make money. Paul Jarvie traces this ambivalence, arguing that there is an 'anti-*Carol*' strain in the book that is at odds with Dickens's critique of capitalism.[15] Some readers agree with a bad-tempered remark attributed to Thomas Carlyle after Dickens's death that Dickens's 'theory of life was entirely wrong. He thought men ought to be buttered up, and the world made soft and accommodating for them, and all sorts of fellows have turkey for their Christmas dinner.'[16] And yet *A Christmas Carol* was very close to Carlyle's *Past and Present*, published the same year, in its attack on the breakdown of the humane relationship between masters and men with the rise of the Industrial Revolution. Dickens did not share Carlyle's reverence for medievalism, however, having a less idealistic view of the feudal system.

In response to this kind of misreading, evident in the *Westminster Review* critique, Dickens was more polemical in the next Christmas book, *The Chimes* (1844). He intended to make 'a great blow for the poor' in a story that he recognized had 'a grip upon the very throat of the time'.[17] Contemporary readers agreed that the book was topical, and many reviewers praised the accuracy of Dickens's satire on political economy and

---

[11] '*A Christmas Carol*', *Weekly Dispatch*, 24 December 1843, 622.

[12] N.U.S., '*A New Spirit of the Age*', *Westminster Review* 41 (June 1844): 357–87.

[13] Lee Erickson, 'The Primitive Keynesianism of Dickens's *A Christmas Carol*', *Studies in Literary Imagination* 30, 1 (Spring 1997): 51–66.

[14] Andrew Smith, 'Dickens' Ghosts: Invisible Economies and Christmas', *Victorian Review* 31, 2 (January 2005): 36–55.

[15] Paul A. Jarvie, '"With what a strange mastery it seized him for itself": The Conversion of the Financier in *A Christmas Carol*', in his *Ready to Trample on All Human Law* (New York: Routledge, 2005), 49–77.

[16] In Sir Charles Gavan Duffy, *Conversations with Carlyle* (London: Sampson Low, Marston and Co., 1892), 75.

[17] *PLets* 4:199–200, 200.

recognizable targets such as the magistrate Sir Peter Laurie, who condemned a destitute woman to death for infanticide. One reviewer, for example, thanked Dickens for 'his last most powerful denunciation of the pharisees of society; for his stout-hearted championship of the weak against the arrogant prosperity of the well-to-do'.[18] Another preferred *The Chimes* to *A Christmas Carol*, seeing it as an 'alarmingly radical' story that laid bare the heart of evil in Victorian society.[19] The book's topicality has been extensively researched by Michael Slater,[20] and other aspects of Dickens's radicalism in *The Chimes* have been examined, as in Michael Shelden's essay on Dickens's support of the free trade movement in the 1840s and Rob Breton's analysis of the story in light of the theories of sociologist Pierre Bourdieu.[21] Studies of Dickens's attacks on statistical thinking and Utilitarian attitudes to human affairs usually focus on *Hard Times*, but *The Chimes* is equally important to discussions of Dickens's social criticism.

By 1845, the reviewers were expecting another Christmas book from Dickens's hands, and the succeeding books were usually compared with the *Carol* and with offerings that were now regularly appearing by other writers such as Thackeray. The 1845 book *The Cricket on the Hearth* was praised for returning to the domesticity of the *Carol* and leaving behind the grim visions of *The Chimes* which, as Dickens's literary adviser and book reviewer John Forster had pointed out, left a 'gloom in the mind' despite the book's happy ending (Figure 13.1).[22] But as usual the criticism veered from Samuel Phillips's view that *The Cricket on the Hearth* was 'a twaddling manifestation of silliness almost from the first page to the last'[23] to the *Critic*'s suggestion that it should be in every household 'to inspire wholesome sentiment and stimulate to practical virtue'.[24]

That the Christmas books did indeed inspire charitable feelings in their readers was recognized at the time[25] and no doubt encouraged Dickens to continue writing for the Christmas season. While this aspect of Dickens's thought was deplored by many in the twentieth century (along with a condemnation of Victorian sentimentality generally), there has been a revival of sympathy with the view that literature can have a moral purpose. Jay Clayton, for example, in distinguishing between affect and emotion, examines how the bells in *The Chimes* affect Toby Veck physically, leading to an emotional response that is tied to the public associations of bells with community belonging and

---

[18] [Review], '*The Chimes: A Goblin Story of Some Bells that Rang an Old Year Out and a New Year In*', *Douglas Jerrold's Shilling Magazine* 1 (January 1845): 87.

[19] [Review], '*The Chimes*', *Tait's Edinburgh Magazine* 12 (January 1845): 60–3.

[20] Michael Slater, 'Dickens (and Forster) at Work on *The Chimes*', *Dickens Studies* 2 (1966): 106–40; 'Carlyle and Jerrold into Dickens: A Study of *The Chimes*', *Nineteenth-Century Fiction* 24 (1970): 506–26; 'Dickens's Tract for the Times', in Slater (ed.), *Dickens 1970* (London: Chapman and Hall, 1970), 99–123.

[21] Michael Shelden, 'Dickens, "The Chimes," and the Anti-Corn Law League', *Victorian Studies* 25 (1982): 329–53; Rob Breton, 'Bourdieu, *The Chimes*, and the Bad Economist: Reading Disinterest', *College Literature* 39, 1 (Winter 2012): 74–93.

[22] [John Forster], '*The Chimes*', *Edinburgh Review* 81 (January 1845): 181–9.

[23] [Samuel Phillips], '*The Cricket on the Hearth*', *The Times* (27 December 1845): 6.

[24] [Review], '*The Cricket on the Hearth*', *Critic* (27 December 1845): 699–700.

[25] See, for example, Margaret Oliphant, who remembered that *A Christmas Carol* 'moved us all in those days as if it had been a new gospel'. See 'Charles Dickens', *Blackwood's Magazine* 109 (1871): 689–90.

FIGURE 13.1 John Leech, 'Trotty Veck', *The Chimes*, wood engraving.

Christmas Books, Oxford Illustrated Dickens, 1954

fellow feeling (Figure 13.2).[26] Heather Anne Tilley has recently argued that *A Christmas Carol* and *The Cricket on the Hearth* encourage their readers to view others sympathetically through the linking of sentiment and vision.[27] Tilley's reading of Bertha's blindness in *The Cricket on the Hearth* defends Dickens against the charge made by some disability theorists that in Bertha and Tiny Tim he is encouraging self-righteous and condescending attitudes to the disabled.

While most readers now dismiss the 1845 and 1846 Christmas books as Victorian sentiment, popular with the public but embarrassingly cloying now, there have been some fine analyses of both *The Cricket on the Hearth* and *The Battle of Life*. Sylvia Manning was

[26] Jay Clayton, 'The Dickens Tape: Affect and Sound Reproduction in *The Chimes*', in *Dickens and Modernity* (Rochester, NY: D. S. Brewer, 2012), 19–39.

[27] Heather Anne Tilley, 'Sentiment and Vision in Charles Dickens's *A Christmas Carol* and *The Cricket on the Hearth*', *19: Interdisciplinary Studies in the Long Nineteenth Century* 4 (2007): <http://www.19.bbk.ac.uk/issue4/HeatherTilley.pdf>.

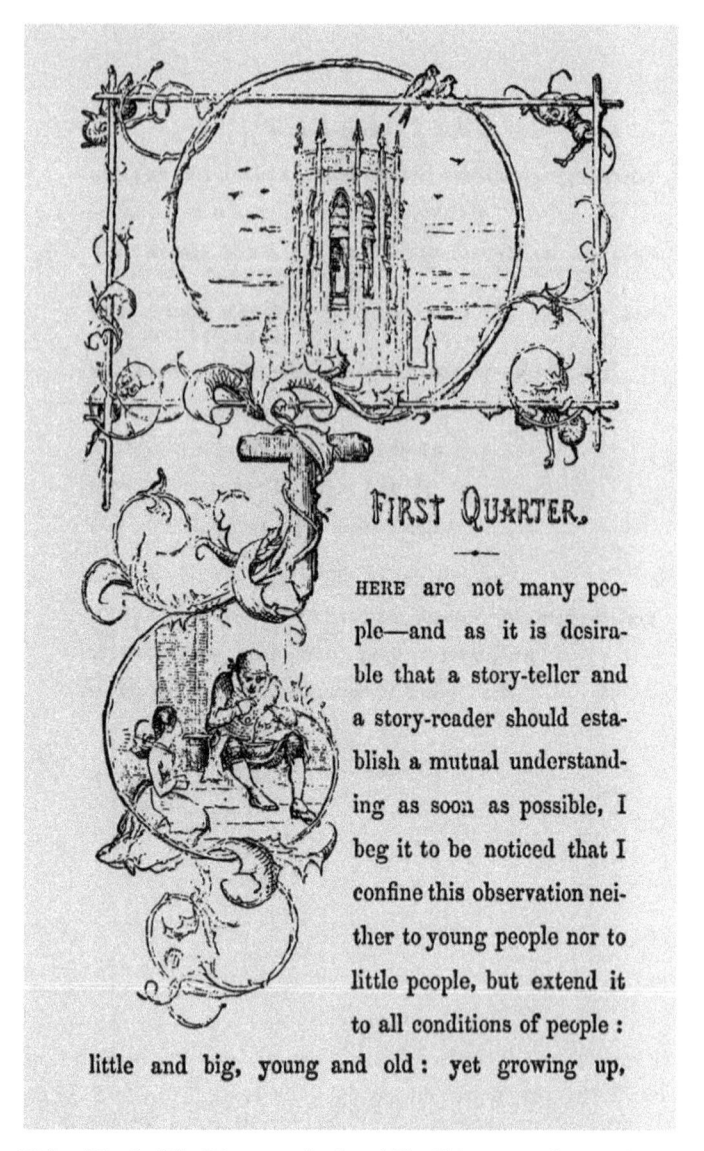

FIGURE 13.2 Richard Doyle, 'The Dinner on the Steps', *The Chimes*, wood engraving.
Christmas Books, Oxford Illustrated Dickens, 1954

the first to discuss at length the January–May marriage plot in *The Cricket on the Hearth*, a topic taken up by Scott Moncrieff in a defence of Dickens's subtle handling of Dot Peerybingle's subconscious doubts about her marriage.[28] *The Battle of Life* (1846) is best known as the least admired of Dickens's works, although it was well received at the time,

---

[28] Sylvia Manning, 'Dickens, January, and May', *Dickensian* 71, 2 (May 1975): 67–74; Scott Moncrieff, '*The Cricket* in the Study', *Dickens Studies Annual* 22 (1993): 137–53.

selling far better than the previous books despite some very scathing reviews. Dickens was unhappy with it, recognizing that its plot could not be worked out in the space of a Christmas book without the time-condensing mechanism of the supernatural. He told a friend that he would like to return to the theme of self-sacrifice, and he did so in *A Tale of Two Cities* 13 years later. *The Battle of Life* has received little critical attention, for many years the only non-biographical study being Katherine Carolan's 1973 analysis of the book's religious elements.[29] More recently, David Chandler helpfully places it in a tradition of other love-triangle stories including Scott's *Ivanhoe* and Boccaccio's story of Titus and Gisippus, which was retold by one of Dickens's favourite authors, Oliver Goldsmith, and which was performed on stage in 1842 under the direction of Dickens's close friend William Macready.[30]

Dickens reluctantly did not write a book for Christmas 1847, but in 1848 *The Haunted Man* marked a return to some of the themes and methods of *A Christmas Carol*. Although many of its contemporary reviewers found it abstruse and incoherent, it has remained of interest for its biographical significance as well as for its artistry, psychological depth, and social comment. John Bowen provides the most comprehensive study of *The Haunted Man* and its exploration of psychic doubling, memory, and social responsibility in a recent wide-ranging essay that draws on the theories of Freud and Walter Benjamin.[31]

The remarkable popularity of *A Christmas Carol* since 1843 has led to the seemingly inexhaustible linking of Dickens with Christmas, a connection which he both acknowledged and tried to ameliorate by not repeating the descriptions of Christmas festivities that were so evocative in the *Carol*. That he 'invented' Christmas as we now know it is a myth put firmly to rest by David Parker in his *Christmas and Charles Dickens*.[32] Parker points out that Dickens described what he saw; in Scrooge, however, Dickens was addressing the increasingly materialistic attitudes of businessmen towards their employees, a breakdown of Christian responsibility for one's fellow man that was so central to Thomas Carlyle's thought. After seeing how the *Carol* did actually instill charitable thoughts in its readers (Carlyle, a dour and careful Scot, was famously moved to host two dinner parties),[33] Dickens adopted the Christmas season as the time best suited to 'awaken some loving and forbearing thoughts, never out of season in a Christian land', as he declared in his preface to the Cheap Edition of the Christmas Books in 1852 (Figure 13.3). In an 1861 letter, Dickens told his correspondent that in 'every one of those

---

[29] Katherine Carolan, '*The Battle of Life*, a Love Story', *Dickensian* 69, 2 (May 1973): 105–10.

[30] David Chandler, ' "Above all natural affections": Sacrifice, Sentiment and Farce in *The Battle of Life*', *Dickensian* 106, 2 (Summer 2010): 139–51.

[31] John Bowen, 'Uncanny Gifts, Strange Contagion: Allegory in *The Haunted Man*', in Eileen Gillooly and Deirdre David (eds), *Contemporary Dickens* (Columbus: The Ohio State University Press, 2009), 75–92.

[32] David Parker, *Christmas and Charles Dickens* (New York: AMS Press, 2005).

[33] Jane Welsh Carlyle, *Jane Welsh Carlyle: Letters to her Family. 1839–1863*, ed. Leonard Huxley (London: John Murray, 1924), 167, 169.

FIGURE 13.3 John Leech, 'Scrooge and Bob Cratchit', *A Christmas Carol*, wood engraving.
Christmas Books, Oxford Illustrated Dickens, 1954

books there is an express text preached on, and the text is always taken from the lips of Christ'.[34] At the same time, however, Dickens distanced himself from hypocritical preachers like Chadband (*Bleak House*) and deplored the pious tracts that were handed out to street waifs like Jo in *Bleak House* or the young Magwitch in *Great Expectations*. When in 1853 he wrote to Elizabeth Gaskell asking for a contribution to the Christmas number that year, he stressed that 'it need *not* be about Xmas and winter, and it need *not* have a moral'.[35]

Many Victorian readers were troubled by this apparent secularity, noted by John Ruskin in his comment to a friend just after Dickens's death that 'his Christmas meant

---

[34] *PLets* 9:556–7, 557.
[35] *PLets* 7:151.

mistletoe and pudding—neither resurrection from dead, nor rising of new stars, nor teaching of wise men, nor shepherds'.[36] In an influential 1972 article, Robert L. Patten offered a useful corrective to this view, interpreting the book as a Christian parable, as do Elliot L. Gilbert and Stanley Friedman. Paul Davis, in his 1990 survey of the *Carol* as a Christmas book and a 'culture text' has identified its Christian iconography and emphasized the centrality of Dickens's religious beliefs to the Christmas works.[37]

Davis's valuable examination of the reception of *A Christmas Carol* and its remarkable transformation into a worldwide industry of adaptations and responses (depending often on the political and economic circumstances of the times) has led to a steady and continuing interest in the *Carol*'s place in the popular imagination and its influence on the Western celebration of the season. In considering the different illustrations for the book that have appeared over the years, Davis draws attention to the ongoing interpretation of the *Carol* for succeeding generations.[38] Fred Guida's seminal survey of adaptations of *A Christmas Carol* [39] has made possible the examination of the vast number of film and stage versions that continue to be created and enjoyed every year. The visual power of the *Carol* has also been a source of interest, as in Joss Marsh's study of the book's origins in the Victorian magic lantern show.[40] Trying to account for the continuing popularity of the *Carol* with readers and viewers has become central in academic studies, with the relationship between Scrooge and the ghosts being seen to mirror that between the reader and text (and reader and Dickens), a central concern as it relates to the development of sympathy. Robert Tracy examines the role of the spectacular in Scrooge's transformation, as do Audrey Jaffe and Emily Walker Heady, readings that take into account the importance of the imagination in Dickens's Christmas writings, both as an antidote to Utilitarian thinking and as a source of sympathy.[41] The versatility of *A Christmas Carol*, its humour and originality combined with its structural completeness and universal appeal, will ensure its lasting place at the centre of the Dickens canon.

---

[36] John Ruskin, *The Works of John Ruskin*, ed. E. T. Cook and Alexander Wedderburn, 39 vols (London: George Allen; New York: Longmans, Green, 1912), 37:7.

[37] Robert L. Patten, 'Dickens Time and Again', *Dickens Studies Annual* 2 (1972): 163–96; Elliot L. Gilbert, 'The Ceremony of Innocence: Charles Dickens' *A Christmas Carol*', *PMLA* 90 (1975): 22–31; Stanley Friedman, '*A Christmas Carol*: Paradox, Puzzle, Exemplum', in his *Dickens's Fiction: Tapestries of Conscience* (New York: AMS Press, 2003), 47–60. Paul Davis, *The Lives and Times of Ebenezer Scrooge* (New Haven: Yale University Press, 1990).

[38] See also Philip V. Allingham, 'Changes in Visual Interpretations of *A Christmas Carol*, 1843–1915: From Realization to Impressionism', *Dickens Studies Annual* 46 (2015): 71–121.

[39] Fred R. Guida, A Christmas Carol *and its Adaptations: A Critical Examination of Dickens's Story and its Productions on Screen and Television* (Jefferson, NC: McFarland, 2000).

[40] Joss Marsh, 'Dickensian "Dissolving Views": The Magic Lantern, Visual Story-Telling, and the Victorian Technological Imagination', *Comparative Critical Studies* 6, 3 (2009): 333–46.

[41] Robert Tracy, '"A Whimsical Kind of Masque": The Christmas Books and Victorian Spectacle', *Dickens Studies Annual* 27 (1998): 113–30; Audrey Jaffe, 'Spectacular Sympathy: Visuality and Ideology in Dickens's *A Christmas Carol*', *PMLA* 109 (1994): 254–65; Emily Walker Heady, 'The Negative's Capability: Real Images and the Allegory of the Unseen in Dickens's Christmas Books', *Dickens Studies Annual* 31 (2002): 1–21.

Christmas Stories

The stories and sketches generally known as Dickens's Christmas Stories have been subject to much misunderstanding and confusion, even to the present day, as a result of their unorthodox publishing history. Originally written for the special Christmas numbers of Dickens's journals *Household Words* and *All the Year Round* from 1850 to 1867, they have since appeared in a variety of largely truncated forms, the first being Dickens's own selection of what he titled 'Christmas Stories' for the 1867 Diamond Edition, published in Boston by Ticknor and Fields. Dickens muddied the waters for later compilers by choosing only nine stories for inclusion and by not adhering to their original chronological order. His editorial statement, that 'they were originally so constructed as that they might express and explain themselves when republished alone', is a long way from the truth of Dickens's original commitment to the Christmas number format, in which his own writings were augmented by contributions by other writers. It is unlikely that Dickens even envisioned his portions being 'republished alone' when he first devised a journal number specifically for Christmas. The first one, in 1850, was not even a special number but just the regular issue for 21 December with the heading 'the Christmas Number'. Until the 1866 number, *Mugby Junction*, all the contributions appeared anonymously, so there has been a history of misattribution that continues to this day. The collaborative nature of the numbers led to their being largely ignored by the critics; only recently has a new interest in collaboration led scholars to examine the numbers as a whole.

To further confuse the public perception of the Christmas Stories, most of them are neither set at Christmas time nor about the Christmas season; and many of them are not stories so much as sketches, monologues, and autobiographical musings similar to Dickens's other journalistic pieces such as those titled *The Uncommercial Traveller*. He selected five such essays from the Christmas numbers for inclusion in the *Reprinted Pieces* volume of the Chapman and Hall Library edition of 1859.[42] Dickens did insist, however, that his contributors appreciate the spirit of the special Christmas number and that each one should be thematically unified and as coherent as such a publishing venture could be. To this end, he sent out circulars each year (after the first few loosely constructed numbers) with his requirements. He would devise a framework story that would allow for the inclusion of other writers' stories and poems. Wilkie Collins became a collaborator for the framework stories, and two numbers (*The Perils of Certain English Prisoners* in 1857 and *No Thoroughfare* in 1867) were written by Dickens and Collins alone. The difficulties involved became increasingly trying, however, and Dickens even made jokes about the trials of editing in the numbers themselves, as in *Somebody's*

---

[42] 'A Christmas Tree' (1850); 'The Poor Relation's Story' (1852); 'The Child's Story' (1852); 'The Schoolboy's Story' (1853); and 'Nobody's Story' (1853). These essays were moved to the Christmas Stories volume in the 1898 Gadshill edition.

Luggage (1862), in which the discarded belongings found under a bed in an inn turn out to contain random manuscripts abandoned by the disconsolate author.

In 1973 Anne Lohrli's edition of the *Household Words* Office Book provided valuable information on the contributors to the Christmas numbers, thereby clearing up many errors of attribution.[43] Also essential to the study of the *Household Words* Christmas numbers is Harry Stone's 1968 compilation of Dickens's contributions to the journal that had not been reprinted. Stone was the first to identify and discuss Dickens's frameworks to the numbers.[44] In recent years, independent editions of the Christmas numbers have started appearing but they are often unreliable.[45] They are, however, making easier the study of the complete numbers, a hitherto unknown area of Dickens studies. The inclusion of the complete numbers in the forthcoming Oxford edition of Dickens's works points to the importance of recognizing that Dickens's contributions must be considered in their original context.

There has been little formal criticism of the Christmas stories until recently, and no consideration at all of the illustrations that appeared for the 1867 Diamond and 1871 Charles Dickens editions (despite Dickens himself appearing in the one for *Mugby Junction*). One important exception is Mirando Haz's illustrated translation of 'A Christmas Tree', Dickens's contribution to the 1850 Christmas number.[46] Haz's illustrations draw attention to the darker aspects of the essay contained in Dickens's often terrifying descriptions of the toys of his childhood. The critical essays that make up this volume also emphasize the nightmarish visions that underpin 'A Christmas Tree' and offer a valuable antidote to the widely held view that Dickens's Christmas writings are sentimental and anodyne. Angus Wilson opened his 1970 biography of Dickens with a description of 'A Christmas Tree' because in its blending of horror and joy he found a microcosm of the Dickens world.[47]

The Christmas story that has attracted the most critical attention is without question the often-reprinted 'The Signal-Man' section from the 1866 Christmas number, *Mugby Junction*. Of particular interest has been the narrator, often misread because of the story's isolation from the framework of *Mugby Junction*, which firmly establishes the narrator of the story as Barbox, newly recovered from a Scrooge-like isolation after suffering a disappointment. Jacques Carre was one of the first to argue that the narrator, the ghost, and the signal-man are the same person, a view taken up or modified by many later

---

[43] Anne Lohrli (compiler), *Household Words: A Weekly Journal 1850–1859. Conducted by Charles Dickens. Table of Contents. List of Contributors and their Contributions Based on the* Household Words *Office Book in the Morris L. Parrish Collection of Victorian Novelists* (Toronto and Buffalo, NY: University of Toronto Press, 1973). See also Ella Ann Oppenlander, *Dickens'* All the Year Round: *Descriptive Index and Contributor List* (Troy, NY: Whitston, 1984); reprinted 2005.

[44] Harry Stone (ed.), *Charles Dickens' Uncollected Writings from* Household Words *1850–1859* (Bloomington and London: Indiana University Press, 1968).

[45] In his foreword to the 2002 Hesperus edition of *The Haunted House*, for example, Peter Ackroyd misdates the number and conflates the Christmas Stories with the Christmas Books.

[46] Charles Dickens, *Un Albero di Natale* (Milan: All'Insegna del Pesce D'Oro, 1981).

[47] Angus Wilson, *The World of Charles Dickens* (London: Martin Secker and Warburg; New York: Viking, 1970).

critics.[48] The ambiguities in the story have led to a variety of theoretical interpretations in recent years, from Marxist and Freudian to structuralist, the latter based on the tripartite aspects of the narrative. A fruitful line of investigation has been the story's exploration of early technology and systems of communication, especially the telegraph, often linked to the ghost story's connection with paranormal visitations. Luke Thurston begins his study of the Victorian and twentieth-century ghost story with an examination of 'The Signal-Man' and the ambiguities inherent in the writing of macabre stories for a season normally associated with cheerful festivities, as observed by the contributors to Mirando Haz's edition of 'A Christmas Tree'.[49] Thurston argues that to Victorian readers, the ghost story was familiar enough to be just a comforting Gothic accompaniment to the Christmas hearth rather than the ontological enquiry it has since become.

Other Christmas numbers have attracted some attention in the twenty-first century. Anthea Trodd has contributed some useful historical background for the 1860 number, *A Message from the Sea*, including a discussion of the international news agency Reuters and the Admiralty's use of messages in bottles. She also provides a helpful discussion of nautical literature as it relates to *The Wreck of the Golden Mary*, the number for Christmas 1856, to argue that Dickens and Collins's collaboration was one of many nautical narratives that sought to re-establish the English sailor as a hero rather than a mutineer, or worse, a cannibal, after the charges made against the Franklin Expedition.[50] Trodd is challenged by Lillian Nayder, whose primary interest has been the relationship between Dickens and Wilkie Collins.[51] Nayder's argument is that *The Wreck of the Golden Mary* is really about the underlying unrest among British sailors in the 1850s but transferred in the number to gold rush fever rather than a class struggle. Nayder is critical of what she sees as Dickens's domineering attitude to Collins, and she argues that Collins undermined Dickens's control of the number by emphasizing class conflict. Nayder's discussions of the collaboration between the two writers are less balanced than Trodd's; she is highly critical of Dickens's attitude to his fellow writers and to women, whom she argues are treated with hostility in *Household Words*, particularly women who aspire to have jobs at sea.[52]

Collaboration and the deflecting of contemporary issues to less volatile settings are discussed in several articles on *The Perils of Certain English Prisoners* (1857), by Dickens and Collins. Dickens's intention in the number was to acknowledge the bravery of the British women in India during the Cawnpore Massacre of 1857, but he

---

[48] Jacques Carre, 'Personnage, sense et idéologie dans "The Signalman" de Dickens', *Langues Modernes* 70 (1976): 359–68.

[49] Luke Thurston, *Literary Ghosts from the Victorians to Modernism* (New York: Routledge, 2012).

[50] Anthea Trodd, 'Messages in Bottles and Collins's Seafaring Man', *SEL Studies in English Literature, 1500–1900* 41, 4 (Autumn 2001): 751–64; 'Collaborating in Open Boats: Dickens, Collins, Franklin, and Bligh', *Victorian Studies* 42, 2 (Winter 1999–2000): 201–25.

[51] See Lillian Nayder, *Unequal Partners: Charles Dickens, Wilkie Collins, and Victorian Authorship* (Ithaca, NY: Cornell University Press, 2002).

[52] Nayder, 'Dickens and "Gold Rush Fever": Colonial Contagion in *Household Words*', in Wendy S. Jacobson (ed.), *Dickens and the Children of Empire* (Basingstoke: Palgrave, 2000), 67–77.

avoided any direct reference to it, wishing not to make 'any vulgar association with real events or calamities'.[53] The story, one of the first fictionalized responses to the Indian Mutiny, was set in the Caribbean, with pirates plundering for treasure standing in for the Indian sepoys. Dickens has been accused of racism in his attitudes to the mutiny, particularly in his letters and the Christmas number. Although he deliberately made the pirates a mixed-race group that includes English convicts, Patrick Brantlinger considers this diversity simply proof of Dickens's antipathy to all non-English races.[54] Michael Hollington defends Dickens on the grounds that both Dickens and Collins were satirizing the views of the first-person narrator, the young marine, Gill Davis.[55] Grace Moore also defends Dickens from the charge of inherent racism, arguing rather that like other English people he fell into Podsnappery over the mutiny.[56] In earlier articles in *Household Words*, Dickens is critical of colonial rule and sympathetic to the Indians.

Several scholars argue that Collins did not share Dickens's antipathy to the native perpetrators of the massacre and redirected the tone of the number away from Dickens's imperialistic stance in his section, chapter two of the number. Lillian Nayder suggests that Dickens resembled Cecil Rhodes in seeing imperialism as a way to solve class unrest in Britain. Gill Davis's resentment against the upper classes is dissolved in their mutual antagonism to the pirates. Nayder sees Collins's section as subversive in drawing attention to the class differences and even finding the British partly responsible for the uprising.[57] Laura Callanan also argues that Collins is more complex in his response, and she points to the homoeroticism of Collins's portrait of Pedro Mendez, the central figure in section two, as taking the reader's attention away from the issue of class.[58]

The Perils of Certain English Prisoners is also an attack on the mismanagement of England's colonial empire, with the bungling Lord Canning, governor-general of India at the time of the massacre, satirized in Commissioner Pordage. William Oddie was the first to examine this satire in detail in 1972,[59] noting that Dickens's response to the events was typical. More recently, Laura Peters has explored the similarity between the attitudes to the empire embodied in the Christmas number and

[53] *PLets* 8: 487–9, 487.
[54] Patrick Brantlinger, 'The Well at Cawnpore: Literary Representations of the Indian Mutiny of 1857', in *Rule of Darkness: British Literature and Imperialism, 1830–1914* (Ithaca, NY: Cornell University Press, 1988), 199–224, 206–8.
[55] Michael Hollington, ' "The Perils of Certain English Prisoners": Dickens, Collins, Morley and Central America', *Dickensian* 101, 3 (Winter 2005): 197–210.
[56] Grace Moore, 'A Tale of Three Revolutions: Dickens's Response to the Sepoy Rebellion', in her *Dickens and Empire: Discourses of Class, Race and Colonialism in the Works of Charles Dickens* (Aldershot: Ashgate, 2004), 113–34.
[57] Nayder, 'Class Consciousness and the Indian Mutiny: The Collaborative Fiction of 1857', in *Unequal Partners*, 100–28.
[58] Laura Callanan, 'The Dialectic of Scapegoat and Fetish: Failed Catharsis in Charles Dickens and Wilkie Collins's "The Perils of Certain English Prisoners" (1857)', in her *Deciphering Race: White Anxiety, Racial Conflict, and the Turn to Fiction in Mid-Victorian English Prose* (Columbus: The Ohio State University Press, 2006), 76–95.
[59] William Oddie, 'Dickens and the Indian Mutiny', *Dickensian* 68, 1 (January 1972): 3–15.

those of contemporary journals such as *The Illustrated London News*, which included eyewitness accounts of the rebellion.[60]

The recent digitization of *Household Words* and *All the Year Round* makes the Christmas numbers more accessible, allowing for greater study of Dickens as an editor and collaborator. Melisa Klimaszewski, for example, has examined Dickens's portions of *The Wreck of the Golden Mary* in light of the contributed stories.[61] Melissa Valiska Gregory, co-editor with Klimaszewski for some of the Hesperus editions of the Christmas numbers, recognizes that Dickens's relationship with his contributors was not always as domineering as critics such as Lillian Nayder have suggested.[62] Fran Baker's excellent edition of Elizabeth Gaskell's contribution, 'The Ghost in the Garden Room', to the 1859 Christmas number *The Haunted House*, provides a detailed examination of Dickens's editing of the story and is a model for what can be done to shed light on Dickens's relationship with his contributors to the numbers, many of them reputable writers such as Eliza Lynn Linton, Amelia Edwards, and Harriet Martineau.[63] Gill Gregory has closely examined Dickens's complicated literary relationship with Adelaide Procter, who contributed poetry to several of the Christmas numbers.[64] Many of the contributed pieces are worthy of further consideration in their own right; others, though underexamined, are vital to our understanding of Dickens's interests and activities, selected by him for their particular relevance. These collaborations are a largely unexplored doorway into Victorian society and culture.

Dickens's numbers began a flood of Christmas periodical publishing that is only now receiving critical attention and which was an essential element of mid-Victorian life. These numbers were immensely popular at the time, *Mrs. Lirriper's Lodgings* reportedly selling 300,000 copies in 1863.[65] Dickens very reluctantly abandoned the numbers in 1868, announcing to his readers in the 28 November 1868 issue of *All the Year Round* that 'the Extra Christmas Number has now been so extensively, and regularly, and often imitated, that it is in danger of becoming tiresome. I have therefore resolved (though I cannot add, willingly) to abolish it at the highest tide of its success'. Dickens often found the contributed stories disappointing because they did not fulfil his thematic

---

[60] Laura Peters, '"Double-Dyed Traitors and Infernal Villains": *Illustrated London News*, *Household Words*, Charles Dickens and the Indian Rebellion', in David Finkelstein and Douglas M. Peers (eds), *Negotiating India in the Nineteenth-Century Media* (New York: St Martin's Press, 2000), 110–34.

[61] Melisa Klimaszewski, 'Rebuilding Charles Dickens's *Wreck* and Rethinking the Collaborative', *SEL Studies in English Literature 1500–1900* 54, 4 (Autumn 2014): 815–33.

[62] Melissa Valiska Gregory, 'Dickens's Collaborative Genres', *Dickens Studies Annual* 41 (2010): 215–36.

[63] Elizabeth Gaskell, *The Ghost in the Garden Room*, ed. Fran Baker, *Bulletin of the John Rylands Library* 86, 1 (Spring 2004).

[64] Gill Gregory, 'Editorial Authority: Charles Dickens', in her *Life and Work of Adelaide Procter* (Aldershot: Ashfield, 1998), 192–250.

[65] From an interview with William Edrupt, the *All the Year Round* office boy. See Philip Collins (ed.), *Dickens: Interviews and Recollections*, 2 vols (London: Macmillan, 1981), 2:195.

requirements for the number,[66] and the difficulties involved in editing the numbers became too onerous. When he was trying to come up with an idea for 1868, he could think of nothing 'which would do otherwise than reproduce the old string of old stories in the old inappropriate bungling way'.[67] Increasingly, the contributed stories weakened his own often brilliant frameworks, especially the monologues of *Somebody's Luggage*, the Lirriper numbers, and Doctor Marigold. At the same time, though, Dickens valued his contributors and was encouraging and helpful to younger writers. As Percy Fitzgerald later wrote, 'it was an object for all to have a seat' in the annual number: 'How far off now seem the days when Boz, so full of fancy and spirit, his imagination at work, touched off those delightful sketches of his, the Christmas "Numbers," as they were called, into which he really put—hence their value—his whole personality and feelings.'[68] As collaborative works, written for his favourite season and expressing his most deeply felt beliefs, these are the essential Dickens, worthy of continued study for the light they shed on Dickens's development over 17 crucial years in his career.

Further Reading

Tatiana A. Boborykina, *The Artistic World of Charles Dickens's Christmas Books: The Dramatic Principle in Prose* (St Petersburg: Hippocrat, 1997)

Philip Collins, '"*Carol* Philosophy, Cheerful Views"', *Études anglaises* 23 (1970): 158–67

The Dickensian. 150th Anniversary of A Christmas Carol, 89, 3 (Winter 1993)

Ruth F. Glancy, *Dickens's Christmas Books, Christmas Stories, and Other Short Fiction: An Annotated Bibliography* (New York and London: Garland, 1985). Supplement I: 1985–2006, *Dickens Studies Annual* 38 (2007): 299–496

T. A. Jackson, 'Dickens and Christmas', in his *Charles Dickens: The Progress of a Radical* (London: Lawrence and Wishart, 1937; New York: International Publishers, 1938), 285–95

John R. Reed, 'Dickens' Christmas Narratives', in his *Dickens and Thackeray: Punishment and Forgiveness* (Athens: Ohio University Press, 1995), 154–68

Brian Sabey, 'Ethical Metafiction in Dickens's Christmas Hauntings', *Dickens Studies Annual* 46 (2015): 123–46

Michael Slater, 'The Christmas Books', *Dickensian* 65, 1 (January 1969): 17–24

Harry Stone, 'The Christmas Books: "Giving Nursery Tales a Higher Form"', in his *Dickens and the Invisible World: Fairy Tales, Fantasy, and Novel-Making* (Bloomington: Indiana University Press, 1979; London: Macmillan, 1980), 119–45

---

[66] In 1852, for example, Dickens complained to a contributor that his story about a highwayman was not satisfactory because the hero turned out not to be a highwayman after all, whereas he wanted to show that the 'bad old days' were a thing of the past. The Revd James White's story appeared anyway. See *PLets* 6:809.

[67] *PLets* 12:166–7, 167.

[68] Percy Fitzgerald, 'Charles Dickens in the Editor's Chair', *Gentleman's Magazine* 250 (1881): 725–42; *The Life of Charles Dickens as Revealed in his Writings*, 2 vols (London: Chatto and Windus, 1905), 1:49–50.

Deborah A. Thomas, *Dickens and the Short Story* (Philadelphia: University of Pennsylvania Press, 1982)

Kathleen Tillotson, 'The Middle Years from the *Carol* to *Copperfield*', in *Dickens Memorial Lectures 1970. Dickensian* 65, supplement (September 1970): 7–19

Catherine Waters, 'Dickens, Christmas and the Family', in her *Dickens and the Politics of the Family* (Cambridge: Cambridge University Press, 1997), 58–88

CHAPTER 14

DAVID COPPERFIELD

PHILIP DAVIS

In chapter 42 David Copperfield thinks of the good that the simpleton, Mr Dick, offers to Dr Strong and his wife, in their separateness:

> I dare say he rarely spoke a dozen words in an hour: but his quiet interest, and his wistful face, found immediate response in both their breasts; each knew that the other liked him, and that he loved both; and he became what no one else could be—a link between them.[1]

It is clear from an often unclear manuscript that in course of composition the clause 'and he became what no one else could be—' was a rapidly added insertion, holding back the ongoing text to take it to a deeper plane than the linear. At first it was simply 'and he was a kind of link between them'. But 'no one' is important in *David Copperfield*, usually by omission, especially in the care of the young David. It amazed the older David that 'nobody should have made any sign in my behalf' when he was sent away from home, at 10 years of age, to work in a factory (*DC* 11, 132). And '[n]o one' ever raised the curtain on that past life of his at Murdstone and Grinby's till he brought himself to do so in writing this book (*DC* 14, 184). That is one of the poignant functions of revision in Dickens: to provide, for the sake of a more caring reality, what *no one else* would otherwise have known to be missing.[2]

Then, when David thinks of Dick filling that space between the Strongs:

> I really feel almost ashamed of having thought that he was not quite in his wits, taking account of the utmost I have done with mine.

---

[1] Charles Dickens, *David Copperfield*, ed. Nina Burgis (Oxford: Clarendon Press, 1981), chapter 42, page 532. Subsequent references are noted parenthetically in the text by *DC* chapter, page.

[2] Grateful acknowledgement to the National Art Library, Forster Collection, Victoria and Albert Museum.

Or that is what Dickens first wrote in the manuscript, working hard to include those characteristically sensitive little words 'really', 'almost', and 'not quite'. But then he changed one further word. He took 'I really feel almost ashamed of having thought that', crossed out 'thought', and put instead 'known' (*DC* 42, 533). As so often in Dickens, it made the wince of having to acknowledge the truth of what one did not want to think all the more painfully registered.

The defence is that Mr Dick's is the 'mind of the heart': 'a subtlety of perception in real attachment, even when it is borne towards man by one of the lower animals' (*DC* 42, 532). Not that Dick is a lower animal: to think so would be like turning against him. For as Thomas Hood said of early Dickens, in a letter to Charles Dilke, 7 November 1839, 'the drift is natural, along with the great human currents, and not against them'.[3] Yet at moments like this with Dick, there is in Dickens an honestly half-ashamed and half-attracted lure towards a second thought which, going against the emotional current, is felt as secret. If Dick is kind but simple—kind even because simple, then what of those who are intelligent? Steerforth said of lower-class, uneducated Ham and Little Em'ly, unkindly:

> 'That's rather a chuckle-headed fellow for the girl; isn't he?' said Steerforth.
> He had been so hearty with him, and with them all, that I felt a shock in this unexpected and cold reply. (*DC* 21, 271)

How could Steerforth put those after-words 'chuckle-headed' so close to the person he has just been so pleasant with?

This chapter, in treating of a novel founded upon a younger and an older view of the same life story, is about the equivocal intelligence of second thought, its place and its pain in relation to both emotional primacies and adult requirements. It derives from work on memory and *David Copperfield* begun by Robin Gilmour and culminating, more recently, in Rosemarie Bodenheimer's *Knowing Dickens*.[4] But the working relation of first to second thoughts also serves to test, deep down within the novelist's own thinking, the whole subsequent conflict in Dickensian literary criticism itself: between the arguably sentimental piety of the liberal-humanist tradition and the postmodern hermeneutics of suspicion and disillusionment.[5]

---

[3] *Memorials of Thomas Hood*, collected, edited, and arranged by his daughter with a preface and notes by his son, 2 vols (London: Edward Moxon, 1860), 2, 41.

[4] Robin Gilmour, 'Memory in *David Copperfield*', *The Dickensian* 71, 375 (1975): 30–42; Philip Davis, *Memory and Writing* (Liverpool: Liverpool University Press, 1983); Rosemarie Bodenheimer, *Knowing Dickens* (Ithaca, NY: Cornell University Press, 2007).

[5] For example, Gareth Cordery's chapter in *A Companion to Charles Dickens*, ed. David Paroissien (Oxford: Blackwell, 2008), 369–89, on Dickens as subversive source for hidden anomalies concerning class, gender, and the meaning of adulthood. On post-humanist criticism as a rigidified form of second-thought suspicion, see Rita Felski, *The Limits of Critique* (Chicago: University of Chicago Press, 2015).

It is also a contribution to the manuscript research begun by Butt and Tillotson.[6] For the second thoughts discussed here include those creatively arising within manuscript revisions made by an artist, in under-cover search of revised improvement. And at moments of heightened sensitivity, that capacity for mental turn-around and verbal delicacy is something the characters themselves possess—in particular David, who goes on to become a writer.

Thus, when Dora on her final sick-bed tells David that she was too young to be a good wife to him, he feels immediately the force of that word 'was': 'she is speaking of herself as past'. He gently responds, 'We have been very happy, my sweet Dora,' protectively pitching the tense between 'were' and 'are'. In reply, it is Dora's turn to revise what is said, fastening this time not upon the verb but on the pronoun: 'I was very happy, very' (*DC* 53, 657).

In years to come, she goes on, speaking of herself now in the third person, she would have so tried and disappointed him 'that you would not have loved her half so well!' Dickens knew how delicate this utterance had to be: on second thought he inserted for 'would not have loved her' 'might not have been able to love her'. Similarly, when David begs his wife not to speak in that way Dickens changed what he had first written, 'Every word is a reproach', to 'Every word seems a reproach' (*DC* 53, 657–8). David knew she did not intend it to be a reproach, just as Dora knew he would not have meant to cease loving her.

Yet that makes it almost harder to bear. It is like what lies behind the instinctive revision Ham makes when he tries to describe his lost love. He cannot bear to say of Little Em'ly simply, 'I loved her', past tense, over and done; he follows it with '—and I love the mem'ry of her'—present tense still, in relation to past (*DC* 51, 631). Dickens inserted such dashes throughout Ham's struggling speech—'I could only be happy—by forgetting of her—and I'm afeerd I couldn't hardly bear as she should be told I done that'—to show how difficult and caring was the formulation, piece by piece, and then added only at proof stage the further explanation via David: 'He was not crying when he made the pauses I shall express by lines. He was merely collecting himself to speak very plainly' (*DC* 51, 630). This in its sensitive emendations is Dickens being a second mind to Ham's heart. It is how he frequently tells himself to be in his working papers: 'Express that, very delicately', underlined, in order to sustain the vulnerable emotional space he wants (*DC* 'Appendix C: The Number Plans', 767).

But for all the protective sensitivity around them, second thoughts in this novel are first experienced in the minds of the characters themselves as painfully obtruding upon ostensibly primal simplicities. 'I couldn't *hardly* bear …' says Ham; but such things are what the emotionally thin-skinned network of *David Copperfield* has to learn to bear

---

[6] John Butt and Kathleen Tillotson, *Dickens at Work* (London: Methuen, 1957). See my 'Deep Reading in the Manuscripts: Dickens and the Manuscript of *David Copperfield*', in Matthew Bradley and Juliet John (eds), *Reading and the Victorians* (Farnham: Ashgate, 2015), 65–77, including analysis of the major non-chronological addition to chapter 4 made when the number seemed too short: the 'perhaps premature' foreview of Little Em'ly on the edge of disaster.

and cope with: 'I was too young'. These are hard truths on second thought, hard to live with or to mitigate, because they seem to go against the primary currents of human love. They are like a version of the Fall repeated within the adult development of each new life—all that was made explicit at the end of the first stage of that second version of *David Copperfield* which was *Great Expectations*: Pip, leaving home, goes on only because unable to turn back, the world of experience all before him.

In that light, the Coleridgean cleric J. C. Hare offers a criticism of the fallen nature of second thoughts, in deliberate opposition to the popular truism that says that 'second thoughts are best'. People claim, he says, that such thoughts are more *like* thoughts, rather than feelings, because they are maturely considered—meaning, more sceptical. But for Hare second thoughts are more like bad thoughts. He resists the anti-Romantic model of adulthood in which thought is only a form of cold disenchantment:

> A second thought is only a half-thought... No second thought ever led a man to do anything generous, anything kind, anything great, anything good. By its very nature it can suggest nothing; except difficulties and hinderances. It objects, it demurs, it pares off, it cuts down.

Second thoughts betray our emotional heritage. They are:

> only fragments of thoughts; that is, they are thought by a mere fragment of the mind, by a single faculty, the prudential understanding; which, though highly useful as a servant, is too fond of putting on its master's clothes.[7]

That single faculty then becomes an independent second mind, sceptical and unfeeling; a second nature that is characteristically suspicious and negative.

In Rosa Dartle for example, second nature lies like a scar over her original features, a tonal deformation of her once-natural voice:

> 'I constantly entreat you,' said Mrs. Steerforth, 'to speak plainly, in your own natural manner.'
> 'Oh! then, this is *not* my natural manner?' she rejoined. 'Now you must really bear with me, because I ask for information. We never know ourselves.'
> 'It has become a second nature,' said Mrs. Steerforth, without any displeasure; 'but I remember—and so must you, I think,—when your manner was different, Rosa; when it was not so guarded, and was more trustful.' (*DC* 29, 370)

The parenthesis '—and so must you, I think,—' is itself an insertion in the manuscript, for a moment changing the centre of gravity. But its appeal goes unanswered, relegated to what the novel elsewhere magnificently describes as the 'possibilities of hidden things' (*DC* 3, 31)—another insertion that by transferred epithet gave to 'the hidden

---

[7] Julius Charles Hare, *Guesses at Truth by Two Brothers*, 2 vols (London: John Taylor, 1827), 2, 95–6.

possibilities of things' a more metaphysical turn in the background of life. The things that do not happen may be as much reality, both in the force of omission and as parallel alternative, as those that do.[8] Otherwise, there is only 'no one' again, nothing but what is.

Without the acknowledgement of possibility even in its loss, a hardened second nature threatens feeling in *David Copperfield*. It becomes, as Hare says, master, not servant:[9]

> Are we then always to halt at our first thoughts? Yes: if we cannot go beyond our second thoughts. These are only good as a half-way house to bait at in the progress to our third thoughts ... For while great practical minds anticipate their second thoughts in their first, great speculative minds take up their first and second thoughts and reconcile them in their third.[10]

And yet what interests Dickens is how he *cannot* stop at first thoughts, however much he—or rather perhaps David Copperfield, standing proxy for him—might want to.

The novel itself feels frightened by the temptation to have bad or underhand thoughts, offered so unconsciously by the very innocence of first-order trust and goodness. The lawyer, Mr Wickfield, warns David against the abuse of the naive kindness of Dr Strong, a man too liable to have faith in those who would be treacherous to him: 'Never be one of those ... He is the least suspicious of mankind ... whether that's a merit, or whether that's a blemish' (*DC* 16, 196–7). Wickfield's daughter, Agnes, tacitly appeals to David 'to deal tenderly' with her father's own weaknesses, 'even in my inmost thoughts, and to let no harsh construction find any place against him' (*DC* 19, 237). But there is here, as later between father and daughter in *Little Dorrit*, a kind of bad angel in Dickens's work relishing these provocations.

The bad angel is what Agnes calls Steerforth when she gently tries to warn David against a hero-worship of him 'rooted in your trusting disposition' (*DC* 25, 314); that same Steerforth who first harmed Rosa Dartle.

> 'Daisy, if anything should ever separate us, you must think of me at my best, old boy...'
> 'You have no best to me, Steerforth,' said I, 'and no worst. You are always equally loved, and cherished in my heart.'
> So much compunction for having ever wronged him, even by a shapeless thought, did I feel within me. (*DC* 29, 373)

For Steerforth, sex has become the secret ulterior motive beneath a social exterior. When next morning, David looks into his friend's bedroom, he seems as innocently asleep as

---

[8] Paraphrasing *DC* 58, 701.
[9] See Iain McGilchrist, *The Master and his Emissary* (New Haven: Yale University Press, 2009).
[10] Hare, *Guesses at Truth*, 2, 98–9.

he was in his schooldays. But '[t]he time came in its season, and that was very soon, when I almost wondered that nothing troubled his repose, as I looked at him' (*DC* 29, 373). It is the word 'almost' again that is the secret sign of this danger-area between these two young men without fathers—innocent Copperfield and duplicitous Steerforth—across which Dickens splits himself, as if those were his own alternatives in argument. David felt bad for having had second thoughts about Steerforth even through the wonderfully good Agnes. He will feel worse later, to think that Steerforth himself had apparently no such inner compunctions.

For David, the age of second thoughts had come prematurely and traumatically. It came with seeing Mr Murdstone, his mother's second husband, almost sexually insinuating a change into his own upbringing:

> He drew her to him, whispered in her ear, and kissed her. I knew as well, when I saw my mother's head lean down upon his shoulder, and her arm touch his neck—I knew as well that he could mould her pliant nature into any form he chose, as I know, now, that he did it. (*DC* 4, 39).

'I knew as well ... as I know, now': it is an adult thought, the thought of an untimely, unnatural severance which means that when his own mother speaks to him intimately, it must now be 'hurriedly and secretly, as if it were wrong' (*DC* 4, 41). Because of the stepfather, her son can no longer rely on her to be straight, or directly herself, with him. Hence the syntax of complication, the qualifications of a previously unequivocal vocabulary. It is a 'strange feeling' on returning from school to be 'going home when it was not home' (*DC* 8, 93); strange, not to be sorry to have to go away again, much as he hates to leave his mother, when already in such a 'home', 'the parting *was there*, every day' (*DC* 8, 104, my italics).

Hare was right. These are disturbing half-thoughts which, helplessly critical of those whom one wants to love uncritically, cannot be kept out of the first love they still cannot wholly sever. David does not want to make qualifications or to have misgivings about goodness. But equally, he comes to have difficulty in bearing a truth that is hurtful. Mr Dick asks David outright what he thinks of him, pointing to his own forehead:

> I was puzzled how to answer, but he helped me with a word.
> 'Weak?' said Mr. Dick.
> 'Well,' I replied, dubiously. 'Rather so.'
> 'Exactly!' cried Mr. Dick, who seemed quite enchanted by my reply...
> 'In short, boy,' said Mr. Dick, dropping his voice to a whisper, 'I am simple.'
> I would have qualified that conclusion, but he stopped me. (*DC* 45, 557)

For all David's scruples, Dickens loves the unqualified comedy that simply wipes away vulnerability just by imperturbably having it. No one will mind if an idiot tries to bring the Strongs back together; it is an idiotic thing to attempt. It is like in *Bleak House* when Inspector Bucket urges the sickening Mr Gridley, whom he has been pursuing for ages, not to surrender, not to give in, even to him.[11] It is not the apparently first consideration that matters any more; it is the energy, the life that can be put into it, however incongruously.

There are such characters so basic to the human structure of *David Copperfield* as to be comically undisturbed by the second thoughts of self-reflection. When Peggotty rather delightedly calls her brother a mere baby for his overwhelming fondness for the orphaned Little Em'ly and Ham, the big soft man, amused that he hardly looks like a babe, happily admits it: '*I* doen't care, bless you!' (*DC* 31, 384). But all this changes when Steerforth elopes with his niece: then there is no escaping the experience of second thoughts. A neighbourhood mother hardly wants her own little one to keep the ribbon Em'ly once kindly gave her: 'It ought not to be, perhaps, but what can I do? Em'ly is very bad, but they were fond of one another. And the child knows nothing!' (*DC* 32, 392). But Mr Peggotty himself can no longer be an innocent baby in this. Even in the midst of his joy at finally being reunited with Em'ly, he cannot but think for a moment backwards to all that has occurred in-between:

> 'You may believe me, when I heerd her voice, as I had heerd at home so playful—and see her humbled, as it might be in the dust our Saviour wrote in with his blessed hand—I felt a wownd go to my art, in the midst of all its thankfulness.'
>
> He drew his sleeve across his face, without any pretence of concealing why; and then cleared his voice.
>
> 'It warn't for long as I felt that; for she was found. I had on'y to think as she was found, and it was gone. I doen't know why I do so much as mention of it now, I'm sure. I didn't have it in my mind a minute ago, to say a word about myself; but it come up so nat'ral, that I yielded to it afore I was aweer.' (*DC* 51, 619)

It is the two-edged thought, *her* wound and *his* thankfulness, that by this stage of the book has become for Dickens almost the nature of adult life itself. It has become 'so nat'ral' that it is no longer easy even for Mr Peggotty to make it go away.

For David himself, growing into adulthood, the second thoughts of compunction, loss, regret, or reproach are irremovable qualifications. They exist in the midst of a complex syntax that seeks the right place for those thoughts within the configuration of what becomes 'my mind on this paper' (*DC* 48, 594–5). For that is remarkably what all the work of writing and rewriting exists to do in this novel—to turn the page itself into a feeling, thinking mind, the representation through this medium of a live nervous system that David Copperfield calls his 'written memory' (*DC* 48, 589; 58, 699). When the author looked at his own words, Dickens felt as though he himself had 'be[en] turned inside-out!'[12]

---

[11] *Bleak House*, ed. George Ford and Sylvère Monod, Norton Critical Edition (New York: W. W. Norton, 1977), chapter 24, page 315.

[12] *The Letters of Charles Dickens*, ed. Madeline House, Grahame Storey, et al., Pilgrim/British Academy Edition, 12 vols (Oxford: Clarendon Press, 1965–2002). Subsequent citations: *PLets* followed by volume: page range, page. Here 6:195.

This complex mental syntax is most necessary and evident at crisis points of recapitulation in the face of potentially broken continuity. So it is at the beginning of chapter 32 when David must cope with the thought of Steerforth's betrayal, through his seduction of Em'ly. Or in chapter 51 when the deserted Ham struggles to convey to Em'ly via David his continuing love without admitting the continuing pain that must for ever accompany it. Or whenever, as in chapters 44 and 48, David has to admit to himself, on paper, painfully critical thoughts about his wife Dora, while nonetheless continuing to love her. Or in chapter 58, with his wanting and not wanting to turn back to Agnes, lest that seems to be only on second thought after the death of Dora.[13] It is in such tender places of aftermath or transition that we most find what the novelist Graham Greene called 'Dickens's secret prose, that sense of a mind speaking to itself with *no one else* there to listen'.[14]

Those secrets of the psyche lie in the coded inclusions, like tiny signs of half-thoughts ('almost', 'hardly') sometimes specially inserted by Dickens in the very midst of writing as though the 'whisper' of a thought (*DC* 58, 700). '[E]ven now' is characteristic, the effect of the young David still vulnerably felt within the older, even as he writes from what could have been a lofty adult height (*DC* 11, 132). These single little words seem to come from a different dimension of mind within the otherwise horizontal line of a sentence. When David thinks of how it was he who had introduced Steerforth into Mr Peggotty's family at Yarmouth, he writes: 'I felt my own unconscious part on his pollution of an honest home' (*DC* 32, 388). And his sorrow at what happened as a result, he goes on, 'may bear an involuntary witness' against Steerforth on Judgement Day (*DC* 32, 388). '[I]nvoluntary' is like 'unconscious': they come on second thought like winces of reluctant entanglement in the complexity of adult life, at once guilty and innocent.[15] When those two states coexist, that is when Dickens knows he is in his human element.

So it is with Dr Strong, forced into explicitness at the suspicions levelled against his much younger wife:

> 'I knew her father well. I knew her well. I had taught her what I could, for the love of all her beautiful and virtuous qualities. If I did her wrong; as I fear I did, in taking advantage (but I never meant it) of her gratitude and her affection; I ask pardon of that lady, in my heart. (*DC* 42, 528)

The parenthesis '(but I never meant it)' is another fine insertion in the manuscript, a sort of verbal intercessor in the way that Mr Dick became a gently physical one. It can hardly be said at the same time, or on the same level, as the other things in the sentence, it is so pinched for room and place; and yet, rather than some lame excuse to be offered afterwards, it is still a sadly implicated part of the story, in the midst of all

---

[13] See my 'Deep Reading in the Manuscripts' for further analysis of these places.
[14] Graham Greene, *The Lost Childhood and Other Essays* (London: Eyre and Spottiswoode, 1951), 53 (my italics).
[15] These insertions are part of what Michael Corballis describes as *The Recursive Mind* (Princeton: Princeton University Press, 2011).

that overcomes good intent. It is about what humans cannot help, about what remains, after all the active efforts and assertions and intentions, residually and fundamentally passive and dependent in a mortal creature. Dickens was a fighter, a self-made man who developed, as a result of his own childhood trauma at the equivalent of Murdstone and Grinby's, 'a passionate resolve, even while he was yielding to circumstances, *not to be what circumstances were conspiring to make him*'.[16] And yet however resolutely he built up his secondary defences and defiant achievements of will, there was something about the collapse back into involuntary dependence and passivity that felt to him more fundamentally true, more ontologically primary.

So it was when Mr Peggotty and Ham visited David at his school, 'ducking at me with their hats and squeezing one another against the wall'. He couldn't 'help laughing; but it was much more in the pleasure of seeing them, than at the appearance they made'. Laughing till there are tears in his eyes, he suddenly breaks down, even as Ham tries to cheer him:

> 'Why how you have growed!'
> 'Am I grown?' I said, drying my eyes. I was not crying at anything particular I knew of; but somehow it made me cry to see old friends. (*DC* 7, 87–8)

'Somehow' is another code-word in the language of secrets, the work done not so much *by* the language, through specific naming, as subconsciously conveyed *through* it. A happy reunion suddenly releases a whole tearful burst of memory in the midst of time. The two from outside remind him of what he was too internally involved in to realize, the subject poignantly turned object to himself: 'Am I grown?' Or there is another collapse, after David flees the factory to make the long lonely journey on foot to find the aunt he has never known:

> Here my self-support gave way all at once; and with a movement of my hands, intended to show her my ragged state, and call it to witness that I had suffered something, I broke into a passion of crying, which I suppose had been pent up within me all the week. (*DC* 13, 163)

Before a startled Aunt Trotwood, his helpless gesture at the end of the journey is the appeal to look at him, at rock-bottom; an inside in exhausted search of some outside for itself. At such moments David has an overflowing sense of his own life story come back upon him, turning to belated tears. These are occasions that strip away the superstructures, and Dickens is glad of their relief. He loves tears and the primary questions they re-create within those that have them: why do people cry when suddenly they are happy? why do tears come only after the worst is over?

---

[16] John Forster, *Life of Charles Dickens*, ed. J. W. T. Ley (London: Cecil Palmer, 1928), 38. See pp. 32–6 for the autobiographical fragment of Dickens's own childhood trauma, a starting point for the writing of *David Copperfield*.

There is deep-rooted in Dickens's mind a basic planning structure. It is shown in a larger-scale revision that took place between manuscript and print late on in the composition of chapter 50. It was only at the proof stage that Dickens decided that Mr Peggotty should not be present when Martha leads David to Em'ly, only to find her already confronted by a jealously vengeful Rosa Dartle. It is a moment that the steadfast man has spent years of recent life in seeking, and yet Dickens, crossing out references to Mr Peggotty accompanying David, will not let him have it straightforwardly. He takes him out, to put him back in only later. It produces a suspense in keeping with Dickens's love of drama, as in all those occasions he wrote 'Not Yet' to himself in his working notes. But what is actually most telling within the large effect is the little in-between addition, made on second thought, that Dickens interpolated in the proof. It could have been no more than a bridging explanation, but as so often, Dickens turns the narrative gap into an opportunity to fill it with something from a deeper level:

> A silence succeeded. I did not know what to do. Much as I desired to put an end to the interview, I felt that I had no right to present myself; that it was for Mr. Peggotty alone to see her and recover her. Would he never come? I thought impatiently. (*DC* 50, 613)

It is Steerforth who can 'pass' carelessly and promiscuously from one situation to another without formal transition (*DC* 20, 249). This is instead like the moment when David first decides to run away from London to his aunt: it only occurs to him as the Micawbers leave, not because he reasons how lonely he will be thereafter but because it was suddenly 'like being that moment turned adrift into my present life, with such knowledge of it ready made, as experience had given me' (*DC* 12, 148). It is about finding the right time, creating the right time, even belatedly, through an intuitive dialectic. First thought: have Mr Peggotty present as he would wish, but on second thought, subtract him; yet on third thought, shift narrative suspense to the level of instinctive moral formality in life—'I had no right ... it was for Mr Peggotty'—and only then let him come in.

At such a moment David cannot be the simple go-between that Mr Dick once was. He has just to stand there, to bear it mentally as unavailing witness, straining to keep open the potential place for Mr Peggotty. As an unknown visitor puts it in chapter 33 of *Dombey and Son*, though for the most part we go on in our clockwork routine, there are moments and thoughts that are (he hesitates to say it, but does) 'a metaphysical sort of thing'.[17] That is what thought, surprisingly to those who did not suppose Dickens a thinker, is at the most of itself in *David Copperfield*—unaffectedly metaphysical. It began when the boy knew that within the physical home there was an invisible separation from his own mother.

But David can no longer be the crying boy who begged his aunt to see his whole story through a single physical gesture. Like Dickens, he has had to grow into becoming a witness not only to others but to himself and his own life: a silently internalized witness,

---

[17] *Dombey and Son*, ed. Alan Horsman (Oxford: Clarendon Press, 1974), chapter 33, page 459. The unnamed character is eventually revealed to be Mr Morfin.

voluntary *and* involuntary without a clear and certain boundary between the two. This rich melding process culminates in 'the blending of experience and imagination' involved in his becoming a writer (*DC* 46, 568). The blending includes the unknowably dense and subtle mix of Copperfield and Dickens himself, to the maximum of possibility and mutation. It makes for a text that can say that it is private, that it is intended for no one else's eyes but its writer's (whoever that exactly is), and that it has meant more to that writer in the writing than any reader can ever know. And yet it can be published externally even as though it had not been so, remaining secretly inside itself in David's own manuscript, beyond the logic of mere contradiction. This is not, as the hermeneutics of suspicion would have it, simply Dickens's manipulation; it is more metaphysical than that. The usual boundaries seem retained at one level, but abolished at another where a greater truth lies, in the place of anomalous refuge between external life and inner thought that writing holds open.

Keeping his worries about his wife and his marriage to himself, David turns to writing in lieu of the impossibility of speaking, to give place to his second-thought secrets: 'I search my breast, and I commit its secrets, without any reservation to this paper.' Or that is what seems to have been first written amidst Dickens's deletions. But then Dickens made another parenthetical insertion, beyond the certainty of control: 'and I commit its secrets, *if I know them*, without any reservation' (*DC* 44, 551). This—the entrée into a language of secrets, itself involving a secret language—is what happens now instead of the earlier relief of tears: so it was with Ham who 'was not crying' but—what was remarkably like and then unlike it—'collecting himself', putting the tears beneath him (*DC* 51, 630). Provoked by the pain of second thoughts and further responses to them, there comes flooding into mind so much psychological material from deep identity as to be beyond conscious control. But not beyond collecting or recollecting, as the thinker tries to become worthy of his emerging thoughts by being able to hold and connect them from below upwards.

No wonder *David Copperfield* in its discovery of the unconscious was one of Freud's favourite books, further remarkable for how un-scared of his own unconsciousness its protagonist becomes. The older David had always worked forwards in remembering—'approaching' and 'going on' are favourite narrative verbs—rather than merely looking backwards. Not settling for second-thought hindsight, he goes through his experience again, at a different level and in a different medium, thereby telling 'how some main points in the character I shall unconsciously develop, I suppose, in writing my life, were gradually forming all this while' (*DC* 11, 144). Not even memory is known in advance.

This is the Dickensian achievement that reaches its maturity in fictional autobiography when it is not a case of complacent self-knowledge, but rather, of whatever 'I shall turn out to be ... these pages must show' (*DC* 1, 1).

> Given what one knows, what one does not know springs up; and I am as absolutely certain of its being true, as I am of the law of gravitation—if such a thing be possible, more so.[18]

[18] *PLets* 3:441.

For Dickens the movement of truly creative art is not from what one does *not* know to what one does, but from what one *does* know to what one does not, and never can wholly.

And the pages mainly show it not through the set stages of first, second, and third thoughts, as in the revised template for chapter 50, but through an intricate 'blending' of times and phases in syntax. It is most clear when sentences are tied together through the interplay of collocations such as: I do not know this/I only know that. The older David at the end of chapter 14 is relieved to have finished describing his time at Murdstone and Grinby's: 'Whether it lasted for a year, or more, or less, I do not know. I only know that it was, and ceased to be; and that I have written, and there I leave it' (*DC* 14, 184). Dickens worked hard in the manuscript to truncate every phrase in that last pained sentence into a basic shorthand that makes more of less ('was', 'ceased to be', 'written'), in order to 'leave it'—not just to the past again like some dead fact but in the unresolved silence of wherever it is that 'it' may still exist. It is like the childhood home when David revisits it years later, and the old spots around it: 'I haunted them, as my memory had often done, and lingered among them as my younger thoughts had lingered when I was far away' (*DC* 22, 272)—as though those young thoughts remain there, shadowy but indelible, and it is them that he is really revisiting. These things are metaphysical. Or again, here is David in chapter 21, on what is (significantly) a return to Yarmouth only for him to find that his childhood sweetheart Little Em'ly is now betrothed to Ham:

> Whether I had come there with any lingering fancy that I was still to love little Em'ly, I don't know. I know that I was filled with pleasure by all this; but, at first, with an indescribably sensitive pleasure, that a very little would have changed to pain. (*DC* 21, 269)

A second-thought man would more crudely have thought, 'Actually I felt jealous, but then I repressed it.' But the order here is, as so often in Dickens, surprised by thought: 'I don't know ... I [do] know ... but'—the 'but' retrieving what was 'first ... indescribably' rather than a later, thinner vocabulary of merely pain or pleasure. The manuscript shows 'at first' was a phrase Dickens added, never wanting to forget that.

It is not that second thoughts autonomously reprove or replace first ones in *David Copperfield*. If a sentence involves hard thoughts about soft feelings, it also has feelings again about those very thoughts. The instinctive feelings in first thoughts themselves react back against the pain of second ones, to become more like thought, in a great re-creation of saturated human mentality, up and down the scale of consciousness, back and forward in experienced time, left and right across cerebral hemispheres, generating too many thoughts in too complex an order to be simply counted or separated. Dickens always wanted more. It is the phrase he inserted for Ham, which Ham asked David to give Mr Peggotty on final parting: the thanks of an orphan, (first) 'as he was ever a father to'; (second) 'ever as a father to'; finally (third) 'as he was ever more than a father to' (*DC* 51, 631).

Dickens wanted what was almost too much for him, sensing that too much made him more delicate, not less. Even in beginning to get over the death of Dora, Dickens's David will write only 'of a kind of sorrow that was not oppressive, not despairing'—and, even then, amend it to 'not *all* oppressive, not *quite* despairing' (*DC* 58, 697; my italics), able to recover life itself only very tentatively. Yet the words speak to each other with something more than suspicion, something other than extenuation, however much they may begin from those grosser intents. What is 'indescribably sensitive' in the writer knows what difference 'a very little' can make at a tipping point.

Apparently little words have to handle a great blending of felt experience: feeler-like adjectives, 'unconscious', 'involuntary', or 'secret'; subordinate clauses and parentheses of 'if', 'that this', 'though', or 'but'; and above all, the adverbs—'almost', 'too', 'perhaps', 'even', 'still', 'hardly', 'not quite', 'somehow'. These are not substantive nouns or main verbs but look like secondary things, and in manuscript (the best clue we have to the secrets of mental composition) often appear as second thoughts. But though subordinate to the words they modify, they are still in front of them, like prior guides adapting to their own adapter role. They are metaphysical masters, half-obscured and half-disguised within these subtle modifiers, trying still to be of service; first things seeking what might remain of their influence in the world, even through the pain and difficulty of an intricate syntax. What is at stake here—for students of syntax or manuscripts, for explorers of psychology through literature, and for further research into complex mental blending—is the making of a model of the human mind, in some of its finest interrelations, through the making of a novel.

Further Reading

Richard J. Dunn (ed.), *David Copperfield: An Annotated Bibliography* (New York: Garland, 1981); supplement with Ann Tandy (New York: AMS, 2000)
Richard J. Dunn (ed.), *Charles Dickens's David Copperfield: A Sourcebook* (London: Routledge, 2003)
Tim Parks, *The Novel: A Survival Skill* (Oxford: Oxford University Press, 2015)
J. P. Stern, *On Realism* (London: Routledge, 1973)
Garrett Stewart, *Novel Violence* (Chicago: University of Chicago Press, 2009)

CHAPTER 15

BLEAK HOUSE

KATE FLINT

I begin, like very many critics of *Bleak House*, at the beginning: with the one-word statement of place—'London'—that opens the first paragraph, and the two-word declaration that begins the second: 'Fog everywhere' (*Bleak House*, chapter 1, page 5).[1] The location established, that first paragraph goes on to specify, more precisely, the legal setting, and then links this, by association if not direct causation, to the confusion, muddiness, and obscurantist properties that stick to the profession of the law for the remainder of the novel.[2] Description, simile, and metaphor merge together: they create, like the diffusive smoke and fog, a novelistic topography that, while highly suggestive, can prove challenging to navigate. Critical approaches are perhaps best seen as something uncomfortably similar to that November mud, gaining their value through accumulation and accretion. *Bleak House* sets up an irresistible lure for Victorian literary scholars—it is, as Simon Joyce remarks, 'perhaps best seen as the Victorianists' white whale, the one text that we are all destined to take a shot at'.[3] Rather as the search for Moby Dick in Herman Melville's 1851 masterpiece is often understood as a quest for meaning in a broader sense, so criticism of *Bleak House* frequently, and understandably, reverts to the topic of interpretation and its limits.

For however compelling very many individual readings of the novel may be, the text itself always seems to exceed and challenge them. The most productive critical approaches to *Bleak House* have a good deal in common: rather than offering an overview, 'as if they

---

[1] *Bleak House*, ed. George Ford and Sylvère Monod, Norton Critical Edition (New York and London: W. W. Norton & Co., 1977). Subsequent references are inserted parenthetically in the text by *BH* chapter, page.

[2] A good deal of *Bleak House* criticism engages at some level with interrelated issues of power, governance, bureaucracy, and law: for a specific focus on the legal system, see Kieran Dolin, 'Law, Literature and Symbolic Revolution: *Bleak House*', *Australasian Journal of Victorian Studies* 12, 1 (2007): 10–18, and Jan-Melissa Schramm, 'Dickens and the National Interest: On the Representation of Parties in *Bleak House*', *Law and Humanities* 6, 2 (2012): 217–42.

[3] Simon Joyce, 'Inspector Bucket versus Tom-all-Alone's: *Bleak House*, Literary Theory, and the Condition-of-England in the 1850s', *Dickens Studies Annual* 32 (2002): 129–49.

were up in a balloon' (*BH* 1, 5), they trace new patterns and connections through the text, and thus become a way of continually reorienting the reader—whether they address the law or evolution, gender and domesticity or sanitary reform, philanthropy or the aristocracy; or whether they deal with emotions (disappointment, frustration, hope) and the creation of affective responses in the reader, including patterns of sympathetic feeling;[4] or whether they take topics, like concealment, deferral, and disclosure; heteroglossia and repetition, that link content and form.

Bleak House itself never lets the reader settle for long. If the novel appears to begin in foggy London, it starts again in chapter 3, with Esther's self-deprecating hesitation—a hesitation so pronounced that one instantly wonders what may consciously or unconsciously be being concealed by this first-person narrator: 'I have a great deal of difficulty in beginning to write my portion of these pages', Esther opens, 'for I know I am not clever' (*BH* 3, 17).[5] If the first chapter opens with atmospheric indistinctness and allusive language, dramatizing the unknowability of the city, then this new voice propels one into uncertainty about Esther's authority, self-knowledge, and hence her very position as narrator. Hilary Schor has complained that this tone represents 'the worst of female self-presentation',[6] but also notes its effectiveness in destabilizing the more impersonal (if decidedly quirky, and recognizably Dickens-like) prose of the novel's early pages. Any criticism of the novel must take into account this deliberate, radical oscillation of point of view, even if—like John Jordan's study of Esther in *Supposing* Bleak House—it makes its own radical choice of concentrating on just one of these narrative voices.[7]

The existence of two separate openings, Matthew Beaumont notes, recalls Dickens's later novella, *George Silverman's Explanation* (1868), with its dithering first-person narrator who cannot quite make up his mind where his own story should begin.[8] For, as Beaumont explains, and as Dickens himself suggests through the allusion to a waddling megalosaurus in the opening paragraph, origins tend not just to be hard to determine, but go back a long way. In the case of *Bleak House*, they include the writer's literary

---

[4] For the place of sentiment and sympathy in *Bleak House*, see Nancy Yousef, 'The Poverty of Charity', in Eileen Gillooly and Deirdre David (eds), *Contemporary Dickens* (Columbus: Ohio State University Press, 2009), 53–75.

[5] Esther's own 'affinity with diffuse forms of vapor, mist, and rain', and its connection with her tentative embodiment as a subject, is discussed in Justine Pizzo, 'Esther's Ether: Atmospheric Character in Charles Dickens's *Bleak House*', *Victorian Literature and Culture* 42 (2014): 81–98.

[6] Hilary Margo Schor, *Dickens and the Daughter of the House* (New York: Cambridge University Press, 1999), 103.

[7] John O. Jordan, *Supposing* Bleak House (Charlottesville: University of Virginia Press, 2010). For other influential criticism that has focused on Esther, her narrative, her apparent self-effacement, manipulation of the reader, and means of establishing quiet authority, see Carolyn Dever, 'Broken Mirror, Broken Words: Autobiography, Prosopopeia, and the Dead Mother in *Bleak House*', *Studies in the Novel* 27, 1 (1995): 42–62 (a psychoanalytic reading informed by the theories of Jacques Lacan), and Robert Newsom, '*Villette* and *Bleak House*: Authorizing Women', *Nineteenth-Century Literature* 46, 1 (1991): 54–81.

[8] Matthew Beaumont, 'Beginnings, Ending, Births, Deaths: Sterne, Dickens, and *Bleak House*', *Textual Practice* 26, 5 (2012): 807–27.

predecessors and contemporaries and his own earlier writing; contemporary events and the debates surrounding them (even if, like the compendious Great Exhibition, it would be anachronistic to place these directly within the novel); and current issues, such as discussions about the condition of metropolitan graveyards, or about the proper recipients of charitable effort. The text raises the question of origins very directly in numerous ways, whilst simultaneously evaluating how much importance they hold: the aristocracy's clinging to tradition, for example, is invariably accompanied by stagnation. *Bleak House* embraces the social and literary implications of orphanhood and illegitimacy. In a psychoanalytic reading, Carolyn Dever argues for the importance of loss and mourning to Esther as this allows her to tell her own story;[9] Jordan extends her implications to embrace the themes of haunting, trauma, and ghosts. Yet origins are seldom singular. 'The text highlights copying as a trope', Eleanor Salotto has reminded us; 'copies scatter the myth of origins. In this connection, it is no accident that Esther's father practices copywriting.'[10]

Behind all of this lack of clarity is the fog and indeterminacy of the opening page: fog that is never simply one thing, but that is both a material sign of the increasing pollution in England's capital, the heart of the Empire—and a metaphor for obscurity and obfuscation. In his eco-critical reading of *Bleak House*, Jesse Oak Taylor makes the point that the two go hand in hand, showing that the 'fog materializes the networks, ideologies, and interconnections of the metropolitan economy that are literally but otherwise invisibly responsible for the fog's material composition.'[11] Fog's diffusion contained a physiological threat, too, since it was believed that thick foggy air played a powerful role in spreading disease[12]—an anxiety, and a thread of connection, made palpable through the unnamed ailment that kills Jo, and sickens and disfigures Esther. Together with the crowded graveyard and its putrefying corpses, disease's transmission is part of Dickens's critique of the 1848 Public Health Act.[13] Jarndyce's East Wind may seem like a quirky means of expressing disappointment and displeasure, but at a moment when disease was thought to be spread by a miasmic cloud—not least from London's East End—it had far more deadly overtones.

---

[9] Dever, 'Broken Mirror', 42.

[10] Eleanor Salotto, 'Detecting Esther Summerson's Secrets: Dickens's Bleak House of Representation', *Victorian Literature and Culture* 25, 2 (1997): 333-49; 341.

[11] Jesse Oak Taylor, *The Sky of our Manufacture: The London Fog in British Fiction from Dickens to Woolf* (Charlottesville and London: University of Virginia Press, 2016), 21-43; 43.

[12] Tina Young Choi, 'Narrating the Unexceptional: The Art of Medical Inquiry in Victorian England and the Present', *Literature and Medicine* 22, 1 (2003): 65-83.

[13] Numerous critical responses address the medical and public health aspects of the novel: see, for example, Laura Fasick, 'Dickens and the Diseased Body in *Bleak House*', *Dickens Studies Annual* 24 (1996): 135-51; Socrates Litsios, 'Charles Dickens and the Movement for Sanitary Reform', *Perspectives in Biology and Medicine* 46, 2 (2003): 183-99; Robert E. Lougy, 'Filth, Liminality, and Abjection in Charles Dickens's *Bleak House*', *ELH* 69, 2 (2002): 473-500. For putrefaction, see Tyson Stolte, '"Putrefaction Generally": *Bleak House*, Victorian Psychology, and the Question of Bodily Matter', *Novel: A Forum on Fiction* 44, 3 (2011): 402-23.

If the thick 'London particular' that Esther mistakes for a great fire on her first visit to the city meant that in literal terms 'scarcely anything was to be seen' (*BH* 3, 29), the problem of seeing one's way clearly applies in immediate terms to the confusions of Chancery, and beyond that to the current and future condition of England. More self-referentially, it stands for the challenges that a text crowded with characters, description, and metaphor poses to our attention, memory, and powers of recombination. Jo's inability to read the shop signs that surround him in the City of London, and Krook's illiteracy, are both circumstantial indicators of limited education, and pointed reminders that one may be surrounded by hieroglyphs that one is unable to decipher.

J. Hillis Miller, in what has remained one of the most influential—and useful—pieces of criticism ever written on *Bleak House*, describes the patterning of the novel as synecdochal, arguing that the narration moves according to a logic of substitution, with a single 'character, scene, or situation' connected to a number of other different parts. Yet even when seen in terms of a pattern of connections, meaning is not always easily discernible—or rather, our tracing of these connections leads to a questioning of 'all interpretation'. The novel, moreover, 'is a complex fabric of recurrences. Characters, scenes, themes and metaphors return in proliferating resemblances'. Meaning, Hillis Miller would have it, is endlessly deferred.[14] Such logic, too, makes it impossible to determine whether one takes an individual character *as* individual, or as in some way representative of a type—what Alex Woloch, writing of the fictional work done by 'minor' characters, terms 'the tension between the authenticity of a character in-and-of-himself and the reduction of the character into the thematic or symbolic field'[15] (the figure of Jo is exemplary here). Or does, say, an orderly, well-run home, like Mrs Bagnet's, function as a synecdoche for the nation, or simply stand as a laudable example of good housekeeping? A further set of ambiguities is created when we turn from the representational to the stylistic. Mr Jellyby opens closet doors in his home, and out tumble 'letters, tea, forks, odd boots and shoes of children, firewood, wafers, saucepan-lids, damp sugar in odds and ends of paper bags, foot-stools, blacklead brushes, bread', and so on (*BH* 30, 373). This ostensibly suggests the nadir of domestic havoc: not just a confusion of possessions out of place, but a confusion of value that can stand in, once again, for our ability to read the condition of the country. On the other hand, it's impossible to deny the writerly and readerly delight to be found in such a cornucopia.

If Hillis Miller construed *Bleak House* as an endlessly open text, D. A. Miller's criticism, which likewise has been enduringly influential, proclaimed it a novel that, read attentively, reveals the structures that underpinned—that, indeed, policed—mid-Victorian Britain.[16] The structures of this disciplinary apparatus are both institutional

---

[14] J. Hillis Miller, 'Introduction' to Charles Dickens, *Bleak House* (Harmondsworth: Penguin, 1971), 12, 34, and 17.

[15] Alex Woloch, *The One vs. the Many: Minor Characters and the Space of the Protagonist in the Novel* (Princeton and Oxford: Princeton University Press, 2003), 15.

[16] D. A. Miller, *The Novel and the Police* (Berkeley and London: University of California Press, 1992), 58–106.

(the law, however imperfect; the police; religion) and ideological—the assumptions and attitudes of those (including contemporary Victorian readers) who play a role in sustaining these systems, and, indeed, whose interpellation within them helps constitute their own sustaining sense of social—and hence, often, personal—identity. The somewhat rigid nature of such a reading, underpinned by the earlier writings of Michel Foucault, is hard to sustain, however, once it's brought into relation with the dialogic nature of Dickens's prose and plots.[17] Mr Gridley, 'the man from Shropshire', whose life has indisputably been ruined by Chancery, proclaims that at the root of his problems lies 'The system! I am told, on all hands, it's the system. I mustn't look to individuals. It's the system' (*BH* 15, 193). But right away, he shows spontaneous and immediate kindness to the children round him—something that cannot easily be reduced to anything systematic. Bruce Robbins offers more flexibility than D. A. Miller when he argues that although individuals may have limited agency within bureaucratic systems, this does not prevent them acting as advocates (and this role of advocacy is also, perhaps, something that the novel sought to instil in the contemporary reader).[18] Esther's delirious dream, when she became a bead on a flaming ring or necklace, and 'when my only prayer was to be taken off from the rest' (*BH* 35, 432) reads like the breaking out of an unconscious desire to be released from the systemic bonds of duty.

Yet what the collision between Gridley's words and actions dramatizes—or what is put into play by D. A. Miller's concern with Victorian Britain's underlying structures—is a further open-ended tension within the novel: a tension that lies at the heart of mid-Victorian debates about liberalism. On the one hand, there's the perceived necessity for the state to intervene in ways that will ameliorate the lives of individuals: not least those who live in the pestilential conditions of such appalling slums as Tom-all-Alone's. As Lauren Goodlad puts it: '*Bleak House* memorably dramatizes the need for pastorship in a society of allegedly self-reliant individuals.'[19] On the other hand, there's a strong emphasis on the need for personal responsibility, aligned with useful social activity and caregiving that should begin, quite literally, at home. The flip side of this is the blinkered selfishness and what amounts to self-destruction in those who, like Skimpole, or even Richard Carstone, refuse not just to assume responsibility for others, but completely lack self-awareness and self-governance. They thereby short-circuit conduits of human affection and sympathy, whether between characters, or between reader and text. Once again, this division of attention—towards a broad picture of society; towards the actions of individuals and their consequences—seems to correspond to (even if it doesn't always neatly map onto) the novel's bipartite split into third-person and first-person narration,

---

[17] Indeed, Jeremy Tambling takes a deliberately contrary line when, in his introduction to a highly useful compilation of important essays on *Bleak House*, he maintains that the novel is, rather, primarily concerned with the unrepresentable and—more controversially—with the ahistorical. 'Introduction', *Bleak House: Charles Dickens*, ed. Jeremy Tambling (New York: St Martin's, 1998).

[18] Bruce Robbins, 'Telescopic Philanthropy: Professionalism and Responsibility in *Bleak House*', in Homi K. Bhabha (ed.), *Nation and Narration* (London: Routledge, 1990), 213–30.

[19] Lauren Goodlad, 'Is there a Pastor in the *House*? Sanitary Reform, Professionalism, and Philanthropy in Dickens's Mid-Century Fiction', *Victorian Literature and Culture* 31, 2 (2003): 525–53; 526.

with Esther's role frequently being to bring home the importance of small-scale, practical interventions and acts of kindness.

However—and there is always a 'however' when one is making critical generalizations about *Bleak House*—the novel does not allow one to believe confidently that even the happiest of homes—such as one is encouraged to think the new Bleak House will be—necessarily offers some kind of totalizing solution to England's woes, even if the novel repeatedly makes it clear that Mrs Jellyby's and Mrs Pardiggle's efforts would be better occupied at home than abroad. Despite Dickens's belief in the rippling-outward effects of local action, *Bleak House* points to no universal panacea, nor, perhaps, does it locate optimism anywhere other than in localized action. Indeed, Emily Heady has shown how Dickens 'uses his familiar critiques of utilitarian and traditionalist ideologies to attack the mother of all Victorian metanarratives: the narrative of progress'.[20]

All the same, if there is frequently a centripetal force at work, encouraging us to acknowledge the sentimental attraction and the neat logic of the domestic, the novel also deploys, time and again, a centrifugal framework that points away from the country. The rest of the world can manifest itself in something as apparently casual as a piece of furniture—the 'Native-Hindoo chair' (*BH* 6, 62) and the prints depicting tea preparation in China that appear among other bric-a-brac in Jarndyce's home, or in something with more obvious metaphoric force: the moment when, at Deal, the 'thick white fog' rises like a Turnerian painting of dawn, revealing a huge number of ships (including a 'large Indiaman' with the sunburnt Allan Woodcourt on board) (*BH* 45, 544), and thus suggesting the global connections that England has to the rest of the world: connections that had been strongly reinforced by the 1851 Great Exhibition.[21]

James Buzard has called our attention to the nationalistic implications of what he terms these 'everything-is-connected arguments',[22] but a further set of connections are brought out when one considers *Bleak House*'s reception and repurposing beyond its native country, and the different ways in which it incorporates references to this wider world. The publication of Hannah Crafts's *The Bondwoman's Narrative* in 2002 showed the indebtedness of this African American writer to Dickens's novel (published in Frederick Douglass's *Journal* between April 1852 and December 1853). Daniel Hack shows how Crafts refashions Dickens in a way that, among other things, makes us consider how readerly sympathy works—whether it depends on, or transcends, local and circumstantial factors. Crafts implicitly asks whether domesticity functions as a truly happy ending, or whether it suggests a quietism, an evasion of a call for political

---

[20] Emily Heady, 'The Polis's Different Voices: Narrating England's Progress in Dickens's *Bleak House*', *Texas Studies in Literature and Language* 48, 4 (2006): 312–39; 315.

[21] For the implicit presence of the Great Exhibition in *Bleak House*, see Phillip Landon, 'Great Exhibitions: Representations of the Crystal Palace in Mayhew, Dickens, and Dostoevsky', *Nineteenth-Century Contexts* 20 (1997): 27–59; Robert Tracy, 'Lighthousekeeping: *Bleak House* and the Crystal Palace', *Dickens Studies Annual* 33 (2003): 25–53.

[22] James Buzard, *Disorienting Fiction: The Autoethnographic Work of Nineteenth-Century British Novels* (Princeton: Princeton University Press, 2005), 114.

action.[23] Hack maintains that Crafts's repurposing of *Bleak House* draws our attention to the relative paucity of references to other ethnicities within Dickens's novel—that is, beyond the mentions of the natives on the banks of the Borrioboola-gha, the far-off focus of Mrs Jellyby's telescopic philanthropy, or the Tockahoopo Indians, to whom Egbert Pardiggle sent pocket money (under, one suspects, moralizing parental duress). I would argue, though, that the existence of Crafts's novel makes us register all the more strongly the terms in which Caddy Jellyby complains of her enslavement to her mother's charitable concerns, that she couldn't be worse off if she ' "wasn't a what's-his-name—man and a brother" ' (*BH* 14, 166), and the remarks made by Harold Skimpole, declaring himself 'truly cosmopolitan', and seeing the labours and effort of others, worldwide, as only serving his own pleasure.

> Take an extreme case. Take the case of the Slaves on American plantations. I dare say they are worked hard, I dare say they don't altogether like it, I dare say theirs is an unpleasant experience on the whole; but they people the landscape for me, they give it a poetry for me, and perhaps that is one of the pleasanter objects of their existence. I am very sensible of it, if it be, and I shouldn't wonder if it were!

Esther observes, in a beautifully succinct put-down, that she 'always wondered on these occasions whether he ever thought of Mrs. Skimpole and the children, and in what point of view they presented themselves to his cosmopolitan mind. So far as I could understand, they rarely presented themselves at all' (*BH* 18, 227). If once again, Dickens is reinforcing the point that one's responsibilities begin at home, he is also satirizing aesthetic escapism (of the type exemplified by Leigh Hunt, the model for Skimpole) and, at the same time as condemning his self-regarding character, in fact getting in a blow for emancipation. As with the morning fog that lifts at Deal, there are moments in *Bleak House* when Dickens alludes to the bonds of sympathy that might usefully be extended beyond England's shores.

Frederick Douglass's Journal was not the only American periodical in which *Bleak House* appeared—part of what Meredith McGill has termed a 'culture of reprinting' made possible by the lack of copyright agreement between Britain and America.[24] Considering the impact of the novel on, say, those who read it when serialized in

---

[23] Daniel Hack, 'Close Reading at a Distance: The African-Americanization of *Bleak House*', *Critical Inquiry* 34, 4 (2008): 729–53. See also Hollis Robbins, 'Blackening *Bleak House*: Hannah Crafts's *The Bondwoman's Narrative*', in Henry Louis Gates and Hollis Robbins (eds), *In Search of Hannah Crafts: Critical Essays on The Bondwoman's Narrative* (New York: Civitas, 2004): 71–86, and Rebecca Soares, 'Literary Graftings: Hannah Crafts's *The Bondwoman's Narrative* and the Nineteenth-Century Transatlantic Reader', *Victorians Periodicals Review* 41, 1 (2011): 1–23. For a yet broader consideration of *Bleak House* and slavery, see Emily Madsen, 'Phiz's Black Doll: Integrating Text and Etching in *Bleak House*', *Victorian Literature and Culture* 41 (2013): 411–33; Rachel Teukolsky, 'Pictures in Bleak Houses: Slavery and the Aesthetics of Transatlantic Form', *ELH* 76 (2009): 491–522.

[24] Meredith McGill, *American Literature and the Culture of Reprinting, 1834–1853* (Philadelphia: University of Pennsylvania Press, 2003).

Harper's New Monthly Magazine (April 1852–October 1853)[25] both form part of the interpretative history of the novel, and is also closely linked to *Bleak House*'s material history. Analysing this materiality also means looking at such things as the advertisements contained between the wrappers of its monthly parts; the impact of reading it in serial form, with the attendant dynamics of deferral and suspense, and the visual amplification provided by Hablot K. Browne ('Phiz's') illustrations—for example, subtly conveying Esther's tendency to self-effacement by almost invariably depicting her bonnet, not her face.[26] A reading of *Bleak House* that pays attention to the objects within it—like that Hindoo chair—could potentially bring out the hidden histories of production and consumption that inhere within apparently inconsequential items, thereby connecting utensils and furnishings with a broader world of commerce and manufacture.

One particular substance, paper, has commanded a great deal of attention. As Hack puts it in *The Material Interests of the Victorian Novel*, '*Bleak House* is less "a document about the interpretation of documents", as J. Hillis Miller argued ... than it is a document about the materiality of documents ... and the interpretation of that materiality'.[27] He extends this observation to handwriting, pointing out the relationship between writing's physical materiality and that of the human body. By extension, again, he shows how '*Bleak House* reduces the difference between texts and bodies'.[28] Both are available to be deciphered, and sometimes almost coalesce, as with Caddy's inkiness. Suzanne Daly has built on Miller's analysis to show that these documents 'frequently function as weapons, deployed with aggressive intent to work material harm'.[29] Dickens, she argues, is concerned with the operations of indirect violence; the paper means through which individuals are harassed and tormented by others; the paperwork that makes and unmakes characters' fates. A great deal of paper, indeed, circulates within the novel (in the law courts, in Krook's rag and bottle warehouse, in the Jellyby household); old clothes bought by Krook are destined for the rag mill (or so a notice in the shop's window tells us) to be turned into paper; the novel itself, of course, is published

---

[25] For *Harper's* reprinting of British literature, see Jennifer Phegley, *Educating the Proper Woman Reader: Victorian Family Literary Magazines and the Cultural Health of the Nation* (Columbus: Ohio State University Press, 2005): 31–69.

[26] See Shayla Alarie, 'Failure in a Successful Interpretation: The Problem of Visual Literacy in Hablot Knight Browne's Illustrations for *Bleak House*', *International Journal of the Book* 7, 4 (2010): 143–59; Donald H. Erickson, '*Bleak House* and Victorian Art and Illustration: Charles Dickens's Visual Narrative Style', *Journal of Narrative Technique* 13 (1983): 31–46; Michael Steig, *Dickens and Phiz* (Bloomington and London: Indiana University Press, 1978): 131–72.

[27] Daniel Hack, *The Material Interests of the Victorian Novel* (Charlottesville and London: University of Virginia Press, 2005), 38. For more on the advertisements, see Emily Steinlight, ' "Anti-Bleak House": Advertising and the Victorian Novel', *Narrative* 14, 2 (2006): 132–62.

[28] Hack, *Material Interests*, 43.

[29] Suzanne Daly, 'Belligerent Instruments: The Documentary Violence of *Bleak House*', *Studies in the Novel* 47, 1 (2015): 20–42; 20. Daly's article also harks back to Bruce Robbins's remark about 'the extraordinary violence of everyday life in *Bleak House*'. Robbins, 'Telescopic Philanthropy', 221. Considering the novel's smoky fogginess, she cites Rob Nixon's term 'slow violence', referring to the tendency of environmental catastrophes to unfold gradually. Rob Nixon, *Slow Violence and the Environmentalism of the Poor* (Cambridge, MA: Harvard University Press, 2011).

on paper. Patrick Chappell takes this material instance of transformation a step further, arguing that paper 'possesses a deep affiliation with *Bleak House*'s structural form', in which characters appear, disappear, reappear, in different combinations. Like paper's forms, some characters are durable, some transient.[30]

Elaine Auyoung proposes less of a hermeneutic approach than a phenomenological one: in other words, rather than regarding *Bleak House*'s abundant accumulation of items as if they were actual things in the world, she asks us to consider them as words working to direct the reader's attention. Despite offering what appear to be densely crowded descriptions, the novel also forces readers to recognize what is *not* made visible, and remains indeterminate. Those characters within the novel who know they only possess partial information are the reader's surrogates: all the same, 'The more that readers find themselves drawn in to the fictional world'—and the proliferation of detail is a seductive lure in this respect—'the more likely they are to find themselves kept out'.[31] Plentiful detail, in other words, helps bring us to a position where we have to recognize how little we know, and form our own connective pathways in order to make sense of it all.

Auyoung's phenomenological emphasis also points us to the role of senses in interpretation. *Bleak House* is full of the dynamics of looking, especially pertinent to recognition and resemblances, whether between live individuals or—in the case of Lady Dedlock—their portraits, circulating in reproducible visual forms, to be hung on the walls of cheap lodgings. Other senses play a central role: sound (the clattering of crockery, the rattling of tin mugs in Mrs Bagnet's kitchen, signalling brisk and cheerful efficiency; the ominous dripping and echoing footsteps at Chesney Wold); taste, smell, and touch, all combined in the terrible stench of cloying burnt chops, the 'stagnant, sickening oil', the defiling 'thick yellow liquor ... which is offensive to the touch and sight and more offensive to the smell' (*BH* 32, 401), that emanates from the self-combusting Krook. Robyn Warhol, while acknowledging the power of sight within the novel to establish spatial relations, shows how Dickens powerfully employs the other senses so that space is constructed through the unseen as well as the seen, through appeals to many parts of the body, moving beyond visual perception to 'visceral apperception'.[32] Others build both on the work of Henri Lefebvre and on Victorian cartography to discuss *Bleak House*'s spaces. Jane Griffith demonstrates how a gendering of space takes place through the double narrative, in which 'Esther is relegated to a perspective in which she merely *sees* urban space cartographically, understanding space as stable'. Only the 'omniscient narrator' (conventionally gendered as male, but, we might point out, far from all-seeing)

---

[30] Patrick Chappell, 'Paper Routes: *Bleak House*, Rubbish Theory, and the Character Economy of Realism', *ELH* 80 (2013): 783–810; 784.

[31] Elaine Auyoung, 'Standing Outside *Bleak House*', *Nineteenth-Century Literature* 68: (2013): 180–200; 200.

[32] Robyn Warhol, 'Describing the Unseen: The Visceral and Virtual Construction of Spaces in *Bleak House*', *Style* 48, 4 (2014): 612–28; 612.

'is permitted an ability to understand urban space as far from stable, but instead as constructed and shaped *by* perspective and sight'.[33]

To walk through a city or to travel to different parts of a country is to make connections through geographic mobility. It is, as we have seen, almost impossible to ignore the emphasis on interconnectedness in *Bleak House*, and few critics seem able to resist quoting the paragraph in chapter 16:

> What connexion can there be, between the place in Lincolnshire, the house in town, the Mercury in powder, and the whereabouts of Jo the outlaw with the broom, who had that distant ray of light upon him when he swept the churchyard step? What connexion can there have been between many people in the innumerable histories of this world, who, from opposite sides of great gulfs, have, nevertheless, been very curiously brought together! (*BH* 16, 197)

Readers are invited to consider the issue of connectivity for themselves, even if they are as confused as Mr Snagsby, unsure whether or not he may be implicated in Krook's spontaneous combustion, for 'He has had something—he don't know what—to do with so much in this connexion that is mysterious, that it is possible he may even be implicated, without knowing it, in the present transaction' (*BH* 33, 407). Raymond Williams describes how this connectivity is simultaneously thematic, and a structural principle: 'unknown and unacknowledged relationships, profound and decisive connections, definite and committing recognitions and avowals are as it were forced into consciousness'.[34]

Some of the curious bringing together is, of course, done by Dickens himself in the course of a complex plot. One can never be certain whether or not a character will reappear. Mrs Pardiggle, for example, evaporates from the novel, having served her role of reinforcing the wrongness of paying more attention to missionary efforts overseas than to one's biological and metaphorical immediate family, but the nurse of Esther's early years re-emerges as the timid wife of the oleaginous preacher Mr Chadband. Trooper George turns out to be the long-estranged son of the Chesney Wold housekeeper, Mrs Rouncewell—but the 'shadowy female figure that flitted past' Mr Bucket and Esther on a London bridge, with a 'profound black pit of water' underneath (*BH* 57, 678), is connected only to all outcasts, all who have committed social or sexual transgressions within the novel. And as Sarah Alexander puts it, connections are more than genealogical: they work 'through legal institutions, documents, disease, items of clothing, economic arrangements, portraits, and most often, through coincidence'.[35]

---

[33] Jane Griffith, 'Such a Labyrinth of Streets: Serialization and the Gendered View of Urban Space in *Bleak House*', *English* 61 (2012): 248–66; 250.

[34] Raymond Williams, *The Country and the City* (Oxford: Oxford University Press, 1975), 155.

[35] Sarah C. Alexander, *Victorian Literature and the Physics of the Imponderable* (New York: Routledge, 2015), 27.

Dickens's contemporary Walter Bagehot, editor of the *Economist*, wrote in 1858 that the novelist's 'genius is especially suited to the delineation of city life. London is like a newspaper. Everything is there, and everything is disconnected.'[36] But in fact the novel seems deliberately designed to dispel this sense of fragmentation—or, as Williams pointed out, to offer a literary construction of a reassurance that it is possible to make some kind of logical sense of 'the sheer rush and noise and miscellaneity of this new and complex social order'.[37] In structural terms, the principle of interconnection suggests the existence of a complex network (or, to borrow George Eliot's metaphor, a pier-glass, or mirror, covered with a myriad scratches), in which placing pressure on one point of the network, or bringing one's attention to bear on one component, sets up different sets of links. These may be internal to the plot's characters and locations, or occur between the resonances of the denotative language and the rich proliferation of metaphors, or reinforce some of its major tenets, such as the importance of responsibility, or stretch way beyond into the social matrix in which the novel both came into being and in which it's been circulated and read. Or, to see it another way, Gordon Bigelow relates the circulatory systems of the novel to questions of economy, both financial and domestic, '*Bleak House* is about circulation without end or essence. It tries to understand the nature of value—economic, linguistic, human—under the conditions of a seemingly infinite market exchange.'[38]

And yet—*Bleak House* manages to resist being stuck within some continually recursive, and self-referential loop. It manifests this resistance on its very last page through a simple act of open-endedness: the '—even supposing—' (*BH* 67, 770) that concludes 'The close of Esther's narrative'. This typographic and rhetorical equivocation undermines the finality of the word 'close'. For nothing, exactly, is concluded by Esther in these words of wishful conjecture, hypothesis, and possibly false modesty, any more than the third-person narrative, despite ending with a hushed, sombre, almost vacant Chesney Wold in a state of 'dull repose' (*BH* 66, 767) ever offers us a settled picture of life in the rest of the country that has been safely secured by the past tense. London, and the steam-hammers, the furnaces, and red-hot iron of the industrial north exist in all the tumult of the present.

Similarly, the novel's prose, taken as a whole, resists being contained, as the chaotic Jellyby closets demonstrate. In particular, Dickens's metaphors operate, as so frequently in his middle and late career, according to an animated, associative logic. But one cannot confidently determine the connections between them, or decide if, indeed, such connections exist beyond the reader's own powers of linkage.[39] For example, in that first

---

[36] Walter Bagehot, 'Charles Dickens' (1858), in Norman St John-Stevas (ed.), *The Collected Works of Walter Bagehot*, 15 vols (London: The Economist, 1865–86), 2: 87.

[37] Williams, *Country and the City*, 155.

[38] Gordon Bigelow, 'Market Indicators: Banking and Domesticity in Dickens's *Bleak House*', *ELH* 67 (2000): 589–615; 591.

[39] For a detailed discussion of Dickens's 'excessive metonymy' in the novel, see Benjamin Joseph Bishop, 'Metonymy and the Dense Cosmos of *Bleak House*', *SEL* 54, 4 (2014): 793–813; 804.

paragraph, Dickens suggests that the thick smoky London air had 'gone into mourning, one might imagine, for the death of the sun' (*BH* 1, 5)—a trope that has encouraged critics to take this as a signal of a preoccupation with entropy, and with the first law of thermodynamics (deduced by chemist James Joule in 1843), and hence with a system characterized by the dissipation of energy.[40] So when we encounter the exhausted Dedlock footmen, in the heat of summer, when 'the solar system works respectably at its appointed distances' (*BH* 48, 572), who 'hang their heavy heads, the gorgeous creatures, like overblown sunflowers' (*BH* 48, 573), we are completely at liberty to trace a scientific, meteorological connection, or to enjoy Dickens's ludic freedom with a typical garden flower. Material signifiers may carry symbolic weight—or they may not. That figure of Allegory on Tulkinghorn's ceiling, pointing away, should be a warning here: although the Roman's outstretched hand must surely mean *something*, the painting is, of course, profoundly silent.

So how, ultimately, might we best make sense of this proliferation of connections that operate in a climate of obscurity? The novel may both contain and critique systems, but it proves remarkably resistant to their application. Probably, indeed, a meta-theoretical approach is ultimately more appropriate than any one line—unless, of course, one takes self-referential refuge in proclaiming it to be a novel about the problems of interpretation. Invoking a familiar Victorian metaphor, Caroline Levine employs network theory to read the social world of *Bleak House* as a set of 'superimposed, conflicting, and overlapping relational webs'.[41] The device of the network proves a highly useful one to apply to the novel. Seeing it in terms of a network is very suggestive—so long as we recognize that such a model involves material objects, appeals to the senses, and ethical and political questions, as well as the relations between characters. Envisaging the novel as a network, one may exert pressure at any point: we might introduce, for example, questions emanating from the developing field of animal studies—what might it mean, say, for Allan Woodcourt to compare Jo's position to that of an 'unowned dog' (*BH* 47, 560)? Each question creates a node from which other connections branch out and flow, especially if one allows for these to function in a rhizome-like fashion, forking and dividing below the surface as well as spreading proliferating pathways among what is visible and legible. Rather than offering containment, this critical model respects *Bleak House*'s apparent inexhaustibility and suggestive powers of recombination.

---

[40] See Barri J. Gold, *ThermoPoetics: Energy in Victorian Literature and Science* (Cambridge, MA: The MIT Press, 2010), 187–224, and Allen MacDuffie, *Victorian Literature, Energy, and the Ecological Imagination* (Cambridge: Cambridge University Press, 2014), 89–113, in which he discusses *Bleak House* as a 'thermodynamic text' (91) both thematically and in terms of its own narrative energies. Also Alexander, *Victorian Literature*, 19–50.

[41] Caroline Levine, 'Narrative Networks: *Bleak House* and the Affordances of Form', *Novel: A Forum on Fiction* 42 (2009): 517–23; 518.

Further Reading

Harold Bloom (ed.), *Charles Dickens's* Bleak House (New York: Chelsea, 1987)

John Butt and Kathleen Tillotson, 'The Topicality of *Bleak House*', in *Dickens at Work* (London: Methuen, 1957), 177–200

Elliot Gilbert (ed.), *Critical Essays on Charles Dickens's* Bleak House (Boston: G. K. Hall, 1989)

Robert Newsom, *Dickens on the Romantic Side of Familiar Things:* Bleak House *and the Novel Tradition* (New York: Columbia University Press, 1977)

Robert L. Patten, '*Bleak House* and the Literary Croesus', in *Charles Dickens and his Publishers* (Oxford: Oxford University Press, 1978), 215–33

Susan Shatto, *The Companion to* Bleak House (London: Unwin Hyman, 1998)

Alexander Welsh, *The Art of* Bleak House *and* Hard Times (New Haven and London: Yale University Press, 2000)

CHAPTER 16

HARD TIMES FOR OUR TIMES

GRAHAME SMITH

In the spirit of Mr Gradgrind, let us begin with a few facts. *Hard Times*, Dickens's tenth novel, is the only one set entirely outside London, and is also the shortest. The book's initial impetus was rooted in the current financial position of the periodical *Household Words*, edited by Dickens and published by Bradbury and Evans. In August 1853 Dickens had completed the massively long *Bleak House,* published serially in 20 parts over 19 months, the final instalment containing what had by then become a tradition for Dickens, a double number. Dickens had planned to take a year away from writing after this huge effort, but a steep fall in the profits of *Household Words* led his publishers to suggest that Dickens should write a new novel to run serially in the magazine. This was the first weekly serial that Dickens had written for 12 years and it caused him immense problems. He began writing on 23 January 1854, and on the 28th he made a brief visit to Preston with his manager W. H. Wills in order to experience for himself the setting and atmosphere of what was a long-running strike. The novel then appeared, without chapter titles, in *Household Words* in 20 weekly instalments, from 1 April to 12 August 1854. Interestingly, its first appearance in volume form, with Bradbury and Evans as the publishers, occurred on 7 August, in other words before the final appearance of the serial itself. It then had the expanded title of *Hard Times for These Times*, was divided into three books, the chapters were given titles, and the work was dedicated to Thomas Carlyle, whom Dickens saw as his master in the field of social analysis. Dickens continued what had become his usual practice of using number plans as a practical aid in his writing, and these, plus the manuscript and the corrected printer's proofs, are held in the Forster Collection in the Victorian and Albert Museum in London. It is worth mentioning that the novel's proofs contain an explanation for Stephen's vow not to strike, which is left as a mystery in the published text.

It is now time that we heard from Dickens himself, in some extracts from the letters published in Volume 7 of the Pilgrim Edition. He confides, in characteristic fashion, to his dear friend Miss Burdett Coutts on 23 January 1854:

> I have fallen to work again. My purpose is among the mighty secrets of the world at present; but there is such a fixed idea on the part of my printers and copartners in Household Words, that a story by me, continued from week to week, would make some unheard-of effect with it, that I am going to write one.[1]

The sense of drama conveyed by this is highly characteristic, with Dickens coming to the rescue and yet again, in the boxing parlance of the day, coming up to the mark. As we have seen, Dickens made a brief visit to Preston, but complains to Forster, on 29 January, that 'I am afraid that I shall not be able to get much here ... there is very little in the streets to make the town remarkable ... It is a nasty place (I thought it was a model town).'[2] Dickens was presumably in search of some kind of atmosphere that he could use for his own creative purposes, but poor Preston seemed unable to provide it. This may be a factor in the strength of feeling expressed in his letter of 11 March to Peter Cunningham when the latter had suggested in a periodical that Dickens's new novel would be set in Preston. Dickens's rebuke is highly revealing of his methods and intentions in writing the book:

> The mischief of such a statement is twofold. First, it encourages the public to believe in the impossibility that books are produced in that very sudden and Cavalier manner ... and Secondly in this instance it has this pernicious bearing: It localizes (so far as your readers are concerned) a story which has a direct purpose in reference to the working people all over England.[3]

Any critical reading of *Hard Times* will clearly need to bear this statement in mind as much as the almost despairing cry to Forster of February 1854: 'The difficulty of the space is CRUSHING. Nobody can have an idea of it who has not had the experience of patient fiction-writing with some elbow-room always, and open places in perspective. In this form, with any kind of regard to the current number, there is absolutely no such thing.'[4] There are some clues here to the special nature of *Hard Times* as a text compared to the novels that preceded and followed it, *Bleak House* and *Little Dorrit*.

Creative agony, that well-known phenomenon and not solely Dickens's preserve, is much in evidence as Dickens tells Forster, on 14 July 1854, that

---

[1] *The Letters of Charles Dickens*, ed. Madeline House, Graham Storey, et al., Pilgrim/British Academy Edition, 12 vols (Oxford: Clarendon Press, 1965–2002). Subsequent citations: *PLets* followed by volume:page range, page. Here 7:255–6, 256.
[2] *PLets* 7:260–1.
[3] *PLets* 7:290–1.
[4] *PLets* 7:282.

> I am three parts mad, and the fourth delirious, with perpetual rushing at *Hard Times* ... I have been looking forward through so many weeks and so many sides of paper to this Stephen business, that now—as usual—it being over, I feel as if nothing in the world, in the way of intense and violent rushing hither and thither, could quite restore my balance.[5]

There is no reason to doubt Dickens's sincerity, but it is more instructive to see Dickens in search of different kinds of information to aid his creative process as when he writes to Wills on 25 January 1854 that he wants '(for the story I am trying to hammer out) the Educational Board's series of questions for the examination of *teachers* in schools'.[6]

Our first question is surely what were the initial critical responses to the novel? It has often been pointed out that it was excluded by F. G. Kitton from the edition of the novels he published in 1897 and only made an appearance in *The Minor Writings* of 1900.[7] This seems like an endorsement of the paucity of comment on *Hard Times* when it first appeared and the generally negative tone of the notices that it did receive. A representative example is provided by Richard Simpson in *The Rambler* of October 1854: 'It is a thousand pities that Mr Dickens does not confine himself to amusing his readers, instead of wandering out of his depth in trying to interest them.'[8] However, there was an exception to these adverse comments, one provided by the great critic of art and society, John Ruskin, in the *Cornhill Magazine* of August 1860:

> The essential value and truth of Dickens's writings have been unwisely lost sight of ... merely because he presents his truth with some colour of caricature ... let us not lose the use of Dickens's wit and insight, because he chooses to speak in a circle of stage fire. He is entirely right in his main drift and purpose in every book he has written.[9]

It is important to begin with Ruskin for a number of reasons, not least because he is taking Dickens seriously although, I would argue, for the wrong reasons. In the brilliant analysis of George Bernard Shaw, for example, it is precisely the 'circle of stage fire' that is the distinctive and special quality in Dickens's embodiment of social and personal evil. But despite his limitations, Ruskin is such an important figure in British culture that his praise of Dickens in general and *Hard Times* in particular marks a significant moment in the novel's appreciation. Another reason for focusing attention on him links to one of the broader themes to be pursued in this chapter, the attempt to discover new lines of enquiry for research. Rather surprisingly Ruskin has recently become an object of media scrutiny in a way not dissimilar to the attention generated by Dickens, although

---

[5] *PLets* 7:369.
[6] *PLets* 7:258.
[7] Paul Schlicke (ed.), *Oxford Reader's Companion to Dickens* (Oxford: Oxford University Press, 1999), 205–8.
[8] 'Review of Hard Times', *The Rambler* NS 2 (October 1854): 361.
[9] 'Unto This Last', *Cornhill Magazine* 2 (August 1860): 159.

for different reasons and with much less intensity. The biography of Ruskin's wife, *Effie Gray* by Suzanne Fagence Cooper,[10] and the film arising from it have brought Ruskin's personal life into sharp focus with their stress on the annulment of the Ruskin marriage on the grounds of his failure to consummate it. It is within this context, perhaps, that Mike Leigh felt emboldened to present Ruskin, the great defender of Turner, as a lisping, upper-class bore in his 2014 film *Mr. Turner*. This exposure of what might once have been considered a private matter is only a pale shadow of the attention devoted to Dickens's relationship with Ellen Ternan, an interest which began in his own lifetime, but has recently been made a matter of widespread media attention through Claire Tomalin's *The Invisible Woman*[11] as well as her more recent biography of Dickens, the former having been, in the time-honoured formula, turned into 'a major motion picture' in 2013. This aspect of Dickens's life has been placed in its historical context with a combination of scholarly detail and incisive wit by Michael Slater in his *The Great Charles Dickens Scandal*.[12] However, leaving aside the rather overheated attention this aspect of Dickens's life has received in some areas of the media, the issue has some bearing on *Hard Times* with its painful emphasis on Stephen's desperate desire to be rid of his alcoholic wife and Bounderby's dismissal of the possibility of divorce for the ordinary people that Stephen represents. What I am suggesting is that there is work to be done in the field of media scrutiny, especially by younger scholars, a point I shall return to in my discussion of the range of effects involved in the appearance of *Hard Times* as a weekly serial in Dickens's own periodical.

Ruskin's response to *Hard Times* is followed by a yawning gap until we get to two very different views of the novel, one by F. R. Leavis well known, the other not at all, at least when it first appeared, that is George Bernard Shaw's Introduction to the so-called Waverley edition of the novel which was published in 1913. Shaw's response is dealt with in the 'DICKENS AND HIS CRITICS' section of the Everyman Edition of *Hard Times*[13] at some length because it is a landmark in Dickens studies, but one that went largely unrecognized given the context in which it originally appeared. Shaw's brilliant comments were republished in *Shaw on Dickens* edited by Dan H. Laurence and Martin Quinn,[14] but again failed to gain the attention they deserved. The heart of Shaw's insights, and this is where he differs most radically from Ruskin, is to grasp that Dickens's understanding of society is expressed in a surreal abandonment of realism. For Shaw, the characters in Dickens's later novels 'utter rhapsodies of nonsense conceived in an ecstasy of mirth. And this begins in *Hard Times* … He even calls the schoolmaster McChoakumchild, which is almost an insult to the serious reader. And so it was to the end of his life'.[15] What

---

[10] Suzanne Fagence Cooper, *Effie Gray: The Passionate Lives of Effie Gray, Ruskin and Millais* (London: Gerald Duckworth & Co. Ltd, 2014).

[11] Claire Tomalin, *The Invisible Woman* (London: Penguin Books, 1990).

[12] Michael Slater, *The Great Charles Dickens Scandal* (New Haven and London: Yale University Press, 2014).

[13] *Hard Times*, ed. Grahame Smith, (London: J. M. Dent, 1994).

[14] Dan H. Laurence and Martin Quinn (eds), *Shaw on Dickens* (New York: Frederick Ungar Publishing Co., 1985).

[15] Ibid. 31.

Shaw is drawing attention to here is Dickens's daring abandonment of conventional realism in the service of his own special brand of social criticism.

The transformation in at least academic views of *Hard Times* was reserved for F. R. Leavis in the so-called 'Analytic Note' on the novel in his *The Great Tradition* of 1948. It is difficult to exaggerate the importance of this intervention although for many it would seem to be based on a false premise, that of 'all Dickens's works it is the one that has all the strengths of his genius, together with a strength no other of them can show—that of a completely serious work of art'.[16] The alternatives here are almost too numerous to enumerate, but for many *Great Expectations*, *David Copperfield*, and *Little Dorrit* would come instantly to mind, although it is important to remember that this position was rectified by the work Leavis published with the active collaboration of Q. D. Leavis in 1970, *Dickens the Novelist*.[17]

It is interesting that major contributions to our understanding of Dickens were made by writers who were not professional academics, such as Edmund Wilson and George Orwell.[18] However, what seems clear is that Leavis was a key factor in helping the scholarly community to grasp that *Hard Times* was worthy of serious attention, an opportunity that was seized by the novelist and critic David Lodge from two different points of view, first in his *The Language of Fiction* and then *Working with Structuralism*.[19] It is also important to draw attention to the value of Philip Collins's insights into Dickens's treatment of education as a theme in *Hard Times*, and the analysis of social issues provided by Raymond Williams is another major contribution.[20] Leaving aside these individual achievements, the general drift of criticism and scholarship focused on *Hard Times* is part of the institutionalization of literary study as it has developed over many years, above all in university departments of English. One result of this has been what might be called the atomization of literary study in scholarly/critical writing. Leavis clearly felt free to range widely throughout the novel, quoting large chunks of the text with little reinforcing analysis. This is not the modern way, an approach where an aspect of the text is usually narrowed down to what seems a manageable portion, be it industrialization, horse-riding, or whatever. An invaluable guide to this material up to 1982 is provided by Sylvia Manning's *Hard Times: An Annotated Bibliography*.[21] Another scholarly work of immense usefulness is Margaret Simpson's *The Companion to 'Hard Times'*.[22] Indeed, it is hard to exaggerate the importance of Simpson's contribution given

---

[16] F. R. Leavis, *The Great Tradition* (London: Chatto & Windus, 1948), 227–8.
[17] Q. D. Leavis and F. R. Leavis, *Dickens the Novelist* (London: Chatto & Windus, 1970).
[18] See Edmund Wilson, 'Dickens: The Two Scrooges', in *The Wound and the Bow* (Oxford: Oxford University Press, 1941) and George Orwell, *The Collected Essays, Journalism and Letters, Volume 1: An Age Like This* (Harmondsworth: Penguin Books, 1970).
[19] David Lodge, *The Language of Fiction* (London: Routledge & Kegan Paul, 1966) and *Working with Structuralism* (London: Routledge & Paul, 1981).
[20] Philip Collins, *Dickens and Education* (London: Macmillan, 1963) and Raymond Williams, 'Dickens and Social Ideas', in Michael Slater (ed.), *Dickens 1970* (London: Chapman & Hall, 1970).
[21] Sylvia Manning, *Hard Times: An Annotated Bibliography* (New York: Garland, 1984).
[22] Margaret Simpson, *The Companion to 'Hard Times'* (Mountfield: Helm Information, 1997).

its detailed examination of all aspects of the novel, providing information and analysis of value to even the most experienced scholar.

But students of *Hard Times* are fortunate in another sense, in their ability to engage with the novel in its Norton Critical Edition edited by Fred Kaplan which appeared in its fourth edition in 2017.[23] There is much to admire here, not least the attractiveness of the volume itself with its high-quality paper, its well-spaced and readable fonts, and its use of a Victorian photograph on its cover. It is indeed such an exemplary union of book design and production that it makes the Norton Critical Edition almost as much a classic as the work it is dealing with. The formula itself is a tried and tested one by now: text, contexts, criticism, chronology, selected bibliography, and so on. And the novel itself is glossed in a series of detailed footnotes. The editor is frank in his acknowledgement of the justness, as he sees it, of the criticisms offered by Joel Brattin of the text produced for the second edition which led to the third and fourth editions reproducing 'the 1854 edition, not exactly warts and all, but with scrupulous fidelity' (*HT* '[Note on t]he Text', 253). There is more to be said later about this question of the text.

The editor's Preface to the fourth edition of the novel differs interestingly from the third in suggesting that *Hard Times* 'sustains its lasting and its ever-changing relevance to our modern world' (*HT* 'Preface', vii). In other words, this edition is concerned to remove the emphasis of the third edition on the novel as eminently teachable which was a recommendation for the academic but not necessarily for the book's status as a work of art. That some important rethinking is going on here is evident although it is also clearly stated that this 'fourth edition ... does not undervalue the traditional discussion that has emphasized the novel as a primer on the factory system' and other related matters (*HT* 'Preface', vii). The choice of the word 'primer' does surely cause a certain unease, a sense that the novel is being appropriated by the academy for utilitarian purposes rather than something more free ranging. For example, the volume's excellent bibliography contains a reference to a seminal essay, Nicholas Coles's 'The Politics of *Hard Times*: Dickens the Novelist versus Dickens the Reformer',[24] the inclusion of a selection from which might have permitted student readers, presumably a crucial part of Norton's hoped for readership, to think about the novel differently from a non-utilitarian standpoint in the way in which Coles challenges assumptions about the value of contextualization: 'The fallacy in the procedure of reading the politics of the novels through Dickens's speeches and journalism is that it ignores crucial differences between these forms of discourse; fiction and journalism use different modes of presentation, which reflect differing imaginative activities, and differing purposes and occasions for writing.'[25]

---

[23] *Hard Times*, ed. Fred Kaplan, Norton Critical Edition, 4th edn (New York and London: W. W. Norton, 2017). Subsequent references are inserted parenthetically in the text by *HT* Book:chapter, page.

[24] Nicholas Coles, 'The Politics of *Hard Times*: Dickens the Novelist Versus Dickens the Reformer', *Dickens Studies Annual* 15 (1986): 145–79.

[25] Ibid., 145–6.

Such an approach might have reinforced an engagement with what is clearly the outstanding piece in the volume's critical section, the essay by George Bernard Shaw. As we have already seen, Shaw argues that *Hard Times* is, amongst other things, a work of the comic imagination of a very peculiar kind: 'Dickens in this book casts off, and casts off for ever, all restraint on his wild sense of humour ... here he begins at last to exercise quite recklessly his power of presenting a character to you in the most fantastic and outrageous terms.'[26] What Shaw is doing is offering, long before Leavis, a way out of the moral fable straitjacket that can only make the novel admirable by sanitizing it of its wilder aspects. This is not to disparage Leavis's achievement in rehabilitating the book. His was a new reading with a vengeance. But in offering such a persuasive social version of the text with an emphasis on moral earnestness he misses aspects of the novel that were evident to Shaw's genius.

This point might be made clearer by reference to the Norton Edition's glossing of chapter VI of the first volume, 'Sleary's Horsemanship'. Nothing at all is said about the Pegasus of the Pegasus's Arms. The note on Childers's similarity to a Centaur omits mention of its traditional association with sexual energy. Cupid is also omitted and there is no comment on Sleary's name with its whiff of gin-sodden tipsiness. In other words, that side of the novel which embodies the hints of rowdyism and frank sexuality present in the life of the circus are omitted, as they so often are in readings of the text that stress its qualities as moral fable or social document. On the other hand, if we are willing to admit that the novel contains a strong element of what might be called comic subversion, then we can see that one of its central aims is to subvert the beliefs of two of its major characters by subjecting them to a gigantic leg-pull. The fact-mongers Gradgrind and Bounderby are undermined by the *imaginative* fiction of which they are a part, undone by the very fairy tales they so much despise. But the irony can be taken one stage further if we accept that by stressing the social dimension of *Hard Times*, the Norton editors have constructed to some degree a utilitarian apparatus around an anti-utilitarian novel. However, the fact remains that the Norton Critical Edition of the novel is an important volume, not the least of its virtues being its impressive bibliography.

The changes in the direction of Dickens studies that I am attempting to clarify are highlighted by a review in the Spring 2006 edition of *The Dickensian* where Stephen Jarvis falls with evident delight on a book by Julian Wolfreys, *The Old Story with a Difference: Pickwick's Vision*, because through it 'one's view of Dickens's text is radically altered' and because it may signal 'a revival of critical interest' in a work that 'has been somewhat ignored by critics'.[27] The desperate search for new readings of established works is to be deplored when it involves forcing them onto a Procrustean bed of inapplicable ideas, but the fresh view inspired by an open mind is hugely enriching and part of the endeavour that keeps literary study alive. On the other hand, I want at this stage to suggest that we may be approaching something like the end of this state

---

[26] *Shaw on Dickens*, 31.
[27] Stephen Jarvis, *Dickensian* 468, 102 (Spring 2006): 60–1.

of affairs given the alternatives to what was once considered conventional publishing that are now on offer. This is clearly a complex field, but one that may open the way to different approaches to even such well-worn territory as critical readings of *Hard Times*. Consider, for example, this passage from a review in *The Dickensian* by Jeremy Clarke of an essay by Wendy Parkins, 'Mobility and Modernity: Reading *Barnaby Rudge*'. Clarke quotes a question posed by Parkins herself: 'Rather than asking, then, what the novel contains … a better question might be: what does the novel unleash or open up?' This leads into Clarke's reading of what he sees as the essence of Parkins's approach:

> There is a great deal of notice taken of what we might call the life of the text outside itself. This includes an awareness of the physical book, monthly part, or magazine, complete with illustrations and adverts, and its presence in the world alone—free of the author himself. Wendy Parkins indeed releases her own idea of the physical text of *Barnaby Rudge* into the hands of William Morris as he reads it to his future wife Jane. This 'primal reading scene' is the device she uses to encourage us to consider the mobility of perspective to which the text is subjected. The physical presence of the book in her scene carries such a strong (indeed a disorientating) analogy with that book on our own lap that it allows her to urge a non-historicist approach to this historical illustration: the mobility of the book keeps it always present.[28]

What we are being presented with is a possible new relationship with the literary text, in our case *Hard Times*, where it is clear that the Norton Critical Edition of the book is about as far removed from the novel's first appearance as it could be. One aspect of this issue is the edition's insistence on its presentation of 'a freshly edited text based on a comparative study of all the relevant versions of *Hard Times*' (*HT* 253). That this is a vexed issue in literary scholarship is demonstrated by The New York Edition of Henry James's fiction, which was published by James in 1907–9 and from which James himself excluded such major works as *Washington Square* and *The Europeans*. In addition, he revised his novels in ways that have been highly controversial, some critics decrying the changes, others expressing approval. The question of what is the 'real' *Portrait of a Lady* for example is clearly far from straightforward. Similarly, if we remember that *Hard Times* made its first appearance in a magazine, the Norton editors' insistence on the primacy of the book may seem at least open to discussion.

This chapter's title, '*Hard Times* for our Times', is of course an adaptation of the long title sometimes used in Dickens's own day, '*Hard Times* for These Times'. To substitute 'our' for 'these' may seem challenging although I hope the change will prove to be justifiable. One reason for making it is to suggest that what follows will open fresh readings of Dickens as a writer and of the text itself. This is a large undertaking, one motivated at least partly by the sheer volume of criticism and scholarship the novel has attracted once its 'greatness' was signalled by F. R. Leavis. It seems quite clear that we are living through, and have been for some time, radical changes in how information is

---

[28] Jeremy Clarke, *Dickensian* 495, 111 (Spring 2015): 64.

disseminated. The electronic media are now a constant presence in our lives, affecting higher education as well as many other aspects of human life. If we are tempted to apply some of these changes to a nineteenth-century writer, in this case Dickens, we need to come to terms with what has become a widespread view expressed, for example, by a leader in the *Independent* newspaper of 14 July 2015: 'Many modern readers forget that Dickens was more like a scriptwriter on *East Enders* than a literary novelist as we think of them today.'[29] It is easy enough to demolish what have become rather fashionable views of a 'Dickens' transmuted to our world of television and much newer forms of media. But it is also possible to maintain critical judgement while exploring some radically new ways of examining Dickens's texts. In the review by Jeremy Clarke quoted above we encountered an emphasis on the book as a physical object, and this is an approach developed with real originality in a University of Buckingham thesis of 2009, '"Making its own history": A Critical and Contextual Reappraisal of *Hard Times*' by Saad Mohammed Kadhum Al-Maliky.[30] Making use of *Dickens Journals Online*, one of the most exciting developments in recent Dickens studies, the thesis demonstrates in minute detail the three ways in which the novel was distributed in *Household Words*. By examining the contexts in which the novel first appeared the writer is able to justify an original approach to this much examined text:

> as successive instalments of *Hard Times* first appeared in the weekly journal, *Household Words* ... they formed a network of discourse complemented by many of the surrounding articles and poems that developed and refined the political and social interests of the novel.[31]

This approach leads to the following Conclusion:

> *Hard Times*, when reappraised in its original journalistic context functions powerfully as a series of magazine articles, written 'for these times' and is highly critical of them, written in the voice of the omni-present 'Conductor' of *Household Words*. Most twentieth-century critics (and even some Victorian reviewers) criticize the novel as an isolated volume of fiction rather than understanding the urgency of its connections to its surrounding context.[32]

For Victorian readers, as opposed to critics and reviewers, 'the individual novel instalment, article, or short story, or poem, was seldom a self-contained verbal entity but part of a broader reading process and a set of reading practices embedded in a specific material framework that shaped responses.'[33] This point becomes even clearer when we are

---

[29] *Independent* (14 July 2015): 2.
[30] Saad Mohammed Kadhum Al-Maliky, '"Making its own history": A Critical and Contextual Reappraisal of Hard Times', University of Buckingham thesis, 2009.
[31] Ibid., ii.
[32] Ibid., 144.
[33] Ibid., 145.

reminded of some of the essays and articles that were appearing at the same time as the novel's instalments and so presumably forming part of the context in which it was being read: 'Frauds on the Fairies', 'On Strike', 'Ground in the Mill'.

That this method is part of a growing movement can be demonstrated by a glance at work being done on *Our Mutual Friend* as part of the 'Dickens Our Mutual Friend Reading Project' organized by Birkbeck, University of London.[34] Putting the novel's serial parts into the context in which they first appeared helps to stress, for example, the importance of Bella Wilfer's domestic role in the novel through the advertisements that formed part of each monthly number.

There is no need to give the minute detail of this experiment, especially when it concerns another novel than ours. However, it does serve to demonstrate that the interest in the text as it appeared to its first readers is becoming fairly widespread. Another example is suggested by the last lines of *Hard Times*, remembering again that these were first read as the conclusion of a story enveloped in the pages of a weekly publication:

> Herself [that is, Sissie] again a wife —a mother—lovingly watchful of her children, ever careful that they should have a childhood of the mind no less than a childhood of the body, as knowing it to be even a more beautiful thing, and a possession, any hoarded scrap of which, is a blessing and happiness to the wisest ... These things were to be.
>
> Dear reader! It rests with you and me, whether, in our two fields of action, similar things shall be or not. Let them be! We shall sit with lighter bosoms on the hearth, to see the ashes of our fires turn gray and cold. (*HT* III:9, 236)

If this passage is read with a contemporary eye it may be that it can help us to connect Dickens meaningfully with the concept and practice of blogging, especially as it is presented by Jill Walker Rettburg in her superb book on the subject, *Blogging*, published in its second edition as recently as 2014.[35] Rettburg presents us with a historical context which suggests that *Hard Times* and perhaps Dickens's work as a whole might be brought into a meaningful relationship with this contemporary form of discourse if only because blogging is usually defined as an interactive phenomenon, with its readers being invited to comment on a piece of writing and to enter into a discussion with other readers and, sometimes, the author. It is also often a non-narrative form of writing composed of sporadic observations or commentaries, rather like a public diary. The more serious examples of blogging are committed to the idea that the readers of blogs can be seen as a kind of community, a social grouping that can act as a possible force for change.

This may seem very far from Dickens and the nineteenth century, then, but blogging in a wider sense can take many forms as, for example, in the work of the London-based commentator who calls himself The Gentle Author and whose delicate and perceptive

---

[34] 'DICKENS OUR MUTUAL FRIEND READING PROJECT', Birkbeck, University of London. <https://dickensourmutualfriend.wordpress.com/>, accessed 21 January 2016.

[35] Jill Walker Rettburg, *Blogging* (Cambridge: Polity Press, 2014).

comments on Spitalfields in London, where he lives, seem not a million miles away from Dickens's *Uncommercial Traveller* essays.[36] If this seems a large claim it is, nonetheless, impossible to exaggerate the charm, interest, and attractiveness of such pieces as 'Vote for the George Tavern' (24 July 2015), 'Scything on Hackney Marshes' (4 August 2015), and 'The Oldest Tree in Bethnal Green' (27 August 2015). That there is a serious purpose at work here is reinforced by the epigraph which appears at the end of every blog: 'In the midst of life I woke to find myself living in an old house beside Brick Lane in the East End of London.'

Obviously, the main emphasis of this approach would be on Dickens's interactivity with his public. And I think it would be fair to say that *Hard Times* provides a particularly good example of what I have in mind, given the complex motives that brought it into being, its brevity, and its weekly publication in Dickens's own periodical. For many this approach might seem bizarre, but no more so than placing Dickens in the context of cinema before that form had come into existence as I suggested in my *Dickens and the Dream of Cinema*.[37]

The book argued that Dickens and his work were among a large number of contributory factors that helped to bring film into existence and, more importantly, that once cinema did exist it was possible to read it back into Dickens's work in illuminating ways. Similarly, Rettberg is at pains to place blogging within a historical context as part of a continuum in which 'blogs have aspects in common with other forms of communication during the last centuries'.[38] Rettberg argues that an essential feature of the blog is that its readers can ask questions of the text in a way that seems akin to readers responding to the serial parts of Dickens's novels while they were being written. And she does, in fact, refer explicitly to Dickens at one point in arguing that the 'best blogs tell stories' and are 'episodic in nature': 'one of the most well-known literary examples of episodic narrative is Dickens's novels, which were first published in weekly and monthly instalments'.[39] Rettberg also tackles the fascinating problems that arise from the hoaxes perpetrated by Kaycee Nicole and lonelygirl15 and the angry responses these revelations provoked in readers. At this point, she draws a distinction between blogs that deceive and novels where we are 'protected, emotionally, by the knowledge that it's just make-believe'.[40] But Dickens's novels were not always simply 'make-believe', of course, and his use of real people in his fiction, however disguised, sometimes provoked anger and distress.

Another link between the serial parts of Dickens's novels and blogging is that both were and are avowedly commercial, a fact disguised by the way in which his work comes to us in volume form. (The advertising breaks in a television adaptation of one of his novels are, of course, another matter.) Perhaps the best way to round off this part of the

---

[36] The Gentle Author@thegentleauthor. Accessed 24 July 2016.
[37] Grahame Smith, *Dickens and the Dream of Cinema* (Manchester and New York: Manchester University Press, 2003).
[38] Rettburg, *Blogging*, 36.
[39] Ibid. 115–16.
[40] Ibid. 133.

discussion is to draw attention to the scholarly and amusing 'blog in honor of Charles Dickens and his world' which can be found at Blogging Dickens 29 August, 2013.[41] The author, Professor Alexis Easley, writes with the ease of one who takes the possibility of blogging on Dickens for granted, not something to make a fuss about, and just one tool amongst others to aid the understanding and appreciation of Dickens's work.

My conclusion is that such modern forms of communication as *Dickens Journals Online* and blogging may suggest new ways of approaching *Hard Times* that could liberate us from the constraints of the formal literary essay as it has been practised for so many years. Thanks to *Dickens Journals Online* we can now read his work in something approaching the form in which it was read by its first readers, an opportunity that may be of particular value to younger scholars.

Further Reading

Peter Ackroyd, *Dickens* (London: Sinclair Stevenson, 1990)

Joseph Butwin, 'Hard Times: The News and the Novel', *Nineteenth-Century Fiction* 32, 2 (September 1997):166–87

Peter Capuano, 'Digital *Dombey*.' Report by Ruth Penny of a lecture at the 2016 Dickens Universe. DICKNS-L-dickns-1@listserv.ucsb.edu

John Drew, *Dickens the Journalist* (Basingstoke: Palgrave Macmillan, 2003)

Paul Schlicke, *Dickens and Popular Entertainment* (London: Allen & Unwin, 1985)

Paul Schlicke (ed.), *Hard Times* (Oxford: Oxford University Press: Oxford World's Classics, 2006)

Michael Slater, *Charles Dickens* (New Haven and London: Yale University Press, 2009)

---

[41] Alexis Easley, 'Blogging Dickens' (29 August 2013). <https://dickens2013.wordpress.com/2013/08/29/15/>. Accessed 21 January 2015.

CHAPTER 17

LITTLE DORRIT

FRANCESCA ORESTANO

Little Dorrit's Faults

Little Dorrit (1855–7; Figure 17.1) did not initially receive the critical accolade other novels by Dickens obtained: too long, too diffuse, too dark, with too many references to contemporary eminent Victorians and to recent scandals that loomed through a '30 years ago' story. The frontispiece by Phiz includes busy crowds, processions, crumbling ruins, and a distant seascape: confusion from bottom to top, a vortex circling in a ring of chained letters the figure of the protagonist. Scathing comments on the writer's art, by James Fitzjames Stephen, aimed at the writer's 'extravagantly high reputation ... rewarded ... at an extravagantly high rate':

> To do his best to persuade his neighbours that the institutions under which they live encourage and permit the grossest cruelties towards debtors and paupers—that their legislature is a stupid and inefficient debating club, their courts of justice foul haunts of chicanery, pedantry, and fraud, and their system of administration an odious compound of stupidity and corruption—is, perhaps, a sufficient responsibility for a man to assume... To the thousands of feverish artisans who read *Little Dorrit*, the Circumlocution Office is a *bona fide* representation of Downing-street.[1]

As in a photographic negative, this passage highlights the issues that produced such a critical reaction: among them, the bankruptcy and scandals touching the Royal British and the Tipperary Banks, the ineffectual efforts of the Administrative Reform Association, to which Dickens had publicly committed himself; the mismanagement

---

[1] [James Fitzjames Stephen], 'The Licence of Modern Novelists' (1857), in Philip Collins (ed.), *Charles Dickens: The Critical Heritage* (London: Routledge, 1997), 367–74.

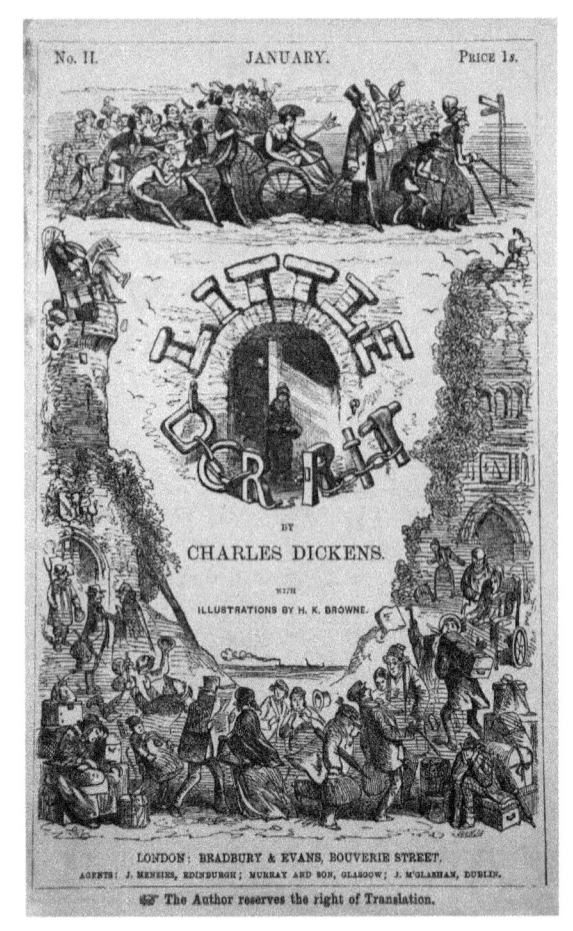

FIGURE 17.1 Hablot K. Browne, wrapper design for January 1856 instalment of Charles Dickens, *Little Dorrit* (London: Bradbury and Evans, 1855–7). 14.4 cm × 22.6 cm. Steel etching.

Courtesy McHenry Library Special Collections, University of California, Santa Cruz

of the Crimean War.[2] In addition to this, the notion that such long novels with convoluted plots were large, loose baggy monsters—as Henry James chose to describe them in 1889—carried weight. In 1904 Gissing commented: 'as a narrative, *Little Dorrit* is far from successful; it is cumbered with mysteries which prove futile, and has no proportion in its contrasting parts'.[3] Yet Gissing would also remark:

> Who, in childhood, ever cared much for *Little Dorrit*? The reason is plain; in this book Dickens has comparatively little of his wonted buoyancy; throughout, it is in a

---

[2] Trey Philpotts, in *The Companion to Little Dorrit* (Mountfield: Helm Information, 2003), provides exhaustive information about the context in which the novel is generated and the historical events in the English and European background.

[3] George Gissing, *Charles Dickens. A Critical Study* (London: Gresham, 1904), 64.

graver key. True, a house falls down in a most exciting way, and this the reader will remember; all else is to him a waste. We hear, accordingly, that nothing good can be said for *Little Dorrit*. Whereas, a competent judge ... will find in it some of the best work that Dickens ever did; and especially in this matter of characterization; his pictures so wholly admirable, so marvellously observed and so exquisitely presented, that he is tempted to place *Little Dorrit* among the best of his novels.[4]

Two elements stand out in this assessment: the unusually grave tone of the narration, prevailing throughout, despite a few scenes of potential comic effect; and the mastery of characterization. Characters, either comic or grotesque, were seen as the quintessence of Dickens's art. With the new century, critical attention would percolate from the outside shell to the inside of his characters, from the mechanic hard without of his comic marionettes, as Wyndham Lewis would have it,[5] to the dark within of personality. Nothing would be lost, however. While G. K. Chesterton agrees with Gissing about the general tone of the novel—'For the first time in a book by Dickens perhaps we do really feel that the hero is forty-five'[6]—the remarks by Osbert Sitwell in 1932 confirm the twofold soundness of Gissing's statement. Sitwell dwells on the one hand on the close similarity of purpose and character between Dickens and Proust, the master of remembrance of things past, and, on the other, on the pure Hogarthian vein of many scenes. Proust, 'thoroughly acquainted with the work of Charles Dickens, ... appreciated it at its true worth'.[7] Moreover, 'often, when it is a visual picture [Dickens] conjures up for us—and indeed, he is a very pictorial writer—we are reminded of Hogarth'.[8] The concept is also fully exploited by Edmund Wilson in *Axel's Castle*, who reiterates that 'it seems plain that Proust must have read Dickens and that this sometimes grotesque heightening of character had been partly learned from him'.[9] The Verdurins are indeed related not only to the Veneerings, but also to the Merdles, the Gowans, and other socially aspiring characters in *Little Dorrit*. The oneiric value both writers assign to Venice is also remarkable.[10]

George Orwell, like other commentators, set his critical acumen on the external detail of character—Doyce the case in point—and on Dickens's ability to anchor Doyce's gestures in our memory, rather than impressing the reader with the technical aspects of

---

[4] Ibid., 98–9.
[5] Wyndham Lewis, 'Long Live the Vortex!', *BLAST: Review of the Great English Vortex* 1 (20 June 1914): 8, and *The Complete Wild Body* (1927), ed. B. Lafourcade (Santa Barbara, CA: Black Sparrow Press, 1982), 279–81.
[6] G. K. Chesterton, *Charles Dickens* (1906; repr. London: Methuen, 1919), 172.
[7] Osbert Sitwell, *Dickens* (London: Chatto & Windus, 1932), 32.
[8] Ibid., 36.
[9] Edmund Wilson, 'Marcel Proust', in *Axel's Castle: A Study in the Imaginative Literature, 1870–1930* (1931; repr. London: Collins, 1969), 111–54; 114.
[10] Francesca Orestano, 'Charles Dickens and Italy: The "New Picturesque"', in Michael Hollington and Francesca Orestano (eds), *Dickens and Italy: 'Little Dorrit' and 'Pictures from Italy'* (Newcastle-upon-Tyne: Cambridge Scholars Publishing, 2009), 49–67.

his inventions.[11] And after remarking on the stylistic hallmark offered by the unnecessary detail, he went as far as equating Dickens's prose with the rococo, with a too rich embroidery, with a wedding-cake:

> As usual, his imagination overwhelms him. The picturesque details [are] too good to be left out... He is all fragments, all details—rotten architecture, but wonderful gargoyles—and never better than when he is building up some character who will later on be forced to act inconsistently... It is because Dickens's characters have no mental life.[12]

Orwell insisted on Dickens's 'monstrosities'.[13] This aspect brings to mind not only the early criticism of *Little Dorrit* by William Forsyth,[14] about the unholy mixture of tragedy and comedy in the novel, but also Voltaire, who deplored the Shakespearian contamination of genres as something monstrous. For Orwell, the fault resides in the mixture of caricature and melodrama. And in the end he complains: 'Who has not felt sometimes that it was "a pity" that Dickens ever deserted the vein of *Pickwick* for things like *Little Dorrit* and *Hard Times*?'[15] Contrary to these remarks, the supposedly decerebrate characters would soon earn the critical foreground *because* of their psychological interest. And *Little Dorrit*—indeed not a novel for children—would be classed among Dickens's finest achievements.

LITTLE DORRIT'S EXCELLENCIES

Edmund Wilson's essay (first composed as a lecture in 1939) focuses on *Little Dorrit* because of the psychological interest offered by the story. Recurring prison images and the 'psychology of Dickens's characters'[16] lead the critic toward the notion of a dramatic dualism—the two Scrooges—informing the life as well as the production of our writer. The biographical context as well as a face-value reading of the autobiographical fragment about the Marshalsea that Dickens entrusted to his friend John Forster prevent Wilson from attending to the wider cultural implications of the inner prison motif—which would become apparent after the paradigmatic *Surveiller et punir: naissance de la prison* (1975) by Michel Foucault. While marking forever all the Dorrit family relationships, the prison motif could be traced to its wider social implications, but Wilson remarks that

---

[11] George Orwell, 'Charles Dickens', in *Critical Essays* (London: Secker and Warburg, 1946), 7–56; 41–2.
[12] Ibid., 48–9; 52.
[13] Ibid., 51.
[14] William Forsyth, 'Literary Style', in Collins (ed.), *Critical Heritage*, 350–2; 350.
[15] Orwell, 'Charles Dickens', 53.
[16] Edmund Wilson, 'Dickens: The Two Scrooges', in *The Wound and the Bow: Seven Studies in Literature* (1941; repr. London: Methuen, 1961), 1–93; 55.

the satire on bureaucracy and 'the Circumlocution office after all, only influences the action in a negative way'.[17]

Lionel Trilling in 1953 would class *Little Dorrit* among the great novels of the last period, and again focus upon the prison motif, seen as the core of the novel, toward which character and society, language and structure, gravitate. Trilling enlarges the reach of the prison beyond individual psychology: *Little Dorrit* contains at once the point of view of imprisoning states of mind *and* the criticism of oppressive institutions, depicted in a truly Kafkian, inescapable way. The prison is at once actuality, symbol, and emblem. Alongside the trauma of Dickens's early childhood, placed foremost in the analysis of a family ensconced within the Marshalsea prison because of the debts incurred by its paterfamilias, Trilling also remarks that 'the Circumlocution office is the prison of the creative mind of England'.[18]

Trilling's essay provides useful critical paths for further investigation: among the fertile hints, the relevance given to themes of childhood and parenthood as sources of psychological states of imprisonment, of the self-tormenting attitude of Miss Wade, and of the 'tragedy of the will' affecting Arthur Clennam. Other critics would associate the pattern of *Hamlet* with Arthur's lot and predicament.[19] Returning from a 20-year residence in China, after the death of his father, Arthur feels that there is something in the family past that cries for revenge—or atonement. Instead of the ghost, the ominous letters in his father's watch, 'DNF', require the family saga to be re-enacted by the son. Against the patriarchal system, Arthur's indecision, and his ineffectual attempts at unveiling the truth about the past, are symmetrically matched by Amy Dorrit's submissive attitude, and by her ability to elude the truth with her father, her siblings, and with Arthur himself.[20]

Other elements of interest pointed out by Trilling are the chain rings of neurosis and guilt; of religious duty and the incarnation of evil in the devilish Rigaud aka Blandois aka Lagnier; cosmopolitanism; the notion that in this novel the 'powers of particularization' are evenly balanced by its 'powers of generalization and abstraction'.[21] Trilling likens the structure of the novel to the expanding circles of a Dantean hell—or rather, perhaps, a Purgatory. In fact, Amy in the guise of a Victorian Beatrice will eventually lead the protagonist towards the exit from the darkening gates, and from the prison of his own mind. After drinking from Lethe—the river of oblivion—and Eunoé—the river of good memories—they can climb to the stars together, toward the light of a better

---

[17] Ibid., 50.

[18] Lionel Trilling, 'Introduction to *Little Dorrit*', in Michael Hollington (ed.), *Charles Dickens: Critical Assessments*, 4 vols (Mountfield: Helm Information, 1995), 3:357–66.

[19] Anny Sadrin, 'Nobody's Fault, or the Inheritance of Guilt', in *Parentage and Inheritance in the Works of Charles Dickens* (Cambridge: Cambridge University Press, 1994), 74–94; Jonathan Arac, 'Hamlet, Little Dorrit, and the History of Character', in *Charles Dickens: Critical Assessments*, 3:402–15.

[20] Patricia Ingham, 'Nobody's Fault: The Scope of the Negative in *Little Dorrit*', in John Schad (ed.), *Dickens Refigured: Bodies, Desires, and Other Histories* (Manchester: Manchester University Press, 1996), 98–116.

[21] Trilling, 'Introduction to *Little Dorrit*', 365.

future. After all the story is not really a tragedy, but rather a 'commedia', albeit infused with sadness and gravity, and a peculiar sense of the implacable passing of time and of the persistence of time past, which causes the happy ending to be a very partial, last-minute redemption.

But the socio-political background against which individuals move has its unavoidable weight of unredeemable negativity. This is so, despite the fact that Dickens's 'Preface' acknowledges that the fiction of the Barnacles and the Circumlocution Office is an exaggeration; that he has done violence to good manners by speaking of the Russian war and of certain banks, and indeed conceiving the extravagant character of Mr Merdle. This apologia built on litotes is followed by his statements about the vanishing of the Marshalsea, whose narrow yard, pent-up inner prison, walls, and rooms in which the debtors lived are mentioned and remembered in detail. Ghosts of places, such as the Old Curiosity Shop, which in the novel of that title ends up as only a mere trace on the pavement, nevertheless exist and resist in their appointed space.

The cosmopolitanism inherent in *Little Dorrit* is also mentioned by Trilling. The deep, knowledgeable nature of Dickens's relationship with Europe, as a traveller and resident abroad, especially in Italy, France, and Switzerland, and his political involvement with Italian exiles and their cause, have been the object of recent collections of essays.[22] Looming in the background of *Little Dorrit* are not only the political condition of Italy, with Austria, Sardinia, France, the Bourbons, and the Pope at war, while Mazzini, the Carbonari, the Giovine Italia, and other supporters of Italian independence were in London and well known to Dickens,[23] but also the larger scene, including China with Canton, the opium trade question, and the Opium War against China in 1855–6. The Orientalist discourse, now viewed from a postcolonial perspective, adds the untold story of the historical confrontation between England and China.[24] These events, while lending political tension to a story in which Dickens is 'deliberately telescoping

---

[22] Anny Sadrin (ed.), *Dickens, Europe and the New Worlds* (Basingstoke: Macmillan, 1999); Michael Hollington and Francesca Orestano (eds), *Dickens and Italy*; Maxime Leroy (ed.), *Dickens and Europe* (Newcastle-upon-Tyne: Cambridge Scholars Publishing, 2013).

[23] Tore Rem, '*Little Dorrit, Pictures from Italy* and John Bull', in *Dickens, Europe and the New Worlds* (Basingstoke: Macmillan, 1999), 131–45; in *Dickens and Italy* see the essays by Sally Ledger, ' "GOD be thanked: a ruin!" The Embrace of Italian Modernity in *Pictures from Italy* and the *Daily News*', 82–92; Valerie Kennedy, 'Dream or Reality? Past Savagery versus Present Civilization in *Pictures from Italy* and *Little Dorrit*', 93–113; Massimo Verzella, 'Dickens, Gallenga, and the Topography of Decay', 134–42; Christine Huguet, 'From Batcheecha to Baptist(e): Dickens's Metaphysical Discourse of Foreignness', 194–204; Gerhard Joseph, '*Little Dorrit*: Cosmopolitanism and Cavalletto', 188–93; David Parker, 'Dickens and the Italian Diaspora', 218–29. Also see Ruth Livesey, 'Europe', in Sally Ledger and Holly Furneaux (eds), *Charles Dickens in Context* (Cambridge: Cambridge University Press, 2011), 203–10.

[24] Jeremy Tambling, 'Opium, Wholesale, Resale, and for Exportation: Dickens and China', *Dickens Quarterly* 21 (2004): 28–43 and 104–13; Louis Lo, 'Calvino's and Dickens's Invisible Cities', in *Dickens and Italy*, 230–43; Robert Tindol, 'Arthur Clennam's Twenty Years in China', in Sajini Mukherji and Saswati Halder (eds), *Jadavpur University Essays and Studies: The Dickens World: Post-Imperial Readings* 28–9 (Kolkata: Jadavpur University Press, 2014–15), 94–106.

periods, events and personages',[25] endow *Little Dorrit* with a spacious geographical quality, a cosmopolitanism that will find adequate contrast and tension in the cultural stronghold of Podsnappery. This tension is also expressed in the novel by two connected tropes: while people like ships at sea cover the whole expanse of the globe, they are also rooted in society, in a world of ascending and descending ladders.[26]

Last but not least, the volume devoted by Philip Collins to the critical reception of the writer's works, where *Little Dorrit* merits nine entries, from the years between 1857 and 1864, has been dramatically expanded by the four volumes of critical assessments edited by Hollington, in which the novel is the subject of seven important contributions, covering the years between 1953 and 1990.[27] Today, after the 2012 bicentenary, it looks as if the negative criticisms of the past may provide the very reasons for a more positive appreciation.

Little Dorrit as Stereoscopic View

Recent criticism confirms the relevance of the issues first detected in *Little Dorrit*. The author and the protagonist are in their 40s: both have travelled a lot, and seen the world. In the United States Dickens has not found the republic of his imagination; in Italy he has seen the ruins of the glorious past, but also corruption and decay, masterpieces of art and abject ignorance, and a grotesque mixture of riches and poverty, of paganism and Christianity. This means that the mind confronting the present is well stored with memories and disenchantment, making the appraisal of the present less absolute, less final. In *Little Dorrit* rather than bold statement we find negotiation, and balance in quiet despair. Nine years after his first journey, Dickens had revisited Italy between October and December 1853: the interplay of his past memories with his second impressions is essential to the conception of the story.

Revisitation generates a kind of stereoscopic effect, when recollections of the past and present perceptions set side by side produce a grotesque effect of mutual overlapping of two differently similar images: an effect all the more haunting if the images of the past have been repressed, modified, or removed—if they have acquired a spectral nature.

---

[25] Charles Dickens, *Little Dorrit*, ed. Harvey Peter Sucksmith (Oxford: Clarendon Press, 1979), 'Introduction', vii–xv. Also see Charles Dickens, *Pictures from Italy*, ed. Kate Flint (London: Penguin, 1998), 'Introduction', vii–xxx.

[26] Robert L. Patten, 'Internationalising Dickens: *Little Dorrit* reconsidered', in Christine Huguet and Nathalie Vanfasse (eds), *Charles Dickens, Modernism/Modernity*, 2 vols (Wimereux: Éditions du Sagittaire, 2014), 1:123–50.

[27] Several collections of essays are recommended as providing modern readings of Dickens's art, such as Paul Schlicke (ed.), *The Oxford Reader's Companion to Dickens* (Oxford: Oxford University Press, 1999); John O. Jordan (ed.), *The Cambridge Companion to Charles Dickens* (Cambridge: Cambridge University Press, 2001); David Paroissien (ed.), *A Companion to Charles Dickens* (Malden, MA: Blackwell Publishing, 2008); Ledger and Furneaux (eds), *Charles Dickens in Context*.

This complexity moulds and directs Dickens's plan of the novel: in fact, granted the overarching effect of the prison motif, one may argue that the real prison of the past, in Book the First, and the prison impressions of Book the Second, merge into one compound of disturbing, uniform pervasiveness, made of sharp detail and deeply affecting awareness. Progress seems denied. My reference to the stereoscope is not casual. In *Little Dorrit*—as elsewhere in Dickens—visual technology is adopted as the metaphorical tool through which narration negotiates its direction and progress—or, rather, it expresses its antagonism to progress and direction.

It is well known that *Little Dorrit* is a rags-to-riches-to-rags story. The initial title, *Nobody's Fault* (related to Dickens's article on the mismanagement of the Crimean War,[28] and probably discarded for the same reason that induced him to call Coketown the place represented in *Hard Times*), well behoves a story that insists on negation. 'How Not to Do It' is the motto of the Circumlocution Office, reflected by Arthur Clennam's attitude, and the almost choral mantra recited by those who invoke erasure of the past in the novel; it also suggests a mature, disillusioned knowledge of the patriarchal system and its more or less subtle ways of ruling individuals and the community. As in *Hamlet* such negativity contains both the weight of the past and a criticism of the present. Four chapters, related to Arthur's abortive romance with Pet Meagles, are entitled 'Nobody's Weakness', 'Nobody's Rival', 'Nobody's State of Mind', and 'Nobody's Disappearance'; and Amy Dorrit is introduced as: 'Oh! She? Little Dorrit? *She*'s nothing.'[29]

The commonplace criticism of the carelessness of the plot, due to the unrelenting schedule of serial publication, has been contested by recent editors of *Little Dorrit*—Harvey Peter Sucksmith and Stephen Wall—who argue, on the basis of Dickens's careful working notes, that the planning was 'organized on binary principles',[30] as the two books' diptych, 'Poverty' and 'Riches', indicates. The two books in fact face each other, hinged by means of a journey from England to Italy that occurs when the imprisonment for debt of William Dorrit is dramatically and suddenly turned into wealth and freedom.

> The presentation of opposed or comparable states allows for many internal echoes, both structural and local... In the plan for the second number the words 'Parallel Imprisonments' (i.e. Mr Dorrit's and Mrs Clennam's) are significantly underlined... It can't therefore be accidental that the second chapter of the first book and the first chapter of the second book have the same title, 'Fellow Travellers' ... Similarly, Book the First ends with Clennam carrying the insensible Little Dorrit out of the Marshalsea ... while Book the Second echoes but improves on this when she and Clennam quietly leave the prison to be married.[31]

---

[28] See Philpotts, *The Companion to Little Dorrit*, 17–18.
[29] Charles Dickens, *Little Dorrit*, ed. Harvey Peter Sucksmith (Oxford: Clarendon Press, 1979), Book I, chapter 3, page 33. Subsequent references are inserted parenthetically in the text by *LD* Book:chapter, page.
[30] Charles Dickens, *Little Dorrit*, ed. Stephen Wall and Helen Small (London: Penguin, 2003), 'Introduction', xi–xxvii; xv.
[31] Ibid., xvi.

Such echoes indeed are manifold and resounding. Dickens's working notes teem with remarks such as 'pave the way' and 'not yet', indicative of his careful planning. Sucksmith confirms that 'a note by Dickens shows that parallel scenes ... were deliberately planned'.[32] This effect of parallelism is sought from the very beginning, when the quarantine to which travellers are subjected is a kind of imprisonment, and the Marseille prison anticipates the Marshalsea; it is doubled in numerous passages that affirm an overwhelming sense of déjà vu and the condition of imprisonment, either material or psychological. This condition infects even the journey to distant places:

> Sitting opposite her father in the travelling-carriage, and recalling the old Marshalsea room, her present existence was a dream. All that she saw was new and wonderful, but it was not real; it seemed to her as if those visions of mountains and picturesque countries might melt away at any moment, and the carriage, turning some abrupt corner, bring up with a jolt at the old Marshalsea gate... only the old Marshalsea a reality. (*LD* II:3, 451)

The description of the eerie effect produced by Italian landscape—so similar to what Dickens would experience on his second journey, so disappointing, and marked by strange tricks of memory—lends to these pages the quality of Giovanbattista Piranesi's series of 16 etchings called *Imaginary Prisons* (1750–61). It's a fantastic sense of being psychologically imprisoned beyond space and time: a nightmare rather than a dream. The sublime unending prison images recur in the unreal oneiric condition of Venice, where Little Dorrit recognizes in her father's mien 'the well-known shadow of the Marshalsea wall... [S]he was not strong enough to keep off the fear that no space in the life of man could overcome that quarter of a century behind the prison bars' (*LD* II:5, 463). The famous passage about Rome again registers the same effect, as Amy contemplates ruins and arches, old temples and old tombs, that

> besides being what they were, to her, were ruins of the old Marshalsea—ruins of her own old life—ruins of the faces and forms that of old peopled it—ruins of its loves, hopes, cares and joys. Two ruined spheres of action and suffering were before the solitary girl often sitting on some broken fragment; and in the lonely places, under the blue sky, she saw them together. (*LD* II:15, 591)

In Dickens's world codes borrowed from pictorial genres, visual culture, and Victorian visual technology are deployed to obtain a maximum of effect. A closer look at mass visual culture in the Victorian age[33] adds a remarkable dimension to criticism by

---

[32] *Little Dorrit*, ed. Sucksmith, 'Introduction', xi.

[33] Jonathan Crary, *Techniques of the Observer: On Vision and Modernity in the Nineteenth Century* (Cambridge, MA: MIT Press, 1993); Carol Christ and John O. Jordan (eds), *Victorian Literature and the Victorian Visual Imagination* (Berkeley and Los Angeles: University of California Press, 1995); Nancy Armstrong, *Fiction in the Age of Photography: The Legacy of British Realism* (Cambridge, MA: Harvard University Press, 1999); Kate Flint, *The Victorians and the Visual Imagination* (Cambridge: Cambridge

indicating the writer's awareness of what would be defined as primacy of perception and techniques of the observer. Such awareness, confirmed by Dickens's mastery of picturesque sketching, by the pictorial and panoramic quality of the text, and the expert command he exerted over his illustrators, is documented by the writer's intentional use of visual strategies in his fiction. Dickens deliberately attended to the dynamics of the eye, infusing realistic descriptions with visual strategies borrowed from the mechanics of the phantasmagoria, the magic lantern-cum-dissolving views, the panorama, the diorama—and the stereoscope.[34]

Little Dorrit is no exception. Dedicated to his friend the painter Clarkson Stanfield, the novel contains an allusion to a painting by J. M. W. Turner, *The Fighting Téméraire*, where the old majestic ship is taken in tow by a modern small steam tug: past and present (*LD* I:13, 142). In 1855 Stanfield made a copy of this painting for Dickens. Other visual references include Mr Meagles's spoils, where 'antiquities from Central Italy' are the product of modern industry (*LD* I:16, 188); the reference to a landscape with cows by Cuyp, a stereoscope device used to suggest the conventional grouping of bovine guests in Mr Merdle's drawing room (*LD* II:12, 544); the character of Henry Gowan, the painter in his studio; Tite Barnacle, eternal sitter to Sir Thomas Lawrence (*LD* I:10, 106); and the naive pastoral fresco varnishing the Plornishes' shop (*LD* II:13, 556).[35]

At a structural level, the notion of linear geometry determining perspective is deployed when Arthur realizes that Pet is in love with Mr Gowan. Even more daringly, to suggest fantastic and disturbing knowledge, Mrs Affery's strange dreams 'hover ... like shadows from a great magic lantern' (*LD* I:15, 172). Light and darkness always carry the inevitable melodrama of moral associations: as in the cover of the monthly issues. 'Eyes', 'gaze', and 'stare', are keywords from the very first chapter.

In addition to these examples, the stereoscope seems to provide the tool through which two parallel views of things past and present, of here and there, can be simultaneously negotiated as one. Presented by Charles Wheatstone in 1838 to the Royal Society, perfected by Brewster, the stereoscope was on display at the Great Exhibition in 1851, soon to become so popular that each respectable Victorian home would have one. Based on the scientific notion of the binocularity of vision, this instrument offered the viewer one in-depth image, resulting from two paired views, often photographs, of the same

University Press, 2000); Daniel A. Novak, *Realism, Photography, and Nineteenth-Century Fiction* (Cambridge: Cambridge University Press, 2008).

[34] Francesca Orestano, 'The Magic Lantern and the Crystal Palace: Dickens and the Landscape of Fiction', in Rossana Bonadei, Clotilde De Stasio, Carlo Pagetti, and Alessandro Vescovi (eds), *Dickens: The Craft of Fiction and the Challenges of Reading* (Milan: Unicopli, 2000), 249–72; Victor Sage, 'Gothic Transformation in *Pictures from Italy*', in *Dickens and Italy*, 144–56; Nathalie Vanfasse, '"A Rapid Diorama": Dickens's Representation of Naples and Florence in *Pictures from Italy*', in *Dickens and Italy*, 68–81; Francesca Orestano, 'Back to Italy: Dickens's Stereoscopic Views', in Leroy (ed.), *Dickens and Europe*, 126–41.

[35] Leonée Ormond, 'Dickens and Contemporary Art', in Mark Bills (ed.), *Dickens and the Artists* (New Haven: Yale University Press, 2012), 35–65.

subject taken at slightly different angles in space, and consequently in time. Thus the stereoscopic image precipitates the separate notions of distant and near, then and now, into one vivid compound—the past, the distant, the blurred, acquire new poignant evidence and distinction of detail. External and internal evidence suggests the prominent role of stereoscopic technology in *Little Dorrit*.

'The Stereoscope' is described in a *Household Words* article by Henry Morley and W. H. Wills, published on 10 September 1853, just a few days before Dickens's second journey to Italy. This article describes the stereoscope in a prose that mingles lucid scientific instruction with the wonders and romance of modern science:

> There is a good deal of romance to be found even in the details of pure science, and a book of wonders could very well be made out of what may be called the social history of optical discoveries... Here is a box... containing any fairy-scene that by the help of photography we may be disposed to conjure up. It is called the Stereoscope. And of what use is its magic? To go no farther than the particular picture just suggested, of very great use... [I]t was invented some years since by Professor Wheatstone to illustrate his discovery of the principles of binocular vision.[36]

To the 1853 article in *Household Words* another piece of external evidence may be added: that of 'the advertisements that appeared in the original serial instalments of Dickens's novels, [which] provide sources for a critique of this Victorian art of seeing'.[37] Advertisements in Dickens's serials allowed readers to complement their purchase by buying interesting objects, manuals, games, books on the art of observing and on eye training. For instance, the booklet 'The Observing Eye' was advertised in the second serial issue of *Little Dorrit* in January 1856. In the same issue, the three-dimensional reality of a stereoscopic photograph is advertised, with, below, 'the Shakespearian quote: "Seems Madam! Nay, it IS!"' (Figure 17.2.)[38] The quotation is taken from *Hamlet*, Act 1, Scene 2, and while summoning the Bard to emphasize the strange effect of the stereoscope, it also confirms critical statements about Arthur Clennam's battle with his own ghost, to gain a clear perception of the past.

Thus the stereoscope not only underpins the narration with its sound scientific technique, but also helps encode memory in the present, fostering that psychological interest remarked by critics who set their focus on duality and binary structure. The theme of memory, already broached by Dickens in *The Haunted Man and the Ghost's Bargain* (1848) with the formulaic recipe of a Christmas story, is revived in the letters from his second journey to Italy, where he realizes that 'le temps retrouvé' never connects precisely backwards into 'le temps perdu'—and the reverse. In *Little Dorrit* memory acquires a kind of viral intensity. Memory—involuntary memory—is what determines

---

[36] Henry Morley and W. H. Wills, *Household Words*, 'The Stereoscope', 10 September 1853, pages 37–42; 37. Subsequent references are inserted parenthetically in the text by *HW*, 'The Stereoscope', date, page.

[37] Gerald Curtis, 'Dickens in the Visual Market', in John O. Jordan and Robert L. Patten (eds), *Literature in the Marketplace* (Cambridge: Cambridge University Press, 1996), 213–49; 214.

[38] Ibid., 217.

FIGURE 17.2 'Little Dorrit Advertiser', insert for part 2, January 1856.

Courtesy McHenry Library Special Collections, University of California, Santa Cruz

the final public undoing of William Dorrit, who, during an elegant banquet in Rome, starts speaking about his former prison. Memory and its remnants in the form of a letter about Arthur's past are eventually destroyed by Little Dorrit, in the gesture that grants her beloved the immersion in the river of oblivion, as well as the life-giving consolations deriving from the thriving condition of his partner Daniel Doyce.

While providing visual evidence of the persistence of memory, the stereoscopic effect legitimizes and dramatizes all kinds of human revisitations of the past. Between Marseille and Marshalsea there is only the gap of a small interval in time, space, and pronunciation; prisons of the past keep pace with the condition of the present, so that the bulky structure of a jail, a lazaretto, a decrepit old house, the foundling institution, the workhouse, while rooted in the past of the characters, are still visible in palaces and in rooms furnished with spiritual iron bars. Sleeves turn into manacles, arresting the fraudulent Mr Merdle even before his bankruptcy. Faces from the past are also of the present, as with Rigaud/Lagnier/Blandois, or with the coexistence of the vanishing Flora and the existing Flora, Arthur's old sweetheart (*LD* I:13, 153).

In the chapter 'APPEARANCES AND DISAPPEARANCES' (*LD* II:9, 510) Dickens encapsulates the connection between optical tools, physiology, science, and romance. Mrs Tickit, the Meagles's housekeeper, tells Arthur about a strange experience that has confused and frightened her. Being sure that Tattycoram, the adopted orphan, was not there, she explains:

> '[W]hen I quivered my eyes and saw her actual form and figure ... I let them close again without so much as starting ... But, sir, when I quivered my eyes again and saw that it wasn't there, then it all flooded upon me with a fright, and I jumped up.' (*LD* II:9, 513)

The eyes of Mrs Tickit have seen two slides, past and present, combined together, and this causes her wonder, as she cannot tell whether five seconds or ten minutes have passed between two ocular 'quiverings'—and whether the person she has seen resides in the past or in the present. The mechanism works in an uncanny fashion, inasmuch as 'when a person does begin thinking of one thing and thinking of another, ... all times seem to be present' (*LD* II:9, 513).

From what we know about Dickens's second time in Italy, juxtaposing past and present generates a kind of oppressive increase in realism. 'The Stereoscope' provides scientific explanation:

> [A] slight—but very sensible—difference exists between the results of the two sights taken from two points in the same head at the same object. The points of sight in the two eyes are of course different, and by the laws of perspective it is easy to determine that the views of the same thing taken from those two points could not be identical. (*HW*, 'The Stereoscope', 10 September 1853, 39)

But the very same instrument plays a 'perverting' trick on visual perception, splitting the firm location of subjectivity: 'If we cheat the eyes in a stereoscope by showing to each eye the picture that belongs only to its neighbour's point of view, everything is perverted' (*HW*, 'The Stereoscope', 10 September 1853, 39). The novel does not gain clarity from the scientific notion it encapsulates, but dwells, rather, upon the uncanny binary option: the 'Parallel Imprisonments' (*LD*, Appendix, 808) and the two sides of the river, with Marshalsea and the house of Clennam, 'two frowning wildernesses of secrets' (*LD* II:10, 526). Firmness of vision is only granted with the final disclosure of Amy's love, a revelation set in visual terms:

> Looking back upon his own poor story, she was its vanishing-point. Everything in its perspective led to her innocent figure.... [I]t was the centre of the interest of his life; it was the termination of everything that was good and pleasant in it; beyond, there was nothing but mere waste and darkened sky. (*LD* II:27, 714)

The visual stance elucidates the discursive form of the novel, described as 'two kinds of novel, two qualities of being: the active and realistic, or the responsive, interiorized, and imaginative'.[39]

Little Dorrit as '*Lieu de Mémoire*'

Analogous with the stereoscope, the notion of '*lieu de mémoire*' deployed by Pierre Nora illustrates the polarity between past and present in *Little Dorrit*, while offering a critical track for further investigation. Nora contrasts memory, 'a perpetually actual phenomenon, a bond tying us to the eternal present', against history, 'the reconstruction, always problematic and incomplete, of what is no longer'.[40] The novel is a metaphorical battlefield in both ways: the image of *The Fighting Téméraire* incarnates the characters of the venerable Casby and Pancks, the modern tug, the ideal cynosure to the theme. On the side of language the signs are no less numerous, earning the novel the definition of a 'stultified, linguistically turbid world',[41] intensely metaphorical, polyphonic, labyrinthine—marked by heteroglossia, as argued by Mikhail Bakhtin.[42] In fact, its language can be described as a hybrid construction, containing 'two utterances, two speech manners, two styles, two "languages", two semantic and axiological belief systems'.[43] This dual capability defines the novel as *lieu de mémoire*—site of memory. Nora remarks that

> memory and history, far from being synonymous, are in fundamental opposition. Memory is life, ... in permanent evolution, open to the dialectic of remembering and forgetting, ... vulnerable to manipulation and appropriation ... At the heart, history is a critical discourse that is antithetical to spontaneous memory. History is perpetually suspicious of memory, and its true mission is to suppress and destroy it.[44]

If memory is affective, visual, and magical, and history thrives on mediation and distance, it is not difficult to spot in *Little Dorrit* the group (mainly the Marshalsea group) of those who keep, endure, cherish, avoid, or even battle against memory; and the group of those who produce history: the Barnacles, Bar and Bishop, the Merdles, and the Meagleses, who aim at 'the conquest and eradication of memory by history'.[45] This is the battlefield entered by Dickens when he wrote a novel about a place that had ceased to

---

[39] Nicola Bradbury, 'Dickens and the Form of the Novel', in *The Cambridge Companion to Charles Dickens*, 152–66.
[40] Pierre Nora, 'Between Memory and History: Les Lieux de Mémoire', *Representations* 26 (Spring 1989): 7–24; 8.
[41] Andrew Sanders, *Dickens and the Spirit of the Age* (Oxford: Clarendon Press, 1999), 132.
[42] Mikhail Bakhtin, 'Heteroglossia in the Novel', in *Charles Dickens: Critical Assessments*, 3:392–401.
[43] Ibid., 398.
[44] Nora, 'Between Memory and History', 8; 9.
[45] Ibid., 8.

exist 20 years before, so relevant to his own individual experience, yet so meaningful in social terms if constructed into a collective memory site. He was, one might say, in advance of his times, in terms of awareness of the value of memory and its epistemological relevance:

> At the end of the last century ... memory appeared at the centre of philosophical thought, with Bergson; at the core of psychological personality, with Freud, at the heart of literary autobiography, with Proust... Our relation to the past is now formed in a subtle play between its intractability and its disappearance, a question of a representation... Ours is an intensely retinal and powerfully televisual memory.[46]

Thus not only is the vanished Marshalsea the deposit of childhood memories that Forster was to inscribe in his historical record of the great writer; the novel is also the medium that aims at inscribing the memory of the vanished prison, of all prisons, onto collective psychology, communal ideas of state, justice, and work, cosmopolitan trends of imperial conquest and gain, tourist hoarding of souvenirs, and poignant visual evidence. The notion of *lieu de mémoire* illustrates Dickens's manipulation of memory and history, two parallel yet distinct and antagonistic ways of accounting for—as Carlyle would say—past and present. The subversive nature of such achievement was underlined in 1937 by Bernard Shaw, who remarked that *Little Dorrit* was a more seditious book than Marx's *Das Kapital*.[47] Dickens indeed was not a prisoner of the past.

Further Reading

Christine Huguet and Paul Vita (eds), *Unsettling Dickens: Process, Progress, and Change* (Wimereux: Éditions du Sagittaire, 2016)
Norbert Lennartz and Dieter Koch (eds), *Texts, Contexts and Intertextuality: Dickens as a Reader* (Göttingen: V&R unipress, 2014)
Brian Rosenberg, *Little Dorrit's Shadows: Character and Contradiction in Dickens* (Columbia: University of Missouri Press, 1996)
Jerry White, *Mansions of Misery: A Biography of the Marshalsea Debtors' Prison* (London: The Bodley Head, 2016)

---

[46] Ibid., 15; 17.
[47] Quoted in Sanders, *Dickens and the Spirit of the Age*, 137.

CHAPTER 18

A TALE OF TWO CITIES

NATHALIE VANFASSE

A Tale of Two Cities is by no means the most popular Dickens novel in France, possibly because it tackles, in what the French may deem a somewhat unsubtle way, a major traumatic episode of French history, namely the Reign of Terror during the French Revolution. In this respect, French translators of *A Tale of Two Cities* are known to have toned down the gruesome and terrifying revolutionary episodes depicted in Dickens's novel to make them more palatable to a French readership, whose collective psyche is still haunted by the trauma that pervades evocations of revolutionary Terror.[1] What this transformation of the original text demonstrates is that translations of *A Tale of Two Cities* not only raise questions regarding interculturality, but also imply memory, and sometimes trauma. In this respect, an extensive study of the novel in the light of French memory, with the help of memory studies and possibly of trauma studies, would certainly yield a deeper understanding of the effects upon the French psyche of the novel's representation of revolutionary Terror.[2] A revealing anecdote seems to corroborate the need for such a memorial and intercultural undertaking. On the occasion of the bicentenary of the Revolution in 1989, the English Prime Minister, Margaret Thatcher, did not just commit a diplomatic faux pas, but revealed an interesting amnesia of sorts on the part of the English government: she offered the French President, François Mitterrand, a copy of *A Tale of Two Cities*!

Now the question of the translation of *A Tale of Two Cities* from English into French can also fruitfully and paradoxically be reversed. One may, indeed, consider the novel as a skilful translation of the French Revolution into English. How did Dickens manage to translate this event for British readers whose imagination was also haunted by the spectre of this disturbing historical episode? For one thing, his transcription of

---

[1] See Christine Raguet, 'Terror Foreign or Familiar—Pleasure on the Edge: Translating *A Tale of Two Cities* into French', *Dickens Quarterly* 26, 3 (September 2009): 175–86.

[2] In this respect, Laurent Bury has studied remembering and dismembering in the novel in *Liberty, Duality, Urbanity: Charles Dickens's A Tale of Two Cities* (Paris: Presses Universitaires de France, 2012), 133–41.

a very French historical event into the English language and culture implied, among other things, the use of a sophisticated Anglo-French parlance in the form of English sprinkled with Gallicisms.[3] This idiom is not just contrived; it also highlights some of the troubling metaphysical questions that the French Revolution raises. Let us take the following dialogue from the famous wine cask scene:

> 'How goes it, Jacques?' said one of these three to Monsieur Defarge. 'Is all the spilt wine swallowed?'
> 'Every drop, Jacques,' answered Monsieur Defarge.
> ... 'It is not often,' said the second of the three, addressing Monsieur Defarge, 'that many of these miserable beasts know the taste of wine, or of anything but black bread and death. Is it not so, Jacques?'
> 'It is so, Jacques,' Monsieur Defarge returned.[4]

'Comment ça va' has come to mean in French 'how things stand in the present circumstances', but in the English transposition of this set phrase, 'How goes it', the verb 'to go' makes the sentence sound stilted. This preserves and highlights the sense of motion contained in the verb 'to go'. Defarge's question somehow seems to already foreshadow the vast crowd movements that will typify the French Revolution as depicted later in the novel. In contrast to this potential movement, the French tag questions and answers *'n'est-ce pas?'* and *'c'est ainsi'*, which would normally be translated into English as 'do they?' and as 'no they don't', are rendered literally in the novel by 'It is not often', 'Is it not so?', and 'It is so', tags emphasizing the verb 'to be'. This unexpected translation emphasizes the duration of the people's wretchedness, thereby foregrounding a condition of stasis, which paves the way for discontent and resentment.

Reverse translation also includes the glossing in English of French revolutionary terms like *'tricoter'* (knitting), *'lanterne de potence'* (swinging lamps), or *'Guillotine'*.[5] These words do not make sense without a background knowledge of their meaning in French culture or of the meaning of the French words they translate. Such is the case with Madame Defarge's knitting. Madame Defarge's needlework clashes with the social and literary model of the Angel in the House, with which Victorian readers were familiar. Her knitting is not connected to the private sphere, but foreshadows her role as the leader of revolutionary women in the Storming of the Bastille (*TTC* II:21 and 22), and later as the head of the French *'tricoteuses'*, whom she epitomizes. However, Dickens chose not to use the French word *'tricoteuse'*, which might have immediately brought to mind the image of French women counting heads at the foot of the Guillotine. Instead, Dickens gradually infuses the English verb with its French meaning that materializes in

---

[3] Sylvère Monod, *Dickens the Novelist* (Norman: University of Oklahoma Press, 1968), 459–60.
[4] *A Tale of Two Cities*, ed. Andrew Sanders, Oxford World's Classics (Oxford: Oxford University Press, 1988), Book I, chapter 5, pages 35–6. Subsequent references are inserted parenthetically in the text by *TTC* Book:chapter, page.
[5] See Nathalie Vanfasse, 'Translating the French Revolution into English in *A Tale of Two Cities*', *Cahiers Victoriens et Édouardiens* 78 (Autumn 2013): n.p. Web. 3 June 2016. Doi: 10.4000/cve.776.

the final image of the Vengeance and her friends sitting with their knitting at the foot of the Guillotine and waiting in vain for Madame Defarge's arrival (*TTC* III:15, 358). These examples clearly bring to light more of the complex intercultural considerations raised by the novel.[6]

In addition to intercultural interpretations, *A Tale of Two Cities* lends itself to interdisciplinary critical readings that engage with the historical, political, philosophical, and sociological issues that it tackles. Let us leave aside the already well-known critical debates as to whether *A Tale of Two Cities* can be considered a historical novel, with some critics claiming that the novel does not contain sufficient historical evidence, and others arguing that Dickens offers a more or less convincing private and personal resolution to the political turmoil of a historically troubled period.[7] Let us consider instead the very materiality of historical evidence and how the novel deals with this issue. For one thing, a close examination of Dickens's manuscript of the novel by Joel Brattin has revealed interesting new interpretations based on textual revisions that bring to light the existence of other doubles for Sidney Carton.[8] But the materiality of paper and documents is tackled in the plot itself, which voices anxiety about the disintegration and disappearance of such historical testimonies, as has been shown by Céline Prest.[9]

In keeping with the conventions of historical novels, the French Revolution in *A Tale of Two Cities* is not just a backdrop; it is part and parcel of a plot that weaves together national history and the individual and fictional destinies of the Manette family. Strikingly, for French readers like myself, Dickens's novel exemplifies a definition of history in keeping with what the famous historian Jules Michelet was to call, in his *History of France* (1869), a 'complete resurrection'.[10] By this, Michelet meant a historical approach that was not just analytical and interpretative, but aimed at re-enacting events in writing. Though theorized by Michelet, this form of Romantic history had already been put into practice earlier by Thomas Carlyle in England—particularly in his *History of the French Revolution* (1837), a book which inspired Dickens's novel.

Besides exemplifying a form of romantic history, *A Tale of Two Cities* also uses a triple temporality that foreshadows the three-tiered view of historical time delineated

---

[6] See Murray Baumgarten, 'Writing the Revolution', *Dickens Studies Annual* 12 (1983): 161–76.

[7] See Irene Collins, 'Charles Dickens and the French Revolution', *Literature and History* 1, 1 (1990): 40–58; Barton R. Friedman, 'Antihistory: Dickens' *A Tale of Two Cities*', in *Fabricating History: English Writers on the French Revolution* (Princeton: Princeton University Press, 1988).

[8] Joel Brattin, 'Sidney Carton's Other Doubles', in N. Vanfasse, M-A. Coste, C. Huguet, and L. Bouvard (eds), *Dickens in the New Millennium, Cahiers Victoriens et Édouardiens* (February 2012): 209–23.

[9] Céline Prest, 'Recalled to Life: Exhuming Documents in *A Tale of Two Cities*', in J.-P. Naugrette et al. (eds), *Charles Dickens: A Tale of Two Cities, Cercles* 31 (2013): 115–24.

[10] Jules Michelet, *Histoire de France*, vol. 1 (Paris: A Lacroix et Compagnie, 1880), iii. 'Plus compliqué encore, plus effrayant était mon problème historique posé comme *résurrection de la vie intégrale*, non pas dans ses surfaces, mais dans ses organismes intérieurs et profonds.' ('More complicated still, more daunting was my historical problem defined as *the resurrection of complete life*, not in its surfaces, but in its inner and deep organisms.' Translation mine; emphasis in the original.)

by French historian Fernand Braudel.[11] Braudel highlights the existence of a slow, geographical evolution of time, alongside the quicker pace of social history, and the even faster momentum of event-driven history. *A Tale of Two Cities* strikingly prefigures these three temporal levels, identifiable in the novel first, as the gradual changes in nature wrought by the growing forests of Norway and France alluded to at the beginning of the novel (*TTC* I:1, 8); then, as the social history of two nations, England and France; and finally, as the accelerations of event-driven history embodied by the revolutionaries—this revolutionary history also standing for what would later be called 'history from below'.

Another interesting interdisciplinary connection established by *A Tale of Two Cities* is the translation or the transposition of time into place, in other words of history into geography. Indeed, the novel maps a historical event onto the geography of two cities. Moreover, this geography—which associates different scales, such as the microcosm of the Faubourg Saint-Antoine quarter with the geography of France and its interactions with the universe—is far from static: it evolves as the Revolution spreads. Sara Thornton and Michael Hollington have looked into this connection of space and time. Thornton considers space not just horizontally but also vertically by showing how *A Tale of Two Cities* superimposes Paris and London stereoscopically, thus delivering a new political message which runs counter to the popular understanding that the novel was primarily hostile to the French Revolution.[12] Hollington associates time and space in *A Tale of Two Cities* via the themes of travel, mobility, and restlessness.[13] Further investigations could involve mobility studies, since the novel is filled with journeys and displacements well worth looking into.[14]

A Tale of Two Cities offers a poetic transfiguration of the French Revolution that is symbolic, epic, fantastic, and at times quasi-hallucinatory.[15] The Storming of the Bastille is a perfect example of such poetic transmutations: the fairly flat French expression '*la prise de la Bastille*'—or 'taking' of the Bastille—is transposed by Dickens into a sustained maritime metaphor in which the charging of the Bastille becomes a stormy seascape à la Turner, foreshadowed by the thundering sea watched by Mr Lorry at Dover in one of the opening scenes of the novel (*TTC* I:4, 22). The verb 'to storm' is used literally and metaphorically by Dickens, who develops the image of a thunderstorm to foreshadow the

---

[11] See Fernand Braudel's preface to *The Mediterranean and the Mediterranean World in the Age of Philip II* (London: Collins, 1972).

[12] Sara Thornton, 'Paris and London Superimposed: Urban Seeing and New Political Space in Dickens's *Tale of Two Cities*', *Études anglaises* 65 (2012–13): 302–14.

[13] See Michael Hollington, *A Tale of Two Cities* (Paris: Atlande, 2012).
Hollington connects the historical notion of Revolution to sundry cyclical movements in space, and he links spatially linear patterns to linearity in time.

[14] On mobility studies, see Jonathan Grossman, *Charles Dickens's Networks: Public Transport and the Novel* (Oxford: Oxford University Press, 2012); Ruth Livesey, *Writing the Stage Coach Nation: Locality on the Move in Nineteenth-Century British Literature* (Oxford: Oxford University Press, 2016).

[15] On patterns of imagery in the novel, see Kurt Tetzeli von Rosador, 'Metaphorical Representations of the French Revolution in Victorian Fiction', *Nineteenth-Century Literature* 43 (1988): 1–23.

coming of the Revolution and its metaphorical rendering as a human wave in a raging sea (*TTC* II:22, 213). This stylistic device partakes of the previously mentioned strategy of translating the French Revolution into English, by using a quintessentially English metaphor: Dickens plays on the double meaning of the word 'storm' in English—namely as a synonym of 'a tempest' but also of the verb 'to charge'. The previous analysis illustrates a well-known interdisciplinary perspective on novel writing, summed up by Pierre Bourdieu's contention that 'literature condenses in the concrete singularity of sentient beings, and of individual adventures—which function both as metaphors and metonymies—the complexity of a structure and of history that scientific analyses laboriously unravel and develop' (translation mine).[16]

A Tale of Two Cities undoubtedly lends itself to connections between literature and other disciplines. It offers an interesting take on legal matters, thus partaking of what is now called the interdiscipline of literature and law, aptly analysed by Christine Krueger.[17] It also tackles professional issues, like Sidney Carton's business as a barrister highlighted by Simon Petch.[18] It can be envisaged as well as a prime meeting point of politics and poetics. If one were to follow the philosopher Jacques Rancière in considering that politics have a quintessentially aesthetic quality, then Dickens's novel produces a deeper and more inclusive reading of common experience than that given by ordinary political discourses.[19] In *A Tale of Two Cities*, politics acquire an aesthetic quality which lies in their contribution to the construction of a community or social body—the French revolutionaries—as well as of a common space—France, and more particularly the Saint-Antoine quarter in which this community evolves.

To better understand Dickens's strategies to make the oppressed and the nameless—in other words the '*Misérables*'—visible, one may resort to another political/poetical perspective, that of the philosopher Hannah Arendt.[20] Indeed, *A Tale of Two Cities* shows the people not as a mere abstraction, but as individuals acting and speaking as distinctive faces, and as a crowd made up of singularities and differences reflecting humanity in its plurality. Dickens also hones in upon the very space that brings these different singularities together: the people's sovereignty is rendered as much by a focus on the Paris quarter of Saint-Antoine as on the representation of the revolutionaries

---

[16] Pierre Bourdieu, *Les Règles de l'art* (Paris, Seuil, 1992), 22. *The Rules of Art: Genesis and Structure of the Literary Field*, trans. Susan Emanuel (Stanford, CA: Stanford University Press, 1996).

[17] Christine L. Krueger, 'The Queer Heroism of a Man of Law in *A Tale of Two Cities*', *Nineteenth-Century Gender Studies* 8, 2 (Summer 2012): n. p. Web. 3 June 2016.

[18] Simon Petch, 'The Business of the Barrister in *A Tale of Two Cities*', *Criticism: A Quarterly for Literature and the Arts* 44, 1 (Winter 2002): 27–42. See also Nathalie Jaëck on the banker Mr Lorry in 'Liminality in *A Tale of Two Cities*: Dickens's Revolutionary Literary Proposal', in Maxime Leroy (ed.), *Charles Dickens and Europe* (Newcastle upon Tyne: Cambridge Scholars Publishing, 2013), 72–84.

[19] Jacques Rancière, *Disagreement: Politics and Philosophy*, trans. Julie Rose (Minneapolis: University of Minnesota Press, 1999); *The Politics of Aesthetics: The Distribution of the Sensible*, trans. Gabriel Rockhill (London: Continuum, 2004).

[20] See Hannah Arendt, *Qu'est ce que la politique?* (1950–9), trans. S. Courtine Denamy (Paris: Le Seuil, 1995), 39–43.

themselves. They, in turn, are represented through a proliferation of anonymous faces interspersed with a few specific portraits, such as those of the Defarges. Dickens's novel exemplifies Hannah Arendt's theory about literature and humanity in dark times, in that it infuses what Arendt calls 'fragments of humanity' into a world that has become inhuman, as much through the inhumanity of the *ancien régime* as through the barbarism of Revolutionary Terror.[21]

The connection between politics and poetics in *A Tale of Two Cities* also implies building the plebeian into the subjects of a political scene, as discussed by political scientist Martin Breaugh. This is achieved by defending the people against the prerogatives of the powerful, thereby giving them a true political status or, as Breaugh puts it, 'human political dignity'.[22]

To further understand Dickens's aesthetic and political stance in *A Tale of Two Cities*, a grammar of compassion, like the one delineated by the French sociologist Luc Boltanski, may usefully be called upon.[23] Boltanski distinguishes three levels in the representation of suffering, namely denunciation—which puts presumed persecutors on trial—emotion and empathy, and aesthetics—in which spectatorship prevails. Dickens makes a subtle and complex use of such a grammar by applying it not only to the ordinary people but also to the very aristocracy that the people overthrow.

Interdisciplinarity applies even further to *A Tale of Two Cities* when one realizes that Dickens's political stance also tackles crucial ethical and philosophical questions involving crime and punishment; or such difficult choices as speaking or being silenced; accepting the order of things or rebelling against it. Dickens delves into these ethical dilemmas only to spell them out in even more problematic terms.[24] In *A Tale of Two Cities*, Charles Darnay's predicament raises, for instance, the question as to whether one should be punished for a crime committed by one's father. Similarly, Doctor Manette's imprisonment at the Bastille is the result of an impossible choice between enduring tyranny to keep a semblance of freedom, or speaking up against it and being locked up forever.

Manette's predicament as an anonymous Bastille prisoner, reduced to being number 'one Hundred and Five North Tower', emphasizes how much identity is at the heart of *A Tale of Two Cities*. The elusiveness and fragmented nature of social identities in *A Tale of Two Cities*, as well as the violence inherent in family names, have been emphasized

---

[21] Hannah Arendt, *Men in Dark Times* (New York: Harcourt, Brace and World, 1968).

[22] See Martin Breaugh, *L'Expérience plébéienne: une histoire discontinue de la liberté politique* (Paris: Payot, 2007), 87–171; *The Plebeian Experience: A Discontinuous History of Political Freedom*, trans. Lazer Lederhandler (New York: Columbia University Press, 2013).

[23] Luc Boltanski, *La Souffrance à distance: morale humanitaire, médias et politique* (Paris: Métailié, 1993); *Distant Suffering: Morality, Media, and Politics*, trans. Graham Burchell (Cambridge: Cambridge University Press, 1999).

[24] On crime and punishment, see also Jeremy Tambling, 'Dickens and Dostoevsky: Capital Punishment in *Barnaby Rudge*, *A Tale of Two Cities*, and *the Idiot*', in *Dickens, Violence, and the Modern State: Dreams of the Scaffold* (New York: St Martin's Press, 1995), 129–54.

by Kamilla Eliott.[25] Eliott focuses on face value, and connects identity in the novel to portraits on promissory notes, French passport descriptions, and photographs. Her study stresses that while the revolutionaries share the same Christian name, 'Jacques' from the French expression, *'Jacquerie'*—meaning popular rebellion—aristocrats in the novel are essentially reduced to their titles. Some of them, like the Marquis, remain nonetheless obsessed with the preservation of their family name, which in this particular case becomes a curse for his nephew, Charles. In *A Tale of Two Cities*, characters are disfigured, refigured, and even prefigured—as is the case at the end of the novel—in an endless process, which precludes any stabilization and finalization of identity.

Also primordial to such complex identity issues as those raised by *A Tale of Two Cities*, is gender. This includes masculinity, women's studies, queer studies, and the history of sexuality situated within prevailing cultural codes. Critics have analysed the complex portrayals of masculinity and femininity offered by Dickens in his novel. They have related these portraits to issues of power and class relations. They have examined them in the light of Victorian patriarchy and domestic norms, and they have also taken into account subjective experiences depicted in the novel. Thus, Lisa Robson studied representations of women in the novel in the light of the Victorian ideal of the Angel in the House.[26] Regarding men in the novel, Richard Dellamora, Lee Edelman, Holly Furneaux, and Christine Krueger have recently explored alternative modes of masculinity in *A Tale of Two Cities*—focusing, in particular, on the characters of Mr Lorry and of Sidney Carton.[27]

Identity in *A Tale of Two Cities* could be tackled in yet another way, following Walter Benjamin, who reflected on ways of giving a voice and appearance to obscure masses who usually form just a seemingly undifferentiated social background, and play what appear to be superfluous and secondary roles.[28] However, giving the voiceless a voice

---

[25] Kamilla Elliott, 'Face Value in *A Tale of Two Cities*', in Colin Jones et al. (ed.), *Charles Dickens, A Tale of Two Cities and the French Revolution* (New York: Palgrave Macmillan, 2009), 87–103.

[26] Lisa Robson, 'The "Angels" in Dickens's House: Representations of Women in *A Tale of Two Cities*', *Dalhousie Review* 72, 3 (1992): 311–33; On women in the novel see also Barbara Black, 'A Sisterhood of Rage and Beauty: Dickens' Rosa Dartle, Miss Wade, and Madame Defarge', *Dickens Studies Annual* 26 (1998): 91–106; Wendy S. Jacobson, '"The World Within Us": Jung and Dr. Manette's Daughter', *Dickensian* 93, 2 (Summer 1997): 95–108; Hilary Schor, '*Hard Times* and *A Tale of Two Cities*: The Social Inheritance of Adultery', in *Dickens and the Daughter of the House* (New York: Cambridge University Press, 1999), 70–98; Michael Slater, *Dickens and Women* (Stanford, CA: Stanford University Press, 1983); Catherine Waters, '*A Tale of Two Cities*', in *Dickens and the Politics of the Family* (Cambridge: Cambridge University Press, 1997), 122–49.

[27] See Lee Edelman, *No Future: Queer Theory and the Death Drive* (Durham, NC: Duke University Press, 2004); Richard Dellamora, *Friendship's Bonds: Democracy and the Novel in Victorian England* (Philadelphia: University of Pennsylvania Press, 2004); Holly Furneaux, 'Charles Dickens's Families of Choice: Elective Affinities, Sibling Substitution, and Homoerotic Desire', *Nineteenth-Century Literature* 62, 2 (September 2007): 153–92; Furneaux, *Queer Dickens: Erotics, Families, Masculinities* (Oxford: Oxford University Press, 2009); Krueger, 'The Queer Heroism of a Man of Law'.

[28] This question also partakes of a sociology that can be traced back to Georg Simmel and is represented today by researchers like Guillaume le Blanc. See Georg Simmel, 'Le Pauvre', in *Sociologie: étude sur les formes de la socialisation* (Paris: Presses Universitaires de France, 2013), 453–90; Guillaume Le Blanc, *Vies ordinaires, vies précaires* (Paris: Le Seuil, 2007).

is easier said than done, as Jules Michelet testified in his book *The People* (1846): 'But [the people's] language, their language, was inaccessible to me. I was unable to make the people speak' (translation mine).[29] As a matter of fact, and contrary to Michelet, Dickens, like Victor Hugo three years later in *Les Misérables* (1862), or later still Émile Zola, did manage to invent a poetics of the people that included giving them a voice of their own.

If we extend the idea of individual identity to that of the French people taken as a whole in *A Tale of Two Cities*, we are led to take a closer look at how Dickens invented strategies to depict the fugitive and unsettling nature of revolutionary crowds. Cates Baldridge, for instance, examines how Dickens subtly discusses and undermines a Victorian liberal ideology based on the primacy of the individual. This was achieved, Baldridge argues, by highlighting some of the positive sides of revolutionary collective action and of collectiveness in general, though not without alluding to their limitations as well.[30] One of these limitations lies in the fact that, as Robert Alter and J. M. Rignall have shown, the protagonists of the French Revolution depicted by Dickens all seem to be trapped in the broader movements of history.[31] Another limitation, pointed out by John Bowen, touches upon the tensions between the one and the many, as well as on mass history's difficulty in representing the many and unnamed.[32]

Such questions could be taken one step further, by comparing Dickens's representation of French revolutionary crowds to those made by historians like George Rudé and Albert Soboul, among others.[33] An interesting literary, cultural, and historical study might even be undertaken on Dickens's French revolutionaries as a superimposition of Victorian representations of French revolutionary crowds with representations of British crowds in the nineteenth century. This could be based on the work of John Plotz, who briefly examines the question of anonymous crowds in *A Tale of Two Cities*, in connection with Wordsworth's poetry on the mystery of London and of urban unknowability.[34] More light might be shed on the way Dickens grapples with the problem of the one and the many, by resorting to Maurice Blanchot's definition, in *The Unavowable Community*, of the people as being powerful precisely through their very elusiveness.

---

[29] Jules Michelet, *Le Peuple* (1846), ed. P. Viallaneix (Paris: Flammarion, 1974), 246. *The People*, trans. and introd. John P. McKay (Urbana: University of Illinois Press, 1973).

[30] Cates Baldridge, 'Alternatives to Bourgeois Individualism in *A Tale of Two Cities*', *Studies in English Literature, 1500–1900* 30, 4 (Autumn 1990): 633–54.

[31] Robert Alter, 'The Demons of History in Dickens' "Tale"', *Novel: A Forum on Fiction* 2, 2 (Winter 1969): 135–42; J. M. Rignall, 'Dickens and the Catastrophic Continuum of History in *A Tale of Two Cities*', *ELH* 51, 3 (Autumn 1984): 575–87.

[32] John Bowen, 'Counting on: *A Tale of Two Cities*', in Colin Jones et al. (eds), *Charles Dickens, A Tale of Two Cities and the French Revolution*, 104–25.

[33] George Rudé, *The Crowd in the French Revolution* (Oxford: Clarendon Press, 1959); Albert Soboul, *The French Revolution 1787–1799: From the Storming of the Bastille to Napoleon* (New York: Random House, 1984).

[34] See John Plotz, *The Crowd: British Literature and Public Politics* (Berkeley: University of California Press, 2000), 39–40; also David Craig, 'The Crowd in Dickens', in Robert Giddins (ed.), *The Changing World of Charles Dickens* (Totowa, NJ: Barnes and Noble, 1983), 104–25.

Useful too might be, in this same light, analyses by Jean-Luc Nancy who, in *Being Singular Plural*, defined crowds as being neither a subsuming entity nor an experience of fusion but a body singularly plural and plurally singular.[35]

Dickens's novel reveals how much crowd movements terrified nineteenth-century English readers, partly because collective representations were infused with dire remembrances of the French Revolution. In *A Tale of Two Cities*, the people are represented at times as being as hideous, ignoble, and grotesque, as in the nineteenth-century French artist Honoré Daumier's caricatures. In such instances, Dickens's novel seems to prefigure Gustave Le Bon's later *Psychology of Crowds* (1895), in which the people are compared alternately to a pack of dangerous animals, to neurotic, capricious, perverse, irrational, or mad beings, or to hysterical madwomen. Deformity prevails here, and the grotesque becomes the dominant representational aesthetics. Such details can be connected to a rising interest in pathological deformities, which developed at the time when the novel was written—an interest later exemplified in France by the work carried out by doctors like Charcot and Richer and summarized in their book *The Deformed and Sick in Art* (1889). The very form of crowds and their transformational power, as defined by Elias Canetti in *Mass and Power* (1960), might also be worth investigating in *A Tale of Two Cities*. Canetti stressed that crowds were not just given entities, but were processes in the form of closed and open multitudes, crowds fleeing, mobilized crowds, festive crowds, rebellious crowds, but also fragmented crowds. Dickens's crowds are also worth relating to the myths and figures of revolutionary crowds, or even to Victorian ethnology.[36]

Preceding comparisons with Daumier's caricatures remind us of the strong visual dimension of Dickens's writing in *A Tale of Two Cities*. For one thing, the influence of Dickens's writing on Eisenstein's cinema has been well documented. Both artists give a striking and epic visual representation of the power of the people. Ana Laura Zambrano has shown that in his film *October* (1928), Eisenstein drew from *A Tale of Two Cities* to stage the Russian people in their Revolution. Like Dickens, Eisenstein resorted to pan and high-angle shots to represent collective fury in his film *Potemkin* (1925). In the famous strike scene of this film, Eisenstein shows the people struggling against the exploitation that alienates them, just as Dickens showed French masses struggling against oppression.[37] The panoramic dimensions of the novel have been further analysed by Robert Alter, who also describes them as picturesque—a quality asserted by Dickens himself in his preface to the novel (*TTC* 'Preface', 3), and which still gives rise to critical interpretations.

---

[35] Maurice Blanchot, *The Unavowable Community*, trans. Pierre Joris (Barrytown, NY: Station Hill Press, 1988); Jean-Luc Nancy, *Being Singular Plural*, trans. Robert D. Richardson and Anne E. O'Byrne (Stanford, CA: Stanford University Press, 2000).

[36] See Fanny Robles, 'Émergence littéraire et visuelle du muséum humain: les spectacles ethnologiques à Londres, 1853–1859', doctorate, Université Toulouse Jean Jaurès, 2014.

[37] Ana Laura Zambrano, 'Charles Dickens and Sergei Eisenstein: The Emergence of Cinema', *Style* 9 (1975): 469–87.

THE CARMAGNOLE.

FIGURE 18.1 Fred Barnard, 'The Carmagnole', 10.7 cm × 13.8 cm. Wood engraving. Illustration for Charles Dickens, *A Tale of Two Cities*. The Household Edition (London: Chapman and Hall, 1873), page 132.

Courtesy Xavier University Library, Cincinnati, Ohio

The visionary intensity of certain scenes of collective violence involves Dickens's staging of rebellious, cruel, terrifying, and anarchic crowds,[38] whose essence was captured in particular by Fred Barnard's illustration of the revolutionary dance, 'La Carmagnole', in the 1873 Household Edition of the novel (Figure 18.1). This, in turn, emphasizes the links between the novel and its illustrations. Philip Allingham has reassessed Hablot K. Browne's ('Phiz') illustrations for *A Tale of Two Cities*.[39] The images, according to Allingham, helped readers remember the details of a novel published over several months as a discontinuous narrative. Illustrations not only reveal Phiz's careful reading of Dickens's text; they actively partake of the very process of reading a novel published

---

[38] See Rignall, 'Dickens and the Catastrophic Continuum of History', 579–80.
[39] Philip V. Allingham. 'Charles Dickens's *A Tale of Two Cities* (1859) Illustrated: A Critical Reassessment of Hablot Knight Browne's Accompanying Plates', *Dickens Studies Annual* 33 (2003): 109–57. On illustrations see also Elizabeth Cayzer, 'Dickens and his Late Illustrators: A Change of Style: "Phiz" and *A Tale of Two Cities*', *Dickensian* 86, 3 (Autumn 1990): 130–41.

in monthly instalments in *All the Year Round*, alongside the non-illustrated weekly instalments.

The novel displays yet another interesting connection with specific images, namely daguerreotypes. Susan Cook has argued that Dickens's style and narrative strategies have the same paradoxical ability as daguerreotypes to capture both past and present in one image, and to encapsulate darkness within light.[40] One thing is certain: the sense of sight is prevalent in *A Tale of Two Cities*, a novel that, according to Catherine Gallagher, depicts the Revolution as an exposure of the private sphere to public scrutiny figured by omnipresent and intrusive gazes and surveillance.[41]

The visual dimension of *A Tale of Two Cities* could also be studied aesthetically and politically, along the lines of recent theories developed by the French philosopher and art historian Georges Didi-Huberman, who maintains in *People Exposed, People as Extras*[42] that the people are either under-exposed and left in the shadow—like Doctor Manette or the brother of Madame Defarge in *A Tale of Two Cities*—or over-exposed through 'spectacularization', which blinds the eye to what is to be seen. This idea of a blinding 'spectacularization' applies, during the Storming of the Bastille, to the revolutionary crowd 'with frequent gleams of light above the billowy heads, where blades and bayonets shone in the sun', 'like a kind of lightning' (*TTC* II:21, 206).

The problem faced by Dickens was that in literature, as in the visual arts, the humble people of the street were often outside the frame. To bring them into focus, Dickens invented a visual poetics of the people, at times lyrical, like the painter Gustave Courbet's *Stone Breakers*—reminiscent of the mender of roads in *A Tale of Two Cities*—at others, cartoon-like, and reminiscent of the grotesque crowds of James Gillray or of Honoré Daumier's engravings. The novelist animated his pictures by using devices like montage that builds the people into an entity made up of a series of views and perspectives on the individuals that constitute it. At times, the narrative zooms in on specific characters; at others, it shows a multitude of faces and bodies. The visual appeal of representations of the people in *A Tale of Two Cities* thus partakes of what Didi-Huberman calls 'the eye of history'.[43]

If sight features prominently in *A Tale of Two Cities* and has given rise to many critical studies, other sense impressions deserve just as much attention, notably sounds and other bodily feelings, as well as the kinaesthetic language associated with them. Through what they reveal and betray, the senses and body language in *A Tale of Two Cities* are so important that, as Michael Hollington aptly maintains, they sometimes even tell a counter-narrative. Hence the importance of studying all five sense impressions in

---

[40] Susan Cook, 'Season of Light and Darkness: *A Tale of Two Cities* and the Daguerrean Imagination', *Dickens Studies Annual* 42 (2011): 237–60.

[41] See Catherine Gallagher, 'The Duplicity of Doubling in *A Tale of Two Cities*', *Dickens Studies Annual* 12 (1983): 125–44. The novel, Gallagher argues, insidiously exposes violence, the better to hide its own violent strategies of exposure.

[42] *Peuples exposés, peuples figurants: l'œil de l'histoire 4* (Paris: Éditions de Minuit, 2012).

[43] Didi-Huberman has published a series of volumes under this general title: *L'Œil de l'histoire*, 6 vols to date (Paris, Éditions de Minuit, 2009–16).

Dickens's novel and not just sight. Hearing, smell, taste, and touch are essential to the understanding of *A Tale of Two Cities*, and they provide new insights into the novel.

In fact, in *A Tale of Two Cities* kinaesthesia, or body language, sometimes produces humour in the novel. This humour is first and foremost dark and caustic, for instance in Dickens's satire of French pre-revolutionary society. The scene where Monseigneur takes his chocolate is, in the light of the people's plight, a grotesque travesty involving 'four men besides the Cook': 'One lacquey carried the chocolate-pot into the sacred presence; a second, milled and frothed the chocolate with the little instrument he bore for that function; a third presented the favoured napkin; a fourth ... poured the chocolate out' (*TTC* II:7, 100).

At other times however, the novel elicits pure laughter, as when young Jerry Cruncher comes running home after having discovered that his father is a resurrectionist—a scene that somewhat prefigures an animated cartoon: 'He [Jerry] had a strong idea that the coffin he had seen was running after him; and, pictured it hopping on behind him, bolt upright, upon its narrow end, always on the point of overtaking him and hopping on at his side—perhaps taking his arm—it was a pursuer to shun' (*TTC* II:14, 155).

Such visual and kinaesthetic qualities open up new possibilities for performances and adaptations of *A Tale of Two Cities*,[44] a novel whose theatrical nature proves ever more complex. This paradoxical theatricality derives partly from the very nature of its subject matter—the French Revolution—an event, in itself, highly dramatic and even melodramatic. As a matter of fact, melodrama features prominently in *A Tale of Two Cities*, especially in the trial scenes. Sally Ledger pointed out that Dickens not only exploits the histrionic potentialities of the judiciary system, but combines the attorney general's posturing and use of technical terms with a masterful use of indirect speech and narratorial intrusions, to produce both a highly dramatic moment and a powerful satire of the legal system and its discourse.[45]

The theatrical nature of the novel also lies in the well-known fact that it was inspired from a play, *The Frozen Deep*, written by Wilkie Collins, assisted by Dickens.[46] In the

---

[44] Regarding performances of the novel, see Charles Dickens, '*The Bastille Prisoner*, in Three Chapters', in *Charles Dickens: The Public Readings*, ed. Philip Collins (Oxford: Clarendon Press, 1975), 279–93. For critical approaches to this question, see Brian Bialkowski, 'Facing up to the Question of Fidelity: The Example of *A Tale of Two Cities*', *Literature/Film Quarterly* 29, 3 (2001): 27–42. See also Charles Barr, 'Two Cities, Two Films', 166–87; Judith Buchanan and Alex Newhouse, 'Sanguine Mirages, Cinematic Dreams: Things Seen and Things Imagined in the 1917 Fox Feature Film *A Tale of Two Cities*', 146–65; Joss Marsh, 'Mimi and the Matinée Idol: Martin-Harvey, Sidney Carton, and the Staging of *A Tale of Two Cities*, 1860–1939', 126–45, all of which can be found in Colin Jones et al. (eds), *Charles Dickens, A Tale of Two Cities, and the French Revolution*. See also Arthur Hopcraft, 'The Spirit of Revolution', *Listener* (18 May 1989): 10–11.

[45] Sally Ledger, 'From the Old Bailey to Revolutionary France: The Trials of Charles Darnay', in *Charles Dickens, A Tale of Two Cities and the French Revolution*, 75–86; for melodrama see also Juliet John, 'Unmasking Melodrama: Sidney Carton and Eugene Wrayburn', in *Dickens's Villains: Melodrama, Character, Popular Culture* (Oxford: Oxford University Press, 2001).

[46] For further information on *A Tale of Two Cities* and *The Frozen Deep*, see Robert Louis Brannan (ed.), *Under the Management of Mr. Charles Dickens: His Production of 'The Frozen Deep'* (Ithaca,

memoranda book he kept in the 1850s, Dickens himself likened his novel to a French drama.[47] In this theatrical light, Anny Sadrin compared the modulations of the performing narrative voice of *A Tale of Two Cities* to those of a professional actor trying different effects upon his audience in a detached, but also, at times, impassioned tone, though, paradoxically, this alternation of detachment and implication was devised by Dickens so as to be cleverly misleading: it in fact proves impossible to perform in spite of its apparent theatricality.[48] Nevertheless, new studies on sights, sounds, and body language in *A Tale of Two Cities* revise this last statement and open up, as we have already seen, new vistas for performances and adaptations of the novel.

At the end of the day, *A Tale of Two Cities*, by its very nature, definitely lends itself to transdisciplinary analysis. Historical, political, psychological, philosophical, visual, physical, and poetical perspectives combine to offer readers and critics fruitful, rewarding, and stimulating research directions, well worth looking into.

Further Reading

Ruth Glancy, '*A Tale of Two Cities*': *Dickens's Revolutionary Novel* (Boston: Twayne, 1991)

Ruth Glancy (ed.), *Charles Dickens's A Tale of Two Cities: A Sourcebook* (Abingdon: Routledge, 2006)

Sylvère Monod, 'Dickens's Attitudes in *A Tale of Two Cities*', *Nineteenth-Century Fiction* 24 (March 1970): 488–505

Andrew Sanders, *The Companion to A Tale of Two Cities* (Boston: Unwin Hyman, 1988)

NY: Cornell University Press, 1966); Malcolm Morley, 'The Stage Story of *A Tale of Two Cities*', *Dickensian* 51 (1954): 34–40.

[47] *Charles Dickens' Book of Memoranda*, ed. Fred Kaplan (New York: New York Public Library, 1981), 5.

[48] Anny Sadrin, '"The Paradox of Acting" in *A Tale of Two Cities*', *Dickensian* 97, 2 (Summer 2001): 124–36. Sadrin likens the alternately detached and involved narrative voice to the manner of other 'performers' like the mender of roads or Sidney Carton.

CHAPTER 19

GREAT EXPECTATIONS

MARY HAMMOND

The Struggle for Life

On the first page of the handwritten manuscript of Dickens's 13th novel *Great Expectations* (1860–1), almost buried under the tangled thicket of black ink corrections and crossings out from which the famous story of Pip the blacksmith's boy finally emerged, one small but vital addition to the final sentence of the third paragraph is faintly visible.[1] In the paragraph as readers now know it, the young orphan Pip, shivering in a bleak Kent churchyard one Christmas Eve in the late 1800s or 1820s, muses on the stones marking the remains of his late parents, alongside: 'five little stone lozenges, each about a foot and a half long, which were arranged in a neat row beside their grave, and were sacred to the memory of five little brothers of mine—who gave up trying to get a living, exceedingly early in that universal struggle' (*GE* I:1, 3).[2]

K. J. Fielding claims that the phrase 'universal struggle' provides hard evidence (rare in Dickens) of the influence of Charles Darwin, who had used it in the third paragraph of chapter 3 of his famous work *On the Origin of Species by Means of Natural Selection: or the Preservation of Favoured Races in the Struggle for Life*, published in November 1859, just a year before the serialization of *Great Expectations* began.[3] While there might be disagreement over the extent of Dickens's engagement with Darwin, few critics would argue with the underlying claim here. It is true that we have no evidence that Dickens actually read *On the Origin of Species* (though we know he had a copy in his library), but the pervasive influence of Darwinian thought on Victorian fiction has become something of a critical truism. In 1983 Gillian Beer made it the subject of her seminal

---

[1] Charles Dickens, manuscript of *Great Expectations*, Townshend Collection, Wisbech and Fenland Museum.

[2] Charles Dickens, *Great Expectations*, ed. Margaret Cardwell (Oxford: Clarendon Press, 1993), I:1, 3. Subsequent references are inserted parenthetically in the text by *GE* volume:chapter, page.

[3] K. J. Fielding, 'Dickens and Science?', *Dickens Quarterly* 13, 4 (December 1996): 200–16, 201–3.

work *Darwin's Plots*, which, while it deals more comprehensively with Dickens's influence on Darwin rather than the other way around, provides a vital backdrop to the literary marketplace in which he was working. As she explains, after *On the Origin of Species* emerged, '[e]veryone found themselves living in a Darwinian world in which old assumptions had ceased to be assumptions, could be at best beliefs, or myths, or, at worst, detritus of the past. So the question of who read Darwin, or whether a writer had read Darwin, becomes only a fraction of the answer'.[4] Darwin's influence, in this view, was out there in the ether, and Dickens had no choice but to breathe it in.

Was this particularly true in the case of *Great Expectations*, which arrived on the scene so soon after Darwin's ground-breaking work? It would seem so. George Levine, while not explicitly citing Darwin, has observed that even 'communication in the novel is "primitive and basic rather than full, complex, or rich in nuance"', and has seen brute nature—the complete failure of civilized rationality—as central to the structuring of the plot.[5] For Goldie Morgentaler, there is evidence throughout Dickens's 13th novel of Darwin's influence, in particular 'the ceaseless and inevitable moving into the future without a glance back to the reassuring reanimation of the past'.[6]

Taking the judicious use of that phrase 'universal struggle' at face value, then, the claim that there is a full thematic engagement in this novel with Darwinian ideas about natural selection in a harsh environment is persuasive, and (despite its pre-industrial setting in the 1810s and 1820s) might even help to explain some of its topicality in its own industrial mid-century moment, and some of its enduring power in the postmodern capitalist Western world. Pip's retrospective narrative is, after all, largely an exploration of the extent to which a human being is formed by his or her environment, or able to transcend it, and with what potential effects. And the very name 'Pip' surely suggests that Dickens had in mind a sort of petri dish plot in which a nascent human seed might be observed developing in response to various conditions. Estella's journey, similarly—a journey which results in her being brutally 'bent and broken ... into a better shape' (*GE* III:20, 480)—raises key questions about the extent to which her cruelty is a result of Miss Havisham's destructive nurturing, or of her nature, which is the consequence of an ill-starred union between a convict and a murderess. On a larger scale too, of course, this is a story about roads taken or not taken, and their consequences, and the extent to which one has free will about such things or is fashioned by one's circumstances. The metaphor of forging (and forcing) matter, human and otherwise, into particular shapes pervades this novel.

But if we return to the manuscript, we might follow a different line of enquiry. The original sentence read 'who gave up trying to get a living exceedingly early in that struggle'.

---

[4] Gillian Beer, *Darwin's Plots: Evolutionary Narrative in Darwin, George Eliot and Nineteenth-Century Fiction* (Cambridge: Cambridge University Press, 1983), 3.

[5] George Levine, 'Communication in *Great Expectations*', *Nineteenth-Century Fiction* 18, 2 (September 1963): 175–81, 176 and 181.

[6] Goldie Morgentaler, 'Meditating on the Low: A Darwinian Reading of *Great Expectations*', *Studies in English Literature, 1500–1900* 38, 4, Nineteenth Century (Autumn 1998): 707–21, 720.

The word 'universal' is added as an afterthought in a lighter ink, using a much finer quill; and quite possibly, therefore, at a later time—or even on a different day (though it is still unmistakably in Dickens's hand). This small correction on the manuscript—insignificant though it might seem—highlights two of the main preoccupations of this chapter. First, though speed was of the essence here Dickens was an obsessive returner to and perfecter of his own creations. In going back to add that word 'universal', arguably to move readers away from a Malthusian-inflected understanding of struggle as pertaining mostly to the labouring poor, he surely knew exactly what he was doing: tapping into powerful prevailing post-Darwinian discourses about the potentially corrosive influence of environment on *all* classes of society. In this period, as Pam Morris suggests, the '[p]ublic perception of a criminal underside to wealth disturbed [the] ... ideological construction of a golden haze of general prosperity interweaving the whole nation into unified contentment'.[7] Struggle, it was becoming clear, defined and affected everyone, and as Chris R. Vanden Bossche argues in Chapter 34 of this volume, for Dickens class was something troublingly unstable.[8]

Second, the novel 'evolved' in Dickens's hands in much the same way as an organism does in nature: as a response to a particular environment; and in this case the environment was not just formed out of mysteriously circulating ideologies but empirical and keenly self-aware. The novel, that is, does not just reflect the contemporary influence of Darwin, as Fielding, Beer, Morgentaler, and others argue, or the dark side of the supposed 'golden age' of the 1850s and 1860s,[9] or 'a personification of the false values of the Victorian dream',[10] or even the fantasy of a 'way out ... and escape from debt or shame' in the colonies[11]—though it almost certainly does all of those things. If we know where to look, it also reflects its author's consummate professionalism in the first multimedia age, giving us a rare insight into what a self-made mid-Victorian middle-class man thought was important, saleable, and topical. *Great Expectations* might even be a special case among Dickens's late works: in 1860 he badly needed a hit if his new journal *All the Year Round* was to weather an alarming recent drop in sales, so he conceived, wrote, and corrected it with multiple different audiences in mind in order to maximize its profits, and as a result it managed to appeal (and continues to appeal) in contexts even he could not have predicted. This was a remarkably modern and prescient way of constructing a work of fiction, and the myriad possibilities it provides for readers (and viewers, and listeners) are a marker of the sophistication of Dickens's mature style, steeped as it was in the Victorian version of what we now call multiplatform publishing.

---

[7] Pam Morris, *Dickens's Class Consciousness: A Marginal View* (Basingstoke: Macmillan, 1991), 106.

[8] See also John H. Hagan, Jr, 'Structural Patterns in Dickens's *Great Expectations*', *ELH* 21, 1 (March 1954): 54–66.

[9] Morris, *Dickens's Class Consciousness*, 103.

[10] Karl P. Wentersdorf, 'Mirror-Images in *Great Expectations*', *Nineteenth-Century Fiction* 21, 3 (December 1966): 203–24.

[11] Raymond Williams, *The Country and the City* (Oxford: Oxford University Press, 1973), 281.

Proliferating Lives

The novel had an enormous amount of work to do on several different levels almost simultaneously if it was to succeed in the way Dickens desired. First, it had to work for the readers of both the English-language serial versions—illustrated in *Harper's Weekly* in the USA, unillustrated for simultaneous publication in *All the Year Round* in Britain. That means it needed not just a small cliff-hanger every three chapters or so to keep readers interested between instalments, but sufficient comic potential to enable its American illustrator to create some convincing caricatures (since American audiences preferred their Dickens funny)[12] and sufficient verbal colour and complexity to enable it to work without them (at least temporarily) for the British. Next came the three-volume English first edition, released in July 1861 just before the serialization ended on 3 August and aimed at subscription library patrons, closely followed by a two-volume illustrated edition overseen by Dickens in 1862, then various one-volume English-language editions which appeared in the UK, USA, and Europe after that. He was aware also that all these versions were likely to have groups of listeners as well as individual readers, as the novel was read aloud in the home, the school, the pulpit, or the workplace. Simultaneously the novel appeared in authorized translations to readers in several European countries including Russia (1861), Denmark (1861), Sweden (1861), France (1862), Holland (1862), Germany (1862), and Poland (1863), so it needed a certain appeal beyond Britain and the USA.[13] Then there were the listeners who, potentially, might one day hear Dickens read it aloud to them; Dickens's reading version was never performed, but the fact that he prepared one indicates that he was at least toying with the idea. In 1860, also, there was always the possibility (ultimately unrealized in the UK in Dickens's lifetime) that an audience might one day watch it performed on stage. Finally—less often, if ever, sanctioned by Dickens, though equally known to and hardly ever prevented by him—there were the readers of regional newspapers in both the UK and the USA who might come across short pirated extracts of little more than a paragraph or so in length among the factual articles in their daily paper.

In fact, Dickens's 13th novel emerged into a marketplace in its own way as diverse and sophisticated as our own: one which its author understood better than almost any of his contemporaries. Traces of his remarkable professional skill and his address to contemporary readers' concerns are recoverable through his masterly structure and his skilful corrections to the manuscript, as I have shown; but thanks to new digital technologies which have enabled us to track the novel across time and space, we can now also understand much more about the variety of contexts and forms in which it

---

[12] The first American illustrations by John McClellan can be found on the Victorian Web: <http://www.victorianweb.org/>.

[13] See Mary Hammond, *Charles Dickens's Great Expectations: A Cultural Life, 1860–2012* (Basingstoke and Burlington, VT: Ashgate, 2015), 151–66 and appendix B.

managed to appeal, and analyse how they may have worked. What Rachel Malik has called its 'capsularity'—by which she means the ways in which the novel's several 'relatively autonomous stories... can be lightly coupled or decoupled by the addition or subtraction of a sentence or even a phrase'[14]—has meant that it is among his most readily adaptable for other formats and other media. This has been particularly true since the advent of film, radio, and television, and much recent scholarship has understandably focused on the ways in which, long after Dickens's death, various segments of the novel have offered themselves for dramatization and rewriting ranging from the reverential to the parodic. But if we consider the capsularity to be an integral part of Dickens's original design, rather than an incidental opportunity for hit-and-run raids by pirates and media producers, new readings of the text itself may become available to us.

Disappearing Lives

A good example of the way in which 'decoupling' works at the level of the plot can be demonstrated by tracking what happens to the novel's themes if we 'decouple' the Estella/romance plotline and privilege the male friendship narrative. If we are to believe both the first mention of Dickens's initial 'very fine, new, and grotesque' yet also 'singular and comic' idea as he described it in a letter to John Forster in September of 1860, and also the evidence provided by the reading version which sidelines Miss Havisham and cuts Estella out completely, the male friendship storyline was Dickens's preferred focus.[15] But which one? According to this letter, it could either be the Pip/Joe relationship which first appeared in Dickens's imagination in a 'singular and comic' fashion, or it could be Pip and Magwitch, whose relationship opens the published story and closes the reading version, which ends with Magwitch's death in prison.[16] It is impossible to tell now which male friendship Dickens had in mind, or which he preferred; the first 'grotesque' germ of the story as he described it to Forster could just as easily have referred to the superficially grotesque character of Magwitch, or to the grotesque behaviour of Pip towards Joe. Perhaps the most important things to note are that Estella was considered utterly dispensable in the reading version, and that each male plot line is capable of sustaining the story without undue emphasis on the other. Their intertwining thickens the brew, certainly, because in some ways the two men are initially dark mirror images of each other: the one homely, honest, and reassuring, the other menacing, criminal,

---

[14] Rachel Malik, 'Stories Many, Fast and Slow: *Great Expectations* and the Mid-Victorian Horizon of the Publishable', *ELH* 79 (2012): 477–500, 479.

[15] Letter to John Forster, mid-September 1860. *The Letters of Charles Dickens*, ed. Madeline House, Graham Storey, et al., Pilgrim/British Academy Edition, 12 vols (Oxford: Clarendon Press, 1965–2002), 9:310.

[16] Jean Callahan, 'The (Unread) Reading Version of *Great Expectations*', in Charles Dickens, *Great Expectations*, ed. Edgar Rosenberg (New York: W. W. Norton, 1999), 546.

and terrifying, and their temporary reversal in Pip's mind (money and status in the dangerous metropolis temporarily trumping rural familial affection) is part of the point. But in the end the mirror dissolves: Pip realizes he loves them both in different ways, and that means one of them is always fairly dispensable by the end since each is equally capable of rendering the moral lesson that goodness is not always apparent to the naked eye (or purchasable), and that a rough exterior is not always synonymous with wickedness (or poverty).

Without Estella, though, Pip's motivations are very different: they spring not from romantic love liberally seasoned with social shame, but from pure greed; and they thus bring into the spotlight Dickens's harsh judgement on social aspiration. In the Estella-less reading version it is Pip's naive and covetous early misreading of Miss Havisham as an example of gentility which makes him want to be a gentleman, and it is his early misreading of Joe's example of true gentlemanliness which leads him to dismiss it contemptuously as brute ignorance. Magwitch's job is simultaneously to provide his fortune (and in so doing to remind him how dirty money can be) and to pick up and develop the 'rough diamond' theme: in Dickens's reading version, Joe disappears after Pip moves to London at the end of Stage 1 and thereafter the plot focuses exclusively on the relationship between Pip and Magwitch.

What happens to what Julian Moynahan has called 'one of the guiltiest consciences in literature' if we remove completely (or prematurely) the constant reminders of Pip's guilt and shame, Joe and Estella?[17] Moynahan himself acknowledges that they are central to this sense of what he calls Pip's inexplicable sense of 'criminality', and there are certainly key moments in the novel in which Pip explicitly juxtaposes his association with criminals with his feelings for one or the other or both of them (not to mention with other frequently excised minor characters such as Biddy and Wemmick). When Joe visits him in London and Pip is so ashamed of his lack of refinement (*GE* II:8, 217–22), the subsequent narrative is shot through with retrospective guilt: 'I lived in a state of chronic uneasiness respecting my behaviour to Joe', he tells us; and, further, that '[m]y conscience was not by any means comfortable about Biddy' (*GE* II:15, 271). We can neither despise nor sympathize with Pip to the same extent without the presence of these characters, and must focus on his actions—his debts, his initial revulsion when he meets Magwitch again, and the snobbish or foolish society he chooses to keep—rather than the interior workings of his conscience.

Where Estella is concerned, too, in losing her we do not simply lose the love interest, but one of Pip's main instruments of self-torture (and one through which or because of which he often also tortures or neglects others). She is crucial to his guilt. While waiting for Estella's coach to arrive after he has been with Wemmick on an idle visit to Newgate prison, for example, he muses:

---

[17] Julian Moynahan, 'The Hero's Guilt: The Case of *Great Expectations*', *Essays in Criticism* 10, 1 (1960): 60–79, 60.

> I thought of the beautiful young Estella, proud and refined, coming towards me, and I thought with absolute abhorrence of the contrast between the jail and her ... So contaminated did I feel, remembering who was coming, that the coach came quickly after all, and I was not yet free from the soiling consciousness of Mr. Wemmick's conservatory, when I saw her face at the coach window and her hand waving at me. What *was* the nameless shadow which again in that one instant had passed? (*GE* II:13, 263)

Neither the brooding sense of his own guilt, nor the final self-awareness that he has been selfish and shallow are quite the same without Joe and Estella. Yet—as Dickens was well aware—even without them there are still drama and pathos and lessons learned aplenty in the remaining capsules. Selfish greed is compounded by—but not dependent on—deliberate cruelty to others.

Plenty of remediators have found this inbuilt capsularity useful. Several stage versions have also—probably quite independently of knowledge of Dickens's reading version—made Pip and Magwitch their central focus and ended with Magwitch's death, among them the first British version by W. S. Gilbert in 1871, and an unperformed version, 'My Unknown Friend', by Shafto Scott in the USA in 1872, though these two did at least put Estella back.[18] A later version, 'Pip's Patron', cut out Miss Havisham as a stage presence instead, and thus—radically diluting the Darwinist subtext—removed from the plot any real sense of the influence on either Pip or Estella of the poisonous environment she creates. Later still, in 1939, Alec Guinness staged a ground-breaking theatrical version in London which also foregrounded the male relationships: this novel seems to have given Guinness an opportunity to write out troublesome women and to posit male relationships as the most natural ones. Miss Havisham is an offstage presence in this adaptation, as in Dickens's own reading version, and while Estella does have a role she disappears to get married after she gets tired of being told what to do, leaving Magwitch to die, Joe and Pip to resolve their differences, and the plot to come to rest full circle with Pip happily resuming his old life as a blacksmith in a comfortable world inhabited exclusively by men. The idea of relentless Darwinian time bending human creatures to its will is entirely lacking in this version, though it did utilize Pip's guilt-ridden introspective narration and was so influential that it was restaged many times in the next two decades and prompted David Lean to create perhaps the most successful film version (albeit with a restored romantic ending) in 1946.

The fact that adaptors—Dickens included—can so easily fade the main female characters in and out in this way is extraordinary. It is difficult to imagine *David Copperfield* (1849–50) without Dora or Aunt Betsey; or even *A Tale of Two Cities* (1859) without Lucie. In *Great Expectations*, Dickens seems to be predominantly concerned with 'man's business': the public worlds of money, social status, character, human (for

---

[18] W. S. Gilbert, *Great Expectations: A Drama in Three Acts with Prologue* (1871). British Library, MS. c.132.g.20; Charles Augustus Shafto Scott, *My Unknown Friend: A Drama, in Three Acts. Being a Dramatized Version of the Novel 'Great Expectations', by the Late Charles Dickens*, Dicks' Standard Plays, Number 412 (London, no date). British Library, X.908.4370.

which read male) destiny as well as with guilt. Like most mid-Victorian men—among them the best-selling author Samuel Smiles, whose books titled *Self-Help* (1859) and *Character* (1871) straddled *Great Expectations* in their publication and associated such desirable traits almost exclusively with men—he probably saw women as equal parts diversion and encumbrance, and was unable to conceive of female power as detachable from sexual desirability. This—arguably—is one of the reasons why Miss Havisham, a rich, powerful, and influential woman too old to be a sex object (and, indeed, bearing the deep scars of a previous male rejection), is so monstrous. Without philanthropy, motherhood, or sex there is nothing left in Dickens's plots for women to do. And perhaps now, at this point in his life more than many others, he was feeling deeply ambivalent about their necessity. He had separated from his wife in 1858 and in 1860 was, possibly, frustrated and annoyed by the reluctance of an 18-year-old actress with whom he was smitten to become his mistress.[19] He was, in addition, reflecting soberly on whether his enormous fame and financial success had made him happy. All these things may have found their way into the very loose 'links' he embedded between the various capsules of the novel, and which enabled them to be so easily detached, jettisoned, and rendered obsolete.

Other characters—usually the minor ones—have suffered similar fates in remediation, and their absence challenges some of our longest-established critical insights. Karl P. Wentersdorf, for example, has offered a reading of the motif of the 'mirror-images' in the novel through which, he explains, since Pip is the 'outstanding example' of a Faustian hero in Dickens, the dark sides of his personality and experience are configured. Such a construction, the dominant means through which Dickens 'gives structure and meaning to his novel', relies on character pairings and contrasts: 'Joe with Orlick, Estella with Biddy, Magwitch with Miss Havisham, Herbert with Drummle, Estella with Clara, Magwitch with Compeyson, Compeyson with Miss Havisham, Miss Havisham with Matthew Pocket, and Jaggers with Wemmick'.[20] So what happens to the Faustian motif—and the related psychological complexity—if most of these pairings are excised or their roles reduced, as they are in many versions (including Dickens's own rewritings) for reading aloud, or for the stage, and later for the screen and the radio? The answer, remarkably, is not much. These characters underline the major themes like visual flourishes of colour and light and shade; they add comic episodes (Wopsle and Trabb's boy) and reinforcement of the main characters' hopes and problems (Wemmick, the Pockets, Clara, Drummle, Compeyson) but they do not in themselves constitute its essential fabric. Even Orlick, who—despite his apparent necessity for Wentersdorf and others as Pip's 'dark double'—is one of the most excised characters from twentieth- and twenty-first-century adaptations, is rarely missed. This is largely because in visual and aural remediations, unlike in the two-dimensional material book (even the illustrated book) and during the moment of silent private reading, adaptors have recourse to mood lighting, gesture, facial

---

[19] Michael Slater, *Charles Dickens* (New Haven and London: Yale University Press, 2009), 492.
[20] Wentersdorf, 'Mirror-Images in *Great Expectations*', 203–4.

expression, music, costume, and set design through which to render the complexity of the main characters and mark the twists and turns of their emotional and psychological journeys. Well-placed shadows can provide sufficient menace in place of Orlick (as they do in David Lean's 1946 film and Mike Newell's 2012 film). A comical musical flourish, a few cartoonish costumes, and a bit of character acting can potentially replace pages of Pumblechook and Wopsle (as they do in numerous TV and radio adaptations). Set and costume designs can suggest the psychological damage and malevolent influence of Miss Havisham, and bind the characters' fates together without the need for all her plot machinations and dialogue (as in Jo Clifford's 2013 London West End adaptation, in which Miss Havisham had little to say but was never offstage, and all the characters' costumes carried a cobweb motif. In several film versions, too, her costume 'functions semiotically to convey to audiences Miss Havisham's situation: that is, the life of an ageing woman who is trapped in, and fixated on, the past').[21]

Another method when one is short of air time is simply to take one strand of the plot and make it central. The earliest film version—made during a period when technology was too rudimentary for a story to last more than two or three reels—focused solely on Pip's encounter with Magwitch ('The Boy and the Convict', 1909). Moving forward in time, the love story was so essential to Hollywood film versions struggling to appeal to female audiences that Estella and Pip constitute the plot's main relationship, with Miss Havisham reduced to performing the role of disapproving, class-obsessed guardian. In these versions (1917 and 1936) Magwitch's escape attempt, recapture, and deathbed scene simply provide the means through which Pip can prove to everyone that he is a good and honourable man despite his class, and enable the happy heterosexual union between Pip and Estella to end the story.

All these capsules and their potential for being de- and re-coupled to create new forms pre-exist in Dickens's version, which was always intended to be far more than 'a book'. While he might not have known the specifics of the entertainment technologies of the future, Dickens, as we have seen, was so well aware of the need for his novels to be adaptable and so visually intuitive himself that, as Grahame Smith suggests, he could even be said to have 'dreamed' cinema some 25 years before its invention.[22] Arguably, *Great Expectations* is one of his most perfect realizations of this talent.

New Lives

But large-scale remediations such as these are by no means the only—or even the main—ways in which the novel's capsularity enables it to serve new purposes and offer

---

[21] Amber K. Regis and Deborah Wynne, 'Miss Havisham's Dress: Materialising Dickens in Film Adaptations of *Great Expectations*', *Neo-Victorian Studies* 5, 2 (2012): 35–58, 36.

[22] Grahame Smith, *Dickens and the Dream of Cinema* (Manchester: Manchester University Press, 2012).

up new readings. As Malik suggests, the capsules can work at the level of the sentence as well as the phrase, the character, or the storyline.

One good—though surprisingly under-explored—example of this practice occurs in the short extracts which appeared in many regional newspapers both during and after the serialization's first run. These are seldom just fillers or adverts for Dickens's novels, though they do sometimes perform those functions. But in many non-metropolitan papers, extracts from *Great Expectations* are also often adopted in the service of the proud expression of regional, and specifically non-London, social identities. The use of extracts from *Great Expectations* in this way in the 1860s serves to highlight the novel's use of London—which was the beating heart of the nation's legal and economic systems and for many people constituted the main drain on rural resources—as a moral problem; and these are things with which regional readers could clearly easily identify. In this period, just a few years after the 1851 census showed that the migration of people from the country to the towns had reached a tipping point, and when rural poverty was just as severe as the far more often publicly discussed urban variety, *Great Expectations*' thematic ambivalence about London, along with its remarkable structural capsularity, were absolute gifts to struggling regional communities looking for some humorous anti-metropolitan ammunition.

There are many examples of extracts reprinted in local papers and they draw on many different parts of the novel, but it might be significant that one of the most commonly reprinted is titled 'Tea at a London Hotel'. It is the episode immediately following the one I have quoted, from chapter 13. Pip, having experienced 'the nameless shadow which again in that one instant had passed' just as Estella arrives in London, is immediately instructed to take her to tea before they travel on together to her new home in Richmond. In the novel, Dickens uses the episode of waiting agonizingly for tea to be served by a reluctant and surly London waiter to underscore through humour Pip's painful sense of his own social inadequacy, powerlessness, and shame in all his dealings with Estella. The shadow of the prison he has just visited hangs over the encounter, exacerbating his sense of nameless guilt. The passage is meant to be funny and painful in equal measure:

> I rang for the tea, and the waiter, reappearing with his magic clue, brought in by degrees some fifty adjuncts to that refreshment, but of tea not a glimpse. A teaboard, cups and saucers, plates, knives and forks (including carvers), spoons (various), salt-cellars, a meek little muffin confined with the utmost precaution under a strong iron cover, Moses in the bullrushes typified by a soft bit of butter in a quantity of parsley, a pale loaf with a powdered head, two proof impressions of the bars of the kitchen fireplace on triangular bits of bread, and ultimately a fat family urn: which the waiter staggered in with, expressing in his countenance burden and suffering. After a prolonged absence at this stage of the entertainment, he at length came back with a casket of precious appearance containing twigs. These I steeped in hot water, and so from the whole of these appliances extracted one cup of I don't know what, for Estella.
>
> The bill paid, and the waiter remembered, and the ostler not forgotten, and the chambermaid taken into consideration—in a word, the whole house bribed into a

state of contempt and animosity, and Estella's purse much lightened—we got into our post-coach and drove away. Turning into Cheapside and rattling up Newgate-street, we were soon under the walls of which I was so ashamed.

'What place is that?' Estella asked me.

I made a foolish pretence of not at first recognising it, and then told her. As she looked at it, and drew in her head again, murmuring 'Wretches!' I would not have confessed to my visit for any consideration. (*GE* II:14, 267–8)

There is no reason for Pip's sense of shame here apart from that niggling feeling that he could have been fairer to Biddy and Joe. He has not yet been made acquainted with the source of his fortune, he has not yet told us that he is living beyond his means, and Estella has not yet started preferring other men. He is hardly a criminal, for whom the very sight of Newgate prison should be fearful and painful. But the shame and the hovering criminality seem integral to the scene, building to the moment—six chapters later—when Magwitch reappears to shatter all his illusions and confirm his worst suspicions about himself as a sham.

What happens to this scene when it is taken out of context and reprinted in a newspaper? A closer look at one example reveals the extraordinary potential of Dickens's writing to furnish multiple different meanings according to their contexts. The *Hampshire Advertiser*, serving England's south coast sea-port and rural farming communities, reprinted this 'Tea at a London Hotel' episode on Saturday 10 August 1861. No introduction, illustrations, or preamble warned readers what they were about to encounter; the extract comprises one small column of about three inches in length among many others, mostly factual, some humorous, on the same page. It is attributed to Charles Dickens's *Great Expectations* only at the end, and the editor's decision about how much of it to print profoundly affects the work it is able to do. This extract cuts off Pip's mention of passing under the walls 'of which I was so ashamed' and instead ends with the line: 'We got into our post-coach and drove away.' The extract is still amusing, but now entirely at the expense of Londoners: Pip's squirming shame, Estella's unwittingly painful dialogue, and the looming prison are all entirely absent. In fact, Pip is here a mere observer, sharing with readers a wry smile at the crooked and incompetent ways of London hoteliers. Yet the extract works; standing alone, detached from its original purpose, and reclaimed by the newspaper in support of their mild contempt for strange metropolitan ways, it is still nonetheless an important thematic capsule, crystallizing for us Dickens's complex feelings about London in this period.

The unobtrusive but potentially enormously revealing appearances of little pirated snippets of Dickens in many regional newspapers between the 1830s and about 1875 is a phenomenon deserving of much more sustained research, one which recent rapid developments in the digitization of nineteenth-century newspapers should encourage, though to date little advantage has been taken of it and what there is remains speculative.[23] Did some readers encounter Dickens only in this way? How did these extracts

---

[23] See Mary Hammond, 'Tracking Pirates Through the Digital Archive: The Case of Dickens', in *The Yearbook of English Studies*, Vol. 45, *The History of the Book* (2015), 178–95.

help to shape cultural knowledge of the Dickens phenomenon? To what other political purposes were they put? All these and other intriguing questions remain as yet unanswered, and in the meantime, the absorption with whole-text analysis continues. Sambudha Sen is only the most recent of those who feel that *Great Expectations* works best as a whole: 'In the final analysis', Sen suggests, 'it is [the] ... bringing together of the gentleman and the criminal, refinement and corruption, the fairy godmother and the witch, which enables Dickens to destabilize the official belief not only in the idea of self-improvement but also in the existence of an internally consistent society capable of sustaining such an improvement.'[24] But as we have seen, the real power of this novel might well lie in its remarkable ability to perform social critique and arouse a smile or a tremor no matter how one slices it: the oppositions are present in essence in each of the capsules. In aggregate they might increase its power, but in this story of a small boy's fairy-tale wish gone horribly wrong in a world from which all magic has faded, Dickens embedded them at the cellular level. Each capsule is a recognizable representative of the whole, yet each is capable of working alone or with a slight mutation in a new environment. This novel has adaptation in its genes; Dickens's last-minute removal at proof stage of the two-word reference to death in the final line of the manuscript's famous rewritten 'happy' ending, 'I saw no shadow of a parting from her [but one]', seems entirely fitting, presaging the remarkable capacity of this novel to survive in environments Dickens would never see.[25]

Further Reading

Jonathan H. Grossman, 'Living the Global Transport Network in *Great Expectations*', *Victorian Studies* 57, 2 (Winter 2015): 225–50

Rachel Malik, 'Horizons of the Publishable: Publishing in/as Literary Studies', *English Literary History* 75 (2008): 707–35

Laurence W. Mazzeno, *The Dickens Industry: Critical Perspectives 1836–2005* (Rochester, NY, and Woodbridge: Camden House, 2011)

Ankhi Mukherjee, 'Missed Encounters: Repetition, Rewriting, and Contemporary Returns to Charles Dickens's *Great Expectations*', *Contemporary Literature* 46 (Spring 2005): 108–33

Robert L. Patten, *Charles Dickens and 'Boz': The Birth of the Industrial-Age Author* (Cambridge: Cambridge University Press, 2012)

---

[24] Sambudha Sen, introduction to Charles Dickens, *Great Expectations* (Dorling Kindersley: Pearson Longman, 2007), xxxviii.

[25] For an excellent discussion of the six different endings, see Edgar Rosenberg, 'Putting an End to *Great Expectations*', in Charles Dickens, *Great Expectations*, ed. Edgar Rosenberg, 491–527.

CHAPTER 20

OUR MUTUAL FRIEND

IAN DUNCAN

Culture and Fancy

OUR *Mutual Friend*, Dickens's last completed novel, received mixed reviews on publication, notoriously from Henry James, who diagnosed the 'permanent exhaustion' of its author's imagination.[1] The novel's critical stock rose in the mid-twentieth century through readings of its symbolism. 'As the fog is the symbol for *Bleak House* and the prison for *Little Dorrit*, so the dust-pile is the symbol for *Our Mutual Friend*', wrote Edmund Wilson, in an essay that set the terms for the revaluation of Dickens's mature works.[2] Recent criticism has analysed the novel's representation of its world through symbolic networks of circulation, exchange, and transformation or transubstantiation, of which the Harmon dust-mounds and River Thames are the main conduits or hubs. Value and waste, life and death, organic and inorganic, persons and things: these are temporary stages rather than fixed categories in *Our Mutual Friend*, as each decays or recycles into the other. Critics have considered this circulatory system as an economy of waste and salvage;[3] as a continuous metamorphosis of organic form;[4] as a flow of energy

---

[1] In *The Nation*, December 1865, reprinted in Philip Collins (ed.), *Dickens: The Critical Heritage* (London: Routledge and Kegan Paul, 1971), 469–73, 469.

[2] Edmund Wilson, 'Dickens: The Two Scrooges', in *The Wound and the Bow* (Boston: Houghton Mifflin, 1941), 75.

[3] See, for example, Nancy A. Metz, 'The Artistic Reclamation of Waste in *Our Mutual Friend*', *Nineteenth-Century Fiction* 34, 1 (1979): 59–72; Efraim Sicher, 'The Waste Land: Salvage and Salvation in *Our Mutual Friend*', in *Rereading the City, Rereading Dickens: Representation, the Novel, and Urban Realism* (New York: AMS Press, 2003), 329–83; Catherine Gallagher, *The Body Economic: Life, Death, and Sensation in Political Economy and the Victorian Novel* (Princeton: Princeton University Press, 2006), 91–110.

[4] Howard W. Fulweiler, '"A Dismal Swamp": Darwin, Design, and Evolution in *Our Mutual Friend*', *Nineteenth-Century Literature* 49, 1 (1994): 50–74; Anna Gibson, '*Our Mutual Friend* and Network Form', *Novel: A Forum on Fiction* 48, 1 (2015): 63–84; Ayşe Çelikkol, 'The Inorganic Aesthetic in Dickens's *Our Mutual Friend*', *Partial Answers* 14, 1 (2016): 1–20.

through states of storage and release.[5] Discussing the last, Allen MacDuffie argues that the novel 'stages a conflict between [an] older model of cyclical decay and regeneration and a modern, entropy-centred economy in which waste represents not an unused potential, but the end of transformation itself'.[6] Both dynamics oppose, in turn, the nineteenth-century novel's formal and ideological commitment to progress, manifest in themes of moral, sentimental, and aesthetic education or culture (*Bildung*).

These contending drives—decay and regeneration, entropy, progress—invest Dickens's treatment of the means and material of culture in *Our Mutual Friend*: books, literacy, and (the main topic of this chapter) the circulation of stories. In one node of this network, the novel tracks the cycle of paper, from its manufacture from salvaged cotton rags, at the paper-mill upriver where Lizzie Hexam works, to its decomposition: the narrator contrasts '[t]hat mysterious paper currency which circulates in London when the wind blows, gyrated here and there and everywhere', with the more efficient scavenger economy of Paris, where 'it blows nothing but dust'.[7] The trope of currency links the paper cycle to the general cycle of economic exchange and transubstantiation, from sublime zenith, 'Shares' (*OMF* I:10, 114), to material nadir, 'Coal-dust, vegetable-dust, bone-dust, crockery-dust, rough dust, and sifted dust—all manner of Dust' (*OMF* I:2, 13)—which may in turn, accumulated in the Harmon mounds, re-enter the cycle and release latent value.[8]

Early on, *Our Mutual Friend* alerts readers to the relation between books as material objects—printed paper, binding—and the sublime edifice of literacy upon which modern civilization is raised: culture, in the sense soon to be celebrated by Matthew Arnold, as 'the study and pursuit of perfection', 'not to be gained without books and reading'.[9] Charley Hexam, son of a waterside scavenger, at first appears to typify a redemptive progress from book to culture, matter to spirit:

---

[5] Gallagher, *The Body Economic*, 91–7; Jessica Kuskey, 'Our Mutual Engine: The Economics of Victorian Thermodynamics', *Victorian Literature and Culture* 41 (2013): 75–89; Allen MacDuffie, *Victorian Literature, Energy, and the Ecological Imagination* (Cambridge: Cambridge University Press, 2014), 122–30.

[6] MacDuffie, *Victorian Literature*, 126.

[7] Charles Dickens, *Our Mutual Friend*, ed. Michael Cotsell, Oxford World's Classics (Oxford: Oxford University Press, 1989), I:12, 144. Subsequent references are inserted parenthetically in the text by *OMF* Book:chapter, page. See Andrew M. Stauffer, 'Ruins of Paper: Dickens and the Necropolitan Library', *Romanticism and Victorianism on the Net* 47 (2007): <https://www.erudit.org/fr/revues/ravon/2007-n47-ravon1893/016700ar/> [Accessed 16 September 2016]; Leah Price, *How to Do Things with Books in Victorian Britain* (Princeton: Princeton University Press, 2012), 219–50; Heather Tilley, 'Waste Matters: Charles Dickens's *Our Mutual Friend* and Nineteenth-Century Book Recycling', in Gillian Partington and Adam Smyth (eds), *Book Destruction from the Medieval to the Contemporary* (Basingstoke: Palgrave, 2014), 152–72.

[8] See Joel J. Brattin, 'Constancy, Change, and the Dust Mounds of *Our Mutual Friend*', *Dickens Quarterly* 19, 1 (2002): 23–30; Virginia Zimmerman, *Excavating Victorians* (Albany: State University of New York Press, 2008), 162–7; Leslie Simon, '*Bleak House*, *Our Mutual Friend*, and the Aesthetics of Dust', *Dickens Studies Annual* 42 (2011): 217–36.

[9] Matthew Arnold, *Culture and Anarchy*, ed. Jane Garnett (Oxford: Oxford University Press, 2006), 35, 53, 120.

There was a curious mixture in the boy, of uncompleted savagery, and uncompleted civilisation. His voice was hoarse and coarse, and his face was coarse, and his stunted figure was coarse; but he was cleaner than other boys of his type; and his writing, though large and round, was good; and he glanced at the backs of the books, with an awakened curiosity that went below the binding. No one who can read, ever looks at a book, even unopened on a shelf, like one who cannot. (*OMF* I:3, 18)

The mixture of inchoate stages of savagery and civilization, rather than their hierarchical layering, hints at a failure of the project of *Bildung* enshrined in those books. Morally Charley remains half-savage or worse, in one of several cases of botched progress or outright regression in *Our Mutual Friend*. Meanwhile Mr Boffin, the 'Golden Dustman', seeks to improve his new status as a man of property by hiring a 'literary man' to read the classics to him. Mr Boffin, who cannot read, locates the book's value in its material condition: 'Eight wollumes. Red and gold. Purple ribbon in every wollume, to keep the place where you leave off' (*OMF* I:5, 52): perhaps this is the annotated, illustrated octavo edition of *The Decline and Fall of the Roman Empire* brought out by John Murray in 1854–62.[10] Mr Boffin's hired reader, the semi-literate ballad-monger Silas Wegg, grapples with printed words as though they are 'things to be subdued',[11] grotesquely mangling his own wares and Gibbon's text alike. The reading course traces its own arc of decline and fall. Sinking from Gibbon and Plutarch to *The Lives and Anecdotes of Misers*, Mr Boffin appears to become what he reads, a degraded version of what he always was—a guardian of the dust-heap. His fraudulent tutor ends up ejected onto a dung-cart.

These failures to rise above base origins belong to the novel's larger critique, well noted by commentators, of formal institutions of literacy and schooling. The critique falls most heavily on young Hexam's schoolmaster, Bradley Headstone, whose own struggle to better himself through education entails a repression rather than sublimation of his native 'wild energy' (*OMF* II:15, 396)—ensuring its eventual murderous outbreak. The failure is rooted in a mechanical, utilitarian discipline of rote-learning that divides knowledge from the imagination and affections, set in opposition to spontaneous, pre-literate practices of thinking and remembering, 'learning by heart', that keep the fancy alive and bear a creative or redemptive charge.[12] Learning by heart and its corollary, storytelling, exemplified in the fireside visions Lizzie Hexam narrates to her brother and the fantastic caprices of Jenny Wren, take us to another strand in the novel's

---

[10] See Price, *How to Do Things with Books*, 1.
[11] Gallagher, *The Body Economic*, 111.
[12] Sarah Winter, *The Pleasures of Memory: Learning to Read with Charles Dickens* (New York: Fordham University Press, 2011), 226–62. See also Catherine Shuman, 'Invigilating *Our Mutual Friend*: Gender and the Legitimation of Professional Authority', *Novel: A Forum on Fiction* 28, 2 (1995): 154–72; Pam Morris, 'A Taste for Change in *Our Mutual Friend*: Cultivation or Education?', in Juliet John and Alice Jenkins (eds), *Rethinking Victorian Culture* (New York: St Martin's Press, 2000), 179–95; David Paroissien, 'Ideology, Pedagogy, and Demonology: The Case Against Industrialized Education in Dickens's Fiction', *Dickens Studies Annual* 34 (2004): 259–82; Gallagher, *The Body Economic*, 111–17.

symbolic network: the circulation of stories within the greater story that is *Our Mutual Friend*.

Our Mutual Friend associates books and schooling with a forced, literal, instrumental acquisition of knowledge, a progress that is no progress, readily harnessed to ambition and deceit. Against this, the novel immerses its characters and readers in the living medium of (to use the contemporary term) 'popular literature', stored in the memory and fancy, renewed in acts of recitation and reinvention: 'old stories' (in Adrian Poole's summary) from which Dickens's 'text is woven', drawn from 'old scripture and prayer-book, ... fairy-tale, nursery rhyme, popular ballad, theatre, newspaper'.[13] These make up the organic tissue of *Our Mutual Friend*, along with other, more properly literary sources—not least among them plots, figures, and motifs recycled from the author's own earlier work. Above all *Our Mutual Friend* draws upon the great European vernacular heritage of folktales, fairy tales, and Mother Goose rhymes, preserved since the seventeenth century in the print collections of Antoine Galland, Mme D'Aulnoy, Charles Perrault, and the brothers Grimm, circulated in chapbooks, penny pamphlets, and the burgeoning popular press, and absorbed through oral narration in childhood, which constitute a common popular culture of poetry and fiction.

In an 1853 *Household Words* article, 'Frauds on the Fairies', Dickens protests against the conscription of 'the fairy literature of our childhood' for didactic purposes. (His immediate target is his former illustrator George Cruikshank, who adapted 'Hop o' my Thumb' for a temperance tract.) The polemic looks forward to the mockery of school curricula in *Our Mutual Friend*:

> In an utilitarian age, of all other times, it is a matter of grave importance that Fairy tales should be respected ... it becomes doubly important that the little books themselves, nurseries of fancy as they are, should be preserved. To preserve them in their usefulness, they must be as much preserved in their simplicity, and purity, and innocent extravagance, as if they were actual fact. Whosoever alters them to suit his own opinions, whatever they are, is guilty, to our thinking, of an act of presumption, and appropriates to himself what does not belong to him.[14]

Fairy tales precede a later—fallen—distinction between hard fact and mere fiction. Located in childhood fancy, they are a kind of natural resource or imaginative commons: a preserve of what nineteenth-century criticism elsewhere recognizes as aesthetic value, free from instrumental use. The main representative of fairy literature in *Our Mutual Friend* is the queer changeling Jenny Wren, the doll's dressmaker. Her relation to fairy literature is organic rather than proprietorial: she appears to be herself a figure from a fairy tale, she identifies other characters as fairy-tale types, and she has the gift of generating (rather than merely citing) rhymes, proverbs, and riddles of her own. Nor is this material exclusively hers, although she is persistently associated with it. The

---

[13] Dickens, *Our Mutual Friend*, ed. Adrian Poole (London: Penguin, 1997), xx, xi.
[14] [Charles Dickens,] 'Frauds on the Fairies', *Household Words*, 1 October 1853, 8:97–100, 97.

novelist keeps invoking fairy literature across *Our Mutual Friend*, along with nursery rhymes and scripture tales, as the stock of a universal popular mythology in Victorian England.

The other custodian of popular literature in *Our Mutual Friend* is Silas Wegg, rascally dealer in a shop-soiled repertoire of parlour songs and street ballads before his appointment as Mr Boffin's reader. Wegg occupies an antithetical relation to the doll's dressmaker. Never appearing together in the same scene, the two figures represent historically distinct conceptions of popular literature as it undergoes momentous transformation in mid-Victorian Britain. The transformation is from an *antiquarian* idea of popular literature as archive of a traditional national culture, typified by the ballad and song revivals of the Romantic era, to a late Victorian *anthropological* idea of popular literature as archive of a universal culture, which may yield a blueprint of human nature—a primitive psychic infrastructure of myth and fable. Appearing in the historical transition between these conceptions, *Our Mutual Friend* resists the gravitational pull of them both. The novel rejects the antiquarian project of national culture, gleefully designating it as rubbish; at the same time it deranges the anthropological ordering of popular culture as a grammar of the human imagination, which would be realized in the decade after Dickens's death. *Our Mutual Friend*'s resistance to these cultural projects, the one residual and the other emergent, in conjunction with its denigration of formal schooling, accounts for much of the novel's signal 'darkness'. The novel keeps intuiting a disintegration of the nineteenth-century idea of culture, more than its transmission through tradition or its regeneration upon a rediscovered ground of human nature.

Dust, Relics, and Wild Tales

Fifteen years before the publication of *Our Mutual Friend*, Henry Mayhew had characterized the 'street-sellers of stationery, literature, and the fine arts' as inveterate hucksters and tricksters, descendants of Autolycus in Shakespeare's *The Winter's Tale*. Silas Wegg's stock in trade is consistent with the repertoire listed by one of Mayhew's informants: 'The Death of Nelson', 'Drink to me only with thine eyes', Scottish and Irish sentimental songs, airs from English operas.[15] Dickens was writing 100 years after Bishop Percy's *Reliques of Ancient English Poetry* had inaugurated the antiquarian assembly of popular and traditional ballads, songs, and tales into the foundation of a national cultural archive, an indigenous resource for the renewal of modern poetic production. Theorized by J. G. Herder in Germany in the 1770s, this nationalist project achieved monumental heft in Romantic-period collections such as Walter Scott's *Minstrelsy of the Scottish Border* (1802–3) and Jacob and Wilhelm Grimm's *Childhood and Household Tales* (*Kinder- und Hausmärchen*, 1812–14). Edgar Taylor's free translation of the latter,

---

[15] Henry Mayhew, *London Labour and the London Poor* (London: Woodfall, 1851), 279.

German Popular Stories (published in successive editions from 1823), proved even more popular than the German original. Ongoing in Dickens's lifetime, this revivalist enterprise would culminate after his death in the founding of the Folk-lore Society (1878) and the publication of Francis Child's *English and Scottish Popular Ballads* (1882–98).

Against the German Romantic hypothesis of the collective, communal origins of popular literature, Percy, Scott, and their followers traced a descent from the ancient bards and minstrels, courtly makers as well as singers of traditional poetry, to the broadside ballads and street songs of modern times—a descent they characterized as the degeneration of a once noble art into vulgar commerce.[16] In Mayhew's summary, 'the ballad-singer and seller of to-day is the sole descendant, or remains, of the minstrel of old, as regards the business of the streets; he is, indeed, the minstrel having lost caste, and being driven to play cheap'.[17] Dickens satirizes this cultural history in Silas Wegg, whose shameless mangling of his wares evinces the textual corruption identified by antiquarian historiography as a symptom of that degeneration. At the same time, Dickens makes Wegg's botched renditions of popular song irresistibly funny: textual corruption expresses a disgraceful, irrepressible vitality, a surplus of amoral comic energy, more than it does lamentable decline. Wegg's recitations channel an irreverent rebuttal of the antiquarians' degenerationist thesis and its premise of an exalted cultural origin.

Elsewhere, Dickens debunks the pretensions of national history:

> REGINALD WILFER is a name with rather a grand sound, suggesting on first acquaintance brasses in country churches, scrolls in stained-glass windows, and generally the De Wilfers who came over with the Conqueror. For, it is a remarkable fact in genealogy that no De Any ones ever came over with Anybody else. (*OMF* I:4, 32)

This pedigree is soon displaced by a more spontaneous onomastic:

> [T]he facetious habit had arisen in the neighbourhood surrounding Mincing Lane of making Christian names for [Mr Wilfer] of adjectives and participles beginning with R. Some of these were more or less appropriate: as Rusty, Retiring, Ruddy, Round, Ripe, Ridiculous, Ruminative; others derived their point from their want of application: as Raging, Rattling, Roaring, Raffish. But, his popular name was Rumty, which in a moment of inspiration had been bestowed upon him by a gentleman of convivial habits connected with the drug market, as the beginning of a social chorus, his leading part in the execution of which had led this gentleman to the Temple of Fame, and of which the whole expressive burden ran:
> 'Rumty iddity, row dow dow.
> 'Sing toodlely, teedlely, bow wow wow.' (*OMF* I:4, 32–3)

---

[16] See Nigel Leask, '"A Degrading Species of Alchemy": Ballad Poetics, Oral Tradition, and the Meanings of Popular Culture', in Philip Connell and Nigel Leask (eds), *Romanticism and Popular Culture in Britain and Ireland* (Cambridge: Cambridge University Press, 2009), 51–71.

[17] Mayhew, *London Labour and the London Poor*, 274–5.

The 'expressive burden'—sheer gleeful noise—releases a giddy, reckless gaiety. Like other Dickens novels, *Our Mutual Friend* delights in such nonsensical declensions. 'Bow wow' recurs in Mr Boffin's sarcastic taunt, 'Mew, Quack-quack, Bow-wow' (*OMF* III:15, 596), adapted from a nursery rhyme, the medium of a proto-human language of infancy. 'Bow-wow' had become a satirical catchphrase in a scholarly debate over the origins of language three years before *Our Mutual Friend* began serialization, when philologist Max Müller dubbed the thesis of an onomatopoeic origin of language (arising from imitation of sounds in the natural world) the 'Bow-wow theory'.[18] 'Bow-wow' is the slogan of language's devolution into babble and noise—and Dickens's burlesque of the degenerationist thesis. *Our Mutual Friend* reduces the antiquarian archive to rubbish, fit only to be scavenged for comic nuggets. It is no accident that the literary classic piled on this dust-heap is miscalled 'Decline-and-Fall-Off-the-Rooshan-Empire', in a scrambled allusion to the Victorian fascination with Roman decadence as a portentous analogue of Great Britain's age of empire.[19] The satiric fallout of Wegg's balladeering includes the repurposing of Roman ballads and songs as historical data, authentic relics of the early Republic, in Barthold Niebuhr's scientific Roman history, appropriated for a British national heritage in Macaulay's *Lays of Ancient Rome* (1842).[20]

Meanwhile, in the mid-1860s, 'popular literature' was undergoing a powerful conceptual transformation: it was being anthropologized. This entailed its conversion from an empirical gathering of the remains of a departed organic culture, around which national life might be sentimentally regenerated, to a universal archive of the human race or species: of culture as such, 'in its wide ethnographic sense', in the phrase of E. B. Tylor,[21] rather than in the pedagogical sense promoted by Arnold. The displacement of antiquarian scholarship by professional formations of anthropology, ethnology, and folklore studies, institutionally consolidated in the last quarter of the nineteenth century, had its roots in the German Romantic sciences of comparative philology and comparative mythology. Scholars such as the Grimms and (in the following generation) Max Müller began to organize the materials of an increasingly global corpus of languages, stories, and customs, mined from modern ethnographic accounts of 'savage' societies as well as from the archaeology of non-classical antiquities, into a grand genealogy of (at first) the Indo-European or Aryan race. *Our Mutual Friend* appeared on the brink of the disciplinary revolution marked by Tylor's *Primitive Culture*, the founding text of the new anthropology in Great Britain, published the year after Dickens's death in 1871. Compiling a database of myths, laws,

---

[18] See Morris, 'A Taste for Change in *Our Mutual Friend*', 108.
[19] Linda Dowling, 'Roman Decadence and Victorian Historiography', *Victorian Studies* 28, 4 (1985): 579–607.
[20] See Peter Hanns Reil, 'Barthold Georg Niebuhr and the Enlightenment Tradition', *German Studies Review* 3, 1 (1980): 9–26.
[21] Edward B. Tylor, *Primitive Culture: Researches into the Development of Mythology, Philosophy, Religion, Art, and Custom*, 2 vols (London: Murray, 1871), 1:1.

customs, ceremonies, arts, and crafts, drawn from all times and places, Tylor and his followers undertook by comparative analysis to discover fundamental laws of human nature according to the developmental paradigm of Darwinian natural history. 'Scientific myth-interpretation', in Tylor's phrase, 'groups and classifies resemblances' in order to discover the universal operations of 'mental law'.[22] This entailed the rejection of degenerationist accounts of popular culture as the debris of a lost archaic high civilization. The materials of popular culture constitute, instead, the prehistoric foundation of a species-wide mentality, a universal 'savage mind', which underlies the recent strata of civilized settlement.

Key to Tylor's project was what he called 'the doctrine of survivals'—the thesis that traces of this primitive mentality persist in modern life, in the form of unconscious, customary, or superstitious habits and practices, including children's games, proverbs, riddles, and jokes. 'In our childhood', Tylor wrote, 'we dwelt at the very gates of the realm of myth.'[23] Andrew Lang's 1873 essay, 'Mythology and Fairytales', applies Tylor's theory to folktales or *Märchen* (a generic term adopted from the brothers Grimm). Lang refutes the degeneration thesis: 'The *Märchen*, far from being the detritus of the higher mythology', are 'remains from the age of totemism and belief magic', 'relics of shamanism'; 'in most cases in which they tally with the higher epic, they preserve an older and more savage form of the same myth, containing more allusions to cannibalism, to magic, or Shamanism, to kinship with the beasts, and to bestial transformations'.[24]

The nexus of mythology, romance, and nursery tale brings us back to *Our Mutual Friend*, and the novel's other great popular archive: that of a pre-literate (rather than illiterate) culture, the culture of childhood, which is on the point of emerging into scientific visibility as a 'culture', thanks in part to Lang and Tylor. In 'Frauds on the Fairies', written before anthropological attention turned to the fairy tale in the 1860s, Dickens does not treat childhood as a culture in this emergent sense. Fairy tales express an unfallen natural condition, affective states of 'simplicity, and purity, and innocent extravagance'; they are 'nurseries of the fancy', which supply a sounder moral basis than didactic programmes for adult life.[25] The fairy-tale allusions scattered throughout *Our Mutual Friend* are a great deal more wild and unruly than Dickens's reflections of a dozen years earlier might lead us to expect—more in tune with the childhood terror he evokes in his autobiographical sketch of 1860, 'Nurses' Stories'. These tales—Bluebeard, Red Riding Hood, and the rest—bristle with sinister violence, including the scenarios of cannibalism and bestial transformation that Lang identifies as memory traces of savage prehistory. The novel's personification of fairy literature, the doll's dressmaker, partakes in this savagery, with her incantation of fantastic threats and her torment of the wretched Fledgby. (She sprinkles pepper on his dressings after he is thrashed by Mr

---

[22] Ibid., 1:254–5.
[23] Ibid., 1:257.
[24] Andrew Lang, 'Mythology and Fairy Tales', *Fortnightly Review* NS 8 (1873): 618–31, 618–19.
[25] [Dickens,] 'Frauds on the Fairies,' 97.

Lammle, in an allusion, perhaps, to European accounts of Native American women's participation in the torture of captives.) Despite her intuitive gifts, Jenny's hermeneutic mastery of the fairy-tale archive is uncertain. 'You are not the godmother at all!' she upbraids the innocent Mr Riah: 'You are the Wolf in the Forest, the wicked Wolf!' (*OMF* III:13, 574). It seems fairy tales may not provide a sure safeguard against the deceits of the adult world.

Unregulated, the corpus of fairy tales spreads chaotically, disruptively, across *Our Mutual Friend*. Jenny's rebuke to Mr Riah identifies him as the devouring wolf of 'Red Riding Hood', one of Dickens's favourite childhood tales.[26] The allusive recurrence of 'Red Riding Hood', outstripping its use by any particular character, grants it something like formal autonomy in Dickens's text, as though it is endowed with independent life. Nor is it the only case. The doll's dressmaker's real name is 'Fanny Cleaver', the narrator tells us: 'but she had long ago chosen to bestow upon herself the appellation of Miss Jenny Wren' (*OMF* II:2, 233). This is the name of Cock Robin's bride in a popular ballad, 'The Courtship and Marriage of Cock Robin and Jenny Wren', absorbed into the nineteenth-century canon of nursery literature and often printed together with another (now more familiar) rhyme, 'The Death and Burial of Poor Cock Robin.' Dickens cites the latter in the description of Mr Venus's taxidermy shop:

> Wegg perceives a pretty little dead bird lying on the counter, with its head drooping on one side against the rim of Mr. Venus's saucer, and a long stiff wire piercing its breast. As if it were Cock Robin, the hero of the ballad, and Mr. Venus were the sparrow with his bow and arrow, and Mr. Wegg were the fly with his little eye. (*OMF* I:7, 78–9)

The perverse hint of eroticism and violence in this tableau touches Jenny herself, with her relish of the torments she will inflict on a future husband. She is not present in the scene; this is not part of her own performance. The allusion to Cock Robin is wielded by the novelist, or, rather, it is wielded *through* the novelist—since the degree to which he may mean something with it remains obscure.

These 'household tales', in short, are only superficially domesticated. Like cats that go out and hunt at night, they retain their wildness. The metaphor of 'vitality', often applied to Dickens's art, provokes us to wonder—in this novel preoccupied with anomalous states of life, death, and suspended animation—how far we may take it literally. Perhaps (the novel knows better than its author) these tales are themselves a kind of artificial wildlife form, charging persons with their uncanny energy rather than the other way around. In a perverse vitalist mutation of aesthetic ideology, they are not for us but for themselves. They *tell us* even as we think we are telling them.

---

[26] See Molly Clark Hillard, *Spellbound: The Fairy Tale and the Victorians* (Columbus: Ohio State University Press, 2014), 173–8, 197–216; also Cynthia DeMarcus, 'Wolves Within and Without: Dickens's Transformation of "Little Red Riding Hood" in *Our Mutual Friend*', *Dickens Quarterly* 7, 1 (1995): 11–12.

'The logic of feeling'

Modern folklore scholars have traced the origins of 'Cock Robin' to the 'early Norse myth about the death of Balder, god of summer sunlight and the incarnation of the life principle'.[27] The degenerationist thesis would gain fresh currency with the archetypalist strain of 'scientific myth-interpretation' that emerged in the twentieth century through J. G. Frazer's grand synthesis of late Victorian anthropology, *The Golden Bough* (multiple editions, 1890–1915). In the wake of Tylor and Lang, Frazer sought to organize the ever-swelling anthropological archive metaphorically around a core set of rites and stories—and ultimately to distil them all into a single, essential story, a *mythos* of sacrifice and regeneration, which is the story of culture as such. *The Golden Bough* was followed by drastic abstractions of the anthropological archive into a finite set of functions, figures, and relations, from Vladimir Propp's *Morphology of the Folktale* (1928) and Stith Thompson's *Motif-index of Folk Literature* (1932–6) to the structural anthropology of Claude Lévi-Strauss (*The Savage Mind*, 1962). The mid-twentieth century saw the rise of an anthropological literary criticism, which sought to subdue literary works to the modernist protocols T. S. Eliot called 'the mythical method', and which acknowledged as its main authority *The Golden Bough*.

Famously, *Our Mutual Friend* anticipated *The Golden Bough* as a source for Eliot's own practice of the mythical method in *The Waste Land*. Betty Higden's praise of Sloppy's newspaper reading, 'He do the Police in different voices' (*OMF* I:16, 198), gave Eliot a working title for his poem. The precedent of *Our Mutual Friend* looms large over *The Waste Land*, with its apocalyptically sombre Thameside setting, its recurrent scenario of death by water, and its preoccupation with a metaphysical economy of waste and salvage, death and regeneration: the 'handful of dust' and 'heap of broken images', 'fragments' the poet has 'shored against [his] ruins'.[28] Eliot's election of *Our Mutual Friend* as a model for *The Waste Land*, subsequently displaced by *The Golden Bough*, would license the symbolist recovery of Dickens's later works mentioned at the outset of this chapter. Mythopoetic readings of *Our Mutual Friend*, in particular, flourished in the third quarter of the twentieth century, yielding (for example) a concordance of mythic motifs in Dickens's novels.[29]

We would do well, however, to be wary of retroactively imposing a later hermeneutic—that of *The Waste Land* and *The Golden Bough*—on *Our Mutual Friend*, which Dickens wrote before the anthropological reformation of culture upon a ground plan of myth. The novel's seething interplay of plots and figures, and echoes of and allusions to other stories, overflows the hold of any archetypal plot or fable upon this

---

[27] Gloria T. Delamar, *Mother Goose: From Nursery to Literature* (Jefferson, NC: McFarland, 1987), 235.
[28] T. S. Eliot, *The Waste Land and Other Poems* (New York: Harcourt, 2014), 30, 46.
[29] Bert G. Hornback, *Noah's Arkitecture: A Study of Dickens's Mythology* (Athens: Ohio University Press, 1972), 169–73.

massive and sprawling text. Other critics, diagnosing a shamanistic and fetishistic—in short 'savage'—cast to Dickens's imagination, have viewed him as more medium than mythographer, channelling rather than interpreting primitive mental states and narrative modes. One early review of *Our Mutual Friend* reports a contemporary characterization of Dickens's tendency to 'give consciousness even to inanimate things' as 'literary Fetishism', while George Henry Lewes aligns the author's mimetic powers with 'the phenomena of hallucination'.[30] Writing shortly after Dickens's death, Lewes sought to analyse this aesthetic:

> The writer presents almost a unique example of a mind of singular force in which, so to speak, sensations never passed into ideas. Dickens sees and feels, but the logic of feeling seems the only logic he can manage. Thought is strangely absent from his works... Compared with that of Fielding or Thackeray, his was merely an *animal* intelligence, i.e., restricted to perceptions.[31]

Such a verdict precludes Dickens from being able to bring the comparative method of 'scientific myth-interpretation' to bear on his own materials and procedures, as George Eliot would do in her great novels of the following decade. Despite the tone of deprecation, Lewes recognizes the distinction of Dickens's art from realist aims and techniques. He likens Dickens's animation of his characters to an experimental scientist's galvanic stimulation of 'frogs whose brains have been taken out for physiological purposes': the electrically convulsed frog may imitate life, but its motions remain isolated and mechanical, lacking 'the distinctive peculiarity of organic action, that of fluctuating spontaneity'.[32] As well as a non-realist rendition of character, Lewes's analogy characterizes the impact of Dickens's fiction upon his readers: physiological rather than intellectual, short-circuiting cognition to press directly on our nerves and feelings.[33]

Dickens himself had invoked this analogy in *Our Mutual Friend*, in which Mr Boffin, preparing for his reading lesson, has the eight volumes of *Decline and Fall* 'ranged flat, in a row, like a galvanic battery' on a side-table (*OMF* I:5, 55). Stored in tales and books, narrative is a kind of electrical energy that flows through storytellers and readers (and auditors) alike. Tales and books, when they work, do something more primitive than educate us: they *possess* us, convulse us, in a sensational agitation of affective states that precedes rational engagement—and may be the condition for reason's healthy or morbid functioning. Commentators have noted the link between Dickens's long-standing

---

[30] E. P. Whipple, 'The Genius of Dickens', *Atlantic Monthly* 19 (May 1867), in Collins (ed.), *Dickens: The Critical Heritage*, 480. For a later example see John Carey, *The Violent Effigy: The Imagination of Charles Dickens* (London: Faber, 1973).

[31] G. H. Lewes, 'Dickens in Relation to Criticism', *Fortnightly Review* 17 (1872); in Collins (ed.), *Dickens: The Critical Heritage*, 569–77, 576.

[32] Ibid., 574.

[33] See Gibson, '*Our Mutual Friend* and Network Form', 63, 80–2; Nicholas Dames, *The Physiology of the Novel: Reading, Neural Science, and the Form of Victorian Fiction* (Oxford: Oxford University Press, 2007), 182–4.

practical interest in mesmerism and his late-career devotion to Public Readings, in which the author's uncanny possession by his characters (murderous Sikes, pathetic Nancy) enabled his hypnotic possession, in turn, of mass audiences.[34]

Nevertheless the most prominent plot in *Our Mutual Friend*, not discussed so far in this chapter, narrates an education: that of Bella Wilfer, raised from mercenary vanity by the combined force of John Harmon's stringent *Bildung* through self-suppression and Mr Boffin's antithetical performance of moral degradation. Bella's education takes place not through books but the men's elaborate play-acting, characterized by Harmon himself as a 'pious fraud' (*OMF* IV:13, 771)—not, in other words, a fiction, in which the subject (Bella) can knowingly participate, but a deception. This is the part of the novel least likely to appeal to modern readers. In a powerful revision of Henry James's complaint, Hilary Schor views the pious fraud as symptomatic of 'Dickens's own weariness of fiction-making': 'Only by the deepest distrust of the magic of fictions can Dickens write his last novel.'[35] At stake here, as throughout *Our Mutual Friend*, is the principle of imaginative commitment to fiction that Coleridge famously characterized as a 'willing suspension of disbelief for the moment'.[36] More than once Dickens's novel designates 'belief' as a crux if not a trick for its characters, and hence also for its readers. Bella, now married to the 'living-dead man' John Harmon, acknowledges the exorbitant measure of belief required to sustain the story she finds herself in:

> 'I believe, John', pursued Bella, 'that you believe that I believe—'
> 'My dear child', cried her husband gaily, 'what a quantity of believing!'
> 'Isn't there?' said Bella, with another laugh. 'I never knew such a quantity! It's like verbs in an exercise. But I can't get on with less believing. I'll try again. I believe, dear John, that you believe that I believe that we have as much money as we require, and that we want for nothing.' (*OMF* IV:5, 687)

Despite Bella's efforts, it is too late for her to choose whether to believe or not. The novel has already locked her into its recursive logic, or rather its grammar, which also secures the contract between reader and author: it is enough that we believe that the author believes in our belief—and vice versa.

Where Bella appeals to grammar, reflexive conjugation, as the system that regulates her role in the story, Mr Boffin, bewildered in the archive of Great Books, resorts to the more primitive reckoning of arithmetic:

---

[34] See Fred Kaplan, *Dickens and Mesmerism: The Hidden Springs of Fiction* (Princeton: Princeton University Press, 1975), 118, 239n.; Alison Winter, *Mesmerized: Powers of Mind in Victorian Britain* (Chicago: University of Chicago Press, 1998), 321–3.

[35] Hilary M. Schor, *Dickens and the Daughter of the House* (Cambridge: Cambridge University Press, 2000), 197, 178.

[36] Samuel Taylor Coleridge, *Biographia Literaria, Or, Biographical Sketches of my Literary Life and Opinions*, ed. James Engell and Walter Jackson Bate, 2 vols (Princeton: Princeton University Press, 1983), 2:6.

What to believe, in the course of his reading, was Mr Boffin's chief literary difficulty indeed; for some time he was divided in his mind between half, all, or none; at length, when he decided, as a moderate man, to compound with half, the question still remained, which half? And that stumbling-block he never got over. (*OMF* III:6, 476)

These are questions we may ask ourselves as we forge our way through *Our Mutual Friend*.

New Directions

Although a great deal has been written on *Our Mutual Friend*, especially in recent years, many paths await further enquiry. Possible new directions include the study of emergent anthropological categories in the novel, such as liminal states and rites of passage, animism and fetishism (in the anthropological rather than Marxist or Freudian sense), and, not least, a historically responsible, comparative account of myth, situating Dickens's work in its European literary and scientific contexts. More work can be done, too, on the relation of Dickens's art to Victorian conceptions of stories and other literary forms as in some sense animate—not just 'organic' (in a loosely analogical sense) but autopoetic, interactively self-maintaining, transmitting themselves across multiple users and functions. Some of the recent insights of 'thing theory' and related critical approaches, redistributing agency away from the human subject, could be brought to bear on poems and narratives, which invest readers with affective and cognitive states they neither have initiated nor can fully control. The Kantian idea of aesthetic autonomy, so influential for the Victorians, emerges contemporaneously and is philosophically entangled with the Romantic conception of life as an autotelic formative force. In locating aesthetic autonomy with childhood fancy, and in weaving together tropes of magical animation and scientific vitalism, Dickens practises a potent alternative to idealist aesthetics, in an art that works resolutely with and through his readers' (and audience's) bodies, as Lewes and others complained.

Our Mutual Friend is one of many nineteenth-century novels in which a will—a script written in the past (by a dead hand)—seeks to determine the lives of characters and hence the narrative of the future. Old John Harmon's will joins the thematic web of ambiguous, mutable states of life and death with that of written and oral transmissions of the past and forecasts for the future in *Our Mutual Friend*. Linked to this, it may be worth exploring the array of potential alternative destinies and counter-histories layered into Dickens's narrative, often articulated by the recurrent motif of the second chance. Deaths that are final and irremediable, whether clean and virtuous (as of little Johnny and old Betty Higden) or the opposite (George Radfoot, Gaffer Hexam), highlight the sequence of variations on death and resurrection that punctuates the story: John Harmon, Rogue Riderhood, and Eugene Wrayburn are gifted with a second chance at their lives, in the most consequential sense, as are, with less attendant violence,

Mr Boffin and Bella. Here as elsewhere (*A Christmas Carol*; *A Tale of Two Cities*) Dickens transmutes traditional Christian motifs into something rich and strange—which may not even be 'Christian' any more, in any doctrinal sense.

Further Reading

Joel J. Brattin and Bert. G. Hornback (eds), *Our Mutual Friend: An Annotated Bibliography* (New York: Garland, 1984)

Katharina Boehm, 'Monstrous Births and Saltationism in *Our Mutual Friend* and Popular Anatomical Museums', in *Charles Dickens and the Sciences of Childhood: Popular Medicine, Child Health and Victorian Culture* (New York: Palgrave Macmillan, 2013), 145–68

Michael Cotsell (ed.), *The Companion to* Our Mutual Friend (Boston: Allen & Unwin, 1986)

Deirdre David, *Fictions of Resolution in Three Victorian Novels:* North and South, Daniel Deronda, *and* Our Mutual Friend (New York: Columbia University Press, 1981)

Sally Ledger, 'Dickens, Natural History, and *Our Mutual Friend*', *Partial Answers: Journal of Literature and the History of Ideas* 9, 2 (2011): 363–78

Helena Michie, '"Who is this in pain?": Scarring, Disfigurement, and Female Identity in *Bleak House* and *Our Mutual Friend*', *Novel: A Forum on Fiction* 22, 3 (1989): 199–212

J. Hillis Miller, *Charles Dickens: The World of his Novels* (Cambridge, MA: Harvard University Press, 1958), 279–327

Mary Poovey, 'Speculation and Virtue in *Our Mutual Friend*', in *Making a Social Body: British Cultural Formation, 1830–1864* (Chicago: University of Chicago Press, 1995), 155–80

Talia Schaffer, 'Salvage: Betty as the Mutual Friend', in *Novel Craft: Victorian Domestic Handicraft and Nineteenth-Century Fiction* (New York: Oxford University Press, 2011), 119–44

Eve Kosofsky Sedgwick, 'Homophobia, Misogyny, and Capital: The Example of *Our Mutual Friend*', in *Between Men: English Literature and Male Homosocial Desire* (New York: Columbia University Press, 1985), 161–79

Garrett Stewart, 'Lived Death: Dickens's Rogue Glyphs', in Daniel Tyler (ed.), *Dicken's Style* (Cambridge: Cambridge University Press, 2013), 231–53

Ruth Bernard Yeazell, 'Podsnappery, Sexuality, and the English Novel', *Critical Inquiry* 9, 2 (1989): 339–57

CHAPTER 21

THE MYSTERY OF EDWIN DROOD

PETE ORFORD

> It's time to stop this Drood debating—
> The Mystery's grown ex(j)asperating.[1]

DICKENS's final work is defined as much by the half that he did not write as by the half that he did. The decision of Chapman and Hall to publish only the remaining chapters left by Dickens after his death, and not to commission an ending by another author, unwittingly threw down a gauntlet to a relentless horde of solutionists all vying to solve the mystery in letters, essays, monographs, novels, plays, screenplays, and musicals.[2] The incomplete status of *The Mystery of Edwin Drood*, far from prohibiting discussion, has multiplied it. Recalling Paul Davis's observation that *A Christmas Carol* has two texts, 'the one that Dickens wrote in 1843 and the one that we collectively remember', we could equally apply his premise of a 'culture-text' to *Edwin Drood*, with provisos.[3] Where the *Carol* is widely known, *Edwin Drood*, for all its many solutions,

---

[1] Dak, 'That Mystery', *The Dickensian*, 8, 12 (December 1912): 326–7.
[2] The final published instalment of *Edwin Drood* contained the following explanatory note from the publishers: 'All that was left in manuscript of EDWIN DROOD is contained in the Number now published—the sixth. Its last entire page had not been written two hours when the event occurred which one very touching passage in it (grave and sad but also cheerful and reassuring) might seem almost to have anticipated. The only notes in reference to the story that have since been found concern that portion of it exclusively, which is treated in the earlier Numbers. Beyond the clues therein afforded to its conduct or catastrophe, nothing whatever remains; and it is believed that what the author himself would have most desired is done, in placing before the reader without further note or suggestion the fragment of THE MYSTERY OF EDWIN DROOD.' Charles Dickens, *The Mystery of Edwin Drood* (London: Chapman and Hall, March–September 1870), No. 6.
[3] Paul Davis, *The Lives and Times of Ebenezer Scrooge* (New Haven and London: Yale University Press, 1990), 4.

remains a curio unfamiliar to the general reader. It owes its identity as culture-text to those dedicated enthusiasts determined to add footnote after footnote to Dickens's plot. The casual reader can thus be deterred from approaching *Edwin Drood* by either one of two extremes: the abrupt brevity of the original text, or the gargantuan length of the culture-text.

Taken alongside the common depiction of the Droodists themselves as squabbling, obsessive fans, the temptation for serious readers of the text is to ignore the solutions and their taint of subjective enthusiasm. This is a mistake. Any solution proposed for *Edwin Drood* is an implicit form of criticism of the Dickensian original. It relies upon, and betrays, the writer's interpretation of structure, characterization, and themes. The unfortunate limitation associated with the solutions is that those who have taken the greatest interest in proposing them are invariably doing so merely to proffer their own ending. As a consequence, subsequent discussion of each solution focuses almost exclusively upon plot, either to identify a corroborating theory or attack a contrary one. But much more can be learned from them and the original by resisting the temptation to view the story purely in terms of its projected outcome. A brief summary of the history of *Edwin Drood* solutions will thus be followed by an exploration of how they have shaped our understanding of Dickens's original text. At the centre of this discussion lies the ongoing subtext of defining the place of *Edwin Drood* in the Dickens canon and the changing perceptions and anxieties surrounding Dickens's genius.

THE HISTORY OF *EDWIN DROOD*

For the sake of clarity, the attempts to solve *Edwin Drood* can be broadly divided into four successive movements: the opportunists, the detectives, the academics, and the irreverent. The opportunists were those writing in the years immediately after Dickens's death. They produced work not with a mind to decipher his intentions, but rather to achieve high sales. The success of Henry Morford's and Thomas Power James's solutions owed less to the quality of the writing and more to who they claimed the author to be: Morford's *John Jasper's Secret* was publicized as the work of Wilkie Collins and Charles Dickens Jnr, while James acted as a medium for the ghost of Dickens himself.[4] But notwithstanding the borrowed authority, their approach to the text was cavalier. While all subsequent solutionists would adhere to the parameters set in Dickens's first half, Morford and James, along with Gillian Vase and Georgie Sheldon after them,

---

[4] Henry Morford, *John Jasper's Secret, Being a Narrative of Certain Events Following and Explaining The Mystery of Edwin Drood* (London: Wyman and Sons, 1872); Thomas Power James, *Part Second of The Mystery of Edwin Drood by the Spirit-Pen of Charles Dickens, Through a Medium. Embracing, also, that part of the Work which was published prior to the termination of the Author's Earth-Life* (Brattleboro, VT: T. P. James, 1874).

introduce new characters and sub-plots to the text.[5] The early responses have far more in common with the many pirated editions of Dickens's other novels which were produced in his lifetime. Indeed, the very first solution by Orpheus C. Kerr had its early instalments published while Dickens was still alive.[6]

The beginning of Droodism as we now think of it originated with a flurry of attempts in the early twentieth century not merely to finish the story, but to do so as Dickens intended. The debate grew through newspaper correspondence and, from 1905 onwards, the publication of *The Dickensian*, which provided dedicated space for detailed Dickensian discussion. While the opportunists had written in isolation from one another, the detectives were frequently responding to one another's theories, generating discussion exponentially. Richard Proctor's *Watched by the Dead: A Loving Study of Charles Dickens' Half-told Tale*, though the first to lay its argument out in a full monograph, might easily have been forgotten were it not for the ensuing arguments about his theories.[7] Over the course of several letters, articles, and monographs, Andrew Lang was the most vocal in support of Proctor's view that Edwin was alive and Bazzard was Datchery, while John Cumming Walters argued just as vehemently that Edwin was dead and Helena was the white-haired detective.[8] While the opinions varied widely, one factor remained constant: the writers insisted that their solutions were true and could be proved to be so. By the time that Howard Duffield was researching his *Edwin Drood* theory in the 1920s and 1930s, this search for evidence had extended well beyond Dickens's text. Duffield's extensive collection, now housed at the Charles Dickens Museum, includes newspaper cuttings about such topics as strangling in twentieth-century America as well as fictional works that describe similar murders. Duffield's own marginalia identify aspects that he felt shed light on the murder of Drood. Instead of being seen as the product of Dickens's imagination, the plot was being treated forensically and thus subjected to the application of evidence from other cases.

Enter the academics. Against such obsessive detective work, Edmund Wilson delivered his seminal lecture *The Two Scrooges* in 1939, in which he argued that the ending of *Edwin Drood* was obvious. Consequently, the quality of the tale lay not in its mystery, but in its portrayal of a guilty man.[9] The task Dickens asked of the reader lay

---

[5] Gillian Vase, *A Great Mystery Solved: A Sequel to The Mystery of Edwin Drood*, 3 vols (London: Remington and Co., 1878); Georgie Sheldon, *The Welfleet Mystery* (London: James Henderson and Sons, 1885).

[6] Orpheus C. Kerr, *The Cloven Foot, Being an Adaptation of the English Novel 'The Mystery of Edwin Drood' by Charles Dickens to American Scenes, Characters, Customs and Nomenclature* (New York: Carleton, 1870).

[7] Richard Proctor, *Watched by the Dead: A Loving Study of Charles Dickens's Half-told Tale* (London: W. H. Allen and Co., 1887).

[8] Both Walters and Lang wrote prolifically on *The Mystery of Edwin Drood*, including numerous letters to the national press. For a fair representation of their main arguments, see John Cuming Walters, *Clues to Dickens's 'Mystery of Edwin Drood'* (London: Chapman and Hall, 1905), and Andrew Lang, *The Puzzle of Dickens' Last Plot* (London: Chapman and Hall, 1905).

[9] Edmund Wilson, 'The Two Scrooges' (1939), in *The Wound and the Bow* (Cambridge, MA: River Side Press, 1941), 1–104.

not in identifying the murderer, but observing him. Philip Collins supported Wilson's theory in 1960, after which completions such as those of Leon Garfield and Charles Forsyte followed suit.[10] The age of wild theories and additional characters had apparently given way to more sober readings. Discussion of *Edwin Drood* moved on to more academic topics. Eve Sedgwick's and John Thacker's analyses—of homosocial and religious themes in the novel, respectively—could not have been produced amidst the hysteria of the detectives.[11] Miriam O'Kane Mara's scholarly reading of colonialism in *Edwin Drood* feels no need to discuss the end of the novel beyond a brief footnote stating simply: 'My reading of *The Mystery of Edwin Drood* begins with the assumption that Edwin's disappearance is a result of his death, and John Jasper is the murderer.'[12]

Yet the creation of weird and wonderful endings for *Edwin Drood* is far from over. The most recent phase of these, running parallel to the academic readings, can be seen either as a reaction against the latter or a gleeful return to the variety of ideas provided earlier by the opportunists. Rupert Holmes's Broadway musical adaptation heralded a deliberate attempt to leave *Edwin Drood* open-ended: 'I wouldn't create my own mock-Dickensian ending for *Drood*. I'd let the audience decide who was the murderer, who was the Detective in Disguise, which pair of lovers had a happy ending.'[13] The incorporation of an audience vote has led to several wilfully anarchic results, such as the marriage of Princess Puffer to Deputy, or the unmasking of Rosa Budd as the killer of Edwin. The story was rendered open to possibility once again, bound by neither the academic view nor the detective's obsession with Dickens's intentions. Carlo Fruttero and Franco Lucentini's *The D Case* continued this creative approach in providing a fictional review of the debate held by the greatest detectives in literary history. The punchline of the tale is the discovery by Hercule Poirot that the entire story is a coded message identifying Wilkie Collins as the murderer of Dickens.[14] Readers are simultaneously informed of all previous theories and taught not to take any of them seriously. By the time screenwriter Gwyneth Hughes adapted the novel for the BBC for the Dickens bicentenary in 2012, she decided that since 'there will never be a definitive answer to the Mystery of Edwin Drood' it would be better instead to write an ending which a modern audience would best respond to.[15] Her adaptation allowed for the variety of outcomes associated

---

[10] Philip Collins, *Dickens and Crime* (London: Macmillan, 1962); Leon Garfield, *The Mystery of Edwin Drood* (London: Andre Deutsch Ltd, 1980); Charles Forsyte, *The Decoding of Edwin Drood* (London: Victor Gollancz, 1980).

[11] Eve Kosofsky Sedgwick, 'Up the Postern Stair: *Edwin Drood* and the Homophobia of Empire', in *Between Men: English Literature and Male Homosocial Desire* (New York: Columbia University Press, 1985), 180–200; John Thacker, *Antichrist in the Cathedral* (London: Vision Press, 1990).

[12] Miriam O'Kane Mara, 'Sucking the Empire Dry: Colonial Critique in *The Mystery of Edwin Drood*', *Dickens Studies Annual* 32 (2002): 233–46, 244.

[13] Rupert Holmes, 'The History of the Mystery', <http://www.rupertholmes.com> <http://www.rupertholmes.com/theatre/essdrood.html>, accessed 29 April 2017.

[14] Carlo Fruttero and Franco Lucentini, *The D Case*, trans. Gregory Dowling (London: Chatto and Windus, 1992).

[15] Gwyneth Hughes, 'Afterword', Charles Dickens, *The Mystery of Edwin Drood* (London: BBC Books, 2012), 279.

with the earlier detective's theories without the anxiety of attempting to determine what Dickens's intentions were likely to have been.

The contrasting approaches of these four groups of *Drood* interpreters herald varied results in the projected plot. Each solution constitutes not merely a writing of a second half, but a rewriting of the first half. In determining how the story should end, each writer implicitly projects his or her interpretation of the characters back on to the original text. As the central protagonist, John Jasper has been most subject to radical reinterpretation through these varied readings. The culture-texts formed by the myriad endings have generated a multitude of Jaspers, of which Dickens's original is just one option. In the hands of the opportunists he was rendered a Gothic villain fit for a Victorian melodrama. The decision, for instance, of James, Vase, and Sheldon to identify the Princess Puffer as the (grand)mother of a woman previously led astray by the choirmaster transformed Jasper from a man torn by his affections for Rosa into a serial womanizer leaving a trail of ruined women in his wake.

The detectives, though keen to keep the story limited to Dickens's cast of characters, focused their energies on the manner and success of the murder, not the motivations of the murderer. He became, like many villains of detective novels, little more than a plot device. It is interesting to note how many solutions relegate Jasper to a minor part as they focus on those uncovering the murder rather than the one who perpetrated it.

It was Wilson who restored attention to Jasper as the conflicted character found in Dickens's text, torn between love for his nephew and lust for Rosa: 'Rosa, even when my dear boy was affianced to you, I loved you madly.'[16] Among the academics, the accounts given of the extent of Jasper's torment and precise motivation became just as diverse as the many plot solutions proposed by the detectives. For Wilson, '[t]he subject of *Edwin Drood* is the subject of Poe's *William Wilson*, the subject of *Dr Jekyll and Mr Hyde*, the subject of *Dorian Gray*. It is also the subject of that greater work than any of these, Dostoevsky's *Crime and Punishment*.'[17] Wilson's *Jekyll and Hyde* theory inspired both Garfield and Forsyte to present Jasper as a split personality. Garfield suggests the choirmaster and the wicked man alternate their control of his body without losing awareness: 'I could do nothing. He [the wicked man] had strangled my poor boy with a black scarf, even as I watched.'[18] In contrast, Forsyte suggests each personality is separate from and ignorant of the other, so that 'Jasper has no knowledge of the murder of Drood', and unwittingly pursues himself as he vows revenge on the killer.[19]

Such readings return us to Dickens's text, looking for clues as the detectives did, but ultimately lead to different conclusions from the same evidence. For just as Dickens left no direct message regarding his intentions about the outcome to the reader, so too

---

[16] Charles Dickens, *The Mystery of Edwin Drood*, ed. Margaret Cardwell (Oxford: Clarendon Press, 1972), 19, 170. Subsequent references are inserted parenthetically in the text by *ED* chapter, page.
[17] Wilson, 'The Two Scrooges', 99.
[18] Garfield, *The Mystery of Edwin Drood*, 316.
[19] Forsyte, *The Decoding of Edwin Drood*, 196.

Jasper never speaks directly to us, but always through a medium: his diary, his opium visions, and the impeccable persona he projects to the inhabitants of Cloisterham. It is only through the external description of his physical actions that we are invited to interpret his inner thoughts. Whether goading Edwin and Neville to disagree, or watching Rosa intently while she sings, his intentions are heavily hinted at without being made explicit. His confrontation with Rosa by the sundial remains teasingly ambiguous as to what it may reveal of his guilt, or awareness of that guilt. He promises to give up the pursuit of Neville as Edwin's murderer, but never confirms whether he himself believes Neville to be guilty. His talk of his 'darling boy' can equally be seen as genuine or as part of the persona he adopts while wooing Rosa:

> Circumstances may accumulate so strongly *even against an innocent man*, that, directed, sharpened, and pointed, they may slay him. One wanting link discovered by perseverance against a guilty man, proves his guilt, however slight its evidence before, and he dies. Young Landless stands in deadly peril either way. (*ED* 19, 172)

The persistent ambiguity of Jasper's words and Dickens's description is one of the greatest provocations to the persistent reinvention of the ending. Dickens almost certainly intended to portray him as the murderer, but that inevitable 'almost' leaves us wondering. The heart of Jasper remains the true mystery of *Edwin Drood*.

THE GENRE OF *EDWIN DROOD*

Behind the central debate about the plot and protagonist rests a yet larger question: just what sort of book is *The Mystery of Edwin Drood*? In order to plan the book's end with confidence, each solutionist has needed to decide upon the style of book they were continuing. Sometimes this decision is subconsciously made, while at other times another novel has been explicitly named as a model for *Edwin Drood*, with any similarities noted in the first half being used to inform a projection of a similar second half. But without an end we cannot confidently define the genre and without an agreed genre we cannot confidently project the ending.

The book's full title, *The Mystery of Edwin Drood*, might suggest that the genre is obvious; but accepting it as a mystery, as the detectives did, is by no means a straightforward undertaking. It is no coincidence that Proctor, Lang, Walters, and others were writing their theories during the golden age of detective fiction. For Dickens's contemporaries, a mystery could mean any range of strange and unsettling tales; but for those writing in the early twentieth century, it meant a story that challenged the reader to guess whodunit. The problem arising from this latter definition is that if Dickens's tale is such a mystery, it is not a very good one. Jasper's guilt is obvious even without the ending, and this lack of the uncertainty required for a successful mystery has been compounded by Forster's statement of Dickens's intent. The book, he wrote, was to show 'the murder of a nephew by his uncle.'[20] Increasingly Dickens's fans felt that the simplicity and obviousness of this ending were an outrage and an attack on Forster's reliability soon followed. Either Forster was making it up, or misunderstanding Dickens, or being lied to by his lifelong friend.[21] Dickens's daughter Kate rebutted such claims and condemned their hypocrisy: 'it is very often those who most doubt Mr Forster's accuracy on this point who are in the habit of turning to his book when they are in search of facts to establish some theory of their own.'[22] But for many Dickensians the alternative was too terrible to consider: that Dickens had written a bad book. For how else could one describe a mystery in which the ending is so obvious? Proctor's book was the first to contain the implicit suggestion that Dickens's story is not a very good one, so long as we assume the ending was to be the obvious one as confirmed by Forster:

> Regarded as a story turning on the murder of a light-hearted lad by a jealous villain of diseased mind, the 'Mystery of Edwin Drood' has scarcely any interest in its main plot; while the accessory details have little meaning. [23]

Instead, Proctor argued that adopting his suggestion for the ending instead of Forster's would mean that we could then—and only then—recognize *Edwin Drood* as Dickens's 'master-plot' in which 'every line is seen to be full of life and light.'[24] The demolition of Dickens was thus an essential selling point for Proctor's book as it suggested that he alone could explain Dickens to readers and save the 'Inimitable's' reputation. Though other detectives would disagree with Proctor's solution, many would adopt this method of attacking the original *Edwin Drood* to champion their own ending. Thus, interpreting Dickens's text as a mystery presented a great challenge for all Dickensians, with the prize being recognition as the critic who best understood the author.

The grounding of all such theories in Dickens's text and style served both to justify the theory being proposed and to advertise the writer's superior comprehension. The irony of course is that such interpretative activity often involved extraordinary contortions of the original text as critics tried to find an ending they considered worthy both of the title of 'mystery' and 'Dickensian'. Felix Aylmer's *The Drood Case* is the second most outlandish theory, arguing that Jasper is trying to save Edwin from Oriental assassins.[25] It is outdone only by Benny Reece's later solution in which all the characters are identified as allegories for the classical gods and 'Helena (Artemis) killed Drood (Orion) when he tried to rape her.'[26] His attempt to find a hidden code within the tale is hardly a response

---

[20] John Forster, *The Life of Charles Dickens*, ed. J. W. T. Ley (London: Cecil Palmer, 1928): 808.
[21] See Gavin Brend, '*Edwin Drood* and the Four Witnesses', *Dickensian* 52, 317 (Winter 1955): 20–4, for a detailed attack on the reliability not only of Forster, but also Charles Alston Collins, Sir Luke Fildes, and Charles Dickens Jnr, who all corroborated Forster's narrative.
[22] Kate Perugini, *Pall Mall Magazine*, 1906, reprinted in W. Robertson Nicol, *The Problem of Edwin Drood: A Study in the Methods of Dickens*, 2nd edn (London: Hodder and Stoughton, 1913): 28–43.
[23] Proctor, *Watched by the Dead*, iv.
[24] Ibid.
[25] Felix Aylmer, *The Drood Case* (London: Rupert Hart-Davis, 1964).
[26] Benny R. Reece, *The Mystery of Edwin Drood Solved* (New York: Vantage Press, 1989), 27.

to the Dickens canon, but rather a product of the Droodist phenomenon. The longer debate wore on, the more extraordinary solutions had to become in order not to have already been discovered.

Wilson's essay cannot be applauded enough for its acceptance of Forster's advice and recognition that too many subsequent interpreters had tried to fit the square peg of Dickens's text into a round hole. However, as already noted (in the section 'The History of *Edwin Drood*'), he nevertheless sought to classify the novel by defining its 'subject' in relation to other nineteenth-century tales of the doppelgänger: *William Wilson, Jekyll and Hyde*, and *Crime and Punishment*. Each of these examples argues for an intentional focus upon Jasper's struggles to be made plain to the reader. But there is also another aim shown here and elsewhere in these reinterpretations: the concern to reinstate recognition of Dickens's genius, as either matching the contemporary work of Dostoevsky and Poe, or anticipating that of Stevenson. As Forsyte states in his introduction, 'Stevenson could hardly have written his story fifteen years later had Dickens completed *Edwin Drood*.'[27] Dickens is positioned in these accounts as the originator, the first to achieve, rather than the one who follows others.

The anxiety beneath such intentions is made more apparent in the course of attempts to classify *Edwin Drood* as a sensation novel. The idea itself is a viable one, but the problem with it arises in relation to the figure of Wilkie Collins. Sensation has for so long been seen as Collins's domain, that for Dickens to have written such a novel cannot be otherwise interpreted than as a deliberate trespass into his protégé's territory. Sue Lonoff clearly laid out the many ways in which *Edwin Drood* can be seen to echo both *The Moonstone* and *The Woman in White*.[28] Ross Murfin duly responded by showing how these two novels in turn echoed *Bleak House*. Both essays raise the question of Dickens's originality: does the suggestion that Dickens imitated Collins diminish his genius, and does the idea that Collins had first imitated Dickens redeem it?[29] Both questions involve Dickens's reputation as the 'Inimitable', whereas recent scholarship is happier with the idea of writers influencing one another at no cost to their reputation.

Furthermore, the fact that both Lonoff and Murfin, like so many before them, drew predominately on two novels by Collins is symptomatic of a larger problem: the selective interpretation of sensation fiction as a genre. Those who dismiss *Edwin Drood* as a poor example of the sensation novel do so because they are using only *The Moonstone* and *The Woman in White* as the basis for their comparison. The effects of such critical selectivity are similarly evident in a damning critique of Thomas Hardy's *Desperate Remedies* by Lawrence O. Jones, who defines the sensation novel as one 'in which the total effect depends on the reader's not knowing the motives and identity of the criminal until the

---

[27] Forsyte, *The Decoding of Edwin Drood*, 104.
[28] Sue Lonoff, 'Charles Dickens and Wilkie Collins', *Nineteenth-Century Fiction* 35, 2 (September 1980): 150–70.
[29] Ross Murfin, 'The Art of Representation: Collins' *The Moonstone* and Dickens' Example', *ELH* 49, 3 (Autumn 1982): 653–72.

end'.[30] Such a narrow definition is only made possible by restricting the cited examples to Collins's two most famous works.

Consideration of a wider range of examples that takes in Mary Elizabeth Braddon and her contrasting model of sensation fiction yields a more nuanced understanding of the genre. Novels such as *Lady Audley's Secret* and *Aurora Floyd* do not attempt to hide the guilty party from the reader's attention, but instead create suspense by encouraging anticipation of the villain's apprehension. If we compare Dickens to Braddon, instead of Collins, his achievement as a sensation novelist can be better appreciated. Dickens does not accidentally reveal Jasper's guilt too soon; instead, he draws the reader into a study of a villain in action. A developing critical awareness of the wider range of sensation writers may yet provide the key to rescuing the reputation of *Edwin Drood*.

Alternatively, Dickens can be compared with himself: whatever genre *Edwin Drood* may be seen to exemplify, it is certainly Dickensian. Philip Collins argues that 'Jasper very clearly continues the development we have traced from Sikes and Rudge [senior] to Jonas Chuzzlewit, [Julius] Slinkton, and Bradley Headstone'.[31] But even drawing on Dickens's own works in an effort to interpret his incomplete novel is not without danger. To begin with, we must recognize of course that Dickens did not write in a vacuum. He knew what his contemporaries in England, France, and the United States were writing, and we cannot rule out external influence in favour of internal influence only. Furthermore, the use of Dickens's earlier texts as a basis for extrapolating interpretations in relation to *Drood* can be misleading. We assume too readily that the use of a previous plot device by Dickens stands as a precedent for his using it again. For example, Proctor's argument for Edwin's resurrection was based upon what he perceived to be 'Dickens' favourite theme' of a wicked man unknowingly being watched by a good man. Ralph Nickleby and Newman Noggs, Seth Pecksniff and old Martin Chuzzlewit, Uriah Heep and Wilkins Micawber: these and many others prove beyond doubt to Proctor that Edwin must be alive and watching Jasper as Datchery. That Collins and Proctor can draw two such different trajectories for Jasper from the evidence of Dickens's earlier work shows the potential not only for suiting the precedent to the theory, but for the multiple possibilities made available by the precedent itself. Jasper as Headstone offers a very different projection from that of Jasper as Pecksniff.

The perception of a parallel between Jasper and Sikes, in particular, becomes coloured by Dickens's performance as the latter in his public reading, thus leading to explorations of Jasper as a portrait of Dickens himself: *Edwin Drood* as the disguised autobiography of its author. The growing awareness of Ellen Ternan's role in Dickens's life has led to a more autobiographical reading of Jasper's attempts to maintain his public image despite his feelings for a younger woman. Later works such as Dan Simmons's *Drood*, and Matthew Pearl's *The Last Dickens*, have accordingly shifted the focus from the work to

---

[30] Lawrence O. Jones, '*Desperate Remedies* and the Victorian Sensation Novel', *Nineteenth-Century Fiction* 20, 1 (June 1965): 35–50, 45.
[31] Collins, *The Decoding of Edwin Drood*, 296.

the author, allowing the mystery of his life to overtake interest in his last novel.[32] Given the anti-climactic lack of a twist in the novel, the personal vicissitudes of Dickens's final years fuel the mystery for these neo-Victorian interpreters of *Edwin Drood*.

THE TRAGICOMEDY OF *EDWIN DROOD*

Let us close by considering two contrasting models for interpreting *Edwin Drood*: *Macbeth* and comedy. The former has been noted before, while the latter has not. The extreme difference between the two models indicates how fluid interpretation of the text has become without a conclusion to define it. To begin with the Scottish play, in an unpublished manuscript Charles E. Carr stressed that '*Macbeth* profoundly influenced *Edwin Drood*.'[33] His case for claiming so lay on three explicit points in the text:

1. The title of chapter 14, 'When Shall These Three Meet Again', is a clear paraphrase of *Macbeth*'s famous opening line.
2. In chapter 10, Crisparkle is said to be 'as confident in the sweetening powers of Cloisterham Weir and a wholesome mind, as Lady Macbeth was hopeless of those of all the seas that roll' (*ED* 10, 80).
3. In chapter 11, the flying waiter's leg is said to be always last to leave the room, 'like Macbeth's leg when accompanying him off the stage with reluctance to the assassination of Duncan' (*ED* 11, 93).

Dickens's homages to Shakespeare have long been noted, but the frequency of the references to *Macbeth* have called attention to further links and encouraged completionists to include additional references to the play.[34] In particular the use of a quotation as a chapter title has proved a gauntlet thrown down, with several completions adopting further *Macbeth* quotations for their own chapters in order to qualify their second half as authentically Dickensian. Garfield takes the prize for persistence with his chapters 26, 'In Thunder Lighting or in Rain', 39 'When the hurlyburly's done', 60 'When the battle's lost and won', and the mischievous 33 'Enter a Porter'. But the references to *Macbeth* in *Edwin Drood* are implicit as well as explicit. Philip Collins notes the thematic parallels of storms, trance-like states, and visions, suggesting that whenever he wrote 'on murder, Dickens was haunted by *Macbeth*'.[35] These moments remind us of the

---

[32] Dan Simmons, *Drood* (London: Quercus, 2009); Matthew Pearl, *The Last Dickens* (London: Vintage, 2009).

[33] Charles E. Carr, *Droodists: Solutions of Charles Dickens's* Mystery of Edwin Drood: *A Critical Survey* (unpublished manuscript, Charles Dickens Museum). The exact date is unknown but internal references date it sometime between 1922 and 1935.

[34] For a longer study of Shakespeare's influence on Dickens, see Valerie Gager, *Shakespeare and Dickens: The Dynamics of Influence* (Cambridge: Cambridge University Press, 1996).

[35] Collins, *The Decoding of Edwin Drood*, 300.

horror of the protagonist's acts, while simultaneously calling for our sympathy with the affliction it causes to the perpetrator. Jasper is, like Macbeth, a man compelled to unnatural murder, killing one supposedly under his protection to further his own aim.

The connections with *Macbeth* then not only suggest a recasting of the tale as a Gothic one, replete with all the generic signatures of crypts, family secrets, damsels in distress, and murderous intent, but as the tragedy of a noble anti-hero. Macbeth's death is simultaneously necessary and to be lamented; Jasper's end, arguably, also seems both just and tragic. While the Scottish king ruminates on 'tomorrow, and tomorrow, and tomorrow', the Kentish choirmaster bemoans '[t]he cramped monotony of [his] existence' (*ED* 2, 11).[36] Both are trapped by fate, rather than masters of their own destiny. Both are haunted by the murder they commit. Their crime *is* their punishment.

The search for a genre to which *Edwin Drood* may be assigned has thus far stretched from whodunit to tragedy, via sensation and autobiography. Varied as they are, they all draw upon the darker side of Dickens. What has consistently been overlooked, and desperately needs to be addressed, is the comedy in *Edwin Drood*. Though Rupert Holmes's musical is decidedly comic, he nonetheless positions this as being in opposition to Dickens's original, which he claims to be 'a very sombre work to be sure'.[37] The spectre of Dickens's death has too easily led us to read *Edwin Drood* in a morbid light, but it was never intended to be his last novel, and our eagerness to read it as such does a disservice to the text. There is a great deal of humour to be explored within it and it is telling that Dickens's contemporaries had no difficulty in appreciating it.

The earliest reviews of *Edwin Drood*, released after the publication of the first instalment, focus on the similarity of Dickens's latest work to his early fiction. Given the five-year hiatus since the last instalment of *Our Mutual Friend*—the longest break between novels in Dickens's career—*The Athenaeum* noted the 'positive pleasure to see once more the green cover in which the world first beheld Mr Pickwick'.[38] Chapter 3's meeting of Rosa and Edwin is not picked apart for dark omens of what is to come, but is seen as a delightful comic passage. For all the subsequent lamentation about *Edwin Drood*'s missing end, it is precisely the lack of further instalments that allows this first review to be so positive in tone. The one-page review pays brief attention to Jasper and far more to Thomas Sapsea and Durdles the stonemason. Subsequent criticism has considered these characters primarily in terms of their role as inadvertent abetters of Jasper's crime. Little to no attention has been given to their comedic role in the text.

When the novel was reviewed again after Dickens's death with only three instalments published, critical attention continued to be paid to the comic characters. A lengthy poetic tribute to Dickens draws attention in its fifth stanza to his last work, citing by

---

[36] William Shakespeare, *Macbeth*, in Gary Taylor, John Jowett, Terri Bourus, and Gabriel Egan, *The New Oxford Shakespeare: The Complete Works, Modern Critical Edition* (Oxford: OUP, 2016), 5.5.18.

[37] Ted Sod, 'A Conversation with Writer/Composer Rupert Holmes', <http://www.broadwayworld.com>, <http://www.broadwayworld.com/article/A-Conversation-with-WriterComposer-Rupert-Holmes-20121017#>, accessed 17 October 2012.

[38] Review of Charles Dickens, *The Mystery of Edwin Drood*, *The Athenaeum*, 2 April 1870, 443.

name Rosa, Canon Septimus Crisparkle, and Luke Honeythunder.[39] Honeythunder has the disadvantage of Sapsea and Durdles in having no immediate connection to the central mystery. He is therefore a character who has been frequently omitted from adaptations and solutions. That Honeythunder, Sapsea, and Durdles were noticed by reviewers at the time, but have been relatively ignored since, forms a key difference in how we read *Edwin Drood* now. On the one hand, such preoccupation among the early critics with the comedic characters is in keeping with the tendency of Dickens's contemporaries to celebrate his earlier work and to lament that his later work 'betray[s] a rather bitter spirit of uncalled-for satire.'[40] On the other hand, if the early critics were too swift to celebrate the comic, later critics have been too swift to dismiss it. Either they have focused on the mystery and the unwritten end, or else in trying to reclaim the surviving fragment as weighty literature they have invariably focused on its tragic elements at the expense of its comic vein.

This is not to say that we should read *Edwin Drood* purely as comedy, with the end reduced to a punchline, nor that any comic moment is somehow less than the tragedy of the main plot. The instances drawn upon throughout this discussion demonstrate the danger of assuming one model alone for interpretative purposes and forcing the whole text to fit that one view. But the emphasis on the plot's end in *Edwin Drood* has eclipsed the comic element in the preceding narrative.

Dickens's novels are less celebrated for their plot than for their characterization and narrative description. Accordingly, it is to these elements, rather than the absent conclusion to the plot, that we should turn our attention in reading *Edwin Drood*. Mrs Billickin, or the Billickin as Dickens terms her, is a marvellous comic creation who suffers for not appearing until the sixth instalment. She receives little mention in criticism and, like Honeythunder, has been cut from all adaptations. Dickens placed Rosa and Miss Twinkleton in her lodgings for a purpose, and that purpose was not to further the plot but to provide a new comic backdrop. Yet even the written solutions, which have to acknowledge all the characters of the first half, have for the most part left the Billickin out. Just as Dickens moves his scene to London, solutionists revert to Cloisterham, taking Rosa back to the cathedral city and the central plot. This is logical if we focus our attention purely on the story's finale, but utterly nonsensical if we consider the plot as a whole.

It is folly to presume that knowing the outcome is equivalent to knowing the second half of the tale. A reader of the serial instalments trying to predict the end of *Great Expectations* based purely upon the first half would no more imagine an entire chapter describing Wopsle's performance of *Hamlet* than a Droodist would be able to anticipate the introduction of the Billickin, based upon the opening five numbers. But Dickens's writing is full of scenes unnecessary to plot, yet wholly necessary to the reader's enjoyment. Comedy, and the resulting scenes which exist purely for their comic purpose, are

---

[39] 'The Late Charles Dickens', *The Period*, 25 June 1870, 84.
[40] 'The Late Charles Dickens', *Illustrated London News*, 18 June 1870, 639.

a fundamental part of the Dickensian experience. We cannot understand *Edwin Drood* properly until we acknowledge and understand this. The tragic tone of the novel needs balance just as much as the subsequent theories of enthusiasts and academics alike can, and should, complement one another. By acknowledging the light as well as the dark, the incidental as well as the fundamental, we can hope to better understand Dickens's final work and its hold on our imagination.

Further Reading

Steven Connor (ed.), *The Mystery of Edwin Drood* (London: Everyman, 1996)

Don Richard Cox, *Charles Dickens's The Mystery of Edwin Drood: An Annotated Bibliography* (New York: AMS Press, 1998)

Wendy S. Jacobson, *The Companion to The Mystery of Edwin Drood* (London: Allen and Unwin, 1986)

David Paroissien (ed.), *The Mystery of Edwin Drood* (London: Penguin, 2002)

CHAPTER 22

'MILESTONES ON THE DOVER ROAD'

Dickens and Travel

MICHAEL HOLLINGTON

WHAT may have been the first significant displacement of Dickens's life away from the dullness of 'Dullborough Town' and the 'cloistered' stuffiness of 'Cloisterham'—two names in his work for Chatham and Rochester, the twin towns in which he grew up—is recorded in *The Uncommercial Traveller* in a thinly disguised piece of autobiography, the account of a stagecoach journey along the Dover Road taken at the age of 10 to join his parents in London in 1822. It is marked by depressing grimness—'[t]here was no other inside passenger, and I consumed my sandwiches in solitude and dreariness, and it rained hard all the way, and I thought life sloppier than I had expected to find it'[1]— so that dullness and stuffiness seem in no way left behind, in a manner we shall find repeated more than once in Dickens's fiction. 'Oh, why are they not driving on! Pray, Pa, do drive on!' sobs Fanny Dorrit at the very end of Part One of *Little Dorrit*,[2] to no avail as far as her father is concerned, for wherever his body goes his mind will remain in the Marshalsea for the rest of his life.

From the frequent mentions in his work of that historic thoroughfare the Dover Road we can gauge the extent of its meaning for Dickens throughout his life. It was the Roman Watling Street, linking Chester via London with the Kent coast, where Julius Caesar first landed in 55 BC. As the main highway to and from the Continent to London it carried in the era of the early Industrial Revolution an exceptional amount of traffic. Eliza Lynn

---

[1] Charles Dickens, *The Dent Uniform Edition of Dickens' Journalism*, ed. Michael Slater and John Drew, 4 vols (London: J. M. Dent, Columbus: Ohio State University Press, 1993–2000). Subsequent references are inserted parenthetically in the text by Dent volume: Title, page. Here, Dent 4: *Uncommercial Traveller* (*UT*), 140.

[2] Charles Dickens, *Little Dorrit*, ed. Harvey Peter Sucksmith (Oxford: Clarendon Press, 1979) I:36, 418. Subsequent references are inserted parenthetically in the text by *LD* Book:chapter, page.

Linton, from whom Dickens bought Gad's Hill Place, records of her childhood there that 'between seventy and eighty coaches passed our house during the day, besides private carriages, specially those of travellers posting to or from Dover,'[3] and there were of course many more travellers on foot. Regiments marched along the Dover Road to embark for India at Gravesend, and sailors 'paid off, rowdy and half-tipsy, made the road really dangerous' at times.[4] Not to mention innumerable tramps, 'ours being a country constantly infested with tramps', Dickens's eldest son recalls. Thus, his reaction on hearing a noise outside Gad's Hill Place 'as if two people were engaged in some violent altercation or quarrel', was that it was merely some 'nomadic gentleman beating his wife up our lane, as was quite the common custom'.[5] It wasn't, in fact—it was Dickens rehearsing to himself his public reading of Bill Sikes's murder of Nancy. He clearly blended in without difficulty into that street 'uproar' on the Dover Road (to remember the last word of *Little Dorrit*) with which he had been familiar since childhood.

Thinking of travellers along the Dover Road in the context of Chaucer's Canterbury pilgrims, it is not difficult, I think, to understand why Dickens tended to imagine this thoroughfare in allegorical terms. The phrase 'the pilgrimage of life', or variants thereof, is a significant one in his work, most notably in the arresting last sentence of chapter 2 of Book 1 of *Little Dorrit* (brilliantly analysed in Jonathan Grossman's book *Charles Dickens's Networks*)[6] which contemplates how, 'journeying by land and journeying by sea, coming and going so strangely, to meet and to act and react on one another, move all we restless travellers through the pilgrimage of life' (*LD* I:2, 26), but earlier in his work, too. *Nicholas Nickleby* had meditated on the moment of Nicholas's waking at Dotheboys Hall to see outside 'the first beam of the sun, which lights grim care and stern reality on their daily pilgrimage through the world'.[7] Even without such explicit allegorical overtones, the word 'pilgrimage' is frequent in Dickens, used to mean, simply, 'travel', in comic contexts just as much as in serious ones, as for instance when Sam Weller goes to find the coward Winkle hiding from the prospect of a duel, and 'set[s] forth on his pilgrimage with a light heart'.[8]

From these and other references (the subtitle of *Oliver Twist*, for instance, or the wanderings of Nell and her grandfather in *The Old Curiosity Shop*) it is easy to see the hold that Bunyan's *Pilgrim's Progress* exercised on Dickens's creative mind. Besides 'pilgrim' and 'pilgrimage', 'progress' also figures prominently in his work to delineate the course of individual lives. Hogarth can be added to Bunyan here, of course, as a determining source, and from the very start of his writing career, in *Sketches by Boz* (*SB*), Dickens takes pains to scrutinize the external signs of everything about him, observing

---

[3] William R. Hughes, *A Week's Tramp in Dickens-Land* (London: Chapman and Hall, 1892), 192.
[4] Ibid., 192.
[5] Charles Dickens, *Interviews and Recollections*, ed. Philip Collins. 2 vols (London: Macmillan/Palgrave, 1981), 1:135.
[6] Jonathan Grossman, *Charles Dickens's Networks* (Oxford: Oxford University Press, 2012), 156.
[7] Charles Dickens, *Nicholas Nickleby*, ed. Paul Schlicke, Oxford World's Classics (Oxford: Oxford University Press, 2009), 13, 146.
[8] Charles Dickens, *Pickwick Papers*, ed. James Kinsley (Oxford: Clarendon Press, 1986), 36, 583.

the marks of upward or downward mobility inscribed on the surface of things in the vast commodity market that surrounded him as he walked the streets of the metropolis. No wonder, as Boz remarks in 'Shops and their Tenants' in his first book, that 'one of our principal amusements is to watch the gradual progress—the rise or fall—of particular shops' (Dent 1: *SB* 61).

Indeed, as an inveterate walker himself, Dickens may often have been reminded of the opening words of Bunyan's allegory—'as I walked through the wilderness of this world'[9]—and the bumpy course of Christian's 'progress' may have been prefigured for his imagination in the ups and downs of the Dover Road. *David Copperfield* is a novel particularly rich in allegorical 'pilgrimages', including that of David as he escapes from Murdstone and Grinby's in London and treks down to Dover. Robbed at the outset of all his possessions, there is an echo of the Book of Job ('naked came I out of my mother's womb, and naked will I return thither')[10] as he sets out on the path of rebirth at Dover, starting from 'Greenwich, which I had understood was on the Dover Road: taking very little more out of the world, towards the retreat of my aunt, Miss Betsey, than I had brought into it, on the night when my arrival gave her so much umbrage'.[11] But David's trials and tribulations along the way are recapitulated in a later work, and a more genteel 'pilgrimage' along the same route, that of the newly rich William Dorrit in *Little Dorrit*, who is 'way-laid at Dartford, pillaged at Gravesend, rifled at Rochester, fleeced at Sittingbourne, and sacked at Canterbury' (*LD* I:18, 614). His spring progress through the Kent landscape is marked by a distinct rhythm of 'rising and falling to a regular measure' as he passes over Shooter's Hill, Gad's Hill, Strood Hill, and so on.

Yet however hard the process of 'progress', all these examples of travel and movement considered thus far have an essentially teleological core—they are about finding or achieving a purpose. Living in Kent as a child, and, much later at Gadshill, as a hugely successful novelist, Dickens was aware that most people passed through the county on their way somewhere else: '[t]here's mile-stones on the Dover road' (*LD* I:23, 263), pronounces the crazed Mr F's Aunt in *Little Dorrit*. But one would be thoroughly mistaken if one studied the theme of movement in Dickens only in this context—there is another side altogether, in which the compulsion to be 'on the move' has no external motive and no purpose beyond itself, to which we must now turn.

'My walking is of two kinds', Dickens writes in 'Shy Neighbourhoods' in *The Uncommercial Traveller*, 'one, straight on end to a definite goal at a round pace; one, objectless, loitering, and purely vagabond. In the latter state, no gipsy on earth is a greater vagabond than myself; it is so natural to me and strong with me, that I think I must be the descendant, at no great distance, of some irreclaimable tramp' (Dent 4: *UT* 119). In recent years, as the result of the frequent application to the novelist of the work of Walter

---

[9] John Bunyan, *The Pilgrim's Progress*, ed. Susan Rattiner (Mineola, NY: Dover Thrift Editions, 2003), 13.

[10] *The Book of Job*, I, xxi. <http://www.kingjamesbibleonline.org/Job>.

[11] Charles Dickens, *David Copperfield*, ed. Nina Burgis (Oxford: Clarendon Press, 1981), 12, 153. Subsequent references are inserted parenthetically in the text by *DC* chapter, page.

Benjamin (a Dickens enthusiast, via his friend Adorno), this latter form of motion has commonly been referred to as *flânerie*, and of course it is chiefly relevant to the London years and the city novels of Dickens. These, by the way, like Anna and Samuel Carter Hall (the latter said to be the original model for Pecksniff) in their 1859 *Book of the Thames, from its Rise to its Fall*, often take the Thames rather than the Dover Road as their central allegory, articulating the passage of human life from the innocence of childhood upstream through the 'deadly sewer' it becomes in the City of London in *Little Dorrit*, where adult corruption thrives, and from thence on out to the sea at Gravesend, a name whose symbolic overtones Dickens never failed to exploit.

That he can reasonably be thought of as a *flâneur*—indeed, may have thought of himself as one, since his friend Albert Smith, with whom he often went out walking on the streets of London, was one of the major importers of the term from Paris—is suggested by a sentence from 'Shops and their Tenants'. 'What inexhaustible food for speculation do the streets of London afford!' (Dent 1: *SB* 61). Here the mental activity of 'speculation', as practised by *flâneurs*, is contrasted with the brain-dead impassivity and indifference of so many city-dwellers: 'we have not the slightest commiseration for the man who can take up his hat and stick, and walk from Covent Garden to St Paul's Churchyard, and back into the bargain, without deriving some amusement—we had almost said instruction—from his perambulation,' and Boz proceeds to bring home his point by providing as if in a kind of mirror a thumbnail *flâneurial* sketch of such people. They are distinguished both from those who move with a purpose—'other people brush quickly by you, steadily plodding on to business, or cheerfully running after pleasure', and from the true *flâneur*, paradoxically busy with 'speculation'—bearing as they do the visible 'marks of weakness, marks of woe' of urban *anomie* that Blake noted in London: '[t]hese men linger listlessly past, looking as happy and animated as a policeman on duty' (Dent 1: *SB* 61).

There are a number of misconceptions abroad about 'Dickens the *flâneur*'—the idea, for instance, that the term can only be used to characterize the gentleman dandy, when in Paris it was equally the favourite pastime of the penniless bohemian or 'vagabond', a term which Dickens often uses of himself when in *flâneurial* mode. It can in fact be used not only to think about both dandyism and vagabondage in Dickens, but also about the writer's very methods of composition, as two familiar passages in the letters suggest. The first conveys how vital it was for Dickens to be *in motion* on busy urban streets in order to compose his books by unveiling the extent of his sufferings in Lausanne, where there is an 'absence of streets and numbers of figures': 'the toil and labour of writing, day after day, without that magic lantern, is IMMENSE!!';[12] and the second describes being 'in a dishevelled state of mind' (a vagabond again, evidently) on the streets of Paris in the early stages of writing *Little Dorrit*: 'motes of new books in the dirty air, miseries of older growth threatening to close upon me'.[13] Chance glimpses and encounters on the streets,

---

[12] Charles Dickens, *The Letters of Charles Dickens*, ed. Madeline House, Graham Storey, et al., Pilgrim/British Academy Edition, 12 vols (Oxford: Clarendon Press, 1965–2002). Subsequent citations: *PLets* followed by volume: page range, page. Here 4:612–14, 612.

[13] *PLets* 7:523.

it would seem, were the genesis of some the later plastic realizations of human character that inhabit Dickens's novels. His novels are not only about being 'on the road', they were in an important sense written 'on the road'.

But to turn back to Bunyan and allegory, perhaps their most important legacy to Dickens's thinking about travel is contained in the dream framework of *Pilgrim's Progress*. 'I lighted on a certain place where was a den', that opening sentence continues, 'and laid me down in that place to sleep: and as I slept, I dreamed a dream. I dreamed, and behold, I saw a man clothed with rags, standing in a certain place, with his face from his own house, a book in his hand, and a great burden upon his back.'[14] This is Christian, about to set forth on his tramping, in a passage which bequeaths to so many of Dickens's actual and imagined journeys the status of dream. An entire chapter in *Pictures from Italy*, for instance, devoted to Venice, is entitled 'An Italian Dream'. And in another of the explicitly designated 'pilgrimages' in *David Copperfield*, that which takes David to Italy at the end of the book after the loss of Dora, Emily, and Steerforth, there is again unmistakable reference to Bunyan—'I roamed from place to place, carrying my burden with me everywhere'—in combination with a revisiting of Dickens's own impressions of Venice and Genoa and elsewhere as David sees himself 'passing on among the novelties of foreign towns, palaces, cathedrals, temples, pictures, castles, tombs, fantastic streets— the old abiding places of History and Fancy—as a dreamer might' (*DC* 58, 696; 697).

These then are some of the contexts I find useful for thinking about Dickens's travel writing, in particular the two central texts *American Notes* and *Pictures from Italy*. A particular word drawn from the lexis of *flânerie* that is often used in connection with the journeys they describe is 'strolling', with its connotations of theatrical itinerancy (*American Notes*, for instance, mentions Le Sage's 'strolling player' as a traveller whose company can be enjoyed). *Pictures from Italy*, indeed, describes the whole year in Genoa as one in which the head of the family proposes 'to stroll about, wherever his restless humour carried him',[15] and uses the word frequently, of Genoa, Modena, and Florence. So there is a very real sense in which these books are about '*flânerie* on tour'.

Yet the other, more teleological aspect of Dickens in motion is also evident. *American Notes*, indeed, contains a fascinating moment of autobiography that seems to confirm the overall hypothesis advanced here, that from childhood onwards Dickens thought in quasi-allegorical terms about life as a 'progress' along roads and paths (exemplified by the Dover Road) towards death. On this occasion, it is a path on water that is the focus, in what is almost a kind of déjà vu experience, described during the return voyage to England: 'I recollect when I was a very young child having a fancy that the reflection of the moon in water was a path to Heaven, trodden by the spirits of good people on their way to God; and this old feeling often came over me again, when I watched it on

---

[14] Bunyan, *The Pilgrim's Progress*, 61.

[15] Charles Dickens, *Pictures from Italy*, in *American Notes and Pictures from Italy*, introd. Sacheverell Sitwell, New Oxford Illustrated Dickens (London: Oxford University Press, 1957), 'Going Through France', 262. Subsequent references to *Pictures from Italy* are inserted parenthetically in the text by *PI* chapter title, page.

a tranquil night at sea.'[16] One can argue, I think, that the passage unlocks some central motifs of the book—in particular, perhaps, its preoccupation with death.

For from the very start of *American Notes* Dickens seems to enter a realm of death—even before going on board the ship that is to take him from Liverpool to Boston, perhaps, for at the dinner the night before there is an unspoken embargo on mentioning the impending journey 'such as may be supposed to prevail between delicate-minded turnkeys, and a sensitive prisoner who is to be hanged next morning'. Once on board the *Britannia* he encounters a long narrow apartment 'not unlike a gigantic hearse', and later sleeps in berths 'than which nothing smaller for sleeping in was ever made except coffins' (*AN* I:1, 14; 10; 11).

In the first of many critical confrontations with American puritanism, Dickens hears a preacher in Boston who clearly borrows his allegorical thinking from Bunyan to construct a land/sea contrast between alternative paths to Heaven or hell, pitting those who come '[f]rom the dreary, blighted wilderness of Iniquity, whose only crop is Death' against those who 'are going—with a fair wind,—all taut and trim, steering direct for Heaven in its glory, where there are no storms and foul weather' (*AN* I:3, 69; 68). At Boston, too, he encounters for the first time the regular funereal atmosphere of American meals—'at every supper, at least two mighty bowls of hot stewed oysters, in any one of which a half-grown Duke of Clarence might be smothered easily' (*AN* I:3, 70)—the denunciation of which grows in intensity as he travels west. On board *The Messenger* on the Ohio river between Pittsburgh and Cincinnati, he satirizes both the food itself (corn-bread is 'almost as good for the digestion as a kneaded pin-cushion') and the company at table: '[u]ndertakers on duty would be sprightly beside them; and a collation of funeral baked-meats, in comparison with these meals, would be a sparkling festivity' (*AN* II:3, 176). Again on the Ohio, but on a subsequent boat, Puritan eating rituals still prevail: '[w]e fed at the same times, on the same kind of viands, in the same dull manner, and with the same observances ... I seriously believe the recollection of these funeral feasts will be a waking nightmare to me all my life' (*AN* II:4, 189).

Thus the structure of *American Notes* can be compared to that of a harrowing of hell. It is a journey towards the emptiness of the prairies—'lonely and wild, but oppressive in its barren monotony' (*AN* II:5, 202)—that involves a crossing of the Mississippi as a kind of Styx, especially at its confluence with the Ohio, where it is 'a breeding-place of fever, ague, and death' (*AN* II:4, 190). The Puritanism that Dickens encounters everywhere—at its sternest at his last port of call before embarking on the return journey, among the Shakers—promotes a paradigm of the trajectory of human life as a journey through a 'vale of tears'. Their view of life is one that 'would strip life of its healthful graces, rob youth of its innocent pleasures, pluck from maturity and age their pleasant ornaments, and make existence but a narrow path towards the grave' (*AN* II:7, 238)—not, manifestly, a moonlight path across water to Heaven.

---

[16] Charles Dickens, *American Notes*, ed. Patricia Ingham (London: Penguin Books, 2000), II:8, 247. Subsequent references are inserted parenthetically in the text by *AN* volume:chapter, page.

For all that, *American Notes* is a book that glories in the sheer thrill of motion, and not only during the *nostos* to England, when the 'splendid' ship on which they sail is seen to ride 'at a furious pace upon the waves, which filled one with an indescribable sense of pride and exultation' (*AN* II:8, 246). Very early on in his travels, arriving in New York on another ship, Dickens passes 'a madhouse' and observes 'how the lunatics flung up their caps, and roared in sympathy with the headlong engine and the driving tide' (*AN* I:5, 89). The city itself is represented as a dynamic vortex of energy constituted in the perpetual motion created by its transport system—'steam ferry-boats', for instance, 'laden with people, coaches, horses, waggons, baskets, boxes: crossed and recrossed by other ferry-boats: all travelling to and fro: and never idle' (*AN* I:5, 89). And although Dickens is (rightly) seen as an intensely visual writer, it is often through sound that he chooses to represent the ceaseless vitality of modern cities in motion, as again in New York, where '[t]he city's hum and buzz, the clinking of capstans, the ringing of bells, the barking of dogs, the clattering of wheels, tingled in the listening ear' (*AN* I:5, 89).

Like *American Notes*, *Pictures from Italy* invokes memories of childhood, this time quite pointedly of deceptive images of the country in which Dickens would spend an entire year in 1844–5 that were first presented him in schoolbooks. Visiting the Leaning Tower of Pisa, he discovers how profoundly he had been cheated in the classroom 'by Mr. Harris, Bookseller, at the corner of St. Paul's Churchyard, London', who had led him to imagine a structure of colossal height: '*His* Tower was a fiction, but this was a reality—and, by comparison, a short reality' (*PI* 'To Rome by Pisa and Siena', 357).

This primary misconception generates a whole sequence of similar mistakes in a book that explores the hazards of interpretation of unfamiliar sights and sounds to which all travellers are prone. Indeed, the whole book can be seen as an exploration of the folly of judging from first impressions. The progress it charts is one that takes the writer from initial revulsion at the sights and sounds of Italy all the way to virtually unconditional love and acceptance of them, as an early passage confides: 'I little thought, that day, that I should ever come to have an attachment for the very stones in the streets of Genoa, and to look back upon the city with affection as connected with many hours of happiness and quiet' (*PI* 'Avignon to Genoa', 283).

But the individual mistakes begin even before Dickens reaches Italy—in Lyon Cathedral, where he imagines a puppet in the mechanical clock to be Satan: ' "Pardon Monsieur," said the Sacristan, with a polite motion of his hand ... "The Angel Gabriel!" '—and continue throughout his time in Italy, beginning perhaps first in Albaro, where he attends a festival in honour of the Virgin Mary at which young men festoon themselves with wreaths of vine-leaves: '[i]t looked very odd and pretty. Though I am bound to confess (not knowing of the festa at that time), that I thought, and was quite satisfied, they wore them as horses do—to keep the flies off' (*PI* 'Lyons', 271; 'Genoa and its Neighbourhood', 287).

A further instance of misapprehension occurs during an impromptu overnight stop at an inn in Stradella in November 1844, when Dickens was en route alone, bound eventually for England and a reading of *The Chimes* to his friends. Here we glimpse how closely this focus on perception and interpretation is linked to cardinal features of

Dickens's imagination, as the narrator describes a yard in which coaches and wagons and firewood and fowls are jumbled together, 'so that you didn't know, and couldn't have taken your oath, which was a fowl and which was a cart' (*PI* 'To Parma, Modena, and Bologna', 315). The confusion of persons and things, the animate and the inanimate, is of course ubiquitous in Dickens, becoming here a technique for the comic examination of how tourists regularly get hold of the wrong end of the stick about what they see and experience. Thus, in apothecary's shops in Genoa regular groups of loungers are to be found, '[s]o still and quiet, that either you don't see them in the darkened shop, or mistake them—as I did one ghostly man in bottle-green, one day, with a hat like a stopper—for Horse Medicine' (*PI* 'Genoa and its Neighbourhood', 297).

We are at no great distance here from the famous Dickens 'animism', the habit of perceiving vitality in all things, deployed here fancifully on numerous occasions to convey the freshness and strangeness of the sights and impressions that travellers seek to expose themselves to. This is true, not only of the gigantic fleas at the Villa Bagnarello in Albaro—themselves animate of course, but here endowed with such fantastic power and energy 'that I daily expect to see the carriage going off bodily, drawn by myriads of industrious fleas in harness', but of the twin leaning towers in Bologna 'inclining cross-wise as if they were bowing stiffly to each other', or of the house of the Capulets in Verona, apparently as committed as ever to the feud that consumed its former inhabitants: 'a distrustful jealous-looking house as one would desire to see' (*PI* 'Genoa and its Neighbourhood', 286; 'Through Bologna and Ferrara', 324; 'By Verona, Mantua, and Milan ...', 337).

We can perhaps see, even in these humorous hyperboles, something of the fundamental ambivalence that surrounds the representation of motion in Dickens. From physical and mental perspectives alike, it involves both exhilaration and torture. Moreover, it is only at certain rare moments in Dickens's writing about travel that actual progress and change are achieved. On many occasions, what is encountered is not difference but sameness. In America, this often takes the form of inferior imitation—a black coachman in Virginia, for instance, is seen as 'faintly shadowing forth a kind of insane imitation of an English coachman' (*AN* II:1, 148)—or at best, mere reproduction of an original at home. Thus the 'park or common in the middle of the town' in which Yale University is situated produces an effect 'very like that of an old cathedral yard in England' (*AN* I:5, 87), and in the 'beautiful country' of rural Ohio, 'the farms are neatly kept, and ... one might be travelling just now in Kent' (*AN* II:6, 208). Likewise in Italy, arriving within sight of Rome, Dickens confesses in mock horrified tones that 'it looked like—I am half afraid to write the word—like LONDON!!!', and later, in St Peter's: 'I felt no very strong emotion. I have been infinitely more affected in many English cathedrals when the organ has been playing, and in many English country churches when the congregation have been singing' (*PI* 'To Rome by Pisa and Siena', 364; 'Rome', 366).

Turning now to the novels, I want first to offer a thumbnail sketch of their treatment of the master theme of motion through Dickens's entire career, dividing them into three categories, before closing with a brief look at how it still figures centrally in his last unfinished book. The first group—books like *Pickwick Papers*, *Nicholas Nickleby*, *The Old*

Curiosity Shop, Martin Chuzzlewit—owe much to the linear structure of the picaresque, bearing clear resemblance to the tradition embodied in Le Sage, Fielding, and Smollett, whose writings Dickens devoured as a child. The second group, which includes some of the works that are nowadays regarded as Dickens's finest achievements—*Bleak House, Little Dorrit, Our Mutual Friend*—gives emphasis to a condition of stasis that prevails in a society governed by ossified legal and political practices, but does so from a viewpoint that insists on the crying need for movement and change. (It is interesting that the first half of the only novel of these three to provide extended treatment of a period 'on the road', closes with Fanny's cry for the coach to drive on quoted at the beginning of this chapter, as if in ironic echo of the implied viewpoint of all three.) And the third—inaugurated most obviously with *A Tale of Two Cities*, but containing also *Great Expectations* and *The Mystery of Edwin Drood*—seems to adopt a circular pattern of travel between two poles, of which London is a constant: London and Paris, London and Rochester, London and the Kent marsh country. Because this group also emphasizes stasis, as if all the toing and froing were pointless, it is perhaps only a sub-group of the second, for as in *Little Dorrit*, the escape from one prison seems to lead simply to another.

In addition to these changing deep structural linear patterns, almost every novel at all stages of his career seems to contain a hastily improvised flight, usually to escape from one form of painful or unsatisfactory situation in the hope of finding a better. Oliver fleeing the Sowerberry household could be said to initiate the series, which nonetheless contains some notable later examples—Nell's flight, or Edith Dombey's, or David's from Murdstone and Grinby. Once again, London is a common denominator of these motifs, though the flights are as often away from it as towards it. One may seek to escape the unfeeling cruelty and indifference of the city in order to find some more secure resting place and sense of identity, as David does, or one may in fact be in search of the very anonymity that the metropolis provides. This is the case when Oliver is 'on the road', at first with no particular goal in mind, until he comes upon a milestone and reads the word 'London'—shades of Mr F's Aunt here—and is reminded of the oral testimony of the old men in the workhouse, that 'no lad of spirit need want in London'.[17]

At a much later point in his career, we find Dickens still ringing changes on this leitmotif. Betty Higden in *Our Mutual Friend* also feels she has 'got to light out for the Territory',[18] as it were, in order to escape the workhouse; she wishes to die (as Tolstoy did) 'on the road'. And finally there is Rosa Bud, once more seeking the anonymity of the city in order to escape the attentions of Jasper in the cramping, stultifying world allegorized in the name Cloisterham.

And then there is the theme of emigration, forced or unforced. It has its joyously comic versions, in the case of Micawber, who makes good in Australia and returns in triumph. Again, the *hie/da* structure is prominent, from the interpolated tale of 'The Convict's

---

[17] Charles Dickens, *Oliver Twist*, ed. Kathleen Tillotson (Oxford: Clarendon Press, 1966), 8, 44.
[18] Mark Twain, *The Adventures of Huckleberry Finn* (Harmondsworth: Penguin, 1985), 369.

Return' in *Pickwick Papers* onwards, and the 'fulcrum' on which Dickens constructed *Great Expectations*, Magwitch's return from Australia to confront the horrified Pip with his real benefactor, is a fine example of the principle of toing and froing that Dickens adopts in his late novels as a cardinal device (Arthur Clennam and John Harmon offer related figures of return from long absences in faraway places). It is capable of generating multiple ironies, including here the paradoxical one that Pip's real 'progress' depends on the confounding of his imaginary one. Thus the relatively simple linearity of the earlier fictions gets more and more complicated in the later work—to get to his goal, for instance, John Harmon has to construct an elaborate new identity, and take part in an entire fictional *Bildungsroman* whose essential focus is Bella. 'And so a man climbs to the top of the tree... only to see that there's no look-out when he's up there!' complains Mr Venus in *Our Mutual Friend*.[19] His comic expression of unrequited love might be used as a leitmotif (originating, not implausibly, in the woes of Dickens's relationship with Ellen Ternan) of what has happened to the idea of 'progress' in the last novels.

Thus the brilliant opening scene of *The Mystery of Edwin Drood* marks an advance on all the previous novel openings after *Dombey and Son* in that we and the protagonist *simply do not know where we are*. London, Blunderstone, Coketown, Marseille, the Kent Marshes, Shooter's Hill: these are all places from whence 'progress' is at least theoretically possible. But how can you get anywhere from a place that is a conundrum hybrid of English cathedral town, Indian palace and parade-ground, and rusty bedpost? When it eventually becomes clear that the real 'objective correlative' of the opening hallucination is an opium den, we are reminded with sharp irony of the 'den' where Christian dreams his dream at the opening of *Pilgrim's Progress*.

Notably, allusion to pilgrimage, allegorical and literal, arising out of Rochester/Cloisterham's situation on the Dover Road, is as prominent as ever. The former mode is recapitulated in the recurrent formula of *Little Dorrit* and *Nicholas Nickleby* in the description of Edwin's father, like Rosa's before him, having gone 'the silent road into which all earthly pilgrimages merge'.[20] The latter is emphasized through constant reference to the immense history of the thoroughfare ('[t]ime was when travel-stained pilgrims rode in clattering parties through the city's welcome shades') and constant contemporary echoes, such as Neville's walking tour (one of several instances in the novel of attempts to control violent passion by channelling it into physical exercise), on which he is resolved to '[t]ravel like a pilgrim, with wallet and staff' (*ED* 19, 168; 14, 123).

Indeed, there are not many characters in the book who do not in some way or another articulate the theme of travel. Concentrating on the lower end of the social scale for a moment, we can mention both 'Deputy', who gets his name from working as a man-servant at the Traveller's Twopenny, and Durdles, who both provides 'Deputy' with an ironic goal in life by turning his vicious stone-throwing tendencies to use, and amusingly

---

[19] Charles Dickens, *Our Mutual Friend*, ed. Michael Cotsell, Oxford World's Classics (Oxford: Oxford University Press, 1998), I:7, 84.

[20] Charles Dickens, *The Mystery of Edwin Drood*, ed. Margaret Cardwell (Oxford: Clarendon Press, 1972), 9, 63. Subsequent references are inserted parenthetically in the text by *ED* chapter, page.

quotes catechism to convey the tenacious hold of 'Tombatism' on his movements, as happens if '[y]ou get among them Tombs afore it's well light on a winter morning, and keep on, as the Catechism says, a walking in the same all the days of your life' (*ED* 4, 30). Not surprisingly, then, in this quasi-allegorical context, his workshop is inhabited by journeymen who appear as 'mechanical figures emblematical of Time and Death' (*ED* 4, 29).

But the metaphor of journeying in the novel is centred on the figure of John Jasper. To stoke up violent envy in Neville Landless—and, in the process, to express and project his own—he presents his nephew Edwin's journey through life as an unproblematic linear progress, consciously or unconsciously quoting the ending of Milton's *Paradise Lost*: 'the world is all before him where to choose'. 'A life of stirring work and interest, a life of change and excitement, a life of domestic ease and love!', he exclaims, implicitly contrasting it with his own, another progress to the top of the tree and no look-out (*ED* 8, 58). Later, to the Princess Puffer, he will describe his path to the presumed murder that is its climax as 'a difficult and dangerous journey ... a hazardous and perilous journey, over abysses where a slip would be destruction' (*ED* 23, 207).

That passage occurs in the very last chapter of the novel, at which Dickens was at work on the day before he died. In a remarkable coincidence, its title—'The Dawn Again'—echoes that of the very first chapter, 'The Dawn'. We are back in the foul opium den, from whence Jasper returns again to Cloisterham to play the organ in the evening. Circularity reigns—Cloisterham to London and back again—as Jasper's life makes no progress. Likewise, in Forster's account of Dickens's collapse at dinner on that same day, 8 June, there is an extraordinary moment that itself takes us right back in circular fashion to the origins of his preoccupation with travel and movement. As they sat down to eat, Dickens told his sister-in-law Georgina Hogarth that he had been feeling very ill for the past hour: 'these were the only really coherent words uttered by him', Forster writes. There followed some fragments of disconnected speech, including a statement 'of his own intention to go immediately to London'.[21] He then stood up, but fell to the ground. Motion and unfulfilled 'progress' along the Dover Road at the last.

Further Reading

A few passages in this chapter rework ideas and phrases in two previously published essays of mine in *Unsettling Dickens: Process, Progress and Change*, ed. Christine Huguet, listed below. They are the Foreword 'On the Road' (13–18) and 'An Ecstasy of Impatience' (101–9), and can be regarded as companion pieces to the present chapter.

Rosemary Bodenheimer, *Knowing Dickens* (Ithaca, NY: Cornell University Press, 2007)

Michael Hollington, 'Dickens the Flaneur', *The Dickensian* 77, 2 (Summer 1981): 71–87

Michael Hollington and Francesca Orestano (eds), *Dickens and Italy*: Pictures from Italy *and* Little Dorrit (Newcastle-upon-Tyne: Cambridge Scholars Publishing, 2009)

---

[21] John Forster, *The Life of Charles Dickens*, ed. J. W. T. Ley (London: Cecil Palmer, 1928), 852.

Michael Hollington, John Jordan, and Catherine Waters (eds), *Imagining Italy: Victorian Writers and Travellers* (Newcastle-upon-Tyne: Cambridge Scholars Publishing, 2010)

Christine Huguet (ed.), *Unsettling Dickens: Process, Progress, and Change* (Paris: Sagittaire, 2016)

Ruth Livesey, *Writing the Stage Coach Nation: Locality on the Move in Nineteenth-Century British Literature* (Oxford: Oxford University Press, 2016)

Charlotte Mathieson, *Mobility in the Victorian Novel: Placing the Nation* (London: Palgrave Macmillan, 2015)

Nathalie Vanfasse, *La Plume et la route: Charles Dickens, écrivain-voyageur* (Aix-Marseille: Presses Universitaires de Provence, 2017)

Stefan Welz and Elmar Schenkel (eds), *Dickens on the Move: Travels and Transformations* (Frankfurt am Main: Peter Lang, 2014)

CHAPTER 23

JOURNALISM AND CORRESPONDENCE

HAZEL MACKENZIE

'THE amount of detail which there is in them is something amazing,—to an ordinary writer something incredible'—this Walter Bagehot writes of Dickens in his well-known dissection of London's 'special correspondent for posterity'.[1] Abundance is intrinsic to Dickens's genius in Bagehot's estimation. It was this profusion of detail in his writing, this talent and appetite for observation, that made him the ideal correspondent for the modern city in all its fragmented glory, not only in his familiar and beloved novels but also in the wealth of other writing that poured from his pen throughout his career. At the same time, it is this abundance—in detail and in output—that has allowed much of this writing to remain under-appreciated even today. Digital technology is set to change that, allowing scholars to engage fully with the abundance that Bagehot so rightly lauded.

Recognition of the significance of Dickens as correspondent both in the public and private spheres is long established among Dickensians. However, the impracticalities of connecting with his non-novelistic writings in a substantive way have meant that beyond a few well-known canonical texts much of this material remains relatively neglected. Digitization has opened up the field, widening access and allowing for concrete and meaningful analysis. James Mussell has written of how 'the increased visibility of nineteenth-century newspapers and periodicals within the emerging digital archive can return the press to its central position in nineteenth-century print culture'.[2] Similarly, digital archives grant scholars the means to appreciate the extraordinary range and wealth of Dickens's writing in different forms, as well as the tools to engage with that writing. Recent projects such as the University of Buckingham's *Dickens Journals Online* and the Dickens Fellowship's *Charles Dickens Letters Project*, as well as the online

---

[1] Walter Bagehot, 'Charles Dickens', in Richard Holt Hutton and Walter Bagehot (eds), *Literary Studies by the Late Walter Bagehot* (London: Longman, Green & Co., 1905), 2:184–220, 194, 197.

[2] James Mussell, *The Nineteenth-Century Press in the Digital Age* (Houndmills: Palgrave Macmillan, 2012), 5.

Pilgrim edition of Dickens's letters and work by the British Newspaper Archive, Gale Cengage, Project Gutenberg, and the Internet Archive, have revolutionized the ways in which readers can interact with these materials. The result is the emergence of a more complex, more multifarious Dickens.

In recent years the orthodox author-centred narrative of Dickens's progression from reporter and sketch artist to mature journalist, editor, and publisher established in the mid- to late twentieth century has been challenged. The collaborative nature of both the earlier and later enterprises, previously subsumed under the 'Charles Dickens' brand, has been demonstrated as have the ambiguities of authorial identity implied by Dickens's negotiation of the roles of journalist, novelist, and editor. Digitization enables the revision to go further, revealing new information as to subject matter, style, trends in editorial policy, and patterns of contribution. It can help to uncover numerous previously unknown contributors and expose editorial choices that shift previous understandings of Dickens's role as editor. In providing readier access to full contents, it derails the tendency towards the canonization of certain articles and letters and the neglect of others, producing a more nuanced contextualization of both canonical and lesser-known texts based upon quantifiable data on genre and subject in both a given year and across the journal's run as a whole. In other words, digitization opens up possibilities for a more intricate consideration of Dickens's rich and profuse output (journalistic and otherwise) and for his varied and diverse engagements with the periodical press—one that destabilizes traditional myths (often self-fashioned) and acknowledges the changeable and sometimes contradictory nature of his fulfilment of these roles.

Percy Fitzgerald, journalist, biographer, and sometime Dickens protégé, wrote of Dickens's magazines *Household Words* (1850-9) and *All the Year Round* (1859-95) that 'without these volumes no one can have an idea of his true character and what he did in his life'.[3] Yet it was not until the second half of the twentieth century that any serious attempt to recover these volumes from the dusty shelves of the archive took place with the pioneering work of Anne Lohrli and Ella Ann Oppenlander. Their comprehensive cataloguing of all currently available information on the journals' content, authorship, and contributor payments provided a strong basis for further scholarship.[4] Perhaps even more significant was the appearance of the *Dent Uniform Edition of Dickens's Journalism* (1994-2000), edited by Michael Slater and John Drew, which contained in four volumes Dickens's journalism from his early sketches to his later essays.[5] Also critical, both to the study of Dickens's career as a journalist and editor and to our appreciation of his skill as a correspondent, was the publication of the Pilgrim Edition

---

[3] Percy Fitzgerald, *Memories of Charles Dickens: With an Account of 'Household Words' and 'All the Year Round' and the Contributors Thereto* (London: Simpkin, Marshall, Hamilton, Kent & Co., 1913), 206.

[4] Anne Lohrli, *Household Words: A Weekly Journal, 1850–1859. Conducted by Charles Dickens* (Toronto: University of Toronto Press, 1973); Ella Ann Oppenlander, *Dickens's All the Year Round: Descriptive Index and Contributor List* (New York: Whitston Publishing Company, 1984).

[5] Charles Dickens, *The Dent Uniform Edition of Dickens' Journalism*, ed. Michael Slater and John Drew, 4 vols (London: J. M. Dent, Columbus: Ohio State University Press, 1993–2000).

of Charles Dickens's *Letters* (1965–2002), which made available some 15,000 surviving letters in its 12 volumes.[6]

In opening up the archive, however, such works could only go so far. The print publication of Dickens's letters was a significant step forward, but the quantity of material was an obstacle to comprehensive study. And, as Michael Slater himself notes, the Dent edition could only go so far in contextualizing the journalism it presented and could do little to illuminate Dickens's role as an editor.[7] The work of Lohrli and Oppenlander in this respect was more productive but in attempting to generate interest in this forgotten area they followed in Fitzgerald's footsteps in presenting the journals as a window into Dickens's character. '[M]ore and more his theme seemed to be himself', writes Oppenlander. The journals are presented as a reflection of that self rather than as a complex collaborative enterprise: 'His imagination for contriving subjects was boundless, but his time limited, so he farmed out his ideas.'[8] Dickens's styling of himself as Conductor, the larger-than-life impresario from whom all took their direction, was seemingly taken at face value. Similarly, early studies of *Sketches by Boz* declared their intention of doing 'little by way of comparing Dickens to his contemporaries' or only sought comparisons among such exemplars as Pierce Egan and Thomas Hood rather than examining the sketches' original newspaper and periodical contexts.[9]

Nonetheless, these monumental works of archival research generated new interest in studying Dickens beyond his novels and this author-centred narrative has been increasingly challenged from a number of different perspectives as a more detailed understanding of Dickens's self-fashioning and the intrinsically intertextual and collaborative nature of the periodical press have emerged. As Robert Patten notes, 'Dickens not only discovered the vocation of authorship but also retrospectively wrote up the story of that discovery.' For Patten, Dickens's successful creation of his authorial persona speaks to his imaginative genius, but contradicts much of Dickens's 'lived experience' as a writer.[10] In his view, the notion of Dickens's wielding the tyrant-like control over his texts that Oppenlander and others propagated is only one of many representations of himself as editor and writer that Dickens crafted.[11] Patten argues that the evidence points to numerous 'conflicting ways in which Dickens imagined himself as playwright, journalist, editor, author, and novelist'.[12] It is the critics who have subsequently attached themselves

---

[6] Charles Dickens, *The Letters of Charles Dickens*, ed. Madeline House, Graham Storey, et al., Pilgrim/British Academy Edition, 12 vols (Oxford: Clarendon Press, 1965–2002). Subsequent citations: *PLets* followed by volume:page range, page.

[7] Michael Slater, 'Foreword' in Ben Winyard and Hazel Mackenzie (eds), *Charles Dickens and the Mid-Victorian Press* (Buckingham: University of Buckingham Press, 2012), i–iv, iv.

[8] Oppenlander, *Dickens's All the Year Round*, 36.

[9] Duane Devries, *Dickens's Apprentice Years: The Making of a Novelist* (New York: The Harvester Press, 1976), ix; Virgil Grillo, *Charles Dickens' Sketches By Boz: End in the Beginning* (Boulder, CO: Colorado Associated University Press, 1974).

[10] Robert L. Patten, *Charles Dickens and 'Boz': The Birth of the Industrial-Age Author* (Cambridge: Cambridge University Press, 2012), 21.

[11] Oppenlander, *Dickens's All the Year Round*, 39.

[12] Patten, *Charles Dickens and 'Boz'*, 23.

to one specific model of authorial identity in order to produce a single cohesive narrative of the great man.

The work of Nikki Hessell and Matthew Bevis on Dickens's early career as a parliamentary reporter points out further complexities. '[M]odern critics', Hessell notes, 'have been largely dismissive of Dickens's reporting precisely because most take it that he cannot be considered to be both accurate and creative.'[13] Hessell follows Bevis in emphasizing the extensive discussion regarding the accuracy of parliamentary reporting during this period and the frequency with which artistic re-creation took the place of word-for-word dictation, concluding that Dickens most likely participated 'in the often creative interpretation that was part of the process of reporting Parliament'.[14] All the same, Hessell argues, an examination of Dickens's early reporting presents 'a radical challenge to our understanding of the style' of reporters such as Dickens, 'because it is essentially about the submersion of individual style'.[15]

In a similar vein, Catherine Waters's study of his later journalism discusses the shared formal characteristics of the journalism of *Household Words* and *All the Year Round* in a manner that goes beyond their superficial designation as 'Dickensy', detailing the 'strategies of defamiliarisation' that Dickens and his contributors employed, and developing a picture of the journals that allows for both Dickens's central role as editor and the power of the individual voices that emerge despite the magazine's policy of anonymous contributions.[16] Waters demonstrates the importance of looking beyond Dickens and certain key contributors if a more nuanced understanding of Dickens and Victorian magazine culture more generally is to be achieved. In the same way, while Lillian Nayder in her study of Dickens and Wilkie Collins ostensibly re-emphasizes the idea of Dickens's tyrannical control over his journals, counteracting late nineteenth-century notions of the contaminating influence of Collins on Dickens's later work, her extended treatment of the collaboration between Dickens and Collins demonstrates the complex combination of comradeship, hostility, pride, and rivalry that went into the production of the magazines.[17]

Alongside this exploration of authorial ambiguity, stylistic conventionalism, and collaborative influence, there has been a move towards recognizing the importance of nation, race, and gender in Dickens's wider writings. Sabine Clemm, in one of the first full-length scholarly studies to focus on *Household Words* as a journal rather than as a vehicle for Dickens's writing, demonstrates that 'the distasteful racism' of Dickens's notorious essay 'The Noble Savage' is not a minor aberration but an integral part of the

---

[13] Nikki Hessell, *Literary Authors, Parliamentary Reporters: Johnson, Coleridge, Hazlitt, Dickens* (Cambridge: Cambridge University Press, 2011), 164.

[14] Matthew Bevis, *The Art of Eloquence: Byron, Dickens, Tennyson, Joyce* (Oxford: Oxford University Press, 2007), 89–90.

[15] Hessell, *Literary Authors*, 16.

[16] Catherine Waters, *Commodity Culture in Dickens's* Household Words: *The Social Life of Goods* (Aldershot: Ashgate, 2008), 13, 17.

[17] Lillian Nayder, *Unequal Partners: Charles Dickens, Wilkie Collins and Victorian Authorship* (Ithaca, NY: Cornell University Press, 2001).

journal's world view.[18] Likewise, Laura Peters argues that the 'Fancy' that Dickens extols, perhaps especially in his journalism, is based on 'the production of an exotic which exhibits racial assumptions' rooted in Dickens's childhood reading: stories of adventures in far-off lands that present anything 'unEnglish' as an exoticized Other, both attractive and repellent.[19] The 'unevenness' of Dickens's treatment of gender in his journalism has also been noticed by Waters and Holly Furneaux. Waters notes that the 'urban streetwalkers' who feature so prominently in Dickens's journalism both 'affirmed and interrogated' gender identities, male and female.[20] Similarly, Furneaux demonstrates the interrogative power of Dickens's depiction of male friendship in her investigation of the depiction of military figures in the Crimean period.[21] Thus the picture of Dickens the journalist and Conductor has deepened as further study has revealed the various layers of discourse and meaning embedded in the journals, often only realizable contextually.

For all this, however, before digitization, when scholars considered Dickens's journalism, or that of *Household Words* and *All the Year Round*, the focus was generally upon a fairly rigid canon of writing. In 1982 Michael Wolff and Joanne Shattock noted that 'for the press as a whole, we appear to have little choice except to be satisfied with a casual or glancing knowledge, believing that anything broader or deeper or more systematic is beyond the bounds of reasonable humanistic ambition'.[22] The digitization of archive material has transformed the limits of reasonable human ambition, making possible the kind of systematic analysis that was previously out of reach. Searchable text generated by optical character recognition means that archives that were too extensive to traverse can now be mapped. The cataloguing of these archives with the storage of information on title, authorship, page length, genre, and subject matter, as in the case of *Dickens Journals Online*, further aids navigation. Material formerly all but inaccessible, not only due to the sheer size of the archive but also due to the difficulty of physically locating hard copies only to be found in certain restricted libraries, can now be accessed, analysed, and brought to bear on our understanding of Dickens as a journalist and an editor. Importantly, however, digitization also enables new ways of marshalling that material, allowing for new patterns to emerge and fresh connections to be made.

In other words, the emergence of a quantifiable literary archive of Dickens's journals can help to refine understanding of their contents. For example, it has long been established that although *All the Year Round* was promoted by Dickens as continuing the 'fusion of the graces of the imagination with the realities of life' that was *Household*

---

[18] Sabine Clemm, *Dickens, Journalism, and Nationhood: Mapping the World in Household Words* (London: Routledge, 2008), 13, 157.

[19] Laura Peters, *Dickens and Race* (Manchester: Manchester University Press, 2013), 1.

[20] Catherine Waters, 'Gender Identities', in Sally Ledger and Holly Furneaux (eds), *Charles Dickens in Context* (Cambridge: Cambridge University Press, 2011), 365–72, 367, 371–2.

[21] Holly Furneaux, *Military Men of Feeling: Emotion, Touch, and Masculinity in the Crimean War* (Oxford: Oxford University Press, 2016), 54–86.

[22] Michael Wolff and Joanne Shattock, 'Introduction', in *Victorian Periodical Press: Samplings and Soundings* (Leicester: Leicester University Press, 1982), xiii–xix, xiii.

Words' modus operandi, there was a shift in the subject matter and focus in the new magazine.[23] John Drew notes that

> There was a marked increase of emphasis on foreign affairs in *All the Year Round* ... Over a representative sample of seven volumes of each periodical, nearly 11 per cent of the non-fiction articles in *All the Year Round* dealt with some aspect of international affairs or cultures, as opposed to 4 per cent in *Household Words*.[24]

Dickens Journals Online's catalogued database of articles, however, provides the basis for establishing trends within the magazines with much greater specificity and ease. It can be seen, for example, that the number of items that dealt with international affairs or foreign cultures in *Household Words* fluctuated between 50 and 80 per volume, and that there was a notable increase in volumes 5 to 12 (1852–6), perhaps due to an increased interest in international relations caused by the Crimean War (1853–6), after which the number of articles moved back to the lower end of the scale.

Similarly, peaks and troughs in the journals' social campaigning can be mapped: 125 articles or works of fiction that dealt with issues of public health and sanitation appeared in the journals between 1850 and 1870. Of these, 87 appeared in *Household Words* and 38 in *All the Year Round*. Although there were clearly more items that dealt with contemporary social problems in *Household Words* than in *All the Year Round* (another long-established difference between the two journals), delving deeper into the statistics shows that *Household Words*' initial enthusiasm for such subjects quickly dampened. The 20 items on public health in the first volume decreased to 13 in the second volume and 5 in the third volume. After volume 10 (1854–5), in which there were 8 articles on matters of public health and sanitation, the figure drops to 1 or 2 articles per volume. Under the wider heading of 'Great Britain: Social Conditions', 259 items appear in this category within the same period, 101 in *All the Year Round*, and 158 in *Household Words*. Of those items, however, 42 appear in the first volume of *Household Words*—thereafter, with exceptions for volumes 5 and 10, the figures are less than 10 per volume. Both sets of figures paint a similar picture: the trend away from social campaigning in *All the Year Round* was already established in *Household Words*' latter years.

Such data, of course, provides little information as to the reasons behind such trends. The resurgence in interest in public health in volume 10 may be attributable to the outbreak of a cholera epidemic in that period, but neither the long hot summer of 1858 and its 'Great Stink', the passage of the 1858 Public Health Act (21 & 22 Vict. c. 97) nor that of the 1866 Sanitary Act (29 & 30 Vict. c. 90), seems to have inspired similar interest. This might be the result of Dickens's own declining interest in the subject due to the long intervals he spent abroad or it may have been caused by other factors. Digital technology

---

[23] Charles Dickens, 'All the Year Round', *Household Words*, 28 May 1859, 19: 601 <http://www.djo.org.uk/household-words/volume-xix/page-601.html>.

[24] John Drew, 'All the Year Round', in Paul Schlicke (ed.), *The Oxford Companion to Charles Dickens* (Oxford: Oxford University Press, 2011), 9–12, 10.

assists in opening up lines of research, but more work is required to provide complete answers.

Another line of research opened up by these figures is the place of poetry within Dickens's journals. Poetry was a major feature of the journals (*Dickens Journals Online* lists 750 published poems between 1850 and 1870, compared to 935 short stories and 1065 instalments of serial fiction), but has yet to be subjected to sustained analysis. Victorian periodical poetry has often suffered from the idea that it was considered to be 'filler' by both editors and readers. For almost the entirety of its run, *Household Words* included in its contents one poem per issue, most of which were original works published for the first time within the magazine. The majority were short lyrics that took up less than a column of print and, as Arthur Adrian argues in his article on 'Dickens as Verse Editor', they were entirely conventional. He sums them up as 'Often sentimental, full of moral observations, not deeply philosophical.'[25] However, since Adrian's article was written more than 50 years ago, little serious work has emerged in this area. Recent re-evaluations of sentimental literature and Linda Hughes's seminal essay on the structural importance of poetry within the periodical have to some extent redressed the dismissive view of some twentieth-century critics regarding periodical poetry, but as yet little attempt has been made to re-evaluate the poetry in Dickens's journals.[26] Not only the poetry itself, but Dickens's relationships with the poets, and how far his editorial control extended to the poetry, remain subjects largely unexamined.[27] Yet when the contents of the magazines are taken collectively, as a project such as *Dickens Journals Online* allows the reader to do, it becomes clear that this poetry was a significant feature within both journals.

Thus in a move away from the necessarily selective practices of the hard-copy anthology, the digital archive allows scholars, as Wolff put it in 1989, to 'study the press on its own terms and not as though it was an anomaly, and for many a regretful, disturbing, even pathological anomaly within the tidy world of traditional letters'.[28] When the archive is contemplated in its sheer abundance, over-generalized statements such as 'Dickens himself wrote much of the original matter' give way to a more nuanced (and accurate) knowledge of the periodicals that does not dismiss the 400-odd other contributors to them, the complexities of collaboration and interconnection alive within the journals, and the skill and finesse required to manage such complexities successfully by both Dickens and his sub-editor.[29] Digitization challenges readers to tackle

---

[25] Arthur A. Adrian, 'Dickens as Verse Editor', *Modern Philology* 58, 2 (November 1960): 97–107, 101.

[26] Linda K. Hughes, 'What the "Wellesley Index" Left Out: Why Poetry Matters to Periodical Studies', *Victorian Periodicals Review* 40, 2 (2007): 91–125.

[27] One notable exception is Gill Gregory's *The Life and Work of Adelaide Procter: Poetry, Feminism, and Fathers* (Aldershot: Ashgate, 1998). See in particular chapter 6 on Dickens and editorial authority (192–250).

[28] Michael Wolff, 'Damning the Golden Stream: Latest Thoughts on a Directory of Victorian Periodicals', *Victorian Periodicals Review* 22, 3 (1989): 126–9, 128.

[29] Patricia Marks, 'Household Words', in Alvin Sullivan (ed.), *British Literary Magazines: The Victorian and Edwardian Age, 1837–1913* (Westport, CT, and London: Greenwood Press, 1984), 170–5, 171.

the difficulties of multi-authorship across platforms: difficulties that Dickens himself as writer and editor tackled with imagination and vigour.

Through computational stylistics and the work of organizations such as the Internet Archive, digital technology also allows scholars to tackle the problem of anonymous publication. Ann Lohrli's publication of the information to be found in the *Household Words*' office book and Jeremy Parrott's recent discovery of Dickens's annotated set of *All the Year Round* might seem to reduce the necessity for such technical tools, but even if the issue of attribution were to be fully resolved, there is in fact still much that such techniques can reveal. The tracing of texts through archives does not simply bring to light attribution but also the afterlives of articles and stories that originally appeared in Dickens's journals, which can help expand understanding of publishing practices and particular relations between various Victorian writers and publishers. Similarly, computational stylistics has much more to reveal than simply who wrote what.

The basis of computational stylistics is the contention that language is more than just 'a cultural artifact': it is 'a distinct piece of the biological makeup of our brains'.[30] Scholars such as Hugh Craig and Arthur Kinney argue that psychology, linguistics, physics, and neuroscience have all shown us that 'each person's processing of language is individually distinct' and that 'word deployment is individual to a high degree'.[31] They argue that each individual has a unique linguistic fingerprint, one that it may be difficult for a reader to perceive but of which a computer can provide a detailed breakdown.[32] More than simply establishing identification, however, Craig and Kinney seek to use this technology to ask a variety of further questions:

> [I]s this work early or late? Is prose dialogue consistently different from speeches in verse? Do playwrights from different classes, with different education, or brought up in different places write differently? Which playwrights are more diverse stylistically across their various works? Which show the widest variation across their characters?[33]

Dickens's young men, writers such as George A. Sala, Percy Fitzgerald, and Edmund Yates, all frequent contributors to *All the Year Round*, were often accused of imitating Dickens's style—how similar exactly are their stylistic fingerprints to Dickens's? How uniform in fact is the style across the journals that Elizabeth Gaskell deemed 'Dickensy'?[34] Does Dickens's stylistic imprint differ in his journalism compared to his fiction? Does it shift over the years? Does the imprint of writers change when writing for *Household Words* and *All the Year Round*? Does Gaskell's writing, for example,

---

[30] Steven Pinker, *The Language Instinct* (London: Penguin, 1994), 18.
[31] Hugh Craig and Arthur F. Kinney, *Shakespeare, Computers, and the Mystery of Authorship* (Cambridge: Cambridge University Press, 2009), 2–3.
[32] Ibid., 9–10.
[33] Ibid., 14.
[34] Elizabeth Gaskell, 'Letter to Charles Eliot Norton, 9 March 1859', in *The Letters of Mrs. Gaskell*, ed. J. A. V. Chapple and Arthur Pollard (Manchester: Manchester University Press, 1966), 534–9, 538.

bear an altered imprint when writing for other publications, or is it consistent across publications? Computational stylistics can provide answers to these questions, which are, arguably, more interesting than simple author attribution.

However, while digitization opens up new ways of reading material, it can, if not used carefully, simultaneously close down other pathways. As Adeline Koh notes, it is important to recognize the manner in which the digital archive can divorce the texts it remediates from the social and material conditions that governed their original emergence. Scholars must be aware of the ways in which the digital environment is shaping readers' experience of the texts and 'the limited ways in which researchers are invited to access and explore these resources', which Koh warns may 'risk the reintroduction of a belle lettristic approach to literature where social, political, historical and ideological conditions are suspended from the reading and production of texts'.[35] For example, a keyword search of a database such as *British Periodicals Collection* will produce a disembodied list of numerous articles from a variety of different publications, immediately divorced from their original context through the very process of the search. Thus, for all its potential, digital technology's ultimate usefulness is determined by how it is used. At the heart of all digital projects is the database. Databases collect information in accordance with certain pre-established rules. While such rules can illuminate material in new ways, they can also be limiting. *Dickens Journals Online*'s database is organized in terms of volume, issue, and article, thus analysis of its contents tends to be shaped by these units. The calendar year, for instance, plays very little part in its organizational structure, which is reflected in the results yielded from the site. This is all to say that the digital scholar must be careful not to create new oversimplifications that reduce the complexity of the material. There must be an awareness of that which digitization does not illuminate and even obscures and that the digital age has its own biases in terms of the information it seeks to gather and reproduce.

Within Dickens Studies, however, digital archives have, so far, rather opened up the exploration of conditions of reading and production than otherwise, as sites such as *Dickens Journals Online* have created opportunities for different ways of reading known material. Key to this is the site's presentation of scanned images of the original magazines alongside searchable text, reinforcing rather than dislocating the materiality of the original. In 2012 *Dickens Journals Online* and the Victorian Studies Centre at the University of Leicester launched a reading project and blog—one of many such projects in recent years that have made use of online editions of Dickens's material. The project invited any and all to read *A Tale of Two Cities* week by week in its original periodical context and then to share responses via the blog. While such a project cannot be seen as authentically re-creating the original readers' experiences of reading the novel, it did suggest fresh perspectives from which to view the novel. Shattock wrote of the experience:

---

[35] Adeline Koh, 'Inspecting the Nineteenth-Century Literary Digital Archive: Omissions of Empire', *Journal of Victorian Culture* 19, 3 (2014): 385–95, 393.

I had thought I grasped the significance of serialization ... But I had never read the individual parts discretely, in a regular, disciplined way... My readerly memory was also caught out by the demands of weekly reading, an experience I was relieved to learn that I shared with fellow bloggers. I was constantly having to leaf back through earlier instalments to be reminded of where I had first met Jerry Cruncher, how the physical similarities of Carton and Darney were first revealed, or whether we had been told that Miss Pross had a brother.[36]

Further, the reading group found that rather than ending on cliff hangers, the instalments frequently ended with little furtherance of the plot and sometimes at an apparently arbitrary point mid-scene. Thus in the course of the project it became evident that the appeal of a novel in serialization was less to do with the pull of the plot, which was oftentimes difficult to remember, and rather lay in the appreciation of the current moment and the rich detail in which it was invoked. Moreover, the project illustrated the 'shared concerns across the fiction and journalism', which were made more than apparent when the novel was read serially in its original magazine context.[37] Such shared concerns of course might also be obvious for the individual reader reading through a bound copy of the original magazine, but digitization allowed readers to come together as a group and share observations and connections almost in real time.

Within the field of digital humanities, such connections and the community they generate are considered to be of key importance. As Jane Dowson notes: 'the digital space takes the reader and researcher from isolation into a community that consists of experts and enthusiasts ... By digitally bringing the material into the public arena with self-declared interests and subjectivities, we shift monolithic narratives to multivocal ones.'[38] *Dickens Journals Online* created an open-access digital archive through the work of over 900 active volunteers, including academics, students, and members of the general public, who dedicated time and effort to creating a searchable archive of readable text. The interaction of these groups, however, was not without contention and it was by necessity hierarchical in nature. Guidelines as to the work asked of volunteers were interpreted variously and to differing effect. Similarly, reading groups, and the web of analysis and commentary generated by them, are not necessarily harmonious forums and social tensions and differing knowledge levels are an intrinsic part of the discussion. But it is perhaps through the experience of negotiating such communities that scholars can come to a fuller understanding of the practices of production and reading that

---

[36] Joanne Shattock, 'The Best of Times: Reading *A Tale of Two Cities* Week by Week', *Journal of Victorian Culture Online*, May 2013, accessed 25 May 2018 <http://jvc.oup.com/2013/05/14/the-best-of-times-reading-a-tale-of-two-cities-week-by-week/>.

[37] Holly Furneaux, 'The Best of Times: Reading *A Tale of Two Cities* Week by Week', *Journal of Victorian Culture Online*, May 2013, accessed 25 May 2018 <http://jvc.oup.com/2013/05/14/the-best-of-times-reading-a-tale-of-two-cities-week-by-week/>.

[38] Jane Dowson, 'Poetry and Personality: The Private Papers and Public Image of Elizabeth Jennings', in Carrie Smith and Lisa Stead (eds), *The Boundaries of the Literary Archive* (Aldershot: Ashgate, 2013), 185–22, 119.

marked the journals' original emergence into the public sphere. For Dickens's imagined community of readers, a hearthside gathering of men and women, was also more complex in actuality than in the imagining. Here again canonization plays a large part, as the conventional understanding of Dickens's imagining of his audience is built on the idealistic constructions of 'A Preliminary Word', the often-quoted address to his readers with which he launched the first instalment of *Household Words*. Instead, scholars might also look to the playful parodies that occasionally appeared as 'Chips', in which Dickens and his team present real and faux interactions with an audience that is portrayed as garrulous, tendentious, and in which the hierarchies between writer and audience are invoked both seriously and in jest.[39] Paradoxically, for all this talk of quantifiable data, digital technology can also help to shift our understanding of Dickens's relationship with his readers from an abstract to a human level, with all the contradiction and conflict that involves.

Much of that which holds true for the journalism also holds true for the letters. Although the surviving correspondence is only a fraction of that which Dickens must have written, owing in part to his deliberate destruction of large quantities of private letters in order to prevent misuse, the number of surviving letters is substantial. Moreover, as David Paroissien notes, 'the subject matter matches the variety of Dickens's correspondents and the interests that energized the century'.[40] Similarly, the tone varies extraordinarily. On the death of his friend William Macready's child, Dickens writes to another mutual friend Daniel Maclise of John Forster's reaction to Macready's loss, noting 'in such an amazing display of grief did he indulge ... such a very gloomy gulf was he sunk up to the chin', revealing quite a different Dickens from the one that wrote to an American fan in 1841, 'I condole with you, from my heart, on the loss you have sustained; and I feel proud of your permitting me to sympathise with your affliction.'[41]

Different collections of the letters have shaped critical understanding of them in different ways, from Mamie Dickens's and Georgina Hogarth's *The Letters of Charles Dickens* (1880) to Jenny Hartley's recent *The Selected Letters of Charles Dickens* (2012). Moreover, there has been a tendency to focus on letters that illustrate particularly well-known relationships, such as his friendships with John Forster, Wilkie Collins, and Angela Burdett-Coutts, as well as those that help to contextualize periods of controversy, such as the breakup of his marriage. Here again abundance can be limiting. The Pilgrim letters project has been invaluable to Dickens scholars in allowing readers an insight into both Dickens's professional practices and his personal life, but the ability to make use of the resource in its print form was limited by its size. The production of a

---

[39] Charles Dickens, 'A Preliminary Word', *Household Words*, 30 March 1850, 1:1 <http://www.djo.org.uk/household-words/volume-i/page-1.html>. For examples of 'Chips' see [Richard H. Horne], 'From Mr. T. Oldcastle concerning the Coal Exchange', *Household Words*, 6 July 1850, 1:352 <http://www.djo.org.uk/household-words/volume-i/page-352.html> or [W. H. Wills], 'Chips: A Card', *Household Words*, 17 May 1851, 3:187 <http://www.djo.org.uk/household-words/volume-iii/page-187.html>.

[40] David Paroissien, '"Faithfully Yours, Charles Dickens": The Epistolary Art of the Inimitable', in David Paroissien (ed.), *A Companion to Charles Dickens* (Oxford: Blackwell, 2008), 33–46, 35.

[41] *PLets* 2:158–9, 393–4.

digital edition in recent years has alleviated this. Moreover, *The Charles Dickens Letters Project*, dedicated to publishing online all Dickens correspondence discovered since the completion of the Pilgrim edition and committed to both rigorous verification and open access, means that all new additions to the archive will be easily accessible. In one recently uploaded letter Dickens writes that

> A certain faculty of remembrance and imitation, and a certain facility of versification, do not make a Poet. Every day of my life, in the daily experience of a Periodical, I see these qualities leading numbers of people hopelessly adrift.[42]

A keyword search for 'poet' reveals 30 results, including letters to Charles Mackay and Robert Lytton, both of whom contributed poetry to the journals (Mackay published 35 poems, Lytton 19, according to *Dickens Journals Online*). To Robert Lytton, Dickens writes:

> It is longer than a piece of Poetry usually is in this limited space of ours; but I cannot call, or think, any thing so very good too long. I made one slight alteration which I hope you will excuse. For 'child of my bowels', I substituted 'child of my bosom.' Your word I very well know to be more in keeping with the speaker, but I think mine the better for the public.[43]

And so from within the archive, relationships emerge and a new picture of Dickens as Verse Editor and correspondent begins to take shape: all with an ease and speed previously unimaginable when presented with the sheer mass of the hard-copy archives. 'Reasonable human ambition' begins to be measured on a new scale.

Dickens as correspondent and journalist wrote with startling imagination and detail about the world around him, investing squalid scenes with beauty, and demonstrating the vitality of the wretched. Technology was not needed to reveal this. Those writings, however, only become richer through the wider contextualization that modern technology provides, through its ability to marshal data, and sharpen the reader's sense of allusion and connection. From within the archive new information emerges and demonstrates, for example, the interest down to the level of the word that Dickens took in the poetry that he published. At the same time, it now seems that the much-vaunted title of 'Conductor' was in fact a fairly common address for the editor of a magazine as digitization means that the curious can easily find the 'Letters to the Conductor' of numerous periodicals with a few simple clicks.[44] Similarly, to search through 15,000

---

[42] '*To* UNKNOWN CORRESPONDENT, [1850–8 JUNE 1870]', *The Charles Dickens Letters Project*, accessed 20 August 2016, <http://dickensletters.com/letters/unknown-correspondent-08-june-1870>.

[43] '*To* THE HON. ROBERT LYTTON, 4 OCTOBER 1861', *The Charles Dickens Letters Project*, accessed 20 August 2016, <http://dickensletters.com/letters/robert-lytton-04-october-1861>.

[44] Periodicals as diverse as the *Ladies Magazine and Museum of Belles-Lettres*, *The Magazine of Natural History*, *The Farmer's Magazine*, *The Floricultural Cabinet*, the *Cornhill Magazine*, and *Good Words*, to name but a few, make reference to the editor as 'Conductor' throughout the nineteenth century.

letters to seek out information on Dickens's practices as a verse editor would have been an incredibly time-consuming enterprise. *Household Words*'s pioneering social investigations may be seen to have tapered out earlier than was once thought, but other areas of interest came to the fore, such as poetry. The engagement of both journals with international affairs is shown to be greater and more intense than previously thought. Similar discoveries undoubtedly await researchers when Dickens's early pieces are analysed in the context of the *Morning Chronicle*. Digitization has allowed a new Dickens to emerge for the twenty-first-century reader: a richer, more complex Dickens and perhaps ironically a more human one.

Further Reading

John M. L. Drew, *Dickens the Journalist* (Houndmills: Palgrave Macmillan, 2003)
Juliet John (ed.), *Dickens and Modernity* (Cambridge: D. S. Brewer, 2012)
Michaela Mahlburg, *Corpus Stylistics and Dickens's Fiction* (London: Routledge, 2013)

CHAPTER 24

CHARLES DICKENS AND THE 'DARK CORNERS' OF CHILDREN'S LITERATURE

MOLLY CLARK HILLARD

Introduction

WITH the 'golden age' of new historical and cultural studies (approximately 1990–2005) came a specialized interest in Dickens's representations of childhood. Some of this scholarship grew around Dickens's life story: his vexed relationship to his childhood and to that of his children. John Forster, the repository of Dickens's secrets, was among the first to connect Dickens's early years to his novels, with his speculation as to 'how far ... childish experiences are likely to have given the turn to Dickens's genius ... [and his musing] to what extent ... compassion for his own childhood may account for the strange fascination always exerted over him by child-suffering and sorrow'.[1] Dickens occasionally hinted at associations between his child and author selves too; in a letter to Angela Burdett-Coutts, for instance, he mused on his own beginnings, 'when I was a very odd little child with the first faint shadows of all my books, in my head'.[2] Other scholarship has arisen from surviving data about Dickens's family circle: the ten children Catherine bore from 1837 to 1852, and Dickens's interactions with and attitudes toward them.[3]

---

[1] John Forster, *The Life of Charles Dickens*, ed. J. W. T. Ley (London: Cecil Palmer, 1928), 553.
[2] Charles Dickens, *The Letters of Charles Dickens*, ed. Madeline House, Graham Storey, et al., Pilgrim/British Academy Edition, 12 vols (Oxford: Clarendon Press, 1965–2002). Here, 8:50–1, 51. Subsequent citations: *PLets* followed by volume:page range, page.
[3] Critical opinion is divided on what we would now call Dickens's 'parenting style'. See, for instance, Michael Slater, *Charles Dickens* (New Haven: Yale University Press, 2010); Claire Tomalin, *Charles Dickens: A Life* (London: Penguin, 2011); and Robert Gottlieb, *Great Expectations: The Sons and Daughters of Charles Dickens* (New York: Picador, 2013). Certainly, he had high hopes for his children,

From our records of Dickens's personal experience there emerges an expansive critical history of childhood and children as they appear in his creative works. For some scholars, such as Laura Berry, Carolyn Dever, Catherine Waters, Hilary Schor, and Holly Furneaux, Dickens contributes to histories and psychologies of the family.[4] For others, Dickens's novels access discourses of children's class and labour; Catherine Gallagher, Gail Turley Houston, and Claudia Nelson are perhaps foremost here.[5] Still others have made Dickensian children central to interventions in Victorian gender and sexuality studies, among them Catherine Robson, James Kincaid, and William Cohen.[6] Their many differences notwithstanding, together these scholars have demonstrated Dickens's shaping epistemologies of both the middle- and working-class Victorian child: the rights and privileges of the former, the wrongs and degradations of the latter. To speak of a 'Dickensian childhood', in other words, is to conjure two very different bodies of imagery: the cosy middle-class childhood of Dickens's 'fireside books' or Christmas publications,[7] and the traumas of his novelistic working-class children, like Oliver Twist, Little Nell, Smike, Jo, and Jenny Wren. Of course, as Robert Newsom suggests,[8] these

naming the boys for authors and poets (dedicated, as it were, like one of his own novels), the girls for his beloved dead sister-in-law, and in one fateful case, for one of his own book characters. Each had his or her own playful nickname. He was undoubtedly involved in their amusements. For at least two years, Dickens's busy Christmas writing routine included the composition, direction, and production of a family theatrical. He collaborated on these (*Tom Thumb*, *Fortunio*, and *The Lighthouse*) with Mark Lemon and Wilkie Collins, and the three men acted together with the children (Forster, *Life*, 573–5). His letters to his wife, friends, and sister-in-law included stories about or messages for the children (*PLets* 6:213–16, 150–1, 354; 7:168–9, 231–2). Yet even sympathetic historians acknowledge that Dickens soured on his children as they neared what he considered a feckless adulthood. The few surviving letters written directly to his children change in tone from affectionate (to the young girls) to stiffly cordial (with the older boys about to strike out on their own). And Dickens's sharpest critics describe the 'monstrous bonhomie' of the Dickens house, a hollow effect carefully cultivated to protect his brand as a prophet of home and hearth. (Matthew Sweet, review of Andrew Lycett, *Wilkie Collins: A Life of Sensation*, in *The Guardian*, 13 September 2013). <https://www.theguardian.com/books/2013/sep/13/wilkie-collins-life-sensation-lycett-review>. Accessed 2 May 2017.)

[4] Laura C. Berry, *The Child, the State, and the Victorian Novel* (Charlottesville: University of Virginia Press, 2000); Carolyn Dever, *Death and the Mother from Dickens to Freud* (Cambridge: Cambridge University Press, 2006); Hilary Schor, *Dickens and the Daughter of the House* (Cambridge: Cambridge University Press. 2007); Catherine Waters, 'Gender, Family, and Domestic Ideology', in John O. Jordan (ed.), *The Cambridge Companion to Charles Dickens* (Cambridge: Cambridge University Press, 2001), 120–35; Holly Furneaux, *Queer Dickens: Erotics, Families, Masculinities* (Oxford: Oxford University Press, 2010); Claudia Nelson, *Family Ties in Victorian England* (Westport, CT: Praeger, 2007).

[5] Catherine Gallagher, *The Body Economic: Life, Death, and Sensation in Political Economy and the Victorian Novel* (Princeton: Princeton University Press, 2009); Gail Turley Houston, *Consuming Fictions: Gender, Class and Hunger in Dickens's Novels* (Carbondale: Southern Illinois University Press, 1994); Claudia Nelson, *Precocious Children and Childish Adults: Age Inversion in Victorian Literature* (Baltimore: Johns Hopkins University Press, 2012).

[6] Catherine Robson, *Men in Wonderland: The Lost Girlhood of the Victorian Gentleman* (Princeton: Princeton University Press, 2001); James Kincaid, *Child Loving: The Erotic Child and Victorian Culture* (New York: Routledge, 1993); William Cohen, 'Manual Conduct in *Great Expectations*', in *Sex Scandal: The Private Parts of Victorian Fiction* (Durham, NC: Duke University Press, 1996), 26–72.

[7] Though, of course, the Christmas stories from 1859 to 1867 did not always have children in mind.

[8] Robert Newsom, 'Fictions of Childhood', in Jordan (ed.), *Cambridge Companion*, 92–105.

apparently very separate bodies could sometimes merge into the traumatized middle-class child, as with Paul Dombey and David Copperfield.

'Children' and 'childhood', then, have received thorough treatment in Dickens studies. It is the subject of children's literature that offers us the freshest avenues of enquiry. In the last two decades or so, we have witnessed the growth and legitimization of the study of children's literature in Australian, British, Canadian, and American academic programmes such as those run by the University of South Australia, University of Canberra, University of Glasgow, Cardiff University, University of British Columbia, University of Pittsburgh, University of Florida, and Rutgers University.[9] That children's literature studies is interdisciplinary, with branches in folklore, education, sociology, and new media, no doubt contributes to its comparatively new-found place in academic curricula and research. Yet among the ground-breaking critical works that might be classified as Victorian children's literary studies—like those of Joseph Bristow, U. C. Knoepflmacher, or Marah Gubar[10]—none treats Dickens explicitly as a producer or consumer of children's media. For good reason, seemingly: while most of Dickens's novels and periodical writing can be classified as 'family reading', only *A Child's History of England* (1851–3) and *Holiday Romance* (1868)[11] were written explicitly for children. Yet it is also undoubtedly true that the children's book market would not have emerged as it did without Charles Dickens, and vice versa. The time is right to consider anew the ways in which Dickens anticipated, participated in, and critiqued Victorian children's literature. To open up this avenue of enquiry, this chapter will take as its broad theme 'Charles Dickens and children's literature'. The capacious term will permit us to range among the following kinds of works in which Dickens was involved: literature written explicitly for children—as well as plots and characters from that literature, audiences for it, and philosophies about it and derived from it; literature that was not originally written for children, but that was later rewritten and remarketed for children (like fairy tales and other folklore); and what we might call 'literature of the child'—novels or periodical materials written for adults, but with significant child characters, or written ironically as if for children, or intertexted with materials from children's literature.

To begin this exploration, we must challenge our enduring bias in thinking that children's literature does not possess the dialogic register of other genres. Dickens, for one, knew better: though he often *tells* his readers that children's literature is a socializing

---

[9] Peter Hunt's work on the field of children's studies is instructive here. See *Children's Literature: The Development of Criticism* (London: Routledge, 1990), *Criticism, Theory, and Children's Literature* (London: Routledge, 1992), and *Understanding Children's Literature* (London: Routledge, 2005).

[10] Joseph Bristow, *Empire Boys: Adventures in a Man's World* (London: HarperCollins Academic, 1991); U. C. Knoepflmacher, *Ventures into Childland: Victorians, Fairy Tales, and Femininity* (Chicago: University of Chicago Press, 1999); Marah Gubar, *Artful Dodgers: Reconceiving the Golden Age of Children's Literature* (Oxford: Oxford University Press, 2009).

[11] [Charles Dickens,] *A Child's History of England i–xxxix, Household Words*, 25 January 1851–10 December 1853. *Dickens Journals Online*, <http://www.djo.org.uk/indexes/articles.html>; Charles Dickens, *Holiday Romance i–iv, All the Year Round*, 25 January 1868–4 April 1868. *Dickens Journals Online*, <http://www.djo.org.uk/indexes/articles.html>.

and humanizing 'nursery of fancy',[12] he *shows* a world in which children's literature is an amorphous network of 'dark corners' of the 'mind', governed by ruthless, working-class bodies.[13] Readers of Dickens soon learn to be on the watch, since, under the influence of children's literary materials, 'reality will take a wolfish turn' at any time.[14] We know that 'shovelling and sifting at alphabeds' might turn up any number of fearful and exhilarating items.[15] These and other tensions in Dickens's fiction and journalism reveal the emerging currency of Victorian children's literature in economic, cultural, and aesthetic terms. Examples follow from Dickens's entire canon, but focus on the years 1849–54, when Dickens's own children ranged from 0 to 16, and therefore when he had a consumer's eye to children's reading materials. If Dickens's production *for* children was limited, his attention *to* children's literature was prodigious.

SHADOWS AND DARK CORNERS: *HOUSEHOLD WORDS* AND *ALL THE YEAR ROUND*

Indeed, the conceit for *Household Words* was indebted to the developing genre of children's literature. Though very little of what appeared in Dickens's magazine was intended explicitly for children, the genres, structures, and ideologies of children's literature pervaded the run of *Household Words*, and, to a lesser extent, *All the Year Round*. In 1850–1, several essays appeared on education, reading materials, and schooling, especially the Ragged Schools (which he visited in philanthropic collaboration with Angela Burdett-Coutts). *A Child's History of England* was serialized 1851–3, concurrently with his writing of child-focused *David Copperfield* and *Bleak House*. 'The Two Guides of the Child',[16] 'A Witch in the Nursery',[17] 'Frauds on the Fairies', and 'The School of the Fairies'[18] were essays on literary fairy tales, while 'Gaslight

---

[12] [Charles Dickens,] 'Frauds on the Fairies', *Household Words*, 10 January 1853. *Dickens Journals Online*, <http://www.djo.org.uk/indexes/articles/frauds-on-the-fairies.html>.

[13] [Charles Dickens,] 'Nurses Stories', in Michael Slater and John Drew (eds), *The Dent Uniform Edition of Dickens' Journalism*, 4 vols (London: J. M. Dent, Columbus: Ohio State University Press, 1993–2000). Here, Dent vol. 4, page 173. Subsequent references are inserted parenthetically in the text by Dent volume: Title, page.

[14] Charles Dickens, *Hard Times*, ed. Fred Kaplan, Norton Critical Edition, 4th edn (New York: W. W. Norton, 2017), II:6, 133. Subsequent references are inserted parenthetically in the text by HT Book:chapter, page.

[15] Charles Dickens, *Our Mutual Friend*, ed. Michael Cotsell, Oxford World's Classics (Oxford: Oxford University Press, 1989), I:5, 50. Subsequent references are inserted parenthetically in the text by OMF Book:chapter, page.

[16] [Henry Morley,] 'Two Guides of the Child', *Household Words*, 7 September 1850. *Dickens Journals Online*, <http://www.djo.org.uk/indexes/articles/two-guides-of-the-child.html>.

[17] [Richard H. Horne,] 'A Witch in the Nursery', *Household Words*, 20 September 1851. *Dickens Journals Online*, <http://www.djo.org.uk/indexes/articles/a-witch-in-the-nursery.html>.

[18] [Henry Morley,] 'The School of the Fairies', *Household Words*, 30 June 1853. *Dickens Journals Online*, <http://www.djo.org.uk/indexes/articles/the-school-of-the-fairies.html>.

Fairies'[19] and 'Harlequin Fairy Morgana!'[20] were essays on the fairy pantomimes; on several other occasions, Dickens or his contributors used fairy tales as the start of homilies on various national discourses, like 'Little Red Working-Coat',[21] 'Wallotty Trot',[22] 'Fairyland in "Fifty-Four"',[23] 'Prince Bull. A Fairy Tale',[24] 'The Thousand and One Humbugs',[25] and 'The Toady-Tree'.[26] The Christmas number was explicitly intended for family reading, for, as Dickens said some years earlier in *A Christmas Carol*, 'it is good to be children sometimes, and never better than at Christmas, when its mighty Founder was a child himself'.[27] *Holiday Romance*, first published in America and reprinted in *All the Year Round* in 1868, perhaps takes this adage the most literally, as the narrators of its four stories are all children. From the preceding list, one can see that children were on the minds of the conductor and his contributors.

Dickens intended from the outset that *Household Words* should reach across ages and classes. This was reflected in the twopenny weekly price, as well as in Dickens's brainstorming missives to Forster. Dickens imagined the work to be a miscellany of current events and literature, united in methodology and theme, as well as by the twin aims of instruction and entertainment. Wanting the journal to be a ubiquitous fixture in all literate homes, Dickens sought an agent 'to bind all this together': 'I want to suppose a certain SHADOW, which may go into any place, by sunlight, moonlight, starlight, firelight, candlelight, and be in all homes, and all nooks and corners, and be supposed to be cognizant of everything ... a kind of semi-omniscient, omnipresent, intangible creature.'[28] Forster diplomatically convinced him that the name was creepy, and that the conceit of a single, unifying character did not have 'a quite feasible look'.[29] Dickens shuffled through several other names in quick succession: 'The Cricket', 'The Robin', 'The Forge', 'The Microscope', 'The Lever', and, hilariously, 'Charles

---

[19] [Charles Dickens,] 'Gaslight Fairies', *Household Words*, 10 February 1855. *Dickens Journals Online*, <http://www.djo.org.uk/indexes/articles/gaslight-fairies.html>.

[20] [Percy Heatherington Fitzgerald,] 'Harlequin Fairy Morgana!', *All The Year Round*, 20 August 1864. *Dickens Journals Online*, <http://www.djo.org.uk/indexes/articles/harlequin-fairy-morgana.html>.

[21] [Henry Morley,] 'Little Red Working-Coat', *Household Words*, 27 December 1851. *Dickens Journals Online*, <http://www.djo.org.uk/indexes/articles/little-red-working-coat.html>.

[22] [George Dodd,] 'Wallotty Trot', *Household Words*, 5 February 1853. *Dickens Journals Online*, <http://www.djo.org.uk/indexes/articles/wallotty-trot.html>.

[23] [W. H. Wills and George Augustus Sala,] 'Fairyland in 'Fifty-Four', *Household Words*, 3 December 1853. *Dickens Journals Online*, <http://www.djo.org.uk/indexes/articles/fairyland-in-fifty-four.html>.

[24] [Charles Dickens,] 'Prince Bull. A Fairy Tale', *Household Words*, 17 February 1855. *Dickens Journals Online*, <http://www.djo.org.uk/indexes/articles/prince-bull-a-fairy-tale.html>.

[25] [Charles Dickens,] 'The Thousand and One Humbugs', *Household Words*, 21 April 1855. *Dickens Journals Online*, <http://www.djo.org.uk/indexes/articles/>.

[26] [Charles Dickens,] 'The Toady-Tree', *Household Words*, 26 May 1855. *Dickens Journals Online*, <http://www.djo.org.uk/indexes/articles/the-toady-tree.html>.

[27] Charles Dickens, *A Christmas Carol and other Christmas Books*, ed. Robert Douglas-Fairhurst, Oxford World's Classics (Oxford: Oxford University Press, 2008), Stave III, 58.

[28] *PLets* 5:621–3, 622.

[29] Forster, *Life*, 512.

Dickens'.[30] Some of these names signal technology, labour, and industry, while others evoke a curious eye turned upon everyday life. In settling on *Household Words*, the sense of penetrating a private space remained; it's clear that in imagining his working-class audience, Dickens wavered between a sympathetic and surveillant gaze. As Forster recalled, by having each item contain 'something of romantic fancy ... with all familiar things, but especially those repellent on the surface, something was to be connected that should be fanciful or kindly; and the hardest workers were to be taught that their lot is not necessarily excluded from the sympathies and graces of imagination'.[31] It is difficult to tell here whether Dickens pictures this readership as composed partly of working-class children and youths, whether he offers the tropes of children's literature as a fanciful corrective to the drudgery of working-class life, or whether he views children's literature as meet entertainment for a childlike people.

In many instances his journals treat fairy tales and other folklore as the nation's best teacher of wonder and delight: an anodyne for the weary body politic. In 'Two Guides of the Child', Henry Morley suggests that fairy tales were a better guide to adulthood than hypotenuses and dead languages. In 'A Child's Dream of a Star', a brother and sister's 'wonder' creates a child's fanciful version of Heaven, enabling the brother to endure the deaths of his family members.[32] In his 1853 *Household Words* article 'Frauds on the Fairies', Dickens calls fairy tales 'the nurseries of fancy', and 'beautiful little stories', and concludes: 'The world is too much with us, early and late. Leave this precious old escape from it, alone.'[33] In 'A Christmas Tree', an 1850 *Household Words* article, the narrator sighs, '[s]he was my first love. I felt that if I could have married Little Red Riding-Hood, I should have known perfect bliss.'[34]

But just as often as they idealized children's literature, his journals recognized the terrifying side of these materials. Richard H. Horne's 'A Witch in the Nursery' details the inappropriate grisliness of nursery rhymes and fairy tales. In his essay 'Nurse's Stories', Dickens remembers the 'utterly impossible places and people, but none the less alarmingly real—that I found I had been introduced to by my nurse before I was six years old ... If we all knew our own minds ... I suspect that we should find our nurses responsible for most of the dark corners we are forced to go back to, against our wills' (Dent 4: 'Nurse's Stories', 173). In this story, the nurse is 'a female bard—descended, possibly, from those terrible old Scalds' (Dent 4: 'Nurse's Stories', 179). She 'made a standing pretence ... that all her ghost stories had occurred to her own relations ... and they acquired an air of authentication that impaired my digestive powers for life' (Dent 4: 'Nurse's

---

[30] Ibid., 512–13.

[31] Ibid., 512.

[32] [Charles Dickens,] 'A Child's Dream of a Star', *Household Words*, 6 April 1850. *Dickens Journals Online*, <http://www.djo.org.uk/indexes/articles/a-childs-dream-of-a-star.html>.

[33] Dickens, 'Frauds on the Fairies'. It is worth noting here that 'Frauds on the Fairies' is a rebuttal to George Cruikshank's *Fairy Library* (1853), a set of four fairy tales rewritten to show the evils of alcoholism.

[34] [Charles Dickens,] 'A Christmas Tree', *Household Words*, 21 December 1850. *Dickens Journals Online*, <http://www.djo.org.uk/indexes/articles/a-christmas-tree.html>.

Stories', 179). And the boy's response to 'the dark corners' is made up of equal parts of horror and *frisson*: to his nurse's tales he is 'indebted for my first personal experience of a shudder and cold beads on the forehead' (Dent 4: 'Nurse's Stories', 173). Likewise, on hearing a tale of supernatural rats, 'the whole of my small listening person was overrun with them. At intervals ever since, I have been morbidly afraid of my own pocket, lest my exploring hand should find a specimen or two of those vermin in it' (Dent 4: 'Nurse's Stories', 178). 'Nurse's Stories' exemplifies the carnivalesque aspect of children's literature—its ludic potential to subvert through humour, fear, and chaos. Dickens, in his periodical writing as in his novels, draws upon his own childhood experiences with his nurse, but also upon the organizing conceit of both Perrault and the Grimms that the origin of children's literature is a working-class woman's imagination, which carries its own terrifying authority.

'Reading as if for Life': *David Copperfield*

In 'A Christmas Tree', published the month after he completed the numbers for *David Copperfield*, Dickens casts a nostalgic eye along tree branches trimmed with the gifts of successive childhood Christmases. As his gaze mounts the tree, what he sees there records a progress in intellectual and artistic endeavour: from an alphabet, to books of fairy tales, to pantomimes, to novels, to histories on the highest branches. One might almost call the essay a précis for the novel, for *David Copperfield* is as much a history of David's experience of reading as it is an autobiography of his life. And, as in 'A Christmas Tree', *Copperfield* presents reading as an evolutionary practice, part of the development from boy to man, from absorber to practitioner. Indeed, as Wu Di says, 'Dickens was concerned throughout his writing life with the complicated reactions of children as readers both in, and of, his works' and presents 'a range of child readers' who are, for better or worse, 'our surrogates in the text'.[35] David moves from the feminine idyll of 'learning the alphabet at [his mother's] knee',[36] and the 'crocodile book' that he reads with Peggotty, to the brutalities of Murdstone's home-schooling. 'Almost stupefied' by draconian pedagogy and perpetual beating, David is sustained by a stash of his dead father's books. Eighteenth-century novels as well as Arabian tales serve to keep 'alive my fancy, and my hope of something beyond that place and time ... This', recalls David, 'was my only and my constant comfort. When I think of it, the picture always rises in my mind, of a summer evening, the boys at play in the churchyard, and I sitting on my bed,

---

[35] Wu Di, 'Child Readers in Dickens's Novels', in Peter Merchant and Catherine Waters (eds), *Dickens and the Imagined Child* (Farnham: Ashgate, 2015), 167–82; 168.

[36] Charles Dickens, *David Copperfield*, ed. Nina Burgis (Oxford: Clarendon, 1981), 4, 45. Subsequent references are inserted parenthetically in the text by *DC* chapter, page.

reading as if for life' (*DC* 4, 48). And of course David does 'read ... for life' in all senses: to preserve his own life, to apprehend others' lives, and to mark his lifespan.

David remembers having 'been ... a child's Tom Jones, a harmless creature ... for a week together' (*DC* 4, 48). And yet, as *Copperfield* unfolds, it's clear that there is nothing harmless about the written word, or about children's absorption of it. If David reads for life, then Tommy Traddles, doodling skeletons all over his textbooks and homework, might be said to read for death. Traddles, like David an abandoned and beaten child, presents us with a competing image of reading and writing to take through *Copperfield*, as Dickens repeatedly reveals the damaging, divisive, and even deathly nature of creative composition. Indeed, David as narrator wields books as a blunt instrument to assert his superiority over others. In recounting his reading to Peggotty, David emphasizes the difference between his literate self and his semi-literate nurse: 'I must have read very perspicuously, or the good soul must have been deeply interested, for I remember she had a cloudy impression, after I had done, that [crocodiles] were a sort of vegetable.' And '"Now let me hear some more about the Crorkindills," said Peggotty, who was not quite right in the name yet' (*DC* 2, 14–15). David's class snobbery in rendering Peggotty's devotion as clownishness, and his childhood feelings of 'comical affection' (*DC* 4, 53) for her, foretell his eventual betrayal of the Peggotty family. When Steerforth coerces David to 'make some regular Arabian Nights of it' (*DC* 7, 79) by telling him stories in their school dormitory, David makes sure we grasp both the homoerotic nature of the relationship unfolding ('it was a tiresome thing to be roused, like the Sultana Scheherazade, and forced into a long story before the getting-up bell rang'; '[w]hatever I had within me that was romantic and dreamy, was encouraged by so much storytelling in the dark', (*DC* 7, 80–1)), as well as its abusiveness: David as storyteller endures victimization together with adulation and pleasure ('But the being cherished as a kind of plaything in my room, and the consciousness that this accomplishment of mine ... attracted a good deal of notice to me ... stimulated me to exertion' (*DC* 7, 81)). David carries the sadomasochistic nature of storytelling—as well as of adaptability to an audience's whims—into adulthood as a model for writing.[37]

Certainly, David learns in boyhood to distinguish gentle, ineffectual writers from those who complete and circulate their written words. Copperfield's and Dickens's synchrony is best illustrated, not through the plot points of David's life story, but through their apprehension of reading and writing, and their observation of readers and writers. Mr Dick, the interminable Memorialist, disseminates his manuscript only by flying its pages on a kite, and headmaster Doctor Strong, compiler of the endless dictionary, carries his drafts no further than the garden, tucked into his hatband. It might be said that David takes these works as manuals for how *not* to be an author. To be sure,

---

[37] This observation is a departure from Mary Poovey's classic argument that compares David's writing with feminine housework; 'The Man-of-Letters Hero: *David Copperfield* and the Professional Writer', in *Uneven Developments: The Ideological Work of Gender in Mid-Victorian England* (Chicago: University of Chicago Press, 1988), 89–125.

Messrs Dick and Strong are both like Dickens—the encyclopedic sweep of Strong's magnum opus, the head of Charles I popping into everything Dick writes (Mr Dick is literally Dick without end/ens)—but also Dickens's *reductio ad absurdum*, for Dickens was defined by his productivity and relentless drive to publish. Young David's watchfulness of writers serves to emphasize the observational nature of his later narrative procedure: spying or peeping in, and looking wilfully or helplessly on as harm comes to others.

Such activity aligns him with the prostitute Martha, ironically, for David's childhood relationship to reading and writing becomes crucial when considering the variously mistreated women in the novel, given that David is often the perpetrator or at least perpetuator of this mistreatment. It is David who offers up Em'ly for Steerforth's delectation because he loves Steerforth. Rosa Dartle is Steerforth's victim of violent and possibly sexual assault, a violation that David refuses to understand. Annie Strong is slandered as a fallen woman because she was, years before, assaulted by Jack Maldon; David circulates this slander. David wilfully mistakes Miss Mowcher for a procuress. And so on. Moreover, David's betrayals occupy both diegetic and extradiegetic spaces: David the child learns the abusive nature of reading, writing, and performance from others. David the narrator earns his livelihood and fame from re-creating these abuses in his writing. The most metafictional of these female characters[38] is Miss Mowcher, who was patterned upon a chiropodist in Dickens's neighbourhood. When the woman recognized herself and wrote a letter of complaint, Dickens prevaricated, assuring her that his characters were composites.[39] But he also quickly switched Miss Mowcher's character plans from the wicked 'goblin pieman' (*DC* 22, 285) he had intended to depict to the misunderstood heroine of the novel's close. This character's 'real' history underscores what Dickens fictionalizes again and again in *Copperfield*: that to produce commercial writing is to 'force into a long story' innocent bystanders.

David *tells* us that there is a sharp, even Wordsworthian, distinction between alphabets and school lessons: 'I seem to have walked along a path of flowers as far as the Crocodile Book, and to have been cheered by the gentleness of my mother's voice and manner all the way. But these solemn lessons which succeeded those, I remember as the deathblow of my peace' (*DC* 4, 46). And yet, witness the crocodile book: 'we returned to those monsters... and we ran away from them, and baffled them by constantly turning... and we went into the water after them... and put sharp pieces of timber down their throats; and in short we ran the whole crocodile gauntlet' (*DC* 2, 15). It is no bad allegory of *David Copperfield*; David returns to and runs away from monsters, baffles pursuit with constant turning, and pursues quarry to waters of river and ocean. Nor is the physical book left behind in childhood, since Peggotty preserves it and places it on David's bedside at key moments of his life: when his mother marries Mr Murdstone (*DC* 2, 22), and

---

[38] The death of Dickens's baby daughter Dora shortly after the death of his pen and ink Dora notwithstanding.

[39] Forster, *Life*, 548.

when she dies (*DC* 8, 99), when David grows condescending to the Peggottys (*DC* 10, 128), when he turns a blind eye to Steerforth's seduction of Em'ly (*DC* 22, 273). Far from anodyne, the child's book is a sharp-toothed reminder of mortality and faithlessness. In the nurse's hands, it becomes a subtle tool of correction and protest.

'Mrs Shipton, and Mother Hubbard, and Dame Durden': *Bleak House*

As in *David Copperfield*, *Bleak House* gazes uneasily upon women in service—unpaid service to men, or paid service to the wealthy. The novel incorporates fairy tale and nursery rhyme into its female plots and character structures, superficially in play, but with underlying dark intent. For instance, Dickens juxtaposes the grand, but stagnant, institutions of the aristocracy and the legal system in these terms: 'Both the world of fashion and the Court of Chancery are things of precedent and usage ... sleeping beauties, whom the Knight will wake one day.'[40] 'Sleeping Beauty' becomes a repeated and extended trope for the slumberous aristocracy.[41] Narrator Esther Summerson contrasts with the torpid nobility and their moribund legal causes by serving as angel in the house, a role she constantly disavows through systemic self-effacement in the novel. Her adumbration is located on multiple registers: plot, narration, orthography, and symbol; one of the most telling ways in which Esther's 'little body ... fall[s]' away (*BH* 3, 27) is through the substitution of her given name with folkloric and nursery rhyme appellations. In welcoming her into her 'rightful' place as housekeeper and lady's companion, John Jarndyce likens her to a variety of children's literary matrons:

> 'You are clever enough to be the good little woman of our lives here, my dear,' [Mr Jarndyce] returned, playfully; 'the little old woman of the Child's ... Rhyme[:] "Little old woman and whither so high/To sweep the cobwebs out of the sky". You will sweep them so neatly out of *our* sky in the course of your housekeeping, Esther...'
>
> This was the beginning of my being called Old Woman, and Little Old Woman, and Cobweb, and Mrs. Shipton, and Mother Hubbard, and Dame Durden, and so many names of that sort, that my own name soon became quite lost among them. (*BH* 8, 90)

---

[40] Charles Dickens, *Bleak House*, ed. George Ford and Sylvère Monod, Norton Critical Edition (New York and London: Norton, 1977), 2, 10–11. Subsequent references are inserted parenthetically in the text by *BH* chapter, page.

[41] The Dedlocks' ancestral home is figured as Sleeping Beauty's castle: 'twining among the balustrades of [the house], and lying heaped upon the vases, there was one great flush of roses ... On everything, house, garden, terrace, green slopes, water, old oaks, fern, moss, woods again ... there seemed to be such undisturbed repose' (*BH* 18, 221–2). And Lady Honoria Dedlock, the mistress of this estate, is its 'exhausted deity' who is routinely 'bored to death' (*BH* 2, 11).

As critics have long since pointed out,[42] these folkloric names, with their associations of old age and maternal surrogacy, transform 24-year-old Esther into a prematurely aged crone, concealing the youth and sexuality she hesitates to claim. In the case of Mother Hubbard, Esther is linked to extended, wearisome labour on behalf of an ungrateful charge.[43] In the case of Dame Durden, Esther is likened to the folksong farmwife who fails to control her 'mating' employees.[44] Esther registers her 'lost' name with covert anger and sorrow, buried in her masochistic sense of 'duty'.

Lest we read Esther as merely an anti-sleeping beauty, her role to 'sweep the cobwebs' from the stagnant institutions in the novel with an abundance of cheerful domestic employment, we are given Lady Dedlock's French maid Hortense as a counterpoint. Ambitious, ruthless, and eventually murderous, she at first seems antithetical to the repressed and dutiful Esther: Hortense 'seems to go about like a very neat She-Wolf imperfectly tamed' (*BH* 12, 143). Throughout, Hortense is figured as a working-class revolutionary: in one weird scene, she walks 'shoeless', like a saboteuse, through grass as if 'she fancies it's blood' (*BH* 18, 231), like 'some woman from the streets of Paris in the reign of terror' (*BH* 23, 286). In spite of national and dispositional distinctions, however, Esther and Hortense are uncannily alike: both are watchful figures who pass judgement on the polite society that marginalizes them, and both are rejected by the chilly Lady Dedlock. John Jordan has even suggested that Hortense becomes Esther's vengeful avatar, committing acts that conveniently sweep antagonists from Esther's path.[45] Indeed, their convergence in the text occasions a violent explosion of narrative energy, which dispels the novel's early stagnancy. Esther's disease and Krook's spontaneous combustion are twin actions that traumatically, but productively, bring change to the deadlocked institutions of the novel. Jack Zipes reminds us that the fairy tale—especially the fairy-tale wolf—was put to use in various political uprisings in Europe in the nineteenth and twentieth centuries:[46] wolfish Hortense may draw upon this tradition, and *Bleak House* is the first of several novels in which Dickens creates lupine characters with rebellious tendencies. In doing so, he suggests that the communal, circulatory vigour of the fairy tale resembles the energy of the mob. And while none of these characters is conventionally heroic, and while their rebellions are nominally quenched, their insurgence is never entirely dissipated.

---

[42] John Jordan, 'Psychoanalysis', in *Supposing Bleak House* (Charlottesville: University of Virginia Press, 2011), 44–66; Elizabeth Campbell, *Fortune's Wheel: Dickens and the Iconography of Women's Time* (Athens: Ohio University Press, 2003); Schor, *Dickens and the Daughter of the House*, 101–23; D. A. Miller, 'Discipline in Different Voices: Bureaucracy, Police, Family, and *Bleak House*', *Representations* 1 (1983): 59–89. Reprinted in *The Novel and the Police* (Berkeley: University of California Press, 1988).

[43] Iona Opie and Peter Opie, *The Oxford Dictionary of Nursery Rhymes* (Oxford: Oxford University Press, 1997), 376–80.

[44] Wiltshire Council, 'Dame Durden', *Wiltshire Community History*, <https://history.wiltshire.gov.uk>. Accessed 2 May, 2017.

[45] Jordan, 'Psychoanalysis', 18–21.

[46] Jack Zipes, *Fairy Tales and the Art of Subversion* (New York: Routledge, 2012), 57–78; 136–67.

With this in mind, Esther's seemingly belittling pet names are worth a second look. Mothers Goose, Bunch, Durden, Hubbard, and Shipton[47] were all characters used in the English pantomime and they are all early forerunners of the panto dame. In fact, there was a widespread conflation of these names in the pantomime and in literature about the pantomime, each name serving to 'embody the spirit and energy of pantomime itself'.[48] Jennifer Schacker has discovered that in England these 'mothers' were often named as the purported 'authors' of fairy tales actually written by the French *conteuses* of pre-revolutionary France. The *conteuses* were the aristocratic women who used salon production of *contes de fées* to articulate subversive ideas about the monarchy and the relation between the sexes.[49] Schacker notes that in eighteenth- and nineteenth-century England, the *conteuses*' identities as writers were erased and supplanted by the images of these other, more folkloric 'mothers'. Nevertheless, Mother Bunch and her ilk retained productive ties to the *conteuses*, making them, ultimately, more subversive figures than they at first appear to be.[50] Given Dickens's involvement with the theatre during the writing of *Bleak House*, it is no stretch to infer that, in associating Esther with Hortense, he had in mind the relationship between these fairy-tale mothers and their long-standing associations with a French insurrectionist spirit, which had existed long before the French Revolution or the Chartist revolutions of 1848.

Esther's disease paradoxically invests her with increased mobility to operate outside the home and the authority to speak truth to power. She becomes—like the children's literature she embodies—fluid, current, and incorporated into multiple cultural spaces. Where Hortense openly revolts, Esther is tacit, insinuating. Rather than the sparkly, artificially bright 'summer's sun' she has been hitherto, she becomes the novel's restless, permanently veiled, dark lady. In Esther Summerson, the fairy tale, like smallpox, like revolutionary fever, seethes within, explodes outward, crosses class boundaries, and is carried inside forever after as an antibody, an anti-body. Esther's little body does fall away, leaving in its place the 'dark corners' of nursery matter.

---

[47] Mrs Shipton was the name given to Ursula Southill or Sontheil, an English soothsayer who reportedly lived in York in the fifteenth century. *Mother Shipton's Prophesies* represents one of the earliest popular books of folklore. *Mrs Shipton's Prophesies* was first published 80 years after her death, but was attributed to her. See Ursula Shipton, *Mrs. Shipton's Prophesies: The Earliest Published Editions of 1641, 1684 and 1686* (Maidstone: George Mann, 1989); William Axton, 'Esther's Nicknames: A Study in Relevance', *Dickensian* 62 (Autumn, 1966): 158–63.

[48] Jennifer Schacker, 'Generic Transformation and the Body of Mother Bunch', unpublished conference paper (2008), 4. See also Jennifer Schacker, 'Fluid Identities: Madame d'Aulnoy, Mother Bunch, and Fairy Tale History', in Ray Cashman et al. (eds), *The Individual and Tradition: Folkloristic Perspectives* (Bloomington: Indiana University Press, 2011), 249–64.

[49] Schacker, 'Generic Transformation', 5.

[50] Ibid., 14–15.

'REALITY WILL TAKE A WOLFISH TURN': *HARD TIMES*

Hard Times, serialized in *Household Words* from April to August 1854, in many ways summed up the magazine's collective thinking about children's literature over the previous five years. One might say that *Hard Times*'s *raison d'être* is to advocate for a humanities-rich education. The utilitarian Gradgrind system makes a business of quashing 'fancy', by which the narrator means a broad sweep of childhood reading material:

> No little Gradgrind had ever learnt the silly jingle, Twinkle, twinkle, little star; how I wonder what you are! No little Gradgrind had ever known wonder on the subject, each little Gradgrind having at five years old dissected the Great Bear like a Professor Owen, and driven Charles's Wain like a locomotive engine-driver. No little Gradgrind had ever associated a cow in a field with that famous cow with the crumpled horn who tossed the dog who worried the cat who killed the rat who ate the malt, or with that yet more famous cow who swallowed Tom Thumb: it had never heard of those celebrities. (*HT* I:3, 13–14)

Gradgrind's philosophy serves to educate the working classes in the McChoakumchild School as well as his own children; in other words, Dickens indicates that all children in an industrial system are gasping for fancy as if for air. The Dickensian narrator suggests that infusing imaginative reading across the entire class spectrum would generate more productive and less dangerously dissatisfied Victorian adults.

Ironically, the narrator invokes this lack of 'fancy' through fairy-tale metaphors:

> The first object with which they had an association, was a large blackboard with a dry Ogre, chalking ghastly white figures on it.
> Not that they knew, by name or nature, anything about an ogre. Fact forbid! I only use the word to express a monster in a lecturing castle ... taking childhood captive, and dragging it into gloomy statistical dens by the hair. (*HT* I:3, 13)

In passages like this, Dickens differentiates between the brick-and-mortar world of Coketown fact and the extradiegetic space where the narrator wields a language peopled with the familiar characters of fancy.[51] At the end of the novel, we see Gradgrind's daughter, a reformed and humanized Louisa Gradgrind, applying the fairy tale with

---

[51] Catherine Gallagher, ' "Relationship Remembered against Relationship Forgot": Family and Society in *Hard Times* and *North and South*', in *The Industrial Reformation of English Fiction: Social Discourse and Narrative Form 1832–1867* (Chicago: University of Chicago Press, 1985), 147–84; 160.

a gentle, reformatory hand: '[A]ll children loving her; she, grown learned in childish lore; thinking no innocent and pretty fancy ever to be despised; trying hard to know her humbler fellow-creatures, and to beautify their lives of machinery and reality with those imaginative graces and delights, without which the heart of infancy will wither up' (*HT* III:9, 236). Sounding much like Dickens's rationale for the *Household Words* venture, Louisa's philanthropy aims to keep the heart of infancy beating in the machine of industry.

But though the narrator bemoans Coketown's absent fancy, he also suggests that fancy should exert its own supervisory function over children and the working classes. The narrator muses: 'there is an unfathomable mystery in the meanest of [wage labourers] … Supposing we were to reserve our arithmetic for material objects, and to govern these awful unknown quantities by other means!' (*HT* I:11, 61) To exemplify those other means, Sissy Jupe reads to her drunken clown father, '[a]bout the Fairies … and the Dwarf, and the Hunchback, and the Genies'. 'They kept him, many times, from what did him real harm' (*HT* I:7, 45; 9, 53). For Dickens, at least in *Hard Times*, fancy ought to be regulatory rather than liberatory.

Dickens approves the power of children's literature when it is derived from *books*, but more than once, *Hard Times* gazes uneasily at workers who rely on word of mouth:

> Not the least eager of the eyes assembled, were the eyes of those who could not read. These people, as they listened to the friendly voice that read aloud … stared at the characters which meant so much with a vague awe and respect that would have been half ludicrous if any aspect of public ignorance could ever be otherwise than threatening and full of evil. (*HT* III:4, 196)

Oral transmission, perhaps, veers too close to the welling up of revolutionary fervour. The dangers of collectivity are always lurking in the corners of *Hard Times*. And while Dickens loved to stir audiences to screams and faintings when he read aloud from his own books, there is a significant difference between the curated affective response of a genteel, ticket-paying audience (who had already read Dickens's work), and the unregulated emotions of working-class crowds. Literacy, then, is offered as government over those 'awful unknown quantities' of labouring 'hands'.

However, there are moments in *Hard Times* when fancy escapes from its regulatory function. At these times, explicitly linked to both sexual and mercantile appetite, fancy threatens to wreak havoc in the urban scene. The narrator often repeats the perception that the Coketown factories become 'Fairy palaces' at night, when they 'burst into illumination' (*HT* I:11, 60). When Louisa Gradgrind applies this metaphor to herself ('There seems to be nothing there, but languid and monotonous smoke. Yet when night comes, Fire bursts out!' (*HT* I:15, 84)), she implicitly correlates the factory fire and that inner fire—mutual to women and wage workers—that threatens domestic and industrial regulation. The fairy-run factory metaphor suggests that when women's and workers' nocturnal time is unregulated, their own to spend as they will, dissent may blaze up.

Critics[52] have long since identified the Sleary Circus as the prime purveyor of fancy in *Hard Times*; many of these[53] argue that Dickens regards the circus with mixed emotions. Certainly, Sleary's is a vital locus of subversion in the novel. It, too, engages in a 'fairy business' which threatens the middle classes both physically and fiscally:

> There were two or three handsome young women among them, with their two or three husbands, and their two or three mothers, and their eight or nine little children, who did the fairy business when required. The father of one of the families was in the habit of balancing the father of another of the families on the top of a great pole; the father of a third family often made a pyramid of both of these fathers ... all the fathers could dance upon rolling casks, stand upon bottles, catch knives and balls, twirl hand-basins, ride upon anything, jump over everything, and stick at nothing. All the mothers could (and did) dance, upon the slack wire and the tight rope, and perform rapid acts on bare-backed steeds; none of them were at all particular in respect of showing their legs ... [T]hey were not very tidy in their private dresses, they were not at all orderly in their domestic arrangements, and the combined literature of the whole company would have produced but a poor letter on any subject. (*HT* I:6, 34)

These pyramids of unregulated, illiterate, and fertile players are linked to fancy broadly and fairies specifically. Though there is usually 'a remarkable gentleness and childishness about these people' (*HT* I:6, 34), they swarm together in unsettling collective action. As ringmaster Sleary points out, ' "They're a very good natur'd people, my people, but they're accuthtomed to be quick in their movementh; and if you don't act upon my advithe, I'm damned if I don't believe they'll pith you out o' winder" ' (*HT* I:6, 36). Far from innocent, this is fantastic violence that the ringmaster barely holds in check. While the factory 'hands' in *Hard Times* are a synecdoche for a population as yet too exhausted to rise up, the circus imagines a future in which working hands may seize upon their masters.

Dickens contemplates not just fancy's hands but fancy's teeth closing upon middle-class prey. The fairy-tale wolf also takes part in the ludic subversions evident in Dickens's oeuvre; his most wolfish characters attack the fences of various middle-class institutions. As with Hortense in *Bleak House, Hard Times* depicts the poor as ravening wolves:

> [T]he poor you will have always with you. Cultivate in them, while there is yet time, the utmost graces of the fancies and affections, to adorn their lives so much in need of ornament; or, in the day of your triumph, when romance is utterly driven out of their souls, and they and a bare existence stand face to face, Reality will take a wolfish turn, and make an end of you! (*HT* II:6, 133)

---

[52] Ibid. 147–84; Anthony Giffone, 'The Sleary Circus', in Vicki K. Janik (ed.), *Fools and Jesters in Literature, Art, and History: A Bio-Bibliographical Sourcebook* (Westport, CT: Greenwood, 1998), 395–9; Margaret Simpson, '*Hard Times* and Circus Times', *Dickens Quarterly* 10, 3 (1993): 131–46.

[53] Gallagher, ' "Relationship Remembered" ', 147–84; J. Hillis Miller, *Charles Dickens: The World of his Novels* (Cambridge, MA: Harvard University Press, 1958), 226–7; Stephen J. Spector, 'Monsters of Metonymy: *Hard Times* and Knowing the Working Class', *ELH* 51, 2 (1984): 365–84.

The 'wolfish turn' here in its broadest sense symbolizes revolutionary violence. If you don't deliver the carefully packaged fancy of literature, *Hard Times* tells us, the poor will devour the rich just as surely as the wolf devours pigs or fair maidens.

Conclusion

In conclusion, while fairy-tale studies, child studies, educational history, book history, and biographical studies all touch upon children's literature as an emerging genre, none fully examines the range of ways in which Dickens's writing may be seen to engage with it. Children's literature—plots and characters from it, philosophies about it or derived from it, and audiences for it—is pervasive throughout Dickens's works, and perhaps especially in his middle period. The foregoing explorations indicate the potential for further work on the subject of Dickens and children's literature. There are many references to works in the early, middle, and late novels that may illuminate his attitudes to and uses of children's literature. Students of Dickens might turn to *The Old Curiosity Shop*, peopled with the characters of fairy tales and legends, where 'things pass away, like a tale that is told'.[54] They might note those moments in *Oliver Twist* in which Oliver appears to conjure up his antagonists through the process of reading.[55] They might reflect that in *Little Dorrit*, Amy's worldly elder sister Fanny is a dancer in the fairy pantomimes, or that Amy communicates with her mentally impaired charge Maggy through fairy-tale analogies.[56] *Great Expectations* includes an extended 'Cinderella' motif, in which Dickens torques, inverts, and recasts the tale into a grotesque pantomimic drag show.[57] Other intertexts in the novel—*Frankenstein, Hamlet, The Tragedy of George Barnwell*, and Morell's tale of 'Misnar's Pavillion'[58]—provide transformation narratives more

---

[54] Charles Dickens, *The Old Curiosity Shop*, ed. Elizabeth M. Brennan (Oxford: Clarendon Press, 1997), 73, 575. For more on this subject, see Molly Clark Hillard, 'Dangerous Exchange: Fairy Footsteps, Goblin Economies, and *The Old Curiosity Shop*', *Dickens Studies Annual* 35 (2005): 63–86.

[55] Charles Dickens, *Oliver Twist*, ed. Kathleen Tillotson (Oxford: Clarendon Press, 1966), 34, 227–8.

[56] Charles Dickens, *Little Dorrit*, ed. Harvey Peter Sucksmith (Oxford: Clarendon Press, 1979), I:9, 95–9; I:24, 284–9.

[57] Charles Dickens, *Great Expectations*, ed. Margaret Cardwell (Oxford: Clarendon Press, 1993). Subsequent references are inserted parenthetically in the text by *GE* volume:chapter, page. While at first Pip sees Miss Havisham as fairy godmother to his Cinderella ('"This is a gay figure, Pip" said she, making her crutch stick play round me, as if she, the fairy godmother who had changed me, were bestowing the finishing gift' (*GE* I:19, 155)), he later comes to recognize that Magwitch in fact embodies an even grislier version of that role. Miss Havisham herself takes a turn as a stagnant Cinderella, ever limping in one shoe, with her clocks stopped at the moment that her intended deserted her. Though Pip would like to see cold Estella as 'the Princess' of Satis House, 'rescue[d]' and transformed into a loving bride (*GE* II:10, 232), Estella is a false heroine compared to the real transformation of village girl Biddy as she comes under Joe's loving influence ('Her shoes came up at the heel' (*GE* I:17, 124)).

[58] Jerome Meckier, *Dickens's Great Expectations: Misnar's Pavilion Versus Cinderella* (Lexington: University Press of Kentucky, 2002); Sir Charles Morell, 'The Enchanters, or The Sultan Misnar of India', in *Tales of the Genii* (London: Simpkin, Marshall, Hamilton, Kent and Co., 1800), 111–28.

suited to an adult audience, but also remind readers that the oldest 'Cinderella' versions are just as gruesome and blood-soaked. Pip comes to learn that his own transformation (characterized by social climbing and familial erasure) and the property he accrues (with its ties to imperial and industrial abuses) is not great, but toxic and filthy.[59] *Our Mutual Friend* fishes the fragments of tales—especially 'Little Red Riding Hood', as I have argued elsewhere[60]—proverbs, ballads, and nursery rhymes from the current of literary history and 'pretty well papers the room' with them (*OMF* I:3, 22).[61] Mr Boffin proclaims that 'it's too late for me to begin shovelling and sifting at alphabeds' (*OMF* I:5, 50); his fanciful conflation of reading materials and dust heaps heralds the central actions of the novel, in which reading, or being read to, leads to the extraction of treasure or revelation of secrets out of which the novel is pieced together.

All in all, children and their literatures are never the light-hearted subjects that even Dickens would have us think them. In his periodical and novel writing, children's literature serves a dual, and seemingly counter-intuitive, function. First, as a tool to prevent the dissolution of the working classes into moral abandonment or mob violence. Second, and paradoxically, as it is absorbed into Dickensian plots it comes to symbolize those very (purported) disaffections of the working classes: physical and sexual hunger, the rage of the dispossessed, carnivalesque and chaotic play, and collective action.

Further Reading

Peter Merchant and Catherine Waters (eds), *Dickens and the Imagined Child* (Farnham: Ashgate, 2015)

Laura Peters (ed.), *Dickens and Childhood* (London: Routledge, 2012)

Harry Stone, *Dickens and the Invisible World: Fairy Tales, Fantasy, and Novel-Making* (Bloomington: Indiana University Press, 1979)

---

[59] For the filthiness of money, see *GE*, I:10, 79 and II:2, 171. See also Elaine Ostry, *Social Dreaming: Dickens and the Fairy Tale* (New York: Routledge, 2002), 1–28.

[60] Molly Clark Hillard, 'Little Red Riding Hood and Other Waterside Characters', in *Spellbound: The Fairy Tale and the Victorians* (Columbus: Ohio State University Press, 2014), 197–216.

[61] Fractured proverbs govern the book titles in each volume, bastardized ballads issue from Silas Wegg, snatches of children's verse bubble up through various characters ('a leg of mutton somehow ended in daygo' (*OMF* I:2, 11); 'Rumty-iddity, Row dow dow' (*OMF* I:4, 33); 'Mew, Quack-quack, Bow-wow!' (*OMF* III:11, 596)). Fanny Cleaver renames herself as the Jenny Wren of nursery rhyme (*OMF* II:2, 233).

PART III
THE SOCIO-HISTORICAL CONTEXTS

CHAPTER 25

THE TROUBLE WITH ANGELS

Dickens, Gender, and Sexuality

JAMES ELI ADAMS

'[E]ARTH seemed not her element, nor its rough creatures her fit companions.' The words describe Rose Maylie in *Oliver Twist*, but Dickens's novels abound with such angelic women, and that heavenly chorus has suggested to many readers that sexuality is not Dickens's element.[1] Indeed, his celebration of other-worldly or childlike femininity, with its corollary anathema of 'fallen' women, has often seemed the quintessence of a fabled Victorian repression, which evaded the complexities and the satisfactions of adult sexual life. Certainly, such emphases chime with Victorian idealizations of domesticity, which obscure or radically simplify the unsettling energies of erotic desire in imagining a tranquil refuge from the wider world. Over the past several decades, however, scholars have elicited a far more complex play of sexuality in Dickens's fiction, prodded most fundamentally by Michel Foucault's example of listening to the apparent silences of a text. Most notably, Eve Kosofsky Sedgwick's ground-breaking work has called attention to the power of homoerotic desire and its violent interdiction in Dickens's representation of social dominance and male rivalry; John Kucich has analysed the work of repression as a structure that generates its own (often violent) erotic pleasures and powerfully shapes social life; Amanda Anderson has analysed 'fallen' women in the novels not merely as anathemas of sexuality but as a more comprehensive preoccupation with compromised agency; Sharon Marcus, Holly Furneaux, and others have explored the queer structures of Dickensian domesticity, which frequently confound 'heteronormative' stereotypes by reserving happiness for households organized by kinship or elective affinities outside marriage.[2]

---

[1] Charles Dickens, *Oliver Twist*, ed. Kathleen Tillotson (Oxford: Clarendon Press, 1966), 29, 187.
[2] Eve Kosofsky Sedgwick, *Between Men: English Literature and Male Homosocial Desire* (New York: Columbia University Press, 1985); John Kucich, *Repression in Victorian Fiction: Charlotte Bronte, George Eliot, and Charles Dickens* (Berkeley: University of California Press, 1987); Amanda Anderson, *Tainted Souls and Painted Faces: The Rhetoric of 'Fallenness' in Victorian Culture* (Ithaca, NY: Cornell, 1993); Sharon Marcus, *Between Women: Friendship, Desire, and Marriage in Victorian*

As this range of work suggests, the play of gender and sexuality in Dickens's fiction leads very quickly to what George Eliot called 'that tempting range of relevancies called the universe'.[3] Hence this chapter focuses on but one thread of its immense subject, approached through the tensions between Dickens's domestic angels and the subtly insistent presence of human reproduction in his novels. Quite apart from the momentous births of Oliver Twist or Paul Dombey or Esther Summerson, Dickens's recurrent attention to pregnancy and breast-feeding sets the action of his novels in a world of fecundity: thus, for example, Mrs Perch in *Dombey and Son* 'being (but that she always is) in an interesting situation' or Mrs Micawber in *David Copperfield*, whose many children are perpetually 'taking refreshment' at her breast.[4] Such figures embody reproductive sexuality as a pervasive, seemingly inescapable force, which might seem the ultimate leveller of social distinction. When the infant Paul Dombey after the death of his mother must be sustained by the wet nurse Polly Toodle, Miss Tox is struck by the notion of 'a little cherub closely connected with the superior classes, gradually unfolding itself from day to day at one common fountain' (*DS* 2, 22): she thinks this 'a privilege' for Polly, but 'common fountain' may suggest instead the common dependence of little cherubs on a maternal body, and the common susceptibility to sexual desire that brings little cherubs into being.

The irony is unsteady, however; while Dickens may mock this view of social superiority, his novels are deeply invested in a moral superiority grounded in the management of sexual desire, a regimen that is central to the articulation of both gender norms and social class. The momentousness of unruly desire is most glaring in the angel/whore dualism in Dickens's fiction, within which even a hint of feminine sexual transgression may bring about a kind of social death. This preoccupation reflects in turn a momentous realignment of long-standing gender norms, which informs a powerful asymmetry in Dickens's representation of gender and sexuality. Woman, traditionally figured as a creature of dangerous, unreflective appetite, becomes in Victorian domestic ideology a figure of selfless, nurturing sympathy and of instinctive modesty and restraint (an unsettled ideal, as many critics have pointed out, which paradoxically seems to require incessant reiteration in Victorian novels). Masculine desire becomes the more disruptive force, which must be controlled by the will, aided by feminine 'influence' and by often virtuoso forms of self-discipline. Thus while representations of femininity tend to be shaped by stark sexual dichotomies—the virtuous and the 'fallen'—masculinity in Dickens tends to be articulated through a broad array of psychic regimens, which are inflected by, and in turn articulate, more intricate social hierarchies.

England (Princeton: Princeton University Press, 2007); Holly Furneaux, *Queer Dickens* (Oxford: Oxford University Press, 2010).

[3] George Eliot, *Middlemarch* (Harmondsworth: Penguin, 1994), 141.

[4] Charles Dickens, *Dombey and Son*, ed. Alan Horsman (Oxford: Clarendon Press, 1974), 31, 423. Subsequent references are inserted parenthetically in the text by *DS* chapter, page. Charles Dickens, *David Copperfield*, ed. Nina Burgis (Oxford: Clarendon Press, 1981), 11, 135. Subsequent references are inserted parenthetically in the text by *DC* chapter, page.

This chapter focuses on three novels from different stages of Dickens's career—*The Pickwick Papers*, *David Copperfield*, and *Our Mutual Friend*—to bring home something of the range in his characterization of sexuality and sexual discipline, as well as some of its consistent preoccupations. *The Pickwick Papers* evokes little sense of character interiority, but this construction allows Dickens to anatomize sexuality itself as largely a surface effect, constructed primarily as a world of collective sexual innuendo and projection, which circulates apart from any evocation of psychic depth in Pickwick himself. In *David Copperfield*, literary character becomes more internalized, not only through first-person narration but as dynamics of sexual suspicion grow more sombre and more momentous. Here the hero's struggle towards self-awareness and self-mastery—articulated largely through his contrasting attachments to Dora and Agnes—erupts with particular intensity in his socio-erotic rivalry with Uriah Heep, one of the most vivid of the character doublings that become so prominent in Dickens's later novels. In *Our Mutual Friend*, fierce male rivalry once again figures centrally, but Dickens divides the novel's interests among three male disciplinary regimens, which are so thoroughgoing that the novel's central preoccupation can seem to be the fashioning of character. In the process, Dickens again presents repression as a marker of class standing, which is ratified in the relative assurance with which a character masters his unruly desires—desires thrown into relief, once again, by contrasting models of femininity.

THE PICKWICK PAPERS

In *The Pickwick Papers*, the sublime innocence of Dickens's protagonist stands out amidst a whirl of sexual innuendo and intrigue. That intrigue takes many forms, from Tracy Tupman's impassioned wooing, in rivalry with that of Jingle, to the insinuating winks of Sam Weller, to scandalous rumours circulated in various contexts. But this sexuality is curiously detached from any evocation of psychic depth; it appears from the very outset as social or literary convention, even cliché, less the quality of an individual agent than a construction of the culture at large. Thus the opening pages introduce Mr Tupman, whose 'ruling passion' even in middle age remains 'admiration of the fair sex' and who seeks 'the fame of conquest'—soon to be echoed in the character of Jingle, a parody of the Byronic lover, with his tales of 'thousands' of conquests in Spain; the 'fat boy' frames Tupman's intrigues with the Gothic invocation, 'I wants to make your flesh creep'; even so minor a character as Mr Smangle, the Fleet prisoner also given to 'many nods and winks, implying profound mystery', regales Pickwick with 'divers romantic adventures ... involving various interesting anecdotes of a thorough-bred horse, and a magnificent Jewess, both of surpassing beauty, and much coveted by the nobility and gentry of these kingdoms'.[5] Only Sam Weller, whose stolen kisses and insinuating

---

[5] Charles Dickens, *The Pickwick Papers*, ed. James Kinsley (Oxford: Clarendon Press, 1986), 1, 5; 8, 119; 44, 683; 41, 643–4. Subsequent references are inserted parenthetically in the text by *PP* chapter, page.

wink—'a wink, the intense meaning of which no description could convey the faintest idea of' (*PP* 52, 802)—suggests a more distinctly embodied desire, but even his eroticism is attached to a literary type, the cockney servant.

The force of sexuality as a social construction is brought home by Mr Pickwick's exposure to the innuendo swirling around him. The trial of Bardell v. Pickwick, in which Pickwick is accused of marital breach of promise, is the epitome of a more subtle and diffuse web of erotic insinuation which discovers transgressive desire in the most banal gestures—such as a note to his landlady reading 'Dear Mrs. B.—Chops and Tomata sauce. Yours, PICKWICK' (*PP* 34, 521). In the eyes of Mrs Bardell's advocate, Sergeant Buzfuz, such notes 'are covert, sly, underhanded communications, but, fortunately, far more conclusive than if couched in the most glowing language and the most poetic imagery ... letters that were evidently intended at the time, by Pickwick, to mislead and delude any third parties into whose hands they might fall' (*PP* 34, 521). The comedy here took added edge from its allusion to recent news, a lawsuit which the Hon. George Norton brought against the Prime Minister of Great Britain, Lord Melbourne, alleging 'criminal conversation'—adultery—with Norton's wife, the Hon. Caroline Norton. But Dickens is interested less in aristocratic licence than in the construction of illicit desire. And in this respect, the interpretative labour of Buzfuz is seconded by a host of figures in the novel, including the narrator. In the famous Eatanswill election scenes, for example, when Pickwick kisses his hand to Mrs Pott, wife of the editor of the *Eatanswill Gazette*, 'this very innocent action', the narrator remarks, 'was sufficient to awaken [the crowd's] facetiousness':

> 'Oh you wicked old rascal,' cried one voice, 'looking arter the girls, are you?'
> 'Oh you wenerable sinner,' cried another.
> 'Putting on his spectacles to look at a married 'ooman!' said a third.
> 'I see him a vinkin' at her, vith his vicked old eye,' shouted a fourth.
> 'Look arter your wife, Pott,' bellowed a fifth;—and then there was a roar of laughter.
> As these taunts were accompanied with invidious comparison between Mr. Pickwick and an aged ram, and several witticisms of the like nature; and as they moreover tended to convey reflections upon the honour of an innocent lady, Mr. Pickwick's indignation was excessive. (*PP* 13, 191–2)

Pickwick's every gesture becomes in its very lack of hidden depth a screen onto which observers are invited to project familiar erotic fantasy. Even the narrator joins in when Pickwick departs from Dingley Dell: he 'kissed the young ladies—we were going to say, as if they were his own daughters, only as he might possibly have infused a little more warmth into the salutation, the comparison would not be quite appropriate' (*PP* 11, 154). The warmth of Pickwickian friendship generates a whisper of incest—an insinuation that of course eludes Pickwick himself; it is the narrator, not Pickwick, who envisions the young ladies as his daughters. In effect, this chorus redoubles the energies most strikingly incarnated in the Fat Boy, who recounts to Mrs Wardle's elderly mother the scene of Tupman wooing Mrs Wardle in the arbour at Dingley Dell, professing, 'I wants to make your flesh creep' (*PP* 8, 119). Which is, in effect, precisely what Buzfuz seeks to accomplish.

In these scenes, sexuality is cut adrift from the psychological depth we associate with high Victorian realism—including later Dickens. It hardly seems to reside in Pickwick, but is instead a collective, public experience, a set of social conventions projected onto a character largely defined through resistance to Buzfuz's hermeneutic of suspicion. In keeping with the melodramatic mode, sexuality becomes externalized as one instance of 'the force of circumstances', which animates so much of the novel's comedy. When Pickwick is served with Mrs Bardell's lawsuit, Tupman recalls an earlier incident, in which Mrs Bardell had fainted and Pickwick was discovered with his landlady 'reclining in his arms'. 'Gracious powers', the innocent Pickwick remarks, 'what a dreadful instance of the force of circumstances!' (*PP* 18, 268–9). The idiom conjures up an agency constraining the character's own, as if circumstances themselves were indicting Pickwick, working in parallel with the wilful sexual projection throughout the novel. In the process, Dickens presents a world in which sexuality does not constitute a private self; indeed, Pickwick's putative desire hardly seems even to belong to him, but is instead a collective, public fantasy.[6]

DAVID COPPERFIELD

The construction of Pickwickian desire, epitomized by Buzfuz's interrogation, comically presumes a psychological depth at odds with the novel's dominant mode of characterization. In Dickens's later fiction, character becomes more deeply internalized, as constructions of sexuality become increasingly sombre and consequential, subject to momentous error, and thereby align sexuality with danger, something to be hidden and avoided—albeit often to little avail. Buzfuz's interrogation is strikingly recalled in an important sub-plot in *David Copperfield*, where sexuality is similarly constructed as a collective fantasy, but now becomes a projection that is far more disturbing in its import, and ultimately redounds on the observer as a form of sexualized shame.[7] This is the plot strand involving Annie Strong, the young wife of David's schoolmaster Dr Strong. Like nearly every character acquainted with the couple, David presumes that Annie is unfaithful to her much older husband (an inference that in itself ratifies the importance of sexuality within marriage). That belief informs his arresting image of Annie in chapter 16, as she listens to her seemingly oblivious husband

> with such a face as I never saw. It was so beautiful in its form, it was so ashy pale, it was so fixed in its abstraction, it was so full of a wild, sleep-walking, dreamy

---

[6] This emphasis reflects Dickens's debt to melodrama, in which, as Juliet John points out, 'emotions do not "belong" to the individual experiencing them but to common experience'. Juliet John, *Dickens's Villains: Melodrama, Character, Popular Culture* (Oxford: Oxford University Press, 2001), 30.

[7] For a fuller comparison of these two episodes, see James Eli Adams, 'Reading with Buzfuz: Dickens, Sexuality, Interrogation', in Eileen Gillooly and Deirdre David (eds), *Contemporary Dickens* (Columbus: Ohio University Press, 2009), 231–44.

horror of I don't know what ... Distinctly as I recollect her look, I cannot tell of what it was expressive ... Penitence, humiliation, shame, pride, love, and trustfulness—I see them all; and in them all, I see that horror of I don't know what. (*DC* 16, 210–11)

Here the very indeterminacy of the image amplifies the sense of interiority already inherent in the first-person narration, attributing to Annie mysterious depths that are alien to the characterization in *The Pickwick Papers*. The 'horror' David detects intimates Annie's consciousness of some form of transgression, which places her within a pattern of feminine purity shadowed by sexual errancy. David's observation of Annie thus anticipates Emily's flight with Steerforth, as well as the more thoroughgoing debasement of Emily's 'shadow', the prostitute Martha Endell, a consummate example of the social death associated with 'fallenness': ' "How can I go on as I am, a solitary curse to myself, a living disgrace to every one I come near! ... Stamp upon me, kill me!" ' (*DC* 47, 583).

Here as throughout Dickens's fiction, the doubling of female characters underscores the momentous stakes of the angel/whore binary, which reflect the irrevocability of sexual transgression. In *David Copperfield*, however, Dickens diverts attention from Annie's sexuality to a dynamic of self-recognition on David's part, in which the most potent locus of erotic energy shifts from a woman's character to the men who observe her. Knowledge itself becomes powerfully sexualized. Tellingly, David is first introduced to the Strongs in chapter 16, 'I am a New Boy in more senses than one', which is centrally concerned with the guilty sexual awareness (and consequent social degradation) that David has derived from his time in Murdstone and Grinby's bottling business. The 'sleepless eyes' of Heep (introduced in the previous chapter) underscore David's worry over the potential exposure of his degrading knowledge, which sets him apart from his new schoolmates: 'How would it affect them, who were so innocent of London life, and London streets, to discover how knowing I was (and was ashamed to be) in some of the meanest phases of both?' (*DC* 16, 196). In his anxiety, David finds a double in Heep, who arouses 'a sort of fascination' (*DC* 16, 200) that leaves David feeling 'attracted to him in very repulsion' (*DC* 25, 328). Just as the naked social ambition of Heep is a foil to David's superior but anxious social standing, so David's preoccupation with sexual transgression is disavowed in the guise of Heep's more overt and self-interested spying. (The same structure may also offer an alibi for the reader, who has been enticed to share in the collective fantasy.)

When in chapter 42 Heep springs his trap to expose (as he imagines) Annie's infidelity, the doubling is made explicit: 'I saw so plainly, in the stealthy exultation of his face, what I already so plainly knew; I mean that he forced his confidence upon me' (*DC* 42, 529). David's inadvertent disclosure of his own suspicion is projected onto Heep as an unwanted intimacy, violently 'forced upon' him, and he slaps Heep as if in response to a sexual advance. But his loss of composure surrenders further mastery to Heep: the clerk 'caught the hand in his, and we stood, in that connexion, looking at each other. We stood so, a long time ...'. When Heep then coyly berates Copperfield for having so lost his self-possession as to strike a social inferior, the turn of the knife is complete: 'He knew me better than I knew myself' (*DC* 42, 530).[8]

Throughout Dickens, such scenes of masculine rivalry capture the often fierce homoerotic energies informing what Eve Kosofsky Sedgwick has influentially analysed as 'homosocial' bonds between men. The sexual energies are made grotesquely clear when Heep's profession of love for Agnes prompts David to imagine 'seizing the red-hot poker out of the fire, and running him through with it' (*DC* 25, 326). In Dickens, the aggression is inflamed by class anxiety; more assured social standing, as we shall see, is distinguished by more assured self-management. But homoerotic rivalry is less fundamental to *David Copperfield* than is the sexualizing of knowledge itself. What is ultimately eroticized in this sub-plot is not so much Annie Strong, who turns out to be a feminine paragon, as the interpretative project, and the peculiar will to power expressed in the two characters' misplaced suspicions. David comes to recognize his inference as a misdirected carnal knowledge, a collective male fantasy that taints the innocent Annie with the stigma of 'fallenness'. In the process, the novel pointedly recasts the erotic comedy of 'circumstances' in *Pickwick*, transforming the earlier sexual innuendo into a psychic drama with potentially devastating social consequences. Annie's climactic declaration of devotion to her husband not only vindicates her fidelity, but offers David a diagnosis of his own waywardness: 'my undisciplined heart'.

That repeated phrase most obviously refers to his choice of Dora, but it resonates far more broadly in Dickens's fiction as a caution for the management of unruly desire. The lapse of such discipline frequently crystallizes as 'fascination', a fixation that is often overtly homoerotic (it recurs, for example, in association with sadistic schoolmasters who delight in flogging their charges).[9] Thus David is fascinated by Steerforth as well as Heep; indeed Heep's 'beastly' character here, too, seems a vehicle for disavowing David's homoerotic desires, which are less troubling when aroused by the charismatic Steerforth, whose charm persists even after death.

Fascination resonates even more widely, however, as it associates erotic life generally with a suspension or derangement of agency. In this regard, David's lapses suggestively shadow the more momentous transgressions of fallen women.[10] For both Emily and David erotic attachment is closely bound up with social ambition. When David falls in love with Dora at first sight, the woman is submerged in the social possibilities she represents, while Emily (like so many fallen women in Victorian fiction) is seduced in large part by the dream of becoming a lady. And this affinity helps to illuminate the peculiar fixation aroused by fallen women in Dickens's fiction. Idealized domestic

---

[8] Here I take issue with D. A. Miller's influential reading of the novel, which takes it to be invested in a fantasy of selfhood as radical privacy: David's self-understanding is emphatically intersubjective, as he recognizes himself, and the desire that rules his project, in the eyes of Uriah Heep.

[9] See Natalie Rose, 'Dickens and Fascination: Flogging and the Fragile Will', *Victorian Studies* 47 (2004–5): 505–33.

[10] Amanda Anderson has suggestively analysed this congruence, but primarily in its bearing on the power of 'coercive narrative forms' rather than David's complicity with Heep, whom her account does not mention. Anderson, *Tainted Souls*, 94–5.

femininity—epitomized by Agnes Wickfield, whom David increasingly invokes as a model for his own discipline—distils a fantasy of the 'disinterested', a world in which selfish desire seems submerged in the steadfast love and integrity of the household 'angel'. This ideal offers a pattern for lovers generally, as it is enforced throughout Dickens at the level of plot. Passion that might further worldly success cannot be love, because it is contaminated by self-interest; hence in Dickensian courtship, protagonists typically must be ruined financially before their passion can be purged of any suspicion of the mercenary.

But the anathema of 'self' makes it difficult to accommodate openly erotic desire, which invariably seems a mode of self-assertion. That logic is particularly striking in David's relation to Agnes, whom he first declares to be his sister—a recurrent Dickensian means of disavowing sexual desire, as with Florence Dombey and Walter Gay—and then transforms into a figure in stained glass gesturing to heaven like a saint.[11] 'There is no alloy of self in what I feel for you', David ultimately professes to Agnes, as if 'what I feel' were evacuated of erotic longing (*DC* 62, 737). Such devotion finds its antitype in the prostitute, who transforms femininity into a commodity, the domestic angel into a creature of untrammelled desire, and the social world into a moral wilderness.

Of course, even Agnes suggests the strains of an idealized femininity, or (put differently) that angelic womanhood is a discipline of desire rather than a transcendence of it. That burden is clearer in the relatively few female characters in Dickens who find an outlet for frustrated desire in a powerfully eroticized anger. Rosa Dartle, Mrs Steerforth's companion, is especially fierce: she is Steerforth's first victim, her scar a testimony to his wilful cruelty even as a child, and thereby aligned with Emily. But the violence has not overcome her desire for Steerforth—'I loved him better than you', she will tell his ageing mother—and she channels that baffled longing into furious attacks on the 'creature' who has displaced her (*DC* 56, 685–6). Her fury culminates in the extraordinary scene in which she confronts the distraught Emily, finally returned from her wanderings, and for five pages excoriates her, '[t]his piece of pollution, picked up from the water-side': 'If I could order it to be done, I would have this girl whipped to death!' (*DC* 50, 613–17). The sadistic attack is all the more unsettling because David is lingering outside the door the whole time, unwilling to intervene, as if he and his narrative were tacitly endorsing the denunciation. Rosa's fury seems to channel not only her own pathological frustration but the deep cultural unease that fallen women arouse throughout Dickens's fiction.

The male erotic rivalry between David and Uriah is similarly entangled in social class, but more clearly illuminates the peculiar tensions besetting social ambition. Upwardly aspiring men in Dickens must master two subtly dissonant challenges. First, they must exhibit the self-discipline that will gain both material security and recognition of their moral character. That moral recognition is the foundation of Victorian reconfigurations of the older, broadly aristocratic ideal of the gentleman. At the same time, that older

---

[11] See Helena Michie, 'From Blood to Law: The Embarrassments of Family in Dickens', in John Bowen and Robert L. Patten (eds), *Palgrave Advances in Charles Dickens Studies* (Basingstoke: Palgrave Macmillan, 2006), 131–54.

ideal persists in the allure of Steerforth and his many kindred spirits in later Dickens—Skimpole in *Bleak House*, James Harthouse in *Hard Times*, Henry Gowan in *Little Dorrit*, Sydney Carton in *Tale of Two Cities*, Eugene Wrayburn in *Our Mutual Friend*. Each of these characters pointedly challenges the middle-class virtues of earnestness and industry. Their languid self-assurance, born of varied experience and material security, seems an attack not merely on earnest striving but on decency itself. Yet the insouciance that is morally reprehensible has a profound erotic appeal, particularly to less privileged men, for whom it seems a latter-day *sprezzatura* radiating both social authority and erotic confidence. As David remarks of Steerforth, 'There was an ease in his manner—a gay and light manner it was, but not swaggering—which I believe to have borne a kind of enchantment with it' (*DC* 7, 89). But how can a life dedicated to disciplined labour ever realize this enchanting 'ease'?

Our Mutual Friend

This challenge lies at the heart of *Our Mutual Friend*, where Dickens more fully explores the burdens of masculinity as an incessant discipline, energized and guided but also imperilled by sexual desire. The novel is built around a male rivalry even more violent than that of David and Uriah, which is evoked in the electric first encounter of the two characters:

> Very remarkably, neither Eugene Wrayburn nor Bradley Headstone looked at all at the boy. Through the ensuing dialogue, those two, no matter who spoke, or whom was addressed, looked at each other. There was some secret, sure perception between them, which set them against one another in all ways.[12]

The riveted, interlocked gazes of melodrama once again evoke an unsettling intimacy. The two men are joined, most immediately, by a struggle for social and erotic dominance. More emphatically even than *David Copperfield*, *Our Mutual Friend* is preoccupied with social mobility. The novel concludes with Twemlow's endorsement of the dramatic social ascent of Lizzie Hexam, and his defence of the 'gentleman' as 'the degree that may be attained by any man' (*OMF* IV:17, 820). Such egalitarianism would ostensibly be affirmed through varieties of masculine self-fashioning, which would enable men of lower birth to claim gentlemanly status. (A woman's ascent remains tied to her marriage.) But Dickens's characterization undermines this ostensible egalitarianism. Far from being a mode of self-fashioning, repression becomes a psychic and social dynamic that affirms a pre-existent class standing. Wrayburn, the born gentleman, manifests that status in

---

[12] Charles Dickens, *Our Mutual Friend*, ed. Michael Cotsell, Oxford World's Classics (Oxford: Oxford University Press, 2008), II:6, 288. Subsequent references are inserted parenthetically in the text by *OMF* Book:chapter, page.

the poise of perfect self-possession; Headstone, the working-class schoolmaster, can never transcend mere self-suppression, the all-too-obvious psychic labour of the pauper lad, which no amount of 'decent' clothing can conceal. Ultimately this hierarchy also will inform different levels of complexity within the three central male characters. Most notably, Wrayburn's virtuosic repression will allow him to embody a psychic division, between cynical idler and earnest lover, that is largely internalized; Headstone's transparency, by contrast, means that his psychic tensions—between the 'decent' and the criminal—will be more obvious, and largely developed through external doubling, as in his juxtaposition with Riderhood. At the same time, however, the 'sure, secret perception' hints at a more fundamental reciprocity: if Headstone recognizes in Wrayburn an index of all he lacks socially, Wrayburn in turn glimpses in Headstone an animating 'fire' that he must acquire in order to escape his own psychic confinement.

Bradley Headstone, the focal point of working-class aspirations, might seem a paragon of Victorian self-help, in the phrase of Samuel Smiles: he is a young man of no means, limited gifts, but great persistence who has ground his way to the modest respectability of 'highly certificated stipendiary schoolmaster' (*OMF* II:1, 216). As this arch phrasing suggests, however, from his first appearance Headstone is doomed to frustration. The narrator lingers over the particulars of Bradley's 'decent' clothing, the repetition of that modifier underscoring the anxious, even compulsive care with which Headstone presents himself to the world. 'He was never seen in any other dress, and yet there was a certain stiffness in his manner of wearing this, as if there were a want of adaptation between him and it, recalling some mechanics in their holiday clothes' (*OMF* II:1, 217). The reference to 'mechanics' recalls *Great Expectations*, where Joe Gargery on his visit to the newly gentrified Pip in London cries out in dismay, 'I'm wrong in these clothes!'[13] But Joe's discomfort marks fidelity to a true self; we are meant to applaud his very lack of social ambition, his awareness that he is out of place in Pip's world of frustrated ambition. Bradley Headstone's hard-won respectability, on the other hand, is presented from the outset as a dangerous masquerade; no amount of discipline can make him at home in the world of the respectable and the decent.

Most critics attribute this disparagement to the 'mechanical' aspects of Headstone's character, his effort to compensate for his lack of intellectual gifts through sheer discipline, drawing on an obvious and apparently debilitating repression: 'I don't show what I feel; some of us are obliged habitually to keep it down. To keep it down' (*OMF* II:11, 344). The obligation, of course, is that of the schoolmaster's calling, and in this emphasis Headstone reproduces a recurrent target of Dickens's satire, the systems of rote learning and unimaginative teaching that had gained new prominence with the creation of national schools. But Headstone is hardly alone in his commitment to repression. 'Cover him, crush him, keep him down!' Rokesmith exhorts himself, referring to his real identity as John Harmon, and Bella recognizes his effort: '"I have noticed ... that

---

[13] Charles Dickens, *Great Expectations*, ed. Margaret Cardwell (Oxford: Clarendon Press, 1993), II:8, 225.

you repress yourself"' (*OMF* II:13, 378; III:9, 521). Even the jaunty Wrayburn, when he is out walking with Lizzie and Riah, shows a 'seeming levity and carelessness' that are just that—'seeming'. When their paths diverge, 'his part was played out for the evening, and ... he came off the stage'—only to mull over more sombre thoughts that he had, for the time, repressed (*OMF* II:15, 406–7). Headstone is set apart, then, not by the fact of repression, but by his ineptitude in executing it, his inability to 'keep it down', which amplifies David's similar anxiety that Heep and others can read his thoughts.

Rokesmith is a subtler case; the energy of his repression is visible, but what it conceals (his actual identity as John Harmon) is not. Wrayburn, however, is the virtuoso of self-management; his discipline is so subtle that it is visible as such only to the narrator and the reader; even his close friend Mortimer Lightwood can register it only in confusing glimpses. Tellingly, these gradations correspond to a social hierarchy: the pauper lad; the disinherited son of a self-made man; the idle younger son of the landed gentry. Repression thus becomes a social grace that reinforces class standing. The erotic allure of Wrayburn's aristocratic panache affects not only Headstone but Lizzie Hexam. His influence on Lizzie may seem perplexing: he is disdainful, cynical, and cruel, savouring his power over a young woman whom he does not love but also does not seem to respect, to the point that even Lizzie at moments fears that the natural endpoint of his attentions will be some form of sexual coercion. But the appeal—and it is unusually emphatic in a Dickens heroine—seems to be that of class itself. To be sure, Lizzie sees in Wrayburn a man worth rescuing; 'She knows he has failings, but she thinks they have grown up through his being like one cast away.' Yet this longing unfolds alongside a fantasy recalling Steerforth's appeal to Emily, of being 'that lady rich and beautiful that I can never come near' (*OMF* II:11, 349). Wrayburn's attentions are 'like glimpses of an enchanted world' (*OMF* II:15, 406). Headstone, in turn, suffers from the sheer visibility of his origins—his awkwardness, his insecurity, his frustration—which the novel suggests are wounds only aggravated by his efforts to conceal them.

The battle, however, is not quite so one-sided as it might seem. In the design of the novel, Wrayburn's poise (like that of Sydney Carton in *Tale of Two Cities*) must be troubled by the energy of unfamiliar desire. His passion for Lizzie ultimately brings him to embrace the middle-class norms he formerly mocked, but the tension is also necessary to produce an internal division that complicates a character otherwise comparatively shallow, too easily reduced to a social type. In this development, Headstone offers an unexpected template: what Wrayburn seems to require is some version of the 'wild energy' that distinguishes Headstone, and is magnified by the very frustration of his desires. We might expect that the 'fire' that breaks out in Headstone's 'terrible' rage will be a focal point of his abjection, as it is an index of his social failings. From Bradley's first appearance, however, this attribute also becomes his lone claim to distinction:

> Suppression of so much to make room for so much, had given him a constrained manner, over and above. Yet there was enough of what was animal, and of what was fiery (though smouldering), still visible in him, to suggest that if young Bradley Headstone, when a pauper lad, had chanced to be told off for the sea, he

would not have been the last man in a ship's crew. Regarding that origin of his, he was proud, moody, and sullen, desiring it to be forgotten. And few people knew of it. (*OMF* II:1, 218)

This smouldering fire will break out to murderous effect. Yet here, at its first mention, Bradley's 'wild energy' elicits a kind of respect. What demeans Bradley, paradoxically, is again his social ambition, his efforts to escape 'that origin of his', which fuels his deference to social constraint, 'suppression of so much'. In another context, the 'fire' that is inflamed by his failing might have flourished, and been a claim to distinction. One such context, a realm freed from the burdens of the decent and the respectable, is life at sea. Another, unexpectedly, is love.

As a man in love, Bradley incarnates the peculiar fascinations of a 'wild energy' that threatens every form of limit or constraint, even one's very sense of self. He thus epitomizes the interplay of passion and repression in Dickens's novels that John Kucich has astutely analysed, in which forms of desire so intense that they threaten self-annihilation are countered by efforts to 'conserve' the self.[14] Outwardly so unprepossessing, even abject, Headstone in his desire burns with such force that his passion for Lizzie seems to transfigure not only his character, but the familiar idioms of love:

> Love at first sight is a trite expression quite sufficiently discussed; enough that in certain smouldering natures like this man's, that passion leaps into a blaze, and makes such head as fire does in a rage of wind, when other passions, but for its mastery, could be held in chains. As a multitude of weak, imitative natures are always lying by, ready to go mad upon the next wrong idea that may be broached ... so these less ordinary natures may lie by for years, ready on the touch of an instant to burst into flame. (*OMF* II:11, 341)

The characterization is powerfully ambivalent: at his first appearance, Headstone was a 'weak, imitative nature'; here he is one of those 'less ordinary natures' that unsettle our preconceptions about passion. We may think we understand the trite expression, 'love at first sight', but when Bradley's 'smouldering nature' leaps into a blaze it transfigures the cliché with an energy that confounds all restraint. Bradley's pursuit of social recognition may seem a feeble conformism, yet it is driven by a vital 'fire', a 'nature' that both lifts him above the 'ordinary' and threatens to destroy him.

Four chapters later, Bradley himself echoes the narrator when he extends this disruptive power to an even more familiar expression: 'I love you.' Here is his remarkable declaration to Lizzie, at the very midpoint of the novel:

> You know what I am going to say. I love you. What other men may mean when they use that expression, I cannot tell; what *I* mean is, that I am under the influence of

---

[14] Kucich, *Repression in Victorian Fiction*, 201–83. Kucich's account has been especially suggestive for my reading of *Our Mutual Friend*.

some tremendous attraction which I have resisted in vain, and which overmasters me. You could draw me to fire, you could draw me to water, you could draw me to the gallows, you could draw me to any death, you could draw me to anything I have most avoided, you could draw me to any exposure and disgrace. This and the confusion of my thoughts, so that I am fit for nothing, is what I mean by your being the ruin of me. (*OMF* II:15, 397)

Both the narrator and Bradley eloquently suggest that the peculiar force of his desire cannot be captured by our usual idioms of love. Those break down along with Bradley's powers of self-suppression. His passion for Lizzie explodes his self-discipline; he is describing a craving that we might now call an addiction. (Sedgwick's influential account of the rivalry finds in Headstone's response to Lizzie a 'terror' at the potentially degrading association, but this misreads as a social anxiety what seems more obviously the deep allure of 'ruin' as an escape from self.) Her very being is his 'ruin': 'I have no government of myself when you are near me or in my thoughts' (*OMF* II:15, 395). And yet Headstone never poses the sort of sexual threat to Lizzie that will become associated with Wrayburn. In effect, Bradley does govern his 'wild energy', but he does so by redirecting it to focus on his rival, where for the time being it can be more safely indulged.

Ultimately, Headstone will surrender all efforts to govern his desire; in his pursuit of Wrayburn, and then Riderhood, he embraces his ruin as an active self-destruction. Yet the sheer blaze of his passion becomes a benchmark of sorts for the failures of self-mastery experienced by men in love throughout the novel. Bradley's language of surrender to tyrannical forces will be echoed by Wrayburn and Rokesmith, and even, in a comic vein, in the sorrows of Mr Venus. Thus Wrayburn finally confesses to Lizzie, 'You don't know how you haunt me and bewilder me' (*OMF* IV:6, 692). One more romantic cliché, perhaps, but one energized by the echo of Headstone's emphasis: 'this and the confusion of my thoughts, so that I am fit for nothing.' All of the men in love are in various ways haunted, a term that suggests longing, memory, confusion, pursuit, and above all death—a recoil from it, and a desire for it.

It may be hard to see Wrayburn's desire for Lizzie placing him in danger of a 'ruin' akin to Headstone's. But his feelings deeply unsettle not only his self-mastery but, increasingly, his very sense of self. Wrayburn's gradual loss of self-possession, however, is crucial to his moral renovation, and his ultimate fulfilment, in two respects. First, his bewilderment registers an energy that requires direction: only through an infusion of the fire that he so conspicuously lacks at the outset can Wrayburn escape from his drifting indolence. Second, Wrayburn's bewilderment helps to rescue him from the suspicion of selfishness that stigmatizes Headstone, and shadows nearly every Dickensian courtship. *Our Mutual Friend* drives home the value of 'disinterestedness' quite explicitly in the elaborate chastening of Bella Wilfer, and also, more darkly, in the Lammles' bitter travesty of a marriage.

The liberating self-transcendence of financial ruin is reinforced by the psychological bewilderment that Bradley Headstone also calls 'ruin'. Wrayburn is troubled by a passion that seems inimical to his worldly interests (as the conclusion of the novel will drive home) but his passion for Lizzie thereby invigorates romantic clichés: it is truly disinterested, like that of Harmon for Bella Wilfer. 'I cannot help it,' Harmon thinks of his passion; 'reason has nothing to do with it; I love her against reason' (*OMF* II:13, 372). Again, the emphasis muffles the worldliness of desire—which is a special challenge here, since marriage to Bella offers Harmon such obvious worldly rewards. 'I cannot help it ... I love her against reason' works to the same effect as the seeming annihilation of the self that would profit from the marriage—that is, the seeming death of Harmon. It also chimes with the masquerade of Boffin, who in denouncing Rokesmith as a fortune-hunter solicits the reader's resistance to that characterization.

A truly selfless desire may be an impossible dream, but it is the special burden of idealized womanhood in Dickens. Here that role falls principally to Lizzie Hexam, who models the selflessness that Bella must be brought to embrace. Thus at their first meeting, Lizzie asks Bella of the experience of love, 'Does a woman's heart ... seek to gain anything?' (*OMF* III:9, 527). The two women are discussing, tellingly, Lizzie's passion for Wrayburn, 'a gentleman far above me and my way of life' (*OMF* III:9, 526). She presumes he does not love her, and she hardly knows him well, but she is entirely devoted to him, to the point of utter self-abnegation, even as she sees no prospect of her love ever being valued or returned:

> I have no more dreamed of the possibility of *my* being his wife, than he ever has—and words could not be stronger than that. And yet I love him. I love him so much and so dearly, that when I sometimes think my life may be but a weary one, I am proud of it and glad of it. I am proud and glad to suffer something for him, even though it is of no service to him, and he will never know of it or care for it. (*OMF* III:9, 528)

Here is 'disinterested' love indeed. Even among the most sympathetic male characters, what comes instinctively to Lizzie is at best the culmination of a long struggle—a struggle, moreover, that endangers their manhood, even their very lives. Masculinity typically is founded on self-assertion; complete selflessness from this vantage is hard to separate from utter passivity, which feminizes men to the point of seeming to emasculate them—witness Bella's father Rumty Wilfer, the 'cherub'. Yet in *Our Mutual Friend* Dickens repeatedly presses this challenge by conjuring up states of near-death or suspended animation, as if trying to imagine an annihilation of self that stops just short of physical destruction. Thus John Harmon, the 'living-dead man' (*OMF* II:13, 373), reflects at length on the near-drowning which enabled his metamorphosis into John Rokesmith, an ordeal so disorienting that, as he recounts it to himself, 'There was no such thing as I, within my knowledge' (*OMF* II:13, 369). When Headstone bludgeons Wrayburn into something like suspended animation, he unwittingly provokes Wrayburn's nearest approximation to Lizzie's selflessness, which lies on the threshold of death. He ultimately awakens to what seems a radically transformed identity, in which a former sense of self is so attenuated that his desire for Lizzie can finally seem truly disinterested. Masculine discipline, paradoxically, culminates in its approach to an idealized femininity.

We arrive, then, at one aspect of a 'queer' Dickens, in which familiar gender binaries are complicated, at times even confounded, by the force of desire. Queer theory suggests many directions for future study of gender and sexuality in Dickens: reconfigurations of friendship, domestic arrangements outside marriage, the erotic energies informing quotidian social forms. More fundamentally, queer theory has encouraged an ongoing interrogation of our very notion of the sexual, and its relation to the more comprehensive category of the erotic. If the erotic, as Sharon Marcus argues (drawing on Roland Barthes), is an 'affective valence' not bound to genital arousal, then our understanding of its force in Dickens will draw on a broader theory of affect, which Holly Furneaux deploys in this volume to understand queer domesticity in Dickens.[15] Finally, Dickensian sexuality may sharpen the challenges of understanding literary character. '[I]t would be something to know where you are hiding', the narrator remarks of the unconscious Rogue Riderhood (*OMF* III:3, 444); a reader might feel much the same in pondering how literary characters can evoke the illusion of a highly individuated, independent life. After a long period of relative neglect, governed by what John Frow has called 'the poles of structuralist reduction and humanist plenitude', the study of character has gained renewed attention of late, in large part through focus on the complex relations between literary form and human selfhood, between 'character' and 'person', in the title of Frow's important study.[16] Representations of sexuality form only one aspect of this larger project, but they clearly have helped to motivate it. How do we recognize and delineate sexual and erotic experience, whether in literary representation or in everyday life? How does an understanding of erotic life inflect our sense of what it is to be human, or plausible, or fantastic, or coherent, or real?

Further Reading

James Eli Adams, 'Victorian Sexualities', in Herbert F. Tucker (ed.), *A New Companion to Victorian Literature and Culture* (Malden, MA: Wiley-Blackwell, 2014), 124–37

Kate Flint, 'Unspeakable Desires: We Other Victorians', in Juliet John (ed.), *The Oxford Handbook of Victorian Literary Culture* (Oxford: Oxford University Press, 2016), 193–210

Ann Heilman and Mark Llewellyn, 'The Victorians, Sex, and Gender', in Juliet John (ed.), *The Oxford Handbook of Victorian Literary Culture* (Oxford: Oxford University Press, 2016), 161–77

Lillian Nayler (ed.), *A Library of Essays on Charles Dickens: Dickens, Sexuality, and Gender* (Farnham: Ashgate, 2012)

---

[15] Marcus, *Between Women*, 114.
[16] John Frow, *Character and Person* (Oxford: Oxford University Press, 2014), 21.

CHAPTER 26

DOMESTICITY AND QUEER THEORY

HOLLY FURNEAUX

There is a strange gap, or misfit, between Dickens's reputation as champion of hearth and home as a panacea to social strife, and the paucity of happy households in his fiction. In *American Notes* one of his grounds for complaint is that the new houses of the new world fail to offer a sufficient bulwark against public struggle:

> Those slightly-built wooden dwellings behind which the sun was setting with a brilliant lustre, could be so looked through and through, that the idea of any inhabitant being able to hide himself from the public gaze, or to have any secrets from the public eye, was not entertainable for a moment. Even where a blazing fire shone through the uncurtained windows of some distant house, it had the air of being newly-lighted, and of lacking warmth; and instead of awakening thoughts of a snug chamber, bright with faces that first saw the light round that same hearth, and ruddy with warm hangings, it came upon one suggestive of the smell of new mortar and damp walls.[1]

The established firesides of England in his wider work, however, similarly fail to deliver comfort. Dickens studies has long been energized by attention to his numerous, vividly realized sites of domestic disharmony, including marital misery and failed parenting.[2] In what follows I turn to a group of difficult women who highlight the failures of domestic ideology. This historically discredited, only partially reclaimed, unharmonious group have been described more or less sympathetically as the shrews, agitating women, and dissenting women of Dickens's canon, that 'gallery of foolish, ridiculous, or

---

[1] Charles Dickens, *American Notes*, ed. Patricia Ingham (London: Penguin, 2000), V:81–2.
[2] Kelly Hager's *Dickens and the Rise of Divorce: The Failed Marriage Plot and the Novel Tradition* (Farnham: Ashgate, 2010), 7, offers a thorough and persuasive exploration of the ways in which 'all of Dickens's novels are concerned—in a multiplicity of ways, both large and small, and in a manner that is alternately comic, tragic, melodramatic, and ironic—with the phenomenon of failed marriage'.

offensive women' as George Gissing put it.[3] This chapter begins with a consideration of Mrs Jellyby of *Bleak House* and Mrs Wilfer of *Our Mutual Friend* as central to Dickens's attention to the critical power of the killjoy, and moves on to a detailed new reading of *Barnaby Rudge*, focusing on the capricious Martha Varden and the dysfunctional household of the Golden Key, to make the case for Dickens's various exposures of the impossibility of domestic ideology. This novel disenchants the tenets on which Victorian ideals of public and private stability and satisfaction rest: paternalism, angelic femininity, and the emotionally regulated home as a bulwark against the aggression of the public sphere. Throughout I will take seriously the contrary affects of Dickens's offensive women and think through the implications of their alienation from domestic ideals for our wider thinking about Victorian domesticity and romance.

Critical recognition of the polymorphous perversity of Dickens's representations of the family, gender, and sexuality has helped to inspire a wider rethinking of the queer content at the heart of Victorian domesticity and desire.[4] Scholarship on the nineteenth-century history of the queer family has enriched our understanding of the period, while offering an urgent political corrective to reactionary positionings of expansive families as recent abominations.[5] This interest in Victorian domesticity as shaped by impulses other than heterosexual desire and reproduction has also informed a wealth of thinking about historical emotions and erotics more difficult to detect from our post-sexological position of fascination with sexuality. While we now think of sexual orientation as a (often *the*) defining facet of identity and the determining factor in our forming of intimacies and families, the Victorian period offers alternatives in, for instance, intrafamilial marriages, companionate non-romantic marriages, and adoption in preference to marriage and reproduction.[6]

---

[3] George Gissing, quoted by Michael Slater, *Dickens and Women* (London: Dent, 1983), 296. Ellen Moers used the term 'agitating women' in an important early exploration of the complexities of the women of *Bleak House*: 'there is more than mockery to Dickens's response to feminist agitation; there is in *Bleak House* a sense of anxiety that approaches respect, and an imaginative concern with the movement of women.' '*Bleak House*: The Agitating Women', *Dickensian* 69 (1973): 13–24, 21. Brenda Ayres chooses the language of religious nonconformity for her thorough study of Dickens's women who reject domestic ideology: *Dissenting Women in Dickens' Novels: The Subversion of Domestic Ideology* (Westport, CT: Greenwood Press, 1998).

[4] Recommended in the growing field of queer Dickens studies are William Cohen's *Embodied: Victorian Literature and the Senses* (Minneapolis: University of Minnesota Press, 2008) and Sharon Marcus's *Between Women: Friendship, Desire and Marriage in Victorian England* (Princeton: Princeton University Press, 2007).

[5] Duc Dau and Shale Preston (eds), *Queer Victorian Families: Curious Relations in Literature* (New York: Routledge, 2015) present Victorian literature as a counter to the restrictive definitions of family, marriage, and parenting now championed by groups like One Million Moms. See also Kelly Hager and Talia Schaffer (eds), *Extending Families*, special issue of *Victorian Review* 39, 2 (2013) and Barry McCrea, *In the Company of Strangers: Family and Narrative in Dickens, Conan Doyle, Joyce and Proust* (New York: Columbia University Press, 2011).

[6] See especially work by Mary Jean Corbett, Holly Furneaux, Helena Michie, and Talia Schaffer detailed in Further Reading.

Queer theories, gender theories, affect theories, and histories of gender, sexuality, emotion, and the family, have underpinned explorations of the expansiveness of Victorian domesticity, able to accommodate a wide range of desires and relationships. These theoretical approaches also offer ways to think through that which cannot be so comfortably accommodated, and to recognize the importance of articulations of domestic and familial discomfort. In this chapter I draw particularly on ideas of the 'affect alien', to use Sara Ahmed's term for those who do not subscribe to the cultural scripts that position marriage, parenting, and the family as central to happiness, and wider queer theories that value the critical power of antisociability and difficult emotion.[7] Sianne Ngai has, influentially, explored 'ugly feelings', including bitterness, disaffection, envy, and hate, as 'interpretations of predicaments' produced by 'state(s) of obstructed agency'.[8] Ngai's work informs my consideration of the negative affects Dickens attributes to an array of outraged and outrageous women characters across his career. By bringing recent approaches to affect into dialogue with Victorian ideals of home, I argue that Dickens's fascination with uncomfortable domestic feelings is part of his wider appreciation of the affective incoherence of the model of paternalist husband and paragon wife. Dickens's awkward women not only express the rage of gendered disempowerment, they also expose the impossible emotional demands, on both women and men, made by domestic ideology.

AFFECT ALIENS: THE JOYS OF DICKENS'S (FEMINIST) KILLJOYS

My attention to Dickens's difficult women is inspired by the enthusiasm of a group of women writers for these awkward characters. Virginia Woolf praised the description of murderess Hortense passionately casting off her shoes in *Bleak House*: 'the maid wading through the long grass is a masterpiece that has always stuck in my mind'.[9] Emily Dickinson and Katherine Mansfield, amongst others, turned to Dickens when describing pain—bodily and mental—and other difficult feelings including loneliness and jealousy.[10] Mansfield invokes Dickens's 'telescopic philanthropist' Mrs Jellyby, also of *Bleak House*, to express her sense of dislocation from her husband, John Middleton Murry, and to articulate concern about the effectiveness of her own mission of writing:

---

[7] Sara Ahmed, *The Promise of Happiness* (Durham, NC, and London: Duke University Press, 2010), 49.

[8] Sianne Ngai, *Ugly Feelings* (Cambridge, MA: Harvard University Press, 2005), 3.

[9] To Ethel Smith, 4 January 1832, *The Letters of Virginia Woolf*, ed. Nigel Nicholson, 6 vols (London: Hogarth Press, 1975–80), 5:2.

[10] I discuss this more thoroughly in '(Re)Writing Dickens Queerly: The Correspondence of Katherine Mansfield', in Ewa Kujawska-Lis and Anna Krawczyk-Łaskarzewska (eds), *Reflections on/of Dickens* (Newcastle-upon-Tyne: Cambridge Scholars, 2014), 121–37.

Murry came to see me late last night, very gay after a dinner at the House with your brother. I had spent a very dull solitary evening finishing a story about a woman who goes to see a friend of hers who has entered a convent—and when Murry came in, twinkling with champagne and smelling of the fleshpots, I felt like Mrs Jellaby [sic] who spent her life, you remember, staring at the ink spots on the wall and writing tomes about some mission that need never have existed. (To Ottoline Morrell, 3 July 1917)[11]

The affective dissonance Mansfield registers between herself and Murry recalls the absolute disconnect Dickens draws between Mrs Jellyby's emotions and those of her husband and children. '[T]oo much occupied with her African duties', her energetic schemes for the well-being of inhabitants of Borrioboola-Gha which involve voluminous correspondence, Mrs Jellyby's hair remains unbrushed, her children tumble unwashed down the stairs, and her bankrupt husband rests, speechless, against the wall in despair.[12]

Though censured by the more ideal heroines of the novel—Esther, Ada, and her daughter Caddy—Mrs Jellyby presents her preoccupation as a coherent emotional strategy through which she maintains her 'serene composure' and 'same sweetness of temper' (*BH* 4, 39, 40). Her main affective mode is extreme distraction and a refusal to relate to her family, which is physically broadcast by her 'handsome eyes' which have 'a curious habit of seeming to look a long way off' (*BH* 4, 37). When asked about her suffering husband, Mrs Jellyby explains the difference in their emotional conditions: 'He has been unfortunate in his affairs, and is a little out of spirits. Happily for me, I am so much engaged that I have no time to think about it' (*BH* 23, 295). She maintains a similar serenity in the approach to her daughter's wedding, responding to preparations with 'a half-reproachful smile like a superior spirit who could just bear with our trifling' (*BH* 30, 372). On being shown her daughter's wedding dress she merely comments that 'at half the cost, this weak child might have been equipped for Africa!' (*BH* 30, 372). Mrs Jellyby thus offers an alternative value system to that of modern capitalism which posits financial success, marriage, and reproduction as goals essential to happiness. She repeatedly describes her mission as a liberation from uncomfortable domestic affects, in this case distress and disappointment at her daughter Caddy's reluctance to act as amanuensis—'"if I were not happily so much engaged... this would distress and disappoint me. But I have so much to think of, in connexion with Borrioboola-Gha, and it is so necessary I should concentrate myself, that there is my remedy, you see"' (*BH* 23, 296).

The mission as proven 'remedy' to the experience of difficult emotion is crystallized in Mrs Jellyby's feeling for it as for a 'favourite child' (a description also used by Dickens to express his affective relationship to his own writing embodied in his feeling for *David Copperfield*): 'Now, if my public duties were not a favourite child to me, if I were not

---

[11] Katherine Mansfield, *The Collected Letters of Katherine Mansfield*, ed. Vincent O'Sullivan and Margaret Scott (Oxford: Clarendon Press, 1984–2008), 1:315.

[12] Charles Dickens, *Bleak House*, ed. George Ford and Sylvère Monod, Norton Critical Edition (New York: W. W. Norton, 1977), 4, 37. Subsequent references are inserted parenthetically in the text by *BH* chapter, page.

occupied with large measures on a vast scale, these petty details might grieve me very much' (*BH* 23, 297). An available, though not Dickens-endorsed reading, is that Mrs Jellyby's mission allows her, ironically, to embody the sweet temper of the angel in the house, by bypassing the domestic emotional circuits that would make her both responsible for, and receptive and vulnerable to, the struggles and pain of her husband and children. Her self-abstraction offers one logical response to the over-determined emotional burdens that wives and mothers were expected to take up, absorbing the ugly feelings of husbands bruised by their public roles and transforming these into domestic bliss while radiating calm order for the benefit of the children. Mrs Jellyby's replacement of the selflessness required by feminine and domestic ideology with the self-fullness of absorption in her 'favourite child' of 'public duties' breaks with what Lisa Downing, in her work on selfish women, has identified as the central 'discourses of what women are supposed to be'.[13] These discourses include the powerful narratives, prevalent in the nineteenth century and now, that women must be complete in their destiny as mothers, 'subject to a psychological need of child bearing in order to justify their own lives', that they are fulfilled by the compliments and attention of men, and, relatedly, that they are 'profoundly social animals, natural carers for others and essentially predisposed to be for the interests of collectivity'.[14] That Mrs Jellyby is profoundly uninterested in the feelings and well-being of her husband and children makes her both a threatening, intriguing, and perhaps even inspiring character.

Mrs Jellyby is the most developed and memorable of an indomitable cast of agitating women in *Bleak House* 'devoted to public objects only'. These include Miss Wisk who 'informed us, with great indignation, before we sat down to [Caddy's wedding] breakfast, that the idea of woman's mission lying chiefly in the narrow sphere of Home was an outrageous slander on the part of her Tyrant, Man' (*BH* 30, 375), and the formidable Mrs Pardiggle who is loathed by her children, forced to contribute all their pocket-money to her philanthropic schemes, and detested by recipients of her chilly charity. Mrs Jellyby was a popular figure in anti-feminist journalism of the later nineteenth century. She was held up as a warning of the domestic dissolutions that would follow bloomerism, the New Woman, professional women, and other forms of female emancipation.[15] J. S. Mill, amongst other gender progressives, saw this part of *Bleak House* as a 'vulgar' 'ridicule [of

---

[13] Lisa Downing, *Selfish Women and Other Inconvenient Deviants*, inaugural lecture, University of Birmingham, 2014, available at <https://www.youtube.com/watch?v=AvXLKhRQv64>.

[14] Ibid.

[15] Kathy Rees discusses the way derogatory references to Mrs Jellyby in the press had established this name as a shorthand for perceived domestic failure. The *Englishwoman's Review* in 1877, for example, expressed the 'fear that women will throw their sympathies into some fanciful Borrioboola-Gha, instead of household management'. Rees details Edmund Gosse's invocation of the character to express his uneasy feelings about his mother and her enthusiasm for evangelical mission work over mothering in 'Reading Edmund Gosse's *Father and Son* (1907) through a Dickensian Lens', *Dickens Quarterly* 33, 3 (2016): 221–41. For a more playful example of the use of this character to discuss neglect see the *Tomahawk*'s response to a (supposed) correspondent who 'writes to us to say that he considers Her Majesty in the light of a "Royal Mrs Jellyby" as she neglects the affairs of her family of subjects to give her undivided attention to "The Late Prince Consort Mania"', 8 June 1867, 54. In 1920 *The Times* critiqued

the] rights of women'.[16] In Mansfield's mournful identification with the character we see the possibility for a reverse discourse, as Mrs Jellyby's rejection of domesticity and embrace of a mission through writing offers a node of connection, albeit an ambivalent one, to a later woman writer with a similarly awkward relationship to marriage, mothering, and domesticity.

More exuberantly, Mansfield also took particular delight in the comedy produced by the dissonance between the feminine ideal and Dickens's figures such as Mrs Wilfer of *Our Mutual Friend*:

> Boge. Have you read Our Mutual Friend? Some of it is really damned good. The satire in it is first chop—all the Veneering business par example—could not be better. I never read it before and am enjoying it immensely—and Mrs Wilfer is after my own heart. I have a huge capacity for seeing 'funny' people you know and laughing and Dickens does fill it at times quite amazingly. (To Murry, 27 and 28 January 1918)[17]

The funniness of both Mrs Wilfer and Mrs Jellyby derives from their emphatic break with the feminine ideal. While Mrs Jellyby's consistent affective relationship to her family is abstraction, Mrs Wilfer's is freezing and petrification. Memorably Mrs Wilfer presents her 'cheek to be kissed', by her daughter, 'as sympathetic and responsive as the back of the bowl of a spoon'.[18] She has a similarly unrelenting approach to her wedding anniversary, which is 'kept morally, rather as a Fast than a Feast, enabling Mrs. Wilfer to hold a sombre darkling state, which exhibited that impressive woman in her choicest colours' (*OMF* III:4, 449). In a parallel to Mrs Jellyby's long-sightedness, Mrs Wilfer embodies the discomfort she is to others in 'a mysterious toothache', experienced on her wedding anniversaries and 'on most special occasions' (*OMF* III:4, 450). Neither Mrs Jellyby nor Mrs Wilfer has any enthusiasm for the affectionate forms of marriage or motherhood, or for comfortable home-making.

In the terms of queer theorist Ahmed they each qualify as an 'affect alien', 'one who converts good feelings into bad, who as it were "kills" the joy of the family'.[19] Ahmed's work is part of a larger body of thinking that values affective resistance to, or variance from, coercive requirements for happiness and optimism that present limited life scripts concerned with marriage, reproduction, and economic productivity as essential to emotional fulfilment. Lauren Berlant, for example, discerns the cruelty within a culturally

---

the press's tradition of presenting Mrs Jellyby as a New Woman, 'Nineteenth-Century Feminism', 5 May 1920, 14.

[16] Quoted by Slater, *Dickens and Women*, 315.
[17] Mansfield, *Collected Letters*, 2:45–6
[18] Charles Dickens, *Our Mutual Friend*, ed. Michael Cotsell, Oxford World's Classics (Oxford: Oxford University Press, 1989) II:8, 310–11. Subsequent references are inserted parenthetically in the text by *OMF* Book:chapter, page.
[19] Ahmed, *The Promise of Happiness*, 49.

mandated optimism that directs us to a uniform 'moral-intimate-economic thing called "the good life"'.[20] A central tenet now of good life consensus, and one promoted by Victorian domestic ideology, is of 'family as a happy object', 'as being what good feelings are directed toward'.[21] Victorian domestic magazines presented women's good cheer as a domestic duty; as *The Ladies Cabinet* put it in 1844, 'her own best ornaments are cheerfulness and contentment', while in 1836 the *Magazine of Domestic Life* prescribed woman's 'special duty' as ensuring the home is a 'place of happiness'.[22] Dickens's difficult women act as affect aliens to puncture the emotional regimes around which fantasies of the good life are organized. Their ugly feelings show up structural inequalities within the prescribed goods of marriage, family, and domestic ideology.

Affect aliens are widespread in Dickens's work. They repeatedly articulate the forms of their disempowerment and through powerful negative affect offer a resistance to the cultural mantras that position their happiness as wives and mothers as inevitable. Dickens's work includes widowed and jilted figures who become entirely characterized by their devastating loss, like, most famously, Miss Havisham of *Great Expectations* and Mrs Gummidge, self-styled 'lone lorn creetur' of *David Copperfield*, who feels that 'everythink goes contrary with me'.[23] Mrs Gummidge meets entreaties 'to cheer up' with the rejoinder, 'my troubles has made me contrary ... I make the house uncomfortable' (*DC* 3, 34). She expresses her discomfort at her socially redundant position as impoverished widow reliant on Mr Peggotty's kindness through grumblings at the physical inconveniences of life in a beached boat, complaints which Mr Peggotty insists on interpreting as resulting from her mourning 'of the old 'un' (*DC* 3, 35). The ugly, stuck feelings of these characters expose the cruelty of an inflexible ideology of marriage as women's sole destiny and source of happiness, a culture inimical to the full personhood of the spinster or widow.[24] The discontent, bitterness, and anger of these

---

[20] Lauren Berlant, *Cruel Optimism* (Durham, NC, and London: Duke University Press, 2011), 2. Given that 'success in a heteronormative, capitalist society equates too easily to specific forms of reproductive maturity concerned with wealth accumulation', Jack Halberstam champions the counterweight of failure and concomitant 'negative affects, such as disappointment, disillusionment, and despair' which can 'poke holes in the toxic positivity of contemporary life'. *The Queer Art of Failure* (Durham, NC, and London: Duke University Press, 2011), 2–3.

[21] Ahmed, *The Promise of Happiness*, 21.

[22] Quoted in Catherine Waters, *Dickens and the Politics of the Family* (Cambridge: Cambridge University Press, 1997), 16. See Waters for a historical overview of the ideal of the home as an '*emotional environment* that would protect and sustain the (male) worker from the damage inflicted by the alienating world of work', 12, emphasis added.

[23] Charles Dickens, *David Copperfield*, ed. Nina Burgis (Oxford: Clarendon Press, 1981), 3, 33. Subsequent references are inserted parenthetically in the text by *DC* chapter, page.

[24] Ronald Frame makes this point in his prequel novel *Havisham* in which he imagines a dialogue between a young Miss Havisham and her father:

'Some man will count himself lucky. When he first sets eyes on you.'
'... So that is what my education's for.'
'It's the prospect for every young woman. To be married. Her responsibility even.'
'Or ...?'
'There is no "or" in your case'. *Havisham* (London: Faber, 2012), 133.

characters have a productive socially critical function. Informed by Ngai's work, I recuperate 'these negative affects for their *critical* productivity', whilst recognizing ambivalence within any 'counter-valorisation' as these sites of ugly feeling do not offer straightforward 'therapeutic "solutions" to the problems they highlight and condense' and 'sentiments of disenchantment' may be just as easily mobilized by opposite ends of the political spectrum.[25]

Other angry single women characters like Miss Wade of *Little Dorrit* and Rosa Dartle of *David Copperfield*, though viewed by other characters as paranoid and of an 'unhappy temper' and sharp to the point of being 'all edge', show finely calibrated social awareness in their killjoy pronouncements.[26] Though warmly welcomed into the family for whom she is a governess, Miss Wade derails her prospective marriage to her employer's nephew: 'Did she presume on my birth, or on my hire? I was not bought, body and soul. She seemed to think that her distinguished nephew had gone into a slave-market and purchased a wife' (*LD* II:21, 650). As part of the novel's wider exploration of the prejudices against illegitimacy (encountered by Miss Wade and Tattycoram) and of the utter disempowerment of women in marriage (particularly in the plot of Pet Meagles's disastrous betrothal to Henry Gowan), Miss Wade's dark perspective is shown to have a logical basis. Similarly, Rosa Dartle raises uncomfortable questions, puncturing the assumption of class superiority in the Steerforth family of which she both is and is not a part as Mrs Steerforth's companion in residence. Responding to James Steerforth's dismissive description of the working-class Peggotty family as 'that sort of people', Rosa asks, '[a]re they really animals and clods, and beings of another order?' (*DC* 20, 251). Her reaction to the casual cruelty of his view that 'like their coarse rough skins, they are not easily wounded' is similarly acerbic: 'It's such a delight to know that, when they suffer, they don't feel! Sometimes I have been quite uneasy for that sort of people; but now I shall just dismiss the idea of them, altogether' (*DC* 20, 251). Although these awkward characters are not endorsed as the novel's heroines, they speak a different kind of sense, often of a type that punctures gender and class hierarchies, and are imbued with memorable vitality. While the affect-alien, killjoy perspective is often framed by a narrative of paranoia or reform, Dickens persistently reinvents women characters who represent an alternative way of being to that mandated by feminine and domestic ideals. Mansfield's sense of Mrs Wilfer 'as after my own heart' shows their emotional resonance, and their power to live affectively beyond the texts in which they first appeared.

---

[25] Ngai, *Ugly Feelings*, 3, 5.
[26] Charles Dickens, *Little Dorrit*, ed. Harvey Peter Sucksmith (Oxford: Clarendon Press, 1979), II:21, 647. Subsequent references are inserted parenthetically in the text by *LD* Book:chapter, page. *David Copperfield*, ed. Nina Burgis (Oxford: Clarendon Press, 1981), 20, 251. Subsequent references are inserted parenthetically in the text by *DC* chapter, page.

Capriciousness: Blocks in the Transmission of Affect in *Barnaby Rudge*

The Varden household, the Golden Key, at the centre of *Barnaby Rudge* accommodates a range of affect aliens. Only Gabriel Varden—master, husband, and father, whose lock-smithing business is advertised in a trade sign that gives the household its name—maintains relentless good cheer. The Golden Key also accommodates Martha Varden, the 'capricious' wife, Miss Miggs, the vinegary servant, and Sim Tappertit, the resentful apprentice, as well as the Vardens' only daughter, the coquettish Dolly. The ugly feelings of the majority of this household, including everyday envy, spite, frustration, and boredom, are, as in Ngai's analysis of these kinds of negative affect, produced by 'situation[s] of restricted agency'.[27]

The affective dissonance of the Varden household is part of the novel's fabric of large- and small-scale emotional disconnects and failures of calibrations in feeling. An interpretation of the anti-Catholic Gordon Riots of 1780, which Dickens presents less as a coherent cause and more as an occasion for outbreaks of inchoate rage and disorder (as with the detail that some of the hanged rioters were found to be Catholic), this is a novel of public and private violence. It variously considers gendered violence, as male bodily integrity is threatened by the loss of limbs, and male necks are longingly sized up by Mr Dennis, the enthusiastic public hangman with an asphyxiation kink. Women, particularly Dolly Varden, endure recurrent attempted rapes and mothers are coerced by threats against their children; Mrs Rudge is victim to extortion through her effort to protect her vulnerable 'foolish' son Barnaby. Within this often Gothicized and melodramatic narrative landscape, an apparently gentler black comedy of domestic disharmony unfolds in the domestic setting of the Golden Key.

Martha Varden, matriarch of the Golden Key, is characterized by emotional contrariness. Though her role under the prevailing domestic ideology is to regulate the emotional temperature of the household by radiating good feeling, she is introduced as 'a lady of what is commonly called an uncertain temper', 'a temper tolerably certain to make every body more or less uncomfortable'.[28] She has a capacity for an extraordinary range of strong feeling and for 'ring[ing] the changes backwards and forwards on all possible moods and flights in one short quarter of an hour; performing, as it were, a kind of triple bob major on the peal of instruments in the female belfry' (*BR* 7, 64). The performance analogy establishes a concern with

---

[27] Ngai, *Ugly Feelings*, 2.
[28] Charles Dickens, *Barnaby Rudge*, ed. Clive Hurst, Oxford World's Classics (Oxford: Oxford University Press, 2003), 7, 64. Subsequent references are inserted parenthetically in the text by *BR* chapter, page.

distinguishing between authentic and theatrical feeling (her genius is also described as exceeding Macbeth's), and the designation of the bell chamber as 'female' points to the novel's concern with the gendered dimensions of emotional repertoire. She operates at variance to an emotional consensus that Ahmed describes as 'sociable happiness': 'to be affected in a good way by objects that are already evaluated as good is a way of belonging to an affective community. We align ourselves with others by investing in the same objects as the cause of happiness'.[29] Rather Mrs Varden's neighbours see her as an affect outsider, believing that her 'uncertainty of disposition [is] strengthened and increased with her temporal prosperity' and that 'a tumble down some half-dozen rounds in the world's ladder—such as the breaking of the bank in which her husband kept his money, or some little fall of that kind— would be the making of her, and could hardly fail to render her one of the most agreeable companions in existence' (*BR* 7, 64–5). She is perceived to have an inverse emotional orientation to 'objects that are already evaluated as good' through the social consensus represented by 'the world's ladder': prosperity, financial security, and, presumably, her husband's satisfaction. Similarly, in domestic interactions, Mrs Varden's spirits are 'capricious' (*BR* 7, 64) and contrary, flowing in inverse direction to those of others around her, particularly her husband, and resisting what Teresa Brennan calls the 'transmission of affect' which binds or blocks a community of feeling as 'the emotions or affects of one person, and the enhancing or depressing energies these affects entail, can enter into another'.[30] Mrs Jellyby and Mrs Wilfer impede affective transmission through their impervious preservation of their respective serenity and 'gloomy majesty' in all circumstances, just as Gabriel Varden's ceaseless good cheer works as an isolated system. Martha's capricious feelings even more vividly dramatize a failure in the transmission of affect by operating in opposition to the emotions of others.

Mrs Varden and Miggs (like Miss Wade and Rosa Dartle) speak to the more subtle violence of the gender and class inequalities at the heart of Victorian domestic ideology. In her first exchange with her husband, Martha Varden highlights his infantilizing breed, albeit 'good-natured', of home discipline which requires her to be 'disposed to talk pleasantly', responding, 'I'm not a child to be corrected one minute and petted the next—I'm a little too old for that, Varden' (*BR* 7, 68). Miss Miggs, 'Mrs. Varden's chief aider and abettor, and at the same time her principal victim and object of wrath' (*BR* 7, 65), expresses the precariousness of the servant's position as both of, and surplus to, the family: 'servitudes was no inheritances' (*BR* 80, 641). When at the end of the novel Mrs Varden is transformed into something much closer to the ever-cheerful wife mandated by domestic magazines—'laughing in face and mood, in all respects delicious to behold'

---

[29] Ahmed, *The Promise of Happiness*, 38.
[30] Teresa Brennan, *The Transmission of Affect* (Ithaca, NY, and London: Cornell University Press, 2004).

(*BR* 80, 638)—a redundant, enraged Miggs articulates the outrageousness of this metamorphosis:

> Times is changed, is they, mim!' cried Miggs, bridling; 'you can spare me now, can you? You can keep 'em down without me? You're not in wants of any one to scold, or throw the blame upon, no longer, an't you, mim? I'm glad to find you've grown so independent. I wish you joy, I'm sure! (*BR* 80, 643-4)

Martha Varden's emotional dependency on Miggs as a form of alter-ego through much of the novel—as Brenda Ayres puts it, 'Miggs often expressed Martha's passion when Martha could not express it herself'[31]—makes a cross-class affective alliance at variance with domestic ideology as a distinctively middle-class value system. Catherine Waters summarizes the way in which domestic ideals 'helped to create a coherent and distinct class identity and to mark clear ideological boundaries that distinguished the middle classes from those social and economic groups above and below them.'[32] Martha's resentment aligns her more with the working-class members of the household, and her expressions of ugly feeling, individually and in concert with Miggs, render the Golden Key deeply uncomfortable, puncturing expectations of the middle-class wife's vocation of sweet ordering, supported by self-sacrificing, unobtrusive, and near-silent servants.

Barnaby Rudge offers a sustained exploration of the porousness of the home and the inseparability of the public and the private presented by John Ruskin as dystopic in his famous delineation of domestic ideology: 'so far as the anxieties of the outer life penetrate into it, and the inconsistently-minded, unknown, unloved or hostile society of the outer world is permitted to cross the threshold, it ceases to be home.'[33] As home—for the Varden family, their servant, and Gabriel's apprentice—and business, The Golden Key exposes the fictiveness of separate spheres ideology both for late eighteenth-century artisans such as Gabriel, and for Victorian men of letters such as Dickens, who worked from a home inhabited by his family and the servants they employed. The emotional tenor of the Varden home is also an anxious mixture, as Mrs Varden and Miggs embody the inconsistent-mindedness and hostility against which Mrs Varden is expected, ideologically, to be a bulwark. As a range of scholars have shown, a separate spheres model does not correlate with the lived experience of the period.[34] In *Barnaby Rudge* Dickens also shows the emotional impossibilities of domestic ideology, the constellation of bad feeling at the Golden Key working to suggest that domestic ideology is an affective regime built on emotions no one really feels.[35]

---

[31] Ayres, *Dissenting Women*, 56.

[32] Waters, *Dickens and the Politics of the Family*, 14.

[33] John Ruskin, 'Of Queens' Gardens', *Sesame and Lilies* (London: George Allen, 1904), 108. First published 1865.

[34] See especially the ground-breaking work of Leonore Davidoff and Catherine Hall, *Family Fortunes: Men and Women of the English Middle Class 1780–1850* (Chicago: University of Chicago Press, 1987); John Tosh, *A Man's Place: Masculinity and the Middle-Class Home in Victorian England* (New Haven: Yale University Press, 2007); Amanda Vickery, 'Golden Age to Separate Spheres: A Review of the Categories and Chronology of English Women's History', *Historical Journal* 36, 2 (1993): 383–414.

[35] I'm inspired by Ngai's reading of Herman Melville's *The Confidence Man* (1857) as exploring a world run on 'a feeling [confidence, trust] that no one actually feels' and 'that no one in the novel can verify or

The woman's soothing, civilizing position—as 'so simply, subtly sweet' in Coventry Patmore's description of 'The Paragon' of the angel in the house—at the heart of Victorian domestic ideology rests on a belief in the entrainment of her emotions. Ruskin similarly casts women as agents of 'sweet ordering':

> If they rightly understood and exercised their royal or gracious influence, the order and beauty induced by such benignant power would justify us in speaking of the territories over which each of them reigned as 'Queens' Gardens'.[36]

Ruskin's language of influence, inducement, and spatial territories presents the emotional comportment of 'sweet order' as transmittable. A poem Ruskin quotes from a knight to his lady further clarifies the transmission model—'from thee all virtues spread | as from a fountain-hedd'[37]—as does his insistence that good women radiate the sense of home: 'wherever a true-wife comes, this home is always around her ... and for a noble woman it stretches far around her'.[38] The true-wife must sympathize with her husband's ugly feelings produced by the inhospitable emotional climate of the public sphere by which, in Ruskin's terms, he is 'wounded', 'subdued', 'misled', and 'always hardened',[39] but she may only enter into those feelings so far as they will not affect, wound, or subdue her. Though understanding negative public affects she must not feel them, instead maintaining and transmitting only good feeling. This is an incoherent model of emotional interaction or influence, in which feeling can only 'spread' and 'stretch' outwards in one direction from the angelic woman; she must be simultaneously immune to the bad feelings brought into the home from outside and those generated by domestic labour while being highly contagious in transmitting her own unaffected good feeling. Even Ruskin sees the catch within his scheme: 'she must—as far as one can use such terms of a human creature—be incapable of error'.[40] A system based on the ideal of an implausibly unerring woman radiating untinctured good feeling is a system in which no one can fully believe, not even those who endorse it, as Ruskin's caveat shows.

As Ayres argues, there is no successfully operating example of feminine perfection in Dickens's fiction.[41] Good women fail to transform the feelings of men who love them and dissenting women reject the model. Extending Ayres's important work, I suggest that Dickens's awkward women illustrate the emotional illogic of domestic ideology by variously embodying its conflicting parts. Mrs Jellyby and Mrs Wilfer have the necessary imperviousness to the feelings of others, and Mrs Jellyby even has the requisite

---

publically prove he possesses, even with the aid of tokens (money, vouchers, receipts) that are essentially abstractions of that unfelt "confidence" and whose values presuppose and depend on it', *Ugly Feelings*, 69.

[36] Ruskin, 'Of Queens' Gardens', 89.
[37] Ibid., 100.
[38] Ibid., 109.
[39] Ibid., 108.
[40] Ibid., 109.
[41] As Ayres puts it, 'the depreciation of the angel's ability to sow and reap goodness is a severe undercutting of ideological dynamics', *Dissenting Women*, 3.

sweetness but can only maintain it by emotional distance rather than proximity to her family. Mrs Varden, on the other hand, is inversely affected by her husband's feelings about his public roles of locksmith and volunteer soldier. While Gabriel delights in these roles, Martha's emotional contrariness raises questions about these activities as public goods, just as the pleasure the neighbours imagine she would take in a slide down the social ladder works to query the consensus of the good life.

RIOTOUS: *BARNABY RUDGE*, FAILED DOMESTICITY, FAILED PATERNALISM

The Varden marriage challenges the end-goals of Ruskinian 'harmony', by which relations between wife and husband will 'aid and increase the vigour, honour and authority of both'.[42] Martha Varden is presented as having no investment in helping to increase Gabriel's authority, viewing his proud position as sergeant in the Royal East-London Volunteers as foolish and 'unchristian' (*BR* 41, 327) and exposing the oppressiveness within his trade. Dickens presents Gabriel's 'sunny heart' and his radiance of 'gladness' as a natural consequence of harmonious lock-smithing work:

> There was nothing surly or severe in the whole scene. It seemed impossible that any one of the innumerable keys could fit a churlish strong-box or a prison-door. Cellars of beer and wine, rooms where there were fires, books, gossip, and cheering laughter—these were their proper sphere of action. Places of distrust, and cruelty, and restraint, they would have left quadrupled-locked for ever. (*BR* 41, 326)

Though Gabriel's good cheer might mean that it 'seemed impossible' to associate his work with prisons, the novel also shows this as a form of false consciousness as Gabriel forged the lock for Newgate, and the products of this trade are shown in especially cruel operation when Miggs becomes a turnkey at Bridewell and torments the inmates by twisting keys into their backs. The Golden Key itself is a site of restraint, from which apprentice Sim gains unauthorized liberties by using his skills to make a duplicate door-key. The range of disaffection within this household demonstrates the difficulty of distinguishing domestic space from 'places of distrust, and cruelty, and restraint', while the rioters—slipping easily from a slogan of 'No Popery' to 'No Property'—imperil the combination of material and emotional comfort. Indeed, the rioters' destruction of alcohol and books, those commodities of cosiness whose security is presented as the 'proper sphere' of Gabriel's trade, is particularly marked in Dickens's account. The 'strong old oaken door, guarded by good bolts and a heavy bar' of the Catholic Haredale family home is swiftly brought down (*BR* 55, 441), and its inner private spaces are sacked: 'Some

---

[42] Ruskin, 'Of Queens' Gardens', 91.

searched the drawers, the chests, the boxes, writing-desks, and closets, for jewels, plate, and money .... Men who had been into the cellars, and had staved the casks, rushed to and fro stark mad, setting fire to all they saw' (*BR* 55, 442). As they infiltrate homes, seizing and smashing goods and burning papers and property, the rioters dismantle a fantasy of secure ownership and home-making through a violently embodied rejection of domestic ideals of sanctuary and retreat from public trouble. The Maypole pub, a central site in *Barnaby Rudge* of warmth, cosiness, and cheer, is similarly eviscerated. Many women, far from acting as agents of social cohesion through sweet ordering, incite and participate in these riots that literally break apart the fabric of the home.

Gabriel Varden's work cannot secure the material possessions of his customers, nor can his emotional labour as benevolent head of the household secure a paternalist ideology. His position as moral centre of the novel, which was originally to have taken his name, is dubious. His flawed relationships as husband, father, and master are part of the novel's wider attention to paternalistic failure on a personal and political level. As Sally Ledger has argued, in *Barnaby Rudge* Dickens 'connects parental tyranny and the despotism of state paternalism', as part of his critique of pre-reform politics, the irresponsibility of the landed gentry and of those in legal authority who lack humanity and morality, like the country magistrate whose lies result in Barnaby's death sentence.[43] Ben Winyard has extended Ledger's argument about the insurrectionary effects of Gabriel's denial of his apprentice Sim Tappertit's 'social and sexual identity as he fixates on Varden's daughter', placing this in a context of the novel's 'private and public paternalism that violently prohibits sexuality and, thus, ironically generates the libidinal excesses it labours to contain'.[44] As Winyard puts it, Varden's 'inability to contain the psychosexual energies that are circulating and fermenting within his own household suggests that paternalism actually incites perversion'.[45]

Gabriel's obstruction of the desires of those in his household directly contributes to the violence of the riots fuelled by the frustrations of his apprentice and of his wife, whose desire for agency and an important role makes her an easy dupe to Lord Chester's self-interested plans for public disorder. Though he is presented as being well intentioned, Gabriel's paternalism results in his infantilization of all members of his household and his consequent failure to recognize their adult desires and his inability to relate to them as complex adults. Dickens presents paternalism as a defunct emotional regime. *Barnaby Rudge* thus dramatizes the affective impossibilities of the two central tenets of domestic ideology: the presumed wisdom and authority of a fatherly figure who always knows best, and the mandated happiness of the home's womanly paragon who has an ability to absorb bad feeling while transmitting only good feeling. Each

---

[43] Sally Ledger, *Dickens and the Popular Radical Imagination* (Cambridge: Cambridge University Press, 2007), 135.

[44] Ibid. 136; Ben Winyard, '"Their Deadly Longing": Paternalism, the Past, and Perversion in *Barnaby Rudge*', in Joseph Bristow and Josephine Mc Donagh (eds), *Nineteenth-Century Radical Traditions* (London: Palgrave Macmillan, 2016), 37–62, 38.

[45] Winyard, '"Their Deadly Longing"', 52.

gendered behaviour results in a limitation of emotional relationship, as only some forms and directions of feeling are permissible, limiting sympathetic identification and understanding as the positions of patriarch and paragon do not allow for an entering into the feelings of others.

The severe doubts raised in *Barnaby Rudge* about the operation of domestic ideology are not allayed by the excessive iterations of the good life with which it ends. Feminine feeling when aligned to the mandated goal of producing household cheer is shown to be no more authentic than earlier performances that cut across domestic ideals. The transformed Mrs Varden uses the same bodily repertoire that Miggs has exposed as fake—'the illnesses of some ladies was all pretensions, and that they could faint away stone dead whenever they had the inclinations so to do' (*BR* 80, 644)—still fainting 'according to the custom of matrons on all occasions of excitement' (*BR* 79, 634). Similarly, Dolly Varden who has apparently repudiated her earlier coquetry in her self-abnegating vow to her husband Joe Willet, 'I will be … your patient, gentle, never-tiring wife. I will never know a wish or care beyond our home and you, and always study how to please you with my best affection and most devoted love' (*BR* 78, 628), is still presented as most appealing in forms of coquetry like making 'believe she didn't care to sit on his side of the table' (*BR* 80, 638). Clearly feminine affectation can be just as much a component of the feminine ideal as a resistance to it, and performed feeling is an endorsed part of domestic ideology. While domestic ideology presumes innate, natural, and authentic gendered behaviours, *Barnaby Rudge* demonstrates that repertoires of fake feeling—such as being overcome, coyness, and coquettishness—are also valued components of femininity, so long as they operate for the emotional comfort and benefit of men.

While fake feminine feeling comfortably underpins women's domestic role, the domestic paternalism that has been shown to be so incendiary persists unreformed. Gabriel's final satisfaction is an obscene intensification of the contentment he has always sustained, showing no awareness of his role in creating the ugly feelings of others as 'the rosiest, cosiest, merriest, heartiest, best-contented old buck' (*BR* 80, 638). Hyperbolic descriptions of happiness combine with an extreme rehearsal of other mandated good life objects—marriage and reproduction. The fecundity of the concluding marriages of Dolly and Joe and Edward and Emma are described in terms of excess, producing 'more small Joes and small Dollys than could be easily counted' (*BR* 82, 658) and a 'family almost as numerous as Dolly's' (*BR* 82, 660). Old Mr Willet, another of the novel's fathers who cannot recognize the adult maturity and sexuality of his child, is almost killed by the arrival of his first grandchild, which he regards as an 'alarming' occurrence (*BR* 82, 659). Mr Willet senior's extreme disconcertment at this fulfilment of the heterosexual, reproductive happy ending highlights the potential array of affective responses, including ugly feelings, produced by the supposedly good life script.

Like those affect-alien characters, Mrs Jellyby and Mrs Wilfer, that resonate with later feminist readers, the counter-domestic affects of *Barnaby Rudge* are not contained by the happily-ever-after structure. The novel has too thoroughly shown the spuriousness of good life narrative conventions, and demonstrated that well-regulated domestic harmony relies on specific gendered performances of emotion. More radically still,

Dickens's work exposes the emotional incoherence of a domestic ideology based on impossible regimes of feeling for both patriarch and paragon.

Further Reading

Mary Jean Corbett, *Family Likeness: Sex, Marriage and Incest from Jane Austen to Virginia Woolf* (Ithaca, NY: Cornell University Press, 2008)

Holly Furneaux, *Queer Dickens: Erotics, Families, Masculinities* (Oxford: Oxford University Press, 2009)

Helena Michie, 'From Blood to Law: The Embarrassments of Family in Dickens', in John Bowen and Robert L. Patten (eds), *Palgrave Advances in Charles Dickens Studies* (New York: Palgrave Macmillan, 2006), 131–55

Talia Schaffer, *Romance's Rival: Familiar Marriage in Victorian Fiction* (Oxford: Oxford University Press, 2016)

CHAPTER 27

PSYCHOLOGY, PSYCHIATRY, MESMERISM, DREAMS, INSANITY, AND PSYCHOANALYTIC CRITICISM

TYSON STOLTE

Despite Dickens's insistence on the truthfulness of his characterization, a claim he makes most vehemently in the preface to the third edition of *Oliver Twist*—'IT IS TRUE', he writes there of Nancy's behaviour—his contemporaries were not always convinced of his ability to represent the mind. George Eliot labelled his a 'false psychology'; George Henry Lewes compared his characters to 'frogs whose brains have been taken out for physiological purposes'.[1] By the first half of the twentieth century, such reactions to Dickens's fiction had become nearly automatic: George Orwell's declaration that 'Dickens's characters have no mental life', for instance, was merely the repetition of a cliché.[2] But even as Orwell wrote, psychoanalytic criticism was discovering in Dickens's fiction powerful representations of the workings of the mind. Over the course of the twentieth century, psychoanalytic critics traced the symptoms of Dickens's traumatic experiences at Warren's Blacking, charted the interplay of desire and repression in the novels, and unearthed the Oedipal relations at the heart of so much of Dickens's fiction. Out of these psychoanalytic readings, moreover, grew another strain of criticism that outlined Dickens's engagement with the psychological theory of the nineteenth century, his wide reading and thinking on such topics as mesmerism, dreams, and insanity. The flourishing scholarly interest in Victorian psychology over the past two decades

---

[1] Charles Dickens, *Oliver Twist*, ed. Kathleen Tillotson (Oxford: Clarendon Press, 1966), lxv; [George Eliot,] 'The Natural History of German Life', *Westminster Review* NS 10 (July 1856): 51–79, 55; George Henry Lewes, 'Dickens in Relation to Criticism', *Fortnightly Review* 17 (February 1872): 141–54, 145.

[2] George Orwell, 'Charles Dickens', in *Collected Essays* (London: Secker and Warburg, 1961), 31–87, 82.

has confirmed both the importance of nineteenth-century mental science to Dickens's writing and the importance of Dickens's writing to nineteenth-century mental science.

As such scholarship has shown, Dickens draws extensively in his fiction on the language and concepts of Victorian theories of mind, charting the interplay of the innate mental faculties and associative links that form David Copperfield's character, for instance, or drawing on the language of double consciousness in his representation of the mysterious John Jasper. Additionally, Dickens frequently published essays on psychological topics in *Household Words* and *All the Year Round*, offering contributors suggestions for revision based on his own reading and thinking on such topics. Nicholas Dames, Jill Matus, Athena Vrettos, and others have produced important recent work that traces Dickens's engagement with nineteenth-century discussions of such diverse topics as memory, the mechanizing effects of habit, and the consequences of trauma.[3] But not nearly enough attention has been paid to Dickens's paramount concern with the larger philosophical context of Victorian psychology, a concern that is apparent in his various interventions on behalf of a soul-based faculty psychology against the encroachment of new materialist theories of mind. It was this debate, however—about the very nature of mind and its relationship to the body—that was most passionately carried on in psychological texts over the course of Dickens's career.

It is in the context of this psychological controversy, I argue, that we must read the complaints of Dickens's contemporaries about his characterization. Lewes's figure for Dickens's mechanical characters, the brainless frog, is drawn straight from the pages of the psycho-physiology Lewes championed against Dickens's soul-based faculty psychology; Lewes's critique is the expression of a psychological objection as much as a literary critical one. Yet Lewes's was a psychological position that Dickens struggled to counter: in the final section of this chapter, I turn to a reading of *Little Dorrit* in order to show how difficult it had become to defend a soul-based psychology by the second half of Dickens's career. In this and other ways, this reading will demonstrate, Dickens's novels have the potential to offer us valuable insight into the struggles that shaped psychology in the nineteenth century.

Dickens and Victorian Psychology

Although there were dissenting voices, readers who insisted on the reality of Dickens's people, the notion that Dickens's characterization never extended beyond externals, that his men and women were little more than bundles of tics and catchphrases, was

---

[3] Nicholas Dames, *Amnesiac Selves: Nostalgia, Forgetting, and British Fiction, 1810–1870* (New York: Oxford University Press, 2001), 125–66; Jill L. Matus, 'Trauma, Memory, and Railway Disaster: The Dickensian Connection', *Victorian Studies* 43, 3 (Spring 2001): 413–36; Athena Vrettos, 'Defining Habits: Dickens and the Psychology of Repetition', *Victorian Studies* 42, 3 (Spring 1999/2000): 399–426.

already firmly established by the end of Dickens's career. John Forster blames the French writer Hippolyte Taine, who insisted in his *History of English Literature* (1856) that Dickens only captures character 'in a single attitude', each character being only 'a vice, a virtue, a ridicule personified', 'an abstraction in man's clothes'.[4] This was a position, Forster complains, that was subsequently 'repeated ad nauseam by others';[5] Lewes's assessment of Dickens's fiction, Forster suggests, is a case in point. Yet what made Lewes in particular an apt 'follower' of Taine,[6] in Forster's words, was not only his dismissive attitude toward Dickens's characterization. In his discussion of Dickens's fiction, Taine had written that Dickens's grotesque and passionate imagination 'is like that of monomaniacs'; Lewes writes that 'there is considerable light shed upon his works by the action of the imagination in hallucination'.[7]

Lewes's position, which Rosemarie Bodenheimer describes as 'couched in the authoritative language of the mental sciences', has been read as an effort to reinforce the boundaries between literature and science, to deny Dickens any standing to comment on psychological topics.[8] Sarah Winter, for instance, calls Lewes's review an effort 'to define both literature and psychology as distinct disciplinary forms of knowledge'.[9] Yet such a move—coming particularly from Lewes, who began his career as a literary critic—hardly seems viable in the generalist scientific culture of the years during which Dickens wrote. As numerous historians of science have shown, novels were considered important means of contributing to psychological debate at mid-century.[10] For all his condescension, then—what Forster labels his 'intolerable assumptions of an indulgent superiority'[11]—Lewes seems ultimately to be making a different move: his discussion of Dickens's fiction, I argue, represents an effort to insist on a different *type* of psychology

---

[4] H. A. Taine, *History of English Literature* (1856), trans. H. Van Laun, 2 vols (Edinburgh: Edmonstan and Douglas, 1871), 2:357.

[5] John Forster, *The Life of Charles Dickens*, ed. J. W. T. Ley (London: Cecil Palmer, 1928), 714.

[6] Ibid., 717.

[7] Taine, *History of English Literature*, 344; Lewes, 'Dickens', 145. Numerous scholars have discussed the way that each of these critics 'pathologizes' Dickens's imagination, in Sarah Winter's words (Sarah Winter, *The Pleasures of Memory: Learning to Read with Charles Dickens* (New York: Fordham University Press, 2011), 3). See, for example, Rosemarie Bodenheimer, *Knowing Dickens* (Ithaca, NY: Cornell University Press, 2007), 3–5; John Bowen, *Other Dickens: Pickwick to Chuzzlewit* (Oxford: Oxford University Press, 2000), 16–17; and Anna Neill, *Primitive Minds: Evolution and Spiritual Experience in the Victorian Novel* (Columbus: The Ohio State University Press, 2013), 66.

[8] Bodenheimer, *Knowing Dickens*, 5.

[9] Winter, *The Pleasures of Memory*, 29.

[10] On the open nature of Victorian psychological debate and the novel's role in shaping psychological knowledge, see Jill L. Matus, *Shock, Memory and the Unconscious in Victorian Fiction* (Cambridge: Cambridge University Press, 2009), 12–14; Neill, *Primitive*, 66; Edward R. Reed, *From Soul to Mind: The Emergence of Psychology, from Erasmus Darwin to William James* (New Haven: Yale University Press, 1997), xi; Graham Richards, *Mental Machinery: The Origins and Consequences of Psychological Ideas, Part 1: 1600–1850* (London: Athlone, 1992), 370; Rick Rylance, *Victorian Psychology and British Culture, 1850–1880* (Oxford: Oxford University Press, 2000), 1–17; and Sally Shuttleworth, *Charlotte Brontë and Victorian Psychology* (Cambridge: Cambridge University Press, 1996), 13–14.

[11] Forster, *Life*, 716.

from that to which Dickens consistently gives voice in his writing, an attempt to delegitimize not literature as a mode of psychological enquiry but the particular conclusions to which such enquiry led Dickens. Key here are the brainless frogs to which Lewes compares Dickens's characters, frogs that also have a place in Lewes's psychological writing: in his 1859 *Physiology of Common Life*, for instance—a book Dickens owned—Lewes turns to such experimental subjects to discuss the automatic actions of the body in sleep, insisting that such reflex actions 'very closely resemble those of animals when the entire Brain has been removed'.[12] Lewes's brainless frogs, in other words, were at the heart of mid-century debate about the nature of thought and the relationship between the mind and body.

Lewes's dismissal of Dickens's characterization, then, needs to be viewed in the context of the broad shift in psychology in the nineteenth century toward more material theories of mind, theories that insisted on the physical roots of consciousness. In the 1830s and 1840s, as Dickens was beginning his career, those studies that insisted on the mind's immateriality seemed to have the upper hand in psychological debate. The mind, these psychologies argued—and it was a diverse group of theories that made such claims—was ontologically distinct from the body and therefore could not be understood by way of the methods of the physical sciences. In the words of John Abercrombie, two of whose books Dickens owned, '[t]he mind can be compared to nothing in nature; it has been endowed by its Creator with a power of perceiving external things; but the manner in which it does so is entirely beyond our comprehension. All attempts, therefore, to explain or illustrate its operations by a reference to any thing else, can be considered as vain and futile'.[13] The body's effects on consciousness couldn't be denied, of course, but such effects were represented as stemming from the conditions of the mind's embodiment in our mortal lives. As the author of 'The Relation of the Will to Thought' puts it, 'consciousness is the function, not of the brain, without a personal self or agent, but of a personal self or agent who in this state of mortality energizes through the brain as his instrument, but is independent of and anterior to its operations'.[14] Such nuances

---

[12] George Henry Lewes, *The Physiology of Common Life*, 2 vols (Edinburgh and London: William Blackwood and Sons, 1859), 2:267.

[13] John Abercrombie, *Inquiries Concerning the Intellectual Powers and the Investigation of Truth*, 10th edn (London: John Murray, 1840), 27. Or, in Lorraine Daston's words, 'Separate ontologies justified distinct methodologies' ('British Responses to Psycho-Physiology, 1860–1900', *Isis* 69, 2 (June 1978): 192–208, 196). The mind was not to be studied through the methods applied to the body. For fuller treatments of the shifts in psychology I discuss here, see especially Edwin G. Boring, *A History of Experimental Psychology*, 2nd edn (New York: Appleton-Century-Crofts, 1950); Daston, 'British Responses'; Thomas Dixon, *From Passions to Emotions: The Creation of a Secular Psychological Category* (Cambridge: Cambridge University Press, 2003); Reed, *From Soul to Mind*; Richards, *Mental Machinery*; Rylance, *Victorian Psychology and British Culture*; and Roger Smith, 'The Physiology of the Will: Mind, Body, and Psychology in the Periodical Literature, 1855–1875', in Geoffrey Cantor and Sally Shuttleworth (eds), *Science Serialized: Representations of the Sciences in Nineteenth-Century Periodicals* (Cambridge, MA: MIT Press, 2004), 81–110.

[14] H. E. M. [Archbishop Manning], 'The Relation of the Will to Thought', *The Contemporary Review* 16 (December 1870): 468–79, 470.

mattered for more conservative thinkers because of the widespread supposition that the mind's immateriality was a necessary condition of its immortality. The corruptible body, after all, could hardly be the vessel in which we would enjoy the future life. Hence the vitriol and anxiety with which conservative writers greeted the physicalist theories which began to dominate the field in the latter part of Dickens's career. Although dualist psychologies persisted, as both Thomas Dixon and Rick Rylance have argued, religiously inclined Victorians felt as though they were increasingly under siege as material theories—those that seemed to make mind a product of the body—proliferated.[15]

Dickens's fascination with psychological subjects has, by now, been well documented. His interest in mesmerism is perhaps most widely known, in large part due to Fred Kaplan's *Dickens and Mesmerism*.[16] Not only did Dickens read widely on the subject, Kaplan has shown, but he even prided himself on his abilities as a mesmeric operator, exercising his talents most notoriously on Augusta de la Rue, a married woman with whose family he became friendly in Genoa. Dickens's library, meanwhile, contained key works by a number of important writers on the mind, such as Abercrombie, John Conolly, E. S. Dallas, John Elliotson, Charles Fourier, David Hume, Lewes, John Locke, Robert Macnish, Dugald Stewart, and Chauncy Hare Townshend.[17] Numerous scholars have also detailed Dickens's friendships and professional relationships with major psychological thinkers of the period, including the heads of asylums, medical practitioners, and psychological theorists, among them Henry, Lord Brougham; William Carpenter; Conolly; and Elliotson.[18] Others have identified the use of Dickens's characters, incidents from his fiction, and his comments as illustrative

---

[15] Dixon, *From Passions to Emotions*, 233–4, and Rylance, *Victorian Psychology and British Culture*, 22.

[16] Fred Kaplan, *Dickens and Mesmerism: The Hidden Springs of Fiction* (Princeton: Princeton University Press, 1975).

[17] As Bodenheimer points out, though, 'Many of the books were presentation copies, so we cannot be sure of what Dickens actually read' (*Knowing Dickens*, 7). For a catalogue of Dickens's Gad's Hill library, see J. H. Stonehouse (ed.), *Reprints of the Catalogues of the Libraries of Charles Dickens and W. M. Thackeray, etc.* (London: Piccadilly Fountain Press, 1935). The fourth volume of the *Pilgrim Letters* also contains an inventory of Dickens's home at Devonshire Terrace in 1844 (*The Letters of Charles Dickens*, ed. Madeline House, Graham Storey, et al., Pilgrim/British Academy Edition, 12 vols (Oxford: Clarendon, 1965–2002), 4:704–26. Subsequent citations: *PLets* followed by volume:page range, page).

[18] Among those who have discussed Dickens's relationships with such figures are Bodenheimer, *Knowing Dickens*, 57; Katharina Boehm, *Charles Dickens and the Sciences of Childhood: Popular Medicine, Child Health and Victorian Culture* (New York: Palgrave Macmillan, 2013), 5, 114; Edwin M. Eigner, *The Metaphysical Novel in England and America: Dickens, Bulwer, Melville, and Hawthorne* (Berkeley: University of California Press, 1978), 183; Lawrence Frank, 'In Hamlet's Shadow: Mourning and Melancholia in *Little Dorrit*', *SEL: Studies in English Literature, 1500–1900* 52, 4 (Autumn 2012): 861–96, 887; Helen Groth, 'Reading Victorian Illusions: Dickens's *Haunted Man* and Dr. Pepper's "Ghost"', *Victorian Studies* 50, 1 (Autumn 2007): 43–65, 44; Kaplan, *Dickens and Mesmerism*; J. W. T. Ley, *The Dickens Circle: A Narrative of the Novelist's Friendships* (New York: E. P. Dutton, 1919); Neill, *Primitive*, 69; Sally Shuttleworth, '"The Malady of Thought": Embodied Memory in Victorian Psychology and the Novel', in Matthew Campbell, Jacqueline M. Labbe, and Sally Shuttleworth (eds), *Memory and Memorials 1789–1914* (London: Routledge, 2000), 46–59, 47; and Graeme Tytler, 'Charles Dickens's "The Signalman": A Case of Partial Insanity?' *History of Psychiatry* 8 (1997): 421–32, 422.

examples in the psychological work of such theorists as Carpenter, James Crichton-Browne, Elliotson, and J. H. Jackson.[19]

Dickens also published numerous essays on psychological topics in both *Household Words* and *All the Year Round*, ranging from discussions of new methods for treating the mentally ill to theories of dreams. These articles, both those written by Dickens himself and those contributed by others, demonstrate a detailed familiarity with the key thinkers of eighteenth- and nineteenth-century mental science: within the pages of these periodicals are to be found citations of or references to such theorists as Abercrombie, Alexander Bain, Brougham, Macnish, and Thomas Reid. Dickens, of course, was no passive editor, often making substantial changes to the articles he published. Dr Thomas Stone's essay 'Dreams', published in the 8 March 1851 issue of *Household Words*, is a case in point. As several scholars have noted, Stone's initial submission was met by a long and detailed letter from Dickens outlining proposed changes, prefaced by Dickens's insistence that '[i]f I venture to say that I think [the article] may be made a little more original, and a little less recapitulative of the usual stories in the books, it is because I have read something on the subject, and have long observed it with the greatest attention and interest'.[20]

But it is Dickens's fiction that offers his most important engagement with and contribution to Victorian psychological debate. The fiction teems with the language of mental science, as in Doctor Manette's explanation, in *A Tale of Two Cities*, of the recurrence of his shoemaking compulsion: 'I believe ... that there had been a strong and extraordinary revival of the train of thought and remembrance that was the first cause of the malady. Some intense associations of a most distressing nature were vividly recalled, I think. It is probable that there had long been a dread lurking in his mind; that those associations would be recalled—say, under certain circumstances—say, on a particular occasion.'[21] Mr Toodle's musing in *Dombey and Son* on his own thought process is equally

---

[19] On Carpenter, see Regenia Gagnier, 'Freedom, Determinism, and Hope in *Little Dorrit*: A Literary Anthropology', *Partial Answers* 9, 2 (June 2011): 331–46, 335; and Matus, 'Trauma': 423; on Elliotson, see Boehm, *Charles Dickens and the Sciences of Childhood*, 5; on Jackson, see Athena Vrettos, 'Dying Twice: Victorian Theories of Déjà Vu', in Amanda Anderson and Joseph Valente (eds), *Disciplinarity at the Fin de Siècle* (Princeton: Princeton University Press, 2002), 196–218, 210; and Anna Neill, 'Evolution and Epilepsy in *Bleak House*', *SEL: Studies in English Literature, 1500–1900* 51, 4 (Autumn 2011): 803–22, 807; on Crichton-Browne, see Gagnier, 'Freedom, Determinism, and Hope in *Little Dorrit*', 335, and Neill, 'Evolution', 807.

[20] Dickens to Dr Thomas Stone, 2 February 1851, in *PLets* 6:276–9, 276. For discussions of Dickens's response to Stone's submission, see Bodenheimer, *Knowing Dickens*, 13–14; Catherine A. Bernard, 'Dickens and Victorian Dream Theory', in James Paradis and Thomas Postlewait (eds), *Victorian Science and Victorian Values: Literary Perspectives* (New York: New York Academy of Sciences, 1981), 197–216; David McAllister, '"Subject to the Sceptre of Imagination": Sleep, Dreams, and Unconsciousness in *Oliver Twist*', *Dickens Studies Annual* 38 (2007): 1–17; and Warrington Winters, 'Dickens and the Psychology of Dreams', *PMLA* 63, 3 (September 1948): 984–1006.

[21] Charles Dickens, *A Tale of Two Cities*, ed. Andrew Sanders, Oxford World's Classics (Oxford: Oxford University Press, 2008), 2:19, 194. Dickens's employment of the language of association should not be read as an indication of his reliance upon or endorsement of the associationist psychology that grew out of the work of Locke and Hume. As Rylance has noted (*Victorian Psychology and British Culture*, 55), the language of association was used by a variety of psychologies in the nineteenth century,

indebted to the concept of the association of ideas: ' "I starts light with Rob only; I comes to a branch; I takes on what I finds there; and a whole train of ideas gets coupled on to him, afore I knows where I am, or where they comes from. What a Junction a man's thoughts is", said Mr. Toodle, "to-be-sure!" '[22] Dickens also often employs the language of physiognomy, as Graeme Tytler and Michael Hollington have shown;[23] and while he was sceptical of phrenology, it nevertheless recurs in his fiction as a source of humour, as in the description, in the second chapter of *Martin Chuzzlewit*, of the after-effects of Pecksniff's fall down his front steps, an accident which leads to 'the development of an entirely new organ, unknown to phrenologists, on the back of his head'.[24]

DICKENS AND DUALISM

As I have suggested, it was psychoanalytic criticism that first subjected the psychological content of Dickens's fiction to serious and sustained scrutiny. This shift away from the more dismissive readings emblematized by Lewes is usually traced to Edmund Wilson's 'Dickens: The Two Scrooges', which made a case for the developing 'psychological interest' in Dickens's later fiction.[25] In the subsequent rush to treat Dickens as a psychological thinker, some psychoanalytic critics attempted to situate him amongst the psychological writings of his contemporaries. Warrington Winters, for instance, paid close attention to Dickens's editorial work on *Household Words*—at least on Stone's article—while Leonard Manheim studied the books catalogued in Dickens's library at the time of his death, noting that the collection 'indicates that [Dickens] had rather more acquaintance with the psychopathology and psychiatry of his age than other men of his education, contacts, and interests'.[26]

Generations of psychoanalytic critics have since offered illuminating and astute readings of Dickens's writing; as Carolyn Dever puts it, psychoanalysis has proven

including the dualist faculty psychology to which Dickens subscribed. I offer a fuller discussion of Dickens's position in this debate elsewhere: see Tyson Stolte, ' "What Is Natural in Me": *David Copperfield*, Faculty Psychology, and the Association of Ideas', *Victorian Review* 36, 1 (Spring 2010): 55–71. For critics who have labelled Dickens an associationist, see Dames, *Amnesiac Selves*; Michael S. Kearns, 'Associationism, the Heart, and the Life of the Mind in Dickens' Novels', *Dickens Studies Annual* 15 (1986): 111–44; and Winter, *The Pleasures of Memory*. Edwin Eigner seems to be the first scholar to have recognized that Dickens—along with the other writers of 'metaphysical fiction' whom Eigner discusses—'reject[ed] Lockean psychology' (*The Metaphysical Novel*, 75).

[22] Charles Dickens, *Dombey and Son*, ed. Alan Horsman (Oxford: Clarendon Press, 1974), 38, 512–13.

[23] Michael Hollington, 'Dickens, "Phiz" and Physiognomy', in Joachim Möller (ed.), *Imagination on a Long Rein: English Literature Illustrated* (Marburg: Jonas, 1988), 125–35; and Graeme Tytler, *Physiognomy in the European Novel: Faces and Fortunes* (Princeton: Princeton University Press, 1982).

[24] Charles Dickens, *Martin Chuzzlewit*, ed. Margaret Cardwell (Oxford: Clarendon Press, 1982), 2, 10.

[25] Edmund Wilson, 'Dickens: The Two Scrooges', in *The Wound and the Bow: Seven Studies in Literature*, new printing with corrections (New York: Oxford University Press, 1947), 1–104, 84.

[26] Leonard Manheim, 'Dickens' Fools and Madmen', *Dickens Studies Annual* 2 (1972): 69–97, 69.

itself to be 'a methodology with considerable explanatory power for the analysis of Dickens's fiction'.[27] But valuable as such work has been, it has often come at the expense of the sort of close attention to context modelled by Manheim. Even Manheim could be condescending toward Victorian psychological theory; others, in praising Dickens's psychological insights, have entirely elided such theory, describing Dickens's positions as *sui generis*, astute intuitions of the truths that Freud would later reveal. Even such praise as Dever's assertion that Dickens was 'a brilliant psychoanalytic thinker, *avant la lettre*', erases from Dickens's intellectual life the hard work of keeping abreast of the latest psychological theory.[28] At times this omission of Victorian mental science is papered over by insisting on psychoanalysis's nineteenth-century roots, as in Dianne Sadoff's argument that '[p]sychoanalysis ... is a nineteenth-century phenomenon', but such claims only justify ignoring the vast and diverse body of Victorian psychological work.[29]

Yet even that more recent body of scholarship that has done so much to parse Dickens's knowledge of and engagement with nineteenth-century mental science has often misrepresented the specifics of Dickens's position in psychological debate, reading his fiction and journalism as replicating the physicalist theories of mind that seemed to be in the ascendant in the second half of his career.[30] What such arguments overlook is how consistently Dickens insisted on the immateriality of mind and its ultimate immortality; his psychological views always tended toward the conventional and the orthodox. We see signs of such orthodoxy in the distinction he so often makes between soul and body, as in the following passage from *Nicholas Nickleby*, which describes the consumption that causes Smike to waste away: 'There is a dread disease ... in which the struggle between soul and body is so gradual, quiet, and solemn, and the result so sure, that day by day, and grain by grain, the mortal part wastes and withers away, so that the spirit grows light and sanguine with its lightening load, and, feeling immortality at hand, deems it but a new term of mortal life.'[31] Dickens's orthodox psychological leanings, his insistence on an immaterial and immortal soul in the face of the advances of a physicalist psychology, are equally on display in both *Household Words* and *All the Year Round*. For example, Stone's article on dreams, the original version of which drew so much feedback from Dickens, acknowledges 'the intimate alliance of the mind with the body', but Stone nevertheless insists on the distinction between the two, describing

---

[27] Carolyn Dever, 'Psychoanalyzing Dickens', in John Bowen and Robert L. Patten (eds), *Palgrave Advances in Charles Dickens Studies* (Houndmills: Palgrave Macmillan, 2006), 216–33, 218.

[28] Dever, 'Psychoanalyzing Dickens', 218.

[29] Dianne F. Sadoff, *Monsters of Affection: Dickens, Eliot & Bronte on Fatherhood* (Baltimore: Johns Hopkins University Press, 1982), 6.

[30] In addition to those critics who read Dickens as an associationist, see, for instance, Louise Henson, '"In the Natural Course of Physical Things": Ghosts and Science in Charles Dickens's *All the Year Round*', in Louise Henson, Geoffrey Cantor, Gowan Dawson, Richard Noakes, Sally Shuttleworth, and Jonathan R, Topham (eds), *Culture and Science in the Nineteenth-Century Media* (Aldershot: Ashgate, 2004), 113–23; and Neill, *Primitive*, 64–5.

[31] Charles Dickens, *Nicholas Nickleby*, ed. Paul Schlicke, Oxford World's Classics (New York: Oxford University Press, 1990), 49, 637. Subsequent references are inserted parenthetically in the text by *NN*, chapter, page.

how in sleep '[t]he lids of the outward senses are closed; a veil is drawn over the immaterial principle of our nature; and mind and body alike, for a period, lie in a state of utter unconsciousness'.[32] Stone goes even further, too, finding in the way 'we always preserve the consciousness of our own identity' in dreams 'a proof of the immateriality of the mind'.[33]

It isn't only through such explicit claims for an immortal soul that Dickens maintains a conservative position in psychological debate. He just as frequently draws attention in his work to the innate qualities that stood, in many conservative psychologies, as a bulwark against materialism, such as the inborn fancy, that 'fire with nothing to burn', that Thomas Gradgrind's educational regimen never quite extinguishes in Louisa.[34] Dickens is clear about the spiritual significance of such innate faculties: Charles Cheeryble describes our '[n]atural affections and instincts' as 'the most beautiful of the Almighty's works' (*NN* 46, 596), words that closely echo Thomas Reid's claim that our faculties are 'the inspiration of the Almighty, no less than our notions or simple apprehensions'.[35] As A. Campbell Fraser explains in 'Sir William Hamilton and Dr. Reid', both Reid and Kant strove to find in '*the original structure of human intelligence*' a 'refuge from skepticism';[36] the faculties, that is, came to stand as evidence of design in more conservative psychologies. Reid, significantly, also takes for granted the mind's immateriality, writing, for example, that '[w]e have reason to believe, that when we put off these bodies, and all the organs belonging to them, our perceptive powers shall rather be improved than destroyed or impaired'.[37]

The importance of innate faculties for Dickens is perhaps clearest in his handling of what, for him, constitute the limit cases of the human: the 'idiot' Barnaby Rudge, for instance, or the blind Laura Bridgman. If, in Barnaby's first appearance in *Barnaby Rudge*, Dickens writes that 'the absence of the soul is far more terrible in a living man than in a dead one; and in this unfortunate being its noblest powers were wanting', Dickens elsewhere describes the God-given mental powers with which even Barnaby is blessed.[38] Of Barnaby's merriment as he and his mother flee to Chigwell, for instance, Dickens writes, '[i]t is something to know that Heaven has left the capacity of gladness in such a creature's breast; it is something to be assured that, however lightly men may crush that

---

[32] [Thomas Stone,] 'Dreams', *Household Words*, 8 March 1851: 566–72, 566.

[33] Ibid., 568.

[34] Charles Dickens, *Hard Times*, ed. Fred Kaplan, Norton Critical Edition, 4th edn (New York: Norton, 2017), I:3, 16.

[35] Thomas Reid, *An Inquiry into the Human Mind on the Principles of Common Sense* [1764], ed. Derek R. Brookes (Edinburgh: Edinburgh University Press, 1997), 215. Many conservative psychologies in the nineteenth century could trace their roots to Reid's Common Sense philosophy. Rylance offers an especially helpful discussion of the origins and nuances of such psychologies.

[36] [A. Campbell Fraser,] 'Sir William Hamilton and Dr. Reid', *North British Review* 10 (1848): 144–78, 157.

[37] Thomas Reid, *Essays on the Intellectual Powers of Man* [1785], ed. Derek R. Brookes (Edinburgh: Edinburgh University Press, 2002), 72.

[38] Charles Dickens, *Barnaby Rudge*, ed. Clive Hurst, Oxford World's Classics (Oxford: Oxford University Press, 2003), 3, 38. Subsequent references are inserted parenthetically in the text by *BR*, chapter, page.

faculty in their fellows, the Great Creator of mankind imparts it even to his despised and slighted work' (*BR* 25, 201). The 'ill-remembered prayer' (*BR* 73, 585) that brings Barnaby solace in his prison cell works to the same effect, seemingly bearing out the claim by Dickens and W. H. Wills in the *Household Words* article 'Idiots' that '[w]hat dim religious impressions [idiots] connect with public worship, it is impossible to say, but the struggling soul would seem to have some instinctive aspirations towards its Maker'.[39] In *American Notes*, Dickens equally accords to Bridgman an 'Immortal soul', and he reproduces within his own pages the declaration of the director of the Perkins Institution and Massachusetts Asylum for the Blind, Dr Samuel Gridley Howe, that 'the immortal spirit which had been implanted within her could not die, nor be maimed nor mutilated';[40] instead, Howe insists of Bridgman's silent conversations with her fellow blind inmates that 'nothing can more forcibly show the power of mind in forcing matter to its purpose' (*AN* I:3, 46).

As is the case for Howe, Dickens's own confidence in the possibility of improving the conditions endured by both Barnaby and Bridgman is founded on the all-important distinction between mind and matter. For Dickens, the disabilities of the pair, just like the madness that also fascinated him, are disorders of the body, not of the soul. As Henry Morley puts it in 'The Cure of Sick Minds', '[i]nsanity is not the immaterial disease of an immaterial essence, but the perverted action of the mind caused by a defect in its instrument'.[41] This link between bodily deficiency and mental debilities motivates Dickens's frequent insistence—in *Dombey and Son*, *Bleak House*, and so on—on the environmental causes of the vice that festers in the nation's unsanitary slums, just as it underlies Morley's claim that 'there is often better mental food in a beefsteak than in a book—that the mind partakes of the body's health or sickness—that whatever weakens one weakens the other, whatever strengthens one strengthens the other'.[42] This is equally the lesson taught in *The Pickwick Papers* by the fate of the author of 'A Madman's Manuscript', for the note appended to that tale tells us that its author slipped into his homicidal madness through the 'fever and delirium' brought on by 'energies misdirected in early life, and excesses prolonged until their consequences could never be repaired'.[43] Dickens's largely sympathetic portrait of Lord George Gordon, that 'poor crazy Lord who died in Newgate' (*BR* 82, 656), similarly seems to stem from his sense that Gordon's actions were the result of 'sheer weakness' (*BR* 36, 292). In his confidence that such weakness could, through proper treatment, at least be ameliorated, Dickens was influenced by the humane reforms in the treatment of the mentally ill instituted by asylum keepers like John Conolly.[44] Having visited Conolly's Park House Asylum, Dickens and Wills write in

---

[39] [Charles Dickens and W. H. Wills,] 'Idiots', *Household Words*, 4 June 1853, 7: 313–17, 315.

[40] Charles Dickens, *American Notes*, ed. Patricia Ingham (New York: Penguin, 2000), I:3, 40, 41–2. Subsequent references are inserted parenthetically in the text by *AN*, volume:chapter, page.

[41] [Henry Morley,] 'The Cure of Sick Minds', *Household Words*, 2 April 1859, 19: 415–19, 417.

[42] Ibid., 417.

[43] Charles Dickens, *The Pickwick Papers*, ed. James Kinsley (Oxford: Clarendon Press, 1986), 11, 166.

[44] On Dickens's representation of madness, his visits to various asylums, and his endorsement of Conolly's reforms, see Richard A. Currie, '*All the Year Round* and the State of Victorian Psychiatry',

'Idiots' that 'the cultivation of such senses and instincts as the idiot is seen to possess'—of the innate material with which these individuals are blessed, in other words—'will, besides frequently developing others that are latent within him but obscured, so brighten those glimmering lights, as immensely to improve his condition, both with reference to himself and to society'.[45] Conolly's views seem equally optimistic and, in psychological terms, equally orthodox. In an 1846 speech, for example, he offers a plea for the 'poor, poor idiot', that 'his soul may be disimprisoned', a plea, to be clear, that registers mental deficiency as a consequence of the weakness of the body, by which the healthy soul is entrapped.[46]

PHYSICALIST PSYCHOLOGY AND *LITTLE DORRIT*

Dickens remained adamant in his endorsement of a dualist psychology throughout his career, but that position became more tenuous with each novel that he wrote. The terms and metaphors on which Dickens drew, shared as they were with more physicalist psychologies, slowly accumulated meanings utterly foreign to his own psychological allegiances. To some degree, this accretion of meaning was strategic: materialist theorists often gained a hearing by appropriating—and then redefining—the language of more generally palatable psychologies.[47] We can catch a glimpse of the consequences of this process in *Little Dorrit*. Dickens there continues to insist on the innate qualities that were among the clearest tokens of an orthodox psychological position. In describing the destructive effects of his childhood, Arthur Clennam assumes a series of such innate qualities, even if they have since been stunted: 'Will, purpose, hope? All those lights were extinguished before I could sound the words.'[48] Further displaying its adherence to the

---

Dickens Quarterly 12, 1 (March 1995): 18–24; Sander L. Gilman, 'Images of the Asylum: Charles Dickens and Charles Davies', in *Disease and Representation: Images of Illness from Madness to AIDS* (Ithaca, NY: Cornell University Press, 1988), 81–97; Richard A. Hunter and Ida Macalpine, 'A Note on Dickens's Psychiatric Reading', *The Dickensian* 53 (January 1957): 49–51; Paul Marchbanks, 'From Caricature to Character: The Intellectually Disabled in Dickens's Novels' (Parts One, Two, and Three), *Dickens Quarterly* 21, 1–3 (March, June, September 2006): 3–13, 67–84, 169–80; Neill, *Primitive*, 78; Susan Shatto, 'Miss Havisham and Mr. Mopes the Hermit: Dickens and the Mentally Ill' (Parts One and Two), *Dickens Quarterly* 2, 2–3 (June, September 1985): 43–50, 79–84; Robert Tracy, 'Treating Mr. Dick: Aunt Betsey as Therapist', *Dickens Quarterly* 30, 2 (June 2013): 114–22; and Tytler, 'Charles Dickens's "The Signalman"'.

[45] [Dickens and Wills], 'Idiots', 313.

[46] Quoted in Patrick McDonagh, '*Barnaby Rudge*, "Idiocy" and Paternalism: Assisting the "Poor Idiot"', *Disability and Society* 21, 5 (August 2006): 411–23, 418.

[47] On the shared language of Victorian psychology, see especially Dixon, *From Passions to Emotions*, and Rylance, *Victorian Psychology and British Culture*. On the prevalent rhetoric of reassurance in Victorian mental science, see Smith, 'The Physiology of the Will'.

[48] Charles Dickens, *Little Dorrit*, ed. Harvey Peter Sucksmith (Oxford: Clarendon Press, 1979), I:2, 20. Subsequent references are inserted parenthetically in the text by *LD*, book:chapter, page.

tenets of an orthodox dualist psychology, the novel is equally persistent in insisting on a Christian universe. After Frederick Dorrit follows his brother into death, for example, Dickens's narrator muses, '[t]he two brothers were before their Father; far beyond the twilight judgments of this world; high above its mists and obscurities' (*LD* II:19, 632). No wonder Dennis Walder writes of this novel, '[t]here is no more profound or original expression of the religious aspect of Dickens's imagination than *Little Dorrit*'.[49]

But the novel's numerous instances of the failure of the will seem to pull in a different direction, threatening to become indistinguishable from the representations of the mind offered in materialist psychologies. Of course, much has been written about what Lionel Trilling called 'the negation of man's will' in this novel, negation perhaps best captured in Clennam's description of the effects of his rigid upbringing: 'I have no will' (*LD* I:2, 20).[50] But while Clennam's comments gesture toward impotence, toward an inability to act, Mrs Tickit's subsequent description of her abstraction in the moments before she caught a glimpse of Tattycoram hints at a different shortcoming, the will's incapacity to control even her wandering thoughts: 'I hardly need to tell you, Mr. Clennam, that I think of the family. Because, dear me! a person's thoughts, … however they may stray, will go more or less on what is uppermost in their minds. They *will* do it, sir, and a person can't prevent them' (*LD* II:9, 512).[51] Far from an isolated example, the condition Tickit describes was one to which Dickens had already frequently returned in the 1850s. Several of the articles he wrote for or published in *Household Words*—'Lying Awake', 'Fly Leaves', 'A Discursive Mind'—similarly trace associative links the will seems powerless to control.[52] In 'Fly Leaves', Chauncy Hare Townshend describes man as 'the slave of association'; the author of 'A Discursive Mind' laments how 'my wretched mind stubbornly refused to yield to my resolve. It was a battle royal between Will and Habit'.[53] Such passages also echo the frustrations Dickens expressed as he struggled to begin *Little Dorrit*: in a letter to Leigh Hunt, for instance, he describes his 'uncontroullable [*sic*] state of being' as he put off work on the novel.[54] These were real anxieties for Dickens, it seems: Forster writes that '[i]t was during the composition of *Little Dorrit* that I think he first felt a certain strain upon his invention which brought with it other misgivings'.[55]

---

[49] Dennis Walder, *Dickens and Religion* (London: Allen and Unwin, 1981; repr. New York: Routledge, 2007), 195.

[50] Lionel Trilling, '*Little Dorrit*', in George H. Ford and Lauriat Lane, Jr (eds), *The Dickens Critics* (Ithaca, NY: Cornell University Press, 1961), 279–93, 282.

[51] I'm not the first to find psychological significance in Tickit's words. Winter describes Tickit as 'a sort of amateur psychologist' (*The Pleasures of Memory*, 32). For other readings that discuss *Little Dorrit*'s engagement with mid-century psychology (including writing on the will), see Gagnier, 'Freedom, Determinism, and Hope in *Little Dorrit*', 334–6, and Frank, 'In Hamlet's Shadow'.

[52] [Charles Dickens,] 'Lying Awake', *Household Words*, 30 October 1852, 6: 145–8; [Chauncy Hare Townshend,] 'Fly Leaves', *Household Words*, 13 September 1856, 14: 201–5; [Sorrell,] 'A Discursive Mind', *Household Words*, 14 November 1857, 16: 477–80.

[53] [Townshend], 'Fly Leaves', 202; [Sorrell], 'A Discursive Mind', 479.

[54] Dickens to Leigh Hunt, 4 May 1855, in *PLets* 7:608–9, 608.

[55] Forster, *Life*, 636.

Hints of the will's inadequacy worried others at mid-century, too. The particular resonances of such images in these years become clear if we return to the brainless frog that was for Lewes the closest approximation to Dickens's characters. As I suggested above, the experiments to which Lewes thus alludes were central to the physicalist psychology of the 1850s, 1860s, and 1870s, perhaps most notoriously in Thomas Huxley's 'On the Hypothesis that Animals are Automata, and its History'. Huxley notes that '[i]f the spinal cord of a frog is cut across, so as to provide us with a segment separate from the brain', the brainless frog will nevertheless make apparently purposive movements in relation to external stimuli: retracting its leg when pricked, for example, or rubbing off acid applied to its side.[56] On the basis of such automatic actions, Huxley makes the case that consciousness is 'a mere symbol' of the physical changes that take place in the nerves and brain.[57] Since the frog's brainless body is able to take purposive action in response to external stimuli, Huxley argues, '[t]he consciousness of brutes would appear to be related to the mechanism of their body simply as a collateral product of its working, and to be as completely without any power of modifying that working, as the steam-whistle which accompanies the work of a locomotive engine is without influence upon its machinery'.[58] Our feeling of volition, then, is only 'the symbol of that state of the brain which is the immediate cause' of any voluntary act.[59]

Such assaults on the will were of the utmost consequence to those who continued to insist on a soul-based psychology, for the will had by mid-century become a last refuge for dualist thinkers who felt under siege, as is suggested in Henry Sidgwick's description of 'the citadel of the will'.[60] As more and more of even our mental life was shown to be the product of automatic processes, more conservative thinkers desperately sought something that transcended—and could hold sway over—the body. Hence William Carpenter's assurance to readers in 'The Physiology of the Will': 'the physiologist sees quite as clearly as the metaphysician that there is a power beyond and above all such mechanism—a *will* which, alike in the Mind and in the Body, can utilize the Automatic agencies to work out its own purposes'.[61] J. M. Capes even more clearly captures the stakes of this question, suggesting that '[i]n Dr. Noble's judgment,... the existence of the *will* in man, whatever may be the case with the emotional and discriminating faculties, is alone sufficient to distinguish him from the lower animals, and to constitute him a religious and responsible agent'.[62] Not just our capacity for ethical action, or even the

[56] T. H. Huxley, 'On the Hypothesis that Animals are Automata, and its History', *The Fortnightly Review* NS 16 (November 1874): 555–80, 566.
[57] Ibid., 560.
[58] Ibid., 575.
[59] Ibid., 577.
[60] Henry Sidgwick, *The Methods of Ethics* (London: Macmillan and Co., 1874), 47. Quoted in Daston, 'British Responses', 194, and Rylance, *Victorian Psychology and British Culture*, 73. See also Daston's and Smith's discussions of the consequences for the will of psycho-physiology.
[61] William Carpenter, 'The Physiology of the Will', *Contemporary Review* 17 (1871): 192–217, 192. Neill quotes a verbatim passage from another of Carpenter's works (*Primitive*, 22).
[62] [J. M. Capes,] 'Noble on the Mind and the Brain', *The Rambler* 9 (May 1858): 353–6, 354. Quoted in Smith, 'The Physiology of the Will', 81.

notion of free will, but the very possibility of immortality seemed to be bound up with the fate of the will in the face of the advances of psycho-physiology.

In the context of such debate, *Little Dorrit*'s oft-discussed hints at a deterministic universe are hard to distinguish from more malicious assaults on the citadel of the will. There seems little room for volition, after all, in Miss Wade's claim that '[i]n our course through life we shall meet the people who are coming to meet *us*, from many strange places and by many strange roads, ... and what it is set to us to do to them, and what it is set to them to do to us, will all be done' (*LD* I:2, 24). But the psychological consequences of this novel's representations of the impotence of the will seem starkest in a set of images on display in Clennam's disappointed musings after his hopes for Pet Meagles have been dashed: 'And he thought—who has not thought for a moment, sometimes—that it might be better to flow away monotonously, like the river, and to compound for its insensibility to happiness with its insensibility to pain' (*LD* I:16, 194–7). The flowing river soon comes to stand in the novel as a figure for thought, for the 'current of ... meditations' (*LD* I:26, 310), finally transforming into a means of representing Clennam's failure, like Mrs Tickit's, to control his associations:

> It was in vain that he tried to control his attention, by directing it to any business occupation or train of thought; it rode at anchor by the haunting topic, and would hold to no other idea. As though a criminal should be chained in a stationary boat on a deep clear river, condemned, whatever countless leagues of water flowed past him, always to see the body of the fellow creature he had drowned lying at the bottom, immovable, and unchangeable, except as the eddies made it broad or long, now expanding, now contracting its terrible lineaments; so Arthur, below the shifting current of transparent thoughts and fancies which were gone and succeeded by others as soon as come, saw, steady and dark, and not to be stirred from its place, the one subject that he endeavoured with all his might to rid himself of, and that he could not fly from. (*LD* II:23, 658–9)

The chained criminal here seems an apt figure for the equally powerless will in theories of psycho-physical parallelism like Huxley's: imprisoned, detached from the current of thought, ultimately unable to alter its flow.

Fittingly, such images of streams and currents also had a place in physicalist psychology. Lewes, for instance, writes in *The Physiology of Common Life* of 'the general stream of Consciousness'.[63] W. K. Clifford, meanwhile, uses such language to make the case for psycho-physical parallelism: 'The mind, then, is to be regarded as a stream of feelings which runs parallel to and simultaneous with a certain part of the action of the body, that is to say, that particular part of the action of the brain in which the cerebrum and the

---

[63] Lewes, *Physiology*, 2:63. Rylance also quotes this passage, and both he (*Victorian Psychology and British Culture*, 11) and Groth ('Reading Victorian Illusions', 48) have noted Lewes's early conceptualization of the stream of consciousness. Rylance, however, suggests that images of 'blending currents and merging streams ... were not uncommon in the science and literature of the period' (*Victorian Psychology and British Culture*, 131).

sensory tract are excited.'[64] But it is the way Lewes employs this figure in 'Consciousness and Unconsciousness' that best expresses the full consequences of *Little Dorrit*'s images of will-lessness: 'Besides the stream of direct stimulations, there is a wider stream of indirect or reproduced stimulations... The term Soul is the personification of this complex of present and revived feelings, and is the substratum of Consciousness (in its general sense), all the particular feelings being its *states*.'[65] Far from the immortal part of us that will enjoy eternity, the soul threatens to become in Lewes's prose utterly ephemeral, no more than the flowing currents of our material existence.

In other words, while Dickens continued to insist on the tenets of a soul-based psychology in *Little Dorrit*—as in the novels that followed it—that position had become murkier, less self-evident, perhaps less convincing by the 1850s.[66] Read alongside the physicalist psychology of mid-century, even Dickens's claims for an immaterial soul become harder to parse, harder to distinguish from the stream of consciousness described by Lewes or Clifford. The novel's ambiguities, then, offer us a glimpse of the frequently noted confusion and nebulousness of Victorian psychological debate, its shifting and opaque battle-lines. But *Little Dorrit* reveals more than merely the fog of intellectual warfare. By examining the hints of various mid-century conceptualizations of volition or the soul in the novel, we can also discern one of the important rhetorical means—the redefinition of key terms—by which a physicalist psychology was able to write more conservative theories of mind out of existence. Lewes's dismissive comments on Dickens's characterization thus come into focus as part of the same project, as an attempt to appropriate Dickens's fiction as yet further evidence of the material basis of mind. Despite the caricatures offered by critics after Dickens's death, Lewes's attack reveals Dickens's place in the thick of psychological debate. But while Dickens's fiction has much to tell us about the state of such debate, the energy Lewes dedicates to neutralizing Dickens's engagements with mental science also stands as a testament to the significance and the value of the psychological meditations Dickens's novels themselves offer.

---

[64] W. K. Clifford, 'Body and Mind', *Fortnightly Review* NS 16 (1874): 714–36, 729.
[65] George Henry Lewes, 'Consciousness and Unconsciousness', *Mind* 2, 6 (April 1877): 156–67, 166.
[66] George Levine's reading of *Little Dorrit* in light of thermodynamics, evolutionary biology, and natural theology shares something in common with my own, especially in its acknowledgement of the way the first two of these bodies of thought seem to preclude voluntary action (*Darwin and the Novelists: Patterns of Science in Victorian Fiction* (Cambridge, MA: Harvard University Press, 1988), 162–4). Yet despite these similarities, Levine and I reach different conclusions about the novel. Dickens, in Levine's reading, follows his images to a secular conclusion, even if such a conclusion runs counter to his initial intentions (*Darwin and the Novelists*, 174); Levine describes Dickens's 'ultimate commitment to the secular' in this text (171), crediting the novel with facing 'the possibility that the religious account could not stand against the pressure of those irrefragable laws' articulated by Victorian science (175–6). I see Dickens as making no such confrontation, but maintaining the psychological position upon which he continued to try to insist for the remainder of his career. Dickens, in my reading, seems unaware of the slipperiness of the psychological language and metaphors he employs in this text.

Further Reading

Karen Chase, *Eros and Psyche: The Representation of Personality in Charlotte Brontë, Charles Dickens, George Eliot* (New York: Methuen, 1984)
Lawrence Frank, *Charles Dickens and the Romantic Self* (Lincoln: University of Nebraska Press, 1984)
L. S. Jacyna, 'The Physiology of Mind, the Unity of Nature, and the Moral Order in Victorian Thought', *The British Journal for the History of Science* 14, 47 (1981): 109–32
John Kucich, *Repression in Victorian Fiction: Charlotte Brontë, George Eliot, and Charles Dickens* (Berkeley: University of California Press, 1987)
Steven Marcus, *Dickens: From Pickwick to Dombey* (London: Chatto and Windus, 1965)
Hilary M. Schor, *Dickens and the Daughter of the House* (Cambridge: Cambridge University Press, 1999)
Sally Shuttleworth, *The Mind of the Child: Child Development in Literature, Science, and Medicine, 1840–1900* (Oxford: Oxford University Press, 2010)
Roger Smith, 'The Background of Physiological Psychology in Natural Philosophy', *History of Science* 11 (1973): 75–123
Tyson Stolte, '"And Graves Give Up their Dead": *The Old Curiosity Shop*, Victorian Psychology, and the Nature of the Future Life', *Victorian Literature and Culture* 42, 2 (June 2014): 187–207
Tyson Stolte, '"Putrefaction Generally": *Bleak House*, Victorian Psychology, and the Question of Bodily Matter', *Novel: A Forum on Fiction* 44, 3 (Fall 2011): 402–23
Alison Winter, *Mesmerized: Powers of Mind in Victorian Britain* (Chicago: University of Chicago Press, 1998)

CHAPTER 28

DICKENS AND ASTRONOMY, BIOLOGY, AND GEOLOGY

JONATHAN SMITH

'DICKENS and science?—the question mark is important', wrote K. J. Fielding in 1996.[1] The long-standing view that Dickens was uninterested in science, Fielding acknowledged, was clearly wrong. He was not prepared, however, to endorse the approaches or the specific arguments of influential studies by Ann Wilkinson, Gillian Beer, and George Levine claiming that Victorian energy physics and Darwinian evolution had played major roles in the narrative structure and thematics of such novels as *Bleak House* and *Little Dorrit*. These scholars' speculative approaches, Fielding complained, 'deal with the history of ideas rather than what happens or is mentioned in the novels', with 'abstractions' rather than 'actualities'.[2] The evidence was too limited and indirect to support their arguments, particularly with regard to thermodynamics, and Robert Chambers's anonymous 1844 best-seller, *Vestiges of the Natural History of Creation*, was a more valid source of evolutionary ideas for Dickens than *On the Origin of Species* (1859).

Fielding's critique was both astute and blinkered. The work of Beer and Levine *could* be fairly positioned in the history of ideas and often *did* rely on evolution and energy being 'in the air'.[3] The evidence connecting Dickens to particular scientific ideas and theories generally *is* indirect. But Fielding's conception of science was, we can now say, quite narrow. Despite his deep knowledge of Dickens's work with *Household Words* and *All the Year Round*, Fielding did not appreciate the roles these and similar popular publications played in the world of Victorian science. Fielding was also unaware that the vibrant world of spectacle and visual display so ubiquitous to Victorian London and so in tune with Dickens's own activities and

---

[1] K. J. Fielding, 'Dickens and Science?', *Dickens Quarterly* 13, 4 (1996): 200–15, 200.
[2] Ibid., 200.
[3] George Levine, *Darwin and the Novelists: Patterns of Science in Victorian Fiction* (Chicago: University of Chicago Press, 1988), 156.

interests emphatically included both elite and popular science. For Fielding, the central questions were about what Dickens said, read, and published in his periodicals, 'rather than what can doubtfully be inferred from his fiction'.[4] Subsequent scholars writing on Dickens and science have generally endeavoured to provide more of the 'actualities' Fielding called for, and they have had a much richer portrait of Victorian scientific culture against which to position the language of the novels. Indeed, recent work by historians of Victorian science has made it possible to see Dickens as quite fully within the world of Victorian science.

DICKENS AND SCIENCE

It was a remark by George Henry Lewes that set the tone for a century of criticism dismissing the notion of any meaningful relationship between Dickens and science. Writing not long after Dickens's death, Lewes described Dickens as 'completely outside' science and 'too unaffected a man to pretend to feel any interest' in it.[5] Lewes, however, was not a fully objective observer on this topic. He had challenged the scientific validity of Krook's spontaneous combustion in *Bleak House*, and he was of course the life companion of George Eliot, one of the period's most scientifically astute novelists. Moreover, his comment has generally been taken out of context. It was not offered as a sweeping assessment of Dickens and science, but rather as part of a portrait of Dickens's intellectual interests in the late 1830s. While Lewes presumably did not see a radical change in Dickens in that regard over the next three decades, the exchange between them over spontaneous combustion alone would have at least qualified Lewes's earlier impression.

Lewes, too, it must be said, did not see Dickens as hostile to science. Yet that was a frequent line of critical discourse on Dickens and science. Eliot biographer Gordon Haight, writing on the spontaneous combustion controversy between Dickens and Lewes, declared Dickens 'indifferent or hostile to the scientific developments of his age'.[6] The case for hostility has generally rested on the sharp satire of utilitarian education in *Hard Times* and the gentler lampoon, in both *The Pickwick Papers* and 'The Mudfog Papers', of scientific societies (particularly the newly formed British Association for the Advancement of Science (BAAS)). The satire of *Hard Times*, however, was much less about science per se than the inhumanity of bureaucratic systems developed and imposed by utilitarian social thought and laissez-faire political economy, with their disregard for feeling and the imagination. As the government officer tells the Coketown schoolchildren:

---

[4] Fielding, 'Dickens and Science?', 200.
[5] George Henry Lewes, 'Dickens in Relation to Criticism', *Fortnightly Review* 17 (1872): 141–54, 152.
[6] Gordon S. Haight, 'Dickens and Lewes on Spontaneous Combustion', *Nineteenth-Century Fiction* 10, 1 (1955): 53–63, 63.

'You are to be in all things regulated and governed,' said the gentleman, 'by fact. We hope to have, before long, a board of fact, composed of commissioners of fact, who will force the people to be a people of fact, and of nothing but fact. You must discard the word Fancy altogether. You have nothing to do with it. You are not to have, in any object of use or ornament, what would be a contradiction in fact. You don't walk upon flowers in fact; you cannot be allowed to walk upon flowers in carpets.'[7]

This is the message that follows the humiliation of Sissy Jupe, who wants representations of flowers on her carpets and who cannot provide the desired definition of a horse ('Quadruped. Graminivorous. Forty teeth') so at odds with her own extensive experience of them (*HT* I:2, 9).

Both the opening chapter of *Pickwick* (April 1836) and 'The Mudfog Papers', which appeared in *Bentley's Miscellany* in October 1837 and September 1838, brilliantly parody the annual meetings of the BAAS and the journalistic accounts of them.[8] As Michael Zerbe has argued, Dickens's satire is in the vein of Swift's lampoon of the Royal Society in *Gulliver's Travels*, highlighting the over-enthusiasm, self-importance, obliviousness to reality, and propensity for proving the obvious of these modern men of science.[9] The title of Samuel Pickwick's paper, 'Speculations on the Source of the Hampstead Ponds, with Some Observations on the Theory of Tittlebats',[10] captures this well, the joke compounded by the fact that the Hampstead Ponds were man-made and thus their source no mystery, and 'tittlebat' was baby-talk for the stickleback, a common British freshwater fish. Both Zerbe and Jay Clayton see genuine concern on Dickens's part with the increasing institutionalization and specialization of science and most of all its potential to become, as Zerbe puts it, 'unmoored' from 'general, public knowledge', but the satire is nonetheless gentle and affectionate.[11] Clayton shrewdly ties Dickens's fascination with the BAAS's peripatetic annual meetings to their staged, very public character, complete with excursions to local sites of scientific interest and elaborate social events—precisely the sort of entertainment that Dickens found irresistibly attractive, both personally and professionally.[12]

---

[7] Charles Dickens, *Hard Times*, ed. Fred Kaplan, Norton Critical Edition, 4th edn (New York: W. W. Norton, 2017), I:2, 11–12. Subsequent references are inserted parenthetically in the text by *HT* Book:chapter, page.

[8] [Charles Dickens,] 'Full Report of the First Meeting of the Mudfog Association for the Advancement of Everything' and 'Full Report of the Second Meeting of the Mudfog Association for the Advancement of Everything', in *The Dent Uniform Edition of Dickens' Journalism*, ed. Michael Slater and John Drew, 4 vols (London: J. M. Dent, Columbus: Ohio State University Press, 1993–2000), 1:513–30, 530–50. Subsequent citations are listed by Dent volume: 'Title', page.

[9] Michael J. Zerbe, 'Satire of Science in Charles Dickens's *Mudfog Papers*: The Institutionalization of Science and the Importance of Rhetoric in Scientific Literacy', *Configurations* 24 (2016): 197–227.

[10] Charles Dickens, *The Pickwick Papers*, ed. James Kinsley (Oxford: Clarendon Press, 1986), 1, 1.

[11] Zerbe, 'Satire of Science', 206; Jay Clayton, *Charles Dickens in Cyberspace: The Afterlife of the Nineteenth Century in Postmodern Culture* (Oxford: Oxford University Press, 2003), 96–7.

[12] Clayton, *Charles Dickens in Cyberspace*, 98–101.

Despite the fact that critics no longer need to defend Dickens from charges of indifference or hostility to science, making that case, and trying to provide an overarching characterization of Dickens's view of science, remains common for those writing about Dickens and science. It was true of Jude Nixon's 2005 thorough and judicious essay on Dickens and science and of Ben Winyard and Holly Furneaux's introduction to a journal issue on *Dickens and Science* in 2010.[13] While that impulse is understandable, it now seems unnecessary. Dickens was not George Eliot when it came to science. But he took an unquestioned interest in science, to some extent in its own right but mainly in terms of its relevance for the public affairs and social questions with which Lewes saw the young Dickens so keenly engaged. Dickens's view of science was neither monolithic nor unchanging, but rather responsive to particular aspects of science, particular men of science, and particular scientific theories. He was drawn to science that stirred the imagination and critical of science that devalued it. His mind was open to new and often unsettling theories and discoveries, but wary of what might justify or increase human suffering. Perhaps most assertively, though, we can say that Dickens, through his editorship of *Household Words* and *All the Year Round*, played a significant role in the popularization of science and the world of popular science. Articles on scientific topics appeared frequently in their pages, and the surveys of both Nancy Metz and Elaine Ostry argue that science and especially individual scientists were generally presented favourably, and in some cases heroically, even though anxieties and criticisms were also expressed.[14] Few of these scientific articles were written by Dickens himself, but the active control he exercised over both publications as editor and 'conductor' justifies the assumption of some degree of familiarity with every article. Care has to be exercised—the perspectives of Dickens's contributors obviously cannot be assumed to be identical with those of Dickens himself—but the periodicals emphatically refute notions of Dickensian lack of interest in science.

DICKENS AND ASTRONOMY

Dickens's engagement with astronomical science generally appears not in the form of observational astronomy, but in relation to theories about the formation and the future of the solar system via the nebular hypothesis and the laws of thermodynamics. According to the former, our planetary system formed from a hot, rotating cloud of

---

[13] Jude V. Nixon, '"Lost in the Vast Worlds of Wonder": Dickens and Science', *Dickens Studies Annual* 35 (2005): 267–333; Ben Winyard and Holly Furneaux, 'Introduction: Dickens, Science and the Victorian Literary Imagination', *19: Interdisciplinary Studies in the Long Nineteenth Century* 10 (2010). doi: 10.16995/ntn.572.

[14] Nancy A. Metz, 'Science in *Household Worlds*: "The Poetic . . . Passed into our Common Life"', *Victorian Periodicals Newsletter* 11 (1978): 121–33; Elaine Ostry, '"Social Wonders": Fancy, Science, and Technology in Dickens's Periodicals', *Victorian Periodicals Review* 34, 1 (2001): 54–78.

nebulous matter that, as it contracted and cooled, spun off material that in turn cooled and condensed to form the planets. In Britain, the nebular hypothesis was regarded with suspicion and concern by the gentlemanly scientific elites, who tended to see it in the same terms as Lamarckian evolutionary theory, as part of the embrace of radical, progressive change that had ushered in the French Revolution.[15] Dickens would have encountered the nebular hypothesis in several of the works of astronomy he owned and in *Vestiges of the Natural History of Creation*. By combining the nebular hypothesis with Lamarckian transmutation, *Vestiges* offered a compelling and comprehensive evolutionary narrative not only of life on earth, but of the universe as a whole. It quickly became a scientific, literary, and cultural sensation, on a par with Dickens's own wildly popular early novels, creating the template for what James Secord has called the 'evolutionary epic'.[16] Dickens was clearly familiar and sympathetic with *Vestiges*: in his favourable review of Robert Hunt's *The Poetry of Science* (1848), he credited *Vestiges* with making a book like Hunt's possible. *Vestiges* had 'created a reading public' that was 'not exclusively scientific or philosophical', and had 'awaken[ed] an interest and a spirit of inquiry in many minds'.[17] Hunt has shown, Dickens wrote, 'that, instead of binding us ... in stern utilitarian chains', science 'offers to our contemplation something better and more beautiful, ... more elevating to the soul, nobler and more stimulating to the soaring fancy'.[18] Dickens also noted with disappointment Hunt's veiled but critical allusions to *Vestiges*, so his own favourable reference to 'that remarkable and well-abused book' suggested a considerable degree of acceptance of *Vestiges*.[19]

No extended critical effort has been undertaken, however, to assess the relevance for Dickens's fiction of his apparent support for *Vestiges*. Lawrence Frank has suggested that the anonymous, third-person narration in *Bleak House* depicts a universe like that described in *Vestiges*, but otherwise even writers on Dickens and Darwin have not really considered how Dickens's sympathy for the more radical evolutionary vision of *Vestiges* might manifest itself in the novels from the mid-1840s on, including his own portrait of radicalism and the French Revolution in *A Tale of Two Cities*.[20]

---

[15] Adrian Desmond, *The Politics of Evolution: Morphology, Medicine, and Reform in Radical London* (Chicago: University of Chicago Press, 1989); Simon Schaffer, 'The Nebular Hypothesis and the Science of Progress', in James R. Moore (ed.), *History, Humanity and Evolution: Essays for John C. Greene* (Cambridge: Cambridge University Press, 1989), 131–64.

[16] James A. Secord, *Victorian Sensation: The Extraordinary Publication, Reception, and Secret Authorship of Vestiges of the Natural History of Creation* (Chicago: University of Chicago Press, 2000), 461.

[17] Dent 2: 'Review: *The Poetry of Science*', 129–34, 131. See also K. J. Fielding and Shu-Fang Lai, 'Dickens, Science, and *The Poetry of Science*', *Dickensian* 93, 1 (1997): 5–10 and Adelene Buckland, '"The Poetry of Science": Charles Dickens, Geology, and Visual and Material Culture in Victorian London', *Victorian Literature and Culture* 35, 2 (2007): 679–94.

[18] Dent 2: 'Review: *The Poetry of Science*', 131.

[19] Ibid.

[20] Lawrence Frank, *Victorian Detective Fiction and the Nature of Evidence: The Scientific Investigations of Poe, Dickens, and Doyle* (Houndmills: Palgrave Macmillan, 2003), 71–98.

The laws of thermodynamics developed on a different path, emerging from efforts to understand and improve engines. The first law, generally referred to in Dickens's day as the 'conservation of force' but known today as 'the conservation of energy', affirms that energy can be converted from one form into another but can be neither created nor destroyed. The second law, however, states that in a closed system any transformation of energy will result in less energy being available for useful work. This reflected the practical reality that no engine is perfectly efficient—some of the energy put into the engine is lost through friction, for example. Total energy is conserved, but some of that energy dissipates (to use a term common to the period) as heat. Applied at the largest scale, the second law implied that the universe would at some point run down, its temperature become uniform and thus its heat incapable of being transformed further into work. The sun's energy, it was similarly realized, was also finite, and thus the death of the sun, as the ultimate source of earthly energy, would leave our planet cold, dark, and dead. Britain's coal supply, which had seemed to place a divine imprimatur on its empire and industrial might, suddenly seemed to be limited, and its profligate or inefficient use became a cause of national concern. Later formulations of the second law associated this dissipation of energy with a concept called entropy, a measure of the system's randomness or disorder, but neither the term 'entropy' nor this way of conceptualizing the second law had become popular in Britain by the time of Dickens's death. The language of conservation and dissipation, of waste and work, and of their practical and, indeed, physical manifestations in both national and everyday life—most vividly, perhaps, in the smoke that poured from factories and urban chimneys—was already commonplace by the early 1850s, and only grew more so over the ensuing two decades as physicists like John Tyndall and William Thomson (the future Lord Kelvin) aggressively popularized them.

The discourse—scientific and popular—of the laws of thermodynamics in the 1850s and 1860s was inextricably tied to industrial capitalism and political economy, and was implicitly religious and explicitly moral. The early British thermodynamicists, as Allen MacDuffie has shown, tended to present as inevitable and 'natural' the very problems that widespread energy consumption was bringing about.[21] If the first law seemed to celebrate transformation and a universe of cyclical processes, the second law reinstated time's arrow, and in a way consistent with Christian eschatology and an end of times, whether that end came with an apocalyptic bang or a whimper. And the language of thermodynamics appropriated words whose common meanings were already weighted with human agency and moral judgement: waste, dissipation, work, efficiency, force, energy. Thermodynamic discourse could add scientific authority to these meanings or (just as easily) obfuscate them.

Probably the first piece of modern scholarship to examine Dickens in relation to science was Ann Wilkinson's 1967 essay on *Bleak House*, which took up precisely this matrix of thermodynamic and moral concerns. The meaning of the novel, Wilkinson

---

[21] Allen MacDuffie, *Victorian Literature, Energy, and the Ecological Imagination* (Cambridge: Cambridge University Press, 2014), 14.

argued, 'resides in the disposition of energies into the productive order—work—or into entropy—chaos'.[22] Setting the example for almost every future study of Dickens and science, Wilkinson mined *Household Words* for evidence of the scientific ideas to which Dickens was exposed. Wilkinson was on especially safe ground in relying on two articles based on Michael Faraday's 1848 Christmas lectures for children, 'The Chemical History of a Candle', for Dickens borrowed Faraday's lecture notes and had a contributor work them up.[23] The first article explained what happens in combustion; the second treated human respiration as an analogous process. Although written from a chemical perspective, these articles, along with others in the early 1850s, reflect interest in the same physical processes that appeared in thermodynamic texts and in *Bleak House*. Curiously, despite the evidence she cites of Dickens's awareness of this nascent thermodynamic discourse, Wilkinson falls back on the notion that Dickens in *Bleak House* 'intuitively apprehended' the laws of thermodynamics.[24]

The next substantive analysis of Dickens and thermodynamics came from George Levine in *Darwin and the Novelists* (1988), in a chapter on *Little Dorrit*. Like Wilkinson with *Bleak House*, Levine argues that *Little Dorrit* 'impl[ies] a world coherent with that asserted by thermodynamics', but that thermodynamics is merely 'an appropriate metaphor' for discussing the novel.[25] The world of *Little Dorrit*, even more than that of *Bleak House*, is a second-law world, full of disorder and decay. The novel 'thematizes failure of energy': if in *Bleak House* individuals like Esther Summerson are able to create order through good work, *Little Dorrit* offers scant sense—the engineer Daniel Doyce being a rare but still only partial counter-example—that humans can bring order and meaning to a decaying and inhospitable natural world.[26] Levine sees a conflict between the thermodynamic vision of decline in the novel and the progressive vision of Darwinism, but he argues that Dickens's willingness to follow these secular visions despite a clear urge to provide a sense of providential design is ultimately more significant.

My own work on thermodynamics in *Our Mutual Friend* took advantage of that novel's later publication date to make the case that there can be no doubt of Dickens's familiarity with thermodynamic concepts.[27] By the early 1860s thermodynamics was being widely popularized, and those popularizations were serving as the basis of many

---

[22] Ann Y. Wilkinson, '*Bleak House*: From Faraday to Judgment Day', *ELH* 34, 2 (1967): 225–47, 247.
[23] [Percival Leigh,] 'The Chemistry of a Candle', *Household Words*, 3 August 1850, 1:439–44 and 'The Laboratory in the Chest', *Household Words*, 7 September 1850, 1:565–9, *Dickens Journals Online* <http://www.djo.org.uk>.
[24] Wilkinson, '*Bleak House*: From Faraday to Judgment Day', 247.
[25] Levine, *Darwin and the Novelists*, 156.
[26] Levine, *Darwin and the Novelists*, 156. Doyce was based on Dickens's friend the mathematician and inventor Charles Babbage; for the underexplored relationship between Babbage and Dickens's fiction, see Jessica Kuskey, 'Math and the Mechanical Mind: Babbage, Charles Dickens, and Mental Labor in *Little Dorrit*', *Dickens Studies Annual* 45 (2014): 247–74, and John M. Picker, *Victorian Soundscapes* (Oxford: Oxford University Press, 2003), 15–40.
[27] Jonathan Smith, 'Heat and Modern Thought: The Forces of Nature in *Our Mutual Friend*', *Victorian Literature and Culture* 23 (1995): 37–69. See also Nancy Aycock Metz, 'The Artistic Reclamation of Waste in *Our Mutual Friend*', *Nineteenth-Century Fiction* 34, 1 (1979): 59–72.

articles in *All the Year Round*. At least nine articles devoted wholly or partly to thermodynamic issues appeared during *Our Mutual Friend*'s serial run or within a year of its commencement, including two based on John Tyndall's *Heat Considered as a Mode of Motion* (1863). '"[I]diots talk ... of Energy"', complains the decidedly unenergetic Eugene Wrayburn in *Our Mutual Friend*'s opening number, setting the tone for a great deal of talk about energy in the novel.[28] Precisely in the middle of the novel, a descriptive passage echoes the famous opening paragraphs of *Bleak House*, with London dark and smoky, choking on soot, the sun 'show[ing] as if it had gone out, and were collapsing flat and cold' (*OMF* III:1, 420). Dickens's thermodynamic vision here is more self-aware than in *Little Dorrit* or even *Bleak House*. While as in those earlier novels Dickens portrays a dark, second-law world of dissipation, decay, and disorder, *Our Mutual Friend*'s optimistic, first-law elements of conservation, transformation, and organization are maintained only with a novelistic sleight of hand. The ruse that brings about much of what's happy in the novel's ending—Mr Boffin's feigned miserliness—is withheld from readers as well as from other characters, only to be justified, by Dickens and his characters, as pious and necessary. That we live in a second-law world, the novel seems to suggest, should condone neither nihilism nor self-interest; we are obliged to work well, to use energy efficiently, as if this were a first-law world.

Two more recent and ambitious literary studies of Victorian energy physics should definitively put to rest any lingering concerns about the validity of treating Dickens's novels of the 1850s and 1860s in relation to thermodynamics. Barri Gold's *ThermoPoetics* has chapters on *Bleak House* and *A Tale of Two Cities*, while Allen MacDuffie's *Victorian Literature, Energy, and the Ecological Imagination* offers chapters on *Bleak House* and *Our Mutual Friend*.[29] Both are able to draw on the rich cultural portrait of Victorian energy physics painted by historians of science over the last generation.[30] This historical work both makes clear just how pervasive and important the discussions of thermodynamics-related issues were in Victorian culture, and it provides the context for appreciating the significance of the articles on these issues in Dickens's periodicals. As MacDuffie pithily puts it, 'Dickens had plenty of access to the kind of discourses that formed the conceptual armature of the thermodynamic research project.'[31]

Gold's analysis of *Bleak House* ultimately reinforces the arguments of Wilkinson and Levine about the novel's differentiation of useful and wasteful workers and the ability of individuals to bring order and improvement to smaller systems, but she also offers new

---

[28] Charles Dickens, *Our Mutual Friend*, ed. Michael Cotsell, Oxford World's Classics (Oxford: Oxford University Press, 1989), I:3, 20. Subsequent references are inserted parenthetically in the text by *OMF* Book:chapter, page.

[29] Barri J. Gold, *ThermoPoetics: Energy in Victorian Literature and Science* (Cambridge, MA: MIT Press, 2010); MacDuffie, *Victorian Literature*.

[30] In particular, Crosbie Smith, *The Science of Energy: A Cultural History of Energy Physics in Victorian Britain* (Chicago: University of Chicago Press, 1998); M. Norton Wise and Crosbie Smith, *Energy and Empire: A Biographical Study of Lord Kelvin* (Cambridge: Cambridge University Press, 1989); Iwan Rhys Morus, *When Physics Became King* (Chicago: University of Chicago Press, 2005).

[31] MacDuffie, *Victorian Literature*, 91.

insights, as in her discussion of characters who operate as 'heat sinks', sucking energy from others.[32] She is also the first critic to examine thermodynamic concepts in *A Tale of Two Cities*—a surprising move given that novel's historical setting—and finds as in *Bleak House* 'a qualified thermodynamic optimism' in that '[s]mall systems, at least, may resist the larger entropic trends, restoring personal energies and securing domestic order'.[33]

MacDuffie stresses the importance to developing thermodynamic discourse in the 1850s and 1860s of the city and the sun. It was the former, London especially, that made resource depletion and pollution visible, creating concerns about the sustainability of a coal-dependent industrial and economic system. Concern over the death of the sun, he contends, was less about cosmic angst than about coal supplies and, more generally, a society that was consuming energy at a rapidly expanding rate. Similarly, early thermodynamic writers tended to obscure the dark implications of the second law or hold out hope that new energy sources would be found, the sun's energy replenished by some newly discovered mechanism. Literary writers like Dickens, MacDuffie argues, were often more willing to confront the unsustainability of the Victorian energy economy, although the authors of these 'alternative thermodynamic narratives' were unable to embrace fully the implications of their critiques.[34] With *Bleak House*, MacDuffie demonstrates that the novel connects its depiction of a world running out of energy to its critique of the economic system, and that this is signalled in the famous opening paragraph, with its reference not only to the death of the sun but to the accumulation of mud 'at compound interest'.[35] Dickens, however, 'backs away from the more radical vision of widespread waste … by corralling energy as a moral signifier, rather than a limited natural resource'.[36] The moral distinctions seen by other critics in the characters' use of energy MacDuffie sees as comparable to the early thermodynamicists' obfuscations of the costs of energy depletion. In the case of *Our Mutual Friend*, MacDuffie reads the novel as a conflict between the differing views of waste offered by sanitary reformers and thermodynamics. Sanitary reformers regarded waste and pollution as solvable problems requiring adjustment to systems that recycled and reused spent materials. The second law, however, exposed this as a fantasy, particularly given the sheer scale of waste being generated in London and other Victorian cities. MacDuffie sees *Our Mutual Friend* as willing to question the sanitarians' fantasy, despite Dickens's sympathy with their cause, but like *Bleak House* beating a retreat into regarding energy as a personal quality rather than a physical commodity.

Bleak House, Little Dorrit, and *Our Mutual Friend* have thus drawn extended attention in relation to the laws of thermodynamics developed and extensively popularized in the same decades. Whereas Wilkinson and even Levine had to rely on loose formulations

---

[32] Gold, *ThermoPoetics*, 194–8.
[33] Gold, *ThermoPoetics*, 183.
[34] MacDuffie, *Victorian Literature*, 15.
[35] Charles Dickens, *Bleak House*, ed. George Ford and Sylvère Monod, Norton Critical Edition (New York: W. W. Norton, 1977), 1, 5.
[36] MacDuffie, *Victorian Literature*, 113.

of Dickensian intuition of thermodynamic concepts or a vague sense of their being 'in the air', more recent critics have been able to draw on the specific and extensive ways in which that was so, ways that obviate the need to appeal to Dickens's artistic intuition. Indeed, we can now see that Dickens helped shape that cultural discourse, both through the novels and through the many articles on thermodynamic topics that appeared in *Household Words* and *All the Year Round*. The language and imagery of dying suns and industrial detritus, of exhaustion and chaos, soot and smoke, of order and disorder, work and waste, which so permeates the novels of these decades, is part of what Dickens saw all around him, and of what he saw and heard and read about almost anywhere he turned.

DICKENS AND BIOLOGY

More than any other science, what we call (but that the Victorians were only just starting to call) biology has drawn attention from Dickens scholars. Much of that, and certainly the most important of that, has involved Darwin. The case for Dickens's familiarity with Darwin's *Origin of Species* is fairly strong: he owned a copy of the second (1860) edition, and *All the Year Round* included three anonymous articles in 1860–1 that extensively explained and commented on Darwin's work.[37] George Levine is surely right that what matters most about these articles is how respectfully, fairly, and fully they presented Darwin's theory, even if they did not explicitly endorse it.[38] And a direct and unambiguous reference to *The Origin of Species* appeared in Dickens's fiction at the first opportunity. The last instalment of *A Tale of Two Cities* appeared in the same month Darwin's book was published, but just over a year later, in the second paragraph of the opening chapter of Dickens's next novel, *Great Expectations*, Pip says his five deceased little brothers 'gave up trying to get a living, exceedingly early in that universal struggle'.[39] The 'universal struggle for life' was a Darwinian phrase, found in the Malthusian chapter on 'Struggle for Existence' in *The Origin of Species*, 'struggle for existence' being a term Darwin said he used in 'a large and metaphorical sense', the economic and metaphorical senses being equally present with the scientific in Dickens's passage as well.[40] Apart from Goldie Morgentaler's, however, no major Darwinian reading of *Great Expectations* has appeared, although many critics have analysed *Our Mutual Friend*, another post-*Origin*

---

[37] J. H. Stonehouse (ed.), *Catalogue of the Library of Charles Dickens* (London: Piccadilly Fountain Press, 1935), 26. 'Species', *All the Year Round*, 2 June 1860, 3:174–8; 'Natural Selection', *All the Year Round*, 7 July 1860, 3:293–9; and 'Transmutation of Species', *All the Year Round*, 9 March 1861, 4:519–21. *Dickens Journals Online* <http://www.djo.org.uk>.

[38] Levine, *Darwin and the Novelists*, 129.

[39] Charles Dickens, *Great Expectations*, ed. Margaret Cardwell (Oxford: Clarendon Press, 1993), 1, 3.

[40] Charles Darwin, *On the Origin of Species by means of Natural Selection*, 2nd edn (London: John Murray, 1860), 62. This is the edition Dickens owned.

novel, in relation to Darwinism.[41] Morgentaler sees *Great Expectations* as significant in Darwinian terms for the way Dickens abandons his usual emphasis on heredity as the determining factor in individual identity, instead examining the role of the individual's ability to adapt to changing circumstance and conditions. Most analyses of *Our Mutual Friend*, on the other hand, have presented that novel as offering a bleak portrait of a Malthusian world now buttressed by Darwin's evolutionary gloss.

In an essay on Darwin and *Little Dorrit*, I have tried to connect Dickens not with the Darwin of *The Origin of Species* but with perhaps the most unlikely Darwinian text of all, his two-volume *Monograph* (1851, 1854) on barnacles.[42] A specialized taxonomic study totalling over 1,000 pages, Darwin's *Monograph* nonetheless had a surprising cultural life in the 1850s, its results popularized in many of the books and articles that fuelled the craze for seaside natural history during that decade. Darwin's elucidation of the barnacle's unusual life cycle and his discovery of the often-bizarre sexual arrangements of some barnacle species made this familiar if mysterious creature a source of entertainment and fascination. As such, barnacles became part of the cultural issues with which such popular seaside writings invariably engaged: idleness and self-improvement, religion and the study of nature, sexuality and sexual display, and the mixing of social classes. Drawing on the discussions and popularizations of Darwin's barnacle work, including an article in *Household Words* itself, I argue that Dickens's depiction of the notorious Barnacle family in *Little Dorrit* suggests familiarity with the results of Darwin's *Monograph*, and engages with many of the same cultural issues addressed in works of seaside natural history.

The most influential discussion of Dickens and Darwin, however, is George Levine's chapter by that title in *Darwin and the Novelists*. Levine sidesteps the limitation of the *Origin*'s late appearance in Dickens's career by talking about general characteristics of Dickens's fictions rather than specific novels, though he draws examples from many of the novels, including ones that pre-date *The Origin of Species*. His opening sentence sets the tone: 'Dickens is the great novelist of entanglement, finding in the mysteries of the urban landscape those very connections of interdependence and genealogy that characterize Darwin's entangled bank.'[43] The worlds of Dickens and Darwin are profuse, complicated, interconnected places, full of diverse and quirky creatures, where

---

[41] Goldie Morgentaler, *Dickens and Heredity: When Like Begets Like* (Houndmills: Palgrave Macmillan, 2000), 163–74. Morgentaler also discusses *Our Mutual Friend* and *The Mystery of Edwin Drood*. See also Howard W. Fulweiler, '"A Dismal Swamp": Darwin, Design, and Evolution in *Our Mutual Friend*', *Nineteenth-Century Literature* 49, 1 (1994): 50–74; Ernest Fontana, 'Darwinian Sexual Selection and Dickens's *Our Mutual Friend*', *Dickens Quarterly* 22, 1 (2005): 36–42; Sally Ledger, 'Dickens, Natural History, and *Our Mutual Friend*', *Partial Answers* 9, 2 (2011): 363–78; Nicola Bown, 'What the Alligator Didn't Know: Natural Selection and Love in *Our Mutual Friend*', *19: Interdisciplinary Studies in the Long Nineteenth Century* 10 (2010) <http://doi.org/10.16995/ntn.567>; Buckland, '"The Poetry of Science"'.

[42] Jonathan Smith, 'Darwin's Barnacles, Dickens's *Little Dorrit*, and the Social Uses of Victorian Seaside Studies', *LIT: Literature, Interpretation, Theory* 10 (2000): 327–47.

[43] Levine, *Darwin and the Novelists*, 119.

even the familiar points to mystery and strangeness. Levine also allows for differences—the essentialism of Dickens's characters is at odds with Darwinian flux and variability, and the sudden changes in Dickensian plots tend to support a much more teleological vision than Darwin's—but the weight of his argument is on how surprisingly similar the Dickensian and the Darwinian are. Levine's analysis elaborates and expands on some comments about Dickens by Gillian Beer in *Darwin's Plots*, a work otherwise focused on realists like George Eliot and Thomas Hardy. Beer, too, had commented on the fecundity and interconnectedness evidenced by both Dickens's novels and *The Origin of Species*, even suggesting that the organization of Darwin's book, 'with its apparently unruly superfluity of material gradually and retrospectively revealing itself as order, its superfecundity of instance serving an argument which can reveal itself only *through* instance and relations', owes much to Dickens's novels, which Darwin read avidly.[44]

This strategy of speaking of the structure and content of Dickens's novels in a general fashion when comparing Dickens's worlds to those of *The Origin of Species* is obviously open to the objection that Dickens's vision in novels like *Bleak House* and *Little Dorrit* could not have been shaped by a book not published until 1859. Fielding was right to note that if we're interested in Dickens and evolution, we ought to look closely at *Vestiges*. Embrace of an evolutionary vision also need not have entailed an embrace of the secular, as Levine has argued: while many orthodox commentators were horrified by what they saw as the heretical in *Vestiges*, their panic was driven by the many readers who clearly thrilled to its combination of progressive change and spiritual rhapsody. Even natural selection, as Bernard Lightman has demonstrated, was incorporated into the very sorts of natural theological frameworks that Darwin sought to overturn.[45] Another too-often-overlooked figure in this regard is Richard Owen. Owen was arguably Britain's leading man of science in the 1850s, famous for his ability to reconstruct extinct animals from fossil fragments. A friend of Dickens, he wrote several articles for *Household Words* and is referred to favourably in others. Mr Venus in *Our Mutual Friend*, the articulator of skeletons whose shop's contents hint at Owen's Hunterian Museum at the Royal College of Surgeons, is sometimes taken to be based on Owen.[46] Although he became a fierce opponent of Darwinism, Owen in the 1840s and 1850s was the chief British exponent of 'transcendental anatomy', the leading theory of the history of life prior to Darwin. In Owen's version, species did not evolve into other species but rather emerged over time as differing approximations of archetypal forms existing in the divine mind. Even those critics who have noted Owen's relationship with Dickens and the importance of transcendental anatomy, however, have not considered how Owen's view of species might connect either to *Our Mutual Friend* or to Dickens's fiction as a whole. More provocatively, Gowan Dawson has recently explored the relationship between the serial

---

[44] Gillian Beer, *Darwin's Plots: Evolutionary Narrative in Darwin, George Eliot, and Nineteenth-Century Fiction*, 3rd edn (Cambridge: Cambridge University Press, 2009), 6 (emphasis in original).
[45] Bernard Lightman, *Victorian Popularizers of Science: Designing Nature for New Audiences* (Chicago: University of Chicago Press, 2007), 7.
[46] Fulweiler, '"A Dismal Swamp"', 63.

publishing of fiction by Dickens and Thackeray in particular and the working methods and publication strategies of Owen and other palaeontologists, but his focus has been on how the serialization of popular fiction influenced and was appropriated by Owen and his peers.[47]

DICKENS AND GEOLOGY

In turning to geology we turn to the branch of science that was the early Victorian period's most popular, even for Londoners. Despite all the attention paid to Dickens and evolutionary biology, Buckland contends that, based on Dickens's review of *The Poetry of Science*, his 'ideal science' was geology.[48] Literary critics, Buckland has rightly complained, 'have not yet given enough emphasis to the scientific elements of the popular shows and entertainments Dickens attended and wrote about throughout his career'.[49] The work of a generation of historians of Victorian geology has shown that the geology of the period was only partly about textual disputes over rival theories of the earth or the accuracy of Mosaic cosmogony, the things on which much previous literary criticism has lingered. A far larger bulk of it involved the details of the stratigraphic column and hence of fieldwork and mapping; the personal relationships among geologists; and the spectacles of visual and material display so popular in London in particular, with competing panoramas vying to produce the most stirring representations of earthquakes and volcanic eruptions.[50] Pompeii, which Dickens of course visited in 1845 and discussed in *Pictures from Italy* (1846), and the work at Nineveh of Austen Henry Layard, the period's best-known archaeologist and a good friend of Dickens, were particularly important, and occupied a visual and material as well as textual presence in Britain. As the example of Vesuvius and Pompeii would suggest, the worlds of geology and archaeology, the latter of which was only just beginning to emerge as a separate discipline, overlapped in this period. The title of Charles Lyell's *Geological Evidences of the Antiquity of Man* (1863) captures this quite well; Dickens owned a copy, and an article summarizing its arguments appeared in *All the Year Round* shortly after the book's

---

[47] Gowan Dawson, '"By a Comparison of Incidents and Dialogue": Richard Owen, Comparative Anatomy and Victorian Serial Fiction', *19: Interdisciplinary Studies in the Long Nineteenth Century* 11 (2010). doi:10.16995/ntn.577; 'Literary Megatheriums and Loose Baggy Monsters: Paleontology and the Victorian Novel', *Victorian Studies* 53, 2 (2011): 203–30.

[48] Buckland, '"The Poetry of Science"', 681.

[49] Ibid., 680.

[50] See especially Ralph O'Connor, *The Earth on Show: Fossils and the Poetics of Popular Science, 1802–1856* (Chicago: University of Chicago Press, 2007) and Martin J. S. Rudwick, *Scenes from Deep Time: Early Pictorial Representations of the Prehistoric World* (Chicago: University of Chicago Press, 1992) and *Worlds Before Adam: The Reconstruction of Geohistory in the Age of Reform* (Chicago: University of Chicago Press, 2008).

publication.[51] In and around London itself, railway cuttings and the diggings for various public works projects like the Thames Embankment meanwhile exposed Britain's own geological and archaeological pasts.

Several critics have taken up this archaeological slant. Lawrence Frank has argued that while *The Mystery of Edwin Drood* is 'a Darwinian narrative', its evolutionary vision is 'modelled upon Lyell's enactment of the reconstruction of the human past as he helped to establish the discipline of prehistorical archaeology' in *Antiquity of Man*.[52] In his embrace of Lyell's approach, Dickens also rejects the older, antiquarian tradition represented by Thomas Wright, some of whose books Dickens also owned.[53] For Frank, *Drood* enacts the story that early archaeology was telling as it established its scientific authority against what it saw as the credulous, speculative, unsystematic work of antiquarians. Virginia Zimmerman also combines geology and archaeology in *Excavating Victorians* (2008), which features a chapter on Dickens that focuses on *Little Dorrit* and *Our Mutual Friend*. Zimmerman argues that the extensive geological and archaeological motifs in these novels serve as 'narrative tools' by which Dickens's characters create stories from recovered fragments of their pasts, the process of personal 'excavation' serving to 'assert the value of the individual in an indifferent world'.[54]

It is Adelene Buckland, however, who has made most extensive use of the historical work on the visual and material culture of Victorian geology. Both in her essay '"The Poetry of Science"' and in its expansion and recasting as a chapter in her book, *Novel Science* (2013), Buckland positions Dickens squarely amidst the world of popular geological display and visual spectacle. Examining *Dombey and Son*, *Bleak House*, and *Our Mutual Friend*, Buckland argues that Dickens's exposure to geologically themed popular entertainments like the panorama, diorama, and cyclorama shapes important elements of these novels, and also, more generally and provocatively, that Dickens's plots are structured spatially and pictorially as these geological displays were. Buckland connects Dickens's dioramic account of his visit to Pompeii and ascent of Vesuvius in *Pictures from Italy* to his depiction of Staggs's Gardens in *Dombey and Son*. The famous image of the Megalosaurus waddling up Holborn Hill in the opening paragraph of *Bleak House* is not an incongruous blast from the past but the sort of thing that Dickens and his readers encountered, textually and visually, in many different venues. *Our Mutual Friend*, appearing as the popularity of the panorama and its ilk waned, and in the aftermath of Darwin's *Origin of Species*, 'marks Dickens's disillusionment with his preferred science of geology' and hearkens back to a time 'when geology had a general appeal that made it accessible to a broad public, and symbolized his hope ... for science-as-entertainment'.[55]

---

[51] Stonehouse, *Catalogue*, 75. 'How Old Are We?', *All the Year Round*, 7 March 1863, 9: 32–7, *Dickens Journals Online* <http://www.djo.org.uk>.

[52] Frank, *Victorian Detective Fiction*, 101.

[53] Stonehouse, *Catalogue*, 120.

[54] Virginia Zimmerman, *Excavating Victorians* (Albany: State University of New York Press, 2008), 144.

[55] Buckland, '"The Poetry of Science"', 690, 692.

Future Directions

Buckland's work makes clear that Dickens, who once seemed 'outside' science, can now be positioned as well within it. What has changed, though, is not our sense of Dickens, but our sense of science. And that is largely the work of historians who have radically altered and broadened our picture of Victorian science. They have done so by focusing on the importance of popular science, of scientific publishing, and of personal friendships and professional networks, among other things. If we cease to think of science as constituted by commitments to large-scale theories promulgated in published form by elite professionals to an audience of fellow elites and the educated intellectuals like George Eliot able to understand and appreciate them, then Dickens, in fact, looks much more typical. Indeed, many of the things we have long known about Dickens that seemed to mark his concern for other things can now be seen as indicators of his engagement with science. In his immersion in popular culture and what Richard Altick called 'the shows of London', and in his proprietorship and editorship of two middle-class periodicals, Dickens was near the centre of popular Victorian science, and that popular science had a relationship with elite science that was multivalent, complex, and two-directional.[56] As Buckland shows, critics who familiarize themselves with this rich body of scholarship by historians of Victorian science can question old truths about Dickens and science and uncover new ones.

Despite the long-common mining of *Household Words* and *All the Year Round* for discussions of science, much work remains to be done, although attention could profitably shift from general surveys endeavouring to capture these periodicals'—and hence Dickens's—overarching view of science to the role of Dickens's periodicals in the popularization of science or of individual disciplines, theories, or scientists. Thermodynamics and Darwinian evolution hardly exhaust the possibilities relevant to the novels; chemistry, electricity, and the various branches of natural history all have a prominent presence in the periodicals. Attention to Darwin has far outstripped that to Owen, Faraday, Babbage, Lyell, Tyndall, Hermann von Helmholtz, Alexander von Humboldt, and Roderick Murchison, among others, yet these other figures appeared with comparable or even greater frequency in the periodicals' pages. Conversely, the burgeoning scholarly interest in the Victorian theatre and Dickens's enthusiastic participation in it offer the potential to open up an area of the scientific spectacle that has been little considered, namely, the various forms in which scientific lectures and displays constituted 'theatre'.

Despite this need for additional focused and detailed studies, it is worth noting that amidst all the books in the Dickens industry with titles like *Dickens and Crime*, *Dickens and Religion*, *Dickens and Women*, and *Dickens and the City*, one on *Dickens and Science*

---

[56] Richard D. Altick, *The Shows of London* (Cambridge, MA: Harvard University Press, 1978).

is conspicuously absent. Such a work is also—surprising as this would have once been to say—long overdue.

Further Reading

Gowan Dawson, *Show Me the Bone: Reconstructing Prehistoric Monsters in Nineteenth-Century Britain and America* (Chicago: University of Chicago Press, 2016)

Catherine Gallagher, *The Body Economic: Life, Death, and Sensation in Political Economy and the Victorian Novel* (Princeton: Princeton University Press, 2009)

Allen MacDuffie, 'Victorian Thermodynamics and the Novel: Problems and Prospects', *Literature Compass* 8, 4 (2011): 206–13

Goldie Morgentaler, 'Meditating on the Low: A Darwinian Reading of *Great Expectations*', *SEL: Studies in English Literature 1500–1900* 38 (1998): 707–21

John Parham, 'Dickens in the City: Science, Technology, Ecology in the Novels of Charles Dickens', *19: Interdisciplinary Studies in the Long Nineteenth Century* 10 (2010). doi: 10.16995/ntn.529

CHAPTER 29

SOCIAL REFORM

DAVID VINCENT

DICKENS learned to write by reporting the greatest constitutional crisis of the nineteenth century. As a young journalist for *The Mirror of Parliament* and *The True Sun* he had a ringside seat as the old order was forced by the threat of revolution to accept the reform of the franchise in 1832. His growing reputation as an accurate and lively recorder of the political process enabled him to move to the parliamentary reporting team at *The Morning Chronicle* where he witnessed the early legislative programme of the new Whig government.[1]

Throughout his ensuing career as a novelist, Dickens was engaged with the fractures and failings of the post Reform Act society. His concerns have generated a contrasting response from critics. Careful empirical studies epitomized by Philip Collins's monographs on education and crime in the early 1960s sought to place the fiction in its social and economic context. Historians were shown how much they could learn from Dickens's dramatization of the misfortunes of the voiceless poor. The subsequent theoretical turn in works such as Catherine Gallagher's *The Industrial Reformation of English Fiction* reversed the preoccupation, focusing on how the engagement with the Condition of England Question created developments and tensions in contemporary treatments of genre and representation.[2]

Amidst these debates, Dickens's social reform agenda remains a stubborn presence. Its sheer scale demands continuing attention from any scholar of early and mid-Victorian Britain. At the same time, historians have learned to pay attention to the narrative strategies that generate their evidence, particularly in the case of a writer whose treatment of specific issues embraced a range of literary forms, including not only the novels but private and public correspondence, recorded speeches, and prolific journalism. Above all, Dickens's fundamental claim that contemporary abuses are best understood and communicated by means of an intense imaginative engagement with

---

[1] Kathryn Chittick, *Dickens and the 1830s* (Cambridge: Cambridge University Press, 1990), 7–17.
[2] Catherine Gallagher, *The Industrial Reformation of English Fiction: Social Discourse and Narrative from 1832–1867* (Chicago: University of Chicago Press, 1985).

individual lives speaks to our own society as much as it did to his contemporaries. Ken Loach's Cannes prize-winner *I Daniel Blake*, for instance, premiered in 2016, is an urgent work of art that sits squarely within Dickens's project.

The Reform Bill and its aftermath had three long-term effects on Dickens's engagement with social reform. In the first instance, his close encounter left him with a lifelong distaste for Parliament as an institution. Whilst he welcomed the defeat of the Tories, he had little respect for the personnel or practices of the Palace of Westminster, before or after the epochal events of 1832. His subsequent national fame gave him opportunity to mix with the ruling elite, but although he formed occasional friendships, most notably with the Whig politician Lord John Russell, and engaged with specific pieces of legislation, he showed no desire to identify with any party. At the centre of his difficulty was a perceived disjunction between the rhetoric and reality of change. The Reform Bill did not sweep away old corruption but rather allowed it to form a new partnership with the rising middle class.

Dickens's alienation from the institution that had provided him with a living whilst he made his first uncertain forays into fiction reached a climax in the aftermath of the Crimean War. Following a highly critical parliamentary report into the management of the conflict, he joined a political organization for the first time, the newly-formed Administrative Reform Association.[3] At its third meeting he delivered a speech where for once he lost control of the hyperbole that generally characterized his public addresses and talked himself into a wholesale rejection of the contemporary democratic process: 'I have not the least hesitation in saying that I have the smallest amount of faith in the House of Commons at present existing [*hear, hear*].'[4] He cited Pepys complaining that nothing was done by Parliament in his time: 'Now, how comes it to pass that after two hundred years, and especially many years after a Reform Bill, the House of Commons is, in the gross, so little changed, I will not stop to inquire.'[5]

Two months later, Dickens began to translate his anger into fiction. In *Little Dorrit*, the exemplar of the new economic morality, the financier Merdle was welcomed with open arms by the established order: 'Admiralty said Mr. Merdle was a wonderful man. Treasury said he was a new power in the country, and would be able to buy up the whole House of Commons.'[6] The machinery of government was shown to be run in the interests of its members whose collective efforts were dedicated to opposing any change: 'Whatever was required to be done, the Circumlocution Office was beforehand with all the public departments in the art of perceiving—HOW NOT TO DO IT' (*LD* I:10, 100).

---

[3] Olive Anderson, 'The Administrative Reform Association, 1855–1857', in Patricia Hollis (ed.), *Pressure from Without in Early Victorian England* (London: Edward Arnold, 1974), 262–88, 265–9.

[4] 'Administrative Reform Association, 27 June 1855', in *The Speeches of Charles Dickens*, ed. K. J. Fielding (Oxford: Clarendon Press, 1960), 197–208, 201.

[5] Ibid., 202.

[6] Charles Dickens, *Little Dorrit*, ed. Harvey Peter Sucksmith (Oxford: Clarendon Press, 1979), I:21, 243. Subsequent references are inserted parenthetically in the text by *LD*, book:chapter, page.

The second conclusion Dickens drew from his parliamentary observations was more a matter of temperament than political analysis. He rapidly concluded that his cast of mind was unsuited to a life of committee rooms and House of Commons benches. As he told the Administrative Reform Association, 'my trade and calling is not politics'.[7] He turned down several invitations to run for Parliament, committing himself to do 'his public service through Literature'.[8] His nervous energy required the instant release of hard writing and fast walking. Preparing for *Little Dorrit*, he described himself 'walking about the country by day—prowling about into the strangest places in London by night—sitting down to do an immensity—getting up after doing nothing ... tearing my hair (which I can't afford to do)—and on the whole astonished at my own condition, though I am used to it'.[9] Pedestrian locomotion was, as we shall see, central to his entire enterprise in the field of social reform.

The third consequence of the Reform Act was the emergence of a new, socially engaged, audience for literature. An expanding reading public had been integral to the collapse of the old regime, and in the aftermath of 1832 it continued to grow.[10] It looked for entertainment, but it now had its own agenda of grievances for which it sought remedies. Most of the respectable working-class audience for Dickens and all of his female readers remained outside the franchise, but they shared a sense that with the defeat of Wellington the old order was now open to enquiry, debate, and change.[11] What Thomas Carlyle termed in 1839 'The Condition of England Question' reflected a broad sense that action had to be taken to counter the growing effects of urbanization and industrialization.

In terms of subject matter, Dickens was not an innovator in the field of social reform. The principal issues with which he was engaged over his writing lifetime—poor relief, education, penal policy, prostitution, public health, the civil service—were already in play. Each had their own trajectory reaching back in some cases to the previous century, and many have continued to be matters of debate and legislation to the present day. The framework of prison reform, for instance, had been established by John Howard more than half a century before Dickens became involved.[12] Public executions were ended in 1868 as a consequence of widespread concern about the threat of public disorder, a cause to which Dickens contributed, but he had initially campaigned for the abolition of the penalty altogether until he realized he had too little political support. The treatment of debtors, where Dickens had a persistent and personal interest, was a topic

---

[7] *Speeches*, 200.

[8] Ibid., 201.

[9] Charles Dickens, *The Letters of Charles Dickens*, ed. Madeline House, Graham Storey, et al., Pilgrim/British Academy Edition, 12 vols (Oxford: Clarendon Press, 1965–2002). 7:626–7, 626. Cited in Claire Tomalin, *Charles Dickens: A Life* (London: Viking, 2011), 257.

[10] David Vincent, 'Dickens's Reading Public', in John Bowen and Robert L. Patten (eds), *Palgrave Advances in Charles Dickens Studies* (London: Palgrave Macmillan, 2006), 177–9.

[11] Humphry House, *The Dickens World* (Oxford: Oxford University Press, 1941), 47.

[12] John Howard, *The State of the Prisons in England and Wales* (Warrington: William Eyres, 1777).

of eighteenth-century fiction, and was partially reformed by the Insolvent Debtors Act the year after he was born.[13]

The conventional historiography of nineteenth-century elementary education has the closest fit with Dickens's career. His very first attempt at fiction was made just after the initial government grant in 1833, and he died whilst Forster's Bill establishing a national system of funded schooling was proceeding through Parliament.[14] But he was responsible neither for identification of illiteracy as a matter of public concern, nor for the sequence of change which embraced an army of voluntary and professional critics and practitioners.

Dickens discovered no new grievances, and proposed few entirely novel solutions. Instead he talked to his audience about matters of shared, urgent, interest. In essence, his engagement with social reform was less a campaign than a dialogue. He enlarged the knowledge of his readers and increased their impatience with the absence of change. He flattered them with the assumption that they stood outside the cast of villains who filled his pages. The corrupt businessmen, brutal or incompetent teachers, self-interested lawyers, callous landlords, self-serving poor-law administrators, ineffective politicians, bigoted clerics, complacent aristocrats, committee-bound philanthropists, were common enemies of both the writer and his readers. Those who bought the monthly serials were at once comforted and infuriated by the vices Dickens exposed. He treated them as equal moral beings, lacking only the range of observation and vocabulary of outrage he brought to his depictions.

By the time of *Little Dorrit*, Dickens's growing fame and vocal criticism of the agents and agencies of the state were generating a reaction from political commentators. The writer and lawyer James Fitzjames Stephen (whose father, the former colonial under-secretary Sir James Stephen, may have been a model for Tite Barnacle of the Circumlocution Office[15]) published an attack in *The Edinburgh Review* of 1857 which focused on the role of a popular novelist engaging with social reform:

> Through novels young people are generally addressed for the first time as equals upon the most interesting affairs of life. There they see grown-up men and women described, and the occupations of mature life discussed, without any *arrière pensée* as to the moral effects which the discussion may have upon their own minds. To an inquisitive youth, novels are a series of lectures upon life, in which the professor addresses his pupils as his equals and as men of the world. There, for the first time, the springs of human actions are laid bare, and the laws of human society discussed in language intelligible and attractive to young imaginations and young hearts. Such teachers can never be otherwise than influential, but in the present day their

---

[13] Margot C. Finn, *The Character of Credit. Personal Debt in English Culture, 1740–1914* (Cambridge: Cambridge University Press, 2007), 25–63.

[14] The grant was agreed on 17 August 1833, and Dickens's first published fiction, 'A Dinner at Poplar Walk', appeared in the *Monthly Magazine* in December 1833; Forster's Bill went into the Committee Stage on 16 June 1870, just a week after Dickens's death.

[15] Michael Slater, *Charles Dickens* (New Haven: Yale University Press, 2009), 428.

influence is enormously increased by the facilities which cheap publication affords to them.[16]

This level of communication was a critical issue for the guardians of the expanding democracy. The process could only be managed if the new or potential electorate would listen with deference to their educated superiors. The threat posed by Dickens was not so much to specific grievances as to the entire mode of public conversation about reform. He gave not only a voice to the dispossessed but a status to the increasing numbers who read about their lives. The consequence was a wholesale breakdown of trust in authority:

> Men of the world may laugh at books which represent all who govern as fools, knaves, hypocrites, and dawdling tyrants. They know very well that such language is meant to be understood subject to modifications; but the poor and uneducated take such words in their natural and undiluted strength, and draw from them practical conclusions of corresponding importance; whilst the young and inexperienced are led to think far too meanly of the various careers which the organisation of society places before them.[17]

Stephen relegated Dickens to a lesser mode of discourse. Novelists, he argued, 'address themselves almost entirely to the imagination upon subjects which properly belong to the intellect'.[18] The claim that in his engagement with social reform Dickens was inferior to the systematic and cerebral critics of his era was and has remained a common response to his writings.[19] In 1858, the journalist Walter Bagehot made a further attempt to put Dickens in his place. He began by observing that 'there is no contemporary English writer, whose works are read so generally through the whole house, who can give pleasure to the servants as well as to the mistress, to the children as well as to the master',[20] and then expelled him from legitimate political enquiry altogether:

> He is often troubled with the idea that he must reflect, and his reflections are perhaps the worst reading in the world. There is a sentimental confusion about them; we never find the consecutive precision of mature theory, or the cold distinctness of clear thought. Vivid facts stand out in his imagination; and a fresh illustrative style brings them home to the imagination of his readers; but his continuous philosophy utterly fails in the attempt to harmonise them,—to educe a theory or elaborate a precept from them. Of his social thinking we shall have a few words to say in detail; his

---

[16] [James Fitzjames Stephen,] 'The License of Modern Novelists', *Edinburgh Review* 106 (1857): 124–56, 125.
[17] Ibid., 131.
[18] Ibid., 125.
[19] John Bowen, 'Dickens and the Force of Writing', in Bowen and Patten (eds), *Palgrave Advances in Charles Dickens Studies*, 255–72, 260.
[20] Walter Bagehot, 'Charles Dickens', in *Literary Studies*, 2 vols (London: Longmans, Green, 1879), 2:184–200, 185.

didactic humour is very unfortunate: no writer is less fitted for an excursion to the imperative mood.[21]

Deploying 'imagination' as a disqualification from polite debate about social reform at once recognized the danger and misread the function of Dickens's enterprise. The tension can be identified in an early excursion by Dickens into 'the imperative mode', his attack on solitary confinement in the account of his visit to America in 1842. Penal policy was an issue of vitriolic controversy. By the 1830s all sides agreed that there needed to be a wholesale reform embodied in large, new, prison buildings. This meant that any decision was both very expensive and largely irreversible—twentieth-century penal reform was severely constricted by the continuing need to house prisoners in Victorian cells. It proved impossible to reach a quiet consensus about the way forward.[22] As Dickens noted in a later article on prisons, '[t]here is a hot class of riders of hobby-horses in the field, in this century, who think they do nothing unless they make a steeple-chase of their object, throw a vast quantity of mud about, and spurn every sort of decent restraint and reasonable consideration under their horses' heels'.[23] Writing up his visit to the Eastern State Penitentiary in Philadelphia, Dickens joined in the chase with enthusiasm, offering not a critique but a wholesale condemnation of the new regime: 'The system here, is rigid, strict, and hopeless solitary confinement. I believe it, in its effects, to be cruel and wrong.'[24]

The publication of *American Notes* coincided with the opening of Pentonville, the first model prison in Britain based on a modified version of the Philadelphia system, and its proponents could not let Dickens's attack stand. The most vigorous rebuttal was made in a book by Joseph Adshead in 1845. In a chapter entitled 'The Fictions of Dickens Upon Solitary Confinement', he argued that the novelist had allowed his storytelling to infect his reportage.

> The flights of fancy may take what altitude they please in works of fiction; the imagination may range discursively in the regions of romance; but the public ought not to be deceived by misstatements in matters of vital importance to the well-being and regulation of society; however pleasing the style, or fascinating the language, if a narrative *which should have the impress of truth* be marked by a departure from it, much as genius may be admired, it must be [a] matter of regret that talent should thus defeat its more noble purpose.[25]

---

[21] Ibid., 2:192.

[22] Philip Collins, *Dickens and Crime*, 3rd edn (Basingstoke: Macmillan, 1994), chapter 3.

[23] [Charles Dickens,] 'Pet Prisoners', *Household Words*, 27 April 1850: 97–103. Subsequent references are inserted parenthetically in the text by *HW*, 'Title', and page.

[24] Charles Dickens, *American Notes*, ed. Patricia Ingham (London: Penguin, 2000), I:7, 111. Subsequent references are inserted parenthetically in the text by *AN* volume:chapter, page.

[25] Joseph Adshead, *Prisons and Prisoners* (London: Longman, Brown, Green, and Longman, 1845), 114.

But for Dickens it was his imagination which in the course of a relatively short visit had allowed him to see through the claims being made for the benefits of solitary confinement:

> I believe that very few men are capable of estimating the immense amount of torture and agony which this dreadful punishment, prolonged for years, inflicts upon the sufferers; and in guessing at it myself, and in reasoning from what I have seen written upon their faces, and what to my certain knowledge they feel within, I am only the more convinced that there is a depth of terrible endurance in it which none but the sufferers themselves can fathom, and which no man has a right to inflict upon his fellow creature. (*AN* I:7, 111)

What was 'written upon their faces' was worth far more than any volume of written reports. It was a matter of how the truth was seen and how it was valued. The empathy of one individual for another was the source of their humanity. The denial of his essential social being was the real measure of the harm that was caused to the prisoner by the system:

> He never hears of wife or children; home or friends; the life or death of any single creature. He sees the prison-officers, but with that exception he never looks upon a human countenance, or hears a human voice. He is a man buried alive; to be dug out in the slow round of years; and in the mean time dead to everything but torturing anxieties and horrible despair. (*AN* I:7, 113)

The argument about prisons, as with other categories of social reform, centred on the heuristic status of evidence. The case for innovation and the estimation of its consequences required the accumulation and appropriate interpretation of relevant information. Dickens's prolonged critique of the court system stemmed in part from the consequences of the 1836 Prisoners' Counsel Act which for the first time allowed the jury to be addressed by a barrister on behalf of a now silenced defendant.[26] Personal testimony was supplanted by actorly professionals with no investment in the truth or the nuances of human conduct. The year of 1836, when Dickens became an 'author' with the publication of *Sketches by Boz*, also saw the creation of the General Record Office (GRO) following the passage of the Registration and Marriage Acts.[27] The Reform Act had set off an 'avalanche of numbers' as statistical societies and government departments began counting the extent of social problems and measuring progress towards their solution.[28] The enterprise sought to combine scale with objectivity. The newly formed

---

[26] Jan-Melissa Schramm, 'The Law', in Sally Ledger and Holly Furneaux (eds), *Charles Dickens in Context* (Cambridge: Cambridge University Press, 2011), 310–17, 312–15; Jan-Melissa Schramm, 'Dickens and the Law', in David Paroissien (ed.), *A Companion to Charles Dickens* (Oxford: Blackwell, 2008), 277–93, 278.

[27] Edward Higgs, *Life, Death and Statistics* (Hatfield: Local Population Studies, 2004), 1–21.

[28] Ian Hacking, *The Taming of Chance* (Cambridge: Cambridge University Press, 1990), 2.

Statistical Society of London stated that 'the first and most essential rule of its conduct' was 'to exclude carefully all Opinions from its transactions and publications—to confine its attention rigorously to facts—and, as far as it may be found possible, to facts which can be stated numerically and arranged in tables'.[29] The staff of the GRO not only managed the decennial census, but also generated copious demographic data based on the improved system of recording. To its surprise, it discovered that the signatures and marks on marriage registers enabled it to construct a stable time series of what later became termed 'literacy'.[30]

In 1837 Dickens went to war with the entire enterprise, publishing a series of sketches in *Bentley's Magazine* purporting to be the reports of the 'Mudfog Association for the Advancement of Everything'. He mocked the reliance on paper-based enquiry. The fascination with counting for its own sake led, for instance, to the discovery that in Yorkshire, a deficiency in chair legs meant that 'ten thousand individuals (one-half of the whole population) were either destitute of any rest for their legs at all, or passed the whole of their leisure time in sitting upon boxes'.[31] Foreshadowing Bumble's calculations in *Oliver Twist* about the relative advantage of moving rather than burying paupers,[32] or Filer's disquisition in *The Chimes* about the excessive costs of boiling tripe,[33] he reported a member's proposal that 'it would be possible to administer—say, the twentieth part of a grain of bread and cheese to all grown-up paupers, and the fortieth part to children, with the same satisfying effect as their present allowance' (Dent 1: 'First Meeting', 526).

The one point of conflict in the proceedings involved Mr Slug, 'so celebrated for his statistical researches', who had been threatened by 'an elderly female, in a state of inebriety' as a consequence of his statistics on the 'the consumption of raw spirituous liquors' (Dent 1: 'First Meeting', 519). Such an encounter with an unruly individual was precisely what the statisticians sought to avoid. Their ambition was the delineation of Adolphe Quetelet's 'l'homme moyen', the average person constructed by summing behaviours and subject to standardized remedies.[34] For Dickens, by contrast, physical contact with individual circumstance was the key to the knowledge that would identify and communicate suffering and abuse. Given the proliferation of official reports after 1832 and the breadth of his journalism, he could not afford to ignore paper-based evidence when it suited his purpose. In a letter to the *Daily News* in 1846 on the evils

---

[29] Prospectus, cited in *Annals of the Royal Statistical Society 1834–1934* (London: Royal Statistical Society, 1934), 22.

[30] David Vincent, 'The Invention of Counting: The Statistical Measurement of Literacy in Nineteenth-Century England', *Comparative Education* 50, 3 (2014): 266–81.

[31] Charles Dickens, 'Full Report of the First Meeting of the Mudfog Association for the Advancement of Everything' [1837], in Michael Slater and John Drew (eds), *The Dent Uniform Edition of Dickens' Journalism*, 4 vols (London: J. M. Dent, Columbus: Ohio State University Press, 1993–2000), 529. Subsequent references are inserted parenthetically in the text by Dent volume: title, page.

[32] Charles Dickens, *Oliver Twist*, ed. Kathleen Tillotson (Oxford: Clarendon Press, 1966), 17, 108.

[33] Charles Dickens, *The Chimes* (London: Chapman and Hall, 1845), 32–7.

[34] Mary Poovey, 'Figures of Arithmetic, Figures of Speech: The Discourse of Statistics in the 1830s', *Critical Inquiry* 19, 2 (1993): 256–76, 268.

of Capital Punishment, for instance, he devoted several paragraphs to a House of Commons Return on 'commitments and executions for murder in England and Wales during the 30 years ending with December 1842'.[35] But he discovered most not by reading but by watching.

In the middle decades of the nineteenth century, the visit was a central device for connecting and learning. Middle-class wives translated their social agenda into a philanthropic endeavour, calling on the homes of the poor under the supervision of local charities, a practice mercilessly parodied in *Bleak House*, where Mrs Pardiggle invades an unwelcoming household of brick-makers.[36] Dickens's own enquiries were made possible by the openness of the developing institutions of relief, instruction, and punishment. It was possible, especially with the range of contacts the novelist possessed, to make repeated calls on workhouses, schools, and prisons and expect to be welcomed and shown round. His long-term friendships with the governors of Coldbath Fields and Tothill Fields prisons gave Dickens access at will.[37] Not until the Prisons Act of 1877 was an attempt made to keep visitors out as well as convicts in. Philip Collins calculated that Dickens knew at least 70 schools from the inside, most in and around London, but some as far away as Yorkshire where he conducted fieldwork for Dotheboys Hall.[38] Ruth Richardson has drawn attention to the first-hand knowledge that lay behind the construction of Oliver Twist's workhouse.[39] Whereas statistical enquiry was confined to professionals and well-educated amateurs, institutional visiting was essentially a democratic practice, as Dickens stressed in his influential account of the Field Lane School in the *Daily News*:

> Before I describe a visit of my own to a Ragged School, and urge the readers of this letter for God's sake to visit one themselves, and think of it (which is my main object), let me say, that I know the prisons of London well. That I have visited the largest of them, more times than I could count; and that the Children in them are enough to break the heart and hope of any man.[40]

Alongside such purposeful encounters, Dickens simply walked, most days and at length.[41] He turned the topography of London, with its abrupt transitions from wealth

---

[35] 'To the Editors of *The Daily News*', 13 March 1846, in *Selected Letters of Charles Dickens*, ed. David Paroissien (London: Macmillan, 1985), 233–5. On Dickens's use of official documents in his writing on education and crime, see Jenny Hartley, *Charles Dickens and the House of Fallen Women* (London: Methuen, 2009), 92.
[36] Charles Dickens, *Bleak House*, ed. George Ford and Sylvère Monod, Norton Critical Edition (New York: Norton, 1977), 8, 98–101. Subsequent references are inserted parenthetically in the text by *BH* chapter, page.
[37] Anne Schwan, 'Crime', in Ledger and Furneaux (eds), *Charles Dickens in Context*, 301–9, 303.
[38] Philip Collins, *Dickens and Education* (London: Macmillan, 1963), 3–4.
[39] Ruth Richardson, *Dickens and the Workhouse: Oliver Twist and the London Poor* (Oxford: Oxford University Press, 2012), 257.
[40] Paroissien, *Selected Letters of Charles Dickens*, 188.
[41] As stressed in Tomalin, *Charles Dickens: A Life*, 45, 309, 320, 375.

to poverty, into a complex text. His service to his readers was to broaden their more limited neighbourhood experience and invite them to consider the contrasts of situation and opportunity. As with his institutional visiting, it was a deceptively amateur activity. In accounts of his pedestrian habits, he celebrated their casual, unplanned nature:

> We have a most extraordinary partiality for lounging about the streets. Whenever we have an hour to spare, there is nothing that we enjoy more than a little amateur vagrancy—walking up one street and down another, and staring into shop windows, and gazing about us as if, instead of being on intimate terms with every shop and house in Holborn, the Strand, Fleet-street and Cheapside, the whole were an unknown region to our wondering mind.[42]

He set off without a map, and returned with an enriched moral cartography. By making the familiar strange he challenged the assumed boundaries of the capital's communities. He connected them by his rambles, and foregrounded the argument underpinning his engagement with social reform, the malign interconnections between the privileged and the dispossessed.

The task of rendering into print his visits, walks, and accompanying conversations raised several difficulties. Dickens could not in practice describe all that he had seen and heard in either the journalism or the novels. It was not just a matter of respecting the otherness of his subject matter. There was no acceptable means, for instance, of communicating the detail of the sexual abuse of women and children, about which Dickens certainly knew a good deal, from his early encounters on the London streets to his systematic interviews with the former prostitutes of Urania Cottage, the transitional refuge he ran with the aid of Angela Burdett-Coutts's money between 1847 and 1858.[43] For all the accusations that Dickens was breaching the walls of polite discourse, he had a clear sense that he was operating above the level of sensationalist fiction in terms of his content and his market. There were limits to what he felt able say to his family readership and to what it wanted to encounter in his pages.[44] The only solution was to adopt the technique familiar in stage melodramas of deploying conventional, abbreviated terminology, and leaving it to the audience to reconstruct the experience as best it could. Thus, for instance, Alice Marwood in *Dombey and Son* is given a dialogue which deprives her character of any sense of the particularity of her life history: 'Wretchedness and ruin came on me, I say. I was made a short-lived toy, and flung aside more cruelly and carelessly than even such things are.'[45]

A second difficulty was making the transition from the journalism, where the immediate findings of his researches were often reported, to the fiction which sought to

---

[42] 'The Prisoner's Van', *Bell's Life in London*, 29 November 1835, cited in Slater, *Charles Dickens*, 53.
[43] Hartley, *Dickens and the House of Fallen Women*, 132–61; Edward F. Payne and Henry H. Harper, *The Charity of Charles Dickens* (Boston: The Bibliophile Society, 1929), 23–51.
[44] House, *The Dickens World*, 215–19.
[45] Charles Dickens, *Dombey and Son*, ed. Alan Horsman (Oxford: Clarendon Press, 1974), 53, 717.

integrate particular social issues into a larger imaginative structure. Chapter 61 of *David Copperfield* illustrates the risks and how they might be resolved. The visit to a lightly fictionalized Pentonville at the end of the novel begins with an apparently superfluous injection of an argument he had just made in *Household Words* (*HW*, 'Pet Prisoners', 99):

> It was an immense and solid building, erected at a vast expense. I could not help thinking, as we approached the gate, what an uproar would have been made in the country, if any deluded man had proposed to spend one half the money it had cost, on the erection of an industrial school for the young, or a house of refuge for the deserving old.[46]

What lifts the novel's episode into a more resonant text than the original journal article is Dickens's triumphant elision of plot and advocacy. Guided by the former brutal teacher, now appropriately transposed into a Middlesex Magistrate, the visiting party makes the astonishing but utterly fitting discovery that prisoner 'Twenty Seven' is none other than Uriah Heep, who had disappeared into the court system earlier in the novel: ' "Well, Twenty Seven," said Mr. Creakle, mournfully admiring him. "How do you find yourself to-day?" "I am very umble, sir!" replied Uriah Heep. "You are always so, Twenty Seven," said Mr. Creakle' (*DC* 61, 729). Heep's long-established, manipulative deference now perfectly illustrates Dickens's fundamental critique of reformative justice, that it was wide open to manipulation by unscrupulous penitents.

By the time of *Bleak House* Dickens had found a way of constructing a narrative in which particular elements of his reform agenda were fully integrated into the plot.[47] The challenge was to locate the appropriate, all-embracing agency of change. His point of departure was not the state but private charity. He was talking to a readership whose lives were suffused in philanthropy. They were either active in the multiplying body of organized giving, or bombarded by individual and collective requests for donations, or the beneficiaries of voluntary relief, whether in cash or kind. In 1850, as Dickens wrote *David Copperfield* and launched *Household Words*, Sampson Low published *The Charities of London*, a guide to the bodies now at work in the capital. He listed almost 500 organizations, describing their purposes, identifying their managing committees, and calculating their income. Together they were raising one and three-quarter million pounds a year, almost five times the current national expenditure on elementary education. 'What an amazing comprehensiveness is here developed in the operations of Christian charity for the relief of suffering and dependent humanity', he observed.[48] By contrast the state was a distant presence in the lives of every sector of society save the criminal and the pauperized. The only regular encounter most adults would make with

---

[46] Charles Dickens, *David Copperfield*, ed. Nina Burgis (Oxford: Clarendon Press, 1981), 61, 727. Subsequent references are inserted parenthetically in the text by *DC* chapter, page.
[47] John Butt and Kathleen Tillotson, *Dickens at Work* (London: Methuen, 1957), 178.
[48] Sampson Low, *The Charities of London* (London: Sampson Low, 1850), 453.

the official world was the figure of the uniformed postman making up to 12 deliveries a day in Dickens's London.[49]

Dickens's response to this industry was fiercely critical. He attacked the 'rapacious benevolence' of otherwise respectable men and women (*BH* 8, 93). In *Bleak House*, Esther and Ada look into Mr Jarndyce's business:

> It amazed us, when we began to sort his letters, and to answer some of them for him in the Growlery of a morning, to find how the great object of the lives of nearly all his correspondents appeared to be to form themselves into committees for getting in and laying out money. The ladies were as desperate as the gentlemen; indeed, I think they were even more so. They threw themselves into committees in the most impassioned manner, and collected subscriptions with a vehemence quite extraordinary. (*BH* 8, 92)

Dickens was both a participant in and a victim of giving. He lived his life in the mainstream of philanthropic endeavour, devoting a decade of energetic commitment to the Urania Cottage project, and, day in and day out, responding to demands on his overpressed time and income.[50] Here he writes to his assistant William Henry Wills in 1852, giving a brief update on his donations:

> We forgot to speak, yesterday, about the begging letters. I send with this a black surtout. That and £2 will be sufficient I think for the Rathbone Place man. £2 for Macpherson, the Orphan[.] £1 for the Needlewoman. And after this, I really must pull up. For I have no funds but my own, in hand or in reversion; and I get these letters by hundreds—not counting those that *you* get.[51]

But as he made clear in his commentary on such correspondence, Dickens himself was never sure about the effect of such charity. His growing fame was measured in the volume of his post. As Low's celebratory guide was published, he wrote of his experiences in *Household Words*: 'For fourteen years, my house has been made as regular a Receiving House for such communications as any one of the great branch Post-Offices is for general correspondence.'[52] His fundamental objection was the corruption of ends by means. The organizational endeavour became an object in itself, the unscrupulous energy traduced basic standards of honourable conduct, and the needs of the poor were subordinated to the sectarian Christianity that framed the philanthropy.

---

[49] Jonathan Rose, 'Education, Literacy, and the Reader', in Patrick Brantlinger and William B. Thesing (eds), *A Companion to the Victorian Novel* (Oxford: Blackwell, 2002), reprinted in Robert L. Patten (ed.), *Dickens and Victorian Print Cultures* (Farnham: Ashgate, 2012), 231–47, 232.

[50] Norris Pope, *Dickens and Charity* (London: Macmillan, 1978), 10.

[51] To William H. Wills, 29 April 1852, in *The Letters of Charles Dickens*, ed. Madeline House, Graham Storey, et al., Pilgrim/British Academy Edition, 12 vols (Oxford: Clarendon Press, 1965–2002). Subsequent citations: *PLets* followed by volume: page. Here 6:654.

[52] [Charles Dickens,] 'The Begging-Letter Writer', *Household Words*, 18 May 1850: 169–72, 169. He further explored this theme in a letter to Edmund Yates, 28 April 1858, *PLets* 8:553.

The problem Dickens faced was the absence of an all-embracing alternative. It was evident to most of his audience that action needed to be taken where philanthropy could or should not go. Sampson Low divided his charities into 18 groups, ranging from 'Medical treatment and Relief' to 'Asylums for the Aged'. In terms of Dickens's agenda of reform, the list excluded policing and prisons where it was now accepted that the state had a monopoly of provision; public health, where the limits of individual endeavour were becoming daily more evident; and the political process itself, in which, as we have seen, Dickens had little confidence. The critique of paper-based bureaucracy applied equally to the private and public sectors. Together with John Stuart Mill he was one of the earliest writers to deploy the phrase 'red tape' as a summary description of organizational inertia, attacking it both in his journalism and, most famously, in the account of *Little Dorrit*'s 'Circumlocution Office' (*LD* I:10, 100–17).[53] The resonance of the term was derived partly from its association with ancient legal documents, which enabled Dickens to emphasize the presence of old corruption in the machinery of the Reform Act State. More generally, as in his critique of the charitable sector, Dickens was turning the energy of modernity back on itself. The rule-bound, document-centred organization was the scalable response to the proliferating needs of an expanding, unnameable, urban population. Dickens's insight, the forerunner of a later industry of organizational sociology, was that it was merely replacing personal with collective self-interest.

Whilst, through the short-lived eruption of the Administrative Reform Association, Dickens was prepared to endorse a manifesto of change, derived in part from the Northcote–Treveleyan Report of 1854, he had no expectation of a third agency of reform, the collective protest of the dispossessed themselves. He had a property-holder's fear of the mob, expressed most directly in *Barnaby Rudge* and *A Tale of Two Cities*,[54] and a deep mistrust of the emerging trade-union movement conveyed through the figure of Slackbridge in *Hard Times*. The absence of an overarching reform programme makes it impossible to place Dickens somewhere on a scale that runs from reactionary to revolutionary. No writer who was so angry about the manifold shortcomings of contemporary social conditions, so dismissive of the construct of the 'Good Old Times', and so contemptuous of both old corruption and new money, can reasonably be seen as a conservative upholder of the status quo.[55] By the same measure, no defender of property rights, no upholder of the identity of interests between employers and employed, and no critic of virtually all the available means of change, including by the victims themselves, can be labelled as some kind of proto-Marxist. He shared the utilitarian endorsement of the pursuit of happiness and the need to subject inherited abuses to enquiry and reform. But his hostility to the mechanical calculation of good and to flagship legislation such

---

[53] See especially [Charles Dickens,] 'Red Tape', *Household Words*, 15 February 1851, 2: 481–4.
[54] Myron Magnet, *Dickens and the Social Order* (Philadelphia: University of Pennsylvania Press, 1985), 5.
[55] On Dickens's 'vigorous reformism ... as an undeclared defense of the status quo', see D. A. Miller, *The Novel and the Police* (Berkeley: University of California Press, 1988), 104.

as the New Poor Law disqualified him from full membership of mid-Victorian middle-class radicalism where he might otherwise have found a home.[56]

Instead he debated with his readership how to grow as a moral agent amidst the corrupting pressures of the age. The issue of schooling illustrates the balance he struck between a programme of reform and a discursive examination of a need for change. Education linked all ranks of society. Every adult, however rich or poor, had been a child whose development could be deformed by mechanical instruction or brutal teachers. Where provision amongst the urban dispossessed was absent or fundamentally inadequate, the consequences would be felt by their prosperous neighbours as a new generation of criminals was called into being. Dickens had limited expectation of the capacity of prisons to rehabilitate hardened malefactors. Only by addressing the early stages of personality formation could crime be kept in check. Thus he visited Ragged Schools, lobbied Angela Burdett-Coutts to support them, and discussed with James Kay-Shuttleworth the possibility of state funding. But in an era when critical steps were being taken to create a systematic, centrally subsidized, and inspected elementary school system, he showed little interest in the legislative process.[57]

The focus was rather what could be learnt from the immense variety of encounters between pupils and instructors. Outside the large public schools, which Dickens ignored, most institutions, from Mr Wopsle's great-aunt's dame school in *Great Expectations* to Dotheboys Hall in *Nicholas Nickleby*, took their identity from a dominant teacher. Thus the narrative drama was driven by the interaction between the flawed adult and the vulnerable pupil. Occasional notice was taken of the emerging structure of inspected schooling, including, for instance, the pupil-teacher system which was shown in *Our Mutual Friend* to be subordinating bright poor children to the 'Gospel according to Monotony'.[58] The broader utilitarian vision of a world of arid facts was attacked in the account of Mr McChoakumchild's establishment in *Hard Times*. But Dickens's own didactic method rested on contrast. In the broad reaches of middle-class education, where in this period there was no question of state intervention, he stressed the range of possible experiences. The key institutions in *David Copperfield*, for instance, were described in opposition to each other: 'Doctor Strong's was an excellent school; as different from Mr. Creakle's as good is from evil' (*DC* 16, 202). The evaluation was based on a double appeal to imagination. The readership learnt an unforgettable lesson through the moving depiction of character distorted, deformed, and occasionally developed in the classroom.

---

[56] Raymond Williams, 'Dickens and Social Ideas', in Michael Slater (ed.), *Dickens 1970* (London: Chapman & Hall, 1970), 77–98, 88–9; Kathleen Blake, '*Bleak House*, Political Economy, Victorian Studies', *Victorian Literature and Culture* 25, 1 (1997): 1–21, 17.

[57] John Manning, *Dickens on Education* (Toronto: University of Toronto Press, 1959), 200–3; Hugh Cunningham, 'Dickens as a Reformer', in Paroissien (ed.), *Companion*, 159–73, 167–8.

[58] Charles Dickens, *Our Mutual Friend*, ed. Michael Cotsell, Oxford World's Classics (Oxford: Oxford University Press, 1989), II:1, 218.

Dickens was further deflected from educational legislation by doubts about the intrinsic value of basic literacy, upon which the emerging state-subsidized system was based, particularly after the 1862 Revised Code.[59] On an individual level he treated the illiterates in his novels such as Joe Gargery or Jo the crossing-sweeper with sympathetic affection, exploring the world view of those excluded from mass communication whilst stressing their consequent vulnerability to exploitation.[60] At the same time he had a deep apprehension of the use the newly educated could make of cheap literature. His campaign against public hangings was based on the harm it did not to those who suffered on the gallows, but to those who came to watch the spectacle, their sensibilities corrupted by the immense trade in execution broadsides.

Over his career his attention shifted to public health as the key reform.[61] Here the metaphor of contagion of the rich by the poor had a physiological basis. In *Bleak House* the 'tumbling tenements' of Tom-all-Alone's are shown to spread infection across society (*BH* 16, 197). What is less clear within the novel is the solution. The only remedial agent is the doctor Allan Woodcourt, a good professional but incapable of responding to the scale of the problem. In an address 'To Working Men' in *Household Words* just after the novel was published, Dickens explained both the urgency of the threat and his role in countering it:

> Long before this Journal came into existence, we systematically tried to turn Fiction to the good account of showing the preventable wretchedness and misery in which the mass of the people dwell, and of expressing again and again the conviction, founded upon observation, that the reform of their habitations must precede all other reforms; and without it, all other reforms must fail.[62]

Through his alliance with his brother-in-law Henry Austin, an influential member of the Health of Towns Association, and his addresses to the Metropolitan Sanitary Association, Dickens was directly involved in lobbying for political reform. In *Household Words* he sought to rouse its unenfranchised readers to unite with the middle class to urge the government to act. However, public health legislation had its own history of innovation and obstruction, and it is impossible to attribute any specific legislation to Dickens. Rather his achievement lay in giving 'Fiction' an entirely new role both

---

[59] Patrick Brantlinger, 'Educating the Victorians', in Ledger and Furneaux (eds), *Charles Dickens in Context*, 219–26, 224; Ruth Tross, 'Dickens and the Crime of Literacy', *Dickens Quarterly* 21, 4 (2004): 235–45.

[60] Mike Baynham, 'Elite or Powerful Literacies? Constructions of Literacy in the Novels of Charles Dickens and Mrs. Gaskell', in Mastin Prinsloo and Mike Baynham (eds), *Literacies, Global and Local* (Amsterdam: John Benjamins, 2008), 173–92, 179–80.

[61] Janis McLarren Caldwell, 'Illness, Disease and Social Hygiene', in Ledger and Furneaux (eds), *Charles Dickens in Context*, 243–49; Lauren M. E. Goodlad, *Victorian Literature and the Victorian State* (Baltimore: The Johns Hopkins University Press, 2003), 87–8.

[62] [Charles Dickens,] 'To Working Men', *Household Words*, 7 October 1854, 10: 169–70, 169.

in describing the need for social reform and engaging the minds and the imagination of a new reading public with the meaning and consequences of preventable misery.

Further Reading

Nina Attwood, *The Prostitute's Body: Rewriting Prostitution in Victorian Britain* (London: Pickering and Chatto, 2011)

Norman Chester, *The English Administrative System, 1780–1870* (Oxford: Oxford University Press, 1981)

M. A. Crowther, *The Workhouse System, 1834–1929: The History of An English Social Institution* (London: Routledge, 2016)

Duane DeVries, *Dickens's Apprentice Years: The Making of a Novelist* (Hassocks: Harvester Press, 1976)

Trevor Fisher, *Prostitution and the Victorians* (Stroud: Sutton, 1997)

Christopher Hamlin, *Public Health and Social Justice in the Age of Chadwick: Britain, 1800–1854* (Cambridge: Cambridge University Press, 1998)

Ian Haywood, *The Revolution in Popular Literature: Print, Politics and the People, 1790–1860* (Cambridge: Cambridge University Press, 2004)

U. R. Q. Henriques, 'The Rise and Decline of the Separate System of Prison Discipline', *Past and Present* 54 (1972): 61–93

Patrick Joyce, *The State of Freedom: A Social History of the British State since 1800* (Cambridge: Cambridge University Press, 2015)

Lynn Hollen Lees, *The Solidarities of Strangers: The English Poor Laws and the People, 1700–1948* (Cambridge: Cambridge University Press, 1998)

Oliver Macdonough, *Early Victorian Government, 1830–70* (London: Weidenfeld and Nicolson, 1977)

Neil J. Smelser, *Social Paralysis and Social Change: British Working-Class Education in the Nineteenth Century* (Berkeley: University of California Press, 1991)

Jeremy Tambling, *Dickens, Violence and the Modern State: Dreams of the Scaffold* (London: Macmillan, 1995)

David Vincent, *Literacy and Popular Culture in England 1750–1914* (Cambridge: Cambridge University Press, 1993)

Anthony S. Wohl, *Endangered Lives: Public Health in Victorian Britain* (London: Dent, 1983)

CHAPTER 30

DICKENS, INDUSTRY, AND TECHNOLOGY

RICHARD MENKE

During Charles Dickens's lifetime, the march of practical knowledge and technology was becoming an inescapable part of daily life in Great Britain. James Watt's epochal improvements to the steam engine and Alessandro Volta's first work on electric batteries had taken place at the end of the eighteenth century. But as a continuing surge of discoveries and inventions turned their pioneering work into projects to be implemented on a vast scale, it was Dickens's generation that came to view its era as an age of steam and electricity. Furthermore, by the time Dickens began writing, it was becoming clear that technological changes would beget further change, as one set of innovations was replaced by the next: the optical telegraph towers of the Napoleonic era by the far more extensive and reliable electric telegraph system; the mail coaches, turnpike roads, and canals of *The Pickwick Papers*, *The Old Curiosity Shop*, and *A Tale of Two Cities*, by the railways that run through *Dombey and Son* or *Our Mutual Friend*. Invention and technological change affected the lives of Victorians of a range of classes and conditions. Industrial innovations and growth in manufacturing were further linked to revolutions in transportation, communication, public health, and sanitation, as well as to urbanization and even to changes in the experiences of space and time. All of these shaped Dickens's world and drew responses in his writing.

As Britain emerged as the world's first great industrial economy, some of the most influential writers of Dickens's age began to consider the machine, as both an idea and a concrete reality, the epitome of what was deplorable about contemporary life. In 'Signs of the Times' (1829), the philosopher, historian, and critic Thomas Carlyle assails the era as an 'Age of Machinery, in every outward and inward sense of that word'.[1] In Carlyle's view, this diagnosis is justified not simply by the revolutionary application of steam power to production and transportation but also by what he considers to be machinery

---

[1] [Thomas Carlyle], ['Signs of the Times'], *Edinburgh Review* 49 (June 1829): 439–59, 442.

in the social realm. Machinery stands first for a distanced, mediated relationship to nature and to the real world; Carlyle notes that modern machines not only weave cloth and speed passengers across land and sea but also chop cabbages and hatch chickens. But Carlyle finds the logic of machinery extending far more broadly to encapsulate relations between human beings. Education reform ('machines for Education'), bible societies ('very excellent machine[s] for converting the heathen'), or parliamentary legislation: such programmes for systematic action or improvement typify many nineteenth-century Britons' approaches to social and moral problems, yet for Carlyle, they represent a profound turn to mere mechanisms.[2] In his account, the machine encapsulates the ascendance of the group over the individual, the turn to institutional change rather than personal initiative, and a view of the world that embraces the material at the expense of the organic and the spiritual. Carlyle's striking critiques here and elsewhere stand behind the social criticism of nearly the gamut of Victorian writers, including Dickens, who hailed Carlyle's *French Revolution* (1837) as a source for *A Tale of Two Cities*.[3]

Other influential Victorian authors often express a similar wariness about machines and technology, although generally in less bombastic terms than Carlyle's. In *The Stones of Venice* (1851–3), the art writer and social critic John Ruskin contrasts the quest for machine-like perfection in modern architecture and manufacturing with the irregularity of Gothic buildings. Ruskin takes the wildness of Gothic architecture as a sign of the freedom of the medieval craftsman, a sharp contrast to the servile status of nineteenth-century workers. Writers concerned about the concrete effects of factory life highlighted the conditions in which the industrial working class lived and worked. Concern about the implications of technological innovation for industrial workers extended far beyond working-class machine breakers or revolutionary socialists such as Karl Marx. Writing in 1848, the philosopher and economist John Stuart Mill considered it 'questionable' whether 'all the mechanical inventions yet made have lightened the day's toil of any human being'. Such innovations had 'increased the comforts of the middle classes' and permitted 'manufacturers and others to make large fortunes', but Mill concluded that their effect on labourers was to allow 'a greater population to live the same life of drudgery and imprisonment'.[4] Yet Mill noted that this immiseration resulted not from technological innovation itself but from a society's choice to value inventions for making fortunes rather than devices that would actually ease the burdens of human labour.

---

[2] Ibid., 443.

[3] See Charles Dickens, 'Preface', in *A Tale of Two Cities*, ed. Andrew Sanders, Oxford World's Classics (Oxford: Oxford University Press, 1988), 29. Subsequent references are inserted parenthetically in the text by *TTC* Book:chapter, page. Charles Dickens to Thomas Carlyle, 24 March 1859 and 30 October 1859, in *The Letters of Charles Dickens*, ed. Madeline House, Graham Storey, et al., Pilgrim/British Academy edn, 12 vols (Oxford: Clarendon, 1965–2002). Here 9:41, 145. Henceforth *PLets* followed by volume:page range, page.

[4] John Stuart Mill, *Principles of Political Economy* [1848], in *Collected Works of John Stuart Mill*, ed. F. E. L. Priestley et al., 33 vols (London: Routledge; Toronto: University of Toronto Press, 1965), 3:756–7.

Like Carlyle, Ruskin, and Mill, Dickens saw industry and mechanical invention as deeply connected to social life and questions of value, and he too could offer harsh criticisms of what he saw as the moral dimension of Victorian industry and technology, most famously in *Hard Times*. Dickens often shares Carlyle's scepticism about institutional machinery, as his attacks on the Court of Chancery and the Circumlocution Office confirm. But Dickens was no technophobe; Ruskin considered him 'a leader of the steam-whistle party par excellence ... his hero is essentially the ironmaster'.[5] While Herbert Sussman's influential *Victorians and the Machine* (1968) emphasized the threat of industrial and transport machinery to Victorian writers' embrace of 'organic' social values, more recent accounts by Tamara Ketabgian and by Sussman himself have stressed the interplay between the technological and literary imaginations, and between the mechanical and the organic in nineteenth-century thought.[6] In fact perhaps no novelist embodies the richness and multiplicity of Victorian thinking about technology and social change better than Dickens himself.

Indeed—thanks to some of the most notable aspects of his writerly sensibility, his development as a novelist, and his work beyond writing fiction—Dickens was particularly well prepared to explore the social and literary possibilities of technological change and the developments that followed in the wake of such innovation. In his writing, the animate and inanimate worlds appear closely linked or even continuous with each other: objects and physical settings are filled with life, while human characters can seem to operate in part through fixed responses and tics that verge on the mechanical—at least according to some of Dickens's critics, Victorian as well as modern. Dickens was also fascinated by the things that connected disparate persons in society, as suggested by a famous narrative question in *Bleak House*: 'What connexion can there be, between the place in Lincolnshire, the house in town, the Mercury in powder, and the whereabout of Jo the outlaw with the broom ...?'[7] Like the links that emerge between the lavish haunts of the Dedlocks and the homeless boy who sweeps the London crosswalks, such connections are not limited to some abstract sense of belonging to a society or a nation; rather, for Dickens they also materialize via infrastructures for communication and movement as well as by the more corporeal connections of sanitation and public health. These connections become more extensive and critical as Dickens shifts from the episodic, picaresque plotlines of his early novels to the complex architectonics of multi-plot works such as *Bleak House*, *Little Dorrit*, or *Our Mutual Friend*, a shift that coincides with the revolutions in transport and communication represented above all by the railway and the electric telegraph. Finally, as a

---

[5] John Ruskin to Charles Eliot Norton, 19 June 1870, in *The Complete Works of John Ruskin*, ed. E. T. Cook and Alexander Wedderburn, 39 vols (London: Allen, 1903–12), 37:7.

[6] Herbert L. Sussman, *Victorians and the Machine: The Literary Response to Technology* (Cambridge, MA: Harvard University Press, 1968), 5. See also the list of 'Further Reading' that accompanies this chapter.

[7] Charles Dickens, *Bleak House*, ed. George Ford and Sylvère Monod, Norton Critical Edition (New York: W.W. Norton, 1977), 16, 197. Subsequent references are inserted parenthetically in the text by *BH* chapter, page.

journalist, editor, and public speaker as well as a novelist, Dickens depended on—and was often fascinated by—the evolving infrastructures for travel and communication. These networks allowed the flow of messages, manuscripts, and publications as well as his own movements through Great Britain, Europe, and North America; moreover, they allowed him to coordinate these two modes of circulation, to travel even while he continued writing and editing.[8]

Dickens's industrial world can be dark, but it is not inherently mechanistic or cold, as a strange episode in *The Old Curiosity Shop* affirms. The novel's main plot commences when Nell and her grandfather flee London and the demonic Quilp for what Nell imagines as a storybook rural England. But what they actually find during their haphazard wandering is far different. In one harrowing scene, Nell and her grandfather arrive in a dirty, noisy, 'great manufacturing town', where they stand on the 'crowded street, ... as strange, bewildered, and confused, as if they had lived a thousand years before, and were raised from the dead and placed there by a miracle'.[9] It's as if the novel had suddenly dropped them from a fairy tale, with its extremes of villainy and innocence, into the world of the early Victorian industrial novel. After spending a rainy day in the midst of a rushing crowd that does not even register their presence, Nell and her grandfather prepare to spend the night sleeping rough. But as they do, they encounter a strange 'black figure' who seems to materialize from their surroundings, 'a man, miserably clad and begrimed with smoke, ... [but] very wan and pallid ... [with] hollow cheeks, sharp features, and sunken eyes' (*OCS* 44, 340). Offering them 'warmth' by a 'fire ... in a rough place' that is still 'safer and better' than the streets, he takes them 'through what appeared to be the poorest and most wretched quarter of the town' to an immense structure where a huge chimney emits a ruddy glare (*OCS* 44, 341).

This is an inhuman landscape, to be sure. The novel never refers to the building as 'a mill' or 'a factory'; it never offers a name that would let Nell or a reader classify the place by its workaday function. Instead, even its elaborate description seems phantasmagoric, hallucinatory, out of scale from the rest of the narrative:

> In a large and lofty building, supported by pillars of iron, with great black apertures in the upper walls, open to the external air; echoing to the roof with the beating of hammers and roar of furnaces, mingled with the hissing of red-hot metal plunged in water, and a hundred strange unearthly noises never heard elsewhere; in this gloomy place, moving like demons among the flame and smoke, dimly and fitfully seen, flushed and tormented by the burning fires, and wielding great weapons, a faulty blow from any one of which must have crushed some workman's skull, a number of men laboured like giants. Others, reposing upon heaps of coals or ashes,

---

[8] For a rich account of Dickens's response to nineteenth-century transportation networks, see Jonathan H. Grossman, *Charles Dickens's Networks: Public Transport and the Novel* (Oxford and New York: Oxford University Press, 2012).

[9] Charles Dickens, *The Old Curiosity Shop*, ed. Elizabeth M. Brennan (Oxford: Clarendon Press, 1997), 45, 346; 43, 337. Subsequent references are inserted parenthetically in the text by *OCS* chapter, page.

with their faces turned to the black vault above, slept or rested from their toil. Others again, opening the white-hot furnace-doors, cast fuel on the flames, which came rushing and tearing forth to meet it, and licked it up like oil. Others drew forth, with clashing noise upon the ground, great sheets of glowing steel, emitting an insupportable heat, and a dull deep light like that which reddens in the eyes of savage beasts. (*OCS* 44, 342)

The first sentence moves from the vast architecture of the place, to the otherworldly sounds and sights of the activities there, to the physical threats they pose to the vulnerable human bodies at work. But it ends with these workers turned not into victims or slaves but into 'giants'; after the long stream of prepositional phrases and dependent clauses that postpone the sentence's action, their human labour itself finally supplies the active verb in the long-deferred main clause. This industrial work may be anonymous and collective, but it is also heroic, part of the gigantism and power of the entire enterprise. Other workers rest as if this were their native world. They feed the flames and draw the hot steel, managing and controlling these fierce elemental creatures. Rather than emphasizing productivity, profit, or the stories of the labourers, Dickens here presents industrialism as an unleashing of coal and steam that invests human beings with their chthonic energies; he offers not a timeless fairy tale but a new myth for the industrial age.

It's unclear how much of this the bewildered travellers actually perceive, although Nell has been admonished to study such things. Earlier in *The Old Curiosity Shop*, when Nell was under the protection of Mrs Jarley, she was publicly scolded by a pompous schoolmistress for working in an itinerant waxwork show:

'Don't you feel how naughty it is of you', resumed Miss Monflathers, 'to be a wax-work child, when you might have the proud consciousness of assisting, to the extent of your infant powers, the manufactures of your country; of improving your mind by the constant contemplation of the steam-engine; and of earning a comfortable and independent subsistence of from two-and-ninepence to three shillings per week? Don't you know that the harder you are at work, the happier you are?' (*OCS* 31, 244)

Treating Nell as something of a wax-work spectacle herself, Miss Monflathers disdainfully contrasts the naughtiness of popular entertainment with industrial productivity, educational discipline, and political economy, an opposition that Dickens will develop further in *Hard Times*. Unlike the tearful Nell, readers can hardly take the speech seriously, especially Miss Monflathers's vacuous fantasy that 'contemplating the steam-engine' will improve the mind of a penniless girl as she advances into a life of respectable work and a meagre but steady income. Miss Monflathers's moralized economics sounds like a parodic distillation of one of Harriet Martineau's *Illustrations of Political Economy* (1832–4), works that sought to assure readers that the laws of the market were immutable and that industrial machinery was beneficial to workers and capitalists alike. (As Elaine Freedgood has pointed out, Martineau's *Illustrations* reached monthly sales figures far higher than those achieved by the serialized novels that Dickens would soon begin publishing.[10]) Here, in a giddily telescoped version of Carlyle's analogy between technophilia and mechanistic views of social life, the image of the quintessential industrial machine incarnates the complacent fantasy that work, mental improvement, and the rejection of fun will somehow come together to transform a marginal 'infant' into a productive economic unit.

But technology and manufacturing figure quite differently when Nell's mysterious rescuer takes her into the factory. He leads Nell and her grandfather to a furnace that blazes night and day, out of natural time, and Nell falls asleep and dreams—safe, warm, and protected. The hot furnace and lulling roar provide a moment of strange comfort in the midst of disorientation and suffering. When she awakes, the man tells her that his duty and great occupation is to watch the fire, his companion since childhood: for him, it is 'a book ... the only book I ever learned to read', with 'many an old story' and 'pictures' of 'strange faces and different scenes'; '[i]t's music' full of 'voices'; 'it's my memory, that fire, and shows me all my life' (*OCS* 44, 344). Although he appears only in a single episode and lacks even a name, Nell's benefactor nevertheless sets a pattern for Dickens's subsequent fire-watchers—although unlike Louisa Gradgrind in *Hard Times* or Lizzie Hexam in *Our Mutual Friend*, he does not find his pastime dismissed by a relative who high-handedly points out that the combustion of coal is simply a physical process. His coal-powered visions are essentially novelistic; his book filled with voices, stories, faces, and scenes sounds like an early Dickens novel. After he reluctantly lets Nell and her grandfather continue on their way, *The Old Curiosity Shop*'s fire-watcher returns to his post to add their stories to his visions. If this episode fabricates a myth of industrialism, it also leaves us with the suggestion that in an age of steam, the novelistic imagination itself may become a by-product of industrial production.

Steam power and Victorian technologies do not always play such a benign role in Dickens's novels, of course. Yet their functions and repercussions are often complex and mixed, not merely negative or inhuman. In *Dombey and Son*, written as the bubble of the 1840s' railway mania was beginning to burst, readers first encounter the railway as its construction consumes an entire London neighbourhood. This impact might remind us that the construction of the railways, the largest infrastructure project ever undertaken in Britain, didn't simply establish fast and regular connections between points on a map but radically remade the geography of city and countryside alike. When we first enter the district of Staggs's Gardens in Camden Town, 'the whole neighbourhood' is in chaos, 'rent' by '[t]he first shock of a great earthquake'. Half demolished but only half reconstructed, the district sceptically prepares to send 'the yet unfinished and unopened Railroad ... from the very core of all this dire disorder ... upon its mighty course of

---

[10] Elaine Freedgood. 'Banishing Panic: Harriet Martineau and the Popularization of Political Economy', in Martha Woodmansee and Mark Osteen (eds), *The New Economic Criticism: Studies at the Intersection of Literature and Economics* (New York: Routledge, 1999), 210–28, 213.

civilisation and improvement'.[11] Only 100 pages afterward, and three months later in the novel's serial run, there's 'no such place as Staggs's Gardens' at all:

> It had vanished from the earth. Where the old rotten summer-houses once had stood, palaces now reared their heads, and granite columns of gigantic girth opened a vista to the Railway world beyond. The miserable waste ground, where the refuse-matter had been heaped of yore, was swallowed up and gone; and in its frowsy stead were tiers of warehouses, crammed with rich goods and costly merchandise. The old by-streets now swarmed with passengers and vehicles of every kind; the new streets that had stopped disheartened in the mud and waggon-ruts, formed towns within themselves, originating wholesome comforts and conveniences belonging to themselves, and never tried or thought of until they sprung into existence. (*DS* 15, 217–18)

'Staggs's Gardens' has become a 'vanished land' that few of the residents of the busy new quarter even seem to remember (*DS* 15, 219). But what a change; now '[b]ridges that had led to nothing, le[a]d to villas, gardens, churches, healthy public walks' (*DS* 15, 218). The march of civilization and improvement, invoked with some irony before, no longer seems so dubious. (In real life, however, Dickens would complain that Camden Town remained in disarray long after the coming of the trains: 'the Railway Terminus Works themselves are a picture of our moral state', he concludes, 'confused and dissipated'.[12])

The arrival of modern transport reshapes culture, commerce, and even chronometry in the former Staggs's Gardens:

> There were railway patterns in its drapers' shops, and railway journals in the windows of its newsmen. There were railway hotels, coffee-houses, lodging-houses, boarding-houses; railway plans, maps, views, wrappers, bottles, sandwich-boxes, and time tables; railway hackney-coach and cab-stands; railway omnibuses, railway streets and buildings, railway hangers-on and parasites, and flatterers out of all calculation. There was even railway time observed in clocks, as if the sun itself had given in. (*DS* 15, 218)

Before the coming of railways, cities and towns had set their own local time based on the position of the sun overhead, an annoyance for railway managers as well as for passengers who had to calculate the times of their connections—and to reset their watches as they went. The rail companies soon decided on a single time scheme for their entire line, a synchronization assisted by the electric telegraph, whose wires often ran along the tracks. 'Railway time' generally meant Greenwich Mean Time, and the railways' uniform time was adopted by many individual local governments, setting the pattern for the eventual move of all of Great Britain onto GMT. The London and North

---

[11] Charles Dickens, *Dombey and Son*, ed. Alan Horsman (Oxford: Clarendon Press, 1974), 6, 65. Subsequent references are inserted parenthetically in the text by *DS* chapter, page.

[12] [Charles Dickens,] 'An Unsettled Neighbourhood', *Household Words*, 11 November 1854, 10:289–92, 291, <http://www.djo.org.uk/household-words/volume-x/page-289.html>.

Western Railway fictionalized here in *Dombey and Son* adopted railway time on its network just months before Dickens began publishing the novel, which makes the novel's reference still timelier.

As even the sun falls into line, Dickens emphasizes the terrific power of railway technology. The 'monster train' joins the giant workers, the oil-licking furnace, and the red-eyed steel among the representatives of a technological sublime that has turned the stuff of old-fashioned fantasy into modern industrial reality:

> Night and day the conquering engines rumbled at their distant work, or, advancing smoothly to their journey's end, and gliding like tame dragons into the allotted corners grooved out to the inch for their reception, stood bubbling and trembling there, making the walls quake, as if they were dilating with the secret knowledge of great powers yet unsuspected in them, and strong purposes not yet achieved. (*DS* 15, 218–19)

These dragons have been tamed, but they have also conquered; the earthquake that destroyed Staggs's Gardens has become the continual quaking of the walls as the engines prepare for their mysterious ends. Eventually, at least one of those dark purposes becomes clear: a locomotive on a line far from Camden will kill Dombey's duplicitous manager James Carker, realizing Dombey's earlier vision of a train as speeding down 'the track of the remorseless monster, Death' (*DS* 20, 276). Disoriented by travel, flight, and the collapse of all his scheming (his watch stops, he cannot remember what day it is), Carker suddenly looks up from the tracks to see his pursuer Dombey—and fails to noticed the engine bearing down on him, blindsided for the last time:

> He heard a shout—another—saw the face change from its vindictive passion to a faint sickness and terror—felt the earth tremble—knew in a moment that the rush was come—uttered a shriek—looked round—saw the red eyes, bleared and dim, in the daylight, close upon him—was beaten down, caught up, and whirled away upon a jagged mill, that spun him round and round, and struck him limb from limb, and licked his stream of life up with its fiery heat, and cast his mutilated fragments in the air. (*DS* 55, 743)

Again the earth shakes under the body of the dragon. The passage takes us into Carker's moment-to-moment consciousness as Dombey's horrified face seems overlaid by the implacable 'red eyes' of the engine. Verbs dominate this sentence's grammar: initially, verbs in the active voice to convey Carker's perceptions and his panic, then passive constructions as he loses his agency and his life, and finally a new set of active, physical verbs as the 'jagged mill' of the train becomes a grammatical subject and violently takes control.

Licking up Carker's life with its heat, the engine becomes a man-eating version of *The Old Curiosity Shop*'s oil-fed furnace. But even here, the railway fulfils a human function as the agent of justice or revenge, as an extension of Dombey's fury or *Dombey and Son*'s design. Making the novel's villain its victim, the locomotive comes as a *machina ex machina*, a device of fateful retribution within the machinery of *Dombey and Son*. If this novel marks Dickens's shift from an early reliance on brilliant improvisation that produced picaresque, episodic fiction based in part on impromptu travel (*The Pickwick Papers, Nicholas Nickleby, The Old Curiosity Shop, Martin Chuzzlewit*) to planned-out novels whose plots are carefully coordinated in space and time (*Bleak House, A Tale of Two Cities, Our Mutual Friend*), the fatal arrival of *Dombey and Son*'s train—on railway time, on schedule, when and where it must be—confirms the change.

Dickens makes other changes at mid-career, as well. His work as founding editor of *Bentley's Miscellany*, as founder and author of *Master Humphrey's Clock*, and (briefly) as founding editor of *The Daily News* demonstrates his long-standing ambition to create a journal and take on the role—and earn the reliable income—of an editor. With the weekly *Household Words*, launched in 1850, he at last created a vehicle that could sustain that desire; Dickens would continue to edit the journal and its successor, *All the Year Round*, for the rest of his life. *Household Words* published short fiction and novels in serial, including Dickens's *Hard Times*, but much of its content would consist of non-fiction articles about contemporary society. Its perspective on social abuses and injustices would be critical, but Dickens also hoped to spread knowledge as well as hopefulness and cheer, seeing *Household Words* as providing an uplifting alternative to the 'villainous literature' of cheap journals.[13] In a 'Preliminary Word' to his journal's first issue, Dickens declares that it will communicate 'the knowledge of many social wonders, good and evil', but he disclaims any 'mere utilitarian spirit'. Rather, *Household Words* would help readers view these wonders by the 'light of Fancy which is inherent in the human breast': 'To show to all, that in all familiar things, even in those which are repellant on the surface, there is Romance enough, if we will find it out'.[14] This programme closely anticipates Dickens's next novels. His Preface to *Bleak House* ends with a similar assertion: 'In Bleak House, I have purposely dwelt upon the romantic side of familiar things' (*BH* Preface, 4). Soon afterwards, Dickens would structure *Hard Times* around the opposition between Fancy and the utilitarian spirit represented by Thomas Gradgrind and his school.

In a rich and complex passage, Dickens singles out new technologies as a specific focus for *Household Words*, and as a model of the numinous possibilities opened up by modern life and modern modes of reading:

> The mightier inventions of this age are not, to our thinking, all material, but have a kind of souls in their stupendous bodies. ... The traveller whom we accompany on his railroad or his steamboat journey, may gain, we hope ... new associations with the Power that bears him onward; with the habitations and the ways of life of crowds of his fellow creatures among whom he passes like the wind; even with the towering chimneys he may see, spirting out [*sic*] fire and smoke upon the prospect. The swart

---

[13] Charles Dickens to Angela Burdett-Coutts, 12 April 1850, *PLets* 6:82–3, 83.

[14] [Charles Dickens,] 'A Preliminary Word', *Household Words*, 30 March 1850, 1:1–2, 1, <http://www.djo.org.uk/household-words/volume-i/page-1.html>.

giants, Slaves of the Lamp of Knowledge, have their thousand and one tales, no less than the Genii of the East; and these, in all their wild, grotesque, and fanciful aspects, in all their many phases of endurance, in all their many moving lessons of compassion and consideration, we design to tell.[15]

Conveyed by steam power and transported by the pages of *Household Words*, the traveller may come to understand both human beings and technology anew. Knowledge and fantasy unite to turn even factory chimneys once again into figures of gigantism, magic, humanity, and storytelling.

These ideas about the spiritual or romantic side of invention may themselves sound airy and fanciful, but in his journals Dickens applied them in highly practical ways, by writing, co-authoring, and commissioning dozens of articles on topics related to industry, transportation, and modern life, including what Dickens called 'process articles', essays that combined the facts about a complex everyday system of production or distribution with a playful appeal to the imagination.[16] (Almost all of the writing in *Household Words* and *All the Year Round* appeared anonymously, although Dickens's own name was featured on every page.) Many of Dickens's own process pieces were collaborative, his sub-editor W. H. Wills often supplying the facts and figures while Dickens added descriptions, metaphors, and mini-narratives that imbued them with humour, whimsy, and a sense of wonder.

Dickens and Wills's first process article, something of a model for many pieces to follow, appeared in the first issue of *Household Words* alongside Dickens's 'Preliminary Word'. 'Valentine's Day at the Post-Office' takes readers to London's General Post Office, where the observers become 'like knights-errant in a fairy tale' as they explore the wonders of Rowland Hill's reformed postal system.[17] As Dickens and Wills note, over the course of a decade of Hill's penny postage, the post office had come to handle four-and-a-half times as many letters as the old system had, while its expenditures had merely doubled. But in *Household Words*, even speed, efficiency, and economies of scale can become the stuff of drama and fantasy. Postal clerks awaken from 'an enchanted state of idleness' to slash open and 'slaughter' sacks of letters; a 'thunder-cloud of newspapers' discharges and threatens to submerge the post office before it too is finally channelled and dispatched via an apparent chaos that is 'really ... a system of admirable order, certainty, and simplicity'. 'Which of us, after this, shall find fault with the rather more extensive system of good and evil, when we don't quite understand it at a glance; or set the stars right in their spheres?' they muse.[18] A modern communication system teaches us

---

[15] [Dickens,] 'Preliminary Word', 1.

[16] See Harry Stone (ed.), *The Uncollected Writings of Charles Dickens: Household Words 1850–59*, 2 vols (London: Allen Lane-Penguin, 1969; Bloomington: Indiana University Press, 1968), 1:53.

[17] [Charles Dickens and W. H. Wills,] 'Valentine's Day at the Post-Office', *Household Words*, 30 March 1850, 1: 6–12, 7, <http://www.djo.org.uk/household-words/volume-i/page-6>.

[18] Ibid., 7, 9, 9.

about the workings of the universe. The fact that this whole adventure takes place on Valentine's Day further links efficient postal processing to romance.

Dickens's journals published process articles, short histories, and informative 'chips' (brief articles that could be used to fill out issues) about subjects such as electric telegraphs, automatic railway signals, power looms, embroidery workshops, the refining of gold and the manufacture of paper, playing cards, paper boxes, plate glass, industrial chemicals—to give just a sampling drawn from the early years. All bring out the everyday wonder of invention and industry, but the pieces written by Dickens himself often go further, reiterating his insistence on the 'souls' of great machines and on the human implications of technologies and practical knowledge. One of his chips notes the 'remarkable truth ... that every Locomotive Engine running on a Railway, has a distinct individuality and character of its own'. Indeed, 'experienced practical engineers' recognize that even engines of the same model made at the same time and at the same factory emerge with their 'own peculiar whims and ways, only ascertainable by experience'. Railway companies must allow for the 'varying shades of character and opinion' of their rolling stock, a policy with a lesson for 'those greater Governments' that deal with 'the finer piece of work called Man'.[19]

Other essays draw attention to more immediate issues of government, applied knowledge, and contemporary life. Again and again, Dickens's journals emphasize the need for sanitary reform, a cause made urgent by the rapid growth of London and other cities. In the 1840s, Dickens read the work of the famous 'sanitarian' Edwin Chadwick and became an ally to the cause of public health (if not a supporter of Chadwick's earlier work on the New Poor Law of 1834, attacked in *Oliver Twist*). His journals would offer a forum for articles on water quality, illness, boards of health, the burial of the dead, and the removal of the filthy Smithfield meat market from central London. More imaginatively, Dickens also incorporates these topics in his fiction, from the contagion, death, and 'waterside pollutions' of *Bleak House*'s 'great (and dirty)' London (*BH* 1, 5), to Pip's first encounter with the sights and smells of London in *Great Expectations*, to the waste economies of the dust heaps and the Thames in *Our Mutual Friend*.

Notwithstanding his sympathetic interest in technology and industry, Dickens found the famous 1851 Great Exhibition less inspiring. A technology and trade show on a vast scale, the Great Exhibition of the Works of Industry of All Nations was housed in the specially built Crystal Palace, whose wrought iron and plate glass made the structure itself a display of cutting-edge materials and construction techniques. In a co-written *Household Words* article, Dickens compared the Great Exhibition to a smaller display of Chinese art, revelling (in a rather Podsnappian vein) in the contrast between British technological progress and the 'perfect Toryism' of a supposedly static, complacent China.[20] But in a private letter, Dickens confessed that the exhibition made him feel

---

[19] [Charles Dickens,] 'Chips: The Individuality of Locomotives', *Household Words*, 21 September 1850, 1:614, <http://www.djo.org.uk/household-words/volume-i/page-614>.

[20] [Charles Dickens and Richard H. Horne,] 'The Great Exhibition and the Little One', *Household Words*, 5 July 1851, 3:356–60, 360, <http://www.djo.org.uk/household-words/volume-iii/page-356>.

'bewildered' and '"used up"': 'I don't say "there is nothing in it"—there is too much.' He offers a story about an 'Infant' who 'strayed' during a school trip there:

> He was not missed. ... this particular Infant went to Hammersmith. He was found by the Police at night, going round and round the Turnpike—which he still supposed to be a part of the Exhibition. He had the same opinion of the police. Also of Hammersmith Workhouse, where he passed the night. When his mother came for him in the morning he asked when it would be over?[21]

A visit to the Exhibition turns urban reality—turnpike, police, workhouse—into yet more display, extending the act of stupefied gawking from machines and manufactures into the social realm. Dickens's response suggests that for him the Great Exhibition ultimately runs counter to the process article's cultivation of informed wonder and to his fascination with the souls of machines.[22] Benumbed by the spectacle, Dickens's lost Infant is primed to see social systems and human beings as nothing more than machines and products on display, a misperception that takes him close to Carlyle's vision of a mechanical age.

In *Bleak House*, written during this phase of Dickens's career but set a generation earlier, technological change counterpoints the insistent stasis exemplified by the Court of Chancery and the world of 'fashion'. From his family seat in Lincolnshire, Sir Leicester Dedlock regards modern Britain's 'Wat Tylerish' tendencies with trepidation and disdain (*BH* 48, 576). But he seems to intuit that it is not a fourteenth-century peasants' insurgency but nineteenth-century capitalism, industry, and social change that represent the real threats to his power and hereditary pride. These threats are unexpectedly personified in the form of Watt Rouncewell, namesake not of the English rebel but of the Scottish engineer, who arrives like a quiet irruption of his 'ironmaster' father's world of steam and invention, of production and reproduction, not to attack the old order but simply to press the claims of social mobility and romantic union (*BH* 28, 346). Yet the Britain of *Bleak House* is on the verge of other techno-cultural changes, as well. Just ahead lies the coming of the railways: 'Preparations are afoot, measurements are made, ground is staked out' from Lincolnshire to London, and Rouncewell Senior's factory is already busy manufacturing iron 'tanks ... boilers ... axles ... wheels ... cogs ... cranks ... [and] rails' (*BH* 55, 654; 63, 742). Journeying north to Rouncewell's factory on horseback, Mr George finds a landscape of 'coalpits and ashes, high chimneys and red bricks, blighted verdure, scorching fires, and a heavy never-lightening cloud of smoke' (*BH* 63, 741).

Even *Hard Times*, Dickens's explicit attack upon the values he saw crystallized in the worst tendencies of Victorian industrialism, confirms the complexity of his views

---

[21] Charles Dickens to the Hon. Mrs Richard Watson, 11 July 1851, *PLets* 6:427–9, 428–9.
[22] On Dickens and the Great Exhibition, see Robert Tracy, 'Lighthousekeeping: *Bleak House* and the Crystal Palace', *Dickens Studies Annual* 33 (2003): 25–53; Deborah Wynne, 'Responses to the 1851 Exhibition in *Household Words*', *Dickensian* 97 (2001): 228–34.

of factory production and technology. Connecting the bumptious industrial magnate Josiah Bounderby with the utilitarian Thomas Gradgrind, the novel aligns the capitalist's treatment of workers as mere labouring units with the educator's view of children as vessels for disjointed fact. The parallel between industrialism and a mechanical approach to education recalls Carlyle's critique of material and social machinery; indeed, Dickens dedicated *Hard Times* to Carlyle, privately assuring him that 'I know it contains nothing in which you do not think with me, for no man knows your books better than I'.[23] Yet for Dickens the problem is less the machines themselves than the more general need for a quickened moral imagination in the industrial world, for the kind of wonder and fellowship epitomized by Sleary's Circus.

Largely a setting for episodes and sub-plots in earlier novels, the industrial town in *Hard Times* now provides the 'key-note' of the story. The narration approaches Coketown with Dickens's customary sense of exoticism and fantasy, if in a mood more ominous than awestruck: the town's palette of 'red and black' resembles 'the painted face of a savage', while 'interminable serpents of smoke' trail from factory chimneys, and 'the piston of the steam-engine work[s] monotonously up and down, like the head of an elephant in a state of melancholy madness'.[24] Monotony provides the dominant motif of Coketown life, the feature that typifies the experience of space and time there:

> It contained several large streets all very like one another, and many small streets still more like one another, inhabited by people equally like one another, who all went in and out at the same hours, with the same sound upon the same pavements, to do the same work, and to whom every day was the same as yesterday and to-morrow, and every year the counterpart of the last and the next. (*HT* I:5, 23)

'Time' may run 'in Coketown like its own machinery; so much material wrought up, so much fuel consumed' (*HT* I:14, 77). Yet the assurance that the novel will pursue its 'tune' after presenting the keynote suggests how the plot will superimpose patterns of change and development over the monotony.

Hard Times carefully distinguishes its workers from the machines they operate:

> It is known, to the force of a single pound weight, what the engine will do; but, not all the calculators of the National Debt can tell me the capacity for good or evil, for love or hatred, for patriotism or discontent, for the decomposition of virtue into vice, or the reverse, at any single moment in the soul of one of these its quiet servants, with the composed faces and the regulated actions. (*HT* I:11, 61)

In fact, this assertion seems misleading insofar as it points to the patient, suffering, faithful workman Stephen Blackpool. Moreover, the repeated treatment of Coketown's

---

[23] Charles Dickens to Thomas Carlyle, 13 July 1854, *PLets* 7:367–8, 367.
[24] Charles Dickens, *Hard Times*, ed. Fred Kaplan, Norton Critical Edition, 4th edn (New York: Norton, 2017), I:5, 23. Subsequent references are inserted parenthetically in the text by *HT* Book:chapter, page.

steam engines as 'melancholy mad elephants' evokes not cold predictability but repressed emotion, the suffering souls in their mechanical bodies—a state similar to that of a human character such as Louisa Gradgrind as she stares out of the window at their fires.[25] Even beyond Dickens's usual animism, the treatment of industrial life in *Hard Times* might suggest the need for an imagination so alert that it can read the moral significance of objects, especially when it comes to creative and created artefacts so close to the human life-world.

Other novels draw machinery still closer to characters and characterization. *Little Dorrit* contrasts the art of governmental inertia with the innovations of the hard-working inventor Daniel Doyce. A 'politico-diplomatico hocus pocus piece of machinery', the Circumlocution Office extends the old patent system's barriers to innovation (described by Dickens in 'A Poor Man's Tale of a Patent') into a general obstructive 'science of government'.[26] *Little Dorrit* is vague about the precise nature of Doyce's mechanical creation, but it consistently describes the rent-collector Pancks as a 'little laboring steam-engine' (specifically, a 'steam-tug' boat) bustling around Bleeding Heart Yard (*LD* I:13, 141, 142). *A Tale of Two Cities*'s Jarvis Lorry professes to separate his warm feelings for the Manettes from his workaday function as the family banker when he tells Lucie Manette to regard him as 'a speaking machine', 'a mere machine' (*TTC* I:4, 25, 26).

The human connections and disconnections enabled by technology are the main focus of Dickens's haunting tale 'The Signal-Man', part of a collection of stories by various hands that is held together by the device of the railway ('Mugby Junction') and which appeared in the Christmas 1866 number of *All the Year Round*. The century's great transport and communication technologies promised (in the phrase of the day) to annihilate space and time. But, following out the subjective effects of speed, Dickens often associates railway travel in particular not with brisk efficiency but with the dreamy sense of becoming spatially and temporally unmoored: 'I am never sure of time or place upon a Railroad. I can't read, I can't think, I can't sleep—I can only dream.'[27] In this late story, the railway visions that accompany the loss of space and time become darker and ghostlier. As a railway signalman, the nameless title character links communication technology with transport, weightless information on electrical wires with careening masses of wood and metal propelled by blazing coal and steam. But he begins seeing ghostly visions, ambiguous signals of events out of time, which will ultimately implicate and doom him. The tale also draws upon the trauma of Dickens's own experience of the 1865 Staplehurst railway crash, from which he emerged badly shaken but able to help attend the wounded and the dying before climbing back into his carriage to retrieve his

---

[25] See Tamara Ketabgian, *The Lives of Machines: The Industrial Imaginary in Victorian Literature and Culture* (Ann Arbor: University of Michigan Press, 2011), 64–70.

[26] Charles Dickens, *Little Dorrit*, ed. Harvey Peter Sucksmith (Oxford: Clarendon, 1979), I:10, 100. Subsequent references are inserted parenthetically in the text by *LD* Book:chapter, page. See [Charles Dickens,] 'A Poor Man's Tale of a Patent', *Household Words*, 19 October 1850, 2:73–5, <http://www.djo.org.uk/household-words/volume-ii/page-73>.

[27] [Charles Dickens,] 'Railway Dreaming', *Household Words*, 10 May 1856, 13:385–8, 385, <http://www.djo.org.uk/household-words/volume-xiii/page-385.html>.

manuscript of the latest number of *Our Mutual Friend*.[28] Eerily enough, Dickens's own death would take place five years to the day after the Staplehurst disaster.

A few months before that uncanny final conjunction of life and technology, in a speech given in a great industrial town, Dickens publicly celebrated the accelerating march of invention, again contrasting it with the kind of cultural stasis—we might call it a deadlock—that he associated with China. Like Carlyle and Ruskin, Dickens turns once more to technology to write about the character of the nation and the age. But, speaking before a group dedicated to adult and industrial education, Dickens explicitly denies the putative opposition between material progress and moral or spiritual value:

> I confess ... that I do not understand this much-used and much-abused phrase, a 'material age' ... For instance: has electricity become more material in the mind of any sane, or moderately insane [*laughter*] man, woman, or child, because of the discovery that in the good providence of God it was made available for the service and use of man to an immeasurably greater extent than for his destruction? Do I make a more material journey to the bedside of my dying parents or my dying child, when I travel there at the rate of sixty miles an hour, than when I travel thither at the rate of six? ... What is the materiality of the cable or the wire, compared with the immateriality of the spark?[29]

Wonder, practical power, and moral meaning come together once again, as weightless electrical flows become part of everyday human dramas. Technological progress means the potential of the spark on the wire to help galvanize the tender deathbed scene.

Dickens's fascination with the strange mutual enmeshment of humanity and technology suggests the potential fruitfulness of contemporary approaches that view this topic from more radical stances: perspectives that centre on inanimate things themselves (as with thing theory); that examine the agency of non-human objects (actor-network theory); that unearth the layers of materiality and function in media objects, including obsolete, odd, or hypothetical ones (media archaeology); that analyse the ways in which technologies and human practices link up to establish enduring ways for a culture to encounter the world (cultural techniques).[30] In fact, even Dickens's electric 'spark' is at once sentimental and impersonal, metaphysical and quite physical, an intangible energy flow that also functions as an object in an enormous, human-made technological network.

---

[28] See Jill L. Matus, 'Trauma, Memory and Railway Disaster: The Dickensian Connection', *Victorian Studies* 43 (2001): 413–36.

[29] Charles Dickens, 'Birmingham and Midland Institute: Annual Inaugural Meeting: Birmingham, 27 September 1869', in *The Speeches of Charles Dickens*, ed. K. J. Fielding (Oxford: Clarendon Press, 1960), 397–408, 404.

[30] See Bill Brown, 'Thing Theory', in Bill Brown (ed.), *Things* (Chicago: University of Chicago Press, 2004), 1–21; Bruno Latour, *Aramis, or, The Love of Technology*, trans. Catherine Porter (Cambridge, MA: Harvard University Press, 1996); Jussi Parikka, *What Is Media Archaeology?* (Cambridge, and Malden, MA: Polity, 2012); Bernhard Siegert, *Cultural Techniques: Grids, Filters, Doors, and Other Articulations of the Real*, trans. Geoffrey Winthrop-Young (New York: Fordham University Press, 2015).

Further Reading

James Buzard, Joseph W. Childers, and Eileen Gillooly (eds), *Victorian Prism: Refractions of the Crystal Palace* (Charlottesville: University of Virginia Press, 2007)

Ian Carter, *Railways and Culture in Britain: The Epitome of Modernity* (Manchester: Manchester University Press, 2001)

Ruth Livesey, *Writing the Stage Coach Nation: Locality on the Move in Nineteenth-Century British Literature* (Oxford: Oxford University Press, 2016)

Richard Menke, *Telegraphic Realism: Victorian Fiction and Other Information Systems* (Stanford, CA: Stanford University Press, 2008)

Herbert L. Sussman, *Victorian Technology: Invention, Innovation, and the Rise of the Machine* (Santa Barbara, CA: Praeger, 2009)

CHAPTER 31

MATERIAL CULTURE

CLAIRE WOOD

CHARLES Dickens imagined a richly populated object world. His fiction, journalism, and non-fiction are crammed with all manner of stuff. There are memorable portrayals of the 'bran-new', indicating Dickens's interest in the plethora of consumer goods made available by industrial advances. Antiquarian, second-hand, and dilapidated objects also stimulated his imagination because they possess a history that may (or may not) be recovered. Descriptions of furniture, household goods, and clothing abound, usually burnished with some resonant detail. Elsewhere Dickens's affinity for the curious and incongruent is expressed in tableaux assembling miscellaneous objects, making pawnbrokers, second-hand stores, and lumber-rooms particular sources of delight. The impulse to order things is observable in the author's personal life, in addition to his art. Friends and family recalled Dickens's extraordinary sensitivity to his material environment and his exacting arrangement of objects within it. Mamie Dickens remembered her father inspecting each room of the house 'and if a chair was out of place... woe betide the offender'.[1] Eliza Lynn Linton claimed that in later life he 'did not stay even one night in an hotel without rearranging the chairs and tables of the sitting-room, and turning the bed'.[2] In his fiction Dickens satirized such tendencies in tyrannically fastidious housekeepers such as Mrs Mac Stinger, whose 'great cleaning days' compel her to 'move all the furniture into the back garden at early dawn, walk around the house in pattens all day, and move the furniture back again after dark'.[3] Yet he was also drawn to scenes of object disorder, in which things appear in chaotic juxtaposition or are put to unorthodox use. In *Bleak House* the Jellybys' topsy-turvy home contains such aberrations as a curtain 'fastened up with a fork' and 'a mug, with "A Present from Tunbridge Wells"

---

[1] Quoted in Rosemarie Bodenheimer, *Knowing Dickens* (Ithaca, NY: Cornell University Press, 2007), 152.
[2] Ibid., 154.
[3] Charles Dickens, *Dombey and Son*, ed. Alan Horsman (Oxford: Clarendon Press, 1974), 23, 319–20. Subsequent references are inserted parenthetically in the text by *DS* chapter, page.

on it, lighted up in the staircase window with a floating wick'.[4] Officially the narrative disapproves of these kludges: the episode criticizes Mrs Jellyby's misguided 'telescopic' philanthropy while neglecting matters (literally) closer to home. At the same time, Dickens is intrigued by such blatant object misuse, which can broaden the function and meaning of things in unexpected ways. Lyn Pykett suggests that 'Dickens is perhaps something of a special case in the extent of his fascination with things, and his ability to suggest the mystery, aura or magic of things, and the way in which they are haunted by history'.[5] Indeed, the nuanced thingfulness of Dickens's art has made his works central to studies of Victorian material culture.

The objects in Dickens's novels exist within a rhetorical hierarchy that invests certain material things with significance while others remain part of the *mise-en-scène*. The ring that Mr Grewgious presents to Edwin Drood exemplifies the former.[6] Originally belonging to the mother of Drood's fiancée, the ring enters the text with much ceremony after being removed from a secret drawer within a locked bureau. Before the box is opened and the object revealed, Grewgious describes the ring's appearance in loving detail and outlines its tragic history. Grewgious fancies a degree of agency in the 'almost cruel' brilliance of the stones, which sparkle defiantly in spite of the death of their mistress.[7] The ring is positioned as a secular relic, removed from the dead mother's hand, but is also poised to begin a new life as a love token that represents Edwin's commitment to Rosa (in fact an uncanny repetition that duplicates the father's gift, as Rosa is the double of her mother). The ring is thus an object endowed with financial and sentimental value; it is a repository of story; it serves to connect characters living and dead along romantic, platonic, and intergenerational lines; and one can speculate that it is likely to have played a significant role in the plot by helping to identify Drood's murderer. On the final occasion that the ring appears in this incomplete novel, it is imbued with even greater allegorical significance. After the couple amicably break off their engagement Edwin resolves to say nothing to Rosa of the 'sorrowful jewels'.

> They were but a sign of broken joys and baseless projects; in their very beauty they were (as the unlikeliest of men had said), almost a cruel satire on the loves, hopes, plans, of humanity, which are able to forecast nothing, and are so much brittle dust. Let them be. He would restore them to her guardian when he came down; he in turn would restore them to the cabinet from which he had unwillingly taken them; and there, like old letters or old vows, or other records of aspirations come to nothing,

---

[4] Charles Dickens, *Bleak House*, ed. George Ford and Sylvère Monod, Norton Critical Edition (New York: Norton, 1977), 4, 39; 4, 40.

[5] Lyn Pykett, 'The Material Turn in Victorian Studies', *Literature Compass* 1 (2003): 1–5, 1.

[6] As such, the ring offers an interesting counterpart to Maria K. Bachman's reading of the locket in *Oliver Twist* as an evocative object that 'links a heterogeneous assemblage of characters' and serves as a repository of 'hidden or obscured (or "unnarrated")' stories. 'Dickens's Evocative Objects: A Tale of Two Lockets', *Dickens Quarterly* 33, 1 (2016): 38–54, 42.

[7] Charles Dickens, *The Mystery of Edwin Drood*, ed. Margaret Cardwell (Oxford: Clarendon Press, 1972), 11, 97. Subsequent references are inserted parenthetically in the text by *ED* chapter, page.

they would be disregarded, until, being valuable, they were sold into circulation again, to repeat their former round. (*ED* 13, 118)

The ring is described as a 'sign' although the meaning that Drood attaches to it is highly subjective. This indicates not only that an object is capable of taking on different meanings in the course of its life cycle, or the progress of the plot, but that its meaning can depend upon who is looking at it. The ring is 'sorrowful' in different ways for Edwin and Grewgious, but both men extrapolate their sense of personal loss to make the jewels symbolic of the human condition. Dickens creates one final associative link by way of simile, connecting the ring to a very different type of material object. As inscribed items, 'old letters' are texts with a legible meaning (although this is, of course, open to interpretation), but can also function as objects (with tactile properties and sentimental associations). The fate imagined for both ring and letters reinforces the long lives of material things, their potential to circulate, and their fluctuating values, meanings, and significance.[8]

More commonly, objects appear within the descriptive set-pieces that give material texture to Dickens's writing. The author was renowned for the quantity and expressive quality of the things he described; in an otherwise mixed review Walter Bagehot praised Dickens's 'power of observation in detail' noting that 'there are pages containing telling minutiæ which other people would have thought enough for a volume'.[9] The presence of many of these objects reflects their prevalence in everyday life, creating an impression of realism, and suggesting something about the 'life that is lived among them'.[10] In the novel these objects are typically overlooked due to the focus on subjects, plots, and the types of objects (like the ring in *Edwin Drood*) that the narrative marks as significant—although Elaine Freedgood has made a persuasive case for 'taking them literally, materially, and then returning them to the novel with lost associations and possibilities restored'.[11] Even without this scrutiny of individual objects, the way in which the author delineates the material world—with irrepressible energy and attention to detail—rewards further investigation. At times Dickens's exuberant cataloguing halts the progress of the narrative and the objects take centre stage. For example, in *Dombey and Son*, the revelation that

---

[8] The passage reflects Dickens's discomfort with the publication of private letters. In his correspondence with R. J. Lane he remarked upon '[t]he extraordinary abuse of confidence in the posting about of private letters which I have of late years constantly observed', which led him to destroy letters from friends and make his own as short as possible. 'To R.J. Lane, 25 February 1864', *The Letters of Charles Dickens*, ed. Madeline House, Graham Storey, et al., Pilgrim/British Academy Edition, 12 vols (Oxford: Clarendon Press, 1965–2002). Subsequent citations: *PLets* followed by volume:page range, page. Here, 10:363.

[9] [Walter Bagehot,] 'Art. IX—Charles Dickens', *The National Review* 14 (1858): 458–86, 466.

[10] J. Hillis Miller, 'The Fiction of Realism: *Sketches by Boz, Oliver Twist*, and Cruikshank's Illustrations', in Ada Nisbet and Blake Nevius (eds), *Dickens Centennial Essays* (Berkeley: University of California Press, 1971), 94.

[11] Elaine Freedgood, 'Commodity Criticism and Victorian Thing Culture: The Case of Dickens', in Eileen Gillooly and Deirdre David (eds), *Contemporary Dickens* (Columbus: Ohio State University Press, 2009), 166.

Solomon Gills's creditors are 'in possession' of his property is forestalled by a lengthy description of the nearby broker's shop:

> There lived in those days, round the corner—in Bishopsgate Street Without—one Brogley, sworn broker and appraiser, who kept a shop where every description of second-hand furniture was exhibited in the most uncomfortable aspect, and under circumstances and in combinations the most completely foreign to its purpose. Dozens of chairs hooked on to washing-stands, which with difficulty poised themselves on the shoulders of sideboards, which in their turn stood upon the wrong side of dining-tables, gymnastic with their legs upward on the tops of other dining-tables, were among its most reasonable arrangements. A banquet array of dish-covers, wine-glasses, and decanters was generally to be seen, spread forth upon the bosom of a four-post bedstead, for the entertainment of such genial company as half a dozen pokers, and a hall lamp. A set of window curtains with no windows belonging to them, would be seen gracefully draping a barricade of chests of drawers, loaded with little jars from chemists' shops; while a homeless hearth rug severed from its natural companion the fireside, braved the shrewd east wind in its adversity, and trembled in melancholy accord with the shrill complainings of a cabinet piano, wasting away, a string a day, and faintly resounding to the noises of the street in its jangling and distracted brain. Of motionless clocks that never stirred a finger, and seemed as incapable of being successfully wound up, as the pecuniary affairs of their former owners, there was always great choice in Mr. Brogley's shop; and various looking-glasses accidentally placed at compound interest of reflection and refraction, presented to the eye an eternal perspective of bankruptcy and ruin. (*DS* 9, 115–16)

The passage illustrates several key features of Dickens's representation of material culture, including descriptive depth, listing, ubiquitous personification, and the blurring of subject and object. Detail is heaped upon detail creating a sense of inexhaustible plurality: dozens of chairs, dining-tables upon dining-tables, and a 'banquet array' of tableware are all reproduced ad infinitum by the parallel arrangement of mirrors. Personification, in the 'gymnastic' arrangement of the furniture and 'genial company' of pokers, makes these objects resident in what John Carey describes as 'the border country between people and things'.[12] References to different body parts—shoulders, legs, bosom, brain, fingers—liken this body of objects to a fragmented human body, 'severed' by the violence of seizure from the domestic space. J. Hillis Miller suggests that in *A Christmas Carol* personification serves to 'reinforce the idea that the inanimate world is not alien or other. It is similar to human beings, friendly to them, continuous with their life and in one way or another ready to serve them'.[13] There is a clear sense of sympathy between objects and subjects here too, particularly in the 'melancholy' trembling of the 'homeless hearth rug' and the clocks that seemed 'as incapable of being successfully wound up, as the pecuniary affairs of their former owners'. However, the narrator

---

[12] John Carey, *The Violent Effigy: A Study of Dickens' Imagination* (London: Faber and Faber, 1991), 101.
[13] J. Hillis Miller, 'The Genres of *A Christmas Carol*', *Dickensian* 89, 431 (Winter 1993): 193–206, 195.

also seems to imagine these objects invested with an independent life—the pokers and hall lamp keep their own company and the displaced window curtains appear to set the stage for a drama that we are not privy to.

The elasticity of subject–object categories in Dickens's work is well established. In the mid-twentieth century Dorothy van Ghent interpreted the author's persistent 'transposition of attributes' between people and things as a response to the dehumanizing processes of industrialism and imperial expansion.[14] For van Ghent there is a threatening quality to this blurring of categories, which imperils the human subject: 'in this universe objects actually usurp human essences; beginning as fetishes, they tend to—and sometimes quite literally do—devour and take over the powers of the fetish-worshiper'.[15] Developing this line of enquiry, Katherine Inglis has explored Dickens's 'automata anxiety', probing the sometimes 'violent relation between indistinct categories of things and people, where the human is vulnerable to mechanical impressions or is reducible to an organic machine'.[16] However, van Ghent's perception of a vampiric object world is only a partial reflection of the varying relationships between subjects and objects in Dickens's work. While likening people to things and things to people can serve to establish the dehumanizing effects of industrialism, as in *Hard Times*, it also does much more—particularly in the comic mode. For example, a richer sense of the affirmative and humorous possibilities underpins Herbert Sussman and Gerhard Joseph's discussion of prostheses in *Dombey and Son*, alongside acknowledgement of the anxiety about prosthetic parts acting independently and 'taking over control from the liberal subject or will'.[17]

In the closing decades of the twentieth century, the 'material turn' in criticism homed in on a particular type of object—the commodity—and explored the power of commodity culture to shape ideologies of gender, class, and nationhood. Drawing upon Marx's theory of commodity fetishism, and influenced by the ideas of Barthes, Baudrillard, and Benjamin among others, the movement was concerned with the commodity, the fetish, consumption, circulation, and spectacle. Thomas Richards locates the advent of the commodity in the second half of the nineteenth century, arguing that,

> in the short space of time between the Great Exhibition of 1851 and the First World War, the commodity became and has remained the one subject of mass culture, the centrepiece of everyday life, the focal point of all representation, the dead center of the modern world.[18]

---

[14] Dorothy van Ghent, *The English Novel: Form and Function* (New York: Rinehart and Company, 1953; repr. Harper Torchbook: 1961), 129.

[15] Ibid., 130–1.

[16] Katherine Inglis, 'Becoming Automatous: Automata in *The Old Curiosity Shop* and *Our Mutual Friend*', 19: *Interdisciplinary Studies in the Long Nineteenth Century* 6 (2008): 1–39. doi:10.16995/ntn.471.

[17] Herbert Sussman and Gerhard Joseph, 'Prefiguring the Posthuman: Dickens and Prosthesis', *Victorian Literature and Culture* 32, 2 (2004): 617–28, 623.

[18] Thomas Richards, *The Commodity Culture of Victorian England: Advertising and Spectacle 1851–1914* (Stanford, CA: Stanford University Press, 1990), 1.

Accordingly, Victorian literature has become an important source for understanding the impact that an emerging commodity culture had upon those who inhabited it. Dickens's works have proved fruitful in this regard for a number of reasons. Not only did he engage extensively with commodity culture, both in his fiction and journalism, but he was deeply ambivalent about its effects. He was interested in the labour and processes involved in manufacturing commodities, and ensured wide-ranging coverage of this topic in *Household Words*. His fiction and journalism are also marked by a fascination with the circulation of commodities, at a local level (via pawnshops, second-hand stores, and household clearances) and transnationally.[19] Furthermore, Dickens's celebrity and close relationship with the literary marketplace have enabled critics to turn from representations of commodity culture in his work to the text as commodity and his attitude towards authorship as a form of production.

Andrew H. Miller helped to establish the groundwork for subsequent literary studies of Victorian consumer culture by tracing the tensions produced in mid-Victorian novels by a 'penetrating anxiety' that 'their moral and social world was being reduced to a warehouse of goods and commodities, a display window in which people, their actions, and their convictions were exhibited for the economic appetites of others'.[20] For Miller, the extensive installation of plate-glass shop windows helped to transform social relationships and the relationship between people and goods.

> The display windows in this nation of shopkeepers thus served as emblems of an economic dynamic which was also and simultaneously libidinal (producing desire and disenchantment), epistemological (concerning the representation of falsehood and truth), and social (marking individual isolation and the possibilities of communal relations).[21]

These dynamics are evident in Dickens's portrayal of Tom Pinch's trip to Salisbury on market day. The scene highlights the contrast between the crowded noisy marketplace, representing an older form of commerce, and the relatively new delights of window shopping. As one of Dickens's wise fools Tom is a credulous observer and consumer, rather than a canny one. In the market, he 'regarded everything exposed for sale with great delight, and was particularly struck by the itinerant cutlery'.[22] After exhausting this scene, he decides to 'regale himself with the shop windows' (*MC* 5, 69). Four extended paragraphs follow. The jewellers' shops (pluralized to further suggest the abundance of

---

[19] Process articles, colonial commodities, and second-hand goods are among the topics explored in Catherine Waters's thoughtful study, *Commodity Culture in Dickens's Household Words: The Social Life of Goods* (Aldershot: Ashgate, 2008).

[20] Andrew H. Miller, *Novels Behind Glass: Commodity Culture and Victorian Narrative* (Cambridge: Cambridge University Press, 1995; repr. 2008), 6.

[21] Ibid., 5.

[22] Dickens, *Martin Chuzzlewit*, ed. Margaret Cardwell (Oxford: Clarendon Press, 1982), 5, 69. Subsequent references are inserted parenthetically in the text by *MC* chapter, page.

the spectacle) seem to have '*all* the treasures of the earth displayed therein' (*MC* 5, 70, my emphasis). Unworldly as he is, Tom is 'almost' compelled by a desire for ownership:

> when he saw one very bloated watch announced as a repeater, gifted with the uncommon power of striking every quarter of an hour inside the pocket of its happy owner, he almost wished that he was rich enough to buy it. (*MC* 5, 70)

Despite the watch's first appearing to be unattractively 'bloated', the middle clause works hard to enchant the commodity. The timepiece possesses an 'uncommon power' that alludes to its properties of novelty and innovation, as well as marking it out as a desirable rarity among the many 'large silver watches hanging up in every pane of glass' (*MC* 5, 70). The participle 'gifted' seems to credit the watch with the responsibility for its own special qualities (thus erasing the talent and labour of the watchmaker) and at the same time evokes a non-monetary form of exchange. The fantasy of possession is completed by conjuring the idea of the watch, in close contact with the body, striking every quarter. Tom is particularly captivated by the bookshops, which transport him back to childhood. The narrator describes 'a pleasant smell of paper freshly pressed ... awakening instant recollections of some new grammar had at school, long time ago, with "Master Pinch, Grove House Academy," inscribed in faultless writing on the fly-leaf!' (*MC* 5, 70). The potent olfactory dimensions of this experience connect Tom with an object possessed in the past and stimulate an acquisitive desire in the present. Gazing at a 'store of books ... whose matter he knew well', Tom 'would have given mines to have [them], in any form, upon the narrow shelf beside his bed at Mr Pecksniff's' (*MC* 5, 70). As Leah Price has shown, books are material objects as well as texts, possessing meaning and function independent of their contents.[23] Already familiar with the 'matter' of these volumes, Pinch is less interested in the knowledge they contain than their tangible possession. Although comically overstated by the narrator, the compulsion to purchase overwhelms any sense of proportion or reality. A book laid open in the window tempts 'unwary men to begin to read ... [it], and then, in the impossibility of turning over, to rush blindly in, and buy it!' (*MC* 5, 70). At the start of the passage the rows of books suggest happiness, but the inability to act upon fantasies of possession leads to disappointment. The narrator archly concludes '[w]hat a heart-breaking shop it was!' (*MC* 5, 70). In contrast to the market's noisy throng of people, window shopping is a solitary pursuit; the street is 'busy' but no human figures are described and there is no social interaction. Yet although the passage attends to the perils of window shopping it also celebrates its pleasures. The commodities on display, such as 'spick-and-span new works from London', connect the people of Salisbury to the wider world (*MC* 5, 70). Although some objects awaken an avaricious appetite, others produce a pleasurable nostalgia. In particular, Tom's reacquaintance with favourite childhood books suggests a different type of engagement with commodity culture, which is imaginative rather than

---

[23] See *How To Do Things with Books in Victorian Britain* (Princeton: Princeton University Press, 2012).

acquisitive. The *Arabian Nights* awakens such a rich train of associations that 'when he turned his face towards the busy street, a crowd of phantoms waited on his pleasure, and he lived again, with new delight, the happy days before the Pecksniff era' (*MC* 5, 71).[24] After this experience Tom has 'less interest' in the chemists' and tailors' shops that follow and considers the displays more dispassionately: the tailors' display of metropolitan waistcoat patterns, for example, 'looked amazing' but 'never appeared at all like the same thing anywhere else' (*MC* 5, 71). This episode shows Dickens's playful examination of the commodity's potential to create a different sort of relationship between subjects and objects. Consumer culture has its dangers, but so too does the marketplace. Significantly it is here that Tom makes a purchase and is duped by 'a pocket-knife with seven blades in it, and not a cut (as he afterwards found out) among them' (*MC* 5, 69).

Miller devotes a chapter of his study to *Our Mutual Friend*, noting within his broader argument that while 'entering imaginatively into the destructive energy of this volatile material world, Dickens also constructs imaginary enclaves from it'.[25] This is interpreted as part of a narrative strategy to resist commodification and although Miller concludes that such efforts are ultimately ineffectual, it registers the possibility that some objects, spaces, and situations may defy the logic of consumer culture. Recognition of the limits imposed by a strict Marxist view of the commodity produced a second wave of criticism, which considered the commodity potential of a broader range of objects and was influenced by Arjun Appadurai's view that the 'commodity phase' is a stage in the social life of a thing.[26] Catherine Waters meditates upon the way that second-hand purchase complicates the sense of what objects tell us about the people who possess them. Focusing on representations of second-hand clothing in *Household Words*, she highlights the way in which these goods disrupt 'the production-to-consumption commodity chain', because they are worn, resold, and worn again.[27] Second-hand clothes are thus a 'paradoxical commodity', retaining the imprint of former owners and possessing the ability to 'undergo multiple stages in their biographical journey'.[28] David Trotter also explores the potential of objects to return to the marketplace, tracing the conversion of household possessions into commodities, and thence into waste-matter, in literary representations of household clearances. Trotter demonstrates the 'pervasiveness and the intrinsic interest of the scene or trope of household clearance' in the work of a

---

[24] Compare the scene from stave two of *A Christmas Carol* when Scrooge observes his younger self reading and suddenly finds 'a man, in foreign garments: wonderfully real and distinct to look at' outside the window. Reconnecting with childhood pleasures aids Scrooge's moral rejuvenation and helps to correct his damaging preoccupation with business. *A Christmas Carol and Other Christmas Books*, ed. Robert Douglas-Fairhurst, Oxford World's Classics (Oxford: Oxford University Press, 2006), 31.

[25] *Novels Behind Glass*, 120–1.

[26] Arjun Appadurai, 'Introduction: Commodities and the Politics of Value', in Arjun Appadurai (ed.), *The Social Life of Things: Commodities in Cultural Perspective* (Cambridge: Cambridge University Press, 1988), 13.

[27] Waters, *Commodity Culture in Dickens's* Household Words, 144.

[28] Ibid., 156.

range of canonical Victorian authors.[29] Although Trotter takes only one example from Dickens—the Satis House auction in chapter 63 of *Great Expectations*—it is worth noting the frequency with which this motif occurs, suggesting Dickens's sense of the inherent instability of property.[30] This is comically expressed in the deeper truth of Augustus Moddle's absurdly dramatic farewell note in *Martin Chuzzlewit*. 'Everything appears to be somebody else's', he concludes. 'Nothing in the world is mine' (*MC* 54, 828).[31] While John Plotz only makes brief reference to Dickens in his study of 'portable property', his sense that 'certain belongings seem dually endowed ... [—] at once products of a cash market and, potentially, the rare fruits of a highly sentimentalized realm of value both domestic and spiritual'—resonates with the multiple values and meanings that objects often hold in Dickens's work.[32] Plotz uses the example of Wemmick's silver mourning rings, noting their status as saleable property, 'portable reliquary', and 'form of domestic retreat' that 'let him recollect, at a touch, the perversely comforting narratives that somehow sustain him'.[33] Attention to the affective and sentimental qualities of items, a more nuanced and often more affirmative sense of the relationship between people and their possessions, and the idea of the object as a repository of story emerged as central themes in thing theory.

Thing theory initially defined itself in sharp contrast to commodity criticism, although as Plotz demonstrates, subsequent critics have produced stimulating work that draws upon the strongest aspects of both traditions.[34] In his seminal study *A Sense of Things* Bill Brown suggested the need for 'a comparably new idiom, beginning with the effort to think with or through the physical object world, the effort to establish a genuine sense of things that comprise the stage on which human action, including the action of thought, unfolds'.[35] Brown advocated an approach that would allow for richer investigation of subject–object relations in literature, and greater attention to the complexities of 'why and how we use objects to make meaning, to make or re-make ourselves, to

---

[29] David Trotter, 'Household Clearances in Victorian Fiction', *19: Interdisciplinary Studies in the Long Nineteenth Century* 6 (2008): 1–19, 17. doi:10.16995/ntn.472.

[30] For example, Dickens portrays the household auction that follows Mr Dombey's bankruptcy with grim delight in chapter 59 of *Dombey and Son* (and the Midshipman narrowly avoids this fate in chapter 9); the Jellyby household is similarly broken up in chapter 30 of *Bleak House*. Given his fictional treatment of the subject, it is intriguing that there was a public sale of Dickens's own domestic belongings after his death. Juliet John offers an account of the auction and its implications in *Dickens and Mass Culture* (Oxford: Oxford University Press, 2010), 246–9.

[31] Moddle refers primarily to his disappointment in love, but the novel shows the statement's relevance to articles of property. When asked by his fiancée to request the price of goods at an Upholstery and Furniture Warehouse, Moddle mournfully suggests 'Perhaps they are ordered already ... Perhaps they are Another's' (*MC* 46, 695).

[32] John Plotz, *Portable Property: Victorian Culture on the Move* (Princeton: Princeton University Press, 2008), 2.

[33] Ibid., xv.

[34] My own study, exploring the ambivalence associated with the commodification of death in Dickens's work, followed this line. *Dickens and the Business of Death* (Cambridge: Cambridge University Press, 2015).

[35] Bill Brown, *A Sense of Things* (Chicago: University of Chicago Press, 2003), 3.

organise our anxieties and affections, to sublimate our fears and shape our fantasies'.[36] Elaine Freedgood's *The Ideas in Things* is another foundational text which explores the 'thing culture' that preceded commodity culture and survived alongside it. Freedgood's approach involves reading objects as a 'collector' rather than an 'allegorist' (in Benjamin's terms), by performing strong metonymic readings that uncover 'the historically and theoretically overdetermined material characteristics of objects ... beyond the immediate context in which they appear' and then returning these objects to the novel with 'a radiance or resonance of meaning they have not possessed or have not legitimately possessed in previous literary-critical reading'.[37]

Thing theory gave fresh impetus to the study of Victorian objects, leading to the recovery of numerous object histories and some fascinating work upon the tactile, bodily, and affective dimensions of material culture.[38] Crucial to the continued vibrancy of the field have been interventions that problematize aspects of thing theory and seek to expand its scope. For example, Clare Pettitt's nuanced reading of Peggotty's workbox in *David Copperfield* explores the potential cultural-social-historical meanings of this object, but also considers the 'importance of time and use when it comes to establishing the meaning of things'.[39] Pettitt emphasizes the need to return meaning to objects in texts with reference to their 'history of consumption and use rather than that of production' and to reinsert such information proportionately, because 'some kinds of description carry more value than other kinds'.[40] Juliet John has furthered this call, arguing for 'more sensitivity to aesthetic texture in our consideration of how literature represents things' while maintaining that 'in Dickens's case, meaning, value and proportion depend upon hierarchical modes of differentiation'.[41] Mindful of Pettitt and John's injunctions to be selective and proportionate in readings of things, I turn in closing to three persistent objects that suggest further possibilities for interpreting the relationship between people and things in Dickens's work.

My first object study examines a talking chair that features prominently in one of the nine interpolated tales in *The Pickwick Papers*. 'The Bagman's Story' relates the tale of Tom Smart's life-changing encounter with a piece of furniture. After several tumblers of hot punch, Tom retires to his bedroom in an old inn and is struck by a 'strange, grim-looking, high-backed chair, carved in the most fantastic manner'.[42] This 'strange

---

[36] Ibid., 4.

[37] Elaine Freedgood, *The Ideas in Things: Fugitive Meaning in the Victorian Novel* (Chicago: University of Chicago Press, 2006), 5–6.

[38] On tactile relationships between subjects and objects see the special journal edition, 'The Victorian Tactile Imagination', *19: Interdisciplinary Studies in the Long Nineteenth Century* 19 (2014). <http://www.19.bbk.ac.uk/87/volume/0/issue/19/> (accessed 24 April 2017)

[39] Clare Pettitt, 'Peggotty's Work-Box: Victorian Souvenirs and Material Memory', *Romanticism and Victorianism on the Net* 53 (2009). doi:10.7202/029896ar.

[40] Ibid.

[41] Juliet John, 'Things, Words and the Meanings of Art', in Juliet John (ed.), *Dickens and Modernity* (Cambridge: D. S. Brewer, 2012), 117.

[42] Dickens, *The Pickwick Papers*, ed. James Kinsley (Oxford: Clarendon Press, 1986), 14, 205. Subsequent references are inserted parenthetically in the text by *PP* chapter, page.

old thing' commands his attention: Tom 'stared at the old chair for half an hour' and 'couldn't take his eyes off it', even when 'slowly undressing himself' (*PP* 14, 205). The chair invades his imagination; when he tries to sleep 'nothing but queer chairs danced before his eyes', and when he looks again the chair undergoes an 'extraordinary change'.

> The carving of the back gradually assumed the lineaments and expression of an old, shrivelled human face; the damask cushion became an antique, flapped waistcoat; the round knobs grew into a couple of feet, encased in red cloth slippers, and the whole chair looked like a very ugly old man, of the previous century, with his arms a-kimbo. No. The chair was an ugly old gentleman; and what was more, he was winking at Tom Smart. (*PP* 14, 205–6)

As Tom watches the antique is transformed from object to subject. The text insists, oxymoronically, that the chair is not *like* a very ugly old man, but '*was* an ugly old man', although readers are left to settle the chair's ontological status for themselves ('said the chair; or the old gentleman, whichever you like to call him' (*PP* 14, 206)). After a lively conversation, replete with furniture puns, Tom and the gentleman-chair make a self-interested pact: to avoid being sold the latter draws upon a seemingly supernatural knowledge of happenings at the inn so that Tom can marry the widowed landlady. The chair lapses into its previous state, Tom enacts the plan, and the story ends abruptly with the conclusion that 'he gave up business many years afterwards, and went to France with his wife; and then the old house was pulled down' (*PP* 14, 213).

This is a light-hearted tale, which does not take itself too seriously. In terms of Dickens's engagement with material culture, however, this talking chair is peculiarly suggestive. It indicates the author's interest in long-lived things and the stories that they might be able to tell. In this case, whether through magical transformation or Tom's drunken fancy, the chair has the opportunity to provide a first-hand account of his acquaintance with two generations of the landlady's family and offers a brief history of his own family of twelve 'fine straight-backed, handsome fellows' (*PP* 14, 208). In this respect, the tale draws upon the tradition of 'it-narrative', a genre of fiction that explores the autobiographies of things, popular in the eighteenth century and persisting into the nineteenth, although object narrators do not converse directly with human subjects as the gentleman-chair does. Freedgood has noted the curious power dynamics associated with these speaking objects, observing that 'they are owned, but they might be said to "own" certain aspects of their possessors ... the commodity exerts a certain ownership in that it "holds" the stories of so many of its owners in reserve; it is a universal heirloom, a keepsake that keeps its owners rather than being kept by them.'[43] The gentleman-chair has this quality, hinting at the family secrets he has access to and boasting of the landlady's grandmother's attachment to him. The prospect of perceiving, sentient objects is comic, but also unnerving. Dickens suggests the potential discomfort

---

[43] Elaine Freedgood, 'What Objects Know: Circulation, Omniscience and the Comedy of Dispossession in Victorian It-Narratives', *Journal of Victorian Culture* 15, 1 (2010): 83–100, 84.

of both parties in replaying a version of this scene in the main narrative, when Mr Pickwick finds himself in the wrong bedroom and observes an unconscious 'middle-aged lady in yellow curl-papers, busily engaged in brushing what ladies call their "back hair"' (*PP* 22, 339).[44] The gentleman-chair lacks Pickwick's delicacy and, in sharing what he has seen, highlights the unwitting intimacy between subjects and objects in the course of everyday use. He gloats that 'hundreds of fine women have sat in my lap for hours together' and implies that he has been privy to numerous other intimacies and indiscretions, responding to Tom's enquiry with 'a very complicated wink' (*PP* 14, 207; 208).

Trotter highlights the importance of genre in considering literary representations of material culture; *Pickwick*'s interpolated tales, with their fairy-tale and Gothic influences, prompt reflection on how objects might behave outside the realist novel.[45] In fairy tales, mundane objects take on special properties and powers. In this case subject–object interaction is enriched by the process of magical transformation, which allows an object to possess the thoughts and feelings associated with subjecthood. During the encounter the gentleman-chair portrays a range of emotions veering from anger to melancholy and the balance of power between Tom and the chair shifts backwards and forwards. The alternative, as Tom's enemies speculate, is that 'Tom invented it altogether' or 'was drunk, and fancied it' (*PP* 14, 213). In this version of events, Tom becomes an avatar for the author, capable of starting objects into life through the power of imagination.

Two bottles of Madeira wine that feature prominently in *Dombey and Son* serve as my second object study. As a long-lived consumable, hoarded for special occasions, the wine illustrates a different aspect of Dickens's engagement with material culture. The first bottle enters the novel with solemn ceremony when Solomon Gills descends to a small cellar and recovers 'a very ancient-looking bottle, covered with dust and dirt' to toast his nephew's start at the Firm of Dombey and Son (*DS* 4, 40). The remaining bottle gestures towards a kind of narrative fulfilment, to be saved until Walter has 'come to good fortune' and 'when the start in life you have made to-day shall have brought you ... to a smooth part of the course you have to run' (*DS* 4, 40). This bottle does not come to light until the final chapter, although Captain Cuttle suggests opening it on the occasion of Walter's departure for Barbados in chapter 19 and to celebrate Florence and Walter's marriage in chapter 57. Yet Sol has the foresight to wait, meaning that when the Madeira is finally uncorked it can be shared in communion with a reformed Mr Dombey. In keeping with the novel's themes of time and timeliness, the old wine is like Sol's investments: 'instead of being behind the time ... he was, in truth, a little before it, and had to wait the fulness of the time and the design' (*DS* 62, 830). Beyond its role in punctuating the plot, the manufacture and transportation of Madeira suggestively parallel the process of character development. The wine was deliberately shipped via

---

[44] Phiz's accompanying illustration, 'The Middle-Aged Lady in the Double-Bedded Room', portrays Pickwick peeping through the bed-curtains so that he appears, like the queer chair, to be a piece of furniture with a human face.

[45] Trotter, 'Household Clearances in Victorian Fiction', 6.

circuitous routes as the agitation of rough seas helped to improve the flavour, just as Dombey is mellowed by his troubles.[46] At the close of the narrative he is white-haired and marked by 'care and suffering', 'but they are traces of a storm that has passed on for ever' (*DS* 62, 829).

Within the novel, the distance that this transnational commodity has travelled and the dangers it has passed through impart a relish to its consumption. 'Think of this wine', Sol enjoins his nephew, 'which has been to the East Indies and back, I'm not able to say how often, and has been once round the world. Think of the pitch-dark nights, the roaring winds, and rolling seas' (*DS* 4, 42). Like many 'spoils of international trade', which Waters suggests reside 'without elaboration, without explanation of the way in which empire underwrites the domestic world of the novel', the more vexed associations of Madeira wine are suppressed.[47] David Hancock notes that 'the rise of the Madeira wine trade roughly parallels the rise of the British and French slave trade' while Freedgood argues that 'some of the cost of the millions of African people who died in the same passage is literally, symbolically, and horrifically recuperated by the extraordinary profits made on this peripatetic aperitif'.[48] However, in the shipwreck tales that Sol and Walter recount as they imbibe, Madeira is distanced from this context and associated with British national identity (albeit with an ironic inflection). The wreck of the *Charming Sally* occurs in the Baltic Sea—a trade route that was significant, but involved relatively small quantities of Madeira.[49] The crew attempts to stave the 500 casks on board, but 'got drunk and died drunk, singing "Rule Britannia," when she settled and went down, and ending with one awful scream in chorus' (*DS* 4, 43).

While foreign consumables are sometimes treated with suspicion in Dickens's work, Madeira functions slightly differently.[50] Indeed, the second bottle casts a beatific light over the closing scenes of *Dombey*, imparting its 'lustre' to those who consume it, so that Captain Cuttle is depicted with 'a very halo of delight round his glowing forehead' (*DS* 62, 828; 829). As a long-lived consumable, Madeira could be kept for several generations, making it easier to naturalize. Asa Briggs notes that Victorian wills refer to 'the disposition of wines and spirits' more frequently than books, suggesting the importance and value (financial and otherwise) placed upon wine.[51] In contrast to other inherited items, such as watches, jewellery, and furniture, wine can only be enjoyed once; the pleasure of drinking it is short-lived in comparison with the length of storage, but if saved too

---

[46] David Hancock, 'Commerce and Conversation in the Eighteenth-Century Atlantic: The Invention of Madeira Wine', *Journal of Interdisciplinary History* 29, 2 (1998): 197–219, 212.

[47] Waters, *Commodity Culture in Dickens's* Household Words, 101, 102.

[48] David Hancock, *Oceans of Wine: Madeira and the Emergence of American Trade and Taste* (New Haven: Yale University Press, 2009), 11; Freedgood, *Ideas in Things*, 50.

[49] Hancock, *Oceans of Wine*, 132.

[50] For example, Grace Moore suggests that Dickens's representation of Rosa, devouring 'lumps-of-delight' in *Drood*, 'points to a subtle threat posed to womanhood by this foreign confectionary', which threatens 'to overrun English values'. 'Turkish Robbers, Lumps of Delight, and the Detritus of Empire: The East Revisited in Dickens's Late Novels', *Critical Survey* 21, 1 (2009): 74–87, 84.

[51] Asa Briggs, *Victorian Things* (London: Penguin, 1990), 40.

long it will spoil. Dickens explores this tension between preservation and consumption elsewhere. *Master Humphrey's Clock* contains a story in which the Guildhall statues of Giants Gog and Magog come to life, the latter moved to laughter by an 'ancient cask' of wine.[52]

> 'To think,' replied the Giant Magog, laying his hand upon the cask, 'of him who owned this wine, and kept it in a cellar hoarded from the light of day, for thirty years,—"till it should be fit to drink," quoth he. He was twoscore and ten years old when he buried it beneath his house, and yet never thought that he might be scarcely "fit to drink" when the wine became so. I wonder it never occurred to him to make himself unfit to be eaten. There is very little of him left by this time.' (*MHC* 1, 19)

The joke, it appears, is on the mortal subject whose lifespan is inferior to that of the wine and the immortal giants who now enjoy it. In contrast to the man's decay, the wine improves when it is 'buried'. Although the queasy comparison between the two invites pause, the discomfort prompted by the wine is existential, rather than related to its origins or composition.

My final object study is drawn from Dickens's life rather than his fiction, although it was incorporated into his life story by Forster. As a real object, instead of an imagined one represented in a literary text, it has a different affective resonance.[53] This example also builds upon Isobel Armstrong's attempts to move beyond the subject–object binary in arguing, with reference to Hannah Arendt's table, for 'the thing as third term, mediating bodies, not preying on them'.[54] In March 1870 Dickens wrote to George Holme to decline the £500 cheque that he enclosed as an expression of gratitude, crediting the influence of Dickens's works with his success in life. Yet deeply moved he proposed an alternative gift in the form of a meaningful material object:

> I have been much affected by what you tell me of the influence of my books upon your life and character. I shall not endeavour to express how deeply I feel such communication at any time, or what an inestimable reward it is to an earnest worker.
>
> This brings me to your generous proposal; which separates you from all my other readers and correspondents.
>
> I do not want money. If I did, I would take it, so offered. Emphatically, I do not. But I should deem it a most precious heirloom, if you would give me something for my dining table or sideboards, which would bear upon it the record that it was presented by one who had been cheered and stimulated by my writings, and who held them

---

[52] Charles Dickens, *Master Humphrey's Clock and A Child's History of England*, introd. Derek Hudson, New Oxford Illustrated Dickens (London: Oxford University Press, 1958), 1, 18. Subsequent references are inserted parenthetically in the text by *MHC* chapter, page.

[53] Pettitt reflects upon the differences between objects in Dickens's life and fiction in 'On Stuff', 19: *Interdisciplinary Studies in the Long Nineteenth Century* 6 (2008): 1–12. doi:10.16995/ntn.474.

[54] Isobel Armstrong, 'Bodily Things and Thingly Bodies: Circumventing the Subject–Object Binary', in Katharina Boehm (ed.), *Bodies and Things in Nineteenth-Century Literature and Culture* (Houndmills,: Palgrave Macmillan, 2012), 24.

among his first remembrances when he became prosperous. No gift could be more acceptable to me; and I should live in it at my usefullest and best, not only among my children, but among their childrens' children, generations hence. I should regard it as my most valuable acquisition in life, and should be correspondingly proud of it.[55]

The passage explores different kinds of value. The money offered, redundant due to Dickens's own prosperity, is eclipsed by the 'inestimable reward' of Holme's testimony. A piece of tableware that records this provenance would make it 'my most valuable acquisition in life' because it is invested with emotional value, regardless of its monetary worth. Indeed, Dickens suggests that such a gift would be entirely removed from systems of economic exchange by becoming 'a most precious heirloom', to be cherished 'generations hence'. Although in his will he rejected commemoration in material form, requesting 'friends on no account to make me the subject of any monument, memorial, or testimonial whatever', Dickens positions this gift as a family memorial.[56] 'I should live in it at my usefullest and best,' he suggests, enchanting the object with his enduring presence in an imaginative reversal of the object–subject transformation of the queer chair. 'The memorial soon came,' Forster notes, in his retelling of this story.

A richly worked basket of silver, inscribed 'from one who has been cheered and stimulated by Mr. Dickens's writings, and held the author among his first remembrances when he became prosperous', was accompanied by an extremely handsome silver centrepiece for the table, of which the design was for [sic] figures representing the Seasons. But the kindly donor shrank from sending Winter to one whom he would fain connect with none save the brighter and milder days, and he had struck the fourth figure from the design. 'I never look at it,' said Dickens, 'that I don't think most of the Winter.' The gift had yet too surely foreshadowed that truth, for the winter was never to come to him.[57]

Two material gifts build a relationship between Dickens and Holme, taking an appropriately communal and convivial form. However, like imagined objects, real things have the capacity to bear multiple meanings and remain open to interpretation. Holme uses the gifts to make his own meaning, absenting winter from the design. But this absence haunted the receiver and, in a deft flourish by Forster, becomes a piece of narrative foreshadowing that pre-empts Dickens's death two months later.

In different ways, these object case studies indicate Dickens's interest in the persistence of material culture over time. The first invites further reflection on things that reside outside the parameters of the realist novel. The second explores the resonances of a commodity that is both long-lived and consumable. The third considers two gifts that were personally significant to Dickens and which he conceived of as heirloom and memorial. Uniting all three objects is their potential to tell or inspire stories. The gentleman-chair

---

[55] 'To George Holme, 14 March 1870', PLets 12: 491–2, 491.
[56] John Forster, *The Life of Charles Dickens*, ed. J. W. T. Ley (London: Cecil Palmer, 1928), 859.
[57] Forster, *Life*, 850.

is a storyteller in his own right, and appears within the storytelling context of an interpolated tale in *Pickwick*. The Madeira inspires a shipwreck tale that juxtaposes the resilience of the commodity with the fragility of human life. Finally, in Dickens's letter to Holmes, we see an object in the process of being storied, this time with the explicit intention of outliving its owner. This reflects Dickens's distinctive way of looking at the material world and ability to start objects into life. Self-consciously referring to his method in 'The Parlour Orator' from *Sketches by Boz*, the writer notes that,

> If we had followed the established precedent in all such instances, we should have fallen into a fit of musing, without delay. The ancient appearance of the room—the old panelling of the wall—the chimney blackened with smoke and age—would have carried us back a hundred years at least, and we should have gone dreaming on, until the pewter-pot on the table, or the little beer chiller on the fire, had started into life, and addressed to us a long story of days gone by. But, by some means or other, we were not in a romantic humour; and although we tried very hard to invest the furniture with vitality, it remained perfectly unmoved, obstinate, and sullen.[58]

While acknowledging the sometimes effortful process of animating the inanimate, Dickens styles himself as conversant with the object world and receptive to the stories it might have to tell.

Further Reading

Holly Furneaux, 'Dickens, Sexuality, and the Body; Or, Clock Loving: Master Humphrey's Queer Objects of Desire', in Juliet John (ed.), *Dickens and Modernity* (Cambridge: D. S. Brewer, 2012), 41–60

Jonathon Shears and Jen Harrison (eds), *Literary Bric-à-Brac and the Victorians: From Commodities to Oddities* (Farnham: Ashgate, 2013)

---

[58] Charles Dickens, 'The Parlour Orator', in Michael Slater and John Drew (eds), *The Dent Uniform Edition of Dickens' Journalism*, 4 vols (London: J. M. Dent, Columbus: Ohio State University Press, 1993–2000), 1: 234–5.

CHAPTER 32

DICKENS AND AFFECT

WENDY PARKINS

A novel, according to James Fitzjames Stephen writing in *The Cornhill* in 1864, is

> an appeal to feelings, and to feelings for their own sake. A novelist never lays down a proposition properly limited and supported. He confines himself to drawing pictures, which act powerfully, but always more or less indistinctly and indirectly, upon the feelings.[1]

Such a powerful vehicle for feelings provided Stephen with a prime example of the dangerous dominance of 'sentimentalism'—the title of his article and a growing concern at this time.[2] Nevertheless, Stephen's denomination of 'sentimentalism' vis-à-vis the novel is at first glance a little misleading. By 1864, sensation fiction had emerged as a striking literary phenomenon and sentimental fiction—with its origins in the eighteenth century—was past its prime, but the capacity of the novel to incorporate conventions of earlier genres was nothing if not capacious and a realist novel of the mid-nineteenth century may well include sentimental elements, as well as, say, aspects of melodrama or satire.[3] Sentimentality in general, however, was of course highly visible across Victorian culture and remains a defining feature of the era in popular memory. As Nicola Bown puts it, 'Its cast of pathetic children, fallen women, faithful animals, lachrymose deathbeds, ... angelic mothers and innocents betrayed—to name only the most obvious topoi of literary and visual sentimentality—is familiar to the point of parody.'[4]

---

[1] James Fitzjames Stephen, 'Sentimentalism', *The Cornhill* 10 (1864): 75.
[2] See Carolyn Burdett, 'New Agenda: Sentimentalities: An Introduction', *Journal of Victorian Culture* 16, 2 (2011): 188.
[3] On the legacies of sentimental fiction in the nineteenth century, see, for example, Valerie Purton, *Dickens and the Sentimental Tradition: Fielding, Richardson, Sterne, Goldsmith, Sheridan, Lamb* (London: Anthem Press, 2012).
[4] Nicola Bown, 'Introduction: Crying over Little Nell', *19: Interdisciplinary Studies in the Long Nineteenth Century* 4 (2007): 1.

Indeed, what primarily concerned Stephen was that 'In almost every subject, in literature, in politics, in religion ... there is abundant evidence that great and increasing weight is attributed to the sentimental view of things', whereby 'tender feelings' are 'indulged in excess' and 'exercise considerably more influence over the conduct of mankind than is desirable'.[5] It was in this context, then, that Stephen turned his attention to 'the influence that novels exercise, not in their proper and natural sphere as amusements and works of art, but as irregular and informal arguments'.[6] (Novels, like Victorian men and women it seems, had a 'proper and natural sphere'.) As Stephen saw it, the problem with the novel's appeal to 'feelings for their own sake' was that, at the same time, the contemporary novel also sought to articulate 'propositions'—distinct political or social views—and such propositions could not be kept separate from the excessive feelings that overflowed promiscuously into areas that should be dealt with rationally and logically. Novels, Stephen continued, 'associate a strong feeling of disgust, or sympathy, or pity, with a particular class of facts; and they suggest to idle readers, or to any reader in an idle mood, conclusions which they do not really prove'.[7]

There is much that is familiar in such criticism of novels and novel readers in the nineteenth century: novels manipulate emotions and attract a certain type of reader—or a certain way of reading[8]—characterized by idleness, where readers may fail to engage their critical faculties and instead read passively or unreflectively, hence becoming easy prey for the manipulation of their feelings (and opinions) by the novelist. 'This explains what is the sting of the imputation of being a sentimental writer', continues Stephen:

> It implies that a man tries to gain his ends not by legitimate means, but by appeals to the passions, by trying to dissuade people from doing what is disagreeable merely because it is disagreeable, and not because it has a general tendency to produce a balance of pain over pleasure, or, in other words, because it is wrong ... A sentimental book is like a cooked account. Its object generally is to make things pleasant, and, as such, it shows that the person who states it, is either weak, ignorant, or fraudulent.[9]

Stephen's assumption that strong feelings make bad (moral/political) arguments, leading readers to draw false conclusions or form erroneous opinions on important issues, provides a provocative starting point for a chapter which considers the significance of affect in the work of Dickens. Looking at examples ranging from his early *Sketches of Young Couples* through to late fiction such as *Our Mutual Friend*, this chapter will consider whether, for Dickens, strong feelings make bad arguments. Emotions frequently have an ethical dimension in Dickens's writing, and the chapter will propose that it may be illuminating to bring a particular understanding of ethics as a matter of

---

[5] Stephen, 'Sentimentalism', 74.
[6] Ibid.
[7] Ibid., 75.
[8] See, for example, Rachel Ablow (ed.), *The Feeling of Reading: Affective Experience and Victorian Literature* (Ann Arbor: University of Michigan Press, 2010).
[9] Stephen, 'Sentimentalism', 76.

'response-ability' (that is, our ability, indeed our obligation, to respond to the needs and rights of others) to the question of how Dickens deploys feelings—whether emotion, affect, sensation, or mood.

There is almost a kind of Levinasian understanding of ethical obligation *avant la lettre* expressed in the work of Dickens. In his extensive writings on ethics, the twentieth-century French philosopher Emmanuel Levinas talked about the 'face' of the 'Other' who summons me to respond, makes an ethical demand on me which places me under an obligation. It is in the literally confronting presence of the Other—whom Levinas also refers to as 'the poor and destitute one'[10]—that our ethical responsibility is, as it were, brought home to us. An ethical impulse, understood as a 'summons to respond' to the Other, may ultimately motivate a politically framed course of action, but it is the recognition of the legitimate claim of the Other that precedes all other obligations or actions arising from this recognition and therefore is best represented in the face-to-face encounter with the impoverished Other, an encounter which occurs repeatedly throughout the work of Dickens and is typically depicted in a highly affective mode.

As John Jordan—similarly drawing on Levinasian ideas—has argued with respect to the character of Jo in *Bleak House*, 'Jo is the figure of absolute alterity to whom we must grant unconditional hospitality if we are to affirm our own humanity.'[11] But it is not only in the later works of Dickens that we see the dramatization of an ethical impulse in this way. In early works such as *Oliver Twist* or *A Christmas Carol*, Dickens foregrounded emotions like pity or compassion to foster a greater awareness of the suffering of others and thus disrupt the reader's self-absorption and provoke an ameliorative response (whether philanthropic, legislative, or merely at the level of everyday behaviour). In a similar—albeit lighter—vein, this chapter will argue that *Sketches of Young Couples*, a little-examined early work of Dickens, is also concerned with the ethical dimension of emotions, particularly the tension between private and public feelings.[12] The chapter will then turn to one of the best-known tropes of Dickensian emotion and affect—the death of the child—to consider whether such incidents are merely opportunities for sentimental indulgence or, again, articulate an ethical imperative of our responsibility for the most vulnerable members of society, taking Little Nell as my primary example. Finally, this essay will look briefly at *Our Mutual Friend* to consider how moods or affects are transmitted between characters and suggest what this may imply about our ethical agency in relation to affect.

In adopting a (roughly) chronological approach, however, there is no intention to suggest that there is a clear and singular line of development in Dickens's work—from emotion to affect, say—or that his mobilization of affect is always and only concerned

---

[10] Emmanuel Levinas, 'Transcendence and Height (1962)', in *Emmanuel Levinas: Basic Philosophical Writings*, ed. Adriaan T. Peperzak, Simon Critchley, and Robert Bernasconi (Bloomington: Indiana University Press, 1996), 18.

[11] John O. Jordan, *Supposing 'Bleak House'* (Charlottesville: University of Virginia Press, 2010), 139.

[12] See Wendy Parkins, 'Emotions, Ethics and Sociality in Dickens's *Sketches of Young Couples*', *Dickens Quarterly* 27, 1 (2010): 3–22.

with the exploration of an ethics of modernity. Such a view would fail to acknowledge the multi-faceted moods and genres of Dickens, from the whimsy of *Pickwick Papers* to the suspense of 'The Signal-Man'. But in tracing a thread whereby a relationship between emotions and ethics, or affect and engagement, may be explored, this chapter will address aspects of Dickens's complex repertoire of feelings at the level of lived experience, or what we might call Dickens's phenomenology of affect.

THE AFFECTIVE TURN

First, however, it is necessary to outline some of the contours of recent theoretical work on emotions and affects. The so-called 'affective turn' is commonly understood to describe a shift in the humanities and social sciences, since the mid-1990s, away from explanatory paradigms derived from semiotics or poststructuralism on the one hand and essentialist understandings of the body and subjectivity on the other. Attention to affect was a means of placing a new and different kind of emphasis on embodied experience and saw scholars drawing on the work of philosophers such as Spinoza and Bergson or, more recently, Deleuze and Guattari. Perhaps the most influential scholar in this field, however, has been Eve Kosofsky Sedgwick, who (initially with Adam Frank) brought the affect theory of psychologist Silvan Tompkins to a wide scholarly audience and sought to show how attention to affect—in both literary and critical texts—could overturn the business-as-usual approach (that Sedgwick, borrowing from Paul Ricoeur, terms a 'hermeneutics of suspicion') in literary criticism and queer theory.[13] Subsequently, in cultural studies and queer theory in particular, the study of affect has often been seen as a way out of an impasse in current theory—between mind and body, social and presocial, structure and individual, power and resistance—and the related binary of politics versus emotion.

Scholarship characteristic of the 'affective turn', however, has not focused solely on affect but also addresses emotions, feelings, sensations, moods, or specific psychic phenomena such as trauma. Moreover, distinctions between affect, emotion, feeling, and mood are far from clear-cut and are debated or redrawn throughout the already extensive scholarly literature. Scholars emphasize different aspects or differentiate between categories of experience to serve their own specific ends, depending on their source material, philosophical inclination, or disciplinary framework. While the distinction between emotion and affect may signal a distinction between voluntary and involuntary, or conscious and pre-conscious feelings, the two may not always be as clearly divided as these oppositions imply, seeping one into the other in their emphasis on an *embodied* response to objects or phenomena encountered by the subject.

---

[13] See Eve Kosofsky Sedgwick and Adam Frank (eds), *Shame and its Sisters: A Silvan Tomkins Reader* (Durham, NC: Duke University Press, 1995) and Eve Kosofsky Sedgwick, *Touching Feeling: Affect, Pedagogy, Performativity* (Durham, NC: Duke University Press, 2003).

Nonetheless, some preliminary attempt to delineate between affects, emotions, and feelings, in particular, should be attempted. A good starting point may be Rei Terada's observation that 'by *emotion* we usually mean a psychological, at least minimally interpretive experience whose physiological aspect is *affect*'.[14] Affect, as a pre-verbal experience of 'embodied intensity',[15] lends itself to being described in terms of a 'force' or 'flow', but, as some critics have pointed out, the danger here is to risk reducing affect to some kind of magical or deterministic phenomenon.[16] Cultural theorists Gregory Seigworth and Melissa Gregg have sought to avoid this pitfall in describing the texture and nuance of affect as a bodily phenomenon that occurs in, and results from, encounter—that is, a necessarily and inevitably social environment:

> affect is found in those intensities that pass body to body [and] is the name we give to those forces—visceral forces beneath, alongside, or generally *other than* conscious knowing ... Affect can be understood then as a gradient of bodily capacity ... that rises and falls not only along various rhythms and modalities of encounter but also through the troughs and sieves of sensation and sensibility.[17]

While acknowledging the difficulties of trying to verbalize or categorize a form of experience that is not entirely contained by cognition or language, then, affect theory does not assume that affect is asocial or innate. At its simplest, what a body reacts to—whether in joy, fear, or disgust—can vary widely from body to body, culture to culture, epoch to epoch. As Jonathan Flatley has noted,

> It is true that affect theorists ... emphasize the extent to which affective phenomena operate according to a logic that is not reducible to the logic of cognition ... In this view, affects and moods may not be *directly* subject to intentions ... but this does not mean that there is *no* way to exert agency in relation to our affects and affective experience, only that such agency is mediated, variable, and situated.[18]

As readers of Dickens, we often become conscious of—if not *self-conscious about*—our own affective reactions, those moments of embodied intensity that we experience that may not necessarily be coterminous with our preferred emotional responses. Episodes like the drunken mob's attack on the Warren in *Barnaby Rudge* (where men 'cast their

---

[14] Rei Terada, *Feeling in Theory: Emotion after the 'Death of the Subject'* (Cambridge, MA: Harvard University Press, 2001), 4, original emphasis.

[15] Brian Massumi, *Parables for the Virtual: Movement, Affect, Sensation* (Durham, NC: Duke University Press, 2002), 28; J. K. Gibson-Graham, *A Postcapitalist Politics* (Minneapolis: University of Minnesota Press, 2006), 203.

[16] See, for example, Ruth Leys, 'The Turn to Affect: A Critique', *Critical Inquiry* 37 (Spring 2011): 434–72.

[17] Gregory J. Seigworth and Melissa Gregg, 'An Inventory of Shimmers', in Melissa Gregg and Gregory J. Seigworth (eds), *The Affect Theory Reader* (Durham, NC: Duke University Press, 2010), 1, 2.

[18] Jonathan Flatley, 'How a Revolutionary Counter-Mood is Made', *New Literary History* 43 (2012): 505, original emphasis.

lighted torches in the air, and suffered them to fall upon their heads and faces, blistering the skin with deep unseemly burns ... [men] rushed up to the fire, and paddled in it with their hands as if in water... On the skull of one drunken lad—not twenty, by his looks—who lay upon the ground with a bottle to his mouth, the lead from the roof came streaming down in a shower of liquid fire, white hot; melting his head like wax'[19]) may make our flesh creep. The Cratchits' loss of Tiny Tim in *A Christmas Carol* ('"My little, little child!" cried Bob. "My little child!" He broke down all at once. He couldn't help it'[20]) may bring a lump to our throat. Such familiar clichés register the way the *body feels* on reading these passages; that is, they signal reactions on an affective level to Dickens's stories. Further, the fact that such reactions may occur on repeated readings—when we already *know* what will happen but register a somatic reaction anyway—attests equally to the power of Dickens's prose and to the body's insistence, sometimes despite our so-called better judgement, on responding to that power.[21]

In the 'affective turn', some have favoured the term 'feelings' in an effort to avoid the difficulty of distinguishing between emotions and affects. As Terada says, '*Feeling* is a capacious term that connotes both physiological sensations (affects) and psychological states (emotions).'[22] Its connotation of the haptic (represented most clearly in the colloquial and often derogatory term 'touchy-feely') also reminds us of the close connection between feelings and the senses, and Teresa Brennan has similarly emphasized the importance of the sensory in this regard, writing that 'feelings [are] sensations that have found the right match in words'.[23] Most recently, however, mood has been added to the repertoire, receiving new attention as a term that describes a state that is not coextensive with feeling, emotion, or affect. As Rita Felski and Susan Fraiman have noted:

> Moods are usually described as ambient, vague, diffuse, hazy, and intangible, rather than intense, and they are often contrasted to emotions in having a longer duration. Instead of flowing, a mood lingers, tarries, settles in, accumulates, and sticks around. It is frequently characterized by inertia.[24]

Being 'in the mood' to read, or in the mood to be moved by our reading, may be just as important as *what* we read in shaping our responses or interpretations to texts.

---

[19] *Barnaby Rudge*, ed. Clive Hurst, Oxford World's Classics (Oxford: Oxford University Press), 2003), chapter 55, page 444. Subsequent references are inserted parenthetically in the text by *BR* chapter, page.

[20] *A Christmas Carol and Other Christmas Books*, ed. Robert Douglas-Fairhurst, Oxford World Classics (Oxford: Oxford University Press, 2008), *A Christmas Carol*, Stave 4, page 73.

[21] It is important to remember that we are talking about *affects* rather than affect as some kind of unitary category (see Sedgwick, *Touching Feeling*, 110). In the work of Silvan Tomkins, for instance, the basic set of affects consists of shame, interest, surprise, joy, anger, fear, distress, disgust, and, in his later writing, contempt (Sedgwick and Frank, *Shame and its Sisters*, 500).

[22] Terada, *Feeling in Theory*, 4.

[23] Teresa Brennan, *The Transmission of Affect* (Ithaca, NY: Cornell University Press, 2004), 5.

[24] Rita Felski and Susan Fraiman, 'Introduction: In the Mood', *New Literary History* 43 (2012): v.

While the scholarship on affects and emotions—encompassing, as we have seen, feeling, sensation, and mood—has already made a noticeable mark on Victorian studies,[25] what, then, can this wealth of theoretical material contribute to our study of Dickens? An author famous for making his readers laugh or cry would seem to make Dickens a crucial case study in this area. Indeed, recent innovative scholarship on 'queer feelings' has already shown some of the potential for expanding the study of Dickens in new and lively directions.[26] In the textual examples that follow, this chapter contributes to the ongoing revaluation of Dickensian feeling which, as Christine Ferguson has argued, 'far from indicating a mawkish abandonment of the political, represents [Dickens's] endorsement of a cultural collectivity. What these scholars share is a desire to expose, challenge, and complicate the conventional assessment of literary affect rather than to abolish the designation out of hand'.[27]

EMOTIONS AND ETHICS

An interesting early example of Dickens's endorsement of a cultural collectivity through a focus on feelings is *Sketches of Young Couples*, a slim volume published to coincide with the marriage of Victoria and Albert in 1840. In these sketches, the companionate form of marriage provides an opportunity to explore the appropriate expression and authenticity of emotions and how social identities—as wives and husbands, mothers and fathers—are built on the performance and circulation of feelings.

In the opening sketch, 'The Young Couple', a surfeit of emotions is depicted in positive terms because the excess of feeling is expressed through, and ordered by, the social forms surrounding a wedding. The Young Couple becomes the nucleus of a social world represented by their immediate neighbourhood; they instigate emotional responses from those around them that link family, friends, neighbours, and servants in what Karen Chase and Michael Levenson have described as the kind of 'continuous social zone' that is typical of Dickens's early fiction.[28] The Young Couple becomes a kind of *tabula rasa* on which both individual and collective fantasies of happiness, harmony, and futurity may be projected. All can feel included through good feelings and/or feeling

---

[25] Examples include special issues of key journals in recent years: 'Victorian Emotions', *Victorian Studies* 50, 3 (2008); 'New Agenda: Sentimentalities', *Journal of Victorian Culture* 16, 2 (2011); 'Rethinking Victorian Sentimentality', *19: Interdisciplinary Studies in the Long Nineteenth Century* 4 (2007); and 'Dickens and Feeling', *19: Interdisciplinary Studies in the Long Nineteenth Century* 14 (2012).

[26] See Holly Furneaux, *Queer Dickens: Erotics, Families, Masculinities* (Oxford: Oxford University Press, 2009) and Ben Winyard, '"Should I feel a moment with you?" Queering Dickensian Feeling', *19: Interdisciplinary Studies in the Long Nineteenth Century* 14 (2012): 1–6.

[27] Christine Ferguson, 'Sensational Dependence: Prosthesis and Affect in Dickens and Braddon', *Lit: Literature Interpretation Theory* 19, 1 (2008): 5.

[28] Karen Chase and Michael Levenson, *The Spectacle of Intimacy: A Public Life for the Victorian Family* (Princeton: Princeton University Press, 2000), 9.

good. 'We smile at such things, and so we should', observes the narrator, simultaneously implying a superior perspective even while perpetuating a collective sentimental fantasy about the wedding as a guarantee of social happiness.[29]

In *Sketches of Young Couples*, feelings circulate in both private and public contexts, across lines of gender or class, and may bring people together in harmonious community or isolate them in solipsistic settings. 'The Couple Who Coddle Themselves', for example, is humorously described in terms of their elaborate arrangements for self-care, home remedies, and a judicious use of flannel. Concerned exclusively with themselves, they indulge both their hypochondria and their gluttony. But the moral is firmly drawn at the end of this sketch. Such 'exclusive habits of self-indulgence', the narrator concludes, cause couples like this to 'forget their natural sympathy and close connexion with everybody and everything in the world around them'; they 'not only neglect the first duty of life, but, by a happy retributive justice, deprive themselves of its truest and best enjoyment' (*SYC* 'The Couple Who Coddle Themselves', 213). 'Coddling', then, with its connotations of infantile pampering, characterizes a couple that has refused to enter the adult realm of responsibility in the ethical sense but instead retreats to a world of their own projection.

This sketch is one of several that examines whether emotional intimacy precludes ethical engagement with society beyond the home. Too much emphasis on feeling (if it is solely inward-directed or if it is given excessive expression that suggests inauthenticity) may be as unethical as too little. What *Sketches of Young Couples* celebrates are authentic forms of intimacy that do not cut the couple off from responding to a wider world of relationship and reciprocity. *Personal* happiness is linked to hospitable engagement with a *social* world both within and beyond the home. The best example of this ethical expression of intimacy is found in 'The Nice Little Couple', a sketch describing the exemplary hospitality of the Chirrups. Their household is notable for its inclusion of Mr Chirrup's 'bachelor friend, who lived with him in his own days of single blessedness, and to whom he is mightily attached' (*SYC* 'The Nice Little Couple', 198). The triangular relationship of 'entire unanimity' which exists between the Chirrups and their unnamed friend represents what Holly Furneaux has seen as the queering of intimacy in Dickens where marriage is deprivileged 'as just one possible choice in determining family'.[30] The inclusion of a third party in the romantic dyad, on terms of everyday intimacy with both members of the couple, provides a model of ethical sociality expressed through good feelings: it is inclusive and responsive to others, rather than exclusive and self-absorbed.

Through a range of contrasting models of marriage, Dickens begins to show how emotions 'provide powerful clues to the ways in which we take ourselves to be implicated in the lives of others'.[31] In *Sketches of Young Couples*, negative portrayals far outweigh

---

[29] Charles Dickens, *Sketches of Young Gentlemen and Young Couples*, introd. Paul Schlicke (Oxford and New York: Oxford University Press, 2012), 'The Young Couple', page 158. Subsequent references are inserted parenthetically in the text by *SYG* or *SYC* 'Title', page.

[30] Furneaux, *Queer Dickens*, 154.

[31] Elizabeth V. Spelman, 'The Virtue of Feeling and the Feeling of Virtue', in Claudia Card (ed.), *Feminist Ethics* (Lawrence: University Press of Kansas, 1991), 226.

the positive, and Chase and Levenson have argued that by the early 1840s Dickens had begun to represent the danger inherent in romantic isolation by depicting 'the withdrawal of the married pair from a broader web of affection' as a problem.[32] The 'limits and exclusions of marriage', Chase and Levenson contend, see a shift from a romantic dyad to a 'flourishing household ... with at least three to break the close circuit of romantic love' as a more ideal form of sociality, a shift already foreshadowed in the idyllic Chirrup household.[33]

SENTIMENT AND SENSATION

While, thus far, Dickensian feeling has been situated in relation to a particular understanding of ethical responsibility, it is far more common for critics to associate Dickens with '*moral* sentiments ... as the source of virtuous action'.[34] In his landmark study, *Sacred Tears: Sentimentality in Victorian Literature*, for instance, Fred Kaplan argued that idealized characters like Little Nell embodied 'Dickens's belief in the moral sentiments' and that, in *The Old Curiosity Shop*, the open expression of emotion in the form of tears communicated moral feeling.[35] In early novels like *Oliver Twist* and *The Old Curiosity Shop*, not only are readers' emotions engaged by the suffering of virtuous children like Oliver and Nell but, in their innate innocence and capacity for strong feelings, these children are themselves vessels of sentiment: their strong feelings—positive or negative—provide a kind of moral compass for evaluating the other characters they encounter, even when the children lack the worldly knowledge to fully understand the events in which they are implicated. More than anything, these child characters are *feeling* subjects who, in turn, call forth strong emotional responses in readers who feel *for* and *with* these characters. This section, then, will reconsider Little Nell—an emblematic figure of Victorian sentimentality most famous for her angelic death—as a character who provokes intense responses from readers that take us beyond emotion and into the intensities of affect.

In *Sacred Tears*, Kaplan argued that Dickens's depiction of the deaths of children like Little Nell 'dramatize[d] his belief ... in sentimentality as morally instructive'.[36] In the case of Nell Trent, however, the death takes place off-stage, as it were; it is only briefly recounted *after* the deathbed scene when Kit, the schoolmaster, and the estranged

---

[32] Chase and Levenson, *The Spectacle of Intimacy*, 92.

[33] Ibid., 94–5.

[34] Fred Kaplan, *Sacred Tears: Sentimentality in Victorian Literature* (Princeton: Princeton University Press, 1987), 40.

[35] Ibid., 40, 45. For a similar, if less sympathetic, argument about the moral significance of tears in Dickens's fiction, see Julian Moynahan, 'Dealings with the Firm of Dombey and Son: Firmness versus Wetness', in John Gross and Gabriel Pearson (eds), *Dickens and the Twentieth Century* (London: Routledge and Kegan Paul, 1962), 121–31.

[36] Kaplan, *Sacred Tears*, 48.

brother of Nell's grandfather approach her bed with 'sobs ... and sounds of grief and mourning'.[37] Instead, it is the spectacle of the already-dead child that carries the sentimental force of this episode, where the extended description of Nell's body is combined with the repeated refrain '[S]he was dead... She was dead... She was dead' (*OCS* 71, 557). Nell may now be immortal, beyond the realm of suffering and more angel than human, but she is still the cause of great sadness and grief. Hers is truly a grievable death and perhaps provided a source of consolation to some of Dickens's contemporary readers craving reassurance about the value of such short-lived lives.

For the feminist philosopher Judith Butler, the question 'what counts as a livable life and a grievable death?' lies at the heart of the ethical foundation of any society because it provides a powerful indication of 'Who counts as human, whose lives count as lives' in a society.[38] Butler's connection of emotion—specifically, grief—with a sense of ethical responsibility on a social level is one that also resonates in Dickens's depiction of vulnerable children throughout his work. In particular, the death of a child provides Dickens's readers with a powerful opportunity to think about (and to feel) whose lives count. For J. F. Stephen, however, the deathbed of Little Nell was a scene of ghoulish salacity: Dickens 'gloats over the girl's death as if it delighted him, he looks at it from four or five points of view, touches, tastes, smells and handles as if it was a savoury dainty which could not be too fully appreciated'.[39] The intensity of feeling surrounding Nell is registered in strongly sensory terms in Stephen's indictment; the scene is (almost literally) distasteful, Stephen charges, with the author vampirically lingering over the child's deathbed—a long way from Kaplan's description of the embodiment of 'moral sentiments' as a 'source of virtuous action' in such scenes. Stephen's view of Nell's death may be at odds with its more familiar reception as a strongly affecting scene of tender sentiment—going even further, in its way, than Oscar Wilde's famous rhetorical laughter over the death of Little Nell—but it is a reminder that emotional excess in Dickens's writing has always been open to a variety of interpretations.

Rather than focusing on Nell's death in isolation, however, it is important to remember how much of the narrative of *The Old Curiosity Shop* is concerned with a child's suffering (mostly Nell's, of course, but also the Marchioness and the schoolmaster's little pupil). In this novel, as in so much of his fiction, Dickens offers searing depictions of a child's *bodily* vulnerability: stripped, starved, beaten, pushed beyond its physical limits, or exposed to the elements—a child's body is rendered defenceless in almost innumerable ways. A child is always vulnerable to violence or ill-treatment, dependent on the care of others, and unable to control or predict how it will be treated. Social class is no protection when it comes to children: think of the physical abuse suffered by David Copperfield in his own home; or Florence Dombey's kidnapping by Good Mrs Brown.

---

[37] *The Old Curiosity Shop*, ed. Elizabeth M. Brennan (Oxford: Clarendon Press, 1998), chapter 71, page 557. Subsequent references are inserted parenthetically in the text by *OCS* chapter, page.
[38] Judith Butler, *Precarious Life: The Powers of Mourning and Violence* (London: Verso, 2004), xv, 20.
[39] Qtd in James A. Colaiaco, *James Fitzjames Stephen and the Crisis of Victorian Thought* (London: Macmillan, 1963), 57.

What the precarious position of the Dickensian child reminds us is that children are always, as Judith Butler puts it, 'given over to the touch of the other, even if there is no other there, and no support for [their] lives, signif[ying] a primary helplessness and need, one to which any society must attend'.[40] The Dickensian child brought into proximity with more powerful others is not only a source of narrative drama or a sentimental tableau, then, but a dramatization of how 'the poor and destitute one' calls us to account; how such proximity renders us responsible, in an ethical sense. The tears or fears that readers experience on behalf of the child, then, are a vital resource for *feeling* that ethical proximity.

Perhaps the starkest example of Nell's vulnerability in relation to those closest to her is the incident in chapter 30 where Nell is left alone one night in her chamber at an unsavoury inn, anxious about the future, after earlier witnessing her grandfather succumb to his gambling addiction once again. Dickens deploys here the familiar Gothic convention of the innocent maiden alone in a threatening environment and the inn is rendered in suitably Gothic terms ('It was a great, rambling house, with dull corridors and wide staircases which the flaring candles seemed to make more gloomy' (*OCS* 30, 236)). After initially waking from a nightmare 'in great terror', Nell eventually sleeps, only to be woken by a 'figure in the room!':

> it crouched and slunk along, groping its way with noiseless hands, and stealing round the bed. She had no voice to cry for help, no power to move, but lay still, watching it…
>
> The dark form was a mere blot upon the lighter darkness of the room, but she saw the turning of the head, and felt and knew how the eyes looked and the ears listened. There it remained, motionless as she. (*OCS* 30, 237–8)

After the figure has stolen Nell's money and left the room,

> The first impulse of the child was to fly from the terror of being by herself in that room—to have somebody by—not to be alone—and then her power of speech would be restored. With no consciousness of having moved, she gained the door. (*OCS* 30, 238)

In this chilling episode, Nell is overwhelmed by the intensity of surprise, fear, distress, and disgust—four of the basic affects named by Silvan Tomkins. Nell's terror renders her unable to speak or move but still able to sense—beyond words or the direct evidence of sight—what the figure is doing ('she *felt and knew* how the eyes looked'). It is an enhanced, embodied response, beyond what the conscious mind can adequately process or understand. Moreover, while it is grammatically correct to refer to the unnamed, unrecognized, ungendered figure here as 'it', the reiteration of the impersonal pronoun throughout this passage reflects Nell's inability to comprehend what she

---

[40] Butler, *Precarious Life*, 32.

witnesses. A confluence of fear and disgust both prevents Nell from identifying the figure as fully human and leaves her unable to withdraw her attention from it. Words and volition fail Nell.[41]

The shocking revelation that it is in fact Nell's grandfather who had entered her room and stolen her money (the revelation of which leaves Nell 'quite dumb, and almost senseless', as she 'staggered forward' to find her grandfather alone in his room counting her money) is one of the most powerful moments of predation in all of Dickens (*OCS* 30, 238). First-time readers of this scene experience a profoundly affective response; it is a scene that has lost none of its power to chill the reader on behalf of the vulnerable child. Such a strongly affective reaction precedes our conscious awareness of what has happened, distracting the reader from drawing the logical inference—while the invasion of Nell's room is taking place—that the problem gambler is the most likely suspect. But what this episode of overwhelming affect also registers—again, beyond Nell's ability to understand in any conscious way—is Nell's unwitting imitation of her grandfather. Like the figure, she too moves mysteriously ('With no consciousness of having moved') and, when she follows it from her room, 'The figure stood quite still, and so did she ... The figure moved again. The child involuntarily did the same' (*OCS* 30, 238). That is, even before Nell comprehends what her grandfather has done, she shares in his shame—unwittingly imitating his creeping behaviour in a way that symbolically represents her inextricable connection with him. What shames him, shames them both, and shame is here 'fleshed out', as it were—performed in the actions of the body in a way the mind may not consciously apprehend. The injustice of Nell's shame does not mean that she cannot experience it in an embodied way, just as she shares her grandfather's fate of poverty and homelessness despite having done nothing to deserve it. Nell's sense of responsibility for her grandfather, rendered almost literally here as her uncanny ability to respond to him, exacerbates her vulnerability and starkly illustrates the high cost that such responsibility may exact from those who would seek to act upon it.

The Gothic elements of this scene not only locate the source of danger to the vulnerable child in those closest to her but also provide a way of expressing what we might call a deeper emotional, or psychological, truth about vulnerability: what it *feels* like to be vulnerable. Variously mobilizing both sentiment and sensation, then, the story of Nell Trent provides a powerful instance of a life that counts, marked by the capacity of that life to move readers first to tears and then to 'a hundred virtues ... in shapes of mercy, charity, and love, to walk the world, and bless it. Of every tear that sorrowing mortals shed on such green graves, some good is born, some gentler nature comes' (*OCS* 72, 563). However unrealistic such sentimental hopes may seem to jaded twenty-first-century readers, the narrator's belief in the indissoluble connection between strong feelings—even grief—and an ethical response to the wider world insists on our responsibilities as feeling subjects even as it shows the suffering to which such a response may expose us.

---

[41] The significance of the use of the impersonal pronoun for the (human) figure in this episode is further emphasized by the fact that the 'summer insect' Nell passes in the passage *is* gendered: 'filling the silent place with his murmurs' (*OCS* 30, 238).

Bad Moods and the Transmission of Affect

But what about the *absence* of strong feeling? Or strong feelings that lead not to mercy, charity, and love but violence, vengeance, and hatred? This final and most speculative section will briefly consider examples of bad feelings and negative affects—and their capacity to transform from one to the other, or to pass from one character to another—in Dickens's last completed novel, *Our Mutual Friend*. While no one could dispute that heightened or excessive emotions and affects are present throughout Dickens's oeuvre, *Our Mutual Friend* is perhaps unique in the way that leading characters are closely identified with a particular affect, emotion, or mood, in the manner of so-called 'flat' characters (think of Bradley Headstone's obsessive rage, Lizzie Hexam's devoted love, Eugene Wrayburn's ennui) but, at the same time, achieve a kind of psychological depth through the representation of their inner conflict or ambivalence. These are characters unknown to themselves in some vital way; they don't consciously understand why they respond in the ways that they do, or what drives them. Dickens seems to be working with a particularly rich repertoire of feelings in this novel and the kind of intense, impulsive responses associated with affects are especially prominent. As Anna Gibson has recently put it, *Our Mutual Friend* is a novel 'populated by characters animated by involuntary reactions and repulsions'.[42]

Theorists of affect, working from the assumption that there is no such thing as a self-contained individual who experiences her unique emotions or affects in isolation from a wider social environment, have talked about the flow, or transmission, of affect arising from our interaction with others, as 'a process that is social in origin but biological and physical in effect'.[43] 'By the transmission of affect', Brennan writes, 'I mean simply that the emotions or affects of one person, and the enhancing or depressing energies these affects entail, can enter into another.'[44] If we think of affect in this way, a number of questions are raised about the extent of our responsibility or agency for what may be transmitted through us, or that we, in turn, absorb from others. If we concede that we have an ethical responsibility towards others, what about others' feelings? And, similarly, what capacity might we have, should we have, to resist being co-opted by the affect or mood of others?

Juliet John has argued that, in Dickens, feelings do not reside *in* characters; rather, a character is a medium through which feeling passes.[45] Whether this understanding of Dickensian character holds in all cases, in *Our Mutual Friend* we can see this character

---

[42] Anna Gibson, '*Our Mutual Friend* and Network Form', *Novel* 48, 1 (2015): 75.
[43] Brennan, *The Transmission of Affect*, 3.
[44] Ibid.
[45] Juliet John, *Dickens's Villains: Melodrama, Character, Popular Culture* (Oxford: Oxford University Press, 2001), 120–1.

dynamic at work in what we might call the 'transmission of affect' that passes from Eugene Wrayburn to Bradley Headstone (and back again), from Eugene Wrayburn to Lizzie Hexam (and back again), and from Bradley Headstone to Lizzie Hexam (and back again). Within this fraught triangle, in every case the feelings or affects that are transmitted do not necessarily return in kind but change from, say, amusement to hatred (Eugene to Bradley) or desire to repulsion (in the case of Bradley and Lizzie), but retain all their intensity as they circulate and transform. The more Bradley desires Lizzie, the more she is repulsed by him. The more Eugene is amused by Bradley's discomfort, the more Bradley hates him, but—in this instance—something of Bradley's obsession also passes *back* to Eugene, who, the reader discovers, has been devoting time and attention to Bradley's pursuit of him that is clearly at odds with Eugene's professed detachment from any emotional investment in this rivalry. When Mortimer Lightwood discovers how his friend has been goading Bradley (by leading him through London streets for hours at night, knowing that Bradley will follow him), Mortimer not only expresses his disapproval of such behaviour but warns Eugene of the danger involved. Eugene, Mortimer believes, bears a responsibility towards Bradley and should not take advantage of the schoolmaster's uncontrollable emotions. Eugene, however, claims that 'goad[ing] the schoolmaster to madness' provides a 'solace' of 'inexpressible comfort' to him, playing up the contrast between his own customary 'coolness' and the 'grinding torments' of the 'white-lipped, wild-eyed, draggled-haired' schoolmaster.[46]

For much of the novel, though, it might be more accurate to describe Eugene Wrayburn in terms of mood rather than affect. If moods 'often manifest themselves as prolonged feeling-states', we could profitably consider the purpose and effect of Eugene's 'cool' mood as a means by which he fosters a certain outlook on, or relationship to, the world around him.[47] Mood, as a kind of 'affective atmosphere' that 'informs our felt connection or lack of connection with others along with our sense of what things mean and how they matter',[48] is more than simply a pose for Eugene, then, and more like a habitus—a habituated mode of inhabiting the world and shaping his sense of place within that world.[49] Eugene's self-described 'susceptibility to boredom' that, he says, makes him 'the most consistent of mankind' (*OMF* I:7, 147), serves a protective purpose, such as when the reader is first introduced to him in chapter 2 at the Veneering dinner party where his cool detachment may be seen as an attempt to insulate himself from the contagion of the morally vacuous society he inhabits. On four occasions in chapters 2 and 3, Eugene is described as 'the gloomy Eugene', establishing this mood as his characteristic disposition and which, like affect, can be contagious: even the cheerful

---

[46] *Our Mutual Friend*, ed. Michael Cotsell, Oxford World's Classics (Oxford: Oxford University Press, 1989), Book III, chapter 10, pages 542, 544. Subsequent references are inserted parenthetically in the text by *OMF* Book:chapter, page.

[47] Felski and Fraiman, 'Introduction', v.

[48] Ibid., vii.

[49] On habitus, see Pierre Bourdieu, *The Logic of Practice* (Cambridge: Polity Press, 1990), 56, and *Pascalian Meditations* (Stanford, CA: Stanford University Press, 1997), 138–41.

Boffin, after his first meeting with Eugene, departs 'with a comfortless impression he could have dispensed with, that there was a deal of unsatisfactoriness in the world' (I:8, 94).

Over the course of the narrative, of course, Eugene will be forced to renounce this mood. As his first sighting of Lizzie proves, he is not immune to responding emotionally to others ('that lonely girl with the dark hair runs in my head', he tells Mortimer; (*OMF* I:13, 162)) and, after surviving Bradley's attack, Eugene is for the first time able to articulate his feelings for Mortimer: 'Touch my face with yours, in case I should not hold out till you come back. I love you, Mortimer' (*OMF* IV:10, 742). Eugene becomes here, quite literally, a man of feeling, in longing for the touch of Mortimer to accompany his declaration of love for his friend. But it is a very different man of feeling who is given the last word in *Our Mutual Friend*, returning us to the issue of sentimentalism with which this chapter began. Twemlow, throughout the novel the elderly embodiment of an earlier time, speaks in defence of the marriage of Eugene and Lizzie in the terms of eighteenth-century sentimental fiction: 'this is a question of the feelings of a gentleman', Twemlow asserts to the disapproving gathering at the Veneerings, going on to enumerate these as 'feelings of gratitude, of respect, of admiration, and affection' (*OMF* IV:17, 819). After all the violence and disharmony of the preceding narrative, *Our Mutual Friend* concludes with a handshake between Mortimer and Twemlow, the benign emotions of friendship and fellow-feeling providing its final image. A sentimental touch, no doubt, but one that does not fully dispel the gloomy mood that has pervaded much of a novel in which the consequences of bad feelings and negative affects linger uncomfortably.

To end this consideration of Dickens and affect with the tendency of bad feelings to linger on after the event is perhaps fitting. Much of the scholarship on affect to date has, after all, focused on the negative: shame, disgust, trauma. Further work remains to be done on the significance of trauma in the life and work of Dickens and, especially, Dickens's emphasis on the vulnerable child as a source of, and possible solution to, childhood trauma. More recently, though, scholars have also turned their attention to happiness, and a future direction in Dickens studies may be to take up some of this work—mainly, thus far, in cultural studies[50]—and pursue its implications for the positive emotions in Dickens (not to mention the happiness that readers continue to derive from his work) and their ethical potential. Beyond the negatively stereotyped connotations of sentimentality—as shallow and self-indulgent feelings, whether heartwarming or maudlin—a more nuanced approach to happiness and its related states may allow a fuller exploration of Dickens's phenomenology of affect.

Further Reading

Michael Bell, *Sentimentalism, Ethics and the Culture of Feeling* (Basingstoke: Palgrave Macmillan, 2000)

---

[50] See, for example, the special issue on 'The Happiness Turn', *New Formations* 63 (Winter 2007–8).

Ann Cvetkovich, *Mixed Feelings: Feminism, Mass Culture, and Victorian Sensationalism* (New Brunswick, NJ: Rutgers University Press, 1992)

William A. Cohen and Ryan Johnson (eds), *Filth: Dirt, Disgust, and Modern Life* (Minneapolis: University of Minnesota Press, 2005)

Jill L. Matus, 'Trauma, Memory, and Railway Disaster: The Dickensian Connection', *Victorian Studies* 43, 3 (2001): 413–36

Sianne Ngai, *Ugly Feelings* (Cambridge, MA: Harvard University Press, 2007)

CHAPTER 33

HISTORY AND CHANGE
Dickens and the Past

DAVID PAROISSIEN

> 'It is in vain, Trot, to recall the past, unless it works some influence upon the present.'
>
> *David Copperfield*, chapter 23 (1849)

The perception of Dickens as a writer indifferent to history took root during his lifetime and has continued unchallenged. Eminent contemporaries like John Forster and George Henry Lewes disparaged those aspects of his work that called for a reflective and analytical engagement with the past. Forster, for instance, expressed impatience with Dickens's only contribution to historical discourse. He dismissed *A Child's History of England* as 'that little book', which 'cannot be said to have quite hit the mark'.[1] Noting that portions of it were 'dictated' and published simultaneously with monthly instalments of *Bleak House*, he assigns Dickens's *History* a secondary status. The novelist's attention, one is left to infer, lay elsewhere: on the composition of the monthly numbers of *Bleak House*, or on editorial duties and the continued management of *Household Words*, in which *A Child's History of England* appeared intermittently between 25 January 1851 and 10 December 1853. Lewes recorded no specific verdict on *A Child's History*, but his summation in 1872 of the novelist's philosophical inadequacies conceivably hints at the mark Forster never defined but believed Dickens missed. 'A man's library', Lewes observed, casting his eyes over Dickens's bookshelves when he first met him, 'expresses much of his hidden life.' Find them, as Lewes did, crowded with three-volume novels, books of travel, and presentation copies but lacking volumes of history, philosophy, and the classics, and you might accept his misleading conclusion. Dickens remained, Lewes later proclaimed, 'completely outside philosophy, science, and the higher literature', to which history belongs.[2]

---

[1] John Forster, *The Life of Charles Dickens*, ed. J. W. T. Ley (London: Palmer, 1928), 571.
[2] George Henry Lewes, 'Dickens in Relation to Criticism', *Fortnightly Review* 17 (1872): 141–54, 152.

Condescension towards Dickens's intellectual status continued well beyond his death in 1870. Initially seconded by distinguished names—John Ruskin, G. K. Chesterton, George Gissing—disdain supplied a context for a further assault on Dickens as a writer unconcerned with the past and indifferent to historiography. Even today neither Peter Ackroyd nor Michael Slater is inclined to grant Dickens much quarter in this respect. The former characterizes *A Child's History* as 'melodramatic and theatrical',[3] while the latter dismisses it as a feeble effort destitute of original research and 'crib[bed]' from secondary sources.[4] Unsurprisingly, his two historical novels receive similar treatment. Echoing and repeating an old charge,[5] Claire Tomalin puts *Barnaby Rudge* (1841) aside, claiming that history was not Dickens's 'territory'.[6] *A Tale of Two Cities* (1859) falls foul in a different way, written off as a pallid shadow of *The French Revolution: A History* (1837), Carlyle's 'wonderful book', to which Dickens admitted he was deeply indebted in his Preface. In both cases, critics drain the novels of historical matter and emphasize personal interests as the 'direct inspiration' of each, works to be read in relation to a schoolboy preoccupation with Newgate prison,[7] filial tensions between fathers and sons,[8] or, in the case of *A Tale of Two Cities*, the reflection of events suggestive of a mid-life crisis.[9]

Connect both novels and *A Child's History* with Thomas Babington Macaulay and Thomas Carlyle, and a different story emerges. Dickens knew each—the two greatest historians of the period—engaged with them intellectually and drew inspiration from their early writing. Working variously—Macaulay invoking the study of history in the cause of parliamentary reform,[10] Carlyle writing in *The Edinburgh Review* and elsewhere—both campaigned to broaden the discipline of history beyond the stiff and archaic limitations of their predecessors. 'Our grand business undoubtedly is', Carlyle proclaimed in 1829, 'not to *see* what lies dimly at a distance, but to *do* what lies clearly at

[3] Peter Ackroyd, *Dickens* (London: Sinclair-Stevenson, 1990), 584.
[4] Michael Slater, *Charles Dickens* (New Haven: Yale University Press, 2009), 323. Compare David Starkey, who sees the work as illustrative of an approach to history 'roundly rejected by modern historians' (introduction in *The History of England by Jane Austen and Charles Dickens* (Thriplow: Icon Books, 2006), xxi).
[5] 'Writings of Charles Dickens', *North British Review* 3 (May 1845): 65–87, 70.
[6] Clare Tomalin, *Charles Dickens: A Life* (London: Viking, 2011), 122. For a survey of the negative assessments of Dickens's treatment of history, see the respective sections of Thomas Jackson Rice, *Barnaby Rudge: An Annotated Bibliography* (New York: Garland, 1987).
[7] John Butt and Kathleen Tillotson, *Dickens at Work* (London: Methuen, 1968), 78.
[8] Steven Marcus, *Dickens: From Pickwick to Dombey* (London: Chatto and Windus, 1965), 184–204.
[9] Michael Hollington, *Dickens: A Tale of Two Cities* (Berlin: Atlande, 2012), 11.
[10] Between 2 March 1831 and 28 February 1832, Macaulay delivered six pro-reform speeches in the Commons, the first of which, Boyd Hilton argues, proved 'A turning point' in the parliamentary debates (*A Mad, Bad, & Dangerous People? England 1783–1846* (Oxford: Clarendon Press, 2006), 432). The exhaustion to which Dickens admits on 7 March 1831 following from 'my week's exertions' points to his role as part of a team of reporters recording this memorable passage in England's history for *The Mirror of Parliament*. Charles Dickens, *The Letters of Charles Dickens*, ed. Madeline House, Graham Storey, et al., Pilgrim/British Academy Edition, 12 vols (Oxford: Clarendon Press, 1965–2002). Subsequent citations: *PLets* followed by volume:page range, page and hn. for headnote, n. or nn. for footnotes. Here, 1: 2n.

hand'. And 'doing', he added, entailed a double obligation: to look ' "before and after" ' and, paraphrasing Goethe, to look calmly at the present,[11] a prescription no less amenable to Macaulay than it was to Dickens on the verge of making a career move that defined him.

Viewing Dickens's writing about history in this context requires further preliminaries. Approximately a year before the passage of the Reform Bill in 1832, Dickens entered the press gallery as a parliamentary reporter. From this unique vantage point, he and his colleagues, young and well educated, looked down on the nation's leaders. Below in a packed House of Commons, Macaulay exchanged views with his High Tory opponents as MPs debated the country's fate at a critical historical moment, one defined by a democratizing impulse at the heart of the drive to extend the electoral franchise and curtail the power of landowners and the aristocracy.

Shortly before, and equally significant as a temporal marker, Dickens had turned 18 and applied for a reader's ticket to the British Museum in order to redress some of the gaps his own fractured education had created. Reading widely and eclectically, he extended his knowledge of English history and politics at a formative period of his intellectual development. Later, Dickens looked back on days passed in the reading-room 'as decidedly the usefullest to himself he had ever passed'.[12] Seated there amidst copies of Britain's leading quarterlies and other materials, not unlike Pip inspired by Mr Pocket, Dickens educated himself 'well enough' so he 'could "hold [his] own" with the average of young men in prosperous circumstances'.[13] In that process he evidently absorbed ideas from both Macaulay and Carlyle about what constituted philosophic history and how it should be written. Perhaps not surprisingly, therefore, it was to history that Dickens turned when he made his first bid for literary recognition with a novel seasoned with ideas about historiography drawn from Macaulay and Carlyle and mediated by Sir Walter Scott. Reading *Barnaby Rudge*, *A Tale of Two Cities*, and *A Child's History* in a context shaped by their views, this chapter argues that Dickens's thoughtful response to the challenge of writing history destabilizes the perception of him as a writer with no interest in the past but his own and one resolutely indifferent to historiography.[14]

---

[11] Thomas Carlyle, 'Signs of the Times', in *Critical and Miscellaneous Essays* (London: Chapman and Hall, 1899), 56–82, 56.

[12] Forster, *Life*, 48.

[13] Charles Dickens, *Great Expectations*, ed. Margaret Cardwell (Oxford: Clarendon Press, 1993), 2:5, 196–7. Compare Forster's judgement: 'No man who knew him in later years, and talked to him familiarly of books and things, would have suspected his education in boyhood, almost entirely self-acquired as it was, to have been so rambling or hap-hazard as I have here described it.' Forster, *Life*, 48.

[14] For a succinct survey of 'old' and 'new' historical approaches to Dickens, see Catherine Robson, 'Historicizing Dickens', in John Bowen and Robert L. Patten (eds), *Palgrave Advances in Charles Dickens Studies* (Basingstoke: Palgrave Macmillan, 2006), 234–54 and Clare Pettitt, 'Dickens and the Form of the Historical Present', in Daniel Tyler (ed.), *Dickens's Style* (Cambridge: Cambridge University Press, 2011), 110–36.

Dickens's letter to John Macrone dated [9] May 1836 offers suggestive evidence for this contention. In it, he affirms his intention to supply Macrone with 'a Work of Fiction (in Three Volumes of the usual size) to be written by me, and to be entitled *Gabriel Vardon, the Locksmith of London*' in return for 'the sum of *Two Hundred Pounds*'.[15] No contract survives, but the letter invites speculation. Why 'written by me', why 'Gabriel Vardon', why identify his occupation, and why link the hero with London? Conventional answers exist. Critics agree that a dignified three-volume historical novel in the format 'hallowed by Scott' would serve as 'the foundation-stone' of the literary career to which Dickens aspired.[16] Also accepted is the attribution of the germ of the novel to a historical incident. The original source remains to be identified, but the affair referred to recounts the bravery of a Moravian blacksmith, who, under threat, refused to strike off the irons of prisoners released from Newgate prison during the Gordon Riots.[17] Both suggestions are helpful but ignore clues that link the projected work, including the hero's name and occupation, with a new concept of history advocated by Macaulay and Carlyle.

In a series of landmark reviews and essays published in late Hanoverian England, historians and essayists put the case that historiography had become too staid and lost its vitality.[18] This had occurred, Carlyle argued, because professionals had shown a 'disproportionate fondness' for 'Senate-houses, ... Battle-fields, nay, even' for 'Kings' Antechambers'.[19] One consequence was that other voices had been marginalized and past lives ignored that deserved recognition. 'Which was the greater innovator, which was the more important personage in man's history?' Carlyle asked. '[H]e who first led armies over Alps, and gained the victories of Cannae and Thrasymene; or the nameless boor who first hammered out for himself an iron spade?'[20] In the course of time, he continued, 'much of this must be amended; and he who sees no world but that

[15] *PLets* 1:150.

[16] Slater, *Charles Dickens*, 64.

[17] John Paul de Castro appears to be the first to link Gabriel Vardon with a Moravian smith. Citing a passage from James Hutton (1715–95), a warden of the Moravian Chapel in Fetter Lane, London, Castro notes how during a meeting of the congregation in June 1780 and with Newgate Prison in flames, '"Br. Liddington, a smith, was sent for, and called out of the meeting in great haste; a party of the mob having come to his house with a number of prisoners whom they had let out of Newgate, to have their irons knocked off: on refusal of which, they threatened immediately to destroy his house; but before he could reach home, they were gone to another smith"'. *The Gordon Riots* (London: Oxford University Press, 1926), 95. Exiles from the Moravian Church, one of the oldest Protestant sects in Europe, had come to England in the early eighteenth century. In 1738 they founded a Moravian Chapel in Fetter Lane and later received recognition by Parliament in 1749.

[18] A survey of the 'peculiarities, the merits, and the defects of the three great British historians' published in the *Gentleman's Magazine* in 1832 illustrates the validity of Carlyle's claim that a preoccupation with 'The "dignity of History" has buckramed up poor History into a dead mummy. There are a thousand purposes which History should serve ... it is an Address ... to our *whole* inner man; to every faculty of Head and Heart from the deepest to the slightest.' *The Collected Letters of Thomas and Jane Welsh Carlyle*, ed. Charles Richard Sanders et al. (Durham, NC: Duke University Press, 1977), 7:52–7, 52.

[19] Thomas Carlyle, 'On History' (1830), in *Historical Essays*, ed. Chris R. Vanden Bossche (Berkeley: University of California Press, 2002), 3–13, 10.

[20] Ibid., 6.

of courts and camps; … will pass for a more or less instructive Gazetteer, but will no longer be called a Historian'.[21]

The belief that historians should broaden their focus received support from Macaulay. Like Carlyle, he complained that history had become ossified and conventional, a discipline borne down by a self-imposed 'code of conventional decencies, as absurd as that which has been the bane of the French Drama'.[22] Improved history therefore would not necessarily omit 'the court, the camp, the senate'. Rather '[t]he perfect historian', he argued, would look below 'the surface of affairs', where 'noiseless revolutions' occur. Urged thus to explore 'even the retreats of misery', historians committed to a new agenda could 'reclaim those materials which the novelist had appropriated'. By judiciously selecting, rejecting, and arranging, they could also show us 'the nation', 'elucidate the condition of society', and illustrate 'the operation of laws, of religion, and of education'.[23]

This same essay published in 1828 and the pivotal reform speech Macaulay gave in the Commons on 2 March 1831 offered further advice relevant both to politicians and to an aspiring novelist. By ignoring 'ordinary men' at work and at pleasure, refusing to 'mingle in the crowds of the exchange and the coffee house', and declining admittance 'to the convivial table and the domestic hearth', historians had turned aside from exploring 'the vast and complex system of society'.[24] In a clear warning to MPs, Macaulay urged them not to follow suit, but rather to recognize that 'a great revolution' has taken place, 'England has grown in population', and

> [a] portion of the community which had been of no account expands and becomes strong. It demands a place in the system, suited, not to its former weakness, but to its present power. If this is granted, all is well. If this is refused, then comes the struggle between the young energy of one class and the ancient privileges of another.[25]

View the artisan hero of Dickens's projected historical novel in this context and teasing hints emerge. If history is to assume the democratic cast Macaulay and Carlyle called for, what better candidate than 'a respectable tradesman', a locksmith from London called Gabriel, whose given name in Hebrew signifies 'God is my strong man'. Humble yet courageous, Dickens's conception of 'the sturdy locksmith'[26] offered an alternative model of heroic conduct, a craftsman with courage and dignity ignored by historians anxious to cultivate an 'elevated' tone and treat only public men and public

---

[21] Ibid., 10.
[22] Thomas Babington Macaulay, review of Henry Neale, *The Romance of History, England*, in *Edinburgh Review* 47 (May 1828): 331–67, 362.
[23] Ibid.
[24] Ibid., 364.
[25] Thomas Babington Macaulay, *The Works of Lord Macaulay. Speeches, Poems and Miscellaneous Writing*, vol. 1. Albany Edition (London: Longmans, Green, 1898): 413–15.
[26] Charles Dickens, *Barnaby Rudge*, ed. Clive Hurst, Oxford World's Classics (Oxford: Oxford University Press, 2003), 64, 510. Subsequent references are inserted parenthetically in the text by *BR* chapter, page.

ceremonies. Specifying the locksmith's place of residence and occupation suggests other considerations. London, Dickens knew, attracted readers; it was moreover his muse, a city whose 'streets and ... figures', he later wrote, 'supplied something to my brain'.[27] The details given in the title also appear timely. Reference to a locksmith who practised his trade in London could divert attention from Birmingham and other Midland towns, where the industry flourished until later in the century. In addition, they would add a hint of local colour.[28]

The germ of the defiant blacksmith Dickens took from history proved equally adaptable to fictional episodes, whose resonances illustrate Macaulay's point about the need for historians to pay attention to life beyond court circles. Varden responds with patience when challenged by his rebellious apprentice, in marked contrast to the other fathers in the novel, who abet rather than allay tension between generations occasioned by changing values. He also proves a model of domestic decorum when tested by his wife. Mrs Varden, the narrator informs us, 'was a lady of what is commonly called an uncertain temper', whose moods and flights her maid exploits (*BR* 7, 64). Most importantly, however, Dickens assigns to Gabriel Varden the role of a surrogate historian, the novel's figure responsible for solving some of the story's mysteries.

An early description of Varden outside his shop in Clerkenwell hints at this agenda. He is portrayed as 'gazing disconsolately at a great wooden emblem of a key' dangling from the house-front. The key swings to and fro 'with a mournful creaking noise, as if complaining that it had nothing to unlock' (*BR* 4, 41); inside, the shop appears dark and dingy, full of tools of 'uncouth make and shape', whose purpose or function remains unclear (*BR* 4, 42). Later, with the business of the day behind him, Varden sets off on his first assignment: an outing to ascertain the progress of a 'wounded gentleman' he had helped to a friend's house the night before.

The hinted mismatch between signs and things and the challenge of reading the past fuse with the efforts of the locksmith to unlock the 'dark' history of Mrs Rudge, 'an old sweetheart' whose behaviour makes no sense. What is the link between her and the 'ill-omened' figure Varden discovers outside her house (*BR* 6, 57)? Why does Mrs Rudge cower in his presence? Why does he haunt the premises and whisper mysterious threats? '"What riddle is this?"' Varden demands (*BR* 6, 56). Later when he joins forces with Mr Haredale, who two decades ago established an annuity to maintain Mrs Rudge, her benefactor exclaims hearing her determination to renounce his support, '"In the name of God, under what delusion are you labouring?"' (*BR* 25, 207).

Coming to grips with the past, in fact, emerges as a principal motif, a point emphasized by the raven in the story, whose hoarse croaks and name—Grip—mock the efforts of both men to comprehend the actions of Mary Rudge. On the occasion of

---

[27] *PLets* 4:612–14, 612.
[28] In 1841 Dickens altered the spelling of 'Vardon' to 'Varden', thereby releasing a pun on the cockney pronunciation of 'warden' (Robert Douglas-Fairhurst, *Becoming Dickens: The Invention of a Novelist* (Cambridge, MA: Harvard University Press, 2011), 293), presumably further affirmation of the importance of a London connection.

her evasive explanation for giving up the annuity she receives, the raven hops onto a table in the chamber where her meeting with Mr Haredale takes place. Assuming 'the air of some old necromancer' intent on 'a great folio volume that lay open on a desk', the bird kept his eye on the book throughout the whole interview, 'listening to everything' 'under the mask of pretending to read hard', and with the air 'of a very sly human rascal' (*BR* 25, 205–8). Subsequently taken to a churchyard by Barnaby, the raven's 'highly reflective state' continues. He walks up and down and appears to study nearby tombstones, markers of past lives, 'with a very critical taste. Sometimes, after a long inspection of an epitaph, he would … cry in his hoarse tones, "I'm a devil, I'm a devil, I'm a devil!" but whether he addressed his observations to any supposed person below, or merely threw them off as a general remark, is a matter of uncertainty' (*BR* 25, 209). Five years later, David Copperfield describes a similar moment of hesitation when he recounts how Mr Dick had questioned the date he had supplied for the execution of Charles I. '[S]orely puzzled' by David's answer, Mr Dick had wondered: '"I suppose history never lies, does it?"' only to be assured by David that it doesn't. As the narrator notes, he was 'ingenuous and young' at the time.[29] Both adjectives undercut Copperfield's youthful confidence and invite a sceptical view of history compatible with the retrospection of an urbane narrator looking back on 'The World as it rolled' by.[30]

History based on a corpus of ascertained facts and committed to a verifiable truth content of course does not lie deliberately. The French Revolution of 1789 refers to a documentary phenomenon; the challenge for historians is how to conduct a responsible enquiry into the circumstances which surround it. They must consider, for example, the contingencies on which events depend, select appropriate materials, and offer a judgement in the fullness of knowledge available at the time. Proceeding in this manner to 'look with reverence into the dark, untenanted places of the Past',[31] this '*thing* now gone silent',[32] historians undertake to reconstruct scenes from former days as part of their duty to the world at large, a point on which Carlyle was explicit. 'History' matters a great deal, he proclaimed in 1833. It 'is the Letter of Instructions, which the old generations write and posthumously transmit to the new, nay it may be called, … the Message, verbal or written, which all Mankind delivers to every man'.[33]

With Carlyle's 'Instructions' in mind as we turn to Dickens's second historical novel, we might ask what stories did he want to deliver about the French Revolution to readers of *All the Year Round* in 1859? Attention to the opening chapters of *A Tale of Two Cities* provides some answers. Taken together, all six chapters of Book I constitute a proem in which Dickens addresses historiographical issues similar to those raised by Macaulay

---

[29] Charles Dickens, *David Copperfield*, ed. Nina Burgis (Oxford: Clarendon Press, 1981), 17, 213–14. Subsequent references are inserted parenthetically in the text by *DC* chapter, page.

[30] One of the novel's 17 trial titles, several of which emphasized the narrator's preoccupation with looking back and disclosing truths learned in the course of a life. Harry Stone, *Dickens' Working Notes for his Novels* (Chicago: University of Chicago Press, 1987), 106.

[31] Carlyle, 'On History', 6.

[32] Thomas Carlyle, 'On History Again' (1833), in *Historical Essays*, ed. Vanden Bossche, 15–22, 16.

[33] Ibid., 15.

during the reform debates and by others in the periodical press in the 1830s. 'It was the best of times, it was the worst of times', begins the novel's oft-quoted first sentence. In seven opposing pairs and 119 words, Dickens deflates the practice of attempting to reduce the past to a series of epochs conveniently characterized by a single dominant idea. The 'noisiest authorities', the sentence concludes, rule out gradations of difference or likeness. Instead, they offer only inflated distinctions, a practice John Stuart Mill had questioned in 1831. In a series of papers published in the *Examiner* under the rubric 'The Spirit of the Age', he ridiculed the 'respect and homage' paid to those who 'bandied from mouth to mouth' such defining phrases as '[t]he wisdom of our ancestors, and the march of intellect'.[34] Carlyle expressed similar reservations. In his *History* of the French Revolution he pointed to the failure of diagnostic descriptions of epochs reductively framed as a contrast between the past and the present. Attempts to characterize French society in the years before the outbreak of revolution, he noted, relied on such rhetorical tropes. '[T]rouble us not with thy prophecies, O croaking Friend of Men', eager to pronounce on the prospect of an 'Age of Hope', he remonstrated in 1837. 'Or is this same Age of Hope itself a simulacrum; as Hope too often is?'[35] Earlier, he had warned against this tendency in 'Signs of the Times'. 'It is no very good symptom either of nations or individuals, that they deal much in vaticination... For here the prophets are not one, but many; and each incites and confirms the other.'[36]

Signs, nevertheless, demand to be read, especially in moments of heightened national tension. Dickens knew this as well as Carlyle and perhaps both took heed of Macaulay's pointed question put before Parliament on 2 March 1831. 'Is it possible that gentlemen long versed in high political affairs cannot read these signs?' he asked, reflecting on the significance of the repeal of Catholic disabilities made law by the Test and Corporation Act of 1828 and the Roman Catholic Relief Act of 1829. The willingness to accept necessary change implicit in the passage of both, he reasoned, 'most clearly indicate[s]' signs 'of which it is impossible to misconceive the import', namely, that if the question of Parliamentary Reform is not speedily settled, 'property, and order, and all the institutions of this great monarchy, will be exposed to fearful peril'.[37]

Successive paragraphs of the opening chapter of Dickens's novel amplify the importance of reading signs correctly. They also address the danger of inattentiveness. When secular authorities in England and spiritual leaders in France misconstrue 'messages', grievances accumulate and strengthen. True, '[m]ere messages in the earthly order of events' in England differed from those in France, a country 'less favoured on the whole as to matters spiritual'; but the momentum of the fourth paragraph leads inexorably to

---

[34] John Stuart Mill, 'The Spirit of the Age 1', *Examiner* 73 (9 January 1831): 20, in *Collected Works of John Stuart Mill*, vol. 22, *Newspaper Writings December 1822–July 1831*, ed. Ann P. Robson and John M. Robson (Toronto: University of Toronto Press, 1986), 227–34, 228.

[35] Thomas Carlyle, *The French Revolution: A History*, Book 2, chs 2 and 3 (New York: Modern Library), 31.

[36] Carlyle, 'Signs of the Times', 56.

[37] Macaulay, *Speeches*, 424.

a 'lesson' that applies equally to the inhabitants of London or Paris.[38] Ignore conditions that cry for correction, irrespective of how they originate, and the probable outcome leads to violence. As the narrator reflects on the continuity of history:

> It is likely enough that, rooted in the woods of France and Norway, there were growing trees, when that sufferer [an actual youth beheaded in Amiens in 1766] was put to death, already marked by the Woodman, Fate, to come down and be sawn into boards, to make a certain movable framework with a sack and a knife in it, terrible in history. (*TTC* I:1, 8)

The arboreal metaphor suggests Carlyle,[39] but the conception of time as a three-dimensional entity,[40] in which the trace of one event leads inevitably to another, pervades the novel. 'All these things, and a thousand like them', the first chapter of Book I concludes, 'came to pass in and close upon the dear old year one thousand seven hundred and seventy-five', the year in which the action of the novel opens. In an earlier leading article published in *Household Words*, Dickens animated a single year, whose task as a 'venerable gentleman' was to characterize the last 365 days before he 'breathed his last'. Using antithesis to indicate contrasting achievements and failures, the 'good old gentleman' 1850 reminds readers of the 'business' he bequeaths to his successor and how events, though unseen and unheard, are always preparing.[41] Now situated within the span of a much greater chronology, another 'dear old gentleman' assumes an identical responsibility on a grander scale.

Viewing past events from a later perspective promotes understanding, a point Dickens the historian emphasizes throughout *A Tale of Two Cities*, determined to make readers aware how the ills endured by 'the wretched millions' (*TTC* II:24, 228) of France arose when the prosperous inflicted ruin and starvation on the whole country. 'Crush humanity out of shape once more, under similar hammers, and it will twist itself into the same tortured forms. Sow the same seed of rapacious license and oppression over again, and it will surely yield the same fruit according to its kind' (*TTC* III:15, 356). Vengeance and retribution, Dickens understood, were long in the making and destined to erupt. So concludes the novel's vatic voice, traces of which had appeared in *Barnaby Rudge*. In a passage describing the behaviour of some of the rioters shortly before their violent death on the scaffold, the narrator of that novel resorts to the same trope. The 'two commonest states of mind' of those brought to this pass, he reflects, are either a display

---

[38] Charles Dickens, *A Tale of Two Cities*, ed. Andrew Sanders, Oxford World's Classics (Oxford: Oxford University Press, 1988), I:1, 7–8. Subsequent references are inserted parenthetically in the text by *TTC* Book:chapter, page.

[39] 'The oak grows silently, in the forest, a thousand years; only in the thousandth year, when the woodman arrives with his axe, is there heard an echoing through the solitudes; and the oak announces itself when, with far-sounding crash, it *falls*. How silent too was the planting of the acorn; scattered from the lap of some wandering wind.' Carlyle, *French Revolution*, 24.

[40] Compare T. S. Eliot, *Burnt Norton*: 'Time present and time past | Are both perhaps present in time future, | And time future contained in time past.'

[41] [Charles Dickens,] 'The Last Words of the Old Year', *Household Words*, 4 January 1851, 2:337–9, 337.

of 'reckless hardihood', or 'an extreme of abject cowardice' painful to behold. 'Such was the wholesome growth of the seed sown by the law, that this kind of harvest was usually looked for, as a matter of course' (*BR* 76, 611).[42]

Dickens's readers, however, often denied that the bloodshed in Paris had a social and political aetiology, blinded, to borrow a phrase from Carlyle, by the 'hysterical ophthalmia' surrounding the French Revolution,[43] an attitude, Dickens believed, that persisted for much of the century. In 'Judicial Special Pleading' (*Examiner*, 23 December 1848), for example, he singled out the lack of 'judicial impartiality' on display during a special commission for the county of Chester, where several Chartist leaders had been brought to trial. On this occasion, Dickens took issue with the presiding judge, when he submitted to the grand jury that the Revolution was no more than 'a mere struggle for "political rights"'. On the contrary, Dickens responded. 'It was a struggle on the part of the people for social recognition and existence. It was a struggle for vengeance against intolerable oppressors. It was a struggle for the overthrow of a system of oppression.'[44] Three years later, he repeated the 'lesson' as a reported exchange between himself and a fellow countryman bound for France. When the traveller, 'flushed—highly respectable—Stock Exchange, perhaps—City, certainly', asserts 'that the French are "no go" as a Nation' and authors of '"that Reign of Terror"', Dickens objects. Noting the inability of 'Monied Interest' to remember what had preceded that 'said Reign of Terror', he remarks how events originate from causes. '[T]he harvest that is reaped, has sometimes been sown,' he lectured.[45] English insularity, however, remained a barrier and ignorance about France persisted when readers, like Mr Podsnap, insisted that other countries were 'a mistake'. With 'a flourish of the arm, and a flush of the face', he and like-minded Englishmen swept foreigners out of sight.[46] The 'Horrors of the French Revolution', against which Edmund Burke and others had declaimed, inaugurated a long spell of British orthodoxy that the only harvest of revolution known in France was a victory for 'disimprisoned Anarchy', an ironical development in a country also guilty of regicide.[47]

---

[42] Compare also how 'bad criminal laws, bad prison regulations, and the worst conceivable police' foster the growth of 'the very scum and refuse of London' (*BR* 49, 393).

[43] Thomas Carlyle, 'Memoirs of Mirabeau' (1837), in *Historical Essays*, ed. Vanden Bossche, 153–217, 158.

[44] [Charles Dickens,] 'Judicial Special Pleading', *The Dent Uniform Edition of Dickens' Journalism*, ed. Michael Slater and John Drew, 4 vols (London: J. M. Dent, Columbus: Ohio State University Press, 1993–2000), 2:140–1. Subsequent references are inserted parenthetically in the text by Dent volume: *Title*, page.

[45] [Charles Dickens,] 'A Flight', *Household Words*, 30 August 1851, 3: 529–33, 529–30.

[46] Charles Dickens, *Our Mutual Friend*, ed. Michael Cotsell, Oxford World's Classics (Oxford: Oxford University Press, 1999), I:11, 128.

[47] Other notable examples of forgetting, Dickens thought, include the government's response to the Monmouth Rebellion in 1685. As he reminded readers in *A Child's History*, 'You will hear much of the horrors of the great French Revolution. Many and terrible they were, there is no doubt; but I know of nothing worse, done by the maddened people of France in that awful time, than was done by the highest judge in England, with the express approval of the King of England, in the Bloody Assize.' In Charles Dickens, *Master Humphrey's Clock and A Child's History of England*, New Oxford Illustrated Dickens (London: Oxford University Press, 1958), 36, 522. Subsequent references are inserted parenthetically in the text by *CH* chapter, page.

The para-textual statement Dickens attached to the first book edition of *A Tale of Two Cities* in 1859 hints at the historiographical challenge such attitudes posed. Writing in November, Dickens affirmed his debt to Carlyle. He also spoke of the effort he had made to represent 'truly' the condition of the French people before or during the Revolution. He achieved this, he explained, by drawing on 'the most trustworthy sources' available to document conditions 'the wretched millions in France' had endured. Most particularly, however, he expressed hope that 'the popular and picturesque means' at his disposal would promote further 'understanding [of] that terrible time' (*TTC* 'Preface' 3).

A concerted effort to reduce the gap between the opening of the serial set in 1775 and readers of *All the Year Round* characterizes the remaining chapters of Book I. Acting to conscript subscribers, Dickens frames Jarvis Lorry as a surrogate historian with a story to tell. The tale itself contains both popular and domestic elements, a story of obvious interest to Lucie Manette, a young orphan summoned to France on the basis of 'intelligence' recently sent to London. As Mr Lorry recounts details about her past, Lucie suddenly exclaims: '"But this is my father's story, sir; and I begin to think"—.' Her intuitive response is correct but only partially. She lacks pertinent facts, most importantly the fact that her father had not died, as she had been brought up to believe. '"I entreat you to tell me more, sir,"' Lucy pleads (*TTC* I:4, 26, 27) and so the '"hard, hard history"' of her father is launched (*TTC* I:6, 46), a story of the Doctor of Beauvais, whose fate is inextricably entangled with a history of France that began one night on 22 December 1757.

A series of pictures follows in the next two Books. Working with what Carlyle described as mere 'thimblefuls' of text at his disposal, Dickens's version of the French Revolution unfolds over 31 weekly numbers. Of these, 19 take place in France, with scenes in Paris predominating. Careful planning enabled Dickens to offer a more extended portrait of France than this reduced scope suggests. Book I combines vignettes of urban life in Paris during the latter part of the *ancien régime*. Book II opens in July 1780 and leads to the storming of the Bastille nine years later. By incorporating into the third Book Dr Manette's description of his abduction and imprisonment by the aristocratic Evrémonde brothers, Dickens extends the chronological coverage to include pictures of life under the Bourbons with selective events in Paris of 'The new era.' This period, the narrator explains, was one in which 'the king was tried, doomed, and beheaded'; and citizens from all over France 'summoned to rise against the tyrants of the earth' (*TTC* III:4, 261–2).

The scenes of revolutionary violence that follow constitute some of the finest of their kind. Both here and in the earlier depiction of the Gordon Riots in *Barnaby Rudge* the rhetoric of Dickens's prose works brilliantly to re-create the nightmarish intensity of figures driven to vengeance and retribution. Less frequently remarked, however, is the deftness with which he conveys the mixed feelings and motives of those involved. For all the blood that flows when Newgate was attacked or when the Bastille was stormed, human feelings and ties of affection mingle with the anarchic energies released on both occasions. Present among the most desperate and abandoned villains in London, some were 'comparatively innocent'. There was more than one woman outside the jail, 'disguised in man's attire, and bent upon the rescue of a child or a brother'. Others also motivated by similar natural feelings included two sons of a man under sentence of death, and condemned to suffer on the scaffold 'on the next day but one' (*BR* 63, 501). Shortly after, the narrator provides a further glimpse into their hearts when they seek in desperation to extricate their father from the burning jail. 'But the anguish and suffering of the two sons ... when they heard ... their father's voice, is past description', a gesture of sympathy for malefactors at odds with the broader censure of the Gordon Riots (*BR* 64, 514).

A more extended treatment of this phenomenon occurs in *A Tale of Two Cities* when the narrator, drawing on details supplied by Carlyle, describes the fate meted out to 'Old Foulon', one of the few historical figures to appear in the novel. Joseph-François Foulon, the man Louis XVI appointed Counsellor of State in 1784 to superintend the country's finances, singularly failed in his duty and earned the people's hatred with a jocular remark. When brought before *Parlement* to explain a fiscal scheme of his, he replied under questioning that if it failed, ' "The people may eat grass." ' A week after the fall of the Bastille he was caught in Paris and summarily lynched. When his body was strung up from a lamp-post, rioters attached an emblematic bundle of grass to his back and hung a garland of thistles and nettles round his neck. Dickens, too, recalls this incident as a 'day's bad work', and elaborates on it in keeping with Carlyle's determination to call upon those whose voices had gone silent and been ignored.

Dickens's solution is to imagine a chorus of speakers and so transform a generic mob into individual figures, women who put aside their 'household occupations' and cry for revenge—for my sister, for my mother, for my withered father, for my dead baby:

> Husbands, and brothers, and young men, Give us the blood of Foulon, Give us the head of Foulon, Give us the heart of Foulon, Give us the body and soul of Foulon, Rend Foulon to pieces, and dig him into the ground, that grass may grow from him! With these cries, numbers of the women, lashed into blind frenzy, whirled about, striking and tearing at their own friends until they dropped into a passionate swoon, and were only saved by the men belonging to them from being trampled under foot. (*TTC* II:22, 215)

Did such a chorus of cacophonous voices occur? Were women seized by fury and whirled around until they fell exhausted in the streets of Paris? Under the accumulating weight of the anaphora, questions like this pale as Dickens finds a way to explore what Simon Schama has termed 'the painful problem of revolutionary violence'.[48] Also worth noting is another component of that bad day's work. After the 'angry blood' of Saint-Antoine cools and darkness falls, those same men and women return home to domestic duties. They form long files outside the miserable bakers' shops and beguile their time by embracing one another and by gossiping. Eventually lights appear in windows, fires are made in the streets, and neighbours cook in common. In defiance of expectations,

---

[48] Simon Schama, *Citizens: A Chronicle of the French Revolution* (London: Penguin, 1989), xvii.

socially transgressive energies transform into domestic virtue and calm; and so self-denial and friendly reciprocity prevail as the artisans of Saint-Antoine rejoin the bourgeois fold. With a Carlylean shift in perspective, the narrative voice moves from ground level to deliver a lofty observation:

> Scanty and insufficient suppers those, and innocent of meat, as of most other sauce to wretched bread. Yet, human fellowship infused some nourishment into the flinty viands, and struck some sparks of cheerfulness out of them. Fathers and mothers who had had their full share in the worst of the day, played gently with their meagre children; and lovers, with such a world around them and before them, loved and hoped. (*TTC* II:22, 217)

So much for barbarian rascality, for men and women seen as beasts. Amidst death and vengeance, neighbourly communion, tenderness, and love flourish, a complication or paradox opponents of the Revolution seemed willing to concede.

The template for historical fiction adapted from practices introduced by Macaulay and Carlyle in the 1830s underwent further evolution during the next decade as experience broadened Dickens's interest in writing history. Travel abroad—North America and later residence in Europe—extended his horizons—as his thoughts turned increasingly to the education of children. Perhaps the clearest expression of this last concern occurs in the response he made in May 1843 to an essay by Douglas Jerrold published in the first number of the *Illuminated Magazine*. 'Elizabeth and Victoria', Dickens enthused, stood out for several reasons. Its topic, 'an ironical description of the "good old days"', illustrated the journal's intention to expose England's 'social abuses and follies' and speak with 'boldness' to 'the masses of the PEOPLE' (Preface). Moreover, the whole, Dickens thought, was 'witty, wise', and 'full of Truth'.[49]

Distaste for the nostalgia speakers had expressed at a fundraising dinner Dickens recently attended in London, and the dawning fear that Charley, his eldest child, might acquire equally false notions about the glories of the past, inform his reaction to Jerrold's satire. Only willed national amnesia, Dickens thought, could portray bygone days as 'the lost Paradise of another age' and assert that we 'shall never see such times again!'[50] Yet the noisy approval he witnessed at the conclusion of the charity dinner was hardly confined to the assembled 'City aristocracy', who had leaped to their feet on hearing the virtues of the past extolled. While Dickens found the 'absurdity' of their response 'too horrible to laugh at', reverence for the past prevailed elsewhere. High Tories maintained a voice in both the Lords and the Commons, and united they stood firm against any further encroachment on what they saw as hallowed privileges and ancient rights. Equally opposed to change were bishops, clerics, and members of the senior common rooms of England's two ancient universities, guardians of institutions, Dickens reminded readers

---

[49] *PLets* 3:481–3, 481 nn. 2, 3.
[50] Douglas Jerrold, 'Elizabeth and Victoria', *Illuminated Magazine* 1 (May–October 1843), 3–8, 4.

of the *Examiner*, 'first established for the Manufacture of Clergymen'.[51] Collectively, these influential constituencies, equal in their determination to put back 'the hands upon the Clock of Time', fell into a category Dickens characterized to Jerrold as 'the Parrots of Society', a myopic cross-section of interests, eager, in the later words of the anonymous narrator of *Bleak House*, to cancel 'a few hundred years of history'.[52] Such falsities unchecked, Dickens feared, threatened a 'horrible result'. 'For I don't know what I should do, if [Charley] were to get hold of any conservative or High church notions; and the best way of guarding against ... [this is] ... to wring the parrots' necks in his very cradle.'[53] A more practical option was to write 'a little history of England' designed to make sure Charley and others did not fix their 'affections on wrong heros, [sic] or see the bright side of Glory's sword and know nothing of the rusty one'.[54]

Although dating the inception of this project remains problematic,[55] no uncertainty obscures the revisionary narrative that began in *Household Words* eight years later. To a friend in Genoa Dickens wrote: 'I don't know whether you have read my Child's History—which contains the Truth respecting certain English Kings, whom it has been thought a kind of religious gentility to lie about.'[56] Particularly telling is the reason he offers for the stubborn failure of truth. Historians, it appears, have 'lied' about the shortcomings of England's hereditary monarchs in deference to deep-rooted religious and social attitudes. Enjoined in public liturgies by clerics beseeching God to 'direct and prosper' 'this kingdom in general' under the stewardship of 'our most religious and Gracious king at this time',[57] congregations throughout the realm had grown accustomed to hold the monarchy in awe, an attitude that had taken root over the centuries, reinforced by an acceptance of what Dickens termed 'accursed Gentility'. So ingrained was 'English Tufthunting, Toad Eating' and servility, he thought, the national psyche persisted in ignoring the role blood played in upholding the gross inequities of a hierarchical system based upon birth rather than upon merit or ability.[58] As Forster observed when citing similar remarks to these made to A. H. Layard in April 1855, this was an 'old belief' of Dickens's, traceable, he thought, to his 'early life', during which time

---

[51] [Charles Dickens,] 'Report of the Commissioners Appointed to Inquire into the Conclusion of the Persons Variously Engaged in the University of Oxford', Dent 2:61.

[52] Charles Dickens, *Bleak House*, ed. George Ford and Sylvère Monod, Norton Critical Edition (New York: W. W. Norton, 1977), 12, 145.

[53] *PLets* 3:481–3, 482.

[54] *PLets* 3:537–9, 539.

[55] *PLets* 3: 482 n. 1.

[56] *PLets* 7:220–1, 221.

[57] Occasional Prayers and Thanksgivings, 'A Prayer for the High Court of Parliament', *The Book of Common Prayer*, 1928 (London: Oxford University Press, 1928), 122.

[58] *PLets* 7:586–8, 587. David Copperfield exposes these attitudes reporting a dinner conversation at the Waterbrooks'. Some ' "low minds" ', one guest avers, ' "bow down before idols ... [b]efore services, intellect, and so on. But these are intangible points. Blood is not so." ' To which another agrees, noting that while some young fellows ' "may be a little behind their station, perhaps, in point of education ... and get themselves and other people into a variety of fixes—and all that—but deuce take it, it's delightful to reflect that they've got Blood in 'em!" ' (*DC* 25, 320). Compare also Dickens's 'The Toady Tree', *Household Words*, 26 May 1855, 11: 385–7.

'certain social directions' were formed, of whose sincerity, Forster concluded, 'there can be no doubt'.[59]

The truths Dickens set out to impart in *A Child's History* offer a vigorous corrective to the habit of English sycophancy, an attitude Dickens deplored. This same 'miserable imbecility', he believed, accounted for the tendency to ignore other aspects of English history. In paying tribute to the 'wrong' heroes, clearly the 'right' ones had suffered neglect, a blind spot he sought to rectify by calling attention to brave and confrontational individuals from humble walks of life, who had defied the united power of secular and religious authorities. Of the many who did, Wat Tyler receives extended praise, a tiler by trade, who, with Jack Shaw and John Ball (both priests), rebelled in opposition to the forest laws and the Poll Tax. Inevitably the people of Essex and Kent proved no match for the martial and legal resources of the establishment; and the rising in 1381 met the inevitable end as 'some fifteen hundred of the rioters were tried ... with great rigour, and executed with great cruelty' (*CH* 19, 297). So Wat Tyler fell, Dickens notes, 'a hard-working man' of 'a much higher nature and a much braver spirit than any of the parasites who exulted then, or have exulted since, over his defeat' (*CH* 19, 297). The fate of Tyler and his followers corroborates another truth about the operation of class, especially in war. While historians make Crécy and Agincourt 'famous in English annals' (*CH* 20, 317), Dickens wrote, 'common men' on either side die in disproportionate numbers to 'knights and gentlemen', who pay a ransom after defeat and go home (*CH* 15, 244).

Respect for those who challenged aristocratic privilege also informs two chapters devoted to the English Civil Wars, a period of national stress from which emerged other heroes to whom 'Englishmen owe a mighty debt' (*CH* 33, 471). Inevitably Oliver Cromwell receives extended treatment. Lacking the preternatural characteristics assigned to him by Carlyle,[60] Dickens's Cromwell appears grounded in domestic virtues, 'a good father and a good husband' (*CH* 15, 244) who brought stability to the country and enhanced England's reputation abroad. 'Although he ruled with a strong hand, ... he ruled wisely, and as the times required' (*CH* 34, 488), he observed. Less famous but also praised were John Pym, John Hamden, William Strode, Sir Arthur Haselrig, and Lord Kimbolton, five MPs whose opposition to the 'illegal acts' of Charles I (*CH* 33, 464) initiated a conflict between the king and Parliament that led eventually to war. Interest in this crucial period was also shared by Forster, a noted historian of the seventeenth century, whose *Arrest of the Five Members by Charles the First*, a more sustained and extensive effort than Dickens's to counter Edward Hyde's partisan history of 'the

---

[59] Forster, *Life*, 826.

[60] To Carlyle, Hampden, Eliot, and Pym were 'right worthy and useful men'; Cromwell stands apart as 'a prophetic man: a man with his whole soul *seeing* and struggling to see'. Lecture VI. Friday 22 May, 1840. 'The Hero as King. Cromwell, Napoleon: Modern Revolutionism.' Thomas Carlyle, *On Heroes, Hero-Worship, and the Heroic in History*, ed. David R. Sorensen and Brent E. Kinser (New Haven: Yale University Press, 2013), 162–95, 171, 177.

"Rebellion",[61] the novelist welcomed in 1860. '[Y]our most excellent, interesting, and remarkable book', he wrote, referring to Forster's study, performs an 'enormous' and dual service. Not only did it treat truths that Clarendon's *Historical Narrative* had suppressed and coloured. It also served as a perpetual reminder to those whom disgust with the failings of 'representative Government' has led to disengagement 'and to the Humbugs at Westminster who have come down—a long, long way—from those men'.[62]

This chapter has sought new contexts for Dickens's writing about history and wrestled with misconceptions about his apparent indifference to the discipline. To the contrary, he was informed about ideas originating with Carlyle and Macaulay, whose early writings challenged accepted historiographical practices and appear to have stimulated Dickens's own thinking. Moreover, by rejecting the urge to look back nostalgically on 'the good old days',[63] he stands with Forster in reminding readers that history should be respected and that telling the 'truth' about the deeds of 'certain English kings' could provoke critical reflection. These suggestions hardly constitute proof of a historiographical revolution or make a case for Dickens's elevation into the pantheon occupied by great historians. They do, however, modify Chesterton's ungenerous contention that as a traveller 'in distant ages' Dickens remained 'a sturdy, sentimental English Radical with a large heart and narrow mind'.[64] 'A talent for History', as Carlyle affirmed in 'On History', 'may be said to be born with us ... In a certain sense all men are historians,'[65] not least of whom is Charles Dickens.

Further Reading

Patrick Brantlinger, 'Did Dickens Have a Philosophy of History? The Case of *Barnaby Rudge*', *Dickens Studies Annual* 30 (2001): 59–74

Owen Dudley Edwards, 'Carlyle Versus Macaulay? A Study in History', *Carlyle Studies Annual* 27 (2011): 177–205

John Gardiner, 'Dickens and the Uses of History', in David Paroissien (ed.), *A Companion to Charles Dickens* (Oxford: Blackwell, 2008), 240–54

Colin Jones, Josephine McDonagh, and Jon Mee (eds), 'Introduction', in A Tale of Two Cities and the French Revolution (London: Palgrave Macmillan, 2009), 1–23

---

[61] Edward Hyde, Earl of Clarendon, *The True Historical Narrative of the Rebellion and Civil Wars in England* (1702–4).

[62] *PLets* 9:244–6, 244–5.

[63] For contributions to *Household Words* that highlight advancement over the past, see [Percival Leigh,] 'A Tale of Good Old Times', 27 April 1850, 1:103–7; [John Forster,] 'New Life and Old Learning', 4 May 1850, 1:130–2; [W. H. Wills,] 'Ten Minutes with Her Majesty', 1 March 1851, 2:529–32; [H. Morley,] 'The City Parliament', 21 August 1852, 5:525–30; [John Forster,] 'Seventy-Eight Years Ago', 5 March 1853, 7:1–6.

[64] G. K. Chesterton, *Charles Dickens: The Last of the Great Men* (New York: Readers Club, 1942), 115.

[65] Carlyle, 'On History', 3.

Gareth Stedman Jones, 'The Redemptive Powers of Violence? Carlyle, Marx and Dickens', in Jones, McDonagh and Mee, A Tale of Two Cities *and the French Revolution*, 41–63

John Lucas, 'Past and Present: *Bleak House* and *A Child's History of England*', in John Schad (ed.), *Dickens Refigured: Bodies, Desires and other Histories* (Manchester: Manchester University Press, 1996), 136–56

'On the Styles of Hume, Gibbon, and Robertson', *Gentleman's Magazine*, 102 (January, February, and April 1832), 17–23; 121–6; 313–17

David Paroissien, '"Dedlocked": The Case Against the Past in *Bleak House* and *A Child's History of England*', in Christine Huguet (ed.), *Charles Dickens: L'Inimitable/The Inimitable* (Paris: Democratic Books, 2011), 123–61

David Paroissien, 'Our Island's Story: Dickens's Search for a National Identity', in Hazel Mackenzie and Ben Winyard (eds), *Charles Dickens and the Mid-Victorian Press, 1850–1870* (Buckingham: University of Buckingham Press, 2013), 297–304

Mark Philip, 'The New Philosophy: The Substance and the Shadow in *A Tale of Two Cities*', in Jones, McDonagh, and Mee, A Tale of Two Cities *and the French Revolution*, 24–40

Andrew Sanders, *The Companion to* A Tale of Two Cities (London: Unwin Hyman, 1988)

David R. Sorensen, 'Carlyle, Macaulay, and the "Dignity of History"', *Carlyle Studies Annual* 11 (1989): 41–52

CHAPTER 34

CLASS AND ITS DISTINCTIONS

CHRIS R. VANDEN BOSSCHE

According to one oft-repeated narrative, the cultural work of the Victorian novel was to produce a subjectivity appropriate to the middle class that rose to a dominant social position in the early nineteenth century. The problem with this narrative is that the rise of the middle class is not a historical fact but a story that the Victorians told about themselves as a way of explaining their historical situation.[1] As Dror Wahrman, David Cannadine, Patrick Joyce, and other social historians have shown, moreover, the Victorians employed a variety of discourses of class each of which privileged a different model of class: not just the tripartite model of aristocracy, middle class, and working class, but also dichotomous models and finely graded hierarchies. Thus, it would be more accurate to say that the mainstream novel—the novel of canonical authors like Dickens, the Brontës, Trollope, and Eliot—employed middle-class discourse. Moreover, given that all class discourses dialogically incorporated oppositional discourses, these novelists did not confine themselves to the discourses of the middle class. Consequently, this chapter will not use class as a category of analysis—a procedure that treats class as something we bring to bear from the outside—and instead will treat it as a discourse through which Victorian authors and readers thought about themselves and sought to come to terms with social being.

This approach means that I do not define class solely as an economically determined category. The idea that class is determined by one's relation to production is itself an element of Victorian discourses about class that often employed the tripartite model that defines class in terms of the source of one's income: the landed class, the moneyed classes, and the working classes. This discourse frequently referred to class interest, a concept implying that individuals who share the same source of income have shared

---

[1] Dror Wahrman, *Imagining the Middle Class: The Political Representation of Class in Britain, c.1780–1840* (Cambridge: Cambridge University Press, 1995), 332–3.

political interests that lead them to promote certain kinds of legislation favouring income from that source, the most notable example being the Corn Laws, which were said to favour the landed interest. As noted above, it is important in this context to keep in mind that the familiar tripartite model of class—aristocracy, middle class, and working class—competed both with a dichotomous model (e.g. the rich and the poor) and a model depicting a finely graded hierarchy.[2]

Consequently, I will not treat Dickens as an author who seeks to promote the interests of his class, but rather an author who employs class discourse. This approach reflects shifts in recent criticism of Dickens. Indeed, there are, surprisingly, few studies of his representations of social class, while much more attention has been paid to the class position from which he wrote. The main debate has been about the extent to which Dickens wrote as a member of, and advocate for, the middle class and to what extent he was a radical and/or a critic of that class.[3] Both sides have tended to assume that Dickens had a particular class identity and thus either wrote on behalf of the middle class or of 'the people' or, in some cases, that he shifted from one to the other over time. The general trend in the late twentieth century was to assume that Dickens, in light of his income and social status, was middle class and thus wrote in the service of middle-class ideology. In the early twenty-first century, drawing on the above-mentioned social histories of class, critics have begun to conceive this question not in terms of Dickens's class identity, but in terms of how he deployed class discourse. This approach enables us to account for his use of radical discourse, as has been so convincingly demonstrated by critics such as Sally Ledger and Sambudha Sen.[4] Future criticism can profitably set aside questions of whether Dickens was radical or middle class and instead explore how he deploys multiple class discourses within a single text as a way to come to terms with the problems of social existence in his time.

All of these Victorian class discourses employ a vocabulary of social exclusion and inclusion. The complexity of the Victorian conception of the gentleman is a result of the way it operates in class discourse as an indicator of social inclusion.[5] The rise of

---

[2] See David Cannadine, *The Rise and Fall of Class in Britain* (New York: Columbia University Press, 1999), 20.

[3] Most accounts identify Humphry House as establishing the orthodoxy of a middle-class Dickens. *The Dickens World*, 2nd edn (London: Oxford University Press, 1942), 152–69. House was in turn disputing T. A. Jackson's argument for a radical Dickens. *Charles Dickens: The Progress of a Radical* (New York: International, 1938). For more recent criticism that treats Dickens as writing from a middle-class perspective, see Knezevic and Sen, cited in notes 10 and 4.

[4] Sally Ledger, *Dickens and the Popular Radical Imagination* (Cambridge: Cambridge University Press, 2007); Sambudha Sen, *London, Radical Culture, and the Making of the Dickensian Aesthetic* (Columbus: Ohio State University Press, 2012). See also Pam Morris, who argues that Dickens both identifies with and seeks to distance himself from the working class because he has an ideal image of himself as gentleman. *Dickens's Class Consciousness: A Marginal View* (New York: St Martin's Press, 1991), 10–14.

[5] See David Castronovo, *The English Gentleman: Images and Ideas in Literature and Society* (New York: Ungar, 1987) and Robin Gilmour, *The Idea of the Gentleman in the Victorian Novel* (Boston: Allen and Unwin, 1981).

the middle-class narrative distinguishes a 'new' class in the middle precisely in order to envision the inclusion of this class in the nation. The Chartist movement similarly sought inclusion of the 'people', the majority of the population that constituted the lower classes. The Latin *gentilis* simply means belonging to the *gens* (people, nation, family), but gentility eventually came to mean belonging to a *good* family, thus dividing the included from the excluded. This meant in turn that, at least in theory, only a son of a gentleman could claim to be a gentleman. From this point of view, aspirations to gentility are not merely a matter of aping the upper classes but of seeking to establish oneself as belonging to society and the nation.

As has been well documented, however, the meaning of the term gentleman had been evolving for some time. Almost from its introduction into English, the word also indicated a man who possessed certain character traits and acted in accord with them. These were, on the one hand, implicitly the traits of those who were well born, but on the other, traits that indicated good character regardless of the status of one's family. Thus, it was possible to observe individuals who behaved like gentlemen though they were not sons of gentlemen and sons of gentlemen who did not behave like gentlemen. The notion that being a gentleman involved one's behaviour, rather than one's birth, gained increasing acceptance in the nineteenth century. In accord with middle-class discourse, the true gentleman was not born but self-made. Thus, the rise of the middle class finds its parallel in the narrative of self-making. As we will see, however, the potential for abuse of the self-making process as well as of the narrative of self-making meant that the word did not entirely lose its connotations of exclusivity.

The fact that class was a term of exclusion and gentleman a term of inclusion may explain why, even as the word gentleman appears thousands of times and constitutes a major thematic element of his novels, Dickens seldom uses the word class in the sense of social class and does not for the most part depict characters as members of a particular social class. Nor does he employ other equivalents for class. The words 'aristocracy' or 'aristocratic' appear about 50 times in his novels while 'upper class' appears four times and 'lower class', 'working class', and the 'poorer class' a total of eight times. The term 'middle class' occurs only once, and in that case ('the Society for Granting Annuities to Unassuming Members of the Middle Classes'[6]) the narrator does not use it to define a group. He uses the term *station* in the sense of social status far more frequently than the word *class*. Yet while the word appears in this sense at least 100 times, he rarely aligns it with the classic tripartite model linking class to the source of one's income. To begin with, it is used by characters more often than by the Dickensian narrator, and when the latter employs it, it is almost always relative, indicating differences in circumstances

---

[6] Charles Dickens, *Our Mutual Friend*, ed. Michael Cotsell, Oxford World's Classics (Oxford: Oxford University Press, 1989), I:17, 211. Subsequent references are inserted parenthetically in the text by *OMF* book:chapter, page.

rather than a specific class status, as in 'Mr. Carker the Junior, Walter's friend, was his brother; two or three years older than he, but widely removed in station.'[7]

Dickens's novels instead employ class discourse dramatically through characterization and plotting rather than through narrative commentary or identification of characters. In his letters, Dickens on occasion employs class discourse in a straightforward way, as when he claimed in 1855 in accord with the recognition that the nation's chief political institutions were still controlled by the aristocracy that England has 'no such thing as a Middle Class'.[8] The fact that Dickens did use the term middle class in his letters in unambiguous fashion makes its absence in the novels all the more striking. In the few instances in which class terms appear in his novels, they are almost always employed by characters to identify someone's social status. So while characters are concerned to make social distinctions, the Dickensian narrator very rarely does so.

Of course, Dickens does indicate with great precision the social location of his characters through their manner of speech, the quality and location of their homes, their profession and income, their social interactions, and the social circles in which they move.[9] The living situation indicates with great specificity how much wealth a character possesses, yet no one set of markers of social location readily maps onto a class identity or more particularly to the tripartite model of lower, middle, or upper class. In accord with his predominant use of middle-class discourse, he does on occasion identify the aristocracy and working classes each acting as a class while his privileging of this discourse accounts for the wide range of social locations of individuals who might be labelled middle class. To take *Dombey and Son* as an example, Dombey, James Carker, John Carker, and Solomon Gills all earn their living from commerce, but Dombey owns a vast enterprise and possesses corresponding wealth, Gills is an artisan, small businessman, and shopkeeper, James Carker is a head clerk who lives in comparative luxury (albeit in part, perhaps, because he is an embezzler), while his brother makes a relatively meagre wage and lives quite modestly. Even less so do they share values, attitudes, or economic interests. This is not to say that class does not figure in Dickens's depiction of society but rather that we find it not in characterization so much as emplotment and discourse.

In accord with a key element of middle-class discourse and the rise of the middle-class narrative, Dickens's novels depict a rising middle class displacing a moribund self-serving aristocracy.[10] This discourse in turn draws on older radical discourses employing

---

[7] Charles Dickens, *Dombey and Son*, ed. Alan Horsman (Oxford: Clarendon Press, 1974), 13, 172. Subsequent references are inserted parenthetically in the text by *DS* chapter, page.

[8] Letter to William Charles Macready, 4 October 1855, in Charles Dickens, *The Letters of Charles Dickens*, ed. Madeline House, Graham Storey, et al., Pilgrim/British Academy Edition, 12 vols (Oxford: Clarendon Press, 1965–2002), 7:714–16, 715.

[9] For a stimulating discussion of class in relation to geographical location, see Franco Moretti, *Atlas of the European Novel 1800–1900* (London: Verso, 1998), 117–33.

[10] See Knezevic, who argues that Dickens was frustrated with the persistence of the patrician elite and the failure of the middle class to displace it. Borislav Knezevic, *Figures of Finance Capitalism: Writing, Class, and Capital in the Age of Dickens* (New York: Routledge, 2003), 17; see chapter 4.

a dichotomous model of class opposing the people to the aristocracy. Over time Dickens shifts from depicting self-interested aristocrats to depicting a self-interested aristocratic class. The earlier novels depict individual aristocrats like Sir John Chester and Sir Mulberry Hawk in terms of middle-class discourse. Beginning with *Bleak House* and its depiction of Chancery, however, he depicts the aristocracy as an extended family that promotes its own interests; unlike Chester and Hawk, Sir Leicester is no villain, but simply a man who typifies his class in his resistance to change and progress. The fact that Dickens makes some aristocrats in the later novels sympathetic is attributable not to a softening of his views but rather the shift in his novels from locating social evil in flaws of character to more deeply systemic problems arising from the promotion of class interest.

In these later novels, Dickens focuses on the aristocracy as a class, rather than on individual aristocrats, by depicting aristocratic families as vast kinship networks. As the narrator of *Bleak House* comments, '[e]verybody on Sir Leicester Dedlock's side of the question, and of his way of thinking, would appear to be his cousin more or less'.[11] The Dedlocks are aligned with two sets of families: the Boodles, Coodles, Doodles, and so on down to the Quoodles and the Buffys, Cuffys, Duffys, down to the Puffys. While these are all presumably different families, the rhyming names suggest their kinship with one another, the focus being on the kinship network rather than on individuals. While the -oodles and -uffys theoretically oppose one another, they are fundamentally the same class for whom it is clear that as far as governing the nation is concerned, 'nobody is in question but Boodle and his retinue, and Buffy and *his* retinue' (*BH* 12, 146). The Barnacles and Stiltstalkings—an extended family related to Lord Decimus Tite Barnacle—function similarly in *Little Dorrit*, as do the St Evrémondes in *A Tale of Two Cities*, in which Darnay's uncle appears through all the early chapters merely as 'Monsieur the Marquis', an epithet that emphasizes his rank rather than his individuality.

Dickens depicts these extended kinship networks not by way of suggesting that the aristocracy values family in accord with the domestic ideal, but rather in accord with contemporary depictions of members of the aristocracy as marrying not for love but in order to advance their political and economic interests.[12] Mr Meagles is quite aware that the Barnacle kin are linked together by such marriages:

[Lord Decimus] married, in seventeen ninety-seven, Lady Jemima Bilberry, who was the second daughter by the third marriage—no! There I am wrong! That was Lady Seraphina—Lady Jemima was the first daughter by the second marriage of the fifteenth Earl of Stiltstalking with the Honourable Clementina Toozellem. Very well. Now this young fellow's father married a Stiltstalking and *his* father married

---

[11] Charles Dickens, *Bleak House*, ed. George Ford and Sylvère Monod, Norton Critical Edition (New York: W.W. Norton, 1977), 28, 347. Subsequent references are inserted parenthetically in the text by *BH* chapter, page.

[12] Chris R. Vanden Bossche, *Reform Acts: Chartism, Social Agency and the Victorian Novel, 1832–1865* (Baltimore: Johns Hopkins University Press, 2014), 14–15.

his cousin who was a Barnacle. The father of that father who married a Barnacle, married a Joddleby.[13]

Although it is a cliché that aristocrats married wealthy members of the middle classes for their money while the latter married aristocrats for their status, Dickens emphasizes the former over the latter by making the aristocrats the primary actors in such courtships. In *Barnaby Rudge*, we learn the motives of the wife of Sir John Chester who gains entry into the 'politest and best circles' of society in exchange for providing him with a 'fortune',[14] but the focus of the plot is on his attempt to force his son to marry for a fortune, not on the possessor of a fortune who seeks a rise in status. In *Dombey and Son* Mrs Skewton, 'sister to the late Lord Feenix', marries her daughter to Dombey (*DS* 21, 286), who is more interested in gaining an heir than a relationship to Feenix. Most tellingly, in *Little Dorrit* the Meagleses actively seek to prevent their daughter from marrying the Barnacle relation Henry Gowan, who is clearly after her money, even as Gowan's mother seeks to disguise his financial motives by claiming that it is the Meagleses who are after the status conferred by the marriage.

Dickens similarly employs class discourse that critiques the aristocracy for claiming that it can best govern the nation because it is disinterested, when it actually is using its political power to advance its own interests. He thus satirizes the Barnacles' claim that 'no *country* which failed to submit itself to those two large families could possibly hope to be under the protection of Providence' and elsewhere concludes: 'Either the *nation* was under a load of obligation to the Barnacles, or the Barnacles were under a load of obligation to the nation. It was not quite unanimously settled which; the Barnacles having their opinion, the *nation* theirs' (*LD* I:25, 295; I:10, 103; emphasis added). Just as they seek kinship alliances in order to enhance their wealth and power, aristocratic families, while claiming that wealth in the form of land frees them from money-grubbing, in fact seek political power in order to obtain pensions and government sinecures for their kin who in turn support them in their quest for greater power and wealth at the expense of the nation as a whole, a process that becomes quite explicit when the narrator of *Bleak House* informs us that when Sir Leicester is in danger of losing his seat in Parliament, members of his family 'feel deprived of a stake in the country—or the pension list' (*BH* 28, 356).

The novels thus invoke a class rhetoric depicting an idle aristocracy that conceals behind a pose of cultivated disinterest an avoidance of working to earn one's living. In *Bleak House* Sir Leicester's family insists that '[i]n any country in a wholesome state, [Sir Leicester's cousin] Volumnia would be a clear case for the pension list' (*BH* 28, 348) and in *Little Dorrit* Mrs Gowan has received an apartment at Hampton Court because she is the widow of a man who, for no apparent reason except that he is related to the

---

[13] Charles Dickens, *Little Dorrit*, ed. Harvey Peter Sucksmith (Oxford: Clarendon Press, 1979), I:17, 199. Subsequent references are inserted parenthetically in the text by *LD* book:chapter, page.

[14] Charles Dickens, *Barnaby Rudge*, ed. Clive Hurst (Oxford: Oxford University Press, 2003), 15, 130. Subsequent references are inserted parenthetically in the text by *BR* chapter, page.

Barnacles, 'had been pensioned off as a Commissioner of nothing particular somewhere or other, and had died at his post with his drawn salary in his hand, nobly defending it to the last extremity' (*LD* I:17, 201). Indeed, the satire of the Circumlocution Office centres on the fact that the Barnacles, in keeping with their name, parasitically use the office to provide income for their family. One aspect of the satire on the principle of 'How not to do it' is that while the occupants of these sinecures, unlike those who receive pensions, are expected to work for their income, the Barnacles studiously avoid doing any work.

In accord with the older conception of gentility, these families claim that birth into the aristocracy or gentry gives them a right to pensions and sinecures and excludes those who are not so born. Thus 'Boodle and Buffy, their followers and families, their heirs, executors, administrators, and assigns, are the *born* first-actors, managers, and leaders, and no others can appear upon the scene for ever and ever' (*BH* 12, 146; emphasis added). The passage cited above, stating that 'nobody is in question but Boodle and his retinue, and Buffy and *his* retinue', goes on to explain the underlying logic by which they alone 'are the great actors for whom the stage is reserved' while the 'People' as mere 'supernumeraries' are excluded from it (*BH* 12, 146). Mrs Gowan laments that her son is 'reduced to court the swinish public as a follower of the low Arts, instead of asserting his *birthright* and putting a ring through its nose as an acknowledged Barnacle', and the Barnacles accordingly 'considered themselves in a general way as having *vested rights*' in the administration of the Circumlocution Office (*LD* I:26, 305; I:10, 103; emphasis added). When they define national priorities by asserting 'that the question was all about John Barnacle, Augustus Stiltstalking, William Barnacle and Tudor Stiltstalking, Tom, Dick, or Harry Barnacle or Stiltstalking, because there was nobody else but mob' they constitute the aristocracy as possessing the sole right of citizenship through the process of excluding the majority of Britons as members of the 'mob' (*LD* I:26, 306).

As with the aristocracy, the actions and behaviours of individualized characters from the lower classes in Dickens's novels are not dictated by their class status, and he does not ascribe any one set of values or characteristics to them. Apart perhaps from a shared use of dialect, criminals and villains such as Bill Sikes and Rogue Riderhood and honest working people such as the Peggottys and Stephen Blackpool have little in common. Nor does he simply divide them into these two categories. One might see in the Peggottys and Blackpool a stereotyped depiction of the working poor who are not only honest but deferential to their social superiors; however, they are far from representative of Dickens's working-class characters. Dickens's labourers, artisans, and servants thus exhibit a wide range of attitudes to social distinctions and their place in the social order.

While Dickens shifts to depicting the aristocracy as a class in his later novels, his depiction of the lower classes acting *as* a class occurs already in *Barnaby Rudge* and is repeated in only two other novels, *Hard Times* and *A Tale of Two Cities*. The difference in his treatment accords with the fact that Dickens's later novels manifest his increasing focus on the view that the problems of British society lay with the aristocracy's hold on political power; these later works do not change the fundamental view that the lower classes act only in response to the actions of the upper classes and cannot act collectively as a class to change the social order and improve their lives.

While the mobs in the historical novels might be seen as seeking political power, the novels depict them as fundamentally reactive. The narrator of *Barnaby Rudge* contends that the 'growth' of the mob participating in the Gordon Riots 'was fostered by bad criminal laws, bad prison regulations, and the worst conceivable police' (*BR* 49, 393). This statement depicts the motive for action not as the desire of the participants to effect a change, but rather as an expression of anger at misgovernment: as a 'great mass [that] never reasoned', they do not have the rational capacity to act on their own behalf (*BR* 53, 421). Indeed, they do not even understand that it is the aristocratic government that oppresses them, which is why they can be led to attack Roman Catholics who have nothing to do with their circumstances. The narrator of *A Tale of Two Cities* provides a similar explanation of the behaviour of the masses during the French Revolution: 'Crush humanity out of shape once more, under similar hammers, and it will twist itself into the same tortured forms. Sow the same seed of rapacious license and oppression over again, and it will surely yield the same fruit according to its kind.'[15] Once again, Dickens depicts the lower classes as reactive—made inhuman by the French aristocracy—rather than as agents seeking to further their own interests. Like the rioters in *Barnaby Rudge*, the denizens of Saint-Antoine are an unthinking mass, incapable of transforming their grievances into rational action. Both novels depict their action as simply a force of nature by comparing them to the surging 'seas' (*BR* 52, 413; *TTC* II:21, 203–11).

In this respect, to act collectively not only fails to promote the interests of the lower classes but actually frustrates them. The rioters in *Barnaby Rudge* become so frenzied that they die in the fires that they themselves have set. While *Hard Times* was inspired in part by the Preston strike of 1853–4, Dickens does not depict the union as striking to improve wages or conditions, but instead as coercing working men to join its membership. The labourers' inability to form a rational plan of action leads them to turn the violence of their anger on themselves by attacking those men who refuse to join the union. In keeping with the Carlylean theme in which the revolution feeds upon itself, the revolutionaries in France pursue 'suicidal vengeance' and themselves fall victim to it (*TTC* III:9, 303; see III:15, 360).

The depiction of working-class action does, nevertheless, evolve in one way in these novels in that Dickens increasingly portrays the lower classes as capable of a rational understanding of the causes of their oppression and consequently as less open to manipulation by the upper classes. Whereas the mob in *Barnaby Rudge* is utterly ignorant of the real sources of their discontent, which enables John Chester to promote his own interest by manipulating them, redirecting their anger from its true source to Roman Catholics, *Hard Times* presents a more sympathetic view of factory labourers and affirms their belief that their 'condition' was 'somehow or other, worse than it might

---

[15] Charles Dickens, *A Tale of Two Cities*, ed. Andrew Sanders, Oxford World's Classics (Oxford: Oxford University Press, 1988), III:15, 356. Subsequent references are inserted parenthetically in the text by *TTC* book:chapter, page.

be'.[16] In accord with upper-class discourse, it depicts the members of the union being manipulated by the oratory of a demagogic union organizer, Slackbridge, who is 'not so honest, ... not so manly ... not so good-humoured' as they are (*HT* II:4, 113). However, they are not being manipulated to serve the interests of another class, as is the mob in *Barnaby Rudge*, for although Slackbridge may not himself be a working man he does not belong to the governing classes. The residents of Saint-Antoine similarly have legitimate grievances and understand that aristocratic control of the government leads to their oppression. If they are manipulated, it is not by an outsider but by Madame Defarge, who makes the anger that she shares with other residents serve her personal desire for revenge for wrongs done to members of her family by the aristocratic Evrémondes. The novel makes no reference to such leaders of the revolution as Robespierre or Marat, who might be regarded as guiding or manipulating the working poor, but nonetheless it does not go so far as to envision the poor as bettering their condition.

If Dickens's novels portray, on the one hand, the aristocracy as a class that seeks to protect its privileged status from which all others are excluded and, on the other hand, the working classes as rebelling against the resulting injustices without aiming, or having the capacity, to achieve social inclusion, they depict the middle-class discourse of self-making as a process of achieving social inclusion. Precisely because middle-class discourse privileges individuals who earn their wealth and position through their own actions rather than obtaining them through class affiliation, the novels do not depict the middle class acting collectively. At the same time, in accord with elements of aristocratic and lower-class discourse critiquing the middle class, they ponder the meaning of social inclusion and the problems that arise in the process of seeking to achieve it.

Because class discourse defined social inclusion in terms established by aristocratic discourse, aspirations to inclusion in Dickens take the form of claiming the status of gentility. In this respect, these characters are not seeking to emulate the aristocracy but to claim the right of inclusion guaranteed by the status of the gentleman. Nicholas Nickleby insists he is the 'son of a country gentleman' in order to assert that he is the 'equal in birth and education' of Sir Mulberry Hawk, not to claim social superiority to the Kenwigs or Crummleses.[17] The word gentleman and its variants (gentlemen, gentlemanly) appear over 5,000 times in the 14 completed novels. To be sure, the vast majority of these instances involve the use of the word merely as a synonym for man, as in the 'gentleman was fast asleep'.[18] That in such cases Dickens does not intend to distinguish gentlemen from ordinary men is evident from the fact that his narrator applies the term

---

[16] Charles Dickens, *Hard Times*, ed. Fred Kaplan, Norton Critical Edition, 4th edn (New York: W.W. Norton, 2017), II:4, 114. Subsequent references are inserted parenthetically in the text by *HT* Book:chapter, page.

[17] Charles Dickens, *Nicholas Nickleby*, ed. Paul Schlicke, Oxford World's Classics (Oxford: Oxford University Press, 2009), 32, 417. Subsequent references are inserted parenthetically in the text by *NN* chapter, page.

[18] Charles Dickens, *Pickwick Papers*, ed. James Kinsley (Oxford: Clarendon Press, 1986), 2, 28.

to individuals regardless of birth, wealth, social standing, occupation, or even moral character, using it, for example, to refer, without explicit irony, to Wackford Squeers and Rogue Riderhood, neither of whom qualifies as a gentleman by any of these standards. In this respect, Dickens's usage is inclusive—all men are gentlemen (and all women gentlewomen)—even as its use in place of the generic *man* suggests the importance of the term for his society. While the Dickensian narrator does not use gentleman as a term of distinction, however, characters in the novels do. Thus Fanny Squeers aspires to marry Nicholas because he is ' "a gentleman's son—(none of your corn-factors, but a gentleman's son of high descent)" ' and in so doing distinguishes him from Matilda Price's fiancé John Browdie (*NN* 9, 104), while *Great Expectations* turns, of course, on how Pip's expectations will transform him from 'a common labouring-boy' into a 'gentleman'.[19]

In accord with the contemporary discourse of the rising middle class, Dickens's novels link the social inclusion entailed in claims of gentility to the ideal of self-making. To claim to be genteel by birth was to claim an arbitrary superiority to others that was belied by myriad examples of aristocratic misdeeds. Self-making thus offered a form of gentility based on what one does, not on being born into a 'good' family. At the same time, however, self-made individuals could be just as self-interested as aristocrats. Moreover, because self-made gentility was based on what one did, it was open to the possibility that the mere performance of self-making could take the place of genuine striving and hard work.

Dickens's protagonists tend to claim the status of the gentleman both through birth and self-making, which accounts for his repeated use of a plot mechanism in which a hero—or in the case of Esther Summerson a heroine—is excluded from the ranks of gentlemen then regains social inclusion through the process of self-making. Birth thus continues to guarantee the authenticity of one's genteel status while exclusion liberates one from the old landed aristocracy so that one can embrace the middle-class ideal of self-making and earn the status of the gentleman. The development of this topos of exclusion and re-inclusion manifests Dickens's continuing attempts to imagine the self-made individual who is neither self-interested nor a fictitious self-invention.

Many of Dickens's protagonists are initially excluded from a genteel patrimony. Oliver Twist is born 'a gentleman's son',[20] but his father's death and the related circumstances of his relationship with Oliver's mother cause the child to grow up an orphan ignorant of his father's status. Esther Summerson's illegitimacy means that in spite of the fact that she is in every other way the equal, or superior, of Ada Clare, she is excluded from consideration as a marriage partner for Richard Carstone, indeed from any marriage at all. Nicholas Nickleby's father, though 'a country gentleman', fails to leave an inheritance sufficient to provide for his family, and his uncle, Ralph, further disenfranchises Nicholas by forcing him to go to work for Wackford Squeers just as Murdstone first displaces David Copperfield's late father and then, after the death of his mother, sends him to labour

---

[19] Charles Dickens, *Great Expectations*, ed. Margaret Caldwell (Oxford: Clarendon Press, 1993), I:8, 61. Subsequent references are inserted parenthetically in the text by *GE* volume:chapter, page.

[20] Charles Dickens, *Oliver Twist*, ed. Kathleen Tillotson (Oxford: Clarendon Press, 1966), 41, 280.

in a manufactory. Nicholas is the last of Dickens's heroes to explicitly claim he is the son of a gentleman, but David Copperfield implies a similar status retrospectively when he titles his narrative 'The Personal History, Adventures, Experience, & Observation of David Copperfield the Younger of Blunderstone Rookery.' Sir John Chester disowns his son and the older Martin Chuzzlewit exiles his grandson because their heirs fail to conform to their marriage plans. The Marquis Saint-Evrémonde's attempted suppression of Charles Darnay leads the latter into exile, and Arthur Clennam's mother sends him to languish in China. For Edward Chester and Charles Darnay, whose families claim aristocratic status, this exile is a happy circumstance, freeing them so they can undertake self-making, earning their own bread (*TTC* II:24, 233). Pip, by contrast, is presumably the son of a labourer or artisan, but nonetheless experiences exclusion when Estella declares him 'a common labouring boy' in response to which he imagines that his great expectations derive from a genteel fairy godmother.

While the discovery or assertion of their genteel birth plays a role in these narratives, the achievement of social inclusion requires adoption of the ideal of self-making. The exception is Oliver Twist, who is restored to his status while he is still a child so that he never has the opportunity to embrace self-making. Dickens instead endows him with an innocence that does not arise from his youth but from his genteel birth, the fact that he speaks a genteel English though surrounded by people who speak working-class dialect or thieves' argot standing in for his genteel instincts. After *Oliver Twist*, however, the protagonists always earn their way to gentility. Nicholas, like Oliver, seems to have inherited the character of the gentleman, which leads him to assault Squeers for his unjust treatment of Smike and Mulberry Hawk for his abuse of his sister, but, more importantly, he earns his way first as an actor and dramatist, then as a clerk, and finally as a partner of the Cheerybles. Edward Chester works on a colonial plantation and Charles Darnay, declaring, ' "I must do, to live, what others of my countrymen, even with nobility at their backs, may have to do some day—work" ' (*TTC* II:9, 119), becomes a teacher and translator. It is Esther Summerson's diligent work as housekeeper and caring for others that leads John Jarndyce to declare her 'true legitimacy' and paves the way to a respectable marriage to the physician Allan Woodcourt (*BH* 64, 753).

In *David Copperfield* and *Great Expectations*, the desire to obtain social legitimacy is complicated by the fact that class discourse defines the gentility of the upper classes as not having to earn a living. While Nicholas Nickleby apparently sees no contradiction between claiming to be the son of a gentleman and earning his way, David Copperfield and Pip, while not claiming genteel parentage, initially seek to establish themselves as gentlemen without self-making. David Copperfield pursues the status of gentleman through a kinship alliance by marrying Dora Spenlow, whose father is an attorney in Doctor's Commons where they 'plume themselves on their gentility', and it is only when forced to do so by the death and financial failure of her father that he embraces the value of self-making and sets to work, first as a shorthand reporter and then as a novelist.[21] Pip

---

[21] Charles Dickens, *David Copperfield*, ed. Nina Burgis (Oxford: Clarendon Press, 1981), 23, 293. Subsequent references are inserted parenthetically in the text by *DC* chapter, page.

initially sees being made a gentleman as an escape from labour, albeit the manual labour of the artisan, his fantasy that he is destined to marry Estella corresponding with David's courtship of Dora. It is only when he learns that his expectations derive from a criminal father figure, not a genteel godmother, that he belatedly begins to earn his way as a clerk in Herbert Pocket's firm.

As these examples indicate, Dickens's novels increasingly raise questions about self-making. Self-making is a complex concept comprising not only the principle of earning one's own way but also of developing qualities intrinsic to the self. While the aspiration to gentility may evince a desire for inclusion, it is also a form of external validation that defines a classed self. Self-making can then become a public performance that displaces development of one's inner talents and personality. Pip's training in becoming a gentleman, for example, focuses precisely on the performance of gentility, in the clothes he wears, table manners, and affiliation with other gentlemen, while his moral development remains stunted.

Not surprisingly then, the novels critique self-made men who are no longer striving to make themselves. While self-making is central to middle-class discourse, Dickens adapts radical critiques depicting those who derive their income from capital—bankers, money-lenders, merchants—as unproductive and self-interested. The elder Paul Dombey does not have to earn his way because he has inherited his business. While he does not claim gentility, the very structure of the firm of Dombey and Son is based on the genteel principle of inheritance: he became 'Dombey' because he was formerly the 'Son'. As with the aristocracy, his aim in marriage is merely the reproduction of himself and his firm, hence his inability to form any kind of meaningful relationship with his wives and children. Similarly, Mr Merdle has married his wife because of her status, which is represented synecdochically by her reduction to 'the bosom'. The character of Josiah Bounderby is summed up in the vision of his self-reproduction through a will

> whereby five-and-twenty Humbugs, ... each taking upon himself the name, Josiah Bounderby of Coketown, should for ever dine in Bounderby Hall, for ever lodge in Bounderby Buildings, for ever attend a Bounderby chapel, for ever go to sleep under a Bounderby chaplain, for ever be supported out of a Bounderby estate, and for ever nauseate all healthy stomachs, with a vast amount of Bounderby balderdash and bluster. (*HT* II:9, 234)

Others like Ralph Nickleby and Ebenezer Scrooge do not seek self-reproduction but rather become self-enclosed through their obsession with reproducing wealth, which leads them to avoid establishing bonds of affection with others. Scrooge's self-making, as revealed by the Spirit of Christmas Past, involves cutting off romance while Ralph Nickleby abandons his wife and child. By contrast, one of the few self-made men that Dickens portrays positively is Ironmaster Rouncewell, who not only is an inventor and industrialist, thus an active maker of things, but also is married and seeks, through assisting his son in marrying Rosa, to bring others into the middle class.

Self-enclosure leads self-made men to view the world entirely in terms of their own self-interest and to deny the reality of others. This is the basic principle of 'Podsnappery' in which 'Mr. Podsnap settled that whatever he put behind him he put out of existence' (*OMF* I:11, 128). These self-made men substitute the narrative of self-making for the actual process of self-development. The most obvious example is Bounderby who can 'never sufficiently vaunt himself a self-made man' but whose narrative of having been 'born in a ditch' and 'fought through' poverty is pure fiction (*HT* I:4, 18). The creation of the fiction of self-making is further linked through the bribes he pays his mother to stay away from him with the process of self-enclosure that denies relationship to others.

In the later novels, this fictional dimension of social inclusion is depicted as the mere circulation of signs. In *Little Dorrit*, Merdle's reputation derives not from an actual fortune but from the circulation of rumours of his wealth: 'All people knew (or thought they knew) that he had made himself immensely rich' (*LD* II:12, 539). Consequently, when he commits suicide and people learn of his fraud, the value of his shares collapses. William Dorrit's claim of gentility, as Dickens's narrator indicates, is a 'ragged old fiction', and he is treated as a gentleman by the other residents incarcerated in the Marshalsea simply because they acquiesce in it (*LD* I:18, 207). There is no indication that his family had previously laid claim to genteel status; on the contrary, 'the more dependent he became on the contributions of his changing family, the greater stand he made by his forlorn gentility' (*LD* I:7, 72). In *Our Mutual Friend*, Alfred Lammle and Sophronia Akersham enter into matrimony because each believes what they have heard circulating at these dinners, that the other is a man/woman 'of property', a rumour, like Merdle's wealth, without foundation (*OMF* I:10, 114). The novel's satire on 'good society' thus suggests that social inclusion involves a shared fiction through which a social group asserts itself as distinctive even though nothing in reality distinguishes these people from other citizens.

The same mediation through which individuals claim to belong to good society also produces the desire for inclusion among those who are excluded from it. Even as the fiction of good society enables its members to feel socially included, it by necessity defines an excluded group that is not acknowledged as belonging to it, hence the conclusion of *Our Mutual Friend* in which the 'Voice of Society' universally condemns Eugene Wrayburn for marrying a woman who is not 'accustomed to Society' (*OMF* IV:17, 818). The fiction of good society works because each individual who attends the Veneerings' dinners acknowledges that every other guest is a member of 'Society'. What occurs, by contrast, when Eugene Wrayburn refuses to acknowledge Bradley Headstone's claim that he has the 'right to be considered … better' than Wrayburn by way of having 'worked his way onward' is that Headstone becomes obsessed with being acknowledged by him (*OMF* II:6, 293). As Eve Kosovsky Sedgwick demonstrates in her classic reading of *Our Mutual Friend*, Headstone's courtship of Lizzie Hexam is mediated by his homosocial rivalry with Wrayburn that aims, in the terms of this discussion, to claim social inclusion by persuading her to prefer him to his rival.[22]

---

[22] Eve Kosofsky Sedgwick, *Between Men: English Literature and Male Homosocial Desire* (New York: Columbia University Press, 1985).

Dickens's novels seem to distinguish between figures like Headstone, who seek social inclusion in response to gestures of exclusion by homosocial rivals, from figures like those discussed in this chapter who begin as members of genteel families and then are exiled from them. What makes *Great Expectations* one of Dickens's most complex examinations of class and its distinctions is that it refuses the distinction between exclusion from a genteel patrimony in the manner of Nickleby and Copperfield and exclusion by homosocial rivals as in the case of Headstone. Pip's fantasy that a fairy godmother is the author of his great expectations is based on the fiction of genteel origins, but, like Headstone, he is born to a family of labourers and his expectations originate with the criminal Magwitch. While the structure of homosocial rivalry, and resulting revenge, persist in his fist-fight with the 'pale young gentleman' for which his reward is a kiss from Estella, his desire to marry her is mediated not by the gentleman but by Estella herself when she excludes him as a 'common labouring-boy' (*GE* I:8, 61). Most significantly, his expectations reverse the narrative of the earlier novels. Rather than being exiled from gentility and then earning his way back, Pip begins as a labourer and then becomes a gentleman through no effort of his own. Although Pip eventually goes to work, he is not restored to gentility through self-making. In terms of one of the novel's principal themes, gentility turns out always to be a forgery.

Great Expectations repeatedly depicts assertions of social distinction as fraudulent. The novel begins with the narrator constructing a fiction that distinguishes him from his birth family through the transformation of the name Philip Pirrip into Pip. This fiction-making is linked to class when he explains to Joe that his lies about his first encounter with Miss Havisham result from wishing that he was not 'common' (*GE* I:9, 71). Yet even as he seeks to set himself apart, his attempts to establish his gentility are fraught with anxiety that he is a fraud. This is why he is so discomfited when Trabb's boy, the shop assistant to the tailor who provides the new suit that will signify his gentlemanly status, recognizing that this status involves exclusion of all who are not genteel, parodies Pip with the repeated ' "Don't know yah" ' (*GE* II:11, 246). It is a short step from refusing to acknowledge the presence of Trabb's boy to refusing to acknowledge his best friend, Joe Gargery.

From this perspective we can see that, in spite of his origins, David Copperfield also remains haunted by anxieties about exclusion. David's insecurity about his status manifests itself in his suspicion that even Steerforth's valet, Littimer, regards him as socially inferior (*DC* 21, 257).[23] In the presence of Littimer, David always feels 'very young', and others frequently refer to him as 'the young gentleman', a locution that on the one hand indicates inclusion in genteel society and on the other implies that he is not yet fully a gentleman. Indeed, as others have pointed out, David's attempts to distinguish himself from Uriah Heep ultimately fail to justify themselves. What presumably distinguishes him is that David moves, after the death of Mr Spenlow and the loss of his

---

[23] See John O. Jordan, 'The Social Sub-Text of *David Copperfield*', in Michael Timko, Fred Kaplan, and Edward Guiliano (eds), *Dickens Studies Annual* (New York: AMS, 1985), 14: 61–92, 67–8.

fortune, from marrying for status to self-making while Uriah shifts from self-making to seeking to coerce Agnes Wickfield into marriage as a means of securing her fortune. Yet, like David, Heep is responding to social exclusion, notably by David himself who refuses to acknowledge him as a fellow gentleman.

David's pursuit of gentility does not arise so much from a belief that he comes from a genteel family—a claim that he never makes explicitly—as from his desire to be acknowledged by the genteel James Steerforth. In turn, it is Steerforth who informs David that the attorneys in Doctors' Commons 'plume themselves on their gentility' and so mediates his courtship of Dora (*DC* 23, 293). David's acceptance of an asymmetrical relationship with Steerforth in which he does all the giving and Steerforth all the taking registers his sense that he never quite belongs to the same social circle even as he aspires to be included in it. David articulates the basis of this asymmetry when he encounters Steerforth in London several years after leaving Salem House and remarks, 'He did not know me, but I knew him in a moment' (*DC* 19, 245). As John Jordan has pointed out, David's need to be acknowledged by Steerforth leads him to be complicit in his friend's mistreatment of their teacher, Mr. Mell, and his seduction of Emily.[24] Dickens's novels increasingly suggest that all forms of inclusion are mediated and that achieving inclusion through acknowledgement by those already included inevitably involves complicity in their acts of exclusion.

The protagonists of these late novels thus eschew social inclusion. In *Our Mutual Friend* Dickens attempts to envision a conversion in which Wrayburn does not seek to bring Lizzie into genteel society but instead accepts his own exclusion by the 'voice of society'. The conclusion of *Little Dorrit*, which depicts Arthur Clennam and Amy Dorrit going down into the 'roaring streets', similarly imagines leaving behind the fictions of gentility of Amy's father and sister (*LD* II:34, 802). Pip's recognition that in striving to be a gentleman he has excluded from his life a 'gentle Christian man' means that he has come to understand that gentility does not arise through the mediation of recognition by an Estella. Yet the concluding scene, whichever version we choose, leaves him still enthralled by the romance of gentility (*GE* III:18, 459).

Further Reading

Gail Turley Houston, *Consuming Fictions: Gender, Class, and Hunger in Dickens's Novels* (Carbondale, IL: Southern Illinois University Press, 1994)
Patrick Joyce (ed.), *Class* (Oxford: Oxford University Press, 1995)
Andrew Sanders, *Dickens and the Spirit of the Age* (Oxford: Clarendon Press, 1999)
Olga Stucherbrukhov, '*Bleak House* as an Allegory of a Middle-Class Nation', *Dickens Quarterly* 23, 3 (2006): 147–68
Chris R. Vanden Bossche, 'Cookery, Not Rookery: Family and Class in *David Copperfield*', in Michael Timko, Fred Kaplan, and Edward Guiliano (eds), *Dickens Studies Annual* 15 (New York: AMS Press, 1986), 87–109

---

[24] Jordan, 'The Social Sub-Text of *David Copperfield*', 68–70.

Chris R. Vanden Bossche, 'Class Discourse and Popular Agency in *Bleak House*', *Victorian Studies* 47 (2004): 7–31

Arlene Young, *Culture, Class and Gender in the Victorian Novel: Gentlemen, Gents and Working Women* (New York: St Martin's, 1999)

CHAPTER 35

RACE, IMPERIALISM, COLONIALISM, POSTCOLONIALISM, AND COSMOPOLITANISM

JAMES BUZARD

For Victorians, race was a concept 'both nebulous and powerful'.[1] They were divided on whether humanity comprised a single race or many races, and on whether racial identities and characteristics were fixed or malleable. In the emerging field of anthropology, monogenists (those believing in a single origin for all) debated polygenists (those believing the different races originated separately), who were determined to treat racial difference as tantamount to *species* difference. Darwin's theory of natural selection, leaked out over many years but authoritatively published in *On the Origin of Species* in 1859, entered the lists on the side of the monogenists but both undermined the biblical origin story they had wanted to uphold and rendered the category of race no less than that of species alarmingly unstable. Nevertheless, for many Victorians, the concept of race came to attain the dignity of scientific fact. George W. Stocking, Jr, notes that 'by the late 1840s, the idea of the Anglo-Saxon "race" was an intellectual commonplace';[2] over the ensuing decades, varieties of 'Teutomania' assured Britons that they bore the blood of the hardy Germanic tribes in their veins, a legacy that might elevate them permanently over the Latin or Celtic races (e.g. the French or Irish). Stocking adds that 'the "racial" nationalism of the revolutionary epoch of 1848 [also] gave the idea of race a greatly heightened saliency'.[3] And of course the persistence of slavery in the United States up to 1865 also kept questions of race current in British media.

---

[1] Laura Peters, *Dickens and Race* (Manchester and New York: Manchester University Press, 2013), 5.
[2] George W. Stocking, Jr, *Victorian Anthropology* (New York: The Free Press, 1987), 62.
[3] Ibid., 63.

So too did the seemingly unstoppable expansion of British power overseas. After the defeat of Napoleonic France in 1815, Britain became the unrivalled global superpower of the nineteenth century. Its settler colonies in North America, Australia, South Africa, and New Zealand absorbed Britain's 'surplus population' and tested the mettle of all those outward-bound Anglo-Saxons, eventually giving rise to a transnational vision of a 'Greater British' brotherhood spanning the globe.[4] At the same time, Britain's imperial experiment in India gave rise to a new interpretation of empire as bearing a mission to civilize the conquered. This interpretation obviously required a degree of openness to the view that the nature of subject peoples was in fact alterable under the guiding hands of European overlords. British expansion also wrought changes in attitudes toward the notion of cosmopolitanism, of what it meant to be 'a citizen of the world'. Romantic celebrations of rooted localism continued to exert force even as new styles of engagement with otherness both at home and abroad virtually forced themselves upon the imperial metropolis, London, and the nation whose capital it was. As Ashis Nandy has put it, '[t]he experience of colonizing did not leave the internal culture of Britain untouched'.[5] Nor did the revolution in transportation—a revolution that Jonathan Grossman has made plain was not limited to the advent of steam power, but already under way in the early nineteenth-century coaching system.[6]

In his non-fictional writings, Charles Dickens expressed various opinions about these matters, some of them extremely distasteful to us today, and certain of his fictions are marred by bigotry. But generally speaking, fiction worth careful consideration is less about the expression of opinion than the staging and probing of possibilities. In Dickens's novels, we encounter an imagination at serious play with the era's contest of conflicting meanings and values for race, empire, colonialism, cosmopolitanism. These concepts become more than a mere list when we appreciate the first and fourth as arising from the geopolitical disruptions wrought by the second and third. In the course of Dickens's career, race acquired its pseudo-scientific authority as an essentially reductive device, capable of shrinking huge and diverse groups, encountered as colonies and empire spread, down to tidy generalizations that implied a justifying narrative of British domination. Meanwhile, cosmopolitanism underwent redefinition from an elite perspective acquired through education and travel to a shared condition of existence in a world increasingly interconnected. In his novels, Dickens tends to satirize or attack the older form of cosmopolitanism in favour of a newer style not fully articulated but glimpsed as a possible way of living with the diversifying and proliferative force of globalization.

---

[4] A classic expression of this vision is in Charles Wentworth Dilke, *Greater Britain: A Record of Travel in English-Speaking Countries during 1866 and 1867* (New York: Cosimo Classics, 2005).

[5] Ashis Nandy, *The Intimate Enemy* (Oxford: Oxford University Press, 1989), 32.

[6] See Jonathan Grossman, *Charles Dickens's Networks: Public Transport and the Novel* (Oxford: Oxford University Press, 2012), 3.

Race and Degeneration

The reductive power of race can perhaps most conveniently be located in the opening passage of Henry Mayhew's encyclopedic *London Labour and the London Poor*, the four-volume edition of which appeared in 1862. Mayhew begins his huge study of the street people of the British metropolis with the following: 'In the thousand millions of human beings that are said to constitute the population of the entire globe, there are—socially, morally, and perhaps even physically considered—but two distinct and broadly marked races, viz., the wanderers and the settlers—the vagabond and the citizen—the nomadic and the civilized tribes.'[7] Over the course of his work, Mayhew exhibits an inconsistency typical of much Victorian discourse on race: sometimes he appears to hold his subjects' race responsible for their nomadic, anti-civilizing, and frequently outlaw tendencies; sometimes he regards their degraded way of life as the result of living conditions for which his more privileged 'settler' readers bear ultimate responsibility. Summing up his account of the London costermongers, Mayhew writes that 'the moral and religious state of these men is a foul disgrace to us, laughing to scorn our zeal for the "propagation of the gospel in *foreign* parts," and making our many societies for the civilization of savages on the other side of the globe appear like a "delusion, a mockery, and a snare," when we have so many people sunk in the lowest depths of barbarism round about our very homes'.[8] This passage Mayhew virtually lifted from Dickens's *Bleak House* (1852), in which the miserable street-sweeper Jo 'sits down to his breakfast on the door-step of the Society for the Propagation of the Gospel in Foreign Parts', a silent rebuke to the misdirected charity of the organization.[9]

During Mayhew's and Dickens's time, Britons became accustomed to hearing that the Anglo-Saxon race possessed qualities of rationality, self-control, and fortitude that both equipped them for world domination and explained and justified their having achieved it. Yet they were unable to avoid the question of whether the character supposedly formed by race could withstand habitual exposure to deleterious conditions. Dickens's portrayal of Jo in *Bleak House* does not explicitly invoke race, but it insistently evokes the question of degeneration. For Jo is English. He is not a charitable object 'softened by distance and unfamiliarity; he is not a genuine foreign-grown savage; he is the ordinary home-made article' (*BH* 47, 564). The dog by Jo's side as he sits at his breakfast is his superior in at least fulfilling the potential of his species, and, by way of reference to this dog, Dickens gives vent to the Victorian middle class's perennial fear of mob violence, suggesting that, however unlikely it may seem, the pitiable figure he depicts in the novel,

---

[7] Henry Mayhew, *London Labour and the London Poor*, 4 vols (New York: Dover Publications, 1968), 1:1.
[8] Ibid., 1:101.
[9] Charles Dickens, *Bleak House*, ed. George Ford and Sylvère Monod, Norton Critical Edition (New York: Norton, 1977), 16, 198. Subsequent references are inserted parenthetically in the text by *BH* chapter, page.

if left unredeemed, may well wind up a criminal brute. 'Turn that dog's descendants wild, like Jo', Dickens writes, 'and in a very few years they will so degenerate that they will lose even their bark—but not their bite' (*BH* 16, 199). Membership in the race of Anglo-Saxons does nothing to halt or hinder Jo's downward, condition-propelled course. Yet in the same novel Dickens features a character—a self-made industrialist—whose 'strong Saxon face' makes him 'a picture of resolution and perseverance', as if race stood guarantor and explainer of his success and self-possession (*BH* 28, 352).

The earlier novel *Oliver Twist* (1838) exhibits a similar instability on race and makes that instability central to its operations. This work is stained by the notorious anti-Semitic stereotype of Fagin 'the Jew', who seems the very type of Mayhew's 'wandering' race of humanity—the Jew as eternal vagabond, roaming among and preying upon the respectable (Christian) 'settlers'. He supervises a youthful band of miscreants and aspires to enlist the orphan Oliver. '[T]he wily old Jew had the boy in his toils', we read, 'and, having prepared his mind, by solitude and gloom, to prefer any society to the companionship of his own sad thoughts in such a dreary place, was now slowly instilling into his soul the poison which he hoped would blacken it, and change its hue for ever.'[10] Of course the project fails miserably. Oliver is proof against contamination by environment and associates, and, while 'race' is not called upon to explain this mysterious imperviousness, a logic involving both race and social class appears to be at work. For we learn that Oliver, who lost his mother on the night of his birth, is buoyed up throughout his many trials by 'dim remembrances of scenes that never were'—that is, by the influence of his dead mother, reaching him from beyond the grave (*OT* 30, 191). The oxymoron 'remembrances of scenes that never were' signals Dickens's attempt to perform the sleight of hand characteristic of race: it bears comparison to the familiar trope of a 'racial memory' in which the history of a people is preserved and to which each member of the race bears a special responsibility.[11] Oliver's never-experienced 'remembrances' participate in a never-quite-believable drama turning upon the question of whether Oliver will lose the way of being that goes with being the descendant of his particular ancestors.

Yet not simply by being the protagonist is Oliver the exception in the novel that bears his name. Virtually everyone else in the work bears the burden of a pitiless environmental determinism. Not only is the novel populated by a host of other English boys not graced with Oliver's exemption from the sway of surroundings; even in the characterization of Fagin, where we might expect to find race triumphantly dominant as the cause of his evil, Dickens leans the other way. We are appalled, but not precisely at what we thought would appal us.

---

[10] Dickens, *Oliver Twist*, ed. Kathleen Tillotson (Oxford: Clarendon Press, 1966), 18, 120. Subsequent references are inserted parenthetically in the text by *OT* chapter, page.

[11] See Walter Benn Michaels, *Our America: Nativism, Modernism, and Pluralism* (Durham, NC: Duke University Press, 1995), 128. For further discussion, see James Buzard, 'Item of Mortality: Lives Led and Unled in *Oliver Twist*', *ELH* 81, 4 (2014): 1225–51.

The mud lay thick upon the stones: and a black mist hung over the streets; the rain fell sluggishly down: and everything felt cold and clammy to the touch. It seemed just the night when it befitted such a being as the Jew, to be abroad. As he glided stealthily along, creeping beneath the shelter of the walls and doorways, the hideous old man seemed like some loathsome reptile, engendered in the slime and darkness through which he moved: crawling forth, by night, in search of some rich offal for a meal. (*OT* 19, 120–1)

Under cover of metaphor, environment sneaks back into relevance: the Jew is the reptile 'engendered in the slime and darkness through which he move[s]'. This easily overlooked emphasis may account for the somewhat sympathetic treatment of Fagin at the end, when he is overcome by fear as he waits out his last night before execution. Learning that he is the product of his environment humanizes the villain, bringing him closer to us than the angelic Oliver ever can be. Still, the overall impression of Fagin is so negative that Dickens later attempted, in *Our Mutual Friend* (1865), to counterbalance him by creating a wholly virtuous Jewish character, Mr Riah (see Weltman's chapter in this collection).

Dickens raised the possibility of degeneration in a number of contexts. In a single work, different characters suggest different answers to the question. In *Martin Chuzzlewit* (1844), one Englishman—Martin—appears to be in danger of succumbing to the character-undermining influence of the American swampland, while another— Mark Tapley—stands firm against it.[12] The 1848 Christmas Book *The Haunted Man* constitutes 'a meditation on the importance of memory' in forestalling debasement and dehumanization.[13] One of Dickens's letters tells us that he planned to launch his magazine *Household Words* with '[a] history of Savages, showing the singular respects in which all savages are like each other; and those in which civilised men, under circumstances of difficulty, soonest become like savages'.[14] This did not materialize, though the 1853 *Household Words* tale 'The Long Voyage' did go some distance toward the goal. This focuses on the phenomenon that for Victorians became a veritable metonym for savagery: cannibalism, here as practised by a British convict who acquires 'an inappeasable relish for his dreadful food'.[15] In both *Dombey and Son* (1848) and *Bleak House*, on the other hand, Dickens had already provided stories in which English heroes rise to the challenge of shipwrecks rather than descending to barbarism. In the latter

---

[12] Dickens also depicts Martin's susceptibility to degeneration in chapter 13: 'And it was strange, very strange, even to himself, to find, how by quick though almost imperceptible degrees he lost his delicacy and self-respect, and gradually came to do that as a matter of course, without the least compunction, which but a few short days before had galled him to the quick.' Dickens, *Martin Chuzzlewit*, ed. Margaret Cardwell (Oxford: Clarendon Press, 1982), 13, 225. Subsequent references are inserted parenthetically in the text by *MC* chapter, page.

[13] Peters, *Dickens and Race*, 12.

[14] *The Letters of Charles Dickens*, ed. Madeline House, Graham Storey, et al., Pilgrim/British Academy Edition, 12 vols (Oxford: Clarendon Press, 1965–2002), 5:621–3, 622. Subsequent citations: *PLets* followed by volume:page range, page.

[15] See [Charles Dickens,] 'The Long Voyage', *Household Words*, 31 December 1853, 8: 409–12, 409.

novel, Allan Woodcourt shows himself '[c]alm and brave, through everything. Saved many lives, never complained in hunger and thirst, wrapped naked people in his spare clothes, took the lead, showed them what to do, governed them, tended the sick, buried the dead, and brought the poor survivors safely off at last!' (*BH* 35, 442).

Two occurrences of the mid-1850s proved especially generative for Dickens's imaginings on race, driving him away from a reformer's focus on changeable environment and toward a view of more or less fixed racial characteristics. The first of these concerned the ill-fated Franklin Expedition, which had vanished on its search for the Northwest Passage. When, in 1854, John Rae published an account arguing that the last survivors of Franklin's group had resorted to cannibalism before perishing themselves, Dickens reacted with outrage at the claim, and he devoted considerable energy to rewriting the story, beginning with two successive numbers of *Household Words*, where he denied the credibility of Rae's Inuit witnesses as 'savages' essentially 'covetous, treacherous, and cruel'.[16] What might they not have done to Franklin's crew in its doubtless desperate condition? For, '[i]t is impossible to form an estimate of the character of any race of savages, from their deferential behaviour to the white man while he is strong ... the moment the white man has appeared in the new aspect of being weaker than the savage, the savage has changed and sprung upon him'.[17] As for the character of the Englishmen involved, Dickens was inspired to develop a few plots in which trial brings out the nobility encoded in the type, even if it has been buried under learned diffidence or selfishness for years. In *The Frozen Deep*, co-authored with Wilkie Collins (1856), the protagonist Richard Wardour, having threatened to murder his rival in love, ultimately gives his life to save that rival on their own Arctic expedition. 'The Wreck of the Golden Mary', Dickens's extra Christmas number for *Household Words* the same year, also co-written with Collins, confronts more directly the spectre of cannibalism. Faced with diminishing supplies, the Captain allays his fellow-survivors' fears by telling them that Captain Bligh, of the Mutiny on the *Bounty*, 'had solemnly placed it on record ... that under no conceivable circumstances whatever would [his] emaciated party, who had gone through all the pains of famine, have preyed on one another. I cannot describe', he adds, 'the visible relief which this spread through the boat'.[18] More indirectly linked to the crisis of the Franklin Expedition is the self-sacrifice, in *A Tale of Two Cities* (1859), of the hitherto useless Sydney Carton, who goes to the guillotine in place of his lookalike Charles Darnay with those unforgettable words, '[i]t is a far, far better thing that I do, than I have ever done; it is a far, far better rest that I go to than I have ever known'.[19]

---

[16] [Charles Dickens,] 'The Lost Arctic Voyagers [I]', *Household Words*, 2 December 1854, 10: 361–5, 362. Quoted in Michael Slater, *Charles Dickens* (New Haven and London: Yale University Press, 2009), 382.

[17] [Dickens,] 'The Lost Arctic Voyagers [I]', 362.

[18] Charles Dickens and Wilkie Collins, 'The Wreck of the Golden Mary', in Charles Dickens, *Christmas Stories*, introd. Margaret Lane, New Oxford Illustrated Dickens (London: Oxford University Press, 1957), 131–60, 152.

[19] Charles Dickens, *A Tale of Two Cities*, ed. Andrew Sanders, Oxford World's Classics (Oxford: Oxford World's Classics, 2008), III:15, 361.

If the Franklin Expedition led Dickens to develop plots in which English blood 'will out' under trial, the so-called Indian Mutiny of 1857 further hardened his view on race when it came to 'savages'. He had already treated certain other races as, if not absolutely unredeemable by Western civilizing efforts, as least so thoroughly degraded as to make the labour of civilizing them next to impossible. In an 1848 essay on a disastrous expedition to the Niger, Dickens wrote that '[b]etween the civilized European and the barbarous African there is a great gulf set' and that the prospect of raising the latter's condition 'is a work which ... requires a stretch of years that dazzles in the looking at'.[20] The 1853 essay 'The Noble Savage' skewered popular interest in indigenous peoples, dismissing them as savages 'highly desirable to be civilized off the face of the earth'. The savage was 'cruel, false, thievish, murderous; addicted more or less to grease, entrails, and beastly customs; a wild animal with the questionable gift of boasting; a conceited, tiresome, bloodthirsty, monotonous humbug'.[21] (Here, Dickens seems to have forgotten his encounter with 'one Pitchlynn, a chief of the Choctaw tribe of Indians' on his American tour of 1842: this man impressed him as 'as stately and complete a gentleman of Nature's making, as ever I beheld'.[22]) Still, in writing that the savage be '*civilized* off the face of the earth', Dickens left space for the possibility that the savage might prove civilizable, if only at the cost of Herculean labour.[23] The Indian Rebellion of 1857, and in particular the 'Cawnpore Massacre' in which a group of English women and children were slaughtered, put paid to any such nuance. In a frequently cited letter of October 1857, Dickens fantasized about being Commander-in-Chief in India and devoting himself 'to exterminate the Race upon whom the stain of the late cruelties rested ... to blot it out of mankind and raze it off the face of the earth'.[24] The ugly 1857 tale *The Perils of Certain English Prisoners* (another joint product with Collins) continued in this genocidal vein, transferring the action to Central America and replacing the Indian antagonist with a 'native Sambo' named Christian George King, whose deep-dyed treachery against his English captives is meant to illustrate the general truth that the savage shows his true, despicable colours whenever he gains the upper hand against his Western betters. For such figures, there can be no *civilizing* them off the face of the earth. 'Believing that I hold my commission by the allowance of God', the Captain Carton of this tale declares, 'I shall certainly use it, with all ... merciful swiftness of execution, to exterminate these people from the face of the earth.'[25] It is almost surprising to see the Captain use

---

[20] [Charles Dickens,] 'Review: *Narrative of the Expedition ... to the River Niger in 1841*', in Michael Slater and John Drew (eds), *The Dent Uniform Edition of Dickens' Journalism*, 4 vols (London: J. M. Dent, Columbus: Ohio State University Press, 1993–2000). Here, Dent 2:125.

[21] [Charles Dickens,] 'The Noble Savage', *Household Words*, 11 June 1853, 7:337–9, 337.

[22] Charles Dickens, *American Notes for General Circulation*, ed. John S. Whitley and Arnold Goldman (London: Penguin Books, 1985), 12, 210–11.

[23] Priti Joshi makes this point in the entry 'Race', in Sally Ledger and Holly Furneaux (eds), *Charles Dickens in Context* (Cambridge: Cambridge University Press, 2013), 292–300, 298.

[24] PLets 8:458–60, 459. Quoted in Slater, *Charles Dickens*, 411.

[25] Charles Dickens and Wilkie Collins, 'The Perils of Certain English Prisoners', in Dickens, *Christmas Stories*, 161–208, 179.

the word 'people'. In his response to the later Morant Bay uprising in Jamaica (1865), Dickens was more muted, but he did sign the petition supporting Governor Eyre's brutal suppression of the revolt. He saw sympathy with the black Jamaicans as another instance of the 'telescopic philanthropy' he had satirized in *Bleak House*, writing in a letter that 'sympathy with the black—or the native, or the devil—afar off, and ... indifference to our own countrymen at enormous odds in the midst of bloodshed and savagery, makes me stark wild'.[26]

One further context demands mention where race is concerned. Dickens was a passionate abolitionist and, though on his 1842 visit to America he scarcely spent any time in slaveholding regions, he included a chapter denouncing slavery in his *American Notes for General Circulation*, published following that trip. He also introduced a sympathetic minor character, the former slave Cicero, into his next novel, *Martin Chuzzlewit* (1844), using him to attack the hypocrisy of the self-proclaimed Land of Liberty. As Mark Tapley puts it, 'they're so fond of Liberty in this part of the globe, that they buy her and sell her and carry her to market with 'em... they can't help taking liberties with her' (*MC* 17, 285). Nevertheless, after 1862 Dickens joined many of his countrymen in supporting the Confederacy, and on his second visit to America in 1868, 'the appearance and behaviour of freed Negroes disgusted him'.[27] Dickens wrote to John Forster of the 'mechanical absurdity of giving these people votes, at any rate at present'.[28] One wonders how much time from 'at present' would have to elapse before Dickens might feel the freed black citizens of the United States worthy of the franchise.

COLONIALISM, EMPIRE, AND THE COSMOPOLITAN

For Dickens as both novelist and parent, the British colonies were first and foremost an available resource. As Grace Moore observes, '[j]ust as in his fiction Dickens often banished troublesome characters like Mr Micawber in *David Copperfield* to the colonies, so he sent his sons out into the Empire in the hope of teaching them to be autonomous and not to depend upon the reputation and generosity of their famous father'.[29] From Jingle and Bob Sawyer of *Pickwick Papers* (1837) (Demerara and Bengal, respectively), through Micawber, little Em'ly, and Martha Endell of *David Copperfield* (1850) (Australia), Dickens availed himself of colonial spaces as repositories for characters needing a fresh start at the end of his novels or deemed no longer containable

---

[26] *PLets* 11:114–16. Quoted in Peters, *Dickens and Race*, 137.
[27] Dickens, *American Notes*, appendix 2, 303.
[28] Quoted ibid.
[29] Grace Moore, 'Empires and Colonies', in Ledger and Furneaux (eds), *Charles Dickens in Context*, 284–91, 284.

at home. The villains Monks (from *Oliver Twist*) and Tom Gradgrind (from *Hard Times*, 1854), abscond abroad to run out their miserable courses beyond sight of British eyes; the 'fallen women' Em'ly and Martha resemble the real-life counterparts whom Dickens and the heiress Angela Burdett-Coutts sought to reform and export to become 'happy wives and mothers in a distant but still British land—Australia or South Africa—where wives were needed'.[30] In such cases, colonial space is imagined as wholly *at the disposal of* Dickens the writer, father, and philanthropist.[31]

Beginning perhaps with *Dombey and Son* (1848), Dickens's novels conduct a series of experiments that suggest an altogether more fraught relationship with colonial and other far-flung places. The posture of regarding the wider world as at one's disposal, an instrument to serve one's interests, is embodied in Mr Dombey, for whom '[t]he earth was made for Dombey and Son to trade in, and the sun and moon were made to give them light. Rivers and seas were formed to float their ships; rainbows gave them promise of fair weather; winds blew for or against their enterprises; stars and planets circled in their orbits, to preserve inviolate a system of which they were the centre'.[32] And though the novel focuses on the 'domestic tyranny' Dombey practises on all around him, we are never quite permitted to lose sight of the global commercial and colonial sphere of action in which Dombey is engaged.[33] Also, since the beginning of his career, Dickens had occasionally treated the situation of the English émigré who does not simply stay put once exported, but who problematically returns to native soil, as do Edmunds in the interpolated tale 'The Convict's Return' in *Pickwick* and Alice Marwood (her moral flaw inscribed in her surname) in *Dombey and Son*.[34] As Moore notes, '[t]he early novels are in fact quite littered with returnees'.[35] After the confidence-shattering crisis of the Indian uprising, however, England's vulnerability to forces beyond it acquires a new edge, in particular in *A Tale of Two Cities* (1859) and *Great Expectations* (1860). In the first, Dickens drew upon Thomas Carlyle's depiction of the French Revolution as an orgy of murderous rage and, whether we read the novel as a straightforward allegory of the Mutiny or not, it is impossible to imagine the Mutiny did not cross Dickens's mind as he wrote.[36] In *Great Expectations*, Dickens would make the illicit returnee central to the

---

[30] Slater, *Charles Dickens*, 269.

[31] Dickens wrote comparatively little about Ireland, but Sabine Clemm argues that it holds a special divided status in *Household Words*, with '"Ireland" ... treated mostly as a physical resource, a collection of agricultural and mineral material' and 'the Irish' as uncomfortably possessing 'the potential to talk back and resist the easy dehumanization that the populations of other British colonies underwent in imperial discourse'. Sabine Clemm, *Dickens, Journalism, and Nationhood: Mapping the World in Household Words* (New York: Routledge, 2009), 81.

[32] Charles Dickens, *Dombey and Son*, ed. Alan Horsman (Oxford: Clarendon Press, 1974), 1, 2.

[33] See Deirdre David, 'Empire, Race, and the Victorian Novel', in Patrick Brantlinger and William B. Thesing (eds), *A Companion to the Victorian Novel* (Oxford: Blackwell, 2005), 84–100, 87.

[34] See Moore, 'Empires and Colonies', 285.

[35] Grace Moore, *Dickens and Empire: Discourses of Class, Race, and Colonialism in the Works of Charles Dickens* (Aldershot: Ashgate, 2004), 13.

[36] For a reading of *A Tale* as an allegory of the Indian Mutiny, see William Oddie, 'Dickens and the Indian Mutiny', *The Dickensian* 68, 366 (January 1972): 3–17. See also Patrick Brantlinger, *Rule of Darkness*, chapter 7, and Moore's corrective account in *Dickens and Empire*, chapter 6.

drama, in the figure of Abel Magwitch, the convict whom the young protagonist, Pip, reluctantly aids at the start of the novel, who later comes back from his Australian 'transportation' to turn Pip's world upside down by revealing himself as the founder of Pip's fortunes. Magwitch is one of nineteenth-century fiction's most powerful embodiments of the idea that empire and colonies involved Britain in processes not solely outward-bound but also recursive, that rather than expressing Britain's supremacy and control, they rendered Britons susceptible to forces flowing back from afar and impossible to deflect. This spectre of 'reverse colonialism' haunts Dickens's final, incomplete novel, *The Mystery of Edwin Drood*, as well, not solely in the figure of the opium-addicted choirmaster John Jasper (Englishman at the mercy of that drug which mighty imperial Britain had forced upon an unwilling Chinese market), but also in the dark-skinned colonial returnees Neville and Helena Landless. Exactly what Dickens intended to do with this brother and sister newly come back from Ceylon must remain unknown, though 'Landless' may signal some plot of disinheritance and restoration; in any case, the brother has ample time to enlist himself among those of Dickens's characters whose circumstances raise that insistent question of degeneration. He tells the Canon Crisparkle, 'I have been brought up among abject and servile dependents, of an inferior race, and I may easily have contracted some affinity with them. Sometimes, I don't know but that it may be a drop of what is tigerish in their blood.'[37] Magwitch, Jasper, and the Landlesses bespeak a globally interconnected world in which influence flows both ways and the saving distinctions—between civilized and savage, high and low, here and there—grow increasingly murky.

In *Bleak House*, Dickens furnished what may have been his strongest, most sustained imaginative response to such a world. To appreciate how, it is necessary to revisit and adjust two influential theses from the 1990s. The first comes from Fredric Jameson and pertained originally to modernism, not the Victorian novel. In the essay 'Modernism and Imperialism' (1990), Jameson characterized modernism as the aesthetic of that phase in an imperial nation's career when daily life in the metropolis has come to feel 'radically incomplete' because of its thoroughgoing dependence on processes and places a world away. Imperialism advances to a point at which 'a significant structural segment of the economic system ... is now located elsewhere ... in colonies over the water whose own life experience [is] unimaginable for the subject of the imperial power'.[38] Art responds by affording the newly inscrutable metropolis the imaginative means to see itself 'by compensation ... formed into a self-subsisting totality'.[39] In the process, as Garrett Stewart writes in commenting on Jameson's essay, a newly hypostatized notion

---

[37] Charles Dickens, *The Mystery of Edwin Drood*, ed. Margaret Cardwell (Oxford: Clarendon Press, 1972), 7, 49. For 'reverse colonization', see Stephen Arata, 'The Occidental Tourist: *Dracula* and the Anxiety of Reverse Colonization', *Victorian Studies* 33, 4 (1990): 621–45.

[38] Fredric Jameson, 'Modernism and Imperialism', in Terry Eagleton, Fredric Jameson, and Edward W. Said, *Nationalism, Colonialism, and Literature* (Minneapolis: University of Minnesota Press, 1990), 50–1.

[39] Ibid., 58.

of literary style becomes the 'figurative register that can only evoke rather than capture the alienating distances on which metropolitan dominance must ground itself'.[40] Modernist style, Stewart summarizes, 'transvalues the vast and shapeless—colonialism's unglimpsed horizons—into sheer perceptual intensity' and substitutes for the vague 'elsewhere' of the colonies evocations of infinity or the metaphysical beyond.[41]

The second 1990s' thesis to concern us here is Edward Said's postcolonial account of the work of 'ideological mapping' done by the English novel in the heyday of empire. Updating the truism that the nineteenth-century novel (before Conrad and Kipling) almost never set its action in the colonies, Said saw the novel as laying out 'a slowly built up picture with England—socially, politically, morally charted and differentiated in immensely fine detail—at the center and a series of overseas territories connected to it at the peripheries'.[42] This distribution of narrative space formed, he claimed, a powerful objective correlative for British ethnocentrism, a sign of British confidence or superiority toward all those regions and peoples outside Britain that afforded the material basis for both the British way of life and its novelistic representation. Seeing novels as thus engaged in the effort to efface the real fact of material domestic dependence on overseas colonies, Said encouraged us to read 'noncollusively', to focus on 'what is unsaid and occluded', on what gets pushed to and even beyond the margins.[43] In treatments of Dickens, this has meant a steep rise in value for all the characters or material objects hailing from the wide beyond and bespeaking that globalized world, from Major Bagstock's unnamed Indian servant, in *Dombey and Son*, to the tamarind and spices in Mrs Crisparkle's cabinet, in *The Mystery of Edwin Drood*.[44]

With regard to Jameson: in an article from 2000, Garrett Stewart was already suggesting that he 'might well be on to something that in fact antedates the arena of his investigation' and that 'the stylistic fallout from colonialism in British fiction is less exclusively modernist than Jameson claims'.[45] I made a similar point in my 2005 book *Disorienting Fiction: The Autoethnographic Work of Nineteenth-Century British Novels*, and more recently Lauren Goodlad has made the backdating of Jameson's 'Modernism and Imperialism' argument central to her own about what she calls *The Victorian Geopolitical Aesthetic* (2015).[46] The disjunction of metropolitan perception and the material basis of its way of life, Goodlad contends, must be located at least half a century

---

[40] Garrett Stewart, 'The Foreign Offices of British Fiction', *MLQ: Modern Language Quarterly* 61, 1 (March 2000): 181–206, 188.
[41] Ibid., 189.
[42] Edward Said, *Culture and Imperialism* (New York: Knopf, 1993), 74.
[43] Suvendrini Perera, *Reaches of Empire: The English Novel from Edgeworth to Dickens* (New York: Columbia University Press, 1991), 2.
[44] On Bagstock's servant, 'the Native', see Grace Moore, *Dickens and Empire*, 58–63.
[45] Stewart, 'The Foreign Offices of British Fiction', 183, 192.
[46] James Buzard, *Disorienting Fiction: The Autoethnographic Work of Nineteenth-Century British Novels* (Princeton and Oxford: Princeton University Press, 2005), see 52–3. Lauren Goodlad, *The Victorian Geopolitical Aesthetic: Realism, Sovereignty, and Transnational Experience* (Oxford: Oxford University Press, 2015), see 29–31.

earlier than Jameson imagined, and materialist criticism must therefore squarely confront rather than dismiss the literary realism of the mid-nineteenth century. This is because

> several forms of global expansion produced the spatial disconnect that Jameson believes was 'new' to the late nineteenth century, including: the slaveholding practices that haunt Collins's *Armadale*; the dizzying settler mobility that Trollope's Barsetshire novels strive to offset; the conquest of Seringapatam which shadows *The Moonstone*; and even the transchannel aesthetic exchange in which Eliot fashioned her distinct literary experiments. Contra Lukács and Jameson, realism's formal vitality does not end in 1848 [as Lukács suggested and as Jameson has tended to accept] but, in many ways, begins in 1857 with the trauma of the Indian 'mutiny'.[47]

One may be persuaded by this claim and still regret that Goodlad's ambitious study features no sustained analysis of Dickens—who still had plenty to contribute after 1857, and without whom any account of a Victorian geopolitical aesthetic is bound to feel incomplete.

With regard to Said, I have argued that the question motivating Said's approach—why don't the novels of the era deal more directly with the offshore material basis of the Victorian way of life?—ought to be replaced by one asking instead *why* novelists working in the period of imperial expansion and consolidation should have devoted the novel to furnishing just such a 'slowly built up' and finely delineated picture of England as Said discerns. Shifting emphasis in this manner allows us to think about the ideological work of the novel as protective rather than simply arrogant; it enables us to conceive of Victorian novels as massive efforts to resist or undo the possible domestic consequence of imperial expansion, namely the evacuation of distinctive cultural identity in the imperial nation—as if the exporting of British institutions and values seemingly anywhere in the world depleted rather than aggrandized Britain, making its way of life tantamount to universally applicable 'civilization' itself.[48] No novel performs this recuperative labour more strenuously than *Bleak House*, in which the national scandal embodied in Jo and the other slum dwellers of Tom-all-Alone's leads the narrator to declare that 'in truth it might be better for the national glory even that the sun should sometimes set upon the British dominions, than that it should ever rise upon so vile a wonder as Tom' (*BH* 46, 553). Through its assault on Mrs Jellyby's telescopic philanthropy, its espousal of Esther Summerson's ethic of the 'circle of duty' that begins with those close at hand and 'gradually and naturally expand[s] itself', its insistence that the horrors of Tom-all-Alone's will work their evil 'through every order of society', its deployment of the tropes of 'consequential ground' and the paradoxical 'Anywhere's nowhere', Dickens presents the nineteenth-century novel just as Said described it, a picture of a social totality densely interconnected down to the seemingly tiniest and most 'throwaway' of

---

[47] Goodlad, *The Victorian Geopolitical Aesthetic*, 31.
[48] See Buzard, *Disorienting Fiction*, 43.

details (*BH* 8, 96; 46, 553; 16, 202; 5, 46). It is a picture visible only if we resolutely turn our backs upon all that lies outside it: the specific community of the British comes into view in all its intricacy of arrangement only if we almost completely occlude the wider, hazy world beyond—that vague domain for which Mrs Jellyby's cherished 'Borrioboola-Gha' seems an appropriately nonsensical label.[49]

In the process of constructing a 'metropolitan autoethnography' of Britain and arguing for the necessity of recognizing national obligations, Dickens mocks the character Skimpole as an embodiment of cosmopolitan ideals that have grown morally and intellectually bankrupt.[50] In *Bleak House*, '[p]roductively being somebody and of some worthy consequence means having a place, and not laying claim to *every* place';[51] yet Skimpole, of the 'cosmopolitan mind', extols the pleasures of being 'bound to no particular chairs and tables, but [able] to sport like a butterfly among all the furniture on hire' (*BH* 18, 227; 218). He is associated with Enlightenment-era blather about the 'Brotherhood of Humanity', failing to perceive that if everyone is your brother no one is, or that admiring someone as 'the child of the universe' will invite the retort, '[t]he universe ... makes rather an indifferent parent, I am afraid' (*BH* 4, 41; 6, 68). It's against the backdrop of this vague and irresponsible universalism that the claims of the national can be made *specific*. Skimpole's attitude toward poor Jo wavers between heartlessness and perverse aestheticism: he argues that the sick child, England's collective responsibility, be sent away rather than cared for; and he 'entertain[s] himself by playing snatches of pathetic airs' about a homeless boy while Jo lies desperate with fever upstairs (*BH* 31, 385; 386).

In his next major novel, *Little Dorrit* (1857), Dickens continued his assault on the exploded cosmopolitan ideal by associating it not only with the morally unmoored aesthete Henry Gowan but also with the book's villain, the loathsome French-English-Belgian Rigaud, who announces himself in no uncertain terms as 'a citizen of the world'.[52] As several critics have contended, however, Dickens appears to be attacking the outmoded notion of cosmopolitanism as an elite perspective acquired through education and travel *in pursuit of* some newer model of cosmopolitan or international interconnection. In her book *Urban Realism and the Cosmopolitan Imagination in the Nineteenth Century* (2011), Tanya Agathocleous acknowledges that *Bleak House* exhibits a deep 'antipathy to the global imbrications of [the] urban space' it represents, but she argues that the novel 'insists that the sympathetic imagination ... must extend beyond the details of city life to embrace a universalist conception of humanity'.[53] Lauren Goodlad's attempt to delineate *The Victorian Geopolitical Aesthetic* has already been mentioned. For

---

[49] See ibid. 116. My argument actually suggests that Dickens not only performs this rendering of British culture but also begins to emphasize its fictionality and even to undermine it.

[50] See ibid., 7, 12.

[51] Ibid., 136.

[52] Dickens, *Little Dorrit*, ed. Harvey Peter Sucksmith (Oxford: Clarendon Press, 1979), I:1, 10.

[53] Tanya Agathocleous, *Urban Realism and the Cosmopolitan Imagination in the Nineteenth Century* (Cambridge: Cambridge University Press, 2011), 110, 112.

critics seeking a new internationalist framework for Dickens, *Little Dorrit* has proved especially fruitful. In *The Powers of Distance: Cosmopolitanism and the Cultivation of Detachment* (2001), Amanda Anderson reads the novel in search of 'a particular form of critical cosmopolitanism ... that allows us to expose naïve forms of cosmopolitanism that fail to take structural economic inequalities into account'.[54] She finds this in the 'detached, suspicious reading of nationalism and provinciality [that] is demanded by this text at every turn'.[55] For Ayşe Çelikkol in *Romances of Free Trade: British Literature, Laissez-Faire, and the Global Nineteenth Century* (2011), *Little Dorrit* explores a Gothic world of 'illicit border-crossings', a 'dystopic vision of free trade in which the uncontainable flow of commodities turns into a nightmare': a cosmopolitanism, in other words, not cultivated but imposed, as an inescapable condition of a post-protectionist reality.[56] Jonathan Grossman's *Charles Dickens's Networks: Public Transport and the Novel* (2012) considers *Little Dorrit* in relation to the nineteenth-century transport revolution and its standardization of time, a phenomenon he insists we see as extending beyond the nation and producing a fully internationalized sense of simultaneity. Standard time 'is premised upon the semi-omniscient awareness that what is going on is going on simultaneously at different places, such that the relation ... between these places now amounts to a zone of human contact, a space shared in time'.[57] While Grossman concedes that a national framework applies to Dickens's novels up to and including *Bleak House*, he maintains that the later texts *Little Dorrit*, *A Tale of Two Cities*, *Great Expectations*, and *The Mystery of Edwin Drood* (he does not mention *Our Mutual Friend* (1865)) require the international perspective first developed in *Dorrit*. 'The whole arc of the book that carries Little Dorrit out of the prison and across Europe', Grossman contends, 'will work to create in her a version of the perspective of international simultaneity upon which the novel has opened.'[58] Dickens enlists his serial readers in the production of this perspective as well, for as Grossman demonstrates, 'to understand the novel's (diachronic) plot, one must retrospectively reconstruct a synchronous international terrain'.[59]

Saree Makdisi's recent *Making England Western: Occidentalism, Race, and Imperial Culture* (2014) offers one more internationalist perspective in its reading of *The Mystery of Edwin Drood*, treated as 'a meditation on imperial culture: on what it means to inhabit empire as an open and continuous space of flows in which a rigid distinction between the familiar and the exotic, the domesticated and the foreign, the metropolis and the periphery, "here" and "there," and ultimately "us" and "them" is unsustainable, insofar as the two spaces, their goods—and, more importantly, their populations—are

---

[54] Amanda Anderson, *The Powers of Distance: Cosmopolitanism and the Cultivation of Detachment* (Princeton and Oxford: Princeton University Press, 2001), 71.

[55] Ibid., 89.

[56] Ayşe Çelikkol, *Romances of Free Trade: British Literature, Laissez-Faire, and the Global Nineteenth Century* (Oxford and New York: Oxford University Press, 2011), 130.

[57] Jonathan Grossman, *Charles Dickens's Networks: Public Transport and the Novel* (Oxford and New York: Oxford University Press, 2012), 185–6.

[58] Ibid., 174.

[59] Ibid., 200.

seen to be interpenetrating and overlapping'.[60] Makdisi insists that we reject now familiar arguments about the novel's supposed representation of a pristine England's invasion by corrupting Asiatic influences. In his account, 'idealized England never existed in the first place'; the modernization process that *produced* 'the West' in the eighteenth and nineteenth centuries was an uneven one inextricably entangled with Orientalism.[61] One comes away from Makdisi's argument feeling a bit like someone who, having been listening to a Victorian-age Teutomaniac on the virtues of pure Anglo-Saxonism, rediscovers Daniel Defoe's satire 'The True-Born Englishman' (possibly 1700). 'Thus from a mixture of all kinds began', Defoe tells us, 'That het'rogeneous thing, an Englishman.'[62] Grossman's and Makdisi's books are likely to have lasting influence in Dickens studies as it continues to explore the Inimitable's relationship to issues of belonging, place, and temporality. Work remains to be done on the interplay of national and transnational sensibilities in Dickens's oeuvre: after *Bleak House* and metropolitan autoethnography, *Little Dorrit* and international simultaneity, perhaps we are ready for new criticism on *Great Expectations* or *Our Mutual Friend* focused on the reciprocal constitutions of home and world.

Further Reading

Timothy Carens, *Outlandish Subjects in the Victorian Domestic Novel* (Houndmills, Basingstoke, and New York: Palgrave Macmillan, 2005)

Sophie Gilmartin, *Ancestry and Narrative in Nineteenth-Century British Literature: Blood Relations from Edgeworth to Hardy* (Cambridge and New York: Cambridge University Press, 1998)

Wendy S. Jacobson, *Dickens and the Children of Empire* (Houndmills, Basingstoke and New York: Palgrave Macmillan, 2000)

Goldie Morgentaler, *Dickens and Heredity: When Like Begets Like* (Houndmills, Basingstoke, and New York: Palgrave Macmillan, 2000)

Suvendrini Perera, *Reaches of Empire: The English Novel from Edgeworth to Dickens* (New York: Columbia University Press, 1991)

Marlene Tromp, Maria R. Bachman, and Heidi Kaufman (eds), *Fear, Loathing, and Victorian Xenophobia* (Columbus: Ohio State University Press, 2013)

---

[60] Saree Makdisi, *Making England Western: Occidentalism, Race, and Imperial Culture* (Chicago and London: University of Chicago Press, 2014), 197.

[61] Ibid., 198.

[62] Daniel Defoe, 'The True-Born Englishman', in *The True Born Englishman and Other Writings*, ed. P. N. Furbank and W. R. Owens (London: Penguin, 1997), 35.

CHAPTER 36

DICKENS, POLITICAL ECONOMY, AND MONEY

AYŞE ÇELİKKOL

INTRODUCTION

SPEAKING on 'The Importance of the Study of Economic Science' in 1854, a political economist lamented Dickens's presumed hostility to that science:

> I cannot but express my deep regret that one to whom we all owe, and to whom we all pay, so much gratitude, and affection, and admiration, for all he has written and done in the cause of good—I mean Mr. Charles Dickens—should have lent his great genius and name to the discrediting of the subject whose claims I now advocate.[1]

The speaker seems surprised that anyone should discredit political economy, as if there were nothing amiss with the science. Earlier in the same year, Dickens had pointed out that 'political economy is a mere skeleton unless it has a little human covering and filling out, a little human bloom upon it, and a little human warmth in it'.[2] Why should Dickens the literary entrepreneur critique the science of wealth? Perhaps the discourse swarmed with too many lifeless abstractions about basic elements of life such as labour and exchange, or perhaps its pessimism about human nature was to blame. Critical as Dickens may have been, his tone remained cordial compared to that of Thomas Carlyle, who had called political economy 'dismal' in 1849:

---

[1] William Ballantyne Hodgson, 'The Importance of the Study of Economic Science as a Branch of Education for All Classes', in *Lectures on Education, Delivered at the Royal Institution of Great Britain* (London: Savill and Edwards, 1854), 298.

[2] Charles Dickens, 'On Strike', *Household Words* 8 (1854): 553–9, 558, accessed 9 June 2016, <http://www.djo.org.uk>.

And the Social Science,—not a 'gay' science, but a rueful,—which finds the secret of this Universe in 'supply and demand', and reduces the duty of human governors to that of letting man alone, is also wonderful. Not a 'gay science', I should say, like some we have heard of; no, a dreary, desolate, and indeed quite abject and distressing one; what we may call by way of eminence, the dismal science.[3]

At the end of the eighteenth century, Thomas Malthus had asserted that poverty and disease would put a check on population growth; in the early nineteenth century, David Ricardo had maintained that the interests of social classes were inherently antagonistic. Political economy no longer reflected the Enlightenment optimism of Adam Smith, for whom individuals served each other's benefit as if an invisible hand were directing their actions. It was in this context that Dickens gained a reputation for trying to discredit political economy.

Exploring recent scholarship, the first section of this chapter, 'Dickens and the Economists: Friction or Affinity?' turns to the perceived friction between Dickens's fiction and political economy and highlights that, contrary to what earlier critics maintained, Dickens upheld some tenets of contemporary political economy, including the need for the pursuit of self-interest. The section 'Professional Authorship in the Credit Economy', exploring the issue of professional authorship, discusses the extent to which Dickens as an author in a competitive literary marketplace experienced and took advantage of the economic system that had come to be dominant by the time he was writing: the credit economy, in which one makes money by borrowing some first. If Dickens was able to dissect and analyse the economic system within which he worked, he did so in part by addressing economic issues such as borrowing and investment thematically in his novels. As 'Literary Form in Light of Economics' illustrates, formal aspects of Dickens's works also reflect his ability to diagnose and weigh the dynamics of economic exchange. From narration to characterization, the form of Dickens's novels alternately exposes, challenges, and puts into practice the logic of capitalism. Literature constitutes an effective medium for this task because the economy, like novels, revolves around fictitiousness. Continuing to emphasize the semiotics of capitalism, the section 'Gender and Sexuality vis-à-vis Capitalism' shows that economic metaphors shape representations of gender and sexuality, which are in turn central to characterization and plot in Dickens's fiction. Just as the exchange of women makes patriarchy possible, the manner in which money circulates shapes the economy: to raise one of these issues is to address the other for Dickens. The final section, 'Dickensian and Economic Unpredictability', proposes that Dickens's attitude toward knowledge and the ways of knowing, like his treatment of women, is shot through with his insights into the economy.

---

[3] Thomas Carlyle, 'Occasional Discourse on the Negro Question', *Fraser's Magazine* 40 (1849): 670–9, 672.

Dickens and the Economists: Friction or Affinity?

Literary criticism in the mid-twentieth century tended to postulate an opposition between political economy and Dickens's writing. In *The Great Tradition*, F. R. Leavis posited that Dickens's humanism countered the mechanistic formulations of the economists. His reading of *Hard Times* celebrates the novel's portrayal of 'sovereign and indefeasible humanity', which proves victorious over the pursuit of self-interest. As Leavis explains, the 'calculating self-interest' associated with the Utilitarians finds an antithesis in the 'vitality as well as goodness' of Sissy.[4] The tendency in twentieth-century literary criticism to pit Dickens's fiction against political economy presupposes a set of binaries, including that between self-interest and altruism, and that between reason and emotion. Consider, for example, the assertion that 'all readers of Dickens will know how deeply hostile he was from the outset of his career to the main tenets of political economy'. This view highlights Dickens's 'politics of sentiment': 'Political economy ... defin[ed] the social world as an atomistic universe of independent, rational actors ... "putting entirely out of sight", as Dickens expressed it in *Oliver Twist*, "any considerations of heart, or generous impulse and feeling."'[5] Philosopher Martha Nussbaum formulates the same opposition when she refers to Mr Gradgrind, who most conspicuously embodies the principle of self-interest in *Hard Times*: 'Many contemporary theories of rationality ... share the goals and policies of Mr. Gradgrind. That is, they make every attempt to cultivate the intellect and none at all to cultivate "fancy" and emotion.'[6] For Nussbaum, Dickens's fiction admirably valorizes what rational discourses would have us forget.

Calling the binary of literature and economics into question, Dickens scholarship in the late twentieth and early twenty-first centuries has focused instead on the author's ability to discern and articulate the logic of capitalism. His insights into the operation of the economy may stem from a structural homology: money and language both evoke questions about the potency of representation. Just as fiction can purport to remain loyal to an underlying truth, monetary instruments such as exchange bills, bank paper, and cheques carry the promise of validity. As Mary Poovey points out, other 'economic genres' that coexist with monetary instruments are similarly in need of establishing their legitimacy: political economists had to convince their audience that their conclusions were sound, just as money issued legitimately had to appear distinct from counterfeits.[7]

---

[4] Frank Raymond Leavis, *The Great Tradition: George Eliot, Henry James, Joseph Conrad* (New York: Penguin, 1983), 229–30.

[5] Norris Pope, '*The Old Curiosity Shop* and the New: Dickens and the Age of Machinery', *Dickens Quarterly* 13, 1 (1996): 3–18, 11, 14.

[6] Martha Nussbaum, *Love's Knowledge: Essays on Philosophy and Literature* (New York: Oxford University Press, 1990), 81.

[7] Mary Poovey, *Genres of the Credit Economy: Mediating Value in Eighteenth- and Nineteenth-Century Britain* (Chicago: University of Chicago Press, 2007), 4.

The interrelation of monetary instruments, political economy, and fiction has been consequential for Dickens scholarship, which has recently been exploring how the author's astute entrepreneurship in the literary market and his interest in political economy simultaneously influenced his literary output.

Dickens is now seen by some as an astute participant in capitalist networks. Critics have argued, for instance, that Dickens used his name as one uses capital and that his novels, like money, created the semblance of reality out of the purely symbolic realm of language.[8] Of course, it is not only the use of language as a symbolic realm that connects Dickens to the economists. Just as Dickens was a willing actor in a literary marketplace shaped by the dictates of capitalism, he was in some ways ideologically aligned with the apologists of that system. He shared with mainstream political economists an ethics of middle-class self-help, though mitigated in his case by a simultaneous call for compassion.[9] Dickens's and the economists' mutual distrust of the landed interest and their implicit preference for the bourgeoisie account for the ways in which Dickens's novels at times advance the economists' premises.

Even *Bleak House*'s Esther, a seeming paragon of altruism and self-effacement, actually embodies the pursuit of self-interest which the political economists notoriously naturalized. Challenging Leavis's assertion that Dickens valorizes self-forgetting, Kathleen Blake offers a reading in which the assertion of selfhood emerges as a primary interest for Dickens, evident in the case of Esther. To be sure, Esther disregards her best interest when she is thankful for being scarred by smallpox, thinking her similarity to her mother is no longer visible. Yet she also regrets the scars out of fear that her beloved Ada will not be able to recognize her. As she tends to displace her erotic feelings onto her relationship with Ada, her fear about Ada's response hints at her desire to attract Allan Woodcourt's interest. Esther is determined to 'win some love', and in that determination we witness her pursuit of self-interest.[10] The criticism of Chancery in the novel befits the class ideology evident in Esther's pursuit of self-interest:

> [I]n attacking Chancery Dickens aligns himself with Utilitarianism and political economy in the open and in good faith. The novel contends against deadlocking hereditary landlords and the class and gender prerogatives they exercise under the law and under Christian auspices. At the most basic level it validates satisfaction of self-interest, and it extends portrayals of self-interest ... from male to female figures.[11]

---

[8] Sean Grass, 'Commodity and Identity in *Great Expectations*', *Victorian Literature and Culture* 40 (2012): 617–41; Tatiana Holway, 'Funny Money', in Eileen Gillooly and Deidre David (eds), *Contemporary Dickens* (Columbus: Ohio State University Press), 169–88.

[9] Kathleen Blake, *Pleasures of Benthamism: Victorian Literature, Utility, Political Economy* (London: Oxford University Press, 2009); see also Michael Shelden, 'Dickens, "The Chimes," and the Anti-Corn Law League', *Victorian Studies* 25 (1982): 329–53.

[10] Charles Dickens, *Bleak House* (New York: Oxford University Press, 1998), chapter 3, page 13, quoted in Blake, *Pleasures of Benthamism*, 24.

[11] Ibid., 29.

If, as Blake argues, the pursuit of self-interest prevails even upon a woman's subjectivity in the novel, this extension is no mean feat, as the putatively universal subjects construed by political economy were implicitly male. Treatises, pamphlets, and essays in periodicals largely ignored domestic labour and exchange and assumed that economic actors had the agency to determine the course of their actions on the 'market', which to them signified a space outside the home. By including the female figure in the category of *homo economicus*, Dickens compensates for one of the major blind spots of political economy.

Dickens's subscription to bourgeois ideology is indeed more explicit in *The Chimes*, which satirizes the selfishness of the landed interest in the character of Sir Joseph Bowley, Member of Parliament, whose words reflect the landed gentry's presumed benevolence: 'My friend the Poor Man, in my district, is my business ... I assume a—a paternal character towards my friend ... I will think for you; I know what is good for you.'[12] Bowley demands that the poor remain entirely dependent on him. As Michael Shelden points out, 'in these attacks on the feudalistic nature of Bowley's tyranny, Dickens goes to the heart of the free trade case against the landed interests, for the free traders considered their battle on protectionism to be ultimately a battle on feudalism.'[13] By turning the feudal landowner into a villain at the height of the Corn Law debates, Dickens sides with the political economists who claim that paternalist benevolence harms the tenants. However critical Dickens may have been of the political economists' stance on the New Poor Laws, his ideas matched theirs when it came to the critique of the landed interest. Recent literary criticism has thus been able to highlight affinities between Dickens's fiction and political economy in part because Dickens upholds the bourgeois values that mainstream political economists helped to construct. Continuing to dwell on Dickens's participation in capitalism, we turn now to explore the ways in which professional authorship allowed him to take advantage of the credit economy.

Professional Authorship in the Credit Economy

Twentieth-century literary criticism has firmly established that fiction-writing was embedded within the market and not exempt from the imperatives of bourgeois ideology. For instance, even as seemingly neutral an entity as the figure of the bright, prolific novelist confirmed the fantasy of autonomous existence cultivated by capitalism.[14]

---

[12] Charles Dickens, 'The Chimes', in *A Christmas Carol and Other Christmas Books*, ed. Robert Douglas-Fairhurst (New York: Oxford University Press, 2008), quarter 2, pages 110–11.
[13] Shelden, 'Dickens, "The Chimes," and the Anti-Corn Law League', 344.
[14] Mary Poovey, *Uneven Developments: The Ideological Work of Gender in Mid-Victorian England* (Chicago: University of Chicago Press, 1988).

If Dickens earned money from writing and capitalized on his name, how did such professionalization reflect the contemporary economic scene, and what did his celebration of his financial independence share with the perspectives of the political economists? To address these questions, literary critics turn to the commodification of literary texts and the contested status of artistic labour in political economy, as well as to Dickens's participation in the credit economy, the system in which economic actors turn profits by first going into debt. In this kind of economy, absence crystalizes into presence: speculative shares have the ability to generate actual wealth. Tatiana Holway notes that

> the dramatic growth of the credit system ... involved ... a tendency toward abstraction in capitalist exchange. Indeed, the detachment from the 'solid ground' of gold appeared to be so complete to some mid-century observers that the entire British economy seemed to be supported by [paper resting on more paper].[15]

It was within this economic system that Dickens navigated the literary marketplace.

The symbolic field in which fiction writers are immersed—language—plays a prominent role in the development of capitalism, and especially the credit economy. To be sure, the texts that lubricate the cogs of the economy appear so natural to us that we barely notice them as language. A bank note, with inscriptions designating its denomination and more, constitutes a form of credit, a promise of value detached from intrinsic worth. Consider, for instance, the moment in which Paul in *Dombey and Son* memorably asks his father, 'what's money?'[16] The answer that Dombey contemplates reveals the extent to which money involves the deferral of value: 'He would have liked to give him some explanation involving the words circulating-medium, currency, depreciation of currency, paper, bullion, rates of exchange, value of precious metals in the market' (*DS* 8, 93). This answer will not do, because it raises more and more questions about the items listed. Elusively, money points to signifiers that in turn point to others. Focusing only on the final component of this list, Dombey's actual answer oversimplifies what money means: '[g]old, and silver, and copper' (*DS* 8, 93). In response, Paul concludes that money is not so powerful after all—it could not 'save ... Mama' (*DS* 8, 94). In this exchange, Dombey and his son both recognize money's relative impotence. If the latter realizes that it cannot give life, the former recognizes that it functions too abstrusely for a little boy to appreciate its worth. Money can be a material object, but it is also a signifier, especially in a credit economy reliant on the documentation of debt.

Language is key to the operation of credit in part because of its prominent display on bank notes, IOUs, and cheques. At the same time, language sustains the credit economy by establishing worthy debtors as trustworthy through business narratives.[17] Dickens

---

[15] Holway, 'Funny Money', 172.

[16] Charles Dickens, *Dombey and Son*, ed. Alan Horsman (Oxford: Clarendon Press, 1974), chapter 8, page 93. Subsequent references are inserted parenthetically in the text by *DS* chapter, page.

[17] Aeron Hunt, *Personal Business: Character and Commerce in Victorian Literature and Culture* (Charlottesville: University of Virginia Press, 2014).

knew full well both the productive operation of credit in such an economy and its reliance on language. Language to him was 'the self-sustaining, self-enhancing source of identity and value'.[18] His name itself was capital in the sense that it was an embodiment of language that generated profits—like money itself. He 'created and recreated' himself through language, just as symbolic inscriptions beget gains in the money market.[19]

Character itself, rather than actual work, sufficed for profits to accrue in a world where being considered debt-worthy guaranteed success. Tatiana Holway connects this economic phenomenon to the unlaborious character of writing in David Copperfield's experience: his rise as professional writer, which indicates the intertwining of literary and monetary success, does not require 'anything that resembles "Work"'. If fortunes accrue magically in *David Copperfield*, that effortless accumulation betrays a credit economy at work: David's earnestness is the character trait that turns into capital, and by extension confers on Dickens himself an aura of authenticity, bestowing on him the credibility necessary for his readers to invest time and money in his work.[20] As literary critics explore, Dickens self-consciously addresses the social and psychological consequences of literary entrepreneurship in his fiction, not only in the conspicuously autobiographical *David Copperfield* but also in novels that do not thematize authorship, from *Hard Times* and *Little Dorrit* to *Great Expectations*.

If Dickens's entrepreneurship in the literary market was subsumed into a larger capitalist framework and dependent on the logic of credit, textuality played a central role in that dynamic. Sean Grass proposes that Dickens managed to turn his identity into a commodity for the market only through the act of first turning it into a text. Dickens's commodification of his own identity resulted in part from writing autobiographically. At the same time, he achieved it through Public Readings of his fiction, in which he became, as Grass explains, 'at once the inventor and embodiment of his writings'.[21] His quest for international copyright worked toward the same end insofar as it cemented the unity of authors and their texts. Grass maintains that *Great Expectations* retraces Dickens's own translation of his identity into a commodity, specifically into texts and things. Operating not unlike Dickens's name, Pip 'circulates through the novel very much like a commodity'. He is 'rented to neighbors and to Miss Havisham, given back to Joe with a "premium", bound apprentice for a fee, and sold finally to Magwitch through Jaggers, though Joe steadfastly refuses the money'.[22] The commodification of the self takes place in an environment in which the subject is readily, though incompletely, textualized. Legal accounts of Magwitch's identity coexist with his own narrative of it; tombstone inscriptions redefine individuals; and of course Pip produces a text standing in for his life. *Great Expectations* reveals the degree to which selfhood develops within exchange

---

[18] Holway, 'Funny Money', 176.
[19] Ibid.
[20] Ibid., 179–80.
[21] Grass, 'Commodity and Identity', 626.
[22] Ibid., 621.

networks that are themselves shaped by the demands of capitalism. Full of references to cannibalism, the novel depicts a market so overpowering that it can swallow up the self.

Like *Great Expectations, Hard Times* reveals the difficulties that surround the act of writing in a commodified literary market. What precisely was a novelist's contribution to the national economy? According to some political economists, it was none, for writing did not constitute productive labour, however valuable it might be artistically, morally, or psychologically. Showing the relevance of the infamous productive/unproductive debate to Dickens's career, Catherine Gallagher argues that in *Hard Times* Dickens opts for the labour theory of value, according to which a commodity's worth depends on the labour that went into its making. In the novel, the factory and the circus are not so antithetical as they may appear: horse-riders are workers, just as everyone else in Coketown seems to be. In suggesting that 'value derives from labor', Dickens replicates the tenets of political economy, and, even more specifically, addresses the value of art amidst other kinds of production, indirectly providing commentary on his own labour. Gallagher writes, 'Dickens wished to prove that the labor of amusers (like himself) is a positive contribution to, rather than a drain on, the wealth of England.'[23]

Dickens once wrote in a letter that he was 'always possessed with the hope of leaving the position of literary men in England, something better and more independent than [he] found it'.[24] The absence of international copyright was not the only challenge confronting him: the very project of writing novels, which featured fictitious characters and events, had become suspect in the age of speculation. At a time when much business revolved around fictitious investments that did not correlate to material projects, whether novelists used language with real-life referents and aspired to verisimilitude mattered more and more. Capitalism had rendered the process of signification replete with anxieties about the virtual: did signifiers actually signify material things?

Fictitiousness was a potential cause for alarm for Dickens as well as the political economists. The finance economy, founded on 'the capacity of speculation to conjure something out of nothing', relied on fictitious resources and investments to generate profit.[25] Poovey argues that Dickens's representation of womanhood also revolved around fictitiousness. Her reading focuses on *Our Mutual Friend*'s Lizzie, who seems to embody the domestic ideal, but nonetheless inspires anxiety. Poovey asks, 'if Lizzie can be like a man when Eugene needs to be pulled out from the water and like a woman when he is ready for a wife, then is it possible that her character is not an expression of some underlying female nature but merely the effect of man's needs?'[26] Just as the figure of the woman lacks an anchor that fixes her identity, the values in the finance economy

---

[23] Catherine Gallagher, *The Body Economic: Life, Death, and Sensation in Political Economy and the Victorian Novel* (Princeton: Princeton University Press, 2006), 78.

[24] Quoted in Robert L. Patten, *Charles Dickens and his Publishers* (London: Oxford University Press, 1978), 12.

[25] Mary Poovey, *Making a Social Body: British Cultural Formation 1830–1864* (Chicago: The University of Chicago Press, 1995), 173.

[26] Ibid.

are not attached to real assets—hence, Poovey argues, both constitute sources of anxiety. This chapter visits the issue of gender in further detail in 'Gender and Sexuality vis-à-vis Capitalism'; here, I only aim to note the extent to which fictitiousness could undermine the seeming stability of gender categories.

Of course, fictitiousness applies not just to the malleability of the female figure, but also to the nature of the novel as a genre. Holway notes that Dickens, responding to the stigma surrounding financial speculation, 'insisted on the factual basis of his representations', claiming that they portrayed reality and were true to life. Yet his engagement of the value—or dangers—of fictitiousness far exceeds such claims to verisimilitude. It surfaces especially in *Little Dorrit*, which, in addition to thematizing speculation in the character of Mr Merdle, reveals the extent to which language 'mimic[s] the structure of credit'.[27] Metonymy (substituting a name for another thing, as a 'suit' for someone in business) and synecdoche (part signifying whole as 'a leg up' for a person/body rising) dominate the representation of financial matters in the novel, with the end result that just one word comes to absorb all: the air in the financial capital of the world is 'laden with a heavy muttering of the name Merdle, coupled with every form of execration'.[28] A single word—the name Merdle—pinpoints the emptiness at the heart of the world of exchange: people project their own fantasies onto that void, which comes to represent investments, gains, returns, and other monetary transactions that have not yet taken place. For Holway, the detachment of the ubiquitous name from the man himself gives rise to a 'disjunction between the nominal attribution and the real situation', which she claims Dickens presents as a crisis.[29] Through the figure of the speculator dallying with fictitious commodities including his own name, *Little Dorrit* critiques the splitting of the signifier and the signified. Once the name floats free of what it is supposed to represent, it points toward economic corruption.

Yet for Poovey, *Little Dorrit* cherishes its own fictitiousness rather than treating it as a threat. Dickens refuses to connect the financial villain to any historical referent such as the embezzler John Sadlier: 'the resemblance between Merdle and Sadlier had the potential to undermine [the] moralizing function—because it might make readers *classify* the novel as a journalistic revelation about contemporary events'.[30] The novel must retain its status as fiction, precisely because it endeavours to assert its generic difference from monetary instruments that create the semblance of being anchored in real value. While Holway's and Poovey's approaches to *Little Dorrit* vis-à-vis the credit economy remain irreconcilable in many ways, they share the common ground that the logic of finance capitalism, in which investments are not anchored to material goods, influenced the way Dickens and his readers thought about fiction. Whether the words on the page

---

[27] Tatiana Holway, 'Imaginary Capital: The Shape of the Victorian Economy and the Shaping of Dickens's Career', *Dickens Studies Annual* 27 (1998): 23–41, 31, 37.
[28] Charles Dickens, *Little Dorrit*, ed. Harvey Peter Sucksmith (Oxford: Clarendon Press, 1979), Book II, chapter 25, page 691.
[29] Holway, 'Imaginary Capital', 39.
[30] Poovey, *Genres*, 375.

portrayed real-life events and persons—or at least captured some kind of underlying 'truth' about them—determined their ethical valence, aesthetic value, and generic status. It seemed that capitalism and literature converged through their mutual preoccupation with the dynamics of signification.

Literary Form in Light of Economics

As literary a topic as it may be, fictitiousness is best understood by reference to economic transactions. This overlap is typical in that economic matters often direct critics' attention to issues lying at the heart of literariness, such as those of form. While this section further explores Dickens's participation in capitalism, it specifically considers how his relation to the economy shaped formal aspects of his novels. Studies of narration and characterization in Dickens's novels figure prominently in what Mark Osteen and Martha Woodmansee have dubbed 'The New Economic Criticism', the school of criticism that interlinks historical and theoretical approaches to economic matters to produce new interpretations of literary texts.[31] Consider, for example, the interlacing of omniscient narration and the first-person point of view in *Bleak House*, which reveals and complicates the connection between the systemic and the personal. Political economy must shuttle between these poles as well. Seeking to formulate abstract laws, the discourse makes claims to universal validity, yet its results must apply to individual circumstances and shed light on them. This bifurcation is most visible in the originary moment of the discourse, as Adam Smith's famous metaphor of the invisible hand explains the interplay between the laissez-faire system and the individual economic actor. For Smith, the connection between part and whole seems unproblematic: in selfishly pursuing their best interest, buyers and sellers serve the common good of the whole. Eleanor Courtemanche finds that *Bleak House* offers a more elaborate, though less sanguine, approach. The double narrators of *Bleak House* problematize the congruence of the systemic and the individual: 'The bird's eye view and the worm's eye view of Smithian theory are ... represented ... as different kinds of narrative voice' and the 'difficulty of bringing them together is dramatized'. Courtemanche finds that the discord between the two perspectives is in part generic, with the omniscient narrator working in the Gothic, and Esther in the realist, mode. Further, while the former 'spiral[s] outwards' in the course of the narrative to reveal connections between people separated by class, the latter moves inward in the sense that Esther must learn to put others' interests aside and work on establishing her own home.[32] The oscillation between the systemic

---

[31] Mark Osteen and Martha Woodmansee (eds), *The New Economic Criticism: Studies at the Interface of Literature and Economics* (New York: Routledge, 1999).

[32] Eleanor Courtemanche, *The 'Invisible Hand' and British Fiction 1818–1860: Adam Smith, Political Economy, and the Genre of Realism* (London: Palgrave Macmillan, 2011), 105, 113.

and the individual is thus altogether more complicated in Dickens than in the case of political economy.

Narration in *Great Expectations* is similarly tangled up in economic matters. For Anna Kornbluh, the peculiarity of the retrospective narration in this novel is key to understanding its engagement of the credit economy. The point in time at which Pip narrates his story is never specified. His past does not extend far enough forward to reach his amorphous present. The absence of a meeting point 'countermands the relentless futurity of investment', thus evoking the speculators' reliance on what the future may bring. While Kornbluh identifies a critique of the logic of credit in *Great Expectations*, like Grass she insists that the self is thoroughly financialized in this novel. She relates Pip's first-person narration to a set of economic developments that cemented the credit economy: the Limited Liability Acts of 1855–6, which 'gave birth to the corporate person as an alter ego bearing sole responsibility for corporate losses, while the persons comprising the corporation bore none'.[33] Just as financial entities became personified through the Limited Liability Acts, inhabiting a 'psychic economy' that functions arithmetically, Pip keeps account of 'his debts to Joe and Biddy, whom he calls "my creditors"'.[34] Subjectivity has turned into a book balance which the narrative maintains by tabulating debts and favours.

If the novelistic fashioning of selfhood tapped into the vocabulary of economic writing, this was perhaps most visible in the fetishization of character reading. Whereas the Limited Liability Acts reinforced impersonality and abstraction in finance, other forces generated an obsession with personhood. As Aeron Hunt shows, family businesses persisted through the late nineteenth century, valorizing 'personalization and embeddedness' even in the age of the Limited Liability Acts. Maintaining one's character remained a central concern in the business world, as myriad kinds of business writing from testimonials to correspondence testify. Insofar as business manuals emphasized the importance of reading character, Dickens's fiction has something in common with them. *Dombey and Son* in particular 'self-consciously highlights its own construction of a version of character as something ... that comes into being through ... interpretation', argues Hunt.[35] Especially important to her analysis is Carker the manager, whose betrayal of Dombey was hinted at throughout the novel. Signs of Carker's disloyalty train the reader to discern character. The very formation and reading of character in fiction replicates the relentless emphasis that business manuals placed on recognizing signs of benevolence and consistency in individuals. The common ground between the discourses of economics and literature thus includes the centrality of interpretation as well as representation. Hence the significance of discourse to a consideration of the economic in Dickens's fiction. To be sure, Dickens was burdened by questions of how much—or how little—money the poor actually had, or how much he himself needed.

---

[33] Anna Kornbluh, *Realizing Capital: Financial and Psychic Economies in Victorian Form* (New York: Fordham University Press, 2014), 54, 52.

[34] Ibid., 58.

[35] Hunt, *Personal Business*, 14, 63.

But he also revealed a deep understanding of the economy's reliance on signs, which ran parallel to the function of literary texts.

Hunt's analysis hints at the degree to which *Dombey and Son* persistently triangulates the literary and the economic with moral considerations. The figure of the woman remains indispensable as the novel maps monetary issues onto a matrix of morals. 'Both a symbol and an agent of moral value', Claudia Klaver proposes, Florence does not cast herself as an economic actor, but nonetheless becomes complicit in capitalist networks.[36] Having considered several of Dickens's novels briefly in the discussions of bourgeois ideology, the semiotics of capitalism, and economies of literary form, we now focus solely on *Dombey and Son* to underline that his notions of gender and sexuality develop through economic tropes.

Gender and Sexuality vis-à-vis Capitalism

As Klaver postulates, *Dombey and Son* arrives at an impasse once Florence gains her father's affections. Up to that point, the novel has constructed a value system in which competition belongs to the realm of capitalism, indicating a kind of value that seems irreconcilable with its moral counterpart. Klaver notes that Florence's status as moral agent is threatened when she becomes potentially involved in a network of competition, having to divide her affections between two men, her father and husband. If the putative opposition between the economic and the moral is to remain intact, the novel must prevent Walter and Dombey from competing for Florence. Klaver proposes that Walter's relative absence from the action in the final chapters owes to the need to rescue the emotional economy of the novel from the claws of competition. She points out that 'the narrative generates a second Florence who can be (and is) claimed as Dombey's sole province'.[37] As the narrator highlights, the granddaughter belongs to Dombey with no risk of competition: 'But no one, except Florence, knows the measure of the white haired gentleman's affection for the girl. That story never goes about ... He hoards her in his heart ... He is fondest of her, and most loving to her, when there is no creature by' (*DS* 42, 833).[38] The economic metaphor penetrates into the most affectionate moment, as if the narrative cannot but gesture toward money as the sole measure and expression of value. Klaver emphasizes the impossibility of maintaining the putative purity of the feminine.

---

[36] Claudia Klaver, *A/Moral Economics: Classical Political Economy and Cultural Authority in Nineteenth-Century England* (Columbus: Ohio State University Press, 2003), 88.
[37] Ibid., 102.
[38] Quoted ibid., 102–3.

Economic networks are so deeply enmeshed with markers and performances of gender and sexuality in Dickens's fiction that new economic criticism and its variants have produced new perspectives on eroticism, desire, and domesticity even as they focus on questions of value, circulation, and self-regulation. Such intertwining is no coincidence, of course, as the exchange of women as commodities remains at the core of any patriarchal order, including modern capitalist ones. Destabilizing gender has significant implications for models of sexuality: for instance, the implication of Florence in economic networks does not just revise traditional femininity but also introduces subversive sexualities, thus affecting the representation of masculinity. Indeed, *Dombey and Son* correlates the transition from one kind of capitalism (mercantilist) to another (finance-based) to a range of experiences of sexuality, specifically to the contrast between asexual stasis and the proliferation of libidinous energy. Dombey, who exports and imports goods in an unadventurous manner, embodies the old order, appearing never to do what the new order requires: to re-invest in the money market or speculate. We have already seen a number of literary critics turning their attention to the emergence of the latter kind of capitalism, characterized by the proliferation of profits that accrue through debt, the re-investment of industrial surplus value in the finance market, and the rise of speculation. For Robert Clark, this new economy mobilized an uncontainable energy that was akin to libidinous desire: under the new economic regime, the threat is that 'all will become venture, all will become risk, and the carker/canker will corner the lot'.[39] It is precisely the energy called upon by finance capitalism that surfaces in the virility of Carker. The need to repress that energy gives rise to Florence's childlike asexuality, claims Clark.

Yet for David W. Toise, Florence has a 'sexual potential' that becomes unleashed 'in her ability to circulate freely', on the streets and across class boundaries.[40] Exploring the impact of the rise of investment capital, Toise traces a shift in notions of value: in the new system, 'money has no inherent value but only has meaning insofar as we give it power to represent a vast network of exchanges. In consequence, value is no longer a tangible aspect of goods but only a contingent meaning given to the object through cash exchange'.[41] Indeed, Gordon Bigelow has made a similar argument with regard to *Bleak House*, claiming that the legal system in that novel has become the equivalent of a self-regulating market in which prices, no longer dependent on inherent value, instead refer to other prices.[42] In *Dombey and Son*, Dombey harbours an older sense of value based on intrinsic worth, Toise claims. Sol Gills's surprisingly lucrative investment, in contrast,

---

[39] Robert Clark, 'Riddling the Family Firm: The Sexual Economy in *Dombey and Son*', *ELH: English Literary History* 51, 1 (1984): 69–84, 82. My own work argues that liberal economics couple with libidinous economies in *Little Dorrit* (*Romances of Free Trade: Laissez-Faire, British Literature, and the Global Nineteenth Century* (New York: Oxford University Press, 2011)).

[40] David W. Toise, '"As Good As Nowhere": Dickens's *Dombey and Son*, the Contingency of Value, and Theories of Domesticity', *Criticism* 41, 3 (1999): 323–48, 336.

[41] Ibid., 325.

[42] Gordon Bigelow, *Fiction, Famine, and the Rise of Economics in Victorian Britain and Ireland* (Cambridge: Cambridge University Press, 2007).

evokes the process of money begetting money as if the commodity form were completely dispensable: '[t]he whisper is that Mr. Gills's money has begun to turn itself, and that it is turning itself over and over pretty briskly' (*DS* 62, 830).[43] Toise argues that Florence's affective energies belong with the newer order that Sol Gills's investment represents. Value is not moored in blood lines, but emerges through affective exchange: 'In [Florence's] sense, families are groups of people who "act" like families.'[44] Circulating freely on urban streets, she creates a family for herself in the world of the Midshipman, turning strangers into loved ones. If capitalism relies on processes of signification, it seems that texts have their own economies, which often correspond to distinct types of sexuality. In the emotional economies Florence concocts, value—abstract and contingent—opens up the potential for a non-traditional domesticity, rehearsed at the Midshipman among those who take up unexpected family roles, such as Captain Cuttle acting as a child.

DICKENSIAN AND ECONOMIC UNPREDICTABILITY

Dickens scholarship has left no economic development unturned: whether correlating the-text-as-signifier to the operation of the credit economy or considering the moral and sexual economies of novels, it has tended to focus on various topics from debt and liability to interest and investment. What if we were to attend not just to the topical content of political economy, but also to its methodologies? Eleanor Courtemache and Mary Poovey have pursued this line of enquiry effectively, showing that literature and the science of wealth were mutually constitutive discourses in the nineteenth century. Unlocking connections between Dickens's fiction and the methods employed by the political economists can produce further insights into their shared epistemologies and ethics.

In *Hard Times* Dickens critiques political economists' presumed claim to know human nature fully. Portraying an impoverished pedagogy, the novel opens with a diatribe on political economy's reliance on facts: '"Fact, fact, fact!" said the gentleman. And "Fact, fact, fact!" repeated Thomas Gradgrind.'[45] Their monomania indicates the danger of subordinating everything else—including the imagination and emotions—to what they call facts, but *what* is it that they call facts? Historically, it was Malthus's use of 'observed particulars' in the form of numbers that had attracted vitriolic reprehension.[46]

---

[43] Quoted in Toise, '"As Good As Nowhere"', 337.
[44] Ibid., 339.
[45] Charles Dickens, *Hard Times*, ed. Fred Kaplan, Norton Critical Edition, 4th edn (New York: W. W. Norton, 2017), Book I, chapter 2, page 11. Subsequent references are cited parenthetically in the text by *HT* Book:chapter, page.
[46] Mary Poovey, *A History of the Modern Fact: Problems of Knowledge in the Sciences of Wealth and Society* (Chicago: University of Chicago Press, 1998), xvi.

Refusing to subordinate such numerical values to any a priori system or law, Malthus had aroused the rage of those who thought providential principles should come first. 'Unsympathetic critics', writes Mary Poovey, 'interpret[ed] the facts he presented as if they had been altogether denuded of theory (and hence morality).'[47] Among those critics were Robert Southey and Samuel Taylor Coleridge, who claimed that Malthus had employed numbers at the expense of 'goodness' and 'principle'.[48] Dickens enlarges that Romantic critique: his target is the use not just of numerical facts, but also of abstractions, which, confusingly, his characters refer to as facts. When Sissy fails to define a horse (we know from Bitzer's response that she should have said, 'Quadruped. Graminivorous' (HT I:2, 9)), Gradgrind says that she is 'possessed of no facts' (HT I:2, 9). In Hard Times, then, facts are not just numerical figures, but also the abstractions that their agglomeration helps to construe.

Dickens identifies the fact-based, fancy-averse universe of Gradgrind and Bounderby with order, an immutable and rigid state that allows for no surprises or ambiguity. Gradgrind's son and daughter, Tom and Louisa, 'have been trained to mathematical exactness' and life, for them, is organized neatly: 'The little Gradgrinds had cabinets in various departments of science too. They had a little conchological cabinet, and a little metallurgical cabinet, and a little mineralogical cabinet; and the specimens were all arranged and labelled' (HT I:3, 17, 14). The size of the cabinets suggests that the elements of the earth, and in fact life itself, are containable—scientific terms capture the essence of matter with precision. Life seems to consist only of matter that can be categorized and named. For Dickens, the epistemology of political economy is a vortex from which there is no escape—even human labour and its products turn into objects of knowledge, and the human subject appears to have no existence apart from what scientists claim to measure. This problem seems to afflict especially the 'Utilitarian economists' who sought to maximize happiness and minimize suffering for the greatest number, thus appearing to employ a calculus of emotions (HT II:6, 133).

Dickens's novel features an epistemology altogether different from the one Dickens ascribes to political economy. Characters must retain their unpredictability. Louisa and Tom, contrary to their father's expectations, must enjoy the circus; Louisa must entertain the possibility of having a lover—or at least we must not be able to tell whether she does—and even as rigid a man as Thomas Gradgrind must become transformed. In this respect, Dickens works against the premises that would come to inform naturalism in the 1860s and 1870s, such as materialistic determinism. While, under that pessimistic genre, human behaviour followed certain immutable laws governed by biology, in Hard Times characters break free of past patterns that could have formed their futures. The real, for Dickens, is a category that matters, but it is full of surprising turns, contrary to what the French realists—or Thomas Hardy—presumed.

---

[47] Ibid., 293.
[48] Ibid., 293, 294.

The novel associates the state of not knowing explicitly with the art of storytelling. Sissy's father, representing the triumph of fancy rather than facts, masters the art: 'And often and often of a night, he used to forget all his troubles in wondering whether the Sultan would let the lady go on with the story, or would have her head cut off before it was finished' (*HT* I:9, 53). *The Arabian Nights*, a mode of entertainment quintessentially divorced from Western modernity, epitomizes the aesthetic of incertitude Dickens holds up in part though the maintenance of novelistic suspense. To assume certainty is morally problematic as well, as it denies the humanity of political economy's subjects. '[N]ot all the calculators of the National Debt can tell me the capacity for good or evil ... in the soul of one of these its quiet servants,' the narrator notes about the labourers (*HT* I:11, 61). With the use of a Christian vocabulary, Dickens evokes free will and the human capacity for transformation and redemption. From the merely human perspective, it is not possible to know all: 'there is an unfathomable mystery in the meanest of them' (*HT* I:11, 56). Through the very act of acknowledging the limits of mortal knowledge, however, Dickens gestures towards a divine power whose knowledge is complete.

Contrary to what Dickens may have assumed, the political economists themselves dwelled on their lack of certainty and at times even foregrounded it. They were ready to accept that 'the science [was] manifestly incomplete', as Thomas Malthus put it in his famous introduction to *Principles of Political Economy*.[49] Indeed, this introduction as a whole bears witness to just how openly political economy—a precursor to fields in the social sciences—admitted the impossibility of imposing order on life. In his discussion of the price of wheat, Malthus reveals that 'truth' elides political economy's effort to capture it:

> Aware, however, of my liability to this error [mistaking correlations for causes] on the one side, and to the error of not referring sufficiently to experience on the other, my aim will be to pursue, as far as I am able, a just mean between the two extremes, and to approach, as near as I can, to the great object of my research—the truth. (17)

Accuracy can only be approached, and that, only as far as the author is able. The admission of errors does not undermine but motivates the search for truth. Admitting the operation of 'unforeseen causes', Malthus draws attention to the shortcomings of political economy (9). His writing reveals both the effort to represent an orderly world and the impossibility of so doing. The world resists the abstractions that the political economist seeks: 'In political economy the desire to simplify has occasioned an unwillingness to acknowledge the operation of more causes than one in the production of particular effects' (5). Induction is always incomplete, as it requires the political scientist to leave out some causes and thereby reach inexact conclusions.

Formally, the mismatch between the messiness of the data and the neatness of the laws gives rise to oscillations between certainty and confusion in Malthus's introduction.

---

[49] Thomas Malthus, *Principles of Political Economy* (London: William Pickering 1836), 12. Subsequent references are cited parenthetically in the text by page number.

Consider, for example, the discussion of the relation between wealth and saving, which was a contested topic in political economy. Did greater saving lead to greater wealth for the nation? Malthus considers Adam Smith's proposition:

> Adam Smith has stated that capitals are increased by parsimony, that every frugal man is a public benefactor, and that the increase of wealth depends on the balance of produce above consumption. That these propositions are true to a great extent is perfectly unquestionable ... But it is quite obvious they are not true to an indefinite extent. (6)

As soon as Malthus sets a rule, he questions it. The contrast between the qualifiers ('to a great extent', 'not true to an indefinite extent') and the expression of absolute certainty ('perfectly unquestionable', 'obvious') reveals a duality that haunts the assertions of political economy: the admission of uncertainty coexists with the endeavour to overcome it. Finally, Malthus asserts that the question of the relation between savings and wealth can be settled by reaching an 'intermediate point' between the extremes. However, the intermediate point is itself elusive, as 'political economy may not be able to ascertain it' (7). He then asserts that 'no general rule can be laid down respecting the advantage to be derived from saving ... without limitations and exceptions' (8). The political economist self-consciously admits the impossibility of deriving flawless abstractions from the data he confronts.

The oscillation that characterizes Malthus's famous meditation on method haunts *Hard Times*. However adamantly Dickens may critique the political scientist's presumed penchant for certainty, he remains ambivalent about life's tendency to upset order. Stephen Blackpool's articulation of the conflict between him and the world in which he finds himself immersed is poignant. Toiling for insufficient wages and burdened by an unloving wife whom he cannot divorce, he says, 'Let 'em [the laws] be. Let everything be. Let all sorts alone. 'Tis a muddle, and that's aw ... awlus a muddle. That's where I stick. I come to the muddle many times and agen, and I never get beyond it' (*HT* I:10, 54). The muddle idealizes the order whose absence it asserts. In the Stephen Blackpool sub-plot, the chaos of life acquires a decidedly negative valence. Yet it is precisely the same chaos that gives rise to unknowability in the plot and produces suspense. The novelist's craft requires the epistemological posture that the proto-social scientist, confronting and admitting inexactness, must also assume. The demands of realism on the one hand and scientific method on the other motivate a victory-averse search for truth, an entity too elusive and too inexact to capture. Dickens scholarship has provided myriad new readings by emphasizing monetary instruments' prerogative to represent. It can attain new insights by exploring the relinquishment and the deferral of knowledge, under the premise that the scientist and the novelist share an ethics and aesthetics of incertitude.

Further Reading

Christopher Herbert, 'Filthy Lucre: Victorian Ideas of Money', *Victorian Studies* 44, 2 (2002): 185–213

Robert L. Patten, *Charles Dickens and 'Boz': The Birth of the Industrial-Age Author* (Cambridge: Cambridge University Press, 2014)

Ruth Richardson, *Dickens and the Workhouse: Oliver Twist and the London Poor* (New York: Oxford University Press, 2012)

Matthew Rowlinson, *Real Money and Romanticism* (Cambridge: Cambridge University Press, 2013)

Garrett Stewart, 'The Foreign Offices of British Fiction', *Modern Language Quarterly* 61, 1 (2000): 181–206.

Peter M. Stokes, 'Bentham, Dickens, and the Uses of the Workhouse', *SEL Studies in English Literature 1500–1900* 41, 4 (Autumn 2001): 711–27

CHAPTER 37

DICKENS AND ANIMAL STUDIES

JENNIFER MCDONELL

During the visit of the Ghost of Christmas Present in *A Christmas Carol* (1843) Scrooge observes his nephew, Fred, entertain his sister and friends with a series of parlour games. They include a pared-down version of the guessing game Twenty Questions, in which it is elicited from Fred that he is 'thinking of an animal', which is:

> rather a disagreeable animal, a savage animal, an animal that growled and grunted sometimes, and talked sometimes, and lived in London, and walked about the streets, and wasn't made a show of, and wasn't led by anybody, and didn't live in a menagerie, and was never killed in a market, and was not a horse, or an ass, or a cow, or a bull, or a tiger, or a dog, or a pig, or a cat, or a bear.[1]

At last Fred's sister guesses that the 'animal' in question is none other than Fred's uncle Scrooge (*Carol*, Stave 3, 60). Dickens himself was adept at variants of Twenty Questions, including Animal, Vegetable, Mineral, in which the answerer tells questioners at the start whether the subject he or she is thinking of belongs to the animal, vegetable, or mineral kingdom.[2] The Victorian enthusiasm for a game based on such straightforward divisions suggests a confidence in taxonomies of the natural world of the same kind that were used to insist on distinct differences of kind between the human and non-human animals, as Linnaeus did in his *Systema Naturae* of 1735. However, distinctions between animals, plants, and minerals were by no means reliable or secure, as eighteenth- and nineteenth-century natural history recognized. The Twenty Questions sequence

---

[1] *A Christmas Carol and Other Christmas Books*, ed. Robert Douglas-Fairhurst, Oxford World's Classics (Oxford: Oxford University Press, 2006). Subsequent references are inserted parenthetically in the text by *Carol*, section, page. Here Stave 3, 60.

[2] For Dickens's enthusiasm for this game see Philip Collins (ed.), *Dickens: Interviews and Recollections*, 2 vols (London: Macmillan, 1981), 1:94, 140; 2:276.

in *A Christmas Carol* similarly reminds readers that even in so seemingly hallowed a domesticated space as the Victorian middle-class home, and on such a quintessentially Dickensian occasion as Christmas, the boundaries separating humans, animals, and things are unstable.

In Dickens's satire of dry-as-dust scientific education in *Hard Times* (1854), the schoolmaster Thomas Gradgrind asks Sissy Jupe, who has grown up with horses in Sleary's circus, to define a horse. When she cannot, Gradgrind addresses the question to his more fact-minded student Bitzer, who readily produces a lifeless definition:

> 'Quadruped. Graminivorous. Forty teeth, namely twenty-four grinders, four eye-teeth, and twelve incisive. Sheds coat in the spring; in marshy countries, sheds hoofs, too. Hoofs hard, but requiring to be shod with iron. Age known by marks in mouth.' Thus (and much more) Bitzer.
>
> 'Now girl number twenty,' said Mr Gradgrind. 'You know what a horse is.'[3]

Later in the novel, however, Bitzer proves no match for a real live dog and dancing horse, exposing the arrogance of Gradgrind's approving remark that Bitzer 'know[s] what a horse is' (*HT* I:2, 10). As well as demonstrating the dangers of over-reliance on useful knowledge at the expense of physical engagement, imagination, and play, the incident also highlights the inherently unstable relationship between 'real' animals and their significations, the literal and the figurative. Dichotomies of reason and feeling, fact and fancy, were commonplace in Victorian print culture, yet as Gillian Beer has influentially argued, literature and science in this period shared 'not only *ideas* but metaphors, myths, and narrative patterns could move rapidly and freely to and fro between scientists and non-scientists: although not without frequent creative misprision'.[4] Dickens was one of Charles Darwin's favourite authors, and Beer has shown that *On the Origin of Species* bears the marks of Dickens's influence, while Darwin's *The Expression of the Emotions in Man and Animals* (1872) makes use of the description of a snarling mob in *Oliver Twist* in arguing that animals not only share emotions with humans, but also the physical means of expressing them.[5] In turn, Darwin and other naturalists appear to have influenced Dickens's work.

While nineteenth-century naturalists, comparative anatomists, and zoologists differed on various aspects of zoological classification and hierarchization, humankind occupied an uncontested position at the apex of the animal kingdom. In this respect, nineteenth-century zoology—including works as different in intent as Bewick's *General History of Quadrupeds* (1790), Darwin's *On the Origin of Species* (1859), or Arabella

---

[3] *Hard Times*, ed. Fred Kaplan, Norton Critical Edition, 4th edn (New York: W. W. Norton, 2017), Book I, chapter 2, pages 9–10. Subsequent references are inserted parenthetically in the text by *HT* Book:chapter, page.

[4] Gillian Beer, *Darwin's Plots: Evolutionary Narrative in Darwin, George Eliot and Nineteenth-Century Fiction* (Cambridge: Cambridge University Press, 1985), 5 (3rd edn, 2009).

[5] Ibid. 6; George Levine, *Darwin and the Novelists: Patterns of Science in Victorian Fiction* (Chicago: University of Chicago Press, 1988), 121.

B. Buckley's popular zoological work for children, *The Winners in Life's Race, or The Great Backboned Family* (1882)—confirmed the unstated assumptions underpinning eighteenth-century systems of classification. These, as Harriet Ritvo points out, ranked animals not according to size, use, geography, or arbitrary factors such as alphabetical order, but according to taxonomical hierarchies which confirmed 'the hegemonic relation of people to the rest of animate nature' as well as 'the relations between human groups'.[6] The same system which placed humankind at the apex of the animal kingdom was used to construct and naturalize hierarchical social distinctions, including divisions between men and women and those between races.[7]

Understanding Victorian perceptions of animals is important to understanding human self-conception in the same period. Sally Ledger has argued that Dickens's many references to animals, particularly in later writings, also need to be understood in relation to nineteenth-century developments in natural history.[8] In particular, Dickens's work needs to be read alongside that of his contemporary, Charles Darwin, who advanced awareness of the fundamental continuity between human and animal species more than any other thinker of the period. Darwin's anti-teleological insights about evolution, common descent, and natural selection challenged powerful religious and secular dismissals of humans' organic relationship with animals and assumptions underpinning inherited mythologies, discourses, and narrative orders. His works presented a new balance between likeness and variability in natural history: in *The Descent of Man*, for instance, Darwin admitted an 'immense' divergence in intellectual power between people and other animals, but nevertheless proposed that the human mind had evolved from animal forebears. Darwin's account itself evolved in relation to the work of other naturalists who recognized similarities between human and non-human animals, including Erasmus Darwin, Alfred Russell Wallace, 'the sponge philosopher' Robert Grant, and Robert Chambers, whose best-seller on transmutationism, *Vestiges of the Natural History of Creation* (1844), provoked fierce partisan debate at the time of its publication. Dickens's *Martin Chuzzlewit* shows his acquaintance with the precursive evolutionary ideas of the German naturalist Johann Friedrich Blumenbach and of James Burnett, Lord Monboddo, both of whom feature in the mock genealogy in the opening chapter of *Martin Chuzzlewit*. In the same novel, Montague Tigg is compared in passing to 'Peter the Wild Boy', the feral child of the Georgian era who provided one of the case studies for Monboddo's argument that humans were unrelated to lower primates.[9] These references are indicative not only of the novel's thematic

---

[6] Harriet Ritvo, *The Animal Estate: The English and Other Creatures* (Cambridge, MA: Harvard University Press, 1987), 15.

[7] Ibid., 15–21.

[8] Sally Ledger, 'Dickens, Natural History, and *Our Mutual Friend*', *Partial Answers: Journal of Literature and the History of Ideas*, 9, 2 (2011): 364. See also Kate Flint, 'Origins, Species and *Great Expectations*', in David Amigoni and Jeff Wallace (eds), *Charles Darwin's* the Origin of Species: *New Interdisciplinary Essays* (Manchester: Manchester University Press, 1995), 152–73.

[9] *Martin Chuzzlewit*, ed. Margaret Cardwell (Oxford: Clarendon Press, 1982), chapter 7, 105. See also James Burnett, Lord Monboddo, *Of the Origin and Progress of Language*, 2nd edn (Edinburgh, 1773–92),

preoccupation with the socially constructed nature of human personality and character but also of a contemporary fascination, which Dickens shared, with human similarities to, and differences from animals.

Monboddo went so far as to argue that orang-utans might possess the capacity for language, and such scientific challenges to distinctions between human and non-human animals are related to more recent debates in literary and cultural studies. Such scholarship often draws on the French philosopher Jacques Derrida's late work on animals, which challenges the construction of the 'human' in opposition to the homogeneous category of 'the Animal', which Derrida designates with a capital 'A' 'in the singular'.[10] The practical consequences of that distinction for both human and animal lives is evident in the terms in which Fred in *A Christmas Carol* distinguishes his uncle from other animals: Scrooge is human because he can live in London without being tethered or slaughtered at market, like the thousands of sheep, pigs, and other animals that were killed weekly at Smithfield in the centre of London.

In light of this long-standing dichotomy, one ongoing challenge for literary animal studies is how to think about animals *as animals* rather than simply as symbols or metaphors to explain primarily human concerns. The latter tendency is apparent in Dickens's character and place names, which frequently enlist animals in the comic task of magnifying human traits: consider Captain Alfred (Ned) Cuttle in *Dombey and Son*, who is devoted to Sol Gills, or Richard Bayham Badger in *Bleak House*, a fashionable Chelsea doctor whose wife had been married to a botanist, Professor Dingo. In the Dickensian aviary we encounter Sir Mulberry Hawk (*Nicholas Nickleby*), Alice Rainbird and Robin Redforth ('A Holiday Romance'), and Jenny Wren, who shares her name with the lover of Cock Robin in the well-known nursery rhyme (*Our Mutual Friend*). In *Great Expectations*, Pip's gentleman's club is called, after Sheridan, the 'Finches of the Grove', while *David Copperfield*'s young hero lives at the bird-less Rookery. In a similar way, animals enter Dickens's fiction and journalism in the culturally ubiquitous form of allegory, fable, proverb, colloquialism, biblical and literary allusion, hymns, nursery rhymes, and popular song. In Victorian representations of animals, as George Levine observes, 'one looks hard to find encounters with animals that register the integrity of the animal itself'.[11] This is related to a broader problem that Levine and others have identified: the impossibility of representing non-human animals in human language, shaped by human intentions and attitudes. What commentators have identified

---

volume 1, 289, 4; A. J. Larner, 'Dickens and Monboddo', *The Dickensian* (Spring 2004): 36–41; and Laura Brown, *Homeless Dogs and Melancholy Apes: Humans and Other Animals in the Modern Literary Imagination* (Ithaca, NY, and London: Cornell University Press, 2010), 55–62.

[10] Jacques Derrida, 'The Animal that Therefore I am (More to Follow)', trans. David Wills, *Critical Inquiry* 28 (2002): 400. See also Jacques Derrida, *The Animal That Therefore I Am*, ed. Marie-Louise Mallett and trans. David Wills (New York: Fordham University Press, 2008); *The Beast and the Sovereign*, volume 1, trans. Geoffrey Bennington (Chicago: University of Chicago Press, 2009), and *The Beast and the Sovereign*, volume 2, trans. Geoffrey Bennington (Chicago: University of Chicago Press, 2011).

[11] George Levine, *Realism, Ethics and Secularism: Essays on Victorian Literature and Science* (Cambridge: Cambridge University Press, 2008), 251.

as 'the animal turn' in recent humanities and social sciences scholarship evinces how 'nonhuman animals have become a limit case for theories of difference, otherness, and power'.[12]

In thinking about the paradox of being 'simultaneously tied-to and separated from animals', as Erica Fudge puts it, we become aware of the limits of our perception, as animal lives 'exceed our abilities to think about them'.[13] Yet this very impasse presents opportunities for literary critics and historians. Animal studies theorists engaged in literary analysis have explored animal-centred reading strategies which demonstrate how paying attention to other animals and their life worlds might help us to think differently about aspects of literary form—such as fable or metaphor—that have been shaped by ideas of human and animal difference or the logic of species differentiation.[14] To read an author like Dickens in an animal-centred way is a very different project from reading Dickens to determine how his work might confirm his popular reputation as an animal lover, particularly as a canophile. That reputation was cemented after Dickens's death through the recollections of John Forster, Percy Fitzgerald, and Mamie Dickens, followed by descriptive studies including Cumberland Clark's *The Dogs in Dickens* (1926) and Mary Macey's catalogue of Dickens's birds (1930), all of which presented Dickens's relationship to animals—real and literary—as of a piece with his progressive humanitarianism.[15] In the twentieth century a slew of articles focused on animal metaphor and characterization in Dickens appeared, particularly in *The Dickensian* and the *Dickens Quarterly*.[16] These commentaries usefully called attention to the prominence of animals in Dickens's fiction, yet the philosophical and ethical questions raised by Dickens's engagement with animals has been less often commented upon. In the light of recent calls for an animal-centric literary criticism which might challenge the anthropocentric underpinnings of so much cultural and literary studies scholarship, the remainder

---

[12] Kari Weil, *Thinking Animals: Why Animal Studies Now?* (New York: Columbia University Press, 2012), 5.

[13] Erica Fudge, *Animal* (London: Reaktion, 2002), 160.

[14] See, for instance, Susan McHugh, *Animal Stories: Narrating Across Species Lines* (Minneapolis: University of Minnesota Press, 2011); Philip Armstrong, *What Animals Mean in the Fiction of Modernity* (New York: Routledge, 2008); Teresa Mangum, 'Narrative Dominion or The Animals Write Back? Animal Genres in Literature and the Arts', in Kathleen Kete (ed.), *A Cultural History of Animals in the Age of Empire*, vol. 5 (Oxford and New York: Berg, 2007).

[15] See John Forster, *The Life of Charles Dickens*, ed. J. W. T. Ley (New York: Doubleday, Doran and Co., 1928), 657–8. On Dickens's dogs see Percy Fitzgerald, *Memories of Charles Dickens* (Bristol: Arrowsmith, 1913), 10–14.

[16] See, for example, Frank A. Gibson, 'Dogs in Dickens', *Dickensian* 53 (Fall 1957): 145–52; Dvora Zelicovici, 'Grip the Raven: A Rehabilitation', *Dickensian* 77 (Fall 1981): 151–3; Mary Rosner, 'Reading the Beasts of *Martin Chuzzlewit*', *Dickens Quarterly* 4, 3 (1987): 131–41; John P. Frazee, 'Of Foxes, Dogs, and the Monthly Cover of *Bleak House*', *Dickens Quarterly* 6, 3 (1989): 112–16, Barbara L. Stuart, 'The Centaur in *Barnaby Rudge*', *Dickens Quarterly* 8, 1 (1991): 29–37; Margaret Simpson, '*Hard Times* and Circus Times', *Dickens Quarterly* 10, 3 (1993): 131–46; Daniel L. Plung, 'Environed by Wild Beasts: Animal Imagery in *David Copperfield*', *Dickens Quarterly* 17, 4 (2000): 216–23. John Carey, *The Violent Effigy: A Study of Dickens' Imagination* (London: Faber and Faber, 1973) is one of the few major early monographs to provide detailed commentary on animals in Dickens's fiction.

of this chapter considers some historically specific ways in which Dickens's texts preserve the traces or tracks of 'real' animals, foreground the medium and processes by which animals are imagined by humans, destabilize anthropocentric assumptions about agency, and represent interspecies 'structures of feeling'—dispositions such as sympathy and sentimentalism—that have been forcefully disavowed as part of modernism's bid for cultural authority over the Victorians.[17]

Literal and figurative representations of animals in Dickens's fiction are not, however, easily disentangled. For one thing, Dickens's deployment of animal figuration can lead us back to the materiality of animals in relation to situated knowledges and practices (in place, time, and social relations) that otherwise may remain invisible. The bird-like Miss Flite, former ward of the state, keeps symbolic caged birds with names including 'Hope', 'Youth', 'Waste', 'Cunning', 'Sheepskin', 'Wigs', and 'Jargon', who are liberated only a few lines after the judgement in *Jarndyce and Jarndyce* is announced.[18] Among the human-made objects and abstract nouns which lend their names to Miss Flite's birds are a number of animal materials: 'Sheepskin', as the narrator reminds us in chapter 10, is the material upon which legal documents are written, while 'Wigs' were often made of horsehair. The circulation of things deriving from animal bodies in Dickens's fiction, including decorative and consumer goods, suggests intersections between animal studies and the emerging field of 'thing theory' or 'object-oriented inquiry', which might be explored in future research.[19] Models may be found in Katherine Grier's work on nineteenth-century American pet-keeping and Kathleen Kete's on pet-keeping in nineteenth-century Paris, which identify a wide range of potentially relevant sources, from newspaper reports and pet-keeping guidebooks to postcards and taxidermy, as well as pet accessories.[20]

The parlour game sequence from *A Christmas Carol* bears comparison to another, more sinister, Christmas scene in *Great Expectations*, one of two dramatic sequences which turn on the consumption of pork in the latter novel. Over dinner,

---

[17] Philip Armstrong has used Raymond Williams's concept of 'structures of feeling', referring to 'lived' or 'practical consciousness' prior to its ideological codification, to clarify how intimately the emergence of dispositions such as sympathy, sentimentalism, and nostalgia for nature has been tied up with human–animal relations in specific historical contexts and mediated through texts. See Armstrong, *What Animals Mean in the Fiction of Modernity*. Key concepts underpinning animal-centred criticism are discussed by Cary Wolfe, 'Human, All Too Human: "Animal Studies" and the Humanities', PMLA 124, 2 (2009): 564–75. For discussion of animal-standpoint criticism see Josephine Donovan, *The Aesthetics of Care: On the Literary Treatment of Animals* (London: Bloomsbury, 2016), 95–111.

[18] *Bleak House*, ed. George Ford and Sylvère Monod, Norton Critical Edition (New York: W. W. Norton, 1977), chapter 14, 180. Subsequent references are inserted parenthetically in the text by BH chapter, page.

[19] See Elaine Freedgood, *The Ideas in Things: Fugitive Meaning in the Victorian Novel* (Chicago: University of Chicago Press, 2006) and Sarah Amato, *Beastly Possessions: Animals in Victorian Consumer Culture* (Toronto: University of Toronto Press, 2015).

[20] See Katherine C. Grier, *Pets in America: a History* (Chapel Hill: University of North Carolina Press, 2006) and Kathleen Kete, *Beast in the Boudoir: Petkeeping in Nineteenth-Century Paris* (Berkeley, CA: University of California Press, 1994).

Wopsle and Pumblechook set Pip an exercise in counterfactual thinking, asking him to imagine what his life would be like as a 'four-footed Squeaker', with Pumblechook vividly evoking how 'the butcher would have come up to you as you lay in your straw … and he would have shed your blood and had your life'.[21] Pip, the human pig who ought to be grateful for Christmas dinner, is conflated with the animal pig who *is* Christmas dinner. This metaphorical transformation resonates with a later scene in which the bills clerk, Wemmick, serves up sausages made from the pig Pip has met on his hobby farm, impressing upon Pip that the meat he had eaten was 'a little bit of *him*. That sausage you toasted was his … Do try him, if it is only for old acquaintance sake' (*GE* III:6, 371). The insertion of the personal pronouns '*him*' and '*his*' (emphasized by Dickens's italicization) erases the hierarchical distinctions that conventionally separate the domesticated animal as an individual 'acquaintance' from the animal as foodstuff destined for human consumption. In so doing, it further confuses the domestic sentiment associated with private space and the instrumental reason associated with public space, a division already allegorized in the sharp contrast between the character traits and values John Wemmick displays at home and in the professional world. The conflation of pig as pet or personage with pig as pork exposes public and private as inseparable, as interconnecting zones of circulation. It is as if an aspect of Smithfield livestock market in the centre of London, which Pip encounters on his arrival in the city, has penetrated the domestic idyll of the 'castle'.

The world's most populous city in Dickens's lifetime, London was as much a city of animals as of people. London's population doubled from 1800 to 1850, and the urban middle classes were exposed increasingly to the real and perceived dirt and disease associated with large numbers of animals confined in overcrowded spaces. The number of urban horses in Britain, for example, increased from about 350,000 in the 1830s to 1,200,000 at the beginning of the twentieth century, most of whom were used to haul omnibuses and other heavy vehicles in the growing towns.[22] In 1870 England, Wales, and Scotland contained 1,064,621 licensed dogs (with the number of unlicensed dogs being inestimably large).[23] In 1850 there were estimated to be 13,000 cows in London; and in 1841 some 2,764 'milksellers and cow keepers'.[24] Other animals roamed freely in the streets, including pigs, as Friedrich Engels describes in his account of Manchester in *The Condition of the Working Class in England* (1845). Enormous numbers of wild birds were snared and sold in the streets as pets—linnets, finches, larks (which were eaten), jackdaws, nightingales, sparrows, and starlings—some of which were subjected to cruel practices such as blinding and tongue splitting.[25] London and other major British cities

---

[21] *Great Expectations*, ed. Margaret Cardwell (Oxford: Clarendon Press, 1993), volume I, chapter 4, 27–8. Subsequent references are inserted parenthetically in the text by *GE* volume:chapter, page.

[22] Ritvo, *The Animal Estate*, 311 n. 1.

[23] See Brian Harrison, 'Animals and the State in Nineteenth-Century England', in *Peaceable Kingdom: Stability and Change in Modern Britain* (Oxford: Clarendon Press, 1982), 83.

[24] Nicholas Daly, *The Demographic Imagination and the Nineteenth-Century City: Paris, London, New York* (Cambridge: Cambridge University Press, 2015), 151.

[25] Ibid., 156.

were in every sense anthrozootic cities: urban environments defined by the close interaction and interdependency of humans and other animals.[26]

Smithfield market—once the site of human executions—was the principal place where London's oxen, sheep, lambs, calves, pigs, and horses had been bought, sold, and slaughtered for nine centuries. It is estimated that some 200,000 head of cattle and 1.5 million sheep were killed at Smithfield every year, and as John Timbs observed in 1855, numerous 'noxious trades' such as 'tainted sausage-makers, slaughter-houses, tripe-dressers, cat's-meat boilers, catgut-spinners, bone houses' thrived in nearby streets.[27] 'The market of the capital of the world' appears in numerous Dickens novels, particularly *Oliver Twist* (1838), *Bleak House* (1853), and *Great Expectations* (1861).[28] The author's descriptions of the market's dirt, noise, overcrowding, and the spectacle of public slaughter illustrate the consequences of such exposure for both animals and people, and his magazine *Household Words* was a significant force in the debates leading up to the *Smithfield Market Removal Act* of 1852, which removed the market to suburban Islington.

The depictions of the interrelationship between species, space, and the senses in the Smithfield environs in Dickens's novels illustrate how human–animal interactions were not only an essential part of London's system of labour and trade but also part of the emotional experience of city dwellers. Consider the *Bleak House* narrator's description of a 'market-day': 'The blinded oxen, over-goaded, over-driven, never guided, run into wrong places and are beaten out; and plunge, red-eyed and foaming, at stone walls; and often sorely hurt the innocent, and often sorely hurt themselves' (*BH* 16, 199). Dickens is alluding to the frequently reported accidents in which distressed oxen escaped from their drovers and ran wild through the congested streets surrounding the market, frightening and sometimes trampling on passers-by.[29] The area around Smithfield had escaped the Great Fire of London, and presented a tangle of narrow streets, alleys, and dead ends, crammed with local trades and industries, through which exhausted animals were driven brutally in large numbers on market days. The narrator also explicitly compares the goaded animals to poor Jo and others like him who are constantly being 'moved on': 'Very like Jo and his order; very, very like!' (*BH* 16, 199). In *Great Expectations* Pip's kinaesthetic experience of animal matter—the filth and fat and blood

---

[26] On the 'anthrozootic city' see Scott A. Miltenberger, 'Viewing the Anthrozootic City: Humans, Domesticated Animals, and the Making of Early Nineteenth-Century New York', in Susan Nance (ed.), *The Historical Animal* (Syracuse: Syracuse University Press, 2015), 262–3.

[27] John Timbs, *Curiosities of London: Rare and Remarkable Objects of Interest in the Metropolis* (London: David Bogue, 1855), 500.

[28] This epithet is used by Dickens and W. H. Wills, *Household Words*, 'The Heart of Mid-London', 4 May 1850, page 123. Subsequent references are inserted parenthetically in the text by *HW*, 'title', date, page.

[29] For a discussion of 'mad bulls' in Dickens's fiction see Trey Philpotts, 'Mad Bulls and Dead Meat: Smithfield Market as Reality and Symbol', *Dickens Studies Annual: Essays on Victorian Fiction* 41 (2010): 25–44. For detailed analysis of 'the Smithfield system' (as it was known) and the production of biopolitical objects in nineteenth-century literature (including Dickens) and food culture see Ted Geier, *Meat Markets: The Cultural History of Bloody London* (Edinburgh: Edinburgh University Press, 2017).

and foam—sticking to him draws attention in a different way to the real and metaphoric relations between the animalized animals (food animals destined for slaughter) and the animalized humans of London's criminal underclass, slums, and workhouses housed in and around Smithfield (*GE* I:1, 163–4). Further, the proximity of Smithfield markets to other sites of death and imprisonment (such as Newgate) and disorder and unruliness (Bartholomew Fair) in *Great Expectations, Oliver Twist,* and *Bleak House* is part of a Dickensian politics of location that connects human and animal imprisonment and oppression.

Writing of animal cruelty at sites such as Smithfield, Hilda Kean highlights the importance of sight in the formation of the modern or 'civilized' subject: 'The very act of seeing became crucial in the formation of the modern person. Who you were was determined by where you were and what you saw—as well as how you interpreted it.'[30] This is evident in the different responses of Sikes and Oliver to Smithfield in *Oliver Twist*: Oliver, who is represented as a gentleman by birth *and* nature, is amazed and sensorily confused by 'the hideous and discordant din', whereas Sikes, who is presented as irredeemably brutal and 'uncivilized', bestows 'very little attention on the numerous sights and sounds', thinking instead of a 'morning dram'.[31] Attitudes towards animal slaughter shifted in this period not only as a result of ethical concern for animal suffering but because animal cruelty was believed to dehumanize humans.[32] Comparisons arise with Dickens's non-fiction writings about animal slaughter, such as 'A Monument of French Folly', in which Dickens recalls his inspection of Parisian abattoirs and praises their humane and efficient operations, but laments such cruel practices as binding the calves' legs, which he attributes to peasant superstition (*HW*, 'A Monument of French Folly', 8 March 1851, 553–8). In the co-written, or 'composite' article as Dickens called such collaborations, 'The Heart of Mid-London', Dickens and W. H. Wills criticize the Smithfield market in terms that reflect the classed dimensions of contemporary debates. Their fictional spokesperson, Mr Bovington—an allusion to John Bull and Britain as a nation of beef eaters—is a new member of the upper classes, whose 'first class character' consists in his humane treatment of his livestock, his concern that they receive the best-quality fodder while at Smithfield, and his desire that they be killed 'comfortably', which he considers no less than his 'sacred duty' (*HW*, 'The Heart of Mid-London', 4 May 1850, 121). Bovington reports that drovers engage in such cruelties as dropping burning pitch on the backs of frantic livestock and implies that their behaviour is akin to that of natives from the 'darkest' parts of the expanding British empire: they 'raved, shouted, screamed, swore, whooped, whistled, danced like savages' (*HW*, 'The Heart of Mid-London', 4 May 1850, 122). Dickens's various representations of Smithfield, taken

---

[30] Hilda Kean, *Animal Rights: Political and Social Change in Britain Since 1800* (London: Reaktion, 2000), 27.

[31] *Oliver Twist*, ed. Kathleen Tillotson (Oxford: Clarendon Press, 1966), chapter 21, 136. Subsequent references are inserted parenthetically in the text by *OT* chapter, page. See pages 369–71 of Tillotson's edition for instalment and chapter divisions in *Bentley's Miscellany* and 1838 three-volume edition.

[32] See Ritvo, *The Animal Estate*, 135.

together, imply that what was at stake in the Smithfield 'abomination' (as it was often called) was the notion of civilization itself. What appears to have most disturbed Dickens and many of his progressive contemporaries about drovers and urban butchers is not the sacrifice of an animal for human consumption as such, but that human and beast appeared to have swapped roles: animal abusers and those that deal in nefarious trades associated with the slaughter of animals take on bestial, brutish characteristics attributed to animals such as bloodthirsty violence and uncontrollable instincts.

Dickens's habitual blurring of the distinction between animal and human is also a blurring of what or who is human and what or who is not. In the fiction, then, animal tropes and metaphors are equally adapted to representing the precariousness of the lives of traumatized and dehumanized children like Oliver, Jo, and Pip, as to marking the radical alterity of humans who prey on children, animals, and women. That Gamfield and Sikes in *Oliver Twist* growl and scowl is an unmistakable sign that they not only share physical and behavioural characteristics with animals but *are* bestial; in turn, the mob that pursues Sikes to his death are described as 'snarling with their teeth and making at him like wild beasts', associating their enraged energy with the animal (*OT* 50, 341). Fagin is controversially racialized as a 'loathsome reptile, engendered in the slime and darkness ... crawling forth, by night, in search of some rich offal for a meal' and has 'fangs as should have been a dog's or rat's' (*OT* 19, 120–1; 47, 317).

In a converse move, animals are figuratively enlisted to elicit sympathy when Dickens addresses moral and social problems such as consumption and hunger. Stray children and women, like dogs, are shown in Dickens's fiction to be equally vulnerable to violation by others: they are subjected to various forms of imprisonment, bodily harm, and death without recourse to social justice, and have a particular interest in food. In *Oliver Twist*, for instance, Sikes's brutalized dog Bull's-eye is metonymically linked to the battered prostitute, Nancy, and the assorted stray children of the metropolis, insofar as they are all cast as victims of Sikes's violence and criminality. The trope of the child as a starving dog recurs in Dickens's fiction. In *Oliver Twist*, for instance, the undertaker's wife Mrs Sowerberry feeds Oliver scraps set aside for her dog, Trip. Addressing readers in the second person, Dickens asks 'well-fed' proponents of Britain's controversial 1834 Poor Law Amendment Act and the system of union workhouses it inaugurated, to witness the spectacle of Oliver tearing at Trip's leftovers like a dog 'with all the ferocity of famine' (*OT* 4, 24–5). Beryl Gray notes that Dickens kept animals, including several large dogs, and had a keen interest in the way they approached food.[33] This observation is on display in *Great Expectations* in Pip's vivid description of the ravenous Magwitch 'gobbling mincemeat, meat-bone, bread, cheese, and pork pie, all at once', with 'strong sharp sudden bites' (*GE* I:3, 19–20). Pip notes how Magwitch 'snapped up, every mouthful ... and he looked sideways here and there while he ate, as if he thought there was danger in every direction ... In all of which particulars he was very like the dog' (*GE* I:3, 19–20). To be subjected to hunger, thirst, and destitution, to be dependent

---

[33] Beryl Gray, *Dogs in the Dickensian Imagination* (Farnham: Ashgate, 2014), 229.

on a more powerful person for food, to be devoid of 'civilized' etiquette associated with eating, is to be reduced to a state that Giorgio Agamben has called 'bare life'—that is to say, life that is wounded, expendable, and endangered. Bare life 'is not simply natural reproductive life, the *zoe* of the Greeks, nor *bios*', Agamben argues, but rather 'a zone of indistinction and continuous transition between man and beast.'[34] Likewise, Dickens's description of human hunger in canine terms suggests the permeability and porousness of species boundaries and destabilizes established cultural hierarchies. As one who is likened to a stray dog, Jo shares the abjection and interstitial agency accorded to stray and unwanted dogs: '[i]t surely is a strange fact', Alan Woodcourt observes, 'that in the heart of a civilised world this creature in human form should be more difficult to dispose of than an unowned dog' (*BH* 47, 560).

In addition to providing glimpses of otherwise occluded animal histories, such as the cruelty suffered by Smithfield livestock or the privations of stray dogs, Dickens's texts display a self-reflexivity about the pitfalls and potential of anthropomorphism, about the way in which zoological language appropriates animals as ciphers and alibis for human concerns. When Boffin recommends bees as models of industry to the congenitally idle Eugene Wrayburn in *Our Mutual Friend*, Wrayburn protests: 'I object on principle, as a two-footed creature, to being constantly referred to insects and four-footed creatures. I object to being required to model my proceedings according to the proceedings of the bee, or the dog, or the spider, or the camel.'[35] But if humans may resist comparison to animals, so too may animals resist being compared to humans—or so Dickens suggests. In a series of four articles for *Household Words* in 1850, Dickens has a disaffected raven address, among other things, the problem of anthropocentric history:

> I want to know who BUFFON was. I'll take my oath he wasn't a bird. Then what did *he* know about birds—especially about Ravens? He pretends to know all about Ravens. Who told him? Was his authority a Raven? I should think not ...
>
> I tell you what. I like the idea of you men, writing histories of *us*, and settling what we are, and what we are not, and calling us any names you like best. What colors do you think you would show in, yourselves, if some of us were to take it into our heads to write histories of *you*? (*HW*, 'From the Raven in the Happy Family [i]', 11 May 1850, 156)[36]

The raven is singling out one of Linnaeus's contemporaries, the French naturalist Georges-Louis Leclerc, Comte de Buffon's *Histoire naturelle, générale et particulière, avec la description du Cabinet du Roi* (1749–1804). This work was enormously influential

---

[34] Giorgio Agamben, *Homo Sacer: Sovereign Power and Bare Life*, trans. Daniel Heller-Roazen (Stanford, CA: Stanford University Press, 1998), 109.

[35] *Our Mutual Friend*, ed. Michael Cotsell. Oxford World's Classics Edition (Oxford: Oxford University Press, 1989), Book I: chapter 8, 93. Subsequent references are inserted parenthetically in the text by *OMF* Book:chapter, page.

[36] This is one of four articles in *Household Words* that turn on the conceit of a talking raven in a 'happy family'.

in the late eighteenth and early nineteenth centuries, including on Cuvier and Lamarck, and Dickens's library at Gad's Hill included Barr's Buffon's *Natural History*.[37] Like Cuvier, Buffon questioned much received wisdom about animals and stressed the importance of animals' habitats, habits, and life cycles, although his attribution of human qualities to particular animals betrays the influence of the language of bestiaries. Turning the tables, Dickens's rebellious raven promises to compile an anthology in which other species will write their 'histories' of humans, warning that the volume will catalogue numerous cruelties inflicted upon animals by humans: a horse will note the indignity of being sent to the knackers, while a donkey will record blows and cudgels (*HW*, 'From the Raven in the Happy Family' [i], 158). The Raven's threat that animals might 'do a Buffon' on humans was anticipated by Balzac, who, as Dickens would almost certainly have known, announced that his *La Comédie humaine* was intended to parallel for the French social world Buffon's classification of the animal kingdom. As if in anticipation of Orwell's *Animal Farm*, this litany of complaints becomes a call to revolution: 'I croak the croak of revolt, and call upon the Happy Family to rally round me' (*HW*, 'From the Raven in the Happy Family' [i], 159).

Even as the raven of *Household Words* provides a channel for Dickens's light-hearted satire of contemporary human manners and political squabbles, his imaginative act of 'becoming animal' entertains the mind-bending thought of what a species-specific history by animals of humans might look like. No less than Montaigne's attempt to imagine how his cat saw him,[38] Dickens's thought experiment anticipates suggestions from recent animal studies scholars that, instead of automatically dismissing anthropocentrism as a form of anthropomorphism, we might consider the potential for anthropomorphism to challenge the rigid distinctions we make between animal and human life.[39] In philosophy, for example, Jane Bennett uses biocentric anthropomorphism to discuss the materiality of non-human experience[40] while Tess Cosslett in literary studies demonstrates how anthropomorphism in late eighteenth- and early nineteenth-century children's writing effectively created a sympathetic equivalence between human and animal suffering.[41]

Dickens evidently had a thing about Ravens. In *Barnaby Rudge*, the entertaining talking raven Grip is Barnaby's 'more knowing' and constant companion.[42] Dickens

---

[37] See J. H. Stonehouse (ed.), *Reprints of the Catalogues of the Libraries of Charles Dickens and W. M. Thackeray* (London: Piccadilly Fountain Press, 1935), 16, 51, 78.
[38] See Derrida's discussion of Montaigne, *The Animal That I am Therefore* (2008), 6.
[39] On the relationship between anthropocentrism and anthropomorphism see Lorraine Daston, 'Intelligences: Angelic, Animal, Human', in Lorraine Daston and Gregg Mitman (eds), *Thinking with Animals: New Perspectives on Anthropomorphism* (New York: Columbia University Press, 2005), 53–4; also Derek Ryan, *Animal Theory: A Critical Introduction* (Edinburgh: Edinburgh University Press, 2015), 36–49.
[40] Jane Bennett, *Vibrant Matter: A Political Ecology of Things* (Durham, NC: Duke University Press, 2010), 99.
[41] See Tess Cosslett, *Talking Animals in British Children's Fiction, 1786–1814* (Farnham: Ashgate, 2006).
[42] This phrase is from Dickens, Letter to George Cattermole, 28 January 1841, *The Letters of Charles Dickens*, ed. Madeline House, Graham Storey, et al., Pilgrim/British Academy Edition, 12 vols (Oxford: Oxford University Press, 1969), volume 2, pages 197–8. Here 197.

explained to readers that this avian character was a composite of two of his own pet ravens, likewise named Grip, both of whom suffered untimely deaths.[43] While at work on the novel's early chapters in March 1841, Dickens wrote a wryly humorous letter to his friend, the illustrator Daniel Maclise, describing in detail the illness, death, and subsequent post-mortem examination of his first Grip. Although Dickens appeared to feel Grip's loss deeply, he did what he often did when faced with the death of an animal, turning the tragedy into an amusing anecdote to entertain friends.[44] Dickens's letters and para-textual commentary on *Barnaby Rudge* document the transformation of the 'real' Grip into 'Grip the clever, Grip the wicked, Grip the knowing', who provides a foil to the 'idiot' Barnaby (*BR* 47, 374–5). For Barnaby, the inter-species affection he and Grip share is foremost: Grip is 'my brother ...—always with me—always talking—always merry' (*BR* 57, 456). Grip's speech is not only a means of communication between himself and Barnaby, but also has a defamiliarizing function, making strange the procedures of human language, including literary language. His humorous mimicry during the Anti-Catholic Gordon Riots of phrases such as 'I'm a devil, I'm a Polly, I'm a kettle, I'm a Protestant, No Popery!' and 'I'm a Protestant kettle' mocks the rote anti-Catholic sloganeering of the rebel crowd (*BR* 57, 455). This bird-talk works through irony, excess, and repetition to produce 'speech' that is characterized by its similarity to, and difference from, human speech.

While *Barnaby Rudge* leaves the fictional Grip alive and well, still energetically conversing, the real Grip has found a different kind of afterlife: Dickens hired a taxidermist to mount the dead bird in a shadowbox of wood and glass which thereafter hung above his desk, an artefact that is now on display in the Free Library of Philadelphia. Dickens also had one paw of a favourite cat, Bob, taxidermied to form part of a letter opener.[45] The ivory blade is engraved 'C. D. In Memory of Bob 1862.' Such objects trouble the boundaries separating the real and the fictional, the figurative and literal, the living and dead. Suspended between life and death, they are 'paralytically animated' as the narrator in *Our Mutual Friend* observes of the preserved animal bodies in Mr Venus's 'little dark greasy shop' (*OMF* I:7, 85, 78). Nor can we easily escape the suspicion that the recuperative work of Mr Venus, modelled on a real taxidermist Dickens knew, is a dark 'other' to the author's novelistic craft as one who animates and reanimates humans, animals, and things.[46] This suspicion is strengthened if we recall Forster's report that 'on Dickens's

---

[43] See 'Preface to the Cheap Edition' (1849), *Barnaby Rudge*, ed. Clive Hurst, Oxford World's Classics Edition (Oxford: Oxford University Press, 2003), 5–9, 5. Subsequent references are inserted parenthetically in the text by *BR* chapter, page.

[44] Similar tendencies are apparent in Dickens's response to the death of his dog, Sultan, whom he had shot: see Philip Howell, *At Home and Astray: The Domestic Dog in Victorian Britain* (Charlottesville, VA: University of Virginia Press, 2015), 47–8. On Dickens's unsentimental anthropomorphism see Gray, *Dogs in the Dickensian Imagination*, 165.

[45] See Mamie Dickens's account of her father's cats in *My Father as I Recall Him* (New York: Dutton, 1896), 80–2.

[46] See Albert D. Hutter, 'Dismemberment and Articulation in *Our Mutual Friend*', *Dickens Studies Annual* 11 (1983): 152.

writing desk there was a French bronze group representing a duel with swords, fought by a couple of very fat toads', an ornament that bears an uncanny resemblance to the 'two preserved frogs fighting a small-sword duel' in Mr Venus's shop window (*OMF* I:7, 77).[47]

The image of battling toads, like the notion of a talking raven, invites us to consider the essentially theatrical dimension of Dickens's animal characters. In *Oliver Twist*, Sikes's dog Bull's-eye becomes another of Dickens's theatrical animals when he leaps to his death from a considerable height in a manner that seems excessive even in a novel that continually brings together the conventions of mimetic representation and theatrical melodrama. In strictly mimetic terms, a dog choosing to jump towards the shoulders of a master who has accidently hung himself, and is swinging in mid-air from a height, makes little sense as an 'imitation' of life. The dog's suicidal leap to his death, narrated as if from the perspective of the spectatorial crowd gathered below, may have had its genesis in the enormously popular but now almost completely forgotten Victorian melodramatic theatrical genre of dog drama, in which trained dogs frequently played a crucial part in the play's action by diving into tanks of water to rescue drowning children or by attacking murderers and villains.[48] Dickens's enthusiasm for all manner of spectacle and entertainment, including performing animals, is well known, and Charley Bates alludes to precisely this kind of theatrical performance when he declares of Bull's-eye: 'He'd make his fortun on the stage that dog would, and rewive the drayma besides' (*OT* 39, 260). It is as if Bull's-eye were conceived of as a parody of sentimental Victorian stories about dogs remaining loyal to their masters even after death.

Writing of Dickens's *Great Expectations*, Ivan Kreilkamp describes animals as the novel's 'sub-proletariat', lacking 'robustness of identity and agency' in the novel's diegesis.[49] More broadly, Kreilkamp argues that pet characters embody minorness in both narrative and generic terms in Victorian fiction, at a time when bourgeois pet-keeping was on the increase.[50] As one of Dickens's most complex animal characters, Bull's-eye complicates Kreilkamp's position. At the simplest level of plot and action, he attacks Sikes, resists drowning by his master, finds his way to Jacob's Island, and leaps to his death rather than be destroyed by Sikes's hand (as is Nancy) or by the state (as is Fagin). In this sense, Bull's-eye can be read as embodying an agency that cannot be fully accommodated within the confines of allegory, as say, an extension of Sikes or a double for Nancy. This agency may be thought of in terms of what Philip Armstrong describes

---

[47] See Forster, *Life*, 654.

[48] On the use of dogs onstage in the nineteenth century, see Richard Altick, *The Shows of London* (Cambridge, MA: Harvard University Press, 1978), 311; Paul Schlicke, *Dickens and Popular Entertainment* (London: Allen & Unwin, 1985), 57; Michael Dobson, 'A Dog at All Things: The Transformation of the Onstage Canine 1550–1850', *Performance Research: A Journal of the Performing Arts* 5 (2000): 116–24, 120–4.

[49] Ivan Kreilkamp, 'Dying Like a Dog in *Great Expectations*', in Deborah Denenholz Morse and Martin A. Danahay (eds), *Victorian Animal Dreams: Representations of Animals in Victorian Literature* (Farnham: Ashgate, 2007), 82.

[50] On pet-keeping, see Howell, *At Home and Astray*; Kete, *Beast in the Boudoir* 1994; and Ritvo, *The Animal Estate*.

as 'feral' eruption, involving animal resistance to 'modernity's attempts at civilization, domestication, captivation or manipulation'.[51] Though not 'feral' in the conventional sense of 'wild', Bull's-eye refuses manipulation and captivity, along with human orderings, especially in his dramatic final leap.

While there is not the space here to rehearse, in full, the range of positions on non-human agency, the argument that animals are agents is becoming ever more commonplace and forms part of a wider posthumanist intellectual project that reconsiders the power and role of non-human forces in both the past and the present. Mobilizing a concept of animal agency in literary interpretation need not require that an animal consciously wills any specific change in the narrative. Indeed, the conventional understanding of agency as a capacity to effect change that combines rational thought with conscious intention itself derives from an anthropocentric paradigm of enlightenment humanism.[52] As such, agency is a conception that is deeply embedded in humanist and Christian conceptions of human exceptionalism. In resisting the classic understanding of agency as rational, intentional, and premeditated, I am guided in my reading of animal and human entanglement in Dickens's work by Vinciane Despret's explication of interagency and *agencement*, a term Despret uses to name the rapport of forces that produces agency.[53] As well as considering Darwin's account of the reciprocity between orchids and their animal pollinators, Despret uses the example of animal resistance to illustrate

> that an animal resisting indeed appears as the very subject of the action, but it is not the same process by which he/she becomes an agent. 'Agenting' (as well as 'acting') is a relational verb that connects and articulates narratives (and needs 'articulations'), beings of different species, things and contexts. There is no agency that is not interagency. There is no agency without *agencement*, a rapport of forces.[54]

Dickens's London, with all its noise, dirt, and danger, can be understood as an interdependent network of objects, animals, and humans responding to the exigencies of environment and the pressures of conflicting agencies. We need only think of Dickens's stylistic habit of animating non-living things that threaten to govern the lives of their owners, to lay to rest the conventional definition of agency based on the subjective experience of autonomous intention. Just as the escaping animals at Smithfield markets and Bulls-eye's actions point to an agency that is overdetermined by a rapport of forces,

---

[51] Armstrong, *What Animals Mean in the Fiction of Modernity*, 227 n. 9.

[52] See Armstrong's discussion of agency (*What Animals Mean in the Fiction of Modernity*, 3). For a detailed discussion of non-human agency in relation to place and space, see Chris Philo and Chris Wilbert, *Animal Spaces and Beastly Spaces: New Geographies of Human-Animal Relations* (London: Routledge, 2000), 15.

[53] Despret is drawing on Deleuze's development of Jakob von Uexküll's notion of *umwelt*, which allows for animal 'point of view'. See 'From Secret Agents to Interagency', *History and Theory* 52, 4 (2013): 31, 37.

[54] Ibid., 44.

the same applies to the actions of Dickens's human characters—no more consistently than the animals do they exhibit rational agency in the classical sense.

If the work of literary criticism consists in introducing 'new objects and new subjects onto a common stage', thereby making 'visible what was invisible', audible what was inaudible, perceptible what was imperceptible, then animals who are everywhere present in Dickens's writing, but largely occluded in Dickens criticism, have a claim to an engaged literary criticism that takes them seriously as literary subjects and as agents in historical processes.[55] As we have seen, systemic violence towards the vulnerable and the beastliness of criminals, unruly mobs, and the ignorant is imagined recurrently in Dickens's fiction through animal metaphor and metonymy, which become fully legible in relation to, among other contexts, contemporaneous perceptions of the continuities and differences between animals and humans. The best-known Dickensian animal characters tend to be hybrid, contradictory, and comic creatures, much like the novels and essays in which they appear. Keith Thomas concludes his influential study of animals and society in England to 1800 by noting that the conflict between 'new sensibilities' towards the natural world, including animals, and the material realities of society with its growing cities and growing population, was not resolved: 'A mixture of compromise and concealment has so far prevented this conflict from having to be fully resolved. But the issue cannot be completely evaded and it can be relied upon to recur. It is one of the contradictions upon which modern civilization may be said to rest. About its ultimate consequences we can only speculate.'[56] Thomas might have made the same observation about England in 1812, the year of Dickens's birth, or 1870, the year of his death, although the forms that those compromises and concealments took are historically specific. Dickens's writing reveals the paradoxical mix of care, sentiment, indifference, and violence that might be said to typify relationships between humans and animals in a society profoundly uneasy about the distinct nature of humanity. The Victorians were what we have become, and the compromises and concealments that characterized their often contradictory attitudes towards animals are an important aspect of their legacy to globalizing modernity.

Further Reading

Linda Kalof (ed.), *The Oxford Handbook of Animal Studies* (Oxford: Oxford University Press, 2016)

Laurence W. Mazzeno and Ronald Morrison (eds), *Animals in Victorian Literature and Culture: Contexts for Criticism* (London: Palgrave Macmillan, 2017)

---

[55] See Jacques Rancière, 'The Politics of Literature', in *The Politics of Literature*, trans. Julie Rose (Cambridge: Polity Press, 2011), 4. Mario Ortiz Robles usefully unpacks Rancière's theorization of the redistribution of the perceptible as a political process with reference to animals. See *Literature and Animal Studies* (New York: Routledge, 2016), 144–5.

[56] Keith Thomas, *Man and the Natural World* (Harmondsworth: Penguin, 1983), 303.

CHAPTER 38

DICKENS AND THE ENVIRONMENT

ALLEN MACDUFFIE

What kind of environmental thinker was Dickens, and how might we read his novels as contributions to a nineteenth-century environmental imaginary? On one hand, he is perhaps the most famous chronicler of the eco-catastrophe that unfolded in English cities in the nineteenth century. Like no writer before or since, Dickens makes palpable the oppressive feel of life lived in intimate contact with various forms of toxic waste:

> Animate London, with smarting eyes and irritated lungs, was blinking, wheezing, and choking; inanimate London was a sooty spectre, divided in purpose between being visible and invisible, and so being wholly neither.... Even in the surrounding country it was a foggy day, but there the fog was grey, whereas in London it was, at about the boundary line, dark yellow, and a little within it brown, and then browner, and then browner, until at the heart of the City—which call Saint Mary Axe—it was rusty-black.[1]

Indeed, so memorably did Dickens describe the 'London particular'—the dense, stifling smog often misleadingly called 'fog'—that his name almost inevitably arises in discussions of nineteenth-century air pollution. He was, as Christine Corton writes, 'in a sense, the creator of London fog in the popular consciousness'.[2] Somewhat less famously, but no less vividly, Dickens also frequently describes the contamination of English waterways, most notably the Thames, which had by mid-century become a 'deadly sewer' (as he writes in *Little Dorrit*) of human and animal waste, industrial

---

[1] *Our Mutual Friend*, ed. Michael Cotsell (Oxford: Oxford World Classics, 2009), Book III, chapter 1, page 420.
[2] Christine L. Corton, *London Fog: The Biography* (Cambridge, MA: Belknap, 2015), 37.

effluents, corpses, and other discarded materials.[3] Take, for example, this passage from *David Copperfield*:

> Slimy gaps and causeways, winding among old wooden piles, with a sickly substance clinging to the latter, like green hair, and the rags of last year's handbills offering rewards for drowned men fluttering above high-water mark, led down through the ooze and slush to the ebb tide. There was a story that one of the pits dug for the dead in the time of the Great Plague was hereabout; and a blighting influence seemed to have proceeded from it over the whole place. Or else it looked as if it had gradually decomposed into that nightmare condition, out of the overflowings of the polluted stream.[4]

It is thanks to such passages that the adjective 'Dickensian' has come to signify, among other things, a kind of overwhelming, almost dystopic, spectacle of urban disorder.

Dickens was also a vociferous supporter of the urban sanitary reform movement, which was rooted in the work of James Kay-Shuttleworth, Southwood Smith, Edwin Chadwick, and other Victorian reformers who strove to reveal the radiating financial, moral, medical, and political consequences of environmental degradation. In a speech delivered to the Metropolitan Sanitary Association in 1851, Dickens indicates the extent to which environmental redress is at the root of his overall social vision: 'I can honestly declare tonight ... that all the information I have since been able to acquire through any of my senses, has strengthened me in the conviction that Searching Sanitary Reform must precede all other social remedies.'[5] Chadwick and other sanitarians were technocrats, and their quasi-utopic belief in the power of technology was problematic in many ways. As historian Bill Luckin argues, for example, massive public works projects like the Embankment of the Thames, which dramatically cleaned up the portion of the river that ran through the city, served as potent symbols of imperial control and technological mastery.[6] But sanitary discourse also helped establish what we call an 'ecological' understanding of both the individual human body and the collective 'social body' as open systems in an ongoing, dynamic interchange with the environment.[7] As Jules Law argues, a project like the Embankment partly came about because of the way the sanitarians helped show how the Thames was 'symbiotically connected to the domestic lives and bodies of ordinary Londoners'.[8]

---

[3] *Little Dorrit*, ed. Harvey Peter Sucksmith (Oxford: Clarendon Press, 1979), Book I, chapter 3, page 29. Subsequent references are inserted parenthetically in the text by *LD* book:chapter, page.

[4] *David Copperfield*, ed. Nina Burgis (Oxford: Clarendon Press, 1981), chapter 47, page 580. Subsequent references are inserted parenthetically in the text by *DC*, chapter, page.

[5] Dickens, 'Metropolitan Sanitary Association: 10 May 1851', in *The Speeches of Charles Dickens*, ed. K. J. Fielding (Oxford: Clarendon Press, 1960), 144.

[6] Bill Luckin, *Pollution and Control: A Social History of the Thames in the Nineteenth Century* (Bristol: A. Hilger, 1986), 17–18.

[7] Mary Poovey, *Making a Social Body: British Cultural Formation, 1830–1864* (Chicago: University of Chicago Press, 1995), 41 and *passim*.

[8] Jules Law, *The Social Life of Fluids: Blood, Milk, and Water in the Victorian Novel* (Ithaca, NY: Cornell University Press, 2010), 50.

On the other hand, we don't tend to think of Dickens as an 'environmental writer', precisely because of his almost exclusive focus on social organization and the built, human-made world. Or, as Robert Patten puts it: 'Nature does not play a large part in his novels, nor in critics' discussions of them. There are, to be sure, moments when Dickens pays tribute to the phenomena of Nature, the almost obligatory set-pieces such as high summer at the Maylies' cottage in *Oliver Twist*, or the countryside around Tong church in *The Old Curiosity Shop*, or the surprisingly lovely appearance of the land around the forge that Pip observes toward the end of *Great Expectations*.' But such scenes, Patten argues, 'are not particularly carefully observed or differentiated'.[9] Rosemarie Bodenheimer makes a similar point, noting that Dickens's 'visual imagination seems to have been fully engaged only by the artifacts of the city'.[10] In short, Dickens seems to be missing that quality we often associate with 'green' writers like Thoreau or Wordsworth—an inclination to appreciate, or defend, or simply describe, the non-human world on its own terms and for its own sake.

Instead, Dickens almost always stylizes non-human nature, either by representing it by way of conventional tropes, as Patten notes, or by thoroughly humanizing it through his powerful anthropomorphic imagination. Take the following three examples, from *David Copperfield*, *A Tale of Two Cities*, and *Martin Chuzzlewit*, respectively, all of which, in slightly different ways, make the power of the natural world less alien or threatening by lending it familiar human shape, emotion, and personality:

> [T]he elms bent to one another, like giants who were whispering secrets, and after a few seconds of such repose, fell into a violent flurry, tossing their wild arms about, as if their late confidences were really too wicked for their peace of mind. (*DC* 1, 5)
>
> The beach was a desert of heaps of sea and stones tumbling wildly about, and the sea did what it liked and what it liked was destruction. It thundered at the town, and thundered at the cliffs, and brought the coast down, madly.[11]
>
> [T]he wind ... slammed the front-door against Mr. Pecksniff who was at that moment entering, with such violence, that in the twinkling of an eye he lay on his back at the bottom of the steps. Being by this time weary of such trifling performances, the boisterous rover hurried away rejoicing, roaring over moor and meadow, hill and flat, until it got out to sea, where it met with other winds similarly disposed, and made a night of it.[12]

The first passage perfectly captures (to my mind) something of the strange, arrhythmic motion of trees in strong gusts of wind; but it functions primarily to evoke the state of

---

[9] Robert L. Patten, '"A Surprising Transformation": Dickens and the Hearth', in U. C. Knoepflmacher and George Tennyson (eds), *Nature and the Victorian Imagination* (Berkeley: University of California Press, 1977), 153–4.

[10] Rosemarie Bodenheimer, 'Dickens and the Art of the Pastoral', *The Centennial Review* 23, 4 (Fall 1979): 452.

[11] *A Tale of Two Cities*, ed. Andrew Sanders (Oxford: Oxford World's Classics, 2008), Book I, chapter 4, page 22.

[12] *Martin Chuzzlewit*, ed. Margaret Cardwell (Oxford: Clarendon Press, 1982), chapter 2, page 9.

David's mind as a child, and his perception of the adult world as collusive, fantastical, and larger-than-life. In the second passage, the beach at Dover doesn't call to mind the chaos of an atomistic universe (as it does for Matthew Arnold), but rather, when read in context, a Carlylean vision of the destructive energies of the revolutionary mob. The winds of history are metaphorically roiling the waters across the channel. And if the comedy in the last passage arises, in part, from the contrast between Pecksniff's overdeveloped sense of personal importance and the wind's rowdy indifference to it, the point is that it delivers to this *specific* character a small but richly deserved come-uppance. The wind may be unmindful of Pecksniff, but it still moves according to the moral weather patterns of Dickens's universe.

For this reason, perhaps, the so-called first wave of eco-critical scholarship, invested as it was in 'eco-mimesis' (the realistic representation of non-human phenomena), had little time for Dickens. Instead, eco-criticism took as its point of departure literature that was interested in either decentring the human from its place of metaphysical centrality, or offering detailed, precisely rendered encounters with the non-human, or making arguments for the protection of wild spaces: texts like Thoreau's *Walden*, Wordsworth's *The Prelude* and "Tintern Abbey", John Clare's lyrics, Ruskin's essays, and Gerard Manley Hopkins's poems. Jonathan Bate's foundational *Romantic Ecology: Wordsworth and the Environmental Tradition* (1991) argued against what he saw as a prevailing New-Historical tendency to read all representations of natural phenomena ideologically, as discursive constructs that find their meaning almost exclusively with reference to human cultural and political concerns. Bate's straightforward but useful intervention was to read nature *as* nature in these texts, and to locate in nineteenth-century British writers like Wordsworth and Ruskin an attempt to approach non-human nature on its own terms: 'this book is dedicated to the proposition that the way in which William Wordsworth sought to enable his readers better to enjoy or endure life was by teaching them to look at and dwell in the natural world'.[13] There is not a word about Dickens in Bate's book, and he merits only a brief mention in that other foundational eco-critical text, Lawrence Buell's *The Environmental Imagination: Thoreau, Nature Writing, and the Formation of American Culture* (1995). In his discussion of how an 'environmentally oriented work' might be defined, Buell uses Dickens primarily to illustrate what such a work *does not* look like. If, Buell argues, one of the definitional criteria is that human history ought to be represented as inescapably entwined with environmental history, then we should be sceptical of a novel like *Martin Chuzzlewit*, where, he notes, the American West is turned into 'little more than a backdrop for Martin's picaresque misadventures'.[14] Dickens is also (almost) nowhere to be found in other major early eco-critical works: neither Karl Kroeber's *Ecological Literary Criticism: Romantic Imagining and the Biology of Mind* (1994), nor Glen A. Love's *Practical Ecocriticism: Literature,*

---

[13] Jonathan Bate, *Romantic Ecology: Wordsworth and the Environmental Tradition* (London: Routledge, 1991), 4.

[14] Lawrence Buell, *The Environmental Imagination: Thoreau, Nature Writing, and the Formation of American Culture* (Cambridge, MA: Harvard University Press, 1996), 7.

Biology, and the Environment (2003) mentions him at all, while three important early essay collections, *Ecocriticism: Landmarks in Literary Ecology* (1996), *The Green Studies Reader* (2000), and *Beyond Nature Writing: Expanding the Boundaries of Ecocriticism* (2001) each include only one passing reference.

But, in a way, Buell's critique also holds the clue to the recent turn towards Dickens in eco-critical scholarship. For even if we concede the (debatable) point that *Martin Chuzzlewit* imagines the American wilderness as a kind of inert background for the staging of Martin's story, it is certainly not the case that Dickens failed to recognize the complex, mutually defining enmeshment of characters and their non-human surroundings. We need only think of the famous opening of *Bleak House* (which has become, as we shall see, a touchstone for eco-critical readings of Dickens) in which smoke, fog, mud, people, horses, dogs, umbrellas, streets, and paving stones have become, in his word, 'indistinguishable', while characters like Krook, Vholes, and Phil Squod appear to be indelibly shaped by their toxically compromised surroundings. Or we might think of the dust heaps, the central symbol of *Our Mutual Friend*, which derive much of their strange power through the way they conspicuously blend the organic and inorganic, the biological and the industrial, the human body and the larger life-world in which it is enmeshed.

The strange sense of a dynamic interchange between the realms of the human and non-human is of course also not new to Dickens's readers and critics. Dorothy van Ghent, for example, in her famous 1950 essay 'A View from Todgers's' wrote about the 'transposition of attributes' that is 'the principle of relationship between things and people in the novels of Dickens'.[15] But this 'transposition' has taken on a new resonance in recent years from environmentally minded critics interested in exploring the ways that the breakdown of seemingly distinct realms or categories (nature and culture, human and non-human, person and thing, subject and object) can help us think past the kind of binary logic that imagines nature as vaguely 'out there', distinct from the human world. The book that perhaps did the most to critique this binary is Timothy Morton's *Ecology Without Nature* (2007), which argues that the tendency to imagine 'nature' as a separate realm is precisely what allows human beings to continue to treat the non-human as an object to be managed and dominated. The perverse result is that what might seem like very different inclinations—the desire to exploit and control the natural world and the desire to protect and appreciate it—actually arise from the same metaphysical assumption of human exceptionalism.

Roughly coincident with Morton's work has been a surge of critical interest in the 'Anthropocene', a stratigraphical category defining the current geological epoch as one shaped by human activity. Timothy Clark argues that it is 'a name for that moment in the history of the earth at which humanity's material impact and numbers become such that the set of discrete and once unconnected individual acts across the globe transmogrifies

---

[15] Dorothy van Ghent, 'The Dickens World: A View from Todgers's', *The Sewanee Review* 58, 3 (July–September 1950): 419.

itself into an entity that is also geological and climatological, transgressing given distinctions of human and inhuman'.[16] Climate change is, of course, the best-known hallmark of the Anthropocene, but it also includes related but distinct phenomena like the acidification of the oceans, the extinction of myriad plant and animal species, and the accumulation of synthetic substances in the soil and groundwater. If Morton's argument is focused on subverting the subject/object dichotomy of Western metaphysics in the name of a more rigorous kind of ecological thinking, the Anthropocene tracks the historical shift through which 'the environment' actually became, to some degree, a human production. Although dating the commencement of this epoch has been a subject of much debate—many would put the pin in the late eighteenth century, with the invention of James Watt's steam engine, while others would go much further back—its effects, most agree, become broadly observable and theorizable during the Victorian period. Indeed, the scientific paper most responsible for popularizing the term, Paul Crutzen and Eugene Stoermer's 2001 essay 'The Anthropocene', references the nineteenth-century scientists George Perkins Marsh and Antonio Stoppani, and their dawning awareness that a new epoch was coming into being.[17] Others have added the Victorian physicist John Tyndall and his work on what would become known as 'the greenhouse effect' to this list of early Anthropocene theorists.[18]

With the contemporary critical emphasis on attending to various violations of the conventional divisions between human and non-human, Dickens's conspicuous anthropomorphism might begin to take on a new kind of expressive significance. That is, if there is a human-centric bias to be found in an imagination that consistently imprints the human upon the non-human, there is also potentially a kind of insight in it as well, if understood as part of a broader cultural moment when the human actually *was* materially imprinting itself upon the non-human world in strange and powerful new ways. Which is not to say that every instance of personification in Dickens's fiction attests to his prescient awareness of the Anthropocene, but that his vivid and transgressive metaphorical imagination may reveal something newly uncertain about the relationship of humans and the non-human world.

Dickens, indeed, seems at times to reveal something of the disturbing, almost occult power of collective human industry to wield forces hitherto only found in (for lack of a better word) 'nature'. Take, for example, our introduction to Staggs's Gardens, home of Polly Toodle, in *Dombey and Son*:

> The first shock of a great earthquake had, just at that period, rent the whole neighbourhood to its centre. Traces of its course were visible on every side. Houses were knocked down; streets broken through and stopped; deep pits and trenches dug

---

[16] Timothy Clark, 'What on World is the Earth? The Anthropocene and Fictions of the World', *The Oxford Literary Review* 35, 1 (2013): 5.
[17] Paul Crutzen and Eugene Stoermer, 'The Anthropocene', IGBP Newsletter 41 (May 2000): 17–18.
[18] Stephanie Pain, 'Before it was Famous: 150 Years of the Greenhouse Effect', *New Scientist* 202, 2708 (13 May 2009): 46–7.

in the ground; enormous heaps of earth and clay thrown up; buildings that were undermined and shaking, propped by great beams of wood. Here a chaos of carts, overthrown and jumbled together, lay topsy-turvy at the bottom of a steep unnatural hill; there, confused treasures of iron soaked and rusted in something that had accidentally become a pond.[19]

It is not, of course, an earthquake that has created this chaos; Dickens here temporarily inhabits the perspective of someone unaware that he is coming upon an urban railway construction site. It's the point of view of an outsider—an outsider to the neighbourhood, of course, but also, in a sense, an outsider to modernity itself, someone who cannot imagine that this chaos could have a human origin. To understand this landscape as the result of a natural disaster is to make a literal miscategorization that functions, in a sense, as an entirely proper *moral* categorization. It suggests that only natural forces *should* be able to inflict this kind of damage upon the world. The ingénue's perspective focuses our attention on the plain fact, rather than the ultimate purpose, of the upheaval, refusing to privilege (at least for this moment) the steamrolling *telos* over the chaos it creates. In the category confusion, we get a picture of human industry not only as a geologic force, but a frighteningly unwitting one that reshapes the landscape in unintended ways. The construction doesn't make 'a pond', but, more ambiguously and indirectly, 'something that had accidentally become a pond'. Dickens's language throughout the passage conveys something of the paradoxical conditions of the Anthropocene through verb forms that suggest a strange and uncertainly distributed agency. For van Ghent, the 'transposition of attributes' expresses 'a world undergoing a gruesome spiritual transformation.' If she and other critics have understood such a transformation primarily through Marxist categories, the Anthropocene concept can now help us see it in historically grounded ecological terms as well. The transformation might now be seen as both the gruesome changes being materially visited upon the external world, and the strange new epistemological ambiguities about the scope and character of human agency.

Thus, where an earlier generation of eco-critics may have passed Dickens by for the lack of 'eco-mimetic' depictions of the natural world, more recent critics see in his very departures from realism one of the keys to his value and interest. As Jesse Oak Taylor writes in his dazzling recent eco-critical reading of *Bleak House*:

> The problem is that Dickens's novel seems so resolutely *un*real, so strangely, *abnaturally* real, thus suggesting a reverse trajectory, whereby the novel questions the nature of the real in the city itself. Indeed, the principal effect of the climate of smog seems to be a breakdown in both the real and our perception of it.[20]

---

[19] *Dombey and Son*, ed. Alan Horsman (Oxford: Clarendon Press, 1974), chapter 6, page 65. Subsequent references are inserted parenthetically in the text by *DS* chapter, page.

[20] Jesse Oak Taylor, 'The Novel as Climate Model: Realism and the Greenhouse Effect in *Bleak House*', *Novel* 46, 1 (2013): 20.

The smog in the opening of *Bleak House* functions both as a blind and a window, disrupting ordinary perception, but enabling forms of what we might think of as ecological insight, including a recognition of the elemental connectedness of humans and non-humans, and even the very existence of something called a 'climate'. That last is Taylor's focus, as he discusses the way Dickens's emphasis on mediation helps make apprehensible environmental phenomena like climate, which cannot be directly experienced by the senses:

> Dickens's fiction abounds with textured materiality such that the imagined reality exceeds any grounding in mimetic accuracy ... Rather than distancing us from the realities of climate change, mediation and modeling provide our only evidence of its existence.[21]

Recent eco-critics also see Dickens's importance as a 'green' writer because of what John Parham terms (following Timothy Clark) his 'ecological imaginary'—his interest in representing a complexly interdependent world.[22] This intermeshment makes its presence felt on both micro- and macro-levels. It appears, of course, on the level of plot, where many of his novels famously work to reveal hitherto unseen or unrecognized connections between people and locations. As Tristan Sipley argues: 'the value of Dickens lies precisely in the way his sprawling fictions avoid fixating on any space in isolation, and instead map the structural relations between spaces, tracing the flow of energy and natural resources as well as the flow of commodities and the circulation of capital over the English landscape'.[23] It also appears on the level of language, where Dickens's vivid metaphors often highlight the kinds of exchange and transformation (monetary, biological, elemental) that define the city environment. For Karen Chase and Michael Levenson, the London of *Bleak House* offers us a vision of the city as a *medium*; it is, in their striking phrase, a 'liquid universe', a place defined by a thick, mingled, and mingling atmosphere of gas, oil, mud, grease, smoke, and slime: the 'foetid effluvia', the 'thick nauseous pool[s]', the 'smears, like black fat', that stick and bind bodies, commodities, and dwelling places.[24] This is much more than a rhetorical emphasis on pollution; it is, as they show, a landmark in environmental representation, the beginning of Dickens's social-*cum*-environmental consciousness about the city as a single integrated ecology: 'a universe of fluids and gases is one that cannot protect

---

[21] Taylor, *The Sky of our Manufacture: The London Fog in British Fiction from Dickens to Woolf* (Charlottesville: University of Virginia Press, 2016), 28.

[22] John Parham, 'Dickens in the City: Science, Technology, Ecology in the Novels of Charles Dickens', *19: Interdisciplinary Studies in the Long Nineteenth Century* 10 (2010). DOI: http://doi.org/10.16995/ntn.529 (accessed 2 June 2016).

[23] Tristan Sipley, 'The Revenge of Swamp Thing: Wetlands, Industrial Capitalism, and the Ideological Contradictions of *Great Expectations*', *The Journal of Ecocriticism* 3, 1 (January 2011): 18.

[24] *Bleak House*, ed. George Ford and Sylvère Monod, Norton Critical Edition (New York: W. W. Norton), chapter 33, page 404; chapter 32, pages 402, 398.

itself with the older barriers of streets, walls, police, and politicians. Contagion can leak through stone'.[25]

Chase and Levenson contextualize Dickens's mid-career turn towards a more systematic mode of ecological thought, which they first mark in the later numbers of *Dombey* and argue finds full expression in *Bleak House*. In his essay 'Early Dickens and Ecocriticism', Troy Boone moves in the opposite chronological direction, attending to the representation of the non-human world in the novels leading up to *Martin Chuzzlewit*, and arguing for Dickens's sensitivity to the non-human, including (and especially) non-human animals.[26] While Dickens's mid- to late-career novels (especially *Bleak House* and *Our Mutual Friend*) have thus far drawn the most attention from environmentally minded critics, the early works hold promising possibilities for further study, especially as our definition of what might *count* as an ecologically significant textual moment continues to broaden.

Dickens's response to the Anthropocene is interesting in part because of how uniquely positioned he was (historically, culturally, and imaginatively) to connect the regional and the global through the city of London. 'The environment' is always at once a local, bodily experienced material habitation, and a larger and more abstract set of interrelated forces and conditions. Dickens's novels often put these two perspectives together stereoscopically, as it were, by focusing on the lived texture of specific city places, while also imagining those places as expressions of much wider economic, demographic, material, and political trends and pressures. Tom-all-Alone's may be peculiarly itself in its look and feel and smell, but it is also the physical manifestation of financial and legal decisions (or indecisions) originating elsewhere. Thus London as it appears in Dickens's later fiction especially can feel simultaneously parochial and planetary, with the exquisitely rendered byways and inns and shops often put in relation to a more totalizing *idea* of the city as a boundaryless, encompassing, even inescapable global system. Even when Sir Leicester retreats to Lincolnshire, he's still, in some sense, in London, just as Mr Dorrit remains trapped in the Marshalsea while roaming the Swiss countryside. The scale and pace and sheer transformational power of industrial development was making it possible to imagine a world in which any kind of truly alternative pastoral space would either entirely disappear from the face of the earth, or exist only as fantasy. The idea of an entirely urbanized planet is a staple of the contemporary environmental imaginary, whether in works of dystopian science fiction like *Blade Runner*, or in non-fiction texts like Mike Davis's *Planet of Slums*, but we see it first coming into being in Dickens's fiction.

---

[25] Karen Chase and Michael Levenson, '*Bleak House*, Liquid City: Climate to Climax in Dickens', in Louise Westling and John Parham (eds), *A Global History of Literature and the Environment* (Cambridge: Cambridge University Press, 2016), 214.

[26] Troy Boone 'Early Dickens and Ecocriticism: The Social Novelist and the Nonhuman', in Ronald D. Morrison and Laurence Mazzeno (eds), *Victorians and the Environment: Ecocritical Perspectives* (New York: Routledge, 2017), 97–113.

The scale and pace of industrial development was also such that the industrially advanced nations had not yet learned how to conceal the pollution they were creating, much less remove it from their own immediate environs. Smog, soot, dust, and refuse were unavoidable and deadly hazards of city experience; they pressed upon the senses and the skin in ways many present-day city-dwellers in the global north simply have never experienced. As the historian Erik Loomis argues, the early twentieth century saw a massive, coordinated campaign of outsourcing pollution to the so-called third world as well as to the poorer regions of the first, thus effectively 'sever[ing] knowledge of the cost of industrialization from their comparatively rich consumers'.[27] Today, climate change seems to be altering this ability to outsource both consequences and awareness, as the deleterious effects of our carbon-intensive economy become, if not exactly more *visible*, then at least more detectable by those who live far from smoke stacks and dumping grounds. Although it's true that the worst effects of drought, rising seas, and so-called 'superstorms' have been and will continue to be visited disproportionately upon vulnerable countries and communities, there is also a dawning sense that no region on earth will be safe from the climate catastrophe. In other words, Dickens's environmental critique of the epicentre of nineteenth-century modernity may resonate with twenty-first-century readers who are becoming increasingly aware of how vulnerable centres of power and capital are now to the chaotic after-effects of 'progress'. The flooding of Wall Street during Hurricane Sandy in 2012 is just one richly symbolic example. Those toxic things that would be buried, or ignored, or pushed out of sight do tend, inevitably, to make their return. As any good reader of Dickens could have told you.

But if we're going to celebrate Dickens for his prescient environmental vision, it is perhaps only fair to point out the limitations and inconsistencies of that vision as well. Consider, for example, the seemingly contradictory positions on industrial technology taken in adjacent novels, *Hard Times* (1854) and *Little Dorrit* (1857). The former reads like a work of dystopian science fiction, so scathing is its depiction of human life subjected to the ruthless logic of mechanization and efficiency. The famous 'melancholy mad elephants'[28] in *Hard Times* are a frightening vision of the way an energy-intensive industrial regime levels the distinctions between the organic and inorganic, the biological and the technological, by reducing both to mere quantities of motive power. Yet what to do, then, with the heroic inventor Daniel Doyce in Dickens's next novel, *Little Dorrit*, 'a smith and engineer ... a very ingenious man' who 'perfects an invention (involving a very curious secret process) of great importance to his country and his fellow creatures' (*LD* I:10, 113)? Doyce describes this mysterious device as 'a great saving and a great improvement' that, we understand, could transform the world were it not for the obstructive Circumlocution Office (*LD* I:10, 114). In other words, *Hard*

---

[27] Erik Loomis, *Out of Sight: The Long and Disturbing Story of Corporations Outsourcing Catastrophe* (New York: The New Press, 2015), 85.
[28] *Hard Times*, ed. Fred Kaplan, 4th edn, Norton Critical Edition (New York: W. W. Norton, 2017), Book I, chapter 2, page 60. Also, II:1, 93; III:5, 203.

Times decries the dehumanizing logic of efficiency embodied in the technology of a rising industrial modernity, while *Little Dorrit* pins its hopes on technological redress, suggesting the problem is with a dehumanizing *inefficiency* and the sclerotic institutions that stifle innovation. If only technology could be unshackled from the restraints of intrusive government agencies, we might get a city that looked like—well actually, it might look something like Coketown.

Similarly, the railroad construction that wreaked such havoc upon Staggs's Gardens in the early part of *Dombey and Son* appears later in that novel as a benevolently transformative agency, bringing order and affluence to the neighbourhood: 'The old by-streets now swarmed with passengers and vehicles of every kind; the new streets that had stopped disheartened in the mud and wagon-ruts, formed towns within themselves, originating wholesome comforts and conveniences belonging to themselves, and never tried or thought of until they sprung into existence. Bridges that had led to nothing, led to villas, gardens, churches, healthy public walks' (*DS* 15, 218). Whereas, in the first description of this scene, the uninitiated's point of view provided a means through which Dickens critically defamiliarized urban construction, here that point of view is recast as hopelessly naive and unimaginative. The *telos* of the project, obscured by the misprision of the initial description, now wholly dominates the scene, seemingly justifying whatever chaos came before. The split vision is striking, and suggests a utopian strain in Dickens's thinking in which environmental damage is not an intrinsic part of industrial development, but merely a temporary, intermediate stage.

This ambivalence towards industrial modernity perhaps can be seen most vividly and perplexingly in the representation of the Court of Chancery in *Bleak House*. On the one hand, the Court is an outmoded, medieval institution that is clearly an impediment to progress. On the other hand, the Court and the case are also persistently linked to the kinds of widespread environmental hazards that are already being produced *by* this new age—most notably the thick smog pervading the atmosphere. Air pollution pre-dates the nineteenth century of course, but Dickens presents it with such apocalyptic intensity that we cannot help but connect it to specifically nineteenth-century concerns about population pressures, resource exhaustion, and atmospheric changes. In other words, in his depiction of the Court there is a deep tension between what we might think of as a 'realist', historically grounded satire of a specific old-fashioned institution, and a symbolically charged, hyperrealist *use* of that institution to represent the entropic forces of the present and future.

To point out these tensions or inconsistencies is not to condemn Dickens for being environmentally blinkered, but rather to suggest that his response to industrial technology is often caught uncertainly between its dystopic effects, and its utopic promise. The promise, indeed, to remediate fully its own dystopic effects. In this, I would argue, he is decidedly our contemporary. Consider the extent to which current discussions of the climate crisis so often involve both scathing condemnations of our fossil-fuel-intensive economic order, and hopeful accounts of the various 'curious secret processes'—carbon sequestration, nuclear fusion, geo-engineering—that would allow us to recover what has been wasted, fix what has been damaged, and save capitalism from itself. Which is not to say such technological remedies are foolhardy or pointless or doomed to failure; it is only that, like Dickens, we have still not figured out whether the optimistic story we are telling ourselves about technological progress is a sustainable one.

Any consideration of technology in Dickens, I would add, edges us toward a long-standing, but potent, critique of his work: namely, his tendency to eschew a systemic or structural diagnosis in favour of moral critique. As George Orwell puts it:

> It would be difficult to point anywhere in his books to a passage suggesting that the economic system is wrong *as a system* ... Bounderby is a bullying windbag and Gradgrind has been morally blinded, but if they were better men, the system would work well enough—that, all through, is the implication.[29]

Like the kind of structural social and economic inequalities Orwell is interested in, environmental crises do not always neatly submit to conventional moral categories, nor can they be confined to the behaviour of specific malignant individuals. They are, instead, the products and unintended byproducts of an entire order, including its patterns of consumption and waste generation; its distribution of wealth and political power; its mechanisms of control over natural resources; its prevailing beliefs about the purpose and value of the non-human; its ethos of conservation, convenience, disposability, instrumentality, and productivity. The climate crisis is happening, in part, because of millions of ordinary acts (lighting a lamp, running an engine) that seem innocuous enough on their own, but have enormous consequences when aggregated across a population and over decades. As the eco-critic Joseph Meeker puts it: 'Environmental guilt is collective, distributed unevenly among the people now living, and those who have lived before. Without a personality to focus upon, ecological crisis presents merely a spectacle of catastrophe.'[30]

Dickens was a master at depicting catastrophic environmental spectacles, but the difficulty with such descriptions, as Meeker suggests, resides in their uneasy relationship to narrative. The passage from *David Copperfield* quoted above doesn't simply describe a toxic landscape; it focuses on items that were once narratively meaningful—the 'rags of last year's handbills offering rewards for drowned men fluttering above high-water mark'—and are now mere detritus. Whatever the stories behind these handbills—the circumstances of each individual drowning, the concerns and motivations of those offering the reward—they are on the verge of becoming altogether illegible and lost in the ooze. Indeed, the history of the locale *itself* is becoming hopelessly muddled and obscure: 'There was a story that one of the pits dug for the dead in the time of the Great Plague was hereabout; and a blighting influence seemed to have proceeded from it over the whole place. Or else it looked as if it had gradually decomposed into that nightmare condition, out of the overflowings of the polluted stream.' It is a nightmare of personal and historical narrative oblivion as much as it is a nightmare of material rot and decay.

---

[29] George Orwell, 'Charles Dickens', in *A Collection of Essays* (New York: Harvest, 1970), 52.
[30] Joseph Meeker, *The Comedy of Survival* (New York: Scribner, 1974), 58.

And all of this matters to the plot of *David Copperfield*, since the very reason David and Mr Peggotty are in this neighbourhood is to follow the prostitute Martha so she can lead them to the wayward Little Emily. David describes Martha this way: 'As if she were a part of the refuse it had cast out, and left to corruption and decay, the girl we had followed strayed down to the river's brink, and stood in the midst of this night-picture, lonely and still, looking at the water' (*DC* 47, 580). It is an arresting image, suggesting Martha paradoxically finds her own reflection in the very opacity of the wastewater. As sympathetic as Dickens is to her plight, the association of her 'polluted' state with the polluted river, the mixing of the moral and material valences of 'corruption', carries with it the implication that she is not so much the victim of this degraded environment, as the embodiment of it. The construction 'as if' tellingly makes such an implication and plausibly denies it in one stroke.

Emily's story—the fallen woman about to descend into prostitution—verges on becoming essentially the same as Martha's, and thus just more undifferentiated refuse in the river. To pull her out of this mess before she plunges in irreversibly is to restore integrity to her story in both senses: she will be saved from depravity, and endowed once again with a distinct, narratable future history. It is no accident that Dickens ultimately ships her off with the Micawbers to Australia, where the cultural mythos of the 'virgin continent' (as it was commonly referred to in the period) once again confounds both the moral and the material, associating the integrity of the person with that of the 'unspoiled' and 'untouched' environment.

The problems with such associations are not hard to see. By playing on the dual moral/material valence of terms like 'pollution', 'corruption', and 'decay', Dickens occludes the actual material problem with the environment, suggesting it is a question of personal rectitude. One can escape being a part of this 'degraded' world by avoiding the kinds of 'degraded' actions that both figuratively and literally lead one there. And by 'being a part' I mean both complicity and identification. After all, we might consider that what is most terrifying about the association of human life with waste is not so much the idea that everyone is responsible for producing it, but that everyone is, at heart, made of the same elemental stuff as the refuse in the river and destined, one day, to join it. This is getting us close to what Morton calls 'the ecological thought' in his book of that name: the perhaps unsettling notion that an individual is not a self-bounded entity, but an open system enmeshed entirely and indissociably with its larger life-world. As he puts it: 'since everything is interconnected, there is no definite background and therefore no definite foreground ... [but] if there is no background and therefore no foreground, then where are we? We orient ourselves according to backgrounds against which we stand out'.[31] Like Martha, Emily is on the verge of *not* standing out against this polluted background, of becoming part of it; but to suggest that such is the condition of the prostitute might distract us from the more disturbing notion that such might actually be the inescapable condition of *all* human beings.

---

[31] Timothy Morton, *The Ecological Thought* (Cambridge, MA: Harvard University Press, 2010), 28–30.

The prostitute or would-be prostitute's story is an extreme case, but we can see the tension between the threat of pollution's elemental entropy and narrative's ordered differentiation in other places in Dickens's fiction as well. One way of thinking about the Jarndyce lawsuit in *Bleak House*, for example, is that it reduces almost all individual life stories to the same entropic plot of expectation, frustration, madness, and death. By endlessly demanding to tell his story, The Man from Shropshire embodies this fate in the very act of trying to escape it (a dynamic played out, in more tragic terms, by Richard Carstone). This obscurity is materialized in the famous opening scene, where the masses of waste-producing passers-by in the streets, undifferentiated in the mud and smoke, have their individual life stories and motivations rendered illegible and irrelevant in a grim Malthusian spectacle. But this is the first page, and, as I have argued elsewhere, the novel strives to pull from this mess legible life histories and stories of moral courage, just as it puts The Man from Shropshire into narrative focus as a character with a name (Gridley) and comprehensible motivations and emotions.[32] Where Chancery produces waste, obscurity, and anonymity, the narrative of *Bleak House* produces order, legibility, and individuation; in this way, pollution appears in the novel not just as a material problem but as a 'toxic' way of seeing other people.

Like the representation of Chancery itself, this is a complicated environmental vision. On the one hand, Dickens wanted to oppose both the institutional structures and the utilitarian (Benthamite and Malthusian) frameworks that would treat people as massed units of breeding, consumption, and energy expenditure. This is an especially important stance at a moment when the blame for overcrowding, disease, and food scarcity was squarely pinned on the poor, who were often imagined as one giant, fecund, wasteful collective. Resisting Malthusianism is then, in this sense, resisting a specific environmental vision that came laden with a noxious, victim-blaming political ideology. It's easy to appreciate Dickens's position, and the politically significant urge to differentiate and individuate through narrative. On the other hand, though, as we have noted, environmental problems like smog, water pollution, or unsustainable resource consumption are not entirely comprehensible without an impersonal, aggregative approach. Chadwick, after all, did as much as anyone to improve sanitary conditions in Victorian London, and he was a thoroughgoing Benthamite whose approach depended upon thinking of people as units of energy expenditure. As with Little Emily in *David Copperfield*, Dickens's individuating narratives in *Bleak House* often work to separate out the pure characters—Esther, Ada, Charley—from the impure Vholes, Smallweed, Skimpole. These latter characters are painted vividly and unmistakably as parasites, drains on the world's resources; as such, they may keep us from noticing the ways that resource consumption and waste is a systemic, statistical problem, shared by everyone. No one can escape the effects of Chancery altogether in this novel, but Dickens suggests there are ways in which one can rise above it and avoid complicity and blame. Esther the

---

[32] Allen MacDuffie, *Victorian Literature, Energy, and the Ecological Imagination* (Cambridge: Cambridge University Press, 2014), 113–14.

housekeeper helps clean up the waste, and gets smudged by it, as it were, but she doesn't herself seem to *produce* it. The metaphorical quarantining effect we noted with Martha in *David Copperfield* is here worked out more in literal ways, as Esther actually checks the spread of disease by containing it within her own body.

I point all this out not to blame Dickens for some perceived lack of environmental awareness, but to suggest how his work can help us see both the possibilities and the obstacles for environmental thought in the nineteenth century. Dickens approached the early stages of the Anthropocene with a startling and unmatched imaginative openness and creative flexibility. His language renders not only the disorienting experience of toxic environments, but, even more fundamentally, the unprecedented, grotesque transformations being visited upon the world through the rise of industrial modernity. His is a metamorphic vision suited to metamorphic times. But Dickens was also a man of his era, and however much we might want to praise the power and reach of his vision, we also must acknowledge the intellectual and ideological conditions through which that vision was shaped.

Further Reading

Karen Chase and Michael Levenson, 'Green Dickens', in Eileen Gillooly and Deirdre David (eds), *Contemporary Dickens* (Columbus: Ohio State University Press, 2009), 131–51

Laurence Coupe (ed.), *The Green Studies Reader: From Romanticism to Ecocriticism* (Howe: Psychology Press, 2000)

Karl Kroeber, *Ecological Literary Criticism: Romantic Imagining and the Biology of Mind* (New York: Columbia University Press, 1994)

Glen A. Love, *Practical Ecocriticism: Literature, Biology, and the Environment* (Charlottesville: University of Virginia Press, 2003)

Benjamin Morgan, '*Fin du Globe*: On Decadent Planets', *Victorian Studies* 58, 4 (Summer 2016): 609–35

John Plotz, 'The Victorian Anthropocene: George Marsh and the Tangled Bank of Darwinian Environmentalism', *Australasian Journal of Ecocriticism and Cultural Ecology* 4 (2015): 52–64

Patricia Yaeger, 'Editor's Column: Literature in the Ages of Wood, Tallow, Coal, Whale Oil, Gasoline, Atomic Power, and Other Energy Sources', *PMLA* 126, 2 (2011): 305–10

CHAPTER 39

DICKENS AND RELIGION

JENNIFER GRIBBLE

THE significance of religion in the work of Dickens was a matter of controversy during his lifetime and remains so. It is complicated, as well, by the various contexts within which he formed views and made pronouncements. There can be no doubt that he considered the New Testament 'the great source of all moral goodness': he often expressed an apparently simple didactic intention 'to lead the reader up to [its] teachings'.[1] He presented each of his sons with a copy, as one by one they left home, and encouraged them to follow their father's practice of daily prayer.[2] In 1846–7, for 'the education of his growing family', he wrote a version of the popular genre of 'harmonization' of the Gospels.[3] Contrary to his instructions, and long after his death, this was published as *The Life of Our Lord*.[4] It has been keenly scrutinized for evidence of the Unitarianism he embraced during the 1840s.[5] Disgruntled with High Church and Evangelical extremes in the Church of England, and attracted by Unitarianism's 'social gospel' and its tradition of theological enquiry, he took out a pew at Edward Taggart's Little Portland Street Chapel.[6] Deviations from what he perceived as the 'great truths of scripture'[7] continued to generate some of his most trenchant satire, provoking the disapproval of earnest clerics.

---

[1] To the Revd David Macrae [1861], *The Letters of Charles Dickens* 9, ed. Madeline House, Graham Storey, et al., Pilgrim/British Academy Edition, 12 vols (Oxford: Clarendon Press, 1965–2002). Subsequent citations: PLets followed by volume:page range, page, and hn. for headnote, n. or nn. for footnotes, with page range given before page cited. Here, 9:556–7, 556.

[2] To Edward 'Plorn' Dickens [? September 1868], PLets 12:187–8, 188.

[3] See Gary L. Colledge, '*The Life of Our Lord* Revisited', *Dickens Studies Annual* 36 (2005): 132–6.

[4] (London: Associated Newspapers, 1934).

[5] Janet M. Larson, *Dickens and the Broken Scripture* (Athens: University of Georgia Press, 1985), 12, argues that 'he does not allow that Jesus is really divine ... yet credulously reports the miracles, the most powerful signs that Jesus is God'. But to the contrary, see, for example, Carolyn W. de la L. Oulton, *Literature and Religion in Mid-Victorian England: from Dickens to Eliot* (Basingstoke: Palgrave Macmillan, 2003), 32.

[6] See John P. Frazee, 'Dickens and Unitarianism', *Dickens Studies Annual* 18 (1989): 119–43.

[7] In the Preface to the Cheap Edition of 1847, in Charles Dickens, *The Pickwick Papers* ed. James Kinsley (Oxford: Clarendon Press, 1986), appendix B, page 887, Dickens defends himself against the charge of anti-Evangelical bias in his depiction of the Revd Mr Stiggins by distinguishing 'between

Each of his children was baptized into the Church of England, and it is evident that by the mid-century, his stated beliefs were aligned with its Broad Church wing of liberal questioning.[8] His quest for 'the True religion'[9] includes a somewhat ambivalent attitude towards Catholicism.[10] His accommodation of 'progressive revelation' in theology[11] is consonant with the openness to 'wonder' reflected in his passionate defence of imagination, his fanciful and visionary transformations of the material world, and his delight in plots that bring to light what is hidden. He immersed himself in developments in the science of the mind while appealing to the Victorian fascination with the supernatural in its many forms.[12]

Dennis Walder, in his ground-breaking *Dickens and Religion*, addressed what K. J. Fielding, in 1963, had described as 'the greatest gap in our knowledge about Dickens'.[13] Setting Dickens's religious formation within its Victorian cultural context, Walder notes how inevitably critical assessment will reflect the assumptions of its own cultural moment.[14] The 'great Christian writer' admired by Dostoevsky[15] has yielded place, in these times of ours, to Dickens the 'radical doubter'[16] and Dickens the 'secular humanist'.[17] And the view persists that being incapable of 'systematic thought', he was

---

religion and the cant of religion, piety and the pretence of piety, a humble reverence for the great truths of scripture and an audacious and offensive obtrusion of its letter and not its spirit'. Subsequent references are inserted parenthetically in the text by *PP* chapter, page.

[8] The term 'Broad Church' became current after the publication of *Essays and Reviews* (1860). See Dennis G. Wigmore-Beddoes, *Yesterday's Radicals: A Study of the Affinity Between Unitarianism and Broad Church Anglicanism in the Nineteenth Century* (Cambridge and London: James Clarke and Co Ltd, 1971) for a discussion of divergences and common ground.

[9] In a dream-vision of his perpetually mourned sister-in-law Mary Hogarth, Dickens asks her 'What is the True religion? ... perhaps the Roman Catholic is the best?' The spirit answers, '[f]or *you*, it is the best!' *PLets* 4:195–7, 196. Michael Slater, *Charles Dickens* (New Haven and London: Yale University Press, 2009), 228, notes that 'this had no effect whatever in modifying the sharp hostility towards Roman Catholicism that was to pervade the pages of *Pictures from Italy*'.

[10] See Michael Wheeler, *The Old Enemies: Catholic and Protestant in Nineteenth-Century English Culture* (Cambridge: Cambridge University Press, 2006), especially on *Barnaby Rudge*, 111–12, 125–35.

[11] A letter to W. W. F. de Cerjat, 28 May 1863, comments on the controversy stirred by *Essays and Reviews*: '[w]hat these bishops and such-like say about revelation, in assuming it to be finished and done with, I can't in the least understand. Nothing is discovered without God's intention and assistance, and I suppose every new knowledge of His works that is conceded to man to be distinctly a revelation by which men are to guide themselves.' *PLets* 10:252–4, 253 n. 2.

[12] See Nicola Bown, Carolyn Burdett, and Pamela Thurschwell (eds), *The Victorian Supernatural* (Cambridge; New York: Cambridge University Press, 2004), 1–12.

[13] (London: George Allen and Unwin, 1981), xiii.

[14] Dennis Walder, *Dickens and Religion* (London: George Allen & Unwin, 1981), 4–6.

[15] *A Writer's Diary*, quoted in Steven Marcus, *Dickens from Pickwick to Dombey* (New York: Simon and Schuster, 1965), 68.

[16] Lance St John Butler, *Victorian Doubt: Literary and Cultural Discourses* (Hemel Hempstead: Harvester Wheatsheaf, 1990), 38.

[17] Vincent Newey, *The Secular Scriptures of Charles Dickens: Novels of Ideology, Novels of the Self* (Aldershot: Ashgate, 2004), 3.

'no theologian',[18] that insofar as his fiction might be said to reveal a theology, it is 'New Testament Lite … a Christianity putting social good works before credal content and demand'.[19]

The essays, speeches, and letters of Dickens express a variety of readily accessible views.[20] Walder persuasively supports Dickens's friend and biographer John Forster, however, in reading his fiction as the most reliable guide to his religious thinking.[21] Engaging with contemporary doctrinal controversies and exploring theological questions made urgent in an age of faith and doubt, the fiction challenges assumptions that he was either uninterested in religious controversy or alienated by it, and that his beliefs were unchanging. But as Walder emphasizes, only 'a patient and informed reading' will disclose the ways in which those beliefs 'are embodied in the texture of his work'.[22] My discussion responds to current, often interrelated, approaches to religion in the novels.

INTERTEXTUALITY

Although Dickens's literary allusions are eclectic, his most profound debt is to the Authorized Version of the Bible and the Church of England *Book of Common Prayer*. Recent scholarship has drawn attention to the Bible's high visibility in Victorian England, and its provision of moral teaching, consolation, and memorable words, for a still predominantly church-going population.[23] Despite, and partly because of, the challenges to its literal truth by evolutionary science and the Higher Criticism, the Bible continued to be disseminated, valued, and widely discussed, throughout Dickens's lifetime. The Society for the Propagation of Christian Knowledge does nothing for Jo the crossing-sweeper of *Bleak House* but produces in vast quantities the bibles from which working-class politicians and middle-class tract-writers alike drew rhetoric and precept.[24] The fiction of Dickens reveals a compendious knowledge of the Bible, its material presence and oral transmission bearing witness to the author's belief in its still-active

---

[18] Gary L. Colledge, *God and Charles Dickens: Recovering the Christian Voice of a Classic Author* (Grand Rapids, MI: Brazos Press, 2005), ch. 3; Linda M. Lewis, *Dickens, his Parables, and his Reader* (Columbia and London: University of Missouri Press, 2011), 17.

[19] Valentine Cunningham, 'Dickens and Christianity', in David Paroissien (ed.), *A Companion to Charles Dickens* (Oxford: Blackwell Publishing, 2008), 258.

[20] See Robert Butterworth, *Dickens, Religion and Society* (Houndmills and New York: Palgrave Macmillan, 2016), 4–25.

[21] Walder, *Dickens and Religion*, 15.

[22] Walder, *Dickens and Religion*, 3.

[23] See Elizabeth Jay, 'The Bible as Intertext', in Rebecca Lemon, Emma Mason, Jonathan Roberts, and Christopher Rowland (eds), *The Blackwell Companion to the Bible in English Literature* (Malden, MA; Oxford and Chichester: Wiley-Blackwell, 2009), 472, and Timothy Larsen, *A People of One Book: the Bible and the Victorians* (Oxford: Oxford University Press, 2011).

[24] George Kitson Clark, *The Making of Victorian England* (London: Methuen, 1962), 147.

role in popular culture. His relationship with the prior text is expressed in a variety of intertextual practices, from direct quotation and rhythmic and verbal echoes, to biblically derived symbols, typology, parables, and themes.

Janet L. Larson, in *Dickens and the Broken Scripture* (1985), establishes, more thoroughly than any scholar to date, the range of his biblical allusions. Her argument that the contrapuntal and sometimes apparently contradictory patterns of meaning his allusions set in play 'seem to reflect the equivocation of a man who wants to be consoling but has no settled belief', for whom the Bible has become a 'locus of hermeneutical instability',[25] responds to nineteenth-century challenges to its authority. Her premise that Dickens's multi-voiced texts reveal a loss of confidence in what Frank Kermode describes as the Bible's 'wholly concordant structure' and 'familiar model of history',[26] is influenced, as well, by the emerging popularity of Mikhail Bakhtin's work at her time of writing. Bakhtin's theorizing of the dialogic[27] continues to generate new readings of Dickens, but Larson's argument has been challenged, particularly by readers who value New Criticism's emphasis on textual coherence.[28] This debate participates in a larger discussion. Writing at the end of the twentieth century, Steven Connor notes a shift in Dickens studies from the valuing of 'moral form' to an interest in 'the spasmodic and adventitious energies of ... content'. Any discussion of Dickens and the Bible must engage with what Connor describes as 'the desire and the thwarting of the desire for narrative forms':[29] an evocative summary of the coherence-resisting slippages and aporias that beset poststructuralist criticism, and the incredulity towards grand narratives maintained by postmodernism. I suggest, in the section 'Interdisciplinary Studies in Literature, Philosophy, and Religion: "The Self in Moral Space"', that notwithstanding Bakhtin's own unresolved attitudes to the authority of form,[30] and to the Bible as intertext,[31] a theological subtext in his early essays and late revisions opens up new ways of reading 'moral form' in relation to Dickens's biblical intertextuality.

Dickens's debt to Wordsworth provides a second intertextual source for his religious thinking, and one that deserves further investigation.[32] He increasingly draws on the words, and the rhythms and cadences, of Wordsworth's blank verse for moments

---

[25] Larson, *Dickens and the Broken Scripture*, 3.
[26] Ibid., 19, quoting Frank Kermode, *The Sense of an Ending: Studies in the Theory of Fiction* (New York: Oxford University Press, 1996).
[27] M. M. Bakhtin, 'Discourse in the Novel', in *The Dialogic Imagination: Four Essays by M. M. Bakhtin*, ed. Michael Holquist and trans. Caryl Emmerson and M. Holquist (Austin: University of Texas Press, 1981). See, in particular, his reading of *Little Dorrit* as an example of the throng of social voices, or *heteroglossia*, he associates with the historical emergence of the novel, 301–8.
[28] Lewis, *Dickens, his Parables, and his Reader*, 24.
[29] Steven Connor (ed.), *Charles Dickens* (London: Longman Critical Readers, 1996), 30.
[30] Ibid., 20.
[31] T. R. Wright, 'The Word in the Novel: Bakhtin on Tolstoy and the Bible', in Mark Knight and Thomas Woodman (eds), *Biblical Religion and the Novel* (London: Ashgate, 2006), 25–38, addresses this problem.
[32] See, however, Dirk den Hartog, *Dickens and Romantic Psychology: The Self in Time in Nineteenth-Century Literature* (Basingstoke and London: Palgrave Macmillan, 1987).

of transcendence, looking beyond the pastoral of earlier novels for the more searching consideration that begins in *Dombey and Son*, of 'what Nature is',[33] and how it might disclose intimations of the numinous. In an apocalyptic vision in *Little Dorrit*, Dickens alludes to the sunset that ends *The Excursion*, 9:590–608,[34] where rays of light reflected from the 'orb of glory' manifest a rapturous and overarching 'unity sublime' (9:608).[35] This contemplative pause in the narrative of Mrs Clennam's and Little Dorrit's release from their respective imprisonments foreshadows the hopefulness of the novel's ending. Allusions to the promise signified in the Bible's 'blessed covenant' give a specifically religious dimension to the visionary moment. The thorns that denote Adam's curse of mortality, sorrow, and the return to dust,[36] are transformed in the 'crown of thorns' that bears witness to the redemptive 'glory' of Christ's crucifixion, and to an end-time foreseen in the Book of Revelation: 'and the city had no need of the sun, neither of the moon, to shine on it: for the glory of God did lighten it, and the lamb is the light thereof'.[37] The reassurance of daily patterns, seasonal renewal, and communal pleasure, provides the correlative for this biblical typology:

> It was one of those summer evenings when there is no greater darkness than a long twilight. The vista of street and bridge was plain to see, and the sky was serene and beautiful. People stood and sat at their doors, playing with children and enjoying the evening; numbers were walking for air; the worry of the day had almost worried itself out, and few but themselves were hurried. As they crossed the bridge, the clear steeples of the many churches looked as if they had advanced out of the murk that usually enshrouded them and come much nearer. The smoke that rose into the sky had lost its dingy hue and taken a brightness upon it. The beauties of the sunset had not faded from the long light films of clouds that lay at peace in the horizon. From a radiant centre, over the whole length and breadth of the tranquil firmament, great shoots of light streamed among the early stars, like signs of the blessed later covenant of peace and hope that changed the crown of thorns into a glory.[38]

---

[33] *Dombey and Son*, ed. Alan Horsman (Oxford: Clarendon Press, 1974), chapter 47, 619. Subsequent references are inserted parenthetically in the text by *DS* chapter, page.

[34] Stephen Wall and Helen Small, *Little Dorrit* (Harmondsworth: Penguin, 1998), 888, footnote the allusion. Dickens owned the 1814 edition, though Michael Wheeler, *Death and the Future Life in Victorian England* (Cambridge: Cambridge University Press, 1990), draws attention to Wordsworth's later 'Christianizing' additions.

[35] *The Excursion* (1814 edition), 9:689, 696, in *The Poetical Works of Wordsworth*, ed. Ernest de Selincourt (London: Oxford University Press, 1953).

[36] *The Holy Bible*, Authorized King James Version (Oxford: Oxford University Press), Genesis 3:18.

[37] *The Holy Bible*, Revelation 21:23. Karl Ashley Smith, *Dickens and the Unreal City: Searching for Spiritual Significance in Nineteenth-Century London* (Basingstoke: Palgrave Macmillan, 2008), 89 and 145, notes these allusions.

[38] Dickens, *Little Dorrit*, ed. Harvey Peter Sucksmith (Oxford: Clarendon Press, 1979), Book II, chapter 31, page 771. Subsequent references are inserted parenthetically in the text by *LD* Book:chapter, page.

In Book the First, the captivity of a group of 'fellow-travellers' in the broiling heat of the Marseille quarantine has introduced 'the prison of this lower world' (*LD* II:30, 741) in its many social and metaphysical dimensions. The thread of biblical allusions that places their 'release' within an interpretative framework provided by the expulsion from Eden, and the building of Babel's Tower, culminates in Revelation's Lake of Fire, imaged in the foul and flaming waters of Marseille Harbour. The serene hopefulness that irradiates the apocalyptic reprise of the novel's urban scenes and domestic spaces, and its structuring binaries of Sunshine and Shadow, through all its 'length' and 'breadth', depends in part on its contrast with the failings and strivings that precede it. Worry, hurry, clouds, murk, the unregenerate evil of the blackmailing Rigaud, even the institutionalized indifference of 'the many churches', and the dehumanizing streets where miserable children huddle together for warmth, are temporarily distanced. Prolonged twilight makes an analogy for what is expected, as yet withheld, in a transformative vastness of reach that recalls dawn while it anticipates the rest to be found at nightfall. The energy that streams 'great shoots of light' from 'a radiant centre' carries the forcefulness of the Wordsworthian vision and of the Genesis *fiat lux*. The 'New Covenant', a key theological concept for Dickens and for Amy Dorrit, can be realized, can only be realized, in the 'as if' of a natural world of time present, and in its intimations of the freedom of time yet to come.

DISCOURSE AND GENRE STUDIES

The novel's generic capaciousness has proved hospitable not only to Bakhtin's dialogic thinking, but also to Foucault's theorizing of the effects of power exerted through discourse. Dickens was an active participant in the social and epistemological contestations of his time, and his appeal to the conscience of 'a Christian people',[39] by turns polemical, sentimental, intellectually rigorous, and imaginatively powerful, was expressed from the vantage point of his religious conviction. Critical enquiry has begun to focus on his engagement with such topical doctrinal disputes as the Doctrine of Original Sin,[40] 1840s Millenarianism,[41] the 1850s debate on Atonement,[42] the 1860s controversy about the Resurrection,[43] and the Doctrine of Anamnesis.[44]

[39] *Dombey and Son* (*DS* 47, 620) provides a well-known example.
[40] See, for example, Oulton, *Literature and Religion in Mid-Victorian England*, ch. 3, and Jennifer Gribble, '"In a State of Bondage": The Children of *Bleak House*', in Peter Merchant and Catherine Waters (eds), *Dickens and the Imagined Child* (Farnham: Ashgate, 2015), 57–76.
[41] Jennifer Gribble, 'Apocalypse Now: Dombey in the Twenty-First Century', in Nathalie Vanfasse, Marie-Amelie Coste, Christine Huguet, and Luc Bonard (eds), *Dickens and the Imagined Child, Cahiers victoriens et édouardiens* (February 2012), 273–84.
[42] Jan-Melissa Schramm, *Atonement and Self-Sacrifice in Nineteenth-Century Narrative* (Cambridge: Cambridge University Press, 2012), 140–8.
[43] Wheeler, *Death and the Future Life*, ch. 6.
[44] Jennifer Gribble, 'Do Not Forget: Memory and Moral Obligation in *Little Dorrit*', in Catherine A. Runcie (ed.), *The Free Mind: Essays and Poems in Honour of Barry Spurr* (Sydney: Edwin H. Lowe Publishing, 2016), 187–98.

Dickens shows a particular relish for the sub-genres of the Gothic and the ghost-story, astutely satisfying popular appetite for beleaguered innocence, imprisoning labyrinths, and buried secrets. The view that 'God has been factored out of the Gothic'[45] is being reassessed as the biblical and theological resonances of his Gothic tropes[46] and 'urban Gothic'[47] come to light. With some backward-looking towards the sinister Catholic 'other' of eighteenth-century Gothic, a distinctly Protestant sensibility begins to inform Victorian Gothic's religious dimension.[48] In *Bleak House*, an implicit association of the Gothic 'Temple' of Chancery with Catholic ritual suggests Dickens's 'Protestant resistance'.[49] And the 'gloomy theology' of Evangelical Protestantism is memorably represented in the Gothic chiaroscuro of the House of Clennam. The domestic ideology promoted in *Household Words* and *All the Year Round* is interrogated in *Dombey and Son* by the biblical parable of the Wise and Foolish Builders,[50] and in *Bleak House* by the parables of the *paroussia*.[51] Haunting legacies are played out in the inheritance plot that surfaces first in *Oliver Twist* and is more searchingly engaged in *Bleak House* and *Little Dorrit*, where the legal terminology of 'testator', 'will', and 'codicil' takes on theological significance. Both the historical and the theological dimensions of inheritance are explored in the Gothic spaces, hauntings, and doublings of *Barnaby Rudge* and *A Tale of Two Cities*. From Jacob's Island to Tom-all-Alone's, Dickens sees polluted and sinister urban space as betrayal of the mutual responsibility entailed in the biblical history of covenantal relationship.

The Gothic progressively accommodates itself to the novel's realist practice; the ghost-story, while drawing on Gothic atmospherics and tropes, typically requires its readership to support a fascination with the supernatural by a modicum of suspended disbelief. What has become known as 'the discourse of spectrality' tracks the metaphor of haunting through the work of Marx, Freud, and Derrida, bringing to light its entertainment of the vagaries of perception as well as its exploration of personal and cultural concerns Victorians were unable to bring to the surface of consciousness. Many reported themselves ghost seers, and Catherine Crowe's *The Night*

---

[45] Nancy Armstrong, 'A Gothic History of the British Novel', in Patrick Parrender, Andrew Nash, and Nicola Wilson (eds), *New Directions in the History of the Novel* (Basingstoke: Palgrave Macmillan, 2014), 103–20, 109.

[46] Robert Mighall, 'Dickens and the Gothic', in Paroissien (ed.), *A Companion to Charles Dickens*, 81–96.

[47] Karl Ashley Smith, *Dickens and the Unreal City* (Basingstoke: Palgrave Macmillan, 2008), explores religious dimensions in Dickens's urban spaces, yet endorses Larson's view that for Dickens the Bible was a 'broken scripture'.

[48] See Victor Sage, *Horror Fiction in the Protestant Tradition* (Basingstoke: Macmillan, 1988).

[49] See Paula Keatley, 'Liberal Protestant Theology in Dickens's *Bleak House*', *Nineteenth-Century Contexts* 39, 2 (2017): 77–86.

[50] Gribble, 'Do Not Forget', 191 n. 11.

[51] Jennifer Gribble, 'Compound Interest: Dickens's Figurative Style', in Daniel Tyler (ed.), *Dickens's Style* (Cambridge: Cambridge University Press, 2013).

Side of Nature, or, Ghosts and Ghost-seers (1848), reviewed by Dickens in February of that year for *The Examiner*, went through 16 editions in six years. Collecting, publishing, and writing ghost-stories, Dickens maintains his scepticism about spectral sightings in the very family magazines that owe a measure of their success to promoting the ghostly.[52] In the later novels, ghosts become projections of a psychic disturbance Dickens associates with the culture's distorted religion, reading its shunning of the 'fallen woman', and its punitive teachings on 'original sin', for example, as misappropriations of the biblical narrative of the Fall. The footsteps that haunt Chesney Wold's Ghost Walk herald the exposure of Lady Dedlock's sexual 'fall' and of Esther's burden of illegitimacy. The ghostly presences that afflict Mrs Clennam's servant Affery prove to be not the result of indigestion (her husband's version of the current 'heavy supper' explanation of spectral sightings),[53] but of repressed memories of the imprisoned 'fallen' woman whose guilt is Arthur Clennam's inheritance.

The four Christmas Books of the 1840s, and the annual Christmas numbers of the family magazines through the 1850s and 1860s, draw on the Christmas tradition of fireside ghost-stories to promote what Dickens came to call his 'Carol Philosophy'. Confiding to Forster that he was 'very loath … to leave any gap at Christmas firesides which I ought to fill',[54] Dickens takes the seasonal opportunity to strengthen the bond with his readership, redirecting the pieties of hearth and home towards the social compassion and beneficent action he finds inherent in the nativity story.

Mr Pickwick's editor interrupts his *Papers* to commend Christmas as:

> a source of such pure and unalloyed delight, and one so incompatible with the cares and sorrows of the world, that the religious belief of the most civilised nations, and the rude traditions of the roughest savages, alike number it among the first joys of a future state of existence, provided for the blest and happy! (*PP* 28, 408)

Readily transportable to the domestic hearth everywhere, this early version of the Dickens Christmas is imperialist in its valorizing of family reunion and collective memory. The rhetoric builds to a climax that baptizes 'even the roughest savages' into the nominal Christianity of 'the most civilized nations', making an emphatic connection between being civilized and going to heaven. Not until *Great Expectations* will Dickens read the Christmas narrative for its potentiality to subvert the comfortable distinction between 'savage' and 'civilized'.

Yet in *A Christmas Carol*, subtitled *A Ghost Story of Christmas*, the genre of the ghost-story and associated Gothic tropes enable a significant development in Dickens's

---

[52] Louise Henson, 'Investigations and Fictions: Charles Dickens and Ghosts', in Bown et al., *The Victorian Supernatural*, 44–61, 60.
[53] Ibid., 48.
[54] 12 September 1847, *PLets* 5:165–6, 165.

thinking about the Christian meaning of the festive season. In a series of Gothic doublings, the Romantic figure of the child brings into association 'the little child' Jesus set 'in the midst' of his followers[55] with the Christ-child of the Christmas narrative, and with the ailing Tiny Tim and the wolfish children of Want and Ignorance lurking beneath the robe of Christmas Present. As the miserly Scrooge laughs and weeps to revisit scenes of his own lonely and neglected childhood, he is made open to Christmas as a celebration of unfolding possibility, social responsibility, and renewing joy. Within his Gothic space, memory and imagination are activated in the looming and dissolves of ghostly visitation: like Wordsworth, Dickens imagines recovered memory as essential to wholeness of being. Inhabiting the liminal space and logic opened up by Victorian dream theory, the Ghosts of Christmas Past, Present, and Yet to Come blur chronological boundaries, and foreshadow the ambitious narratorial overview and reformist agenda of the later novels.

Debate on the *Carol* as 'culture text'[56] centres, currently, on its engagement with other Victorian discourses, and a perceived 'failure to articulate its Christian theodicy'.[57] Scrooge's change of heart continues to be viewed as entangling him in the capitalist system it seeks to redress.[58] His experience of the interrelationship of psychological time with a larger temporality, however, foreshadows an enquiry that dominates the later novels. In a pioneering article, Robert Patten follows the cues of biblical allusion, figuration, and typology, to reflect on the theological sources of Dickens's imagining of time's possibilities in the *Carol*: 'To Christians, the Incarnation and the Passion are a-temporal and simultaneous. The coming of Christ into time redeems time.'[59]

Scrooge is a very different culture hero from Mr Pickwick. Protagonist of the Age of Wonder, Pickwick travels between the pastoral and the carceral: imprisoned in the Fleet, he has 'seen enough'. Scrooge is made to see: not only Want and Ignorance, but the mortality that shockingly confronts him in his own corpse. Patten associates the moment with Rudolph Otto's account of religious experience: 'the *feeling of terror* before the sacred ... the awe-inspiring mystery ... that emanates an overwhelming superiority of power'.[60]

---

[55] 'And He took a little child and set him in the midst of them', Matthew 18:2, a favourite Dickens text.

[56] Audrey Jaffe, 'Spectacular Sympathy: Visuality and Ideology in Dickens's *A Christmas Carol*', in Carol T. Christ and John O. Jordan (eds), *Victorian Literature and the Victorian Visual Imagination* (Berkeley, Los Angeles, and London: University of California Press, 1995), 327–44, 328, reads the tale as 'an exemplary narrative of enculturation into the dominant values of its time'. Jessica Kilgore, 'Father Christmas and Thomas Malthus: Charity, Epistemology, and Political Economy in *A Christmas Carol*', *Dickens Studies Annual* 42 (2011): 143–58, argues, to the contrary, that its cultivation of sympathy attempts to undermine the authority of political economics as paradigm for charitable work.

[57] Stephen Prickett, *Victorian Fantasy* (Hassocks: Harvester, 1979), 61, finds Scrooge's conversion 'strikingly secular' ... 'if we half-expect a Christ Child ... we find only the "wolfish" children'.

[58] Paul A. Jarvie, *Ready to Trample on All Human Law: Financial Capitalism in the Fiction of Charles Dickens* (New York and London: Routledge, 2005), 72–7.

[59] 'Dickens Time and Again', *Dickens Studies Annual* 2 (1970): 163–96, 189.

[60] Ibid., 186.

In *Little Dorrit*, terror becomes premonitory, in a ghostly encounter that recalls Romantic and Gothic indebtedness to Edmund Burke's *A Philosophical Enquiry into the Origins of our Ideas of the Sublime and the Beautiful* (1757). As the Dorrit family, newly released from the Marshalsea, seek shelter in the nightfall of a long and hazardous day on their Grand Tour, they are enclosed by mountain-peaks endowed with uncanny volition: that 'seemed solemnly to recede', bleached 'coldly white', 'like spectres who were going to vanish' (*LD* II:1, 419). Nature's 'overwhelming superiority of power', so benignly manifested in the urban vision of chapter 31, is here acknowledged as mortality's inescapable imprisonment. In the 'Ark' of the Convent of the Great Saint Bernard, a ghoulish representation of survival awaits the party. 'Hunted' and 'haunted' in a visual and audible labyrinth, they meet their ghostly doubles. '[S]ilently assembled in a gated house, half a dozen paces removed, with the same cloud enfolding them, and the same snow flakes drifting in upon them, were the dead travellers found upon the mountain' (*LD* II:1, 421). Syntactically aggregated, the living and the dead make '[a]n awful company, mysteriously come together'. The fearsome life of the undead is enacted in the 'half a dozen paces removed' they share with the living. 'The mother, storm-belated many winters ago, still standing in the corner with her baby at her breast' gives an icy representation to the spectre that haunts the novel, the lost embrace of Arthur Clennam and his outcast mother, a maternal bond made present to him, at last, when Little Dorrit's voice returns its Wordsworthian echoes 'of every merciful and loving whisper that had ever stolen to him in his life' (*LD* II:34, 790).

'The Providential Aesthetic'

In the Victorian debate about origins and destination, while historical and textual criticism is revealing 'God's Book' as a 'palimpsest' of stories of contested origin,[61] evolutionary science is reading in Nature, 'God's second Book', an ever-more unsettling narrative. Yet Dickens continues to find in the natural world a manifestation of divine power and intention. A third approach to his religious thinking is represented in the thesis of Thomas Vargish, that his novels, like others of his time, are shaped by the Providential world view set out in Joseph Butler's *The Analogy of Religion* (1736) and Paley's *Natural Theology* (1802). Vargish suggests that Paley's 'morally lucid pattern' affirms divine oversight and teleology: nature's laws reflect the good order of Providential design, making humankind's relationship with the natural world one of 'moral and ethical responsibility'. The temporal sequence of linear time 'reveals and participates in an order of reality that is transcendent and timeless', referring circumstances and events to 'some ultimate context that has the power to explain them'.[62]

---

[61] Stephen Prickett, *Origins of Narrative: The Romantic Appropriation of the Bible* (Cambridge: Cambridge University Press, 1996), 1–18.

[62] *The Providential Aesthetic in Victorian Fiction* (Charlottesville: University of Virginia Press, 1985), 17, 32.

Dickens affirms this link when he draws on an analogy inherited from his eighteenth-century predecessors, between the novelist as creator and the creator of the cosmos: 'the business of Art ... is to SUGGEST, until the fulfillment comes. These are the ways of Providence—of which ... Art is but a little imitation'.[63] 'Aesthetic', for Vargish, denotes the 'devices and conventions' (including the 'indirectness') through which the novelist conveys Providential design and intention. Assumptions about Providential design underlie discussions of Dickens's use of parable and theodicy,[64] keeping current Connor's questions about the authority of form. George Levine, to the contrary, argues that Dickens, in his commitment to the realist practice and what he sees as the inherently secular form of the novel, is unable persuasively to demonstrate 'a divinely ordered world inside [the] providential plot'.[65]

Providentialist assumptions and analogies permeate Victorian social and economic discourse and policies, as Boyd Hilton has demonstrated.[66] Dickens's confidence in the Providential world view is evident in the structuring biblical allusions through which he invokes the Judaeo-Christian grand narrative of Creation, Fall, Incarnation, Redemption, Apocalypse,[67] the *Heilsgeschichte* or 'salvation history' that preoccupies theological discussion in the wake of the German Higher Criticism. So thoroughly internalized that Dickens needs no signposting in the working notes, salvation history generates plot lines, and guides the formal control of a multiplicity of characters and locations, as he negotiates the constraints of serialized publication. *The Pickwick Papers* has been seen as inaugurating his recognition of the biblical narrative's structuring potentiality.[68]

The framing work of the Judaeo-Christian grand narrative has implications for Dickens's attitudes to the Old Testament and to Judaism. He repeatedly declared his abhorrence of the Old Testament God of vengeance and his confidence in the all-sufficiency of the New Testament: debates between 'Law' and 'Gospel' are staged to dramatic and thematic effect in *Bleak House* and *Little Dorrit*. But it is a whole biblical narrative that drives the momentum of his plots, establishing their typological and thematic connections and continuities. Attempting to ameliorate the anti-Semitism of his portrayal of Fagin in *Oliver Twist* by the creation of the virtuous Riah in *Our Mutual*

---

[63] To Wilkie Collins, 6 October 1859, *PLets* 9:127–8, 128.

[64] See, for example, Kenneth M. Stroka, 'A Tale of Two Gospels: Dickens and John', *Dickens Studies Annual* 27 (1997): 145–69, and Jennifer Gribble, 'The Bible in *Great Expectations*', *Dickens Quarterly* 25, 4 (2008): 232–40.

[65] *Realism, Ethics and Secularism: Essays on Victorian Literature and Science* (Cambridge; New York: Cambridge University Press, 2008), 222.

[66] *The Age of Atonement: The Influence of Evangelicalism on Social and Economic Thought, 1795–1865* (Oxford: Clarendon Press, 1998).

[67] Norman Vance, *Bible and Novel: Narrative Authority and the Death of God* (Oxford: Oxford University Press, 2013), 3–4, notes that the narrative is 'tidied up and formalized' by St Augustine in his *City of God*.

[68] Walder, *Dickens and Religion*, 17–41, discusses this widely contested view.

Friend,[69] Dickens is arguably influenced not only by the advocacy of Jewish admirers, but also by the never-failing appeal to his imagination of God's creative power in the Book of Genesis, and the covenant with the children of Israel recorded in the Pentateuch.

There is further work to be done on Dickens's relationship with Paley,[70] and with Providential Deism more generally.[71] His providential plotting, beginning, as Vargish notes, in a somewhat mechanical distribution of rewards and punishments, becomes more complex. 'The principle of good surviving' in *Oliver Twist*, which concludes in a tendentious attempt to convert Fagin,[72] is more comprehensively imagined in *Little Dorrit*. In *Dombey and Son*, the question of 'survival' reverberates within a mid-Victorian world of chance and change. Mr Dombey's blasphemous appropriation of the Providential world view in chapter 1 authorizes mercantilist prosperity and imperialist ambition. But the sea that floats Dombey's ships dissolves into the terrifying sea of Captain Cuttle's talismanic Psalm 107, maker of shipwreck as well as survival. Its 'wonders of the deep' gather Mrs Dombey into 'the dark and unknown sea that rolls round all the world' (*DS* 1, 11): source of 'mystery' and 'grace' for the children she leaves behind. Birth and death, so often intertwined at this time of high infant and maternal mortality, raise the more poignantly questions about survival in the here-and-now and in a life to come.[73] The mysteriousness of the unknown is compounded for Victorian readers by the aeons of time being opened up in the geological record, and by the railway's acceleration of it. The deathbed scenes that famously made grown men cry have been dismissed by later generations of Dickens readers as religiose and sentimental, though recent 'affect studies' have begun to recuperate 'sentiment', along with 'melodrama', as modes of critical enquiry. The death of little Paul Dombey draws on the conventions of popular deathbed literature in offering its Christian consolation; Mrs Dombey's becalmed drifting is remarkably unconventional in its delicately suggested continuities between the time-bound and the unimaginably timeless. Florence, the 'light spar' to which the dying mother clings, weathers separation and implacable loss to endure as the love that sustains her infant brother. The spar materializes in the piece of wreckage that preserves Walter Gay to salvage Dombey and his House. Whether or not Captain Cuttle's supplications are answered by 'special providence', or by the

---

[69] See Murray Baumgarten, '"The Other Woman"—Eliza Davis and Charles Dickens', *Dickens Quarterly* 30, 1 (2015): 44–63. Harry Stone, 'Dickens and the Jews', in *Victorian Studies* 2, 3 (1959): 223–53, establishes that for the 1867 edition Dickens removed the bulk of the novel's references to Fagin as 'the Jew'.

[70] Paul Schacht, 'Dickens and the Use of Nature', *Victorian Studies* 34 (1990): 77–102, suggests that Dickens never repudiates Paley. Chapter 47 of *Dombey and Son*, however, makes clear his rejection of the Providential Deist views of Adam Smith and Malthus, that poverty is divinely willed and ineradicable.

[71] Charles Taylor, *A Secular Age* (Cambridge, MA, and London: Harvard University Press, 2007), ch. 7, notes Providential Deism's narrowing 'economic view', which begins to exclude 'mystery' and 'grace'.

[72] The Good Friday prayer for the conversion of 'all Jews' (together with 'Turks, infidels, and heretics'), in *The Book of Common Prayer*, would have been familiar to church-going Anglicans. This supercessionism, now officially renounced by both Catholics and Protestants, demonstrably influences Oliver's solicitations for Fagin.

[73] See Wheeler, *Death and the Future Life*, ch. 1, for a full discussion.

'general providence' of divine oversight,[74] the eternal sea, most sustained of all Dickens's Natural-Theological analogies, generates this novel's imagining of what is unpredictable in human voyaging, and the shipwreck, or survival, of its hope. Building on Scrooge's experience of living in a time-bound universe of 'the already here' while expecting judgement in an apocalyptic 'yet to come', *Dombey and Son* anticipates the preoccupation with redemption and resurrection in the later novels.

INTERDISCIPLINARY STUDIES IN LITERATURE, PHILOSOPHY, AND RELIGION: 'THE SELF IN MORAL SPACE'

The 'turn towards the ethical' described by philosopher Martha Nussbaum in 1990[75] has encouraged renewed focus on what theologian Charles Taylor describes as 'the self in moral space': 'my identity is defined by the commitments and identifications which provide the frame or horizon within which I try to determine from case to case what is good, or valuable, or what ought to be done, or what I endure or oppose'.[76] In exploring ways in which Dickens, for example, addresses moral-philosophical questions, Nussbaum shifts the emphasis from the question that has dominated discussion of his 'social gospel': what is it good to do? to the question, what is it good to be?[77]

Taylor's tracing of the historical emergence of the secularization thesis, and the assumptions that continue to lend it authority, makes part of what is currently referred to as 'post-secular studies'. The 'religious turn' in mid-1990s philosophy, and the ongoing interdisciplinary conversation in journals, handbooks, and conferences dedicated to literature and religion,[78] are establishing a climate within which Dickens's religious thinking may begin to attract wider consideration. The question 'where does he locate the good?',[79] although it clearly involves ethical answers, can only be fully addressed,

---

[74] Hilton, *The Age of Atonement*, 91–8 and 211–18, considers Victorian understandings of this distinction.

[75] David Parker, 'Introduction: The Turn to Ethics in the 1990s', in Jane Adamson, Richard Freedman, and David Parker (eds), *Renegotiating Ethics in Literature, Philosophy, and Theory* (Cambridge: Cambridge University Press, 1998), 13.

[76] *Sources of the Self: The Making of the Modern Identity* (Cambridge: Cambridge University Press, 1989), 27.

[77] See, for example, her discussion of *Hard Times* in 'The Literary Imagination in Public Life', in Parker et al., *Renegotiating Ethics*, 225–6.

[78] See Lori Branch, 'Postsecular Studies', in Mark Knight (ed.), *The Routledge Companion to Literature and Religion* (Abingdon and New York: Routledge, 2016), 134–48.

[79] Robert Newsom, 'Religion', in Paul Schlicke (ed.), *The Oxford Reader's Companion to Dickens* (Oxford: Oxford University Press, 1999), 501, answers 'not, very clearly, in religious or moral thought, but rather in immediately and self-evidently useful actions', an opinion he reaffirms in the Bicentenary edition of the *Companion* in 2011.

I have argued, if attention is paid to the Judaeo-Christian moral framework within which Dickens thought and wrote.

New directions for this discussion are suggested by the work of two philosophers who share that framework: Mikhail Bakhtin and Paul Ricoeur. Underlying Bakhtin's theorizing of the dialogic is his elaboration of self/other relationships in terms that challenge 'the politics of alterity'.[80] And in an occasional essay, 'The Economy of the Gift', Ricoeur makes a crucial distinction between 'the logic of equivalence' represented in 'the Golden Rule' (often cited as the essence of Dickens's religion) and 'the logic of superabundance' that informs the Sermon on the Mount,[81] seedbed for Dickens's theological thinking from *Dombey and Son* onwards. Adam Zachary Newton,[82] Alan Jacobs,[83] and Keith Easley[84] have drawn on Bakhtin to explore the intersubjective dynamics of narrative and the collaborative unfolding of character in *Bleak House*. Easley's discussion of Esther Summerson opens up a fresh approach to such critically contested aspects of Dickens's domestic ideology as father–daughter relationships and conduct-book notions of 'duty' and female 'self-sacrifice'. Yet it remains to consider his novels in the light of such specifically theological concepts as 'Creation', 'Incarnation', and 'Grace', as understood by Bakhtin and Ricoeur.

There is no doubt that Amy Dorrit, like Florence before her, is conceived in terms of the Sermon on the Mount's Beatitudes: meek, poor, merciful, pure in heart, a peacemaker, a finder and provider of 'comfort', 'blessed' in her bestowing of 'grace' as unearned gift. Her New Testament goodness not only opposes Mrs Clennam's vengeful Old Testament God, but also her society's 'Gospel of Mammonism'. Her hard-won struggle to assert the sense of self Bakhtin sees as essential to all self–other relationships is not always given its due.[85] Amy's moral integrity negotiates the self-obsessions of her family while rejecting their class-based superiority and learning to claim her love for Arthur Clennam. Raymond Williams, wrestling (as the narrator does) with the nature/nurture conundrum, is content to see Amy's distinctive goodness as 'the kind of miracle that happens, the flowering of love or energy which is inexplicable by the ways of describing people ... we have got used to'.[86] Yet the miracle of the child born into the prison, in a

---

[80] Hilary B. P. Bagshaw, *Religion in the Thought of Mikhail Bakhtin* (Farnham: Ashgate, 2013), provides a useful survey.

[81] See W. David Hall, 'The Economy of the Gift: Paul Ricoeur's Poetic Redescription of Reality', *Literature and Theology* 20, 2 (2006): 189–204.

[82] *Narrative Ethics* (Cambridge, MA: Harvard University Press, 1997).

[83] *A Theory of Reading: The Hermeneutics of Love* (Cambridge, MA: Westview, 2001).

[84] 'Dickens and Bakhtin: Authoring in *Bleak House*', *Dickens Studies Annual* 34 (2004): 185–232.

[85] Larson, *Dickens and the Broken Scripture*, 271, is not unrepresentative: 'Amy belongs to a long line of suffering Dickensian innocents whose strength of renunciation it is hard to judge morally, to distinguish from the weakness of submission to powerful circumstances or the stronger will of others.'

[86] 'Social Criticism in Dickens', *Critical Quarterly* 6 (1964): 224. Generations of critics have wrestled, as well, with this novel's 'intimations of spiritual possibility'. Lionel Trilling, *The Opposing Self* (Cambridge, MA: Harvard University Press, 1950), 57, pronouncing Amy 'the Paraclete in female form ... not only the Child of the Marshalsea, as she is called, but also the Child of the Parable', is disinclined to pursue the 'complicated' question of Dickens's 'relation to the Christian religion', 55.

vernacular nativity scene that updates the iconography of the stable in Bethlehem, is a meditation on Creation, Incarnation, and Grace, that depends on ways of describing people through which Dickens became Inimitable:

> The walls and ceiling were blackened with flies. Mrs Bangham, expert in sudden device, with one hand fanned the patient with a cabbage leaf, and with the other set traps of vinegar and sugar in gallipots; at the same time enunciating sentiments of an encouraging and congratulatory nature, adapted to the occasion.
> 'The flies trouble you, don't they, my dear?' said Mrs. Bangham. 'But p'raps they'll take your mind off of it, and do you good. What between the buryin' ground, the grocer's, the wagon-stables, and the paunch trade, the Marshalsea flies get very large. P'raps they're sent as a consolation, if we only know'd it. How are you now my dear? No better? No my dear, it ain't to be expected, you'll be worse before you're better, and you know it, don't you? Yes. That's right! And to think of a sweet little cherub being born inside the lock! Now ain't it pretty, ain't *that* something to carry you through it pleasant? Why, we ain't had such a thing happen here, my dear, not for I couldn't name the time when. And you a crying too?' said Mrs. Bangham, to rally the patient more and more. 'You! Making yourself so famous! With the flies a falling into the gallipots by fifties! And everything a going on so well! And here if there ain't... your dear gentleman along with Doctor Haggage! And now indeed we *are* complete, I *think!*'... Three or four hours passed; the flies fell into the traps by hundreds; and at length one little life, hardly stronger than theirs, appeared among the multitude of lesser deaths. (*LD* I:6, 62–3)

'Expert in sudden device', loquacious and opportunistic, Mrs Bangham summons to the birth her trajectory of unsanitary London. Fattened on offal and decomposition, the proliferating death-bound flies deliver evolutionary science's grim message of extinction and mystery's unknowable, potential 'consolations'. The gifts the inebriated duo bring are 'tobacco, dirt and brandy'. The interplay of voices, narratorial, 'rallying', and, in the case of the poor gentlewoman in labour, only to be inferred, takes the measure of confinement within the intolerable heat of the prison. The destiny proclaimed for 'The Child of the Marshalsea' confers on the 'famous' mother and displaced father their legendary status. Nature, apparently so careless of the single life, accommodates chance and adaptability, as well as Providence, in the struggle for survival.[87] Robust comedy celebrates the prison's 'moral space', and a communal storytelling that participates in the narrative theology of Dickens and his biblical source-book.

Further Reading

Peter Base and Andrew Stott (eds), *Ghosts, Deconstruction, Psychoanalysis, History* (Houndmills: Palgrave Macmillan, 1999)

---

[87] For a comprehensive theological discussion of these matters, see Jack Mahoney, *Christianity in Evolution* (Washington, DC: Georgetown University Press, 2011).

Jill Matus, *Shock, Memory and the Unconscious in Victorian Fiction* (New York: Cambridge University Press, 2011)

Shane McCorristane, *Spectres of the Self: Thinking about Ghosts and Ghost-Seeing in England, 1750–1920* (Cambridge: Cambridge University Press, 2010)

Andrew Smith, *The Ghost Story, 1840–1920* (Manchester: Manchester University Press, 2010)

CHAPTER 40

DRINKING IN DICKENS

HELENA MICHIE

In *Convivial Dickens: The Drinks of Dickens and his Times* Edward Hewett and William F. Axton take delight in crossing borders.[1] Theirs is a 'crossover book' intended for both academic and non-academic audiences that ends chapters full of serious readings of Dickens's fiction with recipes for milk punch, whisky cobbler, and Smoking Bishop. The term 'convivial' itself, with its origin in the Latin 'con', or together, and 'vivere', to live, invites us to cross over in another sense: we are welcome not only to read about Dickens but also to live and to drink with him. The spirit of conviviality and the spirits that produce that feeling travel across borders from Dickens's texts to Dickens himself, and from the 'Dickens' thus created to readers of those texts. This easy movement is made possible by the popular author, himself something of a crossover figure.[2] Books about eating and drinking, like Cedric Dickens's 1984 *Dining with Dickens*, a collection of recipes from Dickens's novels compiled by one of his descendants, and Susan Rossi-Wilcox's 2005 *Dinner for Dickens*, a study of Catherine Dickens's cookbook, *What Shall We Have For Dinner?* suggest through their use of prepositions a link between the reader and the author of novels filled with characters full of food and drink.[3]

We might even see the impulse to eat and drink *with* Dickens as a form of consuming or incorporating Dickens himself. As one Amazon reviewer of *Dining with Dickens* put

---

[1] Edward Hewett and William F. Axton, *Convivial Dickens: The Drinks of Dickens and his Times* (Athens: Ohio University Press, 1983).

[2] I would like to thank The Dickens Project, with its many academic and non-academic audiences, for teaching me about 'crossover' Dickens. A very early version of this chapter was presented at the 2007 Dickens Universe Conference.

[3] Cedric Dickens, *Dining with Dickens* (Goring-on-Thames: Elvendon Press, 1984); and Susan Rossi-Wilcox, *Dinner for Dickens: The Culinary History of Mrs. Charles Dickens' Menu Books* (Totnes: Prospect, 2005). Examples of identifications resolving into recipes can be found all over the web. The blog Drink Like the Dickens! makes the familiar pun on Dickens's name and links reader and author through 'like' (Adam Selzer, Drink Like the Dickens! [blog], accessed 17 October 2016, <http://dickensdrinks.blogspot.com>). 'Cocktail Hour: Drink What Dickens Drank' uses 'what' in a similar way (Sarah Lohman, 'Cocktail Hour: Drink What Dickens Drank', *Four Pounds Flour: Historic Gastronomy* [blog], 29 October 2009, <http://www.fourpoundsflour.com/cocktail-hour-drink-what-dickens-drank/>).

it, 'If you never cook, still a delightful read, especially during the winter months. The recipe for toast is to be appreciated. The section on Oysters is wonderful. Dickens is definately [sic] more than just a Christmas Goose.'[4] Two things are worth pointing out here: first, the act of reading replaces the act of cooking or eating; the recipes are 'delightful' even if no actual food gets produced. And, second, that by the end of this short review, Dickens has become himself a comestible. If he is 'more than just a Christmas Goose', the logic of this review suggests, it is because he 'is' somehow toast or oysters. Of course, reading Dickens can also quite literally stimulate appetite. Consuming Dickens's novels can, it seems, make readers want to, well, consume. As one anonymous reader of *The Cincinnati Price Current*, a business newspaper, put it in 1908, the '[o]nly objections I've got to Dickens … is that he nearly always makes me hungry, and I've got to hike out to the nearest restaurant and get something to eat.'[5] Here again we have something of a border crossing, this time almost a literal imitation of the Inimitable and his characters.

Other authors were not immune from a particular form of re-enactment centred on food and drink: Louisa May Alcott, whose novels are full of references to early Dickens, recalls in her essay 'Dickens Day' a trip to London in which her thinly disguised heroine, 'Livy', visits the haunts of Sam Weller and Sairey Gamp. When Livy finds herself in the Middle Temple around lunchtime, she tells her companion that she wants 'a Weal pie and pot of porter':

> As she was not fond of either, it was a sure proof of the sincerity of her regard for the persons who have made them immortal. They went into an eating-house, and ordered the lunch, finding themselves objects of interest to the other guests. But, though a walking doormat in point of mud, and somewhat flushed and excited by the hustling, climbing, and adoring, it is certain there wasn't a happier spinster in this 'Piljin Projess of a wale', [sic] than the one who partook of 'weal pie' in memory of Sam Weller, and drank 'a modest quencher' to the health of Dick Swiveller at the end of that delightful Dickens Day.[6]

Here, re-enactment crosses gender and even personal taste, as the avatar for the abstemious Alcott drinks in the sprit of Dickens and of those I am calling his comic or euphoric drunks—the avuncular carousers, the swashbuckling cockneys, the denizens of cosy pubs. Euphoric drinkers become signature Dickens 'characters' featured on dishes, cigarette cards, even Toby jugs shaped like the extraordinarily large heads of Mr Pickwick, Tony Weller, or Sairey Gamp. In those Toby jugs, we drink not only with Dickens but also with (and from) his most engaging characters.

---

[4] D. K. Chef, 'Tasty my dear, very tasty', review of *Dining with Dickens*, by Cedric Dickens, 7 November 2008, accessed 30 August 2016, <https://www.amazon.com/Dining-Dickens-Cedric/dp/0906552311>.

[5] 'Dickens Makes Him Hungry', *The Cincinnati Price Current* 65, 53 (Thursday, 31 December 1908): 847.

[6] Louisa May Alcott, *Shawl-Straps: A Second Series of Aunt Jo's Scrap-Bag* (London: Sampson Low, Marston, & Company, 1895), 303, <http://www.gutenberg.org/files/22022/22022-h/22022-h.html>.

Who, on the other hand, would want to drink out of mugs featuring the faces of Mr Wickfield or Mr Dolls or Mrs Blackpool? These tragic, dysphoric, or serious drinkers are given different histories, personalities, and narrative locations. The difference between comic and serious drinkers is not simply one of tone; 'comic' in the sense I am using it does not mean humorous, although these characters are often hilariously funny. 'Comic' describes a narrative structure in which characters' actions—getting drunk, getting very drunk, falling down—are separated from the possible long-term consequences of those actions. Comic drinkers can commit faux pas, even sometimes have regrets or headaches, but they are not permanently marked as characters or as bodies by drinking. Drinking is quickly relegated to a recent past as the narrative and other characters seem to forget and move on. These figures, I argue, operate in a world outside cause and effect, regulated by what has come to be called 'cartoon physics', the logic that allows cartoon figures to get crushed by buildings, shot, burnt, and torn apart in one episode only to return unscathed in the next.[7] As one non-scholarly source succinctly puts it, '[I]n the world of cartoon physics, there are no hospital bills, no scars, no dismemberment, and, most importantly, no hangovers.'[8] The humour of the comic drinker depends on the reader's ability to forget and to suspend the operations of cause and effect that undergird Dickens's realism. By contrast, Dickens's dysphoric drunks are literally and figuratively marked by their encounters with alcohol and live in a world relentlessly in thrall to cause and effect. Dysphoric drunks drink and fall in a more serious and morally charged way; mostly they drink and—eventually—die.

Scholars of Dickens have paid surprisingly little attention to his representation of alcohol, drinking, or alcoholism, given the sheer amount his characters consume and how many kinds of relations to alcohol he represents. Critics of the early novels tend to celebrate the euphoric drunks as part of a comic spirit. This was especially true in the 1970s and 1980s when psychoanalytically informed critics like Ian Watt and Robert Polhemus emphasized Dickens's oral humour as a form of transgressiveness. For these critics, eating and drinking were largely undifferentiated.[9] Later, more historicist critics

---

[7] See, for example, Alan Cholodenko, 'The Nutty Universe of Animation, The "Discipline" of All "Disciplines," And That's Not All, Folks!' *International Journal of Baudrillard Studies* 3, 1 (January 2006), <http://www2.ubishops.ca/baudrillardstudies/vol3_1/cholodenko.htm>.

[8] 'Cartoon Violence', Cracked (Scripps Co., 2016), accessed 17 October 2016, <http://www.cracked.com/funny-3621-cartoon-violence/>.

[9] See Ian Watt, 'Oral Dickens', *Dickens Studies Annual* 3 (1974): 165–81; and Robert M. Polhemus, *Comic Faith: The Great Tradition from Austen to Joyce* (Chicago: University of Chicago Press, 1980). The slippage between eating and drinking too much is an interesting topic beyond the purview of this chapter. 'Dining' could, of course, be used as a euphemism for drinking, as in 'dining too well'. Andrew Halliday's very amusing essay 'You Must Drink!' parodies the shift in public-house culture from eating and drinking to simply drinking: 'It was different in the old days, when innkeepers wrote over their doors, "Entertainment for Man and Beast." Entertainment for beast may still mean a cozy stall, a feed of corn, and clean straw; but entertainment for man at all houses not hotels, now means, drink, wholly drink, and nothing but drink' (*All the Year Round*, 18 June 1864: 11:437–40, 437). Dickens features certain characters who are overly fond of the solid delights of the table; these are not overeaters in the modern sense but people addicted to pleasure or simply to parsimony and selfishness, such as Mrs Pipchin in *Dombey* or Mr Bumble in *Oliver Twist*.

tend to emphasize specific histories of eating and cookery and their connection to ideas about larger social issues, as Gail Houston does in identifying eating and cookery in Dickens with the 'health of the social body'.[10] Eating in Houston's analysis is linked on the one hand to consumption in all its forms, and on the other to histories of hunger. Annette Cozzi also looks specifically at food in her careful analysis of eating and class in Dickens's novels.[11] Although both critics mention alcohol, their focus is on food and its social meanings. The emphasis on hunger and on class and gender oppression (and occasionally on addiction) provides a stark contrast to the stress on an undifferentiated 'orality' of the earlier critics.

The comic spirit can be as contagious for the more celebratory critics as for the lay writers mentioned above. James R. Kincaid both parodies and takes advantage of the comic possibilities of drink in *Pickwick*: 'Booze. An even slipperier and more reliable oil is alcohol—hot pineapple rum punch, milk punch, porter, brandy and water, gin, wine: the whole novel swims before us in blurry convivial bliss—the book is soused, staggers and speaks with a thick tongue: we won't go home till morning, till daylight doth appear. Everyone has her, or more likely his, arms around everyone else in a tipsy embrace; everyone is always ordering up a double glass of the "invariable", a convivial glass.'[12] Kincaid's own prose suggests a tipsy excess, a fluidity born of appreciatively crossing borders between the critic and his object of study.

Historically, critics have shown less interest in Dickens's serious drunks than in the earlier, funnier, ones. Mr Wickfield, Agnes's alcoholic father in *David Copperfield*, is, for example, dismissed in a footnote and 'as a plot device' in Gareth Cordery's essay on how Dickens uses particular alcoholic beverages to indicate class.[13] More recently, some critics have taken an addiction studies perspective on these dysphoric characters. Robyn R. Warhol and Susan Zieger, who are interested in the historical emergence of the identity categories of the alcoholic and the addict, have turned their attention to early instantiations of those figures in Dickens. These critics, as well as Amanda Claybaugh, are also interested in the relation of alcoholics to narrative, especially, in the case of Warhol, in contrast to contemporary master-narratives of alcoholism (in Alcoholics Anonymous, for example).[14]

---

[10] Gail Turley Houston, *Consuming Fictions: Gender, Class, and Hunger in Dickens's Novels* (Carbondale: Southern Illinois University Press, 1994), 4.

[11] Annette Cozzi, *The Discourses of Food in Nineteenth-Century British Fiction* (New York: Palgrave, 2010), 39–70.

[12] James R. Kincaid 'Fattening up on Pickwick', *Novel: A Forum on Fiction* 25, 3 (Spring 1992): 235–44, 239.

[13] Gareth Cordery, 'Drink in *David Copperfield*', in William Baker and Ira B. Nadel (eds), *Redefining the Modern: Essays on Literature and Society in Honor of Joseph Wiesenfarth* (Madison, NJ: Fairleigh Dickinson University Press, 2004), 59–74, 72.

[14] Robyn R. Warhol, 'The Rhetoric of Addiction from Victorian Novels to AA', in Janet Farrell Brodie, Janet Farrell, and Marc Redfield (eds), *High Anxieties: Cultural Studies in Addiction* (Berkeley: University of California Press, 2002), 197–208; Susan Zieger, *Inventing the Addict: Drugs, Race and Sexuality in Nineteenth-Century British and American Literature* (Amherst: University of Massachusetts Press, 2008),

Some scholars have noticed that Dickens's work displays two contradictory attitudes towards alcohol and those who drink it. David J. Greenman argues that, even in early Dickens, the novelist presents 'both the debilitating and convivial effects of heavy drinking'. Greenman finds what he calls Dickens's 'ambivalence' 'unsettling', noting that he 'seems quite content to play the stern moralist at one moment and the jolly companion the next'.[15] Philip V. Allingham sees both attitudes at work across the Dickens canon and within particular novels. As Allingham puts it in his tantalizingly short piece for The Victorian Web: 'In The Christmas Books, and in particular in *A Christmas Carol* alcohol (taken in moderation, and in company) is benign, but in *Hard Times* Mrs Blackpool's alcoholism, combined with her laudanum addiction, is anything but! Within the same text, we can have contradictory attitudes towards alcohol: for example, Dickens seems to tolerate as harmless dissipation the tippling of Jerry Cruncher in *A Tale of Two Cities*, but condemns Jerry's wife-beating.'[16] While Greenman resolves the contradiction in Dickens's views through recourse to a complicated argument about the supernatural that I discuss in this chapter, Allingham does not, understandably, given the constraints of his piece, explicitly attempt a resolution. He does, however, end with Dickens's own drinking behaviour and with the idea of 'moderation'.

My own argument in what follows draws upon the insights of all three groups of critics I have sketched out here, while attempting to elaborate on the contradictions exposed by the third. I am not so much interested in determining Dickens's own ultimate views on alcohol, drunkenness, or temperance, although these are very interesting issues. I am intuitively dissatisfied with the idea of resolution through the idea of 'moderation', as if wildly differing (and extreme) depictions of drinking can be in a sense averaged out. Instead, I would like to explore the contradiction identified by Greenman and Allingham—and one that has haunted me since I gave a paper on Pickwick in 2007 at the Dickens Conference—as an issue of forgetting.

It is forgetting—alcoholic forgetting—that is, on several levels, the central concern of this chapter. By 'alcoholic forgetting' I do not mean what we would now call blackouts, those occasions in which alcoholics fail to remember what they have done while drinking. There are certainly instances of such forgetting by characters in the novels, and I will be mentioning some of these. My approach, however, is structural and narrative: I am interested how Dickens's texts—from the journalism to the novels, and from the early to the late fiction—compartmentalize the effects of drinking into particular plots and genres. It is as if, in different ways, Dickens's texts create dysphoric drinkers only to forget them in the move between novels, genres, sub-plots, or sentences. In what follows, I look at three different kinds of texts produced at different moments

14; and Amanda Claybaugh, 'Dickensian Intemperance: Charity and Reform', *Novel: A Forum on Fiction* 37, 1/2 (Fall 2003/Spring 2004): 45–65.

[15] David J. Greenman, 'Alcohol, Comedy, and Ghosts in Dickens Early Short Fiction', *Dickens Quarterly* 17, 1 (March 2000): 3–13.

[16] Philip V. Allingham, 'Alcoholic Drink in Charles Dickens' Writings', The Victorian Web, last modified 24 April 2006, <http://www.victorianweb.org/victorian/authors/dickens/pva/drink.html>.

in Dickens's career: a critical essay on temperance-inspired legislation from *Household Words* called 'The Great Baby', the euphoric early novel *Pickwick Papers*, and the later more 'mature' novel and *Bildungsroman*, *David Copperfield*. I hope to show both that they all contain instances of, and are in some sense structured by, alcoholic forgetting and that they forget in different ways, at different levels of plot, genre, character, and sentence. All these levels suggest contradictory relationships to temporality—both to cause and effect and to past, present, and future.

COMIC HAUNTINGS

Part of the critical focus on euphoric drinking has to do with scholarly understandings of Dickens's own attitude towards alcohol; apparently surprisingly abstemious himself, Dickens was famously opposed to, and a satirist of, the temperance movement and its logic. For him, the temperance movement—at least in its severer forms that were the object of his parody in articles like 'Whole Hogs' or his review of George Cruickshank's cartoons 'The Bottle' and 'The Drunkard's Children'—represented an attack on the working class.[17] In his review of 'The Drunkard's Children', Dickens accuses Cruikshank of blaming the poor for the failure of the government to ameliorate the conditions that led to drinking among those Dickens insistently identifies as 'the people'. 'Drunkenness, as a national horror, is the effect of many causes. Foul smells, disgusting habitations, bad workshops and workshop customs, want of light, air, and water, the absence of all easy means of decency and health, are commonest among its common every-day, physical causes. The mental weariness and languor so induced, the want of wholesome relaxation, the craving for *some* stimulus and excitement, which is as much a part of such lives as the sun is ... are its most obvious moral causes.'[18] Oscillating between identification (the human need for light and air) and distance ('such lives'), Dickens sets himself up as a defender not only of working-class lives but also of working-class pleasures. Dickens's critique of the temperance movement is also indicatively anti-paternalist. In his *Household Words* essay 'The Great Baby', Dickens critiques the 1854 Sunday Beer Act (the Wilson Patten Act), which restricted the hours of drinking establishments on Sundays, for treating the working class as 'an abstraction ... a Great Baby, to be coaxed and chucked under the chin at elections ... and stood

---

[17] Dickens, *Household Words*, 'Whole Hogs', 23 August 1851, 3:505–7. Subsequent references are inserted parenthetically in the text by *HW*, 'Whole Hogs', volume: page. For a detailed account of the use and meaning of alcohol and the public house or 'drinking place' to working-class culture in the nineteenth century, see Brian Harrison, *Drink and The Victorians: The Temperance Question in England 1815–1872*, 2nd edn (Keele: Keele University Press, 1994), especially chapter 2.

[18] Dickens, 'Fine Arts', review of 'The Drunkard's Children: A Sequel to the Bottle', by George Cruikshank, *The Examiner* 2110 (8 July 1848): 436.

in the corner on Sundays'.[19] Here at least, he is defending not only the humanity of working-class people but also their status as adults.

As 'Whole Hogs' makes clear, Dickens is also suspicious of the idiom of temperance itself. He notes that temperance, with its connotations of moderation, is 'not an honest use of a plain word' (*HW*, 'Whole Hogs', 3:505). The 'Whole Hog' of the essay's title and central conceit is a figure for going too far; temperance reformers are in reality 'Teetotal', not allowing for 'a hair's-breadth of the tip of either ear of that particular Pig' (*HW*, 'Whole Hogs', 3:505). All forms and all quantities of drink are abstracted into alcohol and forbidden: 'Qualify your water with a tea-spoonful, of wine or brandy—we beg pardon—alcohol—and there is no virtue in Temperance' (*HW*, 'Whole Hogs', 3:505). 'Whole Hogs' also belabours another problem with the term 'Temperance', noting that movement members are far from temperate in their language and tactics: they should, according to Dickens, 'be temperate in many respects—in the rejection of strong words no less than of strong drinks' (*HW*, 'Whole Hogs', 3:506).

The anti-temperance Dickens of his public journalism can easily be absorbed into a discourse of conviviality; even his anti-temperance essays are, however, haunted by the spectre of the dysphoric drinker, and incorporate—if only to forget—the discourse of waste, disease, and death. Nowhere is this clearer than in 'The Great Baby', which begins with what we would now call a pleasure-forward account of drinking culture and ends with the 'horror' of drunkenness:

> It is not necessary for us, or for any decent person to go to Westminster, or anywhere else, to make a nourish [*sic*] against intemperance. We abhor it; would have no drunkard about us, on any consideration; would thankfully see the child of our heart, dead in his baby beauty, rather than he should live and grow with the shadow of such a horror upon him. In the name of Heaven, let drunkards and ruffians restrain themselves and be restrained by all conceivable means—but, not govern, bind, and defame, the temperance, the industry, the rational wants and decent enjoyments of a whole toiling nation! (*HW*, 'Great Baby', 12:4)

Framed by the reassuring idiom of the 'decent', this remarkable purple passage transforms that abstracted and collective 'great baby' into a singular Dickensian dying child—one whose death would indeed be preferable to drunkenness. The working class, that 'toiling nation', have their 'rational wants and decent enjoyments', but only in the face of Gothic possibilities. Those possibilities are dwelt on and then seemingly, quickly, efficiently forgotten as enjoyment replaces horror and death. The word 'intemperance', with which the first sentence of this passage ends, seems radically insufficient to describe the 'horror' which comes after. 'Enjoyment' takes us back to temperate language, but only after we have seen—and perhaps forgotten—the Dickensian dead child. Dickens seems himself to forget one drinking discourse in favour of another.

---

[19] Dickens, *Household Words*, 'The Great Baby', 4 August 1855, 12:1–4. Subsequent references are inserted parenthetically in the text by *HW*, 'Great Baby', volume: page.

Interpolation and Drinking: Alcoholic Temporalities

Pickwick, perhaps Dickens's most beloved novel, is dominated by comic drinkers—comic, that is, in both senses of the term. As Greenman has noted, however, two of the interpolated tales that interrupt the novel's main plot feature 'men in the last stages of alcohol abuse'.[20] Greenman is interested in how those tales of dysphoric drunkenness utilize the figure of the ghost. Arguing that in the early novels Dickens uses alcoholism—and the hallucinations it produces—as a way of explaining what in the later novels will become a more thorough and terrifying commitment to the uncanny, Greenman sees alcoholism as tethered to realism, or at least to realist explanations of what Dickens later refuses to explain. While I agree that in *Pickwick*'s interpolated tales what we would now call *delirium tremens* provides a realist explanation for Gothic events, my emphasis is on the temporal conflicts between the main plot and the interpolated tales, and on how the interpolated tales interrupt the accretive structure of picaresque by invoking other temporalities, other relations to the past, the present, and the future.

The novel's structure is famously episodic as it follows the somewhat undermotivated meanderings of the Pickwick Club. It is also, less obviously perhaps, diurnal. Each short segment records a new adventure of the Club, and most episodes begin with a new day and something of a clean slate. This structure embodies a form of forgetting; although the narrative sometimes indulges in jokes about the previous night's debaucheries, the forward movement of this picaresque plot ensures the ability of characters to begin again with every morning. It is only the darker plotlines—in particular the breach of promise case against Pickwick—that stretch across episodes, allowing actions taken in one part of the story to produce consequences in another. The comedy of *Pickwick*, however, depends on what we might think of as an active forgetting of one of the novel's key narrative components: the interpolated tales. Embedded in the benign narrative structure of night and morning, the tales linger in darkness, in death, and—in particular—in drunkenness.

The first adventure of the Pickwick Club establishes both the comedy and the drinking. The day begins with Pickwick, 'burst[ing] like another sun from his slumbers',[21] and ends in the Bull Inn in Rochester, where the club members have stopped for the night. At the inn, The Pickwickians share several bottles of port with the novel's first (comic) villain, Mr Jingle. Jingle urges his fellow drinkers to pass the port around the 'way of the sun' establishing an ordered cosmos in which drinking aligns with the movement of the universe (port was always passed clockwise). The immediate effects connect Pickwick to that order and to the sun itself:

---

[20] Greenman, 'Alcohol, Comedy, and Ghosts', 4.
[21] Dickens, *The Pickwick Papers*, ed. James Kinsley (Oxford: Clarendon Press, 1986), chapter 2, page 7. Subsequent references are inserted parenthetically in the text by *PP* chapter, page.

> The wine was passed, and a fresh supply ordered. The visitor talked, the Pickwickians listened. Mr. Tupman felt every moment more disposed for the ball. Mr. Pickwick's countenance glowed with an expression of universal philanthropy; and Mr. Winkle, and Mr. Snodgrass, fell fast asleep. (*PP* 2, 7)

Ordered, even ranked in their relation to drink, like the good and bad drunks of Ernest Hemingway's *The Sun Also Rises*, the Pickwickians seem at this moment to be if not at home, at least in their proper place. Pickwick's 'glow[ing]' 'countenance' links him 'to the way of the sun' and to the diurnal rhythms of sleep and waking that shape this novel.

These rhythms of light and dark, night and day, also naturalize Mr Pickwick's first (narrative) experience of extreme drunkenness:

> Mr. Tupman looked round him. The wine which had exerted its somniferous influence over Mr. Snodgrass, and Mr. Winkle, had stolen upon the senses of Mr. Pickwick. That gentleman had gradually passed through the various stages which precede the lethargy produced by dinner, and its consequences. He had undergone the ordinary transitions from the height of conviviality to the depth of misery, and from the depth of misery, to the height of conviviality. Like a gas lamp in the street, with the wind in the pipe, he had exhibited for a moment an unnatural brilliancy: then sunk so low as to be scarcely discernible: after a short interval, he had burst out again, to enlighten for a moment, then flickered with an uncertain, staggering sort of light, and then gone out altogether. His head was sunk upon his bosom; and perpetual snoring, with a partial choke, occasionally, were the only audible indications of the great man's presence. (*PP* 2, 22–3)

Although this passage does suggest that there are 'consequences' to drinking too much, the gentle rhythms of the prose lull us into believing that these consequences are not serious. The repetitive structure of the passage invokes a sense of familiarity: the narrator seems to have seen this form of drunkenness before. Drunkenness happens—not just to Mr Pickwick but also to a large and familiar community of men. The conceit of Pickwick as a 'gas lamp', his 'light' borrowed from the sun of the previous passage, suggests affectionate parody. Not a sun but a gaslight, he flickers and 'goes out'—but not permanently. This is sleep, not death; we will see Mr Pickwick in the morning.

While Pickwick sleeps, fellow club member Mr Winkle gets equally drunk and enters a narrative stream that teases the reader with the solemnities of cause and effect. Challenged to a duel for insulting Dr Snapper, Mr Winkle admits that he cannot remember what he did the night before, searching his own coat for evidence that he was out and about the previous night:

> 'It must be so', said Mr. Winkle, letting the coat fall from his hands. 'I took too much wine after dinner, and have a very vague recollection of walking about the streets, and smoking a cigar afterwards. The fact is, I was very drunk;—I must have changed my coat—gone somewhere—and insulted somebody—I have no doubt of it; and this message is the terrible consequence.' (*PP* 2, 32)

For a moment, it seems drunkenness is taken seriously; it produces 'terrible consequence(s)'. Winkle will have recourse to this idiom a few pages later when he imagines the duel and the shooting skill of the doctor: 'The consequences may be dreadful,' says Mr Winkle. Mr Snodgrass's 'I hope not', is not terribly comforting here; the consequences of drunkenness look as if they might be, in fact, terrible, dreadful—even fatal (*PP* 2, 34). Of course, at the last moment, drunkenness proves inconsequential as the doctor realizes that Mr Winkle is not the man who insulted him. The text that seemingly admonishes Mr Winkle for his forgetting—his drunken blackout—allows us as readers to forget that drunkenness can have effects in the storyworld of the novel and in the real world the novel seals off.

Narrative forgetting is also linked to the idea of recovery, so prominent in the novels' many 'mornings after'. The Wellers, father and son, recover especially easily. After a night of noisy drinking that interrupts Mr Pickwick's sleep, Mr Weller easily washes away the effects of his over-indulgence: 'Early on the ensuing morning, Mr Weller was dispelling all the feverish remains of the previous evening's conviviality, through the instrumentality of a halfpenny shower-bath (having induced a young gentleman attached to the stable-department, by the offer of that coin, to pump over his head and face, until he was perfectly restored)' (*PP* 16, 233–4). The word 'fever', which acts as a sign of danger and disease in other contexts, is passed over quickly, cooled and 'dispelled' by a cheap bath and savvy management. It also does not seem to be contagious across genres in *Pickwick*—as we shall see.

The protections of the comic plot are also afforded to another danger commonly associated with drinking: wife beating. One of the famous conversations about 'widders' between Mr Weller and Sam includes a joke about this topic. In a drunken conversation over beef, bread, and ale, Mr Weller makes fun of Sam for having been 'gammoned' by Jingle. Sam responds with a sly remark about 'widders'—an allusion to his father's second marriage. Mr Weller retorts that 'that's a wery different thing. You know what the counsel said, Sammy, as defended the gen'l'm'n as beat his wife with the poker, venever he got jolly. "And arter all, my Lord", says he, "it's amable weakness." So I says respectin' widders, Sammy, and so you'll say, ven you gets as old as I am' (*PP* 23, 344). Mr Weller is, of course, not represented as beating his own wife—indeed he seems to be in thrall to her powers. Wife beating appears as a topic safely ensconced in one of Weller's comic analogies; what would be shocking in another setting, another genre, another kind of sentence, becomes part of the fabric of *Pickwick*'s comedy.

The Pickwick Papers, however, is not merely a picaresque novel of adventure. Despite its dominant temporal structure, it does not always move relentlessly forward. To quote George Eliot in *Adam Bede*, there are places where the story 'pauses a little'.[22] These pauses take the form of the novel's nine interpolated tales, stories told by the Pickwickians or by characters they meet on their journeys, often at inns and pubs. These tales, embedded in, and to some extent sealed off from, their parent plot, mark the

---

[22] George Eliot, *Adam Bede*, ed. Valentine Cunningham (Oxford: Oxford University Press, 1996), 175.

presence not only of a different genre and a darker tone but also of a different temporality and a different relation to cause and effect.[23]

If we think thematically, four of the tales in particular, 'The Stroller's Tale', 'The Convict's Return', 'The Queer Client', and 'The Story of the Goblins Who Stole a Sexton', feature stories of alcohol abuse. If we think structurally, they differ from the comic novel that hosts them because they follow a different and dysphoric logic. The first of the stories, 'The Stroller's Tale', offers a logic of inevitability at odds with the comic narrative:

> The man of whom I speak was a low pantomime actor; and, like many people of his class, an habitual drunkard. In his better days, before he had become enfeebled by dissipation and emaciated by disease, he had been in the receipt of a good salary, which, if he had been careful and prudent, he might have continued to receive for some years—not many; because these men either die early, or, by unnaturally taxing their bodily energies, lose, prematurely, those physical powers. (*PP* 3, 42)

Gone is the benign spectre of working-class pleasure; the stroller's class inserts him into a master-narrative of drink and decay. The tenses with which his story is told underscore a sense of the inevitable; when we meet him at the beginning of the tale his story is in some sense already over; he has already 'become' 'enfeebled' and 'emaciated'. A more hopeful, optative mode is quickly shut down; if the stroller had been 'more careful and prudent' he might have lived longer—but not much. He is (and has been) doomed to die 'prematurely', the future tense implied as the future is shortened.

The old man who tells the story of 'The Queer Client' introduces the inevitable in another way—in this case before his narrative even begins. When Mr Pickwick observes that the Inns of Court are 'singular old places', the old man counters by identifying them with and as scenes of tragedy. 'Look at them', he says, appropriating the idiom associated with Pickwick's cheer,

> in another light: their most common-place and least romantic: what fine places of slow torture they are. Think of the needy man who has spent his all, beggared himself, and pinched his friends, to enter the profession, which is destined never to yield a morsel of bread to him. The waiting—the hope—the disappointment—the fear—the misery—the poverty—the blight on his hopes, and end to his career—the suicide perhaps, or the shabby, slip-shod drunkard. (*PP* 21, 306)

---

[23] Edgar Johnson was among the first to take these tales seriously. For Johnson, the 'presence of the tales "betrays a vein of morbid horror" ' indicative of Dickens's 'submerged griefs and fears' (*Charles Dickens: His Tragedy and Triumph*, 2 vols (New York: Simon and Schuster, 1952), 1:163). Robert E. Lougy argues in his reading of 'comic' in 'The Parish Clerk' that not all the tales are dark, while Robert L. Patten notes that the difference between the tales and the rest of the novel are analogous to the distinction between literature and life (Lougy, 'Pickwick and "The Parish Clerk" ', *Nineteenth-Century Fiction* 25, 1 (1970): 100–4; and Patten 'The Art of Pickwick's Interpolated Tales', *ELH* 34 1967): 349–66).

The long last sentence of this passage, with dashes between progressively more negative terms, suggests a forward movement, a falling even, into the status of a 'suicide' or 'a drunkard'. The relentless parallel structure of the sentence makes it clear that 'suicide', finally, is a noun. To *be* a suicide rather than to commit suicide is to be robbed even of this final agency. The path from 'waiting' to 'slip-shod drunkard', is a slippery one.

Remembering and Forgetting

If *Pickwick* segregates comic and tragic relations to alcohol explicitly by genre, the later and more fully novelistic *David Copperfield* does so by more subtle contradictions between genre and plot. As with *Pickwick*, the comic and the tragic versions are entangled in different temporalities, different understandings of progress and of the relation of the past to the present and to the future. As a *Bildungsroman*, *Copperfield*'s main plot of David's development is by definition forward looking; borrowing to some extent from the episodic nature of the picaresque, it is, of course, more completely invested in the growth of character. David's single and highly humorous experience of drinking too much is confined to only one night and two chapters; it ends with Agnes's promise not to think of it again. Agnes's father's alcoholism, on the other hand, makes use of a dysphoric temporality and a completely opposite relation to the past, to memory, and to the logic of consequence.[24]

David's night of drunkenness at his housewarming dinner in the company of Steerforth and his two friends experiments with the limits of first-person narration: David is telling in retrospect what his drunkenness might be assumed to cause him to forget. David's initial confusions have to do, appropriately for the genre, with the boundaries of the self:

> Somebody was leaning out of my bed-room window, refreshing his forehead against the cool stone of the parapet, and feeling the air upon his face. It was myself. I was addressing myself as 'Copperfield,' and saying, 'Why did you try to smoke? You might have known you couldn't do it.' Now, somebody was unsteadily contemplating his features in the looking-glass. That was I too. I was very pale in the looking-glass; my eyes had a vacant appearance; and my hair—only my hair, nothing else—looked drunk. (*DC* 24, 308)

While this passage hints of a self-dissolution and of the undoing of the first person that David has so carefully and painfully established, it does so comically, as David takes up a series of narrative positions and points of view, speaking in the first, second, and third person. The description of his drunkenness also, of course, suggests temporal

---

[24] Dickens, *David Copperfield*, ed. Nina Burgess (Oxford: Clarendon Press, 1981). Subsequent references are inserted parenthetically in the text by *DC* chapter, page.

disorientation: the first of three paragraphs to start with 'Somebody', this passage begins a carefully disjointed representation of the four men's journey from David's lodging to the theatre, in which David is consistently surprised by the appearance of new places and people—including, soberly, Agnes, who is at the same play. Drunkenness disconnects cause and effect.

A new chapter set the morning after the debauch opens in the discourse of consequences: 'But the agony of mind, the remorse, and shame I felt, when I became conscious next day! My horror of having committed a thousand offenses I had forgotten, and which nothing could ever expiate—my recollection of that indelible look which Agnes had given me' (*DC* 24, 310). The fear here is not only that he has committed offences, but also that he has forgotten them. The only thing he remembers suggests that consequences are permanent: he recalls Agnes's 'indelible look'.

The novel gives us not only the morning after, but also the morning after that, when David re-enters the world after being nursed through his hangover by his landlady, Mrs Crupp. While that timeline of shame and remorse is inserted carefully into linear time, two days after the party, David notes a disturbance in temporality: 'I was going out at [sic] my door on the morning after that deplorable day of headache, sickness, and repentance, with an odd confusion in mind relative to the date of my dinner-party as if a body of Titans had taken an enormous lever and pushed the day before yesterday some months back' (*DC* 25, 311). It is worth noting the oddness of this timeline: David, worried that Agnes will remember and not forgive, and thus that his sins will be 'indelibly' part of any future he might have with her, is also pushing the episode that he fears will affect the future further back into the past. This may be the beginning of a self-forgiveness that Agnes will convert into her own idiom.

And that idiom turns forgiveness into forgetting. When they finally meet, Agnes initially asks forgiveness from David for presuming to give him advice about associating with Steerforth in the future. David responds in defence of his friend, ' "I will forgive you, Agnes," I replied, "when you come to do Steerforth justice, and to like him as well as I do." ' Agnes's '[n]ot until then?' suggests that this day may be a long way off. It is only after this that David himself asks for forgiveness: ' "And when, Agnes, will you forgive me the other night?" "When I recall it", said Agnes' (*DC* 25, 314). This is, at least as David reads (and recalls) it, not simply a pardon but an absolution. Agnes is saying that she will *not* 'recall' 'the other night'. Of course, this is not quite what Agnes says. One could interpret her comment differently as suggesting that each time Agnes 'recalls' David's drunkenness she will forgive it. Since we do not see into Agnes's thoughts here or elsewhere, we have no access to her own temporalities that David writes into his own narrative. David as character and as narrator seems to take her comments as permission to move on, to write 'that night' off into an episodic past and to interpret it as a stage in his personal development. The exchange between Agnes and David, mediated through the retrospective first person and through the genre of the *Bildungsroman*, suggests that both David's forgetting and remembering are strategic, a possibility that becomes more likely if we compare the representation of David's drunkenness to the depiction of the alcoholism of his future father-in-law.

If Agnes's future husband is granted the protections of the *Bildungsroman*, her father is not. Mr Wickfield enters the text marked by a history of alcohol consumption that is immediately legible to David as narrator: 'He had a very agreeable face, and, I thought, was handsome. There was a certain richness in his complexion, which I had been long accustomed, under Peggotty's tuition, to connect with port wine; and I fancied it was in his voice too, and referred his growing corpulency to the same cause' (*DC* 15, 188). David's education—his *Bildung*—has prepared him to interpret the signs of 'port wine', and to speak in the language of 'cause' and effect. In this case, as in the case of *Nicholas Nickleby*'s Newman Noggs, a man's red face indexes an unalterable past and points to a tragic future.[25] The temporal trajectory of the tragic drunk is so established that David can read a 'growing corpulency' onto a body he has seen for the first time. Facial marks of drunkenness do not always precipitate a tragic plot in Dickens—even in the darker novels. Captain Cuttle of *Dombey and Son* is remarkable for the knobs on his face and for madeira drinking, but we are never invited into a narrative of his past or allowed to think (for long) that his will be a tragic ending.[26] Cuttle is in some ways reminiscent of earlier books and earlier logics, in which drinking is associated with comic language and comic protections.

There are no such safeguards for Mr Wickfield against the effects of liquor or the plotting of Uriah Heep, who preys on his employer's weakness. For those like Cordery who understand Wickfield's drunkenness as simply instrumental on Dickens's part, Wickfield's breakdown—the 'bottom' in AA's drunkalogue[27]—might show Wickfield (and Dickens) going through the motions:

> 'Oh, Trotwood, Trotwood!' exclaimed Mr. Wickfield, wringing his hands. 'What I have come down to be, since I first saw you in this house! I was on my downward way then, but the dreary, dreary, road I have traversed since! Weak indulgence has ruined me. Indulgence in remembrance, and indulgence in forgetfulness. My natural grief for my child's mother turned to disease; my natural love for my child turned to disease. I have infected everything I touched.' (*DC* 39, 493)

Here Wickfield—and perhaps Dickens behind him—is clearly articulating a disease model of alcohol. But that model is also, crucially, a temporal one. Alcoholism is not so much, or not only, about an 'indulgence' in drink, but an indulgence in 'remembering' and 'forgetting'—an indulgence in inappropriate relationships to time.

In a first-person retrospective narrative, the question of memory becomes crucial. Forgetting can happen both on the level of character (David's drunkenness is not mentioned again, either by Agnes or by David) and on the level of narrative. David

---

[25] Dickens, *Nicholas Nickleby*, ed. Paul Schlicke, Oxford World's Classics (Oxford: Oxford University Press, 2008).

[26] Dickens, *Dombey and Son*, ed. Alan Horsman (Oxford: Clarendon Press, 1974).

[27] Robyn R. Warhol and Helena Michie, 'Twelve-Step Teleology: Narratives of Recovery/Recovery as Narrative', in Sidonie Smith and Julia Watson (eds), *Getting a Life: Everyday Uses of Autobiography* (Minneapolis: University of Minnesota Press, 1996), 327–50.

must remember what he can of his drunken night to be able to tell his story, but he can also choose what story to tell. John Jordan has suggested that David's narrative is in fact strategic: that he remembers (and forgets) in order to place himself in the best possible moral light. For Jordan, this self-serving manipulation of narrative is evident, for example, in David's relationship with Steerforth:

> It is important to emphasize that almost never in his narrative does David face up to the possibility of his involvement in Steerforth's [seduction of Emily]. Thus, to the extent that he is complicitous in the crime (and this judgment will vary for different readers), he is also, as the narrator of these events, 'blind, blind, blind' to the motives of his actions as well as to the evasions in his retrospective account of them.[28]

Like Jordan, I am unsure about the extent to which Dickens was aware of, ironic about, or identified with David's evasions—about whether, in other words, David's forgetting is thematized by something I would like, however problematically, to call 'the novel', an entity that includes David, Dickens, and the form and genre in which the story is told.[29] My instinct is to see the Wickfield story as conforming to a particular master-narrative of drunkenness with its own rhythms of cause and effect, remembering and forgetting. That master-narrative returns us to the question of genre. Wickfield's story bears the marks of melodrama; like the interpolated tales in the picaresque, Wickfield's tale of sin and repentance belongs to an embedded genre at odds with, but at the same time constitutive of, the genre of the main story. David's narrative complicity is enabled by the temporality of the *Bildungsroman* and by the narrative exigencies of retrospection. The novel, then, like Mr Wickfield himself, is caught between remembering and forgetting, 'indulging' at different times in each.

This chapter has attempted to bring together the insights of addiction studies with work on Dickens. There is much more that could be done by revisiting some of the older critics on orality who look at other forms of bodily consumption in Dickens. There is a need for more work on Dickens and food, on the mutton chops and loins that are eaten alongside alcoholic beverages, and on the salmon and other foods that are used as euphemisms for drinking but have their own histories and their own temporalities, their own pleasures and dangers (*PP* 8, 117). I would see this not as a psychoanalytic but as a materialist project, attentive, like Elaine Freedgood's *The Ideas in Things*, both to histories of production and consumption and to literary meaning-making.[30] One area of inspiration for this kind of work on food might be the work on food and narrative from the special issue of *Victorian Literature and Culture* on 'Food and the Victorians',

---

[28] John O. Jordan, 'The Social Sub-text of *David Copperfield*', *Dickens Studies Annual* 14 (1985): 61–92, 70.

[29] Ibid., 64.

[30] Elaine Freedgood, *The Ideas in Things: Fugitive Meanings in the Victorian Novel* (Chicago: University of Chicago Press, 2006).

selected articles from which are listed below as further reading. As the editors to the collection point out, Victorian food studies

> may be categorized as having a number of (frequently intertwined strands) ... food as commodity, a significant aspect of the economic life of the period; the social history of food as part of Victorian domestic life ... restaurants and dining out ... food and drink in law and politics; the politics of famine and starvation; and food as an international or imperial phenomenon.[31]

All these approaches would be useful in helping to think systematically through the work of the author who makes readers so hungry.

This piece has also, I hope, contributed to studies of temporality and narration in Dickens. There remains more to be said in the context of a wider and deeper temporality studies that treat time both as a narrative component and as an epistemology. Again, such studies could have a materialist basis, exploring, as does Jonathan H. Grossman, the temporal rhythms of institutions and networks in which Victorian life and Dickens's novels were embedded.

Further Reading

Andrea L Broomfield, *Food and Cooking in Victorian England: A History* (New York: Praeger, 2007)
Lindsey Chappell, 'Dickensian Dimensions of Time', *Victorian Review* 42, 1 (2016): 45–64
Jonathan H. Grossman, *Charles Dickens's Networks: Public Transport and the Novel* (New York: Oxford University Press, 2012)
Gwen Hyman, '"An Infernal Fire in my Veins": Gentlemanly Drinking in *The Tenant of Wildfell Hall*', *Victorian Literature and Culture* 36, 2 (November 2008): 451–70
Ian Miller, 'Feeding in the Workhouse: The Institutional and Ideological Functions of Food in Britain, ca. 1834–70', *Journal of British Studies* 52, 4 (October 2013): 940–62
Tara Moore, 'Starvation in Victorian Christmas Fiction', *Victorian Literature and Culture* 36, 2 (November 2008): 489–506
Kathleen Pacious, 'Misdirections, Delayed Disclosures, and Ethics of the Telling in Charles Dickens's *Our Mutual Friend*', *Narrative* 24, 3 (2016): 330–50

---

[31] Suzanne Daly and Ross G. Forman, 'Introduction: Cooking Culture: Situating Food and Drink in the Nineteenth Century', *Victorian Literature and Culture* 36, 2 (November 2008): 365.

CHAPTER 41

COGNITIVE DICKENS

CHIP BADLEY AND KAY YOUNG

'The old unhappy loss or want of something'
David Copperfield[1]

BROKEN BRAINS, BROKEN ATTACHMENTS

THE work of cognitive literary studies is to explore the relation of how literature 'minds' to how humans mind; that is, it pursues a comparative study of the neurocognitive framework of literary and lived experience. Further, it considers how the study of literature and the mind–brain disciplines might inform and enhance the understandings of each other. Current research in cognitive neuroscience, affective neuroscience, developmental psychology, psychoanalysis, and philosophy no longer imagine an isolated mind or thinking brain separable from our embodied, emotional, relational selves.[2] Our work as cognitive literary theorists should reflect this conception of the integrated mind–brain—as embodied, thinking, feeling, and relational—a conception Dickens seems to anticipate.[3] To 'mind Dickens', then, means to read for more than Dickens's

---

[1] Charles Dickens, *David Copperfield*, ed. Nina Burgis (Oxford: Clarendon Press, 1981), chapter 44, page 552. Subsequent references are inserted parenthetically in the text by *DC* chapter, page.

[2] Antonio Damasio, *Descartes' Error: Emotion, Reason, and the Human Brain* (New York: Avon, 1994); Damasio, *The Feeling of What Happens: Body and Emotion in the Making of Consciousness* (Orlando, FL: Harcourt, 1999); Jaak Panksepp, *Affective Neuroscience: The Foundations of Human and Animal Emotions* (New York: Oxford University Press, 1998). See also Lisa Feldman Barrett, Paula M. Niedenthal, and Piotr Winkielman (eds), *Emotion and Consciousness* (New York: The Guilford Press, 2005) and Luiz Pessoa, *The Cognitive-Emotional Brain: From Interactions to Integration* (Cambridge, MA: The MIT Press, 2013).

[3] William A. Cohen, *Embodied: Victorian Literature and the Senses* (Minneapolis: University of Minnesota Press, 2009); John O. Jordan, *Supposing* Bleak House (Charlottesville: University of Virginia Press, 2011); Kay Young, ' "Wounded by Mystery": Dickens and Attachment Theory', *English* 61, 234 (September 2012): 234–47; Karen Chase, *Eros & Psyche: The Representation of Personality in Charlotte Brontë, Charles Dickens, and George Eliot* (New York: Methuen, 1984).

literary expression of thinking. It means to be alert both to the current research on the integrated mind–brain and to how Dickens reflects, disturbs, and informs those theories through his narrative art. An important focus of this query is to ask what happens when thinking and feeling split? The novels of Charles Dickens find a source of their power in the representation of that problem—as embodied dissociation—and in the recognition of a primary cause for such splitting—the trauma of insecure or broken attachment.

Dorothy Van Ghent's *The English Novel: Form and Function* (1953), one of the great gems of literary criticism on the English novel, offers a remarkably contemporary cognitive study of the 'mindedness' of *Great Expectations*. We turn back to Van Ghent's reading for how her close attention to style leads her to uncover significant functions of consciousness peculiar to Dickens's writing and, too, for how it looks ahead to our focus on that mindedness set in relation to current research in the mind–brain sciences. Van Ghent's discussion of 'Dickens's mindedness' begins from its own return to V. S. Pritchett's *The Living Novel* (1947), with its drilling down to what Pritchett calls 'the distinguishing quality of Dickens's people':

> [T]hey are solitaries. They are people caught in a world of their own. They soliloquise in it. They do not talk to one another; they talk to themselves. The pressure of society has created fits of twitching in mind and speech, and fantasies in the soul … The solitariness of people is paralleled by the solitariness of things. Fog operates as a separate presence, houses quietly rot or boisterously prosper on their own … The people and the things of Dickens are all out of touch and out of hearing of each other, each conducting its own inner monologue, grandiloquent or dismaying. By this dissociation Dickens brings to us something of the fright of childhood.[4]

What is the relation between how Dickens writes dissociation and 'something of the fright of childhood'? Van Ghent takes that question as she works to uncover Dickens's 'technique' and its relation to 'vision':

> Technique is vision. Dickens' technique is an index of a vision of life that sees human separateness as the ordinary condition, where speech is speech *to* nobody and where human encounter is mere collision. But the vision goes much further. Our minds are so constituted that they insist on seeking in the use of language an exchange function, a delivery and a passing on of perceptions from soul to soul and generation to generation, binding them in some kind of order; and they insist on finding cause and effect, or *motivation*, in the displacements and encounters of persons or things. Without the primary patterns of perception we would not have what we call minds. And when these patterns are confused or abrogated by our experience, we are forced, in order to preserve some kind of psychic equilibrium, to seek them in extraordinary explanations—explanations in terms of mutual exchange and cause and effect. Dickens saw his world patently in pieces, and as a child's vision would offer some reasonable explanation of why such a world was that way—and, by

---

[4] V. S. Pritchett, *The Living Novel* (New York: Reynal and Hitchcock, 1947), 88.

the act of explanation, would make that world yield up a principle of order, however obscure or fantastic—so, with a child's literalism of imagination, he discovered organization among his fragments.[5]

Van Ghent suggests no less than a definition of mind here in her consideration of Dickens's technique. What we 'call minds' are, for Van Ghent, chiefly our perceptions, our need to share those perceptions, our desire to derive an order or pattern to our perceptions, and our attributing of cause and effect or motivation to them. Van Ghent derives this definition of mind from how Dickens's art jars us with its strange attributes of vision, fragmented, dissociated, fantastic, and she will add, 'daemonic'[6] and 'nervous'.[7] How difficult it is for Dickens's characters to share perceptions, perhaps most especially when bound to first-person narratives. What is an autobiographical text, after all, but an extended soliloquy? Dickens's first-person narrators prompt us to wonder to whom David Copperfield or Esther Summerson or Pip speak about their perceptions, if there is a listener, and, if there is, is it a listener who understands or cares? More generally, as Dickens readers we must wonder what motivates the often bizarre or illegible acts of others or strange presence of things in the Dickensian world, is there is an order or pattern discernible that makes 'sense' of things, to whom does it fall to try to discern an order or make sense, and if this is possible. Van Ghent derives a final attribute of mind, namely, that when bound to such a dissociated universe, the mind needs to create extraordinary explanations so as to create and maintain 'psychic equilibrium'. Who better to imagine fantastic explanations when reasonable forms of motivation or cause and effect are nowhere to be found than a child? For Van Ghent, the child protagonist becomes the functional means through which Dickens, who 'saw his world patently in pieces', can bring the parts and fragments together through extraordinary feats of magical, associative thinking.

A remarkable close reading of Dickens leads Van Ghent to an understanding of what it means to have a mind—what a mind does, what it needs to do, and what happens to it when those needs aren't met or are perverted or disturbed—that mostly squares with contemporary definitions of mind in the mind–brain sciences. This is what remarkable cognitive readings of the narrative arts can do—help reveal the nature of our narrative minds, how we narrate and why. They help define the nature of mind. Dickens's definition of mind emphasizes the social and environmental dimensions of thought. According to his working definition of mind, social identity and cognitive abilities constitute one another: they can assume the form of what Alan Palmer refers to as 'social minds'[8] or Michael Peled Ginsburg the 'scene of recognition';[9] the relationship

---

[5] Dorothy Van Ghent, *The English Novel: Form and Function* (New York: Rinehart & Company, 1953), 127–8 (emphasis original).
[6] Ibid., 129.
[7] Ibid., 134.
[8] Alan Palmer, *Social Minds in the Novel* (Columbus: The Ohio State University Press, 2010).
[9] Michael Peled Ginsburg, 'Dickens and the Scene of Recognition', *Partial Answers: Journal of Literature and the History of Ideas* 3, 2 (June 2005): 75–97.

between child and family; infant and child mental states; and the orphan's lack of social connections.[10]

Taken alongside recent work on the environmental nature of cognition—especially in terms of architecture[11] as well as interiority and solitude[12]—these critics suggest the ways in which the (neuro)plastic mind can be altered, enhanced, and even wounded in relation to its surroundings. Our interest in attachment arises from this model of socially and environmentally influenced cognition: that mental and emotional states are concomitant with bodily movement through spaces and communities. But if a healthy mind is one that can safely—securely—attach to others and the idea of home, Dickens is drawn to the unhealthy extreme, often writing of broken brains made broken by the trauma of severed attachments: orphanhood (the loss of the parent), vagrancy or picaresque wandering (the loss of home), and death (the loss of relation). Just as the specific stories and traumas of each of Dickens's orphans (in particular, Pip, David Copperfield, and Esther Summerson) remain unique, so too do their impairments: dissociation, faulty Theory of Mind, faulty problem solving, moments of amnesia or of traumatic repetition, and experiences of a 'false self'. Fragmented, dissociative mind states, we suggest, permeate Dickens's art (and we mean by this not just his representations of 'human' minds but more generally how he minds his narrative universe) and reveal a constitution of mind in the way that the lesion method of analysis of an injured or diseased brain reveals to neuroscientists the constitution of the brain. Critics and readers alike have sensed Dickens's interest in depicting the fragmented or dissociative mind: how it is ensnared by memories; how it reflects Victorian understandings of associationist psychology; how it compulsively returns to and works though trauma in dreams; how it is subject to returns of the repressed or suppressed; and how it might accompany states of physical disability or emerge from an interest in evolution and spiritualism.[13] This sample of critical interest suggests the extent to which Dickens both chronicles and

---

[10] Catherine Waters, *Dickens and the Politics of the Family* (Cambridge: Cambridge University Press, 1997); Lynn Cain, *Dickens, Family, Authorship: Psychoanalytic Perspectives on Kinship and Creativity* (Burlington, VT: Ashgate, 2008); Rosemarie Bodenheimer, 'Dickens and the Knowing Child', in Peter Merchant and Catherine Waters (eds), *Dickens and the Imagined Child* (New York: Routledge, 2015), 13–26; Baruch Hochman and Ilja Wachs, *Dickens: The Orphan Condition* (Cranbury, NJ: Fairleigh Dickinson University Press, 1999).

[11] Lauren Cameron, 'Interiors and Interiorities: Architectural Understandings of the Mind in *Hard Times*', *Nineteenth-Century Contexts* 35, 1 (February 2013): 65–79.

[12] Stella Pratt-Smith, 'All in the Mind: The Psychological Realism of Dickensian Solitude', *Dickens Quarterly* 26, 1 (March 2009): 15–23.

[13] Mitsuharu Matsuoka, 'Slips of Memory and Strategies of Silence in *A Tale of Two Cities*', *The Dickensian* 100 (June 2004): 111–20; Sarah Winter, *The Pleasures of Memory: Learning to Read with Charles Dickens* (New York: Fordham University Press, 2011); Ronald R. Thomas, *Dreams of Authority: Freud and the Fictions of the Unconscious* (Ithaca, NY: Cornell University Press, 1990); Warrington Winters, 'Dickens and the Psychology of Dreams', *PMLA* 63, 3 (September 1948): 984–1006; John Gordon, *Sensation and Sublimation in Charles Dickens* (New York: Palgrave Macmillan, 2011); Nancy Engbretsten Lind, '"The Mind of the Heart": Mr Dick's Percipience', *The Dickensian* 108, 486 (Spring 2012): 19–22; Anna Neill, *Primitive Minds: Evolution and Spiritual Experience in the Victorian Novel* (Columbus: The Ohio State University Press, 2013).

incorporates disruptive mental states in the service of narrative. The interwoven threads of narrative mystery (detective fiction), readerly uncertainty (suspicion), and broken attachments (the pang of not knowing yourself or others) all inform Dickens's portraits of the wounded mind.

The social upheavals of nineteenth-century England ('the pressure of society', as Pritchett calls it) makes sense of the Dickensian art of dissociation as a divisive force from *without*. Recent research in attachment theory and its relation to cognition regarding upsetting or ending traditional forms of social affiliation makes sense of dissociated mind states from *within*. Research on topics as diverse as embodied thought, psychoanalytic identity, attachment theory, and emotional life often turn to Dickens because he seems to have understood something in the nineteenth century that we are now corroborating with scientific, psychoanalytic, or philosophical research in the twentieth and twenty-first centuries: that feeling states suffuse, and indeed are, mental states.

How do broken attachments and broken brains converge in 'the fright of childhood'? How do attachment theory and cognitive studies reveal their relation, and how does Dickens? These are the questions that prompt our turn to the mind–brain sciences. While all Dickens's orphan novels may not follow the cognitive model we outline of broken attachment and its mental consequences so closely as they do for *Great Expectations, David Copperfield*, and *Bleak House*, we offer our hypothesis for how Dickens 'minds' as stimulation for future generations of cognitive literary scholars to consider. Such an integrated imagining—not only between literature and the mind–brain sciences but also between thinking, feeling, and embodiment—can only help us better understand what makes the mind and art of Charles Dickens.

Our Cause-Hungry Minds

We infer. This is what human brains do. This is what Van Ghent means when she writes, '[Our minds] insist on finding cause and effect, or *motivation*, in the displacements and encounters of persons or things.' Sometimes with conscious attention, but mostly with unconscious processing, we move through life drawing inferences about the nature of things, most of all, about the nature of ourselves in relation to those other things—cause and effect, self in relation to other, my story in relation to yours. Psychologist of judgement and decision-making, Daniel Kahneman in *Thinking, Fast and Slow* describes our minds as 'hungry for causal stories';[14] this is how we make sense of things. Dickens's orphan protagonists are hungry for the causes of their stories, the desire for what Mr Wickfield in *David Copperfield* will call a 'master motive' (*DC* 42, 526).[15] With

---

[14] Daniel Kahneman, *Thinking, Fast and Slow* (New York: Farrar, Straus and Giroux, 2011), 167.
[15] Daniel N. Stern refers to this as the infant's sense of a 'verbal self'—one that emerges through symbolic representation—in *The Interpersonal World of the Infant: A View from Psychoanalysis & Developmental Psychology* (New York: Basic Books, 1985), 162–84.

some part of their origins unknown, they don't accept that blank space, and so they fill in the space of their empty origins by making inferences.

'There is a deep gap between our thinking about statistics and our thinking about individual cases,' writes Kahneman,

> Statistical results with a causal interpretation have a stronger effect on our thinking than noncausal information. But even compelling causal statistics will not change long-held beliefs or beliefs rooted in personal experience. *On the other hand surprising individual cases* have a powerful impact and are a more effective tool for teaching psychology because the incongruity must be resolved and embedded in a causal story.[16]

Dickens understands and shows us how we infer the general from the particular, how we look for causes, how we need to solve incongruities, mysteries, and the unknown in the stories he tells of his particular orphans and the universes their narratives engender—even if more often than not his orphans get their inferences wrong. As one of the great innovators of detective fiction, Dickens writes to our cause-hungry, inference-making minds: we grasp at whatever scrap of certainty we glimpse in his novels' shadowy realms. What Elaine Auyoung defines as the 'epistemological orientation' of *Bleak House* can be said to stand for Dickens's career as a whole: a constant state of not-knowing, of 'not being in a position to know that something exists'.[17] In *Bleak House*, a novel of opacities, the reader, along with Esther Summerson, must get to the bottom of these mysteries. To solve the mysteries of the plot is to solve the mysteries of one's origins, to perceive one's sense of self implicated by, and subject to, the mysteries of another. For Auyoung, Dickens in *Bleak House* 'self-consciously points up the reader's own condition of dependence upon what does and does not appear on the printed page';[18] this is part and parcel of what Kahneman describes as our hunger for explanation and knowledge.[19]

This explanation-seeking curiosity, which Maria K. Bachman claims 'as [both] a cognitive and affective state',[20] undergirds the Dickens novel. In *Great Expectations*, Pip recounts what the Constables and Bow-street men from London do to solve the case of Mrs Joe's 'blow from behind',[21] 'what I have heard and read of like authorities doing in

---

[16] Kahneman, *Thinking, Fast and Slow*, 174 (emphasis ours).

[17] Elaine Auyoung, 'Standing Outside *Bleak House*', *Nineteenth-Century Literature* 68, 2 (September 2013): 180–200, 182 and 181.

[18] Ibid., 184.

[19] Perhaps serialization speaks to the persistence of our need to infer amidst Dickens's dense, complex novels: just as we perceive an individual narrative more clearly than general data, maybe Dickens crafts his collage-like plots so that we can deduce, in microcosmic detail, from each instalment.

[20] Maria K. Bachman, 'Who Cares? Novel Reading, Narrative Attachment Disorder, and the Case of *The Old Curiosity Shop*', *Journal of Narrative Theory* 37, 2 (Summer 2007): 296–325, 298.

[21] Dickens writes, '[S]he had been knocked down by a tremendous blow on the back of the head, dealt with some unknown hand'; *Great Expectations*, ed. Margaret Cardwell (Oxford: Clarendon Press, 1993), volume I, chapter 15, page 119. Subsequent references are inserted parenthetically in the text by *GE* volume:chapter, page. Mrs Joe's experience of the 'blow from behind' literalizes in its embodiment how Dickens's orphans come to knowledge of the past and, more often than not, its unwelcome truths.

other such cases. They took up several obviously wrong people, and ran their heads very hard against wrong ideas, and persisted in trying to fit the circumstances to the ideas, instead of trying to extract ideas from the circumstances' (*GE* I:16, 121). How we draw our inferences often fits more with what we seek than with what the evidence shows. Or the appearance of things may seem to make an inference obvious, occluding the truth behind that appearance, as Jaggers reminds Pip: 'Take nothing on its looks; take everything on evidence' (*GE* III:1, 334). Like Dickens's orphans, we fill in the blanks of our stories and infer truths or ideas around which we organize our sense of self, our place in the world, and how to be with others in it. And we do so in relation to our longings and our mistaking appearances for evidence. Are you my mother? Are you my benefactor? Are you someone on whom I should model my identity or imagine my future? These are the questions to which the cause-hungry minds of Dickens's orphans seek answers, which is to say, from which they seek to infer a sense of identity and a meaning of life. The individual scenes of seeking in Dickens's novels stand out as strange situations, memorable for how surprising they are as individual cases and for how important they will prove to be in the orphan's resolution-seeking and inference-drawing with regard to his or her individual story.

Signature Repetition

Whom will the orphan child find behind the next door or around the next corner or tombstone? Dickens's adult characters are a collection of bizarre traits, in their extremity and in their consistency. How remarkable for dissociated body parts or tic of language or gesture to roam a narrative universe, as if freed from the whole to which they belong by Dickens's privileging, emphasis, and repetition of description. Dickens's narrative universe is an assemblage of fragments dissociated from some forever lost, but still sought-for and yearned for 'whole'. These dissociated parts await inference-drawing—they are clues-in-waiting. Jaggers repeatedly washes his hands, hands that announce his embodied presence with their scent; Joe will say '[E]ver the best of friends' (*GE* I:18, 140) to Pip, repeatedly, like an epithet that tags their relationship (no matter how mostly one-sided its truth); Wemmick will soften his mouth and speak personally the further he is from the London office and will harden his mouth into a postal slot that speaks only in 'office talk' the closer he is to that office; Miss Havisham will never move from the scene or moment in time of her jilting. Dickens's adult characters are identifiable as characters by the traits that are particular to them, which is to say, his method of characterization is profoundly metonymic. The repetitions of Dickens's characters *are* his characters, and no repetitions are more important than his or her peculiar idiosyncrasies—for these repetitions most distinguish one from another and make visible traces of what lies hidden within (Dickens understood the somatized unconscious before Freud). In an influential reading of *Great Expectations*, Peter Brooks calls our attention to the way in which repetition in the plotting of our lives becomes a kind of 'binding, the creation of cohesion'[22] otherwise absent from psychic life. According to Brooks, this plotting and re-plotting emerges from a tension between an 'official' and a 'repressed' plot;[23] Pip repeatedly repudiates his primal guilt with Magwitch in order to become a gentleman. Along with other critics,[24] Brooks underscores Dickens's sense of the relationship between repetition or metonymy and how we structure our sense of the world. What's traumatic is the frequency with which 'repressed' plots return and impinge upon our meaning-making, inference seeking.

However strange Dickens's metonymic method (for who feels like a repeated assemblage of recurring parts?), our very legibility as ongoing identities to others and others' legibility to us depend on those repetitions and our capacity to read them. Daniel N. Stern, infant psychologist and psychiatrist, calls our attention to the 'signature' quality of character, or how it is that we differentiate between and choose to care about one versus another. His words help us to understand what 'the signatures of Dickens' people'[25] create. Stern writes:

> We see many acts performed by others every day. We attribute motives to them. We observe the manner in which they are accomplished. We grasp the context. But why do we care? How is the what, why, and how of any particular act lit up and selected as worth 'taking in', to internalize, or identify with, or empathize with? ...
>
> The act of another to be identified with must belong to that other specifically. *It must carry their personal signature.* It cannot be any member of a class of acts. The vitality of the forms of the actions of the other must be specific to them. It's what gives it its uniqueness.[26]

Like Van Ghent, Stern draws our attention to primary patterns of perception, but particularizes further from amongst these patterns when he asks the important question, 'Why do we care?' Signature traits act as a mechanism to arouse our interest. 'The selection of a specific other to identify with is primordial', Stern continues. 'That person must have a special relationship to us. We cannot get away from this notion. There must be a way that the behavior of the other has more value because of who they

---

[22] Peter Brooks, *Reading for the Plot: Design and Intention in Narrative* (New York: Vintage, 1984), 123–4.

[23] Ibid., 117.

[24] Lawrence Frank, 'In Hamlet's Shadow: Mourning and Melancholia in *Little Dorrit*', *SEL Studies in English Literature, 1500–1900* 52, 4 (Autumn 2012): 861–96; Jill L. Matus, 'Trauma, Memory, and Railway Disaster: The Dickensian Connection', *Victorian Studies* 43, 3 (Spring 2001): 413–36; John R. Reed, *Dickens's Hyperrealism* (Columbus: The Ohio State University Press, 2010); Athena Vrettos, 'Defining Habits: Dickens and the Psychology of Repetition', *Victorian Studies* 42, 3 (Spring 1999): 399–426, and 'Displaced Memories in Victorian Fiction and Psychology', *Victorian Studies* 49, 2 (Winter 2007): 199–207.

[25] Van Ghent, *The English Novel*, 130.

[26] Daniel N. Stern, *Forms of Vitality: Exploring Dynamic Experience in Psychology, the Arts, Psychotherapy, and Development* (Oxford: Oxford University Press, 2010), 142–3 (emphasis ours).

are to us, in reality or imagination.'[27] He calls those who carry the sense of special value to us 'charged others'.

Dickens presents his protagonist orphans with a vast array of others whose signature traits feel charged. But why they feel charged is a mystery. In part the charge comes from surprise—so strange, so new, so particular—the other's signature qualities demand attention. But Dickens writes into that space of surprise something more: the orphan mind's desire to fill in the specific other with whom to identify or from whom to infer that primordial connection. From the blankness of the most insecure attachment, the posthumous mother, the posthumous father, the posthumous parents, the Dickens orphan moves out into a world of possible attachments, each more strange than the next. What Pip observes, how David infers, what Esther feels, to whom Oliver attaches has everything to do with how their unattached or insecurely attached minds process. The Dickens universe of strange situations reflects the minds of the orphan protagonists who live in mystified relations to themselves, who suffer the 'blow from behind', not knowing from whom they come or where they belong or why they exist. The repetitions, the strange signature traits of Dickens's adult characters make it possible not only for the orphan mind to imagine a possible connection to the other but also to feel in ongoing ways that lost primordial relation—for who repeats without change, growth, or development? Each figure carries the deadliness of repetition without change. But each as well carries the possibility of attachment. So charged are the vast array of others in the Dickens universe because they are so observable in their idiosyncratic repetitions and metonymic presence (through their hands most of all), the orphan protagonist, so unknowing of his or her own story, moves in relation to the strange situation of these charged others with wonder. Are you my mother? Are you my benefactor? Are you a father-figure or a husband? The orphan moves from one charged other to the next, often in fear, always insecure, learning something, inferring something, getting something wrong so as to move on to the next in the hopes of getting something right. From out of a world of strange situations, in which the orphan must engage, one after another, comes a resolution to all that inferring—the story of the orphan's lost attachments and found identity—forged, no longer forgotten, yet still insecure. Why?

The Strange Situation

An infant between the ages of nine and eighteen months old and his mother are alone in an unfamiliar room. The room has toys or other interesting things in it, and the mother lets the young child explore the room on his own. After the child has had time to explore, a stranger enters the room and talks with the mother. Then the stranger shifts attention to the child. As the stranger approaches the child, the mother leaves. After several minutes, the mother returns. She comforts her child and then

---

[27] Stern, *Forms of Vitality*, 143.

leaves again. The stranger leaves as well. A few minutes later, the stranger returns and interacts with the child. Finally, the mother returns and greets her child.[28]

This scenario is called 'The Strange Situation', devised by attachment theorist Mary Ainsworth in 1978, as an instrument by which to assess the secure and insecure attachment styles of mothers and their young. The strange situation is unusual (an unknown room) and briefly stressful (mother leaves) but not overwhelming in its stress (mother returns) or in its unfamiliarity (it's a room with toys). Securely attached children will feel free to explore the room while the mother is present, will cry when she leaves, will hang on tight upon her return, and then will continue to play. They develop a secure base from which to explore the world, confident that there is a caregiver on whom they can depend, both in her ongoing presence and in her attunement to their needs. An insecurely attached child must move out into the world without such a secure base.

Might we imagine the novels of Charles Dickens as narratives of 'The Strange Situation' taken to the extreme? Mostly with no maternal figure with whom to attach or in relation to whom to explore the strange situation, the Dickens orphan must begin life from the strangest situation—motherless. All life is strange when there is no real home, no real mother to come home to. What does the Dickensian strange situation make? Fright, even terror, and the need to engage in a hyper vigilance of care that feels like a relentless emergency: Pay attention! Remember!—This moment!—This figure!—This case!—This particular object!—This peculiar trait!—most of all—This reminder of *the trauma* of what it means to be motherless or fatherless or both. '[S]o new here, and so strange, and so fine—and melancholy—' (*GE* I:8, 60) are the words Pip uses to define Miss Havisham's world and why he can't play there. They capture more generally Dickens's universe of the strangest situation of the motherless. *Great Expectations* thrusts the young Pip into one strange situation after another, one stranger than another, perhaps none stranger than the world of Miss Havisham and her dressing room of arrested bridal preparation, where he is told to play by a figure who lives embalmed by a moment of time, even as her living time passes. We, like Pip, read this old bride as a tableau vivant, stuck at 20 minutes to nine, one shoe still off, a veil not yet properly fixed—'Thou still unravished bride of solitude' transported from Keats's urn to narrative. What travels through time as a preserved object of the ancient, inspiring odes, inspires instead, when described as a living being, horror—'some ghastly wax-work at the Fair'; 'a skeleton in the ashes of a rich dress, that had been dug out of a vault under the church pavement' (*GE* I:8, 59). In *The Forms of Vitality*, Stern writes of the horror of seeing the dead and the infant's seeing of his mother's still face:

> Seeing a dead person is immediately shocking because they do not move, nothing moves, and even the almost subliminal vibrations of tonicity stop. We grasp this in a glance with peripheral vision. Without motion, we cannot read in or imagine mental

[28] Gwen Dewar, 'The Strange Situation Test', accessed 20 May 2016, <http://www.parentingscience.com/strange-situation.html>.

activity underneath, or thoughts, or emotions, or 'will.' That is how we know there is no vital presence.

Similarly, when a mother's face goes 'still face' while facing her infant, i.e., not moving her face at all, not even with the slightest expressions, the baby, or even neonate, becomes upset within seconds. Newborns already have working peripheral vision that is designed to detect motion at a periphery. Accordingly, stillness is registered no matter where their focal vision is on the mother's face.[29]

Stillness. The mother's still face to her infant. A dead body to anyone. The power of Dickens's scene finds its source in how life and death interact. The movement of life meets the stillness of death. The veil of life, like Miss Havisham's 'white veil dependent from her hair' (*GE* I:8, 58), stands next to death. Not underneath the Dickens narrative, and not just in *Great Expectations*, but throughout the Dickens canon, death lies above ground as part of the novel's foreground. It begins rather than ends the narrative; it catalyses the plot with regularity; it counters the comedic tone of vitality and the detective tone of suspense with the quiet knell of stillness, loss, and absence. What is a life that stops time in its stilling of movement? What is a death that continues to live and age? How is the desire to 'see some play' a 'sick fancy'? How does the aliveness of play feel like sick fancy when it is commanded by a stranger who embodies death's presence?

Miss Havisham, this 'impostor of a woman' (*GE* II:14, 266), as Estella comes to call her, acts here the impostor of a mother to young Pip—she is a force of anti-play and anti-life—by seeking Pip's sacrifice, his broken heart, to avenge hers. Likewise, Magwitch acts the impostor of a midwife when Pip's narrative begins in the cemetery of his buried family, and Magwitch turns him upside down and threatens to cut his throat. This is the traumatic birth of Pip and of the novel. Familial scenes as familiar scenes undergo radical de-familiarization. In the absence of parents, in the presence of monstrous surrogates, and in the juxtaposition of graveyard settings with life's progressions, Dickens's orphan child protagonists must try to make their way, essentially alone and unattached, to live and to have a life story. If the test of the strange situation makes attachment style visible, what Dickens's narratives make visible are the cognitive disturbances that accompany separation and loss—his rendering of the psychic experience of the orphan writ large as his narrative art.

ATTACHMENT AND COGNITION

The Dickensian orphan protagonist errs in important ways in his or her assessment of others' characters (exhibits *faulty Theory of Mind*[30]) and is wrong or delayed in

---

[29] Stern, *Forms of Vitality*, 9–10.
[30] Lisa Zunshine defines Theory of Mind as 'our ability to explain people's behavior in terms of their thoughts, feelings, beliefs, and desires ... we ascribe to a person a certain mental state on the basis of her observable action (e.g., we see her reaching for a glass of water and assume that she is thirsty); when we

the judgements s/he makes about how the pieces of the plot come together (exhibits *faulty problem solving*[31]). Clinical psychologists Corine de Ruiter and Marinus H. Van Ijzendoorn refer to 'the freedom to err'[32] (the ability to engage more easily in autonomous exploration and adapt more easily to new ways of imagining) as a defining trait of securely attached children. But Dickens's orphan child is not free to 'engage more easily in autonomous exploration and adapt more easily to new ways of imagining' at home. Instead, pursuit of this 'freedom to err' becomes the orphan's story on the road. For Rosemarie Bodenheimer, 'Dickensian children do not grow older; they just go somewhere.'[33] And what happens when they 'just go somewhere' is to have 'the freedom to err'. The road, the world beyond home, functions as the child's cognitive training ground. For the Dickensian child of broken attachments to ever feel at home in the world and in him or herself, and to ever develop the cognitive capacities for a *dependable Theory of Mind and problem solving*, she or he must learn to whom to attach in the world beyond 'home'. But based on what? How does one choose to whom and to what to attach if the base from which one seeks to do so feels empty or broken or filled with wounds? How to begin?

John Bowlby, the developmental psychologist and analyst whose trilogy *Attachment, Separation,* and *Loss* brought into being the field of attachment theory and with whom Mary Ainsworth worked to test its hypotheses, defines the parent–child attachment, its importance to human development, and the effects of its breaking on the infant/young child from extended separation from or loss of the caregiver parent. In *A Secure Base: Parent–Child Attachment and Healthy Human Development*, Bowlby comes to examine how adverse experiences with parents create 'cognitive disturbances' in the child, where those experiences that are too difficult to bear consciously become 'shut off', or fall into 'amnesia',[34] though they continue to affect the child and his/her development. In addition to these forms of memory loss, the child can feel intense guilt, chronic distrust of others and himself, a tendency to find everything unreal, a sense of inner and

---

interpret our own feelings based on our proprioceptive awareness... when we intuit a complex state of mind based on a limited verbal description... when we compose an essay, a lecture, a movie, a song, a novel, or an instruction for an electrical appliance and try to imagine how this or that segment of our target audience will respond to it; when we negotiate a multilayered social situation... and so forth'. See *Why We Read Fiction: Theory of Mind and the Novel* (Columbus: The Ohio State University Press, 2006), 6.

[31] Mary L. Gick and Keith J. Holyoak, 'Analogical Problem Solving', *Cognitive Psychology* 12 (1980): 306–55; Philip N. Johnson-Laird, *Mental Models: Towards a Cognitive Science of Language, Inference, and Consciousness* (Cambridge, MA: Harvard University Press, 1986); and Keith Oatley and P. N. Johnson-Laird, 'Emotion and Reasoning to Consistency', in Simon C. Moore and Mike Oaksford (eds), *Emotional Cognition: From Brain to Behaviour* (Amsterdam: John Benjamins, 2002): 157–82.

[32] Corine De Ruiter and Marinus H. Van Ijzendoorn, 'Attachment and Cognition: A Review of the Literature', *International Journal of Education Research* 19, 6 (December 1992): 525–39, 534.

[33] Bodenheimer, 'Dickens and the Knowing Child', 20.

[34] John Bowlby, *A Secure Base: Parent–Child Attachment and Healthy Human Development* (New York: Basic Books, 1988), 101–2.

outer fragmentation. He may develop a 'false self',[35] dissociate, experience psychosis, or multiple personality disorder. The mind finds a way to cope—forgetting, inventing through dissociation or multiple instantiations of the self. Fragmenting and turning the sense of guilt on the self enables a child through repression, the imagination, and selection to continue to have a mind and an attachment to the other no matter how faulty that mind or that attachment. We do what we can to go on, to achieve what Van Ghent calls 'psychic equilibrium'. Dickens knows this.

Always the fog, mist, and shadows are near. His protagonists' minds struggle to 'see' (Dickens's favourite verb) the truth of what's before them. But the shadows of the past lie within, and so what lies without seems unclear or occluded. Shut off from scenes and experiences and people, from being too young to remember, or from never knowing, or from amnesia, Esther, Pip, and David struggle to see and to know and to remember what they can't see or know or remember. '[T]his narrative is my written memory' (*DC* 58, 699), Copperfield states, but it is not just that.[36] The scene of Steerforth's drowning, for instance, lives not in his memory but in his dreams and in his associations with storms and the seashore. 'I will try to write it down. I do not recall it, but see it done; for it happens again before me'. *This is trauma.* So shocking, so furious—'like a great tower in a plain, and throwing its forecast shadow even on the incidents of my childish days'—no remove of time separates and comforts David's mind. '[I]t happens again before me' (*DC* 55, 672). Dickens explores how memories and their absence circle in his protagonists' minds. Sometimes a vivid memory enables his characters to see, where other times there is no such seeing, and other moments when the seeing is so real, so powerful, it forces its way forward as if in the here and now when its occurrence was long ago. *This is dissociation.*

'What did I do to her? How did I lose her? Why am I so different from other children, and why is it my fault, dear godmother?'[37] Esther's plea to know something of her mother makes clear the overriding guilt she feels for her loss. 'Why is it my fault?' The sense of internal guilt deepens over time in Dickens's writing career, as the problems of mind become increasingly disturbing, complex, and compelling in his narrative art. The Pip of the forge, the Pip of Satis House, the Pip of London—who is Pip? Why does he feel always ashamed of not being quite right or quite who he is, of being a 'false self'? He floats through the novel's shadowy realms as if in a trance, 'in mortal terror of myself' (*GE* I:2, 15), searching for answers to questions he cannot ask: 'What I wanted, who can say? How can *I* say, when I never knew?' (*GE* I:14, 107). Try as he might to phrase these questions, Pip is caught between the commands of others—'play, play, play!'

---

[35] Ibid., 113.

[36] David's narrative attests to how remarkable he finds his memory, so exact in detail, so certain in recall, most especially during infancy. For John Jordan, the beginning of chapter II is 'as close as Dickens ever comes to presenting a systematic theory of infant memory'. See Jordan, *Supposing* Bleak House, 90.

[37] Charles Dickens, *Bleak House*, ed. George Ford and Sylvère Monod, Norton Critical Edition (New York: W. W. Norton & Company, 1977), chapter 3, page 19. Subsequent references are inserted parenthetically in the text by *BH* chapter, page.

(*GE* I:8, 60); 'Love her, love her, love her!' (*GE* II:10, 240)—and 'the nameless shadow' that lurks 'like a stain that was faded but not gone' (*GE* II:13, 263). This 'stain', which makes Pip feel 'contaminated' with 'Newgate in my breath and on my clothes' (*GE* II:13, 263), is central to Dickens's understanding of the orphan mind, one that seeks out others who might help answer questions central to psychic life: What do I want? How can I say what I want? How can I find the words to express that which I do not already know that I want? The ubiquity of the 'nameless shadow', which follows Pip from Satis House to London, suggests something as to the urgency of these questions which, in order to imagine a future, must return to a past. Does the novel ever really settle on a Pip? The multiple endings seem to suggest not.

The novels of Charles Dickens lead us more generally to infer that while crimes can be solved, the mysteries of identity cannot. Indeed, these mysteries await future generations of Dickens readers: given what we now know, and continue to learn, about the embodied, thinking, feeling, and relational mind, perhaps we may better yet understand opacities like Pip's 'nameless shadow' or David's 'old unhappy loss or want of something'. Our hypothesis as to why such 'shadow[s]' and 'loss' lurk in Dickens's writing is exactly that: a hypothesis, and one attuned to three novels in particular—*Great Expectations*, *David Copperfield*, and *Bleak House*. We invite others to consider other 'signatures of Dickens's people' from across his oeuvre: Agnes and Little Dorrit, Louisa Gradgrind and Sissy Jupe, the Landless twins, Scrooge's sister, and little Paul Dombey. These parentless figures suggest how often the shadows of loss remain in the mist, still invisible, still mysterious, insistent still on making the effects of death—its broken attachments and cognitive disturbances—felt throughout the whole narrative of life.

'When I love a person very tenderly indeed, *it seems to brighten*' (*BH* 3, 17; emphasis ours). These are Esther Summerson's words from just the second paragraph of her self-narrative in *Bleak House*, which means Esther knows that feeling even before she's felt it. She knows love brings the warm light of attachment to the cold dark of being a solitary. This is something like knowing the longing to attach without knowing why or to whom. That longing defines the human-mammalian condition and is the basis of hope. If what is peculiar to Dickens's narrative art is how he embodies the broken brains of broken attachments, what he offers to those breaks is not their 'fix' but the unending desire to mend—the longing to love—which means, in Dickens's universe, the longing to heal.

Further Reading

Rosemarie Bodenheimer, *Knowing Dickens* (Ithaca, NY: Cornell University Press, 2007)
C. B. Cox, 'A Dickens Landscape', *Critical Quarterly* 2, 1 (March 1960): 58–60
Audrey Jaffe, *Vanishing Points: Dickens, Narrative, and the Subject of Omniscience* (Berkeley: University of California Press, 1991)
Mildred Newcomb, *The Imagined World of Charles Dickens* (Columbus: The Ohio State University Press, 1989)

Brian Rosenberg, *Little Dorrit's Shadows: Character and Contradiction in Dickens* (Columbia: University of Missouri Press, 1996)

Evan Thompson, *Waking, Dreaming, Being: Self and Consciousness in Neuroscience, Meditation, and Philosophy* (New York: Columbia University Press, 2015)

Francisco J. Varela, Evan Thompson, and Eleanor Rosch, *The Embodied Mind: Cognitive Science and Human Experience* (Cambridge, MA: The MIT Press, 1991)

PART IV

THE LITERARY AND CULTURAL CONTEXTS

CHAPTER 42

DICKENS'S LANGUAGE

DANIEL TYLER

In *Martin Chuzzlewit*, Dickens twice puns markedly on the word 'dark'. When Tom Pinch tells a tollman that he has left Seth Pecksniff, the tollman and his wife cannot fathom why and so they go 'to bed—metaphorically—in the dark'.[1] The narrative has to sort the idiomatic meaning from the literal one, which, if it stood, would be inconsequential and superfluous. Later, Mr Fips, the mysterious agent of Tom's unknown employer, pays Tom his first wages and leaves him with the words 'Be careful how you go. It's rather dark,' which the narrative invites us to hear differently than is apparently intended: 'So it was dark enough in all conscience; and if Mr. Fips expressed himself with a double meaning, he had good reason for doing so' (*MC* 40, 621). This is a novel that is in many ways about being 'in the dark' in this figurative sense. It is also a novel which parades the confusions, misunderstandings, and falsities of language, so it is not surprising that these expressions of incomprehension have to be extracted from a language that does not make them plain.

The remarkable linguistic inventiveness of Dickens's fiction frequently demonstrates the propensity of language itself to engender an often comic confusion. The novels abound in misunderstandings that arise from ambiguities intrinsic to language. In his fiction, language was not only the medium by way of which Dickens expressed his vision of the world and his critique of its institutions, it was itself one of the institutions upon which he turned his keen eye, comic wit, and lacerating satire. That critique is mounted not only by direct or implied assertion, not only by narrative judgement and characterization, but by the rich verbal invention of Dickens's own prose, which flaunts misunderstandings and demonstrates, time and again, the expressiveness of irregular, unbiddable language, including verbal ambiguities and those contortions of meaning dignified with more formal names: paronomasia (puns), prosopopoeia (personification), and other rhetorical devices.

---

[1] *Martin Chuzzlewit*, ed. Margaret Cardwell (Oxford: Clarendon Press, 1982), 31, 502. Subsequent references are inserted parenthetically in the text by *MC* chapter, page.

The energy of linguistic confusion mobilizes Dickens's early fiction. The vagaries and vaguenesses of language—not only in the uses to which language is put, as with profusions of cant or bombast, but intrinsically—are manifest in the imprecisions of his variegated cast of speakers and in his own linguistic comedy. Some of the most thorough assessments of Dickens's language in twentieth-century criticism were carried out by linguists who emphasized the 'inventive' or 'substandard' language of the fiction.[2] Their aim was rarely to consider these effects in relation to the themes and content of the novels, but rather to study language use as an end in itself. Conversely, studies in the mainstream of literary scholarship have of course been more deeply invested in matters of theme and content—and of form and genre too—but, with exceptions, they have tended to be less likely to focus, close up and sustainedly, on the verbal techniques of Dickens's prose.

As this chapter implies, there are yet gains to be made by scholarship that combines the focus and findings of the linguists with the pursuit of more thematic ends.[3] Some of the early fiction in particular makes verbal and grammatical misunderstandings pivotal to the plots. This is true of *The Pickwick Papers*, a novel rich in verbal comedy of several kinds: for instance, the inflated language applied to Mr Pickwick, the well-known satire of political and journalistic styles, Sam Weller's linguistic resourcefulness, and the narrative voice itself, ever ready with verbal invention of its own. The misunderstanding that so readily attends utterance in the novel is apparent in a scene late on, when Mr Weller, Sam's father, says that the servant girl whom he does not yet know is the object of his son's affection is 'Wery pleasant and conformable':

> The precise meaning which Mr. Weller attached to this last mentioned adjective did not appear, but as it was evident from the tone in which he used it that it was a favourable expression, Mr. Pickwick was as well satisfied as if he had been thoroughly enlightened on the subject.
>
> 'I take a great interest in her, Mr. Weller,' said Mr. Pickwick.
>
> Mr. Weller coughed.

---

[2] Knud Sørensen, *Charles Dickens: Linguistic Innovator* (Aarhus: Arkona, 1985), 12 and *passim*; G. L. Brook, *The Language of Dickens* (London: Deutsch, 1970), 94 and *passim*. In addition to these two works, see Randolph Quirk, *Charles Dickens and Appropriate Language* (Durham: University of Durham, 1959). More recent investigations in the field of corpus stylistics have examined particular examples of Dickens's language structures against the larger body of his work and against the writings of his contemporaries: Masahiro Hori, *Investigating Dickens's Style: A Collocational Analysis* (Basingstoke: Palgrave Macmillan, 2004), and Michaela Mahlberg, *Corpus Stylistics and Dickens's Fiction* (New York: Routledge, 2013).

[3] Studies in the twentieth century that have attended to Dickens's language in depth and at length include Garrett Stewart, *Dickens and the Trials of Imagination* (Cambridge, MA: Harvard University Press, 1975), John Carey, *The Violent Effigy* (London: Faber, 1975), and S. J. Newman, *Dickens at Play* (London: Macmillan, 1981). More recently, a number of works have concentrated on this aspect of Dickens criticism: for example, Joseph Jordan, *Dickens's Novels as Verse* (Madison, NJ; Plymouth: Fairleigh Dickinson University Press, 2012), Daniel Tyler (ed.), *Dickens's Style* (Cambridge: Cambridge University Press, 2013), and Jeremy Tambling, *Dickens's Novels as Poetry* (New York: Routledge, 2015).

'I mean an interest in her doing well,' resumed Mr. Pickwick; 'a desire that she may be comfortable and prosperous. You understand?'
'Wery clearly,' replied Mr. Weller, who understood nothing yet.[4]

This exchange typifies the failures in communication that have dogged the novel, taking in, as it does, vague language use, implication, and innuendo, and a final narrative assertion of incomprehension. In fact it seems not only typical of the many local misunderstandings, but a microcosm of the central plot event: the breach of promise case in which Pickwick becomes embroiled. Mr Weller here goes on to worry about Sam saying something to the girl that might be misconstrued and Sam's being on the end of a 'conwiction for breach' (*PP* 56, 863). The anticipated and actual misunderstandings, of Sam and Pickwick respectively, arise from the instability of language in the world of the novel, so that 'a breach of promise' might take place not because anyone fails to keep their word but because their words keep failing them. A 'breach of promise' proves to be a paradigmatic crisis in a novel where so often language no longer seems to mean what it says.

Since Dickens's first novel depicts a world of confusion, registered as often as not by failures of communication, the novel's own riotous linguistic play is instinct with the world it describes. *The Pickwick Papers* exhibits among others one well-known habit of Dickens's playful prose: animisms that give life to inanimate objects. They are noticeable in the description of the room where the Pickwickians wait for a coach before their journey to Bath:

> The travellers' room at the White Horse Cellar is of course uncomfortable; it would be no travellers' room if it were not. It is the right-hand parlour, into which an aspiring kitchen fire-place appears to have walked, accompanied by a rebellious poker, tongs, and shovel. It is divided into boxes for the solitary confinement of travellers, and is furnished with a clock, a looking-glass, and a live waiter, which latter article is kept in a small kennel for washing glasses, in a corner of the apartment. (*PP* 35, 537)

The adjectives 'aspiring' and 'rebellious' impart a sense of life and contradictory energy to the 'fire-place' and the 'poker', extended when we are told the incongruous fire-place 'appears to have walked' into the travellers' room. The reverse process where life is subtracted from the animate is apparent here too, in this case the 'live waiter'—implicitly distinct from a 'dumb waiter', a piece of furniture present in many Victorian dining rooms—whose humanity is effaced when he is described as an 'article' (and one 'kept in a small kennel' at that).

Dickens's adjectives and his imagery regularly give life to inanimate things. To some extent, this is a property of the language itself; notably so, in the case of catachresis, that is, the application to an object of a word from a different domain, as with 'the face of

---

[4] *Pickwick Papers*, ed. James Kinsley (Oxford: Clarendon Press, 1986), 56, 863. Subsequent references are inserted parenthetically in the text by *PP* chapter, page.

the clock', the 'legs of the chair'; and in words that yield an animating sense over and above a more standard usage: 'gloomy court-yards', lamps that 'dimly blink', a 'lowering sky'.[5] On other occasions, sometimes combining with the former, it is a function of Dickens's image-making: for example, Scrooge's nightgown hangs up 'in a suspicious attitude against the wall',[6] as if to prepare for the tale's more significant ghostly animations; or the 'revolving chimney-pots', seen from the roof of Todgers's in *Martin Chuzzlewit*, which 'seemed to be turning gravely to each other every now and then' (*MC* 9, 132); or Barnard's Inn in *Great Expectations*, which had 'strewn ashes on its head, and was undergoing penance and humiliation as a mere dust-hole'.[7] The equal and yet opposite effect of subtracting life or humanity from what is usually animated is also frequent: Tom Gradgrind as 'the Whelp'; Mrs Merdle as 'the bosom'; Wemmick's mouth turning into a 'post-office'. The deadening effects of such transformations will become characteristic of *Our Mutual Friend* and of the atmosphere of drained vitality that pertains in that novel.

The Pickwick Papers regularly foregrounds other grammatical uncertainties: for example, those attending the antecedents of pronouns. Dickens sometimes clarifies a pronomial uncertainty with a parenthetical insertion—for example, 'he (Mr Trotter)'—but sometimes the uncertainty is imagined rather than real: 'Captain Boldwig was a little fierce man in a stiff black neckerchief and blue surtout, who, when he did condescend to walk about his property, did it in company with a thick rattan stick with a brass ferrule, and a gardener and sub-gardener with meek faces, to whom (the gardeners, not the stick) Captain Boldwig gave his orders with all due grandeur and ferocity' (*PP* 19, 281). This was a stylistic habit that Dickens maintained, albeit with a diminishing frequency, throughout his fiction, but it has not pleased all critics. The linguist G. L. Brook finds such moments 'facetious rather than funny' and wonders why Dickens 'thinks it necessary to warn his readers against a misunderstanding of which no one but a fool would be guilty'.[8] The linguist's priorities are not always equal to the humorist's. Dickens's aim was not simply clarity but to give expression to the verbal mayhem that forever threatens to undermine meaning. In the case of Captain Boldwig's stick, the clarification, which raises rather than clears the possibility that the Captain might have been talking to his stick, adds to the sheen of satire thrown over the characterization. It also builds on the near-personification of 'in company with' to bestow a possible animism on the scene.

---

[5] Respectively, *MC*, 9, 130; *Bleak House*, ed. George Ford and Sylvère Monod, Norton Critical Edition (New York: W. W. Norton, 1977), 32, 392; subsequent references are inserted parenthetically in the text by *BH* chapter, page; *Our Mutual Friend*, ed. Michael Cotsell, Oxford World's Classics (Oxford: Oxford University Press, 1998), I:6, 70. Subsequent references are inserted parenthetically in the text by *OMF* Book:chapter, page.

[6] *A Christmas Carol*, in *A Christmas Carol and Other Christmas Books*, ed. Robert Douglas-Fairhurst, Oxford World's Classics (Oxford: Oxford University Press, 2006), Stave 1, p. 18.

[7] *Great Expectations*, ed. Margaret Cardwell (Oxford: Clarendon Press, 1993), II:2, 171. Subsequent references are inserted parenthetically in the text by *GE* volume:chapter, page.

[8] Brook, *The Language of Dickens*, 53.

More often Dickens uses this kind of clarification—he (Mr Pickwick), she (Mrs Nickleby), he (Mr Swiveller), he (William Barnacle), and so on[9]—as a mock-pedantry in the narrative that shows up the affected scruples, the exaggerated meticulousness, or the sham formality of the character immediately involved. In *Barnaby Rudge*, where more than once the device is taken into a character's direct or reported speech, the conspicuous clarification is more likely to be meaningful than merely absurd. When Sir John Chester speaks of his father having disowned another son, he adds that 'He led a miserable life (the son, I mean) and died early':[10] the parenthetical clarification raises the salient moral likelihood that the father, too, suffered from his own hateful actions. When Miggs seeks to defend Simon Tappertit, arrested for his involvement in the riots, saying 'that temptations had been Simmuns's bane. That it was not his faults, but hers (meaning Dolly's)' (*BR* 70, 562), the explanatory addition preserves what we are to imagine was Miggs's resentful refusal to refer to Dolly by name. (A moment later she pretends to high-mindedness in 'nam[ing] no names'.) What is also at issue here is exactly that Miggs has not been the object of Sim's interest; the added burden of differentiation between Miggs and Dolly that the narrative takes upon itself reinforces the distinction between the two women that is precisely the point. Even when turned to meaningful ends, these clarifications stage the susceptibility to confusion of language. One of the novel's most laughably dull-witted characters causes some puzzlement by way of exactly this grammatical uncertainty. When Mr Willet wakes from a doze to say, 'If he don't come in five minutes ... I shall have supper without him,' the narrative adds, 'The antecedent of this pronoun had been mentioned for the last time at eight o'clock' (*BR* 33, 267). The threat of unintelligibility that Dickens's own prose circumvents—and flaunts—is here taken up, by the very same ambiguity of grammar, into the speech of a confused and confusing landlord. Indeed, since the sense-defying suspension of narration is both bewildering (for Willet's listeners) and in its way a triumph of protraction and recall (on his part), readers of the novel, especially those of its first weekly instalments, might have taken the episode as a miniature of the pleasures and difficulties in keeping up with the novel's involved and extended plot.

The propensity for humour and confusion to emerge from verbal communication, as foregrounded by the novel's style, effects a wider satire. It exposes the complacent rhetoric in legal and political discourse, the lost vigour of conventional language in these arenas that seems to reflect a correspondent waning of ethical vigilance. The solemnity of Pickwick's trial is undermined by numerous puns, as when the magistrate threatens to 'commit' Sam Weller, who responds 'This is a wery impartial country for justice... There ain't a magistrate going, as don't commit himself, twice as often as he commits other

---

[9] Respectively, *PP*, 1, 6; *Nicholas Nickleby*, ed. Paul Schlicke, Oxford World's Classics (Oxford: Oxford University Press, 2009), 28, 358; *The Old Curiosity Shop*, ed. Elizabeth M. Brennan (Oxford: Clarendon Press, 1998), 35, 278; *Little Dorrit*, ed. Harvey Peter Sucksmith (Oxford: Clarendon Press, 1979), I:34, 395; subsequent references are inserted parenthetically in the text by *LD* Book:chapter, page.

[10] *Barnaby Rudge*, ed. Clive Hurst, Oxford World's Classics (Oxford: Oxford University Press, 2003), 32, 261. Subsequent references are inserted parenthetically in the text by *BR* chapter, page.

people' (*PP* 25, 372). In this view, magistrates like politicians are most likely to commit themselves once they start to talk.

The satire on parliamentary oratory that begins with the debate in the first chapter, cleared once it is understood that a word was used only 'in its Pickwickian sense' (*PP* 1, 7), recurs along with the lampooning of local and political journalism, of 'prosy politics', in the episode of the Eatanswill election.[11] There verbal communication has become manifestly fraught, both by way of the self-importance and hyperbolic partisanship of the local press, and in the electioneering itself. The puns that emerge into Dickens's prose at the same time seem more likely to reinforce the described uncertainties of language by suggesting its further faltering than to represent a contrasting virtuosity (though that possibility is also part of the cool comedy here). So when the gathered mob breaks into 'a scene of struggling, and pushing, and fighting', the narrative suggests the occasion exceeds the possibilities of redescription: 'to which we can no more do justice than the Mayor could, although he issued imperative orders to twelve constables to seize the ring-leaders' (*PP* 13, 195), a pun that brings the limitations of narrative art into the frame. As the hustings and hustlings alike subside, the linguistic effects become more pronounced: 'a vote of thanks was moved to the Mayor for his able conduct in the chair; and the Mayor devoutly wishing that he had had a chair to display his able conduct in (for he had been standing during the whole proceedings) returned thanks' (*PP* 13, 196). The chapter ends with the late voters going 'in a body to the poll; and when they returned, the honourable Samuel Slumkey, of Slumkey Hall, was returned also' (*PP* 13, 197). The puns on 'chair' and 'returned' hold up the political and procedural idioms against the ordinary language from which they have come. And especially when the literal meaning follows the political one (as in the case of 'chair' here), a bathetic tone emerges to undermine the political vernacular. The pun on 'returned' that closes the chapter seems to contain also a clinching mastery of language that does now provide a counterpoint to the failed political oratory. Dickens's succinct wordplay brings the chaotic episode with all its bombast and failures of communication to a close with conspicuous neatness.

The sorts of verbal misunderstandings that bemuse Mrs Bardell, prompting her claim against Pickwick, are more likely, in the case of Mrs Lirriper, another landlady at the other end of Dickens's career, to be generated by her than to confound her. Mrs Lirriper's wonderfully idiosyncratic voice runs on under its own impulses, without regard for the norms of grammar and syntax. In the narrative that opens *Mrs Lirriper's Lodgings*, Dickens's round of tales for the Christmas number of *All the Year Round* in 1863, this recollection is exemplary of her manner of speaking:

> I am an old woman now and my good looks are gone but that's me my dear over the plate-warmer and considered like in the times when you used to pay two guineas on ivory and took your chance pretty much how you came out, which made you

---

[11] See Matthew Bevis, *The Art of Eloquence: Byron, Dickens, Tennyson, Joyce* (Oxford: Oxford University Press, 2008), 86–99, for a good account of Dickens's response to parliamentary oratory.

very careful how you left it about afterwards because people were turned so red and uncomfortable by mostly guessing it was somebody else quite different, and there was once a certain person that had put his money in a hop business that came in one morning to pay his rent and his respects being the second floor that would have taken it down from its hook and put it in his breast pocket—you understand my dear—for the L, he says, of the original—only there was no mellowness in *his* voice and I wouldn't let him, but his opinion of it you may gather from his saying to it 'Speak to me Emma!' which was far from a rational observation no doubt but still a tribute to its being a likeness, and I think myself it *was* like me when I was young and wore that sort of stays.[12]

Mrs Lirriper's exuberant idiom strains comprehension as it proceeds, impelled by her train of thought, with its various tangents and distractions, snagged by remembered details and by the landlady's preoccupations with practical affairs. The confused logic of her voice culminates here in the surprising reference to 'that sort of stays', reflecting the insistent concern with ordinary, physical details of one of her profession. It remains an unexpected detail even if it is backed by a heard but unspoken homonym as she remembers at once 'those days' and 'those stays'.

Faint strains on sense are everywhere in this speech, including an uncertainty attendant on many of the pronouns ('it'—what exactly?), because the neuter pronoun, 'it', on each occasion refers to the likeness that is never named as such, but only as 'that's me', an interchange of self and object that runs against the predisposition of grammar to sort animate from inanimate. When Mrs Lirriper refers, with her customary inclusion of extraneous detail that is either explanation or irrelevance, to the 'certain person that had put his money in a hop business that came in one morning to pay his rent and his respects being the second floor', she uses a rhetorical figure known as zeugma or syllepsis, the splicing of syntax into divergent senses, typically pivoting on a polysemous verb (here 'to pay'). The trope is everywhere in *The Pickwick Papers*. Most famously when Pickwick 'fell into the barrow, and fast asleep, simultaneously' (*PP* 19, 280), or when Miss Bolo 'went straight home in a flood of tears, and a sedan chair' (*PP* 35, 553). We also witness Pickwick taking 'a seat and the paper' (*PP* 20, 293) and soon 'rising in person and wrath at the same time' (*PP* 20, 295). There is a still more arresting use of the trope when Bob Sawyer and Ben Allen are sitting together 'discussing minced veal and future prospects' (*PP* 48, 734). Here the figure turns on a usage of 'discuss' to mean to eat, which the *Oxford English Dictionary* dates back to Tobias Smollett and describes as frequently colloquial and humorous, and now archaic.[13] Dickens uses the figure in novel after novel; for example, in *David Copperfield*, David's aunt 'resumed her toast and her discourse together',[14] while in *Martin Chuzzlewit* the figure is extended showily when a

---

[12] 'Mrs Lirriper's Lodgings', *All the Year Round*, Extra Christmas Number, 3 December 1853, X:2. Subsequent references are inserted parenthetically in the text by *ATYR* date, volume:page.

[13] *OED*, sense 6.

[14] *David Copperfield*, ed. Nina Burgis (Oxford: Clarendon Press, 1981), 35, 429. Subsequent references are inserted parenthetically in the text by *DC* chapter, page.

chapter title is given as 'In which Miss Pecksniff makes Love, Mr. Jonas makes Wrath, Mrs. Gamp makes Tea, and Mr. Chuffey makes Business' (*MC* 46), which finds a new sense of 'make' with each nominal object and which faintly echoes its famous Augustan precursor, Pope's 'Dost sometimes Counsel take—and sometimes, *Tea*'.[15]

Garrett Stewart has tracked Dickens's career-long use of this device and the several effects which it yields.[16] Often yoking physical and metaphysical meanings it becomes especially suited to moments where language encounters mortality. It can also be taken as a trope emblematic of storytelling, since its characteristic splits of literal and figurative significations draw attention to the storyteller's attempts to signify meanings that go beyond the material circumstances of the tale. Even when not formulated in a crisply parallel syntactical structure, the simultaneous yoking and forking of literal and figurative meanings that syllepsis concentrates becomes a habit of perception and expression. In this broader sense, what Garrett Stewart calls a 'sylleptic paradigm' or a 'sylleptic tendency' becomes apparent at the climax of Mrs Lirriper's story when the forsaken girl has wandered down to the river and Mrs Lirriper says she 'saw her hands at her bonnet-strings, and I rushed between her and the brink'—that is, of the river and of death—'and took her round the waist with both my arms' (*ATYR* X:7); where such is the latency of meaning in prose like this that even 'took her' might yield the potentially doubled sense, as it were, of 'took her captive and round the waist'.[17]

Martin Chuzzlewit extends the critical recognition of *The Pickwick Papers* that language use and misuse are themselves symptoms of a wider condition. Steven Marcus says of the novel that 'language is one of its subjects' and his point about the wordplay in the first chapter, that it demonstrates 'through a labyrinth of double-entendres, non sequiturs and puns that language is itself essentially deceitful' is applicable to the book as a whole, as I hinted at the outset of this chapter.[18] John Bowen has called the novel 'by some distance the most rhetorically sophisticated of Dickens's early novels', and it is true that the novel, as S. J. Newman neatly puts it, 'wears its art on its sleeve'.[19] The novel recurs repeatedly, in the voices of character and narrative alike, to moral axioms, proverbial wisdom, and an inflated rhetoric that has recourse to superlatives and apostrophe. There is a sustained comic revelry in the fallibility of language—its potential for slippage and humorous or surprising meaning—especially by way of puns and other ambiguities, all

---

[15] Alexander Pope, *The Rape of the Lock*, Canto III, line 8, in *The Twickenham Edition of the Poems of Alexander Pope*, 11 vols, 2: *The Rape of the Lock*, ed. Geoffrey Tillotson (London: Methuen, 1940), 169.

[16] Garrett Stewart, *The Deed of Reading* (Ithaca, NY: Cornell University Press, 2015), esp. 156–66. See also his 'Ethical Tempo of Narrative Syntax: Sylleptic Recognitions in *Our Mutual Friend*', *Partial Answers* 8, 1 (January 2010): 119–45; 'The Ethics of Temporality: A Rejoinder Syllepsis Redux and the Rhetoric of Double Agency', *Partial Answers* 10, 1 (January 2012); and 'Lived Death: Dickens's Rogue Glyphs', in Tyler (ed.), *Dickens's Style*, 231–52.

[17] Stewart, 'Lived Death', 243; *The Deed of Reading*, 161.

[18] Steven Marcus, *Dickens: From Pickwick to Dombey* (London: Chatto and Windus, 1965), 217.

[19] John Bowen, *Other Dickens: Pickwick to Chuzzlewit* (Oxford: Oxford University Press, 2000), 200; Newman, *Dickens at Play*, 105.

the while building a plot on pledges, bonds, and promises, brokered or broken by words themselves.

The world of the novel is again one in which incomprehension is pervasive, as is frequently, sometimes gratuitously, made apparent. When Martin confirms that he is from Europe and is told he is therefore fortunate, he agrees but 'soon discovered that the gentleman and he attached different meanings to this remark' (Martin thinks he is fortunate in hailing from Europe, his interlocutor thinks him therefore fortunate in having the rare chance to meet Elijah Pogram; *MC* 34, 531). In more basic kinds of verbal error, Pecksniff betrays himself when he confuses his grammar: 'But I have ever ... sacrificed my children's happiness to my own—I mean my own happiness to my children's' (*MC* 30, 473), and John Westlock gets his words in a tangle when he reports Mr Fip's visit on business, unintentionally revealing that Ruth and her cookery have distracted his attention: 'The pudding having taken a chair' (*MC* 39, 605).

The propensity to obscurity in language in the novel is accompanied by a sheer linguistic vivacity; though, as critics have noticed, the exuberance of language is primarily confined to the speech and vicinity of the vicious characters. It is as if the potential for comedy, miscommunication, and chaos is made possible by an uneven, fractured language that comes to represent a broken world. As John Bowen says, the novel gives us 'a fallen, un-creating, disseminating word, a text full of deceit, death, hilarity, absence, and aporia'.[20] It is because language is for Dickens, here and elsewhere, a measure of the health—or rather the disrepair—of the nation or of the world of his novels that the novels have proven responsive to critical approaches that recognize in them a commentary on language and on the nature of representation in fiction.[21]

Of course the novel also provides a further subdivision between British English and American English as indexes respectively of the moral life of the two nations. The American chapters of *Martin Chuzzlewit* repeatedly gauge the linguistic perplexities and distortions in speech and print of the people Martin meets, building on Dickens's verbal misunderstandings in the new world documented in *American Notes*. (Indeed, the transition from Dickens's voice to his fictional narrator's between these two texts raises an issue which is beyond the scope of this chapter: there is more to be understood about the relation between Dickens's fictional styles and his other rhetorical performances, such as his letters, travelogues, and speeches.)

The morality of the characters, at home and abroad, is chiefly distinguished by their language use. Pecksniff is 'in the frequent habit of using any word that occurred to him as having a good sound, and rounding a sentence well, without much care for its meaning' (*MC* 2, 14). Here the rhymes of 'word' and 'occurred' and 'sound' and 'round' alert us to Dickens's own ear for the acoustics of his prose in a novel whose sallies at language fly perilously close to its own modes. The heightened, hyperbolic rhetoric surrounding the

---

[20] Bowen, *Other Dickens*, 190.
[21] Notably, J. Hillis Miller, 'Introduction' to *Bleak House*, ed. Norman Page (London: Penguin, 1971), reprinted as 'Interpretation in Dickens' *Bleak House*', in Miller's *Victorian Subjects* (Durham, NC: Duke University Press, 1991), 179–99.

accounts of Tom Pinch suggests that the novel itself participates in the belief in the ineffably good that it also satirizes. So too the speech style of Pecksniff, a bankrupt version of eighteenth-century moralizing, is proximate to the style of the narrative voice, which has a moral earnestness of its own. The remarkably frequent references to the insufficiency of language adequately to capture an elusive (often hyperbolic) reality become a feature of the narrative mode, but they are partly a joke on Pecksniff's own sense of his ineffable moral superiority. By contrast, Tom's virtue is manifest when Mercy Pecksniff suspects him of disingenuous talk and he replies: 'oh can you think, that what I said just now, I said with any but the true and plain intention which my words professed?' (*MC* 37, 581). Since language is the battleground on which the novel's rivalries are drawn, it is no surprise that the architectural plans that Pecksniff hijacks from Martin are for a grammar school.

The expressive power of grammatical irregularities, such as is famously exemplified by Mrs Gamp in *Martin Chuzzlewit*, is pushed to a limit point in the case of ungrammatical speakers like Flora Finching in *Little Dorrit*, where, with combined relish and skill, Dickens retracts most of the punctuation from her speech and has her rattle on as if to parody the quality of self-generating verbal expression that critics have identified behind his own prolific output. Indeed, Horatio Sparkins, Daniel Quilp, Mark Tapley, and Wilkins Micawber are all described as having a remarkable 'flow of language', which seems to banter Dickens's fluency. But Flora's challenge to coherence tops them all, leaving her interlocutors—if they may so be called—mystified. She even occasionally throws off a play on words, as when Clennam asks to see the visitors her father has downstairs: ' "Papa sees so many and such odd people," said Flora rising, "that I shouldn't venture to go down for any one but you Arthur but for you I would willingly go down in a diving-bell much more a dining-room and will come back directly if you'll mind and at the same time *not* mind Mr. F's Aunt while I'm gone" ' (*LD* II:9, 521). The unexpected wordplay (on 'mind') is also accompanied by a rhetorically balanced and near-sylleptic phrasing, since, for Arthur, Flora would go down in a diving bell and not only to a dining room. Earlier, Flora's flurried recollection of Mr Finching's seven proposals yielded a 'triumphant zeugma' as Barbara Hardy calls it: 'he proposed seven times once in a hackney coach once in a boat once in a pew once on a donkey at Tunbridge Wells and the rest on his knees' (*LD* I:24, 275–6).[22]

Her unpunctuated, ungrammatical speech is suggestive even without these occasional flourishes. Consider this example from the chapter of her first appearance in the novel:

> 'Dear dear,' said Flora, 'only to think of the changes at home Arthur—cannot overcome it, seems so natural, Mr. Clennam far more proper—since you became familiar with the Chinese customs and language which I am persuaded you speak like a Native if not better for you were always quick and clever though immensely difficult no doubt, I am sure the tea chests alone would kill *me* if I tried, such changes

---

[22] Barbara Hardy, *Dickens's Creativity* (London: Continuum, 2008), 67.

Arthur—I am doing it again, seems so natural, most improper—as no one could have believed, who could have ever imagined Mrs. Finching when I can't imagine it myself!' (*LD* I:13, 145)

Flora is ridiculous, but not to be despised. Her kindness is real and so is the pain of her experience. Her conversation, especially the characteristic slippage over Arthur's name—'seems so natural, Mr Clennam far more proper'—shows very obviously her inability to come to terms with the passage of time, a difficulty that in its essence she shares with other characters in the novel and which Dickens often takes seriously. It is correlative, after all, to the profound and climactic lapse of Mr Dorrit back to his prison days when still at the Merdle dining table. On more than one occasion, Flora is ushered into the novel to encounter someone under 'altered circumstances' (*LD* I:13, 145; II:17, 599) with which she has difficulty coming to terms (Arthur's and her own, first, and Little Dorrit's later). The slightly wrong-footing juxtaposition of past and present tenses in the speech above—'who could have ever imagined … when I can't imagine'—may be a manifestation of this weakness.

The repeated self-interruption that marks and mars her speech—elsewhere we have 'but that is past and stern reality has now my gracious never mind' (*LD* I:23, 264)—may be understood to register in her conversation the failed coherence of her own life as a narrative sequence. These ruptures in her speech may be understood as the effect of her two painfully curtailed relationships: her attachment to Arthur, cruelly broken at the behest of their parents, and thereafter her marriage to Mr Finching which itself was 'cut short' (*LD* I:24, 275). Who would blame her if these forced dislocations of her affections from their objects produced a corresponding difficulty in maintaining the subject of her sentences? Meaning runs against grammar in this regard when she says: 'the Chinese customs and language which'—that is, now, the language only and not also the customs—'I am persuaded you speak like a Native if not better for you were always quick and clever though'—an elided 'it is' here absents the grammar that would indicate the change of subject to the Chinese language and no longer 'you'—'immensely difficult'. Flora's speech, ungrammatical to the very limit of intelligibility, is stirringly expressive and its feeling radiates into the rest of the novel.

The irregularities and uncertainties of language, pushed to an extreme here, are ordinarily a resource for comedy and for the production of some of Dickens's best effects. One could turn anywhere to find further examples of the way that Dickens mobilizes the features of language I have been discussing, not only to level a criticism of language use nor even to showcase the intrinsic instability of language, as ends in themselves, but to contribute to, to reinforce, occasionally to redirect or to subvert, the purported sense of the prose, the overall meaning and experience of the text. It remains a principal task of literary criticism to make these demonstrations.

In *Our Mutual Friend*, the tricks of language that I have canvassed are so extended that they amount to a desolate vision of national life and the social world. So many interchanges of the animate and the inanimate, and of the living and the dead, take place (at the levels both of plot and language) that the novel seems to drain its world of any quickening vitality. So many surfaces are at odds with the depths they hide, or prove not to have such depths, that reality itself starts to seem shallow, in a world that is morally destitute. The account of the Veneerings in the second chapter is exemplary of the pronounced interchanges of animate and inanimate:

> Mr. and Mrs. Veneering were bran-new people in a bran-new house in a bran-new quarter of London. Everything about the Veneerings was spick and span new. All their furniture was new, all their friends were new, all their servants were new, their plate was new, their carriage was new, their harness was new, their horses were new, their pictures were new, they themselves were new, they were as newly married as was lawfully compatible with their having a bran-new baby, and if they had set up a great-grandfather, he would have come home in matting from the Pantechnicon, without a scratch upon him, French-polished to the crown of his head. (*OMF* I:2, 6)

As their name implies, the Veneerings constitute a surface that is about as lifeless and shallow as their various articles of property. The seamless oscillation in the list of 'brannew' things between the animate and the inanimate reinforces these characteristics and the repetition of the language in the list starts to seem itself mechanically reproducible, rather than vitally organic, and as repeatedly extendable as the Veneering dining table. These effects build to the reference to the great-grandfather clock, called only a 'greatgrandfather' and placed so close to the 'bran-new baby' that it seems another member of the family, an effect clinched by the switch of pronoun from 'its' to 'his'. Dickens retains throughout the novel an ear for the names of things that make them sound like people: a 'modest Dutchman' (for Dutch cheese), Miss Peecher's 'housewife' (a small sewing case, which she both has and is according to the novel's phrasing), and 'Small Germans' (sausages), while conversely the 'Poem on Shakespeare' is used to refer to the man who recites one (*OMF* I:4, 40; II:1, 219; II:8, 315; I:2, 7).

There is a striking proliferation of sylleptic phrasing in the novel; syllepsis is newly mobilized to an extent not seen since *The Pickwick Papers*. For example, we read that Mary Anne 'resumed her seat and her silence' (*OMF* II:11, 340), Mr Wilfer 'recovered his hat and his breath' (*OMF* III:4, 459), and Jenny Wren reprimands her father and asks to 'have your room instead of your company for one half-minute' (*OMF* III:10, 533). Garrett Stewart has shown that this figure, as it often splits the physical from the metaphysical, has an urgency in the chapter detailing Riderhood's 'little turn-up with Death', when he is described as between this world and the other, after being dragged unconscious from the river (*OMF* III:3, 448).[23] Among the many remarkable feats of verbal prestidigitation in that chapter, there is the now-familiar play on an ambiguous pronoun after we read Tom Tootle's report of the accident, that Riderhood 'was slinking about in his boat ... when he come right athwart the steamer's bows and she cut him in two'. The narrative voice explains, 'Mr Tootle is so far figurative, touching the dismemberment, as that he means the boat, and not the man' (*OMF* III:3, 443). Such interchanges of personal

---

[23] Stewart, 'Lived Death', 231–52.

and impersonal pronouns gain an increased pertinence in scenes dealing with death, as when the Inspector earlier clarifies his reference to the lifeless body of Gaffer Hexam, 'I still call it *him*, you see' (*OMF* I:14, 175). There are like occurrences in the novels immediately prior. In *A Tale of Two Cities*, when Doctor Manette is said to have been 'recalled to life', his daughter Lucie shudders as she says, 'I am afraid of it . . . I mean of him. Of my father.'[24] When Pip in *Great Expectations* returns to the forge after the death of Mrs Joe, he 'began to wonder in what part of the house it—she—my sister—was' (*GE* II:16, 278).

The superficial and deadening realities are captured so emphatically, so vitally, in the writing that the ensuing expressiveness of the prose constitutes a central imaginative paradox in *Our Mutual Friend*. Throughout, as in all of Dickens's fiction, grammatical confusions are not merely comic, they do not solely threaten to give the slip to sense; in this case, they deftly and urgently give terrific expression to Dickens's vision of a shattered world; they reinforce the novel's values and its effects. Such effects also cooperate with the novel's depths of feeling. The chapter 'In which the Orphan makes his Will', detailing the last illness of 'Our Johnny', begins with a misunderstanding. Sloppy tells John Rokesmith he put off his visit to wait until the boy was better:

> 'Then he is well now?' said the Secretary.
> 'No he ain't,' said Sloppy.
> Mr. Sloppy having shaken his head to a considerable extent, proceeded to remark, that he thought Johnny 'must have took 'em from the Minders.' Being asked what he meant, he answered, them that come out upon him and partickler his chest. Being requested to explain himself, he stated that there was some of 'em wot you couldn't kiver with a sixpence. Pressed to fall back upon a nominative case, he opined that they wos about as red as ever red could be. (*OMF* II:9, 323)

There is a plaintive humour in the search for the unknown antecedent, as the proliferation of description constitutes a continued deferral of explanation, which nicely captures the ignorance of causes in many such cases on the part of the suffering poor, those who are mere victims. In the account of the orphan's illness, the habitual exchange of animate and inanimate has a sadder and more solemn effect when Sloppy says that 'the mangle seemed to go like Our Johnny's breathing . . . till I scarce know'd which was mangle and which was Our Johnny' (*OMF* II:9, 324).

The chapter's final sentence, announcing the boy's death, is finely phrased, as syllepsis and pronominal uncertainty combine in an undertone. After Johnny passes his Noah's ark and other toys to a fellow sufferer and pledges a 'kiss for the boofer lady', the chapter ends: 'Having now bequeathed all he had to dispose of, and arranged his affairs in this world, Johnny, thus speaking, left it' (*OMF* II:9, 330). The slight dislocation of 'left it' at the end of this final sentence, imparts a light ambiguity to the pronoun so that the line is shadowed by a phantom version of itself, one that reads 'having now

---

[24] *A Tale of Two Cities*, ed. Andrew Sanders, Oxford World's Classics (Oxford: Oxford University Press, 1988), chapter 6, page 50; chapter 5, page 44.

bequeathed all he had to dispose of in this world, Johnny, thus speaking, left it', where 'it' could apply equally to 'the world' and to Johnny's 'all'. This possibility is hidden by the plural 'affairs' in the end, as if the quiet but pointed satire effected by the language of legal procedure, as finally realized, proved more desirable than the possible grammatical and existential ambiguity. The manuscript draft of the novel shows Dickens working his way round these possibilities because, as an alternative to 'arranged his affairs', he tried out 'bequeathed all ~~his property and~~ he had to ~~leave and~~ dispose of', which, as an alternative, would have secured the pun, after supplying the verb that clinches it ('leave') and the singular noun that would have enhanced it ('property'): 'having bequeathed all his property in this world, Johnny, thus speaking, left it'. There remains, nevertheless, the ghost of an effaced sylleptic logic, whereby Johnny 'leaves his property and the world, together', for language is here on the brink of the unsayable, confronted by the instant of death, just as it times his having left the world precisely and yet almost inapprehensibly to the present continuous moment of his 'thus speaking'.[25]

As such writing makes evident, grammatical irregularities and uncertainties are not only a source of comic confusion but of delicacy and eloquence. In exchanges between Rosa Bud and her guardian, Hiram Grewgious, in *Edwin Drood*, the kind of verbal misunderstandings that I have been tracking do not betray villainous motives nor do they suggest a world of unruly incoherence. Instead, they reveal glimpses of more hopeful and generous realities behind Grewgious's self-presentation. Though Grewgious depicts himself as dry and unimaginative, the ambiguities of his language reveal more than he realizes. When he addresses Rosa in the presence of Miss Twinkleton, the schoolmistress, he has to constrain his meaning by a gesture: '"I refer, my dear," said Mr. Grewgious, laying his hand on Rosa's, as the possibility thrilled through his frame of his otherwise seeming to take the awful liberty of calling Miss Twinkleton my dear; "I refer to the other young ladies."'[26] Comparably invigorating misunderstandings pertain when he tells Rosa the story of his coming to offer lodgings to Bazzard, who aspires to be a writer against the wishes of his father. Grewgious says that Bazzard 'imparted his secret',

> 'and pointed out that he was determined to pursue his genius, and that it would put him in peril of starvation, and that he was not formed for it.'
> 'For pursuing his genius, sir?'
> 'No, my dear,' said Mr Grewgious, 'for starvation. It was impossible to deny the position that Mr. Bazzard was not formed to be starved, and Mr. Bazzard then pointed out that it was desirable that I should stand between him and a fate so perfectly unsuited to his formation. In that way Mr. Bazzard became my clerk, and he feels it very much.'

---

[25] *Our Mutual Friend* MS, Pierpont Morgan Library, New York; MA 1202: fol. 200r.
[26] *The Mystery of Edwin Drood*, ed. Margaret Cardwell (Oxford: Clarendon Press, 1972), 9, 67. Subsequent references are inserted parenthetically in the text by *ED* chapter, page.

> 'I am glad he is grateful,' said Rosa.
> 'I didn't quite mean that, my dear. I mean that he feels the degradation.' (*ED* 20, 180–1)

Though Grewgious plays down his kindness and does not intend to impugn Bazzard's lack of gratitude, his language unwittingly betrays them both, especially under the influence of Rosa's generous and humane understanding.

Dickens's ungovernable language has always had these lightly comic and deeply generous and redemptive possibilities. *The Pickwick Papers*, for example, gives us a glimpse of a world where the gap between an aggrandizing language and an ordinary reality proves not to be as wide as the comedy implies. To take a striking example: when Pickwick, at about the time of his entry into the Fleet, starts to live up to his imputed greatness, he encounters Job Trotter, the rascal servant of his adversary, now greatly weakened and in reduced circumstances in the debtors' prison, and tells him to 'Take that, Sir'.

> Take what? In the ordinary acceptation of such language, it should have been a blow. As the world runs, it ought to have been a sound, hearty cuff; for Mr. Pickwick had been duped, deceived, and wronged by the destitute outcast who was now wholly in his power. Must we tell the truth? It was something from Mr. Pickwick's waistcoat-pocket, which chinked as it was given into Job's hand: and the giving which, somehow or other imparted a sparkle to the eye, and a swelling to the heart of our excellent old friend, as he hurried away. (*PP* 42, 659)

Here, the actuality realizes the best possibilities held out by the language. As such, the language has not only staged the confusion, but enabled the imagined reparation. The conflicting impulses of disorder and order animate Dickens's writing from the start. It is a nice touch that the giving of the money 'somehow or other imparted a sparkle to the eye, and a swelling to the heart', not of Job, the grateful recipient, but of 'our excellent old friend', Pickwick. Or as Dickens might have written: 'imparted a sparkle to the eye, and a swelling to his (Pickwick's) heart.' The rewards of generosity are mutual. Fiction, too, can be a transaction of sympathy and generosity, between author and reader, and though language may depict or create confusion, its power is also to repair it.

Further Reading

Robert Alter, 'Reading Style in Dickens', *Philosophy in Literature* 20, 1 (1996), 130–7.
Robert Douglas-Fairhurst, *Becoming Dickens: The Invention of a Novelist* (Cambridge, MA: Harvard University Press, 2011)
Robert Golding, *Idiolects in Dickens: The Major Techniques and Chronological Development* (London: Macmillan, 1985)
Mark Lambert, *Dickens and the Suspended Quotation* (New Haven: Yale University Press, 1981)

Patrick J. McCarthy, 'The Language of Martin Chuzzlewit', *SEL Studies in English Literature, 1500–1900* 20, 4 (Autumn 1980): 637–49

John R. Reed, *Dickens's Hyperrealism* (Columbus: Ohio University Press, 2010)

Brian C. Rosenberg, 'Vision into Language: The Style of Dickens's Characterization', *Dickens Quarterly* 2, 4 (December 1985): 115–24

Garrett Stewart, *Death Sentences: Styles of Dying in British Fiction* (Cambridge, MA: Harvard University Press, 1984)

CHAPTER 43

GENRES

Auctor Ludens, *or Dickens at Play*

ROBERT TRACY

> Energy, balance, outbreak
> At play for their own sake
>
> Seamus Heaney, 'In Time'[1]

In February 1836 Dickens agreed to supply narrative for a series of etchings by Robert Seymour, to appear monthly in 'shilling numbers ... My friends told me it was a low, cheap form of publication, by which I should ruin all my rising hopes'.[2] But *The Posthumous Papers of the Pickwick Club* (April 1836–November 1837) became a great success. Publication in 'Shilling Monthly Parts ... then a very unusual form, at less than one-third of the price ... of an ordinary novel' made Dickens's serial 'easily accessible ... by all classes of society'. That shilling numbers democratized his audience, he declared, was 'consistent with the spirit in which they have been written, and is the fulfillment of a desire long entertained'.[3]

Serial publication altered the author/reader relationship. A novel became a prolonged experience, simultaneously developing in readers' time and in the time scheme of the story. Characters became recurring presences in readers' lives. Dickens could introduce new characters and situations at any point, and gradually reveal his 'design', the word he preferred to 'plot'. Serial publication's necessary discontinuity invited turning discontinuity into a narrative device. In Dickens's novels, these discontinuities take the form of

---

[1] 'In Time' by Seamus Heaney, taken from *New Selected Poems: 1988–2013* by Seamus Heaney (Faber & Faber, 2014) Copyright © The Estate of Seamus Heaney, 2014. Reproduced by permission of Faber & Faber Ltd. Excerpt from "In Time" from SELECTED POEMS 1988–2013 by Seamus Heaney. Copyright © 2014 by The Estate of Seamus Heaney. Reprinted by permission of Farrar, Straus and Giroux.

[2] Charles Dickens, 'Preface to the Cheap Edition, 1847', *The Pickwick Papers*, ed. James Kinsley (Oxford: Clarendon Press, 1986), 884–5. Subsequent references are inserted parenthetically in the text by *PP* chapter, page.

[3] Charles Dickens, 'Address ... to the Cheap Edition', in the National Edition of *The Works of Charles Dickens*, 80 vols (London: Chapman and Hall, 1906–8), 34:433.

interludes: an eccentric character, often tangential to the main action, usually comic in language and appearance, turns up from time to time to amuse the reader and delay the denouement.

Interlude derives from *ludo*, I play; *ludens*, playing. In *Homo Ludens: A Study of the Play-Element in Culture*, Johann Huizinga argues that poetry, music, drama—by implication all arts—originate in our innate ability to play.[4] *Ludens* includes all forms of imaginative activity: making up stories, play and playfulness, acting a part, making music, pretending, sports, daydreaming, amusement—all the impractical, non-utilitarian activities prompted by imagination rather than reason. Dickens, introducing the first issue of his periodical *Household Words* in 1850, anticipates Huizinga: *Household Words* will 'cherish that light of Fancy which is inherent in the human breast' and recognize the 'wild, grotesque, and fanciful'.[5]

A musical interlude provides a shift in tempo or tonality; in theatre an *entr'acte* can alter the mood and action of a play, or introduce an unexpected element. An interlude can be a scene, an episode, or a character not directly part of a novel's or play's main action, often delaying the main action: 'The Murder of Gonzago', *Macbeth*'s drunken porter, 'rude mechanicals' performing 'Pyramus and Thisbe'. Dickens's interludes feature characters with verbal tics, odd behaviour, and curious obsessions, making them recognizable to readers after disappearing for several months. He amuses and distracts himself and his readers by playing in between the intricacies of his own design. Interludic characters comment obliquely on the novel's incidents and design by emphasizing the play element in the whole enterprise of fiction.

While writing *Pickwick Papers*, Dickens had formulated an aesthetic theory of serial publication:

> to place before the reader a constant succession of characters and incidents; to paint them in ... vivid colours ... and to render them, at the same time, life-like and amusing ... publication ... in monthly numbers ... only thirty-two pages in each ... [demanded] that, while the different incidents were linked together ... to prevent their appearing unconnected or impossible, *the general design* [italics mine] should be so simple as to sustain no injury from this detached and desultory form of publication ... over ... twenty months ... every number should be ... complete in itself, and yet ... the whole twenty numbers, when collected, should form one tolerably harmonious whole, each leading to the other by a gentle and not unnatural progress ... no artfully interwoven or ingeniously complicated plot can ... be expected ... if it be objected [that] the Pickwick Papers ... are a mere series of adventures, in which the scenes are ever changing, and the characters come and go like the men and women we encounter in the real world ... they claim to be nothing else. (*PP* 1837 Preface, xcvix)

---

[4] Johan Huizinga, *Homo Ludens: A Study of the Play-Element in Culture*, trans. by the author (London: Routledge and Kegan Paul, Ltd, 1949).

[5] [Charles Dickens], 'A Preliminary Word', *Household Words*, 30 March 1850.

Frequent scene changes, coincidences, and characters randomly entering and departing, remained his method. Twenty years later, his number plans for *Little Dorrit* (1855–7) echo that 1837 preface: 'People to meet and part as travellers do, and the future *connexion* [italics mine] between them in the story, not to be now shewn to the reader but to be worked out as in life. <u>Try this uncertainty and this not-putting of them together, as a new means of interest</u>. Indicate and carry through this intention.'[6] Dickens's May 1857 Preface to *Little Dorrit* describes 'design' as a woven pattern, a tapestry or a rug: 'I may have held its various threads with a more continuous attention than any one else ... during its desultory publication, [but] it is not unreasonable to ask that the weaving may be looked at in its completed state, and with the pattern finished' (*LD* Preface, lix).

In *Pickwick* Dickens varied his narrative as Henry Fielding and Tobias Smollett had done, by interpolating interludic stories not always relevant to the Pickwickians' adventures: 'The Stroller's Tale', 'The Convict's Return', 'The Bagman's Tale'. But when Jingle intervenes between Pickwick and the cabman in *Pickwick* I (April 1836), Dickens discovered a better way of varying a 'desultory form of publication' to be read over 19 months. Jingle, an improvising storyteller, is at this point an *entr'acte*, an interlude, what Roland Barthes calls 'a dilatory area which interrupts the [narrative], suspends it, turns it aside', a formation similar to what Rachel Malik calls a 'capsular narrative ... novelistic digression'.[7] He enlivens the narrative but does not in this chapter advance the plot. A Lord of Misrule, Jingle will appear at intervals to harass Pickwick. His abrupt speech, fantastic stories, and elaborate schemes weave an erratic thread into Dickens's pattern, preserving the design but subtly altering it, like the two themes of a fugue. He and Job Trotter become alternative versions of the two Samuels, Pickwick and Weller: two teams, each inseparable, accused of conspiring to woo ladies. But this is a later development out of the initial ludic intervention: the 'constant succession of characters and incidents', Dickens claimed, were gradually shaped into 'different incidents ... linked together ... to prevent their appearing unconnected or impossible'.

In *Martin Chuzzlewit* Mrs Gamp, *femina ludens*, performs in comic interludes for us, for audiences inside the novel—mothers-to-be, Mr Mould, Mrs Prig—but chiefly to entertain herself. Absorbing us in her self-absorption, she delights us. With her Dickens entertains himself, shows off, varies his grim narrative of Chuzzlewit greed and hypocrisy with comic turns. Gamp first appears in all her garrulous glory in *Chuzzlewit* VIII (August 1843). 'I mean to make a mark with her', Dickens told John Forster.[8] He

---

[6] Charles Dickens, *Little Dorrit*, ed. Harvey Peter Sucksmith (Oxford: Clarendon Press, 1979), 'The Number Plans', page 806. Subsequent references are inserted parenthetically in the text by *LD* Book:chapter, page, or as above.

[7] Roland Barthes, *S/Z*, trans. Richard Miller (New York: Hill and Wang, 1974), 75; Rachel Malik, 'Stories Many, Fast, and Slow', *ELH* 79 (Summer 2012): 477–500, 484–5.

[8] *The Letters of Charles Dickens*, ed. Madeline House, Graham Storey, et al., Pilgrim/British Academy Edition, 12 vols (Oxford: Clarendon Press, 1965–2002). Subsequent citations: *PLets* followed by volume:page range, page, and hn. for headnote, n. or nn. for footnotes, with page range given before page cited. Here, 3:520.

equips her with a gift for monologue, ambitious language slightly above her station—'this Piljian's Projiss of a mortal wale'[9]—peculiar autobiographical details, and anecdotes about pre-natal mishaps. Sly, vicious, selfish, venal, and quarrelsome, a nurse who mistreats her patients, she is a snuffy, gin-soaked harridan moving unsteadily through *Martin Chuzzlewit*. Still, she absorbs us in her self-absorption. In the penultimate chapter old Martin Chuzzlewit advises her to take 'a little less liquor, and a little more humanity, and a little less regard for herself, and a little more regard for her patients, and perhaps a trifle of additional honesty' (*MC* 52, 810). Readers remember her not as a brutal and incompetent nurse, but for her improvised anecdotes and bizarre language.

'Mrs. Gamp was a lady of that happy temperament which can be ecstatic without any other stimulating cause than a general desire to establish a large and profitable connexion' (*MC* 46, 700) with those who might employ her during childbirth, illness, or death. For Dickens that 'connexion' signals three related factors shaping his work: characters from upper and lower social strata; an audience including all classes; and coincidences that bring characters unexpectedly together. In *Bleak House* he encapsulates all three when he asks, 'What connexion can there be, between the place in Lincolnshire ... the Mercury in powder, and ... Jo the outlaw with the broom? ... What connexion can there have been between many people ... who, from opposite sides of great gulfs, have, nevertheless, been very curiously brought together!'[10]

Mrs Gamp is a comic presence and a plebeian voice among the middle-class Chuzzlewits. Mr Mould calls her 'a woman whose intellect is immensely superior to her station in life. That's a woman who observes and reflects in an uncommon manner' (*MC* 25, 407). Closely observing Jonas Chuzzlewit, she records his brutality, his nervous reaction when his father's death is mentioned, and his purchase of poison. She tells Mrs Prig, '[w]hat I knows, I knows; and what you don't, you don't' (*MC* 49, 751). Reading Jonas's character, Gamp prepares Dickens's readers for his exposure, but, as an interludic figure, takes no active role when he is accused of murder.

Dickens's text (chapter 19) and Phiz's etching (p. 313) for Number VIII, '*Mr. Pecksniff on his Mission*' (Figure 43.1), supply a stage set for Mrs Gamp's entrance: shop fronts; signs announce 'MRS. GAMP MIDWIFE' and Sweedlepipe's barber shop ('EASY SHAVING/HAIR DRESSER/BIRD FANCIER'). 'THE ORIGINAL MUTTON PIE DEPOT') next door suggests Sweeney Todd, already an urban legend: Tom Pinch fears 'streets where the countrymen are murdered; and ... have been made meat-pies of, or some horrible thing' (*MC* 36, 576). Her 'MIDWIFE' sign is the only evidence of Mrs Gamp. Dickens and Phiz portray an absence that provokes anticipation, a stage with the major player missing. Pecksniff enters, seeking Gamp to prepare Anthony Chuzzlewit's body for burial. As he tries to rouse her, women gather, thinking him an anxious father-to-be, his wife already in labour. When Mrs Gamp finally shows herself at her window,

---

[9] Charles Dickens, *Martin Chuzzlewit*, ed. Margaret Cardwell (Oxford: Clarendon Press, 1982), chapter 25, page 403. Subsequent references are inserted parenthetically in the text by *MC* chapter, page.

[10] Charles Dickens, *Bleak House*, ed. George Ford and Sylvère Monod (New York: W. W. Norton, 1977), chapter 16, page 197. Subsequent references are inserted parenthetically in the text by *BH* chapter, page.

FIGURE 43.1 Hablot K. Browne, 'Mr. Pecksniff on his Mission', *Martin Chuzzlewit*, steel etching, August 1843.

an impatient audience awaits her, eager to participate in the drama of the moment. 'Is it Mrs. Perkins?' Gamp cries. She knows when her customers are due.

> 'No!' returned Mr. Pecksniff, sharply, 'Nothing of the sort.'
> 'What, Mr. Whilks!' cried Mrs. Gamp. 'Don't say it's you, Mr. Whilks, and that poor creetur Mrs. Whilks with not even a pin-cushion ready. Don't say it's you, Mr. Whilks!'
> 'It isn't Mr. Whilks,' said Pecksniff … 'Nothing of the kind. A gentleman is dead; and some person being wanted in the house, you have been recommended.' (*MC* 19, 312)

After looking 'out of window' with her mourning countenance, Mrs Gamp joins him, now in character for a funeral: 'And so the gentleman's dead, sir! Ah! The more's the pity,' she reflects, 'But it's what we must all come to. It's as certain as being born, except that we can't make our calculations as exact. Ah! Poor dear! ... When Gamp was summoned to his long home, and I see him a lying in Guy's Hospital with a penny-piece on each eye, and his wooden leg under his left arm, I thought I should have fainted away. But I bore up.' (*MC* 19, 312–16)

Dickens endows Mrs Gamp with his own ability to invent fictional characters. He demonstrates how to build a fictional character incrementally when Gamp adds striking but unnecessary details: Mrs Harris's brother-in-law is 'six foot three, and marked with a mad bull in Wellinton boots upon his left arm ... his precious mother havin been worrited by one into a shoemaker's shop' (*MC* 46, 701). Gamp's monologues quickly become dialogues with the fictional Mrs Harris:

> 'If it wasn't for the nerve a little sip of liquor gives me (I never was able to do more than taste it) I never could go through with what I sometimes has to do. "Mrs. Harris," I says, at the very last case as ever I acted in ... "Mrs. Harris," I says, "leave the bottle on the chimley-piece, and don't ask me to take none, but let me put my lips to it when I am so dispoged, and then I will do what I am engaged to do" ... "Mrs. Gamp," she says, in answer, "if ever there was a sober creetur to be got at eighteenpence a day for working people, and three-and-six for gentlefolks—night watching,"' said Mrs. Gamp, with emphasis, '"being a extra charge—you are that inwallable person." "Mrs. Harris," I says to her, "don't name the charge, for if I could afford to lay all my fellercreeturs out for nothink, I would gladly do it; sich is the love I bears 'em".' (*MC* 19, 316)

In *Chuzzlewit* X (October 1843), Mrs Gamp visits Mould the undertaker, the 'connexion' she depends upon for recommendations. In 'a carefully regulated routine', she flatters Mrs Mould and recalls Mould's daughters playing 'at berryins down in the shop, and follerin the order-book to its long home in the iron safe!' (*MC* 25, 404). 'Connexion', Dickens's favourite device of bringing characters coincidentally together in his novels' pattern, lets him juggle the word's alternative meanings: for Gamp a relationship with anyone who might recommend or employ her; for Dickens a nexus between characters to democratize his plot by connecting rich with poor. Gamp is making a connection when Merry Chuzzlewit returns from her honeymoon. Phiz's '*Mrs. Gamp has her eye on the future*' shows her handing Merry a business card. Dickens's text describes her 'leer of mingled sweetness and slyness ... partly spiritual, partly spirituous, and wholly professional and peculiar to her art ... all tending to the establishment of a mysterious and confidential understanding between herself and the bride' (*MC* 26, 422). In *Chuzzlewit* XI (November 1843) and *Chuzzlewit* XV (March 1844) she suspects Jonas, but takes no action. Instead she blames steam engines for causing premature births:

> 'Them Confugion steamers ... has done more to ... bring ewents on at times when nobody counted on 'em (especially them screeching railroad ones) ... I have heerd of one young man, a guard upon a railway ... as is god-father at this present time to six-and-twenty blessed little strangers, equally unexpected, and all on 'em named after the Ingeins as was the cause. Ugh! ... one might easily know you was a man's

invention, from your disregardlessness of the weakness of our naturs, so one might, you brute!' (*MC* 40, 626)

In *Chuzzlewit* XVII (May 1844), Phiz's 'Mrs. Gamp makes tea' (Figure 43.2) depicts her with three potential mothers: 'Mrs. Gamp ... added daily so many strings to her bow, that she made a perfect harp of it; and upon that instrument she now began to perform an extemporaneous concerto' (*MC* 46, 700). Presiding over the tea table, 'she stopped ... to favor the circle with a smile, a wink, a roll of the head, or some other mark of notice ... her countenance was lighted up with a degree of intelligence and vivacity, which it was almost impossible to separate from the benignant influence of distilled waters' (*MC* 46, 705). After the party, she recognizes an opportunity in Jonas's fear lest Chuffey,

FIGURE 43.2 Hablot K. Browne, 'Mrs. Gamp makes Tea', *Martin Chuzzlewit*, steel etching, May 1844.

FIGURE 43.3 Hablot K. Browne, 'Mrs. Gamp propoges a toast', *Martin Chuzzlewit*, steel etching, June 1844.

with his repeated references to 'foul play', might arouse suspicions about Anthony's death. 'Smil[ing] ... and sniff[ing] expressively, as scenting a job', she manipulates Jonas into hiring Betsey Prig and herself to keep Chuffey quiet (*MC* 46, 715).

In *Chuzzlewit* XVIII (June 1844), Phiz's '*Mrs. Gamp propoges a toast*' (Figure 43.3) shows her entertaining Mrs Prig to discuss their new job, with disastrous results:

> 'Mrs. Harris, Betsey—'
> 'Bother Mrs. Harris!' said Betsey Prig.
> Mrs. Gamp looked at her with amazement, incredulity, and indignation; when Mrs. Prig, shutting her eye still closer, and folding her arms still tighter, uttered these memorable and tremendous words:
> 'I don't believe there's no sich a person!' (*MC* 49, 752)

FIGURE 43.4 Hablot K. Browne, Mrs Gamp with a bandbox head dancing with two liquor bottles, one with the head of a teapot, detail of frontispiece to *Martin Chuzzlewit*, 'Tom Pinch at his organ', steel etching, July 1844.

Mrs Harris is Gamp's fiction, invented to celebrate Gamp as heroine of her own life and queen of midwives. When Mrs Prig questions Mrs Harris's reality, she also demolishes Gamp, a creature of words, by leaving her speechless. Gamp is uncharacteristically silent in *Chuzzlewit* XIX–XX (July 1844), when Jonas is accused of parricide, keeping 'two-thirds of herself behind the door, ready for escape, and one-third in the room, ready for siding with the strongest party' (*MC* 51, 780). At Dickens's request, Phiz's frontispiece for the completed novel depicts the characters' futures.[11] Spectral patients and babies watch Mrs Gamp and two animated bottles with teapot and pap cup for heads dancing (Figure 43.4), her head in a bandbox labelled 'GAMP'. Her future seems to be babies, corpses, and gin.

Dickens made his mark with Gamp's comic role, her innovative language, and her natal and pre-natal lore. When Mrs Harris had her first child, 'Mr. Harris who was dreadful timid went and stopped his ears in an empty dog-kennel, and never took his hands away or come out once till he was showed the baby, wen bein took with fits, the doctor collared him and laid him on his back upon the airy stones, and she was told to ease her mind, his owls was organs' (*MC* 49, 748).

An accomplished amateur magician, Dickens could distract an audience with patter, a rapid monologue. Mrs Gamp's patter attracts and simultaneously distracts us from unravelling the novel's 'design' too soon. For most of *Martin Chuzzlewit* she is a 'dilatory area', *femina ludens*, a recurring and entertaining interlude. Gradually introducing

[11] *PLets* 4:140–1, 140.

further details, Dickens enhances her comic role as eccentric monster and rival storyteller, preparing us for her outrage when Betsey Prig challenges Gamp's sustaining fiction. She even makes it into the frontispiece, depicting Tom Pinch at the organ, as a ludic interlude.

Dickens's treatment of Mrs Gamp in an early novel, and Miss Wade in a late novel, reveals how his use of interludes developed. Gamp introduces a comic verbal anarchy into *Martin Chuzzlewit*. Miss Wade introduces an angry social anarchy into *Little Dorrit*. Somebody's illegitimate daughter, shamed by her origin, she rejects friendly overtures as condescending and patronizing, and imprisons herself in resentful solitude. Dickens makes her *non serviam* psychologically believable. She deliberately excludes herself from any participation in the search for the iron box containing documents that explain what Mrs Clennam should 'Not Forget'. Dickens leaves it to the reader to recognize the 'connexion' between Miss Wade's self-isolation and the prison motifs that shape his story.

Little Dorrit I (December 1855) opens with Rigaud, awaiting trial for murder in a French prison. Chapter two introduces 'Fellow Travellers' newly released from quarantine at Marseilles, among them Arthur Clennam, returning home after 20 years of exile; the Meagles family; and Miss Wade. Arthur describes himself to Mr Meagles as 'a waif and stray ... son ... of a hard father and mother ... Austere faces, inexorable discipline, penance in this world and terror in the next' (*LD* I:2, 19–20). Meagles is travelling with his wife, their daughter Pet, and her maid, Tattycoram. When Arthur asks about Tattycoram's name, Meagles explains. Mrs Meagles was moved to tears at the sight of children without parents or identity during a visit to Captain Coram's Foundling Hospital. Mr Meagles suggested taking one of them

> to be a little maid to Pet ... if we should find her temper a little defective, or any of her ways a little wide of ours ... We shall know what an immense deduction must be made from all the influences and experiences that have formed us—no parents, no child-brother or sister, no individuality of home, no Glass Slipper, or Fairy Godmother ... she was called in the Institution, Harriet Beadle ... Harriet we changed into Hatty, and then into Tatty, because, as practical people, we thought even a playful name might be a new thing to her, and might have a softening and affectionate kind of effect ... we gave that name to Pet's little maid. At one time she was Tatty, and at one time she was Coram, until we got into a way of mixing the two names together, and now she is always Tattycoram. (*LD* I:2, 17–18)

Tattycoram's 'droll name' begins with *tatty* (shabby, untidy, scruffy). Coram identifies her as illegitimate. She has been in an orphanage, a kind of prison, without access to the imaginative and playful fancies Dickens champions in *Hard Times* and 'Frauds on the Fairies', and Huizinga praises in *Homo Ludens*. Even the Meagles, intending to be kind, are nevertheless 'practical people' who think a 'playful name' might have a good effect. Their play is hardly 'ludic'.

Mrs Gamp was a sudden inspiration when Dickens had written almost a third of *Martin Chuzzlewit*. But Miss Wade was part of *Little Dorrit* from the start. As a recurring interlude, she embodies Dickens's motifs in *Little Dorrit*: guilt, prison, solitude. 'Reserved Woman. Introduce Miss—Wade?' Dickens asks himself in his first Number Plan (*LD* 'Number Plans', 806). Like Mrs Gamp and Jingle, she immediately energizes the narrative whenever she appears, usually by refusing to interact with the novel's other characters. 'Miss Wade?' is frequent in the *Dorrit* Plans, followed by 'Yes' or 'No'. Neither comic nor playful, she challenges some of Dickens's depictions of benevolent but selective charity, of loyal servants and kind masters. As *auctor ludens*, Dickens distracts us from his own plot to experiment with a fictional character that rejects any supporting role in his story but predicts how it will develop.

'A handsome young Englishwoman, travelling quite alone,' with 'a proud observant face', Miss Wade 'had either withdrawn herself from the rest or been avoided' by them until she suddenly challenges Mr Meagles's readiness to forgive their confinement in quarantine. 'Do you mean that a prisoner forgives his prison? ... If I had been shut up in any place to pine and suffer, I should always hate that place and wish to burn it down, or raze it to the ground' (*LD* I:2, 22). Then she withdraws 'to a remote corner ... as if she were lonely of her own haughty choice'. 'I am self-contained and self-reliant,' her face proclaimed: 'I have no interest in you, care nothing for you, and see and hear you with indifference' (*LD* I:2, 23). She is performing, dramatizing herself as an enigma, inscrutable heroine of her own story. Rejecting Meagles's offer of help with her baggage, she turns on Pet Meagles, whose 'frank face, and wonderful eyes; so large, so soft, so bright' and 'air of timidity and dependence ... gave her the only crowning charm a girl so pretty and pleasant could have been without' (*LD* I:2, 16)—attributes sure to provoke Miss Wade. She frightens Pet by predicting how Dickens will develop *Little Dorrit* with connections and coincidence: 'we shall meet the people who are coming to meet *us*, from many strange places and by many strange roads ... and what it is set to us to do to them, and what it is set to them to do to us, will all be done ... there are men and women already upon their road, who have their business to do with *you* ... they may be coming, for anything you know, or ... can do to prevent it, from the vilest sweepings of this very town' (*LD* I:2, 24–5).

Dickens's notes for *Dorrit* I connect Miss Wade with Tattycoram. Leaving the Meagles family after prophesying those fated future encounters, Miss Wade hears 'an angry sound of muttering and sobbing'. Tattycoram is weeping and raging against her employers: 'Selfish brutes! ... Beasts! Devils!' Miss Wade, who has already been watching this 'sullen, passionate girl', listens with 'a strange attentive smile ... looking at the girl, as one afflicted with a diseased part might curiously watch the dissection and exposition of an analogous case'. Tattycoram's rage gradually 'trail[s] off into broken murmurs', and the angry girl dismisses her complaints as 'all lies ... They are nothing but good to me ... I am afraid of you ... Go away from me, and let me pray and cry myself better!' (*LD* I:2, 25–6). Dickens establishes Miss Wade as a troubling presence, attracted by Tattycoram and her discontent. Self-defined as an outsider among the central characters, she analyses them, and theorizes about their motives and behaviour. Phiz's '*Under the Microscope*' (*LD* I:2, 27) captures Wade diagnosing what she sees: Tattycoram trying to hide her tears, scraps of cloth or paper scattered on the floor (Figure 43.5).

FIGURE 43.5 Hablot K. Browne, 'Under the Microscope', *Little Dorrit*, steel etching, December 1855.

Miss Wade thinks like Dickens. He soon confirms her prophecy about how *Little Dorrit* will develop: 'under the sun and under the stars ... journeying by land and journeying by sea, coming and going so strangely, to meet and to act and react on one another, move all we restless travellers through the pilgrimage of life' (*LD* I:2, 26). Arthur turns Amy Dorrit into a mystery, unaware of an earlier connection between the Dorrit and Clennan families.

In chapter 3, Arthur walks to his mother's house through London on an English Sunday, everything 'bolted and barred' against anything ludic or imaginative that might 'furnish relief to an overworked people. No pictures, no unfamiliar animals, no rare plants or flowers, no natural or artificial wonders of the ancient world—all *taboo*' (*LD* I:3, 29). He receives a frosty welcome from Mrs Clennam. Semi-paralysed, she has been confined to two rooms for 12 years. Chapter 4 ends with Flintwinch, Mrs Clennam's assistant, giving an iron box to Ephraim, his twin. The box will travel from London to Antwerp, where Blandois, also known as Rigaud, will steal it and deposit it with Miss Wade in Calais. Wade delays the resolution of Dickens's complex plot by refusing to admit to Arthur, and later to Meagles, that she has the box. Tattycoram will steal it and bring it to Mr Meagles. The box is Dickens's metaphor for his novel's plot.

Home after 20 years, Arthur confronts Mrs Clennam with unwelcome questions. His dying father, agitated but unable to speak, sent Mrs Clennam his watch and its 'silk watch-lining', with D. N. F. (Do Not Forget) 'worked with beads' (*LD* I:30, 349). 'Is it possible, mother', Arthur asks, 'that he had unhappily wronged any one, and made no reparation? ... If reparation can be made to any one, if restitution can be made to any one, let us know it and make it.' Mrs Clennam responds with vigorous biblical curses: Arthur is 'to be avoided of God and man'. She warns him that 'if you ever renew that theme with me ... I will never see or know you more. And if ... you were to come into this darkened room to look upon me lying dead, my body should bleed, if I could make it, when you came near me' (*LD* I:5, 46–51).

Nineteen months later, serial readers would learn the answers to Arthur's questions in *Dorrit* XIX–XX. 'Do Not Forget', Flintwinch's handover of the box, and Arthur's questions, initiate a complex plot that Dickens himself found elusive. His plan for *Dorrit* XIX–XX includes 'Retrospective', a prequel plot summary he needed to 'work the story round' (*LD* 'Number Plans', 825) by describing events 40 years earlier.

With Miss Wade, Dickens admits an irregular and discordant element into his pattern. As *femina ludens* she rejects participating in the story Dickens is telling. Igor Stravinsky and Benjamin Britten introduce dissonance into their scores; Jacques stands apart from the happy ending of *As You Like It*; Icarus's flailing legs disturb the pastoral idyll in Pieter Bruegel's *Landscape with the Fall of Icarus*. Miss Wade is sure that anyone trying to befriend her is insincere. She has studied how to hate, not how to forgive or tolerate. Dickens challenges himself—and the reader—to comprehend her bitter resentment. As a narrative device, she delays the revelation of Mrs Clennam's secrets and restates Dickens's prison motif. As *auctor ludens* Dickens questions his own authorial control by imagining a fictional character who taunts him by predicting how *Little Dorrit* will proceed by connections and coincidence to the traditional happy ending she scorns.

After Wade debuts in *Little Dorrit* I (December 1855), it is four months in serial readers' time before Tattycoram mentions meeting her near the Meagles's Twickenham house (*LD* I:16, 190–1; Part V, April 1856). In *Dorrit* VIII (July 1856), Tattycoram runs away after a display of 'flaming rage'. Mr Meagles explains that in her passion Tattycoram 'detested us ... When we pretended to be so fond of one another, we exulted over her ... and shamed her ... who were we that we should have a right to name her like a dog or a cat? ... she would fling us her name back again, and she would go ... we should never hear of her again' (*LD* I:27, 314–15). Meagles and Arthur discover her in London with Miss Wade: 'the girl' faces them 'half irresolutely, half passionately; Miss Wade with her composed face attentively regarding her, and suggesting... with extraordinary force, in her composure itself... the unquenchable passion of her own nature.' Miss Wade addresses Tattycoram in a speech mocking Meagles's notions of benevolence:

> 'You can be, again, a foil to his pretty daughter, a slave to her pleasant willfulness, and a toy in the house showing the goodness of the family. You can have your droll name again, playfully pointing you out and setting you apart, as it is right that you should be pointed out and set apart. (Your birth, you know; you must not forget your birth.) You can again be shown to this gentleman's daughter, Harriet, and kept before her, as a living reminder of her own superiority and her gracious condescension. You can recover all these advantages... by telling these gentlemen how humbled and penitent you are, and by going back with them to be forgiven. What do you say, Harriet? Will you go?'
>
> The girl who, under the influence of these words, had gradually risen in anger and heightened in color, answered, raising her lustrous black eyes for the moment, and clenching her hand upon the folds it had been puckering up, 'I'll die sooner!' (*LD* I:27, 319–20)

When Meagles urges Tattycoram to control herself by counting to 'five-and-twenty', she refuses: 'I won't!... I'd be torn to pieces first, I'd tear myself to pieces first!' He implores her: 'consider what is in that lady's heart... that lady's influence over you... is founded in passion fiercer than yours and temper more violent than yours. What can you two be together?' Then he addresses Miss Wade: 'I don't know what you are, but you don't hide, can't hide, what a dark spirit you have within you. If it should happen that you are a woman, who, from whatever cause, has a perverted delight in making a sister-woman as wretched as she is (I am old enough to have heard of such), I warn her against you, and I warn you against yourself' (*LD* I:27, 320–3).

Wade and Tattycoram are believably angry, passionate, and sexual, like Rosa Dartle and Mme Defarge. For post-Freudian readers, Meagles's 'perverted delight' usually suggests that Miss Wade is a lesbian. Does Dickens, a man of the world, use the unsophisticated and impulsive Meagles to hint at what many of his contemporaries could not imagine, others considered unmentionable?

Phiz's '*Five and Twenty*' (*LD* I:27, 322) shows Tattycoram weeping on Miss Wade's shoulder (Figure 43.6). Dickens describes Wade watching her 'with that strange attentive smile, and that repressing hand upon her own bosom, with which she had watched her in her struggle at Marseilles, then put her arm about her waist as if she took possession of her for evermore'. Wade announces that she, like Tattycoram, 'has no name... Her wrong is my wrong'. She taunts Clennam with losing Pet Meagles to his rival, 'your dear friend, Mr. Gowan' (*LD* I:27, 323–4). Her performance shows how carefully she studied Tattycoram, how eager she is to share her own misery, to have an ally against a hostile world. But Dickens reassures readers. 'Dear kind Master, dear kind Mistress, take me back again', Tattycoram will cry in *Dorrit* XIX–XX (June 1857) after leaving Miss Wade, 'and give me back the dear old name! Let this [the iron box] intercede for me. Here it is!' (*LD* II:33, 787). Wade has had her say about illegitimacy and condescension, and about

FIGURE 43.6 Hablot K. Browne, 'Five and twenty', *Little Dorrit*, steel etching, December 1855.

selectively benevolent patrons of the deserving poor. With Miss Wade, Dickens plays against the comforting *persona* he projected in earlier novels.

In *Dorrit* XIII (December 1856) Tattycoram is briefly seen in Twickenham. Then Arthur finds her by chance in London, leading Rigaud/Blandois to meet Miss Wade, another connection, intensified when the two women lead him to Casby, whose daughter Arthur once courted. After a brief comic interlude featuring Mr F's Aunt, Casby admits handling Wade's trust fund, but claims not to know where she lives. Arthur's nocturnal adventures in *Dorrit* XIII continue, to find Mrs Clennam welcoming Blandois and ready to act as his banker. One of the 'vilest sweepings' of Marseille has reappeared in connection with Mrs Clennam.

Miss Wade makes her fifth appearance in *Dorrit* XVI (February 1857). Arthur seeks the iron box; she denies having it. Her Calais lodgings are a metaphor for the wasteland of her angry life:

> A dead sort of house, with a dead wall over the way and a dead gateway at the side, where a pendant bell-handle produced two dead tinkles, and a knocker produced

a dead flat surface-tapping … the door jarred open on a dead sort of spring; and [Arthur] closed it behind him as he entered a dull yard, soon brought to a close at the back by another dead wall, where an attempt had been made to train some creeping shrubs, which were dead; and to make a little fountain in a grotto, which was dry; and to decorate that with a little statue, which was gone. (*LD* II:20, 635)

Dickens's number plan for *Dorrit* XVI, Book II, chapter 19 asks, 'After the death of the [Dorrit] brothers … Carry through Miss Wade and Tattycoram? <u>Yes.</u> Gowan and his wife? <u>No. Except through Miss Wade</u> [/] <u>The History of a Self Tormentor</u>. From her own point of view. Dissect it' (*LD* 'Number Plans', 822). As first written, Miss Wade tells Arthur her 'History [as] a Self-Tormentor', stressing her anger and shame at being illegitimate, her rejection of friendly overtures, and her belief that offers of friendship are insincere and patronizing. After reading the proofs, Forster suggested that Miss Wade instead write her 'History' specifically for Arthur to read. Dickens was unsure:

> I don't see the practicability of making the History of a Self-Tormentor, with which I took great pains, a written narrative. But I do see the possibility of making it a chapter by itself, which might enable me to dispense with the necessity of the turned commas. Do you think that would be better? I have no doubt that a great part of Fielding's reason for the *introduced* [italics mine] story, and Smollett's also, was, that it is sometimes really impossible to present, in a full book, the idea it contains (which yet it may be on all accounts desirable to present), without supposing the reader to be possessed of almost as much romantic allowance as would put him on a level with the writer. In Miss Wade I had an idea, which I thought a new one, of making the *introduced* [italics mine] story so fit into surroundings impossible of separation from the main story, as to make the blood of the book circulate through both. But I can only suppose, from what you say, that I have not exactly succeeded in this.[12]

For *introduced* read interlude. Notes added to the *Dorrit* XVI number plan record Dickens's division of Arthur's visit to Calais into two chapters (20 and 21), 'getting the Self-Tormentor Narrative by itself' as a written narrative (*LD* 'Number Plans', 822). In the revised text, Miss Wade tells Arthur she has *written* 'The History of a Self-Tormentor' for him 'to tell you what my life has been … that you may comprehend … what I mean by hating' and understand 'what my life has been' and 'with what care I have studied myself, and people about me'. Arthur's Calais visit ends when Tattycoram appears, and admits her visit to Twickenham. 'Is that your fidelity to me?' Miss Wade asks angrily. 'Is that the common cause I make with you?' 'As each of the two handsome faces looked at the other, Clennam felt how each of the two natures must be constantly tearing the other to pieces.' 'You are as bad as they were, every bit', Tattycoram replies. 'But I will not be quite tamed and made submissive' (*LD* II:21, 640-3).

---

[12] *PLets* 8:279–80.

In the proofs Forster read, Miss Wade *tells* Arthur her story just before Tattycoram's entrance and the quarrel about her revisiting Twickenham. After Dickens revised the episode, Wade hands Arthur several written pages, the women quarrel, and Arthur reads 'The History' on the boat to England, but does not react. As a monologue, Wade's tirade resembles her remarks in *Dorrit* I about prisoners hating their prison, and about Meagles's 'practical' charity in *Dorrit* VIII. But what motivates Miss Wade to write anything for Arthur to read? She despises his passivity, and lies to him about the iron box. How could he respond to her autobiography? Leaving Miss Wade self-imprisoned in hatred and in her barren setting restates the prison motif. The 'blood of the book' does circulate through the written interlude, as Dickens intended, but perhaps not as forcibly as when spoken in anger. Like Mrs Gamp, Wade is a self-dramatizer, as Dickens recognized in initially presenting her 'History' as an oral performance. When she last appears, in *Dorrit* XIX–XX, denying to Meagles that she has the iron box, Tattycoram takes it, with its evidence of Mrs Clennam's crimes, to London.

Spoken or written, Wade voices Dickens's protest against contemporary attitudes. Esther Summerson, also illegitimate, remembers being told, 'Your mother, Esther, is your disgrace, as you were hers' (*BH* 17, 213). Self-defined as tainted, Miss Wade rejects friendship. She hates herself for loving Henry Gowan. Like Mrs Clennam, who will also try to control the telling of her own story, Wade is self-imprisoned in resentment, in self-isolation. She hires Blandois to spy on Gowan's and Pet's marriage. She recognizes Tattycoram's repressed rage at the Meagleses for making her their servant and giving her an absurd name. Why does she describe how to hate to Arthur? Why taunt him with failing to attract Pet? Her lessons on hating prepare us for the revelations about Mrs Clennam's cruelty, despite her refusal to participate in the plot she predicted.

In one last interludic device, Blandois, the Flintwinches, and Mrs Clennam vie with and interrupt each other to tell the story in the iron box, the prequel to *Little Dorrit*. The story comes out like a serial, in instalments narrated by several voices (*LD* II:30, 741–65). Mrs Clennam describes her guilt and fear of damnation during her own childhood 'of wholesome repression, punishment, and fear', paralleling Miss Wade's conviction that she too is tainted by her parents' sin. Wade's lesson in hating helps us understand Mrs Clennam's hatred when, a year after marriage, she discovered that her husband had 'sinned against the Lord' by earlier marrying a 'creature of perdition ... a singing girl'. Arthur is their child. Mrs Clennam, and the uncle who controlled the family business, demanded that Arthur's father abandon the singing girl, marry Mrs Clennam, and surrender Arthur to her custody. Threatened with disinheritance, he obeyed. The Clennams settled into a loveless marriage, leaving the singing girl to 'the just dispensation of Jehovah', death in a lunatic asylum. Mrs Clennam's punitive theology justified raising Arthur 'strictly' until he turned 20, when she sent father and son to manage family business interests in China.

Even after Blandois confronts her with her own misdeeds, and Little Dorrit has read an account of them, Mrs Clennam claims divine approval for her cruelty towards Arthur's mother: 'she did wrong me! ... I was stern with [Arthur] ... knowing ... that there was an angry mark upon him at his birth ... I have seen him, with his mother's face ... and trying to soften me with his mother's ways that hardened me' (*LD* II:31, 768–9). Her history of self-torment is another lesson in how to hate.

Mr Clennam first met Arthur's mother in Frederick Dorrit's 'idle house where singers, and players, and such-like children of Evil, turned their backs on the Light and their faces to the Darkness ... secretly pining ... for those accursed snares which are called the Arts'. In old age, the uncle who had forced Mr Clennam to abandon his wife felt some remorse. His will left a thousand guineas to the singing girl, and the same sum to 'the youngest daughter [Frederick] might have at fifty, or (if he had none) his brother's youngest daughter, on her coming of age' (*LD* II:30, 757), legacies Mrs Clennam has withheld from the beneficiaries, including, with imaginative accuracy, William Dorrit's 'youngest daughter', Little Dorrit herself.

A few pages later, the 'shadow ... of the prison-buildings' in the Marshalsea makes Blandois's summary of Mrs Clennam's crimes 'too dark' for Little Dorrit to read until she moves to a sunlit window, leaving Mrs Clennam in darkness. Hoping to retain Arthur's 'respect', she persuades Amy to conceal Arthur's own story from him, at least until she is dead. But she continues to claim divine approval: 'Even now, I see *you* shrink from me, as if I had been cruel ... I have been an instrument of severity against sin. Have not mere sinners like myself been commissioned to lay it low in all time?' (*LD* II:31, 770). *Little Dorrit* ends with Arthur unaware of his parentage or of Mrs Clennam's crimes. At Little Dorrit's request, he burns Blandois's summary on their wedding day, without reading it. He may never read his own story. It is Dickens as *auctor ludens*, playing a prank on readers expecting to learn how his characters later fared.

The energy Dickens introduced into serial publication with interludic characters like Jingle and Mrs Gamp, and the opportunities for psychological analysis Miss Wade and Tattycoram offer, invite further critical attention to Dickens's interludes and their function in serial publication. Serials are popular again. Elena Ferrante's *L' amica geniale* (2011–14) is four annual instalments of a single novel about Neapolitan life; the Norwegian writer Karl Ove Knausgård's autobiographical *Min Kamp* runs to six volumes (2009–11). Television has revived serials: *Upstairs, Downstairs; House of Cards; Mad Men; Downton Abbey*; BBC versions of novels by Dickens and Trollope. A less successful revival was the BBC's short-lived *Dickensian*. The idea was to detach Dickens's characters from the novels in which they appear and recycle them: in the first episode, Inspector Bucket investigates the murder of Jacob Marley with Bill Sikes as prime suspect. Dickens as interactive Virtual Reality may be next. There I decline to go.

Further Reading

M. M. Bakhtin, *The Dialogic Imagination: Four Essays*, ed. Michael Holquist, trans. Michael Holquist and Caryl Emerson (Austin: University of Texas Press, 1998)

Donald Fanger, *Dostoevsky and Romantic Realism: A Study of Dostoevsky in Relation to Balzac, Dickens, and Gogol* (Cambridge, MA: Harvard University Press, 1966)

Vladimir Yakovlevich Propp, *The Russian Folktale*, ed. and trans. Sibelan Forrester (Detroit: Wayne State University Press, 2012)

Victor Shklovsky, *The Theory of Prose*, trans. Benjamin Sher (Elmwood Park, IL: Dalkey Archive Press, 1990)

Michael Steig, *Dickens and Phiz* (Bloomington: Indiana University Press, 1978)

CHAPTER 44

DICKENS AND THE THEATRE

JOHN GLAVIN

Dickens's Engagements with Victorian Theatre

THEATRE arcs through the whole of Dickens's adult life, from the famous missed audition at Covent Garden in 1832, when he was still a very young man, to the final Readings that hastened his death in 1870. That larger arc divides roughly into three segments.

In the 1830s Dickens regularly reviewed professional performances in a wide variety of journals. At the same time he staged private and distinctly amateur theatricals with friends and family at home. This practice continued for several decades, often to mark family events like birthdays or seasonal holidays. During this decade he also began with some success to write for the professional theatre. In September 1836 his two-act farce *The Strange Gentleman* ran for almost 60 performances. This was followed by a more ambitious two-act musical burletta, *The Village Coquettes*, a popular though not a critical success. And finally, he wrote the one-act burletta *Is She His Wife?*[1] At that point his increasingly brilliant success as a writer of fiction seems to have brought to an end any further thought of the professional theatre.

In the second unit, starting in the mid-1840s and continuing until 1858, he turned to serious amateur theatre, what he called a sham theatre: 'The real Theatre is so bad, that I have always a delight in setting up a sham one.'[2] And for a period of about 15 years he was regularly involved with increasingly elaborate performances involving both

---

[1] John Glavin, 'Dickens and Theatre', in *The Cambridge Companion to Charles Dickens*, ed. John O. Jordan (Cambridge: Cambridge University Press, 2001), 189–203, 191.

[2] *The Letters of Charles Dickens*, ed. Madeline House, Graham Storey, et al., Pilgrim/British Academy Edition, 12 vols (Oxford: Clarendon Press, 1965–2002). Subsequent citations: *PLets* followed by volume:page range, page, and hn. for headnote, n. or nn. for footnotes, with page range given before page cited. Here, 7:641.

amateurs and professionals in full-length plays performed mostly for charity. These performances have been covered in detail by the major biographies as well as in more specialized studies such as Robert Louis Brannon's *Under the Management of Mr. Charles Dickens* and Lillian Nayder's *Unequal Partners: Charles Dickens, Wilkie Collins, and Victorian Authorship*.[3]

The third phase involves the celebrated series of public, for-profit Readings that Dickens inaugurated in 1858, effectively displacing the other forms of theatrical engagement. They have been brilliantly examined by Malcolm Andrews in *Charles Dickens and his Performing Selves*, one of the truly indispensable Dickens studies.[4] We return to Andrews's invaluable analysis to conclude this chapter.

Dickens is nowhere more recognizably Victorian than in this fascination with the theatre. Happily, the last 20 years have generated a remarkable about-face in attitudes toward and knowledge of nineteenth-century performance. Until Oscar Wilde and George Bernard Shaw the Victorians contributed little to the next century's repertory, with the always notable exception of Gilbert and Sullivan. As a result, twentieth-century text-oriented criticism tended typically to ignore that theatre or to treat it as a trivial mélange of farce and melodrama, of little interest to serious critique. However, building on the path-breaking work of Michael R. Booth, particularly *Victorian Spectacular Theatre, 1850–1910*, the current generation of theatre historians has enabled us to recover much of the dynamism of the gaslight stage.[5] Notable in this regard is the work of Tracy C. Davis, *The Economics of the British Stage 1800–1914* and Jacky Bratton, *The Making of the West End Stage*, building on pioneering work in the collection of essays edited by Bratton and Ellen Donkin, *Women and Playwriting in Nineteenth-Century Britain*.[6] At the same time literary critics sympathetic to the theatre have shown how writers in a wide range of genres could find themselves invigorated and challenged by the theatre as a model for other sorts of text, beginning with Elaine Hadley's widely influential *Melodramatic Tactics* and continuing into the twenty-first century with David Kurnick in *Empty Houses: Theatrical Failure and the Novel* and Sos Eltis with *Acts of Desire*.[7] Because of Dickens's sustained investment in adapting Shakespeare, we are also particularly indebted to the brilliant investigations of Richard W. Schoch, especially

---

[3] Robert Louis Brannon, *Under the Management of Mr. Charles Dickens* (Ithaca, NY: Cornell University Press, 1975). Lillian Nayder, *Unequal Partners: Charles Dickens, Wilkie Collins, and Victorian Authorship* (Ithaca, NY: Cornell University Press, 2002).

[4] Malcolm Andrews, *Charles Dickens and his Performing Selves: Dickens and the Public Readings* (Oxford and New York: Oxford University Press, 2006).

[5] Michael R. Booth, *Victorian Spectacular Theatre, 1850–1910* (Boston, MA: Routledge and Kegan Paul, 1981).

[6] Tracy C. Davis, *The Economics of the British Stage, 1800–1914* (Cambridge: Cambridge University Press, 2000). Jacky Bratton, *The Making of the West End Stage* (Cambridge: Cambridge University Press, 2000). Jacky Bratton and Ellen Donkin, *Women and Playwriting in Nineteenth-Century Britain* (Cambridge: Cambridge University Press, 1999).

[7] Elaine Hadley, *Melodramatic Tactics: Theatricalized Dissent in the English Marketplace, 1800–1885* (Stanford, CA: Stanford University Press, 1995). David Kurnick, *Empty Houses: Theatrical Failure and the*

Shakespeare's Victorian Stage: Performing History in the Theatre of Charles Kean and *Not Shakespeare: Bardolatry and Burlesque in the Nineteenth Century*.[8]

Their project enables us now to view theatre going as a central experience for all but the abject in nineteenth-century England, not just in London, and certainly not just for the more comfortable classes. As Tracy C. Davis's comprehensive data proves, by the mid-nineteenth century it is not too early to use the term 'entertainment industry'.[9] Dickens was an ardent friend and supporter to many individuals in that industry. He was particularly close to William Macready, after whom he named a daughter, Kate Macready Dickens. But while an enthusiastic amateur actor and manager, he seems to have loathed the professional theatre itself. Not so surprising when one recalls that Macready also loathed it. In fact, we cannot talk accurately about Dickens and theatre without balancing both attraction and rejection.

It is Bratton who has most clearly helped us to place Dickens accurately in the theatre of his time. 'Dickens', she argues, paraphrasing his own 1858 speech to the Royal Theatrical Fund, 'came to expect and anticipate that everything he wrote was, in effect, written for the stage as well as the page.'[10] By the mid-1840s he had become, in her phrase, the 'Victorian Shakespeare ... one of the major foundations of the modern West End.'[11] The novels were routinely adapted to the stage—with and without his cooperation—almost from the moment they appeared in print. (These adaptations have been exhaustively studied by H. Philip Bolton in his magisterial *Dickens Dramatized*.[12]) But even more significantly: 'Here was the writer whom the public wanted to shape and embody their everyday lives and aspirations in ideal and fantastic forms. The Lyceum and the Adelphi [leading playhouses of the day] were more than willing to collaborate with him.'[13]

Bratton's argument situates Dickens at the cross-hairs of what she has influentially termed *intertheatricality*, arguing that 'all entertainments, including drama, that are performed within a single theatrical tradition are more or less interdependent'.[14] As Eltis extends this argument, it ramifies into a Bottom-like catalogue of 'plays and performances' that cut across 'dramatic genres ... in melodramas, farces, tragedies, problem plays, society dramas, musical dramas, and propagandist sketches ... common to "high" and "low" forms of theatrical entertainment'.[15] But as Bratton makes clear, the

---

Novel (Princeton: Princeton University Press, 2012). Sos Eltis, *Acts of Desire: Women and Sex on Stage, 1800–1930* (Oxford: Oxford University Press, 2013).

[8] Richard W. Schoch, *Shakespeare's Victorian Stage: Performing History in the Theatre of Charles Kean* (Cambridge: Cambridge University Press, 1998). Richard W. Schoch, *Not Shakespeare: Bardolatry and Burlesque in the Nineteenth Century* (Cambridge: Cambridge University Press, 2002).

[9] Davis, *The Economics of the British Stage*, 354.
[10] Bratton, *The Making of the West End Stage*, 179.
[11] Ibid., 37.
[12] H. Philip Bolton, *Dickens Dramatized* (Boston: G. K. Hall, 1987).
[13] Bratton, *The Making of the West End Stage*, 180.
[14] Ibid., 37.
[15] Eltis, *Acts of Desire*, 2.

intertheatrical extends beyond that which is staged to what is read: Dickens, 'the greatest Victorian author wrote for the stage only indirectly; but his work is nevertheless radically part of it. In literary terms, Dickens is the lost leader, the major modern dramatist sought for in vain by Macready and his supporters.'[16] There was almost never a time during Dickens's writing life when what he wrote was not also appearing in adaptation on the stage.

But intertheatricality is a dual carriageway. Dickens served up to his readers what he saw around him in London life, but he also simultaneously served up that life in forms he observed on, and borrowed from, the London stage: from Alfred Jingle the Stroller in his first novel; through Daniel Quilp, Edmund Kean's Richard III, scaled down to pint size; to Lady Dedlock, minted from melodrama; to John Jasper's opium dreams, spangled with the exotic glamour of spectacular theatres like that of Charles Kean.[17] Which means that his original audiences were also likely to read the novels intertheatrically: that is, in large part derived from and dependent on the fullest range of the then current theatrical repertoire, a repertoire that Dickens himself was at the same time reshaping.[18] The missing major titles in the Victorian dramatic canon turn out to be titles we already know: *Oliver Twist, Martin Chuzzlewit, The Chimes, A Tale of Two Cities*, in fact the entire oeuvre. A fact, of course, not missed by savvy theatre managers ever since. Nor should it be overlooked by savvy Dickensians, who can find in intertheatricality a rich field for further critical enquiry.

Why then did Dickens not write also directly for the stage? Why is his stage history a history of adaptation? As Robert Douglas-Fairhurst sagely observes: 'Anyone glancing at the posters for St. James's Theatre in 1836 [where *The Strange Gentlemen* was pulling in audiences] would have seen that transforming himself from sketch writer to novelist and from reporter to editor, were only two of the possible futures [Dickens] was contemplating for himself. A third was playwright.'[19] As Dickens later wrote in a letter to John Forster: 'I have often thought, that I should certainly have been as successful on the boards as I have been between them.'[20] Why did this multi-talented writer, addicted to theatre, obsessed with performance, write no plays after 1837?

In the late 1830s, recently married, Dickens needed a steadier income than any aspiring theatre-outsider could expect. And yet, by the mid-1840s, the date of the letter to Forster, when the economics didn't any longer matter, why does Dickens write as having renounced playwriting? That de facto renunciation, almost parallel to the comparable rejection of life in the theatre by Nicholas Nickleby, speaks powerfully to what it meant in the early nineteenth century to be a man of the theatre, whether manager or playwright.

---

[16] Bratton, *The Making of the West End Stage*, 180.
[17] Glavin, 'Dickens and Theatre', 196–202.
[18] Bratton, *The Making of the West End Stage*, 37.
[19] Robert Douglas-Fairhurst, *Becoming Dickens: The Invention of a Novelist* (Cambridge, MA: Harvard University Press, 2011), 225.
[20] *PLets* 4:244–6, 244.

By the end of the 1830s the disorderly Georgian theatre, patronage-driven, exploitative on every side, was finally giving way to what would become, after the dissolution of the Patents (exclusive royal licences to theatres to present serious spoken dramas), the West End, the fully professional and professionalized theatre of the Victorian and post-Victorian era. By 1843, with the Theatres Regulation Act, British theatre had become another, indeed an iconic, instance of Victorian capitalism. 'With this change, the evolution of the present corporate economy can be traced through theatre; indeed entertainment may be among the first sectors of the British economy to evince the organizational characteristics of centralized management and integrated production and management and distribution.'[21] The theatre, with the Patent system dissolved, became for the first time—in our sense—professional. Macready's endless imbroglio with the Patent holders and the hobo theatre of the Crummles alike swiftly gave way to an enterprise reorganized around a now fully professional actor-manager: figures like Henry Irving, George Alexander, Charles Wyndham, and Herbert Beerbohm Tree. Unlike their eighteenth-century predecessors such as David Garrick, the Victorians were even more important as managers than as actors, and all of the men on this list were ultimately knighted, a key indicator of their now fully professional status. These are the figures Dickens self-consciously emulated when he prominently labelled the performances of *The Frozen Deep* UNDER THE MANAGEMENT OF MR. CHARLES DICKENS at *his* Tavistock House Theatre. But that new professional structure made it virtually impossible any longer, as it were, to dabble in theatre.

The new Victorian theatre is both dominated by, and exemplified in, the fully professional Dion Boucicault, the triple threat as playwright, manager, and actor. He dominated the theatre with the quality captured in the title of his early enormous success *London Assurance* (1841). Even Dickens's restive auxiliary, Wilkie Collins, clearly committed to the writing of plays, was constrained to stage them largely in the amateur not the professional theatre, except as adaptations of his previously published and successful fiction. Of course, the new theatre business was as volatile as the old one, with figures as significant as Madame Vestris and her husband Charles Mathews—well known to Dickens—suffering not only bankruptcy but, in her case, imprisonment for debt.[22] A fully capitalized theatre was not, of course, a stranger to risk.

This new form of professional enterprise emerged in the theatre just when Dickens, as Douglas-Fairhurst shows, was settling on what became his own profession, writer/editor. By 1850 Dickens had, of course, succeeded in making himself into another sort of Victorian manager, the editor-in-chief of a mass circulation periodical. 'For the rest of his life', Michael Slater recounts, 'he was to spend a high proportion of his working hours "conducting" and writing for *Household Words* and its successor *All The Year Round*.'[23] Boucicault then is not Dickens's double, he is Dickens's path not taken, pursuing on the

---

[21] Davis, *The Economics of the British Stage*, 181.
[22] Ibid., 187–8.
[23] Michael Slater, *Charles Dickens* (London and New Haven: Yale University Press, 2009), 306.

stage the same kind of new enterprise that Dickens pursued on the page. One literally excluded the other.

Dickens's 'Sham' Theatre

But Dickens's turn away from the professional stage involves more than a simple choice between equally plausible career paths. In her superb *Knowing Dickens* Rosemary Bodenheimer calls attention to a number of passages from the letters of the mid-1850s that suggest that Dickens realized he could not make for himself a life on or back stage.[24] We've already seen the most telling: 'The real Theatre is so bad, that I have always a delight in setting up a sham one.' The distinction here is crucial: real/bad vs sham/delight. He claimed, 'I would rather, by a great deal, act.'[25] But throughout his fiction the real (professional) theatre is routinely presented as in some sense bad, for men—not so for women. His first villain is the vagrant actor Jingle, who must be humiliated before being redeemed at *Pickwick*'s conclusion. Nicholas Nickleby vehemently denounces the folly of his time in the theatre, time squandered when he should have been working to protect his sister. In *Bleak House*, William Guppy makes a fool of himself ogling Esther Summerson from the pit every time she attends the theatre. Nothing is more damning or demeaning than Wopsle's hapless riverside *Hamlet* in *Great Expectations*. And it is of course in that same theatre that Pip is dangerously spied on by Compeyson, the enemy of Abel Magwitch. In very different ways for men up and down the social and moral scale, the theatre becomes a site, and indeed a sight, of risk, distress, and shame.

In part, perhaps, this connection between theatre and degraded or endangered men emerges from the low social status actors endured throughout the Georgian era. Even someone as distinguished as David Garrick was forced to kneel and beg pardon from the bullying balconies when they felt he had offended them. In Dickens's early years it was still not possible for a gentleman to be a professional actor, or for even the most distinguished actors to be recognized as gentlemen—a situation which the déclassé Macready deplored with an ever-increasing bitterness. Arriviste Dickens understood this very well. But, as we've seen, that stigma was evaporating in the 1840s. During Dickens's adult life actors came to enjoy the same status as gentlemen in the other, more traditional professions. All those knighthoods! Dickens could have been part of, and profited from, that change. That he chose not to, despite his passion for performing, suggests that this theatre-borne anxiety roots not in his milieu but in Dickens's experience of himself.

As he observed more than once, Dickens valued acting because it 'enables me, as it were, *to write a book in company* instead of in my own solitary room, and to feel its

---

[24] Rosemarie Bodenheimer, *Knowing Dickens* (Ithaca, NY, and London: Cornell University Press, 2007), 110–11.
[25] *PLets* 8:623–4, 624.

effect coming freshly back upon me from the reader'.[26] Almost every word here matters, but for the Dickens Theatre the key word must be 'back'. Professional actors often talk about the feel of the house: how scenes play differently on different nights; how the successful actor must adjust each performance to match that audience's mood, tone, attitude. Lines get unintended laughs, intended effects don't come off. Here, for example, is the great Uta Hagen, the original Martha of Edward Albee's *Who's Afraid of Virginia Woolf*, and the author of an indelible book on acting: 'The way an audience reaches out to me, when I am presenting a character ... I believe to be the true realm of the actor, rather than reaching out to them, and hitting them over the head with my "interpretation".'[27] In effect, the 'vulnerable' (Hagen's term) performer is in dialogue with and also dependent on the (Dickens's word) 'company'. But in Dickens's sense company refers not to strangers, potentially indifferent or even hostile strangers (let alone, in the usual theatrical sense, to the other actors), but to one's guests, those enjoying one's hospitality, bound by rules of civility. What Dickens wants from his acting, his book in company, then, is the assurance that his audience will reliably give 'back' to him nothing but, and therefore freshly, what he transmitted.

From readers of the written word that much-needed reassurance is necessarily delayed, and diffused, and often risky. Only from the sham audience, his own audience, can Dickens feel confident of getting what he needs: control. Dickens's sham theatre founds itself in and on this need for control. That need colours virtually every account he offers of his amateur productions. But nowhere is it more remarkably, indeed somewhat alarmingly visible than in the almost manic way in which he approached and supervised the 1857 Tavistock House production of Collins's *The Frozen Deep*, examined in detail by Robert Louis Brannan in *Under the Management of Mr. Charles Dickens*. Dickens literally dominates everything. He rewrites Collins's script; he designs and oversees the extension of the playing space out from the house's school room. He persuades Clarkson Stanfield to go back to his earlier life as a scene painter, and similarly dictates William Telbin's lighting effects. (It is hard for us now to imagine the special effects skilled managers of gaslight could produce.) He casts and directs the actors, and even selects the exceptionally distinguished audience whom he invites individually with personal letters. And then of course he plays the lead. 'Dickens assumed the responsibility for every detail of the performance. Both he and his audiences knew that he bore this responsibility, and that prominent people were coming to see a production by Dickens, not a play by Collins.'[28] As the reviewer for *The Leader* (cited by Brannan) recognized: 'Mr. Dickens ... is a genuine manager'—precisely the claim Dickens made of and for himself: 'I have arranged to do it in my own way.'[29]

Of course he enjoyed a similar kind of control at the journals he edited. Tellingly, Lillian Nayder sees that power as gendered and sexual: 'Dickens's periodicals were ... a

---

[26] *PLets* 8:367–8, 367.
[27] Uta Hagen, *Respect for Acting* (New York: Macmillan, 1973), 213.
[28] Brannon, *Under the Management of Mr. Charles Dickens*, 50.
[29] *PLets* 8:208–9, 209.

harem where writers were expected to submit to Dickens's will', as his wife and children were similarly expected to submit at home.[30] But the management of the editorial staff and the management of the stage differ from each other in a quite significant way. In an oft-quoted letter to Mrs Richard Watson he offers what seems to emerge as the exemplary paradigm for the theatre he manages: 'doing that Richard Wardour part. It was a good thing to have a couple of thousand people all rigid and frozen together, in the palm of one's hand—as at Manchester—and to see the hardened Carpenters at the sides crying and trembling at it night after night'.[31] A 'couple of thousand people', 'night after night': clearly what we have here is not an actual memory, not the reconstruction of a specific experience, but a kind of prescription for, or even better a kind of dream vision of the ultimately satisfying sham performance. Both audiences, those out in the house and those at the sides, are necessary to make the experience so particularly fulfilling.

But the thousands and the carpenters function in radically different ways, just as they display entirely different emotions. Submitting to his power, the audience congeals, 'in the palm of one's hand'. He forces them into a version of the frozen deep he is simultaneously playing on the stage. And for them, he appears to feel a sort of condescension; their response makes them indistinguishable, 'a couple of thousand', hardly worth counting, numbed, entrapped.

For those carpenters, however, his condescension deepens to contempt. The 'hardened' theatre professionals are unmanned by what they watch, crying and trembling, responding to Dickens's masterful playing, supremely aware and in control. The carpenters present the degraded alternative, the impotent theatre professionals, banished to the sides, his foils. Onto them, for Mrs Watson's instruction—she is a kind of third audience here—he projects what happens to men who make the mistake of taking theatre for real. Unlike them, Dickens (to paraphrase William Butler Yeats) does not break up his lines to weep.

Rather, like Richard Wardour at that moment within the play, where he sacrifices himself for the woman he loves, he is supremely in control. The frozen audience guarantees that control, even as it melts the carpenters. As commentators have noted, Wardour was a key role for Dickens, the prototype of Sydney Carton, the most fulfilling theatrical experience of his life. It was perhaps the only time he got out of acting everything he looked for, and looked for in vain, off the stage, to be at once, and publicly, overcome with emotion and entirely in control: 'a strange feeling ... a conviction of its being actual Truth without its pain'.[32]

But this line between the bad real and the fulfilling sham theatres was, in Richard Sennett's terms, always a border for Dickens, never a boundary.[33] It was not a firmly policed wall of separation and exclusion but a membrane, porous and fluid, through which frequent and easy exchanges passed. Through adaptation Dickens regularly

---

[30] Nayder, *Unequal Partners*, 158.
[31] *PLets* 8:487–9, 488.
[32] *PLets* 8:255–6, 256.
[33] Richard Sennett, *The Craftsman* (New Haven and London: Yale University Press, 2008), 227.

entered the professional theatre, as source and at times as adviser. And though after his first flutter in 1836–7 he never stepped into the West End as performer, playwright, or manager, its forms became his sources, and its professionals were throughout his life his friends, associates, and, often, colleagues. That dynamic and inexhaustibly fruitful interchange was fundamental to the working of his imagination, not only on the stage but also on the page.

Dickens and Theatricality

In one sense we have already answered the question: what might it mean to describe Dickens's fiction as theatrical? The novels and stories rely heavily on genres originating in the theatre, particularly on melodrama, burlesque, pantomime, and spectacle. In another way, also briefly mentioned, the novels are theatrical because they are so regularly and complexly involved in a dialogue with Shakespeare. This includes not only plot and character but also what Valerie Gager, the leading authority on the connection, calls 'quotations, allusions, or echoes'.[34] Those linguistic traces are literally innumerable. Scarcely a page of Dickens does not borrow from one of the plays, either explicitly or through some half-buried allusion. *Little Dorrit* is unimaginable without *King Lear* and *Hamlet; Dombey and Son* equally unimaginable without *Othello* and *King Lear*. George Gissing saw Mistress Quickly and Juliet's Nurse as the undoubted forebears of Sairey Gamp.[35] It does not require a talent like Gissing's to spot Shylock inside Fagin or Falstaff in Wilkins Micawber.

But these are not merely debts to texts, they are also debts to performance. Dickens did not just read Shakespeare, he saw him. What's more he saw him at a time when the texts used in performance were rapidly changing, from the drastically abridged versions common to the Georgian stage, to the increasingly more textually faithful scripts of the mid- and later Victorian stages. Thus he knew the tradition of an effeminate Romeo—surely a source for Nickleby's self-condemnation—and the genteel Othello of the Georgians who did not slap Desdemona but brushed her face with a feather. Moreover, he knew the plays not only in their legitimate stagings but also in their popular burlesque forms, the source of his own *O'tello The Irish Moor of Fleet Street*. Rather than claiming Dickens knew his Shakespeare, then, it is more accurate to insist Dickens knew his Shakespeare and everyone else's.

Nevertheless, because theatrical can mean so many different, even contradictory things, there is also a sense in which Dickens's fiction is not theatrical, even a sense in which it is anti-theatrical. Especially if we take theatre in the sense it carried at its origin. In the City Dionysia, the annual theatre festival in Athens, according to Andrea Wilson

---

[34] Valerie L. Gager, *Shakespeare and Dickens: The Dynamics of Influence* (Cambridge: Cambridge University Press, 1996), 3.

[35] Ibid., 8.

Nightingale, the spectator entered a space of alterity seeing for a spectacle he was not accustomed to view, crossing a line between the customary and the other.[36] Athenian audiences met 'multiple perspectives that challenged their individual points of view'.[37]

This model of theatre enjoys an extended and splendid history, highlighted most recently by paradigms like Jerzy Grotowski's Poor Theatre and Bertolt Brecht's highly influential practice of *Verfremdungseffekt*, the alienation that turns the audience from what it came in knowing toward a radically alternative account of experience. It also matches a recurring motif in Dickens's fiction, where with some regularity, a character, removed from the customary, sees for her- or himself possibilities unavailable to ordinary sight. Nowhere does Dickens realize this re-vision more hauntingly than in the Preface to *Little Dorrit*. The text of the novel complete, the narrator belatedly seeks out the grounds of the 'extinct Marshalsea jail', now a 'butter-shop', 'every brick of the jail' apparently 'lost'. But as he allows himself to engage the experience of this empty stage in dialogue with 'the smallest boy I ever conversed with', more and more of the past slips into and displaces the present until, desolated, he 'stand[s] among the crowding ghosts of many miserable years'.[38] It is bravura prose, but what seems most notable here, what makes it theatrical rather than novelistic, is the speaker's insistence that what happens to him is not merely a personal recollection. This is not Marcel Proust and the madeleine. Just the reverse: the same thing, the Preface insists, will happen 'to whoever goes into Marshalsea Place', Marshalsea Place as public theatre.

Something quite similar, though less public, happens in *Bleak House* chapter 36, when Esther, contemplating the Ghost's Walk from Lawrence Boythorn's grounds, encounters Lady Dedlock. She first sees only the great lady she has met before, but the scene then gradually transforms until she recognizes Lady Dedlock as her mother. And the same sort of thing recurs repeatedly in *A Tale of Two Cities*, perhaps Dickens's most fully theatricalized novel—which is why, of course, it is the most easily and successfully adapted to stage and screen. The great courtroom scenes obviously function as theatre, but so do even the most private moments, like the first encounter between Lucie Manette and her father in the room above the wine shop with its carefully staged sequence from shop, to staircase, to garret (chapters 5 and 6). All such scenes are characterized by the recognition of alterity: a hidden and crucial reality emerges to transform understanding through the shared experience of witnessing.

Tellingly, however, this does not happen inside any of Dickens's actual theatres. Those theatres are more or less all like Wopsle's waterside folly. Access to what Nightingale or Grotowski or Brecht would call theatre, witnessing to alternative, underlying truth, happens for Dickens only, as we have seen, in a pseudo-theatre, another sort of sham.

---

[36] Andrea Wilson Nightingale, *Spectacles of Truth in Classical Greek Philosophy: Theoria in its Cultural Context* (Cambridge and New York: Cambridge University Press, 2004), 51.
[37] Ibid., 58.
[38] *Little Dorrit*, ed. Harvey Peter Sucksmith (Oxford: Clarendon Press, 1979), Preface, lix–lx. Subsequent references are inserted parenthetically in the text by *LD* Book:chapter, page.

And yet there is a rich, complex, and revealing sense in which Dickens's fiction can indeed be labelled theatrical. In his recent, well-received study of performance, *Why Acting Matters*, the critic and historian David Thomson offers a radically unorthodox model of acting. In his account acting becomes 'a gesture toward resemblance', a resemblance that functions simultaneously in two directions.[39] The actor resembles the role she is playing but she also resembles the role we can call herself, the self the audience knows something about apart from, perhaps before, this particular experience of theatre. By emphasizing resemblance Thomson upends Konstantin Stanislavski's insistence on the intense identification of the actor with the role, the so-called Method elucidated in manuals like Uta Hagen's. Hagen argues for a craft that relies on *transference*: 'finding of the character within ourselves, through a continuing and overlapping series of substitutions of our experiences and remembrances'.[40] Reviewing her career high points, Saint Joan, Blanche in *Streetcar*, Martha in *Virginia Woolf*, and Natalya in *A Month in the Country*, Hagen insists: 'I always felt that it was *me* on stage ... not *she*.'[41] So thoroughly did she become identified with the part in her own mind and for the audience (she hoped) that any sense of a real Uta Hagen, apart from the part, evaporated. But for Thomson that identification flattens the power of theatre: 'the proximity and pulse of someone pretending for me', an excitement that can take hold only if I remain always aware that I am watching what he calls 'uncanny pretending'.[42]

Watching that pretending is not Samuel Taylor Coleridge's iconic *willing suspension of disbelief*. In Thomson's model, the audience maintains belief and disbelief in tension, as equal vectors. That brings this model of acting intriguingly close to what the psychoanalyst Adam Phillips calls 'flirting'. 'Flirting ... can make us wonder which ways of knowing, or being known, sustain our interest, our excitement in other people ... flirtation puts in disarray our sense of an ending. In flirtation, you never know whether the beginning of the story ... will be the end.'[43] Seen in this way, acting, like flirting, becomes a 'version of the experimental life'.[44] Whatever else the actor is doing with her scene partners on the stage, she is also at the same time 'flirting' with the members of the audience, who are, in effect, flirting back. As a result, whatever the plot of the particular play, as theatre it communicates to an audience the thrilling, liberating awareness that one need not be oneself, indeed that there may perhaps be better (or even more painful) possibilities in life than being oneself. Responding to 'real and fake at the same time',[45] the audience delights in this inviting doubleness. A doubleness which is not, as the antitheatrical Puritans claim, duplicity—because it does not intend to trick us into an act of faith. This, as it were, double-take is, of course, another sort of alterity, but it is far from

---

[39] David Thomson, *Why Acting Matters* (New Haven and London: Yale University Press, 2015), 12.
[40] Hagen, *Respect for Acting*, 34.
[41] Ibid., 28.
[42] Thomson, *Why Acting Matters*, 25–6.
[43] Adam Phillips, *On Flirtation* (Cambridge, MA: Harvard University Press, 1994), xviii–xix.
[44] Ibid., xxiv.
[45] Thomson, *Why Acting Matters*, 33.

the alterity that Nightingale locates in the Athenian theatre. That alterity claims to reveal to the audience the real truth. In Thomson's view (and by extension Phillips's), the deep point of performance—why acting matters—is to expose 'the myth of fact',[46] to insist there can be 'no question of an ultimate and reliable reality'.[47]

Turned into print, gesture toward resemblance captures in a remarkable way 'the pulse and pressure' of Dickens's characteristic theatricality: to be simultaneously both the self, recognizable, impressive, and the other, the chosen role, affecting and effective. Nowhere does this dynamic surface more memorably than in the indelible scene of Trabb's Boy in chapter 30 of *Great Expectations*, a paradigmatic instance of *uncanny pretending*. In a sequence of three appearances the Boy stages the snobbery that Pip relishes but also needs to keep unspoken and implicit. If the scene consisted only in the Boy's cruelly accurate imitation of Pip, we'd have satire but not, in our sense, theatricality. Merely imitating or disguising oneself as another almost invariably in Dickens leads to failure and exposure, and often connects to crime: Bradley Headstone pretending to be Rogue Riderhood in order to murder Eugene Wrayburn; Hortense pretending to be Lady Dedlock. One-on-one performances like these, looking alike, hiding behind assumed identity, distort or even strangle the energies, the free play, and the liberation that a flirtatious theatricality is designed to generate. Because they aim to deceive, we might adapt Thomson and call them (merely) canny pretending, one step away from the pseudo-spectacular theatre of John Jasper's soul-killing opium den.

In contrast, the Boy appears not once but three times in this brief sequence, in steadily varying ways. He plays different parts (like Sloppy the orphan in *Our Mutual Friend* doing—that is, reading news accounts of crime and performing—the Police in different voices), and at each point he only gestures toward resemblance; he never makes himself in any sense one with what he is playing. He starts out as the awed townsman, but in two different modes, and then, to culminate, plays Pip himself. His blue bag is as mutable as the Boy, cleverly whirling about as shifting metaphor rather than single object, and also a stable pointer to his own origins. In this way, turning the street into a sort of box set, with multiple entrances, receding toward the back, the protean Boy holds Pip as mortified spectator to his own interior monologue, a gesture which offers Pip the potential of metanoia, the chance to see the resemblance between what he is watching and what he thinks and desires. Captured, Pip does not turn away; he does not even register the possibility that he could cease partnering this performance—drop into a shop, turn round, call for the Boy to stop. Though he feels only anger at and contempt for the Boy, he cannot deny his sense that what he sees is his, specifically and pointedly his, own 'disgrace'.[48]

Trabb's Boy eerily calls up the god Dionysus hauntingly rendered by the poet-dramatist-classicist Anne Carson in her 2015 translation of Euripides' *Bakkhai*:

---

[46] Thomson, *Why Acting Matters*, 42.
[47] Ibid., 26.
[48] *Great Expectations*, ed. Margaret Cardwell (Oxford: Clarendon Press, 1993), volume II, chapter 11, page 246. Subsequent references are inserted parenthetically in the text by *GE* volume:chapter, page.

Dionysus-Bacchus, the god of the theatre. Paralleling Thomson, she argues in her preface that the key Dionysiac (that is: the key theatrical experience) is not self-realization but ecstasy, literally standing outside oneself.[49] *Bakkhai* violently dramatizes that model. Dionysus teases out a new self from within Pentheus, the King of Thebes, a self that before the theatrical encounter was never performed. This both thrills and threatens Pentheus, and in the tension between those conflicting emotions the king perishes. Reworked as comedy, this encounter closely parallels Trabb's Boy taunting Pip. (Pip doesn't die; mocked and derided, he simply flees.) Like shape-shifting Dionysus, the Boy (nameless, he is a kind of god, a divine imp perhaps) performs for Pip both the self-image he harbours, the gentleman, and also the reality he projects, the snob who is really a sham, Magwitch's sham. And at the same time he also personifies what Pip could and should have been—Gargery's Boy the blacksmith, just as this boy is Trabb's: Pip as he could have been if he had not been caught up in the manipulations of Miss Havisham and Magwitch. A boy who might in some healthy way actually have learned how to play as Trabb's Boy plays in his polymorphous gesture toward resemblance.

Of course Pip, like Pentheus, at this point can't play; he rejects all the possibilities demonstrated in this supremely theatrical encounter. This is why, with mordant irony, Dickens sends him immediately afterward to Wopsle's *Hamlet*, to the theatre, not the theatrical. A theatre in which he will later be spied on and entrapped by his inexpungable past (*GE* III:8, 379–85). But it is also the Dionysiac Boy who in the third volume will rescue Pip from Orlick, in an incendiary scene that could have been lifted directly from *Bakkhai*—it wasn't—at the point at which Pip can finally make use of everything the Boy has to offer.

Trabb's Boy epitomizes a recurring scene, a recurring character, major as well as minor, and indeed a recurring plot in Dickens's fiction, in which roles performed through affective gesture make available to spectators an alternative, preferable reality while keeping the performer recognizable as the self. These performances reappear so often and so variously throughout Dickens's career, as elegy, tragedy, comedy, satire, and farce, that, regrettably, the remainder of the chapter itself becomes only a gesture toward resemblance.

In *The Old Curiosity Shop* Dick Swiveller's treatment of 'the Marchioness' inverts, comically, sublimely, Trabb's Boy's bitter and satiric performance with Pip: a literal swivelling on which the orphan girl is spun in delightedly dizzying circles, from nameless, to Marchioness, to Sophronia Sphynx, to Mrs Swiveller, by the force of Dick's centring, encompassing play. Theatricality as sheer flirtatious game; flirting as sheer theatricality. 'Jenny Wren' in *Our Mutual Friend* is of course a sort of stage name for Fanny Cleaver, whose dolls' dressmaking is itself a gesture toward resemblance. Her elegiac 'Come up and be dead' creates a kind of consolatory outcasts' theatre of antiphrasis, in which standard meanings and their realities are creatively, therapeutically reversed. On a much larger scale, in the same novel, Boffin, by playing the miser, drives the comedic

---

[49] Euripedes, *Bakkhai*, a new version, trans. Anne Carson (London: Oberon Books, 2015), 5–8.

plot of *Our Mutual Friend*. It is crucial that all along this performance has been shared with Mrs Boffin, his delighted co-conspirator and preferred audience. It would be an entirely different matter if he had performed only for the self, like the Veneerings before their marriage. In a novel which takes shape as a virtual anthology of performance tropes, Boffin reverses John Harmon-Rokesmth's fruitless, secretive, and unconvincing attempt to collapse one role into another. Surely the uncharacteristic, ham-fisted prose of his ten-page soliloquy in Book II, chapter 13—Pay Attention John Harmon!—must be on Dickens's part intentionally implausible, exposing the inevitable failure of performing a self only for the self. On the other hand, Boffin's free and generous play contrasts Bradley Headstone's villainous impersonation of Riderhood, where resemblance becomes its demonic double, duplicitous impersonation, which in Dickens always fails.

On an even larger scale, Sydney Carton, Dickens's supremely theatrical hero, begins and ends his role in *A Tale of Two Cities* with gestures toward resemblance, the initial gesture liberating Darnay and the final one condemning himself to the scaffold, but at the same time displacing Darnay at the centre of Lucie's emotional life. The poor girl in the tumbril functions as a kind of body double for Lucie, who not only knows of but will never forget this performance. Between these twinned performances, with enormous subtlety Dickens delineates a character that can *only* function theatrically, who can realize the possibilities of self only for and through the man he resembles. And this crucial dependence differentiates him from Dickens's supremely theatrical heroine, though this claim may come as a surprise: Little Dorrit. Amy Dorrit lives out an almost unending series of gestures toward resemblance. She thrives by performing for different specific audiences the roles they need her to embody and through which she accomplishes her own desire to be needed and of use: Little Dorrit, the Child of the Marshalsea, Little Mother, My Child, Miss Dorrit. The only role she steadfastly refuses is Nurseling of the Faeries—she is not going to stoop to pantomime. When Mrs Merdle quite rightly sniffs of her in contrast to Fanny: 'not professional' (*LD* I:20, 234), she is absolutely on target. Superficial, narcissistic, Fanny is of the professional theatre, all cheap glam. Amy is the real thing, not of the theatre but essentially theatrical.

Relying on contemporary theorists like Thomson and Carson to frame Dickens's theatricality may appear inexcusably ahistorical. But their accounts of theatricality chime remarkably with the theatricality Dickens himself knew, admired, and practised. When Thomson offers examples of acting as its most sublime, he names Sir Laurence Olivier, Marlon Brando, *and* Edmund Kean, the greatest actor of the first half of the nineteenth century.[50] Later, referring to Dickens's own performances, he groups him with 'Garrick and Kean'.[51] Indeed, Garrick can be said to have inaugurated, and Kean to have concluded, a theatrical version of the late baroque aesthetic of affective gesture, inevitable in enormous playhouses where what was heard would always be less effective

---

[50] Thomson, *Why Acting Matters*, 20.
[51] Ibid., 141.

than what was seen. This was also Dickens's theatre, 'famous for the range of emotions [the actor] could evoke in the spectator in rapid succession not by words but by gesture and facial expression'.[52] And it is also the aesthetic Dickens made his own in the final celebrated Readings.

DICKENS'S READINGS: THE IDEAL OF THEATRICALITY

Those Readings, our final focus, have been brilliantly examined by Malcolm Andrews in *Charles Dickens and His Performing Selves*, indispensable for all Dickens studies.[53] Andrews shows in painstaking detail how carefully Dickens distinguished his performances from the ordinary readings by authors, practised by contemporaries like William Makepeace Thackeray, and the multi-character one-man shows of Charles Mathews, Dickens's early idol. Unlike either, Dickens was uncannily able to appear both as himself, in evening dress standing at his specially designed reading desk, and—by rapid changes of voice and gesture—the wide range of characters in the text under performance. In these Readings, clearly, Dickens was finally able to achieve and sustain the ideal of theatricality he had been pursuing all his life, which he could only fleetingly experience playing Wardour, that thrilling combination of unchecked power and emotional intensity (even working susceptible audience members to hysteria). It is no wonder that the Readings virtually took over the final decade of his life; indeed, in their exhausting demands they finally took his life. Reading a book in company satisfied the appetite that could only be tantalized by writing a book in company. In these last years devoted to sheer theatricality Dickens may be said to have finally found the experience of self for which he had been working and searching all his life.

A final counsel: if the editors had chosen to call this chapter 'Dickens, the Drama, and the Dramatic', it would have produced a very different argument indeed. Dickens is theatrical but he is not dramatic.

FURTHER READING

Edwin M. Eigner, *The Dickens Pantomime* (Berkeley: University of California Press, 1988)
Robert Garis, *The Dickens Theatre: A Reassessment of the Novels* (Oxford: Clarendon Press, 1965)

---

[52] David Bindman and Malcolm Baker, *Roubiliac and the Eighteenth-Century Monument* (New Haven and London: Yale University Press, 1995), 37. Bindman and Baker's magisterial study of English funerary and memorial sculpture takes as its subtitle: *Sculpture as Theatre*. Twin arts, not one wordless and the other speaking but both primarily dependent on gesture.

[53] Andrews, *Charles Dickens and his Performing Selves*, particularly chapter 4, 'Celebrity on Tour', and chapter 5, 'Performance'.

Juliet John, *Dickens's Villains: Melodrama, Character, Popular Culture* (Oxford: Oxford University Press, 2001)

Tore Rem, *Dickens, Melodrama, and the Parodic Imagination* (Brooklyn, NY: AMS Press, 2002)

Paul Schlicke, *Dickens and Popular Entertainment* (London: Allen and Unwin, 1985)

Deborah Vlock, *Dickens, Novel Reading, and the Victorian Popular Theatre* (Cambridge: Cambridge University Press, 1998)

CHAPTER 45

DICKENS'S VISUAL MEDIATIONS

HELEN GROTH

Dickens's seminal place in the history of Victorian visual culture is uncontested. Contemporaries, such as George Henry Lewes, described Dickens as a 'seer of visions', who, like 'no other sane mind' he had observed, possessed a 'vividness of the imagination approaching so closely to hallucination'.[1] The work of filmmakers spanning from D. W. Griffiths through to Alfonso Cuarón and Mike Newell attests to the enduring impact of what Sergei Eisenstein seminally identified as the 'extraordinary plasticity' and 'optical quality' of Dickens's prose on the history of cinema.[2] Critics working at the meeting point of literary and visual cultural history have long acknowledged this and other inter-medial aspects of his work.[3] Dickens's creative collaborations with illustrators, the vivid phantasmagoric nature of his prose, and evocative reliance on optical metaphors that assumed his readers were, amongst other things, familiar with popular visual entertainments, such as the kaleidoscope, the panorama, and dissolving slides of contemporary magic lantern spectacles, have been interrogated and debated by a range of critics working in the cognate fields of the history of illustration, popular visual culture, pre- and early cinema, as well as film adaptation.[4] The

---

[1] George Henry Lewes, 'Dickens in Relation to Criticism', *Fortnightly Review* 11 (February 1872): 141.
[2] Sergei Eisenstein, 'Dickens, Griffith, and Film Today', in *Film Form: Essays in Film Theory* (San Diego: Harvest, 1977), 195–205, 201.
[3] Of the many works I could cite, a few which focus on visual mediation: Grahame Smith, *Dickens and the Dream of Cinema* (Manchester: Manchester University Press, 2003); John Glavin (ed.), *Dickens on Screen* (Cambridge: Cambridge University Press, 2003); Kate Flint, *The Victorians and the Visual Imagination* (Oxford: Oxford University Press, 2000).
[4] Again there are too many to cite but here are an exemplary few: Joss Marsh, 'Dickens and Film', in John O. Jordan (ed.), *The Cambridge Companion to Charles Dickens* (Cambridge: Cambridge University Press, 2001), 204–24; Joss Marsh, 'Dickensian "Dissolving Views": The Magic Lantern, Visual Story-Telling, and the Victorian Technological Imagination', *Comparative Critical Studies* 6, 3 (2009): 333–46; Carol T. Christ and John O. Jordan (eds), *Victorian Literature and the Victorian Visual Imagination* (Berkeley: University of California Press, 1995).

visual, as all these scholars variously concur, is a vital and dynamic aspect of Dickens's enduring relevance to our understanding of the entangled histories of literary and visual mediation.

Recent theories and histories of mediation and technologies of writing offer us yet another way of understanding Dickens's contribution to the histories of visual and print media. In light of recent critical debates about technologies of writing, storage, and inscription generated by a diverse array of critics, including Friedrich Kittler, Nancy Armstrong, Daniel Hack, and Richard Menke, this chapter reconsiders Dickens's assimilation of technologies of visual mediation into his writing as an integral dimension of his assertion of the Victorian novel's distinctive capacity to both store and represent the complex and uneven developments of its age.

Dickens was acutely aware of a range of medial techniques for transforming the transient flickers of optical phenomena into a series of material inscriptions permanently recorded on paper and mass-produced in the form of the modern industrial novel. When he writes in *Pictures from Italy*, for example, of the 'rapid and unbroken succession of novelties' passing before his eyes that his mind arrests at intervals before they dissolve 'like a view in a magic-lantern', he reveals his interest not only in the nature of perception, but in how the mind mediates ephemeral inchoate visual impressions, transforming them into decipherable signals and storing them as retrievable communicable knowledge.[5] This process of transmission and storage of memorable images was a vital one for Dickens, intimately linked to his conception of how those selected images might consequently be channelled through print media and impressed on the malleable minds of a mass readership. Read from this perspective the famous moments in *Bleak House, Great Expectations, Dombey and Son*, and *Our Mutual Friend* where the narrative voice evokes an all-seeing eye that oscillates between panoramic overview and a microscopic focus on the particularities of London's crowded streets, courts, and dwellings also becomes synonymous with the avid collection, communication, and virtuosic mastery of data. Shifting the theoretical ground from questions of surveillance, adaptation, and illustration to questions of mediation and storage, as this chapter advocates, generates new ways of thinking about Dickens's experimental and conceptual engagement with the new visual media that were gradually transforming how people read, saw, and imagined the world around them. Drawing on Hablot Knight Browne's iconic illustrations for *Bleak House, Dombey and Son*, and *Little Dorrit* as exemplary instances of Dickens's visual conception of the mediation of his work, this chapter expands to consider the ways in which the visual functions as a generative catalyst for memorable images designed to be inscribed, stored, and adapted as required, in much the same way as Browne's illustrations. This is the visual plasticity Eisenstein praises and that has ensured the enduring cinematic and televisual afterlives of Dickens's novels.

---

[5] *American Notes and Pictures from Italy*, introd. Sacheverell Sitwell, New Oxford Illustrated Dickens (London: Oxford University Press, 1957), 'An Italian Dream', 329–36, 329.

Illustration as Mediation

As we know, thanks to the extensive research of scholars, including one of the editors of this handbook, Robert L. Patten, the enticing visual distillations of Dickens's plots featured on the novel and serial wrappers that encased each new offering were often prompted by nothing more than a suggestive title in the case of serial publication and were in circulation long before the completion of the entire manuscript. Taking their initial cue from Dickens's verbal accounts of his works in progress, George Cruikshank, Hablot Knight Browne, and later Luke Fildes, produced illustrations characterized by a technically virtuosic, yet economic style and a keen awareness of graphic traditions. The process of condensing information about the plot, in the case of some of Hablot Knight Browne's most recognizable illustrations for *Dombey and Son*, *Bleak House*, and *Little Dorrit*, also evolved over time, moving from emblematic typologies to more pictorially expressive evocations of characters and scenes that experimented with the illusionistic effects of chiaroscuro.[6] As Patten suggestively puts it in relation to the latter: 'Light and dark, the essentials of etching, take on huge symbolic significance, not only in the dark plates, but also in the more "realistic" ones. Sources of light—candles, lamps, sun and moon—may indicate genuine material and immaterial illumination, but such lights may also, like will-o'-wisps, be deceiving.'[7] Phantasmal in theme and form, maybe, and yet these images are also, irrefutably, concrete in their visual mediation and durable storage of Dickens's preliminary anecdotal distillations of key characters and scenarios.

In the case of Browne's illustrations for *Bleak House*, the combined series of wrapper and in-text illustrations operate on multiple levels. They parallel Dickens's prosaic creation 'of assemblages of concrete images whose meanings are non-discursive and represent a poetry of external things', to quote Donald Ericksen.[8] Yet they also vary dramatically in mode and style. Browne's wrapper, in contrast to the numerous dark plates that distinguish his illustrations for this novel, is an exercise in the art of compression; an entangled series of scenes of frantic activity enframe the static solidity of a sketchily rendered Bleak House. Images of communication of all kinds move the reader's eye around the frame—spoken, written, and manically physical—as opposed to the stillness of the house around which all this visual noise swirls. In contrast, the haunting stasis of one of Browne's most memorable dark plates 'Tom-all-Alone's' captures the desolate silence, the moral failure at the core of the elaborate legal, social, and economic systems that the novel so densely elaborates (Figure 45.1). All human connection falls away and the reader is left to contemplate the darkness within. This transition in illustrative mode was both aesthetic and technological, as Browne changed from a more traditional

---

[6] Donald H. Ericksen, 'Bleak House and Victorian Art and Illustration: Charles Dickens's Visual Narrative Style', *Journal of Narrative Theory* 13, 1 (Winter 1983): 31–46, 35.

[7] Robert L. Patten, 'Illustrators and Book Illustration', in Paul Schlicke (ed.), *The Oxford Companion to Charles Dickens: Anniversary Edition* (Oxford: Oxford University Press, 2011), 292.

[8] Ericksen, 'Bleak House and Victorian Art and Illustration', 36.

FIGURE 45.1 Hablot K. Browne, 'Tom all Alone's', steel etching, *Bleak House*, April 1853.
Courtesy of Special Collections, McHenry Library, University of California, Santa Cruz

etching technique to a wet-plate process halfway through the volume. In the process the 'close up' physiognomic intimacy of the Hogarthian tradition on which Browne had previously relied is replaced by a photographic style of mediation resulting in images encoded by a more literal referential connection to the social realities that the novel so capaciously represents.

Nancy Armstrong argues that this shift further blurred the lines between the visual data Browne's images drew into the reading experience and what she describes as Dickens's 'stereoscopic' rendering of the 'gothic city': both novelist and illustrator point to a 'contemporary world' that can no longer be captured by 'the older iconographic tradition'.[9] While Browne's dark plates, which chart Lady Dedlock's agonized fall from

---

[9] Nancy Armstrong, *Fiction in the Age of Photography: The Legacy of British Realism* (Cambridge, MA: Harvard University Press, 2002), 138.

the domestic splendour of Chesney Wold to the destitution of 'Tom-all-Alone's', are notably bereft of human presence, they provide an insight into Browne's attempt to move beyond physiognomic details that, to quote Armstrong, 'could no longer carry an iconic meaning in and of themselves ... but instead receive their meaning from the visual context which inflects them'.[10] Experimenting with how to register the radical instability of this 'visual context', however, required new forms of documentation and very different observational practices.

Browne's dark plate for 'Tom-all-Alone's' materializes the novel's sustained interrogation of how information and meaning can be derived from apparently obscure data in often unexpected ways. The disintegrating surfaces of the old court refuse easy access to the uninitiated eye. Open windows suggest habitation, but remain opaque, buildings crowd, vacant shop fronts loom, and the narrow path between them suggests a hidden sinister presence, invisible from the relative safety of the street outside. What Browne's visual realization of Dickens's allusive description of this same scene achieves, then, is to place the stress on the process of seeing or detecting, rather than what is actually seen. As the opening paragraph of chapter 46 grimly details:

> Darkness rests upon Tom-all-Alone's. Dilating and dilating since the sun went down last night ... For a time there were some dungeon lights burning, as the lamp of Life burns in Tom-all-Alone's, heavily, heavily, in the nauseous air, and winking—as that lamp, too, winks in Tom-all-Alone's—at many horrible things. But they are blotted out.[11]

This brief series of images insists on a new set of visual conventions inaugurated by a modern industrial environment saturated with ambiguous or conflicting data that confronted the observer with the precarious and partial nature of human perception. To see and to write was to enter into a new system of information gathering driven by the desire to collect more, which, in turn, registered the instability of existing forms of mediation and storage. Ink, for example, is both a medium for images and writing, as well as the means of blotting out horrible truths in the above quotation. The use of dilation is striking here as well, evoking multiple associations with contagion, the steady creep of spilt ink across previously legible script and the dilation of a pupil, potentially blinded by too much light. In this sense, image and text reflect a heightened awareness of the logic of accumulation that the novel simultaneously represents and enacts at the level of form.

The frenetic accumulation of documents, as Daniel Hack, has argued, drives *Bleak House* in particular at both thematic and structural levels.[12] Developing this argument further, Hack emphasizes the 'epistemological implications' of Dickens's insistence on

---

[10] Ibid.

[11] *Bleak House*, ed. George Ford and Sylvère Monod, Norton Critical Edition (New York: W. W. Norton, 1977), 46, 551. Subsequent references are inserted parenthetically in the text by *BH* chapter, page.

[12] Daniel Hack, *The Material Interests of the Victorian Novel* (Charlottesville: University of Virginia Press, 2005), 44–5.

'writing's materiality' in this novel, that is, the descriptive attention given to different forms of script, handwriting, documents, print, modes of inscription, ink, and paper, which takes place alongside the persistent confusion of interpretative and observational 'protocols' used to encode and evaluate them.[13]

Browne's illustrations are integral to the shift in systems of knowing that Dickens thematically materializes not only in *Bleak House*, but also in *Dombey and Son* and *Little Dorrit*. Produced during the most successful phase of Browne and Dickens's collaboration, the illustrations in these novels synchronize with Dickens's vigorous ambition for the novel more generally as 'a medium and information system in an age of new media' to quote Richard Menke.[14] Browne's wrapper design for *Dombey and Son* (Figure 45.2) visualizes the novel in precisely this way: all is connected in a system driven by the accumulation of ever more precarious piles of data. Even Dickens, who judged 'the cover very good', thought there was 'perhaps a little too much in it'.[15] Like the circular format of Browne's wrapper design for *Bleak House*, scenes of frenetic activity swirl around a relatively stable centre, in this case, a sign advertising the firm of 'Dombey and Son' hanging tenuously between two figures perched on a ladder balancing on a stack of cards on one side, and the equally unreliable grasp of a figure clutching onto a pile of books on the other. Unread books, documents, signs, and cards clutter the frame, serving every purpose other than their intended one, as sources of truth, information, and knowledge. The novel this wrapper advertises, by implication, is the alternative to this confusion of data. It is a coherent system, an alternative medium that opens the covers of the shut ledgers, reports, journals, and cheque-books, that provides, in other words, legible information. Browne's wrapper plays with the motif of information, the sheer visual dynamism of the framing narration of key events in the novel. Dombey's delusional empire thrives on the exploitation of others, then descends into chaos, and concludes with the reclaiming of the domestic as the primary site of reparatory meaning. The wrapper design encourages the reader to recognize the unstable foundations of capital, law, and social convention. Enthroned atop a cash box, Dombey is oblivious to what lies beneath, 'DEALINGS' quite literally pierced and shot through with self-interest and reduced to a disarticulated set of letters provisionally held together with a large pin.

Dickens's opening characterization of Dombey drives home the false consciousness that the novel intends to expose:

> The earth was made for Dombey and Son to trade in, and the sun and moon were made to give them light. Rivers and seas were formed to float their ships; rainbows gave them promise of fair weather; winds blew for or against their enterprises; stars

---

[13] Ibid., 45.

[14] Richard Menke, *Telegraphic Realism. Victorian Fiction and Other Information Systems* (Stanford, CA: Stanford University Press, 2008), 3.

[15] *The Letters of Charles Dickens*, ed. Madeline House, Graham Storey, et al., Pilgrim/British Academy Edition, 12 vols (Oxford: Clarendon Press, 1965–2002), 4:618–20, 620.

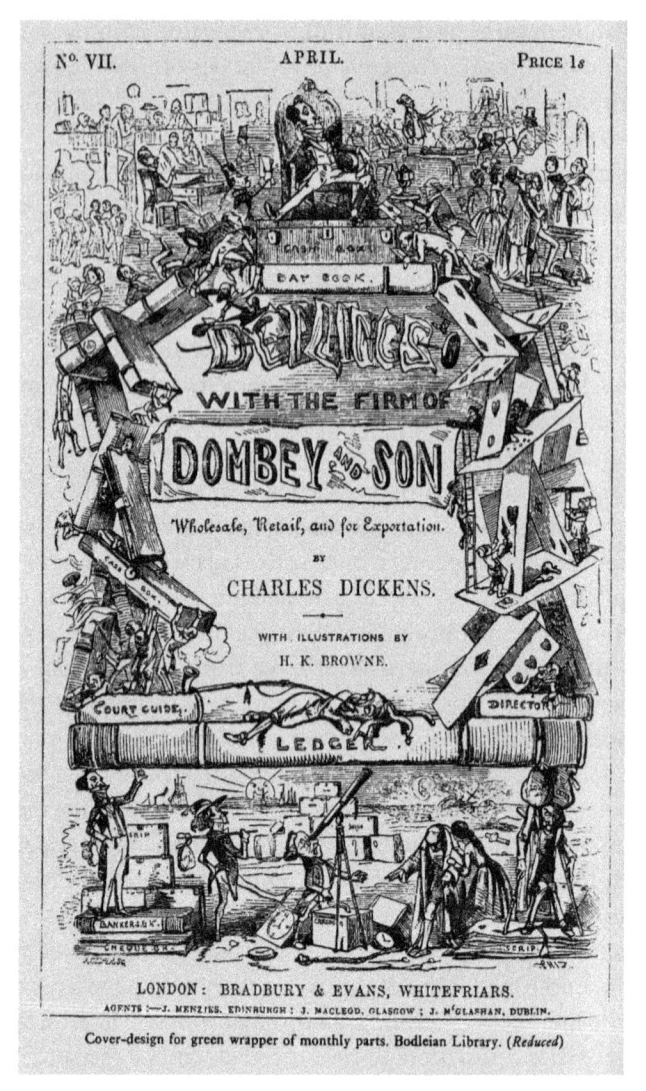

FIGURE 45.2 Hablot K. Browne, wrapper design for *Dombey and Son*, steel etching, October 1846.

and planets circled in their orbits, to preserve inviolate a system of which they were the centre.[16]

The global over-reach of Dombey's hubris is visualized here in the hyperbolic naturalization of the voracious consumption and circulation of capital, with its ships, railway, and communication networks. All is out of order in this world where seas and rivers

---

[16] *Dombey and Son*, ed. Alan Horsman (Oxford: Clarendon Press, 1974), 1, 2. Subsequent references are inserted parenthetically in the text by *DS* chapter, page.

take shape around the mechanical emissaries of international trade, where rainbows bend and winds blow according to the regulated rhythms of industrial production. The privileged insight of free-indirect style exposes Dombey's distorted world view for all to see: a narcissistic subjectivism that misidentifies itself as objective fact. Coming so soon after Browne's circular wrapper design, the listing rhythms of Dickens's prose here echo the accumulative dynamism of the former reinforcing the image and idea of a global system that has corrupted and brutalized filial bonds. By so doing Browne's images and Dickens's prose offer the reader parallel pathways into a new way of imagining and visualizing the dramatic transformation of the world around them; a modern world that required new ways of reading and seeing that registered both the differences and affinities between alternative modes of information delivery.

Dombey and Son also signalled a shift in Dickens's writing practices towards a more carefully orchestrated pre-planning of individual monthly numbers. The consequence of this change was a more unified and focused novel that presaged the complexity of social representation to be found in later novels, such as *Little Dorrit, Our Mutual Friend*, and *Great Expectations*. Raymond Williams reflects in his introduction to the novel on these unifying techniques in his observation of the parallel to be drawn between the above passage and the reflections on 'the monstrous delusion' of Dombey's life, 'swelling with every grain of sand that shifted in its glass' (*DS* 47, 618).[17] In the parallel passage that Williams identifies, the narrator calls on the hard data of the physical sciences to argue for the necessary changes required to see differently, more systematically, and with the benefit of accurate information:

> Those who study the physical sciences, and bring them to bear upon the health of Man, tell us that if the noxious particles that rise from vitiated air, were palpable to the sight, we should see them lowering in a dense black cloud above such haunts, and rolling slowly on to corrupt the better portions of a town. But if the moral pestilence that rises with them, and in the eternal laws of outraged Nature, is inseparable from them, could be made discernible too, how terrible the revelation! Then should we see depravity, impiety, drunkenness, theft, murder, and a long train of nameless sins against the natural affections and repulsions of mankind, overhanging the devoted spots, and creeping on, to blight the innocent and spread contagion among the pure. Then should we see how the same poisoned fountains that flow into our hospitals and lazar-houses, inundate the jails, and make the convict-ships swim deep, and roll across the seas, and over-run vast continents with crime. (*DS* 47, 619–20).

The physical sciences may have the power to identify the threat and record the scale of 'noxious particles' in the 'vitiated air' above London, but it is the novelist who can circulate that information in a meaningful way, revealing their symbiotic connection 'to the moral pestilence that rises with them'. The drive to expose, to reveal, to make visible, accelerates the rhetorical momentum of this paragraph, which sets up one of the more

---

[17] Raymond Williams, Introduction, *Dombey and Son* (London: Penguin, 1970), 11–34.

striking visual images of the novel in the first sentence of the following paragraph: 'Oh for a good spirit who would take the house-tops off' (*DS* 47, 620). Tantalized by the possibility of unmediated surveillance, the reiterated collective 'we see' in this passage takes allegorical flight in a typically Dickensian convergence of the material and the metaphysical. In this scenario the 'good spirit' who reveals all is the mystified novelist, an all seeing I who gives the 'we' 'one night's view of the pale phantoms rising from the scenes of our too-long neglect' (*DS* 47, 620).

Integral to this visualization of global pestilence at an intimate local level, in individual houses inescapably and irredeemably networked to a global systemic pestilence of both material and moral kinds, is the novelist's ambition to generate images that demand attention and retention. Dickens's relish for the spectacular is in this sense of a piece with his assertion of the capacity of 'fictional realism' to store and transmit 'daily discourse', as Richard Menke has argued, 'in an age busy producing alternatives to it'.[18] In the pages that follow, the private world of the Dombey household is exposed to view with renewed relish. Awkward, brittle, and excruciating, a sequence of 'private' conversations between Dombey, his wife Edith, and daughter Florence, with his confidential clerk James Carker as the 'medium of communication', are revealed in relentless fictional detail (*DS* 47, 626). Browne's image of 'Florence and Edith on the staircase' follows the most melodramatic of these, in which Carker articulates his true function in the house 'for the humiliation of Mrs. Dombey' and Edith matches his scorn, silently and spectacularly divesting her body of the last tokens of marital possession: 'From each arm, she unclasped a diamond bracelet, flung it down, and trod upon the glittering heap' (*DS* 47, 630–1). Positioned in the shadows slightly below and to the side, rather than above the staircase, the reader witnesses Edith's final act of divestment of the trappings of the marriage—the rejection of Florence. Chiaroscuro encodes the women, Florence's gown is predominantly white and Edith's mainly black. Florence moves upwards, reaching out, while Edith retreats into the shadows of the 'gallery of communication that opened at some little distance on the staircase', which the narrator informs us 'was only lighted on great occasions' (*DS* 47, 631). The sketchiness of Browne's style here infuses the scene with indeterminacy, lines of sight blur, the details of figures and paintings on the wall dissolve into the surrounding gloom, just as Edith desires to do. In the final sequence Florence faints at the sight of her mother's 'haggard face and staring eyes' (*DS* 47, 632). Like one of the phantasmagoric figures that populate Florence's dreams, Edith spreads her hands over her eyes, shudders, and crouches down against the wall, then crawls 'by her like some lower animal', and finally springs up and flees away (*DS* 47, 632).

Free indirect discourse blurs the lines here between Florence's haunting dream-like perception of her stepmother and the narrator's visualization of Edith crawling away 'like some lower animal', taking the reader back to Dickens's reflections on the descriptive limitations of the physical sciences that serve as the prelude to this scene (*DS* 47, 619). Amplified by Browne's dark illustration, Dickens makes the 'noxious' particles

---

[18] Menke, *Telegraphic Realism*, 11.

that 'strike our children down' 'palpable to the sight', animating with the poetic force of his novelistic style what the physical sciences alone cannot do (*DS* 47, 619–20). Writing in the same year on the subject of Leigh Hunt's *Poetry of Science*, Dickens transforms science into a generative revelatory machinery that destroys to reveal and illuminate new truths:

> Caverns in rocks, choked with rich treasures shut up from all but the enchanted hand, Science has blown to atoms, as she can rend and rive the rocks themselves; but in those rocks she has found, and read aloud, the great stone book which is the history of the earth, even when darkness sat upon the face of the deep. Along their craggy sides she has traced the footprints of birds and beasts, whose shapes were never seen by man. From within them she has brought the bones, and pieced together the skeletons, of monsters that would have crushed the noted dragons of the fables at a blow.[19]

Adelene Buckland has drawn attention to the metaphoric complexity of this passage, observing how Dickens manipulates the geological image of 'the great stone book' to characterize science as 'reading aloud', conveniently seizing upon the performative aspects of the popular science of the period, which aligned with his own interests in spectacle, showmanship, and the pleasures of the imagination.[20] In the process of this metamorphic transformation Dickens also highlights two other facets of the revelatory force of the 'physical sciences' that align with his abiding interest in forms of mediation and information storage. Geological discovery has exposed the earth's archival riches. Stored deep within its recesses, durably inscribed on and through its geological layers, are the traces of 'footprints of birds and beasts', visual markings of long gone beings 'never seen by man'.

STORING UP VISUAL DATA

By opening up a visual archive in his novels, analogous to the one that he evokes in his reflections on 'The Poetry of Science', Dickens generates an imaginative counter-narrative with the power to reanimate forgotten lives as well as the fragments of long extinct species, like the Megalosaurus who waddles up Holborn-hill in the opening paragraph of *Bleak House*. In this potently anachronistic image the geologist aligns with the novelist, revealing rare sights that require new forms of mediation. To return to Richard Menke's argument in *Telegraphic Realism*, but with a greater stress placed on

---

[19] Charles Dickens, 'The Poetry of Science', *The Examiner*, 9 December 1848. Reprinted in *The Nonesuch Papers: Collected Papers I* (London: Bloomsbury, 1937), 178–81, 179.

[20] Adelene Buckland, 'The Poetry of Science: Charles Dickens, Geology, and Visual and Material Culture in Victorian London', *Victorian Literature and Culture* 35, 2 (2007): 679–94, 681.

the visual, Dickens implicitly and explicitly asserts the novel as an alternative system for storing and transmitting images, and for rendering visible what other information systems could not, a character's inner thoughts or the secret workings of social, legal, or economic structures.[21] Revealing London's geological substrata and the traces of the otherwise forgotten species that live there involves Dickens in a process of microscopic visualization typified by the extraordinary description of Stagg's Gardens in the sixth chapter of *Dombey and Son*, which is followed by Browne's illustration of the brutal mobbing of the 'charitable grinder' and his merciful rescue by the long-suffering Polly Toodle. Browne's illustration is a dark chaotic rendering of brutalized bodies and moral debasement inseparable from the chapter's opening image of the rending and fragmentation of the 'great earthquake' caused by the 'unfinished and unopened Railroad' blasting its way through suburban London:

> Everywhere were bridges that led nowhere; thoroughfares that were wholly impassable; Babel towers of chimneys, wanting half their height; temporary wooden houses and enclosures, in the most unlikely situations; carcases of ragged tenements, and fragments of unfinished walls and arches, and piles of scaffolding, and wildernesses of bricks, and giant forms of cranes, and tripods straddling above nothing. There were a hundred thousand shapes and substances of incompleteness, wildly mingled out of their places, upside down, burrowing in the earth, aspiring in the air, mouldering in the water, and unintelligible as any dream. (*DS* 6, 65)

In this modern technological version of nature's rending and riving the rocks of London, to adapt Dickens's geological metaphor from 'The Poetry of Science', images are layered on top of one another through a relentless enumeration of detail. Traces of life, discarded artefacts, carcases of houses, dismembered forms wildly mingled, and burrowing into the depths of the earth as if in flight from the horrors of the surface, are captured here in Dickens's typically capacious sentences, self-consciously mediated in a compressed, highly memorable form.

This dream-like mingling of wild incomplete shapes is echoed in visual form in the literal human chaos of Browne's illustration of the crowd of bodies surrounding the miserable Robin Toodle whose 'social existence had been more like that of an early Christian, than an innocent child of the nineteenth century' (*DS* 6, 69). Faces and bodies merge in a dark swirl of frantic bodies in the centre of the image and while the title, 'Polly rescues the Charitable Grinder', identifies the central subjects, the prevailing impression is one of a random anonymous crowd indifferent to the fate of any single individual child, an uncivilized entity that turns back the clock on human history, becoming animal in its bestial violence. John Plotz encapsulates this violent aspect of 'mundane outdoor life' in London in these decades as increasingly characterized by such 'random encounters with strangers, inexplicable aggregations, sudden eruptions of violence, and permanent sites

---

[21] Richard Menke sets out his case for the novel as an alternative information system and as a register of shifting understandings of information in his introduction to *Telegraphic Realism*, 4–10.

for encountering others *en masse*'.[22] Like Browne's dark plates in *Bleak House*, physiognomic detail is of less interest than capturing the radical instability of the urban environment. Surfaces shift, lines trail off at the edges of the image implying more of the same, an implied dilation of ink that mediates yet another scene of urban isolation, seemingly different, yet ultimately continuous with the desolate alienation of Tom-all-Alone's and the dark images that illustrate *Little Dorrit*, Browne's final collaboration with Dickens.

Browne's wrapper design for *Little Dorrit* is sparser and more stylized than his wrappers for either *Bleak House* or *Dombey and Son* (see Figure 17.1). It follows the same circular design, with a series of visual vignettes featuring an array of frenetic scenarios derived from the novel whirling around Amy Dorrit's back-lit diminutive figure peering out from the shadowy archway encircled by her name in chains, a dark focal point in a starkly illuminated space. The surrounding illustrations transition from the explicit political allusions of the images above Amy Dorrit, in which a daydreaming Britannia is drawn along by a ragged assortment of fools, bureaucrats, and a blind woman slowly tapping out the path, to crumbling edifices on both sides, none too subtly materializing the decay of social foundations that the novel records in such forensic detail. An old man perched atop one tower reads the newspaper as all crumbles beneath him, to drive the message of the knock-on effects of social irresponsibility home, just in case the reader/viewer was in danger of missing the point. The bottom half of the wrapper is busier and more illustrative of the novel. Mrs Clennam appears in one corner malevolently ensconced in her wheelchair, alongside the equally malign Jeremiah Flintwinch, while Arthur Clennam stands benignly amidst a crowd of figures on the move, talking, dealing, carting, travelling, waiting expectantly to be transported elsewhere, or asleep from sheer exhaustion.

Writing of the crowded pages of *Little Dorrit*, Daniel Novak has observed that what photography and realism had in common was 'not necessarily their fidelity to detail but rather their inability to present these details in any coherent form'.[23] Novak cites the following review from the *Spectator*, which also nicely captures Dickens's contemporary critics' frustration with his impulse to mediate and store too much data in his novels:

> So crowded is the canvas which Mr Dickens has stretched and so casual the connexion that gives to his composition whatever unity it has, that a daguerreotype of Fleet Street at noon-day would be the aptest symbol to be found for it; though the daguerreotype would have the advantage in accuracy of representation.[24]

Like a daguerreotype, Dickens's prose indiscriminately captures and stores a moment in time, like a photographer's image perfectly timed to capture the highest definition

---

[22] John Plotz, *The Crowd: British Literature and Public Politics* (Berkeley: University of California Press, 2000), 1.

[23] Daniel Novak, *Realism, Photography, and Nineteenth-Century Fiction* (Cambridge: Cambridge University Press, 2008), 63.

[24] Anonymous Review, 26 September 1853, 924: quoted ibid.

image of the bustle of Fleet Street. The location of the photograph seems pointed here too, aligning Dickens's prose images with the world of newspaper, commerce, and the circulation of information. Dickens's prose and Browne's illustrations do not have to be realistic to be photographic, they only need to be part of the same circuitry of mass communication, where data collection prevails over the making visible of details hidden from plain sight—the invisible dreams and thoughts of individual characters.[25] They also have to be memorable, because this is a novel preoccupied with legacy, inheritance, and the dangers of forgetting.

The first image we have of Arthur Clennam sets his capacity to remember against the amnesiac repetitions of modern time, measured out in standardized minutes, hours, days, and weeks. Chapter 3, entitled 'Home', begins with an arresting image of London that immediately alienates and disrupts any comforting notions of return. This is a city that demands that its occupants forget and move on:

> IT was Sunday evening in London, gloomy, close and stale. Maddening church bells of all degrees of dissonance, sharp and flat, cracked and clear, fast and slow, made the brick and mortar echoes hideous. Melancholy streets in a penitential garb of soot, steeped the souls of the people who were condemned to look at them out of windows, in dire despondency. In every thoroughfare, up almost every alley, and down almost every turning, some doleful bell was throbbing, jerking, tolling, as if the Plague were in the city and the dead-carts were going round. Everything was bolted and barred that could by possibility furnish relief to an overworked people. No pictures, no unfamiliar animals, no rare plants or flowers, no natural or artificial wonders of the ancient world—all *taboo* with that enlightened strictness, that the ugly South Sea gods in the British Museum might have supposed themselves at home again. Nothing to see but streets, streets, streets.[26]

Like a daguerreotype, this image of the city offers a single view. Guided by the perspective of the narrative voice, the eye of the reader scans the scene, moving along each anonymous street looking for signs of life and finding none. Negation, syntactically encoded through the repetition of 'no' and 'nothing', defines the contents of the image, what is included, and excluded from the frame, and thus what is remembered, and what is forgotten. Home in this image is a misplaced memory, associated with homesick South Sea gods, stored against their will in the nation's definitive imperial archive, the British Museum.

A page later, these same church bells produce a very different effect on Arthur Clennam, whose memory is triggered by being drawn back into the familiar soundscape of London. His listing of fragments of childhood memory follows, an assemblage of details tenuously unified by arbitrary Sunday rituals. Images of past Sundays

---

[25] Novak also discusses George Eliot's famous criticism of Dickens in her 'Natural History of German Life' (1859), 63.

[26] *Little Dorrit*, ed. Harvey Peter Sucksmith (Oxford: Clarendon Press, 1979), I:3, 26–9. Subsequent references are inserted parenthetically in the text by *LD* Book:chapter, page.

are mediated through grim decelerating adjectives—a 'dreary Sunday' when a 'horrible tract' had scared him 'out of his senses', a 'sleepy Sunday' when he had been marched to chapel 'morally handcuffed to another boy', an 'interminable Sunday' tortured by his unrelenting stern Bible-reading mother, and a 'resentful Sunday' sullenly contemplating his ignorance of the 'beneficent history of the New Testament': 'There was a legion of Sundays, all days of unserviceable bitterness and mortification, slowly passing before him' (LD I:3, 30–1). Like a sequence of magic lantern slides projected on a screen in his mind, Arthur Clennam's memory images forth experiences of past Sundays in a series of illuminated transparencies, a process that aligns with Walter Benjamin's much quoted observations on memory: 'Language has unmistakably made plain that memory is not an instrument for exploring the past but its theatre. It is the medium of past experience, as the ground is the medium in which dead cities lie interred.'[27]

While the data points may be scattered and the record incomplete, Dickens's language here transforms Arthur's memory into a medium that captures and stores moments in time that will be progressively recovered and illuminated for the reader as the narrative progresses. Only a few pages later, this first image of his stern unrelenting mother reading her Bible on an interminable Sunday afternoon is reanimated through association with another arresting tableau from Arthur's childhood memory, summoned by the sight of his mother 'propped up behind with one great angular black bolster, like the block at a state execution in the good old times':

> She and his father had been at variance from his earliest remembrance. To sit speechless himself in the midst of rigid silence, glancing in dread from the one averted face to the other, had been the peacefullest occupation of his childhood. She gave him one glassy kiss, and four stiff fingers. (LD I:3, 33–4)

While acoustically rich, the power of this image lies in its distillation of the horror of Arthur's childhood, caught between two hostile parents, silenced and yet bearing the burden of mediation nevertheless. Mother, father, and child are frozen in time, arrested in a stylized family portrait worthy of the rigidity of early daguerreotype family portraits.

While Browne's illustrations for *Little Dorrit* lack the complexity and ingenuity of his extraordinary dark plates for *Bleak House*, the dark plate technique still effectively materializes the gloomy interiors that form the backdrop for Arthur Clennam's melancholic return home. In the first plate Browne provided for the second monthly instalment of the novel, 'The Room with the Portrait', Arthur enters the deserted room once inhabited by his father. Emerging from the gloom, a sketchily rendered version of Clennam senior's portrait faintly gestures towards the symbolic power this image is given in the scene it illustrates: 'His picture, dark and gloomy, earnestly speechless on the wall, with the eyes intently looking at his son as they had looked when life departed from them, seemed to urge him awfully to the task he had attempted' (LD I:5, 54). The

---

[27] Walter Benjamin, *Selected Writings*, ed. Michael W. Jennings, Howard Eiland, and Gary Smith, 4 vols (Cambridge, MA: Harvard University Press, 1999), 2:61.

shards of sunlight illuminating the papers, open ledgers, and untouched quill on his father's desk are similarly true to the text's stress on failed communication, of messages unsent, discarded, or forgotten. Even the chiaroscuro effect created by this form of natural illumination returns the reader to the text's monochromatic visual cues:

> Arthur looked through the whole house. Dull and dark he found it. The gaunt rooms, deserted for years upon years, seemed to have settled down into a gloomy lethargy from which nothing could rouse them again. The furniture, at once spare and lumbering, hid in the rooms rather than furnished them, and there was no color in all the house; such color as had ever been there, had long ago started away on lost sunbeams—got itself absorbed, perhaps, into flowers, butterflies, plumage of birds. (*LD* I:5, 54)

Drained of life and colour, this home that is not a home is encoded with signs of precariousness. As Jeff Nunokawa argues so compellingly, everything that is taken is taken away again in this novel which is so sensitive to the 'rule of exchange': 'such sensitivity condemns any acquired property to an eventual loss as sure as the night that follows day; like dust to dust, anything that was once in circulation must be returned there'.[28] A home transformed into a medium of commerce provides little comfort or stability. Reduced to black and white, the limited palette of factual information and company ledgers, Browne's illustration and Dickens's prose drive home the associations of sterility and parasitism that cluster around Mrs Clennam's extortionate domestic economy.

By contrast, Dickens insists on the novel as a medium of an alternative domestic economy, a dynamic and panoramic means of communicating the complexity of an intimate social system under threat. In contrast to the black and white rationalism of global capitalism, colour is aligned with local and idiosyncratic expressions of family and relationship in this novel. This is vividly realized in the characterization of Mrs Plornish's decoration of the shop parlour of 'Happy Cottage' in 'Bleeding Heart Yard':

> Mrs. Plornish's shop-parlour had been decorated under her own eye, and presented, on the side towards the shop, a little fiction in which Mr. Plornish unspeakably rejoiced. This poetical heightening of the parlour consisted in the wall being painted to represent the exterior of a thatched cottage; the artist having introduced (in as effective a manner as he found compatible with their highly disproportionate dimensions) the real door and window. The modest sun-flower and holly-hock were depicted as flourishing with great luxuriance on this rustic dwelling, while a quantity of dense smoke issuing from the chimney indicated good cheer within, and also, perhaps, that it had not been lately swept. A faithful dog was represented as flying at the legs of the friendly visitor, from the threshold; and a circular pigeon-house, enveloped in a cloud of pigeons, arose from behind the garden-paling. On the door (when it was shut), appeared the semblance of a brass plate, presenting the

---

[28] Jeff Nunokawa, *The Afterlife of Property: Domestic Security and The Victorian Novel* (Princeton: Princeton University Press, 1994), 22.

inscription, Happy Cottage, T. and M. Plornish; the partnership expressing man and wife. No Poetry and no Art ever charmed the imagination more than the union of the two in this counterfeit cottage charmed Mrs. Plornish. (*LD* II:13, 556)

Transformed into her own private panorama, Mrs Plornish's shop-parlour responds to debt and absence with visual plenitude. Sunflowers and hollyhocks supplant traces of dust and decline. Counterfeit, and yet more authentic than Mrs Clennam's sterile domestic capital, Mrs Plornish's property cannot be exchanged in Dickens's alternative system of value. It is also hard to divorce this scene, as Grahame Smith has noted, from the popular nineteenth-century visual entertainments that Dickens relished, and more particularly in this case, the *trompe-l'œil* effects of the panoramas and panoramic theatre sets of the period.[29] Enacting the perceptual logic of the panoramic experience, Mrs Plornish prefers illusory simulation to the grim realities of Marshalsea Prison. Like Dickens himself, who reacted to John Banvard's astonishing 'The America Panorama'— a moving panorama that captured over 3,000 miles of spectacular scenery—with delight, Mrs Plornish immerses herself in the pleasures of visual mediation.[30]

Dickens's friendship with Clarkson Stanfield, who adapted the moving panorama format for the theatre, also drew him into the orbit of new forms of visual storytelling that aligned with his own experiment with the visual potential of the novel form, as many, including Smith, have noted. Both moving panoramas and dioramas are also invoked as opening up new channels for information to flow out to audiences beyond a metropolitan well-travelled elite in Dickens's travel writing and journalism.[31] Paralleling Mrs Plornish's invention of her own alternative visual economy, Dickens's earlier reflections on the great moving panoramas and dioramas of the age in 'Some Account of an Extraordinary Traveller' marvelled at the creation of 'new worlds' that literally expanded the scale of the ordinary and everyday:

> It is a delightful characteristic of these times, that new and cheap means are continually being devised, for conveying the results of actual experience, to those who are unable to obtain such experiences for themselves; and to bring them within the reach of the people—emphatically of the people; for it is they at large who are addressed in these endeavours, and not exclusive audiences ... Some of the best results of actual travel are suggested by such means to those whose lot it is to stay at home. New worlds open out to them, beyond their little worlds, and widen their range of reflection, information, sympathy, and interest. The more man knows of man, the better for the common brotherhood among us all.[32]

---

[29] Smith, *Dickens and the Dream of Cinema*, 164.
[30] Grahame Smith discusses Dickens's reaction to John Banvard's panorama, *Dickens and the Dream of Cinema*, 33.
[31] This cross-pollination has been discussed at great length by a range of critics, including Adelene Buckland in 'The Poetry of Science' and by Kate Flint in *The Victorians and the Visual Imagination*, chapters 1 and 6.
[32] Charles Dickens, 'Some Account of an Extraordinary Traveller', *Household Words*, 20 April 1850: 73–7, 77.

Vicarious tourism, as Adelene Buckland argues, is integral to Dickens's encouragement of an expansive world view.[33] The associative listing of the cognitive and affective processes that these expansive visual media make possible, however, suggests a more systemic rewiring or networking of individual minds into more collective globally connected forms of knowing and seeing that the collaboration between Browne and Dickens likewise explores and materializes. Dickens's observers ideally become more reflective, more informed, more sympathetic, and more interested, world citizens rather than passive consumers, with the capacity to reproduce and remediate what they know in new forms—like Mrs Plornish and her domestic panorama.

New visual technologies consequently create new 'discourse networks' or systems for writing down, and storing information, to reframe Dickens's observations in Friedrich Kittler's terms.[34] Whether in the form of a dark plate illustration, a daguerreotype or photograph, a magic lantern slide, a diorama, or moving panorama, new technologies structure the way the eye and mind make meaning and remember. Eye and mind, in this sense, are interconnected medial systems, as Laura Otis reminds us: 'No mind can be abstracted from the information system that feeds it, and rather than passively receiving data, the mind controls the circuits that monitor its own environment.'[35] To return then to where this chapter began, rethinking the visual in Dickens, less in terms of illustration and adaptation, and more in terms of mediation and data storage, opens up new ways of reading both his illustrative collaborations and his prodigious fascination with the optical illusions generated by new visual media. How, for example, could approaching the role of the visual in the Christmas Books be reconceived in terms of mediation or data storage? Read through this lens, these ritualized circular narrations not only invite nostalgic recalibrations of modern scenarios of alienated labour and family life, but also feed into and reflect Dickens's sustained engagement with new forms of mediating and visualizing data in his fiction and non-fiction. At the centre of Dickens's deeply experimental and imaginative engagement with the visual, however, is a definitely modern understanding of the novel as a multi-medial system with seemingly infinite potential to open the eyes and minds of the readers it drew into its parallel new worlds.

Further Reading

Collette Colligan and Margaret Linley (eds), *Media, Technology, and Literature: Image, Sound, Touch* (Farnham: Ashgate, 2011)

Lisa Gitelman, *Always Already New: Media, History, and the Data of Culture* (Cambridge, MA: MIT Press, 2007)

---

[33] Buckland, 'The Poetry of Science', 684–5.

[34] Friedrich Kittler, *Discourse Networks 1800/1900*, trans. Michael Metteer with Chris Cullens (Stanford, CA: Stanford University Press, 1990), section 1.

[35] Laura Otis, *Networking: Communicating with Bodies and Machines in the Nineteenth Century* (Ann Arbor: University of Michigan Press, 2011), 3.

Allen MacDuffie, *Victorian Literature, Energy, and the Ecological Imagination* (Cambridge: Cambridge University Press, 2014)

Leah Price, *How to Do Things with Books in Victorian Britain* (Princeton: Princeton University Press, 2012)

Matthew Rubery, *The Novelty of Newspapers and the Invention of the News* (Oxford: Oxford University Press, 2009)

PART V
DICKENS RE-VISIONED

CHAPTER 46

DICKENS'S WORLD-SYSTEM

Globalized Modernity as Combined and Uneven Development

PAUL YOUNG

INTRODUCTION

DICKENS's world has long been associated with a systematic coherence. Seminal studies by Humphry House and J. Hillis Miller claim respectively that Dickens produced a 'complete world', and that the world he rendered stands as 'the totality of all things as they are lived in by all human beings collectively'.[1] But these works are notable for the fact they suggest Dickens plots a markedly English world, with London's metropolitan topography all but filling his literary map. It is a world, then, but not in a properly global sense. And the consequential implication that 'English literature is mainly about England' profoundly limits such scholarship. So argues Edward W. Said, who endorses Raymond Williams's claim that the mid-nineteenth century marked 'the decisive period in which the consciousness of a new phase of civilization was being formed and expressed' in Britain, and that in *Dombey and Son* Dickens captured the 'transforming, liberating and threatening' character of this shift. But why, Said complains, does Williams make this claim '*without* reference to India, Africa, the Middle East, and Asia, since that is where transformed British life expanded to and filled'. Elaborating the point, and stressing his central argument, Said proposes Dickens belongs to a Western literary canon that 'makes constant references to itself as somehow participating in Europe's overseas expansion, and therefore creates what Williams calls "structures of feeling" that support, elaborate, and consolidate the practice of empire'. Accordingly, he continues, we should read Western literature with regard to 'the dynamic global environment created by

---

[1] Humphry House, *The Dickens World* (Oxford: Oxford University Press, 1941), 224; J. Hillis Miller, *Charles Dickens: The World of his Novels* (Oxford: Oxford University Press, 1958), xv.

imperialism, itself revised as an ongoing contest between north and south, metropolis and periphery, white and native'. Only then, he explains, can we comprehend how metropolitan consent was gained 'and continuously consolidated for the distant rule of native peoples and territories'.[2]

Said and other postcolonial scholars have drawn compelling links between culture and overseas expansion. But as the above-cited analysis suggests, this work has tended to privilege imperialism's drive towards geopolitical domination over and above its economic imperatives. Economic historians have expressed frustration that postcolonial specialists have not done more 'to place economy and culture in the same analytic frame'.[3] To do so in a nineteenth-century British context, recent historical work makes clear, is to recognize that the Victorian economy was marked by a web of trading relationships and allied movements of capital and people that incorporated but went well beyond empire. Noting the loss of America meant that 'the Empire never recaptured the position of importance in Britain's economic life it had held before 1776', P. J. Cain highlights Britain's central position in a global economy that grew tenfold in the second half of the nineteenth century, 'as a truly multilateral network of world trade emerged for the first time'.[4] In his field-defining history *The Empire Project: The Rise and Fall of the British World-System, 1830–1970*, John Darwin likewise points to an 'extraordinary range' of relationships that developed as nineteenth-century Britain's economic and geopolitical interests extended across 'a global realm among whose key provinces were Canada, Argentina, India, Australia, Southern Africa, China and the Middle East', as well as Europe and the United States.[5] This expansion was driven, he emphasizes, 'not by official designs but by the chaotic pluralism of British interests at home and of their agents and allies abroad'.[6]

As a result of the wide-ranging, contingent way in which the Victorians penetrated the world, Darwin cautions against the notion that Britain's global presence was defined by 'the exercise of *sovereign* power, or the unfettered enjoyment of imperial *rule*'.[7] Nevertheless, he concludes, what made 'Britain *the* great power of the nineteenth-century world' was the way in which it projected 'its influence all over the world and with particular force into those regions where it met least resistance from an organised state, an existing "high culture" or a developed economy'.[8] And in a remark that invites further exploration of the way in which Britain's worldwide influence gripped in imaginative

---

[2] Edward W. Said, *Culture and Imperialism* (London: Vintage, 1994), 14, 59.
[3] Gary B. Magee and Andrew S. Thompson, *Empire and Globalisation: Networks of People, Goods and Capital, c.1850–1914* (Cambridge: Cambridge University Press, 2010), 14.
[4] P. J. Cain, 'Economics and Empire: The Metropolitan Context', in Andrew Porter (ed.), *The Oxford History of the British Empire: The Nineteenth Century* (Oxford: Oxford University Press, 1999), 31–52 (31, 42).
[5] John Darwin, *The Empire Project: The Rise and Fall of the British World-System, 1830–1970* (Cambridge: Cambridge University Press, 2009), 1, 4.
[6] Ibid., 3.
[7] Ibid., xi.
[8] Ibid., 37, 49.

and ideological as well as material terms, Darwin suggests Britain's unrivalled albeit at times collaborative and at times contested capacity to shape and profit upon international economic development was underwritten by British 'cultural confidence bred by a sense of enduring "centrality" in a globalised world'.[9]

Taking up this invitation, and thus focusing on the genuinely global as well as economically driven character of Victorian expansion, this chapter considers how Dickens's work can be understood with relation to Britain's principal position within a growing and increasingly interconnected world economy. Consequently, it proposes that Dickens should be read as 'world literature', in the sense that his writing constitutes '*literature of the world-system*—of the modern capitalist world-system, that is'. This bald yet compelling definition of world literature, set out recently by the Warwick Research Collective (WReC), revolves around the twofold contention that: one, capitalism is 'the substrate of world-literature'; and two, modernity constitutes 'world-literature's subject and form—modernity is both what world-literature indexes or is "about" and what gives world literature its distinguishing formal characteristics'.[10] In what follows WReC's explication of world literature is drawn upon to consider afresh Williams's claim that Dickens registers and encodes industrial capitalism as 'a new phase of civilization' in British life. Where Said turns to 'empire' in order to link literature with expansionism, therefore, this study turns to the 'modern capitalist world-system' in order to consider how Dickens furnished literary form to the global. Perhaps more than any other English writer of the period, it argues, Dickens crafted an aesthetic that was acutely attentive towards the wide-ranging, empowered, profitable yet inherently uneven, unequal way that Britain in general, and London in particular, worked at the heart of nineteenth-century globalized modernity. While this line of analysis shows how Dickens countered simplistic, celebratory accounts of imperially driven globalization, however, the chapter contends that his novels and journalism tied Britain's own socio-economic progress to industrial capitalism's inexorably expansionist logic. It closes, then, by suggesting that Dickens's metropolitan, racially discriminative perspective on the modern world-system served to sanction and sustain the imperial forms of primitive accumulation, exploitation, and violence that were so central to the way in which the Victorians penetrated and networked the world.

Venture Capitalism and Globalized Gammon

In Dickens's fiction the kind of systemic 'cultural confidence' that Darwin ties to Britain's central position within a globalized world appears embodied in the bald, red-faced

---

[9] Ibid., 7.
[10] WReC, *Combined and Uneven Development: Towards a New Theory of World-Literature* (Liverpool: Liverpool University Press, 2015), 8, 15.

personage of Paul Dombey. On the birth of his son at the start of the novel the shipping magnate's expansionist excitement knows no bounds:

> The earth was made for Dombey and Son to trade in, and the sun and the moon were made to give them light. Rivers and seas were formed to float their ships; rainbows gave them promise of fair weather; winds blew for or against their enterprises; stars and planets circled in their orbits, to preserve inviolate a system of which they were the centre.[11]

Highlighting this passage in order to elaborate his criticism of Williams, Said remarks: 'Dombey's egoism recalls, mocks, yet ultimately depends on the tried and true discourses of imperial free trade, the British mercantile ethos, its sense of all but unlimited opportunities for commercial advancement abroad.'[12] While Said tends to focus upon issues of territorial conquest and control, then, here he correctly identifies Dombey as the personification of a global force that stretched far beyond Britain's colonial possessions. Darwin underscores the historical significance of this point when he identifies Britain's deep-sea merchant marine as the 'jewel in the crown' of 'a vast abstract realm of assets and interests' stretching well beyond those parts of the world coloured red on Victorian maps; this global network cohered around London and comprised infrastructure projects including railways, harbour-works, plantations, and mines, financial services including banks and insurance agents, as well as shipping firms.[13] Yet the complex, abstract character of these worldwide operations raises another important point concerning *Dombey and Son*: the firm's labyrinthine global transactions, celebrated as 'prodigious ventures', result in 'ruinous consequences' for those involved (*DS* 53, 714). Set against Said's suggestion that the novel validates Dombey's discursive register, then, we might rather say that the expansionist economic discourse it invokes is 'tried' by the novel, in a manner that drives home the point it is manifestly not 'true'.

At least, not true in the sense that it fails to make good on the smooth delivery of tremendous profits it promises for the shipping firm's owner and those who have invested in his House. Yet at the same time true in the normative, binding sense that here, as elsewhere in his writing, Dickens is at pains to reveal the dangerously deceptive way in which globally oriented visions and their associated speculative schemes shape and move a future-focused, money-motivated society. The development of nineteenth-century financial capitalism is particularly salient in this regard; as Ayşe Çellikol has recently argued, the portrayal of 'corrupt adventurers who float shares of fake business ventures' allowed mid-Victorian novelists including Anthony Trollope as well as Dickens to expose and critique an expansionist financial economy in which 'signifiers

---

[11] *Dombey and Son*, ed. Alan Horsman (Oxford: Clarendon Press, 1974), chapter 1, page 2. Subsequent references are inserted parenthetically in the text by *DS* chapter, page.
[12] Said, *Culture and Imperialism*, 14.
[13] Darwin, *The Empire Project*, 10.

mattered more than the things they claimed to represent'.[14] Thus the Anglo-Bengalee Disinterested Loan and Life Insurance Company in *Martin Chuzzlewit*, with its 'substantial and expensive' offices that prove little more than an 'ornamental', 'poetical', and 'inventive' means of parting the British public from their savings; or *David Copperfield's* Aunt Betsey, who takes her 'pigs' to 'foreign market' with disastrous consequences; or *Little Dorrit's* 'multitude' who 'worship' Merdle's 'world-wide commercial enterprise and gigantic combinations of skill and capital', in spite of—or rather precisely because of—the fact that 'nobody knew with the least precision what Mr. Merdle's business was, except that it was to coin money'; or 'us smaller vermin' in *Our Mutual Friend*, whose delusional reverence is inspired not so much by the figure of the financier as by the immaterial financial mechanisms—'Shares. O mighty Shares!'—through which his 'mysterious business' schemes exert their exploitative social hold.[15]

Such financial schemes, Çellikol notes, index 'the capitalist tendency to build a world of abstraction'.[16] But Dickens was also concerned with the ideologically charged, textually energized drives that encouraged his fellow Britons to invest their labour as well as their pecuniary resources in expansionist enterprise. The millions of Victorians who left home for Britain's settler colonies and the United States, James Belich notes, were pulled by a 'paradise complex' promoted by 'booster literature', the wealth of 'books, pamphlets, newspaper and journal articles, lectures, and advertisements' he identifies as 'one of the largest genres in nineteenth-century English literature'.[17] In *Martin Chuzzlewit* an American 'paradise' takes shape as the appropriately named 'Eden', a 'flourishing', 'architectural' city on paper that in reality becomes 'the dread of some rapacious animal or human enemy' in the midst of a malarial swamp (*MC* 21, 353–4; 23, 378). And significantly it is the swamp that subdues Martin and Mark Tapley rather than vice versa. Not only did he undercut the exaggerated claims of booster literature, then, but Dickens also opened up only to turn down the literary opportunity for an adventurous confrontation between heroic settlers and their hostile environment. In *Dombey and Son* Walter Gay's boyhood yearning for 'a life of adventure' sees him following his fictional forebear Robinson Crusoe to sea. Far from setting the stage for a Robinsonade, however, the shipwreck that (inevitably) follows leaves Walter adrift—in narrative as well as geographical terms—until he is plucked from the ocean by a China trader

---

[14] Ayşe Çellikol, 'Globalization and Economics', in Juliet John (ed.), *The Oxford Handbook of Victorian Literary Culture* (Oxford: Oxford University Press, 2016), 124–41 (137–8).

[15] *Martin Chuzzlewit*, ed. Margaret Cardwell (Oxford: Clarendon Press, 1982), chapter 27, pages 430, 429. Subsequent references are inserted parenthetically in the text by *MC* chapter, page; *David Copperfield*, ed. Nina Burgis (Oxford: Clarendon Press, 1981), chapter 35, page 438. Subsequent references are inserted parenthetically in the text by *DC* chapter, page; *Little Dorrit*, ed. Harvey Peter Sucksmith (Oxford: Clarendon Press, 1979), Book II, chapter 12, page 539, Book I, chapter 33, page 386. Subsequent references are inserted parenthetically in the text by *LD* Book:chapter, page; *Our Mutual Friend*, ed. Michael Cotsell, Oxford World's Classics (Oxford: Oxford University Press, 1989), Book I, chapter 10, page 114. Subsequent references are inserted parenthetically in the text by *OMF* Book:chapter, page.

[16] Çellikol, 'Globalization and Economics', 137.

[17] James Belich, *Replenishing the Earth: The Settler Revolution and the Rise of the Anglo-World, 1784–1939* (Oxford: Oxford University Press, 2009), 153–4.

returning to London (*DS* 4, 43). If it is right to suggest that the adventure story serves as a fictional correlative to booster literature, charging 'England's will with the energy to go out into the world and explore, conquer, and rule', therefore, the broader point to obtain from both *Martin Chuzzlewit* and *Dombey and Son* is that Dickens is concerned to dissipate rather than stoke such hyperbolic expansionism.[18] It is a point underscored when Mr Gregsbury, 'the great member of Parliament' in *Nicholas Nickleby*, is moved by the technologically advanced transportation network that binds together 'the peaceful industrious communities of our island home' to pontificate upon 'the boundless prospect of conquest and possession—achieved by British perseverance and British valour—which is outspread before me'. 'Gammon' is the prosaic retort to such confidence in Britain's industrialized, imperial capacity to penetrate and dominate the world.[19]

'Gammon' is also Mr Weller's reaction to charitable overseas aid, in the form of the 'noble society for providing the infant negroes in the West Indies with flannel waistcoats and moral pocket handkerchiefs'; for, as he bluntly surmises, 'what's the good o' flannel veskits to the young niggers abroad?'[20] Dickens was equally dismissive when it came to the somewhat less selfless conviction that the global extension of Britain's economic relations would see his own nation profit at the same time as it shaped the express emergence of a progressive, peaceful and inclusive modern world. He used 'The Niger Expedition', a review essay for *The Examiner* newspaper published in 1848, to pour scorn upon the idea that Britain's technologically enhanced capacity to cross oceans and open up foreign markets was matched by the capacity of non-European peoples to respond rationally to modern commercial culture. Transportation advances may well have compressed global space and time, he acknowledged, but he warned those Exeter Hall philanthropists who called for 'the railroad Christianisation of Africa and the abolition of the Slave Trade' of the 'great gulf set' '[b]etween the civilized European and the barbarous African'.[21] It was *Bleak House* where Dickens furnished fictional form to such sentiments, memorably dismissing Mrs Jellyby's Borrioboola scheme to effect 'the general cultivation of the coffee berry—*and* the natives' as an interventionist form of 'telescopic philanthropy' that remained blind to the socio-economic problems on its doorstep.[22] 'The Niger Expedition' anticipated the domestically oriented moral of that later novel, urging that Britain must right its local wrongs before it turned to global

---

[18] Martin Green, *Dreams of Adventure, Deeds of Empire* (London: Routledge and Kegan Paul, 1980), 3.

[19] *Nicholas Nickleby*, ed. Paul Schlicke, Oxford World's Classics (Oxford: Oxford University Press, 2009), chapter 16, pages 189, 192, 193. Subsequent references are inserted parenthetically in the text by *NN* chapter, page.

[20] *Pickwick Papers*, ed. James Kinsley (Oxford: Clarendon Press, 1986), chapter 27, pages 403–4. Subsequent references are inserted parenthetically in the text by *PP* chapter, page.

[21] Dickens, 'Review: Narrative of Expedition to River Niger', *The Dent Uniform Edition of Dickens' Journalism*, ed. Michael Slater and John Drew, 4 vols (London: J. M. Dent, Columbus: Ohio State University Press, 1993–2000), volume 2, pages 124–5. Subsequent references are inserted parenthetically in the text by Dent volume: 'The Niger Expedition', page.

[22] *Bleak House*, ed. George Ford and Sylvère Monod, Norton Critical Edition (New York: W. W. Norton, 1977), chapter 4, page 35. Subsequent references are inserted parenthetically in the text by *BH* chapter, page.

problems: 'The work at home must be completed thoroughly, or there is no hope abroad' (Dent 2: 'The Niger Expedition', 125).

Whether in the guise of globe-trotting commercial transactions, overseas financial investments, settler emigration, colonial conquest, or the imperial civilizing mission, therefore, Dickens's representation of industrial capitalist expansion as a misguided, overconfident, dangerous affair constitutes a 'general repudiation of "the global" as an unmappably vague and destructive realm, lacking in coordinates and subject to the pitiless law of entropy'.[23] This is the argument advanced by James Buzard, in an engaging, influential reading of *Bleak House* as a reaction against the Great Exhibition of 1851, the event that prompted so many Victorian commentators to celebrate British-led capitalism's irresistible capacity to shape a world after its own image. Buzard labels such imperial universalism as 'metropolitan anticulture', contending that along with other nineteenth-century novelists Dickens's 'autoethnographic' fiction plotted national culture as a distinctive and bounded life-world diminished not enhanced by such expansionism. The moral associated with the urban horror of Tom-all-Alone's—'it might be better for the national glory even that the sun should sometimes set upon the British dominions, than that it should ever rise upon so vile a wonder as Tom' (*BH* 46, 553)—thus bears testament to Buzard's insistence that Dickens sought at once to raise and to 'manage the possibility that worldwide empire amounts not to a nation-expanding or nation-aggrandizing process, but to a nation-erasing one'.[24] Setting his argument against Said's claim that nineteenth-century British novels furnished form to an outward-facing 'desire to conquer and control', Buzard reads Dickens as a 'defensive rather than smug' writer, albeit one whose inward-facing efforts to trace the 'centripetal force' tying his nation together tend towards 'cultural protectionism or "little Englandism"'.[25]

Buzard is certainly correct that Dickens had no truck with triumphalist accounts of a *Pax Britannica* or Victorian new world order, wherein 'the global' emerged as a space distinguished by the free-flowing, fast-acting, all-encompassing force of British-led industrial capitalist civilization. One significant conclusion to be drawn concerning my contention that Dickens's writing constitutes literature of the modern world-system, therefore, is precisely the fact that it recognizes, records, and rejects—as 'gammon'—this system's exaggerated yet empowered discursive articulation. But in making the case for Dickens as a writer concerned to secure the 'conceptual boundaries' of Britain's small-c culture against such a vision of globalized modernity, Buzard acknowledges that this narrative endeavour concerned a nation whose rapidly developing economy was embroiled in a web of 'far-flung investments of capital and personnel' that marked quotidian metropolitan existence. Did not the British way of life 'revolve around *tea*, after all?' Buzard asks, in rhetorical echo of David Copperfield's bafflement with a tea-loving old lady's 'indignation at the impiety

---

[23] James Buzard, *Disorienting Fiction: The Autoethnographic Work of Nineteenth-Century British Novels* (Princeton: Princeton University Press, 2005), 113.
[24] Ibid., 52.
[25] Ibid., 13, 43, 55.

of mariners and others, who had the presumption to go "meandering" about the world' (*DC* 1, 2).²⁶ Tea gives the lie to any clear-cut distinction between the local and the global, refusing that the latter constitutes an 'unmappably vague and destructive realm' by making manifest the fact that, for better or for worse, international 'meandering'—'traveling, purchasing, cultivating, and colonizing the world'²⁷—is bound up with the everyday, material reality of what it is to be British. And it is in this sense that Copperfield's local/global perspective gives the lie to an ethnographic world view built around 'a "culturalist" world order in which all inhabited space is broken into separate, incommensurable, but functionally equivalent cultures'.²⁸ For as Anna Lowenhaupt Tsing notes, such ethnography obscures the fact 'that all human cultures are shaped and transformed in long histories of regional-to-global networks of power, trade, and meaning'.²⁹

Where Buzard reads Dickens with regard to a repudiation of 'the global', therefore, Copperfield's local/global perspective and Tsing's ethnographic injunction raise the question of how his writing might also be understood to rid 'the global' of its scare quotes. Which is to say, how might it be understood to plot a more materialist account of those 'regional-to-global networks of power, trade, and meaning' that shaped and transformed Victorian life? Here Tsing's own work in *Friction: An Ethnography of Global Connection* is helpful, since it introduces the metaphor of friction in order to contest late twentieth-century celebrations 'of a new era of global motion' in which the 'flow of goods, ideas, money, and people would henceforth be pervasive and unimpeded'. Set against this 'imagined global era', Tsing's focus upon the 'messiness of capitalism in the Indonesian rainforest' illustrates her broader point about the particular, contingent way in which a universalizing mode of production connects the world:

> Capitalism only spreads as producers, distributers, and consumers strive to universalize categories of capital, money, and commodity fetishism. Such strivings make possible globe-crossing capital and commodity chains. Yet these chains are made up of uneven and awkward links.³⁰

Then as now: Tsing's insistence upon global capitalism's messy, frictional, uneven character finds its echo in Darwin's emphasis on Victorian expansion as 'unfinished, untidy, a mass of contradictions, aspirations, anomalies'; it urges that the categories of the local and the global are understood in dialectical relation; and it opens up a way of reading Dickens that is attentive towards the fact that 'friction gets in the way of the smooth operation of global power', even as it 'makes global connection powerful and effective'.³¹

---

[26] Ibid., 55, 57.
[27] Julie. E. Fromer, *A Necessary Luxury: Tea in Victorian England* (Athens: Ohio University Press, 2008), 185.
[28] Buzard, *Disorienting Fiction*, 34.
[29] Anna Lowenhaupt Tsing, *Friction: An Ethnography of Global Connection* (Princeton: Princeton University Press, 2005), 3.
[30] Ibid., 4.
[31] Darwin, *The Empire Project*, xi; Tsing, *Friction*, 6.

Grounding Globalization

In order to develop such a reading it is instructive to return to *Dombey and Son*, wherein 'hints of adventurous and romantic story' are afforded by the institutions, businesses, and tableaux surrounding Dombey's London offices: Guildhall, the Royal Exchange, the Bank of England, the 'rich East India House', 'pictures of ships speeding away full sail to all parts of the world', 'outfitting warehouses ready to pack off anybody anywhere', and 'little timber midshipmen ... outside the shop-doors of nautical instrument makers'(*DS* 4, 36). As indicated, the maritime misadventures endured by both Dombey and Walter Gay tell a very different story about Britain's position in the world from the richly rewarding narratives suggested by these edifices and symbols. But here Dickens's concern with the imaginative excesses of an expansionist superstructure should not obscure the bigger, baseline picture: namely, that London's built environment bears emphatic witness to Britain's economic power and global span. And this point brings to the fore the fact that while 'capitalism is under the impulse to eliminate all spatial barriers, to "annihilate space through time" as Marx puts it ... it can do so only through the production of a fixed space'. Elaborating this critical tension, which is central to the reason that friction not freedom of movement defines capital's global circulation, David Harvey writes that economic development is dependent upon and thus restricted by material and political frameworks: 'The building of fixed physical infrastructures to facilitate the movement as well as support the activities of production, exchange, distribution and consumption'; and 'the construction of territorial organization, primarily (though not solely) state powers to regulate money, law and politics and to monopolize the means of coercion and violence according to a sovereign territorial (and sometimes extra-territorial) will'.[32] All of which draws attention to the significance of fixed space to an understanding of how global connections take shape in Dickens's work.

In *Dombey and Son* this significance is perhaps best illustrated by leaving the East India House—'teeming with suggestions of precious stuffs and stones, tigers, elephants, howdahs, hookahs, umbrellas, palm trees, palanquins, and gorgeous princes of a brown complexion sitting on carpets' (*DS* 4, 36)—and going down to the India Docks, to Captain Cuttle's residence 'on the brink of a little canal ... where there was a swivel bridge which opened now and then to let some wandering monster of a ship come roaming up the street like a stranded leviathan' (*DS* 9, 117). Much as *Bleak House's* waddling Megalosaurus works in temporal terms to complicate the teleological narrative of Victorian Progress, so the spatial traction of this monstrous analogy disrupts overly fluid accounts of globalized modernity. But even as it does so, this amalgamation of canal, bridge, ship, and street breaks down any clear-cut distinction between the land and the water; and, by extension, the local and the global. What follows develops this

---

[32] David Harvey, *Spaces of Hope* (Berkeley: University of California Press, 2000), 59–60.

infrastructural imbrication, as Dickens moves from 'slopsellers' shops, with Guernsey shirts, sou'wester hats, and canvas pantaloons' to 'anchor and chain-cable forges, where sledge hammers were dinging upon iron all day long':

> Then came rows of houses, with little vane-surmounted masts uprearing themselves from among the scarlet beans. Then, ditches. Then, pollard willows. Then, more ditches. Then, unaccountable patches of dirty water, hardly to be descried, for the ships that covered them. Then, the air was perfumed with chips; and all other trades were swallowed up in mast, oar, and block making, and boat building. Then, the ground grew marshy and unsettled. Then, there was nothing to be smelt but rum and sugar. (*DS* 9, 117–18)

The sights, sounds, and smells of this scene embed far-reaching, complex processes of production, exchange, distribution, and consumption within a riverside environment that simultaneously facilitates and frustrates capitalism's drive to eliminate spatial barriers; while a web of topographical detail pulls the local and the global together, therefore, it is a laboured and awkward rather than an easy and smooth assemblage. This is what Tsing means when she states, 'Friction refuses the lie that global power operates as a well-oiled machine.'[33] And this is how Dickens gives frictional form to a modern world-system that grips precisely because it is grounded.

Albeit that it is afloat as well as grounded. Elsewhere in his novels activities on and about the Thames afforded Dickens further opportunities to plot the expansionist enterprise that cohered around the capital city's fluid as well as fixed space. In *The Old Curiosity Shop*, then, Daniel Quilp profits upon British imperial activity through the diverse occupations he pursues from the counting-house on his riverside wharf; and his activities cast in microcosmic relief the wide-ranging, empowered way in which the Victorians sought to profit upon the world:

> He collected the rents of whole colonies of filthy streets and alleys by the waterside, advanced money to the seamen and petty officers of merchant vessels, had a share in the ventures of divers mates of East Indiamen, smoked his smuggled cigars under the very nose of the Custom House, and made appointments on Change with men in glazed hats and round jackets pretty well every day.[34]

Around Quilp's wharf the 'water and all upon it was in active motion', but once more Dickens is drawn to friction in order to describe the action: a fleet of barges move in a 'wrong-headed, dogged, obstinate way, bumping up against the larger craft, running under the bows of steam-boats, ... and being crunched on all sides like so many walnut-shells'; while a 'great steam ship' moves slowly like a 'sea monster' through 'a forest of masts', 'as though she wanted room to breathe' (*OCS* 5, 46). In *Our Mutual Friend* such

---

[33] Tsing, *Friction*, 6.
[34] *The Old Curiosity Shop*, ed. Elizabeth M. Brennan (Oxford: Clarendon Press, 1998), chapter 4, page 34. Subsequent references are inserted parenthetically in the text by *OCS* chapter, page.

ponderous power is cast in the terrific terms of the sublime, as Eugene and Mortimer experience first-hand the infrastructural scale and frictional force of river-borne operations flanked by colossal wharves and warehouses: 'all the objects among which they crept were so huge in contrast with their wretched boat as to threaten to crush it' (*OMF* I:14, 171).

While in the above examples it is the slow, laborious power of the world-system that dominates, on other occasions Dickens picked up the pace as he described the frenetic energy of the Thames, with river-life lending itself particularly well to the hurrying, pressing, pushing, crowding, miscellaneous prose style through which Williams proposes Dickens captured the experiential essence of urban modernity:

> Little steam-boats dashed up and down the stream incessantly. Tiers upon tiers of vessels, scores of masts, labyrinths of tackle, idle sails, splashing oars, gliding row-boats, lumbering barges; sunken piles, with ugly lodgings for the water-rat within their mud-discoloured nooks; church steeples, warehouses, house-roofs, arches, bridges, men and women, children, casks, cranes, boxes, horses, coaches, idlers, and hard-labourers: there they were, all jumbled up together, any summer morning, far beyond Tom's power of separation. (*MC* 40, 622)[35]

In this scene too, from *Martin Chuzzlewit*, we note again how topographic confusion—of land and water, labour and leisure, architecture and transport, stasis and movement—suggests the chaotic, uneven, yet powerful imbrication of the local and the global. And this point builds upon the fact that Dickens has already introduced the 'devious mazes' that link this riverside space with London's fruit-brokers: 'All day long, a stream of porters from the wharves beside the river, each bearing on his back a bursting chest of oranges, poured slowly through the narrow passages' (*MC* 9, 129). Such quotidian viscosity brings with it pressure for change, notwithstanding those 'ancient inhabitants' in the neighbourhood who 'were much opposed to steam and all new-fangled ways' (*MC* 9, 131). So whether depicted in frenetic or ponderous terms, friction is not simply an inherent feature of London's position within the world-system; it is also a force that opens up new routes and forms of interconnection, speeding up rather than smoothening out global power through a variety of ongoing infrastructural developments. In *Little Dorrit* Dickens expanded this point when he invited his readers to imagine the Thames 30 years or so earlier, allowing him to pull into focus the fixed and fluid space of globalized modernity in its most up-to-date instantiation: 'no small steam-boats on the river, no landing-places but slippery narrow stairs and foot-causeways, no railroad on the opposite bank, no hanging bridge or fish-market near at hand, no traffic on the nearest bridge of stone, nothing moving on the stream but watermen's wherries and coal-lighters' (*LD* II:9, 514). If river-borne technology and riverside infrastructure enabled

---

[35] Raymond Williams, 'Notes on English Prose: 1750–1950', in *Writing in Society* (London: Verso, 1983), 94.

Dickens to track capitalism's drive to 'annihilate space by time', then, so too it allowed him to chart the historical momentum of a system that, in Marx's equally memorable formulation, was driven by the need to 'nestle everywhere, settle everywhere, establish connections everywhere'.[36]

Representations of the frictional force and historical dynamism generated by fixed and fluid space on and around the River Thames thus illustrate particularly powerfully how Dickens can be read with regard to the global extension of industrial capitalist modernity. And this makes material sense, given that the Thames served as the principal metropolitan conduit for the goods, technologies, people, and information around which nineteenth-century British global expansion cohered. But so too in a literary sense these riverside scenes suggest the need for further critical work on the way in which Dickens's writing might be understood with regard to a frictional aesthetic that grounded globalization, dramatizing the dialectical interplay of the local and the global in a way that captured the energy of the modern world-system as it pulsed through Britain and beyond. Where the first section of this chapter discussed how Dickens repudiated globalization as a smoothly powerful success story, then, its second section proposes that at the same time his novels revealed frictionally forceful, historically dynamic, materially significant global connections within the metropolitan topographies he represented. In its third and final section attention turns to the way in which Dickens can be read in terms of what for WReC constitutes the distinguishing feature of the modern world-system and thus world literature: for while friction marks the way in which we should understand global connections to take shape in Dickens's fiction, the theory of 'combined and uneven development' allows us to consider his work with relation to industrial capitalism's divisive, violent impact upon the world.

Unequal and Violent

Explicating the theory of combined and uneven development, which in its earliest iteration is associated most prominently with Trotsky, WReC write that it was 'devised to describe a situation in which capitalist forms and relations exist alongside "archaic forms of economic life" and pre-existing social and class relations'.[37] As such, they continue, in a passage worth citing at length, the global articulation of the capitalist mode of production gives the lie to the twinfold idea that: one, 'modernity' is a phenomenon that occurs first in one place and then—perhaps—in another; and two, there could ever exist 'some sort of "achieved" modernity, in which unevenness would have been superseded, harmonised, vanquished or ironed out':

---

[36] 'The Communist Manifesto', in *Karl Marx: Selected Writings*, ed. David McLellan (Oxford: Oxford University Press, 1977), 221–47 (224).
[37] WReC, *Combined and Uneven Development*, 11.

'Modernity' does not mark the relationship between some formations (that are 'modern') and others (that are not 'modern', or not yet so). So it is not a matter of pitting France against Mali, say, or New York City against Elk City, Oklahoma. Uneven development is not a characteristic of 'backward' formations only. Middlesbrough and North East Lincolnshire are in the United Kingdom as well as London and the Home Counties—and London, itself, of course, is among the more radically unevenly developed cities in the world. To grasp the nettle here involves recognising that capitalist development does not smooth away but rather *produces* unevenness, systematically and as a matter of course. Combined *and* uneven: the face of modernity is not worn exclusively by the 'futuristic' skyline of the Pudong district in Shanghai or the Shard and Gherkin buildings in London; just as emblematic of modernity as these are the favelas of Rocinha and Jacarezinho in Rio and the slums of Dharavi in Bombay and Makoko in Lagos, the ship graveyards of Nouadhibou and the Aral Sea, the vast, deindustrialised wastelands north, east, south and west, and the impoverished and exhausted rural hinterlands.[38]

Then as now: underscoring the fact that this analysis of the contemporary world pertains too to that of Dickens, WReC collaborator Pablo Mukherjee concludes that if nineteenth-century industrial capitalism furnishes 'a world-systemic framework for the literature of the Victorian period', then critics should pay particular attention to the 'globally entrenched but uneven' development of this system.[39] So while we have seen already how Dickens's novels can be read with regard to the untidy, frenzied, protean power of British-led globalization, we now look to these works in order to offer some preliminary evaluation of WReC's contention that the novel serves paradigmatically as 'a literary form in which combined and uneven development is manifested with particular salience'.[40]

Here the notion that capitalist development '*produces* unevenness, systematically and as a matter of course' is again well served by Dickens's representation of London's riverside life, marked topographically by the enduring—rather than decreasing—interplay of technological progress and sweated labour, rationalized business practices and haphazard economic opportunism, industrial advance and environmental degradation, expansive commodification and resource scarcity, heightened global connectivity and inadequate sanitation. Thus, in *Oliver Twist*, Dickens introduces his 'visitor' to a 'wholly hidden' yet intricately networked metropolitan locality on the Thames, 'where the buildings on the banks are dirtiest and the vessels on the river blackest with the dust of colliers':

> Jostling with unemployed labourers of the lowest class, ballast-heavers, coal-whippers, brazen women, ragged children, and the very raff and refuse of the river,

---

[38] Ibid., 12–13.
[39] Pablo Mukherjee, 'Introduction: Victorian World Literatures', *The Yearbook of English Studies* 41, 2 (2011), 3.
[40] WReC, *Combined and Uneven Development*, 16.

he makes his way with difficulty along, assailed by offensive sights and smells ... and deafened by the clash of ponderous waggons that bear great piles of merchandise from the stacks of warehouses that rise from every corner.[41]

In *David Copperfield* the triumphal march of capitalist progress is recast as a Thameside 'nightmare' of failed speculation and urban degeneration, in a scene where the ongoing 'glare of sundry fiery Works' illuminates rotting 'carcases of houses' and 'rusty iron monsters of steam-boilers, wheels, cranks, pipes, furnaces, paddles, anchors, diving-bells, windmill-sails' that sink inexorably back into the river. Beneath the 'cavernous shadow' of London's first iron bridge, the fallen figure of Martha attempts suicide, so that up-to-date engineered infrastructure and age-old patriarchal oppression come together in an image that refutes modernity's hypothetical drive towards universal autonomy and betterment (*DC* 48, 580). In *Our Mutual Friend* Gaffer Hexam's peripheral, precarious efforts to eke out an existence in the midst of the 'slime and ooze' of the River Thames stand in stark contrast with the 'spick and span', 'varnish and polish' novelty of the Veneerings. But Dickens's concern is to insert his '[h]alf savage' yet 'business-like' activities into 'these times of ours' (*OMF* I:1–2; II:8). And in so doing, to enfold the pre-modern within the modern, the primal within the progressive, and the barbaric within the civilized.

Dickens's depictions of the Thames thus register modernity's unevenly developed as well as frictionally forceful momentum. And away from the Thames his novels extend this world-systemic logic throughout the nation, in a manner that furnishes form to Neil Smith's definition of uneven development as 'social inequality blazoned into the geographical landscape, [as well as] the exploitation of that geographical landscape for certain socially determined ends'.[42] Hence the 'rows and rows of old women, seated on inverted baskets shelling peas' who work amidst 'the perfume of the fruits and flowers [... and] the magnificence of the pine-apples and melons' in Covent-Garden Market (*MC* 40, 621); or the railway journey that affords Mr Dombey 'glimpses of cottage-homes, of houses, mansions, rich estates, of husbandry and handicraft, of people, of old roads and paths ... miserable habitations far below ... deformity of brick and mortar penning up deformity of mind and body' (*DS* 20, 276); or the crossing kept clear by Jo, 'the outlaw with the broom', who solders the socio-economic circuitry of urban modernity notwithstanding that he knows only that 'it's hard to keep the mud off the crossing in dirty weather, and harder still to live by doing it' (*BH* 16, 197); or 'the hardest working part of Coketown', built in 'a violent hurry for some one man's purpose', and distinguished by an 'unnatural family' of 'stunted and crooked' industrialized architecture that appears to 'put out a sign of the kind of people who might be expected to

---

[41] *Oliver Twist*, ed. Kathleen Tillotson (Oxford: Clarendon Press, 1966), chapter 50, page 338. Subsequent references are inserted parenthetically in the text by *OT* chapter, page.

[42] Neil Smith, *Uneven Development: Nature, Capital, and the Production of Space* (Athens: The University of Georgia Press, 2008), 206.

be born in it';[43] or 'a neighbourhood which looked like a toy neighbourhood taken in blocks out of a box by a child of particularly incoherent mind, and set up anyhow':

> here, one side of a new street; there, a large solitary public-house facing nowhere; here, another unfinished street already in ruins; there, a church; here, an immense new warehouse; there, a dilapidated old country villa; then, a medley of black ditch, sparkling cucumber-frame, rank field, richly cultivated kitchen-garden, brick viaduct, arch-spanned canal, and a disorder of frowziness and fog. (*OMF* II:1, 219)

The point to underscore is that these landscapes reveal industrial capitalism's systematic drive to commodify human and extra-human nature precisely because of the disordered, incongruous, asymmetrical way in which they take shape. And we note besides how the above examples attest to a powerful synergy between this socio-economic reality and Dickens's writing style, which Daniel Tyler defines with regard to 'its syntactical and grammatical irregularities, its temporal confusions and shifts of tense, its rhythms, its clipped sentences, its combination of detailed realism and hallucinatory vision, ... its odd collocations'. That this 'energetic and uneven prose' is so well suited to an energetic and uneven modern world-system gives weight to Tyler's claim that 'the attention of the critic may be rewardingly directed towards the way Dickens writes inseparably from what he writes about'.[44]

While in the aforementioned 'The Niger Expedition' Dickens expressed hope that modernity's work 'at home' might be thoroughly, evenly completed, therefore, the form as well as the content of his fiction can be understood to have laid bare the structural logic of a socio-economic system that contradicted such an expectation. Dickens's striking capacity to reveal the inherently uneven impact of industrial capitalism upon modern landscape and life in this way bears powerful testament to the 'truly disruptive' energy that Sally Ledger associates with 'a radical political writer on the side of the poor and dispossessed'.[45] At least, it does so at a national level. On an international level, however, Dickens's representations of non-European peoples complicated this radical political position, because they suggested such putatively primitive beings were either profoundly ill suited or wholly unsuited to the modern world-system. Where on the domestic front Dickens traced industrial capitalism's uneven development in a manner that showed how modernity failed the poor and dispossessed, therefore, on the global stage he figured racial difference in a manner that suggested non-Europeans failed modernity.

---

[43] *Hard Times*, ed. Fred Kaplan, 4th edn, Norton Critical Edition (New York: W. W. Norton, 2017), Book I, chapter 10, page 56. Subsequent references are inserted parenthetically in the text by *HT* Book:chapter, page.

[44] Daniel Tyler, 'Introduction', in Daniel Tyler (ed.), *Dickens's Style* (Cambridge: Cambridge University Press, 2013), 1–25 (4, 1).

[45] Sally Ledger, *Dickens and the Popular Radical Imagination* (Cambridge: Cambridge University Press, 2007), 2.

Here it is important to note from the outset that Dickens used his fiction as well as non-fiction to protest vociferously against the combined and uneven barbarity of 'new world' slavery, usefully defined as 'the first and least-camouflaged expression' of the 'continuing and relentless process whereby capitalist accumulation battens on pre-capitalist modes of exploitation'.[46] Thus *American Notes* devoted an entire chapter to the atrocities of a system overseen by those 'who, when they speak of Freedom, mean the Freedom to oppress their kind, and to be savage, merciless, and cruel';[47] *Martin Chuzzlewit* mounted a sustained and hard-hitting attack on slavery as the inexcusably violent 'liberty' at the heart of American Liberty (*MC* 17, 285); and *Bleak House* ridiculed as utterly repellent Mr Skimpole's 'cosmopolitan mind' as it contemplated the 'poetry' of slaves on American plantations (*BH* 18, 227). This forthright condemnation of a system that so explicitly and so brutally prized profit over people stands in stark contrast with Dickens's friend Thomas Carlyle, whose 'Occasional Discourse on the Negro Question' demanded in 1849 that the 'Saxon British' join America, take up the 'beneficent whip', and re-enslave 'Black Quashee' in the West Indies.[48]

But although Dickens's abolitionism registered that black slaves were kin to their white owners, it was for him a distant, troubling kinship. Grace Moore remarks upon Dickens's 'fundamental inability to envisage the slave as a man and a brother', drawing attention to his readiness in *American Notes* and elsewhere to indulge a grotesque panoply of racist stereotypes that she contrasts with his serious domestic commitment to represent the 'urban poor' on an 'equal footing'.[49] Hence a slave in *Martin Chuzzlewit* is at once a 'man and a brother' and 'a man of colour', so that the horror of his scarred, battered body is tempered by the humour of Martin's reaction to 'the blackest [face] that was ever seen' (*MC* 17, 284). Similarly, in *Dombey and Son*, Major Bagstock's relentless beating of his non-European retainer produces a pointed critique of British imperialism. Yet as he shrinks from Bagstock's blows, 'like a shrivelled nut, or a cold monkey' into his 'outlandish', ill-fitting European clothes, so too 'the Native' bears striking testament to the fact that Dickens was quite prepared to mobilize the comic potential of racial difference in a manner that worked counter to the idea of common humanity and developmental potential (*DS* 20, 278–9).

Away from his fiction, the 'active disdain' that Priti Joshi associates with Dickens's attitude towards the 'dark races' of the earth is at its most virulent in the writing he did not intend to reach the public domain.[50] Publicly Dickens exercised more restraint, yet

---

[46] Robin Blackburn, *The Making of New World Slavery: From the Baroque to the Modern, 1492–1800* (London: Verso, 1997), 554.

[47] *American Notes*, ed. Patricia Ingham (London: Penguin, 2000), volume II, chapter 9, page 250. Subsequent references are inserted parenthetically in the text by *AN* volume:chapter, page.

[48] [Thomas Carlyle], 'Occasional Discourse on the Negro Question', in John Plunkett, Ana Parejo Vadillo, Regenia Gagnier, Angelique Richardson, Rick Rylance and Paul Young (eds), *Victorian Literature: A Sourcebook* (Basingstoke: Palgrave Macmillan, 2012), 236–8 (238).

[49] Grace Moore, *Dickens and Empire: Discourses of Class, Race and Colonialism in the Works of Charles Dickens* (Aldershot: Ashgate, 2004), 56.

[50] Priti Joshi, 'Race', in Sally Ledger and Holly Furneaux (eds), *Charles Dickens in Context* (Cambridge: Cambridge University Press, 2011), 292–300 (297). Dickens's outrage at the Indian 'Mutiny'

consistently set such dark races apart from their white, civilized counterparts. In 'The Niger Expedition' Dickens extended the possibility that world history might eradicate the 'great gulf' he identified between Europeans and non-Europeans. But he invoked deep geological time as he charted the long, slow stretch of 'progressive changes' that were first required (Dent 2: 'The Niger Expedition', 125). Elsewhere he threw into doubt the prospect of such improvement ever occurring. 'Some Account of an Extraordinary Traveller', a piece on the global scope of London's panoramas that appeared in *Household Words* in 1850, featured scenes of American 'progress' interspersed with the corpses of 'fast-declining Indians' and 'the doomed negro race'. Lamenting the sight, Dickens's 'traveller', Mr Booley, concludes that these and all other such primitive peoples 'must be surely and inevitably swept from the earth' as they are caught up in 'the eternal current of progress setting across this globe in one unchangeable direction'.[51] Three years later, in 'The Noble Savage', Dickens adopted a far less melancholic register as he declared the savage 'something highly desirable to be civilised off the face of the earth', before cataloguing the bestial, bloodthirsty drives associated with these 'howling, whistling, clucking, stamping, jumping, tearing' abominations. Such animated prose seemed at once to rule out racial advance and legitimize imperial force. Yet Dickens reached the pointed if strained conclusion that there was 'no greater justification for being cruel to the miserable object' in question, 'than for being cruel to a WILLIAM SHAKESPEARE or an ISAAC NEWTON' (*HW*, 'The Noble Savage', 11 June 1853, 337–9).

This public caution against across-the-board campaigns of imperial violence, alongside his forthright abolitionism and his stated albeit far less emphatic belief that savages might—eventually—become civilized, has led Moore to describe 'Dickens's sporadic outbursts of prejudice against non-whites' as 'knee-jerk' discrimination, 'lacking the force of a coherent argument' and set apart from Carlyle's 'systematic racial programme'.[52] While there were certainly substantive differences between the two writers, however, both men promoted the idea that race served—perhaps fatefully and certainly for the long term—to inhibit the possibility of modernity's even development on an inclusively global scale. And they did so as an imperially expanding modern world-system embraced, imposed, and exploited uneven development across the planet. So although Dickens did not actively promote systematic racialized subjugation and violence as an economically rational end, the political and aesthetic energy he invested in racial difference should nevertheless be read with regard to the systematic way in which, as Immanuel Wallerstein has it, 'genetic and/or long-lasting "cultural" traits'

---

of 1857 saw him call privately for the extermination of the '[Hindoo] Race from the face of the earth' (cited in Moore, *Dickens and Empire*, 94). And in 1865 he elaborated his public declaration of support for Governor Eyre's brutal suppression of the Morant Bay rebellion in personal correspondence that heaped scorn upon those who expressed 'sympathy with the black—or the native, or the devil' (cited in Laura Peters, *Dickens and Race* (Manchester: Manchester University Press, 2013), 137).

[51] Charles Dickens, 'Some Account of an Extraordinary Traveller', *Household Words*, 20 April 1850, pages 73–7. Subsequent references are inserted parenthetically in the text by *HW*, 'title', date, page.

[52] Moore, *Dickens and Empire*, 166.

have positioned ethnic groups within historical capitalism 'as under classes, as inferior beings, and therefore as deserving ultimately of whatever fate comes their way'.[53]

Conclusion

'Despite the reassurances of public oratory, the spread of capitalism has been violent, chaotic, and divisive, rather than smoothly all-encompassing.'[54] As this chapter has demonstrated, the distinction that Anna Tsing here identifies between the rhetoric and the reality of the modern world-system holds true for the nineteenth century as much as the twenty-first. And as it has also made clear, Dickens's writing captured this distinction with relation to life within Victorian Britain, working as it did to expose and critique globalized 'gammon' at the same time as it grounded—formally as well as through its content—the extensive, complex, dynamic, and uneven way in which his own nation was centrally caught up with globalized modernity's ongoing, far-reaching, money-making developments. If, following Buzard, we accept that 'the global' appears in Dickens as 'an unmappably vague and destructive realm', therefore, we must also recognize that he plotted the resolutely material, productive, chaotic, and divisive impact of globalized modernity upon Victorian life. There are two key points to be made in concluding this chapter, then, that might guide future readings of Dickens as 'world literature' in the context of combined and uneven development: first, as already indicated, we should look to the dialectical interplay of the local and the global in order to discuss how Dickens gave fictional, frictional form to a nation that was working variously, awkwardly but forcefully to move goods, peoples, technologies, services, finances, and ideas around the world; second, and building upon this point, we should engage with the idea that while it pointedly mocked exuberant imperial ambition, Dickens's writing nevertheless served in its own less triumphalist but no less significant way to endorse a world view that 'saw Britain's fate as tied up with its overseas interests and assumed, for example, the unchallengeable right of British migrants abroad to seize and fill up the lands of indigenous peoples'.[55] Such work will elaborate the tension this chapter identifies as central to Dickens's depiction of Victorian Britain in an age of heightened global connectivity and intensified world-level forces: he attacked the uneven development of capitalist modernity at home at the same time as he naturalized and energized expansionist imperatives and attitudes that underpinned Britain's dominant position within an uneven modern world-system. This tension is helpful to keep in mind with regard to Chapter 47, which turns to consider how Dickens's global circulation has seen readers,

---

[53] Immanuel Wallerstein, *Historical Capitalism* with *Capitalist Civilization* (London: Verso, 1995), 78, 122.
[54] Tsing, *Friction*, 11.
[55] Darwin, *The Empire Project*, 15.

critics, and writers from around the world take up, repurpose, and resist his metropolitan Victorian perspective on globalized modernity.

Further Reading

Tayna Agathocleous, *Urban Realism and the Cosmopolitan Imagination in the Nineteenth Century: Visible City, Invisible World* (Cambridge: Cambridge University Press, 2011)

Elaine Freedgood, *The Ideas in Things: Fugitive Meaning in the Victorian Novel* (Chicago: The University of Chicago Press, 2006)

Lauren M. E. Goodlad, *The Victorian Geopolitical Aesthetic: Realism, Sovereignty, and Transnational Experience* (Oxford: Oxford University Press, 2015)

Stephen Shapiro, *The Culture and Commerce of the Early American Novel: Reading the Atlantic World-System* (University Park: The Pennsylvania State University Press, 2008)

CHAPTER 47

DICKENS'S GLOBAL CIRCULATION

REGENIA GAGNIER

In 2009, the British Academy funded a pilot project on the Global Circulation of Charles Dickens's Novels. This was a pilot for a much larger project on the Global Circulation of Literature and Culture that is being given electronic infrastructure and a special site within Wiley Blackwell's electronic peer-reviewed journal *Literature Compass*. The Global Circulation Project (GCP) is a global map and dialogue on how key anglophone works, authors, genres, and literary movements have been received, imitated/mimicked, adapted, syncretized, or remediated outside Britain, Europe, and North America, and, conversely, how key works from outside these areas have been received, imitated/mimicked, adapted, syncretized, or remediated within anglophone literary traditions.[1] The GCP asks: How, and under what conditions, does one culture use another? What forms of intertextuality, adaptation, translation, etc. are generated through both voluntary and coercive processes of transculturation? The research questions for the British Academy grant included:

- How has Dickens been received, imitated/mimicked, adapted, or syncretized outside Britain, Europe and North America?
- What forms of intertextuality have been generated with indigenous cultural forms?
- What is the role of Dickens's Britain in the imaginary of other cultures?

Over the last century, the cultural and educational impacts of empire and global markets in cultural commodities have globalized 'English Literature' and its major authors.[2] Yet the prevailing scholarly commentary on major writers has stayed resolutely anglophone if not nationally oriented. The pilot project studied in an

---

[1] *The Global Circulation Project* of *Literature Compass*, <http://onlinelibrary.wiley.com/journal/10.1111/(ISSN)1741-4113/homepage/global_circulation_project.htm>.

[2] See the essay by Paul Young on 'Dickens's World-System', also in this volume.

interactive mode the global circulation of the novels of Charles Dickens outside Britain, Europe, and North America. The grant allowed the investigators to spend some time in the California Dickens Project's Ada B. Nisbet archive.[3] Nisbet (now deceased) was a noted Dickens scholar and former professor at the University of California, Los Angeles. At the time of her death, she was engaged in compiling an international guide to research on Dickens that would have included contributions from scholars in every part of the globe, locating and giving accounts of editions, manuscripts, bibliographies, biographies, critical books, articles, films, and plays relating to Dickens and his impact on other creative writers throughout the world. Michael Hollington's two volumes of essays on the reception of Dickens in Europe exploited the European materials in the Nisbet archive.[4] Beginning with the Nisbet archive but then extending to new networks, the GCP's specialists in literary and cultural translation focused on areas outside Europe and North America. Whereas Nisbet's was very much a project of the last century, an international appreciation of Dickens, the GCP is a global dialogue in which the contributions of other cultures are as significant as the Western author, in which the forms of circulation rather than the original novels are the primary interest. Nisbet was a Dickensian; the GCP includes literary historians and analysts of cultures in contact. Perhaps more boldly, the GCP understands our own and other cultures comparatively, through the processes of transculturation and the diverse ways of engaging with authors such as Dickens whose works have circulated globally under uneven and unequal conditions of production, distribution, and consumption.

While Dickens can be seen to register on every current definition of 'world literature', we might nonetheless abandon terms like 'influence', 'originality', and 'impact' in favour of circulation, transculturation, appropriation, use, revoicing, reaccentuation, indigenization, and (re)mediation. This chapter historicizes both Dickens and the genre of the novel, showing that diverse societies caught between traditional cultures and the forces of modernization, as Dickens's society was, give rise to formal similarities in their literatures. 'Dickensian' novels, 'Dickensian' characters, 'Dickensian' affect, 'Dickensian' institutions, and so forth are thus less derivative than similar, strategic aesthetic responses to similar social conditions. The first section, 'Local Dickens in Popular Culture', shows that 'Dickens' is continuously re-created in the processes of cultural translation both within evolving media in his own (British) culture and also within transcultural contexts. The second section, 'Global Dickens', turns to the circulation of Dickens outside Britain, Europe, and North America.

---

[3] For the Nisbet Archive, see John O. Jordan, 'Global Dickens', *The Global Circulation Project of Literature Compass* 6, 6 (2009): 1211–23. See also The California Dickens Project, <http://dickens.ucsc.edu/index.html>.

[4] See Michael Hollington (ed.), *The Reception of Charles Dickens in Europe*, 2 vols (London: Continuum, 2013).

Local Dickens in Popular Culture

In considering Dickens in 2012, the bicentennial of his birth, we began with current activities in the UK, where he and 'Dickensian' are popular cultural currency. Vice-Chancellor Steven Schwartz of Macquarie University in Australia prompted debate in the British *THE* (*Times Higher Education*) with one of many defences of the humanities in times of economic cutbacks, citing Orwell on Dickens's 'consciousness that society is wrong somewhere at the root'. Schwartz states, 'If there are some authors university graduates should be familiar with, then Dickens and Orwell must surely be among them. They matter today perhaps more than ever. Education was in the beginning, and remains today, moral—to make people wiser, to act in more noble ways, to help to make our world a better place. Dickens reveals this to us in his brilliant fiction and he will continue to do so for generations to come.'[5] Schwartz discussed the limitations of Gradgrind's reduction to scientific and technological instrumentalism. This is the popular view of Dickens as humanistic writer currently deployed in debates on the funding of the humanities within Higher Education.

Other local events in the UK and France included a massive travelling conference, 'Tale of Four Cities', between Paris, Boulogne/Condette, Chatham/Rochester, and London, including a 'Global Dickens' conference at the Museum of London; a Wreath-laying at Westminster Abbey, where the actor-director Ralph Fiennes read the death of Jo the crossing-sweep and the then Archbishop of Canterbury Rowan Williams reflected on Dickens's role in the modern world; a reception at Mansion House for academics, curators, actors, and producers of Dickens throughout the culture industry hosted by the Lord Mayor of London; and many more conferences and workshops continuing throughout the Bicentenary. The British Council, whose mission is to represent British culture internationally, hosted a Global Readathon of 24 hours reading of 24 Dickens works in 24 countries. Sixty-six countries responded to their Call, with 3 million hits from China alone. The British Council urged education ministers throughout the world to invite their schools to participate in the Bicentenary by asking pupils, 'What would Dickens write today?' This was refined, tellingly, in the course of the longitudinal event, to 'Where would he be writing from?', suggesting that there might be conditions in which 'Dickensian' works arise, a suggestion that will be addressed at length below. *Sketches by Boz* evolved as a model for the schoolchildren, who produced sketches of their own local markets in the morning, *porteños* in Buenos Aires, housing projects, and other 'Dickensian' scenes collected by the Council.

Within other lay circles, the Dickens Fellowship, founded in 1902, continued its activities; and any discussion of Dickens's global circulation should note the popular activity of the Fellowship founded, as stated in their Constitution:

---

[5] Steven Schwartz, quoted in John Elmes, 'The Scholarly Web', *Times Higher Education* (23 February 2012),<https://www.timeshighereducation.com/the-scholarly-web/419065.article>.

to knit together in a common bond of friendship, lovers of that great master of humour and pathos, Charles Dickens;

to promote the knowledge and appreciation of his works;

to spread the love of humanity, which is the keynote of all his works; and to exercise such charitable support as would have appealed strongly to the heart of Charles Dickens;

to take such measures as may be expedient to alleviate those existing social evils, the amelioration of which would have enlisted his support.[6]

By 1903, 15 branches of the Fellowship had been established, whose early function notably included free meals offering good fellowship to the homeless and downcast. A 1911 meeting of the Melbourne Fellowship Branch reported: 'Had Dickens an important influence on Australian democracy, its founders and its fruits? This was the question answered at a remarkable meeting of the Melbourne Branch of the Dickens Fellowship.'[7] By 1950, there were over 200 branches worldwide, which then began to decline somewhat, probably due to the decline of British hegemony worldwide. Still in 2017, there were 61 branches throughout the world including 3 in Australia, 1 in New Zealand, 21 in the United Kingdom, and 23 in the United States.

In terms of traditional 'influence' and literary appreciation, Dickens has historically been the most popular creative writer in English after Shakespeare. Although such figures are very hard to verify, Wikipedia's List of Bestselling Books names *A Tale of Two Cities* as the 'best-selling novel of all time' with 200 million copies sold.[8] More reliable data comprise the Unesco Index Translationum—World Bibliography of Translation 1978–present, in which Dickens is the 25th most translated author in the world, the ninth most translated author in China, for example, and the fourth in Egypt. Of all Victorian novelists, with 2,152 translations since 1978, he is second only to Arthur Conan Doyle with 2,512, followed by Robert Louis Stevenson with 2,085.[9]

From Dostoevsky, Galdós, Joyce, Kafka, Faulkner, Nabokov, and Beckett to Lao She, Anand, Kumar, Naipaul, Ngugi, Soyinka, Dabydeen, Carey, Mistry, and Rushdie, writers have written of the impact of Dickens on their own creative practice. Dickens has served as representative of the 'English Book', panoramic and demotic styles, model depictor of the masses, the city, the suffering of children, and critic of poverty and injustice. Film auteurs from Eisenstein, Griffith, and Chaplin to Lean, Polanski, Greene, and Burstall have adapted the novels according to their own cultural moments and locations. Eisenstein said that Griffith discovered the technique of montage from his reading of Dickens.[10] After Dickens, a literature grew up of street children in Argentina

---

[6] 'Constitution of the Dickens Fellowship', <http://www.Dickensfellowship.Org/Constitution>.

[7] Anon., 'Dickens Fellowship', *Dickensian* 7, 9 (September 1911): 231.

[8] Wikipedia, 'List of Best-Selling Books', <https://en.wikipedia.org/wiki/List_of_best-selling_books#>.

[9] Unesco, 'Unesco Index Translationum—World Bibliography of Translation', <http://Portal.Unesco.Org/Culture/En/Ev.Php-url_Id=7810&Url_Do=Do_Topic&Url_Section=201.Html>.

[10] Jay Clayton, *Dickens in Cyberspace: The Afterlife of the Nineteenth Century in Postmodern Culture* (New York: Oxford University Press, 2003), 156.

and Brazil and a genre of sociological 'homages' to *Oliver Twist*, as in the Uruguayan Armónía Somers's *Un retrato para Dickens* (1969).[11]

Jay Clayton's *Charles Dickens in Cyberspace* (2003) began to track the popular consumption of Dickens abroad and on the internet. In terms of material culture, Clayton notes the proliferation of pubs and inns with Dickensian brands: Olde Curiosity Shoppes, Dickens Inns, Artful Dodger Pubs (in Exeter, Philadelphia, Saskatoon), Great Expectations (Maternity Shop, Dallas), Great Waxpectations (Richmond), Baked Expectations (Winnipeg), Great Hair-Spectations (Brooklyn), Grape Expectations (Manhattan), Great Expectorations (Saturday Night Live), Gretz Expectations (of a hockey hero). Clayton also notes the commercialization of Christmas, widely attributed to Dickens despite the charitable sentiments of his most famous story on the topic. And he notes the innovations in print culture and history of the book attributed to Dickens: monthly numbers, annual Christmas stories, uniform editions, international copyright, Public Readings, all of which Clayton designates in our contemporary terms as Dickens's 'cultural bandwidth'.[12] In *Charles Dickens and 'Boz': The Birth of the Industrial-Age Author* (2012), Robert Patten writes of the 'proliferation' of Dickens's writing and its various 'spin-offs'.[13] Yet until now studies of Dickens's reputation and cultural impact have focused chiefly on Britain, the USA, and Europe.[14] The remainder of this chapter will place Dickens within broader world literatures.

GLOBAL DICKENS

Dickens seems to span all current senses of world literature: world literature as the best, as early envisioned by Goethe and Hesse's *Weltliteratur*; as bearer of universal values, as envisioned by Rabindranath Tagore's *vishva sahitya*; as circulating in translation/remediation; in relation to power and domination (e.g. in relation to postcolonial studies); in relation to globalization; and in relation to commodification and circuits of production and consumption, serialization and adaptation.[15] Dickens spans all senses of world literature from the original 'masterpiece' sense of world literature as the best to the

---

[11] Beatriz Vegh (ed.), 'Dickens in Latin America: Views from Montevideo', *Dickens Studies Annual* 36 (New York: AMS Press, 2005).

[12] Clayton, *Dickens in Cyberspace*, 52, 199–200.

[13] Robert L. Patten, *Charles Dickens and 'Boz': The Birth of the Industrial-Age Author* (Cambridge: Cambridge University Press, 2012).

[14] See also Mary Hammond, *Charles Dickens's Great Expectations: A Cultural Life, 1860–2012*, Ashgate Studies in Publishing History (Farnham: Ashgate, 2015). The book historian Mary Hammond has done a detailed study of one novel, showing Dickens as a savvy manipulator of media as well as the object of extensive remediation, including films, translation, graphic novels, and mashups.

[15] See Mark Wollaeger with Matt Eatough (eds), *The Oxford Handbook of Global Modernisms* (Oxford: Oxford University Press, 2012). Theo D'haen, David Damrosch, and Djelal Kadir (eds), *The Routledge Companion to World Literature* (London: Routledge, 2012).

most popular or best-selling, breaking down the distinction between elite and popular cultures, as we shall demonstrate. If our account of Dickens thus far seems familiar to Anglophone readers, we may now ask, how might we *defamiliarize* an author so present to many of us?

We can see a different Dickens in cultural translation, if we look in terms of the phenomenology of 'his' circulation rather than the ontology of his masterpieces. Even further, we might abandon notions of originals, derivatives, influence, impact, diffusion, innovation, and rather think in terms of circulation, appropriation, use, indigenization, and (re)mediation. In his own day, not all of Dickens's contemporaries agreed that he was 'the best', nor was his reputation in the early twentieth century assured even in England—consider the role of the Leavises in rehabilitating him. Yet perhaps 'he', or 'Dickens', is continuously re-created in the constant processes of cultural translation both within evolving media in his own (British) culture and within transcultural contexts. We might consider that, if there is a 'mimetic desire' of one culture towards another, it often goes both ways, or more ways than two, in the process we have come to call, after the great Cuban anthropologist Fernando Ortiz, 'transculturation'.[16] As we turn to Dickens in global contexts, we historicize both social and generic differences, drawing attention to the specificity of local contexts. Yet we also ask whether there are shared experiences that underwrite formal resemblances, for instance whether there is a 'Dickensian' novel, 'Dickensian' characters, 'Dickensian' affect, 'Dickensian' institutions. The goal is that we should not impose our meanings and interpretations of Dickens on other writers or cultures, but rather see how they may have used Dickens for their own purposes within their own specific contexts.

Lydia Wevers of Wellington has studied the archives of the Wellington Pickwick Club of New Zealand, emphasizing the synchronicity of Dickens and the British empire.[17] The Pickwick Club was founded with the arrival of the first anglophone settlers to New Zealand on Wakefield's policy, young men aged 21–45, who used Dickens's fiction as they settled to confirm their identity in a land new to them. They asked, What makes an Englishman? According to Wevers, they tried to materialize Dickens's world in New Zealand society, reconstructing his physical habitats, environments, and forms of social life. Unlike Australia's history of convict deportation, the comparatively gentrified New Zealand settlers relied on Dickens to make their new home more *heimlich*.

Simultaneously, Dickens himself was deeply interested in Australasia. *The Pickwick Papers* were published in Australia in 1838, a mere year after they appeared in Britain. In Australia, Dickens was a novelist less of settlement and identity than of movement and immigration. Grace Moore begins her nuanced study of Dickens and empire with the famous quote from Forster on Dickens's children, 'Charley is in the Far East, Sydney is at sea, Walter in India, Alfred in Australia, whither he is planning to send another

---

[16] Fernando Ortiz, *Cuban Counterpoint: Tobacco and Sugar*, trans. Harriet de Onís (New York: Knopf, 1947).

[17] Lydia Wevers, 'Dickens in New Zealand', *The Global Circulation Project of Literature Compass*, 11, 5 (2014): 321–7.

boy',[18] showing how intimate the empire could be for British with children abroad. With the gold-rushes of 1850 in New South Wales and Victoria, the Australian population trebled, and, with the simultaneous California gold-rushes in North America, had enough purchasing power to revive the British economy. This process of globalization was not lost on Dickens, whose *Household Words* published over 100 articles on Australia from 1850 to 1859.[19] For him even more than most, Australia was ceasing to be a distant colony—transportation of convicts ended mid-century—and coming to be a site of adventure, wealth, and the future, with an increasingly self-governing urban middle class. Reciprocally, the great Australian writer Henry Lawson (1867–1922) saw Dickens as a 'father figure', whose work guided Lawson as he struggled with Australian identity between the bush of its native peoples and the new urban environments where were concentrated most of the immigrant population.

Dickens's very popularity would have consequences in Australasia, as in Africa, under decolonization. 'Classic' Victorian novels on school syllabi could become obstacles for modern Australian writers like Peter Carey, who dramatizes his agonistic relationship with Dickens in his neo-Victorian *Oscar and Lucinda* and *Jack Maggs*.[20] To the Dickens afterlives in Australasia mentioned by John Jordan in 2009, we can add Richard Flanagan's *Wanting* (2008), the story of Sir John and Lady Jane Franklin's tenure in Tasmania, in which Dickens appears as a character, and the New Zealander Lloyd Jones's *Mister Pip* (2007), each of them showing the complex intertextualities of transculturation.[21] The dominance of British publishing houses in Australasia for the first half of the twentieth century, with corresponding sensitivities on the parts of domestic talent, further complicated Dickensian afterlives.

In Africa, the 1880s saw the consolidation of colonialism, more intense dissemination of printing presses, and many pamphlets of Dickens's writings distributed by missionaries. By 1890, Dickens and Shakespeare were favourites of colonial readers. During decolonization, each emerging nation produced novelists who had read some version of Dickens as a child, and most of them acknowledged it later in life. The Nigerian Amos Tutuola (1920–97) was often called a 'successor to Dickens'; the Ghanian Ayi Kwei Armah (b. 1939) followed Dickens in depicting the poor in cities; the Ethiopian Berhane Mariam Sahle Sellassie (b. 1936) translated Dickens; the South African Es'kia

---

[18] Grace Moore, *Dickens and Empire: Discourses of Class, Race and Colonialism in the Works of Charles Dickens* (Aldershot: Ashgate, 2004), 1.

[19] Wendy Jacobson (ed.), *Dickens and the Children of Empire* (New York: Palgrave, 2000). Cathy Waters, *Commodity Culture in Dickens's Household Words: The Social Life of Goods* (Aldershot: Ashgate, 2008). It should also be noted that in Robert Aguirre's extensive research on the Victorians and Latin America, Dickens's *Household Words* is repeatedly cited expressing views on British expansion. See Robert Aguirre, *Informal Empire: Mexico and Central America in Victorian Culture* (Minneapolis and London: University of Minnesota Press, 2005). *Mobility and Modernity: Panama in the Anglo-American Imagination, 1840–1903* (Columbus: Ohio State University Press, 2017.

[20] Peter Carey, *Oscar and Lucinda* (London: Faber and Faber 1988). *Jack Maggs* (London: Faber and Faber, 1997).

[21] Richard Flanagan, *Wanting* (New York: Knopf, 2008). Lloyd Jones, *Mister Pip* (London: John Murray, 2007).

Mphahlele (1919–2008) adapted *Tale of Two Cities* for the stage and cited Dickens in his theory of 'Engagement'; and the Kenyan Ngugi wa Thiong'o's (b. 1938) later novels are often compared to Dickens in his representation of the ideological state apparatuses of neocolonialism, in the institutions of business, school, church, and law as well as in the haunting subjectivities of Ngugi's masterpiece *A Grain of Wheat*.[22]

B. Venkat Mani and others have distinguished between the Old World Literature in its European instantiations and the New World Literature of post-war decolonization, tracing the 'bibliomigrancy' or material history of books as the great German Reclam Series gave way to Heinemann's introduction of African literature to Europe and the USA at the time of emerging nations.[23] As these novelists and writers were beginning to circulate outside Africa, South Africans in the 1950s performed a revolutionary *Tale of Two Cities* in black townships; by the 1970s students at Lovedale College reading *Oliver Twist* demanded more, forming a committee to ask for more lessons, more food, and more and better books (152 were expelled).[24] *Oliver Twist* was required reading in all secondary schools in Ghana. In the Great Nairobi Literary Debates of 1968–9, Ngugi and his colleagues argued that African literature and orature should be

---

[22] See Rand Bishop, *African Literature, African Critics: The Forming of Critical Standards, 1947–1966* (New York: Greenwood Press, 1988). Robert Fraser, *The Novels of Ayi Kwei Armah* (London: Heinemann, 1980); David I. Ker, *The African Novel and the Modernist Tradition* (New York: Peter Lang, 1997). Neil Ten Kortenaar, 'Fictive States and the State of Fiction in Africa', *Comparative Literature* 52 (2000): 228–45. Bernth Lindfors, *Comparative Approaches to African Literatures* (Amsterdam: Rodopi, 1994). Greenwell Matsika, 'Dickens in Africa: "Africanizing" *Hard Times*', in Jacobson, *Dickens and the Children of Empire* (2000), 173–83. Neil McEwan, *Africa and the Novel* (London: Palgrave, 1983). Ode Ogede, *Intertextuality in Contemporary African Literature: Looking Inward* (Lanham, MD: Lexington Books, 2011). Stephanie Newell, *Literary Culture in Colonial Ghana: 'How to Play the Game of Life'* (Bloomington: Indiana University Press, 2001). *Readings in African Popular Fiction* (Bloomington: International African Institute in association with Indiana University Press, 2002). *West African Literatures: Ways of Reading* (New York: Oxford University Press, 2006). Pushpa Naidu and Siga Fatima Jagne Parekh (eds), *Postcolonial African Writers: A Bio-Bibliographical Critical Sourcebook* (Westport, CT: Greenwood Press, 1998). Paul Rich, 'Liberal Realism in South African Fiction, 1948–1966', *English in Africa* 12 (1985): 47–81. Carol Sicherman, 'Ngugi's Colonial Education: "The Subversion … Of the African Mind"', *African Studies Review* 38 (1995): 14, 16, 34.

I have relied on published research more for Dickens in Africa because the Nisbet archive has very little on Africa. When the archive ended, there were eight translations into Afrikaans, but there were no Bantu languages and no North African Dickens material in the file for French. A letter to Ada Nisbet from Dr A. M. L. Robinson, Chief Librarian, South African Public Library of 21 November 1966 in reply to Nisbet's request stated, 'Our closeness to the British publishing world prevents the production in this country of any English edition which would not be economic and as far as African languages are concerned I fancy it has generally been felt that the background and reading interests of the Africans are such that translation would not be justified.' This is one of the few depressing items in the archive. Another is from Mrs E. T. Wilcox, then Humanities Editor at Harvard University Press, who wrote to Nisbet that Harvard was not interested in publishing Nisbet's collection on Dickens's global circulation insofar as 'Contributors would be almost totally unknown to the American community' (17 February 1970, and see ensuing correspondence with John H. Fisher, Executive Secretary MLA, 21 April 1970).

[23] B. Venkat Mani, 'Bibliomigrancy: Book Series and the Making of World Literature', in D'haen et al., *Routledge Companion to World Literature*, 283–97.

[24] Archie L. Dick, *The Hidden History of South Africa's Book and Reading Cultures* (Toronto: University of Toronto Press, 2012), 140–2. Jordan, 'Global Dickens', 8.

central in African curricula, so that they could 'produce students who can by starting from their own environment, freely link the rural and urban experiences of Kenyan and African literature to that of García Márquez, Richard Wright, George Lamming, Balzac, Dickens, Shakespeare and Brecht'. In 1986, Ngugi acknowledged Dickens's influence in *Decolonizing the Mind*. In *Hidden History: South Africa's Book and Reading Cultures* (2012), Archie L. Dick concludes, 'as a kind of cross-over author, Dickens has been read and enjoyed for more than a hundred years by rich and poor, black and white, conservative and liberal South Africans. The influence of his books and their multiple interpretations still await assessment'.[25]

In other societies in transition, Dickens's 'cross-over' capacities varied. Former Soviet satellite countries such as Bulgaria, Czechoslovakia, East Germany, and Poland have been extensively covered in Michael Hollington's *Reception of Charles Dickens in Europe* (2013), a two-volume collection providing the first comprehensive survey of Dickens's European reception.[26] Ewa Kujawska-Lis has shown that while Dickens was consistently the most popular English writer in Poland, he was a problem for the Communists who came into power in the 1950s.[27] Dickens's novels criticized capitalism and were sympathetic to workers and the poor, but he did not advocate systemic revolution. Their solution was to navigate readers away from Dickens the idealist Christian to Dickens the revolutionary. In support of this, they were able to show that Dickens portrayed the uglier truths of capitalism: debtors' prisons, bleak orphanages, factory children, poverty, and exploitation. He also portrayed the rise of a new social class, the bourgeoisie; the unequal and exploitative division of wealth between it and the working poor; the tragedy of the lower-middle class and those dispossessed of their land and labour. Importantly, he was also able to show the processes of reification, how humans become products of economic systems. In promoting this Dickens, the Party emphasized his early works as masterpieces, especially *Sketches by Boz*, and slighted the later works as resigned and gloomy.

Similarly in China, Dickens was consistently popular from his first translation by Lin Shu (1852–1924) in 1907, who knew no language but Chinese and worked with an amanuensis, Wei Yi, who knew English, to the Cultural Revolution of 1966–76. Lin Shu's translations, which were essentially retellings of the plot, raised issues (debated in China at the time) of translation that are still important today, questions of aesthetic fidelity versus purposive adaptation suiting the needs of the target culture. Klaudia Hiu Yen Lee has recently studied these early translations 1895–1915.

In the beginning, Dickens's Chinese translators appreciated his 'cries of grievance' on behalf of the common people above his particular literary style.[28] In 1925, Wu

---

[25] Dick, *The Hidden History of South Africa's Book and Reading Cultures*, 141.
[26] Hollington, *The Reception of Charles Dickens in Europe*.
[27] Ewa Kujawska-Lis, 'The Transformations of Charles Dickens in Early Socialist Poland', *The Global Circulation Project of Literature Compass* 10, 4 (2013): 396–405.
[28] Zhen Tong, *Dickens in China* (Xiangtan: Xiangtan University Press, 2008). H. C. Chuang, 'Dickens in Chinese': 5. Nisbet Archive, UC Santa Cruz.

Kuang-chien, one of Dickens's first literary critics in China, called for *Hard Times* to be required reading for 'everyone studying social problems'.[29] After the establishment of the People's Republic in 1949, Dickens remained popular for supplying 'valuable documents about a capitalist society'.[30] Under the Communists, scholarly eulogies were tempered by criticism of his compromises with the bourgeois world view: his 'realist exposition [was] damped by idealist morality'.[31] Yet it was only with the Communists that appreciation of Dickens's later, pessimistic novels *Bleak House, Little Dorrit, Great Expectations*, and *Our Mutual Friend* grew, as giving realistic expression to the disenchantment of the capitalist world.

During the Great Proletarian Cultural Revolution, little was officially printed about Dickens or any other Western writers, but between 1907 and 1966, Dickens was probably the most—Chuang said 'only'—influential English writer, and that was not due to style, except insofar as he opened paths to vernaculars that were central to China's modernization during the Republican period, but especially to his politics of representing the poor. The classic modern novelist and dramatist Lao She (b. Beijing 1899, d. 1966) was influenced by Dickens in *The Rickshaw Boy* (1936) and the play *Teahouse* (1957), importantly for representing characters not previously represented in Chinese literature, but also for his exuberant rhetoric, dialects, melodramatic plotting, galleries of grotesques, and the literature of the street. Like many of the reformers of the May Fourth and New Culture Movements and after, Lao She had considered the role of Western-influenced ideologies of individualism in China's future, and in the *Rickshaw Boy* came to reject the idea that individualism was meaningful in an unjust society, concluding that no matter how virtuous and industrious an individual might be, social conditions and prejudices could make individual progress impossible. Lao She's earlier works such as *Zhang de Zhexue* (The Philosophy of Old Zhang) (1926) and *Zhaozi Yue* (Zhao zi says) (1927) also show his reworking of Dickens in the wit, the vivid caricatures of his relatives portrayed as petty bourgeois, and the overwhelming sensationism of the Beijing (then Beiping) street scenes.

As Lao She's memorable presentations of Beiping suggest, Dickens's 'Britain' did not figure prominently in the symbolic imaginary of China except as an objective correlative of market society; more precisely, for purposes of fiction, his 'Britain' loomed largest in the synecdoche of his 'London'. As late as 1983 Yang Xianyi, the distinguished translator and General Editor of *Chinese Literature*, claimed in the *Times Literary Supplement* that 'even today most Chinese people probably still view remote English society through Dickensian characters'.[32] When schoolchildren read *Oliver Twist*, the title was not transliterated, as is customary in Chinese translation, but was *Orphan in the Foggy City*. It was Dickens's London that captured the imagination of non-European cultures,

---

[29] Chuang, 'Dickens in Chinese', 21. Nisbet Archive, UC Santa Cruz.
[30] Ibid. 28, citing Hai Kuan, Postscript to translation of *Dombey and Son*.
[31] Chuang, 'Dickens in Chinese', 32, citing Yang Yao-min, 'The Creative Process and Ideological Characteristics of Dickens', *Wenxue Pinglun* 6 (1962): 39.
[32] Xianyi Yang, 'English Literature in Translation', *TLS* (24 June 1983): 670.

less than his Britain. Britain generally, like the West generally, meant either Progress in terms of science, technology, and democratization, and/or Decadence in terms of its reduction of values to material wealth. Of his translation of *David Copperfield* in 1907, Lin Shu noted: 'The malpractices among the common folk during the time when England was half-civilized are clearly exposed to the readers' eyes... There is no need for us to be so enamoured with the West as to assume that all Europeans seem to be endowed with a sense of propriety and a potential for talent, and are superior to Asians.'[33] Lu Xun, the most highly acclaimed of modern Chinese reformist writers, used the term 'grabbism' (拿来主义, *nalai zhuyi*) or 'borrowing' to denote how the Chinese reformers would use Western literature: they would grab what they needed and discard what they considered useless or negative for their purposes as they reformed China.

One Dickens film adaptation is worth noting for its illustration of *nalai zhuyi*: an unusually leftist Hong Kong production of *Great Expectations* in 1955 (when Hong Kong was officially politically distinct from mainland China), *Guxing Xuelei* or 'An Orphan's Tragedy' from Zhonglian Film Studio. After 1949, Chairman Mao Zedong advised that in educating the masses of Chinese peasantry into literacy, and in re-educating the formerly privileged into respect for the masses, it was best to emphasize 'model' characters in literature and drama, especially models of soldiers, peasants, workers, sometimes of teachers and doctors. In the 1955 film 'An Orphan's Tragedy'—as in Latin America, Dickens was often influential for his concern with children as casualties of cultures in transition—a young Bruce Lee starred as Pip; women characters were rearranged to delete resentment and provide 'models' (i.e. no Miss Havisham, a weak Estella, a key role for Biddy or *Bei'er*); and the great expectation is not Pip's individual desire to be a gentleman, but rather the village's desire that he succeed in being a doctor for them. *Fu Qun* (Pip) meant 'return to/recover the public'; *Fan Tiansheng* (Pip's father!) meant 'born in the field, deep roots in the masses'.[34]

Other recent work on Chinese translation of Dickens also shows examples of difference from the source. Klaudia Hiu Yen Lee has shown how the London labyrinth of *Little Dorrit* is replaced in the Chinese version with organized horizontal architecture, and the Marshalsea is not a labyrinth but a flat, real prison, which she attributes to the control and balance favoured in Chinese aesthetics.[35] Lee argues that in *David Copperfield* Dickens's subjective, psychological sense of self is translated into the traditional Chinese sense of one's position in relation to others.[36] Lin Shu and Wei Yi's translation (1907) of *The Old Curiosity Shop*, entitled *The Biography of Filial Daughter Nell*,

---

[33] Kirk A. Denton, *Modern Chinese Literary Thought* (Stanford, CA: Stanford University Press, 1996), 86.

[34] Ting Guo, 'Dickens on the Chinese Screen', *The Global Circulation Project of Literature Compass* 8, 10 (2011): 795–810. Hong Kong: Zhonglian Dianyi Qiye Youxian Gongsi, 'Guxing Xuelei, an Orphan's Tragedy [Great Expectations]' (1955).

[35] Klaudia Hiu Yen Lee, 'Cross-Cultural Adaptation of the Dickensian Spatiality: The Case of *Little Dorrit*', *English: Journal of the English Association* 62 (2013): 6–21.

[36] Klaudia Hiu Yen Lee, 'Cross-Cultural Encounters: The Early Reception of Charles Dickens in China (1895–1915)'. Ph.D. Dissertation, University of Nottingham, September 2012.

emphasizes traditional Chinese virtues of filial piety and protection of family from debt and shame. And with *Tale of Two Cities* (1859) published in the important journal *The Justice* by the reformer Liang Qichao in 1913, revolutionary politics came to the fore. In her interpretations of the Chinese translations, Lee emphasizes the 'paratexts' or 'off-texts', including directive titles, subtitles, prefaces, and translators' notes. The new, and first complete, Chinese translation of all Dickens's novels published in 2012 is raising fascinating issues in the aesthetics and politics of translation.[37]

While much circulation of British literature, including Dickens, was triangulated between Europe, Japan, and China,[38] the Japanese had their own distinctive interests in Dickens. Japan and Russia have historically been the most active in translating foreign literatures. From the first Japanese translations of British fiction with *Robinson Crusoe*, of interest for its representation of the technological Western entrepreneur at a time when Japan's standing in the world was internally perceived to have declined, through the Meiji Restoration in the second half of the nineteenth century, the Meirokushi (reforming literati) had also grabbed what they found useful in European culture. By the 1880s, Japanese writers were interested in translations that also showed emotion and romance in Western writers, indicating that the latter were not exclusively practical, technological, and materialist. *Oliver Twist* was translated in 1885 and noted for the 'minute descriptions and the sincerity of [Dickens's] social criticism', and in 1911 Toshihiko Sakai (堺 利彦, Sakai Toshihiko), a precursor of the Japanese socialist movement, translated *Oliver Twist* 'for Charles Dickens's sympathy for the weak and the low and his ironical treatment of the high and the powerful'.[39]

Yet the Meiji literati tended to prefer European literatures over the traditionalism and what they perceived as the moralism of the Victorians. They were unmoved by the 'Christmas' sentiment so attractive to the English-speaking colonies, and Dickens's dense symbolic prose of the later novels was difficult to translate. By the 1890s, they turned to Naturalism on the Continent rather than Dickensian realism. However, from the first translation in 1882 of Dickens's 'Sketches of Young Couples', translated as 'Couples in the Western World', gender critique and liberalization were central to Meiji reform, and many writers were interested in Dickens's representations of gender and domesticity. In 1892, chapter 44 of *David Copperfield*, 'Our Housekeeping', was translated for domestic suitability, and from 1905 there were many 'Nelliads' (like the *Robinsonnades*) on girls and girlhood. In the late twentieth century, Dickens went through a reassessment in Japan, in which interest developed in his depictions of criminals and morbid psychology, and the perceived pessimism of his later works became more attractive.

---

[37] *Complete Works of Charles Dickens*, ed. Zhaolin Song (Hangzhou: Zhejiang Gongshang University Press, 2012).

[38] Ting Guo, 'Translating a Foreign Writer: A Case Study of Byron in China', *The Global Circulation Project of Literature Compass* 7, 9 (2010): 883–99.

[39] Masaie Matsumura, 'Dickens in Japan', Nisbet Archive, UC Santa Cruz, 1983. For an extended study of 'Dickens in Japan' see Matsumura in vol. 4 of Hollington (ed.), *Charles Dickens: Critical Assessments*, 541–61.

Recently, with the enormous popularity of graphic novel adaptations of Dickens throughout anglophone countries (classiccomicsstore.com lists many editions of *A Tale of Two Cities, David Copperfield, Great Expectations, A Christmas Carol, Barnaby Rudge, Nicholas Nickleby*), mangaka (manga writers) are beginning to adapt Dickens in the popular graphic form in Japan and Korea's Tsai Fong Books.[40]

The novel as a modern form was introduced into India by the British following the 1835 English Education Act, which gave rise to intense debate on the literatures appropriate for purposes of colonization. According to Priya Joshi's *In Another Country: Colonialism, Culture, and the English Novel in India* (2002), there was a disjunction between the prescribed 'good' novels introduced by the colonial authorities and their pervasive rejection by Indian readers in favour of Marie Corelli, Francis Marion Crawford, W. H. Ainsworth, Charles Garvice, George Payne Rainsford James, and George W. M. Reynolds, whose *Pickwick Abroad* (1839) was favoured over the original (1837). Dickens appears less often than these, as do Thackeray, Meredith, Eliot, the Brontës, and Austen. Stuart H. Blackburn also conducted a survey of public libraries across different regions of the subcontinent and developed a 'masterlist of all the European authors available to Indian readers in the nineteenth century', and a shortlist of 'vendible' authors whose works were available in multiple copies. The result was 207 mostly British authors. He narrowed this list down to authors who were available in nearly all the libraries, ending with 21 authors who were widely available to Indian readers from 1850 to 1901. Dickens appeared in 13 out of 14 catalogues.[41]

Joshi concluded that 'The British novel of "serious standards" was introduced in India in the nineteenth century as a means of propagating and legitimating Englishness in the colony. Yet the fiction consumed most voraciously—discussed, copied, translated, and "adapted" most avidly into [22] Indian languages, and eventually into the Indian novel—was not the novel of "serious standards" but the work of what are often considered minor British novelists.... Despite this apparent "neglect of serious reading", the Indian novel ascended to "serious standards".'[42]

An example of a modern Indian novel of serious standards influenced by Dickens is Mulk Raj Anand's classic *Untouchable* (1935). Anand (1905–2004), known as India's Dickens, transposed the crossing-sweep Jo of *Bleak House* into the caste of his untouchable Bakha, showing the full subjectivity—again, going well beyond what Dickens had been able to represent of the inarticulate Jo—of one who cleaned up human excrement and was therefore untouchable by humans. Anand's remarkable novel was legendarily edited by Gandhi, whose agitation for the emancipation of the caste concludes the novel. After independence, the Indian-born Canadian Rohinton Mistry (b. 1952) was

---

[40] I am grateful to the manga expert Dr Tara-Monique Etherington (University of Exeter) for this information.

[41] Stuart H. Blackburn and Vasudha Dalmia (eds), *India's Literary History: Essays on the Nineteenth Century* (Delhi: Permanent Black, 2004).

[42] Priya Joshi, *In Another Country: Colonialism, Culture, and the English Novel in India* (New York: Columbia University Press, 2002), 5.

compared repeatedly to Dickens, one of his favourite writers, for his humour and strong emphasis on plot and character, and Vikram Seth's (b. 1952) *A Suitable Boy* participates in both Dickensian and Bengali popular traditions of three-decker realistic family sagas.

Versions of Jo the sweep appear also in modern Arabic fiction, where Dickens, again, was influential in representing the poor. Dickens was first translated into classical Arabic in 1912, on the occasion of the first Centenary, beginning with *David Copperfield* and then with redacted children's stories in capsule form of David, Little Nell, Oliver, Pip, Paul Dombey, Smike, Little Dorrit, and Jo the sweep. Between 1912 and 1920, Dickens was used by educators to signify social criticism, freedom from oppression, defences of the poor and inarticulate. In a 49-page Introduction to *A Tale of Two Cities* Muhammad al-Sibaci writes that he hopes that his translation might contribute to a more equal, democratic Egypt, and later Egypt's Chief Controller of Education expresses hope that his translations of Dickens will serve the same purpose of social and moral reform.[43] Nur Sherif saw the influence of Dickens in the Egyptian Taha Hussein's (1889-1973) *The Tortured on the Earth* (1949), banned on its first appearance under monarchy, and in Youssef Idris's (b. 1927) *The Language of Pain* (1965), in which, Nur writes, 'Dialogue is not used on a single occasion, as this action is not dramatized. What we are given is simply a dumb show [of life simply endured] ... the burden of their existence which they had resignedly carried about with them.... The silent forgotten millions of have-nots.'[44]

As the modern realist novel grew in Arabic from the 1950s with Naguib Mahfouz and others, Dickens remained largely in abridged and simplified forms. F. H. Mikdadi has argued that in the second half of the twentieth century, Arabic novelistic interest was primarily in events and their effects on protagonists (i.e. on plot) and in the moral to be extracted (often this latter was rhymed). In the translations of *David Copperfield* that Mikdadi studies, descriptive and subjective passages are omitted; David's sufferings are events, shown from an external perspective. Dora's death is abstracted as event: girl dies, dog dies, without the sentiment. Mikdadi emphasizes that, as elsewhere in world literatures, Dickens's unhappy children are central in the Arabic adaptations of the novels. The later novels have not yet been translated into Arabic.[45]

Although this chapter has focused on Dickens outside Britain and the Commonwealth, Europe, and North America, one triangulated relationship is particularly illustrative of bibliomigrancy, that between Dickens, Galdós, and Dostoevsky. In Hispanic literary studies, Galdós's translations and transformations of Dickens are well known; however, as Galdós read Dickens, Dickens read the Spanish ur-novelist of the *Quixote*, Miguel de Cervantes, and the overlapping, rhizomatic traditions are evident. Dickens was the most translated of all foreign fiction writers in the Hispanic world, especially *Oliver Twist*, *David Copperfield*, and *A Christmas Carol*, in Argentina and Mexico as well as Spain. As Galdós perceived, both his and Dickens's societies were in transition between old aristocratic orders and new economic ones; they both were experiencing

---

[43] Nur Sherif, *Dickens in Arabic 1912-1920* (Beirut: Beirut Arab University, 1974).
[44] *About Arabic Books* (Beirut: Beirut Arab University, 1970), 18.
[45] F. H. Mikdadi, 'David Copperfield in Arabic', *Dickensian* 75, 388 (Summer 1979): 85-94.

the worst excesses of capitalism and its correlative impoverished populations; but both societies were Christian, and their authors offered similar liberal solutions to social problems in charity, pity, and altruistic love. Galdós read Dickens's 'solution' to the social problem of new versus old world and translated it through the *lazarillo* figure of Spain's picaresque tradition, from the anonymous Spanish novel *Lazarillo de Tormes* (1554), in which a servant becomes the sacrificial provider for the master through the servant's charity and pity. Galdós saw in Dickens's characters from Little Nell to Little Dorrit *lazarillo* figures, who minister to grandfather and father—captives of a mythic Old Order of family, status, and patronage—as sacrifices to a new economic order that in particular sacrificed women and girls. Galdós repeatedly worked through this narrative and cultural formation in *El abuelo* (1897), *Marianela* (1878), and *Misericordia* (1897).[46]

In one of the most stunning triangles in world literary history, Dostoevsky, who read Dickens while imprisoned in Siberia, constructed his own version of the sacrificial victim in *The Insulted and Injured* (1861), in which Helen/Nelly appears as one of his earliest 'thinking children', those children *sans* childhood, old before their time, and victims sacrificed to elders who should have protected them. Following Dickens's/Galdós's depiction of the arrogance of the world's elite (insult) and its exploitation of the poor (the injured), Dostoevsky was able to show the sexual abuse and child prostitution that Dickens himself could not depict. Tolstoy, Dostoevsky, Gorky, Gogol, Turgenev all saw Dickens as the model of a Christian (or, under the Soviets, humanist) writer, and it is noteworthy that of all the cultures that adapted Dickens to their own purposes, only Russians, who began translating Dickens as early as the 1830s, loved the late, bleak novels even more than the more accessible, more easily translated, and more optimistic early ones. Dickens was translated into the 16 languages of the republics of the USSR, and great critics and translators like Chernyshevski, Gorky, Vvdenski, and Viktor Shklovsky held Dickens as a 'landmark in the cause of democratic literature'.[47] Emily Finer, who has studied Dickens's circulation during the Soviet period, confirms his popularity throughout the USSR, peaking in the 1950s and 1960s with anniversaries and new editions. She attributes this consistency to his critiques of capitalism, particularly in relation to children (hence his being a core component of school curricula); his attacks on state institutions and bureaucracies ('Bar, Barnacles, and Bank' as Dickens calls them in *Little Dorrit*, that is, legal, political, and economic institutions); and his potential as a model for the Soviet writer. Intriguingly, Finer's recent research is beginning to reassess the Soviet canon as being rooted in European modernisms and avidly westernizing.[48]

Now if we consider the transculturation of Dickens, he has 'meant' both migration and settlement, class warfare, revolution, critique of neocolonial ideological state

---

[46] Stephen Gilman, *Galdós and the Art of the European Novel: 1867–1887* (Princeton: Princeton University Press, 1981).

[47] Igor Katarsky, 'Dickens in Russia', ed. Academy of Sciences of the USSR Institute of World Literature (Nisbet Archive, UC Santa Cruz, 1983): 97a. With Rodney L. Patterson and Mira Perper.

[48] Emily Finer, 'Dickens in Twentieth-Century Russia', in Hollington (ed.), *The Reception of Charles Dickens in Europe*, 103–20.

apparatuses, care of orphans/children, critique of capitalism, socialism, gender and domestic relations, sociology and psychology of crime and deprivation, and Christian solutions to social divisions and suffering. In global literary histories, he has 'meant' realism, romantic realism, industrial fiction, metropolitan fiction, dialect, demotics, and the vernaculars of the street. He has represented extreme psychology and individual identity, for which the *muletilla* (in Galdós, 'tagging' for Katherine Mansfield in New Zealand), a pet word or phrase repeated inadvertently revealing a character's 'tic' or deep psychology, was much adapted. He has also represented the divisions between country and city, as in Henry Lawson's studies of an Australian national ethos torn between its traditions of the bush and its rapid centralization in cities.

We may conclude, though this is by no means the conclusion of work that will need to progress through dialogue in many languages, that cultural translation gives perspective on authors, works, genres, cultures, and most importantly ourselves and our own critical limitations. Although this chapter has synthesized some of the global circulation of Dickens's novels, we hope for a dialogue and dialectic between the local complexity of close studies by scholars within their own literatures and the perspective that such synthetic overviews can bring. We are urged to think in terms not of originality but of circulation, appropriation, use, and their corollaries of transculturation, triangulation, revoicing, reaccentuation, indigenization, (re)mediation. This may distance (defamiliarize (after Shklovsky) or make strange) anglophone Dickensians from Dickens as an English author deep within his native environment, and deep within his own aesthetic, but the losses are offset by seeing him as an author of diverse meanings in other cultures going through similar social changes and in other literary histories. Societies caught between traditional cultures and forces of modernization give rise to 'Dickensian' social problem novels, comic and tragic 'Dickensian' characters and caricatures, 'Dickensian' affect and sentiment, neocolonial 'Dickensian' institutions and so forth, as creative literatures worldwide continue to represent our processes of world-making and unmaking.

Further Reading

Regenia Gagnier, 'Introduction: Victorian Studies, World Literatures, and Globalisation', *The State, or Statelessness, of Victorian Studies*, Special Issue *Critical Quarterly* 55 (2013): 1–8

Regenia Gagnier, 'Global Studies', in Dino Franco Felluga, Pamela K. Gilbert, and Linda K. Hughes (eds), *The Encyclopedia of Victorian Literature* (Oxford: Blackwell Publishing, 2015), 649–60

Juliet John, 'Global Dickens: A Response to John Jordan', *The Global Circulation Project of Literature Compass* 9, 7 (2012): 502–7

John O. Jordan and Nirshan Perera (eds), *Global Dickens* (New York and London: Ashgate, 2012)

Margaret Mendelawitz, *Charles Dickens' Australia: Selected Essays from* Household Words *1850–1859*, 5 vols (Sydney: University of Sydney Press, 2011)

CHAPTER 48

ADOPTING AND ADAPTING DICKENS SINCE 1870

Stage, Film, Radio, Television

SHARON ARONOFSKY WELTMAN

In March 1832, a bad cold kept the 20-year-old aspiring actor Charles Dickens from his audition at Covent Garden, forcing him to postpone trying out until the following season. In the intervening time, his first story appeared in print. The result? He dropped his initial plans for a theatrical career, and we have *David Copperfield, Bleak House*, and *A Christmas Carol*.[1] Yet Dickens never stopped performing. He was such a ham that Mamie Dickens described her father's acting out his remarkable characters as he wrote them, examining his own expressions in a mirror, then laughing and scribbling in response.[2] This well-known story tells us that, for Dickens, performance was integral to the very act of writing. Throughout his life, he continued to write, direct, produce, and perform in theatricals. His wildly popular and financially successful Public Readings of his own work in several extended tours through England, France, and the United States, in which he again acted every character, helped determine which of his novels we still read and study.[3] Stage adaptations of Dickens's novels appeared in theatres all over Great Britain and America within weeks of the books' publication. In London alone, three different adaptations of *Pickwick Papers* (1836–7) ran simultaneously before its serialization had even finished. Although such pirated dramatizations irked Dickens (he collected no royalties from them because there were no copyright protections addressing theatrical adaptation for authors of novels), they reinforced the exuberant popularity of his fiction during his lifetime and disseminated his work beyond his readership. Like

---

[1] Robert L. Patten, *Charles Dickens and 'Boz': The Birth of the Industrial-Age Author* (Cambridge: Cambridge University Press, 2012), 49.
[2] Mamie Dickens, *My Father as I Recall Him* (New York: E. P. Dutton, 1900), 49–50.
[3] Malcolm Andrews, *Charles Dickens and his Performing Selves* (Oxford: Oxford University Press, 2006), 56.

his own Readings, the scenes selected for dramatization while he was alive helped to fix which remained popular after his death in 1870 and which texts became canonized.[4]

After 1870, the voracious appetite for staging Dickens expanded further: over 1,000 new plays adopted from Dickens were mounted by the end of the nineteenth century. More than 3,000 separate productions have been documented between 1834 and 1984,[5] and that number has continued to rise. The adaptation of Dickens's books to stage, film, radio, and television has shaped and continues to shape the reception of his work, how we interpret his writing, even what we think of as 'Dickensian'. Every year, new film or television versions or parody appropriations of *A Christmas Carol* (1843) appear, while many community theatres depend upon their annual productions of this story to help fund the rest of the year's repertoire. *Oliver Twist*, *A Christmas Carol*, *David Copperfield*, *A Tale of Two Cities*, and *Great Expectations* have been adapted so many times that each has become what Paul Davis calls a *culture text*:[6] nowadays, without even reading *Oliver Twist*, the public repeatedly encounters Oliver asking for more—perhaps as an orphaned kitten in Disney's *Oliver & Company*, or as Stewie suddenly transported to the parish Workhouse in an episode of *Family Guy*, or as a headline about industry woes or financial institution bail outs.

In this chapter, I briefly address the plenitude of adaptations from Dickens's fiction to performance media since his death in 1870 (with a nod to a few earlier plays that impact later works). I consider not only how adaptations serve as interpretations of the source texts but also how each new adaptation reconfigures previous ones. In other words, they all add to what Sarah Cardwell names the *metatext*.[7] Whether the term is Davis's *culture text* or Cardwell's *metatext*, the accretion of source-plus-adaptations is always in the process of being created as each additional reworking enlarges our sense of what *Oliver Twist* or *A Christmas Carol* can be. I discuss what makes Dickens's fiction, conceived through performance, so suitable for rendering into such varied embodied forms as theatre, cinema, TV, and radio. Through a miniature case study of the 1980s, I investigate how Dickens helps us to think about theories of adaptation and Dickens's utility for negotiating a wide array of ideological positions worldwide. Finally, in the chapter's second half, I examine chief examples of one representative novel—*Oliver Twist* (1837–9)—the second-most adapted of his works.

---

[4] I developed some material here to lead the 2014 NEH Summer Seminar for College and University Teachers 'Performing Dickens: *Oliver Twist* and *Great Expectations* on Page, Stage, and Screen' at UC-Santa Cruz, sponsored by the Dickens Project. I thank the brilliant participants: Kirsten Andersen, Daniel Brown, Patrick Fleming, Joshua Gooch, Taryn Hakala, Carrie Han, Mary Isbell, Rob Jacklosky, Douglas Kirshen, Rebecca O'Neill, Rebecca Richardson, Julianne Smith, Mary-Antoinette Smith, Adena Spingarn, Linda Willem, and Steven Willis.

[5] H. Philip Bolton, *Dickens Dramatized* (London: Mansell, 1987), 19, vii.

[6] Paul Davis, *The Lives and Times of Ebenezer Scrooge* (New Haven: Yale University Press, 1990), 4.

[7] Sarah Cardwell, *Adaptation Revisited: Television and the Classic Novel* (Manchester: Manchester University Press, 2002), 25.

Adapting Dickens

The Dickens adaptation industry has spawned its own growth economy in critical scholarship. Entire books have been devoted to the afterlife of a single Dickens text, not only Davis's *The Lives and Times of Ebenezer Scrooge*, which details the rewriting, staging, and filming of Dickens's most adapted work, *A Christmas Carol*,[8] but others as well, such as Mary Hammond's authoritative *Charles Dickens's Great Expectations: A Cultural Life, 1860–2012* (2016), chronicling the previously untold reception and adaptation history of Dickens's 13th (and third most adapted) novel. Marc Napolitano's book *Oliver! A Dickensian Musical* (2014) provides a detailed biography of just one very influential musical stage adaptation of the novel *Oliver Twist*. The larger cultural landscape has been examined by such scholars as Dianne Sadoff in *Victorian Vogue* (2009), Jay Clayton in *Dickens in Cyberspace* (2003), and John Glavin in *Dickens on Screen* (2003). Indeed, there is a special relationship between Dickens and cinema. In a sense we can say that Dickens (and adaptation) presided over the inception of both narrative filmmaking and film theory, with the foundational American silent film director D. W. Griffith and the pioneering Soviet practitioner and theorist Sergei Eisenstein each directly addressing the influence of Dickens's storytelling techniques on their new medium. As Eisenstein so famously points out, Griffith attributes his invention of montage to Dickens's narrative use of parallel action; that is, scenes representing simultaneous events involving different sets of characters intercut sequentially.[9] In *Dickens and the Dream of Cinema* (2003), Grahame Smith argues that Dickens's prose is proto-cinematic, providing a blueprint for an incipient medium; in other words, as his title asserts, Dickens essentially dreams up cinema before its invention.[10]

So rich is the adaptation history of *A Christmas Carol* in particular and so relentless is its re-appropriation to new forms that any effort at comprehensive documentation is doomed to be perpetually out of date. Philip Bolton, who counts only the most straightforward adaptations, documents 357 plays, films, radio dramas, and teleplays of *A Christmas Carol* between 1843 and 1984,[11] the majority after 1950.[12] Even catalogues of adaptations compiled by dedicated groups of volunteers, such as those on Wikipedia or IMDb, necessarily leave out more than they can include. Beyond the nearly annual new films directly sourced by the story, there are many more inspired by it; think of *It's a Wonderful Life* (1947), *Scrooged* (1988), or *Ghosts of Girlfriends Past* (2009). Even a

---

[8] See also Fred Guida's *A Christmas Carol and its Adaptations: A Critical Examination of Dickens's Story and its Productions on Screen and Television* (Jefferson, NC, and London: McFarland, 2000).

[9] See Sergei Eisenstein, 'Dickens, Griffith, and Film Today', *Film Form* (1949; repr. New York: Harcourt Brace, 1977).

[10] Grahame Smith, *Dickens and the Dream of Cinema* (Manchester: Manchester University Press, 2003), 47.

[11] Bolton, *Dickens Dramatized*, 234–67.

[12] Ibid., 416.

pornographic film adaptation, *The Passions of Carol*, appeared in 1975.[13] And then every year there are the Christmas television specials that rework elements of Dickens's plot or characters in surprising ways. Perhaps the earliest example is the 25 December 1953 episode of *Topper* entitled 'Christmas Carol',[14] in which the resident ghosts of the socialite couple always haunting Topper now morph into the spirits of Christmas Past and so on. Abundant retellings on television series situate their existing characters within Dickens's plot, usually with a twist: just a few examples are *Bewitched*, 'Humbug Not to Be Spoken Here' (1967); *The Odd Couple*, 'Scrooge Gets an Oscar' (1970); *A Different World*, 'For Whom the Jingle Bell Tolls' (1989); *Roseanne*, 'Halloween IV' (1992); *Northern Exposure*, 'Shofar, So Good' (1994); *Martin*, 'Scrooge' (1996); and *Doctor Who*, 'Christmas Carol' (2010).[15] Jules Styne of Broadway fame composed the TV-musical *Mister Magoo's Christmas Carol* (1962), based on the theatrical cartoon character; this animated special was so successful that it spawned the 1964 television cartoon series *The Famous Adventures of Mr. Magoo*, in which the title character inhabits other classic tales.[16]

Many popular Dickens dramatizations—like David Lean's films *Great Expectations* (1946) and *Oliver Twist* (1948) or the West End/Broadway musical *Oliver!* (1960/3)—have grown into much studied classics in their own right. High culture adaptations, such as Albert Coates's opera *Pickwick* (1936) and Arthur Benjamin's opera *A Tale of Two Cities* (1949–50), were mounted by esteemed British opera companies, Sadler's Wells and Covent Garden respectively.[17] Experimental works have also succeeded, such as Rupert Holmes's 1985 Broadway musical *Drood*, in which the audience chooses the solution to the novel's mysteries. In fact, the 1980s provides a fascinating glimpse of the variety of Dickensian stage and screen adaptations. Lauded innovations during this period include the Royal Shakespeare Company's eight-and-a-half-hour production of *Nicholas Nickleby* in 1980, which transferred to Broadway in 1981 and was then mounted in Sydney in 1983, Melbourne in 1984, and the Adelaide Theatre Festival in a production by the Australian Opera and the Sydney Theatre Company in 1985. In the filmmaker Christine Edzard's two-part epic *Little Dorrit* (1987), each nearly three-hour movie gives a different but overlapping perspective on the multi-plot story, one following Arthur Clennam and the other Amy Dorrit. Less critically successful but innovative nonetheless is the 2015 BBC television series *Dickensian*, which weaves together plots from many

---

[13] Laura Helen Marks, 'Resexualizing Scrooge: Gender, Spectatorship, and the Subversion of Genre in Shaun Costello's *The Passions of Carol*', in Whitney Strub and Carolyn Bronstein (eds), *From Porno Chic to the Sex Wars: The Destabilization of American Culture and Politics in the 1970s* (Amherst and Boston: University of Massachusetts Press, 2016).

[14] Michael Pointer, *Charles Dickens on the Screen: The Film, Television, and Video Adaptations* (Lanham, MD: Scarecrow Press, 1996), 99.

[15] For more examples, see Pointer, *Charles Dickens on the Screen*, 99–104, and Noel Murray, '"You will be visited by 69 spirits": 23 TV episodes based on "A Christmas Carol"', *TV Club* (20 Dec 2010), <http://www.avclub.com/article/you-will-be-visited-by-69-spirits-23-tv-episodes-b-49218>.

[16] In this 18-part series, Mr Magoo entered many familiar stories, playing Victor Frankenstein, Ishmael from *Moby Dick*, Watson from *Sherlock Holmes*, Friar Tuck from *Robin Hood*, and all seven dwarves from *Snow White*.

[17] My thanks go to Matthew Ingleby for pointing me to these two operas.

Dickens novels. We see the doomed courtship of a young Miss Havisham from *Great Expectations*, who is best friends with an as yet unmarried Honoria (later Lady Dedlock from *Bleak House*), occupying the same time frame as characters from *Pickwick Papers, Oliver Twist, The Old Curiosity Shop, A Christmas Carol*, etc., all living and interacting in close proximity in 'London'.

What makes Dickens so eminently adaptable in both traditional and edgy forms? One hint comes in Neil Sinyard's argument that the Royal Shakespeare *Nicholas Nickleby* and Edzard's *Little Dorrit* demonstrate Dickens to be 'the most relevant and trenchant of social commentators in a Thatcher (and Reagan) era that openly espoused the virtues of self-interest and so-called "Victorian values"'.[18] It may also be that Dickens's interest in social justice has made his writing perennially relevant, and that the 1980s merely serve as a test case for the range of adaptations he generates. But these experimental examples are only the cutting edge of that decade's profusion of Dickens dramatizations; there are many others that seem more interested in lush costuming than social protest. Many detractors see the heritage film and television genre as neoconservative, packaging upper-class privilege for middle-class viewers who, as Dianne Sadoff says, find themselves 'applauding private ownership of stately mansions' as part of a kind of patriotism or as compensation for their own lack of material wealth.[19] In contrast to Sinyard's opinion of experimental Dickens adaptations, Robert Hewison critiques the heritage industry as a manifestation of a Thatcherite agenda.[20] As Julie Sanders explains about the act of adapting canonical texts generally, reproducing the original while altering it (as all adaptations do) is simultaneously 'inherently conservative' and 'oppositional, even subversive' in that the adaptation itself helps to maintain the source's canonical status while altering it hints at the original's imperfect fit for the current climate.[21]

Perhaps in part because of the mixed politics of adaptations in the 1980s, the decade was a boom time for Dickens in much of the English-speaking world. CBS produced a made-for-TV *A Tale of Two Cities* in 1980; Disney made a six-part *Great Expectations* for television in 1989; there were two Broadway musicals, the successful *Drood* and the failed *Copperfield* (1980); Clive Donner directed George C. Scott starring in TV-movies of both *Oliver Twist* in 1982 and *A Christmas Carol* in 1984. Australia's Burbank Studios produced at least four animated features (*David Copperfield* in 1983, *The Old Curiosity Shop* and *A Tale of Two Cities* in 1984, and *Pickwick Papers* in 1985), while the Australian Broadcasting Company produced a six-hour *Great Expectations: The Untold Story* in 1987, concentrating on what Magwitch's life might have been like down under. BBC produced the most serial adaptations in that ten-year span, usually between seven and

---

[18] Neil Sinyard, 'Dickens on Television', <http://www.screenonline.org.uk/tv/id/1420996/>.

[19] Dianne Sadoff, *Victorian Vogue: British Novels on Screen* (Minneapolis: University of Minnesota Press, 2009), xvii.

[20] Robert Hewison, *The Heritage Industry: Britain in a Climate of Decline* (London: Methuen, 1987); for a succinct history and placement of the debates, see Belén Vidal's *Heritage Film: Nation, Genre, and Repesentation* (New York: Columbia University Press, 2012).

[21] Julie Sanders, *Adaptation and Appropriation* (London and New York: Routledge, 2005), 9.

12 episodes each; a sampling includes *A Tale of Two Cities* (1980), *Great Expectations* (1981), *Dombey and Son* (1983), *Oliver Twist* (1985), *Bleak House* (1985), *Pickwick Papers* (1985), and *David Copperfield* (1986).[22] Dickens's original publication in serial format seems ready-made for the television mini-series. Rachel Malik argues that Dickens's multiform publication strategy (serial, volume, etc.) and his readership of 'sophisticated genre switchers' promotes the adaptability of his writing to ever new instruments.[23]

While this chapter concentrates on Britain and America, Dickens has been frequently adapted worldwide. Australia, India, and Japan have robust film industries of long standing; in each we find significant cinematic appropriation of Dickens. I have already mentioned a number of Australian adaptations. In India, Gyan Mukherjee's *Kismet* (1943), which 'held the record for the longest run of an Indian film in a single theatre for more than three decades',[24] includes several elements inspired by *Oliver Twist*:[25] a 'lovable rogue' pickpocket,[26] an illegitimate child, a locket yielding family secrets that resolves the plot. *Oliver Twist* even more clearly inspired *Q&A* (2005), the debut novel by Indian author and diplomat Vikas Swarup that features a Fagin-like character, Maman, who leads a gang of child-beggars, providing them with food and shelter, but often at the cost of their eyesight, since blinded they bring in more money. *Q&A*, in turn, was adapted into the Oscar-winning film *Slumdog Millionaire* (2008) directed by Danny Boyle.[27] In 2016, *Great Expectations* became *Fitoor*, a Bollywood film directed by Abhishek Kapoor. A similar story of influence has been traced by Masaie Matsumura from Dickens's novel *Nicholas Nickleby* to Natsume Sōseki's classic novel *Botchan* (1906), which adopts scenes and characterizations from the Yorkshire school chapters of *Nicholas Nickleby*;[28] *Botchan* has been adapted several times to the screen, as a film in 1935 and 1953, as a made-for-TV movie in 2016, and a television anime series in 1986, always retaining its Dickensian elements. Repeatedly filmmakers in India and Japan have found in Dickens—or a mediated Dickens—a means for depicting the plight of children and their need for champions.

---

[22] 'EVERY Charles Dickens adaptation', <http://www.imdb.com/list/ls006348409/>, 25 December 2011. Accessed 2 June 2016. BBC has remade many of these same novels in subsequent years. For the most comprehensive discussion of the Australian Broadcasting Company's *Great Expectations: The Untold Story*, see John O. Jordan, '*Great Expectations* on Australian Television', in John Glavin (ed.), *Dickens on Screen* (Cambridge: Cambridge University Press), 45–52.

[23] Rachel Malik, 'Stories Many, Fast and Slow: *Great Expectations* and the Mid-Victorian Horizon of the Publishable', *ELH* 79, 2 (Summer 2012): 477–500; 483, 479.

[24] 'Kismet', National Film Archive of India, <http://nfaipune.nic.in/kismet.htm>.

[25] Vijay Mishra, *Bollywood Cinema: Temples of Desire* (London and New York: Routledge, 2013), 30.

[26] 'Kismet', National Film Archive of India, <http://nfaipune.nic.in/kismet.htm>.

[27] For more on the relationships between *Oliver Twist*, *Q&A*, and *Slumdog Millionaire*, see Jerod Ra'Del Hollyfield, *Framing Empire: Victorian Literature, Hollywood International, and Postcolonial Film Adaptation*, diss., Louisiana State University, 2011.

[28] My thanks to Akiko Takei for alerting me to this text at the 2016 Dickens Society Symposium. Masaie Matsumura, 'Japan', in Paul Schlicke (ed.), *The Oxford Companion to Charles Dickens: Anniversary Edition* (Oxford: Oxford University Press, 2011), 307.

John Jordan describes the importance of Dickens as a vehicle for protest in apartheid-era South Africa. For example, 'soon after the imposition of apartheid as official government policy, Ezekiel [Es'kia] Mphahlele adapted *A Tale of Two Cities*, Dickens's novel of revolution, 'and staged theatrical performances of it in black townships'.[29] *Oliver Twist* also has a long tradition of social critique in South Africa, extending into the 1970s and beyond. Jordan states that 'after reading the novel, students at historically black Lovedale College formed a committee to ask for more lessons, more food, and more and better books', resulting in expulsions and incarceration.[30] *Oliver Twist* remains important in this context: the 2004 independent South African film *A Boy Called Twist* owes a debt to David Lean's *Oliver Twist*, borrowing its structure from the earlier film. But its shift in setting and sensibility (the Rastafarian Fagin populates his den with children of the AIDS epidemic) works both to highlight the novel's relevance and to attach movie-goers to pressing social issues. These South African instances are just a few that demonstrate the global breadth of Dickens's adaptability, not only to performance but also to different national or cultural situations, often—as John Jordan points out—in situations in dire need of social action.[31]

Four other examples show Dickens as a lens for interpreting the postcolonial world. Alfonso Cuarón's 1998 *Great Expectations* relocates Dickens's story to the contemporary American south. Cuarón's personal background makes this shift particularly interesting from a postcolonial perspective: from Mexico himself, Cuarón sets the Victorian novel in another geographical area formerly colonized by Spain; he also is something of an interloper in Hollywood and his stylish postmodern look is associated by critics with his outsider standing. The 2011 drama *Great Expectations* by British playwright Tanika Gupta places the action in Calcutta and puts Dickens's narrative within India's traditional caste system, remaining otherwise remarkably faithful to Dickens's text. In 2012, BBC aired *The Mumbai Chuzzlewits*, a three-part radio series by Ayeesha Menon. Pointing to the utility of adaptations for simultaneously examining what Dickens tells us about our present and what transposing his characters to the current moment reveals about the source, *The Guardian* states 'modern-day Mumbai is as obsessed with status, social hierarchy and making money as Victorian Britain ever was'.[32] Though the point is well taken, it is as easily said of Dallas or New York. A final instance illustrating the cultural utility of *Oliver Twist* is *Asking for More: Dickens in Nigeria* (2012), an original play created and performed by an ensemble of Nigerian immigrants in Lowell,

---

[29] John O. Jordan, 'Global Dickens', *Literature Compass* 6, 6 (2009): 1211–23, doi: 10.1111/j.1741-4113.2009.00664.x.

[30] John O. Jordan, 'Postcolonial Dickens', in David Paroissien (ed.), *A Companion to Charles Dickens* (Malden, MA, and Oxford: John Wiley & Sons, 2008), 486–500: 499.

[31] Jordan, 'Global Dickens'.

[32] Elisabeth Mahoney, 'Radio Review: The Mumbai Chuzzlewits', *The Guardian* (Sunday 1 January 2012) |<https://www.theguardian.com/tv-and-radio/2012/jan/01/radio-review-mumbai-chuzzlewits-dickens>. Accessed 16 June 2016.

Massachusetts.[33] The play portrays a Nigerian student falling asleep in class to dream of asking for more, emphasizing the meaningfulness of Dickens's portrayal of deprivation for an immigrant community.[34]

The LGBT community has also found *Oliver Twist* useful as a resource for cultural work. Though neither met with wide release, two film adaptations have resituated the novel within the gay world. *Twisted* (1996), written and directed by Seth Michael Donsky, was selected for several important film festivals and in 2012 for the permanent collection at the New York Museum of Modern Art.[35] Set among a population of New York City drag queens, *Twisted* uses the lens of *Oliver Twist* to deal with prostitution, racial identity (Oliver is black), and drug abuse. The *Los Angeles Times* praised its innovative use of the novel's melodrama and its invoking silent film adaptations by inserting artful intertitles.[36] *Twist* (2003), a Canadian film directed by Jacob Tierney, depicts a Toronto underworld of male prostitution and exploitation. Seen from the point of view of a character renamed Dodge, it has not met with the same critical success despite praise for some strong performances and clever reimagining.[37]

Though theatre and film are largely visual media, not all performances are visual. Radio adaptations of Dickens began with the medium itself. The first radio adaptation of any Dickens novel is the 'Barkis is Willing' segment from *David Copperfield* in 1923. In the beginning they were simply prose readings by an individual rather than fully adapted radio dramas enacted by a cast. A milestone was *Great Expectations* read in 16 instalments from January to April 1930 by V. C. Clinton Baddeley, so successful that he followed it with one-man versions of many more of Dickens's novels, continuing to adapt and perform them on the radio until 1947.[38] Theatre actors moved seamlessly into radio. A good example is the music hall star Bransby Williams, who from 1896 performed serious monologues of Dickens's characters on stage (as well as spoofing celebrated actors such as Irving performing Fagin) and then reprised his monologues on radio.[39] Fully fledged radio plays adapting

---

[33] The creator/actors were Olisa Adigwe, Prince Emenogu, Michael Enagbare, Robert Omoyeni, Anastasia Onyenho, Monica Swaida, and Lucy Zorokong; the play was conceived by Robert Omoyeni, directed by Obehi Janice, and produced by the Nigerian Association of Merrimack Valley at the University of Massachusetts, Lowell. 19 October 2012. <http://library.uml.edu/media/campusvoices/dickensnigeria.html>. Accessed 17 July 2016.

[34] My thanks to Diana Archibald for speaking about this production.

[35] Seth Donsky's official web page, <http://www.sethmichaeldonsky.com/screenplays.php>. Accessed 26 August 2016.

[36] Kevin Thomas, 'A "Twisted" Tale of Souls Rising Above Corruption', *Los Angeles Times* (12 December 1997). <http://articles.latimes.com/1997/dec/12/entertainment/ca-63147>. Accessed 26 August 2016.

[37] Ruthe Stein, 'FILM CLIPS / Also opening today: Twist'. *San Francisco Chronicle* (23 July 2004). <http://www.sfgate.com/movies/article/FILM-CLIPS-Also-opening-today-2706163.php>. Accessed 26 August 2016.

[38] F. Dubrez Fawcett, *Dickens the Dramatist on Stage, Screen, and Radio* (London: W. H. Allen, 1952), 214–15.

[39] Paul Schlicke, *The Oxford Companion to Charles Dickens: Anniversary Edition* (Oxford: Oxford University Press, 2011), 597.

Dickens's fiction often featured fabulous theatre and film casts; Lionel Barrymore played Scrooge in live radio broadcasts annually from 1934 to 1953. On the rare occasions he had to miss a performance, other stars such as Orson Welles (in 1938) or John Barrymore stepped in. In 1950 the Theatre Guild on the Air produced a well-known *David Copperfield*, condensed to less than one hour, starring Boris Karloff as Uriah Heep and Richard Burton as David. The same novels were adapted to the radio many times. Between 1947 and 1952, Dubrez Fawcett reports four radio broadcasts of *A Tale of Two Cities*: a 12-part series, a children's version, a 'complete play', and an eight-part series.[40] Although of course television broadcasts superseded radio by the 1950s and 1960s, radio drama has never gone away. One niche for radio Dickens is the Evangelical Christian market. Focus on the Family Radio Theatre offers both a 90-minute *A Christmas Carol* (originally airing in 1996, the organization's first radio dramatization) and a 14-part *Oliver Twist* (which aired starting 13 October 2012 and won a 2014 Audie Award for Best Radio Drama). In addition to broadcasting these productions on their many radio stations, Focus on the Family sells them as CDs with a bonus DVD that promotes ultra-conservative values, proof that Dickens can be employed in service of a variety of political agendas, just as well today as in the 1980s.

Although I have endeavoured to sketch the dizzying enormity of the task, to survey meaningfully the wealth of adaptations of Dickens since his death is impossible. Instead, in the remainder of this chapter I discuss the Anglo-American adaptation lineage of one novel, *Oliver Twist*. I examine key moments in its transmediation from the Victorian melodrama theatre to the silent screen, to the commercial stages of Broadway and the West End, to radio and to television. *Oliver Twist* is a fitting case study on adaptations of Dickens because in a sense it is itself a kind of adaptation, growing out of a range of earlier writings, genres, and conventions, including plays. It was first published serially, with each instalment designed as an aesthetic object at once distinct from those that went before and building upon them to make up part of the larger whole. Each number was embedded in the journalistic paratext of essays, poems, and advertisements surrounding them on the pages of *Bentley's Miscellany*, edited by Dickens. Then it was revised and adapted for volume publication and performance by Dickens himself. His famed reading version of Nancy's murder was a performance so intense it caused women to faint and—because it raised his blood pressure so high—may have hastened Dickens's death from a stroke at 58. Moreover, *Oliver Twist* is self-consciously designed like a stage melodrama, as the narrator explains in the opening paragraphs of Chapter 17.[41]

---

[40] Fawcett, *Dickens the Dramatist*, 216.

[41] Charles Dickens, *Oliver Twist*, ed. Kathleen Tillotson (Oxford: Clarendon Press, 1966), chapter 17, 105–6. Subsequent references are inserted parenthetically in the text by *OT* chapter, page. See pp. 369–71 of Tillotson edition for instalment and chapter divisions in *Bentley's Miscellany* and 1838 3-vol. edition.

Oliver Twist

As important as it is to value adaptations as fully realized art objects independent of their sources, it is also vital to recognize how adaptations help us to see the source texts' interpretative problems and opportunities. The same issues that concern literary critics also challenge adapters and performers alike. With *Oliver Twist*, these complications include anti-Semitism and the novel's depiction of Sikes's brutally murdering Nancy. The problem of Fagin is born of Dickens's use of the stereotype of the 'stage Jew' in creating the character (another example of the novel's inherent theatricality), but it persists for every actor taking on the role, wherever perpetuation of racism is reviled. The choices adapters make to soften the depiction of Fagin also sharpen current readers' focus on the anti-Semitism in the novel. Later, Dickens himself recognized its offensiveness to Jews, brought to his attention by a letter from a Jewish acquaintance and admirer named Eliza Davis. In response, he deleted from his next edition of *Oliver Twist* hundreds of instances of his calling Fagin 'the Jew' in an effort to decouple Fagin's villainy from his identity as a Jewish character. The difficulty of Nancy's gruesome death also remains intractable: it is more vicious in the novel than in any stage or screen adaptation, due probably to the difference between how the mind's eye individually interprets and processes a description of violence and the graphic image palpably thrust before viewers who cannot control what they see. In prose we read of Nancy's hair clinging to the club that bashes in her head, of so much blood that the dog walking through it leaves prints. We see none of this in Roman Polanski's 2005 film, for example. Instead, the camera presents the subtler image of blood seeping under the door, even though Polanski is notorious for creating films ruthlessly realistic in their depiction of gory violence.

These critical/performance problems arise in the novel's earliest adaptations. Because Dickens published his books serially, they were often (just as we saw with *Pickwick*) performed before Dickens had written—let alone printed—the concluding episodes. The final instalment of *Oliver Twist* appeared in *Bentley's Miscellany* in April 1839; Bolton lists ten stage productions that preceded that date.[42] Best known is George Almar's *Oliver Twist: A Serio-Comic Burletta*, which premiered at the Surrey Theatre in the autumn of 1838. In witnessing a performance, Dickens was so embarrassed that he lay down in the corner of his box during the first scene and did not rise again until the final curtain fell.[43] Nevertheless, it played for months, and it became the adaptation most frequently mounted throughout the rest of the nineteenth century.[44] These earlier stagings of the incomplete novel helped cement in the public consciousness what episodes would become favourites in later renditions, so that, for example, the novel's short paragraph

---

[42] Bolton, *Dickens Dramatized*, 104.
[43] Phillip Cox, *Reading Adaptations: Novel and Verse Narratives on the Stage, 1890–1840* (Manchester: Manchester University Press, 2000), 121.
[44] Sue Zemka, 'The Death of Nancy "Sikes," 1838–1912', *Representations* 110, 1 (Spring 2010): 29.

without dialogue describing the fun of teaching Oliver to pick pockets becomes a fully articulated and choreographed scene with dialogue and stage business in Almar, and it remains an indispensable part of most important subsequent adaptations.[45] We see it in the 1922 silent film starring Jackie Coogan and Lon Chaney, the 1948 Lean standard, and the musical *Oliver!*, which transforms the moment into the hilarious song and dance 'You've Got to Pick a Pocket or Two'.

Oliver Twist was Dickens's most frequently adapted novel in the nineteenth century; more than 200 versions were performed in England or America by 1900,[46] with 35 more produced in London or New York by 1920.[47] It also inspired burlesques such as *Oliver Twist; or Dickens Up a Tree* (1905) at the Royal Pavilion and *Oliver Twisted*, licensed for performance in London in 1916.[48] Cinematic versions of *Oliver Twist* were among the earliest films ever made. Not even two years after the Lumière brothers displayed some of the first projected film in December 1895, the first movie adaptation of any of Dickens's works, 'The Death of Nancy Sykes', appeared in 1897. Sue Zemka notes that after this 'thirty-seven-foot short' initiated Dickens on screen, 'Nancy was murdered on celluloid at least ten more times before sound films.'[49] The early cinematic choice to dramatize the ruthless extract surely owes something to Dickens himself having adapted it for his own enormously popular reading tours.

Early film adaptations of *Oliver Twist* were often directly taken from the contemporary stage. Bolton explains that 'actresses would step back and forth between the two media. Playwrights became screenwriters. Plays became films.'[50] The stage-to-screen pipeline was an important part of maintaining Dickens's relevance while legitimizing the new medium. A key example is *The Tale of Two Cities*, which was adapted to the stage by Frederick Longbridge and Freeman Wills as *The Only Way*, first performed at the Lyceum on 16 February in 1899, starring John Martin-Harvey as Sidney Carton.[51] Martin-Harvey continued in the role of Carton in stage performances literally thousands of times; in 1927 the play was filmed—starring Martin-Harvey—by Herbert Wilcox productions, with Wilcox directing, and with a scenario by one of the original playwrights, Freeman Wills. The same permeability between stage and screen is true of *Oliver Twist*. Marie Doro played Oliver in the 1912 centennial Broadway revival of J. Comyns Carr's melodrama *Oliver Twist* at the New Amsterdam Theater; in 1916, Doro re-created the title character on screen in a Paramount *Oliver Twist* directed by James

---

[45] George Almar, *Oliver Twist: A Serio-Comic Burletta, in Four Acts*, French's Standard Drama, No. 228 (New York: Samuel French, 1864?), 11–12.

[46] Bolton, *Dickens Dramatized*, 104–5.

[47] Ibid., 106.

[48] *Oliver Twist; or Dickens Up a Tree* (1905) was written by W. Pink with music by S. Baker. Bolton, *Dickens Dramatized*, 105, 137, 141.

[49] Zemka, 'The Death of Nancy "Sikes"', 30.

[50] Bolton, *Dickens Dramatized*, 106.

[51] He would play Magwitch in a 1935 adaptation *The Convict* (later renamed *The Scapegoat*) by Dickens's granddaughter Ethel Dickens. Mary Hammond, *Charles Dickens's Great Expectations: A Cultural Life, 1860–2012* (New York and London: Routledge, 2016), 100.

Young. Carr's popular play was revived often, and he was the first playwright to adapt *Oliver Twist* for radio broadcast in 1937, a version still presented on air as late as 1953.[52]

It may surprise some twenty-first-century readers to know that Oliver was typically played by a woman on stage and screen in the late nineteenth and early twentieth centuries, but Marie Doro's performance was the rule rather than the exception. Women playing boys was a long-standing convention of melodrama that carried over from drama to early cinema.[53] For example, in Dickens's lifetime, Miss Carson originated Oliver in C. Z. Barnett's 1838 adaptation. After Dickens's death, Jenny Lee acted the role of the little crossing sweep Jo from *Bleak House* on stage and screen around the world for decades, starting from the J. P. Burnett play *Poor Jo* in 1874 in San Francisco,[54] with several runs in Australia and England, continuing to 1922 when, in her mid-60s, Lee reprised poor Jo at London's Lyric Theatre in a benefit for the Charles Dickens Memorial House.[55] Although actresses performing boys in melodrama largely disappeared from film in the 1920s, they continued on stage until at least until 1933, when Betty Bligh played Oliver at the Lyceum.[56] In a sense the tradition reasserts itself in the 1968 film *Oliver!*: the orphan's songs are voiced not by the young actor Marc Lester, who played the title character, but rather by the singer Kathe Green. *Olivia Twist* (2014), made in conjunction with the British Youth Film Academy, flips the protagonist's gender outright.

By 1922, the boy-actor Jackie Coogan played Oliver and Lon Chaney played Fagin in a silent *Oliver Twist* directed by Frank Lloyd. The visually striking Lloyd movie was lost for 50 years and only released on DVD in 2009; the intertitles were re-created for the film by Chaney. Here we see his Fagin continuing the Victorian stage fun of the pickpocket scene, making the villain simultaneously repulsive and attractive. Music would help negotiate this tension: it is vital to remember that silent films were never silent but always accompanied by musicians who played the same kind of underscoring they had performed for stage melodrama to augment the emotional content. With the innovation of synchronized sound, silent films that had been based on stage plays were in turn remade into talkies.[57] Most important in the twentieth-century lineage of *Oliver Twist* on film is David Lean's critically acclaimed but controversial 1948 film. Like Lloyd's,

---

[52] Carr's adaptation was first produced by Herbert Beerbohm Tree at His Majesty's Theatre, London, 1905. Bolton, *Dickens Dramatized*, 107.

[53] See Laura Horak, *Girls Will Be Boys: Cross-Dressed Women, Lesbians, and American Cinema, 1908–1934* (New Brunswick, NJ: Rutgers University Press, 2016).

[54] Julianne Smith, 'J. P. Burnett's Bleak House: A Drama in Three Acts', Streaky Bacon A Guide to Victorian Adaptations, <http://www.streakybacon.net/j-p-burnetts-bleak-house-a-drama-in-three-acts-by-julianne-smith/>.

[55] She performed the role at London's Globe in 1876, toured Australia, returned to London's Strand Theatre in 1885, and then revived it at Drury Lane in 1896; Shafto Justin Adair Fitz-Gerald, *Dickens and the Drama: Being an Account of Charles Dickens's Connection with the Stage and the Stage's Connection with Him* (New York: C. Scribner's Sons, 1910), 246–8.

[56] Bolton, *Dickens Dramatized*, 106.

[57] The first sound *Oliver Twist* was the 1933 movie directed by William J. Cowan, with Dickie Moore playing Oliver.

David Lean's adaptation owes much both to Victorian stage versions and their realization of George Cruikshank's original illustrations.

In a popular theatrical effect, Victorian actors would freeze in tableaux to create exact replicas or 'realizations' of familiar images, often ending a scene.[58] So well known were Cruikshank's etchings for *Oliver Twist* that Victorian political cartoons mocking prominent Jewish politicians invoked the illustrator's rendition of Fagin.[59] More than 100 years after the publication and first stage performances of *Oliver Twist*, David Lean's film represents Fagin, played by Alec Guiness, as a realization of Cruikshank's illustrations. Guinness's outrageously large prosthetic nose provoked accusations of anti-Semitism and demonstrations in Berlin. This was in the immediate wake of the Second World War and the systematic genocide enabled in part by the use of propaganda, which Guinness's appearance shockingly resembled. Twelve minutes, primarily of Guinness in profile, had to be eliminated before the film could be released in the United States.[60]

Drawing on both Dickens's novel and David Lean's film, Lionel Bart's musical *Oliver!* opened in London in 1960, a tremendous hit starring Ron Moody as Fagin and Georgia Brown as Nancy. Bart (who not only composed the music but also wrote the lyrics and the book) borrowed much of Lean's condensation of the story, dropping the Maylie plot; he moreover musicalized scenes highlighted in the film, such as the pickpocketing game. But what is different from Lean's controversial movie—and from Dickens's novel—is the depiction of Fagin, now a lovable scamp and the chief nurturer of the boys, instead of a villain corrupting children and inciting murder. There is probably a biographical factor in Bart's choices regarding Fagin. A Jewish teen from London's East End when he first saw Lean's *Oliver Twist*, Bart may have wanted to recuperate Fagin.[61] People who experience the musical *Oliver!* (or its imitations, such as Disney's *Oliver & Company*) before they read the novel often find that it forever softens Dickens's Fagin in their own imaginations. The musical highlights the ambiguous and even tender aspects of the novel's character. These moments permitted Lionel Bart to birth a Fagin who is recognizable as Dickens's wily fence without being an anti-Semitic caricature. Unlike Dickens, Lionel Bart never mentions that Fagin is a Jew. His Jewish identity on stage is entirely a result of performance, including the instrumental underscoring and vocal embellishments in klezmer and cantorial musical styles. Stage actors such as Clive Revill (who opened the Broadway premiere in 1963), Jonathan Pryce, Rowan Atkinson, and Omid Djalili have varied widely in how they perform Fagin's Jewishness. Pryce, for example, elected to empty out the role of any stereotypes in his 1994 performance,

---

[58] Martin Meisel, *Realizations: Narrative, Pictorial, and Theatrical Arts in Nineteenth-Century England* (Princeton: Princeton, 1983), 247–65.

[59] 'Fagin's Political School' (*Punch*, 9 November 1867) depicts Disraeli corrupting the young Parliamentarians.

[60] Joss Marsh, 'Dickens and Film', in John O. Jordan (ed.), *The Cambridge Companion to Charles Dickens* (Cambridge: Cambridge University Press, 2001), 218–19.

[61] Jack Gorman, *Knocking Down Ginger* (London: Caliban Books, 1995), 138; Napolitano records additional accounts of how *Oliver!* was conceived (*Oliver!* 44–8).

stating 'Yes, I played a Jewish character, but what do you need to see to know that he's Jewish?'[62] Ron Moody, who in 1960 originated the role in London with a Yiddish accent and Yiddish-inflected mannerisms, did not make the 1963 transfer to New York in part because David Merrick, the Broadway producer, believed his highly ethnic portrayal would be seen as anti-Semitic, despite Moody's being Jewish himself.

When the musical was remade into Carol Reed's 1968 Oscar-winning film *Oliver!*, Moody portrayed a toned-down Fagin for the much broader film audience. Now the interconnections between Bart's musical and Lean's 1948 film become even more obvious. John Romano points out that the director 'Reed stole shot for shot Lean's version for the narrative portions of the musical. The story boards are the same.'[63] As Marc Napolitano observes, the back-and-forth connections between stage and screen melodrama adaptations of *Oliver Twist* are far more convoluted than the blatant borrowing of shots and perspectives: the director of the film *Oliver!* was the son of Sir Herbert Beerbohm Tree, who initially mounted J. Comyns Carr's 1905 *Oliver Twist*, which we have discussed as a basis of the 1916 silent film, playing the role of Fagin;[64] Oliver Reed, who plays Sikes in the film *Oliver!*, was Tree's grandson (and director Carol Reed's nephew).

These interconnections extend also to television. The BBC continued their long history of adapting Dickens serially from their supremacy in radio to TV.[65] But they did not adapt *Oliver Twist* into a television mini-series until relatively late, in 1962. Only after the spectacular success of *Oliver!* on the London stage stirred such excitement did the BBC air a 13-part drama written by Constance Cox, who had already adapted an 11-episode *Bleak House* for BBC in 1959. Neil Sinyard explains that the violence of Cox's dramatization of *Oliver Twist* generated discussion in Parliament because of the 'brutal murder of Nancy (Carmel McSharry) by Bill Sikes (Peter Vaughn) in its final episode', as people weighed the timing of broadcast for family viewing against a reluctance to sanitize Dickens's 'harsh vision of social cruelty and injustice'.[66]

The musical *Oliver!* has had a pervasive influence on other adaptations of *Oliver Twist*. Perhaps most transparent is *Oliver & Company* (1988), the Disney animated musical film. A tiny kitten, Oliver is befriended by a gang of adolescent dogs who snatch sausage links from New York street vendors. Billed on the packaging as 'inspired' by *Oliver Twist*, it is greatly indebted to the intermediate *Oliver!* One example is Dom DeLuise's portrayal of Fagin as a victim of Sikes, with no mention of the gang-leader's Jewish identity. Another is the cartoon's treatment of Nancy, now a buxom red-furred Afghan hound named Rita reminiscent of the movie-musical *Oliver!*'s red-headed actress Shani Wallis

---

[62] Sharon Aronofsky Weltman, '"Can a Fellow Be a Villain All his Life?": *Oliver!*, Fagin, and Performing Jewishness'. *Nineteenth-Century Contexts* 33, 4 (September 2011): 371–88; 377.

[63] Gerhard Joseph, 'Dickens, Psychoanalysis, and Film: A Roundtable', in John Glavin (ed.), *Dickens on Screen* (Cambridge: Cambridge University Press, 2003), 18.

[64] Napolitano, *Oliver!*, 183.

[65] Bolton, *Dickens Dramatized*, 107.

[66] Neil Sinyard, 'Dickens on Television', <http://www.screenonline.org.uk/tv/id/1420996/>.

in a low-cut red dress.[67] In the cartoon's planning stages, she was to be killed by cruel Dobermans whom she stalls to save Oliver's life as he escapes. Patrick C. Fleming's research into the Disney archives reveals how that scenario was abandoned as Rita's part gradually became much smaller. A subsequent Story Outline describes her merely bandaged in the final scene. In the final cut, the Dobermans never hurt Rita at all.[68] The film's title, *Oliver & Company*, pays tribute to Bart's adaptation; the score of *Oliver!* includes many musical numbers to be performed by 'Oliver and Company'.

The influence of the musical *Oliver!* extends even to Tim Burton's 2007 film version of Stephen Sondheim's *Sweeney Todd: The Demon Barber of Fleet Street*.[69] Critics often comment on its Dickensian qualities. *The New York Times*, for example, likens Burton's London to the set in the movie *Oliver!*[70] Burton ages down the character of Toby, Todd's apprentice, from the adolescent of the stage musical to the boy of the film, going so far as to include a line (not in Sondheim's musical play) about how young Toby came from the workhouse. This is most likely a reverberation from the 1936 non-musical film *Sweeney Todd* directed by George King, which interpolates a whole scene from Dickens. Just as the Beadle apprentices Oliver to the undertaker Mr Sowerberry in *Oliver Twist*, in King's *Sweeney Todd* the Beadle delivers Toby from the Workhouse to Todd. Equally surprising is that a Beadle appears in *Sweeney Todd* at all. In *Oliver!* (as in *Oliver Twist*), Mr Bumble puffs his own importance, propels the plot, and adds immeasurably to the humour. His significance is signalled by his several songs: 'Oliver!', 'I Shall Scream', and 'Boy for Sale'. In contrast, *Sweeney Todd*'s Victorian source, the novel *The String of Pearls* (1846–7), includes only an unnamed, unimportant Beadle, who appears briefly to investigate a mysterious stench. Yet Sondheim's musical expands the character to Dickensian proportions. He too puffs his own importance, propels the plot, and adds to the humour and horror, singing 'Ladies in their Sensitivities' and 'Sweet Polly Plunket'. According to the *Minneapolis Star-Tribune*, Timothy Spall, who plays the Beadle in Burton's film, comes 'straight out of a Dickens illustration'.[71] So powerful is Dickens's effect on our sense of what seems Victorian that playmakers and filmmakers change their adaptations of other Victorian novelists to be more Dickensian.

Timothy Spall is of course no stranger to playing a character from Dickens, having portrayed an unusual Fagin in the 2007 BBC television production, written by Sarah Phelps and directed by Coky Giedroyc. The novel's Fagin is a Jew only because the narrator and other characters say so. The character himself performs no aspect of being Jewish: he has no Yiddish accent, observes no Jewish rituals, and abides by no specifically

---

[67] Thanks to Rebecca Gorman O'Neill for pointing out how Rita's chest fur mimics a full-breasted silhouette.

[68] Patrick C. Fleming, 'Dickens, Disney, Oliver, and Company: Adaptation in a Corporate Media Age', *Children's Literature Association Quarterly* 41, 2 (2016): 182–98; 192–3.

[69] For a detailed analysis of *Sweeney Todd*'s debt to *Oliver!*, see Sharon Aronofsky Weltman, 'Boz versus Bos in *Sweeney Todd*: Dickens, Sondheim, and Victorianness', *Dickens Studies Annual* 42 (2011): 55–76.

[70] See <http://movies.nytimes.com/2007/12/21/movies/21swee.html?ref=movies>.

[71] See <http://www.startribune.com/entertainment/movies/12672012.html>.

Jewish religious commandments. Instead, he eats sausages and spurns the '[v]enerable men of his own persuasion' who come to offer comfort to the condemned at the novel's end (*OT* 52, 361). But Spall's Fagin wears a yarmulke, says Hebrew blessings over his food, and pointedly does not eat the sausages he cooks for the children. For Dickens, genuine piety would have rendered Fagin incapable of vile acts, as we see in the Jewish character of Riah in *Our Mutual Friend*. The BBC's point in making Fagin religiously observant is to motivate his criminal actions by depicting what would have been his persecution as a Victorian Jew. This concept culminates in the surprising interpolation of Shylock's forced conversion scene from *A Merchant of Venice*. However, it backfires, merging British literature's two most famous—and villainous—Jewish characters. The BBC's choice makes Fagin's fraught Jewish identity (still intertwined with his perfidy) no longer an aspect of ethnicity or racial identity but rather a matter of religious practice, something Dickens himself considered a 'very indecent and unjustifiable thing' to do.[72]

The feature of the 2007 BBC mini-series that has garnered the most commentary is the race-blind casting of Nancy, portrayed by Sophie Okonedo, of Nigerian-Jewish descent. She is generally mentioned as the first black actress playing Nancy on the screen.[73] But is she? Rita in *Oliver & Company* was voiced by the African-American singer-actor Sheryl Lee Ralph, best known at that time for originating the role of Deena Jones in the Broadway musical *Dreamgirls* (1981). Okonedo's casting recalls the first choice of the film *Oliver!*'s director Reed, who wanted Shirley Bassey for the part of Nancy, but 'Columbia vetoed her because it was felt that a black Nancy would alienate filmgoers in the American South'.[74] Nevertheless, Okonedo is the first black actress to visibly perform Nancy in a major screen adaptation. There is no suggestion in the novel or in the dramatization's plot that the character is of African or Afro-Caribbean ancestry, but there is also no compelling plot reason why she should not be black. The notion of race-blind casting—a long-time practice in the professional theatre in London and New York—assumes that viewers do not necessarily read the performers as raced. However, since the BBC has a long tradition of highly faithful adaptations, in which almost documentary attention to historical accuracy in costuming and sets is expected, casting Okonedo as Nancy has suggested to some an untold backstory that would account for her blackness in a predominantly but not completely white Victorian London underworld.[75] As in the novel and most adaptations (other than Disney), Nancy is brutally murdered by Bill Sikes, her lover. Her being the only black character focuses attention on the unmentioned fact of race and adds a racial interpretation to

---

[72] To Eliza Davis, 10 July 1863. *The Letters of Charles Dickens*, ed. Madeline House, Graham Storey, et al., Pilgrim/British Academy Edition, 12 vols (Oxford: Clarendon Press, 1965–2002), vol. 10:269–70, 270.

[73] Rachel Carroll, 'Black Britain and the Classic Adaptation: Integrated Casting in Television Adaptations of *Oliver Twist* and *Little Dorrit*', *Adaptation* 8, 1 (2015): 16–30; 17–20.

[74] Robert Moss, *The Films of Carol Reed* (New York: Columbia University Press, 1987), 251.

[75] Benjamin Poore, '"I have been true to you, upon my guilty soul I have!" Negotiating Nancy, "Hyperauthenticity" and "Hyperfidelity" in the 2007 BBC Adaptation of *Oliver Twist*', *Journal of Adaptation in Film and Performance* 3, 2 (2010): 157–70; 166–8.

that event: she is the only female character in a romantic relationship that crosses racial lines. Okonedo's race becomes a signifier carrying a hint of the Tragic Mulatta, bringing Dickens suddenly into comparison with other Victorian authors such as the playwright Dion Boucicault, who wrote *The Octoroon* (1859).[76] Phelps has said that her motive in creating the 2007 BBC Nancy as black was that she was sick of seeing all-white casts in period drama, implicitly acknowledging the problem of classic television adaptions promoting a vision of nineteenth-century London without non-white inhabitants.[77] This *Oliver Twist* eliminates what for Dickens was Fagin's racial difference and deflects it onto a newly legible racial difference for Nancy. It not only emphasizes Dickens's not having included a black character (and having never explored the Tragic Mulatta plot in his novels) but also focuses renewed critical attention on his having identified Fagin as racially rather than religiously a Jew.

Conclusion

As Julie Sanders points out, 'adaptation becomes a veritable marker of canonical status, prolonging the life of the source',[78] and it is possible to argue that Dickens persists so strongly in contemporary culture in part through his rich legacy of adaptation and performance. How does Dickens help us to theorize adaptation? How do adaptations give us a better understanding of the novelist's works? Adaptations of Dickens to the stage, cinema, television, and radio show us that his writing was from the beginning engaged with other forms: born of performance, crafted serially, rendered visually, and experienced audibly. Adaptations continue to proliferate beyond what I have discussed here into new media, expanding both the content and the forms that constitute the *metatext*. No matter the medium, adapters serve as interpreters of Dickens, not only choosing to dramatize what interests them but also offering in that set of choices a particular vision of what each novel means, at least for the moment. So long as actors are involved, they make performance choices that reveal problems and possibilities within both adaptation and source. Dickens's rich legacy of adaptation also demonstrates his fiction's flexibility as a vehicle to comment on contemporary cultural, political, and social concerns. Related to the nexus of interdependent forms in the novels' creation is

---

[76] The nineteenth-century trope of the Tragic Mulatta depicts a woman passing as white who often does not know of her mixed racial ancestry until it suddenly and tragically comes to light, forcing her into slavery; or she knows and finds her liminal position between identities too painful to survive. For more information, see Werner Sollers, *Neither Black nor White Yet Both: Thematic Explorations of Interracial Literature* (New York: Oxford University Press, 1997); Jennifer Devere Brody, *Impossible Purities: Blackness, Femininity, and Victorian Culture* (Durham, NC: Duke University Press, 1998); and Kimberly Snyder Manganelli, *Transatlantic Spectacles of Race: The Tragic Mulatta and the Tragic Muse* (New Brunswick, NJ, and London: Rutgers University Press, 2012).

[77] Poore, '"I have been true to you"',166.

[78] Sanders, *Adaptation and Appropriation*, 9.

that the texts and pieces of novels read aloud by Dickens or staged even in his lifetime later become the most canonical and influential of his works.

Further Reading

Pamela Atzori, 'Dickens in Television', in Michael Hollington (ed.), *The Reception of Charles Dickens in Europe*, 2 vols (London: Bloomsbury, 2013), 594–9

Linda Hutcheon, *A Theory of Adaptation* (New York and London: Routledge, 2006)

Thomas Leitch, *Film Adaptation and Its Discontents* (Baltimore: Johns Hopkins University Press, 2007)

Joss Marsh, *Starring Charles Dickens: Multi-Media 'Boz' and the Culture of Celebrity* (New York and London: Routledge, forthcoming, 2019)

Streaky Bacon: A Guide to Victorian Adaptations. <http://www.streakybacon.net/>.

Tony Williams, 'Modern Stage Adaptations', in Sally Ledger and Holly Furneaux (eds), *Charles Dickens in Context* (Cambridge: Cambridge University Press, 2011), 59–66

CHAPTER 49

CROWDSOURCED DICKENS

Adapting and Adopting Dickens in the Internet Age

JULIET JOHN[*]

Since the publication of Paul Schlicke's ground-breaking *Dickens and Popular Entertainment* in 1985, Dickens's relationship with popular culture has become an increasingly prominent area of Dickens studies.[1] Work on Dickens and popular culture splinters into three sub-fields: Dickens's relationship with Victorian popular culture, Dickensian 'afterlives' or posthumous remediations, and, in recent years, 'global' Dickens. Research on Dickensian afterlives has overwhelmingly tended to focus on Dickens's posthumous relationship with the screen and on the re-presentation of versions of Dickens's works since his death. The 2012 Bicentenary celebration website was perhaps the first major attempt to map the myriad of local, amateur, and hitherto unregulated Dickensian afterlives online and in communities. It made manifest the fact that cultural analysis of 'the Dickensian' today cannot simply be a matter of analysing artistic texts or even screen adaptations. Jay Clayton's *Charles Dickens in Cyberspace* and my own *Dickens and Mass Culture* have both touched on the ways in which a consideration of less familiar cultural spaces—and indeed a new sense of cultural space—alters, extends, and complicates our sense of Dickens's significance in today's popular imagination.[2] However, both were published before the bicentenary started the work of mapping the new Dickens terrain and brought its possibilities and challenges quite so

---

[*] I am grateful to Emma Curry, John Drew, Pete Orford, Rachel Stevens, Alex Werner, Ben Winyard, and Claire Wood, for sharing with me the unpublished information informing this article, to James Bennett, Patrick Fleming, Ruth Livesey, and Gillian Gordon for research leads, and to John Jordan and Bob Patten for meticulous feedback on drafts.

[1] (London: Allen & Unwin, 1985).

[2] Jay Clayton, *Charles Dickens in Cyberspace: The Afterlife of the Nineteenth Century in Postmodern Culture* (Oxford: Oxford University Press, 2003); Juliet John, *Dickens and Mass Culture* (Oxford: Oxford University Press, 2003).

clearly into focus.[3] Since the Bicentenary, papers on Dickensian 'ephemera'—or Dickens outside the usual textual or critical landscape—are beginning to spring up, focusing on a diverse range of topics: the internet, digital humanities, celebrity culture, Dickensian organizations, museums and monuments, heritage sites and entertainments, festivals, new readerships, and ways of reading. As Linda Hutcheon argues in the Preface to the First Edition of her influential *A Theory of Adaptation*, 'Adaptation has run amok. That's why we can't understand its appeal and even its nature if we only consider novels and films.'[4] This chapter offers a first attempt at theorizing this new adaptive landscape in relation to Dickens. It employs the idea of 'crowdsourcing' as an umbrella term to analyse a range of Dickensian appearances in new cultural space(s) which claim partnership, cooperation, or indeed a merging between cultural consumers and producers.[5] While internet projects which define themselves as 'crowdsourced' are a main focus, the idea of crowdsourcing is also employed more elastically to examine a variety of self-proclaimed populist or participatory projects in order to revisit what we think we know about Dickens's cultural reach in a new media era.

What follows seeks to temper or perhaps reshape the optimism that characterizes so much new work which sees the internet as facilitating Dickens's original utopian and inclusive vision of popular culture. It examines the evidence produced by a range of populist Dickensian ventures since the bicentenary to argue that the internet has facilitated not an extension of Dickens's audience or new 'crowds', but a reconfiguration of communication structures which allows 'clubs' to feel newly empowered. Dickens remains the most adapted author of all time for the screen, but this broader appeal has not been replicated, in terms of numbers of participants, by internet ventures, particularly those which have 'grass roots'. The most successful Dickensian populist projects, in terms of reaching 'crowds' of people, have benefited from 'top down' infrastructure or finance. Nonetheless, the internet has allowed smaller groups to revel in their sense of autonomous or (literally) ec-centric worldbuilding, rejecting the tyranny of numbers which associates value with larger cultural impact.

The literary club has always defied the logic that numbers equate to cultural influence in the industrial era, and its relationship to crowds both actual and imagined is a topic largely neglected by both literary studies and new media theory. Where there has been impactful new thinking on the effect of the internet in facilitating new political groups (including terrorists) and on the ways in which a new digital 'ecology' has been hijacked not simply to spread 'fake news' but to destabilize the authority of any news, the concept

---

[3] Claire Wood's paper, 'Making the Bicentenary Count', at the BAVS 2013 annual conference at Royal Holloway, outlined the difficulties of her postdoctoral work 'mapping' global bicentenary activity. This research was funded by the AHRC Cultural Engagement Fund and the Archives and Records Association.
[4] In Linda Hutcheon and Siobhan O'Flynn, *A Theory of Adaptation*, 2nd edn (London: Routledge, 2013), xiii–xviii (xiii).
[5] I am grateful to Bob Patten for suggesting the title of this chapter.

of the literary club has understandably seemed less urgent.[6] This neglect is symptomatic of a larger neglect of the effect of the internet on the literary marketplace, whose clubs are not necessarily counter- or sub-cultural, and whose members consist of a relatively small pool. However, the fact that online literary culture is of relatively little interest to politicians and corporations can enable literary groups or clubs to experience affective empowerment through what we could call micro-worldbuilding, specifically because of their seeming irrelevance to modern culture. Moreover, the affective and communicative ecosystem which underpins the 'worldbuilding' function of canonical global literature can tell us a great deal about modern myth-making.

This chapter seeks to shed light on the ways in which the concepts of crowds and clubs function dialogically in the industrial and digital eras to generate and sustain a process of cultural worldbuilding. Whereas in the early days of mass culture, for example, Dickens's utopian impulse was to generate a crowd of readers through shared fantasies of cultural belonging, as mass culture has become both more global and more diverse in an internet era, Dickens internet groups project fantasies of themselves as a crowd before celebrating their literal ec-centricity to a culture dominated by numbers. The cultural confidence of canonical literary groups does not stem simply from a fringe mentality, however: theirs is an ephemerality rooted in a sense of relation to cultural myths that have affected crowds of people across space and time. In this respect, numbers mark time and not just the market.

Sourcing Dickensian Crowds

The yoking together of the idea of Dickens and the idea of 'crowdsourcing' has become familiar in recent years in Dickens studies, where a congruence is often assumed between Dickens's optimistic vision of an inclusive popular culture and the technological possibilities of the internet. Dickens believed that popular culture enabled connection (and connection to Dickens), as the famous 'Preliminary Word' to *Household Words* puts it, between 'many thousands of people, of both sexes, and of all ages and conditions, on whose faces we may never look ... to bring the greater and the lesser in degree, together, ... and mutually dispose them to a better acquaintance and a kinder understanding'.[7] Enthusiasts for crowdsourcing—or for internet projects which are dependent on the labour or cooperation of large numbers of the public—see it as a potential means

---

[6] See Carol Cadwalladr's *Observer* article 'Google, Democracy and the Truth about Internet Search' (4 December 2016), <https://www.theguardian.com/technology/2016/dec/04/google-democracy-truth-internet-search-facebook> (last accessed 29 May 2017) based on Jonathan Albright's research and Katharine Viner's A. N. Smith lecture, 'The Rise of the Reader: Journalism in the Age of the Open Web' (9 October 2013), <https://www.theguardian.com/commentisfree/2013/oct/09/the-rise-of-the-reader-katharine-viner-an-smith-lecture> (last accessed 29 May 2017).

[7] 1 (30 March 1850): 1.

of empowering people outside the machinery of money or power, of enabling a new populism, a way of bypassing the labyrinthine structures of the global culture industry. Dickensians have embraced the idea of crowdsourcing, and more broadly the internet, as enabling the inclusive relations between academic and/or literary culture and the general public which Dickens himself envisaged. In her excellent article in the journal *19*, for example, reflecting on the *Our Mutual Friend* Dickensian Twitter experiment at Birkbeck, Emma Curry explains that the project facilitated a kind of crowdsourced close reading (close tweeting, perhaps), by creating a shared 'creative space in which readers can collate, discuss, and imaginatively respond to a multiplicity of perspectives on the novel's plot, structure, and characterization'.[8] In 2016, the *Placing Literature* 'crowd-sourcing project', which aimed 'to plot every novel, short story and poem in the world that takes place in real locations', added a Dickens collection, run by the Dickens Society. The site's explanation of its decision to devolve direction of Dickens activity to the Society must win the award for the number of times the term 'crowdsourcing' and its derivatives can be used in a brief project description: 'I guess you'd call the group effort a kind of crowdsourced, crowd-sourced project. Although, some contributors are sharing responsibility for mapping specific novels–which would be crowdsourcing a crowdsourcing of a crowd-sourced project.' No wonder the writer's 'head hurts'.[9] Writing ostensibly on the *Our Mutual Friend* and University of Leicester *Tale of Two Cities* on-line reading projects, Ben Winyard claims that 'reading the Dickensian serial digitally can be seen as giving life to Dickens's vision of the radical communality of reading' but reserves the idea of crowdsourcing for *Dickens Journals Online* (*DJO*), described as a 'crowdsourced text-correcting project'.[10] An interview in the *Daily Mail* with Dickensian Pete Orford to publicize his website, *The Drood Enquiry*, was entitled 'A very modern ending for Dickens' final unfinished work as academics turn to crowd-sourcing to complete *The Mystery Of Edwin Drood*'.[11] *The Drood Enquiry*'s website appeals directly to 'the public' to help solve the mystery of Edwin Drood.[12] James Mussell sums up the groundswell of optimism about the cultural potential of digital technology in his foreword on 'Social Media' to the *Journal of Victorian Culture*'s 'Digital Forum'. Social media, Mussell posits, 'represent an important opportunity to engage with audiences for academic

---

[8] Emma Curry, 'Doing the Novel in Different Voices: Reflections on a Dickensian Twitter Experiment', *19: Interdisciplinary Studies in the Long Nineteenth Century*, 21 (2015), <http://www.19.bbk.ac.uk/articles/10.16995/ntn.736/> (last accessed 10 July 2016]).

[9] *Placing Literature: Where Your Book Meets the Map*, <https://placingliterature.wordpress.com/2016/04/04/new-dickens-collection-in-progress/> (last accessed 2 September 2016).

[10] Winyard, '"May We Meet Again": Rereading the Dickensian Serial in the Digital Age', *19: Interdisciplinary Studies in the Long Nineteenth Century* 21 (2015), <http://www.19.bbk.ac.uk/articles/10.16995/ntn.736>/ (last accessed 2 September 2016).

[11] (5 January 2015), <http://www.dailymail.co.uk/news/article-2897308/A-modern-ending-Dickens-final-unfinished-work-academics-turn-crowd-sourcing-complete-Mystery-Edwin-Drood.html#ixzz4DA35mZdf> (last accessed 10 July 2016).

[12] <http://www.droodinquiry.com/home> (last accessed 10 July 2016).

research. These might be existing audiences, or new audiences beyond the academy'. He reasons optimistically that:

> As the essence of most social media is interaction, these resources allow audiences to become collaborators, active participants in ongoing research. These modes of communication have their own discourses, and social media platforms have been embraced as a way of breaking down academic hierarchies or divisions between those within a particular group and those hitherto excluded.[13]

Mussell tempers this optimism with an acknowledgement that 'such interactions are sometimes viewed with suspicion', citing the saying: ' "If you're not paying for it, you're the product" '. Elsewhere, he has written of the ways in which Facebook 'markets mutuality'.[14] This tension between an optimistic view of popular culture which believes in its potential to undermine hierarchies and a more negative view which sees this as an impossibility in the context of global capitalism has of course been central to debates and theories of popular culture since Adorno's demolition of *The Culture Industry* and the advent of Cultural Studies.[15] Dickens's hopeful vision of popular culture has seemed naive in the context of the dominant chorus of post-Victorian voices arguing for the necessary entrapment of popular culture in today's developed global cash nexus. The internet has not fundamentally changed the contours of debate about the political possibilities of popular culture, but it has perhaps enabled a debate to continue, offering glimmers of hope for those who continue to want to believe in the power of grassroots and popular movements as well as in the ability of the internet to facilitate what Dickens called 'connexion' and community.

Crowdsourcing is not, however, in its origins a 'grassroots' or 'bottom up' phenomenon. The term—let alone the practice—is more semantically slippery than its popular usage, particularly in Dickens studies, can acknowledge. The *OED*, which added the term as recently as 2013, defines crowdsourcing as 'The practice of obtaining information or services by soliciting input from a large number of people, typically via the Internet and often without offering compensation.' It attributes its first use to Jeff Howe, writing in *Wired* magazine in June 2006: 'The rise of crowdsourcing ... Smart companies in industries as disparate as pharmaceuticals and television discover ways to tap the latent talent of the crowd ... It's not outsourcing; it's crowdsourcing.'[16] According

---

[13] 'Digital Forum: Social Media', *Journal of Victorian Culture* 17, 3 (2012): 347.
[14] ' "Scarers in Print": Media Literacy from *Our Mutual Friend* to Friend Me on *Facebook*', *Gramma* 21 (2013): 163–78 (174).
[15] See Theodor W. Adorno and Max Horkheimer, 'The Culture Industry: Enlightenment as Mass Deception', in *Dialectic of Enlightenment*, trans. John Cumming (1944; London: Verso, 1979), 120–67. A collection of Adorno's essays on 'the culture industry', including a reappraisal of the earlier essay of that name, is available as *The Culture Industry: Selected Essays on Mass Culture*, ed. J. M. Bernstein (London: Routledge, 1991).
[16] (179:1) <http://www.oed.com.ezproxy01.rhul.ac.uk/view/Entry/376403?redirectedFrom=crowdsourcing#eid> (last accessed 2 September 2016). The original article, 'The Rise of Crowdsourcing' (1 June 2006) can be found at <http://www.wired.com/2006/06/crowds/> (last accessed 2 September 2016).

to this definition, the crowd is more resource than source (in the sense of originator or agent); it is subject to sourcing rather than generative of it. While the idea that members of a crowd might contribute their labour voluntarily (with or without payment) to help with a larger project from one perspective lends itself to utopian ideas of community and mutual generosity that go beyond the cash nexus, from another, it raises fears of exploitation, of paternalism, and of a Victorian reliance on a politically problematic 'charity'. 'Crowdfunding', a subspecies of crowdsourcing which invites members of the public to donate money to assist with a larger task, perhaps magnifies the paradoxes and contradictions that attend crowdsourcing. It seems likely that the Arts and Humanities will be increasingly reliant on such forms of labour and funding in an age of austerity and utility—indeed *DJO* encourages financial donations. However, the debates surrounding both crowdsourcing and crowdfunding make clear the difficulty of establishing the unfettered mutuality that Dickens sought when he wrote of bringing 'many thousands of people... to a better acquaintance and a kinder understanding'.

It is perhaps easier to establish that the acts of communal kindness attempted by Dickensian crowdsourcing internet ventures are propelled by generous and un-commercial impulses, than that they are properly communal. The research for this chapter has taken me to many Dickens internet sites. The V&A's 'Deciphering Dickens' 'crowdsourced' manuscript project, led by Bill Sherman and John Bowen, is typical of the 'uncommercial' model underpinning many of these ventures, in that it asks the public to donate free labour and the enterprise is not for profit.[17] But none of these ventures is profit-driven—even the biggest, *Dickens Journals Online*, asks the public for labour and voluntary subscriptions simply to fund the remarkable work of the very small inhouse team in allowing free online access to Dickens's journalism to a global audience. Though the idea of a 'gift economy', functioning as 'an alternative regime to capitalism', is fraught with difficulty, literary crowdsourcing projects lend the concept more validity than fan studies, its original home within Cultural Studies.[18]

The notion that Dickensian crowdsourcing projects garner 'crowds' in the sense of numerous members of the public, however, seems more difficult to verify than their uncommercialism. When we turn our attention to the size and composition of Dickens online 'communities', interviews with the orchestrators of some of the most high-profile Dickensian online group ventures suggest that there is more distance between Dickens's desire to use his writings to bring together a crowd (in the sense of a large number) of people from diverse backgrounds and the reality today. Emma Curry reports of the *Our Mutual Friend* reading project that there were just two tweeters who did not have

---

[17] <https://www.vam.ac.uk/info/deciphering-dickens> (last accessed 30 May 2017).

[18] See Roberta Pearson's discussion of 'the gift economy' in 'Fandom in the Digital Era', *Popular Communication* 8 (2010): 84–95 (87). She traces its origins to Lewis Hyde's anthropological study *The Gift: Imagination and the Erotic Life of Property* (New York: Random House, 1983) and offers Suzanne Scott's article 'Repackaging Fan Culture: The Regifting Economy of Ancillary Content Models' as an example of scholarship promoting the idea—see Scott, *Transformative Works and Cultures* 3 (2009), <http://journal.transformativeworks.org/index.php/twc/article/view/150/122> (last accessed 6 October 2016).

any connection with academia—the person who played Mrs Boffin, who found out about the project through Twitter; and the person who was planning to play the Man in the Moon, who worked for NASA at the Jet Propulsion Lab (but did not in the end tweet). 'Other than that', she concludes, 'everyone was connected to a university in some way, and all the blog posts were contributed by academics' (Emma Curry, email interview, 21 June 2016). There was a degree of disappointment that the project facilitated less public engagement than envisaged. Ben Winyard elaborates: 'We had very little interaction with the *OMF* blog in terms of people writing comments (fewer than 40 comments across the entire 18-month project), while the very small number of people who did comment were almost all academics or graduate students.' There was, however, 'definitely more public interaction with the *TOTC* blog, although, again, the vast majority of those people were academics or grad students', with three key 'non-academic contributors' (Ben Winyard on the Leicester *Tale of Two Cities* and Birkbeck *Our Mutual Friend* Reading Projects, email interview, 22 June 2016). Similarly, Claire Wood reports of the *Placing the Author* postcard project that 'although the definition of academic/non-academic isn't clear cut', the participants could broadly be categorized as follows:

- Undergraduate students: 8
- Postgraduates, postdocs, and academics: 17
- Speakers (a mix of Ph.D.s, ECRs and academics: 8
- Non-academics: 3
- Total: 36

Though there were only two Dickensian participants (one academic and one non-academic), once again expectations of non-academic reach were disappointed, 'in part', Wood argues,

> due to limited resource—there wasn't any funding to do paper-based marketing for the Postcard Project, so we relied on using Twitter and various online mailing lists to publicise the project. Our team of 3 conference organisers and 3 undergraduate assistants then took it in turns to upload the postcards (essentially working for free).
>
> With a bit more money we'd have sent postcard-leaflets to a variety of tourist sites, which I think would have helped in terms of building our non-academic audience. (Claire Wood, email interview, 1 July 2016)

Wood's sense that greater resource and the capacity to use paper-based media would have allowed for an increase in non-academic involvement confirms a pattern evident elsewhere. Perhaps the most successful 'crowdsourced' Dickens project in terms of both its academic and non-academic influence has been the *Dickens Journals Online* project, which recruited about 1,000 volunteers to its text-correcting project, mostly non-academic, and has received approximately 1.4 million page views. What is interesting is not only that the relatively high profile of this venture had a knock-on effect on interest in the *Tale of Two Cities* reading project, according to Winyard, but that the recruitment of large numbers of public volunteers on *DJO* was in no small part enabled by an article in the 'old' media. In 2011, a piece in *The Guardian* by the Director of *DJO* John Drew, 'Calling All Dickens Detectives', asked, 'Can you help?' announcing that 'No qualifications are needed to become a *DJO* online editor.'[19] Again, Pete Orford who runs *The Drood Enquiry* website claims a degree of non-academic involvement in the reading project on *Drood*, with contributors 'both commenting and following' and 25,000 visitors attending the Dickens museum exhibition, partly attracted by the website and publicity surrounding it. The projects were no doubt also given a boost by the January 2015 article about the project in the *Daily Mail*. Though many readers 'consume' their newspapers online today, the brands (and consequent readership) of the *Daily Mail* and the *Guardian* have been built up over many years, and draw on a print history and professional infrastructure pre-dating the internet.

Whereas it is commonplace among Dickens internet enthusiasts, therefore, to herald the internet as offering a new, alternative means to attempt to realize Dickens's utopian ideal of cultural community, the truth is that we live in an inter-medial age in which old and new media are mutually entangled, and in which resource and infrastructure are required to generate as well as to sustain any 'crowd' of non-academic participants. The success of *Dickens Journals Online* was interestingly sustained not only by mainstream press publicity, but by the generosity of the Leverhulme Trust, a British research charity founded by the Victorian industrialist William Hesketh Lever (whose profits from the mass market funded his paternalism). This funding helped to sustain an inhouse team that 'mediated' volunteer involvement. As its Director John Drew explains:

> it was hugely important that Hazel [Mackenzie] and Ben Winyard were working as Leverhulme-funded post-docs on the project; ... their ability to respond to volunteers' e-mails within hours and often minutes, was crucial to the success of the enterprise... We also needed to engage 'supervolunteers' (who had proved their skills, accuracy & commitment) to help monitor the work of new volunteers:—but it was an important finding of the project that volunteers should not be enabled to talk to one another directly about their work/its quality, but that this should *always* be mediated—with great tact—via the project team.
>
> (Email interview, 1 July 2016)

Dickensian public engagement projects that have been able to draw a (numerous) crowd have thus depended on a top down infrastructure, even if it taps into a pre-existing popular interest in Dickens. In other words, the crowd has to be created, in the first instance at least, before it can become creative. Thus the *Placing Literature* website, which has garnered 3,656 contributions to date, was founded by a writer and a doctoral student, and funding originated from the Connecticut Department of Economic

---

[19] (4 August 2011), <https://www.theguardian.com/books/booksblog/2011/aug/04/charles-dickens-journals-online-project> (last accessed 10 July 2016). The online article followed a letter published in the newspaper two days earlier.

Development, Connecticut Office of the Arts. Dickens activity on the site is propelled by Emily Bell, a committed postdoctoral student from the University of York researching Dickens's afterlives and representing the international membership of the Dickens Society.[20] The 'City Reads' projects in London and Portsmouth were sponsored by their respective city councils, enabling the London *Oliver Twist* read to reach 12,000 Facebook active participants. The British Council's remarkable Bicentenary programme successfully staged a Global Read-a-thon, in which on Dickens's birthday, readers of Dickens all over the world were filmed reading their favourite passages from his novels, and a *Sketching the City* writing project, through which teenagers and high school children in global cities were encouraged to write contemporary sketches of their own cities which were inspired by *Sketches by Boz*. Similarly, Punchdrunk Enrichment and the Arcola Theatre took theatre into four international cities (Melbourne, Singapore, Penang, and Karachi). These were just some of the strands to a large-scale global programme of diverse cultural activity. Its success can be evidenced in qualitative as well as quantitative terms. The British Council's own evaluation report contains a great deal of evidence of the transformative nature of its activities on individuals and some startling statistics: its Read-a-thon, for example, involved 2 million participants, 208 events were held across 68 countries with an audience reach of 92 million people worldwide, and the estimate of its potential international press audience was 60,384,462.[21]

Such a programme was clearly not possible without a serious level of planning, coordination, and investment, not just from the British Council but between the Council and its many partners, including, in Britain, Film London, the BFI, the Charles Dickens Museum, Penguin, Arcola Theatre, Punchdrunk Enrichment, and London and Portsmouth Councils. International partners included Penguin India, the Bronx Museum, the National Academy of Performing Arts (Pakistan), the Ministry of Education and Culture (Azerbaijan), School of the Arts (Singapore), and the National Play Writing Festival (Australia). 'Many of these partnerships', according to the British Council report, have continued (5). The reach of the British Council's global directive crowdsourcing realized Dickens's international vision for his writing to reach 'every nation upon earth', shaping the crowd into a community.[22] The Council is an established charity which is sponsored by the British Foreign and Commonwealth Office. Its mission to 'create the basis of friendly knowledge and understanding between the people of the UK and the wider world' has much in common with Dickens's own aspirations.[23] As the British Council also aims to promote British work in education and the arts, however, its activities, like those of Dickens—or any national cultural body which aims to shape international opinion—could also be subject

---

[20] (Accessed 5 October 2016.) The website was set up by Andrew Bardin Williams and Kathleen C. Williams.

[21] '*Reinventing Heritage*: Evaluation Report', 16, 14. Privately circulated. Subsequent references are inserted parenthetically in the text by page number.

[22] Dickens, 'A Preliminary Word', *Household Words*, 1.

[23] <https://www.britishcouncil.org/arts/about> (last accessed 5 October 2016).

to the suspicions of cultural imperialism which tend to shadow orchestrated international cultural activity.

One community-building international Dickens project which was celebrated in the press is the first production of *Oliver!* in Arabic in the summer of 2015 in Amman, which brought together about 100 Syrian and Jordanian children. The project is intended as 'a bridge between Syrian and Jordanian communities' and to ease tensions arising from the large influx of Syrian refugees. The team behind it comprised a British couple, Charlotte Eager (a film producer and former journalist) and William Stirling (a scriptwriter), and their co-producer, Georgie Page. Though the team was not the first to see parallels between Dickens's London and developing cities today and the idea of *Oliver!* as a community-building text is also hardly new, the novelty of the Amman production was its focus on breaking down barriers between different communities. Eager explains: 'They were shy and nervous six months ago—they stood on opposite sides of the room… These were kids who had lost everything. Some of their school friends had been killed. Their relatives are scattered in Turkey, Lebanon, and Germany. But *Oliver!* has created a whole new community. They say: "We're the Oliver! family now".[24]

This was not, however, a grassroots project. Stirling needed, and won, the backing of Cameron Mackintosh, who controls most of the show's stage rights, before the show could take shape. Although, according to its producers, this was the first Arabic production of *Oliver!*, the project was the brainchild of an all-British team who recruited 'top Arab talent to steer the show'.[25] These were Egyptian, rather than Jordanian and Syrian, their links to UNICEF, Disney, and the Egyptian media bringing considerable external cultural capital to the enterprise. In an article on the project for *Newsweek*, Eager is open about the project's dependence on what she specifically calls 'patronage': 'the production was under the patronage of Jordan's Queen Rania' and 'the Jordanian business and diplomatic communities paid for much of the production'. The production which had started in a community centre in a poor area ended up 'grander' than Eager had expected, taking place in Amman's Royal Cultural Centre.[26]

What is interesting is that despite Eager's clarity about the fusion of patronage, privilege, and grassroots enthusiasm which allowed the production to happen, the English-language press coverage presented it as a nostalgic fairy tale of benign British cultural paternalism crystallizing local enthusiasm in a venture propelled mainly by goodwill. Even the left-leaning UK newspaper *The Guardian* omits any mention of the multiple layers of Arab patronage underpinning the show.[27] The project was in fact a paternalistic

---

[24] Mark Tran, 'Oliver! with a twist: musical swaps Dickensian London for modern Amman', *The Guardian* (24 August 2015), <https://www.theguardian.com/world/2015/aug/24/oliver-musical-london-modern-amman-syria-refugees-jordan> (last accessed 5 September 2016).
[25] Ibid.
[26] Charlotte Eager, 'Teaching "Oliver!" to the Children of Syrian Refugees in Jordan', *Newsweek* (8 September 2015) <http://europe.newsweek.com/teaching-oliver-syrian-refugees-332657?rm=eu> (last accessed 5 September 2016).
[27] Only articles by Eager herself in *Newsweek* and *The Financial Times* seem to give a full account of the production—Charlotte Eager, 'The first Arabic production of "Oliver!"', *Financial Times* (2 October

variant of what media theorist Henry Jenkins calls 'convergence culture', where 'bottom up' and 'top down' forces coalesce in cultural production.[28]

The idea that Dickens can forge affective community and social inclusivity is key, not just to the coverage of this Arabic production of *Oliver!*, but to the broader portability of the Dickens brand. The front cover of the British Council's Dickens 2012 Evaluative Report (significantly entitled *Re-Inventing Heritage*) declares its intention 'to re-think and re-interpret the figure whose global appeal spans across people, places and fiction' (1). The Council's bicentenary emphasis on 'how a writer can have an influence on social justice and reform' is typical of many modern remediations of the idea of Dickens and his works. Most do not engage in specifics about Dickens's politics or Victorian legislation but focus on his empathy for the dispossessed and moral disapproval of their social neglect. The major exhibition of the bicentenary year, for example, was the Museum of London's *Dickens and London* exhibition. In *Fulfilled Expectations*, its 'Summative evaluation of *Dickens and London* at the Museum of London' (May 2012),[29] one of the main 'outcomes of the visit' was in the area of what the report calls 'Moral impact': 'Many visitors left the exhibition struck by Dickens' sense of social justice', it concludes, citing one who realized that 'He really cared about the poor and had some very strong moral views' (Vox pop; *Fulfilled Expectations*, 12).

The Museum of London's summative report is measured, however, in evaluating the complex nature of the exhibition's undoubted success: it attracted large numbers of visitors (just under 100,000), to the extent that it was literally 'crowded at times';[30] but 'visitors with less existing knowledge struggled to engage fully' (6). Strikingly, 74 per cent of visitors were 'intellectually motivated'. 'The Amusements of the People' section, dedicated to Dickens's commitment to popular culture, along with the section on 'Dickens and the Modern Age' were relatively unsuccessful, whereas the section on 'Home and Hearth' attracted a 'relatively large number' of visitors (24-7). A 'star exhibit' was his writing desk, attracting 65 per cent of visitors. It is tempting to conclude from this that visitors sought a conventional image of Dickens with which they were already familiar, one which fossilized associations between Dickens and domesticity as well as of authorship. However, a curious fact is that Dickens's manuscripts were 'overlooked by visitors' (45); staggeringly, 'no visitors' were 'observed engaging deeply with the *David Copperfield* manuscript', for example. Moreover, one of the more successful exhibits was William Raban's documentary film of contemporary London, *The Houseless Shadow*, voiced over by an actor reading Dickens's 'Night Walks' (28–9).

2015), <http://www.ft.com/cms/s/2/007396b6-681d-11e5-a57f-21b88f7d973f.html#axzz4JOmR9Tsp> (last accessed 5 September 2016).

[28] Jenkins, *Convergence Culture: Where Old and New Media Collide* (New York: NYU Press, 2008).
[29] Privately circulated. Subsequent references are inserted parenthetically in the text by page number.
[30] The number of 100,000 is cited by Joanna Robinson, 'Digitalizing Dickens: Adapting Dickens for the Bicentenary', *Dickens Quarterly* 31 (2014): 42–61 (50), quoting from an email that the exhibition curator Alex Werner had written her on 18 October 2013.

One of the Curator's aims was that 'visitors would after visiting the exhibition read a Dickens work rather than just view one of the latest TV adaptations'.[31] It is notable that 'Night Walks' itself, along with 'classics like *Oliver Twist* and *Great Expectations*', were the main sellers (books 'selling out on a daily basis'), a fact which suggests that a certain cultural idea of Dickens—whether taken from a documentary or from the circulatory adaptive context of post-Victorian mass culture—is as important in shaping interest in him as the range of his novels. Joanna Robinson in fact goes as far as to suggest in her analysis of the bicentenary that 'creative reimagining' of Dickens's work 'through adaptation' was more important than the texts themselves: 'interpretations of the novels came to count for more than the original texts'.[32] She deconstructs the 'relevance' rationale often given for modern remediations of Dickens to argue that relevance is a construct rather than a quality of the texts themselves. Whilst the fact that none of Dickens's novels has ever been out of print should perhaps soften the idea that the texts themselves are entirely without relevance, it is true that the texts themselves are far from the sole driver of the posthumous Dickens industry. It is notable that the 'Charles Dickens Fan Club' site, for example, is populated by images, videos, polls, a Charles Dickens wall, 'wallpapers, 'icons', a quiz, and a forum—there is very little on the actual novels. The site is significantly dedicated to 'His Work and his World', and though it boasted only 1,588 fans at the time of this research, its focus on a multi-media Dickens 'world' typifies the metamorphic energies of today's Dickensian afterlives. The 'dark Dickens' app developed by Robinson for the Bicentenary, for example, is just one of 145 Dickens apps available via the app store as this chapter goes to press, many but not all of which are versions of his texts.

Clare Parody uses the term 'worldbuilding' to describe the ways in which successful media franchises, like the Harry Potter franchise, use electronic products alongside books to allow readers, consumers, and fans to engage with a 'world' generated through the text-product circulation.[33] The Dickens 'world' differs from the franchises which have sprung up in the new media era in that it has evolved over time rather than been generated by a guiding corporation or living authors. While this is true and dilutes or disperses the profits of the Dickens industry, this does not amount to what Robinson calls 'the lack of a definite "Dickens" brand'.[34] The combination of strength and flexibility in Dickens's 'brand' has allowed it to sustain Dickens's central position in the global cultural consciousness. The brand is not 'definite' only in the sense that it is not owned by one company. It was masterminded, as I argued in *Dickens and Mass Culture*, by Dickens himself, through his intuitive understanding of the importance of 'worldbuilding' to the cultural consciousness through the portability of his characters, his engagement with all the adaptive media at his disposal, and his intuition of the visual technologies of the future (film, photography). Thus when people respond to Dickens today, they

---

[31] Robinson, 'Digitalizing Dickens', 56 n. 5, citing Werner's email of 18 October 2013.
[32] Ibid., 45.
[33] Parody, 'Franchising/Adaptation', *Adaptation* 4 (2011): 210–18 (212).
[34] Robinson, 'Digitalizing Dickens', 49.

are responding not just to Dickens's texts but to a sense of a Dickens world which has been built up over time and across media. It is in this intersection between time and the market that cultural traditions evolve and grow.

From Crowds to Clubs: Eccentricity, Worldbuilding, and the Literary in the Digital Age

This chapter has in part sought to temper the general optimism which has regularly seemed to suggest that digital media can enable crowdsourced Dickens projects to achieve Dickens's own utopian vision of a cultural community which is sociologically inclusive and empowering to large numbers of 'the people'. It functions partly to soften the seductive enthusiasm of the wave of new media theorists who celebrate the internet as inaugurating, in the words of Linda Hutcheon, 'a major democratizing shift in media production'.[35] I am not alone in urging caution as new media studies has moved beyond either blanket optimism or pessimism about the possibilities for popular culture in an internet age, scholars like Matt Hills, Roberta Pearson, and James Bennett, to name just a few, refining binary ways of thinking about the political and commercial synergies of the new media landscape.[36] The media analytics work on the news of scholars like Jonathan Albright, as I have mentioned, is in the vanguard of research into the ways in which the internet complicates received models of power dynamics.

However, there is a relative scarcity of significant work on literary and historical cultures and their modern afterlives in the digital age. Fandom and celebrity studies have been in the vanguard of attempts to reconfigure our understanding of modern cultural formations and the role of the popular therein, pioneering concepts like the 'acafan' (academic who celebrates their fandom in their academic work), the 'fan-scholar' (who brings critical theory to his/her fandom), and the prosumer (cultural consumer who also produces, for example, the fan). While both fields have a great deal to offer Dickens studies, Dickens studies can return the favour. And offer some challenges, a small number of which I will touch on here.

Fan and celebrity studies are not naive about the fact that both fandom and celebrity pre-date the digital as well as the screen age. But nonetheless, the focus of both fields is overwhelmingly on the twentieth and twenty-first centuries and there are very few studies, if any, that trace either concept through vastly different periods, with different

---

[35] Preface to the 2nd edition, *A Theory of Adaptation*, xxv.
[36] See, for example, Matt Hills, *Fan Cultures* (London: Routledge, 2002); Roberta Pearson, 'Fandom in the Digital Era'; James Bennett, ' "Get Internet Famous! (Even if you're Nobody)": Multiplatform Fame and the Television Personality System in the Digital Era', in his *Television Personalities: Stardom and the Small Screen* (London: Routledge, 2011), 168–89.

underpinning structures of communication and finance. My own *Dickens and Mass Culture*, for example, while exploring Dickens's relations with mass culture from his own time to the present day, deliberately marginalized new media. The reason for this was that I did not believe when that book went to press in 2009 that new media had been a major vehicle of Dickens's 'mass' popularity. In terms of numbers, television, film, and print cultures were (and remain) the main vehicles of Dickens's engagement with large numbers of people. In the numbers game, as I have argued in this chapter, the internet enables large numbers of people to engage with Dickens mainly when the mechanism is intermedial (e.g. the British Council's Readathon) and when the project is supported by 'top down' infrastructure. The backing of Dickens internet projects tends to come from what might be best termed patronage, as opposed to the commercial conglomerates that back major screen and publishing production. New media theory assumes that 'top down' forces in digital production are more nakedly those of the capitalist culture industry which Adorno so despised and has given far less attention to the charitable infrastructure, no less complex and problematic as Victorianists will be aware, which can attend the digital transmission of literary culture.

The oddity about literary culture in the twenty-first century is that it can be global, pervasive, and culturally prominent without affecting the numbers of people associated with, for example, popular international television franchises like *The X Factor* or *Keeping Up with the Kardashians*. It is more persistent and residual than prominent in today's global mass cultural landscape. Dickens creates particular challenges for media theory: the first self-made media celebrity of the mass cultural era, as I have argued elsewhere, famous enough in his own time for fights to break out in the streets over tickets to see him, and remaining famous enough since his death to adorn the £10 note for a decade in the 1990s. The paradox about this most famous of authors, however, is that though his celebrity is undiminished, the internet is not in fact awash with Dickens fans (as evidenced by the relatively small number of self-declared Dickens fans signed up to the Dickens fan club website); here, the bookish ground is ceded to fans of Harry Potter and Sci-Fi.[37]

This is partly because Dickens's enduring fame has made him respectable, of course, and seemingly adrift from the mass culture he helped to create. Dickens still affects large numbers through book sales, TV, and film adaptations (he remains the most adapted author for the screen of all time), but grassroots and 'fan' activity is numerically limited. There are more reasons for this than the restrictions of this chapter will let me explore, but if new media alone has not in fact led to radically new crowds of people engaging with Dickens nor to fundamentally new hierarchies in the literary cultural sphere, this does not mean, however, that its populist possibilities have been chimeric. While digital Dickens has not on its own given us new crowds, or restored a sense of the crowd as source, it has given us new groups or even new clubs—small, localized special interest

---

[37] Sherlock Holmes is also a significant and interesting nineteenth-century presence though fan attention centres on the BBC's modern *Sherlock* series and its transmedia spin-offs.

groups who are able to build their own 'world' through their interest in Dickens and to delight in the literal ec-centricity of that world. The exuberant pleasure of the *Our Mutual Friend* tweeters and bloggers as they revelled in their parts, for example, clearly bred a sense of empowerment and autonomy enabled by the electronic media and magnified by an awareness of the project's position outside the cultural or commercial mainstream. This building of community is an important form of worldbuilding which taps into the mass intermedial environment whilst defining itself as proud to be small, marginal, and uncommercial.

Cultural dynamics have evolved so much since the early nineteenth century, when small literary groups could exert major cultural influence, that online literary communities today can embrace their 'special interest' status whilst celebrating inclusivity: simply put, online literary clubs are inevitably inclusive rather than exclusive because relatively few people want to belong to 'ec-centric' groups. Dickensian groups are thus typical in that they are often run by people who could be seen as elite—often but not always academics—because of the 'cultural capital' they possess, but are in fact open to all comers and conscious of their own lack of greater market 'relevance' or 'impact'. The dynamics here offer a paternalistic variant of the pattern observed by Jenkins in relation to the co-option of participatory online activity by commodity culture: though conceding that grassroots agency is thereby appropriated, he notes that nonetheless the alliance of the corporate and the participatory 'can also increase the diversity of media culture, prompting opportunities for greater inclusiveness'.[38] The fact that 'the opportunities for greater inclusiveness' created by Dickens special interest groups are not always seized by large numbers of the public engenders not a feeling of failure but a festive, even carnivalesque sense of communal identity among group members. This is not principally because these groups offer a Dickensian version of what Richard Burt calls 'Scholckspeare' (or 'mass-media driven ephemera of the trivial and discardable'),[39] though there can be some of this; but the carnivalesque of the new Dickensian club comes from a celebratory sense of autonomous worldbuilding which rejects the tyranny of numbers and the cultural logic which associates value with its larger (in its literal sense) impact.

Such clubs are not confined to the internet of course, but the internet now allows us to participate vicariously in the joys of the manifold activities of the local Dickensian group. Claire Wood's research on bicentenary activity brought many community and 'grassroots' projects into focus, her favourite of which was 'the Pickwick Bicycle Club ride to the Birthplace Museum on historical cycles in Portsmouth' (Figure 49.1).[40] This photo sums up the point of the new Dickens club—wilfully oblivious to the presence of a multi-storey car park in the background, on a concrete tarmac built for many cars with

---

[38] 'Interactive Audiences', in *Henry Jenkins: Fans, Bloggers and Gamers: Exploring Participatory Culture* (New York: New York University Press, 2006), 134–51 (151).

[39] Richard Burt (ed.), *Shakespeare after Mass Media* (New York: Palgrave Macmillan, 2002), 'Introduction', 1–32 (15).

[40] I am grateful to Claire Wood for sharing this image with me in an email of 1 July 2016.

FIGURE 49.1 The Pickwick Bicycle Club's bicentenary ride to the Birthplace Museum on historical cycles in Portsmouth. Unidentified photographer.

Courtesy of the Pickwick Bicycle Club

its flagrant yellow '£6' sign demanding money for city space, the club parades its right to define its own world view and the persistence of individuality in a world of standardization. It presents a paradoxical parade of ephemerality rooted in longevity. It in fact asserts its right to override the mass cultural context, to supplant the power of the crowd with the will of the group. And yet I do not think this is necessarily nostalgic or elitist—the photograph symbolizes the collective belief in the singular energies of the eccentric and the right of such groups to celebrate their proudly minority status in an age of reproduction. The work of David Muggleton in 'post-subcultural studies' has urged us to rethink notions like 'sub-culture' and 'counter-culture' as outdated in a postmodern era, too reliant on monolithic concepts of culture and its others—not cognizant enough of fragmentation, flux, and fluidity in social structures.[41] The activities of the Pickwick Bicycle Club, like those of the tweeters, in most ways so different from those of the youth cultures that form Muggleton's subject, in other ways confirm and extend his critique of the ideas of sub- and counter-culture, offering fertile new scope for work on minority cultural groupings. Dickensian clubs do not position themselves against or outside mainstream culture, but rather create and celebrate their autonomous and self-defining

---

[41] See David Muggleton and Rupert Weinzieri (eds), *The Post-Subcultures Reader* (Oxford: Berg, 2003). This work follows up theoretical questions emerging from Muggleton's *Inside Subculture: The Postmodern Meaning of Style* (Oxford: Berg, 2002).

acts of worldbuilding. The participatory nature of the group is, in other words, born of a festive disregard of the social world which disregards it; the group does not ultimately define itself against other cultures but defines itself in terms of itself. This is perhaps more true of special interest literary groups than it is of youth movements. While today's Dickensian grassroots clubs have benefited from the technologies of the modern era and rely on the fragmentation and flux that Muggleton associates with postmodernism, they partake of the mood of the pre-industrial and pre-disciplinary era, promoting an attitude to identity and social structures that is as well described as 'picaresque' as postmodern (though the diverse terms share an interesting consonance).

There are of course class implications underpinning what I have been saying, as there are in the fact that so few lovers of Dickens seem keen to define themselves as 'fans'. To think in terms of picaresque worldbuilding can be a luxury afforded to those who have not had to experience the real-world effects of hierarchy and disempowerment; to celebrate autonomy and self-definition can be a symptom of the individualism traditionally associated with middle-class cultures. However, though there is no denying that Dickensian special interest groups today are resoundingly middle-class, in today's advanced if not decadent commodity culture, the relationship between class and cultural politics is hugely fraught. Many who actively broadcast their appreciation of Dickens seem happier to define themselves as 'enthusiasts' or 'lovers' of Dickens than 'fans'. This is indeed in large part a rejection of the mass cultural associations of fandom: what so many admire in Dickens is his 'worldbuilding' ability to capture individual essence and agency. Though fan studies has moved beyond the idea of a fan as subjugating him/herself to a mass grouping, there remain nonetheless connotations of dependent veneration and hierarchy about self-defining as a fan which is at odds with the eccentric ethos of the Dickensian. There is an analogy between the presence of the Dickens enthusiast in a mass cultural age and the presence and necessity of Dickens's minor characters in his novels: they reject secondariness, asserting a sense of primariness in their own worlds and thus exuding an autonomous aesthetic energy.[42]

Dickens's idea of mass culture did not accept a binary model of cultural relations and is indeed an anticipatory variant of Henry Jenkins's idea of 'convergence culture'. Nor did Dickens accept the synonymity of class and cultural politics. While he would have been dismayed by the idea that his future 'fan' base would turn out to be middle-class and wilfully marginal, his ability to appeal to large numbers of people has in fact been sustained by neither academics and cultural producers nor by 'fans'—more by the large numbers of the public who enjoy his stories, a largely middle-brow grouping which has been under-theorized in contemporary cultural theory. However much he sought to influence large numbers of people, his global ambitions did not preclude a delight in the local, the eccentric, and the communal. In fact, the health of the one depended on the other; just as Dickens's cultural theory and practice in many ways attempted to merge

---

[42] See Alex Woloch, *The One vs. the Many: Minor Characters and the Space of the Protagonist in the Novel* (Princeton: Princeton University Press, 2003).

the two, his longevity has depended on an ecosystem in which the club and the crowd depend on each other in fantasy as well as in reality. He would have delighted in the Pickwick Bicycle Club. The text which first made him a star was of course *The Pickwick Papers* (or properly titled, *The Posthumous Papers of the Pickwick Club* (1836–7)), a work which celebrated 'the club' and the random, undisciplined social structures which allowed for its picaresque goings-on. *The Pickwick Papers* looks fondly on the world of 'the just past', as Ruth Livesey has argued, as the world of the crowd looked poised to occlude the world of the club.[43] It is an example of ' "the strange mutability of human affairs" ',[44] in Mr Pickwick's words, and indeed of the strange mutability of the media, that the technological invention that is so often celebrated as empowering 'the crowd' has allowed for the carnivalesque resurgence of a new kind of club.

Further Reading

Carolyn Burdett and Hilary Fraser (eds), 'The Nineteenth-Century Digital Archive', *19: Interdisciplinary Studies in the Long Nineteenth Century* 21 (2015) <http://www.19.bbk.ac.uk/90/volume/2015/issue/21/>

Thomas Leitch (ed.), *The Oxford Handbook of Adaptation Studies* (Oxford: Oxford University Press, 2017)

Julie Sanders, *Adaptation and Appropriation*, 2nd edn, The New Critical Idiom (London: Routledge, 2016)

---

[43] *Writing the Stage Coach Nation: Locality on the Move in Nineteenth-Century British Literature* (Oxford: Oxford University Press, 2016).

[44] *Pickwick Papers*, ed. James Kinsley (Oxford: Clarendon Press, 1986), chapter 2, page 17.

Index

Note: Figures are indicated by an italic *f* following the page number. Footnotes are indicated by n. following the page number.

À Beckett, Gilbert 38, 92
Abercrombie, John 391–3
Ackroyd, Peter 11, 13–14, 157, 201n., 485
acting 676–7
  by CD 671–3, 679, 738
    missed audition 666, 738
actor-network theory 450
adaptations 738–55, 769
  Barnaby Rudge 734
  Bleak House 742–3, 749, 751
  CD's adaptations of Shakespeare 667
  Christmas Carol 171, 199, 734, 739–42, 746
  David Copperfield 734, 739, 742–3, 745–6
  film 277, 279–81, 732, 739–45, 747–9, 769
  global circulation 725, 732, 734–5
  graphic novels 734
  Great Expectations 276–7, 279–81, 732, 734, 739–45
  Little Dorrit 741–2
  Martin Chuzzlewit 744
  musical 740–2, 748, 750–2, 765
  Mystery of Edwin Drood 302–3, 309–10, 741–2
  new media 756–73
  Nicholas Nickleby 734, 741–3
  Old Curiosity Shop 742
  Oliver Twist 739–54
  Pickwick Papers 738, 741–3, 747
  radio 277, 280–1, 739–40, 744–6, 749, 751
  Tale of Two Cities 271–2, 675, 734, 739, 741–4, 746, 748
  television 177, 277, 281, 302–3, 664, 683, 739–43, 746, 751–4
  theatre 171–2, 302, 309, 668–9, 673–5, 738–41, 744–5, 747–51

Addison, Joseph 30, 86
Administrative Reform Association 245, 421–2, 432
Adorno, Theodor W. 315, 760, 769
  Old Curiosity Shop 135–6, 140–1, 147, 149, 151
Adrian, Arthur A. 330
Adshead, Joseph 425
adulthood 210
  David Copperfield 212–14
aesthetic autonomy 297
affect 468–83
  affective turn 471–4
  Barnaby Rudge 380–4
  CD's relationship to his own writing 375
  cognitive studies 618
  deathbed scenes 592
  domestic ideology 374, 377, 380–4
  emotions and ethics 474–6
  gender and sexuality 371
  public readings and performances 350
  sentiment and sensation 476–9
  transmission of 480–2
affect aliens 374–80
Africa 728–30
afterlives 740, 756
  global circulation 728
  journal articles and stories 331
  Martin Chuzzlewit 166, 171–5
  see also adaptations
Agamben, Giorgio 560
Agathocleous, Tanya 529
agreements
  vs contracts 126, 129
  Nicholas Nickleby 119–24, 131

INDEX

Aguirre, Robert 728n.
Ahmed, Sara 374, 377, 381
Ainsworth, Mary 622, 624
Ainsworth, William Harrison 37, 84n., 137, 155, 734
Alain 191
Albert, Prince 67, 81, 474
Albright, Jonathan 768
alcohol 597–612
Alcott, Louisa May, 'Dickens Day' 598
Alexander, George 670
Alexander, Sarah 229
allegory
   Bleak House 231
   David Copperfield 345
   Great Expectations 556
   Mystery of Edwin Drood 305
   Old Curiosity Shop 134–7, 141, 144, 150
   Oliver Twist 107, 117
   Pickwick Papers 98, 99
   Sketches by Boz 89
   Tale of Two Cities 525
   travel 313–17, 320–2
Allen, Michael 13–15
Allingham, Philip V. 269, 601
All the Year Round 325–31, 336
   CD as professional author 43, 46–7, 51–2
   CD as public figure 65, 66
   CD's reading 26n., 29n., 33n., 38, 38n., 40, 40n.
   children's literature 340–1
   Christmas Stories 200, 204–5
   digitization 40, 204
   Great Expectations 275–6
   'Harlequin Fairy Morgana!' 341
   industry and technology 444, 445, 449
   language 636–7, 638
   Mrs. Lirriper's Lodgings 47, 51, 204–5, 636–8
   'Mugby Junction' stories 200–2, 449
   'New Uncommercial Samples: Mr. Barlow' 26n., 29n.
   psychology 389, 393, 395
   religion 587
   science 404, 407, 411, 413, 416, 418
   'The Signal-Man' 201–2, 449, 471
   Tale of Two Cities 270, 490, 494
   and the theatre 670
   title 31
   'The Uncommercial Traveller' *see* 'Uncommercial Traveller, The'
Almar, George 747–8
Alter, Robert 267, 268
Altick, Richard D. 418
Amateurs, Company of 32, 40, 56, 67
amateur theatre, CD's participation in 666, 671–4
ambiguities, grammatical 631, 634–8, 641, 643–4
America *see* United States of America
American Notes for General Circulation
   Bridgman 397
   CD as public figure 73
   CD's reading 34, 36
   domesticity 372
   language 639
   Martin Chuzzlewit 167, 176
   prisons 425
   race 523, 524
   slavery 524, 718
   travel 316–18
Anand, Mulk Raj, *Untouchable* 734
Anderson, Amanda 357, 363n., 530
Andrews, Malcolm 667, 680
animal studies 550–65, 574
animisms 319, 438, 449, 455, 633–4
anonymous publication 331
Anthropocene 570–1, 572, 574, 580
anthropocentrism 554–5, 560–1, 564
anthropology 289, 291–3, 517
anthropomorphism 560–1, 568, 571
anti-Catholicism 153, 156–65
antiquarianism 289–91, 417
antisociability 374
Appadurai, Arjun 459
'Appeal to Fallen Women, An' 69
Apperley, Charles James ('Nimrod') 92, 103–4
apps 767
Arabian Nights, The 30, 547
Arabic adaptations 735, 765–6
archaeology 416–17
Arcola Theatre 764
Arendt, Hannah 264–5, 465
Argentina 735

aristocracy 501–12
    Bleak House 221–2, 346
    CD mixes with 54
    Dombey and Son 188
    history 486, 498
    and morality 364
    Our Mutual Friend 367
    patronage 57
    Pickwick Papers 96–7
    Reform 486
    Tale of Two Cities 265, 266
Armah, Ayi Kwei 728
Armstrong, Isobel 465
Armstrong, Nancy 683, 685, 686
Armstrong, Philip 555n., 563–4
Arnold, Matthew 286, 291, 569
Asking for More: Dickens in Nigeria 744–5
associationism 393–4, 616
astronomy 407–13
Athenaeum, The 30, 92–3, 96, 309
Atkinson, Rowan 750
attachment theory 613–17, 621, 624
    and cognition 623–6
    strange situation 621–3
Austen, Jane 45, 181–2
Austin, Henry 434
Austin, John 128n.
Australia 727–8, 741–3, 749
author, CD as professional 43–58
    credit economy 533, 536–41
autobiographical fragment 24
    city 108
    class 113
    David Copperfield 215n.
    identity 114
    image of CD 74
    Little Dorrit 248
    Warren's Blacking 10–20
Auyoung, Elaine 228, 618
Axton, William F. 597
Ayler, Felix, *The Drood Case* 305
Ayres, Brenda 373n., 382, 383

Bachman, Maria K. 453n., 618
Bacon, James 129n.
Baddeley, V. C. Clinton 745
Bagehot, Walter 60, 230, 324, 424–5, 454

Bain, Alexander 393
Baker, Fran 204
Bakhtin, Mikhail 98, 100, 258, 584, 586, 594
Baldridge, Cates 267
ballads 288, 289–91, 292
Balzac, Honoré de 140, 561
Banks, Percival 86n.
Banvard, John 697
Barham, Richard Harris ('Thomas Ingoldsby') 38
Barnaby Rudge 153–65
    adaptations 734
    affect 472–3
    animal studies 560–1
    Catholicism and Gashford 156–64
    CD as professional author 46
    CD as public figure 65
    CD's reading 37
    class 506, 507–8, 509, 511
    contract 85, 125, 129n., 130f, 153
    critical interpretations 154–6
    domesticity and queer theory 373, 380–7
    history and change 485, 486–7, 488–90, 492–3, 494–5
    illustrations 160–1, 161f
    language 635
    and *Martin Chuzzlewit* 175–6
    and *Master Humphrey's Clock* 139
    negotiations 132
    originally *Gabriel Vardon* 153
    psychology 396–7
    questions raised 240
    religion 587
    sexuality 385
    social reform 432
Barnard, Fred 269f, 269
Barnett, C. Z. 749
Barrow, Thomas Culliford 84
Barrymore, John 746
Barrymore, Lionel 746
Bart, Lionel 750, 751, 752
Barthes, Roland 371, 456, 649
Bartholomew Fair 99
Bassey, Shirley 753
Bastille 265, 270, 494–5
Bate, Jonathan 569
Battle of Life, The 51, 191, 195–7

778 INDEX

Baudelaire, Charles 94–5, 140
Baudrillard, Jean 456
Bayley, F. W. N. 103
Beadnell, Maria 82–3
Beaumarchais, Pierre 102
Beaumont, Matthew 151, 221
Beer, Gillian 273–5, 404, 415, 551
'Begging-Letter Writer, The' 71, 431
Belich, James 707
'Bellamy's' 89
Bell's Life in London 40, 45, 87
Benjamin, Arthur 741
Benjamin, Walter
  commodity culture 456
  flânerie 314–15
  memory 695
  Old Curiosity Shop 135–6, 142, 151
  Pickwick Papers 98
  Tale of Two Cities 266
Bennett, James 768
Bennett, Jane 561
Bentley, Richard
  Barnaby Rudge 125
  CD as public figure 64
  CD's contracts with 81, 84, 125–6, 127f, 128–9, 130f
  CD's finances 44–5
  CD's relationship with 128–9, 132, 137
  Oliver Twist 125
Bentley's Miscellany 125
  Ainsworth's *Jack Sheppard* 37
  CD as professional author 46
  CD as public figure 64–5
  CD's reading 37–8, 40
  CD's resignation 129, 137
  industry and technology 444
  Oliver Twist 746, 747
  science 406
  social reform 427
Bergson, Henri 259, 471
Berlant, Lauren 377–8
Berry, Laura 338
Bevis, Matthew 327
Bewick, Thomas, *General History of Quadrupeds* 551
Bewitched 741
Bible 156n., 581, 589n.

David Copperfield 314
  influence on CD 33–6
  intertextuality 583–6
  Little Dorrit 595
  Providential world view 591, 592
Bigelow, Gordon 230, 544
Bildung see self-formation
Bildungsroman
  city 108
  David Copperfield 608–11
  Martin Chuzzlewit 169, 177
  Our Mutual Friend 321
biographers/biographies
  marriage breakup 21, 23
  Warren's Blacking 11–15, 18, 23
biology 413–16
Birkbeck College University of London 759, 762
Black, John 84n.
Blackburn, Stuart H. 734
Blade Runner 574
Blake, Kathleen 535–6
Blake, William 45, 50, 315
Blanchot, Maurice 267
Bleak House 220–32
  adaptations 742–3, 749, 751
  affect 470
  animal studies 553, 555, 557–60
  and *Barnaby Rudge* 154
  CD as professional author 46, 48, 50, 57
  CD as public figure 62, 68
  CD's reading 26n., 34–5, 40
  charity 376, 428, 430–1, 708
  children's literature 340, 346–8
  and *A Child's History of England* 484
  class 365, 505–7, 510–12
  cognitive studies 614, 616–18, 621, 625–6
  and Collins's novels 306
  connections 650
  and *David Copperfield* 212–13
  domesticity and queer theory 373, 373n., 374–6, 381, 383–4, 386
  empire 526, 528–9, 530–1
  environment 570, 572–4, 576, 579–80
  gender and sexuality 358
  global circulation 731, 734–6
  and *Hard Times* 234

history 497
illustrations 50, 227, 683–7, 685f, 693, 695
industry and technology 438, 444, 446–7
language 634
law 128
and *Little Dorrit* 663
material culture 452–3, 460n.
political economy 535, 541, 544
psychology 376, 397
race and degeneration 519–22, 524
religion 156, 198, 583, 587, 591, 594
science 404–5, 408–12, 415, 417
serial publication 227, 233–4, 484
social reform 428, 430–1, 434
theatre 671
theatricality 675
transport 447
travel 320
visual mediations 683, 684–7, 691, 693
world-system 708, 709, 711, 716, 718
Bligh, Betty 749
blogging 242–4, 332, 762, 770
'Bloomsbury Christening, The' 83
Blumenbach, Johann Friedrich 552
'Boarding-House, The' 39
Boccaccio, Giovanni 197
Bodenheimer, Rosemarie 133n., 208, 390, 568, 624, 671
body and mind, relationship between 391–2, 395–400
Boltanski, Luc 265
Bolton, Philip 667, 740, 747–8
Bookchin, Murray 107
Book of Common Prayer 33–6, 156n., 583, 592n.
'Book of Memoranda' 54
Boone, Troy 574
Booth, Michael R. 667
Boucicault, Dion 670, 754
Bourdieu, Pierre 194, 264
bourgeois ideology 535–6, 731
Bowen, John
  Barnaby Rudge 155
  Deciphering Dickens project 761
  Haunted Man 197
  Martin Chuzzlewit 166–7, 170, 175, 639
  Nicholas Nickleby 121

  Oliver Twist 105, 113
  Pickwick Papers 98, 638
  Tale of Two Cities 267
Bowlby, John 624
Bowles, Emily 764
'Boy and the Convict, The' (film version of *Great Expectations*) 281
Boy Called Twist, A 744
Boyle, Danny 743
Boyle, Mary 39
Bradbury and Evans 233
Braddon, Mary Elizabeth 307
Brannon, Robert Louis 667, 672
Brantlinger, Patrick 155, 203
Brattin, Joel 238, 262
Bratton, Jacky 667, 668–9
Braudel, Fernand 263
Breaugh, Martin 265
Brecht, Bertolt 675
Brennan, Teresa 381, 473, 480
Breton, Rob 194
Brewster, David 254
Bridewell prison 384
Bridgman, Laura 396, 397
Briggs, Asa 464
Bright, John 68
Bristow, Joseph 339
British Academy 722
British Association for the Advancement of Science (BAAS) 405–6
British Council 724, 764, 766, 769
British history 484–500
British Museum 30, 486
'Broker's Man, The' 90
Brontë sisters 501
Brook, G. L. 634
Brooks, Peter 619–20
Brougham, Henry, Lord 98, 392–3
Brown, Bill 460
Brown, Georgia 750
Brown, Nicola 468
Browne, Hablot K. ('Phiz') 684, 698
  Barnaby Rudge 160–1, 161f
  Bleak House 227, 683–7, 685f, 693, 695
  Caswall's *Sketches of Young Ladies* 80
  CD as professional author 50
  Dombey and Son 683–4, 687–93, 688f

Browne, Hablot K. (*cont.*)
  Little Dorrit 245, 246f, 657, 658f, 660, 661f, 683–4, 687, 693–6
  Martin Chuzzlewit 650, 651f, 653–5, 653–5f
  Master Humphrey's Clock 138
  Old Curiosity Shop 148f
  Pickwick Papers 95, 98–9, 104, 463n.
  Sketches of Young Couples 81
  Sketches of Young Gentlemen 81
  Tale of Two Cities 269–70
Browning, Elizabeth Barrett 39
Browning, Robert 53
Buckland, Adelene 416–18, 691, 698
Buckley, Arabella B., *The Winners in Life's Race* 551–2
Buell, Lawrence 569, 570
Buffon, Comte de (Georges-Louis Leclerc) 560–1
Bulgaria 730
Bulwark, or Reformation Journal, The 159
Bulwer Lytton, Edward
  CD's reading 37, 39
  CD's rewrite of *Great Expectations* 49
  and Forster 53
  Guild of Literature and Art 57
  Paul Clifford 37
  poetry 39
Bunyan, John, *The Pilgrim's Progress* 36, 313–14, 316, 321
Burdett-Coutts, Angela
  CD's marriage breakup 22, 23
  charity 63, 68–9
  empire 525
  letters from CD 234, 334, 337, 444n.
  Ragged Schools 340, 433
  Urania Cottage 429
bureaucracy 249
Burke, Edmund 493, 590
Burnett, Fanny Dickens 9, 14, 17–20
Burnett, James, Lord Monboddo 552–3
Burnett, J. P. 749
Burney, Frances 45
Burns, Robert 39
Burt, Richard 770
Burton, Richard 746
Burton, Tim 752

Buss, Robert William 95
Butler, Joseph, *The Analogy of Religion* 590
Butler, Judith 477–8
Butler, Samuel, *Hudibras* 94
Butt, John E. 155, 191–2, 209
Buzard, James 225, 527, 709–10, 720
Byron, Lord 39, 45

Cain, P. J. 704
Callanan, Laura 203
Canada 745
Canetti, Elias 268
Cannadine, David 501
cannibalism 521–2, 539
Canning, Lord 203
Capes, J. M. 400
capitalism 533, 534–7, 539
  Bleak House 375, 447
  Christmas Carol 193, 589
  environment 577
  gender and sexuality 543–5
  global circulation 730, 731, 736
  Great Expectations 274
  Hard Times 448
  Old Curiosity Shop 136, 142, 146–8
  popular culture 760, 761, 769
  theatre 670
  thermodynamics 409
  world-system 705–7, 709–12, 714–18, 720
capital punishment 422, 428, 434
Cardwell, Margaret 168
Cardwell, Sarah 739
Carey, John 455
Carey, Peter 728
caricatures 94–5, 99, 235, 268
Carlton Chronicle 45, 86n., 89
Carlyle, Thomas 197
  Christmas Carol 193
  'The Condition of England question' 422
  and Cromwell 498
  Hard Times dedicated to 233, 448
  history 485–6, 487–8, 490, 491, 493, 496, 499
  History of the French Revolution 262, 437, 485, 491, 492n.
  lieu de mémoire 259

INDEX

machinery 436–7, 438, 441, 447, 448, 450
Past and Present 193
political economy 532–3
race 718
Tale of Two Cities 437, 494–5, 508, 525, 569
carnival 98–102
carnivalesque 343, 353, 770, 773
Carolan, Katherine 197
Carpenter, William 392–3, 400
Carr, Charles E. 308
Carr, J. Comyns 748–9, 751
Carre, Jacques 201–2
Carson, Anne 677–8, 679
Carson, Miss (actress) 749
cartoon physics 599
Castro, John Paul de 487n.
Caswall, Edward ('Quiz') 80–1
catachresis 633–4
Catholic Emancipation Act (1829) 158–9
Catholicism 153, 156–65, 582, 587
Cattermole, George 50, 138, 143*f*, 145, 146*f*
cause-hungry minds 617–19
Cawnpore Massacre 202, 523
Cazamian, Louis 191
celebrity studies 768–9
Çelikkol, Ayşe 530, 706–7
Cervantes, Miguel de
  CD compared with 86
  CD's reading 37
  Combe's and Rowlandson's *Doctor Syntax's Tour in Search of the Picturesque* 94
  Don Quixote 37, 98, 100–1, 103, 735
Chadwick, Edwin 446, 567, 579
Chambers, Robert, *Vestiges of the Natural History of Creation* 404, 408, 415, 552
Chandler, David 197
Chaney, Lon 748, 749
change 484–500
Chapman, Edward 80n., 94
Chapman and Hall
  CD as professional author 43
  CD's relationship with 125, 126, 128, 132
  Christmas Stories 200
  letters of CD 73
  Martin Chuzzlewit 166
  Master Humphrey's Clock 138

Mystery of Edwin Drood 299
Nicholas Nickleby 67, 125, 128, 131, 137
Old Curiosity Shop 134
Pickwick Papers 84, 92, 96, 125, 131
Pickwick Portrait Gallery 97
Sketches by Boz 80n., 85–6, 87
Sketches of Young Gentlemen 81
Sketches of Young Ladies (Caswall) 80
Squib Annual of Poetry, Politics, and Personalities 92
Chappell, Patrick 228
Charcot, Jean-Martin 268
charity
  begging letters 71, 431
  Bleak House 376, 428, 430–1, 708
  CD as public figure 62, 68–72
  CD's donations of *The Old Curiosity Shop* to American schools for the blind 145
  Christmas Books 194
  Christmas Carol 192, 195, 197, 726
  Pickwick Papers 708
  social reform 340, 428, 430–2
  Urania Cottage 69–70, 429, 431
  world-system 708
Charles Dickens Fan Club 767
Charles Dickens Letters Project 324, 335
Charles I 498
Chartism 81, 146, 155–6, 493, 503
Chase, Karen 474, 476, 573–4
Chatham 312
Chaucer, Geoffrey, *The Canterbury Tales* 313
Chesterton, G. K.
  Barnaby Rudge 154
  CD's engagement with history 485, 499
  Christmas Books 191, 192
  Little Dorrit 247
  Martin Chuzzlewit 167
  Old Curiosity Shop 149
  Pickwick Papers 97, 98
  Sketches by Boz 81
Child, Francis, *English and Scottish Popular Ballads* 290
Childers, Joseph W. 132n.
childhood, cognitive studies 614–26
child labour 63
children's hospitals 70–1

children's literature 337–53
  anthropomorphism 561
  Bleak House 346–8
  David Copperfield 343–6
  Hard Times 349–52
  Household Words and *All the Year Round* 340–3
'Child's Dream of a Star, A' 342
Child's Fairy Library, The 26
Child's History of England, A 339–40, 484–6, 493n., 497–8
'Child's Story, The' 26n., 200n.
Chimes, The 191, 193–5
  CD as professional author 51
  CD's reading to his friends 318
  illustrations 51, 195f, 196f
  political economy 536
  social reform 427
  theatre 669
China 250, 730–3
Chittick, Kathryn 82
Chitty, Joseph 126n.
Christmas 63, 197, 588, 726
  see also Christmas Books; Christmas Stories
Christmas Books 191–9
  CD as professional author 51
  CD as public figure 62–3
  CD's reading 37
  drinking 601
  ghost stories 588
  illustrations 51
  visual mediations 698
  see also *Battle of Life, The*; *Chimes, The*; *Christmas Carol, A*; *Cricket on the Hearth, The*; *Haunted Man and the Ghost's Bargain, The*
Christmas Carol, A 191–5, 197, 199
  adaptations 171, 199, 734, 739–42, 746
  affect 470, 473
  animal studies 550–1, 553, 555
  Catholicism 165
  CD as professional author 47, 51
  CD as public figure 62–3, 71
  children's literature 341
  class 512
  commercialization of Christmas 726

  drinking 601
  global circulation 734, 735
  illustrations 51, 198f, 199
  language 634
  and *Martin Chuzzlewit* 176
  material culture 455, 459n.
  and *Our Mutual Friend* 298
  public readings and performances 71, 192
  religion 588–9, 593
  as two texts 299
Christmas Stories 62, 200–5, 341
'Christmas Tree, A' 200n., 201–2, 342–3
  CD's reading 26n., 28n., 29n., 34
Chuang, H. C. 731
cinema *see* film
circulation, global 722–37, 743–4
city
  Bleak House 220–1, 230
  environment 566–8
  Old Curiosity Shop 107–8, 111, 113–15
  Oliver Twist 106–18
  see also London; Paris
city-in-literature 175
City Reads projects 764
Clare, John 569
Clarendon, Earl of (Edward Hyde) 498–9
Clark, Cumberland 554
Clark, Robert 544
Clark, Timothy 570–1, 573
Clarke, Jeremy 240–1
class 501–16
  Barnaby Rudge 162, 381–2
  Bleak House 365, 505–7, 510–12
  children's literature 340
  Christmas Stories 202
  David Copperfield 344, 363–5
  domesticity and queer theory 379, 381–2
  and drinking 600, 607
  gender and sexuality 358, 359
  Great Expectations 275, 281, 366, 510–12, 514–15
  Hard Times 365, 507–9, 512–13
  and history 498
  Household Words readership 341, 342
  imperialism 203
  Little Dorrit 365, 505–7, 511, 513, 515

Old Curiosity Shop 144, 145, 147
Oliver Twist 112, 113, 114, 117
Our Mutual Friend 365–7, 503n., 513–15
Pickwick Papers 103
popular culture 772
Tale of Two Cities 266, 365, 505, 507–8, 511
see also aristocracy; middle class; working class
Claybaugh, Amanda 600
Clayton, Jay 194–5, 406, 726, 740, 756
Clement XIII, Pope 158
Clemm, Sabine 327, 525n.
Clifford, C. K. 401–2
Clifford, Jo 281
Close, Anthony 100
clubs, in popular culture 757–8, 768–73
Coates, Albert 741
cognitive disturbance 624–5
cognitive studies 613–27
   attachment and cognition 623–6
   broken brains, broken attachments 613–17
   cause-hungry minds 617–19
   signature repetition 619–21
   strange situation 621–3
Cohen, William 145, 338
Cohn, Elisha 177
Coldbath Fields prison 428
Cole, Sir Henry 66–7
Coleridge, Samuel Taylor 39, 45, 296, 546, 676
Coles, Nicholas 238
collaborations 330–1
   CD as professional author 51, 52–3
   Christmas Stories 200, 202–5
   with Collins see under Collins, Wilkie
   Household Words 445
   with Wills 397–8, 445–6, 558
Collins, Philip
   Hard Times 237
   Little Dorrit 251
   Mystery of Edwin Drood 302, 307–8
   religion 157
   social reform 420, 428
Collins, Wilkie
   and *Bleak House* 306
   collaborations with CD 52, 327
      Christmas Stories 200, 202, 203

The Frozen Deep 21, 52–3, 271, 522, 670, 672–3
The Perils of Certain English Prisoners 52, 200, 202–4, 523
The Wreck of the Golden Mary 52, 202, 204, 522
Fruttero and Lucentini's *The D Case* 302
Household Words 66
The Lazy Tour of Two Idle Apprentices 21
letters from CD 334, 591n.
The Moonstone 52, 306, 307
and *The Mystery of Edwin Drood* 300, 306, 307
theatre 338n., 670, 672–3
The Woman in White 52, 66, 306–7
colonialism see empire
Combe, William 94
comedy
   Barnaby Rudge 380
   Christmas Carol 199
   David Copperfield 212, 213
   drinking 598–9, 600, 602–3, 604–8, 610
   Great Expectations 276, 277, 280, 281, 282
   Hard Times 239
   interludes 648
   language 631–2, 635–6, 638–9, 641, 643–5
   Little Dorrit 247, 248, 250
   Martin Chuzzlewit 167, 639, 650, 656
   Mystery of Edwin Drood 308, 309–10
   Our Mutual Friend 291, 643
   Pickwick Papers 98, 101, 360–1, 635–6, 638
   Tale of Two Cities 271
   travel writing 319
commodity culture 456–9
communication 436, 438–9, 445–6, 449
   blogging 243, 244
   'The Signal-Man' 202
Communist Party 730, 731
Company of Amateurs 32, 40, 56, 67
comparative studies 150–1
computational stylistics 331–2
Conan Doyle, Arthur 725
connections 649, 650, 652, 656–9, 661
Connor, Steven 584, 591
Conolly, John 392, 397–8
Conrad, Joseph 527

consumption 597–612
contracts
    vs agreements 126, 129
    CD's 56, 124–6
        Barnaby Rudge 85, 153
        with Bentley 81, 84, 125–6, 127f, 128–9, 130f
        Forster's negotiations 53
        Nicholas Nickleby 119–24, 129, 131–2
        Pickwick Papers 95, 125
        reneged 44, 84, 85
Convict, The 748n.
Coogan, Jackie 748, 749
Cook, Susan 270
Cooper, Suzanne Fagence 236
Copperfield (1980 Broadway musical) 742
copyright
    CD as professional author 47, 57
    CD as public figure 64
    Christmas Carol 171
    Martin Chuzzlewit 171
    Nicholas Nickleby 129
    Oliver Twist 125
    political economy 538, 539
    Sketches by Boz 85
    theatrical adaptations 738
    United States 176, 226
Coram, Thomas 70
Cordery, Gareth 208n., 600
Corelli, Marie 734
Cornhill Magazine 235
correspondence see letters
Corton, Christine 566
cosmopolitanism 518, 529–31
    Bleak House 226
    Little Dorrit 249–51, 259
Cosslett, Tess 561
countryside
    environment 568
    Oliver Twist 106, 116–18
Courbet, Gustave, Stone Breakers 270
Court Journal 86
Courtemanche, Eleanor 541, 545
Cowan, William J. 749n.
Cox, Constance 751
Cozzi, Annette 600
Crafts, Hannah, The Bondwoman's Narrative 225–6

Craig, David 107
Craig, Hugh 331
Crawford, Francis Marion 734
credit economy 533, 536–41
Crichton-Browne, James 393
Cricket on the Hearth, The, 51, 191, 194–6
Crimean War 68, 246, 252, 328–9, 421
Critic 194
Cromwell, Oliver 498
crowds
    CD's fear of the mob 432
    in popular culture 757–68
    Tale of Two Cities 266–70
crowdsourcing 756–73
Crowe, Catherine 587–8
Cruikshank, George 684
    'The Bottle' 602
    CD as professional author 50
    and Cervantes 100
    'The Drunkard's Children' 602
    Fairy Library 342n.
    'Hop o' my Thumb' adaptation 288
    Oliver Twist 109, 110f, 116f, 750
    Quiz, Jun.'s Characteristic Sketches of Young Gentlemen 81
    and Seymour 92
    Sketches by Boz 82, 83, 84, 85f
    theatrical performances 172
Crutzen, Paul 571
Cuarón, Alfonso 682, 744
cultural studies 471, 482, 760–1
culture
    commodity 456–9
    global circulation 722–8, 731–3, 736–7
    material 227–8, 286, 452–67
    Our Mutual Friend 285–92
    popular 756–73
    technology 450
    world-system 704–5, 710
culture texts 300, 303, 589, 739
Cunningham, Peter 234
curiosity 140–4
Curry, Emma 759, 761–2
Cuvier, Georges 561
Czechoslovakia 730

daguerreotypes 270, 693–5, 698
Daily Mail 763

Daily News, The 17–18
   CD as professional author 44, 51
   CD as public figure 65
   CD's reading 40
   Dickens, John 44
   industry and technology 444
   letters from CD 427–8
   tribute to CD 60
Daleski, H. M. (Bill) 102, 168
Dallas, E. S. 392
Daly, Suzanne 227
Dames, Nicholas 389
Dante Alighieri 249
Darwin, Bernard 97
Darwin, Charles 404, 413–15, 417–18
   animal studies 552, 564
   CD's influence on 551
   The Descent of Man 552
   The Expression of Emotion in Man and Animals 551
   influence on CD 551
   Monograph 414
   On the Origin of Species 273–4, 404, 413–14, 517, 551
Darwin, Erasmus 552
Darwin, John 704–5, 706, 710
Daston, Lorraine 391n.
Daumier, Honoré 268, 270
David Copperfield 207–19
   adaptations 734, 739, 742–3, 745–6
   affect 477
   animal studies 553
   Catholicism 165
   CD as professional author 46, 49, 58
   CD as public figure 74
   CD's affective relationship to his own writing 375
   CD's reading 28, 30, 31–2, 33–4, 39, 39n.
   children's literature 340, 343–6
   class 507, 510–12, 514–15
   cognitive studies 614, 616, 617, 621, 625, 626
   Copperfield as a 'posthumous child' 93
   Dickens and London exhibition, Museum of London 766
   domesticity and queer theory 378, 379
   drinking 600, 602, 608–11
   empire 524
   environment 567, 568–9, 577–8, 579, 580
   gender and sexuality 358, 359, 361–5
   global circulation 732, 733, 734, 735
   history and change 484, 490, 497n.
   language 637
   literary entrepreneurship 538
   maintenance 186
   material culture 461
   political economy 538
   psychology 217, 219, 361, 389
   quality 237
   separate spheres model 382
   Shakespearian influence 674
   social reform 430, 433
   Talfourd as model for Tommy Traddles 96
   travel 314, 316, 320
   trial titles 490n.
   Warren's Blacking 12, 17
   world-system 707, 709–10, 716
Davis, Eliza 747
Davis, Mike 574
Davis, Paul 199, 299, 739–40
Davis, Tracy C. 667–8
Dawson, Gowan 415–16
death penalty 422, 428, 434
deaths and deathbed scenes
   children, and affect 470, 476–7
   David Copperfield 209
   'The Death of Nancy Sykes' (1897 film short) 748
   Dombey and Son 592
   Great Expectations 281
   Old Curiosity Shop 145, 146f, 165, 476–7
   religion 592
debtors, and social reform 422–3
de Cerjat, W. W. F. 582n.
Deciphering Dickens project 761
Defoe, Daniel 30, 36, 531
degeneration and race 519–24
de la Rue, Augusta 392
Deleuze, Gilles 471, 564n.
Dellamora, Richard 266
DeLuise, Dom 751
Derrida, Jacques 553, 587
de Ruiter, Corine 624
design (plot), and serial publication 647–9, 655

desire 358
  David Copperfield 363, 364
  Our Mutual Friend 365, 367–71
  Pickwick Papers 360
Despret, Vinciane 564
detective fiction 303, 304–5
development
  of CD's world-system 703–21
  of CD's writing 82
    Barnaby Rudge 153, 154
    Christmas Books 191
    and development of CD himself 132–3
    Martin Chuzzlewit 166, 169, 175–6
Dever, Carolyn 222, 338, 394–5
Devonshire Terrace 25
DeVries, Duane 81
Dexter, Walter 73
Di, Wu 343
Dibdin, Charles, *The Waterman* 99–100
Dick, Archie L. 730
Dickens, Alfred (CD's brother) 19
Dickens, Anna (née Weller) 18
Dickens, Catherine (née Hogarth)
  CD's autobiographical fragment 20n.
  CD's courtship 83
  children 18, 337
  cookbook 597
  illness and death of Fanny Dickens 19
  letters from CD 83
  marriage breakup 10–11, 20–3, 69, 75, 82, 280
  A New Piljians Projiss 172
Dickens, Cedric, *Dining with Dickens* 597–8
Dickens, Charles Culliford Boz (CD's eldest son) 17–18, 20n., 313, 496, 497
Dickens, Charles John Huffam
  acting 671–2, 673, 679, 738
    missed audition 666, 738
  affective relationship to his own writing 375
  alcohol, attitude towards 602
  as animal lover 554, 559, 561–3
  autobiographical fragment *see* autobiographical fragment
  bicentenary celebrations 4–5, 724, 756–7, 764, 766–7, 770
  'brand' 767
  calls himself Dick 113

capitalism 535, 536, 541
childhood 114, 337
  effects 215
  fairy tales 293
  image 74
  Noah's ark toy 34
  reading 26–30
  school 28–9
  toys 201
  Warren's Blacking 9–19
  see also autobiographical fragment
children 337, 340
  Dora's death 345n.
  empire 524, 727–8
  names and nicknames 338n.
  religion 581, 582
contracts *see under* contracts
correspondence *see* letters
courtship of Catherine 83
as crossover figure 597, 730
death 322
  on anniversary of Staplehurst disaster 450
  memorial service 60–1
  posthumous tributes 59–61, 60*f*
  public sale of CD's belongings 460n.
development of writing 82
  Barnaby Rudge 153, 154
  Christmas Books 191
  and development of CD himself 132–3
  Martin Chuzzlewit 166, 169, 175–6
'Dignity of Literature' debate 56
editorships *see* editorships
education 486
family theatricals 338n.
finances *see* finances of CD
flânerie 90, 140
as gentleman 502n.
global circulation 722–37
image of 61–2, 74–5
journalism *see* journalism
letters *see* letters
library 25–6, 41*f*, 41, 561
marriage breakup 10, 11, 20–3
  and Burdett-Coutts 69
  Great Expectations 280
  letters 11, 20, 22–3, 334

public image 75
re-creation of early marriage 82
material culture 452, 465–6, 467
name as capital 535, 538
novelist as creator 591
parliamentary reporting 89, 98, 157, 327, 420, 485n., 486
at play 647–65
as professional author 43–58, 64
pseudonyms 80, 93
as public figure 59–76
public readings *see* public readings and performances
reading 25–42, 392, 394, 484, 561
religious beliefs 581–3, 589n., 594
reputation *see* reputation of CD
role of the writer 64
speeches *see* speeches
and theatre 666–80
travels 315–19, 496
see also *American Notes for General Circulation*; *Pictures from Italy*
'Twenty Questions'-type games 550
walking and *flânerie* 90, 140, 315–16, 428–9
writing desk 563, 766
Dickens, Edward Bulwer Lytton ('Plorn', CD's son) 33–4
Dickens, Elizabeth (née Barrow, CD's mother) 13n., 14, 16–19, 20n.
Dickens, Ethel (CD's granddaughter) 748n.
Dickens, Frederick (CD's brother) 17–19
Dickens, John (CD's father)
CD's work at Warren's Blacking 13n., 14, 16, 17, 20n.
Daily News 17–18
imprisonment 11, 13, 13n., 17, 19, 89, 102–3
journalism 17–18, 44
piano studies of Fanny Dickens 18
unreliability 18
Dickens, Kate Macready (CD's daughter) 305, 668
Dickens, Letitia (CD's sister) 18–19
Dickens, Mary ('Mamie', CD's daughter)
CD as professional author 49
CD's acting 738
CD's love of animals 554
CD's material environment 452

letters of CD 73, 334
parents' marriage breakup 21
Dickens and London exhibition, Museum of London 766–7
Dickens Fellowship 724–5
Charles Dickens Letters Project 324, 335
Dickensian (television series) 664, 741–2
Dickensian, The (journal) 239–40, 301, 554
Dickens Journal Online (DJO) project 241, 244, 324, 328–33, 759, 761–3
poetry 335
Dickens Quarterly 554
Dickens Society 759, 764
Dickinson, Emily 374
Didi-Huberman, Georges 270
Different World, A 741
digital media 756–73
digitization
of CD's journals 40, 204, 241, 244, 324–5, 328–36
of nineteenth-century newspapers 283
Dilke, Charles Wentworth 20
'Dinner at Poplar Walk, A' 49, 83, 423n.
dioramas 697, 698
disability 145, 195
discourse
class as a 501–16
religion 586–90
Dissent 156–7
dissociation 614, 616–17, 619, 625
Dixon, George 68
Dixon, Thomas 392
Djalili, Omid 750
Doctor Marigold's Prescriptions 48, 54
'Doctors' Commons' 89
Doctor Who 741
Dolby, George 71
Dombey and Son 179–90
adaptations 743
affect 477
animal studies 553
capitalism 543–5
CD as professional author 46, 49–50
CD's reading 27, 28, 29, 31, 35–6, 37, 38
class 504, 506, 512
drinking 610
eating 599n.

Dombey and Son (cont.)
  empire 525, 527
  environment 571–2, 574
  gender 358, 364, 543–5
  global circulation 735
  home 115
  housekeeping 186–7, 452
  illustrations 683, 684, 687–91, 688f, 692–3
  lost child 111, 112
  and *Martin Chuzzlewit* 176
  material culture 452, 454–6, 460n., 463–4, 467
  metaphysics 216
  political economy 537, 542–5
  psychology 393–4, 397
  race and degeneration 521
  railways 103
  religion 585, 586n., 587, 592–3, 594
  science 417
  serial publication 689
  sexuality 358, 364, 543–5
  Shakespearian influence 674
  social reform 429
  transport 103, 436, 441–4
  travel 320–1
  visual mediations 683, 687–91, 692–3
  world-system 703, 706, 707–8, 711–12, 716, 718
  writing of 18
domestic ideology 372–87
  affect aliens 374–9
  Barnaby Rudge 380–7
  see also home
Donkin, Ellen 667
Donner, Clive 742
Donsky, Seth Michael 745
Doro, Marie 748, 749
Dostoevsky, Fyodor 735, 736
  admiration for CD 582
  Crime and Punishment 303, 306
  The Insulted and Injured 736
  and *The Old Curiosity Shop* 151
  Pickwick Papers 100
Douglas-Fairhurst, Robert 669, 670
Douglass, Frederick 225–6
Dover Road 312–16, 321, 322
Downing, Lisa 376

Dowson, Jane 333
Doyle, Richard 196f, 196
dreams 388, 393
  Barnaby Rudge 164
  Bleak House 224
  CD's, of Mary Hogarth 165, 582n.
  Oliver Twist 116
  Pickwick Papers 93
  trauma 616
  and travel 316
  Victorian dream theory 589
Drew, John J. L. 15, 325, 329, 763
drinking 597–612
  alcoholic temporalities 604–8
  comic hauntings 602–3
  remembering and forgetting 608–12
Dr Marigold's Prescriptions 205
Drood (1985 Broadway musical) 741, 742
Drood Enquiry, The 759, 763
'Drooping Buds' 70
dualism 392, 394–400
Duffield, Howard 301
Duncan, Ian 137

Eagar, Charlotte 765
Easley, Alexis 244
Easley, Keith 594
East Germany 730
eating 597, 611–12
eco-criticism 147, 569–70, 572–4, 577
ecology 567, 571–4, 577–8
eco-mimesis 569, 572
economics 532–49
  Bleak House 230
  literary form in light of 541–3
  unpredictability 545–8
  world-system 704–5, 711
  see also finances of CD; money
Edelman, Lee 266
Edinburgh Review, The 485
editorships 325–31, 335–6
  CD as professional author 43, 44, 46, 51–2
  CD as public figure 64–6
  CD's reading 37–8, 40
  Christmas Stories 205
  control 672–3
  industry and technology 439, 444–5

psychology 393, 394
science 407, 418
and the theatre 670
see also *All the Year Round*; *Bentley's Miscellany*; *Daily News, The*; *Household Words*
education *see* schools and education
Edwards, Amelia 204
Edzard, Christine 741, 742
Egan, Pierce 87, 96, 103, 326
Egypt 735
Eigner, Edwin 394n.
Eisenstein, Sergei 268, 682, 683, 725, 740
'Election for Beadle, The' 89
Eliot, George 230, 358
  Adam Bede 606
  CD's 'false psychology' 388
  class 501
  Household Words 51
  and Lewes 405
  science 295, 405, 407, 415, 418
  serial publication 45
Eliot, T. S. 173, 294, 492n.
Elliotson, John 392, 393
Elliott, Kamilla 266
Eltis, Sos 667, 668
Emerson, Sir James 52-3
emigration 320-1
emotions 469-77, 480-2
  Barnaby Rudge 380-7
  Bleak House 375-6
  David Copperfield 208, 209
  domesticity and queer theory 374-87
  and ethics 474-6
  see also feelings
empire 518, 524-31
  Bleak House 225
  global circulation 727-8, 734
  Great Expectations 275
  Little Dorrit 259
  Our Mutual Friend 291
  The Perils of Certain English Prisoners (CD and Collins) 203-4
  thermodynamics 409
  world-system 704-9, 712, 719, 720
Engels, Friedrich 556
English Civil War 498-9

English Education Act (1835) 734
Englishwoman's Review, The 376n.
entropy 409, 410, 412
environment 566-80
  degradation 147, 397, 566-7, 571-80
  Great Expectations 274, 275
equity 120, 123, 126-9
Ericksen, Donald 684
ethics
  and affect 469-71, 474-80, 482
  and emotions 474-6
ethnicity *see* race and ethnicity
Euripides, *Bakkhai* 677-8
Evening Chronicle 40, 45, 84n., 89
Evening Standard 170
evolution 404, 408, 413-15, 417
  animal studies 552
  and religion 583, 590
Examiner, The 497
  CD as public figure 65
  CD's review of Crowe's *The Night Side of Nature* 588
  'Judicial Special Pleading' 493
  Mill's 'The Spirit of the Age' 491
  'The Niger Expedition' 708-9, 717, 719
  'The Poetry of Science' 691, 692
  Sketches by Boz 86
  world-system 708

Facebook 760, 764
factories 437, 439-40, 447-8
'Fairyland in "Fifty-Four"' 341
fairy tales 26-7, 352-3
  Bleak House 346-8
  Hard Times 349-52
  journalism 340-3
  material culture 463
  Our Mutual Friend 288-94
family
  Austen's novels 181
  Dombey and Son 179-90
  domestic ideology and queer theory 372-87
  Goldsmith's *The Vicar of Wakefield* 180-1, 189
  Nicholas Nickleby 120-1, 123-4, 132
  see also marriage

Family Guy 739
Famous Adventures of Mr. Magoo, The 741
fan studies 761, 768–9, 772
Faraday, Michael 410
Faulkner, William 173, 173n.
Fawcett, Dubrez 746
feelings 468–82
  see also emotions
  ugly 374, 376, 378–80, 382, 386
Felski, Rita 473
femininity 357, 358, 359
  Barnaby Rudge 383, 386
  David Copperfield 362, 363–4
  Dombey and Son 543, 544
  domesticity and queer theory 376–7, 383, 386
  Our Mutual Friend 371
  Tale of Two Cities 266
Ferguson, Christine 474
Ferrante, Elena, *L'amica geniale* 664
Field, Kate 71
Fielding, Henry 102, 649, 662
  CD compared with 86
  CD's reading 36–7
  financial difficulties 44
  as influence on CD 96
  Joseph Andrews 36, 100
  picaresque 320
  Tom Jones 37
Fielding, K. J. 273, 275, 404–5, 415, 582
Fiennes, Ralph 724
Figaro in London 92, 95, 102
Fildes, Sir Luke 50, 61, 684
film
  adaptations 277, 279–81, 732, 739–45, 747–9, 769
  CD's influence on 243, 268, 682–3
finances of CD
  Barnaby Rudge 125
  contracts with Bentley 125
  early sketches 81
  Master Humphrey's Clock 138
  Nicholas Nickleby 128, 131
  Oliver Twist 125
  Pickwick Papers 125
  professionalism 44, 47, 56

Finer, Emily 736
first-person narratives 615
Fitoor 743
Fitzgerald, Percy
  All the Year Round 331
  CD's journals 325, 326
  CD's love of animals 554
  Christmas Stories 205
  Pickwick Papers 97
Flanagan, Richard, *Wanting* 728
flânerie 90, 140, 315–16, 428–9
Flatley, Jonathan 472
Fleet prison 99, 102–4
Fleming, Patrick C. 752
Fletcher, John 53
'Flight, A' 493n.
fog/smog 566
  Bleak House 220–3, 225–6, 572–3, 576
folklore 352–3
  Bleak House 346–8
  Hard Times 349–52
  journalism 340–3
  Our Mutual Friend 288–94
Folk-lore Society 290
food 597, 611–12
forgetting, alcoholic 601–4, 606–12
Forster, John
  Arrest of the Five Members by Charles the First 498–9
  autobiographical fragment 11–12, 248, 259
  CD archive 43, 54
  CD as professional author 53–4
  CD's childhood 74, 337, 486
  CD's children 727–8
  CD's death 322
  CD's early sketches 82, 85
  CD's engagement with history 484, 497–8
  CD's love of animals 554
  CD's marriage breakup 21, 22
  CD's reading 26, 28, 30
  CD's religious beliefs 583
  CD's writing desk 562–3
  Child's History of England 484
  Chimes 194
  on criticisms of CD 390
  Daily News 17

'Dignity of Literature' debate 56
Examiner 65
grief on death of Macready's child 334
history 498–9
Holme's gift to CD 466
Household Words 341, 342
illness and death of Fanny Dickens 19
importance to CD 53
letters from CD 12, 73, 334
   Arrest of the Five Members by Charles the First 498–9
   Bentley 128
   biography 73
   Christmas 588
   editing 51
   finances 44–5
   Great Expectations 277
   Hard Times 234–5
   Household Words 341
   illness and death of Fanny Dickens 19
   Little Dorrit 662
   marriage breakup 22, 23
   Marshalsea Prison 64
   Martin Chuzzlewit 166, 171, 649
   Master Humphrey's Clock 138
   public readings 71
   race 524
   reading 30, 39
   theatre 669
   weekly publication 48
Little Dorrit 399, 662, 663
London Shakespeare Committee 32
Mystery of Edwin Drood 304–5, 306
A New Piljians Projiss 172n.
Pickwick Papers 93–4, 100
Royal Literary Fund 57
Smollett's influence on CD 96
theatrical performances 172
Warren's Blacking 9, 11–12, 14–15, 15n., 17, 20
Forster, E. M. 172–3
Forsyte, Charles 302, 303, 306
Forsyth, William 248
Fortunio 338n.
Foucault, Michel 224, 248, 357, 586
Foulon, Joseph-François 495
Foundling Hospital 70

Fourier, Charles 392
Fraiman, Susan 473
Frame, Ronald, *Havisham* 378n.
France
   animal slaughter 558
   CD's travels 318
   history 490–6
   see also French Revolution
   Paris 263–4, 315, 494
   Tale of Two Cities 260–72
Frank, Adam 471
Frank, Lawrence 408, 417
Franklin Expedition 522–3
Fraser, A. Campbell 396
'Frauds on the Fairies' 288, 292, 340, 342
   CD's reading 36
   and *Hard Times* 242
   and *Little Dorrit* 656
Frazer, J. G. 294
Frederick Douglass's Journal 225–6
Freedgood, Elaine
   it-narratives 462
   Master Humphrey's Clock, 139–40
   material culture 454, 461, 462, 464, 611
Freeman, James 68
French Revolution 490–6
   Tale of Two Cities 260–72, 508–9
Freud, Sigmund 217, 259, 395, 587, 619
Friedman, Stanley 199
'From the Raven in the Happy Family' 560–1
Frost, Thomas 86n.
Frow, John 371
Frozen Deep, The (CD and Collins) 21, 52–3, 271, 522, 670, 672–3
Fruttero, Carlo, *The D Case* (with Lucentini) 302
Fudge, Erica 554
Furneaux, Holly
   children 338
   gender and sexuality 357, 371
   journalism 328
   Master Humphrey's Clock 139
   queer theory 475
   science 407
   Tale of Two Cities 266
Fyfe, Paul 169, 177

Gad's Hill Place
  burning of letters 74
  charity 71
  Dover Road 313, 314
  Fildes's 'The Empty Chair' engraving 61
  library 25, 41f, 41, 561
  marriage breakup 21
  Shakespearian connection 30–1
Gager, Valerie L. 674
Galdós, Benito Pérez 735–6, 737
Gallagher, Catherine 270, 338, 420, 539
gambling 141–2, 144, 147
Gamp, Sarah ('Sairey') 40, 50, 72, 170–3, 598, 638, 640, 674
  illustrations 651f, 653f, 654f, 655f
  interludes 649–56, 657, 663, 664
Gandhi, Mohandas Karamchand 734
Garfield, Leon 302, 303, 308
Garrick, David 670, 671, 679
Garvice, Charles 734
Gaskell, Elizabeth
  CD's reading 38
  CD's request for Christmas story 197–8
  computational stylistics 331–2
  Cranford 186, 189
  'The Ghost in the Garden Room' 204
  'Half a Lifetime Ago' 38n.
  Household Words 51, 66
  North and South 38, 51
  serial publication 45
'Gaslight Fairies' 340–1
Gay, John, *Beggar's Opera* 103
gender 357–71
  Bleak House 228
  and capitalism 533, 539–40, 543–5
  David Copperfield 361–5
  Dombey and Son 179, 186–8
  domesticity and queer theory 372–86
  early sketches 90
  Great Expectations 279–80
  Household Words 202
  housekeeping 186
  journalism 328
  Our Mutual Friend 365–71
  Pickwick Papers 359–61, 362
  social reform 422
  Tale of Two Cities 266

General Record Office (GRO) 426–7
genres 647–65
  drinking 601–2, 606–8, 611
  material culture 463
  Mystery of Edwin Drood 304–10
genre studies 586–90
gentility 503, 507, 509–15
Gentle Author (blogger) 242–3
Gentleman's Magazine 487n.
gentlemen 502–3, 509–15
  and actors 671
  CD as 502n.
geology 416–17
George Silverman's Explanation 221
gesture 677–80
Ghana 729
Ghosts of Girlfriends Past 740
ghost stories 587–90
  see also *Christmas Carol, A*; 'Signal-Man, The'
Gibbon, Edward, *The Decline and Fall of the Roman Empire* 287, 295
Gibson, Anna 480
Giedroyc, Coky 752
gift economy 761
Gilbert, Elliot L. 199
Gilbert, W. S. 279
Gilbert and Sullivan 667
Giles, William 28–9, 81n.
Gillray, James 270
Gilmour, Robin 208
Ginsburg, Michael Peled 615
Gissing, George
  CD's engagement with history 485
  CD's women characters 373
  Little Dorrit 246–7
  Pickwick Papers 97
  Sketches by Boz 81
  theatre 674
  Warren's Blacking 14
Glance at the Intrigues of the Jesuits, A (Anon) 163
Glavin, John 131n., 740
global circulation 722–37, 743–4
Global Circulation Project (GCP) 722–3
globalization 518, 711–14, 728
global modernity, as combined and uneven development 703–21

global perspective 525, 528, 529–31
  see also empire
Global Read-a-thon 764, 769
Goethe, Johann Wolfgang von 726
Gold, Barri J. 231n., 411–12
Goldsmith, Oliver
  The Bee 29
  Boccaccio's story of Titus and Gisippus 197
  carnivalesque drinking 99
  CD compared with 86
  financial difficulties 44
  A History of England 30
  She Stoops to Conquer 102
  The Vicar of Wakefield 30, 180–2, 189
Goodlad, Lauren 224, 527–9
Gordon, Lord George 155, 157, 160, 163–4, 397
Gordon Riots 153–8, 160–4, 487, 494–5,
      508, 562
Gosse, Edmund 376n.
Gothic 587–90
  architecture 437
  Barnaby Rudge 155, 380
  Bleak House 541
  CD's marriage breakup 22
  drinking 603, 604
  Little Dorrit 530
  Mystery of Edwin Drood 309
  Old Curiosity Shop 137, 141–2, 145,
      147, 478–9
  Pickwick Papers 463
  'The Signal-Man' 202
Gower Street, London 13n.
Grant, Robert 552
Grass, Sean 538, 542
Gray, Thomas, 'Elegy Written in a Country
      Churchyard' 39
'Great Baby, The' 602–3
Great Exhibition 66–8, 222, 225, 254,
      446–7, 709
'Great Exhibition and the Little One, The' 446
Great Expectations 273–84
  adaptations 276–7, 279–81, 732, 734, 739–45
  animal studies 553, 555–6, 557–8, 559, 563
  CD as professional author 46, 48, 49, 50
  CD as public figure 65
  CD's reading 26, 31, 32, 34, 35, 37, 38
  children's literature 352–3

  class 275, 281, 366, 510–12, 514–15
  cognitive studies 614, 616–23, 625–6
  and *David Copperfield* 210
  disappearing lives 277–81
  and *Dombey and Son* 689
  domesticity and queer theory 378
  empire 525–6, 530, 531
  environment 568
  global circulation 731, 732, 734, 735
  illustrations 276
  industry and technology 446
  language 634, 643
  literary entrepreneurship 538, 539
  material culture 460
  new lives 281–4
  political economy 538–9, 542
  popular culture 767
  proliferating lives 276–7
  quality 237
  religion 197, 588
  science 413–14
  social reform 433
  struggle for life 273–5
  theatre 671
  theatricality 677–8
  travel 320–1
  visual mediations 683
Great Ormond Street Hospital for Sick
      Children 70–1
'Great Winglebury Duel, The' 87
Green, Kathe 749
Greene, Graham 214
Greenman, David J. 601, 604
Gregg, Melissa 472
Gregory, Gill 204, 330
Gregory, Melissa Valiska 204
Grener, Adam 169, 177
Grier, Katherine 555
Griffin, Susan M. 160
Griffith, D. W. 682, 725, 740
Griffith, Jane 228
Grillo, Virgil 81
Grimaldi, Joseph 125
Grimm, Jacob and Wilhelm 289–92, 343
Grossman, Jonathan H. 103, 518, 612
  Little Dorrit 313, 530, 531
  Old Curiosity Shop 139

Groth, Helen 401n.
Grotowski, Jerzy 675
'Ground in the Mill' 242
Guardian, The 763m 765
Guattari, Félix 471
Gubar, Marah 339
Guida, Fred 199
Guild of Literature and Art 57
guilt 278–9
Guinness, Alec 279, 750
Gupta, Tanika 744
Guxing Xuelei ('An Orphan's Tragedy') 732

Hachette, Louis 80n.
Hack, Daniel 225, 227, 683, 686–7
Hadley, Elaine 667
Hagen, Uta 672, 676
Hager, Kelly 372n.
Haight, Gordon S. 405
Hakala, Taryn 172
Halberstam, Jack 378n.
Hall, Anna 315
Hall, Samuel Carter 171, 315
Halliday, Andrew 599n.
Hamden, John 498
Hammond, Mary 740
Hampshire Advertiser 283
Hancock, David 464
Hannoosh, Michele 95
Hard Times 233–44
  animal studies 551
  CD as professional author 46, 48, 50, 54
  CD as public figure 65
  CD's reading 35
  children's literature 349–52
  class 365, 507–9, 512–13
  Coketown name 252
  drinking 601
  editions 236, 238–40
  empire 525
  environment 575–6
  global circulation 731
  industry and technology 438, 440, 441, 444, 447–8
  literary entrepreneurship 538, 539
  and *Little Dorrit* 656
  material culture 456

  political economy 534, 539, 545–7, 548
  psychology 248, 396
  science 405–6
  social reform 432–3
  world-system 716–17
Hardy, Barbara 168, 640
Hardy, Thomas 45, 306, 415, 546
Hare, Julius Charles 210, 211, 212
'Harlequin Fairy Morgana!' 341
Harper's New Monthly Magazine 227
Harper's Weekly 276
Hartley, Jenny 334
Harvey, David 711
Haselrig, Sir Arthur 498
Hatten, Charles 180n.
Haunted House, The 204
Haunted Man and the Ghost's Bargain, The 51, 191–2, 197, 255, 521
Haz, Mirando 201, 202
Heady, Emily Walker 199, 225
Health of Towns Association 434
'Heart of Mid-London, The' (CD and Wills) 558
Hemingway, Ernest, *The Sun Also Rises* 605
Herder, J. G. 289
Hervey, Thomas K., *The Book of Christmas* 92
Hesse, Hermann 726
Hessell, Nikki 327
heteroglossia 258
Hewett, Edward 597
Hewison, Robert 742
Higden, Betty 294
Hill, Jane Seymour 49
Hill, Rowland 66, 74, 445
Hills, Matt 768
Hilton, Boyd 591
historical novels *see Barnaby Rudge*; *Tale of Two Cities, A*
historiography 485–7, 494, 499
history 484–500
Hoffmann, E. T. A. 101
Hogarth, Catherine *see* Dickens, Catherine
Hogarth, George 44, 84
Hogarth, Georgina
  CD's death 322
  CD's letters to 32
  CD's marriage breakup 21–2
  publication of CD's letters 73, 334

Hogarth, Mary 64, 96, 165, 582n.
Hogarth, William 86, 313
  and Browne 685
  carnivalesque drinking 99
  and Cervantes 100
  influence on CD 96
  Little Dorrit 247
  A Rake's Progress 103
Holbein, Hans, *The Dance of Death* 30
Hole, S. R., Revd. 74
Holiday Romance 339, 341, 553
Hollington, Michael
  global circulation 723, 730
  Little Dorrit 251
  Old Curiosity Shop 145, 151
  Perils of Certain English Prisoners 203
  physiognomy 394
  Tale of Two Cities 263, 270
'Holly Tree Inn, The' 37
Holme, George 465–6, 467
Holmes, Rupert 302, 309, 741
Holway, Tatiana 537, 538, 540
home
  Bleak House 225
  Dombey and Son 115, 179–80, 181–90
  Goldsmith's *The Vicar of Wakefield* 180–1, 182, 189
  Old Curiosity Shop 115
  as sanctuary 115
  see also domestic ideology
'Home for Homeless Women' 69
homeless child 109
homoeroticism 357, 363
homonymy 637
Hong Kong 732
Hood, Thomas
  on CD 208
  Master Humphrey's Clock 134n., 135
  Old Curiosity Shop 142, 147
  Sketches by Boz 326
Hook, Theodore 96–8
Hopkins, Gerard Manley 569
'Horatio Sparkins' 89
Horney, Richard H., 'A Witch in the Nursery' 340, 342
hospitals, children's 70–1
House, Humphry 73, 157, 502n., 703

Household Words 325–31, 336
  animal studies 557, 558, 560–1
  'The Begging-Letter Writer' 71, 431
  CD as professional author 43, 44, 46, 51–2
  CD as public figure 65–6, 68, 69, 70, 71, 75
  CD's hostility towards women 202
  CD's marriage breakup 22
  CD's rationale 334, 350
  CD's reading 26n., 27, 28n., 29, 29n., 30n., 32n., 34, 36–40
  children's literature 340–2
  'A Child's Dream of a Star' 342
  Child's History of England 484, 497
  'The Child's Story' 26n., 200n.
  Christmas Stories 200–4
  'A Christmas Tree' *see* 'Christmas Tree, A'
  digitization 40, 204
  drinking 602
  'Drooping Buds' 70
  'Fairyland in "Fifty-Four"' 341
  'A Flight' 493n.
  'Frauds on the Fairies' *see* 'Frauds on the Fairies'
  'From the Raven in the Happy Family' 560–1
  Gaskell's *North and South* 38
  'Gaslight Fairies' 340–1
  globalization 728
  'The Great Baby' 602–3
  Hard Times 233, 234, 241
  'The Heart of Mid-London' (CD and Wills) 558
  history and change 492, 493n., 499n.
  'The Holly Tree Inn' 37
  'Home for Homeless Women' 69
  'Idiots' (CD and Wills) 397–8
  industry and technology 442n., 444–6, 449n.
  Ireland 525n.
  'The Last Words of the Old Year' 67–8, 492
  launch 87n.
  The Lazy Tour of Two Idle Apprentices 21
  'Little Red Working-Coat' 341
  'The Long Voyage' 521
  'The Lost Arctic Voyagers' 522n.
  'Lying Awake' 399
  material culture 457, 459

796 INDEX

Household Words (cont.)
  'A Monument of French Folly' 558
  'The Noble Savage' 327–8, 523, 719
  'On Strike' 242, 532n.
  'Our School' 32n.
  'Out of the Season' 27
  'Personal' 75
  'Pet Prisoners' 430
  play 648
  poetry 39
  political economy 532n.
  'A Poor Man's Tale of a Patent' 449
  'A Preliminary Word' 334, 444–5, 648, 758
  'Prince Bull. A Fairy Tale' 341
  psychology 389, 393, 394, 395–6, 397, 398, 399
  race and degeneration 521, 522, 523
  'Railway Dreaming' 449n.
  'Red Tape' 432n.
  religion 587
  'The School of the Fairies' 340
  science 404, 407, 410, 413–15, 418
  social reform 430, 431, 432n., 434
  'Some Account of an Extraordinary Traveller' 697, 719
  'The Stereoscope' (Morley and Wills) 255, 257
  and the theatre 670
  'The Thousand and One Humbugs' 341
  title 31, 341–2
  'The Toady Tree' 341, 497n.
  'To Working Men' 434
  'The Two Guides of the Child' 340
  'An Unsettled Neighbourhood' 442n.
  'Valentine's Day at the Post-Office' (CD and Wills) 445–6
  'Wallotty Trot' 341
  'Where We Stopped Growing' 30n.
  'Whole Hogs' 602–3
  'A Witch in the Nursery' 340, 342
  world-system 719
  'The Wreck of the Golden Mary' (CD and Collins) 52, 202, 204, 522
housekeeping
  David Copperfield 186
  Dombey and Son 186–7, 452
  material culture 452

Houseless Shadow, The 766
Houston, Gail Turley 338, 600
Howard, John 422
Howe, Jeff 760
Howe, Samuel Gridley 397
Hughes, Gwyneth 302–3
Hughes, Linda K. 330
Hugo, Victor 86, 151, 267
Huizinga, Johann 648, 656
human and animal studies 550–65
Hume, David 392
Hunt, Aeron 542, 543
Hunt, Leigh 53, 172, 226, 399, 691
Hunt, Robert, The Poetry of Science 408, 416
Hussein, Taha, The Tortured on the Earth 735
Hutcheon, Linda 757, 768
Hutton, James 487n.
Huxley, Thomas 400, 401
Hyde, Edward (Earl of Clarendon) 498–9

I Daniel Blake (Ken Loach film) 421
identity
  cognitive studies 619–21, 626
  Tale of Two Cities 265–7
'Idiots' (CD and Wills) 397–8
Idris, Youssef, The Language of Pain 735
illiteracy see literacy/illiteracy
Illuminated Magazine 496
Illustrated London News, The 71–2, 204
illustrations 682
  Barnaby Rudge 160–1, 161f
  Bleak House 227, 683–7, 685f, 693, 695
  CD as professional author 46, 50–1
  Chimes 195f, 196f
  Christmas Carol 198f, 199
  Christmas Stories 201
  Dombey and Son 683–4, 687–93, 688f
  early sketches 81, 82, 85f, 86
  Great Expectations 276
  Little Dorrit 245, 246f, 657, 658f, 660, 661f, 683–4, 687, 693–6
  Martin Chuzzlewit 650, 651f, 653–5, 653–5f
  Master Humphrey's Clock 138
  as mediations 684–91
  Old Curiosity Shop 134, 135f, 143f, 146f, 148f
  Oliver Twist 750, 752
  Pickwick Papers 92–5, 98–9, 104, 463n.

Sketches by Boz 50, 85f
Tale of Two Cities 269f, 269–70
image of CD 61–2, 74–5
imperialism *see* empire
imprisonment *see* prisons
Inchbald, Mrs, *Collection of Farces* 28
Independent 241
India 518, 734–5, 743–4
Indian Mutiny 203–4, 523, 525, 528, 718–19n.
industrial age 436–51
    CD as professional author 49
    CD as public figure 63, 67
    Dover Road 312
    education 349, 350
    and the environment 566–7, 570, 574–6
    Hard Times 349, 350
    material culture 456
    Old Curiosity Shop 146–7
    social reform 422
    thermodynamics 409, 412
    world-system 705, 708, 709, 714–17
inferences 617–20
influences on CD 25–42
information
    illustration as mediation 684, 686–7, 689, 691
    storing up visual data 692, 694, 696–8
Inglis, Katherine 145, 456
innovation *see* inventions
inns 97, 102–4
insanity 388, 397–8
Insolvent Debtors Act 423
institutionalization of literary study 237
interculturality 260, 262
interludes 648–64
international perspective *see* empire; global perspective
internet 756–73
interpolated tales
    drinking 604–8, 611
    Master Humphrey's Clock 138
    Pickwick Papers 101, 649
interpretation 220
intertextuality 26–9, 31–40
    Great Expectations 352
    journalism and correspondence 326
    religion 583–6

transculturation 728
intertheatricality 668–9
inventions 436–8, 449–50, 575–6
Ireland 525n.
Irving, Henry 670
Irving, Washington 40, 86, 100, 102
Is She His Wife? 666
Italy
    CD's travels 316, 318–19
    Little Dorrit 251, 252–3, 255, 257
    see also *Pictures from Italy*
it-narratives 462
It's a Wonderful Life 740

Jackson, J. H. 393
Jacobs, Alan 594
Jaffe, Audrey 137, 199, 589n.
Jamaica, Morant Bay uprising 524, 719n.
James, George Payne Rainsford 734
James, Henry 240, 246, 285, 296
James, Thomas Power 300, 303
Jameson, Fredric 526–8
Janes, Dominic 147
Japan 733–4, 743
Jarvie, Paul 193
Jarvis, Stephen 239
Jenkins, Henry 766, 770, 772
Jerrold, Douglas 66, 171–2, 496, 498
Jesuit riots *see* Gordon riots
Jesuits Exposed, The (Anon) 159
Jewusiak, Jacob 169–70, 177
Jingle, Alfred 57, 96, 97, 103, 359, 524, 604, 606, 669, 671
    illustration 94
    interludes 649, 657, 664
John, Juliet 461, 480, 756, 769
Johnson, Edgar 11–12, 193, 607n.
Johnson, Samuel, *Lives of the Poets* 38
Jones, Lawrence O. 306–7
Jones, Lloyd, *Mister Pip* 728
Jonson, Ben 40, 172
Jordan 765
Jordan, John O.
    adaptations 744
    Bleak House 221–2, 347, 470
    David Copperfield 515, 611
    global circulation 728

Joseph, Gerhard 456
Joshi, Priti 718, 734
Joule, James 231
journalism 17, 324–31, 333–4, 335–6
   animal studies 553, 558–9
   anti-Catholicism 157
   CD as public figure 64–6
   children's literature 340–3
   Christmas Stories 200
   drinking 602–3
   and *Hard Times* 238, 241
   history 493, 497
   industry and technology 439
   material culture 457
   and *Pickwick Papers* 98
   Reform Bill 89
   social reform 420, 427, 429–30, 432
   theatre reviews 666
   world-system 708–9, 717, 719
   see also *All the Year Round*; *Bentley's Miscellany*; *Daily News, The*; *Household Words*
Journal of Victorian Culture 759
Jowett, Benjamin 60–1
Joyce, James 151
Joyce, Patrick 501
Joyce, Simon 220
'Judicial Special Pleading' 493

Kadhum Al-Maliky, Saad Mohammed 241
Kahneman, Daniel 617–18
kaleidoscope 682
Kant, Immanuel 396
Kaplan, Fred 238, 392, 476–7
Kapoor, Abhishek 743
Karloff, Boris 746
Karpenko, Lara 145
Kay-Shuttleworth, James 433, 567
Kean, Charles 669
Kean, Edmund 679
Kean, Hilda 558
Keats, John 45, 622
Kelvin, Lord (William Thomson) 409
Kent, Charles 71, 72
Kenton, Charles 73
Kenya 729–30
Kermode, Frank 584
Kerr, Orpheus, *The Cloven Foot* 301

Ketabgian, Tamara 438
Kete, Kathleen 555
Kidd, William 81
Kilgore, Jessica 589n.
Kimbolton, Lord 498
kinaesthesia 270–1, 272
Kincaid, James R. 168, 338, 600
King, George 752
Kinney, Arthur F. 331
Kinsley, James 103
Kipling, Rudyard 527
Kismet 743
Kittler, Friedrich 683, 698
Kitton, F. G. 171, 235
Klaver, Claudia 543
Klimaszewski, Melisa 204
Knausgård, Karl Ove, *Min Kamp* 664
Knezevic, Borislav 504n.
Knight, Charles 33
Knoepflmacher, U. C. 339
Knowles, James Sheridan 37, 67
Koh, Adeline 332
Kolle, Anne (née Beadnell) 82–3
Kolle, Henry 82–3
Korea 734
Kornbluh, Anna 542
Kracauer, Siegfried 136
Kreilkamp, Ivan 563
Kroeber, Karl 569
Krueger, Christine 264, 266
Kucich, John 357, 368
Kujawska-Lis, Ewa 730
Kumbier, William 170
Kurnick, David 667

labour theory of value 539
labyrinth, urban
   Martin Chuzzlewit 174, 175
   Oliver Twist 108, 111
Ladies Cabinet, The 378
Lamarck, Jean-Baptiste 408, 561
Lamb, Charles 53
Lamert, James 13n.
Landor, Walter Savage 53
Lane, R. J. 454n.
Lang, Andrew 292, 294, 301, 304
language 631–46
Lao She 731

Larson, Janet L. 156, 581n., 584, 594n.
'Last Cab Driver, and the First Omnibus Cad, The' 88
'Last Words of the Old Year, The' 67–8, 492
Laurence, Dan H. 236
Laurie, Sir Peter 194
law
  Bleak House 220
  vs equity 126–9
  legal satire 137, 147
  Nicholas Nickleby 119, 120, 123
  Old Curiosity Shop 147–9
  Pickwick Papers 147
  Tale of Two Cities 264, 271
Law, Jules 180n., 567
Lawson, Henry 728, 737
Layard, Austen Henry 416, 497
Lazarillo de Tormes (Anon) 736
Lazy Tour of Two Idle Apprentices, The 21
Lean, David 279, 281, 741, 744, 748–51
Leavis, F. R. 236–7, 239–40, 534–5, 727
Leavis, Q. D. 237, 727
Le Bon, Gustave 268
Leclerc, Georges-Louis, Comte de Buffon 560–1
Ledger, Sally 271, 385, 502, 552, 717
Lee, Bruce 732
Lee, Jenny 749
Lee, Klaudia Hiu Yen 730, 732, 733
Leech, Anne 172
Leech, John 50, 74, 172, 195f, 198f
Lefebvre, Henri 228
legal satire 137, 147
Leigh, Mike 236
Leigh, Percival, 'The Chemical History of a Candle' 410
Lemon, Mark 172, 338n.
Lesage, Alain René 30, 40, 320
Lester, Marc 749
letters 324–6, 334–6
  Bentley 128
  biographers' access to and use of 12, 13
  brother's marriage 18, 19
  CD as professional author 43–5, 52–3, 58
  CD as public figure 71, 72–4
  on CD's children 338n.
  CD's discomfort with publication of 454n.
  CD's reading 27–8, 29, 30, 32, 33, 35, 38

Child's History of England 497
Chimes 193
Christmas Books 197
Christmas Stories 205
class 504
early sketches 82–3
flânerie 315
to Forster *see under* Forster, John
Great Exhibition 446–7
Hard Times 234–5
history 487, 496, 497
Household Words 521
from Italy 255
Little Dorrit 315, 662
marriage breakup 11, 20, 22–3, 334
Martin Chuzzlewit 649
Master Humphrey's Clock 137–8
material culture 465–6, 467
pets 562
political economy 539
publications 73
Queen Victoria's wedding 81
race and degeneration 521, 523, 524
religion 581n., 582n., 591
role of the writer 64
social reform 420, 427–8, 431
theatre 666, 669, 673
Levenson, Michael 474, 476, 573–4
Lever, William Hesketh 763
Leverhulme Trust 763
Levinas, Emmanuel 470
Levine, Caroline 231
Levine, George
  animal studies 553
  Great Expectations 274
  Little Dorrit 402n., 410
  religion 591
  science 404, 411–15
Lévi-Strauss, Claude 294
Lewes, George Henry
  CD's engagement with history 484
  Child's History of England 484
  Our Mutual Friend 295, 297
  psychology 388, 389, 390–1, 392, 394, 400, 401–2
  science 405, 407
  theatrical performances 172
  visual mediations 682

Lewis, Wyndham 247
Liang Qichao 733
library, CD's 25–6, 41f, 41, 561
Library of Fiction 45
lieu de mémoire, Little Dorrit as 258–60
Life of Our Lord, The 33n., 581
Lighthouse, The 338n.
Lightman, Bernard 415
Limited Liability Acts (1855–6) 542
Lindsay, Jack 154
Linnaeus, Carl 550
Lin Shu 730, 732
Linton, Eliza Lynn 204, 312–13, 452
literacy/illiteracy
  Bleak House 223
  David Copperfield 344
  Hard Times 350
  Oliver Twist 109
  Our Mutual Friend 286, 287, 292
  social reform 423, 427, 434
literary clubs 757–8, 770, 772
Literature Compass 722
Little Dorrit 245–59
  adaptations 741–2
  advertisements 255, 256f
  CD as professional author 45–6, 50, 64
  CD as public figure 63
  CD's reading 38–9
  children's literature 352
  class 365, 505–7, 511, 513, 515
  cosmopolitanism 529, 530, 531
  and *David Copperfield* 211
  and *Dombey and Son* 689
  domesticity and queer theory 379
  environment 566, 574, 575–6
  excellencies 248–51
  faults 245–8
  global circulation 731, 732, 735, 736
  and *Hard Times* 234
  illustrations 50, 245, 246f, 657, 658f, 660, 661f, 683–4, 687, 693–6
  industry and technology 438, 449
  interludes 649, 663–4
    Miss Wade 656–63, 664
  language 635, 640–1
  as '*lieu de mémoire*' 258–9
  literary entrepreneurship 538

London 315
  political economy 540, 544n.
  psychology 248–9, 253, 255, 259, 389, 398–402
  quality 237
  religion 584n., 585–8, 590–2, 594–5
  science 404, 410–12, 414–15, 417
  serial publication 252, 649, 659
  Shakespearian influence 674
  social reform 421–2, 423, 432
  as stereoscopic view 251–8
  theatricality 675, 679
  travel 312–14, 320–1
  visual mediations 683, 684, 687, 693–8
  Wade, Miss 249, 379, 381, 401
    illustrations 658f, 661f
    interludes 656–63, 664
  world-system 707, 713
  writing 315
'Little Red Working-Coat' 341
Livesey, Ruth 773
Lloyd, Frank 749
Loach, Ken 421
Locke, John 392
Lodge, David 177, 237
Lohrli, Anne 201, 325–6, 331
London
  animals 556–9, 564
  Barnaby Rudge 489
  Bleak House 220, 222–3, 230, 231
  environment 566–7, 573–4, 579
  flânerie 315, 428–9
  geology 416, 417
  Great Expectations 282–3
  Little Dorrit 315
  Martin Chuzzlewit 174–5
  Oliver Twist 106–15, 320
  race 519
  Tale of Two Cities 263
  and travel 320
  world-system 703, 705, 711–16
'London Recreations' 89
London Shakespeare Committee 32, 67
Longbridge, Frederick 748
'Long Voyage, The' 521
Lonoff, Sue 306
Loomis, Erik 575
'Lost Arctic Voyagers, The' 522n.

lost child 111–12
Lougy, Robert E. 168, 607n.
Louis XVI 495
Love, Glen A. 569–70
Lover, Samuel 38
Low, Sampson, *The Charities of London* 430–2
Lucas, John 170, 175
Lucentini, Franco, *The D Case* (with Fruttero) 302
Luckin, Bill 567
ludens 647–65
Lu Xun 732
Lyell, Charles, *Geological Evidences of the Antiquity of Man* 416–17
'Lying Awake' 399
Lytton, Robert 335

Macaulay, Thomas Babington 291, 485–91, 496, 499
MacDuffie, Allen 286, 409, 411–12
Macey, Mary 554
machinery 436–41, 446–9
Mackay, Charles 335
Mackenzie, Hazel 763
Mackintosh, Cameron 765
Maclise, Daniel 50, 81n., 334, 562
Macnish, Robert 392, 393
MacPike, Loralee 151
Macrae, David 581
Macready, William Charles
  child's death 334
  Goldsmith's retelling of Boccaccio 197
  inscribed copy of *Sketches of Young Couples* 81n.
  letters from CD 27, 70, 504n.
  and Shakespeare 33
  theatre 668, 669, 670, 671
Macrone, John 80, 83–5, 84n., 86n., 487
madness 388, 397–8
Magazine of Domestic Life 378
magic lanterns 682, 683, 695
Mahfouz, Naguib 735
Mahony, Francis ('Father Prout') 37
maintenance
  David Copperfield 186
  Dombey and Son 180, 182–4, 186–8
Maitland, Frederic William 128n.

Makdisi, Saree 530–1
Malik, Rachel 277, 282, 649, 743
Malthus, Thomas 532–3, 545–8, 592n.
management 188–90
Manheim, Leonard 394, 395
Mani, B. Venkat 729
Manning, Archbishop, 'The Relation of the Will to Thought' 391n.
Manning, Sylvia 195, 237
Mansfield, Katherine 374–5, 377, 379, 737
manuscript revision *see* revision
Mao Zedong 732
Mara, Miriam O'Kane 302
Marcus, Sharon 357, 371
Marcus, Steven 12, 102, 155, 175, 638
marriage
  Austen's novels 181
  CD's marriage breakup 10, 11, 20–3
  and Burdett-Coutts 69
  Great Expectations 280
  letters 11, 20, 22–3, 334
  public image 75
  re-creation of early marriage 82
  Dombey and Son 181–2
  Martin Chuzzlewit 177
  see also family
Marriage Act 426
Marseille prison 253, 256
Marsh, George Perkins 571
Marsh, Joss 199
Marshalsea prison
  CD as professional author 54
  imprisonment of John Dickens 11, 13, 13n., 17, 19, 89, 102–3
  Little Dorrit 64, 248–50, 252–3, 256–9, 312, 574
    class 513
    global circulation 732
    religion 590, 594, 595
    theatricality 675
    visual mediations 697
  Pickwick Papers 103
Martin (television series) 741
Martin Chuzzlewit 166–78
  adaptations 744
  animal studies 552
  CD as professional author 46, 49
  CD's reading 29, 34, 40

Martin Chuzzlewit (cont.)
    class 511
    environment 568, 569, 570, 574
    Gamp, Sarah ('Sairey') 40, 50, 72, 170–3,
        598, 638, 640, 674
      illustrations 651f, 653f, 654f, 655f
      interludes 649–56, 657, 663, 664
    illustrations 650, 651f, 653, 653–5f, 654, 655
    interludes (Mrs Gamp) 649–56, 657,
        663, 664
    language 631, 634, 637–8, 639–40
    material culture 457–9, 460
    phrenology 394
    race and degeneration 521, 524
    Shakespearian influence 674
    theatre 669
    travel 320
    world-system 707, 708, 712, 716, 718
    see also Gamp, Sarah ('Sairey')
Martineau, Harriet 38, 204, 440–1
Martin-Harvey, John 748
Marx, Karl
    la bohème 55
    commodity culture 456, 459
    Das Kapital 259
    'discourse of spectrality' 587
    technology 437
    world-system 711, 714
Marxism 572
masculinity 358
    David Copperfield 363
    Dombey and Son 544
    Our Mutual Friend 365, 370–1
    Tale of Two Cities 266
Master Humphrey's Clock 134, 137–40
    Barnaby Rudge 153
    CD as professional author 46, 49
    CD as public figure 65
    industry and technology 444
    material culture 465
    Old Curiosity Shop see *Old Curiosity
        Shop, The*
material culture 227–8, 286, 452–67
materialism 389, 391–2, 396–9
Mathews, Charles 670, 680
Matsumura, Masaie 743
Matus, Jill 389
Matz, B. W. 97, 102

Maxwell, Richard 151
Mayhew, Edward 37–8
Mayhew, Henry 38, 92, 289–90, 519–20
McCann, Andrew 147
McClellan, John 276n.
McGill, Meredith 226
McSharry, Carmel 751
Meckier, Jerome 167
media archaeology 450
media theory 769
mediations, visual 682–99
    illustrations 684–91
    storing up visual data 691–8
'Meditations in Monmouth Street' 90
Meeker, Joseph 577
Melbourne, Lord 360
Melville, Herman 220, 382–3n.
memory 389
    cognitive studies 625
    David Copperfield 208, 213, 215, 217–18
    and drinking 601–4, 606–12
    Haunted Man and the Ghost's Bargain 255
    Little Dorrit 255–6, 258–60
    Tale of Two Cities 260
    visual mediations 694–5, 698
Mendelssohn, Felix, 'Birmingham' sketch 9,
    10f, 15
Menke, Richard 683, 687, 690–1, 692n.
Menon, Ayeesha 744
Meredith, George 39
Merrick, David 751
mesmerism 296, 388, 392
Message from the Sea, A (CD and Collins) 52, 202
metatext 739, 754
Method acting 676
metonymy
    animal studies 559, 565
    Bourdieu on 264
    cognitive studies 619–21
    Little Dorrit 540
    Oliver Twist 559
    thing theory 461
Metropolitan Sanitary Association 434, 567
Metz, Nancy Aycock 167–8, 171, 407
Mexico 735
Michelet, Jules 262, 267
middle class 501–4, 506, 509–10, 512
    Barnaby Rudge 382

charity 428
children 338
earnestness and industry 365
education 433
Great Expectations 275
Hard Times 351
industry and technology 437
Old Curiosity Shop 145, 147
Oliver Twist 117
Our Mutual Friend 367
political reform 434
popular culture 772
radicalism 433
social reform 421, 433, 434, 438
Mikdadi, F. H. 735
Mill, John Stuart 376–7, 432, 437–8, 491
Miller, Andrew H. 457, 459
Miller, D. A. 223–4, 363n.
Miller, J. Hillis 82, 168, 223, 227, 455, 703
Miller and his Men, The 28
Milton, John, *Paradise Lost* 38, 322
mind and body, relationship between 391–2, 395–400
Mirror of Parliament, The 420
Mister Magoo's Christmas Carol 741
Mistry, Rohinton 734–5
Mitterrand, François 260
modernism 526–8, 555
modernity
  affect 471
  animal studies 564
  as combined and uneven development 703–21
  environment 572, 576
  Martin Chuzzlewit 167
  Old Curiosity Shop 136, 138, 142, 144, 151
  social reform 432
Moers, Ellen 373n.
Monboddo, Lord (James Burnett) 552–3
Moncrieff, Scott 196
money 532–49
  Christmas Carol 193
  Nicholas Nickleby 120, 121, 123, 124, 131, 132
  Old Curiosity Shop 142
  see also economics; finances of CD
Monmouth Rebellion 493n.
Monod, Sylvère 167
Montaigne, Michel de 561

Monthly Chronicle 86n.
Monthly Magazine
  'The Bloomsbury Christening' 83
  'A Dinner at Poplar Walk' 49, 83, 423n.
  Sketches by Boz 45
  'The Steam Excursion' 83
monthly numbers *see* serial publication
'Monument of French Folly, A' 558
mood 469–74, 480–2
Moody, Ron 750, 751
Moore, Dickie 749n.
Moore, Grace 203, 464n., 524–5, 718–19, 727
Moore, Thomas, *Irish Melodies* 39
Moran, Maureen 162
Moretti, Franco 108
Morford, Henry, *John Jasper's Secret* 300
Morgentaler, Goldie 274–5, 413–14
Morley, Henry 38, 342
  'The Cure of Sick Minds' 397
  'The Stereoscope' (with Wills) 255, 257
Morning Chronicle, The 336
  CD as public figure 64
  CD's early sketches 84n.
  CD's reading 40
  CD's resignation 84
  CD's review of 'The Bloomsbury Christening' dramatization 83
  and *Pickwick Papers* 98
  Reform 420
  Sketches by Boz 45
Morris, Pam 275, 502n.
Morton, Timothy 570–1, 578
Moscheles, Ignaz 9
motion 314–19
Moynahan, Julian 278
Mphahlele, Es'kia 728–9, 744
Mrs. Lirriper's Lodgings 47, 51, 204–5, 636–8
Mr. Turner (Mike Leigh film) 236
'Mudfog Papers, The' 405–6, 427
'Mugby Junction' stories 200–2, 449
Muggleton, David 771–2
Mukherjee, Gyan 743
Mukherjee, Pablo 715
Müller, Max 291
multimedia publishing 275, 276–7
Mumbai Chuzzlewits, The 744
Murfin, Ross 306
Murray, John 1

Murray, Lindley, *English Grammar* 28–9
Museum of London, *Dickens and London* exhibition 766–7
musicals 740–2, 748, 750–2, 765
Mussell, James 324, 759–60
Mystery of Edwin Drood, The 299–311
   adaptations 302–3, 309–10, 741–2
   CD as professional author 46, 50, 57
   empire 526, 527, 530–1
   genre 304–8
   history 300–4
   illustrations 50
   language 644–5
   material culture 453–4, 464n.
   popular culture 759
   psychology 389
   science 417
   tragicomedy 308–11
   travel 320–2
Mytton, Jack 104
'My Unknown Friend' (unperformed stage version of *Great Expectations*) 279

Nabokov, Vladimir 151
Nancy, Jean-Luc 268
Nandy, Ashis 518
Napolitano, Marc 740, 751
narrative
   Bleak House 221, 223, 230
   drinking 599, 601, 611–12
   first-person 615
   Little Dorrit 247
   Martin Chuzzlewit 169, 170, 176
Nassau Senior 193
Nayder, Lillian 21n., 202–4, 327, 667, 672–3
nebular hypothesis 407–8
Nelson, Claudia 338
networks 231
New Criticism 584
Newell, Mike 281, 682
Newgate prison 83, 485
   Barnaby Rudge 155, 384, 487, 494–5
   Great Expectations 278–9, 282–3
Newman, S. J. 638
new media 756–73
New Piljians Projiss, A 172
New Poor Law (1834) 62, 63, 105, 433, 446, 536, 559

Newsom, Robert 12, 338, 593n.
newspapers, extracts of CD's novels in 282–4
New Sporting Magazine 92
Newton, Adam Zachary 594
'New Uncommercial Samples: Mr. Barlow' 26n., 29n.
New York Tribune 22
New Zealand 727
Ngai, Sianne 374, 379–80, 382–3n.
Ngugi wa Thiong'o 729–30
Nicholas Nickleby 119–33
   adaptations 734, 741–3
   animal studies 553
   betrayal of the social contract 122–4
   business and social contracts 119–22
   CD as professional author 46
   CD as public figure 62, 66–7
   CD's reading 28–9, 31
   class 509–12, 514
   contracts, equity, and the law 124–30
   drinking 610
   and early sketches 81
   global circulation 734, 735
   language 635
   psychology 395–6
   Shakespearian influence 674
   social reform 433
   theatre 669, 671
   travel 313, 319, 321
   world-system 708
   writing 137
Niebuhr, Barthold 291
'Niger Expedition, The' 708–9, 717, 719
Nightingale, Andrea Wilson 674–5, 677
Nightingale, Florence 68
'Night Walks' 766, 767
Nisbet, Ada B. archive 723, 729n.
Nixon, Jude V. 407
Nixon, Rob 227n.
'Noble Savage, The' 327–8, 523, 719
'Nobody's Story' 200n.
Nora, Pierre 258
Northcote–Treveleyan Report (1854) 432
Northern Exposure 741
Norton, Caroline 360
Norton, George 360
No Thoroughfare (CD and Collins) 52, 200
Novak, Daniel 693

novels, Stephen on 468, 469
Nunokawa, Jeff 696
nursery stories/rhymes 26–7, 352–3
   Bleak House 346–8
   Hard Times 349–52
   journalism 340–3
   Our Mutual Friend 288–94
'Nurse's Stories' 292, 342–3
Nussbaum, Martha 534, 593

October (Eisenstein film) 268
Odd Couple, The 741
Oddie, William 203
Oe, Kenzaburo, Legion of Quilp 151
Okonedo, Sophie 753–4
Oldbuck, Jonathan 93
'Old Couple, The' 90
Old Curiosity Shop, The 134–52
   adaptations 742
   affect 470, 476–9
   allegory and capitalism 134–7
   capitalism and the law 146–9
   Catholicism 165
   CD as professional author 46–7, 49
   CD as public figure 65
   CD's reading 32, 36–7
   children's literature 352
   city 107–8, 111, 113–15
   curiosity, gambling, temporality 140–4
   dwarf and wax-work girl 144–5
   environment 568
   failed rescue and comparative studies 149–51
   global circulation 732–3
   illustrations 134, 135f, 143f, 145, 146f, 148f
   industry and technology 439–41, 443
   language 635
   and Little Dorrit 250
   and Pickwick Papers 102
   theatricality 678
   transport 436
   travel 313, 319–20
   Warren's Blacking 15n.
   world-system 712
Oliphant, Margaret 194n.
Oliver! 740–1, 748–53, 765–6
Oliver & Company 739, 750, 751–2, 753
Oliver Twist 105–18
   adaptations 739–54
   affect 470, 476
   animal studies 557–9, 563–4
   CD as professional author 44–6, 50, 55–6
   CD as public figure 62–3, 65
   CD's reading 36–7
   children's literature 352
   city 106–18
   class 507, 510–11
   cognitive studies 621
   contract 125
   copyright 125
   country 116–18
   in Darwin's work 551
   and early sketches 85
   eating 599n.
   empire 525
   environment 568
   gender and sexuality 357–8
   global circulation 726, 729, 731, 733, 735
   homages 726
   illustrations 50, 109, 110f, 116f, 750, 752
   London 106–15, 320
   material culture 453n.
   negotiations 132
   New Poor Law 446
   political economy 534
   popular culture 764, 767
   psychology 110, 117
   public readings and performances 307, 313, 746, 748
   race and degeneration 520–1
   religion 587, 591–2
   Shakespearian influence 674
   social reform 427, 428
   source-material 101
   Thackeray's criticism 55
   theatre 669
   travel 313, 320
   world-system 715–16
Oliver Twisted 748
Oliver Twist; or Dickens Up a Tree 748
Olivia Twist 749
online resources 324–5
   see also digitization
Only Way, The 748
'On Strike' 242, 532n.
opera 741
Oppenlander, Ella Ann 325, 326

Orford, Pete 759, 763
orphanhood 213, 218, 222, 616–26
Ortiz, Fernando 727
Orwell, George 237
   Animal Farm 561
   on CD 577, 724
   CD's psychology 388
   Little Dorrit 247–8
Osteen, Mark 541
Ostry, Elaine 407
O'tello The Irish Moor of Fleet Street 674
Otis, Laura 698
Otto, Rudolph 589
Our Mutual Friend 285–98
   affect 469, 470, 480–2
   animal studies 553, 560, 562
   Birkbeck Reading Project 242
   CD as professional author 46, 48, 50
   CD as public figure 62
   CD's reading 26, 34, 36, 39
   children's literature 353
   class 365–7, 503n., 513–15
   culture and fancy 285–9
   and *Dombey and Son* 689
   domesticity and queer theory 373, 377, 379, 381, 383, 386
   dust, relics, and wild tales 289–93
   empire 531
   environment 566, 570, 574
   gender and sexuality 359, 365–71
   global circulation 731
   history and change 493n.
   illustrations 50
   industry and technology 438, 441, 446
   language 634, 641–4
   'logic of feeling' 294–7
   material culture 459
   and *The Mystery of Edwin Drood* 309
   new directions 297–8
   political economy 539
   popular culture 759, 761–2, 770
   race and degeneration 521
   religion 591–2
   Riah 753
   science 410–15, 417
   serial publication 242
   social reform 433
   Staplehurst disaster 450
   theatricality 677, 678–9
   transport 436
   travel 320–1
   visual mediations 683
   world-system 707, 712–13, 716, 717
'Our Parish' sketches 89–90
'Our School' 32n.
'Out of the Season' 27
Ovid 29
Owen, Richard 415
Oxford Movement 157

Page, Georgie 765
Paley, William, *Natural Theology* 590, 592
Palmer, Alan 615
Palmer, Samuel 50
panoramas 682, 683, 696–8
parallelism, in *Little Dorrit* 253, 254, 257, 259
Parham, John 573
Paris 263–4, 315, 494
Parker, David 197
Parkins, Wendy 240
parliamentary reporting 89, 98, 157, 327, 420, 485n., 486
'Parliamentary Sketch, A' 89
'The Parlour Orator, The' 467
Parody, Clare 767
Paroissien, David 334
paronomasia *see* puns
Parrott, Jeremy 66n., 331
Passions of Carol, The 741
pastoral conventions 116–18
patent system 449
paternalism 384–7
Patmore, Coventry 39, 383
Patten, Robert L.
   Barnaby Rudge 175–6
   CD as professional author 49
   Christmas Carol 199
   environment 568
   global circulation 726
   illustrations 684
   journalism and correspondence 326
   moral code in literature 131n.
   Nicholas Nickleby 121
   Old Curiosity Shop 139
   Oliver Twist 108
   Pickwick Papers 97–8, 607n.

religion 589
   Sketches by Boz 84
   Warren's Blacking 15n.
patterns 649, 652, 659
Paxton, Joseph 67
Paz, D. G. 156
Pearl, Matthew 307
Pearson, Roberta 768
Peel, Sir Robert 170, 171
penal reform 422, 425–6, 428, 430, 432–3
Penn, Richard 92
Pentonville prison 425, 430
Pepys, Samuel 421
Percy, Bishop, *Reliques of Ancient English Poetry* 289, 290
performance 271–2, 738
   see also public readings and performances
Perils of Certain English Prisoners, The (CD and Collins) 52, 200, 202–4, 523
Perrault, Charles 343
'Personal' 75
personification *see* animisms
Petch, Simon 264
Peters, Laura 203, 328
'Pet Prisoners' 430
Pettit, Clare 461
Phelps, Sarah 752, 754
phenomenology 228
philanthropy *see* charity
Phillips, Adam 676, 677
Phillips, Samuel 194
Phiz *see* Browne, Hablot K.
photography 693–4, 695, 698
phrenology 394
physiognomy 394
picaresque
   cognitive studies 616
   David Copperfield 608, 611
   Martin Chuzzlewit 569
   Pickwick Papers 102, 604, 606, 773
   popular culture 772
   Spanish literature 736
   travel 320
Pickwick (1936 opera) 741
Pickwick Bicycle Club 770–1, 771f, 773
Pickwick Club, New Zealand 727
Pickwick Papers, The 92–104
   adaptations 738, 741–3, 747

affect 471
carnival and Cervantes 97–102
CD as professional author 45, 46, 47, 50, 57
CD as public figure 66
CD's reading 27, 36–7
Chapman and Hall 84, 92, 96, 125, 131
contract 95, 125
drinking 600, 602, 604–8
and early sketches 80, 82, 84, 85, 86
empire 524, 525
gender and sexuality 359–61, 362, 363
global circulation 727
illustrations 463n.
inns and prisons 102–4
interludes 647, 648
   Jingle 649, 657, 664
Jingle, Alfred 57, 96, 97, 103, 359, 524, 604, 606, 669, 671
   illustration 94
   interludes 649, 657, 664
   language 632–3, 634, 635–6, 637, 638–9, 642, 645
and *Master Humphrey's Clock* 137, 138, 139
material culture 461–3, 467
and *The Mystery of Edwin Drood* 309
and *The Old Curiosity Shop* 147
popular culture 770–1, 771f, 773
psychology 361, 397
religion 156, 581–2n., 588, 589, 591
science 405, 406
serial publication 95–6, 647–8, 747
Seymour 84, 92–5, 97–8, 102, 647
theatre 671
transport 436
travel 93, 102–3, 313, 319, 321
Warren's Blacking 15
world-system 708
writing and reception 95–7
see also Jingle, Alfred
Pictures from Italy 1
   CD as public figure 73
   geology 416, 417
   religion 161, 164, 582n.
   travel 316, 318–19
   visual mediations 682
Piggott, Gillian 151
pilgrimage 313–14, 316, 321

808　INDEX

'Pip's Patron' (stage version of *Great Expectations*) 279
piracy 276–7, 283, 301, 738
Piranesi, Giovanbattista, *Imaginary Prisons* 253
Pius VII, Pope 158
Placing Literature project 759, 763–4
Placing the Author postcard project 762
plagiarism 46–7
play 647–65
Plotz, John 267, 460, 692–3
Poe, Edgar Allan, *William Wilson* 303, 306
poetry
　CD's journals 330, 335–6
　CD's reading 38–9
'The Poetry of Science' 691, 692
Poland 730
Polanski, Roman 747
Polhemus, Robert M. 173, 599
political commentary/journalism 89, 98, 157, 327, 420, 485n., 486
political economy 193, 409, 532–49
political reform 434, 485
　see also Reform
politics 421–3
　Barnaby Rudge 153, 155–6, 162–4
　Bleak House 225
　CD refuses to stand for election 68, 422
　and class 502
　Hard Times 238
　Little Dorrit 250
　Tale of Two Cities 262, 263, 264–5, 270
Pollock, Sir Frederick 128n.
pollution 566–7, 573, 575–9
　see also fog/smog
Poole, Adrian 288
Poole, John 172
Poor Jo 749
Poor Law Amendment Act (1834) 62, 63, 105, 433, 446, 536, 559
'Poor Man's Tale of a Patent, A' 449
'Poor Relation's Story, The' 200n.
Poor Theatre 675
Poovey, Mary 344n., 534, 539–40, 545–6
Pope, Alexander 38–9, 638
Pope, Norris 534n.
popular culture 756–73

popular science *see* science, popular
postal system 66–7, 74, 445–6
post-secular studies 593
Potemkin 268
'Preliminary Word, A' 334, 444–5, 648, 758
Prest, Céline 262
Preston 233, 234
Price, Leah 458
Prickett, Stephen 589n.
'Prince Bull. A Fairy Tale' 341
Prisoners' Counsel Act (1836) 426
prisons
　Bastille 265, 270, 494–5
　Bridewell 384
　Coldbath Fields 428
　Fleet 99, 102–4
　Little Dorrit 248–50, 252–3, 256–9
　Pentonville 425, 430
　Pickwick Papers 102–4
　reform 422, 425–6, 428, 430, 432–3
　Tothill Fields 428
　see also Marshalsea prison; Newgate prison
Prisons Act (1877) 428
Pritchett, B. S. 614, 617
Procter, Adelaide 204
Proctor, Richard, *Watched by the Dead* 301, 304, 305, 307
professionalism of CD 43–58, 64
professional theatre
　CD's attitude towards 668
　CD's reviews 666
　in CD's writings 671
　CD's writings for 666
　development 670
progress 313–14, 316, 321
pronouns 634, 635, 637, 642–3
Propp, Vladimir 294
prosopopoeia *see* animisms
prostitution
　Old Curiosity Shop 144
　Oliver Twist 55, 108
　social reform 429
　Urania Cottage 69–70, 429, 431
Protestantism 165
　Barnaby Rudge 153, 156, 157–9, 164
　Bleak House 587
Proust, Marcel 247, 259, 675

Providentialism 590–3, 595
Provident Union of Literature, Science, and Art 56–7
Pryce, Jonathan 750–1
psychiatry 394
psychoanalytic criticism 388–9, 394–5
psychology 388–94
  Barnaby Rudge 396–7
  Bleak House 376, 397
  CD's childhood 15, 388
  crowds 268
  David Copperfield 217, 219, 361, 389
  Dombey and Son 393–4, 397
  dualism 394–8
  Great Expectations 280, 281
  Hard Times 248, 396
  Haunted House 197
  high Victorian realism 361
  Little Dorrit 248–9, 253, 255, 259, 389, 398–402
  Mystery of Edwin Drood 389
  Nicholas Nickleby 395–6
  Old Curiosity Shop 140
  Oliver Twist 110, 117
  Our Mutual Friend 369
  Pickwick Papers 361, 397
  Tale of Two Cities 393
  urban environment 107
public figure, CD as 59–76
public health 436, 438
  Bleak House 222
  journalism 329
  social reform 432, 434, 446
Public Health Act (1848) 222
Public Health Act (1858) 329
public readings and performances 667, 738–9
  affect 350
  CD as professional author 53–4
  CD as public figure 71–2
  Christmas Carol 71, 192
  Great Expectations (prepared but never performed) 276
  influence 755
  Martin Chuzzlewit 171–2
  mesmerism 296
  Oliver Twist 307, 313, 746, 748
  political economy 538
  theatricality 680

publishing industry 43–7, 57
Punch 170, 171, 173n.
Punchdrunk Enrichment 764
puns 631, 635–6, 638, 644
Pykett, Lyn 453
Pym, John 498

queer theory 357, 371–87
  affect 471, 474, 475
  affect aliens 374–9
  Barnaby Rudge 380–7
  Master Humphrey's Clock 139
Quetelet, Adolphe 427
Quinn, Martin 236

Raban, William 766
race and ethnicity 517–18
  Bleak House 226
  and degeneration 519–24
  Indian Mutiny 203
  journalism 327–8
  Oliver Twist adaptations 753–4
  world-system 717–19
radio adaptations 277, 280–1, 739–40, 744–6, 749, 751
Rae, John 522
Ragged Schools 63, 69, 340, 428, 433
'Railway Dreaming' 449n.
railways 436, 438, 442–3, 446, 449
  Bleak House 447
  Dombey and Son 103, 441–4, 572, 576
  Staplehurst disaster 75, 449–50
Rainof, Rebecca 177
Ralph, Sheryl Lee 753
Rambler, The 235
Rancière, Jacques 264, 565n.
Read-a-thon 764, 769
reading, CD's 25–42
  history 484
  natural history 561
  psychology 392, 394
reception
  Barnaby Rudge 153
  Battle of Life 195
  Bleak House 225
  Chimes 193–4
  Christmas Carol 191–3, 197

reception (*cont.*)
  Cricket on the Hearth 194
  early sketches 82, 86
  Hard Times 235, 236–7
  Haunted Man 197
  Little Dorrit 245–8
  Martin Chuzzlewit 166–70
  Mystery of Edwin Drood 309–10
  Old Curiosity Shop 134, 135–6, 137, 139
  Oliver Twist 105
  Our Mutual Friend 285, 295
  Pickwick Papers 96, 97
  Tale of Two Cities 260
recycling 285, 294
'Red Tape' 432n.
Reece, Benny 305
Reed, Carol 751, 753
Reed, Oliver 751
Rees, Kathy 376n.
Reform 420–2, 426, 486
  early sketches 79, 89–90
  Macaulay 485n., 486
  Tale of Two Cities 491
regional newspapers, extracts of CD's novels in 282–4
Registration Act 426
Reid, Thomas 393, 396
religion 581–96
  Barnaby Rudge 153–4, 156–65
  Bleak House 198
  CD's reading 33–6
  Christmas Books 197–9
  discourse and genre studies 586–90
  Great Expectations 198
  interdisciplinary studies 593–5
  intertextuality 583–6
  Little Dorrit 249
  Old Curiosity Shop 141
  Providential world view 590–3
  thermodynamics 409
  see also Catholicism; Protestantism
repression 357, 359, 365–8
reprints 47, 86, 226
reproduction of social ties
  Austen's novels 181, 182
  Dombey and Son 180, 182, 186–90
  Goldsmith's *The Vicar of Wakefield* 181

reputation of CD
  Christmas books 191
  early sketches 80
  and Forster's biography 11
  Mystery of Edwin Drood 305, 306, 307
  Old Curiosity Shop 46
resemblance, and acting 676–9
responsibilities 224, 226, 230
Rettburg, Jill Walker 242, 243
reviews *see* reception
Revill, Clive 750
Revised Code (1862) 434
revision
  David Copperfield 207–9, 213, 216–19
  early sketches 82, 86–7
  Great Expectations 273, 274–5, 276, 280, 284
  Old Curiosity Shop 134–5
  Oliver Twist 747
Reynolds, George W. M., *Pickwick Abroad* 734
Rhodes, Cecil 203
Ricardo, David 533
Rice, Thomas J. 154
Richards, Thomas 456
Richardson, John 96, 99
Richardson, Ruth 428
Richer, Paul 268
Ricoeur, Paul 471, 594
Rignall, J. M. 267
Ritvo, Harriet 552
Robbins, Bruce 224, 227n.
Robinson, Joanna 767
Robles, Mario Ortiz 565n.
Robson, Catherine 144–5, 338
Robson, Lisa 266
Roche, Antonin 80n.
Rochester 312
Roman Catholicism *see* Catholicism
Roman Catholic Relief Act (1829) 491
Romano, John 751
Roscoe, Thomas 101
Roseanne 741
Rossi-Wilcox, Susan 597
Round of Stories by the Christmas Fire, A 51
Rowlandson, Thomas 94, 103
Rowlinson, Matthew 142
Royal British Bank 245
Royal Literary Fund 57

Royal Shakespeare Company 741, 742
Royal Society 406
Roylance, Mrs 13n.
Rudé, George 267
rural depictions
   environment 568
   Oliver Twist 106, 116–18
Rushdie, Salman 151
Ruskin, John
   CD's engagement with history 485
   Christmas Books 198–9
   domestic ideology 382, 383, 384
   environment 569
   Hard Times 235, 236
   media scrutiny 235–6
   The Stones of Venice 437, 438, 450
Russell, C. W. 192
Russell, Lord John 421
Russia 736
Rylance, Rick 392, 401n.

Sadoff, Dianne F. 395, 740, 742
Sadrin, Anny 272
Said, Edward W. 527–8, 703–6, 709
Sakai, Toshihiko 733
Sala, George A. 331
Salotto, Eleanor 222
Sanders, Andrew 113–14, 157
Sanders, Julie 742, 754
Sanitary Act (1866) 329
sanitation 329, 436, 438
   Our Mutual Friend 412
   social reform 446, 567, 579
Scapegoat, The 748n.
Schacht, Paul 592n.
Schacker, Jennifer 348
Schaffer, Talia 177
Schama, Simon 495
Schlicke, Paul 3, 137, 171, 756
Schoch, Richard W. 667–8
'Schoolboy's Story, The' 200n.
'School of the Fairies, The' 340
schools and education
   CD as public figure 62–3, 69
   CD's education 486
   Hard Times 349–50
   Our Mutual Friend 287–8, 366

Ragged Schools 63, 69, 340, 428, 433
   social reform 423, 428, 433–4, 496
Schor, Hilary Margo 137, 221, 296, 338
Schwartz, Steven 724
Schwarzbach, Fred 82
science, popular 404–19
   astronomy 407–13
   biology 413–16
   geology 416–17
Scott, George C. 742
Scott, Shafto, 'My Unknown Friend' 279
Scott, Sir Walter 132
   Barnaby Rudge 154, 155
   CD's reading 37
   financial difficulties 44
   friendship with George Hogarth 44
   historiography 486, 487
   Ivanhoe 197
   Minstrelsy of the Scottish Border 289, 290
   The Antiquary 93
Scrooged 740
Sebald, W. G., *Austerlitz* 149–50
second thoughts 208–19
Secord, James 408
Sedgwick, Eve Kosofsky
   affective turn 471
   gender and sexuality 357, 363, 369
   Mystery of Edwin Drood 302
   Our Mutual Friend 513
Seigworth, Gregory J. 472
self-formation (*Bildung*)
   David Copperfield 610
   Oliver Twist 107–15
   Our Mutual Friend 286, 287, 296
self-help 533–6
Sellassie, Berhane Mariam Sahle 728
Sen, Sambudha 284, 502
Sennett, Richard 673
sensation 468, 476–9
sensation fiction 306–7
sentimentality 468–9, 470, 476–9, 482
serial publication
   Barnaby Rudge 139
   Bleak House 227, 233–4, 484
   CD as professional author 43, 45, 46, 48
   CD as public figure 64, 66–7
   Child's History of England 340

serial publication (*cont.*)
  cognitive studies 618
  Dombey and Son 689
  Great Expectations 275–6
  Hard Times 233, 236, 242–3, 349
  illustration as mediation 684
  interludes 647–64
  Little Dorrit 252, 649, 659
  Martin Chuzzlewit 176
  Old Curiosity Shop 137, 139
  Oliver Twist 746
  Our Mutual Friend 242
  Pickwick Papers 95–6, 647–8, 747
  religion 591
  and scientific findings 415–16
  Tale of Two Cities 269–70, 332–3
  and television mini-series 743
  writing process 747
Seth, Vikram, *A Suitable Boy* 735
Sewell, William, *Hawkstone* 162
sexuality 357–71
  Barnaby Rudge 385
  capitalism 533, 543–5
  children 338
  David Copperfield 361–5
  domestic ideology 374
  Our Mutual Friend 365–71
  Pickwick Papers 359–61, 362
  see also queer theory
Seymour, Robert 46, 100
  Pickwick Papers 84, 92–5, 97–8, 102, 647
Shakespeare, William
  CD's adaptations 667
  CD's involvement in
    commemorations 66–7
  collaboration with Fletcher 53
  global circulation 725, 728
  Hamlet 31, 32, 674
    and *Great Expectations* 671, 678
    and *Little Dorrit* 249, 252, 255
  Henry VIII 53
  influence on CD 28, 30–3, 96, 674
  Macbeth 28, 31–2, 308–9, 648
  The Merchant of Venice 31, 753
  The Merry Wives of Windsor 32, 172
  Othello 31, 674
  Pickwick Papers 101
  Romeo and Juliet 31, 674
  Two Noble Kinsmen 53
  The Winter's Tale 289
Shakespeare Foundation Schools 31
Shakespeare Memorial Theatre 67
sham theatre, CD's participation
  in 666, 671–4
Sharpe, Sutton 129n., 130*f*
Shattock, Joanne 328, 332–3
Shaw, George Bernard 235–7, 239, 259, 667
Shelden, Michael 194, 536
Sheldon, Georgie 300, 303
Shelley, Percy 45
Sherif, Nur 735
Sherman, Bill 761
Shillibeer, George 88
'Shops and their Tenants' 37, 314, 315
'Shy Neighbourhoods' 314
al-Sibaci, Muhammad 735
Sidgwick, Henry 400
'Signal-Man, The' 201–2, 449, 471
signature repetition 619–21
Simmel, Georg 107
Simmons, Dan 307
Simpson, Margaret 237–8
Simpson, Richard 235
Sinyard, Neil 751
Sipley, Tristan 573
Sitwell, Osbert 247
sketches, early 79–91
  see also *Sketches by Boz*; *Sketches of Young Couples*; *Sketches of Young Gentlemen*
Sketches by Boz 79–80, 81–90
  bicentenary celebrations 724, 764
  'The Boarding-House' 39
  CD as professional author 45, 46, 50, 57
  CD as public figure 64
  CD's reading 37, 39
  early studies 326
  global circulation 730
  Hogarth's influence 313
  illustrations 50, 85*f*
  material culture 467
  'The Parlour Orator' 467
  Pickwick Papers advertisement 93
  'Shops and their Tenants' 37, 314, 315
  social reform 426

Sketches of Young Couples 80, 81, 90, 733
  affect 469, 470, 474–6
Sketches of Young Gentlemen 80, 81
Sketching the City project 764
Slater, Michael 11
  CD's childhood 15
  CD's journalism and editorships 325, 326, 670
  CD's marriage breakup 21
  CD's religious beliefs 157, 582n.
  Child's History of England 485
  Chimes 194
  Ternan 19, 236
slavery 718
Slumdog Millionaire 743
Smiles, Samuel 280, 366
Smith, Adam 533, 541, 548, 592n.
Smith, Albert 315
Smith, Arthur 22
Smith, Grahame 281, 697, 740
Smith, Karl Ashley 587n.
Smith, Neil 716
Smith, Southwood 567
Smithfield market 157, 446
  animal studies 553, 556, 557–9, 560, 564
Smithfield Market Removal Act (1852) 557
smog/fog 566
  Bleak House 220–3, 225–6, 572–3, 576
Smollett, Tobias 637, 649, 662
  carnivalesque drinking 99
  CD compared with 86
  CD's reading 37
  financial difficulties 44
  Humphry Clinker 37
  influence on CD 96
  Peregrine Pickle 37
  picaresque 320
  Roderick Random 37, 93, 100
Soboul, Albert 267
social inclusion 502–3, 509–11, 513–15
social media 759–60
social reform 420–35
  public health 432, 434, 446
  sanitation 446, 567, 579
social ties
  Austen's novels 181–2
  Dombey and Son 180–2, 184, 186–90

Goldsmith's *The Vicar of Wakefield* 181–2
Society for the Propagation of Christian Knowledge 583
solitary confinement 425–6
'Some Account of an Extraordinary Traveller' 697, 719
Somebody's Luggage 54, 200–1, 205
Somers, Armónía, *Un retrato para Dickens* 726
Sondheim, Stephen 752
Sorrell, 'A Discursive Mind' 399
Sōseki, Natsume, *Botchan* 743
soul
  of machines 446, 447
  psychology 389, 395–6, 398, 400, 404
South Africa 729, 730, 744
Southey, Robert 546
Soviet Union 736
Spain 735–6
Spall, Timothy 752–3
Spectator, The 29, 30
speeches
  CD as public figure 72
  CD's reading 31, 32, 37, 39
  environment 567
  Hard Times 238
  industry and technology 439, 450
  Old Curiosity Shop 141–2
  Shakespeare references 31, 32
  social reform 420, 421, 422
  on theatre 668
Spinoza, Baruch 471
spontaneous combustion 40, 229, 347, 405
Sporting Magazine 92
sports 95, 104
Squib Annual of Poetry, Politics, and Personalities, The 92
stage adaptations *see* theatre: adaptations of CD's works
Stanfield, Clarkson 33, 50, 254, 672, 697
Stanislavski, Konstantin 676
Stanley, Very Reverend Arthur 59
Staplehurst rail disaster 75, 449–50
Starkey, David 485n.
Statistical Society of London 427
'Steam Excursion, The' 83
Stephen, James Fitzjames 245, 423–4, 468–9, 477

Stephen, Sir James 423
stereoscopes 263
stereoscopic view, *Little Dorrit* 251–8
Stern, Daniel N. 617n., 620–3
Sterne, Laurence 37, 96–7, 100
Stevenson, Robert Louis 151, 303, 306, 725
Stewart, Dugald 392
Stewart, Garrett 137, 526–7, 638, 642
Stirling, William 765
Stocking, George W., Jr 517
Stoermer, Eugene 571
Stone, Frank 50, 172n.
Stone, Harry 201
Stone, Marcus 50
Stone, Thomas, 'Dreams' 393, 394, 395–6
Stoppani, Antonio 571
Strange Gentleman, The 666, 669
strange situation 619, 621–3
String of Pearls, The 752
Strode, William 498
Styne, Jules 741
subject–object relations 456, 460, 463, 465
Sucksmith, Harvey Peter 252, 253
Sue, Eugene, *The Wandering Jew* 159
Sunday Beer Act (1854) 602
Sunday Under Three Heads 156
Surtees, R. S. 92, 95, 97
Sussman, Herbert L. 438, 456
Swarup, Vikas, *Q&A* 743
Sweeney Todd (George King, 1936) 752
Sweeney Todd: The Demon Barber of Fleet Street (Tim Burton, 2007) 752
Swift, Jonathan 36, 406
Swinburne, Algernon 172
Switzerland 17
syllepsis 637–8, 640, 642, 643–4
synecdoche 540
Syria 765

Taggart, Edward 581
Tagore, Rabindranath 726
Taine, Hippolyte 390
Tale of Two Cities, A 260–72
   adaptations 271–2, 675, 734, 739, 741–4, 746, 748
   and *The Battle of Life* 195
   and Carlyle 437, 494–5, 508, 525, 569
   CD as professional author 46, 48, 50

   CD as public figure 65
   CD's reading 35
   class 266, 365, 505, 507–8, 511
   drinking 601
   empire 525, 530
   environment 568–9
   gender and sexuality 367
   global circulation 725, 729, 733–5
   history and change 485–6, 490–6
   illustrations 269f, 269–70
   industry and technology 449
   language 643
   online project 332–3
   and *Our Mutual Friend* 298
   popular culture 759, 762
   psychology 393
   race and degeneration 522
   religion 587
   science 408, 411–13
   social reform 432
   theatre 669
   theatricality 675, 679
   transport 436
   travel 263, 320
Talfourd, Sir Thomas Noon 96
Tambling, Jeremy 107, 111, 138, 224n.
Tatler, The 29
Tauchnitz, Bernard 80n., 176n.
taverns 97, 102–4
Taylor, Charles 593
Taylor, Edgar, *German Popular Stories* 289–90
Taylor, Jesse Oak 222, 572–3
'Tea at a London Hotel' (extract from *Great Expectations*) 282–3
technology 436–51
   computational stylistics 331–2
   and the environment 575–7
   Hard Times 575–6
   Little Dorrit 575–6
   'The Signal-Man' 202
   see also digitization
Tegg, Thomas 86n.
Telbin, William 672
telegraph 436, 438, 442
teleology 314, 316
television adaptations 177, 277, 281, 302–3, 664, 683, 739–43, 746, 751–4

temperance movement 602–3
temporality
  drinking 602, 604–10, 612
  Old Curiosity Shop 142–3
Tennyson, Alfred, Lord 39
Terada, Rei 472, 473
Ternan, Ellen
  in biographies of CD 11–12, 12n.
  CD's marriage breakup 21
  CD's public image 75
  CD's reading 27–9
  Great Expectations 280
  media attention 236
  Mystery of Edwin Drood 307
  Our Mutual Friend 321
Ternan family 21
Test and Corporation Act (1828) 491
Thacker, John 302
Thackeray, William Makepeace
  CD's reading 38
  Christmas Books 194
  Christmas Carol 63, 176, 192
  'Dignity of Literature' debate 56
  Oliver Twist 55
  Pickwick Papers 102
  public readings 680
  serial publication 45
  Vanity Fair 38, 55
Thames, River
  Little Dorrit 315, 566
  Old Curiosity Shop 145, 148
  Our Mutual Friend 285, 294, 446
  pollution 566–7
  travel 315
  world-system 712–16
Thatcher, Margaret 260
theatre 666–81
  adaptations of CD's works 171–2, 276,
    279–81, 302, 309, 668–9, 673–5, 738–41,
    744–5, 747–51
  CD's adaptations of Shakespeare 172, 667
  CD's attendances 28
  CD's engagements with Victorian
    theatre 666–71
  CD's readings *see* public readings and
    performances
  CD's 'sham' theatre 671–4
  CD's toy theatre 28

Company of Amateurs 32, 40, 56, 67
dog drama 563
Every Man in his Humour (Jonson) 172
fairy-tale characters 348
family theatricals 338n.
The Frozen Deep (Collins with CD) 52–3
The Merry Wives of Windsor
  (Shakespeare) 172
scientific lectures and displays 418
see also public readings and
  performances
Theatres Regulation Act (1843) 670
theatricality 674–80
theology 581–96
theories of mind 389, 616, 623–4
see also psychology
thermodynamics 231, 407, 409–11
Thief, The 83
thing theory 460–1
  animal-derived objects 555
  Dombey and Son 186
  Master Humphrey's Clock 139–40
  Our Mutual Friend 297
  technology 450
Thomas, Keith 565
Thompson, Stith 294
Thomson, David 676–9
Thoreau, Henry David 568–9
Thornton, Sara 263
'Thousand and One Humbugs, The' 341
Thurston, Luke 202
Ticknor and Fields 200
Tierney, Jacob 745
Tilley, Heather Anne 145, 195
Tillotson, Kathleen 81–2, 155, 209
Timbs, John 557
Times, The
  anti-Catholicism 159
  Bleak House 376–7n.
  CD's marriage breakup 22
  tribute to CD 59, 60, 74
Tipperary Bank 245
'Toady Tree, The' 341, 497n.
Toise, David W. 544–5
Tolstoy, Leo 320
Tomahawk 376n.
Tomalin, Claire 236, 485
Tomkins, Silvan 471, 473n., 478

INDEX

Tom Thumb 338n.
topicality
   Barnaby Rudge 155
   Chimes 194
   Great Expectations 274
   Sketches by Boz 88–90
Topper 741
Tothill Fields prison 428
Townshend, Chauncy Hare 392, 399
'To Working Men' 434
Tracy, Robert 199
trade-union movement 432
transcendental anatomy 415
transculturation 722–3, 727–8, 736–7
translations
   CD as professional author 47
   global circulation 722–3, 725–8, 730, 732–7
   Great Expectations 276
   Sketches by Boz 84
   Tale of Two Cities 260–1
transnationalism 225–6, 250–1, 457, 464
transport 436, 438–9, 441–3
   Old Curiosity Shop 139
   revolution 518, 530
   Sketches by Boz 88
   world-system 708
   see also railways; travel
trauma studies 260
travel 312–23
   CD's 315–19, 496
      see also American Notes for General Circulation; *Pictures from Italy*
   Pickwick Papers 93, 102–3, 313, 319, 321
   Tale of Two Cities 263, 320
   see also railways; transport
Tree, Sir Herbert Beerbohm 670, 749n., 751
tributes to CD, posthumous 59–61, 60*f*
Trilling, Lionel 249–50, 399, 594n.
Trodd, Anthea 202
Trollope, Anthony 45, 501, 706
Trotsky, Leonid 714
Trotter, David 459–60, 463
True Sun, The 15, 420
Tsing, Anna Lowenhaupt 710, 712, 720
Turner, J. M. W. 236, 254, 258, 263
Tutuola, Amos 728

Twist (2003 Canadian film) 745
Twisted (1996 film by Seth Michael Donsky) 745
Twitter 759, 761–2, 771
'Two Guides of the Child, The' 340
Tyler, Daniel 717
Tyler, John 32
Tyler, Wat 498
Tylor, E. B. 291–2, 294
Tyndall, John 409, 411, 571
Tytler, Graeme 394

Uexküll, Jakob von 564n.
ugly feelings 374, 376, 378–80, 382, 386
uncertainty
   Dickensian and economic 545–8
   grammatical 631, 634–8, 641, 643–4
'Uncommercial Traveller, The' 200, 312
   and blogs 243
   CD as public figure 65
   in CD's reading 26n., 28n., 33n., 40n.
   'Shy Neighbourhoods' 314
Unesco Index Translationum—World Bibliography of Translation 725
Union of Soviet Socialist Republics 736
Unitarianism 153, 581
United States of America
   adaptations 744–5, 746, 748–51, 753
   Bleak House 225–7
   CD's travels 317–18, 319
   copyright 176, 226
   Great Expectations 276
   Little Dorrit 251
   Martin Chuzzlewit 167, 176, 569, 570, 639, 707
   prisons 425
   slavery 517, 524, 718
   world-system 704, 707, 718, 719
   see also American Notes for General Circulation
University of Buckingham *see Dickens Journal Online (DJO)* project
University of Leicester 332, 759, 762
'Unsettled Neighbourhood, An' 442n.
upper class *see* aristocracy
Urania Cottage 69–70, 429, 431
urban depictions *see* city; London; Paris

urban labyrinth
   Martin Chuzzlewit 174, 175
   Oliver Twist 108, 111
urban studies 175
utilitarianism 432, 433
   Bleak House 535
   Hard Times 534, 546

'Valentine's Day at the Post-Office' (CD and Wills) 445–6
Vance, Norman 591n.
Van Ghent, Dorothy
   cognitive studies 614–15, 617, 620, 625
   environment 570, 572
   Martin Chuzzlewit 174–5
   material culture 456
Van Ijzendoorn, Marinus H. 624
Vargish, Thomas 590–1, 592
Vase, Gillian 300, 303
Vaughn, Peter 751
Verfremdungseffekt 675
Vestiges of the Natural History of Creation (Chambers) 404, 408, 415, 552
Vestris, Madame 670
Victoria, Queen 54, 68, 81, 474
Victorian Britain
   aesthetic autonomy 297
   All the Year Round 65
   Anthropocene 571
   aristocracy 364
   associationist psychology 616
   Bleak House 223–5
   CD's effect on modern views of 752
   charity 68, 70
   children 338
   Christmas 63
   class 501–3
   coincidence 169
   dog drama 563
   domestic ideology 373–4, 378, 381, 383
   dream theory 589
   environment 566–80
   food studies 611–12
   gender and sexuality 280, 357, 358
   global circulation 731–2, 733
   Great Expectations 275, 282
   Household Words 65

   industry and technology 436–51
   literature *see* Victorian literature
   magazine culture 327
   Martin Chuzzlewit 168, 173, 177
   Master Humphrey's Clock 139
   material culture 453, 456–7, 461, 464
   natural history 551–7, 565
   Old Curiosity Shop 139, 147, 149
   Oliver Twist 105
   parlour games 550, 551
   political economy 545
   popular literature 289
   psychology 388–95
   public discourse 55
   race 517, 519, 521
   religion 583, 589, 590–2
   Roman decadence, fascination with 291
   schooling 63, 69, 141
   science 404–19
   sentimentality 194, 195, 468
   short stories 204
   Sketches by Boz 87
   social reform 420–35
   social upheavals 617
   stereoscope 254
   supernatural 582, 587
   Tale of Two Cities 260, 266, 267
   theatre 666–71
   world-system 704–21
Victorian literature
   adaptations 752
   animal studies 551, 553, 563
   anti-Catholicism 160, 162–3
   Bleak House 220
   children's 339–40
   city 107–8, 114
   class 501
   commodity culture 457, 460
   context 241–2
   empire 527, 528
   Forster 11
   gender and sexuality 361
   global circulation 722–37
   journals 331
   Old Curiosity Shop 137, 149
   Our Mutual Friend 297
   progress, commitment to 286

Victorian literature (*cont.*)
  'The Signal-Man' 202
  Sketches by Boz 87
  thing theory 186
  visual mediations 683
  world-system 705, 706, 709, 715
Victorian studies 474, 722–37
Village Coquettes, The 666
'Violated Letter' 22
Virgil 29
visual culture 404, 416–17
visual mediations 682–99
  illustrations 684–91
  storing up visual data 691–8
visual qualities
  Bleak House 228
  Little Dorrit 247, 252–8
  Tale of Two Cities 268–71
Volta, Alessandro 436
Voltaire 40, 248
Vrettos, Athena 389

Wade, Miss 249, 379, 381, 401
  illustrations 658*f*, 661*f*
  interludes 656–63, 664
Wahrman, Dror 501
Walder, Dennis 137, 156, 399, 582–3
Walkingame, Francis, *The Tutor's Assistant* 29
Wall, Stephen 252
Wallace, Alfred Russell 552
Wallerstein, Immanuel 719–20
Wallis, Shani 751
'Wallotty Trot' 341
Walters, John Cumming 301, 304
Warhol, Robyn R. 228, 600
Warren, Jonathan 14
Warren, Robert 14–15
Warren's Blacking 9–20
  CD as professional author 54
  and CD's marriage breakup 22–3
  early sketches 89
  Mendelssohn's 'Birmingham' sketch 9, 10*f*, 15
  psychoanalytic criticism 388
Warwick Research Collective (WReC) 705, 714–15
waste 285–6, 294, 409, 412, 566, 577–80

Waters, Catherine
  children 338
  domesticity and queer theory 378n., 382
  journalism 327, 328
  material culture 459, 464
Watkins, John 39
Watson, Mrs Richard 673
Watson, Robert 159
Watt, Ian 107, 599
Watt, James 436, 571
Watts, Isaac, *Divine Songs, Attempted in Easy Language for the Use of Children* 29
Watts-Dunton, Theodore 62
Wei Yi 730, 732
Weller, Christiana 18
Weller, Mary 26
Welles, Orson 746
Welsh, Alexander 12, 115, 137, 171n., 177
Wentersdorf, Karl P. 280
Werner, Alex 766n.
West, Charles 70
Westminster Review 193
Wevers, Lydia 727
Wheatstone, Charles 254, 255
'Where We Stopped Growing' 30n.
White, Revd James 205n.
Whittington, Dick 27
'Whole Hogs' 602–3
wife beating 606
Wilcox, Herbert 748
Wilde, Oscar 303, 477, 667
Wilkinson, Ann Y. 404, 409–12
will 398–402
Williams, Bransby 745
Williams, Raymond
  Bleak House 229
  city 107
  Dombey and Son 689
  Hard Times 237
  religion 594
  'structures of feeling' 555n.
  world-system 703, 705, 706
Williams, Rowan 724
Williams, Samuel 135*f*
Willis, Nathaniel Parker 83
Wills, Freeman 748

Wills, William Henry
   collaborations with CD 397–8, 445, 558
   Hard Times 233, 235
   letters from CD 44, 74, 235, 431
   'The Stereoscope' (with Morley) 255, 257
Wilson, Angus 201
Wilson, Edmund 237
   Christmas Carol 192
   Little Dorrit 247, 248–9
   Mystery of Edwin Drood 301–2, 303, 306
   Our Mutual Friend 285
   psychology 394
   Warren's Blacking 12
Wilson Patten Act (1954) 602
Wilt, Judith 158
Winter, Maria 35
Winter, Sarah 390
Winters, Warrington 394
Winyard, Ben 385, 407, 759, 762–3
Wirth, Louis 107
'Witch in the Nursery, A' 340, 342
Wolff, Michael 328, 330
Wolfreys, Julian 239
Woloch, Alex 223
Wood, Claire 762, 770
Woodmansee, Martha 541
Woolf, Virginia 374
Wordsworth, William 45
   environment 568, 569
   The Excursion 585
   influence on CD 584–5, 586, 590
   Lyrical Ballads 79
   memory 589
   The Prelude 39, 569
   Tintern Abbey 569
   urban unknowability 267
workhouses 428
working class 501–4, 507–9
   Barnaby Rudge 162, 382
   Bleak House 347
   children 338
   children's literature 340
   David Copperfield 379
   drinking 602–3
   Hard Times 349, 350
   Household Words readership 342
   industry and technology 437
   Old Curiosity Shop 144
   Oliver Twist 113
   Our Mutual Friend 366
   Sketches by Boz 79, 90
   social reform 422
worldbuilding 767–73
world literature 705, 709, 714–15, 720
   global circulation 722–3, 726–7
world-system 703–21
   grounding globalization 711–14
   unequal and violent 714–20
   venture capitalism and globalized gammon 705–10
Wreck of the Golden Mary, The (CD and Collins) 52, 202, 204, 522
Wright, Thomas 417
writer, role of the 64
Wu Kuang-chien 730–1
Wyndham, Charles 670

Yang Xianyi 731
Yates, Edmund 331
Young, James 749
'Young Couple, The' 90

Zambrano, Ana Laura 268
Zerbe, Michael 406
zeugma (syllepsis) 637–8, 640, 642, 643–4
Zieger, Susan 600
Zimmerman, Virginia 417
Zipes, Jack 347
Zola, Émile 267
Zunshine, Lisa 623–4n.